THE CAMBRIDGE
HISTORY OF
Hellenistic Philosophy

THE CAMBRIDGE
HISTORY OF
Hellenistic Philosophy

*

Edited by

KEIMPE ALGRA
LECTURER IN ANCIENT PHILOSOPHY,
UNIVERSITY OF UTRECHT

JONATHAN BARNES
PROFESSOR OF ANCIENT PHILOSOPHY,
UNIVERSITY OF GENEVA

JAAP MANSFELD
PROFESSOR OF ANCIENT AND MEDIEVAL PHILOSOPHY,
UNIVERSITY OF UTRECHT

MALCOLM SCHOFIELD
PROFESSOR OF ANCIENT PHILOSOPHY,
UNIVERSITY OF CAMBRIDGE

CAMBRIDGE
UNIVERSITY PRESS

PUBLISHED BY THE PRESS SYNDICATE OF THE UNIVERSITY OF CAMBRIDGE
The Pitt Building, Trumpington Street, Cambridge, United Kingdom

CAMBRIDGE UNIVERSITY PRESS
The Edinburgh Building, Cambridge CB2 2RU, UK   www.cup.cam.ac.uk
40 West 20th Street, New York, NY 10011–4211, USA   www.cup.org
10 Stamford Road, Oakleigh, Melbourne 3166, Australia

First published 1999

Printed in the United Kingdom at the University Press, Cambridge

Typeface TEFF Renard 9.5/12.75 pt   *System* QuarkXPress® [SE]

A catalogue record for this book is available from the British Library

Library of Congress cataloguing in publication data
The Cambridge history of Hellenistic philosophy / edited by Keimpe
Algra . . . [et al.].
p.   cm.
Includes bibliographical references and index.
ISBN 0 521 25028 5 (hardback)
1. Philosophy, Ancient.   I. Algra, Keimpe, 1959–.
B171.C36 1999   180–dc21   98–36033 CIP

ISBN 0 521 25028 5 hardback

Contents

Preface xi

[v]

Preface

Not so many decades ago Hellenistic philosophy was widely regarded as a dark age in the history of thought: it was a period of epigoni, a period of post-Aristotelian depression. The age produced nothing worth pondering and little worth reading. Moreover, there was little enough to read: few texts from the period survive in their entirety; and the fragments and testimonies to which we are now reduced derive for the most part from jejune epitomators or hostile commentators. An historian of philosophy would be best advised to doze through the Hellenistic period – indeed, why wake up before the birth of Plotinus?

Fashions change, and this dismal and depreciatory assessment is now universally rejected. Hellenistic philosophy was not dull: on the contrary, it was a bright and brilliant period of thought. The Hellenistic philosophers were not epigoni: on the contrary, they opened up new areas of speculation and they engaged in debates and discussions which were both passionate and profound. It cannot be denied that time has served the period badly. If the textual situation is less desperate than has sometimes been pretended, it remains true that for the most part we are obliged to reconstruct the thought of the Hellenistic philosophers from later reports – and these reports are indeed often thin or confused or biassed. But such difficulties no longer daunt – rather, they add a certain piquancy to the study.

The revived interest in the Hellenistic period has caused a spate of publications – articles and monographs and books pour from the learned presses, and some of them are distinguished contributions to scholarship. But for the most part they deal with particular problems or specific aspects of the matter; and a good, full, general treatment of Hellenistic philosophy is not easy to discover. It may thus seem opportune to essay a general history of the subject – and that is what this volume attempts to do. Not that it represents, or pretends to determine, an orthodoxy. Indeed, there are few interesting claims about Hellenistic philosophy which are not controversial, and few areas where any scholar would be inclined to say: There we have it. This *History of Hellenistic Philosophy*, then, is not definitive. Nor did the editors seek to persuade the contributors to disguise their discords: the riding of hobby-horses was discouraged, and a contributor who proposed to offer a novel or a bold interpretation was asked to confess the fact and to provide references to rival views; but no doctrinal uniformity was imposed, and readers of the *History* will occasionally find an interpretation commended on one page and rejected on another.

The phrase 'Hellenistic philosophy' consists of two disputable words. The Hellenistic period conventionally begins with the death of Alexander the Great and ends with the battle of Actium some three hundred years later. The *History*, for reasons which are explained in the Epilogue, has a slightly more modest chronological scope: it starts, in effect, from the last days of Aristotle (who died a year after Alexander) and it stops in about 100 BC. In consequence, it says nothing – save incidentally – about certain figures who standardly count as Hellenistic philosophers: Posidonius is not among its heroes; Philodemus and the Epicureans of the first century BC, do not appear in their own right; Aenesidemus and the revival of Pyrrhonism are not discussed.

Any division of any sort of history into chronological segments will be arbitrary, at least at the edges, and it would be absurd to pretend that philosophy changed, abruptly or essentially, in 320 BC and again in 100 BC. Equally, any history must choose some chronological limits; and the limits chosen for this *History* are, or so the editors incline to think, reasonably reasonable – at least, they are more reasonable than the traditional limits. It may be objected that the word 'Hellenistic' is now inept. (In truth, some historians dislike the word *tout court*.) But there is no other word with which to replace it, and it is used here without, of course, any ideological connotations – as a mere label, a sign for a certain span of time.

The term 'philosophy', too, is not without its vagaries – what people have been content to name 'philosophy' has changed from age to age (and place to place), and at the edges there has always been a pleasing penumbra. The *History* has, in effect, adopted something like the following rule of thumb: anything which both counted as philosophy for the Hellenistic Greeks and also counts as philosophy for us is admitted as philosophy for the purposes of the *History*; and in addition, a few other items which find themselves on the margins of the subject – the sciences, rhetoric and poetics – have been considered, though less fully than they might have been in a history of the general intellectual achievements of the period. Other principles might have been followed: the editors claim that their rule of thumb is no worse than any other.

Then there is the question of order and arrangement. In effect, any historian of Hellenistic philosophy is confronted by a difficult choice: to write by school or to write by subject? Each choice has its advantages and its disadvantages. Writing by school – Part I: the Epicureans, Part II: the Stoa . . . – allows for a systematic and coherent presentation of the main 'philosophies' of the period; and since those philosophies were – or at least purported to be – systematic, such a presentation is in principle desirable. On the other hand, the Hellenistic period was also characterized by vigorous debate and discussion among the partisans of the different schools of thought: if systems were built, they were also attacked – and defended, redesigned, attacked again . . . A history which proceeds school by school will find it relatively hard to bring out this dynamic aspect of its subject and hence it will tend to disguise the very aspect of Hellenistic philosophy which has contributed most to the revival of its fortunes.

Writing by subject has, evidently enough, the opposite features: the cut and thrust of debate is more readily exhibited and explained – but the school systems will be presented in fragmented fashion. The editors decided, without great confidence, to prefer subjects to schools: readers who require an account of, say, Stoicism may, without great labour, construct one for themselves by studying a discontinuous selection of sections of the *History*.

If a history is to be written by subject, then how is philosophy best divided into its component subjects? It would have been possible to take one of the ancient 'divisions' of philosophy, and to let it give the *History* its structure. Indeed there was, in later antiquity, a standard division, for

> most, and the most important, authors say that there are three parts of philosophy – ethical, physical, logical.[1]

Ethics comprehended political theory as well as moral philosophy; physics included most of what we should call metaphysics, as well as philosophy of science and philosophical psychology; and logic embraced not only logic in the broadest of its contemporary senses but also epistemology – and sometimes even rhetoric.

Numerous texts acknowledge the tripartition as a feature of Hellenistic philosophy. Thus according to Sextus Empiricus,

---

[1] Sen. *Ep.* 89.9; cf. e.g. Apul. *Int.* 189, 1–3.

> there has been much dispute among the Dogmatists about the parts of philosophy, some saying that it has one part, some two, some three; it would not be appropriate to deal with this in more detail here, and we shall set down impartially the opinion of those who seem to have dwelt upon the matter more fully ... The Stoics and some others say that there are three parts of philosophy – logic, physics, ethics – and they begin their exposition with logic (although there has indeed been much dissension even about where one should begin). (S.E. *PH* II.12–13)

Elsewhere Sextus goes into the details; and he reports that 'implicitly, Plato was the originator' of the tripartition, although 'Xenocrates and the Peripatetics introduced it most explicitly – and the Stoics too stand by this division' (*M* VII.16).[2]

The reference to Plato is a matter of piety rather than of history; and most scholars are content to ascribe the formal origin of the division to Xenocrates. The Peripatetics acknowledged a three-fold division, but not a literal tripartition; for they preferred to split philosophy itself into two parts, theoretical and practical (which corresponded roughly to physics and ethics), and to deem logic to be not a part but a tool or instrument of philosophy.[3] As for the Stoics, Zeno and Chrysippus and many of their followers did indeed subscribe to the tripartition; but

> Cleanthes says that there are six parts – dialectic, rhetoric, ethics, politics, physics, theology – although others, among them Zeno of Tarsus, say that these are not parts of philosophical discourse but rather parts of philosophy itself. (D.L. VII.41)

Other Schools, and individuals, might acknowledge three parts in principle while in practice 'rejecting' one or another of them – usually logic. Thus the Epicureans 'rejected logical theory', in the sense that they thought that it was somehow superfluous or useless (S.E. *M* VII.14). Nonetheless, they studied what they called 'canonics', a subject which covers much of what their rivals subsumed under logic, and which they chose to regard as a part of physics (D.L. X.30).

Sextus decided to follow the order: logic, physics, ethics. And this was the usual practice. But, as Sextus insists, there was dissent on this matter too, and most of the possible permutations had their advocates. To be sure, it is not clear what the dissension was about. Sometimes the question at issue seems to be pedagogical: in which order should a student of

---

[2] See also S.E. *M* VII.1–19; D.L. VII.39–41; Plut. *Stoic.Repug.* 1035A (further texts in Hülser 1987–8, 12–22): discussion in Hadot 1979; Ierodiakonou 1993b; Dörrie and Baltes 1996, 205–31.   [3] See Barnes *et al* 1991, 41–3.

philosophy be taught the three parts of the subject? Sometimes it is rather systematical: what are the logical relations among the parts, which presuppose which? Sometimes, again, it appears to have had a normative colouring: which part is the culmination, the summit, of the philosophical ascent? Connected to these issues were certain similes or analogies. Thus philosophy was likened to an orchard: the trees are physics, the fruit is ethics, and the fencing is set up by logic. Or to an egg: ethics the yolk, physics the white, logic the shell. Or to an animal: physics the flesh and blood, logic the bones, ethics the soul.[4]

What was the importance, inside Hellenistic philosophy, of this tripartition? It might be thought, first, to have had a certain negative significance, inasmuch as it served to exclude various intellectual disciplines from the study of 'things human and divine' and hence to determine the bounds of philosophy proper. Thus the tripartition might seem to leave no place for mathematics, say, or for medicine; or for astronomy, music, rhetoric, grammatical theory . . . But this is not so. Some philosophers, to be sure, would have no truck with rhetoric; but the Stoics treated it as a philosophical discipline – and they had no difficulty in subsuming it under logic, as the companion to dialectic. Again, astronomy was usually taken to be a technical discipline to which philosophers had no professional access; but the cosmological parts of physics in fact brought philosophers into contact with the heavens – and the Epicureans found much to say on the matter. In truth, the tripartite scheme was a fairly elastic sausage-skin: you might stuff it with what you would.

Secondly, and more obviously, the tripartition might be thought to have given a structure to the enquiries of the Hellenistic philosophers. No doubt the subject – like a well planted orchard or a good egg – had a unity and an internal coherence; but it also had its compartments, and you might research here rather than there, write or teach on this aspect rather than on that. This, to be sure, is true; the ancient 'doxographies' reveal it in its most jejune form; and the titles of numerous Hellenistic works offer a meatier indication. But it would be a mistake to insist on the point. Readers of Plato sometimes ask themselves: What is this dialogue – the *Republic*, the *Phaedrus* – about? to what part or branch of philosophy does it pertain? And they quickly see that the question has no answer: the dialogue advances whithersoever reason leads it, unconstrained by school-masterly notions of syllabus and timetable. And the same, it is reasonable to think, was often the case in Hellenistic texts. Read the

---

[4] See esp. S.E. *M* VII.17–19 (where the simile of the body is ascribed to Posidonius); D.L. VII.40.

surviving fragments of Chrysippus, and guess from which works they derive: where the answer is known (which, to be sure, is not often), you will be wrong as often as right.

Yet if the ancient tripartition was not universally recognized, if the contents of its constituent parts were not uniformly determined, and if ordinary philosophical practice allowed a fair amount of seepage from one part to another, nonetheless – to return to Seneca – 'most, and the most important, philosophers' accepted it. And we might have based this *History* upon it. In fact, we decided to prefer a modern to an ancient division. To be sure, the standard tripartition Seneca refers to is reflected in the general structure we have imposed on the material. But its detailed articulation does not purport to follow an ancient pattern, and some of our topics and subtopics were not known to the Hellenistic world. (Epistemology, for example, was not a branch, nor yet a sub-branch, of ancient philosophy.)

The choice of a modern rather than an ancient principle of division was determined by a prior choice of the same nature. In general, we may look at a past period of thought from our own point of view or we may try to look at it from the point of view of the thinkers of the period itself; that is to say, we may consider it as an earlier part of the history to which we ourselves now belong, or we may consider it as it appeared at the time. The two approaches will produce, as a rule, two rather different histories; for what then seemed – and was – central and important may, with hindsight, seem and be peripheral, and what was once peripheral may assume, as the subject develops and changes, a central importance. Each approach is valuable. The two cannot always be followed simultaneously. Most contemporary historians of philosophy, for reasons which are both various and more or less evident, have adopted the former approach. The *History* is, in this respect, orthodox. But it is a mitigated orthodoxy: several of the contributors have followed – or hugged – the ancient contours of their subject; and the faculty of hindsight is a subjective thing – some readers of the *History* will doubtless find it antiquated rather than contemporary in its implicit assessment of the centre and the periphery of philosophy.

A pendant to these remarks. It would be satisfying were the number of pages allotted to a subject a rough measure of its weight or importance. The *History* does not distribute its pages according to such a principle; for the nature of the evidence imposes certain constraints. Where the evidence is relatively extensive, a longer discussion is possible; and where the evidence is relatively sparse, a longer discussion is desirable. A topic for which we have only a handful of summary reports focused on what the ancients thought, not why they thought what they thought, can hardly be given a generous allowance of space, however important it may seem to us (or have seemed to them). The exigencies of the evidence have not determined the distribution of pages among subjects; but they have powerfully and inevitably influenced it.

*

The *History* has been written by specialists: it has not been written for specialists. Nor, to be sure, has it been written for that mythical personage, General Reader. The editors imagine that any serious student, amateur or professional, of ancient philosophy might find a history of Hellenistic philosophy useful and interesting; and they have supposed that a similar, if less direct, interest and utility might attract students of classical antiquity who have no special concern for philosophy and students of philosophy who have no special concern for classical antiquity.

Such hopes have determined the degree of technical expertise which the *History* expects of its readers – expertise in the three pertinent disciplines of philosophy, history, and philology. From a philosophical point of view, some of the issues discussed in the *History* are intrinsically difficult and dense. No account of them can be easy, nor have the contributors been urged to smooth and butter their subjects. But in principle the *History* does not presuppose any advanced philosophical training: it tries to avoid jargon, and it tries to avoid knowing allusions to contemporary issues. For quite different reasons, the history of the period – its intellectual history – is not easy either. Here too the *History* in principle offers a text which supposes no prior expertise in the chronicles and events of the Hellenistic period. Those historical facts (or conjectures) which are pertinent to an understanding of the discussion are, for the most part, set down in the Introduction; and in general, the *History* itself purports to supply whatever historical information it demands.

As to philology, the nature of the evidence makes a certain amount of scholarship indispensable: as far as possible, this has been confined to the footnotes. On a more basic level, there is the question of the ancient languages. In the footnotes there will be found a certain amount of untranslated Greek and Latin; but the body of the *History* is designed to be intelligible to readers whose only language is English. Any passage from an ancient author which is cited is cited in English translation. (If a Greek or Latin word appears in the main text, it serves only to indicate what lies behind the English translation.) Technical terms – and technical terms were common enough in Hellenistic philosophy – form a problem apart.

In most cases a technical term has been given a rough and ready translation; in a few cases a Latin word or a transliterated Greek word has been
treated as a piece of honorary English: every technical term is introduced
by a word or two of paraphrase or explication when first it enters the discussion.

Principles of this sort are easy to state, difficult to follow with consistency. There are, no doubt, certain pages where a piece of philosophical
jargon has insinuated itself, where an historical allusion has not been
explained, where a morsel of ancient terminology remains unglossed. The
editors hope that there are few such pages.

*

The several chapters of the *History* are largely independent of one another:
the *History* will, we imagine, sometimes be used as a work of reference;
and it is not necessary to begin at page 1 in order to understand what is
said on page 301. Occasional cross-references signal interconnections
among the chapters, so that a reader of page 301 might find it helpful (but
not mandatory) to turn back or forward in the volume. The requirement
of independence leads to a small amount of repetition: the odd overlap-
pings among the chapters may detract from the elegance of the *History* but
they add to its utility.

The footnotes serve three main functions: they quote, and sometimes
discuss, ancient texts – in particular, esoteric or knotty texts; they provide
references to ancient passages which are not explicitly quoted; and they
contain information, for the most part sparing, about the pertinent modern literature on the subject. The Bibliography serves to collect those
modern works to which the footnotes refer: it is not a systematic bibliography, let alone a comprehensive bibliography, of Hellenistic philosophy.
Printed bibliographies are out of date before they are published; and any
reader who wants a comprehensive list of books and articles on
Hellenistic philosophy may readily construct one from the bibliographical journals.

The *History* was begun more years ago than the editors care to recall. It
was inaugurated in a spirit of euphoria (occasioned by a celebrated sporting triumph). Its career was punctuated by bouts of depression (which
had nothing to do with any sporting disasters). Twice it nearly suc-
cumbed. The editors therefore have more cause than most to offer thanks:
first, to the contributors, some of whom must have despaired of ever seeing their work in print; secondly, to the University of Utrecht, its
Department of Philosophy, the Netherlands Organization for Scientific

Research (NWO), and the C. J. de Vogel Foundation for their generous financial aid; thirdly, to the Cambridge University Press – and in particular to Jeremy Mynott and to Pauline Hire – for their patience, encouragement and optimism. In addition, we would like to express our gratitude to Stephen Chubb for his translation of chapters 2, 3, 18, and parts of chapter 21; and we would like to record that without the unstinting technical support of Han Baltussen and Henri van de Laar the *History* would never have reached the public.

KA · JB · JM · MS
Utrecht, September 1997

PART I

INTRODUCTION

*

Sources

JAAP MANSFELD

1 Why so much has been lost

We know a good deal about Hellenistic[1] philosophy, but by no means as much as we would like to know. The reason is that with very few exceptions no works written by the Hellenistic philosophers themselves survive. The situation is therefore quite different from that in which we find ourselves with regard to the great classical philosophers, Plato and Aristotle. Plato's complete works have been preserved. Much of Aristotle's vast output has perished, but the philosophically more important part of his writings is still available. The reason for the preservation of these Platonic and Aristotelian corpora is that these works continued to be taught and studied in the philosophical schools. Treatises of Aristotle were taught by the late Neoplatonists as a preparation for the study of a set of dialogues by Plato, and those of his works which were not part of the curricula have mostly perished. The professional teachers of philosophy themselves were required to have perfect knowledge of practically everything these great masters had written.

But by the end of the third century AD the schools (in the sense both of institutions and schools of thought) which had been founded in the early Hellenistic period had died out.[2] The works of Epicurus and his immediate followers, or of the great early Stoics for example, were no longer taught, though a preliminary instruction in the views of the main schools could still be part of a decent pagan education in the fourth and to a much lesser extent in the fifth and sixth centuries AD.[3] The institutional basis

---

[1] For the nineteenth-century origin of this problematic denomination and periodization see Bichler 1983, Isnardi Parente 1985–6. For *belles-lettres* the classical period is the 5th century, for philosophy the 4th, for medicine the 5th/4th century BC. For mathematics it is the 3rd/2nd century BC, i.e. the early Hellenistic period (most of the works of Euclid, Archimedes and part of Apollonius having been preserved, as well as opuscula by other authors); for the traditions involved see Knorr 1989, esp. 224–45 on Pappus and Eutocius.

[2] On the philosophical recession in the third century AD see Longinus at Porph. *VP* 20, Saffrey and Westerink 1968, xli–xlii.   [3] For the survival of doxographical literature see below, n. 65.

which would have ensured the preservation of the Hellenistic philosophers disappeared.

From the second to the fourth centuries AD the originally humble vel-
lum (or papyrus) codex, the forerunner of our book, gradually replaced
the papyrus scroll as the vehicle for higher forms of literature[4]. The works
that were taught to students and studied by the professors themselves
were carefully and systematically transcribed, and in sufficient numbers.
The enormous mass of works that were no longer taught were either not
transcribed at all and so eventually perished along with the fragile
material on which they had been written, or transcribed in quantities that
were not sufficiently large to warrant their survival, though works that
were popular for other reasons had good chances to survive. Libraries
tend to deteriorate and – much worse – burn.[5] In order to explain Plato
and Aristotle, as the expression was, 'from themselves',[6] that is to say
from what is stated in their own writings, there was no need to adduce the
works of the Hellenistic philosophers. These thinkers and their later followers had often enough criticized Plato and Aristotle, or attempted to
work out ideas which they believed to be better, and in some cases
undoubtedly were better. But from the first centuries BC and AD onwards,
the professors of Aristotelian and Platonic philosophy had taken some of
these criticisms and alternatives into account in their oral or written comments and commentaries on individual works. Useful ideas worked out
by philosophical rivals had been incorporated in updated versions of the
Platonic system, and the ingenuity of Plato's exegetes had found intima-
tions of, and so a legitimation for, these ideas in Plato's own works. The
commentaries on the great classical philosophers were quite effective in
protecting students against the impact of potentially destructive doctrines of rival schools. What the average student should know about
Stoicism or Epicureanism, to mention only the more important currents,
was found in elementary handbooks or in the Platonic and Aristotelian
commentary literature itself. Doing philosophy had more and more
turned into exegesis, that is to say into the study and interpretation of the
works of the great classics.[7] The actual practice of teaching and doing phi-

---

[4] Up-to-date overviews in Cavallo 1989, 1994. For the disappearance of literary works that were
no longer taught see Irigoin 1994, 72–6.

[5] For the history of transmission in general see Reynolds and Wilson 1978, Wilson 1983.

[6] Cf. Schäublin 1977, and e.g. Procl. *TP* 1.2, p. 10.1–4.

[7] P. Hadot 1987, Sedley 1989a, 97–103, Barnes et al. 1991, 4–7, Baltes in Dörrie and Baltes 1993,
162–6, Erler 1993. For Demetrius of Laconia's exegesis of Epicurus see Puglia 1988, and the
comments of Roselli 1990, who compares Galen's practice. For the commentaries on Aristotle
see the papers in Sorabji 1990, with useful bibliography 484–524; for those on Plato Westerink
1990, lxi–lxxvi, Dörrie and Baltes 1993, 20–54, 162–226. For what should be taught and how
see I. Hadot 1990, 1991, Mansfeld 1994b.

losophy therefore hardly encouraged the study of the original works written by representatives of other schools of thought. Accordingly, in the later exegetical literature concerned with Plato and Aristotle the doctrines of the Hellenistic philosophers that could not be assimilated survive, if at all, in a fossilized form, that is to say as objections or alternatives that were worth remembering precisely because they had been neutralized, and so provided useful material for training one's students.

II Primary sources

The extant primary sources are very few. Epicureanism has fared comparatively well, because we still have three didactic letters written by Epicurus himself as well as a collection of aphorisms, the so-called *Key Doctrines* (*KD*), all preserved in Diogenes Laertius book x.[8] The letters are the *To Herodotus*, dealing with physics, the *To Pythocles*, dealing with cosmology and meteorology, and the *To Menoeceus*, dealing with ethics. It is important to recognize that these letters do not work at the same level. In the proems to the first two Epicurus makes a distinction between those who diligently study all his works and others who for one reason or other are not in a position to devote their life to the study of nature. For the latter the (lost) so-called greater *Greater Abstract* (from the multi-book treatise *On Nature*) had been especially written (*Ep. Hdt.* 35), whereas the *Ep. Hdt.* has been composed as an *aide-mémoire* for the accomplished Epicurean who no longer needs to go into the details (cf. *Ep. Hdt.* 83). At *Ep. Pyth.* 84–5 Epicurus says that a succinct account of cosmo-meteorology will be useful both for beginners and for those who are too busy to study the subject in depth. The *Ep. Pyth.* therefore is on the same level as the lost *Greater Abstract*, while the *Ep. Hdt.* is an entirely different sort of work. We are not in a position to read it with the eyes of its original public, because only (quite large) fragments of a number of books of the *On Nature* have been preserved among the remains of the library at Herculaneum.[9] The *Ep. Men.* is directed at young as well as at old readers, so presumably is a combination of introduction and *aide-mémoire*, though the protreptic element predominates. The *KD* is a sort of catechism.[10]

The remaining scraps of primary material are scanty indeed. Diogenes

---

[8] Another collection, the so-called *Gnomologium Vaticanum* (not to be confused with the other *Gnom. Vat.* edited by L. Sternbach 1963), first published by Wotke 1888, contains fragments of Epicurus (among which several sayings from the *KD*), and others, among whom Metrodorus. Further fragments, among which again several from the *KD*, are incorporated in the inscription of Diogenes of Oenoanda; text in M. F. Smith 1993.   [9] See below, n. 20.

[10] For the role of such compendia in the Epicurean community see I. Hadot 1969a, 53–4, I. Hadot 1969b, see below, p. 670.

Laertius has preserved catalogues of the works of the more important Hellenistic philosophers,[11] but these are not always complete. For Epicurus, for instance, we are only given a selection, while the full and systematic bibliography of Chrysippus breaks off half way because the unique ancestor from which our extant manuscripts derive had already been damaged. For Stoicism we have the *Hymn to Zeus* by Cleanthes preserved in Stobaeus.[12] We also have the remains of part of Chrysippus' *Logical Investigations* (*PHerc.* 307)[13] and fragments of anonymous treatises, preserved in the library at Herculaneum. A large number of fragmentary scrolls containing the doctrines of minor Epicureans have also survived at Herculaneum. Further papyrus fragments have been found in Egypt.[14] Other first-hand evidence for the Hellenistic philosophers consists of verbatim quotations in a variety of authors, a number of whom only cite in order to refute. Pyrrho did not write anything, so for early Pyrrhonism we mainly have to rely on his disciple Timon, of whose works only fragments are extant. All our other evidence is at one or more removes from the originals and consists of various forms of reportage.

iii Secondary sources

For our information about Hellenistic philosophy we are therefore for the most part dependent on peripheral sources.[15] In this section, I shall briefly enumerate the more important among the works and authors that are involved. The earliest evidence is from about the mid-first century BC, and the fact that it is at our disposal at all is in two cases due to events which were rather unfortunate for those concerned.

In 46 BC the great rhetorician, orator and statesman Cicero, who had studied philosophy and read philosophical literature during his whole active life and already published works on political philosophy from a

---

[11] Similarly, Soranus is said to have composed a *Lives of Physicians and Schools and Writings*, ten books, *Suda* 1.4, 407.23-4. The more important catalogues are at D.L. vi.80 (Diogenes the Cynic), viii.4 (Zeno), vii.162 (Aristo), vii.166 (Herillus), vii.167 (Dionysius), vii.174-5 (Cleanthes), vii.170 (Sphaerus), vii.189-202 (Chrysippus), x.24 (Metrodorus), x.25 (Polyaenus), and x.27-8 (Epicurus).

[12] Nothing is known about its *Sitz im Leben*; I suspect that it may have served as an easily memorized compendium of Stoic thought. This would help to explain why it has been preserved. At any rate Cleanthes' four lines of prayer to Zeus-and-Destiny according to Epictetus will be always 'ready at hand' (*procheiron*), Epict. *Diss.* iii 22.95, iv 4.34; *Ench.* 53. For this technical term see I. Hadot 1969a, 58 n. 107.   [13] Preliminary text at *FDS* 698.

[14] Eventually, this material will be better accessible in the *CPF* which for pieces whose author is known proceeds in alphabetical order.

[15] Glucker 1991 has carried out the interesting experiment of reconstructing in outline what would be our view of Plato if only the late derivative reports were still extant.

mostly Platonic and Stoic point of view, was forced to retire from the political scene. He had just written a short tract entitled *Stoic Paradoxes*, six rhetorical essays on philosophical issues. Because he wanted to continue to be of service to society, or at least to the 'good people', he decided to bring Greek philosophy to the Roman world by composing a series of philosophical treatises.[16] Some of these are dialogues in which issues in systematic philosophy are set out and discussed from the points of view of the major Hellenistic schools, namely by Epicurean, Stoic and Academic speakers. But in most of his other works too Cicero attempted to present the divergent options fairly fully, so that the reader would be in a position to make up his own mind. As a rule he does not take sides, though he indicates which point of view seems most plausible to him, or most useful – at least for the time being.

These works, the sequence of which by and large conforms to that of the parts of philosophy, but which fail to provide a complete treatment, were written in an unbelievably short span of time, from 45 to 43 BC. He started by writing a pamphlet, the *Hortensius* (lost), in which he warmly recommended the study of philosophy. Next came the *Academics*, of which two different editions were published. We still have the first part of the first book of the second edition, and the second book of the first; the former gives an overview of the three main divisions of philosophy, namely logic, physics, ethics, and the latter deals with epistemological questions from Stoic and sceptic angles. Next are the still extant five books of the *On the Chief Ends of Good and Evil*. In 44 BC, he first wrote the *Tusculan Disputations* in five books, consisting of disputes about questions of major practical importance between an anonymous and dominating master (Cicero himself) and an anonymous respondent. In the last book, for instance, the master argues that all the philosophers worth the name are agreed, or almost, that virtue is sufficient for happiness, but does so without committing himself on the nature of either happiness or virtue. Next is the *On the Nature of the Gods*, in three books, with one large and several small gaps in the third book which contains the Academic counterarguments against the Stoic position. This work is not a theological treatise only, but also an important source for Stoic physics and cosmology

---

[16] Cicero describes the works he had written and still plans to write in the autobibliography at *Div.* II.1–4; cf. also the excursus at *ND* 1.6–7, and see P. L. Schmidt 1978, Steinmetz 1990. Rawson 1975, 230–48, Schofield 1986b, 48–51, and Powell 1995a, 7–11 are useful brief surveys. MacKendrick 1989 is a detailed study of the corpus, with summaries of each work and discussion of sources and influences; Görler and Gawlick 1994 is an overview of the corpus (including the rhetorical treatises) and an up-to-date introduction to the philosophy. For *Tusc.* see also Douglas 1995.

because of the central role that the gods play in the Stoic conception of the cosmos.[17] The *On Divination* in two books follows; divination was an important issue in Stoic philosophy and a fact of Roman life. Book one argues pro, book two contra. The more technical *On Fate*, which treats a closely related topic, the arguments pro and contra determinism, survives only in mutilated form. Two rather literary essays, *On Old Age* and *On Friendship*, have also survived. Cicero further wrote the *Topics*,[18] a treatise on various forms of argument which is more rhetorical than logical. Finally he wrote the *On Duties* in three books, dedicated to his profligate son. This is a treatise, and a sternly moralistic one, in which he declines to furnish arguments against the rather dogmatic stance adopted. It should finally be added that the rhetorical treatises composed by Cicero in his youth and middle age are interesting sources for certain aspects of Hellenistic philosophy too, and of course also for the history of rhetoric.

Cicero was not the only person to promote philosophy in the Rome of his day. His younger contemporary Lucretius (died before 50 BC) wrote an epic poem in six books entitled *On the Nature of Things*,[19] which may have been published from his papers after his death. It deals with the whole of physics (including e.g. psychology and history of civilization) from the Epicurean point of view and is in fact an attempt to convert its readers to what we may call the gospel of Epicurus. It is one of the most important sources for Epicurean philosophy still extant.

We also have the carbonized remains of the philosophical library of a villa near Herculaneum, which was buried and thus preserved by an eruption of the Vesuvius in AD 79 and dug up in the eighteenth century.[20] The majority of these scrolls had been brought to the villa by a professional philosopher, the Epicurean Philodemus who was a contemporary of Cicero, or been produced there under his supervision or by his successors.[21] Needless to say, they have been very much damaged, firstly by nature, then not only by the patient human attempts to unwind and preserve them but also by stupidity and neglect. Apart from important

---

[17] See below, pp. 758–62.   [18] Not on a boat; see Immisch 1928.

[19] *De Rerum Natura* translates *Peri Phuseōs*, the title traditionally given to works by Presocratic philosophers such as that of Empedocles (much admired by Lucretius) or to treatises dealing with the philosophy of nature, like Epicurus' own *On Nature*. Note that Cic. *Acad.* II.73 translates Metrodorus of Chius' title as *De natura*.

[20] Short overview of the contents with references to the literature in Dorandi 1995b; catalogues of the papyri: Gigante 1979, Capasso 1989.

[21] See Cavallo 1983, 58–65, 1984, 6–23, who further points out that the Epicurus scrolls have to be dated to the third–second centuries and will be copies of the holdings of the school at Athens; those with the works of Demetrius of Laconia date to the second–first centuries BC and are contemporary with the author.

remains of works by Epicurus and several other Epicureans (Carneiscus, Polyaenus, Polystratus, Demetrius of Laconia), the library comprises quite a number of writings composed by Philodemus himself.[22] It would seem that several of these are based on memoranda of lectures (*scholai*)[23] of Philodemus' masters. In some cases even parts of the drafts survive.[24] These books provide us with important insights into the discussions which took place both inside the Epicurean school and with opponents, e.g. the Stoics, and so are an important source of information for Hellenistic Stoicism too. Philodemus wrote among other things on signs, theology, ethical subjects, literary theory and rhetoric. Of particular relevance are the remains of his historical treatise, entitled *Arrangement of the Philosophers* (Σύνταξις τῶν φιλοσόφων), especially the two books dealing with the Academics and the Stoics. Of great interest too is his polemical treatise *On the Stoics*.[25]

Among the many works of the Jewish exegete of the Old Testament, Philo of Alexandria (died after AD 40), there are also several philosophical treatises which contain a considerable amount of information on Hellenistic philosophy. Two of these, *On the Eternity of the World* and *That Every Good Man is Free*, are extant in Greek; the other two, *On Providence*[26] and *Alexander or Whether Irrational Animals Possess Reason*, in a very literal sixth-century Armenian translation. Philo discussed topics which were of interest to an orthodox Jewish audience, and in some ways his position is comparable to that of Cicero *vis-à-vis* his Roman public. Like other Jews before and a whole crowd of Christian authors after him, he was convinced that the Greek philosophers had been either directly inspired by God or cribbed their doctrines from the Old Testament. Accordingly, their views could be used to interpret the Old Testament (as Philo did in his treatises devoted to the exegesis of the 'books of Moses') or to discuss issues which arose in the context of its interpretation.[27] For this reason, commentaries and homilies by learned Christians on individual books and passages of the Old as well as the New Testament may contain sections that are of interest for the historiography of philosophy, including Hellenistic philosophy, as long

---

[22] For modern editions see list of editions of sources and fragments, and bibliography. The villa also seems to have possessed a text of Lucretius, see Kleve 1989; but the fragments are minimal.

[23] The Epicurean Diogenes of Tarsus wrote a treatise entitled *Epilektai Scholai* or *Epilekta*, in at least twenty books; see D.L. x.97,120,136,138. On *scholai* see Sedley 1989a, 103–4; cf. also Quint. *Inst.* 1. 7.   [24] Dorandi 1991d; cf. also Manetti 1994 on the *Anon. Lond.*

[25] See Dorandi 1990a and 1990b; texts: Dorandi 1982b, 1991b, 1994b.

[26] Several passages in Greek from *Prov.* II have been preserved by Eusebius.

[27] Mansfeld 1988a, Runia 1990, Runia 1993; in general Ridings 1995.

as one does not forget that these works have been composed from a particular point of view.

The date of the remains of a more general work, or works, by a certain Arius Didymus remains uncertain;[28] it may be as late as the third century AD. A systematic treatment of Stoic and of Peripatetic ethics which with some confidence may be attributed to him has been preserved in Stobaeus. Substantial fragments of his treatment of the physics of Aristotle (and his followers) and of the physical doctrines of the more important Stoics have been preserved by Eusebius and Stobaeus.[29] The title or titles of the work or works are not certain; fragments are quoted as from the *On Sects*, or *Abstract(s)*. One of the problems is that *epitomē* ('abstract') may pertain either to an abridgement of Didymus' work or to abstracts made from, or representing, the originals themselves.

Frequent references to Hellenistic philosophical doctrines are found in the voluminous writings of Plutarch (after 45–after 120). Of special importance are treatises such as the *On Moral Virtue*, and the polemical works against the Stoics and the Epicureans[30] which contain numerous verbatim quotations. The anti-Epicurean treatises are the *That Epicurus Makes a Pleasant Life Impossible*, the *Reply to Colotes* and the *Is 'Live Unknown' a Wise Precept?*. The treatises directed against the Stoics are the *On Stoic Self-Contradictions*, the *Against the Stoics on Common Conceptions*, and an abstract of the *The Stoics Talk More Paradoxically than the Poets*. The even more voluminous extant works of Galen (*c.* 130–*c.* 210) are also peppered with references and verbatim quotations (but the special treatises which he devoted to Stoic and Epicurean philosophy are lost).[31] Of major importance is his great treatise *On the Doctrines of Plato and Hippocrates*, in which he argues against Chrysippus' philosophy of mind and ethics, and attempts to pin down his opponent by verbatim quotation on a fairly generous scale.[32] At *PHP* VIII.2.12–14, Galen describes his method by saying that he does not explain 'every expression, as writers of commentaries do',

---

[28] The identification of Arius Didymus with the Stoic Arius, court philosopher to the emperor Augustus, has been challenged by Heine 1869, 613–14 and Göransson 1995, 203–26.

[29] Moraux 1973, 259–443, Kahn 1983, Long 1983a, Hahm 1990; for the physical fragments Diels 1879, 69–87, 447–72, and Moraux 1973, 277–305 (on the Peripatetic section only). Göransson 1995, 206–7, 219–26, argues that the attribution to Didymus of the section on Stoic ethics is less certain than that of the section on the Peripatos, and that the provenance of the majority of the anonymous fragments in Stobaeus attributed to Arius Didymus by Diels is problematic. The latter argument is answered by Runia 1996a, cf. in general Mansfeld and Runia 1997, 238–64.

[30] Babut 1969, Hershbell 1992a, 1992b. A number of philosophical works by Plutarch have been lost; see list in Einarson and De Lacy 1967, 2.   [31] Titles at *Lib. Prop.* XIX 47–8.

[32] Vegetti 1986, Tieleman 1996; in general Hankinson 1992. Much remains to be done on Galen as a source for Greek philosophy.

but only 'those statements which give consistency to the doctrine'. A selective use of the commentary method by a person who did write a number of commentaries dealing with every expression, namely on Hippocratic works. Galen is also our major and in many cases only source for Hellenistic medicine,[33] and his essay *On Sects for Beginners* is still a most useful introduction to the doctrines of the principal medical schools. Another important source for Hellenistic medicine is the second part of the so-called *Anonymus Londinensis*,[34] to be dated to the second century AD, and information on the Dogmatists and Empiricists is also found in the proem of Celsus *De Medicina*, written in the early first century.[35]

Much information, though relatively little verbatim quotation (at least of Hellenistic philosophers, Timon excepted), is to be found in the works of the Neopyrrhonist philosopher-cum-physician Sextus Empiricus (probably second century AD). These are the treatise *Outlines of Pyrrhonism* in three books and the composite work *Adversus mathematicos*, consisting of a treatise (now) in six books *Against the Professors* (of grammar, mathematics etc., *M* I–VI) and of the remaining books of the original *Adversus mathematicos*, viz. two *Against the Logicians* (*M* VII–VIII), two *Against the Physicists* (*M* IX–X) and one *Against the Ethicists* (*M* XI).[36] From the titles of *M* VII–XI it is clear that Sextus' approach is not only polemical but also systematic. His aim is not to tell us what certain historical figures believed (and then to show the weaknesses of these beliefs), but rather to tell us what, in general, the Dogmatists believe and then to show the weaknesses of Dogmatism. Yet the Stoics are his most cherished opponents (*PH* I 65).

One of our most precious sources is the already-mentioned treatise in ten books of the otherwise unknown Diogenes Laertius (probably *c.* 230), entitled *Lives and Maxims of those who Have Distinguished themselves in Philosophy and the Doctrines of Each Sect*.[37] The Minor Socratics are treated in book II, the Academics up to Clitomachus in book VI, the Peripatetics up to

---

[33] Deichgräber 1930, W. D. Smith 1979, von Staden 1982, von Staden 1989, Lloyd 1991b, von Staden 1991. On the various connections of the Hellenistic schools with Hippocrates and Hippocratic medicine see Kudlien 1989.

[34] Text: Diels 1893; new edn in preparation, see Manetti 1986.

[35] Commentary by Mudry 1982; see also Deuse 1993.

[36] For the original form of *M* and the suggestion that the actual books VII–XI were originally VI–X see Blomqvist 1974, who hypothesizes that the original *M* I–V are lost. But the argument of Cortassa 1989 that the actual books III–IV originally were one and that the lost books of *M* are fewer is more plausible. On Sextus see Annas 1992b, Classen 1992, Decleva Caizzi 1992b, Döring 1992, Hülser 1992, Ioppolo 1992, Isnardi Parente 1992, Sedley 1992a. Note that in these papers Sextus' systematic presentations have been carved up according to prosopography and philosophical school, though Decleva Caizzi sketches a programme for the study of Sextus as an author. For a bibliography of the important writings on Sextus and related sceptic themes by K. Janáček see Barnes 1992, 4298–9.

[37] Martini 1899, 82–3, 86–7. For Soranus' similar title see above, n. 11.

Demetrius and Heraclides in book v, the Cynics up to Menedemus in book VI, the Stoics in book VII (which originally ended with Cornutus),[38] the Pyrrhonists in book IX, and Epicurus and the Epicureans in book x.[39] From the sequence of schools treated it is clear that Diogenes' approach is more historical in our sense of the word than for instance that of Sextus.

Other authors and books may be treated more briefly. A rather interesting little handbook of uncertain date is pseudo-Andronicus *On the Affections and the Virtues*,[40] which provides parallels for the treatment of Stoic ethics in Diogenes Laertius and Arius Didymus and for the mix of Stoic and Peripatetic ethics at Cic. *Inv.* II.159–78. The works of Seneca and Epictetus may be used, though with caution, for the understanding of early Stoic ethics. A rather orthodox line seems to be followed by the first century AD Stoic Hierocles.[41] In the *Attic Nights* of Aulus Gellius (second century AD), a work written to amuse and instruct rather than for purposes of serious study, we nevertheless find useful information concerning Stoicism and Pyrrhonism.[42] Among the works of Alexander of Aphrodisias (died after AD 200) three treatises must be singled out because a Peripatetic alternative to Stoic doctrines is offered: the *On Mixture*, the *On Fate*, both extant in Greek, and the *On Providence* which survives in Arabic.[43] These should be used with some caution because it is not always certain that the Stoicism Alexander criticizes is Hellenistic. The learned Christian Clement of Alexandria (later part of the second century AD), whose attitude to Greek philosophy is indebted to that of Philo,[44] has worked important bits of information into the extant eight books of his *Strōmata* ('*Patchworks*');[45] book VIII consists of abstracts,[46] most of which deal with philosophical themes. Other works by Clement are also relevant in this respect, as are those of the learned Origen (*c.* 185–*c.* 250).[47] The multi-book *Praeparatio Evangelica* of another not less learned Christian, Eusebius of Caesarea (*c.* 260–*c.* 340), who was sitting in a splendid library, is a huge anthology of verbatim excerpts from a plurality of authors, with comments and connecting passages by Eusebius himself. In this way, passages from among others Arius Didymus, Diogenianus,

---

[38] Mansfeld 1986, 358–60, Dorandi 1992a.

[39] Minor Socratics: Giannantoni 1986b, Knoepfler 1991; Academics: Long 1986a, Dorandi 1992b; Peripatetics: Moraux 1986, Sollenberger 1992; Cynics: Goulet-Cazé 1992; Stoics: Mansfeld 1986; Pyrrhonists: Barnes 1992; Epicurus: Mansfeld 1986, 373–9. On Diog. Laert. in general see Schwartz 1905, Mejer 1978, Mejer 1992. The manuscript tradition has been sorted out by Knoepfler 1991, but see Dorandi 1995c for additional information.

[40] Text in Glibert-Thirry 1977; both longer and shorter versions were in circulation.

[41] The text of the papyrus has been newly edited with commentary by Bastianini and Long 1992.

[42] Goulet 1989.

[43] On Alexander see Sharples 1987; texts in Todd 1976, Sharples 1983, Ruland 1976.

[44] Lilla 1970, Runia 1993, 132–56. Cf. also Spanneut 1957, Le Boulluec 1994.

[45] Méhat 1966.   [46] Nautin 1976.   [47] Dorival 1992.

Numenius and Aristocles have been preserved which are important for the history of Hellenistic Stoicism, Pyrrhonism, and Academic scepticism. The first two books of the huge and invaluable anthology of Ioannes Stobaeus (fifth century), which survives only in mutilated form, are called *Eclogae physicae et ethicae* ('*Selections Dealing with Physics and Ethics*'). This systematically structured work has preserved much of Arius Didymus and Aëtius, but in the *Eclogae* as well as in the following books, the so-called *Florilegium*, other precious texts too have been preserved; we may recall, for instance, Cleanthes' *Hymn* (*Ecl.* 1.1.12).

One of the factors involved in the survival of these secondary sources is the popularity of an author as a literary model and/or his usefulness for Christian writers. Cicero and Plutarch, who were more famous for their non-philosophical works, were much admired, and Cicero's philosophical works proved useful to the Latin Fathers of the West.[48] Philo survived because he was used and admired by some of the learned Christians of the East.[49] Yet a good number of Plutarch's so-called *moralia*, as well as some of Cicero's *philosophica*, have been lost, and there are gaps in the corpus of Philo's writings too.

IV *Quellenforschung*

Understandably, scholars would like to go back from these secondary sources to (the) original works, or at least to intermediary secondary sources closer in time to these originals and so, supposedly, truer to them. Because from a historical point of view the information provided by the original work of a philosopher is to be preferred to a later rendering, rehash, or reinterpretation, however competent or philosophically interesting, much work has been done to ferret out the lost original sources of the derivative sources for Hellenistic philosophy which we still have. We may for example ask ourselves whether Lucretius versified extant and/or lost works by Epicurus, or also used works by younger Epicureans. This is important for our view of Epicurus as well as of Lucretius. The rediscovery of Theophrastus' previously lost *Metarsiology*, one of the works used in Epic. *Ep. Pyth.*, has shown that certain passages in Lucretius may derive from the *Greater Epitomē*.[50] It is also worth our while to try to find out to what extent Seneca may have used particular works of Chrysippus

---

[48] For Cicero see Hagendahl 1958, 399–401, 1967, 52–168, 486–553, Ogilvie 1978, 59–72, MacKendrick 1989, 258–60; for Lucretius Hagendahl 1958, 9–88, Ogilvie 1978, 15–16; for Seneca Lausberg 1970, 14–35, Hagendahl 1967, 676–9, Trillitzsch 1971, Vol. I 120–85, Vol. II 362–83, Ogilvie 1978, 72.   [49] Runia 1993, 16–30.
[50] Mansfeld 1992b (J. Schmidt 1990, 34–7 is out of date).

directly.[51] This kind of inquiry has been traditionally called *Quellenforschung* (or *Quellenanalyse, Quellenkritik*), derived from the German word for source, *Quelle*. This enjoys a bad reputation today, especially among students of ancient philosophy,[52] though our scholarship is still much dependent on the results of the largely forgotten investigations carried out in the nineteenth and early twentieth centuries.[53] But one instance which does not know itself is as much *à la mode* as ever, the quest for the historical Socrates. Yet the only Socrates available is a *plurale tantum*, namely Plato's + Xenophon's + Aeschines' etc., etc., to be augmented with a crowd of Socrateses according to the various receptions in the Hellenistic and later schools. In biblical scholarship the method is as alive as ever, for example in the study of the synoptic Gospels and the Pentateuch. As a matter of fact, *Quellenforschung* is a relative of another genealogical method which today is still considered to be indispensable, namely stemmatology, or the establishing of a family tree for a plurality of extant manuscripts containing a text, or a corpus of texts, though we have become aware of the phenomenon of so-called open transmission.[54] An often used method (deriving from New Testament studies) is that of the printing of similar texts in parallel columns.[55]

We may distinguish between two main models, or forms, of *Quellenforschung*. The first is the tracing back of a single extant work, for instance the *Iliad* or the *Odyssey*, to a plurality of sources; the hypothesis that these epics have been combined from a number of independent shorter poems, to which other material was added later, was already formulated in the seventeenth century. The second is the tracing back of a plurality of extant texts, or parts thereof, to a hypothetical single source. Just as all lagers are the offspring of *Pilsener Urquell*, so a plurality of manuscripts may derive from a single lost ancestor, the so-called archetype.[56] An exceedingly influential instance of this second type of *Quellenforschung* is the reconstruction of the lost source commonly called Aëtius, which

---

[51] Fillion-Lahille 1984, 51–118.

[52] In other areas of classics it can still, or again, be practised quite successfully; see e.g. Brunt 1980 (ancient historians), Cameron 1993 (Greek anthology).

[53] For precedents and parallels in Old Testament studies see Ackroyd 1970, Kraus 1982, Smend 1984, for New Testament studies Evans 1970, 265–77, Kümmel 1970, Mansfeld and Runia 1997, 95–7.

[54] Diels 1879, 40 combines the direct, indirect and MSS traditions of ps.Plutarch in a single stemma. Cf. also Bernheim 1908, 396, 400, 403 (on texts), and 420 (on MSS). See further Mansfeld 1998.   [55] Mansfeld and Runia 1997, 88–94, 116–20.

[56] Mansfeld and Runia 1997, 88, 91. A comparable application of this geneticist paradigm is the construction of the family tree of Indo-European languages and the hypothesis of a common lost mother tongue (and lost intermediary ancestors of e.g. the group of Germanic, or Celtic, languages). This began with Schlegel 1808 and esp. Bopp 1816; see e.g. Timpanaro 1972.

according to Diels' analysis is the ancestor, or source of, the extant *Placita* of pseudo-Plutarch and of the parallel sections in Stobaeus and Theodoret.[57]

These two forms may be combined in several ways. A plurality of sources may for instance be posited for (parts of) a particular book of Philodemus, or Cicero, or Lucretius, or Philo, or Sextus, or Diogenes Laertius, and sections in these authors which are very much similar may then be traced back to single sources that have been lost.[58] This procedure may be of help in understanding passages which remain in part obscure when studied in isolation, and also in eliminating errors. Furthermore, noticing correspondences brings out the differences much more clearly, and so helps to determine the stance of an individual author. It goes without saying, however, that pinpointing a source, or shared tradition, is not equivalent to interpreting a thought. Source-criticism should be no more than an unavoidable means to an end, that is, the understanding of ideas in philosophy.

We should moreover not overlook that (to mention only one instance) an author such as Cicero, though not a professional philosopher, really knew a lot of philosophy by heart, as it were.[59] He has one of his speakers (Cotta) address his opponent as follows:

I have memorized all your arguments, and in the right order. (*ND* III.10)

---

[57] Diels 1879, Runia 1989, Mansfeld 1990a, 1992c, Laks 1996; Diels' reconstruction revised in Mansfeld and Runia 1997. On the *Plac.* see below; the Arabic translation of pseudo-Plutarch (not of Aëtius!) has been edited and translated by Daiber 1980; the Greek text has been newly edited by Mau 1971, and edited and translated with some comments by Lachenaud 1993. The variety of *Quellenforschung* practised by e.g. Corssen 1878, a pupil of Usener just like Diels, has been far less successful because it does not much more than substitute one name, e.g. Posidonius, for another, e.g. Cicero, or (when a plurality of sources is postulated) is based on the assumption of contradictions in the text. This is pseudo-precision, and highly subjective. But exceptions exist; cf. below, n. 59 *ad fin.*

[58] For instance the Epicurean doxographies in Phld. *Piet.* (*PHerc.* 1428) and Cic. *ND* I (below, text to n. 80), and sections in Cic. *ND* III and S.E. *M* IX dealing with the gods (see below, p. 475), have so much in common that a shared source is plausible. Baltes, in Dörrie and Baltes 1993, 165–6, points out that interpretations of individual Plato passages in Cicero, Philo, Seneca and Plutarch can only be explained against the backdrop of a commentary tradition.

[59] So rightly Boyancé 1936, but note that his argument against *Quellenforschung* (cf. above, n. 57) is based on Cicero and literature related to Cicero alone, and that he has its history begin with Madvig's edn. of *Fin.* of 1839 (Madvig, followed by others, took *Ad Att.* XII.52.3 too literally, where Cicero seems to say that his works are mere 'transcripts', *apographa*; the text moreover is corrupt). Yet Boyancé accepts that in certain privileged cases source-critical comparison is useful, a point often missed by his followers, e.g. Lévy 1996. On the correct and incorrect uses of *Quellenanalyse* Bernheim (1908) 358–503, 529–70 is still very much worth reading; see esp. 404–13 on how to reconstruct lost sources ('Nachweis verlorener Quellen'), with references to predecessors of Boyancé dealing with the sources of Livy, or the traditions of Carolingian literature. See now the judicious remarks on the main source (Panaetius' Περὶ τοῦ καθήκοντος) in relation to *Off.*, and on Cicero's own contributions, in Dyck 1996, 18–21, and his commentary, *passim.*

The practice of memorizing the main points of a speech in the right order was taught in the rhetorical schools, which makes Cotta's statement dramatically credible. Cicero writes to his friend Atticus for books and has his own libraries. Nevertheless, in some cases his sources were things he knew and remembered, or believed he knew and remembered, rather than things he had just looked up or was directly translating, or paraphrasing, from a book in front of him, though he often did translate or check. But his attitude towards his sources was quite free; speaking of his treatment of Stoic ethics, he points out:

> I shall follow them [. . .] not as a translator but shall, as I am wont to do, draw from these sources what seems right, using my own judgement and making my own decisions. (*Fin.* III.7)

So *Quellenforschung*, even when done properly, may remain somewhat inexact.

v Genres

History of philosophy not as philosophy but as history, or as the ideal of an impartial and exact rendering of what earlier philosophers said rather than an interpretation, evaluation or even critique of what they said, implied or meant, is not an ancient genre. In fact, the methodological principle involved was first clearly formulated and applied in the nineteenth century. In antiquity history of philosophy was part of philosophy, just as, at least in certain cases, the history of medicine was part of medical science. The previous history of philosophy and medicine was seen as important from a systematic and scientific rather than a purely historical point of view. This is in agreement with the growing 'classicist' tendency, beginning in the first century BC, to appeal to famous figures from the distant past – this not being 'past', *passé*, *vergangen*. Such a systematic approach to one's philosophical predecessors is already found in Plato, and on a much larger and far more influential scale in Aristotle. Originality or novelty (*kainotomia*) was a dirty word; the various philosophical schools tended to consider themselves (or were considered by others) to belong with the general tradition of Greek philosophy and to depend on past masters.

We should therefore look a bit more closely at the various ancient genres which, in a loose sense of the word, we may call historiographic, or which contain material that is important for the history of philosophy: (i) doxography, (ii) biography, (iii) literature on sects (*Peri Haireseōn*), (iv) literature on the successions of the philosophers in their respective schools

(*Diadochai*), (v) collections of maxims (*gnōmai*), apophthegms, anecdotes, pronouncement stories (*chreiai*), and brief abstracts,[60] and (vi) introductions (*Eisagōgai*). It should however be borne in mind that these genres are not rigidly distinct.[61]

VI Doxography

The widely used and frequently misused modern term doxography was coined by Diels for a genre he reconstructed and which he believed to be reliable because he regarded Theophrastus' lost *Physical Tenets* (*Physikai doxai*) as the ultimate ancestor of the tradition.[62] This genre was, in his view, to be sharply distinguished from fanciful biography. There is some truth to this distinction,[63] but as we shall see it does not hold generally. Unavoidably Diels also had to allow for a mixed bio-doxographic genre. Doxography according to him is the systematic description of the tenets (*placita*, *doxai*, *areskonta*), or doctrines, of the philosophers.

But Diels is responsible for a confusion. The genre he derives from Theophrastus, which deals with collections of briefly formulated tenets from a systematic point of view, should not right away be put on a par with the often extensive description of the doctrines of a single philosopher, or school, such as we find in the individual books of Diogenes Laertius' treatise, or in Cicero. Oddly enough, Diels neglected to inquire for what purposes these collections of contrasting *doxai* had been assembled.[64] From the extant *Placita* of pseudo-Plutarch (restricted to tenets in the fields of natural philosophy) and related large and smaller excerpts in other authors which he very successfully traced back to a single lost work,[65] it is already quite clear that such tracts are concerned with

---

[60] The distinction between a *gnōmē* and an apophthegm/anecdote is that the latter links the maxim to a specific person; the *chreia* often develops this further into a little story (Nassen Poulos 1981). Useful survey of Greek collections of *gnōmai* in Küchler 1979, 236–61; for the problems involved in the reconstruction of the gnomic traditions, for which the material surviving in Arabic appears to be indispensable, see Gutas 1975. Full and exemplary treatment at Berger 1984, 1049–74, 1092–110. In anthologies material could survive anonymously; see e.g. the cento of fragments of Epicurus at Porph. *Marc.* 27–32 which presumably derives from a florilegium.

[61] In general see Berger 1984, 1036–48, and for the genres mentioned in the text Mansfeld 1986, 303–10.

[62] Diels followed his *Doktorvater* Usener, oblivious of the fact that Theophrastus too had a sort of *Doktorvater*, viz. Aristotle. For the correct title of Theophrastus' treatise (called *Physikōn Doxai* by Usener and Diels) see Mansfeld 1990a, 1992c, and for Diels' method Mansfeld and Runia 1997, 64–110.

[63] D.L. III.47 distinguishes the *bios* 'life', from the *doxai* 'doctrines', of Plato, and VII.38 the *bios* of Zeno from the *dogmata* of the Stoics.   [64] Mansfeld 1990a, 1992c.

[65] See above, pp. 14–15. We may note in passing that the *epitomē* of ps.Plutarch is extant, while Aëtius and his predecessors are lost; clearly, shorter works have a better chance to survive.

problems and the alternative solutions to these problems provided by the philosophers of nature, and in some cases doctors and astronomers. In the *Placita* literature the tenets are more important than the names of those said to have held them. Names often occur in systematic rather than chronological order, the system of arrangement being that of the tenets, and name-labels may be attached in a cavalier way. It may happen that tenets which we can check because the original ultimate sources (e.g. Plato, Aristotle) survive have been compressed and modified almost beyond recognition. Caution is therefore an absolute must whenever no such check is possible. The problems themselves (coinciding with chapters or parts of chapters) are arranged according to a systematic pattern based on standard topics and check-lists of questions relating to these topics. For instance on the gods the following questions are asked: do they exist? what are they, i.e. what do they consist of? how are they, i.e. what are their attributes (e.g. what is their shape)? where are they?, etc.[66]

I see no objection to calling Aëtius a doxographer and would provisionally define a doxographer of the Aëtian type as someone who provides materials for discussion both for the purpose of training and as a starting-point for further research. The author of an earlier collection which according to Diels is Aëtius' source and which was used by e.g. Varro and Cicero however, seems to have had an axe to grind and been a person of sceptic leanings, desirous of producing deadlocks through the disagreement of the tenets (*diaphōnia*). Such a diaphonic structure is still clearly recognizable in Aëtius. I believe that this earlier work, or rather (one of) its predecessor(s), was already used by Chrysippus.[67]

This brings us to doxography at one remove, namely the exploitation of doxographic materials relating to a definite issue in physics, psychology, theology and metaphysics. In fact, collections of the Aëtius type were widely utilized. They offered a frame of reference and enabled philosophers or scientists to provide an overview of and arguments against those views they wanted to discuss. Various motives could be involved: rejection, appropriation, revision, supplementation or complete replacement. Ethical doxographies were compiled for the same end. To give one example, Plutarch, before arguing in favour of his own view concerning moral virtue, writes:[68]

---

[66] Aët. 1.7, 11.4.15–17. These types of questions derive from Aristotle; see Mansfeld 1992c, 70–109, also for their impact on the treatment of philosophical issues in the later literature.

[67] Mansfeld 1989c.

[68] The doxography follows. The extensive doxography concerned with the *telos* at Clem. *Strom.* 11.127.1–133.7 is structurally different from the brief one at Cic. *Fin.* 11.34–5 and the fuller one at *Fin.* v.16–23; for those in Cicero see Algra 1997.

It is better to give a brief overview of the (tenets) of the others, not so much for the sake of the record as that my own view may become clearer and more firmly established when these others have been presented first. (*Virt. Mor.* 440e)

Readers were obviously familiar with this technique. Aristotle is the important pioneer; he used his own collections of *doxai* which most of the time he used as a prelude to working out an original solution, in physics as well as in ethics. Epic. *Ep. Pyth.* applied the method in a way which is different from Aristotle's, because for certain problems in cosmo-meteorology he allowed for sets of equally feasible solutions, rejecting only those which flatly contradicted the phenomena.[69] Wilamowitz, referring to Woltjer's book on Lucretius, once suggested that apart from the Peripatetic doxographic tradition one should also allow for and try to reconstruct an Epicurean tradition. I believe that this split is unnecessary and that the differences can be explained in terms of the specific use made of the available material.[70]

The *Placita* of pseudo-Plutarch and its relatives and predecessors were used by numerous authors, from at least Chrysippus to Philoponus. But the sections in their works based on or inspired by doxographic overviews of the Aëtius type should as a rule *not* be called doxographic. This also holds for comparable sections in Sextus (and presumably Aenesidemus), who needed doxographic collections of opposed views to produce suspension of judgement. The same goes for Philo, who selects tenets according to agreement or disagreement with Scripture, and also for a number of Christian authors, who may argue that all the pagans were wrong, or that some among them were right to some extent. The use of a doxography as a first orientation may encourage an author to look up an original text, and to quote or paraphrase a passage or a few pages. To give an example, Cicero when writing *Tusc.* checked Dicaearchus' own formulation of his view on the existence and location of the soul and its regent part (*Tusc.* I.21).

VII On sects

The other historiographic genres dealing with the philosophies of the past are more difficult to determine because clear examples are no longer extant, or at least not completely extant.[71] The treatise of Diogenes

---

[69] See below, pp. 288–9, 505–7.

[70] Von Wilamowitz-Moellendorff 1881, 2 n. 1, Woltjer 1877; Mansfeld 1994a.

[71] Useful overview of genres, authors and titles at Mejer 1978, 60–95.

Laertius seems to be a combination of a variety of genres: biography, doxography (though not according to the Aëtian pattern), literature dealing
with successions and with the sects, and collections of maxims and anecdotes which are not a historiographic genre in the proper sense of the
word.[72] This odd medley of the insipid and the invaluable has often puzzled scholars, but here the young Cicero provides us with the key.[73] At
Inv. II.116-48, he deals with the interpretation of written documents such
as wills and laws, which often allow of more than one interpretation. We
are told how to tackle this problem; the most important piece of advice
runs as follows:[74]

> One ought to estimate what the writer meant *from the rest of his writings
> and from his acts, words, character and life*, and to examine the whole docu-
> ment which contains the ambiguity in question in all its parts, to see if
> any thing agrees with our interpretation or is opposed to the sense in
> which our opponent interprets it. (*Inv.* II.117)

The backdrop of Cicero's advice is much wider and pertains to the study
of written documents in general, especially in the fields of literature and
philosophy. The study of the life, activities and sayings of a philosopher
was regarded as an indispensable preliminary to that of his writings. In
those cases where no books were available the 'life' itself, including acts
and apophthegms etc. and in some cases private documents, had to
suffice. Conversely, if biographical data were unavailable they were made
up from what a person wrote, or from what others were supposed to have
written about him. Practices such as these gave ancient biography, or at
least part of it, its bad name.[75] But I am not now concerned with the reliability of the protean genre from a historical point of view but with its his-
toric function. Life and work, or teaching, have to be in agreement; in
some cases the works may have been used to (re)construct the relevant
aspects of the 'life', but the biography itself, be it detailed or compressed,
was certainly believed to be needed to understand the works and doctrines.[76]

---

[72] On these as important ingredients in the biographies of philosophers see Gallo 1980, 13, Nassen
  Poulos 1981; in general Arrighetti 1994. For the fictitious aspect of certain types of *chreia* see
  Glucker 1988. Cf. also above, n. 60. Interesting hypothesis concerning Diogenes' method of
  composition in Goulet 1997.

[73] Mansfeld 1994b, 177-82.

[74] Cf. Cic. *Part. Or.* 132, which is less clear. A more conventional treatment at e.g. [Cic.] *Rhet. Her.*
  I.19-20, II.14, Cic. *De Or.* I.139-40, Quint. *Inst.* VII.5.5-6; cf. Leeman and Pinkster 1981,
  237-8.

[75] Leo 1901, 104-8, Dihle 1970, 104-7, Arrighetti 1987, 141-8, 164-7, Momigliano 1993, 70.
  Canfora 1993 is a fine pastiche of a dubious ancient biography.

[76] See further Arrighetti 1994, Mansfeld 1994b, 177-91.

The literature *On Sects*, a Hellenistic genre, dealt with the doctrines of the important philosophical and medical schools. Lost works with this title are attributed to various people by Diogenes Laertius, and have been used by him at one or more removes. The first to write a book on the philosophical sects seems to have been Hippobotus.[77] Important philosophers, e.g. the Stoic Panaetius (D.L. 11.87) and the Academic sceptic Clitomachus (D.L. 11.92) wrote works with this title. Galen's extant *On Sects for Beginners* belongs with this genre, but also with another, the *Eisagōgai* or *Introductions* literature. The remains of Arius Didymus' work(s) presumably belong here as well, and we may perhaps believe that it/they compared the doctrines of the main schools in the domains of logic, ethics and physics respectively.[78] A brief abstract (not ethical but epistemological) is cited at Stob. 11.1.17 as 'Of Didymus: from the On Sects' (Διδύμου ἐκ τοῦ Περὶ αἱρέσεων). One aim of this type of literature seems to be to offer reasonably objective information on the divergent views. But it could also serve to set off the doctrines more sharply against each other by way of a sort of blow-up of a chapter, or a set of chapters, in Aëtius. Another aim could be to defend the views of a particular school against those of the others. The word *hairesis* (usually translated 'school' or 'sect') means 'choice' or 'option', then also 'what is chosen'.[79] A choice for something as a rule also is a choice against something else, but a more or less impartial overview of the options that are open is also an option.

A number of Cicero's philosophical works are composed according to this contrasting pattern too. In *ND*, for instance, the different views of the Epicureans and the Stoics on the gods are treated in the first part of *ND* i and in ii respectively, and the Academic speaker argues against in the second part of i and in iii. *ND* i moreover includes at its beginning a doxography, or a survey of the contrasting tenets of the philosophers starting with Thales about the gods from an Epicurean point of view (*ND*

---

[77] Remains of Hippobotus in Gigante 1983c. On medical works entitled *Against the Sects*, *On the Empiricist Sect*, and *On the Sect of Herophilus* see von Staden 1982, 77–80. Porph. *In Ptol. Harm.* 3.1–12 says that there are numerous *haireseis* of musical theorists, the most prominent being the Pythagorean and the Aristoxenean; 5.11–13 cf. 25.4–6 he cites the *On the Difference of the Pythagorean Musical Theory from the Aristoxenean* by Didymus 'the musician', on whom see Barker 1989, 230.

[78] Cf. above n. 28 and text thereto. The main mistake of Giusta 1964–7, which contains much useful material, is that he believes in the existence of a lost ethical doxography parallel to the physical doxography of Aëtius.

[79] How 'choice' could come to mean 'school of thought' – for which see Glucker 1978, 166–93 – and then 'school' *tout court* is illustrated e.g. at Alb. *Intr.* 150.15 H., where the person who has decided to become a Platonist is indicated as τὰ Πλάτωνος αἱρούμενος 'one who takes Plato's side' (see LSJ *s.v.* αἱρέω b.2); cf. also Cic. *ND* 1.85.

I.18–43),[80] ostensibly intended to shore up the argument that the *doxa* of Epicurus is the only correct one, but simultaneously providing a thoroughly doxographic introduction to the subject of the treatise. Accordingly, *ND* is not a representative of a 'pure' genre. The questions concerned with 'existence', 'what-it-is', 'how-it-is' which to a large extent determine the structure of the discussion in this work are familiar from the doxographies of the Aëtius type as well. The Greek term for such a general issue is *thesis*, the Latin *quaestio infinita*, i.e. an issue, or problem, which is not restricted to individuals or particulars. When you have such a *quaestio*, the views about its solution will inevitably differ.[81]

Though some among Cicero's treatises in the field of ethics, i.e. *Tusc.* and especially *Off.*, are more one-sided, the major work *Fin.* is devoted to the exposition and critical comparison of the various views. The overviews of the doctrines of the schools in D.L. II–X, I believe, are also indebted to the literature *On Sects*, for traces of comparison (*sunkrisis*) are still visible.[82] Though the sceptically inclined Cicero and the more irenic Diogenes Laertius want to inform their public rather than to take sides in the dispute, preferences may be expressed (Cicero is very critical of Epicureanism and not always fair,[83] Diogenes favours it). Yet it is important to acknowledge that the works *On Sects* are written from the point of view that the doctrines are significantly divergent, that the views of the schools are in many ways opposed to each other, and that – as Cicero approvingly says – this makes philosophy a really worthwhile and ongoing affair:

> In Greece itself philosophy would never have been held in such high honour, if it had not derived its vitality from the disputes and disagreements among its greatest practitioners. (*Tusc.* II.4)[84]

Again and again, Cicero highlights the disagreements of the philosophers, both from one school to another or within one and the same

---

[80] Largely paralleled in Phld. *Piet.* (*PHerc.* 1428); see Diels 1879, 531–50, Henrichs 1974, and above, n. 58. Obbink (1996) argues that Philodemus is Cicero's immediate source, but this cannot be proved, and *Piet.* may even have been written later than the *ND*.

[81] Mansfeld 1990a, 3193–208, or 1992c, 70–93. On the *thesis* see Throm 1932.

[82] E.g. D.L. II.86–90 (with reference to Panaetius, *On Sects*) and X.136–8, critical comparison of the Epicureans and the Cyrenaics; VII.121 versus X.119, on the question whether the philosopher should behave as a Cynic; VII.127, contrast between Stoics and Peripatetics which recalls the argument of Cic. *Fin.* III–V.

[83] He sometimes exploits the vulgar misunderstanding of the ethics and fails to take notice of developments in the school; see Erler 1992b. But his treatment of Epicurus in *Tusc.* v.26, 31, 73–5, 88–9 is quite fair.

[84] This point is applied to different views among the Christians by Orig. *Cels.* III.12 (who adduces the philosophical as well as the medical sects); cf. further Greg. Thaum. *Or. Pan.* XIV.170–2 (text in Crouzel 1969). The biblical proof-text is *Gal.* 5:20.

school.[85] Depending on the personal preferences or school allegiance of the author who is involved, this attitude may lead to subjective reporting, or even to the defence of a specific doctrine. Differences of opinion within one school are also believed to be relevant. They are reported on a large scale e.g. in D.L. VII, on the Stoics. The author of the ethical doxography *apud* Stob. II.7, p. 42.5–6 explicitly says that he intends to report them. In the physical fragments of Arius Didymus differences between individual Stoics are sometimes noted. The fact that in the ethical part the Stoics and the Peripatetics are discussed *per se* but also occasionally compared to each other conforms to the 'on sects' scheme of exposition. Numenius' treatise on the differences between the Academics and Plato makes disagreement its main theme and then argues for a return to the earlier doctrine of Pythagoras-cum-Plato.

Accounts of doctrines in logic, physics and ethics in the literature *On Sects* may to some extent be based on *Introductions* to (*Eisagōgai*) or *Brief Accounts* (*Epitomai*) of (parts of) the philosophical sub-disciplines written by members of the school at issue.[86] Arguably, one of the motives behind Diogenes Laertius' transcription of Epicurus' *Letters* is that no better or more authoritative *epitomai* of Epicurean doctrine were available. His account of Stoic philosophy seems to a large extent to be dependent on introductory tracts written by teachers of Stoic philosophy. Chrysippus himself already wrote *Eisagōgai*,[87] though these were not always brief.

VIII Successions

Another originally Hellenistic genre is the literature on the *Successions (of the Philosophers) (Diadochai)*.[88] Of these too there are no pure instances or large portions extant, though Philodemus' books on respectively the Academics and the Stoics (which also contain little biographies) come quite close.[89] Aristotle already speaks of a 'succession' in the field of

---

[85] E.g. *De Or.* III.61, III.67, *Leg.* 1.55, *Acad.* II.118, II.129, *Fin.* III.44, V.16, *Tusc.* 1.18, 1.79, V.11, *ND* 1.2, 1.5. Cf. also Cassius' letter to Cicero, *Ad Fam.* XV.19.3, which shows that these disagreements were well known to members of the Roman intelligentsia.

[86] References to Stoic logical *Eisagōgai* e.g. S.E. *M* VIII.428, Gal. *Inst. Log.* XIX.5K; on Epicurean compendia see Angeli 1986, on introductory medical textbooks Kollesch 1966 and 1973, 13–46, on handbooks in general Fuhrmann 1960, on *Epitomai* in general Mansfeld and Runia 1997, 183–5; also cf. Mutschmann 1911a, 96, Schäfer 1959.

[87] E.g. *ap.* Athen. 464d, *Eisagōgē* to the Treatment of Good and Evil; *Epitomē* of Interrogation and Inquiry, one book and *Epitomē* of Reply, one book, *apud* D.L. VII.191.

[88] The first to write a work with this title was Sotion; texts in Wehrli 1978. See further von Kienle 1961, Glucker 1978, 161, 343–4, Giannattasio Andria 1989, Mansfeld 1992a, 20–43. Brent 1993 and 1995, 475–501 is inadequate.   [89] Texts: Dorandi 1991b, 1994b.

rhetoric (*Soph. El.* 34.183b17–33),[90] by which he means that a pupil takes over from the master, though not necessarily in an institutional sense. The motivation for writing history of philosophy in this manner mainly derives from the institutional practice of the established philosophical schools, starting with the Academy. In these schools the head of the association had a successor (*diadochos*) who was appointed or chosen. Retrospectively, such lines of succession were also constructed for the Preplatonic period, and these successions of Preplatonics were in various ways linked with the later philosophical schools.[91] This entails that a 'succession' could also be postulated in cases where a real or purported doctrinal affinity was found, or believed to exist. The notion of succession is important for the idea of a school, and may therefore play a decisive part in the literature *On Sects*. We may observe that the ancients more often than not emphasized continuity, while modern historians are accustomed to think in terms of different historical periods.

In the field of philosophy there are two alternative models – either two (e.g. at D.L. 1.13) or three successions comprising the whole of Greek philosophy from Thales and Pythagoras to the Hellenistic period (subsequently, later philosophies could be conveniently appended).[92] We have the Ionian line, starting with Thales and including the 'Socratics', namely the so-called minor Socratics and the Academy, Peripatos, Cynics and Stoa. The Italian line, starting with Pythagoras, includes the Early Pyrrhonists and Epicureans. We may find a third line too, called Eleatic, which begins with Xenophanes and also includes the Pyrrhonists and Epicureans. Some philosophers were considered to be outside these lines (οἱ σποράδην).[93] The standard division according to lines of succession consequently emphasizes a contrast between the principal dogmatist Hellenistic schools, namely Epicureans and Stoa, and somewhat to our surprise rather strongly opposes Early Pyrrhonism to Academic scepticism, and the Cyrenaics to the Epicureans.

The work of Diogenes Laertius, of which I have already suggested that it belongs in large part to the literature *On Sects*, is from beginning to end structured according to lines of succession.[94] The learned doctor Soranus is said to have written a book entitled *Successions of the Physicians*.[95] There are even occasional references to successions in

[90] Cf. also *Met.* A.1.993b14–19, on other genres.
[91] For the similar practice of the Hellenistic medical schools and/or medical historiography see e.g. [Gal.] *Int.* xiv.683–4κ.   [92] Von Kienle 1961.   [93] E.g. D.L. viii.91–ix.20.
[94] The Ionian succession and sects are treated in books ii–vii, the Italian(-cum-Eleatic) in books viii–x.
[95] Scholion to Oribasius, *CMG* vi.3.132. This may be identical with the work cited above, n. 11.

Aëtius (e.g. 1.3.1–9) which Diels either ignored or declared to be later accretions.

These works contain information on and anecdotes concerned with the lives of the philosophers; therefore they are often believed to be less reliable than doxographies. There is some truth in this. But the *Diadochai* of Alexander Polyhistor (to mention only one instance) contained a substantial summary concerned with doctrines attributed to the (Early) Pythagoreans.[96] That this account has no historical basis is less important than the fact that works of this kind may contain more than biographic facts, or pseudo-facts, and gossip. The information on the history of the schools of Plato and Zeno preserved by Philodemus, which occasionally includes brief accounts of major doctrines, is certainly quite invaluable. So is much of what is found in Diogenes Laertius.

ix Biography

References to the rather fluid genre of biography have already been made in the previous sections. The *bios* ('life') of a philosopher may be part of a 'succession', or series of 'lives' (e.g. Diogenes Laërtius' *On Cleanthes* as part of the Stoic *diadochē*), but may also exist individually, or form the introduction to the collected works of an author. The earliest examples in the field of philosophy seem to be lost writings about Plato by his early pupils; the one by Hermodorus is cited not only for biographic details but also for specific doctrines.[97] The reason why I have said that biography is fluid is that its ingredients may vary. Diogenes Laertius, for instance, includes the doctrines of the Stoa in the *bios* of its founder, but adds the common doctrines of the Cynics after the sequence of their individual biographies.[98] In other 'lives', the doctrinal element may be poor, or even absent.[99]

An interesting feature of 'lives' (especially in the context of a succession) is that various alternative versions of a person's affiliations, schooling and personal fortunes may be given. Here not merely 'antiquarian' interest but the desire not to lose information that may be relevant is at work. The alternatives may in some cases be capable of an explanation (Zeno of Citium as a Cynic or as a decent person, perhaps even a sort of

---

[96] Quoted D.L. VIII.24–35.

[97] Speusippus, *Eulogy of Plato*, D.L. v.5; Hermodorus, *On Plato*, Phld. *Acad. Hist.*, col. 6.34, D.L. II.106, III.6, Simp. *Phys.* 247.33–48.18, 256.32–57.4.   [98] D.L. VII.38, VI.103.

[99] On Antigonus of Carystus, not interested in doctrines, see Dorandi 1995a who corrects von Wilamowitz-Moellendorff, 1881.

Platonist, depending on the preferences of the reporter or constructor of a succession).[100] The modern historian should tread carefully and not attempt, at least not always, to cut knots or appeal to development. The fact that the Church eventually chose to accept four not always mutually compatible 'lives' of Jesus[101] from the number that were available shows the same tendency at work. By preserving such alternatives, or varieties, as are not patently wrong you may at least be certain of preserving what is useful. In Diogenes Laertius (but also in others, e.g. pseudo-Soranus' 'life' of Hippocrates)[102] this conservative fondness for alternatives entails the presence of explicit references to a plurality of traditions, or more or less recherché sources for the cited bits of information.

x Fragments

Where originals are lost, and the extant derivative literature involves compression and may entail a certain amount of distortion, priority should clearly be given to surviving verbatim quotations, although we can almost never be certain that their wording is exact. Secondary sources may quote from the work of a philosopher they are discussing, or paraphrase (a part of) it. As a rule, such quotations (*marturia*, *laudationes*) are given to underpin an argument that is being propounded. In order to evaluate quotations with regard to the information provided on the philosopher at issue, one should not only look at the so-called (immediate) context, but take the specific purpose of the quoting author into account and keep in mind that ancient authors may well be concerned with making a point rather than providing information. It is of course well known that words may be quoted without regard to their original environment; even quotations in verse may be adapted to a new context. Furthermore, from the point of view of an ancient author involved in explaining or paraphrasing a person's doctrine it may be useful to ascribe to him views you want to refute but which he never may have held, at least not in this form, or views which you may regard as a welcome consequence of what he said though actually he never expressed them.

The concept of a fragment is ill defined, and such definitions as may be believed to exist are not consistently heeded. Usener in his edition of the remains of Epicurus, followed by his pupil Diels in his editions of the

---

[100] Mansfeld 1986, 317–28.

[101] For the gospels in the context of the traditions of Greek biography see Cancik 1984b, 94–6, Berger 1984, 1231–45, Aune 1987, 46–76.

[102] Text: *CMG* IV 175–8, transl. in Rubin Pinault 1992, 7–8.

remains of the philosophers who wrote in verse and of the fragments of the Presocratics, introduced a useful distinction between (1) verbatim quotations and (2) what (regardless of the genre involved) they called 'testimonia', or secondary evidence.[103] Today such testimonia (again regardless of the genre involved) are often treated as reliable 'fragments' in those cases where a name or name-label is added in the source. To a certain extent, this may be justifiable as a salutary reaction to the vagaries of the *Quellenforschung* which tended to trace back sections in derivative sources to primary sources on speculative grounds. Yet a preliminary observation must be made. The attribution of particular tenets or doctrines to, say, Cleanthes or Posidonius is from a historical point of view less suspect than one to e.g. Zeno, because Zeno, as founder of the school, may serve as a *nom de plume* for the Stoics in general. A second observation is that collections of testimonia-with-labels of Hellenistic philosophers may provide a distorted impression because views of individuals are noted especially in those cases where they are different, or to some extent different, from those of the founder, or the majority of the members, of a particular school. Here the distinction of genres becomes particularly important. Testimonia about individual Stoics derived from the *Placita* literature of the Aëtius type as a rule emphasize disagreement, whereas strings of *laudationes* concerned with Stoics in Diogenes Laertius and Arius Didymus, though scrupulously listing differences, may place the emphasis on fundamental agreement in doctrine and so suggest that disagreement is for the most part merely verbal.

A further note of warning should be sounded. Modern collections of 'fragments' of individual philosophers, or of philosophers belonging to a particular school or brought together under a specific denomination, are to be used with caution. This also holds for the collected fragments of physicians. Usener's collection of Epicurean fragments and testimonia is an in many ways unsurpassed example of the method. But it is not only now out of date and incomplete; a more serious defect is its tendency to lump the testimonia together in a systematic way without regard for their provenance and eventual relations to one another. Von Arnim's collection of the fragments of the Early Stoics, also out of date, is much less good than the splendid works of Usener and Diels.[104] Though von Arnim indicates what he considers to be the relative importance of testimonia and fragments by means of a confusing variety of type-faces, his – far too

---

[103] Usener 1887, Diels 1901, 1903.
[104] Von Arnim 1903–5. For Usener and Diels see previous note.

systematic – arrangement of chunks of text fails to give preference to verbatim quotations. He often ascribes common Stoic views to Chrysippus, thereby demoting him to a *nom de plume*. In actual practice, users may tend to consider any item to be found in Usener or von Arnim[105] a fragment to be put on a par with any of the others. For the purposes of research as contrasted with a first orientation or with teaching, existing and future collections of fragments should be used as inventories or 'databases' which direct us to the sources which should really be consulted, and which should both be studied in themselves and carefully compared with each other.[106]

A word may be added on a technique of composition often found in derivative sources, namely the cento method. This is not a modern invention but a method recognized and discussed in antiquity.[107] In prose works the cento (*kentron*, 'patchwork') is a collection of quotations and/or paraphrases, sometimes pertaining to a single author and/or source, more often to a plurality of authors and/or sources, and serving a definite end. This aim may be made explicit by means of exegesis, or the cento itself may be subservient to larger interpretative purposes. In a sense, a string of *laudationes* collected to prove that Epicurus is immoral (D.L. x.3–9) is a cento. The first book of Hippolytus' *Refutation of All Heresies* is a cento compiled from various sources, of both the doxographic and the *On Sects* type, with an emphasis on succession comparable to that of Diogenes Laertius. Diogenes' own book is to some degree a cento – mainly of other centos, as it would appear. Galen, in the *PHP*, constructs centos of quotations from Chrysippus interspersed with much exegesis in order to prove him one-sided, or wrong. Clement of Alexandria in his *Patchworks* (*Strōmateis*) provides numerous centos adducing, and explaining, the views of poets and prose-writers, philosophers and others, on a great number of issues. Little or no work has been done on the comparison of centos dealing with the same issues to be found in various extant secondary sources. Unfortunately, the prosopographic and systematic arrangement of existing collections of fragments successfully obliterates those centos which cite a wide range of views.

---

[105] Or in the excellent collections of Deichgräber 1930, Long and Sedley 1987, and von Staden 1989. On fragments see the papers collected in Most 1996 and Burkert 1998.
[106] The naive view is expressed by Kristeller 1993, 2, who says that the 'fragments and summaries preserved by later authors' have been 'carefully assembled by modern scholars whose work is like that of the archeologists who reconstruct the cities and monuments of Antiquity out of ruins either preserved or unearthed'.   [107] Le Boulluec 1982, Mansfeld 1992a, 152–65.

XI Tradition and reception

In a number of ways, the concepts of 'tradition' or 'history of tradition' are more convenient from a methodological point of view than 'source' and 'source-criticism'. When one speaks of a tradition, one is of course also thinking of the hypothetical primary sources of extant derivative sources, but need not be too specific about these sources. It is for example clear that Cicero works within a tradition, or a plurality of traditions, and that only in some cases may we speak of sources used, or consulted. History of tradition can be usefully applied in the study of genres; one may speak of traditions concerned with successions or schools, of a doxographic tradition, and so on.

The Neoplatonist idea that the lower forms of reality receive what transcends them on their own level, formulated in the Middle Ages as 'whatever is received is received according to the character of the receiver' (*Quidquid recipitur ad modum recipientis recipitur*), may be converted into a formula defining reception. Inevitably, traditions are involved with reception, because topics of interest may have been formulated in a different way or because a later author, especially if he belongs to a different school, reads through coloured glasses and so provides coloured information. Reception is already an issue in Aristotle himself, because he tends to interpret his predecessors in terms of his own system. There is a Stoic reception of Heraclitus and an Epicurean of Atomism, as well as a so-called Middle Stoic[108] reception of Early Stoicism and a Neopyrrhonist[109] reception of Early Pyrrhonism and Academic scepticism. The pythagoreanizing Platonist Numenius finds fault with the reception of Plato in the sceptical Academy and even to some extent in the early Academy. Likewise, there is a Galenic reception of the treatises in the *Corpus Hippocraticum* and of Plato's dialogues which we can check, and of the Hellenistic physicians which we cannot check in the same way because their works are lost. Instances could be provided *ad lib*. What is handed on, looked for or rediscovered changes as it changes hands. Ancient philosophy in relation to its past, or pasts, is to a large extent a history of receptions and interpretations. Our sources for Hellenistic philosophy must be evaluated from this point of view as well.

Just as history of reception is more useful than history of tradition, so history of tradition is more useful than *Quellenforschung*. But a history of

---

[108] Seneca, Epictetus, Marcus Aurelius.   [109] Aenesidemus, Agrippa, Sextus Empiricus.

reception which keeps aloof from history of tradition and *Quellenforschung* will be blind. Conversely, *Quellenforschung* is feasible only in the context of the history of tradition, just as history of tradition is in that of the history of reception.

2

Chronology

TIZIANO DORANDI

I Introduction

During the years immediately following the deaths of Plato (348/7 BC) and Aristotle (322/1 BC) Athenian philosophical life was dominated by four large schools: the Academy, the Peripatos, the Stoa and the Garden (*Kēpos*) of Epicurus. Alongside these were the Pyrrhonian sceptics, named after their founder Pyrrho of Elis, and certain representatives of the so-called minor Socratic schools – in particular the Cyrenaics, the Dialecticians and the Cynics.

The reconstruction of the chronology of the members of all these schools up to about 100 BC presents a series of difficulties, which often make dating proposals necessarily vague or at least subject to possible changes as studies develop. In the following pages I do not intend simply to reproduce the lists of scholarchs who succeeded each other as heads of individual schools, but rather to give a concise bird's-eye sketch of the principal events in the lives of the more important personalities in correlation with the more secure dates in the chronology.[1]

II The Academy

On Plato's death (348/7) he was succeeded as head of the Academy by his nephew Speusippus, who held the post until 339/8 (Lysimachides' archonship), when Xenocrates of Chalcedon was chosen by the younger members of the Academy as his successor. The third scholarch was Polemo of Athens, chosen in 314/3, the year of Xenocrates' death. Young, rich and dissolute, Polemo was converted to philosophy after listening to a lecture by Xenocrates on temperance (*sōphrosunē*). His chronology should be

---

[1] For the Stoa, Academy and Garden I have mostly used (but also revised) the evidence in Dorandi 1991c. J. D. Morgan has enabled me (*per litteras*) to correct some imprecisions. I am very grateful for his help. Some of the dates are still provisional and will perhaps have to be changed once the complete results of Morgan's research have been published.

examined alongside those of Crantor of Soli in Cilicia and of Crates of
Athens, both important members of the Academy, connected with Polemo
by their school ties and by friendship.[2] A reliable passage in the *Chronicle* of
Eusebius/Hieronymus[3] records the year of Polemo's death as 270/69. He
was succeeded as head of the school by Crates, on account of Crantor's pre-
mature death, probably in 276/5 (Philocrates' archonship).[4] Crates' date of
death remains uncertain because of a lacuna in Diogenes Laertius' text
(D.L. IV.23). If one accepts Jacoby's restored version, Crates would have
died between 268 and 264 BC (128th Olympiad).[5] Crates' period as scholarch was, in any case, of short duration.

In the same period appears the figure of Eratosthenes of Cyrene, pupil
in Athens of the Stoic philosopher Aristo of Chios, but also of Arcesilaus.
His chronology is disputed: he went to Alexandria as librarian to Ptolemy
III Euergetes (246–221 BC) and lived there at least until the end of the
reign of Ptolemy V Epiphanes (205/4–181/0 BC), if the information that he
died aged eighty is reliable.[6]

After Crates, probably between 268 and 264, Arcesilaus of Pitane in
Aeolia took on the scholarchate (headship, or direction, of the school), following its refusal by a certain Socratides, who had been elected by the *neaniskoi* of the Academy. Arcesilaus, after studies with Theophrastus, turned
to the Academy of Polemo, Crates and Crantor. Ancient sources name him
as someone who inaugurated a new era in Academic thought, taking a
position close to that of the Pyrrhonists. Arcesilaus' chronology is tied to
that of his successor Lacydes of Cyrene.[7] From Apollodorus and Diogenes
Laertius[8] we learn that the beginning of Lacydes' headship of the school
fell in 241/0 and that this philosopher held the post for thirty-six years
until 206/5; in the last ten years, because of serious illness, Lacydes
effectively had to delegate the running of the school to a council of *presbuteroi*.[9]

We are informed by Apollodorus' *Chronicle*[10] about the events in the
Academy during the years of Lacydes' direction of the school and immediately following his death.[11] Telecles and Euander, who had with other
students taken part in the council running the Academy during Lacydes'
illness, kept hold of its control after the latter's death without proceeding

[2] Dorandi 1991c, 3–6.   [3] Eus./Hieron. *Chron.*: Ol. 127.3 (p. 130.21 Helm).
[4] I believe that the evidence in Phld. *Acad. Hist.* col. Q.2–5 refers to him, not to Polemo or Crates.
[5] Jacoby 1902, 344.
[6] Pfeiffer 1968, 152–70. For membership of the Academy, see Krämer 1983, 152–4, 164–8, 169,
172.   [7] I have here modified what I wrote in Dorandi 1991c, 7–10.
[8] Phld. *Acad. Hist.*, col. 27.1–7 and D.L. IV.61.   [9] Görler 1994b, 830–1.
[10] Phld. *Acad. Hist.*, col. 27.7–28.34.   [11] Dorandi 1991b, 65–8.

to formal election of a new scholarch. On Telecles' death in 167/6 (Nicosthenes' archonship), Euander continued on his own for a few years. He was succeeded by Hegesinus, and he in turn by Carneades of Cyrene. Besides Telecles, Euander and Hegesinus, Apollodorus cites as students of Lacydes Paseas, Thrasys and Aristippus. As students of Telecles, Euander and Hegesinus there were in addition Agamestor, Eubulus of Erythrae, Eubulus of Ephesus and Moschion of Mallos who died in 185/4 (Eupolemos' archonship). Eubulus of Erythrae died during Alexander's archonship (174/3) and his Ephesian namesake three months later. The Arcadian Agamestor died during Xenocles' archonship (168/7) after the battle of Pydna. A certain Apollonius, student of Telecles, died during Epainetos' archonship (159/8). Finally, a young Eubulus, Apollonius' brother, died during the archonship of Aristophon (143/2), the successor to Theaetetus (144/3).

On the other hand, information relating to the biography of Carneades of Cyrene, the other major representative of the Academy after Arcesilaus, is scarce. Diogenes Laertius quotes Apollodorus as saying that Carneades was eighty-five when he died in 129/8, so he was born in 214/13.[12] There were two significant episodes in his life. (1) He participated, along with the Peripatetic Critolaus of Phaselis and the Stoic Diogenes of Seleucia, in the mission sent in 156/5 to Rome to defend the Athenian cause in the affair of the city of Oropos. With his ability in dialectic Carneades managed to persuade the Roman Senate to decree the annulment of the 150 talent fine imposed on the Athenians.[13] (2) He decided to retire from the headship of the Academy for health reasons in 137/6. The subsequent succession of events up to the death of Clitomachus of Carthage and the headship of Philo of Larissa is fairly intricate.[14] Carneades was succeeded by his namesake Carneades, son of Polemarchus: he died in 131/0 when the elder Carneades was still alive, and was succeeded by Crates of Tarsus. With the elder Carneades' death in 129/8 Clitomachus, who had opened his own school in the Palladium a little before the succession of Carneades the younger, re-entered the Academy (probably by force) and two years later, on the death of Crates, effectively took over as head. Clitomachus (born in Carthage, 187/6) had originally come to Athens at the age of twenty-four, in 163/2, and four years later, in 159/8, started attending the lectures of the elder Carneades.[15] His reasons for founding his own

---

[12] D.L. IV.65.   [13] The sources are collected in Mette 1985, T. 7a–k.
[14] Dorandi 1991c, 11–16.
[15] These dates are only approximate, because of the problems connected with exclusive *versus* inclusive reckoning.

school, nineteen years later, in 140/39 (Hagnotheos' archonship) are obscure. He remained head of the Academy until his death in 110/09, during Polycletus' archonship. Clitomachus was succeeded by Philo of Larissa.

Two other protagonists in this period of the history of the Academy were Boethus of Marathon and Melanthius of Rhodes. Boethus of Marathon was a student of Aristo of Ephesus and of Eubulus of Ephesus; he died ten years after the elder Carneades, in 120/19, during the archonship of Eumachos. We do not know his date of birth, but he may have lived for a long time, in view of the fact that Eubulus died before 168/7.[16] We know that Melanthius was the tutor of Aeschines of Naples and that the latter also attended the lectures of the elder Carneades; it is therefore possible to place the *floruit* of Melanthius around 150 BC.[17]

Metrodorus of Stratonicea and Charmadas are more important. We know that Metrodorus, after being Epicurus' pupil, went to the Academy where he became the pupil of the elder Carneades, and was regarded as the only true interpreter of what Carneades really thought.[18] Charmadas' chronology is difficult to determine. If we accept that Charmadas was the anonymous philosopher described by Apollodorus as 'naturally endowed with a good memory' (φύσει μνήμων), we have the following dates:[19] he went to Athens at the age of twenty-two in 142/1 (Aristophantos' archonship) and studied with Carneades of Cyrene for seven years. He would therefore have been born in 164/3. From Cicero's evidence in *De Oratore* II.360 we can deduce that Charmadas had already died by 91 BC.[20]

Between the end of the second and the beginning of the first century BC, the Academy went through a period of crisis as an institution, which coincided, paradoxically, with a splendid flowering of thought, associated with the names of Philo of Larissa and Antiochus of Ascalon.

The chronology of Philo, the last head of the official Academy, is fairly certain.[21] He was born in 154/3 (Aristaichmos' archonship). In 130/29, during Nicomachus' archonship, he went to Athens where during the period up to 120/19 he was a student of Clitomachus and an unidentified Apollodorus. On Clitomachus' death, in 110/09, Philo became scholarch. He remained in Athens until 88, at which point he fled to Rome where he died, probably in 84/3 (Nicetes' archonship).

---

[16] Cf. Dorandi 1991b, 71–2.   [17] Cf. Dorandi 1991b, 74–5.

[18] D.L. x.9 and Phld. *Acad. Hist.*, col. 24.9–16. Cf. Glucker 1978, 107–8, 113 n. 54 and 303.

[19] Phld. *Acad. Hist.*, cols. 31.33–32.10; I here follow a suggestion of J. Morgan.

[20] Cf. Dorandi 1991b, 75–6.

[21] The data which I here provide are slightly different from those in Dorandi 1991c, 17–20, because I have in the meantime endorsed some suggestions made by J. Morgan.

Antiochus was born in Ascalon between 130 and 120; in 69, when he was accompanying L. Lucullus in the military campaign against Mithridates, he was already an old man. In Athens he was a student of Philo of Larissa and of the Stoics Mnesarchus and Dardanus. The crucial point of his career was undoubtedly his 'conversion', which led him to found his own school called the Old Academy, in opposition to the Academy of Philo, who had no successor. The centuries-old history of the school founded by Plato – the Academy in the true sense of the word – ends with Philo; a new phase of Platonism began with Antiochus. The break with Philo occurred at some time we cannot determine during the nineties.[22] From *c.* 87 to 84 Antiochus seems to have been at Alexandria, where he got to know Lucullus; but in 79 Cicero heard his lectures at Athens in Ptolemy's Gymnasium (*Ptolemaeum*). From 74 to 69 he accompanied Lucullus in the war against Mithridates and he died in *c.* 68.[23]

The theory[24] that Charmadas might have run the Academy for a few years after Philo's flight to Rome is disputable.[25]

iii The Peripatos

The history of Aristotle's school from the death of its founder to the first century BC is sparsely documented in the ancient sources.[26] In 323, on the death of Alexander the Great, Aristotle was forced to leave Athens and fled to Stagira, where he died in 322/1. Theophrastus remained at Athens as his successor in charge of the Peripatos for another thirty-six years until he died in 288/7 or 287/6.[27]

Demetrius of Phalerum, born *c.* 350 BC, was an accomplished politician. His chronology does not exclude the possibility that he was in direct contact with Aristotle, though the sources only name him as a student of Theophrastus. It is difficult to determine with any certainty his relationship with the Peripatos. In 322, after the battle of Crannon, Demetrius took part in the Athenian mission to Antipater of Macedon. In 317 he was summoned to govern the city in the name of Cassander with legislative powers. Demetrius replaced the democratic system with one based on property qualifications and ruled Athens under the titles of 'curator of the city' (ἐπιμελητὴς τῆς πόλεως) and *stratēgos*. He achieved an important reform

[22] I accept the findings of Glucker 1978, 15–21 (modified at Dorandi 1991c, 19 n. 7, 30, 34, 60 and 74).   [23] Cf. Glucker 1978, Barnes 1989c and Görler 1994b, 939–45.

[24] Glucker 1978, 109–11.   [25] Cf. Ferrary 1988, 472 n. 122.

[26] For a summary, cf. Sollenberger 1992, 3842–4.

[27] For the life and chronology of Theophrastus see Regenbogen 1940, 1355–61.

of the law on Platonic–Peripatetic principles. In 309/8 he was archon[28] and remained in power until 307, when he fled into exile upon the capture of Athens by Cassander's foe Demetrius Poliorcetes. Accordingly he went first to Thebes, and then (after Cassander's death in 297) to Egypt, where he sought asylum from Ptolemy I Soter, and remained until his death *c.* 282 BC.

Strato, son of Arcesilaus or Arcesius, born at Lampsacus between 340 and 330, was elected to succeed Theophrastus as scholarch of the Peripatos. It is not impossible that he might have known Epicurus during his period of teaching in Lampsacus between 310 and 306. Strato went to Athens (date unknown) where he attended Aristotle's school. After the master's death he left the Peripatos for a time and went to Egypt to the court of Ptolemy I Soter, who entrusted him with the education of his son, Ptolemy II Philadelphos. He returned to Athens on Theophrastus' death (288/7 or 287/6) and was chosen as successor in preference to Neleus, probably because of his seniority. He remained as scholarch for another eighteen years, until 270/69 or 269/8.

With Praxiphanes, native of Mytilene but for a long time inhabitant of Rhodes, we move on to the second generation of Peripatetics who were students of Theophrastus only. Praxiphanes' birth has been placed within the last quarter of the fourth century BC. The possibility that he might be the person similarly named in a contemporary Greek inscription from the island of Delos must be dismissed.[29] The chronology of Hieronymus of Rhodes, possibly introduced to philosophy by the same Praxiphanes on his native island, can be placed in the first twenty-five years of the third century BC. Other students of Theophrastus were Duris of Samos (who lived between *c.* 350–330 and some date after 281) and his brother Lynceus.

The third scholarch of the Peripatos was Lyco. Born in the Troad, he succeeded Strato in 270/69 or 269/8 and remained in the post for forty-four years, until 226/5 or 225/4. Since we know that he died aged seventy-four (D.L. v.68), his date of birth must be 300/299 or 299/8. In Diomedon's archonship (248/7 or 245/4) this philosopher was honoured at Athens for contributing to an *epidosis*, and, at an uncertain date, also by the Delphic Amphictiony.[30]

We know very little of Aristo of Ceos, probably born around 250. Doubts remain about whether he was elected scholarch. But we have much more, and more detailed information about Prytanis, son of

[28] Sollenberger 1992, 3825 n. 160. Cf. Tracy 1994, 151–61.

[29] *IG* xi[4].613.10. Cf., most recently, Salvadori Baldascino 1990.

[30] Cf., respectively, *IG* ii[2] 791d29 = *SIG*[3] 491 (Lyco fr. 13 Wehrli) and *SIG*[3] 461 (Lyco fr. 14 Wehrli), on which see Habicht 1989, 9 (= 1994, 166) and Sollenberger 1992, 3823, n. 152.

Astykleides and a native of the city of Carystus in Euboea.[31] His chronology revolves around October 225 BC, when he was honoured by the Athenians on the occasion of his participation in a mission to Antigonus Doson.[32] In 223 he was employed by Doson to draft a constitution for Megalopolis (Plb. v.93.8). Since his students included the poet Euphorion of Chalcis, the start of his teaching career can be put between 260 and 255. The information in the so-called *Vita Hesychii* of Aristotle, which puts him among the scholarchs of the Peripatos, is certainly false.[33] The same holds true for Phormion. His chronology has been fixed around 195 on the basis of information in Cicero (*De orat.* II.18.75) that he made a speech at Ephesus 'on the functions of a commander-in-chief and military matters in general' before the exiled Hannibal.

I shall omit from consideration other people who had a real or supposed relationship with the Peripatos – Satyrus of Callatis Pontica, Hermippus of Smyrna, Sotion of Alexandria, Heraclides Lembos, Antisthenes of Rhodes, Agatharchides of Cnidus and Athenodorus – since this would involve dealing with learned men rather than with philosophers in the strict sense.

In the period from the death of Lyco (226/5 or 225/4) to Critolaus of Phaselis (already scholarch in 156/5), there is a gap in the ancient sources regarding the succession of scholarchs of the Peripatos. Even if it is granted that one of these was Aristo of Ceos, there can be no reliability attached to other names detailed in the *Vita Hesychii*, which include Lyciscus, Praxiphanes and Hieronymus, as well as Prytanis and Phormion.[34] We lack solid information about Critolaus' birth and death. It is only certain that he took part in 155 in the famous Athenian delegation to Rome together with Carneades and Diogenes of Seleucia. This date allows us to establish that Critolaus must already have been scholarch at that time. If one believes pseudo-Lucian ([Luc.] *Macr.* 20), according to whom Critolaus lived to be eighty-two, his date of birth ought to be put before 200 BC. We know virtually nothing about the chronology of Critolaus' students: Diodorus of Tyre, his successor as scholarch, Calliphon and Aristo the Younger.

IV The Stoa

Reconstruction of the chronologies of Zeno of Citium and Cleanthes of Assos, respectively the founder of the Stoic school and his first

---

[31] Kassel 1991.   [32] Cf. Moretti 1967, nr. 28.
[33] [Hesych.] *Vita Arist.* 9 (p. 82 Düring = p. 26 Gigon).   [34] Brink 1940, cols. 908–14.

successor,[35] has to rely above all on dates drawn from the *Stoicorum Historia* of Philodemus,[36] considered together with the first sections of another work by Philodemus, *De Stoicis*,[37] and with information taken from pseudo-Lucian, Valerius Maximus, Censorinus and Diogenes Laertius.[38]

From Philodemus in particular it seems that Zeno died in Athens during the archonship of Arrheneides and that his successor Cleanthes, born during Aristophanes' archonship (331/0), was head of the Stoa for thirty-two years, dying during Jason's archonship. Pseudo-Lucian, Valerius Maximus and Censorinus put Cleanthes' age at ninety-nine, while Diogenes Laertius claims he lived as long as Zeno. On the basis of accurate determination of the years in office of the archons Aristophanes (331/0), Arrheneides (262/1) and Jason (230/29), it is possible to work out from Philodemus' evidence that Cleanthes was born in 331/0, became scholarch of the Stoa in 262/1 on the death of Zeno, and died in 230/29. This would mean that Cleanthes lived to be 101. If we add to this inference Diogenes Laertius' statement that Zeno and Cleanthes lived to be the same age, and the information contained in an incompletely preserved passage of Philodemus' *De Stoicis*,[39] according to which some people also made Zeno live to be 101,[40] we may conclude that in ancient times parallel chronologies were circulated for Zeno and for Cleanthes. But they cannot be reconciled with each other. In particular, we should keep in mind the report, which deserves credence, that according to Persaeus Zeno lived to the age of seventy-two (D.L. VII.28). The following conclusions can therefore be reached: Zeno was born in 334/3 (according to Persaeus) or at a date we cannot determine (if we follow the evidence of Apollodorus in Philodemus); Cleanthes was born in 331/0 (Aristophanes' archonship). On Zeno's death in 262/1 (Arrheneides' archonship), Cleanthes became scholarch and continued in the post until his death in 230/29 (Jason's archonship).[41]

According to ancient sources Zeno, during an enforced stay in Athens brought about by a shipwreck, read Xenophon's *Reminiscences of Socrates* and became a pupil of the Cynic Crates and of Stilpo.[42] In *c.* 300 he opened his own school in the *Stoa Poikilē* ('portico with frescos'). What little we know of the life of Cleanthes of Assos has an anecdotal flavour: he

[35] Dorandi 1991c, 23–8.
[36] Phld. *Stoic. Hist.*, cols. 28–9. For the text, cf. Dorandi 1991c, 23–5.
[37] Phld. *De Stoic.*, cols. 1–8.
[38] [Luc.] *Macr.* 19; Val. Max. VIII.7 exc. 11; Cens. 15.3 and D.L. VII.176.
[39] Phld. *De Stoic.*, col. 5.9, via Apollodorus of Athens.   [40] Cf. Dorandi 1982b, 111 and n. 89.
[41] The chronology of Zeno remains controversial; cf. Lefèvre 1995 and Knoepfler 1995, 159.
[42] D.L. VII.1–2.

was a fighter in his youth; because he was very poor he had to work nights in order to attend Zeno's lectures; and he became an enthusiastic and loyal student.

Among those of Zeno's pupils who were highly regarded but did not become scholarchs were Persaeus of Citium, Aristo of Chios, Herillus of Carthage, Dionysius of Heraclea Pontica, called *Metathemenos*, and finally Sphaerus of Borysthenes.

Zeno's favourite student was Persaeus. An unfavourable source claims that he was born a household slave and was taken on and introduced to philosophy by Zeno.[43] From the evidence of Diogenes Laertius VII.6, who puts his *floruit* at 260–256, it has been deduced that Persaeus was born in 307/6.[44] Invited by Antigonus Gonatas of Macedon to go to his court at Pella, Zeno refused for reasons of age and in his place sent his students Persaeus and Philonides of Thebes. Persaeus arrived in Pella probably around 274.[45] After Antigonus recaptured Corinth *c*. 244, Persaeus was given control of the city in the capacity of *archōn*. Persaeus died in 243, courageously defending the fortress of Corinth against the attack of his old student Aratus of Sicyon. Another unfavourable source claims he actually managed to escape and rejoin Antigonus.[46]

The ancient sources, in particular Diogenes Laertius (VII.160–7), classify the three Stoic philosophers Aristo, Dionysius of Heraclea and Herillus, as unorthodox or dissidents. No chronological data survive concerning Aristo's life. We know only that he was a pupil of Zeno and of the academic Polemo. He was friendly with Persaeus and Sphaerus and opposed to Arcesilaus. The enmity implicit in his confrontations with Chrysippus has contributed to a distorted picture of his views.[47] We also have little biographical information about Herillus. Originally from Carthage, he studied at Athens under Zeno and became famous for founding a sect under his name, the *Herilleioi*.[48] The figure of Dionysius, called *Metathemenos*, is more complex. After having been a pupil of Heraclides Ponticus at Heraclea, he studied at Athens with Alexinus and Menedemus and, later, with Zeno. According to information in Athenaeus (VII.281e), he died at a great age; Diogenes Laertius states that he died of starvation at eighty (D.L. VII.167). Bearing in mind his contact with Heraclides, we can assume that he was born *c*. 330–325 and died *c*. 250 BC. He caused a sensation by leaving the Stoa in favour of the Cyrenaic or Epicurean school, on account of serious illness. Another

[43] Phld. *Stoic. Hist.*, col. 12.   [44] Jacoby 1902, 368–9.

[45] I agree with Grilli 1963, 289–91 (= 1992, 471–2).   [46] Deichgräber 1937, cols. 926–7.

[47] Ioppolo 1980a, 19–38.   [48] Ioppolo 1985b.

student of Zeno of Citium was supposedly a Zeno of Sidon, but his existence has recently been put in doubt.[49]

A pupil first of Zeno of Citium and then, after his death, of Cleanthes was Sphaerus of Borysthenes. Sphaerus' chronology, connected with that of Cleomenes III of Sparta (*c.* 260–219 BC), is controversial.[50] In 235, Cleomenes became king of Sparta and was supported in his revolutionary programme of reform by Sphaerus. The project lasted until 222, when after the defeat at Sellasia Cleomenes was forced to flee to Egypt, to the court of his patron Ptolemy III Euergetes. After Euergetes' death in 222/1, he was kept under house arrest by Ptolemy IV Philopator, and after a desperate escape he committed suicide in 220/19. Given that Cleomenes was born *c.* 260, his teacher Sphaerus must have been born around 285, which is consistent with the information that he was also Zeno's student. There is a problem concerning his trip to Egypt to see a Ptolemy who could be identified as Philopator.[51] It is likely that Sphaerus went with his patron Cleomenes during his exile in 222. Therefore his possible dates are as follows: born around 285; went to Athens *c.* 265, where he was able to attend the lectures of Zeno (died 262/1) for a short time; joined Cleomenes in Sparta in *c.* 240; followed the Spartan king into Egyptian exile in 222.

Cleanthes' successor and the third scholarch of the Stoa was Chrysippus of Soli in Cilicia – famous in ancient times for being the 'second founder' of Stoicism. His chronology is based on Apollodorus' calculations as recorded in Diogenes Laertius, which place his death at the age of seventy-three during the 143rd Olympiad (208–204).[52] The data found in pseudo-Lucian (that he died aged eighty-one) and in Valerius Maximus (that Chrysippus wrote a series of *Logical Investigations* at the age of eighty) are less credible.[53] His date of birth has been placed between 281 and 277. This takes away any basis for the claim that Chrysippus also studied with Zeno, though he may well have been a student of Cleanthes.[54] He went to Athens probably around 260 and would also have been able to attend the courses of Arcesilaus and his successor Lacydes. Some chronological detail exists concerning Aristocreon, Chrysippus' nephew. Between 229 and 190, Aristocreon was in Athens where he was honoured with the *proxenia* and where we still find him in 184/3 (Charicles' archonship).[55] After

---

[49] Gigante 1983b, 168–70.   [50] I summarize the conclusions of Hobein 1929, cols. 1683–7.
[51] Cf. D.L. VII.17. Festa 1935, II.178 note *d*, thinks there is an error in Diogenes Laertius and that Sphaerus was invited to Egypt by Ptolemy II Philadelphos.   [52] D.L. VII.184.
[53] [Luc.] *Macr.* 20; Val. Max. VIII.7 ext. 10.
[54] D.L. VII.179; the first derives from Alexander Polyhistor, the second from Diocles.
[55] Cf. *IG* II² 786 = *SIG*³ 475 and *IG* II² 785 = *SIG*³ 474, on which see Habicht 1989, 13–14 (= 1994, 170).

Chrysippus, the direction of the school of the Stoa passed to Zeno of Tarsus, of whose life we know nothing.[56]

The chronology of Diogenes of Seleucia, who was Zeno of Tarsus' successor as scholarch, is based on little and rather uncertain information.[57] The only authenticated date in his life is 155, the year in which he took part, with Carneades and Critolaus, in the aforementioned mission to Rome. From Cicero's *De senectute*, 23 it is possible to deduce that Diogenes had already died by 150. Since pseudo-Lucian ([Luc.] *Macr.* 20) claims that he lived to be eighty, his date of birth has consequently been put around 240 BC. But this chronology clashes with the dates for Mnesarchus and Dardanus and with the crucial events in the life of Antiochus of Ascalon. The date of Diogenes' death can reasonably be put forward at least a decade, to around 140. The birthdates of Mnesarchus and Dardanus can therefore be placed in 160 or a little later, so that, at the time of Antiochus' 'conversion', they would be over sixty but not over eighty, as would be the case if Diogenes' death was put *c.* 150. This superior hypothesis also accords with Diogenes' participation in the mission of 155; Diogenes, born around 230, would have arrived in Rome aged just over seventy.[58]

As Ferrary has inferred,[59] and as I have demonstrated on the basis of a new reading of a passage in Philodemus' *Stoicorum Historia*,[60] after Panaetius' death Mnesarchus and Dardanus were not joint scholarchs. On the death of Diogenes of Seleucia there was not so much a progressive crumbling of the Stoic school's original unity as the co-existence in Athens of several parallel courses of lectures. It is probable that, after Diogenes, the official post of scholarch passed to Antipater of Tarsus; but at the same time Mnesarchus too was teaching philosophy. Something similar probably happened in 129, when Antipater died: Panaetius assumed the official headship of the Stoa while Dardanus in his turn gave lectures, possibly on an independent footing.[61]

Panaetius was born in Rhodes around 185–80 and died in 110/09. Re-examination of two Greek inscriptions[62] has allowed a better assessment of the dates of the central years of his life.[63] *IG* II[2] 1938 confirms Panaetius' presence in Athens around 150, probably in 149/8 (Lysiades' archonship), where he was at the school under the headship of Diogenes of Seleucia (died *c.* 140). From *ILind* 223 we learn that some time before

---

[56] Von Fritz 1972.   [57] Dorandi 1991c, 29–34.   [58] Dorandi 1991c, 31–4.
[59] Ferrary 1988, 457–64.   [60] Phld. *Stoic. Hist.*, col. 52.
[61] This is how I would modify the details in Ferrary's reconstruction.
[62] *IG* II[2] 1938 and *ILind* 223.   [63] Dorandi 1991c, 35–42.

(possibly around 155) Panaetius was still at Lindos on Rhodes, having been awarded the post of *hierothutēs* of Poseidon Hippios. The documented presence of Panaetius at Rhodes midway through the second century, and the start of the mission to the East with Scipio in 140,[64] would put Panaetius and Scipio's first meeting at about 146, bearing in mind that from 151 to 146 Scipio was fully committed to the campaigns in Spain and Africa.[65] This allows the definitive exclusion of the supposed involvement of Panaetius, along with Polybius and Scipio, in the third Punic war (149–146). I would redefine his principal dates thus: at an uncertain date between 185 and 180 Panaetius was born at Rhodes. After Crates of Mallos returned from the mission to Rome in 168, Panaetius might have attended his courses at Pergamon. Half way through the century, back in Rhodes, he was elected to be *hierothutēs* of Poseidon Hippios in Lindos. He went on to Athens to complete his studies, and here worked with Diogenes of Seleucia and Antipater of Tarsus (from *c.* 155 onwards). In Athens he took on the position of *hieropoios* for the celebrations of the *Ptolemaia* in 149/8. After 146 he met Scipio and joined him in the mission to the East in 140–38. In the following years he moved between Rome and Athens, where he worked with Antipater. In 129, the year in which Scipio and possibly also Antipater died, Panaetius was elected scholarch. He died in 110/09. The theory of Philippson and Pohlenz that he died in 100/99 has been proved groundless.[66]

I can give no more than a brief account, finally, of Posidonius.[67] Most of the available dates are untrustworthy. Only the years 86 (Marius' last consulate), when he was sent from Rhodes as an ambassador to Rome (Plu. *Mar.* 45.7), and 60, when Cicero sent him a first draft in Greek of his writings about his own consulate (Cic. *Att.* II. 1.2), seem secure. Alongside these dates one can also consider the information that Posidonius was the pupil of Panaetius (died 110/09),[68] that he may have taken part in a second diplomatic mission to Rome in 51,[69] and pseudo-Lucian's information that he lived to be eighty-four.[70] Hence, one may calculate that he died between 45 and 43 BC (Cic. *Tusc.* V.107). Nevertheless, the standard chronology accepted for Posidonius takes his dates to be 135–51 BC.[71]

---

[64] The data appear in Cichorius 1908, 204–5. The recent attempt by Mattingly 1986 to bring it back to 143/2 is not convincing. Against, see Ferrary 1988, 399 n. 4.

[65] Astin 1967, 297 and n. 4.   [66] Cf. Garbarino 1973, 387–90 and Ferrary 1988, 395–400.

[67] I can refer only to recent literature: Laffranque 1964, 45–97 and Kidd 1988, 1–58.

[68] Cic. *Div.* I.3 and *Off.* III.8. Cf. Kidd 1988, 12–13.

[69] According to the evidence of the *Suda* (T. 1 E–K). Cf. Kidd 1988, 3–4.   [70] [Luc.] *Macr.* 20.

[71] Kidd has raised an opportune *caveat* 1988, 8–9.

Laffranque has cautiously proposed an alternative: *c*. 142–59/8 or, more probably, *c*. 130–40.[72]

v The Garden

The chronology of Epicurus (342/1–271/0)[73] – the founder of the other great Hellenistic school of philosophy, Epicureanism – is founded principally on Apollodorus' synchronisms as recorded in Diogenes Laertius x.14–15. He was born on the twentieth of the month of Gamelion (24 January 341)[74] in the year of Sosigenes' archonship (342/1). At the age of thirty-two (310/09) he opened a school of philosophy at Mytilene and at Lampsacus and taught there for five years, until 305/4. He then moved to Athens, where he founded the Garden and where he died, aged seventy-two, during Pytharatus' archonship (271/0). According to other sources, among them Heraclides Lembus in the *Epitomē* of Sotion (D.L. x.1), Epicurus was born at Samos as the son of Neocles, who belonged to a group of Athenian colonists who had been sent to the island in 352,[75] and was only eighteen (323) when he went to Athens. After the expulsion of the Athenian colonies from Samos at the hands of Perdiccas, the philosopher moved to Colophon (after 322), where he met his father; he directed a school there for a few years and then returned to Athens during Anaxicrates' archonship (307/6). The discrepancy between the two sources regarding Epicurus' year of arrival in Athens – 305/4, according to Apollodorus, 307/6, according to Heraclides – is only slight and can be disregarded. From Epicurus' own testimony we learn that he claimed to have begun his philosophical studies at the age of fourteen (327).[76] Around 290 there was the serious episode of the apostasy of Timocrates,[77] brother of Metrodorus and student of Epicurus, who abandoned the Garden and launched a long defamatory campaign against his master.[78] The chronology of Metrodorus of Lampsacus is closely related to that of Epicurus; he died aged fifty-three, seven years before his friend (278/7), and was therefore born in 331/0.[79]

Among the members who comprised Epicurus' first circle of friends and disciples and who attended his school, we have the names of Pythocles,

[72] Laffranque 1964, 47–8. Cf. the *Tableau chronologique* between 139–40.
[73] Cf. Dorandi 1991c, 45–54.
[74] The debate over the exact date of his birth was definitively resolved by Alpers 1968.
[75] Cf. Philippson 1935. [76] D.L. x.2. Cf. Steckel 1968, col. 580.
[77] Cf. Sedley 1976a, 127–32, 151–4, esp. 152 n. 27.
[78] For a detailed discussion, cf. Schmid 1962 = 1984, 151–6 and Steckel 1968, cols. 579–93. The commentary of Laks 1976 is also useful. [79] Cf. D.L. x.23.

Polyaenus, Colotes and Idomeneus, four people whom Epicurus met during his stay in Lampsacus. The information that Pythocles died aged eighteen, in 289, is false. Pythocles was actually born around 324, was seventeen
or eighteen in 307/6 when Epicurus came to Lampsacus, and was still alive
in 292/1, aged thirty-two.[80] Polyaenus died before Epicurus, between 290
and 280.[81] We know very little about Colotes: it seems he was born about
320 and that after 268 he wrote his *On the Impossibility of Living on the
Principles of the Other Philosophers*, dedicated to King Ptolemy II Philadelphos (282–46) and designed as a critique of Arcesilaus, the Academy's
scholarch since *c.* 268–4. There is better documentation concerning
Idomeneus. He was born around 325 and was about fifteen when he met
Epicurus at Lampsacus. In the period between 306 and 301 he was
involved in political activity in his own city, as a court dignitary, while his
commitment to Epicureanism is to be dated after 301.[82]

Epicurus' first successor as scholarch was his old pupil from Mytilene,
Hermarchus.[83] On the basis of Epicurus' will,[84] in which he speaks of
those who alongside himself and Hermarchus 'chose to grow old in philosophy', it has been deduced that the two men were contemporaries. The
only certain date for Hermarchus' life is 267/6, the year in which he wrote
his letter to an otherwise unknown Theopheides on rhetorical arguments.[85] At a date around 250 for which we have no precise evidence,
Polystratus became scholarch following the death of Hermarchus.[86] We
know virtually nothing of his life. The most important question which
has occupied commentators is whether he was an immediate pupil
(*akroatēs*) of Epicurus.[87] We may infer with some caution that he had
already died by 219/18 (Menecrates' archonship).

The chronology of Dionysius of Lamptrai and Basilides of Tyre, respectively the Garden's third and fourth scholarchs, is relatively certain.
Dionysius of Lamptrai was scholarch from at least *c.* 219/18 (Menecrates'
archonship) until 205/4 (Isocrates' archonship), the year in which
Basilides of Tyre succeeded him in the position.[88] Between Basilides and
Apollodorus of Athens, who belonged to a later generation and was the
teacher of Zeno of Sidon, there is a gap in time which leads one to suspect

[80] Sedley 1976b, 43–8.
[81] Sedley 1976b, 48. Cf. Tepedino Guerra 1991, 25–6 and 141 (comm. on fr. 10).
[82] Angeli 1981.   [83] Cf. Longo Auricchio 1988.
[84] D.L. x.20. Cf. Longo Auricchio 1988, 25–7 and 115–16.
[85] Cf. Phld. *Rhet.* II, *PHerc.* 1674, cols. 44.19–23 and *Rhet.* III, *PHerc.* 1506, cols. 44.26–33. The let-
       ter is dated to the archonship of Menecles. Cf. Dorandi 1990c, T 37–8.
[86] Indelli 1978.   [87] Capasso 1982.
[88] Cf. Phld. *PHerc.* 1780, pz. VIIm* 13.17 and VIIIr 1–6, on which see Dorandi 1991c, 49–50.

the existence of at least one other intermediate scholarch: the name of
Thespis may be suggested. But the chronology and development of the
events of this time still remain obscure.[89] The figures of Philonides of
Laodicea-on-the-Sea and of Protarchus of Bargylia appear in the same
period. Philonides, whose anonymous life is preserved in *PHerc.* 1044,
remains famous for his mathematical studies.[90] Protarchus' *floruit* is put
at *c.* 150–120;[91] he was not a scholarch of the Garden.

A prominent figure in the school was Apollodorus of Athens, the so-
called *Kēpoturannos* ('Garden-Tyrant'). He was probably born at the
beginning of the second century and assumed the headship of the
school towards the middle of the century, holding the post until
approximately 110. The important figure of Demetrius of Laconia, an
Epicurean whose huge literary output is well known thanks to the
papyri of Herculaneum, also belongs to the second century. Demetrius
taught at Miletus but never became scholarch. His chronology is connected with that of Zeno of Sidon who was his somewhat younger contemporary. He lived roughly between 150 and 75.[92] On Apollodorus'
death, the headship passed to Zeno of Sidon. This philosopher, born
around 150, remained in Athens as scholar during the tyranny of
Aristion in 87, where Cicero studied with him in 79/8 (Cic. *Tusc.*
III.17.38). He died probably a few years later (around 75).[93] After Zeno
the school at Athens continued until the middle of the century, under
Phaedrus and Patro. Phaedrus' chronology has been reconstructed
fairly securely by Raubitscheck[94] on the basis of inscriptions.[95] A member of a distinguished Athenian family, Phaedrus, ephebe in 119/18, was
born *c.* 138.[96] He was in Athens in 93;[97] in 88 he fled to Rome, where he
taught philosophy and met Cicero, Atticus, and Appius and Lucius
Saufeius. He returned to Athens after the restoration of Sulla (86) and
here became scholarch at an advanced age on the death of Zeno of
Sidon. According to the evidence of Phlegon of Tralles,[98] he died in
70/69 leaving Patro as his successor.

---

[89] Dorandi 1991c, 50–1.

[90] See the edition of Gallo 1980, 21–166. This chronology has been better defined thanks to a more
precise dating of *IG* II² 1236: cf. Habicht 1989, 18–22 (= 1994, 174–8).

[91] Fraser 1972, I.423–4.   [92] Useful criticism in Angeli and Colaizzo 1979, 50–1.

[93] Angeli and Colaizzo 1979.

[94] Raubitscheck 1991 (= 1949), 337–44. Cf. also Gigante 1983a, 33–4. Sbordone's contribution
1968, is not convincing.   [95] In particular *IG* II² 1008, 3513, 3897 and 3899.

[96] The information about the ephebe comes from a secure restoration of *IG* II² 1008, line 125.

[97] Cf. Cic. *Leg.* 1.53, when L. Gellius was in Athens *after* his praetorship (*ex praetura*), which he had
held in 94.   [98] Phleg. Trall. *FGrHist.* 257 fr. 12 par. 8.

VI Pyrrhonists

I shall say something about the two representatives of Pyrrhonism for whom we possess chronological details: Pyrrho of Elis and Timon of Phlius.

The birthdate of Pyrrho of Elis, the founder of scepticism, can be placed between 365 and 360 BC. It is difficult to establish the reliability of the information that he was a student of Bryson, which is based on a dubious passage in Diogenes Laertius.[99] From around 334 to 324 he took part, with Anaxarchus, in Alexander the Great's oriental campaign. On returning from Asia, Pyrrho settled in Elis and began teaching. If we believe the account in Diogenes Laertius IX.62, Pyrrho lived to be ninety; he would therefore have died between 275 and 270 BC.[100]

Timon of Phlius, after studies with Stilpon of Megara around 300, became a follower of Pyrrho.[101] He lived the life of an itinerant Sophist in Chalcedon, Propontis and in Alexandria in Egypt, but moved to Athens c. 275, where it seems he died aged ninety. He had a good relationship with the kings Antigonus Gonatas and Ptolemy II Philadelphos. These dates allow us to put his chronology approximately between 325 and 230 or 225 BC.

After Timon, the other major representative of Pyrrhonian scepticism is Aenesidemus (first century BC). Even in ancient times there were questions raised as to whether there was a connection between the ancient school and Aenesidemus' revival, and whether the original Pyrrhonist tradition had continued, even if its representatives achieved little prominence, or whether it survived in this period only underground. Diogenes Laertius IX.115–16 reproduces the terms of the debate, between those who denied any linear succession (Menodotus) and those who had reconstructed an uninterrupted chain of successors (Hippobotus and Sotion),[102] running from Timon to Aenesidemus: first immediate pupils of Timon, Dioscurides of Cyprus, Nicholochus of Rhodes, Euphranor of Seleucia and Praylus of the Troad; Euphranor was supposedly teacher of Eubulus of Alexandria, who was in turn the teacher of Ptolemy of Cyrene,[103] the teacher of Sarpedon and Heraclides; and Heraclides was, finally, the teacher of Aenesidemus. Diogenes Laertius' list contains all the characteristics of a fictitious *diadochē* ('succession') and offers no proof of the existence of an actual Pyrrhonian sect involving Pyrrho, Timon and

---

[99] D.L. IX.61. Cf. Decleva Caizzi 1981a, 132–5.   [100] Decleva Caizzi 1981a, 146–7.
[101] Di Marco 1989, 1–5.   [102] Hippob. fr. 22 in Gigante 1983c; Sotion fr. 33 Wehrli.
[103] Restorer of scepticism, according to Menodotus.

Aenesidemus. Further confirmation of this assessment can be found in Aenesidemus' *Pyrrhonian Discourses*, which indicate a rebirth of Pyrrhonism only in the second half of the first century BC, with Aenesidemus.[104]

VII Minor Socratics

To conclude, I will give no more than a brief account of the chronology (running approximately from 320 to 250 BC) of the main representatives of the so-called Minor Socratic schools: Dialecticians (or 'Megaric'), Cyrenaics and Cynics. Their chronology is actually almost contemporaneous with that of certain members of the major philosophical schools and their histories often intersect in a series of sometimes controversial relationships.

The Dialectical (or 'Megaric') school[105] was given its name by Dionysius of Chalcedon, whose *floruit* can be placed at 320; he was more or less the contemporary of Euphantus, born before 348. More important are Diodorus Cronus, active in Athens and Alexandria between 315 and *c.* 284[106] (his contemporary was Aristides the Dialectician), and Stilpo, who lived *c.* 360–280. Alexinus (*c.* 339–265), a younger figure, is well known for a debate on rhetorical questions with the Epicurean Hermarchus, dated – with certainty – to 267/6, and for his attacks on Zeno of Citium. Philo the Dialectician was a student of Diodorus Cronus between 310 and 300, and a contemporary of Zeno of Citium. Between 280 and 275 Panthoides, whose lectures were attended by the Peripatetic Lycon, was active; while the *floruit* of Aristotle and Artemidorus is put at around 250. The first is known for having contributed to the overthrow of the rule of Abantidas of Sicyon, the second for attacking the Stoic Chrysippus.

The Cyrenaic philosophers traced their ancestry to Aristippus of Cyrene, who lived in the last decades of the fifth century and the first half of the fourth. An important place among them is occupied by his daughter Arete and his grandson of the same name, who was effectively the creator of Cyrenaic philosophy. We have some chronological details about Antipater of Cyrene (*c.* 350–250) and Aristotle of Cyrene, a contemporary of Stilpo (*c.* 360–280), whose membership of the Cyrenaic school has been put in doubt. The *floruit* of Hegesias has been placed around 290, while Theodorus the Atheist lived *c.* 340–250.

---

[104] Decleva Caizzi 1992a and Mansfeld 1995.

[105] On the existence and name of this school, cf. Cambiano 1977 and Sedley 1977. Against this, see Döring 1989. Like Giannantoni 1990, IV 41–50, I am inclined to accept Sedley's hypothesis regarding the 'Dialectical' school. For the chronology of these philosophers I follow Sedley 1977, 107 n. 23. Cf. also the useful chronological table *ibid.* 82.

[106] This chronology is reconstructed in Sedley 1977, 78–80 and 107–9.

Diogenes of Sinope, founder of the Cynic *hairesis*, lived approximately between 412–403 and 324/1.[107] Crates of Thebes (*c.* 368/5–288/5) was his disciple; he was joined in his philosophical studies by his wife Hipparchia of Maroneia and his son Metrocles. The philosopher Menedemus, the butt of attacks by the Epicurean Colotes in his two works *Against Plato's Lysis* and *Against Plato's Euthydemus*,[108] was about ten years younger.

Menedemus of Eretria, philosopher and politician (he was *proboulos* of his city), was head of a philosophical school there and lived to the age of eighty-four, from 345/4 to 261/0.[109] Menedemus was a pupil first of Stilpo at Megara, then of Polemo and Theophrastus at Athens.

VIII Survey

A. THE ACADEMY

c. 408 Birth of Speusippus

396/5 Birth of Xenocrates at Chalcedon

c. 390 Birth of Heraclides Ponticus

c. 370 Xenocrates goes to Athens

367 or 361 Xenocrates accompanies Plato on his second or third trip to Sicily

c. 365 Heraclides enters the Academy

361/0 Heraclides Ponticus made head of the Academy

348/7 (Theophilos' archonship) Death of Plato; Speusippus becomes scholarch

339/8 (Lysimachides' archonship) Death of Speusippus; Xenocrates becomes scholarch. Heraclides leaves Athens and returns to Heraclea Pontica

331 Chaeron becomes ruler of Pellene

322 Xenocrates' mission to Antipater in Macedonia

316/15 Birth of Arcesilaus (Hermippus in D.L.)

314/13 Death of Xenocrates; Polemo becomes scholarch

c. 310 Death of Heraclides Ponticus

276/5 (Philocrates' archonship) Death of Crantor

275–273 Birth of Eratosthenes of Cyrene

270/69 Death of Polemo; Crates becomes scholarch

268–264(?) Death of Crates; Arcesilaus becomes scholarch after Socratides refuses office

post 246 Eratosthenes is summoned to Alexandria in Egypt by Ptolemy III Euergetes

241/0 Death of Arcesilaus; Lacydes becomes scholarch

214/13 Birth of Carneades of Cyrene

206/5 (Callistratos' archonship) Death of Lacydes

post 205/4 Death of Eratosthenes

---

[107] I agree with Giannantoni 1990, IV 421–2.

[108] For the identity of the philosopher and a summary of the argument, cf. Giannantoni 1990, IV 581–3 and Gigante 1992, 71–8.   [109] Cf. Knoepfler 1991.

187/6 Birth of Clitomachus in Carthage

185/4 (Eupolemos' archonship) Death of Moschion

174/3 (Alexander's archonship) Death of Eubulus of Ephesus and Eubulus of Erythrae

168/7 (Xenocles' archonship) Death of Agamestor

167/6 (Nicosthenes' archonship) Death of Telecles

164/3 Birth of Charmadas

163/2 Clitomachus goes to Athens

159/8 (Epainetos' archonship) Death of Apollonius

154/3 (Aristaichmos' archonship) Birth of Philo at Larissa

143/2 (Aristophon's archonship) Death of Eubulus

142/1 (Aristophantos' archonship) Charmadas, aged twenty-two, goes to Athens

140/39 (Hagnotheos' archonship) Clitomachus founds his own school in the Palladium

137/6 Carneades of Cyrene retires as scholarch; the younger Carneades becomes scholarch

131/0 (Epicles' archonship) Death of the younger Carneades; succeeded by Crates of Tarsus

130/29 (Nicomachus' archonship) Philo goes to Athens

130/29–110/09 Philo studies with Clitomachus and with an unknown Apollodorus

c. 130–120 Birth of Antiochus of Ascalon

129/8 (Lyciscus' archonship) Death of Carneades of Cyrene; Clitomachus re-enters the Academy

127/6 Death of Crates of Tarsus; Clitomachus becomes effective scholarch of the Academy

120/19 (Eumachos' archonship) Death of Boethus of Marathon

110/09 (Polycleitus' archonship) Death of Clitomachus; Philo becomes scholarch of the Academy

ante 91 Death of Charmadas

c. 90 Antiochus founds the 'Old Academy'

88 Philo establishes himself at Rome

87–84 Antiochus at Alexandria in Egypt

84/3 (Nicetes' archonship) Death of Philo (in Rome?)

79 Antiochus returns to Athens

c. 68 Death of Antiochus

B. THE PERIPATOS

372/1 or 371/0 Birth of Theophrastus

ante 350 Birth of Eudemus of Rhodes

c. 350 Birth of Chamaeleon and of Demetrius of Phalerum

c. 350–281 Lifespan of Duris and of Lynceus of Samos

348/7 On Plato's death, Theophrastus (?) and Aristotle go to Assos to see Hermias of Atarneus

345/4 Theophrastus transfers to Mytilene on Lesbos with Aristotle

343/2 Aristotle is summoned by Philip II to Mieza to be Alexander's tutor

c. 340 Birth of Clearchus of Soli

340–330 Birth of Strato of Lampsacus

337/6 Theophrastus and Aristotle return to Athens. Aristotle opens his school in the
      Lyceum
323/2 Aristotle is forced to leave Athens and flees to Stagira
322/1 Death of Aristotle; Theophrastus becomes scholarch for 36 years. Strato goes to
      Egypt to the court of Ptolemy I Soter; Eudemus returns to Rhodes
317–307 Demetrius of Phalerum becomes governor of Athens
307   Demetrius of Phalerum forced into exile (he goes to Alexandria in Egypt) after
      297; maybe in 295, when Demetrius Poliorcetes marched northward
300/299 or 299/8 Birth of Lyco
post 297 Demetrius of Phalerum exiled from Thebes
288/7 or 287/6 Death of Theophrastus; Strato becomes scholarch for 18 years. Neleus
      returns to Scepsis
post 283 Death of Demetrius of Phalerum
281   Chamaeleon's mission to Seleucus I
270/69 or 269/8 Death of Strato; succeeded by Lyco, scholarch for 44 years
260–255 Prytanis' floruit
c. 250 Birth of Aristo of Ceos and of Phormion
247 or 244 Lyco honoured at Athens (*IG* II² 791)
226/5 or 225/4 Death of Lyco; Aristo of Ceos becomes scholarch
225   Prytanis' mission to Antigonus Doson
223   Prytanis redrafts the constitution of Megalopolis
c. 200 Birth of Critolaus of Phaselis
195/4 The elderly Phormion speaks before Hannibal at Ephesus
155   Critolaus' mission to Rome
c. 118 Death of Critolaus

c. The Stoa

334/3 Birth of Zeno (according to Persaeus)
?   Birth of Zeno (according to Apollodorus)
330–325 Birth of Dionysius of Heraclea
331/0 (Aristophanes' archonship) Birth of Cleanthes (according to Apollodorus)
307/6 Birth of Persaeus of Citium
c. 285 Birth of Sphaerus of Borysthenes
280–276 Birth of Chrysippus
c. 274 Persaeus arrives in Pella at the court of Antigonus Gonatas
c. 265 Sphaerus goes to Athens
262/1 (Arrheneides' archonship) Death of Zeno (according to Apollodorus);
      Cleanthes becomes scholarch
260–256 Persaeus' floruit
c. 250 Death of Dionysius Metathemenos
c. 244 Persaeus becomes archon of Corinth
243   Death of Persaeus
c. 240 Sphaerus goes to Sparta to Cleomenes III
c. 230 Birth of Diogenes of Seleucia
230/29 (Jason's archonship) Death of Cleanthes (according to Apollodorus)
229–209 Aristocreon at Athens
c. 222 Sphaerus follows Cleomenes III to Egypt

208–204 Death of Chrysippus, aged 73

c. 185–180 Birth of Panaetius at Rhodes

184/3 (Charicles' archonship) Aristocreon honoured in Athens

c. 170 Birth of Mnesarchus and of Dardanus

post 168/7 Panaetius studies with Crates of Mallos at Pergamon

ante 155 Panaetius becomes *hierothutēs* of Poseidon Hippios at Lindos

155 Diogenes of Seleucia, Carneades the Elder and Critolaus of Phaselis sent on diplomatic mission to Rome

post 155 Panaetius studies with Diogenes of Seleucia at Athens

c. 150–140 Death of Diogenes.

149/8 Panaetius is *hieropoios* in Athens on the occasion of the celebration of the *Ptolemaia* (they presumably honoured Ptolemy III)

post 146 Panaetius meets Scipio Aemilianus (in Rome?) for the first time

140–138 Panaetius accompanies Scipio during his diplomatic missions to the East and to Greece

c. 138–129 Panaetius travels between Rome and Athens

c. 130 Birth of Posidonius

130/29 Death of Scipio and of Antipater of Tarsus; Panaetius becomes scholarch.

110/09 Death of Panaetius. Mnesarchus and Dardanus are *principes Stoicorum* in Athens; Mnesarchus *vigebat*

post 88 Death of Dardanus and of Mnesarchus

60 Cicero sends to Posidonius a *hypomnēma* in Greek of his work on his consulship

51 (?) Posidonius' second mission to Rome

D. THE GARDEN

342/1 (Sosigenes' archonship) Birth of Epicurus

331/0 Birth of Metrodorus

328/7 Epicurus begins philosophical studies aged fourteen

c. 325 Birth of Idomeneus and Hermarchus (?)

c. 324 Birth of Pythocles

323–321 Epicurus is ephebe in Athens

c. 320 Birth of Colotes

320–311 Epicurus in Colophon (?)

311/10–307/6 Epicurus teaches at Mytilene and at Lampsacus; comes into contact with Colotes, Hermarchus, Idomeneus, Pythocles and Polyaenus

307/6 or 305/4 Epicurus in Athens; founds the Garden. Pythocles aged seventeen or eighteen

c. 306–301 Idomeneus is court dignitary at Lampsacus

301/0 (Clearchos' archonship) Epicurus writes Book XIV of the *On Nature*

300/299 (Hegemachos' archonship) Epicurus writes Book XV of the *On Nature*

296/5 (Nicias' archonship) Epicurus writes Book XXVIII of the *On Nature*

c. 290 Timocrates' apostasy

290–280 Death of Polyaenus

278/7 (Democles' archonship) Death of Metrodorus

271/0 (Pytharatus' archonship) Death of Epicurus

post 268 Colotes writes *On the Impossibility of Living on the Principles of the Other Philosophers* dedicated to King Ptolemy II Philadelphos

c. 250 Death of Hermarchus; Polystratus becomes scholarch; birth of Basilides (?)
219/18 (Menecrates' archonship) Death of Polystratus; Dionysius of Lamptrai
        becomes scholarch
205/4   (Isocrates' archonship) Death of Dionysius; Basilides becomes scholarch
c. 175 Death of Basilides; Thespis (?) becomes scholarch
?   Apollodorus succeeds Thespis (?) as scholarch
c. 150 Birth of Zeno of Sidon and of Demetrius of Laconia
138   Birth of Phaedrus
119/18 (Hipparchos' archonship) Phaedrus is ephebe
c. 100 Zeno of Sidon becomes scholarch
88   Phaedrus in Rome
c. 75   Death of Zeno of Sidon; Phaedrus becomes scholarch
70/69   Death of Phaedrus; Patro becomes scholarch

E. THE PYRRHONISTS

365–360 Birth of Pyrrho
334–324 Pyrrho and Anaxarchus follow Alexander the Great into Asia
c. 325   Birth of Timon
275–270 Death of Pyrrho
c. 275   Timon sets up in Athens
c. 230 or 225 Death of Timon

F. THE MINOR SOCRATICS

c. 412–403 Birth of Diogenes of Sinope
c. 368–365 Birth of Crates of Thebes
c. 360   Birth of Stilpo of Megara
c. 360–280 Aristotle of Cyrene
c. 350–250 Antipater of Cyrene
ante 348   Birth of Euphantus
345/4   Birth of Menedemus of Eretria
c. 340–250 Theodorus the Atheist
c. 339   Birth of Alexinus
c. 324–321 Death of Diogenes of Sinope
c. 320   *floruit* of Dionysius of Chalcedon and Euphantus
c. 315–284 Diodorus Cronus active in Athens and Alexandria; *floruit* of Aristides
310–300   Philo the Dialectician studies with Diodorus Cronus
c. 290   *floruit* of Hegesias
c. 288/5   Death of Crates of Thebes
c. 284   Death of Diodorus Cronus
c. 280   Death of Stilpo
c. 280–275 *floruit* of Panthoides
267/6   (Menecles' archonship) *Letter* by Hermarchus to Theophides against Alexinus
c. 265   Death of Alexinus
261/0   Death of Menedemus of Eretria
c. 250   *floruit* of Aristotle the Dialectician and Artemidorus

Appendix
Successions of scholarchs

Year	Academy	Lyceum	Stoa	Kepos
348/7–339/8	Speusippus			
339/8–314/13	Xenocrates			
322/1–288/7 or				
287/6		Theophrastus		
?–262/1			Zeno	
314/13–270/69	Polemo			
307/6–271/0				Epicurus
288/7 or				
287/6–270/9 or				
269/8		Strato		
c. 271/0–250				Hermarchus
270/69–268–264	Crates			
270/69 or				
269/8–226/5 or				
225/4		Lycon		
268–264–241/0	Arcesilaus			
262/1–230/29			Cleanthes	
c. 250–*ante* 220/19				Polystratus
241/0–226/5 or				
225/4	Lacydes			
230/29–208–204			Chrysippus	
226/5 or 225/4–?		Ariston		
226/5 or 225/4–				
167/6	Telecles and			
	Euander; Hegesinus			
ante 220/19–201/0				Dionisius
208–205–?			Zeno of Tarsus	
201/0–*c.* 175				Basilides
c. 175–?				Thespis (?)
?–150–140			Diogenes	
167/6–137/6	Carneades I			
?–*c.* 100				Apollodorus
c. 155		Critolaus		

[53]

Year	Academy	Lyceum	Stoa	Kepos
150–140–129/8			Antipater	
137/6–131/0	Carneades II			
131/0–127/6	Crates of Tarsus			
129/8–110/9			Panaetius	
?–c. 110		Diodorus of Tirus		
127/6–110/9	Clitomachus			
110/9–84/3	Philo			
c. 100–c. 75				Zeno of Sidon
c. 75–70				Phaedrus

3

Organization and structure of the philosophical schools

TIZIANO DORANDI

Before tackling in detail the issue of the organization and structure of the philosophical schools, both in the Hellenistic period and more generally, one must try to find an answer to the question of what a philosophical school was. This is a difficult question, which has not yet found an answer that copes satisfactorily with all the problems it poses.[1]

Until recently the theory of Wilamowitz prevailed, according to which the philosophers' schools were religious societies (*thiasoi*), dedicated to the worship of the gods, or the Muses in this particular case.[2] Wilamowitz started from the presumption that all such ancient societies had cult characteristics and that, for this reason, they were recognized by Athenian law, giving them the status of legal bodies. From an outsider's viewpoint the philosophical schools would therefore have appeared to be religious societies devoted to the worship of the Muses, while internally they would have developed functions like those of modern universities. In the Academy and Peripatos, above all, there would have been activity in scientific research and teaching based on a division of duties between teachers old and young, and carried out in a series of public lectures and private seminars.

Wilamowitz's theory has attracted criticism and objections. In particular, it has been discovered that certain elements which for Wilamowitz were typical of a *thiasos* (statues of the Muses and their worship) were shared by other institutions like the gymnasia and children's schools, and were therefore not by themselves enough to support the identification of philosophical schools as religious societies.[3] To state that the philosophical schools were institutions of common ownership in which the scholarch (the head of the school) was the single owner of the property and all the fixtures has become unacceptable;[4] nor is there clear, concrete proof to lead one to say that the philosophical schools were organized like

---

[1] For the *status quaestionis* see Isnardi Parente 1974b; 1986, 350–7; and Natali 1991, 93–120.
[2] Wilamowitz 1881, 181–6, 194–7, 263–88.   [3] Gomperz 1899.
[4] Gottschalk 1972, 320, 329.

thiasoi devoted to the worship of the Muses. Still less does the assumption that the schools resorted to this device to obtain the status of a legal body bear up, since such a concept was foreign to the Greek world. So it has been assumed that the philosophers' schools were instead secular institutions with educational aims directed towards propagation of useful knowledge. They would have been supported by private funds and have had nothing to do with the state and therefore no need for any authorization for their existence and activity.[5]

But there is no lack of support for Wilamowitz's theory, particularly as regards the Academy. There would seem to be no serious reason to oppose the recognition of *thiasos* characteristics in the Athenian philosophical schools. If anything, the need for the legal and religious device of an association (*koinon*) devoted to the Muses, developed with time in the case of the Academy: some think it might have become necessary in the second phase of the school's history, at the point when there was the prospect that a poor non-citizen philosopher such as Xenocrates would become scholarch.[6] As far as the Peripatos goes, the theory[7] that it was a permanent foundation much like elementary schools or funeral associations seems to be the correct one. The Peripatos was created out of the legacy of Aristotle, who had as his aim not the provision of education for the young nor the worship of the Muses, but rather the fulfilment of the ideals of the theoretical life (*bios theorētikos*), the shared pursuit of philosophy (*sunphilosophein*) which was one of the methods he indicated for spending periods of leisure (*scholē*) with one's friends (Arist. *EN* IX.1172a1–8).

It seems clear from what has been said above that there is a general interest in the initial foundation of the schools, particularly the Academy and the Peripatos. From Wilamowitz on, the Academy has been seen as the prototype for every school, and reconstructions of all other schools (primarily the Peripatos) have been modelled on the blueprint of its organization and structure. But it is also evident that the schools did not always have the same characteristics and organization, nor could such characteristics and organization (nor their aims) be the same for all the schools for the whole of their long existence.

For example, despite interesting points of similarity, there are important differences between the Academy and Peripatos, on the one hand, and Epicurus' Garden[8] on the other. Its organization, more than that of

---

[5] Lynch 1972, 105–34 and Wehrli 1976, 129–30.   [6] Isnardi Parente 1986, 350–7.
[7] Natali 1991, 93–120, following the findings of Veyne 1976, 241–4.   [8] Cf. Clay 1983b, 277–8.

any other school, was based on principles of emulation, commemoration and imitation.[9] Since one of the great aspirations of Epicurean philosophy was the imitation of divinity, the emulation of those who had reached a state of maximum perfection in imitating the gods – Epicurus, Metrodorus, Hermarchus and Polyaenus (the so-called leaders or *kathēgemones*) – was, for students in the Garden, a primary and vital consequence. Already among the first generations of Epicureans the idea of *kathēgemones* gave rise to an ideal model of a 'shared life' (*contubernium*), which took shape as 'many members of one body' (Sen. *Ep.* 33.4). There was no attempt to achieve a meticulous hierarchical organization in which *philosophoi*, *philologoi* ('scholars'), *kathēgētai* ('professors') and *sunētheis* ('intimates') were distinguished.[10] The ideal of freedom of speech (*parrhêsia*) between teachers and students, the basis of a common lifestyle inspired by the pedagogical aims of friendship, kindliness and goodwill prevailed. That lifestyle was founded on the practice of common celebration, with festivals and feasts, of holidays kept in memory of Epicurus and other friends and family who had died prematurely, like Metrodorus, Polyaenus and Epicurus' brothers.[11] We know of at least five cults celebrated within the school: the annual funeral cult which Epicurus had established in memory of his parents and brothers; the two celebrations of Epicurus himself – an annual one, on the twentieth day of the month of Gamelion, his birthday, and one on the twentieth of each month, in honour also of Metrodorus. There was also a day devoted to commemorating the birthdays of Epicurus' brothers, in the month of Poseideon, and a day for Polyaenus, which occurred in the month of Metageitnion.

We also have some interesting information on the internal organization and lifestyle of the Academy and Peripatos. A famous fragment of the comic playwright Epicrates[12] describes how Plato, Speusippus and Menedemus tried to distinguish and define the various species of animals and plants. Aristotle's writings speak of the use made by the philosopher of tablets, anatomical charts, diagrams and other teaching aids in his lectures.[13] In the last century there was a desire to find in these accounts, and especially in that of Epicrates, confirmation of the suggestion that the Academy and Peripatos were prototypes of modern universities. Plato was seen as the first organizer of scientific research in the Academy, and it was assumed that the school had regular programmes and seminars in which students were assigned research projects under the guidance of

[9] Cf. Clay 1983b, 264–70.
[10] De Witt 1936, rightly criticized by Gigante 1983a, 110–13. Cf. Clay 1983b, 269–70.
[11] Clay 1986, 11–28.   [12] Fr. 10 Kassel–Austin.   [13] Jackson 1920, 191–200.

their master.[14] But these are dangerous theories, fully rebutted by successive critics and with little plausibility since they are tied too closely to modern culture, experience and modes of thought. From a later period, we do have a report about Carneades' lectures (scholai) being written up and read (and criticized) at a next meeting.[15] Unfortunately we know nothing about the Stoa.

The individual institutions were run by a scholarch (prostatēs, archōn) who could be chosen or appointed in different ways: the previous scholarch could nominate his successor directly, before his death (Plato chose Speusippus, Strato Lyco, Epicurus Hermarchus);[16] the election could be decided by a free vote (Xenocrates was elected as Speusippus' successor; Socratides as Crates' successor).[17] A scholarch could refuse the job in favour of another member of the school (Socratides gave way to Arcesilaus). As a rule the scholarch stayed in the job until his death: there were two significant exceptions to this, both in the Academy: Lacydes and Carneades of Cyrene retired from running the school while they were still alive because of their health.[18] But there are no examples of joint scholarchs. The case of Mnesarchus and Dardanus, thought to have been joint successors to Panaetius as head of the Stoa, is based on false premisses.

In some schools there was in use a distinction between younger students (neaniskoi) and older ones (presbuteroi), perhaps corresponding to a different level of attainment.[19] What is also significant is that, at least in the cases of the Academy and the Garden, the schools were open to female students: Axiothea and Lasthenia were pupils of Plato and Speusippus; Batis, Boidion, Demetria, Edia, Leontion, Mammarion, Nikidion, and Themista were active members of the Garden.[20] Diogenes Laertius credits Theophrastus with two thousand students: it is difficult to establish whether this number stands for the total number of the philosopher's students during his whole period of teaching, or the usual attendance at his lectures.[21]

We know that Plato, Xenocrates and Polemo took up residence in the garden of the Academy and that, during Polemo's time as scholarch, some

---

[14] On this question, see Isnardi Parente 1974b, 862–70.

[15] Phld. Acad. hist., cols. 22.35–23.3, cf. Mansfeld 1994b, 193.

[16] Cf. D.L.iv.1 (Speusippus); D.L. v.62 (Lyco); D.L. x.17 (Hermarchus).

[17] Phld. Acad. hist., cols. 6.41–7.14 (Xenocrates); 18.1–7 (cf. D.L. iv.32: Arcesilaus).

[18] Cf. D.L. iv.60 and Phld. Acad. hist., col. 27.1–7 (Lacydes); cols. 24.28–25.16; 25.39–26.4 (Carneades).

[19] We have definite information about the Academy: Phld. Acad. hist., cols. 6.41 and 18.6 (cf. Athen. ii.59d–f) and the Peripatos: D.L. v.53, 70–1.   [20] Cf. Dorandi 1991a.

[21] On this question, cf. Sollenberger 1992, 3828.

students followed their master's example.[22] The members of the Garden also lived within their school's grounds.

The methods of upkeep of the schools took different forms. The system practised by Epicurus is well known: free donations (*suntaxeis*) were given to the Garden by influential persons, sometimes at the request of Epicurus himself. If Diogenes Laertius' account is to be trusted, Speusippus used to demand an honorarium from his students (D.L. iv.2); the Stoics Cleanthes, Chrysippus and Diogenes of Seleucia required payment for their lectures.[23] But it is not certain, in the cases of the Academy and the Stoa, that the payment of fees was actually intended for the upkeep of the school. Perhaps it was geared to the actual or presumed personal needs of individual scholarchs.

I have already called attention to the fact that all the schools without exception underwent an evolution, not only in thought but also in structure, over the centuries of their existence, although it is not always clearly documented. I have traced the principal directions taken by individual schools in the pages devoted to their chronologies,[24] but it would be wise to note here some important points concerning possible influences on the outward form of their organization and structure. In the case of the Academy there is a point of demarcation at the moment when Speusippus died and Xenocrates succeeded as scholarch. But the situation becomes more complicated – and more interesting – in the period from the death of Arcesilaus to Antiochus: Lacydes and Carneades of Cyrene resigned as scholarchs while they were still alive. This brings us to the schism in the time of Clitomachus and the birth of the 'Old Academy' of Antiochus of Ascalon and his brother Aristus in opposition to the sceptically-oriented Academy of Philo of Larissa. The Peripatos, after Lyco, witnessed a rapid decline to the point where under Diodorus of Tyre the school had practically disappeared as an institution. It recovered its prestige only in the first century BC with Cratippus of Pergamon. In the Stoa, after the first skirmishes of the separatist movements,[25] there is a report suggesting that in the time of Antipater and Panaetius courses of instruction were offered alongside those given by the official scholarch. It is no accident that during this time at least two Stoics of note, apart from Antipater and Panaetius, were active in Athens, i.e. Dardanus and Mnesarchus (Cicero describes them as 'leaders of the Stoics', *principes Stoicorum*, Cic. *Acad.* ii.69); these men were roughly contemporary with

---

[22] Dillon 1990 (1983).
[23] Cleanthes: Phld. *Stoic. hist.*, col. 19; Chrysippus: Plu. *Stoic. Rep.* 1043e; Diogenes of Seleucia: Cic. *Acad.* ii.98.   [24] See above, pp. 31–54.   [25] See above, p. 41.

Panaetius.[26] Even in the Garden, at least from the second half of the second century BC, there was no unity of thought or institution: even if certain 'dissident' groups, like the Epicureans who ran a school at Rhodes, are excluded, one can identify the presence of strong personalities within the ambit of the mother school – Zeno of Sidon, Demetrius of Laconia and Phaedrus – symptomatic of a situation of unease and indeed fragmentation of its original unity.

One should not overlook the other serious problem: secession by certain members of a particular school in favour of a rival or else to found a school of their own. In the case of the Academy the most striking instance was undoubtedly that involving the young Aristotle who, on Plato's death, left the Academy and opened his own school in the Peripatos a few years later (335/4). Not long before that (339/8), Menedemus of Pyrrha and Heraclides Ponticus had also left the Academy on the election of Xenocrates as scholarch. Some centuries later there were episodes involving Clitomachus, returning to the fold of his mother school after having run an establishment of his own; Metrodorus of Stratonicea, who moved to Epicureanism; Dion of Alexandria and Cratippus of Pergamon, who became Peripatetics; and the very serious case of Antiochus of Ascalon. I know of no such instances in the Peripatos, but in the Stoa there are the cases of Aristo of Chios, of Dionysius *Metathemenos* ('Turncoat') who at the end of his life went over to the Garden, of Herillus of Carthage, and of Chrysippus who left Cleanthes to study with Carneades and Lacydes but returned to the Stoa to become its third scholarch. Examples of schism also took place in the Garden: in Epicurus' lifetime Timocrates, brother of Metrodorus, not only left the school but took part in a defamatory campaign against Epicurus, which proved very damaging.[27] Philodemus informs us of a whole series of 'dissident' Epicureans (called by him *sophistai*) who lived between the second and first centuries BC and were especially active in the centres of Cos and Rhodes:[28] there are references to doctrines of a group of Epicureans involved in discussions about the status of rhetoric as an art (*technē*), about the topic of anger, and about questions of theology – we find the names of Nicasicrates, possibly the head of the school at Rhodes, Timasagoras, Antiphanes and Bromius.

We also have information about the existence of philosophical schools

---

[26] The theory of Ferrary 1988, 449–64, that one could already at this moment speak of the presence of three different currents of thought, owing allegiance to Diogenes of Seleucia, Antipater of Tarsus and Panaetius of Rhodes, is perhaps a bit hazardous. However, it seems evident that the Stoa's internal unity had already lost its coherence by this point.

[27] Cf. Angeli 1993, 13–17.   [28] Cf. Longo and Tepedino 1981 and especially Sedley 1989a.

outside Athens, but it is hard to say whether they were actual branches. With regard to the Academy, a significant case is that of the Assos school, created by the intervention of Hermias of Atarneus, where we find Erastus, Coriscus, Aristotle and possibly Theophrastus.[29] More doubtful is the presence of a branch of the Academy in Alexandria, supposedly run for a certain time by Zenodorus of Tyre.[30] We know that Epicurus, in the early years of his teaching, had opened a school at Lampsacus, which continued to flourish after his departure for Athens.[31] Demetrius of Laconia successfully ran a school at Miletus and possibly also one in Italy.[32] The highly significant case of Philodemus, who left Athens to go to Italy, first to Rome then to Herculaneum, lies outside the chronological limits of this study. We are also told of the existence of a Stoic school at Rhodes, run by Posidonius.[33] Also interesting is the fact that not only many scholarchs but also a large number of students came from peripheral geographical regions of the Mediterranean basin, often far away from Greek influence: the coasts of Asia Minor, Africa, the interior of Syria and Mesopotamia.[34]

Beside this kind of organized and institutionalized school (*scholai*, *diatribai*), there were also groups of people who got together to practise philosophy in an apparently less rigidly structured form, which could be defined as a 'pseudo-school' or, better, 'philosophical tendency' (*agōgai* or *haireseis*).[35] The so-called minor Socratic schools (Cyrenaics, Dialecticians, Cynics) and Pyrrhonism should be considered as fitting under this heading.

The modern reader at this point might demand a reply to more specific questions: what did it mean to be a member of a school? Was there a registration fee (with or without tax)? Could one pass freely from one school to another, in order to pursue courses with different teachers, with different methods, ideas and programmes? Furthermore, could a philosopher begin to teach freely in a specific public place (e.g. the *Stoa Poikilē* or one of the many Athenian gymnasia, the *Lacydeum* or the *Ptolemaeum*) or did he have to be authorized by somebody? This question is closely tied to

---

[29] Phld. *Acad. hist.*, col. v. Cf. Dorandi 1991b, 31–3.

[30] Phld. *Acad. hist.*, col. 23.2–3. Cf. Dorandi 1991b, 70, n. 239.   [31] Cf. Angeli 1981 and 1988b.

[32] Puglia 1988, 37–48 and Romeo 1988, 25–32.   [33] Moretti 1976.

[34] Early evidence can be found from lists of the students of Plato, Arcesilaus, Carneades and Antiochus (?) handed down at Phld. *Acad. hist.*, cols. 6.1–20; 20.4–44; 22.35–24.16 (cf. 32.32–42); 34.3–16, or those of the students of Zeno of Tarsus, Diogenes of Seleucia and Panaetius: Phld. *Stoic. hist.*, cols. 48; 51–2; 63–8.

[35] *Agōgē* probably had the same original meaning as the later *hairesis* (Glucker 1978, 165). The semantic development and history of the term *hairesis* has been traced by Glucker 1978, 159–225.

that already discussed concerning the legal status of the philosophical schools. These questions cannot, in my opinion, be given a specific or definitive answer because of an almost total lack of ancient sources which might throw light on them. We read that Arcesilaus, through innate modesty, urged his disciples to follow the courses of other teachers and on one occasion actually accompanied one of his pupils who came from Chios and recommended him to the Peripatetic Hieronymus (D.L. iv.42). The same Arcesilaus at one point decided to leave Theophrastus' school for Crantor's (D.L. iv.29–30). From two passages in the *History of the Stoa* by Philodemus it seems possible to deduce that, at least from the time of Antipater and Panaetius, there were series of introductory lectures in the school, parallel to those of the scholarchs, given to the most advanced members.[36] If the expression *scholastikai esthētes* of which Diogenes Laertius speaks in the *Life of Bion* really carries the sense of 'scholars' (i.e. philosophers') clothing', we have a curious testimony that in at least some schools a particular kind of clothing was required or adopted.[37] But nothing more precise has been discovered.

[36] Phld. *Stoic. hist.*, cols. 60 and 77, 1–3. This seems to be the meaning of the verb προεξάγειν. Cf. Dorandi 1994a, 167–9.   [37] On this last point see Capasso 1980.

PART II

LOGIC AND LANGUAGE

*

4

Introduction

JONATHAN BARNES

1 A map of logic

The Stoics were the innovative logicians of the Hellenistic period; and the leading logician of the school was its third scholarch, Chrysippus. Most of this section of the *History* will therefore describe Stoic ideas and Stoic theories. Its hero will be Chrysippus.

Logic is the study of inference, and hence of the items upon which inference depends – of propositional structure (or 'grammar'), of meaning and reference. That part of their subject which the Hellenistic philosophers called λογική (*logikē*) was a larger discipline;[1] for *logikē* was the science which studies λόγος in all its manifestations,[2] and logic is included in *logikē* as a part. Indeed as a part of a part. For the Stoics divided *logikē* into two subparts, rhetoric and dialectic; and logic is a part of dialectic.[3]

The founder famously distinguished rhetoric from dialectic by a gesture:

> When Zeno of Citium was asked how rhetoric differed from dialectic, he closed his hand and then opened it again, saying 'Thus'. With the closing he aligned the rounded and brief character of dialectic, and by opening and extending his fingers he hinted at the breadth of rhetorical power. (S.E. *M* 11.6–7)

The gesture is picturesque, and it caught the imagination;[4] but the thought behind it was neither original nor enlightening. There were also formal definitions:

---

[1] On the parts of philosophy see the Preface pp. xiii–xvi; see also Hadot 1979, Ierodiakonou 1993b and Dörrie and Baltes 1996, 205–31.

[2] See e.g. [Plu.] *Plac.* 874e. (But note Hülser 1987–8, LXXXII.)

[3] D.L. VII.41 (ἔνιοι); Sen. *Ep.* 139.17. Other divisions of λογική are recorded: D.L. VII.41; cf. Hülser 1987–88, LXXIX–XC.

[4] Other reports in Cic. *Fin.* 11.17; *Orat.* 113; Quint. *Inst.* 11.7; cf. Varro *apud* Cassiod. *Inst.*11.2; Cic. *Brut.* 309. Compare Zeno's more complicated gesture designed to illuminate the stages of knowledge: Cic. *Acad.* 11.145.

Dialectic is the science of conversing correctly where the speeches involve question and answer – and hence they also define it as the science of what is true and false and neither. (D.L. VII.42)

The first of these definitions, frequently repeated,[5] is the prose version of Zeno's gesture. The second[6] is elsewhere ascribed to Posidonius (D.L. VII.62): a shorter version – 'the science of what is true and false' – is also attested (Cic. *Acad.* II.91), and scholars commonly suppose that Posidonius enlarged and ameliorated a definition which had been standard in the Old Stoa.[7]

However that may be, a science 'of what is true and false' is a science which *discriminates* the true from the false;[8] and it is a science whose subject-matter recognizes no limits 'for all objects are perceived by way of the study of λόγοι'.[9] But dialectic is neither a superscience nor an omniscience: it enables us to discriminate truth and falsity on any question whatever inasmuch as its methods and theorems are 'topic neutral'; and by the same token it cannot, by itself, discriminate among the truths and falsities of physics or ethics.

> ... dialectic is an art, but it does not effect anything on its own unless it is linked to propositions (λόγοι) from ethics or physics, as some of the Stoics maintained. (Phld. *Rhet.* I, *PHerc.* 1427, col. VI.10–18)

Dialectic permeates all areas of inquiry, but as a collaborator or an ancillary.

Dialectic was subdivided: one part studied signifiers or utterances, the other part studied things signified or 'sayables' or 'objects'.[10] The first subdivision contained a farrago: the nature of language, the parts of speech, virtues and vices of language, poetics, ambiguity, music, definitions and divisions, etymology. The second subdivision was further divided into two parts. One of these parts concerns 'presentations' and the other 'sayables'. The former part is essentially epistemology. The study of 'sayables' is essentially logic: it includes the study of the different kinds of sayable and their parts (grammar and semantics), and also the study of arguments and argument-forms.[11]

---

[5] See *PHerc.* 1020, col. I, 25 (= *FDS* 88, p. 90); Cic. *De Orat.* II.157; Sen. *Ep.* 89.17; cf. D.L. VII.47, 48.

[6] Found also at S.E. *PH* I.94; *M* XI.187 (cf. *Suda s.v.* διαλεκτική, without reference to the Stoics).

[7] See e.g. Long 1978c, 103–5.

[8] So Diogenes of Babylon: Cic. *De Orat.* I 1.157; cf. D.L. VII.47; Phil. *Cong.* 18. Note also Chrysippus, *apud* Plu. *Stoic. Rep.* 1037b.

[9] D.L. VII.83: the text of this paragraph is corrupt; for suggestions see von Arnim 1903–24, II.40; Gigante 1960; Long 1978c, 122 n. 9; Egli 1981, 24.

[10] The distinction is certainly Chrysippean: D.L. VII.62; cf. D.L. VII.43; Sen. *Ep.* 139.17; S.E. *PH* II.214 (ascribed to τινες); *Suda s.v.* διαλεκτική (no ascription).   [11] See D.L. VII.43–4.

The matter can be exhibited thus:

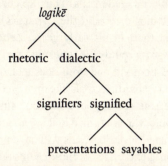

This is only one among several Stoic maps of logic.[12] Moreover, sections marked clearly on a map may be muddy on the terrain. Nonetheless, the map shows how the discipline of logic fits within the Stoic classification of the sciences: logic is a part of a part of the dialectical part of *logikē*.

11 The value of logic

Late authors report a dispute about the status of logic: is it a part of philosophy, or is it an instrument of philosophy? The Stoics took the former side, the Peripatetics the latter; and the discussion, the significance of which is greater than it may seem, was conducted with some subtlety.[13] The dates of the war are uncertain – but there is reason to think that it was not Hellenistic.[14] However that may be, logic, whether part or instrument, was surely an indispensable aspect of philosophical study. After all, if the case for logic was not self-justified,[15] an argument from authority was available: Plato and Aristotle and their followers, and Socrates himself, had all been passionate for dialectic; and, as Chrysippus urged,

> had they spoken of these subjects only in passing, one might perhaps dismiss this area of philosophy; but since they have spoken so carefully on the matter, as though dialectic were among the greatest and most indispensable of capacities, it is not plausible that they should make such a great mistake, given the general qualities which we observe in them. (Plu. *Stoic. Rep.* 1046a)

---

[12] In particular, the place of epistemology and of the theory of definition within λογική were disputed (see Hülser 1987-8, XXXIII–LXXXVI).

[13] Texts in Hülser 1987-8, 22-39 (add Elias *APr.* 134.4-138.13); discussion in Lee 1984, 44-54; see also Barnes *et al.* 1991, 41-8; Barnes 1993d.

[14] Sen. *Ep.* 138.21-9 (on which see Kidd 1978b) shows that this sort of issue was known to Posidonius; but the debate itself probably presupposes the renascence of Aristotelianism at the end of the first century BC. [15] E.g. Epict. *Diss.* II.25.1-3.

And yet, as Chrysippus' apologia insinuates, not all thinkers were impressed by the subject's credentials. Thus Epicurus and his followers 'rejected' dialectic;[16] and so too did the Cyrenaics[17] and the Cynics.[18] Some have suspected that, in his early years, Zeno himself dismissed logic.[19] His pupil Aristo certainly did, offering a series of similes to show that dialectic does us no good and even does us harm: dialectical arguments are like spiders' webs, dialectic is like mud on the pavement, studying dialectic is like eating crabs, young dialecticians are like puppies.[20] Logic is useless – people who are skilled in it are no more likely to *act* well; and logic is pernicious – clever logicians will have no difficulty in acting badly with a good conscience. Each of these claims is plausible.

Yet according to orthodox Stoicism, dialectic is not only an essential element of philosophy: it is actually an ἀρετή, a virtue or excellence;[21] and therefore the only dialecticians are Sages and gods.[22] The virtue has a negative and a positive aspect. Dialectic ensures that you will not be deceived by captious argumentation: so Chrysippus asserted,[23] so Zeno had taught.[24] Dialectic also ensures that you will guard the knowledge which you have acquired; for it will equip you with the capacity to conduct valid arguments and to present cogent proofs.

Did the Stoics themselves exhibit the virtue of dialectic? They were notorious for their syllogizing.[25] They were criticized for ignoring substance and fiddling with logical form; for ignoring the useful parts of dialectic and elaborating empty theories; for ignoring scientific methodology and worrying over abstract proof.[26]

Our sources frequently present Stoic arguments in a formal dress which hugs the contours of Stoic hypothetical syllogistic;[27] and the secondary evidence is confirmed by several of the scanty fragments of the Stoics

---

[16] D.L. x.31; Cic. *Fin.* 1.22; Sen. *Ep.* 89.11; S.E. *M* VII.15; Hier. *Ruf.* 1.30. See e.g. Long 1971d, 114; Long and Sedley 1987, I.101. On Metrodorus see Spinelli 1986; Tepedino Guerra 1992.

[17] D.L. II.92; Sen. *Ep.* 89.12; S.E. *M* VII.11; cf. Them. *Or.* XXXIV.5. [18] D.L. VI.103.

[19] See the *mot* in Stob. II.2.12; and note that Zeno rejected the ἐγκύκλιοι τέχναι (D.L. VII.32), which may have included logic (Hülser 1987–8, LXXX–LXXXI, 444–5).

[20] Stob. *Ecl.* II.2.14, 18, 22; 25.44 (and note Zeno's simile at II.2.12); all perhaps from Aristo's Ὁμοιώματα, on which see Ioppolo 1980a, 50–1. Logic no good: Stob. II.1.24; D.L. VII.160 (see Ioppolo 1980a, 63–9); harmful: S.E. *M* VII.12; Sen. *Ep.* 89.13.

[21] See esp. D.L. VII.46–7; also Cic. *Fin.* III.72; [Plu.] *Plac.* 874e. Cf. Long 1978c, 107–8; Atherton 1993, 53–5. [22] D.L. VII.83; Alex. *Top.* 1.19: Long 1978c. Gods: Plu. *De E* 387d.

[23] *PHerc.* 1020, col. II, III (*FDS* 88) – if the text is Chrysippean. [24] Plu. *Stoic. Rep.* 1034e.

[25] E.g. Quint. *Inst.* x.1.84; XII.2.25; Hipp. *Ref.* 1.21.1; Aug. *CD* VIII.7. For Zeno's snappy style, βραχυλογία, see D.L. VII.18, 20; Cic. *ND* II.20–2: Schofield 1983. Note that even the Roman Cato went in for crisp syllogisms: Cic. *Parad.* 3 (cf. Sen. *Ep.* 82.9).

[26] E.g. Cic. *Tusc.* v.5.9; Gal. *PHP* v.225; Cic. *Top.* 6.

[27] See e.g. Plu. *Stoic. Rep.* 1034ef (Zeno); Nemes. 78–9 (Cleanthes); Cic. *Div.* 1.83–4 (Chrysippus, Diogenes, Antipater).

themselves. Here is one example, taken from Chrysippus' *Logical Investigations*:

> If there are passive predicates, then there are also passives of passives; and so *ad infinitum*. But this is not so. Neither therefore is the first. If there are plural predicates, then there are also plurals of plurals; and so *ad infinitum*. But this is not so. Neither therefore is the first. (*PHerc.* 307, col. II.17–26)

Two arguments in *modus tollens*, which is the second Stoic 'indemonstrable', each of which is given quasi-schematic form or presented as a λογότροπος.

Most philosophers produce arguments, and some of their arguments are likely to exemplify *modus tollens*: there is nothing noteworthy in the fact that Chrysippus argues in this way. The noteworthy fact is this: the Stoics used such arguments explicitly, self-consciously, deliberately; they were concerned, in their philosophical writings to apply the argument forms which their dialectical studies had investigated and approved.[28] The Stoics studied logic fervently and they used it sedulously.

III The history of Hellenistic logic

1: Chrysippus

Chrysippus was the chief figure in Stoic logic:

> So renowned was he in dialectical matters that most people thought that if dialectic existed among the gods it could not be anything but Chrysippean dialectic. (D.L. VII.180)

A literary critic who had little time either for Stoicism or for logic admitted that 'no one brought greater precision to the dialectical arts' than Chrysippus.[29] What exactly did Chrysippus do?

We know little of Chrysippus' *modus operandi*; for few logical fragments have survived. But the *Logical Investigations*,[30] rigorously presented and densely written, abrupt and compact in form, strong and substantial in matter, invite stylistic comparison with Aristotle's *Analytics*. No doubt there were also less forbidding works; but when the thin and flaccid

---

[28] Contrast Aristotle, on the surface of whose writings there is scarcely a trace of the categorical syllogism.

[29] D.H. *Comp.* 31. On the pre-eminence of Chrysippus see Frede 1974a, 26–9, 31.

[30] *Logika Zētēmata*, *PHerc.* 307. Text in Marrone 1997 (see also Hülser 1987–8, 812–31). See Marrone 1982, 1984, 1992, 1993; Sedley 1984; Barnes 1986b.

reports in the secondary sources vex or depress, recall that the original pages which they wanly mirror were firm and full.

On the nature and extent of Chrysippus' logical interests we have more evidence; for Diogenes Laertius, observing that his 'books have a very high reputation', determined 'to record the list of them arranged by subject' (VII.180). The catalogue is only partially preserved. It was divided into three parts: logic, ethics, physics. It began with logic; the ethical part starts at VII.199; and the text breaks off in the middle of an ethical title. The three main parts of the list were themselves divided and subdivided, on thematic or philosophical principles. The list surely came from Apollonius of Tyre, who 'published the table of the philosophers of Zeno's school and of their books'.[31]

The logical section lists at least 130 works, amounting in all to over 300 books.[32] Nonetheless, it does not tell us exactly how much Chrysippus wrote on logic: the final sentence of the logical section is crucially corrupt; the section on ethics contains several titles which suggest a logical content;[33] and other sources offer a few supplementary titles.[34] However that may be, it is plain that Chrysippus wrote at vast length on logic: almost half of his writings fell within the logical part of philosophy;[35] and these writings must have been about twenty times as long as Aristotle's *Organon*.

The titles themselves give an idea of the range and balance of Chrysippus' logical interests.[36] The first of the five *topoi* or areas into which the logical section of the catalogue is divided contains a single subordinate σύνταξις or group, the titles in which were introductory. The second area is 'concerned with objects (πράγματα)', that is to say, with the items which are signified by words and sentences: five groups include works on the different types of assertibles, both simple and complex, and on their parts. The third area, with three groups, is given to expressions or λέξεις: the issues include the parts of speech, and amphiboly. The final area, 'concerned with arguments and modes', is the largest: ten groups

---

[31] Str. XVI.2.24 [757C]. Apollonius dates from the first century BC; the other Stoic book-catalogues may also be his (Zeno: D.L. VII.4, Aristo: VII.163, Herillus: VII.166, Dionysius: VII.167, Cleanthes: VII.174-5, Sphaerus: VII.178). See: Goulet 1989-94, I, 294; Dorandi 1990a, 2334-5; Hahm 1992.   [32] The MSS of D.L. VII.198 give the figure of 311.

[33] E.g. Περὶ τῆς διαλεκτικῆς, Περὶ τῶν ἀντιλεγομένων τοῖς διαλεκτικοῖς (D.L. VII.202): Hülser 1987-8, 184-7, prints most of the first ethical *topos* among his dialectical fragments.

[34] Note esp. the Introduction to Syllogisms (S.E. *M* VIII.224), and the three books on Syllogistic (Gal. *Lib. Prop.* XIX.47; *Inst. Log.* XIX.9), neither of which is readily identified with any title in D.L.'s list.   [35] In all he wrote 705 books: D.L. VII.180.

[36] But titles must be used with caution: see Nachmanson 1941. D.H. *Comp.* 31-2 shows how misleading Chrysippean titles could be. See also Barnes 1996b.

subdivide its contents, which deal with two main areas – different types of argument and syllogism, and the exposition and resolution of logical puzzles and *aporiai*.

Three aspects of logic appear to have engaged Chrysippus' especial attention. First, he wrote twelve works in 23 books on the Liar paradox; seven works in 17 books on amphiboly; another nine works in another 26 books on other conundrums. In all, twenty-eight works or 66 books – more than a sixth of his logical *oeuvre* – were given over to puzzles. The importance of puzzles within Stoic logic has often been observed: the Chrysippean catalogue measures this importance. Secondly, there are some eighteen works in 35 books on the various forms of inference and of syllogism which the Stoics recognized and investigated. These works correspond, as it were, to Aristotle's *Prior Analytics*: they will have presented, explained, and defended the theory of hypothetical syllogistic and the system of the 'five indemonstrables' which was the centrepiece of Chrysippus' logical achievement. Thirdly, there are some twenty works in 46 books on the elements of arguments: on the various forms of complex assertible (five works in 12 books on conditionals); on simple assertibles; on predicables and terms. Thus Chrysippus devoted as much paper to the elements of arguments as to the arguments themselves: his work here has no real parallel in the Peripatetic tradition, and his reflections in this area (which is now called 'philosophical logic') were no less remarkable than the formal system of inference which he developed.

2: *After Chrysippus*

Chrysippus was pre-eminent, but he was not authoritative: there were conflicts within the Stoa, some of them over logic. Thus Cicero informs us that 'two of the leading dialecticians, Antipater and Archedemus, both men of the greatest subtlety,[37] disagree on many issues' – and Cicero plainly has logical disagreements in mind (*Acad.* II.143). We may suppose that Stoic logic changed and developed, at least in minor ways, in the course of its long career. There is nothing remarkable about this supposition (nor is it often remarked).

Diogenes of Babylon professed himself a teacher of dialectic (Cic. *De Orat.* II.157), on which he wrote a handbook (D.L. VII.71).[38] His *Handbook on Utterance* may have been a more ambitious work: it probably lies behind Diocles' account of Stoic 'grammar' in D.L. VII.55–8, and it perhaps

[37] Reading *spinossisimi* (Hermann) for the transmitted *opiniossisimi*.
[38] No doubt there were other logical writings: D.L.'s Life of Diogenes, which will have included a bibliography, is lost.

served as the model for the grammatical Handbook ascribed to Dionysius Thrax.[39]

Antipater was keen on sophisms,[40] and he discussed the Master Argument 'not only in his *On Possibles* but also in a special work *On the Master Argument*' (Epict. *Diss.* II. 19.9). He maintained 'against the opinion of everyone' (Apul. *Int.* 200.17) that there are valid arguments which have a single premiss.[41] And he devised a 'more concise' method of analysing syllogisms by way of the themata (Gal. *PHP* v 224).

Of Archedemus, who disputed with Antipater, we know a work *On Utterance* (D.L. VII.55) and an *On Possibles* (Epict. *Diss.* II.19.9); he classified assertibles (D.L. VII.68); and he referred to predicables as sayables (Clem. *Strom.* VIII.9.26.4). There is similarly meagre information about Crinis: a *Handbook on Dialectic* (D.L. VII.71), in which he divided assertibles into simple and compound (D.L. VII.68), explained the idea of a 'quasi-conditional' (D.L. VII.71), gave a formal definition of argument (D.L. VII.76), and analysed the concept of a partition or μερισμός (D.L. VII.62).

The only other major figure[42] is Posidonius. It is clear that logic mattered to him;[43] but of the few scraps of information which have come to us only one excites. In his *Introduction to Logic* Galen discusses what he calls a 'third kind' of syllogism, alongside Peripatetic categoricals and Stoic hypotheticals: they are 'relational syllogisms'. At the end of his account Galen makes reference to Posidonius (xviii.8), and some scholars infer that Posidonius invented relational syllogistic. But the text is corrupt: Posidonius' contribution was probably modest.[44]

3: Before Chrysippus

One or two of Chrysippus' book-titles insinuate a complex debate: *Against the Objections to the claim that the same argument can be organized in a syllogistic and a non-syllogistic schema* (D.L. VII.194); *Against the objections to the work against cutting indefinites* (D.L. VII.197). Two titles refer explicitly to Philo of Megara (*Against Philo's On Signs, Against Philo's On Schemata*: D.L. VII.191, 194[45]); and others perhaps refer to other 'Megarics'. One title may

---

[39] See Hagius 1979.   [40] Posidon. *apud* Sen. *Ep.* 137.38–40; and the anecdote in Athen. 186c.

[41] Varro *Sat.* fr 291; Apul. *Int.* 200.15–19; Alex. *APr.* 8.14–9.8; S.E. *PH* II.167; *M* VIII.443.

[42] Four minor names: Dionysius of Cyrene; Apollodorus of Seleucia; Diodotus, who taught Cicero logic (Cic. *Brut.* 309); and Lucius Aelius Stilo Praeconinus, who was perhaps the first Latin logician (Gell. XVI.8.2; cf. I.18.1: Goetz 1894).   [43] See esp. Kidd 1978b.

[44] See Barnes 1993a. Kidd 1978b, 277–9, Kidd 1988, 692–6, and Hülser 1987–8, 1484–7, argue for a generous attribution.

[45] Philo's works are known only from these Chrysippean titles. For *On Signs*, Περὶ Σημασιῶν, see Ebert 1987, 108–9; 1991, 60–1. *On Schemata*, Περὶ Τρόπων, must have discussed argument-schemata, as its position in the catalogue shows.

advert to Theophrastus: the *Solution according to the Older Philosophers* (D.L. VII.197) discussed an earlier solution to the Liar paradox, and the only earlier philosopher we know to have written about the Liar is Theophrastus (D.L. V.49).

No title mentions any earlier Stoic. Yet Chrysippus' predecessors had studied logic. Zeno offers an uncertain case. The catalogue of his writings (D.L. VII.4) contains a few items which fall under the general heading of *logikē*, but none which indisputably concerns itself with logic (thus *On Signs* may have discussed conditional propositions[46] – but its primary subject was no doubt epistemological). The biographical evidence links Zeno with Diodorus and Philo and with Stilpo, and we are informed that he 'used to solve sophisms himself, and he urged his pupils to learn dialectic, since it had the power to do this' (Plu. *Stoic. Rep.* 1034e). A further text puzzles rather than enlightens:

> What are the theorems <of the philosophers>? . . . As Zeno says, they are concerned with knowledge of the elements of λόγος – knowledge of what each of them is, of how they relate to one another . . . (Epict. *Diss.* IV.8.12)

Are the 'elements of λόγος' the elements of reasoning, so that a Zenonian philosopher must grasp the first principles of logic and their interrelations? Or are they rather the 'parts of speech'?[47] We may be sure that Zeno recognized the existence and the importance of logic, in some fashion or other; but there is no reason to believe that he made any serious contribution to the discipline.[48]

For Cleanthes there are several book-titles: *On Reason* (three books), *On Properties*, *On the Puzzles*, *On Dialectic*, *On Schemata*, *On Predicables* (all in D.L. VII.174–5); and *On Possibles* (Epict. *Diss.* II.19.9). The last work discussed Diodorus' Master Argument, and perhaps reflected more generally on the logical modalities. *On the Puzzles* will have dealt with other logical conundrums; and *On Dialectic* was perhaps the first textbook in Stoic logic. More intriguing are two other titles. *On Predicables* must have discussed 'sayables' or λεκτά.[49] As for *On Schemata* or Περὶ Τρόπων, the title is ambiguous; but if the word τρόπος is used in its technical sense, then Cleanthes discussed logical forms.

Finally, Sphaerus: the catalogue in D.L. VII.178 contains seven or eight items of logical relevance. Two of them recall Cleanthine titles: *Handbook*

<hr>

[46] Under the influence of Philo, according to e.g. Rist 1978a, 391; Ebert 1991, 65.

[47] Different interpretations in e.g. Graeser 1975, 11–13; Hagius 1979, 1–26; Long and Sedley 1987, II.190. Cautious comments in Pearson 1891, 58–9; Hülser 1987–8, 82–3.

[48] So e.g. Frede 1974a, 14; Long 1978c, 105. The contrary view is urged by Rist 1978a; see also Hülser 1987–8, XLVI; Ebert 1991, 56.   [49] On Clem. *Strom.* VIII.9.26.4 see below, p. 210.

on Dialectic (two books), and *On Predicables*; one anticipates Chrysippus: *On Ambiguities*.

From this brief survey, two banal conclusions: first, Chrysippus had Stoic predecessors; secondly, his Stoic predecessors were far less prolific than he.

What of the outside world? There is no need to mention the Epicureans: rejecting dialectic, they did not attempt to advance it. (But Philodemus' work *On Signs* shows that later Epicureans could interest themselves in such things as the truth-conditions of conditional propositions.) Nor will the Academy detain us; for there is no evidence that any Academician laboured at logic. The Lyceum is another matter.

Of course, Aristotle's successors studied logic – it was part of their inheritance; and we know of works by Theophrastus, Eudemus, Phanias, Strato. But for Phanias there is only a single dubious report; Strato's interests do not seem to have gone beyond the subject-matter of Aristotle's *Topics*; and Eudemus' name is almost always conjoined with that of Theophrastus, from whom, in logic, we can no more separate him than we can Rosencrantz from Guildenstern. Peripatetic logic in the Hellenistic period is for us the logic of Theophrastus.[50]

His logical oeuvre filled some forty works in some eighty books.[51] Almost half the titles are Aristotelian or semi-Aristotelian; so, doubtless, were the contents; and for the remainder, it is usually easy to find a plausible Aristotelian link.[52] But Theophrastus was no lackey: Alexander frequently cites him; Galen wrote a commentary in six books on his *On Affirmation* (*Lib. Prop.* xix.47); Porphyry probably wrote a commentary on the same work (Boeth. *Int.*[2] 217.26–8): there must have been some matter there. Moreover, there are two interestingly unAristotelian titles: *Topics Reduced*, in two books (D.L. v.42), perhaps attempted to reduce to categorical syllogisms the various argument-forms which are collected in Aristotle's *Topics* (a papyrus fragment illustrates what Theophrastus had in mind).[53] *On the Liar*, in three books (D.L. v.49), was the first serious investigation of a celebrated paradox. In addition, and most significantly, Theophrastus is known to have worked in the area of hypothetical syllogistic.

---

[50] In general see Barnes 1985, 559–60. For Phainias see Wehrli 1969c (he wrote a *Cat.*: Phlp. *Cat.* 7.20); for Strato see the catalogue in D.L. v.59. (Note also the titles for Heraclides, D.L. v.88, one or two of which might betray a logical interest.) For Eudemus see Wehrli 1969b. On Theophrastus' logic the pioneering work of Bochenski 1947 is still indispensable; see also Graeser 1973; Repici 1977; Barnes 1983b, 1985. Texts in Fortenbaugh 1992b.

[51] See D.L. v.42–50 (full details in Fortenbaugh 1992b). Counting cannot be accurate; but the total is surely greater than Bochenski 1947, 27–32, or Graeser 1973, 1–3, allow.

[52] See the remarks in Bochenski 1947, 52, 66, 110, 125–6; cf. Barnes 1983b, 305.

[53] *PSI* 1095 (= Appendix 2 in Fortenbaugh 1992b): see Solmsen 1929; Bochenski 1947, 25, 119–20.

If Chrysippus read Theophrastus' *On the Liar*, did he also read other works by Theophrastus and did he read Aristotle's *Organon*?

The *Organon* was known outside the Lyceum: Epicurus referred to the *Analytics*;[54] Eubulides criticized Aristotle's views on the conversion of categorical propositions.[55] And in his *Dialectic* Chrysippus adverted in general terms to Aristotle's logic (Plu. *Stoic. Rep.* 1045f–1046a). The later commentators on Aristotle's work frequently report debates between Stoics and Peripatetics and frequently state or imply that Aristotle influenced the Old Stoa.

But Chrysippus' *Dialectic* refers to Plato and Polemo, Strato and Socrates, alongside Aristotle, a constellation which hardly suggests that Chrysippus had his mind on technical logic or the *Analytics* – nor does the text imply acquaintance with any of Aristotle's writings. And the numerous passages in the commentators either do not purport to give information about the Old Stoa[56] or else indulge in patent fantasy.[57] In short, the present state of our evidence gives no reason to believe that Chrysippus cared for, or was influenced by, the formal logic of the Lyceum.

Finally, what of the 'Megarics'? Three things emerge from the mists. First, the 'Megarics' were puzzle-mongers. Of Eubulides it is said that

> he put forward many arguments in dialectic – the Liar, the Deceiver, the Electra, the Veiled Man, the Heaper, the Horns, the Bald Man. (D.L. II.108)

And the evidence associates these and other conundrums with all the Megarics. Secondly, for Diodorus and Philo at least, puzzle-mongering was a mode of philosophizing: the Master Argument was rightly taken to have serious philosophical implications; and we know that both men said subtle things about conditional propositions and about modality. Thirdly, there are a few hints of a more general interest in philosophical logic: Philo put out a book *On Schemata*;[58] the obscure Clinomachus wrote on 'assertibles and predicables and the like' (D.L. II.112);[59] and Menedemus ruminated on different types of proposition (D.L. II.135).

What did the Stoics make of this? On the one hand, Chrysippus dismissed some of it as *vieux jeu*:

---

[54] Phld. *Ad Cont.*, *PHerc.* 1005, fr.111.9–10: Angeli 1988a, 166–7, 233–40.

[55] See Alexander's essay *On Conversion* and Themistius' *Reply to Maximus on the Second and Third Figures*: the two works survive only in Arabic (texts in Badawi 1971, translation of Themistius in Badawi 1987).

[56] E.g. Alex. *APr.* 402.1–405.16, an essay on negation: see Lloyd 1978b; Barnes 1986a.

[57] E.g. Alex. *APr.* 284.10–17, on the θέματα.   [58] Above, p. 72.

[59] A 'pioneering study of propositional logic', according to Sedley 1977, 76; but we know nothing about the work apart from the reference in D.L.

What a fate has befallen the arguments of Stilpo and Menedemus. They were greatly renowned for wisdom and now their arguments have come to be regarded as something shameful: some of them are pretty crude and others evidently sophistical. (*On the Use of Reason*, *apud* Plu. *Stoic. Rep.* 1036f)[60]

So much for Stilpo, the most popular philosopher of his age.

On the other hand, there is Zeno's pupillage with Diodorus Cronus; and there are the Chrysippean titles which refer to Philo and his friends. Moreover, we know that the Old Stoa was exercised by the Master Argument, and wrote at length on it. It seems likely that the Stoics inherited from the Megarics their general interest in logical puzzles, and that Stoic work on the modalities was influenced by Megara. Beyond that the evidence will hardly take us.[61]

---

[60] And from the Περὶ βίων: some people 'are misled by the Megaric arguments and by other more numerous and more powerful arguments' (Plu. *Stoic. Rep.* 1036e).

[61] For a sober assessment see Frede 1974a, 22–3. On the thesis of Ebert 1991, that the 'Dialecticians' invented some main elements of Stoic logic, see e.g. Barnes 1993d.

5

Logic

JONATHAN BARNES (I), SUSANNE BOBZIEN (II AND
III.1–7) AND MARIO MIGNUCCI (III.8)

i The Peripatetics

Late antiquity learned two logics: categorical syllogistic and hypothetical
syllogistic. Categorical syllogistic studies categorical arguments. An argument is categorical if all its components (its premisses and its conclusion)
are categorical propositions. A proposition is categorical if it 'says one
thing of one thing' – or better, if it is simple in the sense of not containing
two or more propositions as components. Hypothetical syllogistic
studies hypothetical arguments. An argument is hypothetical if at least
one of its components is a hypothetical proposition. A proposition is
hypothetical if it contains at least two propositions as components.

It is a plausible guess that this terminology was developed in the
Hellenistic Peripatos. The phrase 'hypothetical argument' is attested for
Chrysippus (D.L. VII.196);[1] Galen says that 'the ancients' spoke of hypothetical propositions (*Inst. Log.* III.3), Alexander that they spoke of
'mixed' syllogisms (*APr.* 262.31–2); and 'the ancients' in such contexts are
usually the Peripatetics.[2] Philoponus says that Theophrastus used the
phrase 'wholly hypothetical syllogism' (*APr.* 302.9).

Categorical syllogistic was thought of as essentially Peripatetic, hypothetical syllogistic as essentially Stoic;[3] and although it was known that
the Stoics and Peripatetics had disputed with one another in logic no less
than in ethics and physics, it was often supposed that the two syllogistics
were partners, each adequate in its own area. This irenic view is misleading. The Peripatetics thought that their categorical syllogistic embraced
the whole of logic: any argument which submitted to formal treatment at
all submitted to categorical syllogistic. And the Stoics held the same for
their hypothetical syllogisms. The two systems regarded themselves as

---

[1] But the sense of the phrase in Chrysippus is uncertain, and some connect it with the 'speech act'
of supposition (τὸ ὑποθετικόν): below, p. 201.   [2] See Barnes 1990a, 71–3.
[3] But some Arabic texts appear to show that there was a Peripatetic form of hypothetical syllogistic: Maróth 1989.

rivals; and behind the texts there is a genuine and philosophical rivalry, between 'term' logic which supposes that relations among terms are the fundamental logical relations and 'sentence' logic which assumes that it is sentences on which logic must ground itself.[4]

Peripatetic logic in the Hellenistic period is the logic of Theophrastus. His work on categorical syllogistic is a pendant to the past: he introduced some new terminology;[5] he supplemented some of Aristotle's proofs; he tidied up Aristotle's messy remarks about the supplementary moods in the first figure;[6] and above all he proposed major alterations to Aristotle's modal syllogistic. The alterations turned on his application to modal propositions of the '*peiorem*' rule:[7] 'Eudemus and Theophrastus say that . . . in all combinations the conclusion follows the inferior and weaker of the premisses' (Alex. *APr.* 124.8–13). The possible is 'weaker' than the actual, the actual than the necessary: hence in a mixed modal syllogism the modality of the conclusion must be at least as 'weak' as the modality of the 'weaker' of the two premisses. Theophrastus' adoption of the rule, together with other pertinent innovations, enabled him to purge Aristotle's modal syllogistic of some of its confusions and contradictions.[8]

Several texts prove that Theophrastus discussed hypothetical syllogisms, thereby keeping, vicariously, a promise which his master had made (Arist. *APr.* 50a39–b2). The extent and significance of his discussion are controversial: it has been held, at one extreme, that he anticipated the central parts of Stoic logic, and, at the other, that his work did not properly bear upon hypothetical syllogistic at all;[9] and the ancient texts do not speak with one voice.[10]

He certainly said something about hypothetical propositions.

In hypotheticals in which the antecedent is not only true but also evident and non-controversial, they use the connective 'since' instead of 'if', the quasi-conditional instead of the conditional (hence the moderns call

---

[4] On this see Barnes 1983b, 279–83.

[5] E.g. he called propositions such as 'Some man is just' 'indeterminate', by contrast with propositions such as 'Socrates is just', which he called 'determinate'. Ammon. *Int.* 90.12–20 uses the word ἀόριστος – compare the Stoic terminology at D.L. VII.70.

[6] Alex. *APr.* 69.26–70.21; see Barnes *et al.* 1991, 136 n. 157.

[7] So called from the scholastic tag: *peiorem semper sequitur conclusio partem.* Texts in Fortenbaugh 1992b, T105–7; see Barnes *et al.* 1991, 113 n. 58. On Theophrastus' modal logic see esp. Bochenski 1947, 73–102.

[8] But Theophrastus' system, insofar as we can reconstruct it, has internal incoherences of its own: Bochenski 1947, 100–1.

[9] E.g. on the one hand Prantl 1855, I.379, on the other Ebert 1991, 15–19.

[10] Theophrastus 'mentioned' hypothetical syllogisms (Alex. *APr.* 326, 21–2); he discussed the 'elements' of the subject (Boeth. *Hyp. Syll.* 1.1.3); he wrote 'lengthy treatises' on the matter (Phlp. *APr.* 242.18–21).

such propositions quasi-conditional). Theophrastus, in the first book of his *Prior Analytics*, explains the reason for this usage. (Simp. *Cael.* 552.31–553.4)

The context and the point of Theophrastus' remarks are lost; but it is clear that, in a logical text, he displayed an interest in the differences between two propositional connectives.

At *Inst. Log.* III.3–5, Galen reports that 'the ancients' called conditional propositions 'hypothetical by connection (κατὰ συνέχειαν)' and disjunctive propositions 'hypothetical by division (κατὰ διαίρεσιν)' or simply 'divisive'. The ancients are contrasted with 'the moderns', to whom the standard Stoic nomenclature is ascribed. In such contrasts the ancients are often the old Peripatetics: if that is Galen's contrast here, then (since the terminology is not Aristotelian) we have a trace of Theophrastan usage,[11] and Theophrastus distinguished two sorts of compound proposition.

Perhaps he also held that there were *only* two sorts of logically interesting compound proposition. In the later Peripatetic tradition we frequently find the following line of argument:[12] 'A compound sentence either connects its components, in which case it is conditional, or else it separates them, in which case it is disjunctive. Hence there are only two sorts of logical compound.' This argument, with all its horrid confusions, seems to go back to Eudemus (Boeth. *Hyp. Syll.* 1.3.3); and it was perhaps endorsed by Theophrastus.

Other texts set Theophrastus' interest in compound propositions in a broader logical context. One such text concerns 'wholly hypothetical syllogisms'.[13] Alexander affirms that

wholly hypothetical syllogisms, too, can be reduced to the three categorical figures, as Theophrastus has proved in the first book of his *Prior Analytics* (Alex. *APr.* 326.20–2)

and he proceeds to explain how the reduction is to be done (326.22–328.7). Alexander's discussion is based on Theophrastus; but he does not simply paraphrase Theophrastus' work,[14] and we know that other logicians had worked on the topic.[15] How much can we ascribe to Theophrastus himself?

---

[11] So Bochenski 1947, 108–9, a conclusion widely accepted.
[12] So e.g. Alcin. *Didasc.* 158; Gal. *Inst. Log.* III.1; Alex. *APr.* 11.20; Boeth. *Hyp. Syll.* 1.i1.5, 3.2. See Sullivan 1967, 24–30; Barnes 1983b, 284 n. 2; 1985, 567.
[13] Detailed discussion in Barnes 1983b.
[14] He explicitly notes one point of disagreement: 328.2–5.
[15] See Alcin. *Didasc.* 159: Barnes 1983b, 297–8.

Two points are certain. First, Theophrastus developed a reasonably detailed *theory* of wholly hypothetical syllogisms. Secondly, he denied that they constituted an independent body of logical science – rather, they are in some sense reducible to categorical syllogisms. One point of uncertainty concerns the very subject matter of the theory. Alexander's illustrative examples are all arguments with *two* premisses, each premiss (and the conclusion) being a conditional proposition of the form 'If *p*, then *q*', where '*p*' and '*q*' may be affirmative or negative but are not themselves hypothetical propositions. Alexander says that these are 'simple' arguments, and he adverts to other, 'compound' arguments; but he does not say what a compound argument would look like, nor does he indicate whether Theophrastus had made this distinction.

But this is not the only element of uncertainty. Alexander says that

an argument of the following sort is wholly hypothetical:
   If A, then B.
   If B, then C.
   Therefore if A, then C.
(Here the conclusion too is hypothetical.) E.g.:
   If he is a man, he is an animal.
   If he is an animal, he is a substance.
   Therefore if he is a man, he is a substance. (*APr.* 326.22–5)

Some scholars construe the letters in Alexander's schema as term-letters (so that the schematic sentences are elliptical), thus supposing that the conditional sentences of wholly hypothetical arguments must all have the specific form 'If x is F, then x is G'. This construe, which greatly limits the scope of wholly hypothetical syllogistic, is supported by two facts: first, Philoponus and Boethius clearly use term-letters rather than sentence-letters in *their* formulations of wholly hypothetical syllogisms;[16] and secondly, a reduction to categorical syllogisms then becomes much easier to imagine (indeed, Alexander's first illustration will appear to be little more than a terminological variant on *Barbara*, for which see note 132). On the other side, the straightforward reading of Alexander's schemata takes the letters as sentence-letters, and Alexander never hints at any restriction on the sort of conditionals with which wholly hypothetical syllogistic may operate. The problem is of some importance and our evidence does not allow a definitive solution.

However that may be, it is plausible to suppose, on the evidence sup-

---

[16] See e.g. Phlp. *APr.* 302.22; Boeth. *Hyp. Syll.* 1.9.2–3. On the issue see Barnes 1983b, 290–5: *contra*, Ebert 1991, 17 n.16.

plied by Alexander, that Theophrastus attempted to survey the possible kinds of simple wholly hypothetical syllogisms; that he arranged them into three figures according to the structure of their premisses; that he proved that second and third figure syllogisms can be derived from first figure syllogisms;[17] and that he remarked upon an 'analogy' between conditional and categorical propositions:

> being a consequent or apodosis is analogous to being predicated, and being antecedent to being a subject – for in a sense it *is* a subject for what is inferred from it. (Alex. *APr.* 326.31–2)

According to Alexander, this analogy formed the basis of Theophrastus' reduction; but how the reduction proceeded Alexander does not say – nor indeed is it clear in what sense Theophrastus intended the word 'reduce'.[18]

The attempted reduction shows that Theophrastus was still working within an Aristotelian framework; and his general approach to wholly hypothetical syllogisms was evidently modelled on Aristotle's way with categoricals. Nonetheless, the discussion of these arguments goes beyond anything in the *Organon*.

On Aristotle's unkept promise to say how many kinds of hypothetical syllogism there are (*APr.* 50a39–b2), Alexander comments thus:

> He postpones them, as though intending to discuss them more carefully; but no book of his on the subject is in circulation. (Theophrastus mentions them in his own *Analytics*; and so do Eudemus and certain others of Aristotle's associates.) He means hypothetical arguments (A1) by way of a continuous proposition (also called a conditional) and an additional assumption, and those (A2) by way of a divisive or disjunctive proposition. (And also (A3) those by way of a negative conjunction, if they are really different from the others.) In addition to these, there are (B4) the arguments from proportion and (B5) those which they call qualitative (those deriving from the more and the less and the equally) and (B6) any other kinds of argument based on a hypothesis which there may be (they have been discussed elsewhere). (*APr.* 390.1–9)

How did Alexander know which types of hypothetical syllogism Aristotle had intended to discuss? Perhaps he hunted for hints elsewhere in Aristotle's work – and in fact most of the items which he lists can be found, in one form or another, in the *Topics*. But there is a more plausible

---

[17] Alex. *APr.* 327.33–4: Alexander does not illustrate; but see Boeth. *Hyp. Syll.* III.1–6, which carries out the analyses in tedious detail.

[18] On the Peripatetic conception of reduction see Barnes 1983b, 286 n. 3.

explanation. Alexander reports that Theophrastus had kept Aristotle's promise for him: it is tempting to infer that Alexander's guess about what Aristotle had intended to do was based on his knowledge of what Theophrastus had in fact done. Hence Alexander's list of hypothetical syllogisms is a list of the types of argument which Theophrastus discussed.[19]

Wholly hypothetical syllogisms are not explicitly named; but they are no doubt alluded to in (B6), where Alexander must be referring to *APr.* 325.31–328.7. Item (B5) or 'qualitative' arguments – the phrase is Aristotle's: *APr.* 45b17 – are explained elsewhere as arguments in which

> since items of such-and-such a sort are so-and-so, then items which are similarly (or more, or less) such-and-such share the same quality. (*APr.* 324.19–22)

For example: health is more likely to produce happiness than is wealth; but health does not: therefore wealth does not. Arguments from proportion, (B4), have the general form 'As A is to B, so C is to D; but A stands in the relation R to B: therefore C stands in R to D'.

Items (A1) and (A2) are more exciting. Alexander uses the terminology which Galen ascribes to 'the ancients' in order to characterize arguments of the general form 'If A, then B; but C: therefore D' and 'Either A or B; but C: therefore D'. Two instances of (A1):

(1) If p, then q
p
Therefore q

(2) If p, then q
not-q
Therefore not-p

Two instances of (A2):

(3) Either p or q
p
Therefore not-q

(4) Either p or q
not-q
Therefore p

Item (A3) – which has only a tentative status in the list[20] – indicates the general form 'Not both A and B; but C: therefore D'. For instance:

(5) Not both p and q
p
Therefore not-q

---

[19] So Prantl 1855, I.379; Barnes 1985, 563–4.   [20] For the text see Barnes 1985, 566 n. 16.

If we allow that Theophrastus said *something* about such arguments, two questions arise. First, what exactly did he say about them? To this question our texts offer no response; but if he discussed them in detail, and if his discussion (like his account of wholly hypothetical syllogisms) was modelled on Aristotle's categorical syllogistic, then we can make a romantic guess.[21]

Secondly, did Theophrastus thereby invent Chrysippean logic?[22] After all, the argument-forms (1)–(5) are identical with, or at least intimately related to, the five 'indemonstrables' on which Chrysippean logic was grounded,[23] and Theophrastus flirted with (1)–(5) long before Chrysippus courted his indemonstrables. Nevertheless, it is plain that even if Theophrastus discussed (1)–(5), he did not anticipate Chrysippus' achievement. There are several minor reasons for this answer. (Thus it is not clear that Alexander wishes to ascribe (A3) to Theophrastus at all.) And there is a major reason: even if Theophrastus had explicitly recognized all of (1)–(5), his Aristotelian approach to the study and organization of argument-forms would have given his discussion of mixed hypothetical syllogisms an utterly unStoical aspect.[24]

II The 'Megarics'

Apart from the various logical puzzles and sophisms, there are only two topics on which we can be sure of a positive contribution to logic[25] by the 'Megarics'.[26] These are the positions of Diodorus Cronus and of Philo on the theory of conditionals and on modal logic. Why the discussion of these topics came down to us, we can only divine. Certainly both involve notorious difficulties. Again, they were topics which were extensively and intensely discussed in Hellenistic logic; so much so that the disputes became part of the general knowledge of the intelligentsia of the time (e.g. S.E. *M* 1.309–10). In addition, the theory of modalities was believed to have far-reaching results for other areas of philosophy.

The passages on the conditional and on modal logic, together with some scattered testimonies, allow one to draw some conclusions about 'Megaric' logic in general: The treatment of conditionals and modalities implies that – like most Hellenistic philosophers – the 'Megarics' worked

---

[21] See Barnes 1985, 571–3.

[22] So Prantl 1855, 1.379; and see also Bochenski 1947, 9; Graeser 1975, 42, 46. *Contra* e.g. Sandbach 1985, 18.   [23] See below, pp. 127–31.   [24] See Barnes 1985, 574–6.

[25] Logic in the narrow sense, i.e. not including contributions to the study of ambiguity.

[26] On the extent to which it is legitimate to speak of a 'Megaric' (or Dialectical), 'school', see above, p. 47 n. 105.

with a concept of proposition that differs from ours in that it allows truth-values to change over time. We may also conjecture that Philo and Diodorus distinguished between simple propositions, like 'It is day', and complex or non-simple propositions which are composed from simple ones, for instance disjunctions and conditionals. But although we can confidently assume that the truth-conditions of non-simple propositions were examined, we know the 'Megaric' views only in the case of the conditional.

*

In the debate about the conditional (συνημμένον) the point of disagreement concerned the question of what the right truth-conditions of a conditional were (Cic. *Acad.* 11.143). This controversy was played out against the background of a common acceptance of what counts as a conditional, and what its function is. Conditionals were understood to be non-simple propositions containing one proposition as antecedent and one as consequent. The antecedent has the particle 'if' prefixed to it; the standard form is 'If p, q'. A conditional serves to manifest the relation of consequence (ἀκολουθία): it announces that its consequent follows from (ἀκολουθεῖν) its antecedent (S.E. *M* VIII.110–12).[27]

Philo's criterion for the truth of a conditional is truth-functional. It was later generally accepted as a minimal condition for the truth of a conditional. Philo maintained that a conditional is false precisely when its antecedent is true and its consequent false, and true in the three remaining cases: whenever the antecedent is false, and when both antecedent and consequent are true (S.E. *M* VIII.113–17; *PH* II.110). Thus this concept of a conditional comes very close to that of modern material implication. (It is not quite the same, since Hellenistic truth is relativized to times.) Philo's suggestion is remarkable in that it deviates noticeably from the common understanding of conditional sentences and requires abstraction on the basis of the concept of truth-functionality.

Remarkable as it is, Philo's view has the following two drawbacks: first, as in the case of material implication, for the truth of the conditional no connection at all between antecedent and consequent is required. Thus, for example, during the day 'If virtue benefits, it is day' is Philonian true. This introduces a variant of the so-called 'paradoxes of material implication'. Sextus' presentation shows that the ancients were aware of this

---

[27] The term ἀκολουθία was also commonly used for the relation between premisses and conclusion in a valid argument.

problem. Secondly, due to the time-dependency of Hellenistic propositions, Philo's criterion implies that conditionals can change their truth-
value over time: for instance, 'If it is day, it is night' is true at night, but
false in the daytime. This is counter-intuitive as regards the ordinary use
of if-sentences. Moreover, if the concept of a conditional is meant to provide for logical consequence between premisses and conclusion, this leads
to the result that arguments could in principle change from being valid to
being invalid and vice versa.

For Diodorus, a conditional proposition is true if it neither was nor is
possible that its antecedent is true and its consequent false (S.E. *M*
VIII.115–17; *PH* II.110–11). The reference to time in this account ('was ... is
possible') suggests that the possibility of a truth-value change in Philo's
truth-condition was one of the things to be improved on.

We do not know whether Diodorus had his own modal notions in mind
when talking about possibility in his criterion, or just some pre-technical,
general concept of possibility,[28] or whether he perhaps even intended to
cover both.[29] If one assumes that he had his own modal notions in mind
when giving this account, the truth-criterion for the conditional stands in
the following relation to Philo's: a conditional is Diodorean true now precisely if it is Philonian true at all times. Diodorus has, as it were, quan-
tified the Philonian criterion over time. The conditional 'If I walk, I move'
is now true because at no time is the antecedent true and the consequent
false. Thus for Diodorus, a conditional cannot change its truth-value. If it
is true (false) at one time, it is true (false) at all times. If on the other hand
one presumes that Diodorus had some unspecified general concept of possibility in mind when producing his account, the criterion would be correspondingly less specific. However, it would presumably still be a
minimal requirement that it is never the case that the antecedent is true
and the consequent false.

Diodorus' criterion bears some resemblance to the modern concept of
strict implication. In particular, it shares some of its disadvantages in that
we encounter a parallel to the 'paradoxes of strict implication'. As in
Philo's case, no connection is required between antecedent and consequent. This time, whenever either the antecedent is impossible or the
consequent necessary, the conditional will be true, regardless of whether
there is any relevant connection between the two constituent propositions. So for instance 'If the earth flies, Axiothea philosophizes' would be

[28] For Diodorus' modal concepts see below. The verb used here for being possible, ἐνδέχεσθαι
differs from the word used for possibility in Diodorus' modal theory, which is δυνατόν.
[29] The latter is argued for in Denyer 1981b, 39–41; cf. also Sedley 1977, 101–2.

Diodorean true, since the antecedent was considered impossible (D.L. VII.75). Again, Sextus' example for the Diodorean criterion (S.E. *PH* II.111) suggests that there was some awareness of these paradoxes.

*

Modal logic is the second topic where we have evidence about the positions of Philo and Diodorus and their influence on the Stoics.[30] Although the modalities were discussed under the heading of 'On things possible', the Hellenistic modal systems were each built on a set of four modalities: possibility, impossibility, necessity and non-necessity. The matter of dispute was which system was the right one, that is, which one adequately described the modalities inherent in the world. In connection with this, an extra-logical concern provided additional fuel to the debate: the belief that if propositions about future events that will not happen turn out to be impossible, the freedom and choices of individuals would be curtailed.[31]

For the 'Megarics' the modalities were primarily properties of propositions or of states of affairs. There is no discussion of modal propositions, i.e. of propositions of the type 'It is possible/possibly true that it is day'. Philo's concept of possibility has survived in four sources[32] but only in Boethius are the accounts of all four modal notions reported:

> Possible is that which is capable of being true by the proposition's own nature . . . necessary is that which is true, and which, as far as it is in itself, is not capable of being wrong. Non-necessary is that which as far as it is in itself, is capable of being false, and impossible is that which by its own nature is not capable of being true. (Boeth. *Int.* 2.11.234)

So according to Boethius the basic feature of Philonian modalities is some intrinsic capability of the propositions to be or not to be true or false. That this feature is intrinsic is plain from the phrases 'own nature' and 'in itself'. In Simplicius both phrases are used to characterize Philonian possibility (Simp. *Cat.* 195); hence both phrases may have originally applied to all four accounts.

In all sources the concept of possibility stands out, and so it seems likely that Philo built his set of modal notions on a concept of internal

---

[30] For a detailed discussion of Philo's and Diodorus' modal theory cf. Kneale-Kneale 1962, 117–28; Bobzien 1993.

[31] This is a variation on the problem of logical determinism which is known from Arist. *Int.* IX. Several of the 'Megaric' sophisms touch upon this issue – so the Mower Argument (for which see Seel 1993), the Lazy Argument (for which see Bobzien 1998, 180–233), and the Master Argument.

[32] Alex. *APr.* 184; Phlp. *APr.* 169; Simp. *Cat.* 195–6; Boeth. *Int.* 2.11.234–5.

consistency, as given in his account of possibility. Philo's modal concepts are thus defined by resort to another, perhaps more basic, modal concept. As to the kind of consistency Philo had in mind, we learn nothing more. Notwithstanding this, there can be little doubt that Philo's modal concepts satisfy a number of basic requirements which normal systems of modern modal logic tend to satisfy as well. These requirements are:

(i) Every necessary proposition is true and every true proposition possible; every impossible proposition is false and every false proposition non-necessary.

According to Philo's accounts, a proposition that is not capable of falsehood must be true; one that is true must be capable of being true, etc.

(ii) The accounts of possibility and impossibility and those of necessity and non-necessity are contradictory to each other.

This can be directly read off the definitions.

(iii) Necessity and possibility are interdefinable in the sense that a proposition is necessary precisely if its contradictory is not possible.

This holds for Philo's accounts, if one neglects the difference in the two phrases 'in itself' and 'by its nature' or assumes that originally both were part of all the definitions. Then a proposition is not capable of being false precisely if its contradictory is not capable of being true, etc.

(iv) Every proposition is either necessary or impossible or both possible and non-necessary, that is, contingent.

In Philo's system this amounts to the fact that every proposition is either incapable of falsehood, or incapable of truth, or capable of both. The fact that Philo's modal accounts – and those of Diodorus and the Stoics, as will be seen – satisfy these four requirements is of course no proof that the ancients consciously reflected upon all of them, regarding them as principles with which they had to comply.

We know a little more about Diodorus' modal theory.[33] Still, again only Boethius reports all four definitions of Diodorus' modal notions:

> Possible is that which either is or will be <true>; impossible that which is false and will not be true; necessary that which is true and will not be false; non-necessary that which either is false already or will be false. (Boeth. *Int.* 2.11.234–5)

---

[33] Our sources are Epict. *Diss.* 11.19; Cic. *Fat.* 12, 13, 17; *Fam.* ix, 4; Plu. *Stoic. Rep.* 1055e–f; Alex. *APr.* 183–4; Phlp. *APr.* 169; Simp. *Cat.* 195; Boeth. *Int.* 2.11.234, 412.

Two of these modal accounts are disjunctions, the other two are conjunctions. Provided that Diodorus accepted the principle of bivalence, these definitions, too, satisfy the modal requirements (i) to (iv).

Apart from that, Diodorus' modalities are of a very different kind from Philo's. There is no modal expression hidden anywhere in his accounts. Instead, which Diodorean modality a proposition has depends wholly on the range of truth-values it has at present and in the future. For instance, if a proposition is always true from now on, it is now both necessary and possible; if it is, from now on, sometimes true but not always, it is possible, but not necessary. Hence it is not the case that for Diodorus every proposition is either necessary (and possible) or impossible (and non-necessary). There are propositions that are contingent in the sense of being both possible and non-necessary, namely all those which will change their truth-value at some future time. The proposition 'It is day' is such a case.[34]

We do not know what exactly motivated Diodorus to introduce these modal notions.[35] But we know that Hellenistic philosophers generally regarded Diodorus' modal notions as jeopardizing freedom – since they rule out the possibiliy that something that never happens, or is never true, is nonetheless possible. For example, if 'Dio goes to Corinth' is and will always be false then 'Dio goes to Corinth' is impossible, and then, or so the thought went, it is impossible for Dio to go to Corinth.[36]

*

Diodorus' definition of that which is possible can be split into two distinct claims: first that everything that either is or will be true is possible, and second, that everything that is possible either is or will be true. The first statement was not questioned by Hellenistic philosophers. It is the second claim that was and is considered counterintuitive and in need of justification; it is this claim which Diodorus attempted to back up with his Master argument (Alex. *APr.* 183.34–184.6; Epict. *Diss.* II.19.1).

Despite being widely known in antiquity, the argument has not come down to us; all we have is a brief passage in Epictetus:

[34] The dependence of the Diodorean modal concepts on truth-values implies that a proposition can change its modality, from possible to impossible and from non-necessary to necessary. For instance, 'Artemisia is five years old' is now possible, because it is now true. But it will at some future time be impossible, namely once Artemisia has reached the age of six, since from then on it will never be true again.

[35] According to Aristotle, some 'Megarics' maintained that the possibility of an event implies its actuality (Arist. *Metaph.* Θ.3.1046b29–32). Perhaps Diodorus endeavoured to keep the spirit of this concept of possibility.

[36] For a comparison between Philo's, Diodorus' and Chrysippus' modalities, see below, pp. 120–1.

The Master argument seems to have been developed from the following starting points: There is a general conflict between the following three <statements>: (I) every past true <proposition> is necessary; and (II) the impossible does not follow from the possible; and (III) something is possible which neither is true nor will be true. Being aware of this conflict, Diodorus used the plausibility of the first two <statements> in order to show that (IV) nothing is possible that neither is nor will be true. (Epict. *Diss*. II.19.1)[37]

This is usually understood as implying that the argument was grounded on statements (I) and (II), and had (IV), which is the contradictory of (III), as conclusion. And this is about as far as the passages lead us. But how did the argument run?[38] A viable reconstruction has to satisfy a number of more or less trivial conditions. It must make use of the principles (I) and (II) handed down in Epictetus; in addition to these, it must make use solely of premisses plausible to the Stoics; and it must appear valid. For we know that different Stoic philosophers attempted to refute one or other of the principles in Epictetus, but we do not hear of anyone questioning the truth of any other premiss or the validity of the argument. Moreover, the reconstruction must employ only the logical means and concepts available in antiquity; in particular the notions of proposition, consequence, and modalities used must fit in with the logic of the time, and it must be possible to formulate the argument in ordinary language. Finally, the restored argument must not have a complexity which precludes its presentation at a social gathering, since people enjoyed discussing the Master argument over dinner (e.g. Plu. *Quaest. Conv.* 615a; Epict. *Diss*. II.19.8).

In line with Diodorus' modal definition, the general conclusion of the argument (IV) may be reformulated as

(IV′) If a proposition neither is nor will be true it is impossible.

The first principle is not so readily comprehensible. It runs

(I) Every past true <proposition> is necessary.

The Greek term used for 'past', παρεληλυθός, is a standard Stoic expression for past propositions, meaning not that the proposition itself subsisted in the past, but that it is in some sense about the past.[39] The principle occurs also in Cicero, together with some explication:

---

[37] There is some additional information in 19.2–9.
[38] Cf. Giannantoni 1981c and R. Müller 1985, 232–4 for a historical overview and extensive bibliographies.   [39] Cf. below, pp. 95–6.

> All true <propositions> of the past are necessary . . . since they are unal-
> terable, i.e. since past <propositions> cannot change from true to false.
> (Cic. *Fat.* 14)

From this passage we may infer that it was a peculiarity of all past true
propositions that they cannot change their truth-value to falsehood; and
that because of this they are necessary. This suggests that the past true
propositions at issue do not include all propositions in the past tense, but
that they were those propositions which correspond to some past state or
event. For instance, the true past proposition 'I went to Athens' corresponds to the event of my having gone to Athens. It can never become
false. Assume that I went to Athens last month. Then the proposition 'I
went to Athens' is not only true now, it will also be true tomorrow, the
day after, and in fact always from now on. The truth of the proposition is
based on the fact that there has been a case of my going to Athens, and –
whatever happens from now on – this cannot unhappen. (One may bring
out this feature more clearly by reformulating the proposition as 'It has
been the case that I went to Athens'.) On the other hand the proposition
'You have not been to Athens' does not correspond to a past state or event.
Suppose that up to now you never went to Athens. Then the proposition
is true now. Now suppose in addition that you will go to Athens next
week. After you have gone there, the proposition 'You have not been to
Athens' is no longer true. Hence it is not necessary. We may hence refor-
mulate principle (i) as

(i′) Every true proposition that corresponds to a past state or event is necessary.

The second principle that functions as a premiss in the argument is

(ii) The impossible does not follow from the possible,

The principle was accepted by Aristotle and by almost all logicians
Hellenistic and modern alike.[40] At least by the Stoics it was understood
as

(ii′) An impossible proposition does not follow from a possible one.

This amounts to the statement that if a proposition is impossible and follows from some other proposition, then this other proposition is impossible, too.

The following reconstruction assumes that the argument rests on a

---

[40] The exception is Chrysippus, see below, pp. 116–17.

couple of further principles, which might have been generally understood as valid and thus not worth mentioning, or else which might have been generally accepted by the Stoics, and because of this omitted by Epictetus. The first additional principle is

(v) If something is the case now, then it has always been the case that it will be the case.

For instance, if I am in Athens now, then it has always in the past been the case that I would be in Athens (at some time). This principle gains historical plausibility from the fact that we find a version of it in Aristotle, and that another version of it was accepted by the Stoics.[41]

The second supplementary principle is

(vi) If something neither is nor will be true, then it has been the case (at some time) that it will never be the case.

This theorem is based on the idea that if some proposition presently neither is nor will be true, and you step back in time, as it were, then the formerly present 'not being true' turns into a future 'not going to be true', so that from the point of view of the past, the proposition will never be true, and the corresponding state of affairs will never obtain. This is assumed to hold at least for the past moment that immediately precedes the present. This principle has some plausibility to it. However there is no unambiguous evidence that it was discussed in antiquity.[42]

Fallacies and sophisms were generally presented by means of an example which stands in for the general case, and it is a plausible guess that this was so for the Master argument as well. A suitable example can be found in Alexander – the proposition 'I am in Corinth.' The argument then starts with the assumption that

(1) the proposition 'I am in Corinth' neither is nor will ever be true.

and the conclusion to be demonstrated is that

(C) the proposition 'I am in Corinth' is impossible.

By principle (vi) it follows from (1) that

(2) it has been the case (at some time) that I will never be in Corinth.

Using principle (i), that all past truths are necessary, it follows from (2) that

---

[41] See Arist. *Int.* IX.18b9–11; Cic. *Div.* 1.125; cf. Cic. *Fat.* 19 and 27.
[42] Becker 1960, 253–5 adduces a few passages in which some ideas that are related to the principle are expressed.

(3) the proposition 'It has been the case (at some time) that I will never be in Corinth' is necessary.

But since necessity of a proposition is equivalent to the impossibility of its contradictory, from (3) it follows that

(4) the proposition 'It has always been the case that I will be in Corinth (at some time)' is impossible.[43]

Now, according to principle (v), it holds that

(5) if I am in Corinth, then it has always been the case that I will be in Corinth (at some time).

This is equivalent to

(5′) the proposition 'It has always been the case that I will be in Corinth (at some time)' follows from the (initial) proposition 'I am in Corinth'.

This makes it possible to apply principle (ii), that the impossible follows from the impossible, to (4) and (5′), so that one obtains as a result that

(C) the proposition 'I am in Corinth' is impossible.

And this is precisely what the Master argument was meant to show. Moreover, this argument appears indeed to be valid.

Where does the argument go wrong? The ancients went in for criticizing principles (i) and (ii), and one may indeed wonder whether (i) covers cases of the kind to which it has been applied above. But there are also a couple of things questionable with principles (v) and (vi). With a certain continuum theory of time, one could state that (vi) does not hold for those (rather few) cases in which the proposition at issue has started to be false only at the present moment.[44] More importantly, (v) and its variants seem to smuggle in a deterministic assumption.

III The Stoics

If Aristotelian logic is essentially a logic of terms, Stoic logic is in its core a propositional logic. Stoic inference concerns the relations between items having the structure of propositions. These items are the assertibles (ἀξιώματα) which are the primary bearers of truth-value.[45] Accordingly,

---

[43] Assuming that the proposition 'It has always been the case that I will be in Corinth (at some time)' in (4) is at least equivalent to the contradictory of the proposition 'It has been the case (at some time) that I will never be in Corinth' from (3).   [44] Cf. Denyer 1981b, 43 and 45.

[45] In a derivative sense, presentations (φαντασίαι) can be said to be true and false: Chrysippus

Stoic logic falls into two main parts: the theory of arguments (λόγοι) and the theory of assertibles, which are the components from which the arguments are built.

1: Assertibles

What is an assertible? In order to answer this, it is best to look at the various definitions or accounts of 'assertible' that have survived. What appears to be the standard definition states that

(1) an assertible is a self-complete sayable that can be stated as far as itself is concerned.[46]

This definition places the assertible in the genus of self-complete sayables,[47] and so everything that holds in general for sayables and for self-complete sayables holds equally for assertibles. According to the definition, what marks off assertibles from other self-complete sayables is 'that (i) they can be stated (ii) as far as they themselves are concerned'.

Assertibles can be asserted or stated, but they are not themselves assertions or statements. They subsist independently of their being stated, in a similar way in which sayables in general subsist independently of their being said. This notwithstanding, it is the characteristic primary function of assertibles to be stated. On the one hand, they are the only entities which we can use for making statements: there are no statements without assertibles. On the other, assertibles have no other function than their being stated.[48]

There is a second account of 'assertible' which fits in well with this. It determines an 'assertible' as

(2) that by saying which we make a statement[49] (D.L. vii.66; cf. S.E. *M* viii.73; 74).

'Saying' here betokens the primary function of the assertible: one cannot genuinely say an assertible without stating it. To say an assertible is more than just to utter a sentence that expresses it. For instance, 'If it is day, it is light' is a complex assertible, more precisely a conditional, that is composed of the two simple assertibles, 'It is day', which comes in as

---

Logika Zētēmata, *PHerc.* 307, iii.13–14 (Hülser 1987–8, 818; revised text in Marrone 1993); S.E. *M* vii.244–5); and in a different sense so can arguments (see below, p. 126).

[46] Tὸ μὲν ἀξίωμα . . . εἶναι λεκτὸν αὐτοτελὲς ἀποφαντὸν ὅσον ἐφ' ἑαυτῷ (S.E. *PH* ii.104: cf. D.L. vii.65).   [47] For self-complete sayables see below, pp. 202–3.

[48] In that respect, assertibles differ from propositional content or the common content of different sentences in different moods. For a propositional content is as it were multifunctional: it can not only be stated, but also asked, commanded etc. In contrast, assertibles are unifunctional: one cannot ask or command them etc.   [49] ὃ λέγοντες ἀποφαινόμεθα.

antecedent, and 'It is light', which comes in as consequent. Now, when I utter the sentence 'If it is day, it is light' I make use of all three assertibles. However, the only one I actually assert is the conditional, and the only thing I genuinely say is that if it is day, it is light.

This suggests that the phrase 'can be stated' is sufficient to delimit assertibles from the other kinds of self-complete sayables. But what then is the function of the remaining part of definition (1), the phrase (ii) 'as far as itself is concerned'? In fact it does not serve to narrow down the class of assertibles any further. Rather it is meant to pre-empt a misinterpretation: the locution 'can be asserted' could have been understood as too strict a requirement, that is, as potentially throwing out some things which for the Stoics were assertibles. For there are two things that are needed for a statement of an assertible: first the assertible itself, secondly someone who can state it. According to Stoic doctrine, that someone would have to have a rational presentation in accordance with which the assertible subsists.[50] But there are any number of assertibles that subsist even though no one has a suitable presentation.[51] In such cases, one of the necessary conditions for the 'assertibility' of an assertible is unfulfilled. Here the qualification 'as far as the assertible itself is concerned' comes in. It cuts out this external, additional condition. For something's being an assertible it is irrelevant whether there actually is someone who could state the assertible.

In the two accounts of 'assertible' presented so far, the expression 'to state' (ἀποφαίνεσθαι) has been taken as basic and has not been explicated; nor do we find an explication of it elsewhere. But there are two further Stoic accounts of 'assertible', and they suggest that 'statability' was associated with another essential property of assertibles, namely that of having a truth-value. In a parallel formulation to account (2), we learn that

(3) assertibles are those things saying which we either speak true or speak false (S.E. *M* VIII.73)

and several times we find the explication that

(4) an assertible is that which is either true or false (e.g. D.L. VII.65; cf. 66).[52]

From (3) and (4) we can infer that truth and falsehood are properties of assertibles, and that being true or false – in a non-derivative sense – is both

---

[50] Cf. below, pp. 211–13.   [51] See above, p. 93 and below, p. 211.

[52] This account (4) also occurs in the form of a logical principle, '(5) every assertible is either true or false' (Cic. *Fat.* 20; [Plu.] *Fat.* 574e). This is a logical metatheorem which is usually called 'principle of bivalence'.

a necessary and a sufficient condition for something's being an assertible. The exact relation between truth, falsehood and 'statability' we are not told. But it seems safe to assume first that one can only state something that has a truth-value, and second that one can only speak true or false if one 'says' something that is itself either true or false, that is, only if one 'says' an assertible.

*

From what has been said so far, one can see that assertibles resemble modern propositions in various respects. There are however essential differences. For instance, true and false assertibles differ in their ontological status. According to a passage in Sextus Empiricus, a true assertible is opposed to something – i.e. something false – and is real (ὑπάρχειν), whereas a false assertible is opposed to something – i.e. something true – but is not real (S.E. *M* VIII.10). A difficulty here is what is meant by 'being real'. Perhaps assertibles that are real serve at the same time both as true propositions and as states of affairs that obtain, whereas there is no corresponding identity between false propositions and states of affairs that do not obtain, since the Stoics did not allow anything like 'states of affairs that do not obtain'.

The most far-reaching difference is that truth and falsehood are temporal properties of assertibles. They can belong to an assertible at one time and not belong to it at another time. This becomes obvious for instance by the way in which the truth-conditions are determined: the assertible 'It is day' is true when it is day (D.L. VII.65). This understanding of 'true' is certainly close to everyday use: we might say that it is true now that it is raining, implying that it might be false later. So, when the Stoics say '*p* is true' we have to understand '*p* is true now'.

A modern proposition is often taken as containing no indexicals. Examples of such propositions, say 'Two plus two equals four' or 'Rain occurs in England on 5/6/94' given that they are true, do not allow a serious question: and *will* they be true? (The present tense used in them is the a-temporal present.) With an assertible like 'Dio is walking' on the other hand, such a question does make sense: as with Hellenistic examples for propositions generally, it contains no definite time. This assertible now concerns Dio's walking now; uttered tomorrow it will concern Dio's walking tomorrow, etc. This 'temporality' of (the truth-values of) assertibles has a number of consequences for Stoic logic.

In particular, assertibles can in principle change their truth-value: the assertible 'It is day' is true now, false later, true again tomorrow, and so forth. In fact it changes its truth-value twice a day. Assertibles which do (or can) change their truth-value the Stoics called 'changing assertibles' (μεταπίπτοντα). The majority of Stoic examples belong to this kind.

A temporal concept of truth raises questions about the status of tense and time in relation to assertibles. The Stoics standardly distinguished past, present, and future assertibles. They were expressed in past, present, or future tenses. Examples are 'Socrates walked', 'It is night', 'Dio will be alive.' A passage in Sextus (S.E. *M* VIII.255) makes the distinction between something being in the past or in the future and a statement being made about something past or about something future, and makes clear that past and future assertibles are not themselves past or future, but about past or future. They subsist in the present just as present assertibles do. For they have their truth-value in the present, when they are asserted. 'Being (about the) past', 'being (about the) future' etc. were hence considered as properties of the assertibles themselves and not merely as context-dependent parts of the linguistic structure of the sentences which express these assertibles.[53]

2: Simple assertibles

The most fundamental distinction of assertibles was that between simple (ἁπλᾶ) and non-simple (οὐχ ἁπλᾶ) ones (D.L. VII.68–9, S.E. *M* VIII.93, 95, 108). Non-simple assertibles are those composed of more than one assertible, which are linked by connective particles, like 'either ... or ...', 'both ... and ...'.[54] Simple assertibles are defined negatively as those assertibles which are not non-simple. There were various kinds of simple and of non-simple assertibles. Before I turn to them, a few preliminary remarks are in order.

We are nowhere told what the ultimate criteria for the distinctions are. But it is important to keep in mind that the Stoics were not trying to give a grammatical classification of *sentences*. Rather, the classification is of *assertibles*. So the criteria for the distinctions are not merely grammatical, but at heart logical or 'ontological'. This leads to the following complication: the only access there is to assertibles is by way of language. But there is no one-to-one correspondence between assertibles and declarative sentences. For Chrysippus one and the same sentence (of a certain type) may express an assertible or a self-complete sayable that belongs to different

---

[53] This view that time is – in some way – a property intrinsic to the assertibles leads to several difficulties; one being the problem of the status of time-indexicals in assertibles (e.g. in 'I will be alive tomorrow'); another the relation between a future assertible stated now and a corresponding present assertible, stated at the relevant future time.   [54] See below, p. 103.

classes – although one may 'reveal itself' more readily than the other.[55] Equally, two sentences of different grammatical structure may express the same assertible.

This view of the relation between assertibles and sentences offers a gloomy prospect for the development of a logic of assertibles. How can we know which assertible a sentence expresses? Here the Stoics seem to have proceeded as follows: aiming at the elimination of (structural) ambiguities they embarked upon a programme of standardization of language such that it became possible (or easier) to read off from the form of a sentence the type of assertible expressed by it.

*

I now turn to the various types of simple assertibles. Our main sources for them are two lists, one in Diogenes Laertius (D.L. vII.69–70), the other in Sextus Empiricus (S.E. *M* vIII.96–100), and a handful of titles of works by Chrysippus. At first glance, the lists in Sextus and Diogenes do not match very well: Diogenes enumerates six kinds of simple assertibles, three affirmative, three seemingly negative; Sextus gives only three kinds, which show strong parallels to Diogenes' affirmative ones. But the names differ in two of the three cases, and their accounts differ, to various degrees, in all three cases. Diogenes lists negations (ἀποφατικά), denials (ἀρνητικά), privations (στερητικά), categorical (κατηγορικά), catagoreutical (καταγορευτικά), and indefinite (ἀόριστα) assertibles. Sextus lists indefinite (ἀόριστα), definite (ὡρισμένα), and middle (μέσα) ones.

The accounts in Diogenes show a greater degree of uniformity and are more grammatically orientated. They apply exclusively to simple assertibles. The accounts in Sextus on the other hand are rather 'philosophical' and do not necessarily apply to simple assertibles only. There are good reasons for assuming that the list in Sextus is earlier than that in Diogenes. But it is likely that both lists were developed in the third and second centuries BC, and the two sets of concepts are in fact perfectly compatible.[56] Chrysippus wrote three books about negations and seven

---

[55] Cf. e.g. Chrysippus *Logika Zētēmata*, *PHerc.* 307, xI.19–30 (Hülser 1987–8, 826; revised text in Marrone 1993).

[56] First, neither of the lists is introduced as an exhaustive disjunction: Sextus introduces the classification with τινὰ μέν . . . τινὰ δέ instead of τὰ μέν . . . τὰ δέ (S.E. *M* vIII.96); Diogenes starts with ἐν δὲ τοῖς . . . (D.L. vII.69). Then, although Sextus does not list different types of 'negative' assertibles, he discusses Stoic negation (ἀπόφασις) in S.E. *M* vIII.103–7, that is immediately after his threefold distinction and immediately before talking about non-simple assertibles, to which he turns with the words 'now that we have touched upon the simple assertibles to some degree . . .' (S.E. *M* vIII.108). Finally, we find traces of most of the kinds of assertibles in Chrysippus, with names from the sets of *both* authors.

about indefinite assertibles, one book on catagoreuticals and at least one
book on privations (D.L. VII.190, Simp. *Cat.* 396.19–21); he wrote about
definite assertibles (D.L. VII.197) and used in his writings the term
'definite' in the way it is determined in Sextus.[57] There are no traces of
the terms 'categorical' and 'middle'; and there is no evidence that
Chrysippus discussed denials.

*

Examples of Sextus' middle and Diogenes' categorical assertibles are of
two kinds: 'Socrates is sitting' and '(A) man is walking'. The rather
unhelpful name 'middle' is based on the fact that these assertibles are neither indefinite (since they define their object) nor definite (since they are
not deictic) (S.E. *M* VII.97). Why in Diogenes the assertibles are called
'categorical' remains in the dark. They are defined as those that consist of
a nominative case (ὀρθὴ πτῶσις), like 'Dio' and a predicate, like 'is walking' (D.L. VII.70). It is noteworthy that assertibles of the type '(A) man is
walking' are extremely rare in Stoic logic: besides the example in Sextus
there seems to be only one other example, namely the second premiss and
the conclusion in the No-one fallacy (D.L. VII.187).

*

The next class of simple assertibles, that is, definite and catagoreutical
ones, have in their standard linguistic form a demonstrative pronoun as
subject expression. A typical example is 'This one is walking.' According
to Sextus Empiricus, a definite assertible is defined as one that is uttered
along with reference or *deixis* (δεῖξις) (S.E. *M* VIII.96). What do the Stoics
mean by '*deixis*' here? Galen (*PHP* II.2.9–11) cites Chrysippus talking
about the *deixis* with which we accompany our saying 'I', which here can
be either a pointing at the object of *deixis* (ourselves in this case) with
one's hand or finger, or making a gesture with one's head in its direction.
So, ordinary *deixis* seems to be a non-verbal, physical act of pointing at
something or someone, simultaneous to the utterance of the sentence
with the pronoun. Further information is provided by a *scholium* to
Dionysius Thrax, namely that

> every pronoun is fully defined either through *deixis* or through *anaphora*,
> for a pronoun either signifies a *deixis*, like 'I', 'you', 'this one', or an *anaph-
> ora*, as in the case of 'he' (αὐτός)

---

[57] Cf. Chrysippus *Logika Zētēmata*, *PHerc.* 307, v.14,17 (Hülser 1987–8, 820; revised text in
Marrone 1993).

and that

> every *deixis* is primary[58] knowledge and knowledge of a person that is present. (ΣDThrax 518–19)

Here *deixis* and *anaphora* are contrasted with each other, from which one may infer that definite assertibles, which require *deixis*, do not include those in which a pronoun is used anaphorically.[59] Moreover, we learn that besides 'this one' and 'I', 'you' can be used along with *deixis*. And thirdly, we learn that *deixis* is always direct reference to an object that is present. This suggests that if, say, I point at a statue of Hipparchia and utter 'This one is a philosopher', I have not performed a genuine *deixis*. (Whereas, if I had said 'This one is a statue of a philosopher' I would have.) '*Deixis* by proxy' seems to be excluded.

Despite these clarifications of the Stoic concept of *deixis*, there remain difficulties with definite assertibles: first, how does one identify a particular definite assertible? Certainly, the sentence (type) by which a definite assertible is expressed does not suffice for its identification. For example if I have my eyes closed while someone utters the sentence 'This one is walking', thereby pointing at someone, I do not know which assertible was stated. For the sentence 'This one is walking' uttered, say, while pointing at Theo expresses a different assertible than when uttered while pointing at Dio.[60]

However, we have every reason to believe that when now I utter 'This one is walking' pointing at Dio, and when I utter the same sentence tomorrow, again pointing at Dio, the Stoics regarded these as two assertions of the same assertible. Thus, regarding the individuation of definite assertibles, the easiest way to understand the Stoic position is to conceive of a distinction between '*deixis* type' and '*deixis* token': a '*deixis* type' would be determined by the object of the *deixis* (and is independent of who performs an act of *deixis* when and where): whenever the object is the same, the *deixis* is of the same type; and the tokens are the particular utterances of 'this one' accompanied by the physical acts of pointing at that object. Hence we should imagine there to be one assertible 'This one is walking' for Theo (namely with the *deixis* type pointing-at-Theo), and one for Dio (with the *deixis* type pointing-at-Dio).

But now the question arises: how does a definite differ from the corresponding middle assertible – e.g. 'This one is walking (pointing at Dio)'

---

[58] 'First-hand' or 'prior' or 'primary' – the Greek word is πρῶτος.

[59] For the Stoic treatment of cases of anaphora see below, pp. 104–5.

[60] Our texts suggest that the Stoics identified a particular definite assertible when it is used, by the accompanying act of pointing; and when it is mentioned, by the addition of a phrase like 'pointing at Dio' just as I did above (cf. Alex. *APr.* 177.28–9).

from 'Dio is walking'? Are they not rather two different ways of expressing the *same* assertible? Not for the Stoics. For we know that in the case of the assertibles 'Dio is dead' and 'This one is dead (pointing at Dio)' at the same time one could be true, but the other not (see below p. 116). What is it then that distinguishes them? Some information about the difference between middle and definite assertibles can be obtained by scrutinizing the case in which their truth-values differ.

In a passage that reports Chrysippus' rejection of the modal theorem that from the possible only the possible follows[61] we learn that the assertible 'This one is dead (pointing at Dio)' cannot ever become true, since so long as Dio is alive it is false, and thereafter, once Dio is dead, instead of becoming true, it is destroyed. The corresponding assertible 'Dio is dead', on the other hand, does – as expected – simply change its truth-value from false to true at the moment of Dio's death. The reason given for the destruction of the definite assertible is that once Dio is dead the object of the *deixis*, i.e. Dio, no longer exists.

Now, for an assertible destruction can only mean ceasing to subsist. When an assertible ceases to subsist, that implies that it no longer satisfies all the conditions for being an assertible. And this should have something to do with its being definite, that is, with its being related to *deixis*. So one could say that in the case of definite assertibles, assertibility or statability (being ἀποφαντόν) becomes in part point-at-ability, and Stoic point-at-ability requires intrinsically the existence of the object pointed at. This is not only a condition of actual statability in particular situations – as is the presence of an asserter; rather it is a condition of identifiability of the assertible; of its being this assertible.[62]

*

Next the indefinite assertibles. In Sextus, they are defined as assertibles that are governed by an indefinite part of speech or 'particle' (S.E. *M* VIII.97). According to Diogenes they are composed of one or more indefinite particles and a predicate (D.L. VII.70). Such indefinite particles are 'someone' (τις) or 'something' (τι). Examples are of the type 'Someone is sitting.'[63] Again, Sextus presents special truth-conditions: the indefinite

---

[61] The passage is quoted in full, below, p. 116.

[62] Diogenes Laertius' catagoreutical assertibles are defined as being composed of a deictic nominative case and a predicate (D.L. VII.70). This implies that the object of the *deixis* must be referred to by a deictic pronoun in the nominative. The catagoreuticals might then simply have formed a subclass of Sextus' definite assertibles.

[63] The Stoics had both simple and non-simple indefinite assertibles and Sextus' account of indefinite assertibles seems to cover both kinds. For the latter see below, pp. 111–14.

assertible 'Someone is sitting' is true when a corresponding definite assertible ('This one is sitting') is true, since if no particular person is sitting, it is not the case that someone is sitting (S.E. *M* VIII.98). This truth condition, in connection with the requirement of existence of the object of *deixis* for the subsistence of a definite assertible, gets the Stoics into trouble. Assertibles like 'Someone is dead', it seems, can never be true – since no assertible 'This one is dead' can ever be true. The Stoics could have easily mended this by expanding the truth condition to '. . . if a corresponding definite *or middle* assertible is true'. The indefinites are the Stoic counterpart to our existential propositions, and their classification on a par with the other simple assertibles leads to some complications when it comes to the construction of non-simple assertibles.[64]

We do not know how the Stoics classified simple assertibles that are expressed by sentences with more than one noun expression, like 'This one loves Theo', 'Aspasia loves this one', 'Leontion loves someone' etc. The accounts in Diogenes make one think that the criterion for classification may have been always the subject expression. At any rate, examples of these kinds are extremely rare in Stoic texts.[65]

*

The most important kind of negative assertible is the negation. For the Stoics, a negation is formed by prefixing to an assertible the negation particle 'not:' (οὐχί, οὐκ etc.) as for instance in 'Not: it is day'. The negation is truth-functional: the negation particle, if added to true assertibles, makes them false, if added to false ones makes them true (S.E. *M* VIII.103).

Every negation is the negation of an assertible, namely of the assertible from which it has been constructed by prefixing 'not:'. The assertible 'Not: it is day' is the negation of the assertible 'It is day'. An assertible and its negation form a pair of contradictories (ἀντικείμενα):

> Contradictories are those <assertibles> of which the one exceeds the other by a negation particle, such as 'It is day' – 'Not: it is day.' (S.E. *M* VIII.89)

This implies that an assertible is the contradictory of another if it is one of a pair of assertibles in which one is the negation of the other (cf. D.L. VII.73). Of contradictory assertibles precisely one is true and the other false.[66]

---

[64] See below, pp. 111–14.   [65] Cf. also Brunschwig 1994b, 66–7; Ebert 1991, 117–18.

[66] The concept of contradictoriness is pertinent to various parts of Stoic logic, e.g. to the truth-conditions for the conditional and to the accounts of the indemonstrable arguments; see below, p. 106 and p. 127.

Why did the Stoics insist on having the negation particle prefixed to the assertible? If we assume that they were looking for a standardized formulation for the negation of an assertible which expresses its contradictoriness, this becomes readily comprehensible. In order to obtain an assertible's contradictory, the scope of the negation particle has to encompass the whole assertible which it negates. This is achieved with a minimum of structural ambiguity if one places it right in front of this assertible. A negation particle elsewhere in a sentence – especially in its common place before the predicate – can easily be understood as forming a negative assertible that is not contradictory to the original assertible. For instance, in the view of some Stoics, 'Callias is walking' and 'Callias is not walking' could both be false at the same time: namely in the case that Callias does not exist (Alex. *APr.* 402.3–19).[67] This explains why the Stoics did not call negative assertibles of this kind negations, but rather affirmations (Apul. *Int.* 191.6–15; Alex. *APr.* 402.8–12): for them in the above example it is affirmed of Callias that he is not walking.

Although in Diogenes Laertius the negation is introduced as one of the types of simple assertibles, the Stoics equally prefixed the negation particle to non-simple assertibles in order to form complex negations. The negation of a simple assertible is itself simple, that of a non-simple assertible non-simple. Thus, differently from modern logic, the addition of the negative does not make a simple assertible non-simple. The negation particle 'not:' is not a propositional connective (σύνδεσμος), for such connectives bind together parts of speech and the negation particle does not do that.

An interesting special case of the negation is the 'super-negation' (ὑπερ ἀποφατικόν) or, as we would say, 'double negation'. This is the negation of a negation, for instance 'Not: not: it is day'. This is still a simple assertible. Its truth-conditions are the same as those for 'It is day'. It posits 'It is day', as Diogenes puts it (D.L. VII.69).

*

Diogenes' list contains two further types of negative assertibles: denials and privations. A denial consists of a denying particle and a predicate, the example given is 'No one is walking' (D.L. VII.70). That is, this type of assertible has a compound negative as subject term. Unlike the negation particle, this negative can form a complete assertible if put together with a predicate.

The truth-conditions of denials have not been handed down, but they seem obvious: 'No one φ's', should be true precisely if it is not the case

---

[67] Cf. Lloyd 1978b.

that someone φ's. Denials must have been the contradictories of simple indefinite assertibles of the kind 'Someone φ's'. But why do they form an extra class? Would not the negations of indefinite assertibles, like 'Not: someone φ's' have sufficed? Possibly the Stoics who introduced denials pursued a chiefly grammatical interest in classifying assertibles. Alternatively, they may have aimed at differentiating them from categorical assertibles: although grammatically they could be seen as consisting of a nominative and a predicate, they do not have existential import.[68]

*

Finally, the privative assertible is determined as a simple assertible composed of a privative particle and a potential assertible, like 'This one is unkind' (D.L. VII.70, literally 'Unkind is this one', a word order presumably chosen in order to have the negative element at the front of the sentence). The privative particle is the *alpha privativum* 'α-' ('un-'). It is unclear why the rest of the assertible, '(-)kind is this one' is regarded merely as a potential assertible. For e.g. in the case of the negation proper, in 'Not: it is day', 'It is day' is referred to simply as an assertible.

3: Non-simple assertibles

The analogue to the modern distinction between atomic and molecular propositions is the Stoic distinction between simple and non-simple assertibles. Non-simple assertibles are those that are composed of more than one assertible or of one assertible taken twice (D.L. VII.68–9; S.E. *M* VIII.93–4) or more often. These constituent assertibles of a non-simple assertible are put together by one or more propositional connectives. A connective is an indeclinable part of speech that connects parts of speech (D.L. VII.58). An example of the first type of non-simple assertible is 'Either it is day, or it is light'; one of the second type 'If it is day, it is day'.

Concerning the identification of non-simple assertibles of a particular kind, the Stoics took what one may call a 'formalistic' approach, for which they were often – and wrongly – rebuked in antiquity.[69] In their definitions of the different kinds of non-simple assertibles they provide the characteristic propositional connectives, which can have one or more parts, and determine their position in (the sentence that expresses) the non-simple assertibles. In this way it is shown how the connectives are syntactically combined with the constituent assertibles; their place relative to (the

---

[68] Cf. Ebert 1991, 122. The Stoics can thus express all four basic types of general statements, e.g. 'Someone φ's', 'No one φ's' and 'No one does not φ'.   [69] Cf. e.g. Gal. *Inst. Log.* IV.6; III.5.

sentences expressing) the constituent assertibles is strictly regulated. The advantage of such a procedure is that once one has agreed to stick to certain standardizations of language use, it becomes possible to discern logical properties of assertibles and their compounds by looking at the linguistic expressions used.[70]

Non-simple assertibles can be composed of more than two simple constituent assertibles (Plu. *Stoic. Rep.* 1047c–e). This is possible in two ways. The first has a parallel in modern propositional logic: the definition of the non-simple assertible allows that its constituent assertibles are themselves non-simple. An example of such a non-simple assertible is 'If both it is day and the sun is above the earth, it is light'.[71] The type of non-simple assertible to which such a complex assertible belongs is determined by the overall form of the assertible. The above example, for instance, is a conditional. The second type of assertible with more than two constituent assertibles is quite different. Conjunctive and disjunctive connectives were conceived of not as two-place functors, but – in line with ordinary language – as two-or-more-place functors. So we find disjunctions with three disjuncts: 'Either wealth is good or <wealth> is evil or <wealth is> indifferent' (S.E. *M* VIII.434; S.E. *PH* II.150).

It is worth noting that all non-simple assertibles have their connective or one part of it prefixed to the first constituent assertible. As in the case of the negation, the primary ground for this must have been to avoid ambiguity. Consider the statement

'p and q or r'.

In Stoic 'standardized' formulation this would become either

Both p and either q or r

or

Either both p and q or r.

The ambiguity of the original statement is thus removed. More than that, the Stoic method of pre-fixing connectives can in general perform the function brackets have in modern logic.[72]

The avoidance of ambiguity must also have been one reason behind the Stoic practice of eliminating cross-references in non-simple assertibles.

[70] See Frede 1974a, 198–201.

[71] Cf. S.E. *M* VIII.230 and 232, 'If it is day, <if it is day> it is light.'

[72] In this respect one might rightly consider the Stoic formulation as a fore-runner of Polish notation; cf. Ebert 1991, 115–16.

Instead of formulations of ordinary discourse like 'If Plato walks, he moves' and 'Plato walks and (he) moves', the subject term is repeated in full: 'If Plato walks, Plato moves', 'Plato walks and Plato moves.'[73] This practice of elimination is not reflected upon in our sources, but its regular occurrence leaves no doubt that it was exercised intentionally – perhaps to simplify the application of formal logical procedures.

Truth-conditions for the non-simple assertibles are given separately from their definitions. They suggest that the Stoics were not aiming at fully covering the connotations of the connective particles in ordinary language. Rather they lend themselves to the interpretation that the Stoics attempted to filter out the essential formal characteristics of the connectives. Leaving aside the negation – which can be simple – only one type of non-simple assertible, the conjunction, is truth-functional. In the remaining cases modal relations (like incompatibility), partial truth-functionality and basic relations like symmetry and asymmetry, in various combinations, serve as truth-criteria.[74]

For Chrysippus we know of only three types of non-simple assertibles: conditionals, conjunctions, and exclusive-cum-exhaustive disjunctive assertibles. Later Stoics added further kinds of non-simple assertibles, although the number seems always to have been fairly small. Besides the three Chrysippean kinds, we find a pseudo-conditional and a causal assertible, two types of pseudo-disjunctions, and two types of dissertive assertibles. It is quite possible that the main reason for adding these was logical, in the sense that they would allow the formulation of valid inferences which Chrysippus' system could not accommodate. A certain grammatical interest may have entered into it, but this alone could not account for all the choices and omissions made.[75]

*

The conjunction (συμπεπλεγμένον or συμπλοκή) seems generally to have been regarded as unproblematic. One account runs 'A conjunction is

---

[73] Cf. D.L. vii.77, 78, 80; S.E. *M* viii.246, 252, 254, 305, 308, 423; S.E. *PH* ii.105, 106, 141; Gell. xvi 8.9; Gal. *Inst. Log.* iv.1; Simp. *Phys.* 1300; Alex. *APr.* 345; Cic. *Fat.* 12–13; see also below, pp. 111–14 on indefinite non-simple assertibles.

[74] In addition to the direct determination of the truth-conditions, we frequently find another way of providing truth-conditions, namely by stating what a particular non-simple assertible 'announces' (ἐπαγγέλλεσθαι) (D.L. vii.72; Epict. *Diss.* ii.9.8). Occasionally, as in the case of the conditional, this 'announcement' covers only the uncontested main features of the truth-criterion (D.L. vii.71).

[75] The most comprehensive list of Stoic non-simple assertibles is provided in D.L. vii.71–4. Other important texts are Gell. xvi.8.9–14; Gal. *Inst. Log.* iii, iv and v, and various passages in Sextus Empiricus.

an assertible that is conjoined by certain conjunctive connective particles, like "Both it is day and it is light." (D.L. VII.72). Like a modern conjunction, the Stoic one connects whole assertibles: it is 'Both Plato walks and Plato talks', not 'Plato walks and talks'. Unlike modern conjunction, the conjunctive assertible is defined and understood in such a way that more than two conjuncts can be put together on a par (cf. Gell. XVI.8.10). The standard form has a two-or-more part connective: 'both . . . and . . . and . . . . . .' (καί . . . καί . . . καί . . .). The truth-conditions, too, are formulated in such a way as to include conjunctions with two or more conjuncts. A conjunction is true when all its constituent assertibles are true, false if one or more are false (S.E. *M* VIII.125,128; Gell. XVI.8.11). The Stoic conjunction is therefore truth-functional.[76]

For Stoic syllogistic the negated conjunction (ἀποφατικὴ συμπλοκή) D.L. VII.80) is of chief importance, since only when negated is the conjunction suitable as a 'leading' premiss.[77] Typically of the kind 'Not: both *p* and *q*'. Some more complex arguments have conjunctions with negated conjuncts as minor premiss.[78]

*

The conditional (συνημμένον) was defined as the assertible that is formed by means of the linking connective 'if' (εἰ) (D.L. VII.71). Its standardized form is 'If *p*, *q*', with *p* as the antecedent and *q* as the consequent.

In Chrysippus' time the debate about the truth-conditions of the conditional – which had been initiated by the logicians Philo and Diodorus – was still going on. There was agreement that a conditional 'announces' a relation of consequence, namely that its consequent follows (from) its antecedent (D.L. VII.71). It was what it is to 'follow' and the associated truth-conditions that were under debate. A minimal consensus seems to have been this: the 'announcement' of following suggests that a true conditional, if its antecedent is true, has a true consequent. Given the acceptance of the principle of bivalence, this amounts to the minimal requirement for the truth of a conditional that it must not be the case that the antecedent is true and the consequent false – a requirement we find also explicitly in our sources (D.L. VII.81). It is equivalent to the Philonian criterion.

We know that Chrysippus offered a truth-criterion that differed from Philo's and Diodorus' (Cic. *Acad.* II.143), and we can infer that

---

[76] See also Brunschwig 1994c, 72–9.   [77] See below, p. 121. Cf. also Sedley 1984.
[78] For the indefinite conjunction see below, p. 113.

Chrysippus' alternative was the one which Sextus reports, without naming an originator, as third in his list which starts with Philo and Diodorus. For it is presented as Stoic in D.L. VII.73 and alluded to as Chrysippean in Cic. *Fat.* 12.[79]

Sextus ascribes the Chrysippean criterion to those who introduce a connection (συνάρτησις) (S.E. *PH* II.111); this connection can only be that which holds between the antecedent and the consequent. The requirement of some such connection must have been introduced to avoid the paradoxes that arise from Philo's and Diodorus' positions. A look at the criterion itself shows that the connection in question is determined indirectly, based on the concept of conflict or incompatibility (μάχη): it states that a conditional is true precisely if its antecedent and the contradictory of its consequent conflict (D.L. VII.73). According to this criterion, for example, 'If the earth flies, Axiothea philosophizes' – which came out as true for both Philo and Diodorus – is no longer true. It is perfectly compatible that the earth flies and that it is not the case that Axiothea philosophizes.

For a full understanding of Chrysippus' criterion, one has to know what sort of conflict he had in mind. But here our sources offer little information. We find the shift to a modal expression in some later texts, according to which two assertibles conflict if they *cannot* be true together. This confirms that the conflict is some sort of incompatibility. Then there is a brief passage in Alexander (Alex. *Top.* 93.9–10) which has been interpreted as saying that two assertibles p, q conflict precisely if, assuming that p holds, q fails to hold *because p holds*.[80] However, the passage need not be of Stoic origin, and due to the condensed form of the text the interpretation inevitably remains speculative.

It is inappropriate to ask whether Chrysippus intended empirical, analytical or formal logical conflict: a conceptual framework which could accommodate such a distinction is absent in Hellenistic logic. Still, we can ask whether kinds of conflict that we would place in one or the other of those categories would have counted as conflict for Chrysippus. We can be confident that formal incompatibility would count. Assertibles like 'If it is light, it is light' were regarded as true (Cic. *Acad.* II.98; S.E. *PH* II.111) – presumably because 'It is light' and 'It is not the case that it is light' are incompatible, contradictoriness being the strongest possible conflict between

---

[79] Cf. Frede 1974a, 82–3. Sextus mentions a fourth type of conditional, which is based on the concept of *emphasis* (S.E. *PH* II.112). Its truth-conditions are that the consequent has to be potentially included in the antecedent. It is unclear who introduced this conditional. Cf. Frede 1974a, 90–3; Croissant 1984. [80] Cf. Barnes 1980, 170.

two assertibles. Equally, some cases that some may describe as analytical incompatibility were covered: for instance 'If Plato is walking, Plato is moving' and 'If Plato is breathing, Plato is alive' were regarded as true.

The question then boils down to the point whether any cases of what one might label 'empirical' incompatibility would count as conflict for Chrysippus.[81] There are a number of true conditionals where it is hard to decide whether the connection is empirical or logical, for instance, 'If it is day, it is light' and 'If there is sweat, there are invisible pores'. But some instances of empirical incompatibility were accepted by some Stoics: so conditionals with causal connections of the kind 'If someone has a wound in the heart, that one will die' were considered true.[82]

The connection expressed in theorems of divination on the other hand seems to have been an exception (Cic. *Fat.* 11–15). Such theorems are general statements which give in their 'consequent' the predicted future type of event or state, and in their 'antecedent' a sign of the event, to which the diviner has access. Chrysippus accepted that such theorems, if genuine, held without exception, and hence that in all instantiations the 'consequent' is true when the 'antecedent' is true. Nevertheless, he claimed that they would not make true conditionals.[83] Instead, he maintained that the diviners would formulate their theorems adequately if they phrased them as negated conjunctions with a negated second conjunct; i.e. if instead of 'If p, q' they said 'Not: both p and not q'.[84] Given that the conjunction and the negation are truth-functional, the resulting non-simple assertible is equivalent to a Philonian conditional.

*

Grounded on the concept of the conditional, the Stoics introduced two further kinds of non-simple assertibles (D.L. VII.71, 72). Both were probably added only after Chrysippus. Their accounts and truth criteria are in principle open to interpretation with Philo's, Diodorus', or Chrysippus' truth criterion for the conditional as their basis. Yet the presentation of Chrysippus' conditional in the same section in Diogenes suggests that it was his conditional these later Stoics had in mind.

---

[81] Scholars are divided on this point. Cf. e.g. Frede 1974a, 84–9; Donini 1974–5; Bobzien 1998, 156–70.

[82] S.E. *M* VIII.254–5; cf. *M* v.104, where the heartwound is referred to as cause (αἴτιον); cf. also Alex. *APr.* 404.21–4.

[83] This implies that Chrysippus thought that there was no conflict in the required sense between the sign of a future event and the non-occurrence of that event. Perhaps he assumed that there was no causal connection, either direct or indirect, between sign and future event, let alone any logical link.

[84] Cicero's example for a theorem of the diviners is in fact a negated *indefinite* conjunction. For these, see below, pp. 113–14.

The first, called 'pseudo-conditional' (παρασυνημμένον), is testified at the earliest for Crinis and has the standardized form 'Since (ἐπεί) p, q'. (D.L. VII.71). The truth-criterion for such assertibles is that (i) the 'consequent' must follow (from) the 'antecedent' and (ii) the 'antecedent' must be true (D.L. VII.74).[85]

The second kind is entitled 'causal assertible' (αἰτιῶδες) and has the standard form 'Because (διότι) p, q'. The name is explained by the remark that p is, as it were, the cause/ground (αἴτιον) of q.[86] The truth-condition for the causal assertible adds simply a further condition to those for the pseudo-conditional ((i) and (ii)). It is the element of symmetry that is ruled out for causal assertibles: the extra condition is (iii) that if p is the ground/cause for q, q cannot be the ground/cause for p, which in particular implies that 'Because p, p' is false. This condition makes some sense: 'being a cause of' and 'being a reason for' are usually considered as asymmetrical relations. In contrast, assertibles of the kind 'Since p, p' are true pseudo-conditionals, and it is possible that both 'Since p, q' and 'Since q, p' are true.

*

The Greek word for 'or' (ἤ) has several different functions as a connective particle, which are distinct in other languages. It covers both the Latin *aut* and the Latin *vel* and also both the English 'or' and the English 'than'. Not surprisingly, it plays a role as a connective in at least three different types of non-simple assertibles.

Chrysippus and the early Stoics seem to have concentrated on one type of disjunctive relation only: the exhaustive and exclusive disjunctive relation, called 'διεζευγμένον', here rendered 'disjunction'. This is the only disjunctive that figures in Chrysippus' syllogistic. In Diogenes it is defined as 'an assertible that is disjoined by the disjunctive connective "either", like "Either it is day or it is night."' (D.L. VII.72). As in the case of the conjunction, the disjunctive connective was understood as being able to have more than two disjuncts, and there are examples of such disjunctions (Gell. XVI 8.12; S.E. *PH* I.69; S.E. *M* VIII.434). Thus the connective was 'either . . . or . . . or . . . . . .' (ἤτοι . . . ἤ . . . ἤ . . .) with its first part ('either') prefixed to the first disjunct.

---

[85] It has been suggested that 'Since p, q' is an economical and appropriate way of expressing Stoic sign-inference (so Burnyeat, 1982c, 218–24; Sedley, 1982c, 242–3). For a sign is the antecedent in a sound conditional which both begins and ends with truth, and is revelatory of its consequent (cf. S.E. *PH* II.101,104.106).

[86] The Greek αἴτιον covers both physical causes and grounds, reasons, explanations.

The formulation of the truth-conditions raised some difficulties, not least due to the fact that more than two disjuncts were allowed. Gellius presents them as follows:

> But (i) all the disjuncts must be in conflict with each other and (ii) their contradictories . . . must be contrary to each other. (iii) Of all the disjuncts one must be true, the remaining ones false. (Gell. XVI.8.13)

First a non-truth-functional criterion is given ((i)–(ii)), which is then immediately followed by something like a truth-functional criterion (iii). This could be either an alternative truth-criterion; or – similar to the case of the conditional – just an uncontested minimal requirement, perhaps to permit one to single out some false disjunctions more readily.[87]

It certainly was a necessary condition for the truth of the disjunction that precisely one of its disjuncts had to be true and all the others false. But most sources imply that this was not sufficient. The criterion they state is stricter and typically involves the term 'conflict', which is already familiar from the conditionals. The criterion is in fact a conjunction of two conditions ((i) and (ii)). First, the disjuncts must be in conflict with each other; this entails that at most one is true. Secondly, the contradictories of the disjuncts must all be contrary to each other; this ensures that not all of the contradictories are true, and hence that at least one of the original disjuncts is true. The two conditions may be contracted into one as 'necessarily precisely one of the disjuncts must be true'. As in the case of the conditional, a full understanding of the truth-criterion would require one to know what kind of conflict the Stoics had in mind.

*

According to Gellius the Stoics distinguished two kinds of the so-called 'pseudo-disjunction' (παραδιεζευγμένον).[88] Regarding their standard form, most examples are formed with 'either . . . or . . .' or, occasionally, just with '. . . or . . .' and some have more than two pseudo-disjuncts. Thus apparently the two types of pseudo-disjunctions are indistinguishable in their linguistic form from disjunctions (and from each other). Thus – unlike the case of the other non-simple assertibles – it becomes impossible to tell from the language whether an assertible is a pseudo-disjunction or a disjunction, and hence which truth-conditions it has to satisfy.

---

[87] It is unclear whether the disjunction was ever understood as truth-functional. Reference to the truth-values of the constituent disjuncts is made repeatedly (Gell. XVI.8.13: S.E. *PH* II.191; D.L. VII.72).

[88] Gell. XVI.8.14. Cf. Proculus (*floruit* 1st century AD) in the *Digesta Iustiniani Augusti* 50.16.124. Other sources mention just one kind, e.g. Ap. Dysc. *Conj.* 219.12–24.

If we follow Gellius (XVI.8.13–14), the truth-criteria for the two types of pseudo-disjunctions are simply the two halves of the truth-condition for the genuine disjunction: One kind is true if its pseudo-disjuncts conflict with each other, which entails that at most one of them is true. The other kind is true if the contradictories of its pseudo-disjuncts are contrary to each other, which entails that at least one of the pseudo-disjuncts is true.[89]

*

As mentioned above, the Greek word for 'or' (ἤ) serves another purpose: that of the English word 'than'. Accordingly, we find a further kind of non-simple assertible which is sometimes discussed in the context of the disjunctives. This is the comparative or dissertive[90] assertible, formed by using a comparative or dissertive connective (διασαφητικὸς σύνδεσμος). Diogenes reports two types (D.L. VII.72–3), with the connectives 'more (or rather) ... than ...' (μᾶλλον ... ἤ ...) and 'less ... than ...' (ἧττον ... ἤ ...). These are two-part connectives, again with the characteristic part prefixed to the first constituent assertible, thus allowing the identification of the type of assertible.

The truth-conditions for these two types have not survived in Diogenes, but the treatment of such assertibles by the grammarians offers some help. One text describes the comparative statements as 'when two are posited and one of them is stated', another the connective as 'as if it became the umpire of the disjunctive'.[91] This suggests that the comparative assertibles stand to the disjunction as the pseudo-conditional to the conditional: the truth-conditions would be equivalent to those of 'Both either p or q and p' (p μᾶλλον q) and 'Both either p or q and q' (p ἧττον q).

*

The definition of the non-simple assertibles implies that they take any kind of simple assertibles as constituents, and that by combining connectives and simple assertibles in a correct, 'well-formed' way, all Stoic non-simple assertibles can be generated. But apparently this is not so: non-simple assertibles that are composed of simple indefinite ones raise

---

[89] This latter type has the modern inclusive disjunction with the connective 'v' as its truth-functional counterpart.

[90] The Greek names for these assertibles are διασαφοῦν τὸ μᾶλλον ἀξίωμα and διασαφοῦν τὸ ἧττον ἀξίωμα (D.L. VII.72–3). Cf. Sluiter 1988.

[91] Ὅταν τῶν δύο προτεθέντων τὸ ἕν εἴρηται (*Epimerismi ad Hom.* 189); ὡσεὶ ἐπικριτικὴ γενομένη τῆς διαζεύξεως (Ap. Dysc. *Conj.* 222.25–6). Moreover, the dissertive statement is said to ἐππαγγέλλεται ... 'τοῦτο ... οὐ τοῦτο' (*ibid.* 223.1).

some special problems. Unlike the case of definite and middle assertibles, one can conceive of two different ways of putting together indefinite ones.

First, following Stoic formation rules to the letter, by combining two simple indefinite assertibles into a conjunction or a conditional, one obtains assertibles like

If someone is breathing, someone is alive.
Both someone is walking and someone is talking.

According to Stoic criteria these would be true, respectively, if 'Someone is breathing' and 'Not: someone is alive' are incompatible and if 'Someone (e.g. Diotima) is walking' is true and 'Someone (e.g. Theognis) is talking' is true. However, complex assertibles with indefinite pronouns as grammatical subject more commonly tend to be of the following kind:

If someone is breathing, that one (he, she) is alive.
Someone is walking and that one is talking.

Here the truth-conditions are different from those in the previous case. For the second 'constituent assertible' is not independent of the first. As a matter of fact, we find no Stoic examples of the first type of combinations of indefinite assertibles but quite a few of the second (D.L. VII.75; 82; Cic. *Fat.* 15; S.E. *M* XI.8, 10, 11; cf. 1.86). The second type was explicitly dealt with by the Stoics and it seems that the terms 'indefinite conjunction' and 'indefinite conditional' were reserved for it.[92] In order to express the cross-reference in the second constituent assertible to the indefinite particle of the first, 'that one' (ἐκεῖνος) was standardly used (D.L. VII.75; 82; Cic. *Fat.* 15; S.E. *M* XI.8, 10, 11).[93]

The Stoics were certainly right to single out these types of assertibles as a special category. Plainly, the general problem they are confronted with is that of quantification. The modern way of wording and formalizing such statements, which brings out the fact that their grammatical subject expressions do not have a reference ('For anything, if it is F, it is G', (x) (Fx -> Gx)), did not occur to the Stoics. We do not know how far they 'understood' such quantification as lying behind their standard formulation. Three things suggest that at least they were on the right track.

*

[92] Cf. Cic. *Fat.* 15. On the other hand, 'indefinite disjunctions', i.e. assertibles of the kind 'Either someone φ's or that one ψ's' are not recorded.

[93] Note that in non-simple assertibles composed of two definite assertibles we have οὗτος twice, and not a cross-reference with ἐκεῖνος or any other pronoun; see e.g. S.E. *M* VIII.246.

First, in the context of the Stoic theory of definition and division we are told that the assertible 'Every human being is a rational, mortal animal' was reformulated in standardized form as 'If something is a human being, that thing is a rational, mortal animal' (S.E. *M* xi.8–9). That is, in general,

All S are P

became

If something is S, that thing is P.

The term used for such universal assertibles seems to have been 'universal' (καθολικόν) (S.E. *M* xi.8–11; Epict. *Diss.* ii.20.2–3).

Secondly, the same passage also tells us something about what the Stoics regarded as the truth-conditions of such statements: indefinite assertibles have non-indefinite ones 'subordinated' to them. These are all those definite and middle assertibles that differ from the indefinite only with respect to their subject. The indefinite conditional is false if (at least) one of the subordinated conditional assertibles is false (S.E. *M* xi.9, 11) and a sufficient condition for falsehood is that at least one of the subordinated conditionals has a true antecedent and a false consequent (*ibid.* 10). From this we can infer that indefinite conditionals are true if all their subordinated conditionals are true. There is some evidence that negative universals were subjected to a corresponding reformulation. A passage in Epictetus (*Diss.* ii.20.2–3) implies that the negative universal 'No S is P' became 'If something is S, not: that thing is P'.

Cic. *Fat.* 11–15 suggests that, parallel to the distinction between conditionals and negated conjunctions, the Stoics distinguished a weaker type of universal statement, namely of the kind

Not: both something is S and that thing is not P.

Such negated conjunctions would cover mere universality, as in 'All cats in this street are tabbies'.

We have seen that in their classification of simple assertibles the Stoics could fit in all four types of general statement without specific subject expression.[94] But we learn of no standard formulations for Aristotelian particular statements of the kinds

Some S are P
Some S are not P.

[94] See above, pp. 100–3 and esp. n. 68.

Still, since the *negated* indefinite conjunction stands in for a universal, it is possible that the Stoics thought of such particulars as indefinite conjunctions. In that case we only have to remove the prefixed negation in the negated indefinite conjunction and we obtain the two types of particulars

Both something is P and not: that thing is S
Both something is P and that thing is S.

Here the standard truth-conditions for indefinites apply: there must be at least one subordinated assertible that is true – for instance 'Both Diotima is P and not: Diotima is S'.

Thirdly, one reason for the importance of indefinite conditionals and indefinite negated conjunctions was no doubt the need to obtain certain types of valid arguments by means of which one can infer a singular case from a universal. For instance, the Stoics used arguments of the kind

If someone φ's, that one ψ's.
Now Dio φ's.
Therefore Dio ψ's.

These arguments will be discussed later.

The Stoic accounts of assertibles, simple and non-simple, reveal many similarities to modern propositional logic. It is tempting to draw further parallels with the modern propositional calculus, but one can easily go too far. There can be little doubt that the Stoics attempted to systematize their logic. But theirs is a system quite different from the propositional calculus. In particular, Stoic logic is a logic of the validity of arguments, not a system of logical theorems or tautologies, or of logical truths.[95] Of course, the Stoics did have logical principles, many of them parallel to theorems of the propositional calculus. But, although they had a clear notion of the difference between meta- and object language,[96] apparently logical principles that express logical truths were not assigned a special status or dealt with any differently from logical meta-principles. A survey of the principles concerning assertibles may be useful. First, there is the principle of bivalence (Cic. *Fat.* 20), which is a logical meta-principle. Then, corresponding to logical truths we find:

– the principle of double negation, expressed by saying that a double-negation (Not: not: *p*) is equivalent (ἰσοδυναμεῖν) to the assertible that is doubly negated (*p*) (D.L. VII.69);

– the principle that all conditionals that are formed by using the same assertible twice (διαφορούμενα) (like 'If p, p') are true (Cic. *Acad.* II.98; S.E. *M* VIII.281, 466);

– the principle that all disjunctions formed by a contradiction (like 'Either p or not: p') are true (S.E. *M* VIII.282, 467).

No principles of commutativity have survived in explicit formulations, and they may not have been expressed as principles. However, the accounts of the indemonstrable arguments tend to have symmetry of conjunction and disjunction 'built in' so that no extra rules are required.[97] Moreover, at least some later Stoics may have dealt with relations like commutativity and contraposition via the concepts of inversion (ἀναστροφή) and conversion (ἀντιστροφή) of assertibles (Gal. *Inst. Log.* VI.4). Inversion is the change of place of the constituent assertibles in a non-simple assertible with two constituents. Thus, with σ_1, σ_2 standing for the parts of the connective, 'σ_1 p, σ_2 q' is inverted to 'σ_1 q, σ_2 p'. Commutativity could thus have been expressed by saying that in the case of conjunction and disjunction inversion is sound or valid. In a conversion the two constituent assertibles are not simply exchanged, but each is replaced by the contradictory of the other. So 'σ_1 p, σ_2 q' is converted to 'σ_1 not: q, σ_2 not: p'. The Stoics seem to have recognized that conversion holds for the conditional; that is, they seem to have accepted the principle of contraposition (cf. D.L. VII.194). Moreover, a passage in Philodemus suggests that some Stoics may have explicitly stated the principle (Phld. *Sign.*, *PHerc.* 1065, XI.26–XII.14).

A final question concerns principles regarding the interdefinability of connectives. There is no evidence that the Stoics took an interest in reducing the connectives to a minimal number. For the early Stoics we also have no evidence that they ever attempted to give an account of one connective in terms of other connectives, or that they stated logical equivalences of that kind.[98]

4: Modality

As the previous sections have illustrated, the Stoics distinguished many different types of assertibles: simple and non-simple, definite and indefinite, negative, conjunctive etc.; these were generally identifiable by their form. In addition, the Stoics classified assertibles with respect to certain

---

[97] See below, p. 128.

[98] The passage Cic. *Fat.* 15 that is sometimes cited in this context states that there is a logical *difference* between a conditional and a negated conjunction with a negated second conjunct (cf. also Frede 1974a, 103–4).

of their properties which were not part of their form. The most prominent ones, after truth and falsehood, were the modal properties possibility, necessity etc.

Two further such properties were plausibility and probability: an
assertible is plausible (πιθανόν) if it induces assent to it (even if it is false),
like 'If someone has given birth to (τίκτειν) something, she is its mother';
for a bird who lays or gives birth to (τίκτειν) an egg is not its mother (D.L.
VII.75). We would expect this rather to be discussed in the context of epistemology. An assertible is probable or reasonable (εὔλογον) if it has
higher chances of being true, like 'I shall be alive tomorrow' (D.L. VII.76;
cf. ibid. 177).

*

Stoic modal logic[99] developed out of the debate over the 'Megaric' modalities, in particular over Diodorus Cronus' Master argument and the threat
of logical determinism.[100] Cleanthes, Chrysippus and Antipater wrote
about possibility and all three attacked the Master argument. Cleanthes
rejected its first premiss, that true past propositions are necessary.
Chrysippus had a go at the second premiss, i.e. the principle that from the
possible only the possible follows (Epict. *Diss*. II.19.1–5, 9). A passage in
Alexander gives us the details:

> But Chrysippus says that nothing precludes that something impossible
> follows something possible.... For he says that in the conditional 'If Dio
> is dead, this one is dead', which is true when Dio is pointed at, the ante-
> cedent 'Dio is dead' is possible, since it can at some time become true
> that Dio is dead; but 'This one is dead' is impossible; for once Dio has
> died, the assertible 'This one is dead' is destroyed, since the object of the
> *deixis* no longer exists. For <in the present case> the *deixis* is of a living
> being and in accordance with <its being a> living being. Now, if – him
> being dead – the 'this one' is no longer possible, and if Dio does not come
> into existence again so that it is possible to say of him 'This one is dead',
> then 'This one is dead' is impossible. This assertible would not be impos-
> sible, if at some later time, after the death of that Dio about whom the
> antecedent was said when Dio was alive, one could say of him again 'this
> one'. (Alex. *APr*. 177.25–178.4)

Chrysippus' argumentation is in short as follows: First, the assertible 'Dio
is dead' is possible, since it will be true at some time. Secondly, the assert-

---

99 For a detailed discussion of Stoic modal logic see Frede 1974a, 107–17, Bobzien 1986, 40–120,
　　Bobzien 1993.
100 For the 'Megaric' modalities and the Master Argument see above, pp. 86–92.

ible 'This one is dead (pointing at Dio)' is impossible. For any assertible that neither is nor can ever be true is impossible. And 'This one is dead (pointing at Dio)' is necessarily either false (namely as long as Dio is alive) or destroyed (namely when Dio is dead, since then there is nothing to point at any more). Thirdly, the conditional 'If Dio is dead, this one is dead' (pointing at Dio) – as long as it subsists – is true:[101] any conditional of the form 'If x is φ-ing, this one (pointing at x) is φ-ing' is a true conditional, according to all three Hellenistic truth criteria for conditionals.[102] Finally, if a conditional is true, its consequent follows from its antecedent. Hence Chrysippus provided a case of a conditional in which the consequent assertible, which is impossible, follows from the antecedent assertible, which is possible. Whatever we may think about it, Chrysippus must have been sufficiently content with his rejection of the Master argument; for he developed his own system of modal notions, which soon became the Stoic one.

*

Stoic modal logic is not a logic of modal propositions, e.g. propositions of the type 'It is possible that it is day' or 'It is possibly true that it is day', formed with modal operators which qualify states of affairs, or propositions. Instead, their modal theory was about non-modalized propositions like 'It is day', insofar as they are possible, necessary and so on. (This is well illustrated in the Alexander passage, *APr.* 177–8, quoted above.) The modalities were considered – primarily – as properties of assertibles and, like truth and falsehood, they belonged to the assertibles at a time; consequently an assertible can in principle change its modal-value. Like Philo and Diodorus, Chrysippus distinguished four modal concepts: possibility, impossibility, necessity and non-necessity. Although the concept of contingency (in the sense of that which is both possible and non-necessary) was important for the Stoic debate about determinism, we do not find a special term for it. The discussion of contingent assertibles was usually conducted in terms of two sub-groups, assertibles that are both false and possible and assertibles that are both true and non-necessary.[103]

For the Stoic system of modal notions, the situation with the sources is

---

[101] At the point when Dio dies, the antecedent assertible turns true. The consequent, instead of turning true as well, is destroyed, and together with it – or so Chrysippus must assume – the whole conditional is destroyed, i.e. ceases to subsist.

[102] See above, pp. 84–6 and pp. 106–8.

[103] Cf. Cic. *Fat.* 13. For the relevance to the debate about determinism see Bobzien 1997a, 75–6.

bad but not hopeless; besides several passages that deal with some of the
Stoic modalities[104] there are two reports of a set of Stoic modal definitions, one in Diogenes Laertius (VII.75) and one in Boethius (*Int.* 2. 11.
234.27–235.4 Meiser); although the reports differ in various respects, they
in fact present the same account. By adding up all the bits and pieces, and
making the plausible assumption that the Stoic modal notions, too, fit the
four requirements of normal modal logic[105] it becomes possible to
restore as follows the definitions given in Diogenes and Boethius:[106]

> A *possible* assertible is one which (A) is capable of being true and (B) is not
> hindered by external things from being true;
>
> an *impossible* assertible is one which (A′) is not capable of being true <or
> (B′) is capable of being true, but hindered by external things from being
> true>;
>
> a *necessary* assertible is one which (A′), being true, is not capable of being
> false or (B′) is capable of being false, but hindered by external things
> from being false;
>
> a *non-necessary* assertible is one which (A) is capable of being false and (B)
> is not hindered by external things <from being false>.

We can be confident that this set of modal concepts was Chrysippus'; for
we know that Chrysippus' modal concepts were meant to improve on
Diodorus' (Cic. *Fat.* 12–14) and in Plutarch (*Stoic. Rep.* 1055d–f.) we find
remnants of Diogenes' accounts, with identical formulations, ascribed to
Chrysippus.

The definitions of possibility and non-necessity are conjunctions; in
their case, two conditions (A and B) have to be fulfilled. The definitions of
necessity and impossibility, on the other hand, are disjunctions; in their
case one of two alternative conditions has to be satisfied (A′ or B′); in this
way in effect two types of necessity and impossibility are distinguished.
Diogenes' example, 'Virtue benefits' (D.L. VII.75), most probably illustrates necessity of the first type; his example 'The earth flies'. (*ibid.*) illustrates impossibility of the first type.

The first parts of all four definitions (A, A′), conjuncts and disjuncts

---

[104] Plu. *Stoic. Rep.* 1055d–f; Cic. *Fat.* 12–15; Epict. *Diss.* II.19.1–5, 9; Alex. *Fat.* ch. 10.

[105] See p. 87.

[106] This reconstruction is based on Frede 1974a, 107–14, Bobzien 1986, 45–56. The possibility
definition (δυνατὸν μὲν <ἐστιν ἀξίωμα> τὸ ἐπιδεκτικὸν τοῦ ἀληθὲς εἶναι τῶν ἐκτὸς μὴ
ἐναντιουμένων πρὸς τὸ ἀληθὲς εἶναι) could also be translated as 'A possible assertible is one
which is capable of being true, when external things do not prevent its being true' (cf. e.g.
Mates 1961, 41); the same holds for the non-necessity definition. However, this interpretation
is logically and historically less satisfactory (cf. Bobzien 1986, 40–4, 51–3).

alike, very much resemble Philo's modal definitions;[107] this can hardly be a coincidence. Chrysippus must have chosen Philo's accounts as the basis for his own.

In the case of possibility and non-necessity the second parts (B) add a further condition. These conditions feature 'external things' (τὰ ἐκτός) that do not prevent the assertibles from having a certain truth-value. The affirmative counterparts to these conditions (B′) specify the second type of Chrysippean necessity and impossibility. Here the external things have to prevent the assertibles from having a certain truth-value. We have no examples of such external things, but ἐκτός should refer to something external to the logical subject of the assertible. Things that prevent truth should include ordinary, physical hindrances: for example, a storm or a wall or chains that prevent you from getting somewhere; the surrounding ocean that prevents some wood from burning. It is harder to imagine what counted as external hindrances for something's being false. Presumably they were things that externally forced something to be the case. Locked doors might force Dio to be or remain in a certain room; and hence prevent 'Dio is in this room' from being false. The accounts leave us in the dark about another aspect of the external hindrances, namely at what time or times they are taken as being present (or absent). Knowledge of this is essential for an adequate understanding of the modalities. At first blush one might think that the circumstances are meant to hinder just at the time of utterance of the assertible. But that is unlikely. For it would have the curious effect that, say, the assertible 'Sappho is not reading' is necessary at a time at which someone keeps her from reading (e.g. by temporarily hiding all reading material), but three minutes later, that hindrance being removed, the same assertible would no longer be necessary; and a few minutes later it could be necessary again etc.[108]

The passage in Alexander quoted above (Alex. *APr.* 177–8) suggests that for the possibility of an assertible, the requirement of absence of hindrances is not restricted to the time of its utterance; but rather covers present plus future time – relative to the utterance of the assertion. For we learn that for Chrysippus 'Dio is dead' is possible (now) if it can be true at some time (ποτέ, 177.29–30); equally, that 'this one is dead (pointing at Dio)', which is impossible, would not be impossible (now) if, although being false now, it could be true at some later time (ὕστερόν ποτέ, 178.1–4).

---

[107] For Philo's modal accounts see above, p. 86.
[108] Certainly, this would clash with the Stoic assumption that that which is necessary is – in some sense at least – always true (Alex. *Fat.* 177.8–9).

If one reads 'can be true' as short for Chrysippus' requirement 'is capable of being true and not prevented from being true', it seems that an assertible is possible for Chrysippus if (A) it is Philonian possible and (B) there is some time from now on at which it is not hindered from being true. For instance, 'Sappho is reading' is Chrysippean possible, as long as Sappho is not continuously prevented from reading. Correspondingly an assertible falls under the second part of the definiens of the impossible if (B′) it is capable of being true, but is from now on prevented from being true – as in the above example, if Sappho were suddenly struck by incurable blindness or died. Chrysippean necessity of the second type (B′) would require continuous prevention of falsehood; non-necessity at least temporary absence of such prevention. For example, 'Sappho is reading' is non-necessary as long as she is not continuously externally forced to read.[109]

*

So we can see that Chrysippus took a middle position between Philo and Diodorus, combining elements of both modal systems. A comparison between Diodorus and Chrysippus shows that all assertibles that are contingent for Diodorus are contingent for Chrysippus as well: 'It is night' was contingent for Diodorus, since there are present-or-future times at which it is true, and present-or-future times at which it is false. The same assertible is contingent for Chrysippus (Alex. *APr.* 178.5–8), since there are both present-or-future times at which it is not hindered from being true, and times at which it is not hindered from being false. But for Chrysippus, in addition, there are assertibles that neither are nor will ever be true, but are still possible; namely all those that are false but are at some present-or-future time not hindered from being true. So, if Hipparchia never read Plato's *Symposium*, 'Hipparchia reads Plato's *Symposium*' would still not have been Chrysippean impossible; but it would always have been Diodorean impossible.

Contrasting Chrysippus with Philo, fewer assertibles are possible: for instance 'This wood is burning' (namely the piece of wood that is and will be at the bottom of the sea until it decomposes) is Philonian possible; but it is not Chrysippean possible, since there is a lasting circumstance (the sea or its wetness) which prevents the assertible from being true.

---

[109] Some later Stoics seem to have considered the modalities as merely epistemic (Alex. *Fat.* 176.14–24); according to them, possible is that which as far as we know is not externally prevented from being the case.

Why did Chrysippus add the Philonian requirement to his definitions? The answer should be that there are assertibles that are not in any way hindered by external circumstances from having a certain truth-value, but which Chrysippus nevertheless must have wanted not to be contingent: think of assertibles like 'This triangle has three sides' or 'This square is round'. For such assertibles the first disjuncts of the necessity and impossibility accounts were required.

5: Arguments

The second main part of Stoic logic is their theory of arguments. Arguments (λόγοι) form another subclass of complete sayables (D.L. VII.63); they are neither thought processes nor beliefs, nor are they linguistic expressions; rather, like assertibles, they are meaningful, incorporeal entities (S.E. *PH* III.52; *M* VIII.336). However, they are not themselves assertibles, but compounds of them.

An argument is defined as a compound or system of premisses (λήμματα) and a conclusion (ἐπιφορά, συμπέρασμα) (D.L. VII.45). Premisses and conclusion, in turn, are self-complete sayables, standardly assertibles, which I shall call the 'component assertibles' of the argument. The following is a typical Stoic argument:

P$_1$ If it is day, it is light.
P$_2$ But it is day.
C   Therefore, it is light.

It has a non-simple assertible (P$_1$) as one premiss and a simple assertible (P$_2$) as the other. The non-simple premiss, usually put first, was referred to as the 'leading premiss' (ἡγεμονικὸν λῆμμα). The second or the last premiss was called the 'co-assumption' (πρόσληψις). It is usually simple; when it is non-simple, it contains fewer constituent assertibles than the leading premiss. The co-assumption was introduced by 'but' (δέ) or 'now' (ἀλλὰ μήν), and the conclusion by 'therefore' (ἄρα).

All accounts of 'argument' have in common that they talk about a plurality of premisses – and indeed, it was the orthodox Stoic view that an argument must have more than one premiss.[110] We are not told why. Thus, for the Stoics, compounds of assertibles of the kind

p; therefore *p*
p and *q*; therefore *p*
p; therefore either *p* or *q*

---

[110] The exception is Antipater who admitted single premiss arguments; see below, p. 155.

are not arguments. On the other hand,

If $p, p; p$; therefore p

counts as an argument – and as valid at that.

A passage in Sextus defines 'premisses' and 'conclusion': the premisses of an argument are the assertibles that are adopted by agreement for the establishing of the conclusion; the conclusion is the assertible that is established by the premisses (S.E. *M* VIII.302; cf. *PH* II.136).[111] 'Premisses' and 'conclusion' are thus determined as relative terms that depend on each other. The account of 'premisses' illustrates clearly that for the Stoics the theory of argument is still embedded in the dialectical practice of conducting arguments by question and answer.

A difficulty with this account is that it seems to imply that something only counts as an argument if the premisses – at the very least – appear true to the discussants. This apparently rules out arguments with evidently false premisses and with premisses the truth of which is not or not yet known. In this way a whole range of arguments seems to be precluded from being recognized as such by the Stoics: indirect proof, theories grounded on hypotheses, 'thought experiments', arguments concerning future courses of actions etc.

Perhaps not all Stoics shared this account of 'premiss'. It is also possible that difficulties like the above gave rise to the development of the Stoic device of supposition or hypothesis (ὑπόθεσις)[112] and hypothetical arguments (λόγοι ὑποθετικοί): the Stoics thought that occasionally 'it is necessary to postulate some hypothesis as a sort of stepping-stone for the subsequent argument' (Epict. *Diss.* 1.7.22 tr. Oldfather).[113] Thus, one or more premisses of an argument could be such a hypothesis in lieu of an assertible; and it seems that hypothetical arguments were arguments with such hypotheses among their premisses.[114] Hypotheses as premisses apparently were phrased as 'Suppose it is night' (ἔστω νύξ) instead of 'It is night', by which an assertible is expressed (Epict. *Diss.* 1.25.11–13;

---

[111] 'Established' (κατασκευαζόμενον) should not mean 'validly derived' here, since that would exclude the existence of invalid arguments.

[112] Hypothesis is one of the kinds of self-complete sayables on which see below, pp. 202–3.

[113] Chrysippus wrote a considerable number of books on hypotheses and hypothetical arguments (D.L. VII.196; 197; cf. D.L. VII.66). The placement of the book-titles after those about changing arguments, which Epictetus repeatedly mentions together with the hypothetical arguments, as well as the book-titles on hypothesis and exposition (ἔκθεσις) in the same section render it likely that Chrysippus' hypothetical arguments were those Epictetus talks about. Cf. also Bobzien 1997b.

[114] The range of examples for Stoic hypotheses fits well the above-mentioned types of arguments in which assertibles would not do as premisses; e.g. 'Suppose that the earth is the centre of the solar sphere' (Ammon. *Int.* 2.31–2); 'Suppose it is night' (while it is day) (Epict. *Diss.* 1.25.11–13).

Ammon. *Int.* 2.31–2). These premisses could be agreed upon *qua* hypotheses; that is, the interlocutors agree – as it were – to enter a non-actual 'world' built on the respective assumption, but they remain aware of the fact that this assumption and any conclusions drawn hold only relative to the fact that this assumption has been made.[115]

*

The most important distinction of arguments is that between valid and invalid ones. The Stoic general criterion was that an argument is valid (συνακτικός, περαντικός) if the corresponding conditional formed with the conjunction of the premisses as antecedent and the conclusion as consequent is correct (S.E. *PH* II.137; cf. S.E. *M* VIII.415; *PH* II.249). If the assertible 'If (both P_1 and ... and P_n), then C' is true, then the argument 'P_1; ... P_n; therefore C' is valid. Diogenes Laertius' report of the criterion for invalidity of arguments (D.L. VII.77) implies that the criterion for the correctness of the conditional was the Chrysippean one: an argument is valid provided that the contradictory of the conclusion is incompatible with the conjunction of the premisses. Thus there is some similarity between the Stoic concept of validity and our modern one. But it must be kept in mind that the conditional has to be true according to Chrysippus' criterion, which as we have seen, is not necessarily restricted to logical consequence.[116] This brings out a shortcoming of the Stoic concept of validity: for what is needed is precisely logical consequence. It is thus unfortunate to have the same concept of consequence for both the relation between antecedent and consequent in a conditional, and the relation between premisses and conclusion.[117] In any event, the concept of conflict is too vague to serve as a proper criterion for validity.

Perhaps the Stoic classification of invalid arguments may shed some further light on their general concept of validity. Sextus tells us about some Stoics who distinguished four ways in which arguments could be invalid (*M* VIII.429–434; *PH* II.146–51): first, in virtue of disconnectedness (διάρτησις), that is, when the premisses lack communality or connectedness with one another and with the conclusion, as in

---

[115] Cf. Epict. *Diss.* 1.25.11–13; on Stoic hypotheses and hypothetical arguments in general see Bobzien 1997b.

[116] See above, p. 106. Note also that the Stoic validity criterion differs in both content and function from the modern principle of conditionalization. For the Stoics, the truth of the conditional is a criterion for the validity of the argument, not vice versa; moreover, the conditional must be constructed from a Stoic argument, which implies that its antecedent must be a conjunction.

[117] One result of this is that true arguments in *modus ponens* inevitably turn out redundant. See S.E. *M* VIII.441–2 and Barnes 1980, 173–5.

If it is day, it is light.
Now wheat is being sold in the market.
Therefore it is light.

Secondly, in virtue of surplus or redundancy (παρολκή), that is, when something is added extrinsically and superfluously, as 'virtue benefits' in the following argument:

If it is day, it is light.
Now it is day.
And also virtue benefits.
Therefore it is light.

Thirdly in virtue of being propounded in an incorrect (μοχθηρός) form, as for example, in

If it is day, it is light.
Now it is light.
Therefore it is day.

Finally in virtue of omission or deficiency (ἔλλειψις) as in

Either wealth is good or wealth is bad.
But wealth is not bad.
Therefore wealth is good.

Here, what is claimed to have been omitted is the disjunct '(or) wealth is indifferent' in the leading premiss, and accordingly the negated conjunct '(and) neither is wealth good' in the co-assumption, such that the proper conclusion would have been 'Therefore wealth is indifferent'.

This fourfold distinction is unsatisfactory from the point of view of modern logic: the examples of redundancy and of omission seem to be perfectly valid;[118] the example of disconnectedness seems to be nothing but a special case of invalidity due to an incorrect form (and so would be examples of omission, say, of a whole premiss). This makes the Stoic authors look rather bad logicians. We could reprove them and leave it at that. Alternatively, if we acknowledge that Hellenistic theory of argument developed out of the practice of dialectical debate, and is still entrenched in that context (recall the account of premisses and conclusion in Sextus), we can at least get an idea of what those Stoics were after. First, one may notice that Sextus reports that 'invalid arguments *come*

---

[118] The fourth, illustrating omission, appears to confound the truth of the leading premiss (and the way the proponent got it wrong) with the validity of the argument.

about in four ways' rather than 'they distinguished *four kinds* of invalid arguments',[119] and they come about 'in virtue of' (κατά) disconnectedness etc., which might hence be external to them. So we should expect what follows not to be entirely a matter of formal logic. Indeed, all four ways in which invalid arguments come about seem to be connected with the *intention* of the proponent of the argument. The four ways make most sense if one understands them as four ways of criticizing an argument by indicating how to *mend* it such that the argument that is intended or appropriate in the particular discourse comes out right. We have to assume that in the cases of redundancy, omission and disconnectedness the proponents do not get the form wrong; rather, they envisage the right form, but add something superfluous, leave something out, or put in the wrong assertible or assertibles 'in that form', as it were. Whereas in the case of the incorrect form, leaving out, adding, or replacing something does not help, since the proponent envisages the wrong form and would justify the argument by referring to the validity of arguments of that form: in this case the proponent would have to understand that the form is not correct.

How does Chrysippus' notion of validity square with this conception of invalidity? Tested against his general criterion of validity, incorrect form, disconnectedness and omission (of a straightforward case – one would hope he did not accept the example in Sextus) would turn out as invalid, too. But what about redundancy? One can imagine why redundancy was seen as an obstruction to validity. It is not only that, if one propounds an argument and adds irrelevant premises, it might obfuscate the deductive structure of the inference; also, one might claim that the conclusion does not in any true sense follow *from* the irrelevant premises. We know that Chrysippus wrote two books about redundancy; they are listed in the context of his works on syllogistic (D.L. VII.195). But when we look at his validity criterion, certainly at first sight it would not outlaw redundancy: if a conjunction of assertibles $(P_1, P_2 \ldots P_n)$ conflicts with another assertible (not:C), then it will certainly also conflict with it when any further conjunct whatsoever is added. This, however, might not in fact be so, if Chrysippus' concept of consequence resembled the – implicit – concept of conflict we find in Alex. *Top.* 93.9–10.[120] For if 'conflict' means that 'P_1 and P_2 and ... P_n conflict with not:C since, *because* P_1 and P_2 and ... P_n, not:C fails to hold', the addition of a further conjunct might cancel the

---

[119] M VIII.429; 'to come about' (γίνεσθαι) recurs three times, and equally in the *PH* passage.
[120] See above, p. 107.

conflict. Supposing that the above conflict holds, '$P_1 \ldots$ and P_n and P_{n+1}' might nonetheless not conflict with 'not:C', since P_{n+1} is not one of the factors *because of which* 'not:C' fails to hold. That is, the 'because' would prevent the addition of irrelevant conjuncts. In this way the idea of the relevance of the premises to the conclusion, as a condition for 'proper following from', would be part of the validity criterion.

*

In addition to validity, the Stoics assumed that arguments could have the properties of truth and falsehood. An argument is true (we would say 'sound') if, besides being valid, it has true premises (D.L. VII.79, cf. S.E. *M* VIII.418); an argument is false if it is either invalid or has a false premiss (D.L. VII.79). The predicates of truth and falsehood are here based on the concept of truth of assertibles, but are used in a derivative sense. The relevance of truth and falsehood of arguments is epistemic rather than logical: only a true argument guarantees the truth of the conclusion.

But the Stoics went further in assuming that arguments could also have modal properties: like assertibles, arguments can be possible, impossible, necessary and non-necessary (D.L. VII.79). The modal predicates, too, can only be used in a derivative sense here. The motivation behind such a classification is easy to make out; again, it is in the first place epistemic. The time dependency of assertibles affects the arguments. Since the concept of truth of arguments is based on that of truth of assertibles, and the latter can change their truth-value, so can arguments. For instance, the argument

If it is day, it is light.
Now it is day.
Therefore it is light.

will be true in the daytime but false at night.[121] It seems that arguments with premises that did (or could) change truth-value were called 'changing arguments' (μεταπίπτοντες λόγοι) (Epict. *Diss.* I.7.1; III.21.10). Chrysippus or some later Stoic wrote five books about changing arguments (D.L. VII.195-6). Now, if like the Stoics one is interested in knowledge gained by inference, one would focus on conclusions on which one can always rely, that is, on true arguments of which one can be sure that they are always true – or at least from the time onwards at which the argument was propounded. It is hence plausible to assume that the modalities

---

[121] Two of several passages that take into account truth-value changes of arguments are S.E. *M* VIII.418 and *PH* II.139. There the provisos 'given it is this night' and 'it being day' are added when a particular truth-value of an argument is stated.

of arguments were introduced in order to have available a way of referring to arguments which do not change truth-value. For this purpose the Chrysippean modal accounts[122] could have been used: for example, a necessary argument would be one that either cannot be false or can be false but is hindered by external circumstances from being false, and accordingly for the three remaining modalities.

6: Syllogistic

More important for logic proper are the divisions of valid arguments. These are based primarily on the form of the arguments. The most general distinction is that between syllogistic arguments (συλλογιστικοὶ λόγοι) or syllogisms (συλλογισμοί) and those called 'valid in the specific sense' (περαντικοὶ εἰδικῶς). The latter are concludent (i.e they satisfy the general criterion of validity), but not syllogistically so (D.L. vii.78). Syllogisms are, first, the indemonstrable arguments, that is, those that are valid in virtue of having one of a limited number of basic forms, and secondly those that can be reduced to indemonstrable arguments by the use of certain rules called 'θέματα'.[123]

The indemonstrable syllogisms are called 'indemonstrable' (ἀναπόδεικτος) because they are not in need of proof or demonstration (ἀπόδειξις) (D.L. vii.79), since their validity is obvious in itself (S.E. M ii.223). The talk of five indemonstrables alludes to classes of argument, each class characterized by a particular argument form in virtue of which the arguments of that class are understood to be valid. Chrysippus distinguished five such classes; later Stoics up to seven.

The Stoics defined the different kinds of indemonstrables by describing the form of an argument of that kind. The five Chrysippean types were described as follows.[124] A first indemonstrable is an argument that is composed of a conditional and its antecedent as premises, having the consequent of the conditional as conclusion (S.E. M viii.224; D.L. vii.80). An example is

If it is day, it is light.
It is day.
Therefore it is light.

A second indemonstrable is an argument that is composed of a conditional and the contradictory of its consequent as premises, having the

---

[122] For Chrysippus' modal accounts see above, p. 118.
[123] For a comprehensive discussion of Stoic syllogistic and its relation to modern logic see Bobzien 1996.   [124] For the terminology used cf. the section on non-simple assertibles.

contradictory of its antecedent as conclusion (S.E. *M* VIII.225; D.L. VII.80), e.g.

> If it is day, it is light.
> Not: it is day.
> Therefore not: it is light.

A third indemonstrable is an argument that is composed of a negated conjunction and one of its conjuncts as premises, having the contradictory of the other conjunct as conclusion (S.E. *M* VIII.226; D.L. VII.80), e.g.

> Not: both Plato is dead and Plato is alive.
> Plato is dead.
> Therefore not: Plato is alive.

A fourth indemonstrable is an argument that is composed of a disjunctive assertible and one of its disjuncts as premises, having the contradictory of the remaining disjunct as conclusion (D.L. VII.81), e.g.

> Either it is day or it is night.
> It is day.
> Therefore not: it is night.

A fifth indemonstrable, finally, is an argument that is composed of a disjunctive assertible and the contradictory of one of its disjuncts as premisses, having the remaining disjunct as conclusion (D.L. VII.81), e.g.

> Either it is day or it is night.
> Not: it is day.
> Therefore it is night.

Each of the five types of indemonstrables thus consists – in the simplest case – of a non-simple assertible as leading premiss and a simple assertible as co-assumption, having another simple assertible as conclusion.[125] The leading premisses use all and only the connectives that Chrysippus distinguished.

The descriptions of the indemonstrables encompass many more arguments than the examples suggest, and this for three reasons. First, in the case of the third, fourth and fifth indemonstrables the descriptions of the argument-form provide for 'commutativity' in the sense that each time it is left open which constituent assertible or contradictory of a constituent

---

[125] The forms of the first and second indemonstrables correspond to the basic argument-forms later named *modus (ponendo) ponens* and *modus (tollendo) tollens* and those of the fourth and fifth to the basic argument-forms later called *modus ponendo tollens* and *modus tollendo ponens*.

assertible is taken as co-assumption. For instance, if we symbolize the constituent assertibles in a fourth indemonstrable as d_1, d_2 (disjuncts one and two), the two sub-types covered are of the following kind:

Either d_1 or d_2; now d_1; therefore not d_2.
Either d_1 or d_2; now d_2; therefore not d_1.

Secondly, the descriptions are all given in terms of assertibles and their contradictories, *not* in terms of affirmative and negative assertibles. In all five cases, the first premiss can have any of the four combinations of affirmative and negative assertibles: for instance in the case of the first and second indemonstrable (if we symbolize affirmative assertibles by p, q, negative ones by not: p, not: q):[126]

if p, q if not: p, q if p, not: q if not: p, not: q.

Thus, putting together these two points, we have four sub-types under the first and second description of indemonstrables and eight in the case of the third, fourth, and fifth, thirty-two subtypes in all.

The third reason for the multitude of kinds of indemonstrables is the fact that the descriptions, as formulated, permit the constituent assertibles of the leading premisses to be themselves non-simple. And indeed, we have an example in Sextus which is called a second indemonstrable and which is of the kind[127]

If both p and q, r; now not:r; therefore not: <both p and> q.

In addition to describing the five types of indemonstrables at the meta-level, the Stoics employed a second way of determining their basic forms of arguments, namely by virtue of modes (τρόποι). A mode is defined – rather vaguely – as 'a sort of scheme of an argument' (D.L. VII.76; S.E. *M* VIII.227).[128] Diogenes Laertius adds the example

If the first, the second; now the first; therefore the second.

This is an example of the (or a) mode of the first indemonstrable. It differs from a first indemonstrable in that ordinal numbers have taken the place of

---

[126] Where not indicated otherwise, p, q, r, etc. symbolize affirmative and negative simple assertibles alike.

[127] S.E. *M* VIII.237; the text requires emendation: in the conclusion the first conjunct of the leading premiss has to be added, as is clear from 236.

[128] In later authors, τρόπος and the Latin translation '*modus*' are frequently used as synonyms either for 'indemonstrable' or for 'basic kind of indemonstrable' (e.g. Phlp. *APr.* 244.9, 12, 3; 245.23, 26, 33; Cic. *Top.* 54–7; Martianus Capella IV.414–21), whereas the term 'indemonstrable' is not used at all in these texts. In contrast, what was called τρόπος by the early Stoics is then called *forma* in Latin (e.g. Martianus Capella IV.420) and in Greek probably σχῆμα (Phlp. *APr.* 246.10–12).

the antecedent and consequent assertibles of the leading premiss, and the same ordinals are re-used where the antecedent and consequent assertibles recur in co-assumption and conclusion. It is always whole assertibles that correspond to the ordinals – as opposed to terms that correspond to the letters in Aristotelian logic. A mode is syllogistic when a corresponding argument with the same form is a syllogism. There can be little doubt that the modes played a prominent role in the Stoic theory of arguments. They feature in at least seven of Chrysippus' book titles (D.L. VII.193–5). But their exact status in Stoic logic is hard to make out. It seems that modes, and parts of modes, performed at least three distinct functions.

First, the modes functioned as forms in which the different indemonstrables – and other arguments – were propounded (S.E. *M* VIII.227; *PH* II.292). If for instance one wants to propound a first indemonstrable, the mode provides a syntactic standard form in which one has (ideally) to couch it. This is similar to the requirement of couching non-simple assertibles in a certain form, for example, of expressing a conjunction by using 'both . . . and . . .'.[129] When employed in this way, the modes resemble argument-forms: the ordinal numbers do not stand in for particular assertibles; rather, their function is similar to that of schematic letters. So, any argument that is propounded in a particular syllogistic mode is a valid argument, but the mode itself is not an argument. The logical form presented by a syllogistic mode is the reason for the particular argument's formal validity. In this function the modes can be used to check the validity of arguments.

In the two other ways in which modes and ordinal numbers are employed the ordinals seem to stand in for assertibles and the modes are used as abbreviations of particular arguments rather than as argument forms. In the analysis of complex syllogisms, for purposes of simplicity and lucidity, ordinals may stand in for simple assertibles, in the sequence of their occurrence in the argument (S.E. *M* VIII.235–7). And in the so-called 'mode-arguments' (λογότροποι) the constituent assertibles are given in full when first occurring, but are then replaced by ordinal numbers, as in

If it is day, it is light.
Now the first.
Therefore the second.

Here, too, the function is mainly one of abbreviation (D.L. VII.77). There are however a couple of pertinent questions on which the texts provide no

---

[129] See above, p. 103.

unambiguous information. First, it cannot be made out with certainty what kind of assertibles may correspond to the ordinals in the modes. On the one hand, in all our sources the ordinals correspond exclusively to simple affirmative assertibles. This holds even in those cases in which the illustrative arguments are indemonstrables with negative or non-simple assertibles as constituents in the leading premiss, such as

If both p and q, r; but not:r; therefore not: both p and q.[130]

On the other hand, two Chrysippean book-titles imply that one and the same argument can be classified in several modes (D.L. VII.194). Chrysippus may – but need not – have maintained that examples like the above could be classified not only in the mode

If both the first and the second, the third;
but not the third;
therefore not both the first and the second.

but also in the mode

If the first, the second; but not the first; therefore not the second.

A related point is the question of whether there was one (typical) mode for every basic type of indemonstrable, that is, one that fits all first indemonstrables, one that fits all second indemonstrables etc. Alternatively, there could have been several (typical) modes for each type of indemonstrable; that is, as many as there are subtypes. Again, the sources provide no answer; but if there were just one mode for each basic type of indemonstrable, this would raise a number of problems.[131]

*

For a full understanding of Stoic syllogistic it is essential to know what made Chrysippus choose the five types of indemonstrables; however, the sources do not permit a clear answer. All we are told expressly is that the indemonstrables were thought to be evident and hence not in need of demonstration, and that all other syllogisms could be reduced to them (D.L. VII.78; cf. above). And we can infer from the presentation of the

[130] Cf. S.E. *M* VIII.236, quoted below, p. 140; see also Martianus Capella IV.420. I use p, q, r for affirmative simple assertibles in this case.
[131] E.g. in the case of the third, fourth, and fifth indemonstrables, commutativity would not be catered for. For instance, how could
Either p, q; q; therefore not: p,
which is a fourth indemonstrable according to the general account, fit the mode
Either the first or the second; the first; therefore not the second?

types of indemonstrables that their evident validity is grounded on their form. No doubt the five types of indemonstrables are basic arguments and evident 'in some respects'. But so are other types of arguments.

In which respects then are all and only indemonstrables evident? We may approach this question in the first place negatively, by listing some ways of being basic and evident which Chrysippus cannot have had in mind. First we can see that all indemonstrables (and consequently all Stoic syllogisms) relate whole assertibles, and not terms as Aristotelian syllogisms do. These latter, which consist of three different categorical general statements,[132] did not count as syllogisms, let alone as evident for the early Stoics. Second, it seems that Chrysippus was not entertaining the idea of minimizing connectives. Third, Chrysippus cannot have been concerned to minimize the number of types of indemonstrables: for, with the help of the first *thema*,[133] second indemonstrables can be reduced to first ones (and vice versa), and fifth to fourth ones (and vice versa), and this can hardly have escaped his attention. Fourth, Chrysippus seems not to have aimed at deducing the conclusions from premisses of the minimum possible strength. For any conclusion one can draw by means of a first or second indemonstrable (with a leading premiss 'If p, q'), one could also draw from a corresponding third indemonstrable (with a leading premiss 'Not: both p and not:q'). The extra requirement in the truth-criterion for the conditional – compared with the negated conjunction – that is, the element of conflict, seems completely irrelevant to the conclusions one can draw in Chrysippus' syllogistic.

For a conjecture as to what Chrysippus' positive criteria were it may help to consider the following points: in the indemonstrables – and consequently in all syllogisms – all and only the Chrysippean connectives ('and', 'if', 'or') and the negation ('not') are used to construct non-simple assertibles. Among these non-simple assertibles Chrysippus distinguished a particular class entitled 'mode-forming' or 'grounding assertibles' (τροπικὸν ἀξίωμα). These were apparently conditionals, disjunctions and negated conjunctions.[134] All the indemonstrables have as leading premiss such a 'mode-forming' assertible.

On the assumption that Chrysippus restricted the connectives to those mentioned above, the way the Stoics thought about the indemonstrables

---

[132] A paradigm form is *modus Barbara*: A holds of every B; B holds of every C; therefore A holds of every C.   [133] See below, p. 138.

[134] Later logicians, in particular Peripatetics, would refer to such premisses as 'hypothetical propositions' (ὑποθετικαὶ προτάσεις). Accordingly, they often called standard Stoic arguments 'hypothetical', as opposed to the Aristotelian 'categorical' ones. This use of 'hypothetical' is not to be confused with Stoic 'hypothetical sayables' and 'hypothetical arguments', see above, p. 122 and Bobzien 1997a.

may have been like this. Of all non-simple assertibles, the mode-forming ones stand out in that they permit the construction of formally valid arguments. In the most basic cases they make it possible to infer, with a simple assertible as co-assumption, another simple assertible as conclusion. Thus one obtains exactly the five types of indemonstrables, with all the above-mentioned subtypes. Perhaps the deductive power of the indemonstrables was somehow thought to be grounded on the mode-forming assertibles.

But still, why single out the valid arguments composed of a mode-forming premiss and two simple assertibles? There are certainly other syllogisms that are fairly short and simple. What the indemonstrables seem to have in common (and not to share with others) is that no one could reasonably doubt their validity, simply because understanding the connectives that are used in their leading premisses implies knowing the validity of the corresponding forms of the indemonstrables. (Understanding 'Not: both p and q' implies knowing that if one of them holds, the other does not; understanding 'If p, q' implies knowing that (i) if p holds, so does q, and (ii) if q doesn't hold, neither does p; and understanding 'Either p or q' implies knowing that (i) if one of them holds, the other does not, and (ii) if one of them does not hold, the other does.)

This kind of criterion would for instance fail the following two candidates for indemonstrability, although they are simple and evident in some ways:

p, q, therefore p and q

would not rank as an indemonstrable since understanding p does not imply knowing that if q then 'p and q'. And

If p, q; if q, r; therefore if p, r

would not rank as an indemonstrable since understanding 'if p, q' does not imply knowing that if 'if q, r', then 'if p, r'.

*

The situation is slightly complicated by the fact that Chrysippus talked about a syllogism which he called 'fifth indemonstrable with several <disjuncts>' (ὁ πέμπτος διὰ πλειόνων ἀναπόδεικτος) (S.E. *PH* I.69). It is of the following kind (S.E. *PH* I.69; cf. *PH* II.150; *M* VIII.434; Phlp. *APr.* 246.3–4):

Either p or q or r
Now, neither p nor q
Therefore r.

Its form obviously differs from the form of the fifth indemonstrables as given above, which have two disjuncts only in their leading premiss. Some have thought, therefore, that this is a Stoic complex argument, to be analysed into two fifth indemonstrables. However, such a reduction does not work. Syllogisms of this form cannot be reduced in Chrysippus' system.[135] This might have been the reason why Chrysippus regarded such arguments as indemonstrables. However, as the name implies, he did not introduce them as 'sixth indemonstrables'; rather they are a special version of the fifth, that is, they *are* fifth indemonstrables.

If we take this seriously, we have to revise our understanding of the fifth indemonstrable. In line with the account we should assume that the leading premiss in a fifth indemonstrable has two-or-more disjuncts, and that the 'basic idea' which one grasps when one understands the disjunctive connective is 'precisely one out of several' rather than 'precisely one out of two'. This understanding of the major premiss of the fifth indemonstrables has the consequence that one also has to modify one's understanding of the co-assumption: its description 'the contradictory of one of its disjuncts' becomes a special case of 'the contradictory of one-or-more of its disjuncts', the added possibility coming down to 'the conjunction of the negation of all but one of them'. There was a standard way of expressing such co-assumptions, namely by 'neither . . . nor . . .' (οὔτε . . . οὔτε . . .) (e.g. S.E. *PH* 1.69; cf. *PH* 11.150; *M* viii.434; Phlp. *APr.* 246.3–4).

If Chrysippus allowed non-simple conclusions in indemonstrables, we could have a further kind of 'syllogism with several disjuncts' in the case of the fourth indemonstrables – which, too, is irreducible in Chrysippus' syllogistic:

Either *p* or *q* or *r* . . .; *p*; therefore neither *q* nor *r* . . . .[136]

There could also be third 'indemonstrables' with three or more conjuncts.[137] However these would be analysable into indemonstrables.

*

In Cicero and a number of later Latin authors we find a list of seven basic syllogisms which most probably is of Stoic origin (Cic. *Top.* 53–7; Boeth. *Cic.Top.* 355–8; Martianus Capella iv.414–21; Cassiod. *Inst.* 11.3.13). In addition, we find mention of basic syllogisms other than Chrysippus' indemonstrables in Galen (Gal. *Inst. Log.* v.3–4; vi.7; xv.1–11; cf. xiv.4–8;

---

[135] For the Stoic method of reduction see below, pp. 137–48.   [136] Cf. Gal. *Inst. Log.* xv.9.
[137] Cf. Cic. *Top.* 54.

10–11) and in a *scholium* to Ammonius (ΣAmmon. *APr.* XI.3–4; 13–36). They, too, may be of Stoic origin. Most of these texts adopt the Peripatetic terminology and refer to the basic syllogisms as hypothetical syllogisms. The presentation of the list of seven varies slightly from one source to another, but the first five types tend to correspond closely to the Chrysippean indemonstrables.[138]

Difficulties arise with the sixth and seventh types of argument. Both have a negative conjunction with two conjuncts as leading premiss; they are of the kinds

Not: both p and q; now p; therefore not:q (6th)
Not: both p and q; now not:p; therefore q (7th)

The problem is obvious: the sixth looks exactly like a Chrysippean third indemonstrable whereas the seventh, as it stands, is patently invalid. If one wants to make sense of them, perhaps the best guess is that the sixth and seventh basic syllogisms were those with pseudo-disjunctions as leading premiss.[139] For, with one exception, the additional basic hypothetical syllogisms in Galen and in the scholium are all of that kind, and several later sources suggest they are or should be formulated as (negated) conjunctions.[140]

*

Not all Stoic syllogisms, or formally valid arguments, are indemonstrables. Non-indemonstrable syllogisms can be more complex than indemonstrables in that they have more than two premisses; but they can also have just two premisses. For example, in our sources we find Stoic non-indemonstrable syllogisms of the kinds:

If both p and q, r; not r; p; therefore not:q (S.E. *M* VIII.234–5)
If p, p; if not:p, p; either p or not:p; therefore p (S.E. *M* VIII.281, 466)
If p, if p, q; p; therefore q (S.E. *M* VIII.230–2).

The Stoics distinguished and discussed a number of special cases of syllogisms, both indemonstrable and non-indemonstrable. First, there is the class of indifferently concluding arguments (ἀδιαφόρως περαίνοντες); as example we get

---

[138] Cf. Ierodiakonou 1993a.   [139] For the Stoic pseudo-disjunction see above, p. 110.

[140] Cf. Gal. *Inst. Log.* v.1 (παραπλήσιον διεζευγμένῳ) and XIV.6 and 11 for the sixth indemonstrable and Ap. Dysc. *Conj.* 219.18–19 and *Digesta Iustiniani Augusti* 34.5.13. § 6 for the seventh (cf. also Phlp. *APr.* 246.5–6). Perhaps the leading premiss of the seventh was originally 'Not: both not: p and not: q' and the second and third negation dropped out in the process of copying – as has been suggested by Becker 1957b, 47.

Either it is day or it is light.
Now it is day.
Therefore it is day. (Apul. *Int.* 201.4–7; Alex. *Top.* 10.10–12)

This argument is of the kind

Either *p* or *q*; *p*; therefore *p*.

The name of these arguments is presumably based on the fact that it is irrelevant for their validity what comes in as second disjunct. Often mentioned in tandem with the indifferently concluding arguments are the so-called 'duplicated arguments' (διαφορούμενοι λόγοι) (Apul. *Int.* 201. 4–7; Alex. *Top.* 10.7–10; *APr.* 18.17–18). It seems that their name rests on the fact that their leading premiss is a 'duplicated assertible', that is, composed of the same simple assertible, used twice or several times (Cf. D.L. VII.68–9; S.E. *M* VIII.95, 108). The standard and only example is

If it is day, it is day.
Now it is day.
Therefore it is day.

It is of the kind

If *p*, *p*; *p*; therefore *p*

and is a special case of the first indemonstrable. It is uncertain whether the use of the negation of the simple assertible was allowed, e.g. whether this argument was duplicated:

Either *p* or not:*p*; *p*; therefore *p*.

Such an example occurs in Alexander (*APr.* 19.3–10) but it is not called duplicated.[141]

A third type of syllogism were those with two mode-forming premisses (οἱ διὰ δύο τροπικῶν), that is, arguments composed of two mode-forming assertibles as premisses and a simple assertible as conclusion: the examples we get are of the kind

If *p*, *q*; if *p*, not:*q*; therefore not:*p*.

A Stoic example is

---

[141] The Aristotle commentators characterized both the indifferently concluding arguments and the duplicated ones as those in which one premiss is identical with the conclusion, and usually argued that this fact is the reason why they were not syllogisms (Alex. *APr.* 18.12–18; Ammon. *APr.* 28.9–13; Phlp. *APr.* 33.23–6). They seem to have been unaware of their special characteristics and as a consequence the two types seem to have occasionally been confounded (ΣArist. *Top.* 294b23–9 Brandis).

If you know that you are dead, you are dead.
If you know that you are dead, not: you are dead.
Therefore not: you know that you are dead. (Orig. *Cels.* VII.15)

A related type of syllogism is that with three mode-forming premisses: the examples are all of the kind

If *p*, *p*; if not: *p*, *p*; either *p* or not:*p*; therefore *p* (S.E. *M* VIII.281, 466),

that is, containing only one constituent assertible (and its negation), used several times. Generally, such syllogisms may have been of the kind

If *p*, *q*; if *r*, *q*; either *p* or *r*; therefore *q*.

This is a simple constructive dilemma, which was used, for example, in paradoxes. The examples in Sextus would then be a special case of this kind. (A passage in Alexander (*APr.* 164.27–31) suggests that the Stoics distinguished further types of syllogisms.)

*

Arguments of all these kinds were syllogisms. And, since Diogenes reports that all syllogisms are either indemonstrable or can be reduced to indemonstrables (D.L. VII.78), this means that – if they were not indemonstrables themselves – these arguments, too, could be reduced to indemonstrables. The Stoic expression for reducing arguments was to analyse (ἀναλύειν) them into indemonstrables (D.L. VII.195; Gal. *PHP* II.3.188–90; S.E. *M* VIII.235; 237). What is the purpose of such a reduction or analysis (ἀνάλυσις)? It is a method of proving that certain arguments are syllogisms or formally valid, by showing how they stand in a certain relation to indemonstrables. This relation between the argument-to-be-analysed and the indemonstrables is basically either that the argument is a composite of several indemonstrables, or that it is a conversion of an indemonstrable, or that it is a mixture of both. The analysis or reduction was carried out by means of certain logical meta-rules which determined these relations. They were called *themata* (θέματα), sometimes translated as 'ground-rules'. They were argumental rules, i.e. rules that can only be applied to arguments. They reduce arguments to arguments, not, say, assertibles to assertibles.[142] Our sources suggest that there were four of them (Alex. *APr.* 284.13–17; Gal. *PHP* II.3.188 De Lacy). We know further that the Stoics had some logical meta-rules, called 'theorems' (θεωρήματα), which were relevant for the analysis of arguments (D.L.

---

[142] Cf. on this point Corcoran 1974b and Bobzien 1996.

VII.195; S.E. *M* VIII.231; *PH* II.3; cf. Orig. *Cels.* VII.15.166–7). Since the *themata* were regarded as sufficient for the analysis of all non-indemonstrable syllogisms (D.L. VII.78), the function of some of the theorems was presumably to facilitate or speed up the analysis.

It is important to see that Stoic analysis is strictly an upwards method (to the indemonstrables), rather than a downwards method (from the indemonstrables). Analysis always starts with a given non-indemonstrable argument, and with the question whether it can be analysed into indemonstrables by means of the *themata*. There are no signs that the Stoics ever tried to establish systematically (or otherwise) what kinds of formally valid non-indemonstrable arguments could be *deduced* or *derived* from their set of indemonstrables by means of the *themata*.

Related to this point is the fact that Stoic analysis was carried through with the arguments themselves, not with argument-forms or schemata, although, of course, the analysis depends precisely on the form of the arguments. This might strike one as odd, since it appears to imply that analysis had to be carried out again and again from scratch, each time the (formal) validity of a non-indemonstrable argument was in question. But this need not have been so: the Stoics seem to have introduced certain meta-rules, which would state that if an argument is of such and such a form, it is a syllogism or it can be analysed into indemonstrables in such and such a way (cf. S.E. *PH* II.3 together with Orig. *Cels.* VII.15.166–7). Moreover, at least in complex cases, the modes were employed in order to facilitate the reduction; that is, ordinal numbers were used as abbreviations for constituent assertibles (S.E. *M* VIII.234–6).[143] This abbreviation brings out the form of the argument and makes it easier to recognize which *thema* can be used.

*

How did Stoic analysis work in detail? How did the *themata* and theorems function, that is, how were they applied to arguments? Let us look first at the first *thema*. It ran:

> When from two <assertibles> a third follows, then from either of them together with the contradictory of the conclusion the contradictory of the other follows. (Apul. *Int.* 209.10–14)

Here – as in the case of the last three indemonstrables – a formulation is chosen that leaves the order of the premisses undetermined. The rule may be presented formally as

[143] On this point see above, p. 130. Cf. also Frede 1974a, 136–44.

$$\frac{P_1, P_2 \vdash P_3}{P_1, \text{ctrd } P_3 \vdash \text{ctrd } P_2} \quad (T_1)$$

'ctrd' stands for 'contradictory', '$\vdash$' for 'therefore'; $P_1, P_2 \ldots$ mark places for assertibles that function as premisses. In an application of the rule the argument-to-be-analysed (or the original argument) would occupy the bottom line, the syllogism into which it is analysed the top line. For instance, if we have a non-indemonstrable argument of the kind

p; not:q; therefore not: if p, q

this can be reduced to a first indemonstrable of the kind

If $p, q; p$; therefore q

by employing the first *thema* as follows: When from 'p' and 'if p, q' 'q' follows (this being the indemonstrable), then from 'p' and 'not: q' 'not: if p, q' follows (this being the non-indemonstrable argument). Or formalized:

$$\frac{\text{If } p, q; p \vdash q}{p; \text{not:}q \vdash \text{not: if } p, q} \quad (T_1)$$

In all cases in which such a procedure leads to one of the five indemonstrables, the original argument is a syllogism.

By using the rule on all possible kinds of simple non-indemonstrable arguments, one obtains four new types of syllogisms, namely those of the kinds (with the indemonstrables into which the arguments are analysed in brackets)

p, not:$q \vdash$ not: if p, q	(first or second)
$p, q \vdash$ not: either p or q	(fourth)
not p, not $q \vdash$ not: either p or q	(fifth)
$p, q \vdash$ both p and q	(third)

These arguments may be called 'simple non-indemonstrable syllogisms'. In fact, no such arguments are handed down. As will be seen, the first *thema* can be used in one and the same reduction in combination with one or more of the other rules of analysis; it can also be employed several times in the same reduction.[144]

*

[144] For the analysis of some arguments with more than two premisses a more general version of the first thema is required; a passage in Galen (*Inst. Log.* VI.5) suggests that there was such a rule. It could have run: 'When from two or more assertibles something follows, then from all but one of them together with the contradictory of the conclusion, the contradictory of the remaining one follows.'

It will be helpful to consider the meta-rule which was known as a 'dialectical theorem' (S.E. *M* VIII.231) before the discussion of the remaining three *themata*. This theorem presumably did the same work as the second, third, and fourth *themata* together.[145] Sextus preserves the rule, which ran simply:

> When we have (the) premisses which deduce some conclusion, we potentially have that conclusion too in those premisses, even if it is not expressly stated. (S.E. *M* VIII.231)

As it stands, this theorem does not fully determine a method of analysis. It is only a general presentation of a principle. But the Sextus passage illustrates how the analysis works, by applying it to two arguments (S.E. *M* VIII.230–8). In the second example the analysis is carried out first with the mode of the argument, then by employing the argument itself. Let us look at the former, which begins by presenting the mode of the argument-to-be analysed:

> For this type of argument is composed of a second and a third indemonstrable, as one can learn from its analysis, which will become clearer if we use the mode for our exposition, which runs as follows.
>
>> If the first and the second, the third.
>> But not the third.
>> Moreover, the first.
>> Therefore not: the second.
>
> For since we have a conditional with the conjunction of the first and the second as antecedent and with the third as consequent, and we also have the contradictory of the consequent, 'Not: the third' we will also deduce the contradictory of the antecedent, 'Therefore not: the first and the second', by a second indemonstrable. But in fact, this very proposition is contained potentially in the argument, since we have the premisses from which it can be deduced, although in the presentation of the argument it is omitted. By putting it together with the remaining premiss, the first, we will have deduced the conclusion 'Therefore not: the second' by a third indemonstrable. Hence there are two indemonstrables, one of this kind
>
>> If the first and the second, the third.
>> But not: the third.

---

[145] This can be inferred from the facts that it allows reduction of the same arguments as the so-called 'synthetic theorem' which was used by the Peripatetics (cf. Mignucci 1993, 218–21), and which in turn did the work of the second to fourth themata (Alex. *APr*. 284.10–17). We are told that Antipater facilitated Stoic analysis (Gal. *PHP* 11.3.190). Perhaps it was he who introduced the synthetic or the dialectical theorem.

Therefore not: the first and the second.

which is a second indemonstrable; the other, which is a third indemonstrable, runs like this

Not: the first and the second.
But the first.
Therefore not: the second.

Such is the analysis in the case of the mode, and there is an analogous analysis in the case of the argument (S.E. *M* VIII.235–7).

The general procedure of reduction by means of the dialectical theorem then is as follows: take any two of the premisses of the argument-to-be-analysed and try to deduce a conclusion from them, by forming with them an indemonstrable. Then take that 'potential' conclusion and look whether by adding any of the premisses, you can deduce another conclusion, again by forming an indemonstrable. (The old premisses are still in the game and can be taken again, if required, as is plain from Sextus' first example, S.E. *M* VIII.232–3.) Proceed in this manner until all premisses have been used at least once and the last assertible deduced is the original conclusion. In that case you have shown that the original argument is a syllogism.

Thus, the dialectical theorem turns out to be a rule for chain-arguments by which a complex non-indemonstrable is split up into two component arguments. The theorem should suffice to analyse all composite arguments, i.e. all arguments with any of the following as underlying or 'hidden' structures. (A triangle gives the form of a simple two-premiss argument with the letter at the bottom giving the place of the conclusion. $P_1 \ldots P_n$ give the places of the premisses, C that of the conclusion of the argument-to-be-analysed; P_{n*} that of a premiss that is a 'potential conclusion' and hence does not show in the argument-to-be-analysed. The type of argument-to-be-analysed has been added underneath each time.)

type (1)   (three premiss arguments)

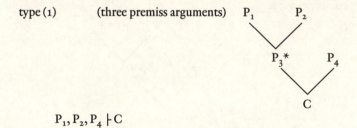

$$P_1, P_2, P_4 \vdash C$$

The argument in the above quotation for instance, is of this type.

type (2)   (four premiss arguments)

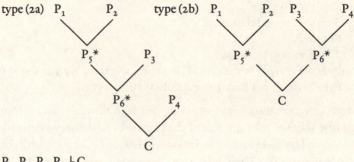

$$P_1, P_2, P_3, P_4 \vdash C$$

One can analyse all the expansions of these types which one gains by adding further two-premiss syllogisms which have one of the explicit premisses as conclusions. These conclusions would thereby become 'potential', i.e. would no longer appear in the argument to be analysed, and would accordingly get an '*'. As is clear from Sextus' first example of analysis (S.E. *M* VIII.232–3), the dialectical theorem also covers inferences in which the same premiss is implicitly used more than once, but occurs only once in the original argument. The most basic type of these is:

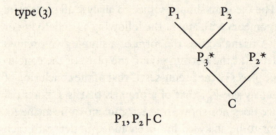

$$P_1, P_2 \vdash C$$

Sextus' first example, which is of the kind 'If p, if p, q; $p \vdash q$', is of this type. A more complex case is

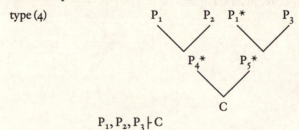

$$P_1, P_2, P_3 \vdash C$$

Again, all expansions and variations of these types, and moreover all their combinations with type (1) can be analysed by repeated use of the theorem. If one takes together the first *thema* and the dialectical theorem, with their help at least all Stoic syllogisms of which we know can be analysed into Stoic indemonstrables.

*

Next I consider the second, third, and fourth Stoic *themata*. Formulations of the third *thema* have survived in two sources (Simp. *Cael.* 237.2–4; Alex. *APr.* 278.12–14). The second and fourth are not handed down. However, a tentative reconstruction of them and of the general method of analysis by means of the *themata* is possible, since there are a number of requirements which these three *themata* have to satisfy; they are:

– the second, third, and fourth *themata* together should cover the same ground as the dialectical theorem[146]

– the *themata* have to be applicable, in the sense that by using them one can actually find out whether an argument is a syllogism

– they have to be simple enough to be formulated in ordinary Greek

– the second *thema*, possibly in tandem with the first, is said to reduce among others the indifferently concluding arguments and the arguments with two mode-premisses[147]

– the third and fourth *themata* should show some similarity or should be used together in some analyses (Gal. *PHP* 11.3.188 De Lacy).

The following is a reconstruction which satisfies these requirements reasonably well.[148]

*

The two formulations of the third *thema* that have survived in Alexander and in Simplicius present in fact two different versions of it. Alexander has

> When from two <assertibles> a third follows, and two external assumptions syllogize one of the two, then the same <i.e. third> one follows from the remaining one and the external ones that syllogize the other. (Alex. *APr.* 278.12–14)

---

[146] See previous note.

[147] Gal. *PHP* 11.3.188 De Lacy; Alex. *APr.* 164.27–31. For these kinds of arguments see above, pp. 135–7.

[148] For details of this reconstruction of Stoic analysis see Bobzien 1996; for alternative reconstructions cf. Frede 1974a, 174–96 and Ierodiakonou 1990, 60–75.

And Simplicius reads

> When from two <assertibles> a third follows, and from the one that fol-
> lows <i.e. the third> together with another, external assumption,
> another follows, then this other follows from the first two and the exter-
> nally co-assumed one. (Simp. *Cael.* 237.2–4)

Both formulations reveal that, like the dialectical theorem, the third
thema is a kind of chain-argument rule which allows one to break up a
complex argument into two component arguments. But the two versions
of the *thema* differ essentially, in that in Alexander the assumptions or premisses that are taken 'from outside' (ἔξωθεν) deduce one of the premisses
of an argument that deduces the conclusion of the argument-to-be-
analysed; whereas in Simplicius the external premiss comes in, together
with the conclusion of another inference, in order to deduce the conclusion of the argument-to-be-analysed. Formally this difference between
Alexander and Simplicius can be made clear as follows: ($P_1, P_2 \ldots P_3 \ldots$
give the places for non-external premisses, $E, E_1, E_2 \ldots$ for external premisses, C for the conclusion of the argument-to-be-analysed).

Simplicius' version:
$$\frac{P_1, P_2 \vdash P_3 \qquad P_3, E \vdash C}{P_1, P_2, E \vdash C}$$

Alexander's version:
$$\frac{P_1, P_2 \vdash C \qquad E_1, E_2 \vdash P_1}{P_2, E_1, E_2 \vdash C}$$

By comparing these versions, one can see that they allow us to reduce
exactly the same arguments, and that they differ only with respect to the
premisses that count as 'external'.[149] I assume that Chrysippus' version of
the third *thema* was closer to Simplicius' version.[150]

For the analysis of arguments with more than three premisses one
needs an expanded version of the third *thema*, in which one of the component arguments has more than two premisses. One obtains such an expansion if one modifies Simplicius' version in such a way that the second
component argument can have more than one 'external premiss'.[151]

[149] For example, one can get from Simplicius' to Alexander's version by substituting E_1 for P_1, E_2
for P_2, P_1 for P_3 and P_2 for E.
[150] For a detailed discussion of this point see Bobzien 1996, 145–51.
[151] Chrysippus' book title 'On the <question of> which <premisses> syllogize something together
with another <assumption> or with other <assumptions>' (D.L. VII.194) – which is part of a
group of titles on arguments and their analysis – might refer to the third *thema*. It has 'with
another <assumption> or with other <assumptions>' instead of Simplicius' 'with another
<assumption>', that is, it would refer to a plural of external premisses.

Perhaps Simplicius mentioned only one external premiss because the example he uses has only one. The expanded version of the third *thema* then runs:

> When from two assertibles a third follows, and from the third and one or more external assertibles another follows, then this other follows from the first two and those external(s).

Or formalized:　　　(T_3)　　$P_1 P_2 \vdash P_3 \quad P_3, E_1 \ldots E_n \vdash C$

$$\overline{P_1, P_2, E_1 \ldots E_n \vdash C}$$

There are two types of composite arguments the reduction of which is not covered by the third *thema*, namely first those in which there are no 'external' premisses, but instead one of the premisses used in the first component argument is used again in the second component argument; and secondly those in which both a premiss of the first component argument and one or more external premisses are used in the second component argument. One may conjecture that the remaining two *themata* covered these two cases. They hence could have run:

the second *thema*:

When from two assertibles a third follows, and from the third and one (or both) of the two another follows, then this other follows from the first two.

formalized:　　　(T_2)　　$P_1, P_2 \vdash P_3 \quad P_1, (P_2,) P_3 \vdash C$

$$\overline{P_1, P_2 \vdash C}$$

the fourth *thema*:

When from two assertibles a third follows, and from the third and one (or both) of the two and one (or more) external assertible(s) another follows, then this other follows from the first two and the external(s).

formalized:　　　(T_4)　　$P_1, P_2 \vdash P_3 \quad P_3, P_1, (P_2,) E_1 \ldots E_n \vdash C$

$$\overline{P_1, P_2, E_1 \ldots E_n \vdash C}$$

Each of the second to fourth *themata* thus has a typical kind of argument to which it applies; but they can also be used in combination or more than once in one reduction. Going back to the types of arguments distinguished when discussing the dialectical theorem one can see that arguments of type (1) take the third *thema* once; those of types (2a) and (2b)

take it twice. More complex ones – without implicitly multiplied premisses – take it more often. Arguments of type (3) take the second *thema*
once; those of type (4) take the fourth and third each once. More complex
arguments may take combinations of the second, third, and fourth *themata*. Occasionally the first *thema* is needed in addition. Taken together the
second, third, and fourth *themata* cover precisely the range of the dialectical theorem.

*

How were the *themata* applied? Before I describe the general method of
analysis, here are a few examples. First, take again the second example
from the Sextus passage (S.E. *M* VIII.230–8, used there to illustrate the
dialectical theorem). The argument-to-be-analysed is of the kind

> If both p and q, r; not:r; $p \vdash$ not:q.

It has three premises and takes the third *thema* once. By simply 'inserting' this argument into the *thema* we obtain:

When from two assertibles
  i.e. If both p and q; not:r
a third follows
  i.e. not: both p and q (by a second indemonstrable)
and from the third and an external one
  i.e p
another follows
  i.e. not: q,   (by a third indemonstrable)
then this other
  i.e. not: q
also follows from the two assertibles and the external one.

Or, using the formalized version of the *thema*:

$$\frac{\text{If both } p \text{ and } q, r; \text{not:}r \vdash \text{not:both } p \text{ and } q \quad \text{Not:both } p \text{ and } q; p \vdash \text{not:}q}{\text{If both } p \text{ and } q, r; \text{not:}r; p \vdash \text{not:}q} \quad (\text{T}_3)$$

Examples of the use of the second *thema* we obtain from some of the special types of non-indemonstrable arguments. Indifferently concluding
arguments like

> Either it is day or it is light.
> Now it is day.
> Therefore it is day.

use the second *thema* once and reduce to one fourth and one fifth indemonstrable

$$\frac{\text{Either } p \text{ or } q; p \vdash \text{not:} q \text{ Either } p \text{ or } q; \text{not:} q \vdash p}{\text{Either } p \text{ or } q; p \vdash p} \quad (T_2)$$

Syllogisms with two mode-premisses like those of the kind

If p, q; if p, not:q; therefore not:p

take the first *thema* twice, the second once and reduce to two first indemonstrables. The analysis works again step by step from the bottom line
(a) to the top line (d):

(d) p, if p, not:$q \vdash$ not:q

$$\rule{5cm}{0.4pt} \quad (T_1)$$

(c) If p, q; $p \vdash q$ $p, q \vdash$ not: if p, not:q

$$\rule{5cm}{0.4pt} \quad (T_2)$$

(b) If p, q; $p \vdash$ not: if p, not:q

$$\rule{5cm}{0.4pt} \quad (T_1)$$

(a) If p, q; if p, not:$q \vdash$ not:p

In general then, the method of analysis into indemonstrables by means of
the *themata* appears to have worked as follows. In a very first step, you
check whether the argument-to-be-analysed, or original argument, happens to be an indemonstrable. If so, it is valid. If not, the next thing to do
is to try to pick from the set of premisses of the argument-to-be-analysed
two from which a conclusion can be deduced by forming an indemonstrable with them.

If the original argument is a syllogism, this conclusion, together with
the remaining premiss(es) (if there are any), and/or one or both of the premisses that have been used already, deduces the original conclusion –
either by forming an indemonstrable or by forming an argument that by
use of the four *themata* can be analysed into one or more indemonstrables.
Hence you see whether one of the remaining premisses plus this conclusion yields the premisses to another indemonstrable (in which case you
apply the third *thema*); if there are no remaining premisses, or none of
them works, you look whether one of the premisses already used in the
first step is such a premiss (in which case you apply the second or the
fourth *thema*).

If the second component argument thus formed is an indemonstrable
too, and all premisses have been used at least once and the last conclusion

is the original conclusion, the analysis is finished, the original argument a syllogism. If not, the same procedure is repeated with the argument which is not an indemonstrable (i.e. the second component argument, which has the original conclusion as conclusion); and so forth until the premisses of the second component argument imply the original conclusion by forming an indemonstrable with it.

If at any point in the analysis no indemonstrable can be formed, the first *thema* might help: namely if the negation of the conclusion would produce a premiss you need, i.e. a premiss which together with one of the available premisses makes up a pair of premisses for an indemonstrable. If at any step the application of none of the *themata* leads to two premisses that can be used in an indemonstrable, the argument is not a syllogism.

This method of reduction is practicable and easy. All one has to know is the *themata* and the five types of indemonstrables, plus those four types of simple arguments which can be reduced to indemonstrables. The number of steps one has to go through is finite; they are not very many, even in complex cases. The method appears to be effective, the system decidable.

*

Stoic syllogistic is a system consisting of five basic types of syllogisms and four argumental rules by which all other syllogisms can be reduced to those of the basic types. In Sextus Empiricus (*PH* II.156; 157; 194) we find Stoic claims that can be understood as the assertion of some kind of completeness in their logical system. We learn that the valid non-indemonstrable arguments have the proof of their validity from the indemonstrables (194), that the indemonstrables are demonstrative of the validity of the other valid arguments (156) and that those other arguments can be reduced (ἀναφέρεσθαι) to the indemonstrables (157).

The implication that the proof of the validity of the non-indemonstrables is given by reduction is confirmed by Diogenes (D.L. VII.78) who reports that all syllogisms are either indemonstrables or can be reduced to indemonstrables by means of the *themata*. We may then assume that the claim of 'completeness' in Sextus is that (at least) all non-indemonstrable syllogisms can be reduced to indemonstrables by the *themata* (or by related theorems). One could take this as the – trivial – claim that the *themata* (or theorems) lay down or determine whether an argument is a syllogism. But this is unlikely. Rather, we should assume that the Stoics had – independently of the *themata* – some pretechnical notion of syllogismhood, and that the indemonstrables plus *themata* were devised in order to 'capture' this notion; perhaps also to make it more pellucid and precise.

This is a plausible assumption. It leaves us with the following problem: how can we find the independent Stoic criteria for syllogismhood? that is, how can we decide which peculiarities of the Stoic system preceded their choice of logical rules and which peculiarities are simply a result of their introducing these rules? The paucity of evidence does not allow us to fully answer this question. *A fortiori*, we cannot decide whether the Stoics achieved completeness, i.e. were successful in devising their rules in such a way that they adequately covered their pretechnical notion of syllogism-hood; and consequently, whether they were successful in demonstrating the completeness of their syllogistic.

Still, it is possible to determine a number of features of the Stoic system that are relevant to its completeness, and thus to narrow down consider-ably the number of possible interpretations of what completeness they wanted. It is safe to assume that the Stoic system shared the following condition of validity with modern semantic interpretations of formal logic: it is necessary for the validity of an argument that it is not the case that its premises are true and its conclusion is false. Accordingly, it is a necessary condition for formal validity (syllogismhood) that no syllogism or argument of a valid form has true premises and a false conclusion. To this we can add a number of necessary conditions for Stoic syllogismhood which are not requirements for formal validity in the modern sense, and which show that the class of Stoic syllogisms can at most be a proper sub-class of valid arguments in the modern sense.

First, there is a formal condition which restricts the class of syllogisms not by denying validity to certain arguments, but by denying the status of argumenthood to certain compounds of assertibles. Stoic syllogistic is interested in formally valid *arguments*, not in *propositions* or *sentences* that are logically true. And their concept of argument is narrower than that of modern logic: an argument must have a minimum of two premises and a conclusion. That is, Stoic syllogistic considers (tests etc.) only arguments of the form

$$\Delta \vdash A$$

in which Δ is a set of premises with at least two (distinct) elements. Stoic syllogistic does not deal with arguments of the forms

$$\vdash A \qquad A \vdash B \qquad \text{or} \qquad \Delta \vdash.$$

A consequence of this is that there is no one-to-one correspondence between valid arguments and logically true conditionals. Such a corre-spondence exists only between a proper subclass of the latter – those which have the form 'If both A and B and . . ., then C' – and valid arguments.[152]

Second, there is the restriction of validity through the requirement of non-redundancy of the premisses:[153] an argument is invalid according to redundancy if it has one or more premisses that are added to it from outside and superfluously (S.E. *M* 11.431). For cases of non-indemonstrable arguments one may interpret the clause 'from outside and superfluously' as meaning that there is no deduction in which this premiss, together with the others of the argument, deduces the conclusion.[154] The requirement of non-redundancy leads to the exclusion, for instance, of the following kinds of arguments from being syllogisms:

p; q; therefore p

If p, q; p; r; therefore q

although they are valid in all standard propositional calculi.

A third restriction known to us – independently of the *themata* – concerns the wholly hypothetical 'syllogisms'. (Their prototype is 'If p, q; if q, r; therefore if p, r'.) There are some hints that the Stoics considered such arguments as valid but not as syllogisms.[155] We do not know whether this restriction was part of the Stoic pretechnical notion of a syllogism, or whether these arguments were excluded because they were not analysable in the system.

In addition to these three requirements the Stoics apparently maintained that an argument cannot have two identical premisses. That is, compounds of assertibles of the form

$\Delta, A, A \vdash B$

were, it seems, considered as a non-standard way of putting the argument

$\Delta, A \vdash B,$

that is, as an argument in which the same premiss is stated twice rather than in which two premisses of the same form and content are stated.[156]

---

[152] For instance, although any conditional of the form 'If A, A' is true for the Stoics, there is no valid argument of the form 'A $\vdash$ A', since no compound of assertibles of that form is an argument.

[153] For redundancy see above, p. 125.

[154] So the premiss 'Either p or not: p' is not redundant in the argument 'If p, p; if not: p, p; either p or not: p; therefore p' since there is a deduction of the conclusion in which it is used. Namely when one considers the argument as a special case of the simple constructive dilemma.

[155] Cf. for instance Frede 1974b, n. 5 (b) and (c); see also Alex. *APr.* 262.28–31. For the status of wholly hypothetical 'syllogisms' in Stoic logic see above, p. 133 and below, p. 156.

[156] At least this is implied by a passage in Alexander (Alex. *APr.* 18.2–7), which is most certainly Stoic, and which maintains that an 'argument' of the form 'A, not: not: A $\vdash$ B' is in actual fact of the form 'A $\vdash$ B', and hence no argument at all.

Hence there can be no 'structural rules' which allow us to indiscrimi-
nately eliminate or introduce doublets of premisses – as there often are in
rule-deductive systems.

We are now in a position to examine whether the Stoic system of syllogisms, as containing indemonstrables and *themata*, captures the – at least
partly – pretechnical notion of syllogismhood as determined by the three
requirements stated. And we can see that their system does not permit
reduction of any of the arguments that are precluded by them from being
syllogisms. First, no one- or zero-premiss arguments are reducible, since
every indemonstrable has two premisses, and every *thema* can be applied
only to arguments with two or more premisses. Secondly, redundant
arguments cannot be reduced: the indemonstrables have no 'redundant'
premisses, and the *themata* require that all premisses of the argument-to-
be-analysed are components of the indemonstrables into which it is analysed – either as premiss or as negation of a conclusion. Thirdly, no wholly
hypothetical 'syllogisms' are indemonstrables, nor can they be reduced to
indemonstrables; for the last three *themata* require that one splits off one
two-premiss argument each time they are used, and this two-premiss
argument must contain at least one simple proposition,[157] because it
must be either an indemonstrable itself or reducible into one by the first
thema. And any reduction to an indemonstrable by means of a single application of the first *thema* also requires that the argument-to-be-analysed
contains at least one simple proposition. So far then Stoic syllogistic coincides with what might have been their pretechnical concept of syllogismhood.[158]

7: *Arguments valid in the specific sense*

Finally, the second group of valid arguments distinguished by the Stoics,
the arguments called 'valid in the specific sense' or 'specifically valid' (D.L.
VII.78). The surviving information on these arguments is sparse and many
details are under dispute. At least two subclasses were distinguished. One
were the so-called 'subsyllogistic arguments' (ὑποσυλλογιστικοὶ λόγοι),

---

[157] Or a substitution instance of a simple proposition.

[158] Can we state positively what the claim of completeness could have been? Maximally, the claim
could have been that the class of arguments that either are indemonstrables themselves or can
be analysed into indemonstrables by means of the *themata* contains precisely all arguments of
the form '$\Delta \vdash A$', with $\Delta = \{P_1 \ldots P_n\}$ and $n \geq 2$, which (i) because of their form can never have
true premisses and a false conclusion, (ii) contain – as relevant to their form – only the Stoic logical constants 'not . . .', 'either . . . or . . .', 'if . . . then . . .', 'both . . . and . . .', (iii) contain no premiss doublets and no redundant premisses, and (iv) are not wholly hypothetical, and (v) are, or
are composed of, nothing but self-evidently valid arguments. Perhaps a proof of this kind of
completeness is possible.

another the arguments named 'unmethodically concluding' (ἀμεθόδως περαίνοντες). There might have been a third group; there might have been more. How was the validity of the specifically valid arguments explained or justified? At D.L. VII.79 we read that all (valid) arguments were constructed by means of the indemonstrable syllogisms. If we take this at face value, the validity of the specifically valid arguments might have been grounded on or justified by the validity of syllogisms. This justification one would expect to vary from subclass to subclass.

*

Only two short passages explicitly talk about subsyllogistic arguments (Alex. *APr.* 84.12–14; Gal. *Inst. Log.* XIX.6), and a further passage briefly discusses them without naming them (Alex. *APr.* 373.28–35). From these texts it emerges that a subsyllogistic argument differs from a corresponding syllogism only in that one (or more) of its component assertibles, although being equivalent to that in the syllogism, diverges from it in its linguistic form. Examples are of the types

> '*p*' follows from '*q*'; but *p*; therefore *q*. (Alex. *APr.* 373.31–5)

instead of a first indemonstrable and

> It is false that 'both *p* and *q*'; but *p*; therefore not: *q*. (D.L. VII.78)

instead of a third indemonstrable. We may assume that the reason why subsyllogistic arguments were not syllogisms was that they did not share their canonical form. This distinction displays an awareness of the difference between object- and meta-language: a conditional is indeed not the same as a statement that one assertible follows from another. The validity of a subsyllogistic argument might have been established by constructing a corresponding syllogism and pointing out the equivalence to it.[159]

The unmethodically concluding arguments are slightly better attested.[160] Stoic examples are:

> Dio says that it is day.
> But Dio speaks truly.
> Therefore it is day.

---

[159] Training in recognizing which kinds of assertibles were equivalent to which seems to have been part of some Hellenistic logic courses (cf. Gal. *Inst. Log.* XVII.5). The manuscript text of the first Galen passage mentioned (Gal. *Inst. Log.* XIX.6) is corrupt. It can be read as implying that the Stoics distinguished a further class of specifically valid arguments which were linguistic mutations of syllogisms. Cf. Barnes 1993d, 38–43; 52.

[160] Gal. *Inst. Log.* XIX.6; Alex. *APr.* 21–2; 68–9: 345–6; *Top.*14–15; [Ammon.] *APr.* 70.11–15; Phlp. *APr.* 35–6.

and

> It is day.
> But you say that it is day.
> Therefore you speak truly.[161]

These arguments, as they stand, are not Stoic syllogisms. They are neither indemonstrables nor can they be reduced to them. For they contain no non-simple assertible as component. What was the reason for their validity? Perhaps they were dubbed 'unmethodically concluding' because there is no formal method of showing their validity; but even then their validity must have been justified somehow – and if we take the remark at D.L. VII.79 seriously, these justifications should have involved some suitably related syllogisms.

We have no direct evidence for a way of detecting 'corresponding syllogisms', as in the case of the subsyllogisticals. One foolproof method is of course to add as leading premiss a conditional formed by the conjunction of the premisses as antecedent and the conclusion as consequent (and to conjoin the former premisses). For instance, add:

(p and q->r)   If you say that it is day and you speak truly, then it is day.

to the conjunction of the premisses and the conclusion

(p and q)   You say that it is day and you speak truly.
(r)   Therefore it is day.

This operation makes any argument into a syllogism, namely into a Chrysippean first indemonstrable. But, obviously, this cannot be the method devised to justify the validity of the unmethodicals. For it would equally work for invalid arguments.

Still, this might be a step in the right direction. First, Chrysippus used just such a first indemonstrable (with 'it is light' instead of 'it is day') in the discussion of the Liar,[162] as a parallel argument to

> If you say that you are lying and you speak truly, you are lying.
> But you say that you are lying and you speak truly.
> Therefore you are lying.[163]

---

[161] Alex. *APr.* 345.24–30; 22.17–19. The first example occurs with 'you' instead of 'Dio' in Gal. *Inst. Log.* XVII.2.   [162] For the Stoic discussion of this paradox see below, p. 165.

[163] Cic. *Acad.* II.96. Equally, the second example is parallel to the second argument of the paradox of the Liar, cf. [Acro] *Scholia vetustiora in Horatii Epist.* II.1.45 (= *FDS* 1215): *dico me mentiri et mentior verum igitur dico*; see also Placidus *Liber Glossarum* 95.14 (= *FDS* 1217). The liar might thus have provided the context in which these examples arose. Cf below, p. 166.

So after all, there is some indication that the Stoics adduced syllogisms that correspond to unmethodicals.[164] Still, the Stoics must have ensured somehow that invalid arguments could not be justified as valid by forming a parallel syllogism with such a conditional added as leading premiss. To achieve this they might simply have stipulated that the added conditional must be true. For the truth of a conditional formed by the conjunction of the premisses of an argument as antecedent and the conclusion as consequent is nothing but the Stoic general criterion for the validity of an argument.[165]

But we are still left with the question: what was the ground for the validity of the unmethodicals? For, although the conditional, if added, makes the unmethodical into a formally valid argument, it does not provide a reason or explanation for its validity. The reason for the validity – and for the truth of the added conditional – should rather be the truth of one or more 'universal' assumptions on which the argument is based, and which have not been made explicit in the argument. And indeed Galen reports that the Stoic Posidonius called at least some of the unmethodicals 'concludent on the basis of the power of an axiom' (Gal. *Inst. Log.* XVIII.8). Moreover, both Alexander (e.g. Alex. *APr.* 344–5) and Galen (*Inst. Log.* XVII.1–4) state that the arguments the Stoics call unmethodicals depend on some universal statement or principle. Now it is likely that they took over the idea of an implicit universal assumption from the Stoics together with the category of unmethodicals. For the Stoics, universal propositions are standardly formulated as conditionals.[166] In our example a plausible candidate for such a universal would be:

(*u*) If someone says something and that thing obtains, that one speaks true.

However, note that if one actually added such a Stoic universal to an unmethodical, one would not get a formally valid argument or syllogism; and that there is no reason to think that the Stoics wanted it to be added.

An argument would then be unmethodically concluding if the following requirements are fulfilled:[167] a corresponding syllogism can be constructed by adding a conditional formed with the conjunction of the premisses as antecedent, the conclusion as consequent. This conditional must be true, and it is true, since the unmethodical argument is valid. However, it does not provide any reason for the argument's validity.

---

[164] *Pace* Barnes 1990a, 81.   [165] See above, p. 123.   [166] See above, p. 113.
[167] For different views see Frede 1974a, 121–3; Barnes 1990a, 78–81.

Rather, the ground for its validity is the truth of some universal assumption which is not made explicit in the argument.

*

There are a number of arguments which were regarded as valid by some Stoics, some of which might have been counted as specifically valid arguments.

There are first Antipater's single-premiss arguments (μονολήμματοι). The orthodox Stoic view was that arguments must have at least two premisses. However, Antipater admitted single-premiss arguments, and he presumably regarded at least some of them as valid. If we trust Apuleius, Antipater adduced arguments like

You see.
Therefore you are alive. (Apul. *Int.* 200.15–18)

Another example is 'You are breathing. Therefore you are alive' (Alex. *Top.* 8.19). What reasons he had for admitting such arguments, we are not told. But it is unlikely that Antipater proposed that these arguments were syllogisms (as Alex. *Top.* 8.16–17 has it). For they are certainly not valid in virtue of their form. Thus Antipater might have thought of them as unmethodically concluding, perhaps with a non-explicit assumption of the kind 'If someone is breathing, that one is alive.'[168]

Secondly, there are the arguments with an indefinite leading premiss and a definite (or middle) co-assumption, which were mentioned earlier in the context of non-simple assertibles.[169] Chrysippus' work 'Of arguments constructed from an indefinite and a definite <premiss>' (D.L. VII.198) may have dealt with such arguments. A typical example is

If someone walks that one moves.
This man walks.
Therefore this man moves.[170]

Despite the similarity, this is not a straightforward first indemonstrable, as would be

If Plato walks, Plato moves.
Plato walks.
Therefore Plato moves.

---

[168] Cf. Alex. *Top.* 8.20–22 where '<someone> who is breathing is alive' (ὁ ἀναπνέων ζῇ) and 'Everyone who is breathing is alive' (πᾶς ὁ ἀναπνέων ζῇ) are given as alternative reasons for the concludency of the single-premiss argument: the first is a later Stoic non-standard formulation of universals, the second is Peripatetic.   [169] Above, p. 114.

[170] Aug. *Dial.* III.84–6 Pinborg; cf. Cic. *Fat.* 11–15.

Preoccupied with linguistic form as the Stoics were, they must have noticed this. So if they did not simply smuggle such arguments into the class of syllogisms, how did they justify their validity? Presumably by referring to the truth-conditions of the leading premiss. Since its truth implies the truth of all subordinated assertibles, one can always derive the particular conditional one needs ('If this one walks, this one moves') and thus form the needed syllogism, in this case a first indemonstrable. This relation between the indefinite conditional and the corresponding definite and middle ones might have been counted as an implicit assumption by which validity was justified (but which if added would not make the argument formally valid). For similar reasons one may conjecture that Stoic arguments of the kind

If someone φ's, *p*; this one φ's; therefore *p*[171]

were regarded as unmethodically concluding.

Although it is unlikely that the early Stoics discussed Aristotelian logic, later Stoics were confronted with Peripatetic forms of arguments, in particular with categorical 'syllogisms' and wholly hypothetical 'syllogisms'.[172] We know that some 'moderns' (νεώτεροι) – who may well have been Stoics – claimed that the unmethodically concluding arguments resembled categorical 'syllogisms' (Alex. *APr.* 345.13–17).

For the Stoics, following their policy concerning the formulation of universal statements, an argument in *modus Barbara*

'A holds of every B; B holds of every C; therefore A holds of every C'

becomes:

If something is A, that thing is B.
If something is B, that thing is C.
Therefore, if something is A, that thing is C.

This is still not a Stoic syllogism. So, if anything, categorical 'syllogisms' could only have had the status of specifically valid arguments.

There is no direct evidence that the Stoics discussed wholly hypothetical 'syllogisms', i.e. arguments of the type

If *p*, then *q*; if *q*, then *r*; therefore if *p*, then *r*.

There are two such examples that use typically Stoic constituent sentences.[173] All one can say is that wholly hypothetical 'syllogisms' should

---

[171] Cf. S.E. *PH* II.141; *M* VIII.313.

[172] For these kinds of argument see above, p. 150. Here I put 'syllogism' in quotes to indicate that although the Peripatetics considered them syllogisms, presumably the Stoics did not.

[173] ΣAmmon. *APr.* XI.1–3: Alex. *APr.* 374.23–35. Ironically, the latter is employed to discredit this type of argument.

not have counted as syllogisms, since they cannot be analysed into indemonstrables by the *themata*. One would expect them to have been mentioned, had they been regarded as syllogisms. But if the Stoics reformulated *modus Barbara* in the way suggested, and considered the resulting arguments valid, they must also have considered wholly hypothetical 'syllogisms' as valid.

8: Paradoxes

In the Stoic classification of arguments sophisms, the ancient counterparts of modern paradoxes, are put under the head of false arguments. A false argument is an argument which either has something false in its premisses or is formally incorrect (D.L. VII.79). What makes a false argument a sophism is that its conclusion is evidently false and it is not clear on what the falsity of the conclusion depends (Gal. *Pecc. Dig.* v.72–3). As Sextus explains, in a sophism we are solicited to approve a clearly false conclusion by having endorsed premisses which look plausible and seem to yield the unacceptable conclusion (S.E. *PH* II.229).

To understand the meaning of this characterization it must be remembered that sophisms are supposed to be part of a (real or fictitious) discussion. One is asked to accept some propositions from which an overtly false conclusion is derived, and in this way the answerer is left in the embarrassing position of admitting a completely unacceptable statement. The many situations described by Plato in the *Euthydemus* caricature this sort of context.

This account explains the role that, according to the Stoics, dialectic should play regarding sophisms. It should not only distinguish sophistical from good arguments but also be able to solve them by showing what is wrong with them in such a way that any embarrassment is dispelled (S.E. *PH* II.229, 232). Their being classified among false arguments offers an indication of what one must look for in solving them: either the conclusion does not follow from the premisses or at least one of the premisses is false.

The Stoic characterization of paradoxes looks traditional and reminds us of the Aristotelian definition of contentious deductions at the beginning of the *Topics* (100b23–6). This impression is reinforced by Galen when he points out that sophisms resemble true arguments and stresses that a trained dialectician, being acquainted with good arguments, can easily detect and solve bad ones (Gal. *Pecc. Dig.* v.73). Quintilian echoes this way of thinking when he reports that a training in solving paradoxes is part of the formation of the Stoic wise man because he cannot be mistaken even in trifles (Quint. *Inst.* 1.10.5), and so does Seneca when he dismisses people who consume their time in examining the Liar paradox (*Ep*. 45.10). Even apart from this practice, the general definition of a sophism seems to reflect the style of the Platonic–Aristotelian tradition rather than the role that paradoxes played in the philosophical debate with which the early Stoics were confronted. We will see in a moment that the picture is much more complicated than one might expect.

*

Our sources offer a rather confused report of a classification of paradoxes. According to Diogenes Laertius sophisms are first divided into those depending on utterance and those depending on states of affairs (D.L. VII.43–4). This distinction reminds us of the division of refutations into refutations depending on language and refutations independent of language, which constitutes the leading distinction of Aristotle's treatise dedicated to paradoxes (Arist. *SE* 165b23–4.). Nothing is said about the Stoic sophisms depending on utterance but we may guess that they had to do with language and ambiguity, and the analysis of amphibology reported by Galen may give an idea of the way in which they were presented.[174]

We have no definition of the second group of sophisms either, but a list of them is given, which includes some of the most important and famous paradoxes such as the Liar, the Sorites, the Veiled Man, the Horned Man, the Not-someone, the Mower.[175] Diogenes' list is interrupted in its middle by a different classification of sophisms, according to which they may be either defective or aporetic or concludent. It is not clear what Diogenes hints at by defective and concludent arguments. Probably, there is here the superimposition of two different and possibly unrelated classifications of sophisms. This impression is reinforced by the fact that Diogenes elsewhere mentions among the aporetic arguments paradoxes which are here distinguished from the aporetic ones.[176] Moreover, Cleanthes dedicated a work to the aporetic arguments and, more conspicuously,

---

[174] Gal. *Soph.* XIV.595–8. See also Atherton 1993.

[175] D.L. VII.44. Diogenes' list is interesting for at least two reasons. The names of the arguments are in the plural (ψευδομένους λόγους, αωρίτας ἐγκεκαλυμμένους, κερατίνας and so on), and this may be taken as an allusion to different versions of the same argument. Moreover, beside the 'Lying arguments', other less-known arguments are quoted, i.e. Truth-telling arguments (ἀληθεύοντας <λόγους>) and Denying arguments (ἀποφάσκοντας <λόγους>). There are reasons to believe that these are versions of the Liar (cf. Clem. *Strom.* v.1.11.6 and Epict. *Diss.* III.9.21).

[176] Among the aporetic arguments D.L. VII.82 lists the versions of the Veiled Man, the Disguised Man, the Sorites, the Horned Man and the Not-someone arguments, while Luc. *Symp.* 23 quotes as aporetic the Horned Man, the Sorites and the Mower.

Chrysippus is reported to have written an *On the Aporetic Arguments of the Dialecticians* in five books.[177]

It might be that the Stoics had a technical and refined definition of aporetic arguments. Late sources hint at complicated characterizations of arguments where the aporetic ones seem to be to some extent related to the presence of a vicious circle of the sort which occurs in the Liar paradox.[178] But there is no evidence that this classification of paradoxes goes back to the early Stoics, and it seems to be based on external and logically unimportant features of the arguments involved.[179] At any rate, the terminology of 'aporetic argument' seems to be old. The Greek ἄπορον was translated by Cicero as *inexplicabile*[180] and in the Latin medieval tradition as *insolubile*. This does not mean that ancient logicians, and in particular the Stoics, were pessimistic about the solution of some paradoxes. The number of works dedicated by Chrysippus to the Liar paradox may show that in some cases he was not happy with his own solution, but not that the Liar or any other important paradox was considered unsolvable by him. The aporetic character ascribed to certain sophisms depended primarily on the impression they made on people to whom they were directed. Aporetic arguments were those in which it is very difficult for the answerer to see where the fallacy lies, since both the premises and the logic of the argument appear to be acceptable, although something wrong is derived. In the very end it may be that the difficulty for the answerer to get free of the paradoxes becomes a difficulty also for the experienced logician who tries to solve the paradoxes and detect their fallacies. But it is not because of this that some paradoxes received their qualification of aporetic.[181]

*

It is sufficient to describe briefly the puzzles mentioned by Diogenes to be aware that the Stoics dealt with the most difficult paradoxes that have intrigued philosophers and logicians ever since. At least two different versions of the Veiled Man are known. In the more popular one, Callias is asked whether he knows that Coriscus is a cultivated person. When Callias answers affirmatively a veiled man is shown to him so that Callias cannot

---

[177] D.L.vii.175 and 198.   [178] *Rh. Gr.* iv, 154.2–25 and vii, 1.163.4–19.

[179] It may be interesting to observe that some of the arguments logically related to the Liar paradox are labelled by Gellius (v.10.1–16) as 'convertible arguments'.   [180] Cic. *Acad.* ii.95.

[181] This interpretation is indirectly confirmed by Alexander of Aphrodisias (fr. 1.91.1–4, text in Vitelli 1902) where he says that if one both claims that an argument is about aporetic material and gives a solution of it, then the argument is aporetic not in itself but with respect to the skilfulness of the listener.

recognize him and say whether he is cultivated or not. Since it turns out
that the veiled man is Coriscus the conclusion is drawn that Callias both
knows and does not know that Coriscus is cultivated.[182] The puzzle is well
known to modern logicians and it has to do with substitutivity in opaque
contexts. Eubulides, a disciple of Euclid of Megara, is said to have dealt
with this paradox,[183] and Aristotle discusses it (*SE* 179a33ff.); but there is
no testimony to the way in which the Stoics faced it, although we know
that Chrysippus dedicated to it a treatise in two books (D.L. VII.198).

Among the titles of Chrysippus' works we find also a treatise on the
Disguised Argument (Περὶ τοῦ διαλεληθότος, D.L. VII.198), and the
hypothesis has been made that it does not refer to a version of the Veiled
Man but to a puzzle, hinted at by Plutarch, concerning the wise man who,
on the one hand, can hardly be aware of being such from the very begin-
ning of his being wise, and, on the other hand, should not be unaware of
his state since he is wise (Plu. *Virt. Prof.* 75c-e). But the fact that a
Disguised Argument is mentioned among the puzzles considered by
Eubulides (D.L. II.108) and referred to in connection with Timon (Clem.
Strom. V 1.11.5) points to an origin which is outside Stoic philosophy and
offers reason to consider it as a version of the Veiled Argument, as the
Electra evidently is.[184]

Another argument mentioned by Diogenes is the Not-someone
(Οὔτις). It is not clear why such a name was given to this puzzle[185] but its
content is described by several sources in more or less the same way. As
Diogenes puts it (D.L. VII.82), it consists of two premises one of which is
an indefinite and the other a definite assertible and one of its possible
forms is as follows:

If anyone is in Athens, he is not in Megara
Man is in Athens

Man is not in Megara[186]

where 'Man' must be taken as a general term denoting a particular entity.
Interpreted in this way the argument is sound,[187] and the false conclusion

[182] [Alex.] *SE* 125.13–18.
[183] D.L. II.108. However, D.L. II.111 attributes the Veiled argument to Diodorus Cronus.
[184] For the Electra see Luc. *Vit. Auc.* 42–3. Before having recognized Orestes Electra knew and did
not know her brother.
[185] Simp. *Cat.* 105.7–20 and Phlp. *Cat.* 72 not. crit. ad lin. 4 have different explanations. Remember
however that a concept for the Stoics is a Not-something (οὔ τι): D.L. VII.61. See below, 411.
[186] This is Simplicius' formulation (*Cat.* 105.7–20). See also Elias *Cat.* 178.1–12.
[187] For this reason I do not think that we need to change συνακτικός into συναπτικός in D.L.
VII.82, as Frede 1974a, 57 n. 10 has suggested.

simply shows that a general term cannot be taken as referring to a particular. It has been suggested that the puzzle was used by the Stoics to prove that the Platonic conception of universals is false.[188] We know that Chrysippus dealt with it in at least two, and possibly three, works (D.L. VII.197).

The Horned Argument was famous among the Ancients and its paternity has been attributed both to Eubulides or to Diodorus Cronos.[189] Its formulation is very simple and consists of the following argument:

If you have not lost something, you have it

You have not lost horns

_____

You have horns[190]

Gellius has an interesting point about this puzzle, which looks quite naive especially in comparison with the others. He claims that the argument has to do with the rule of dialectical inquiry according to which one should not answer in a way that is different from the way in which the question is put. But this rule cannot be observed in the case of the Horned Argument otherwise one cannot escape the conclusion. To the question: 'Does one have what one has not lost?' the answer cannot simply be 'Yes' or 'No'. To get free from the Horned Argument one should rather answer: 'I have everything I had, if I have not lost it.' But in this way the answer is not simple (Gell. XVI.2.1–13).

Far more interesting is the Liar paradox. We will discuss later the formulation that the Stoics favoured. For the present it is sufficient to point out that various versions of it were known. One popular variant of it was the so-called Crocodile. A crocodile kidnaps a child and he proposes the following pact to its parent: I will give you back your child if you guess what I intend to do with him. If the parent says that the crocodile will eat the child, then he cannot have his child back. But the same happens if he chooses the other horn of the dilemma. Therefore, he will never get his child back (Luc. *Vit. Auc.* 41–2). The same holds in the case of the daughter of a seer taken by bandits.[191] It is not clear whether all these cases are equally strong. However, they share to some extent with the proper Liar paradox what is called the self-reference of the truth value of the critical propositions implied by the arguments.

The traditional ascription of the Liar paradox to Epimenides has no

[188] Cf. Sedley 1985, 87–92.   [189] D.L. VII.187 and II.111.   [190] D.L. VII.187.
[191] *Rh. Gr.* VII, 1. 162.11–163.1.

support in the texts.[192] Diogenes claims that this paradox was dealt with
by Eubulides (D.L. ii.108), and some form of it was perhaps known to
Aristotle, when he considers a series of cases in which contradictory statements appear *prima facie* to be true of the same thing. He claims that the
problem can be solved by distinguishing different aspects or senses
according to which the predicates are true of their objects. The same solution is applied by him to the case of a person who promises that he will not
keep his oaths and to the case of a person who apparently at the same time
tells the truth and a falsity (Arist. *SE* 180a23–b7). However, Aristotle
should not have had in mind the real paradox as it is formulated today and
as the Stoics probably thought of it, otherwise his solution would have
been clearly inadequate.

The Sorites, which we will discuss later, was also known to Eubulides
(D.L. ii.108). It has sometimes been claimed that this paradox was known
to Zeno of Elea when he stated that if a bushel of grain makes a noise falling from a given distance, then any part of it however small must make a
noise. But Aristotle's criticism makes it clear that what is in question is
Zeno's belief in a law of proportionality, which has no relation to the
Sorites (Arist. *Phys.* vii.250a19–25).

*

It is a common view that Eubulides proposed his paradoxes without trying to solve them and his approach is normally contrasted with the Stoic
attitude where a strong attempt at solving them can be detected. This
opinion is connected with another view according to which Eubulides
had invented his paradoxes to show that the world of experience is
contradictory or that plurality is inconsistent, according to the Eleatic
positions to which his master, Euclid, subscribed. This picture looks
attractive, but there is no evidence to support it. We do not know on what
assumptions Eubulides' interest in the paradoxes was based nor is it clear
what use he made of them. It may be that he invented and discussed them
just for their own sake and this view fits the picture that Sextus gives of
him by putting him in the company of those who cultivated only logic
among the philosophical disciplines (S.E. *M* vii.13).

Although we cannot say what use Eubulides made of the paradoxes he
invented, subsequent philosophers became increasingly aware of their
importance in philosophical debate. Diodorus Cronus, a pupil of
Eubulides, surely used and debated some of the paradoxes he heard from

[192] Cf. the texts assembled at DK 3 B1 and Mates 1961, 84.

his master, and he passed them to Arcesilaus and the Academics, who applied them against the Stoics.[193] The Academics used the Sorites to undermine the Stoic distinction between apprehensive and non-apprehensive presentations (S.E. *M* VII.415–21), and, according to Sextus, they had recourse to the Veiled argument to the same effect (*M* VII.410). The Stoics themselves exploited paradoxes to criticize other philosophical positions, as the case of the Not-someone argument shows.

It is plausible to think that the Stoics formulated some of their doctrines with an eye to avoiding paradoxes. It is a characteristic Stoic view that a man who becomes wise achieves this state instantaneously, that is, by performing a single virtuous action. Before this last performance he is just as vicious as every non-wise man (Plu. *Comm. Not.* 1063a–b). This strange and extreme doctrine, according to which Plutarch can ironically say that the Stoic wise man is the man who was the worst in the morning and becomes the best in the evening (Plu. *Virt. Prof.* 75d–e), is probably the result of protecting the distinction between wisdom and vice from soritical attack. If the border-line between the two states is sharp, in the sense that there is a fixed point which makes the non-wise wise, 'being wise' is not a soritical predicate, i.e. it cannot be treated in the way in which a predicate such as 'few' can be treated, and therefore no soritical argument can be brought against it.

Paradoxes were used as powerful weapons in philosophical debate and this helps to explain Chrysippus' concern for them. He had to deal with them to defend the major points of his philosophy from Academic attacks. However, to account for the astonishing number of works that he dedicated to paradoxes, as is shown by the catalogue of his writings,[194] one must probably consider also the interest that he had for them as a logician. There are clues that Chrysippus was to some extent aware of the formidable logical and philosophical problems which lay behind some of the paradoxes.

*

We cannot analyse all the paradoxes dealt with by the Stoics, and we shall examine in some detail only two of them, the Liar paradox and the Sorites. What is probably the oldest formulation of the Liar can be found in Cicero:

> Clearly it is a fundamental principle of logic that what is pronounced (this is what they call 'assertible' (ἀξίωμα), that is 'ecfatum') is either true

---

[193] Sedley 1977, 89–96.
[194] D.L. VII.196–8. Sections five to nine of the logical writings are dedicated to paradoxes.

or false. Then, are the following assertibles true or false: 'If you say you are speaking falsely and you tell the truth about it, you are speaking falsely *** you are telling the truth'? You claim that these assertibles cannot be explained. (Cic. *Acad.* II.95)

The personal pronoun 'you' at the end of the translation addresses the Stoics and we may think that the formulation of the Liar refers directly to the Chrysippean one. '*Mentiri*' is normally rendered by 'to lie', which is, of course, a possible translation. But one might also render the Latin by 'speaking falsely', as the Greek ψεύδεσθαι which is behind the Latin allows. The advantage of this translation is that we avoid all the problems connected with the psychological act of lying. What we say by lying may be true if our beliefs are false. By taking '*mentiri*' as 'speaking falsely' we are faced with the simpler situation of someone who utters false assertibles, and this is a necessary condition for constructing the paradox.

Unfortunately, there is a lacuna in the text between 'you are speaking falsely' and 'you tell the truth', and it has been filled up in various ways by the editors. Three solutions have been proposed which are relevant for the philosophical understanding of the paradox:

(I) *si te mentiri dicis, mentiris et verum dicis* [If you say you are speaking falsely, you are speaking falsely and you are telling the truth][195]

(II) *si te mentiri dicis idque verum dicis, mentiris <an> verum dicis?* [If you say you are speaking falsely and you tell the truth about it, are you speaking falsely or telling the truth?][196]

(III) *si te mentiri dicis idque verum dicis, mentiris <et, si te mentiri dicis, idque mentiris> verum dicis* [If you say you are speaking falsely and you tell the truth about it, you are speaking falsely; and if you say you are speaking falsely and you tell the truth about it, you are telling the truth].[197]

None of these proposals is satisfying. To get (I) one must not only add *et*, but also delete *idque verum dicis*, which is attested by all MSS, and this is a strange way to fill up a lacuna. If (II) is adopted it becomes difficult to understand the meaning of the expression: 'are the following assertibles true or false' which introduces (II) since (II) is a question and it does not make sense to ask of a question whether it is true or false. With (III) no logical paradox arises. To prove this claim we must consider what the sen-

---

[195] On the basis of an old correction of the Codex Vossianus and by deleting '*idque verum dicis*'. See Plasberg 1922, *ad loc.*

[196] By analogy with Gell. XVIII.2.10. Cf. Reid 1885, 290–1; Rüstow 1910, 89.

[197] For the text see Hülser 1987–8, 1708–12, following a note of Plasberg 1922, *ad loc*; Barnes 1997.

tence by which the paradox starts refers to. Let us give a name to the 'you' of whom Cicero is speaking and call her 'Calpurnia'. Suppose that Calpurnia says:

(a)   *mentior* [I am speaking falsely]

This assertible, like the Greek ψεύδομαι, may be taken to have different truth conditions according to different situations to which it may be related. To decide whether (a) is true or false we must establish to what assertibles (a) refers. It may be that (a) refers to a finite set Φ of assertibles which does not include (a). In this case no paradox arises and (a) will be true if all assertibles in Φ are false and will be false if at least one of them is true. But it may be that the set of assertibles with respect to which we evaluate (a) includes (a) itself. In this case we can get a paradox if either (a) is the only assertible uttered by Calpurnia or all assertibles in Φ are false. If Φ contains at least one true assertible, (a) is simply false and no paradox arises.

Let us now return to the passage in Cicero and assume that he is spelling out a real paradox. It is hard to believe that he is considering the case that (a) refers only to itself, because this condition is not normally meant by (a) and it is usually added as an explicit statement by people who present the paradox in this way. Therefore, Cicero must say something to mean that the non-empty set of assertibles to which Calpurnia is referring is entirely constituted by false assertibles. A little reflection shows that this condition is not implied by (III). Given that Φ is not empty the second conjunct of (III) means:

(III*) If you say that you are speaking falsely in all your statements and you thereby speak falsely, then you are telling the truth

and the truth of the antecedent of this conditional implies that not every statement of yours is false. From this the truth that all your statements are false, which alone makes the consequent of (III*) true, does not follow.

An alternative way to fill up the lacuna and get a real paradox is by means of:

(IV) (α) *si te mentiri dicis idque verum dicis, mentiris <et* (β), *si mentiris,> verum dicis* [(α) If you say you are speaking falsely and you tell the truth about it, you are speaking falsely, and (β) if you are speaking falsely, you are telling the truth].

From a palaeographical point of view the corruption can easily be explained. Moreover, (IV) represents an adequately paradoxical formulation of the Liar. Suppose as before that Calpurnia by uttering (a) refers to whatever she is saying. In (α) Calpurnia says that whatever she is saying is false and that in saying so she tells the truth. Therefore (*a*) is false, being something she has said. But if all her utterances are false and she speaks falsely by stating (*a*), as is stated by (β), she tells the truth about it, and consequently (*a*) is true. A contradiction is generated. The difference between (III) and (IV) is that in (III) the two conjuncts are independent assertibles, while in (IV) the antecedent of (β) is supposed to be the same as the consequent of (α). This allows us to say that the claim that (*a*) is false, as is implied in the antecedent of (β), is made under the condition that Calpurnia is saying that she is speaking falsely and that she is telling the truth. This implies that every statement different from (*a*) Calpurnia may have made and (*a*) itself are false. Therefore, (*a*) is true. The reasoning becomes really paradoxical.

This interpretation is confirmed by the way in which the puzzle is presented by Gellius (XVIII.2.9–10). What is interesting in his formulation is that the hypothesis that I am really speaking falsely is stated first, that is, as a condition for the paradoxical assertible. In other words, Gellius states two clauses, i.e.:

(*b*)   I am really speaking falsely (*mentior*)

and

(*c*)   I say that I am speaking falsely (*dico me mentiri*)

These two clauses are also present in other versions of the paradox.[198] Why is the assumption that I am really speaking falsely made explicit? The reason, I believe, depends on the implicit interpretation of (*a*). If (*a*) had to be interpreted as an immediately self-referring assertible, there would be no need to add condition (*b*) to get the paradox. On the other hand, by taking (*a*) as including other assertibles different from (*a*), condition (*b*) is required for the construction of the paradox. Therefore, the Gellius formulation of the Liar confirms our interpretation of the Cicero passage and the filling up of the lacuna proposed in (IV).

Actually, after this discussion one might be tempted to propose an even more conservative version of the *Academica* text, simply reading

(v) *si te mentiri dicis idque verum dicis, mentiris <et> verum dicis* [If you say you are speaking falsely and you are telling the truth about it, you are speaking falsely and you are telling the truth].

---

[198] Cf. [Acro] *Scholia vet. in Horatii Epist.* II 1.45 (= *FDS* 1215); Anon. *in SE Paraph.* 25, 58.29–33 (= *FDS* 1218).

If Calpurnia utters (a) and what she is saying is the case, in the sense that it refers to a set of false assertibles among which there is (a) itself, then she is really speaking falsely because all assertibles to which (a) refers are false and (a) is one of them. But, by the same token, she tells the truth because she is really speaking falsely, it being the case that all assertibles to which (a) refers and (a) itself are false. The conclusion is that (IV) or (V) may be taken as a way to formulate the Stoic version of the Liar, which is a real paradox.

*

Had Chrysippus a solution for the Liar paradox? To judge from the number of works he dedicated to the subject one has the impression that he at least attempted to give an answer to this puzzle. This impression is confirmed by a passage in Plutarch where he claims that Chrysippus' solution of the Liar was in overt contrast to some usual views about logic (Plu. *Comm. Not.* 1059d–e). Plutarch makes two points against Chrysippus: (i) he refused to qualify as false the conjunction of a contradictory pair, i.e. admitted that there is at least one contradiction (the conjunction of an assertible with its denial) which is not false; (ii) he would have admitted arguments with true premises which are sound from a logical point of view and nevertheless have false conclusions.

*

Perhaps the first Plutarchan objection may be expanded as follows. The Liar paradox shows that the Liar's critical assertible, namely

(a)*   I am speaking falsely

is, or better entails, a contradiction, since it turns out that it is at the same time true and false. However, Chrysippus denied that this assertible is false, and in this way he would have accepted a contradiction which is not false. The second criticism can be reconstructed along the same pattern. In the Liar there is a sound argument by which one can show that (a)* is false. Chrysippus would have maintained that (a)* is not false. In this way he would have subverted the notion of sound inference, by admitting correct inferences in which the premises are true together with the negation of the conclusion.

What emerges from Plutarch's arguments is that Chrysippus, possibly in contrast to other members of his school, maintained that the Liar's critical assertible, our (a)*, cannot be qualified as false. By considering this claim in the light of the subsequent discussion of the Liar paradox in the

Middle Ages, we may appreciate its philosophical relevance: Chrysippus cannot be ranged among the forerunners of the so-called *restringentes*, that is, the people who believed that (*a*)* is a false assertible on the grounds that it yields a contradiction. From this perspective Plutarch's criticism, although clumsily constructed, has a philosophical respectability.

Shall we range Chrysippus among the *cassantes*, i.e. people who believed that the Liar's critical statement is not an assertible because it is meaningless? This interpretation has been widely adopted and might be defended by the observation that if Chrysippus denied that (*a*)* is false, he surely could not have believed that (*a*)* is true. Therefore, he ought to have admitted that (*a*)* is neither true nor false, so that it is not an assertible. This interpretation finds indirect confirmation in Alexander of Aphrodisias. Commenting on an Aristotelian *locus* where, by attributing a predicate to a subject, the conclusion can be drawn that the subject has contrary predicates (Arist. *Top*. 113a24–32), he explicitly reports that the *locus* may be used to prove that (*a*)* is not an assertible, since if one assumes that (*a*)* is an assertible a contradiction follows, namely that (*a*)* is both true and false (Alex. *Top*. 188.19–28). Unfortunately, Alexander does not tell us who were the people who used this sort of *reductio ad impossibile*. Clearly, he is not referring to the standard Peripatetic view about the Liar.[199] May we say that he is hinting at the Stoic view?

This question seems to have an affirmative answer if we consider Cicero's testimony. He attacks Chrysippus, with a strategy which is not very different from that used by Plutarch, by showing that his solution of the Liar is inconsistent with other major tenets of Stoic logic. His point is as follows:

> If assertibles of this sort cannot be explained and for them there is no criterion[200] according to which you can answer the question whether they are true or false, what happens with the definition of an assertible as that which is true or false? (Cic. *Acad*. II.95)

I take 'assertibles of this sort' to refer to sentences such as (*a*)*, the critical statement of the Liar paradox. If so, Cicero's text contains an important piece of information, since it implies that (*a*)* not only cannot be said to be false, as Plutarch reports, but also cannot be said to be true; for otherwise it is difficult to see why (*a*)* is said to be inconsistent with the definition of

---

[199] E.g. [Alex.] *SE* 170.29ff. commenting on *SE* 180b2–7. Alexander of Aphrodisias apparently had a different view (fr. 1, text in Vitelli 1902).

[200] The Latin is *'iudicium'* which is a translation for the Greek 'κριτήριον'. Elsewhere 'κριτήριον' is rendered by *'terminatio'* (Cic. *Fin*. v.27) or *'norma'* (*Acad*. 1.42).

an assertible. This interpretation is confirmed by what Cicero goes on to say about Epicurus and the Stoics. The latter behave incoherently. On the one hand, they attack Epicurus for having allowed exceptions to the Principle of Bivalence and, on the other, they are themselves adopting the view that there are assertibles such as the Liar which are not subject to the laws of logic. Cicero is alluding to Epicurus' claim that the Principle of Bivalence admits exceptions, since it does not hold for future contingent assertibles.[201] The Stoics, while criticizing Epicurus, allowed the same for another kind of assertible, namely for assertibles such as $(a)*$.[202]

Then is Chrysippus a forerunner of the Mediaeval *cassantes*? On reflection, the passage in Cicero does not warrant this conclusion. Typical of the solution proposed by the *cassantes* was the view that $(a)*$ is not an assertible, since it is meaningless. The idea which emerges from the Ciceronian passage is the opposite: while in Alexander and for the *cassantes* $(a)*$ is not an assertible, Cicero seems to imply that the Stoics considered it to be an assertible, and for this reason he finds that their position is inconsistent. Moreover, Cicero offers a reason why Chrysippus believed that $(a)*$ is neither true nor false: because there is no criterion for assigning one of these truth-values to it. Of course, to make the argument work, one should not take the criterion of which Cicero is speaking to be an epistemological criterion. We cannot infer that $(a)*$ is neither true nor false from the fact that we do not know whether it is true or false. To make the reasoning work we must take 'criterion' as referring to the objective conditions for assigning a truth-value to an assertible independently of our capacity to recognize them. Therefore, what is implicit in Cicero's point is that an assertible such as $(a)*$ was said by Chrysippus to be neither true nor false, because there is no criterion for attributing a truth-value to it, namely because its truth-conditions are not given.

If this interpretation is accepted it seems that the Stoic approach to the Liar contained an important idea. What makes an assertible such as $(a)*$ paradoxical is not its own form or intrinsic structure, but the truth conditions which allow its evaluation. Since truth-conditions may change according to the history of the external world, it may happen that the same assertible is evaluated as false or paradoxical according to different external situations. Of course, this approach to the Liar would imply a revision of the notion of an assertible, and Cicero is right in pointing to the inconsistency between the standard Stoic definition of an assertible and the Chrysippean view about the Liar. It is reasonable to think that

---

[201] See below, pp. 517–18.   [202] Cic. *Acad.* II.97.

Chrysippus was aware of the problem and that he had an answer to it, even if we do not know it.

*

Let us now consider the case of the Sorites.[203] Its name comes from 'σωρός', 'heap' or 'pile', and according to Galen the argument was called this way 'after the matter which first led to this question, I mean the heap' (Gal. *Med. Exp.* XVI.2). His way of presenting the argument probably reflects the way in which it originally had been expounded. Is a single grain of wheat a heap? The answer is: 'No'. Are two grains a heap? The answer is again: 'No'. Going on by adding one grain to the previous quantity we never reach a heap. As Galen explains, the reason why one never gets a heap is that if one denies that a certain amount of grains is a heap, one cannot allow that that amount plus a single grain becomes a heap (*Med. Exp.* XVII.1–3).

The ancient authors were well aware that the argument had a general form and could be applied to many things. For the same reason which forces us to conclude that there are no heaps, compels us to state that there are no waves, no flocks of sheep, no herds of cattle, no open seas, no crowds. And for the same reason we must deny that there is boyhood, adolescence and manhood or seasons (Gal. *Med. Exp.* XVI.1). In the Galen text the form of the ascending Sorites is presented: even if we add millions of grains one by one to a given collection that is not a heap, we never reach a heap. The ancients knew also the descending form of the Sorites. The most famous version of it is the Bald Man. Consider a man with luxuriant hair and everybody will agree that he is not bald. Take a hair away. He is still not bald. By repeating the operation we reach a moment when our poor man has no hair at all and is not yet bald (Gal. *Med. Exp.* XX.3).

Given the variety of the forms in which the Sorites was presented, we are entitled to look for the logical structure which is common to all of them. The argument is surprisingly simple. Consider a collection of grains of wheat formed by one single grain. Call it a_1. Clearly, it is not a heap. For the sake of simplicity, omit the negative way in which the case of the heap is expressed and simply state

(1) $F(a_1)$

This assertible is supposed to be true by hypothesis. Consider now a second collection a_2 formed by two grains of wheat, and a series of these col-

---

[203] Cf. Barnes 1982b, Burnyeat 1982b, Williamson 1994.

lections such that each of them differs from the immediately preceding one only by having one grain more. So we get a succession of individuals

(*) $\langle a_1, a_2, a_3, \ldots, a_n \rangle$

This succession need not be infinite. It is enough that it is sufficiently large to allow us to state that, e.g., its last element is not F (or that it is a heap in this case). Therefore, we assert

(†) $\neg F(a_n)$

This statement is also true by hypothesis. For a sufficiently large n it is difficult to deny that a_n is a heap. Thirty million grains of wheat reasonably form a heap of wheat, and if you are uncertain let us increase n as much as you like. At the end we should get a heap, if there are any heaps in the world.

To get the paradox we need a second assumption, namely that in general if a_j ($j=1, 2,\ldots, n$) is F, then a_{j+1} is also F. For instance, if the collection of j grains of wheat is not a heap, neither is the collection of $j+1$ grains. In other words, we assume that each pair of contiguous elements of the succession (*) is constituted by elements which cannot be distinguished as far as F is concerned. Call this thesis the 'Indiscriminability Thesis'. We can express it by means of:

(IT) $\forall a_j (F(a_j) \rightarrow F(a_{j+1}))$

It is easy to see that by using (1) and an appropriate number of instances of (IT) we reach the negation of (†). We can construct the following argument:

(SR)   (1) $F(a_1)$ by hypothesis
        (2) $F(a_1) \rightarrow F(a_2)$ by (IT)
        _____

        (3) $F(a_2)$ by *modus ponens*
        (4) $F(a_2) \rightarrow F(a_3)$ by (IT)
        _____

        (5) $F(a_3)$
         .   .
         .   .
         .   .

        (p) $F(a_{n-1})$ by *modus ponens*
        ($p+1$) $F(a_{n-1}) \rightarrow F(a_n)$ by (IT)
        _____

        ($p+2$) $F(a_n)$

Thus, we have a contradiction because $(p+2)$ is the negation of $(\dagger)$. The same pattern applies to the descending Sorites.

Let us call (1) the *categorical premiss* or *assumption* of the argument and (2), (4), $(p+1)$ the *conditional premisses*. Clearly, premisses such as (3), (5), (p) are not proper assumptions of the argument, since they are obtained by *modus ponens* and may be eliminated. Let us call them the *intermediate premisses*. (IT) does not work as an explicit premiss of the argument. It has the function of ensuring that we can rely on the conditional premisses – we need it to justify them. In this respect our reconstruction of the argument is near to the Galen text, where the idea that for each case one is allowed to assert F of it is justified by the remark that one single grain of wheat added to a non-heap of wheat cannot provide a heap. This is the same as our thesis (IT).

It is obvious that neither the categorical nor the conditional premisses of our argument are logical laws. Their truth, or at least plausibility, depends on the choice of predicate F and individuals $a_1, \ldots, a_n$. As we have seen, the individuals must be ordered and form a series and the predicate must apply to them. This is meant by a passage of Galen where he says that a soritical argument may be construed when we have to do with anything 'which is known from its name and idea to have a measure of extent or multitude, such as the wave, the open sea, a flock of sheep and herd of cattle, the nation and the crowd' (Gal. *Med. Exp.* XVI.1). What 'is known from its name and idea to have a measure of extent or multitude' is the soritical predicate as applied to an ordered series of individuals $a_1, \ldots, a_n$. They must be such that a measure can be applied to them, and this in effect means that they can be counted. There is no reason to think that soritical predicates themselves must represent quantitative notions,[204] and our sources make it clear that purely qualitative concepts were also submitted to soritical treatment. Sextus, for instance, reports that Chrysippus had to defend the notion of apprehensive presentation from soritical attacks (*M* VII.416–17). What is peculiar to soritical predicates is rather that they apply to an ordered series of individuals in such a way that they satisfy (IT).

It should be clear that (SR) is not a single argument but a succession of arguments. However, a passage of Diogenes Laertius suggests that the Stoics sometimes presented the Sorites in the form of a single argument. The version reported by him is as follows:

> It is not the case that two are few and three are not also; it is not the case that these are few and four are not also (and so on up to ten thousand). But two are few: therefore ten thousand are also. (D. L. VII.82)[205]

---

[204] *Pace* Burnyeat 1982b, 318–20.   [205] Reading μυρίων and μύρια instead of δέκα and δέκα.

We know that Chrysippus in some cases reformulated conditionals as negated conjunctions,[206] and this may mean that the Stoics took the conditionals of the Sorites as weak implications, approximately what we call 'material implications'. It may be pointed out that the type of conditional involved in the Sorites does not substantially affect the logical structure of the argument. The only condition which is required to originate the paradox is that the conditional admit the application of *modus ponens*. By applying this rule several times we are able to get the conclusion of (SR).[207]

*

Once the structure of the Sorites is exposed, it is easy to see on what its force is based. When premiss (1) and thesis (IT) are stated, the argument becomes straightforward, because it is simply based on *modus ponens*, which is one of the most elementary rules of deduction. Therefore, from the point of view of logic nothing suggests that argument (SR) is formally invalid.

On the other hand, a contradiction arises, and we must suppose that there is something wrong with (SR). Since the inconsistency does not apparently depend on the logic of the argument, it must depend on the premisses which are assumed. Premiss (1) seems to be based on immediate observation, and therefore can hardly be rejected. The intermediate premisses depend on *modus ponens*, and they are as safe as their premisses. Thus, we must look at one of the conditional premisses, and since they are justified by (IT) we must discharge (IT). If (IT) is false, its negation is true, and this allows us to reject one of the conditional premisses of (SR). There is a grain of wheat which makes a heap out of a collection that is not a heap, and there is a hair whose subtraction makes a non-bald man bald. That would be plausible if we take 'heap' to mean: 'a collection of n elements', where n is a fixed number. Therefore, while a collection of n-1 grains is not a heap, a collection of n grains is a heap. But this does not seem to be the meaning we attribute to a word such as 'heap', nor in general to soritical predicates. These predicates are intrinsically imprecise and vague and so we may think that it is for this reason that they cannot admit the sharp treatment imposed by logic. It is only when we make the soritical predicates precise that we can avoid the paradox.

---

[206] Cic. *Fat.* 15.

[207] If one wants to remain strictly faithful to the Stoic formulation of the argument (IT) must be presented as

(IT)* $\forall a_j \neg (F(a_j) \wedge \neg F(a_{j+1}))$

and a rule based on the third indemonstrable must be substituted for *modus ponens* to get the paradox.

Is it along these lines that the Stoic analysis of the paradox developed? To answer this question we must consider the evidence at our disposal, which is rather disappointing. Comparing the Stoic attitude to paradoxes with that of the sceptics, Sextus says that in the case of a Sorites Chrysippus recommended us to refrain from assenting to at least some premisses put forward by the adversary (S.E. *PH* II.253–4). The point is repeated to some extent by Sextus elsewhere (*M* VII.416) and on the same lines Cicero reports that according to Chrysippus the wise man must stop answering before entering the dangerous area of the argument (*Acad.* II.93).

There is a standard interpretation of these texts which consists in saying that after all the Sorites is a *reductio ad absurdum*. Deduction (SR) ends in a contradiction. Therefore, at least one of its premisses is false, and of course this means that one of the conditional premisses is so. Since the wise man knows by logic that one of the premisses is false he must refuse to assent to it. But the predicates of the assertibles in question are to some extent vague and he is not able to locate where the false premiss lies. This is the background against which one is asked to understand Chrysippus' suggestion: the wise man should start answering some of the clear cases and refrain from committing himself on the non-clear cases. If he does not stop soon enough he will be led to admit something false. To use Cicero's words, the wise man 'like a clever charioteer, will pull up [his] horses, before [he] gets to the end, and all the more so if the place where the horses are coming to is steep' (*Acad.* II.94).

In the end, this interpretation consists in attributing to Chrysippus a denial of (IT), and this means that there are no predicates which make adjacent pairs of individuals indistinguishable and there is a magic grain of wheat which turns a collection of grains into a heap. If this was the Chrysippean answer to the Sorites why did he order his sage to keep silent after a few questions, and not rather suggest that he use an exact definition of the notion of a heap? One might try to answer this objection by pointing out that the notion of a heap is imprecise, not because it does not imply a limit in itself, but because nobody knows where it is. By adding grains to a collection step by step we do indeed reach a point where this collection becomes a heap, but nobody knows where this point lies. But from this perspective the objection that Cicero raises against Chrysippus is legitimate. If the wise man has to stop answering 'a little while before [he] come[s] to many' and withhold his assent before things become obscure, the wise man is compelled to withhold his assent even from things which are perfectly clear and safe (Cic. *Acad.* II.93–4).

One could try to defend Chrysippus' position from this objection by taking his view not as an epistemic but as an ontological one. To make the point clear let us first determine what is obscure in a soritical argument. Cicero clearly says that the wise man should at a certain moment stop answering questions such as 'Are three few?' Therefore he must refrain from assenting to some of the intermediate premisses of (SR). Then the whole point is: on what does the obscurity of these intermediate premisses depend? The traditional answer is: it depends on one of the preceding conditional premisses, for which it is not clear whether it is true or false, although in itself it is either true or false. But to avoid the consequence that in this way the wise man is obliged to refrain from assenting to true assertibles, one could reason in a different way. The obscurity of the intermediate premisses cannot depend on the preceding conditional premisses. It is for exactly the same reason that we accept that if two grains do not form a heap, then three grains do not form one either, and that if two million grains do not form a heap, then two million and one grains do not form one either, since, to make the point with Galen: 'I know of nothing worse and more absurd than that the being and not-being of a heap is determined by a grain of corn' (Gal. *Med. Exp.* XVII.3). In this way our intuitive notion of a heap is preserved.

The obscurity of some of the intermediate premisses of (SR) might be based on the idea that soritical predicates make the assertibles of which they are part behave in a special way with respect to truth and falsity. The idea is that to claim that one grain is not a heap of wheat is pretty true, as well as to state that, say, 10,000 grains are a heap. But what happens with, let us say, 5,000 grains? Are they a heap or not? One might claim that if saying that one grain is not a heap is completely true, to claim that 5,000 grains are not a heap is less true, although it is not yet completely false. With respect to deduction (SR) the situation might be as follows. Suppose that one is asked to admit $F(a_1)$, e.g., that one grain of wheat is not a heap. The answer is of course: 'Yes', because $F(a_1)$ is simply true, let us say 100 per cent true. Then take premiss (2), the first conditional premiss, which is supposed to be absolutely true by the indiscriminability thesis. By *modus ponens* we immediately get (3), $F(a_2)$. Now $F(a_2)$ is also true, but perhaps a little less than $F(a_1)$, let us say 99 per cent true. Two grains of wheat are not a heap, but not as truly as before. By repeating the procedure a sufficient number of times we get assertibles which are less and less true.

From this perspective soritical predicates admit of degrees of truth, in the sense that they are more or less true of the objects to which they apply. These degrees vary in a continuous way. What happens when we submit assertibles formed by these predicates to the laws of logic is that the laws of logic hold, but locally, that is, in the short distance. If we apply *modus ponens* in a chain like (SR), we can safely do so only if we do not repeat the process too many times. That is all.[208] It is enough to stop in due time. In due time for what? For not deriving a false assertible, or an assertible which is so little true as to become obscure, from completely true premisses. Then Chrysippus' suggestion becomes clear: stop the process before the dark precipice of assertibles which are so little true that they are almost false. And if we interpret it in this way, we can also answer Cicero's objection: the wise man never refrains from assenting to simply true assertibles. He is allowed to suspend his judgement when confronted by assertibles which are less than simply true. This way of solving the Sorites paradox has a price: we must give up the idea that *modus ponens* preserves truth in the long run. Its repeated application in a deductive chain may create problems when soritical predicates are involved. The evidence of which we dispose does not allow us to ascribe this view to Chrysippus. However, it is consistent with the statements that our sources attribute to him and allows us to reject Cicero's objections.

If we take this approach to Chrysippus' position we can conclude that his view about the paradoxes is much more modern than the view represented in the Aristotelian tradition. His solution of the Liar paradox requires a reform of his notion of an assertible, since he seems to admit assertibles which are neither true nor false. On the other hand, if his way out of the Sorites was based on a limitation of the range of application of *modus ponens*, it is not too bold to conclude that he was aware that an answer to the main paradoxes implies that we must give up some of our common-sense beliefs. It is not without sacrifices that we resolve paradoxes.

---

[208] As is well known, it is not difficult to give a precise semantic basis to the idea we are proposing.

6

Language

DIRK M. SCHENKEVELD AND JONATHAN BARNES (I.2)*

I Linguistics

1: The study of language

In the classical period, the Greek language was studied by philosophers, sophists and rhetoricians, and the contributions of Aristotle and Theophrastus in particular are very valuable. But only in the Hellenistic era does grammar show significant development and almost becomes a discipline in its own right. Although their origin as students of poetry is never forgotten, grammarians now start to be acknowledged as teachers and scholars in the fields of phonology and morphology. To some extent they also study syntax and pragmatics, while semantics provides, as it were, their basic approach. This development is the result of the concurrence of three kinds of linguistic analysis: in philosophy, rhetoric and scholarship. Students of each of these disciplines look at language from their own specific point of view and in a different context. Thus, philosophers, especially Stoics, are interested in the nature of language and its relationships to reality and knowledge, and analyse speech in the context of their study of logic, which analysis has its consequences for their physics and ethics. Rhetoricians are more concerned with ways of manipulating people by means of language; and scholars develop tools for language analysis in order to edit and explain the texts of Homer and other poets. These different concerns greatly advance the study of language although the complete emancipation of grammar as a discipline to be studied for its own sake, like mathematics, is not achieved in this period.[1]

The extent of the evolution is well demonstrated by the use of the very word γραμματική. To Plato τέχνη γραμματική means 'the art of putting

---

* J. Barnes' contribution runs from p. 193 to p. 213.
[1] Varro's approach in *De lingua latina* x (*c.* 50 BC) may have been the exception; cf. D. J. Taylor 1987b, 188–9.

together letters'[2] but to Dionysius Thrax it is '(the art of) grammar'.[3] He defines τέχνη γραμματική[4] as 'the practical study of the normal usages of poets and prose writers' and distinguishes six parts, all of them related to the exegesis of literature. After him, Asclepiades of Myrlea makes a useful distinction between three parts: in the 'more special' part the grammarian is concerned with textual criticism and explanation, in the 'historical' one with *realia* and also with lexicography, while in the 'technical' part we find the systematic description of language, 'grammar' in the modern sense. This technical part not only describes the parts of speech (μέρη λόγου), phonology included, but also looks at how to achieve correct Greek in pronunciation, orthography and inflection.[5] The term γραμματικός then denotes the scholar (and teacher) of grammar as well as of textual criticism and related subjects, and 'scholar' is, therefore, often a more correct modern translation than 'grammarian'.[6]

This situation, however, is not reached before the end of the second century BC or even later. Before this time, grammarians (scholars), like Aristophanes of Byzantium and Aristarchus of Samothrace, do not write separate treatises on grammar, and their grammatical knowledge and competence can only be inferred from their works on Homer and other authors. Rhetorical writings on e.g. tropes and figures also deal with matters of language.[7] As to philosophers, from Epicurus and the Peripatos after Theophrastus no particular works on linguistic topics are known, though Epicurus expresses some views on language in his *Letters* and also – at greater length – in his *On Nature*.[8] The Stoics are known to have treated many grammatical aspects in a systematic way in their τέχναι περὶ φωνῆς and their treatises on σημαινόμενα are also important in this respect. In both categories we possess no originals, however, the expositions in D.L. VII being our main source. Later grammatical writings help to fill this gap only to a limited extent.

This picture of the growth of grammar deliberately ignores the once popular view of a fundamental opposition between philosophical, largely

---

[2] Plato *Soph.* 253a, *Crat.* 431e. To Aristotle (*Int.* 17a6) 'questions of language, in so far as they were not of a mere logical nature, had to be relegated to rhetoric and poetics' (Pfeiffer 1968, 76).

[3] More general is Eratosthenes' definition of γραμματική as the perfect skill in writing, cf. Pfeiffer 1968, 162.

[4] *Technē* § 1 Uhlig. The quotation in S.E. *M* 1.53. proves this part to be genuinely Dionysian. From § 6 onwards the *Technē* is now considered to be of later date (Kemp 1991, 307–15) and we can only guess what may have been there originally (Schenkeveld 1995, 41–52).

[5] Siebenborn 1976, 32–3.

[6] See Pfeiffer 1968, 156–9 on the meanings of the terms φιλόλογος, κριτικός, and γραμματικός.

[7] Most of them are now lost and have to be reconstructed with the help of later treatises.

[8] In the reconstruction of book XXVIII by Sedley, 1973; see also Tepedino Guerra 1990.

Stoic grammar with Pergamene grammar as its offshoot on the one hand, and technical, Alexandrian grammar on the other, an opposition intensified by an alleged controversy between analogists and anomalists. Modern research has shown that the latter controversy, if not totally an invention of Varro, was of limited importance only,[9] and the topic of analogy versus anomaly will be dealt with below (p. 183) in its proper context. For the rest, no fundamentally different approaches between philosophers and grammarians to technical matters, such as the distinction of parts of speech, can be detected.[10]

*

The question of how language, or languages, came into being is a different one from that about the relationship, original or later, between the form and the meaning of words. However, the questions are to some extent related and a view on the origin usually implies an opinion about the original relationship but not the other way round.[11]

About the origin of language two views prevailed. One is that language gradually and naturally (φύσει) evolved in a collective of men, whereas the second opinion is that some individual (god or man), or individuals, invented language and put names to things (θέσει). The other question about the relation between form and meaning (ὀρθοέπεια, or ὀρθότης τῶν ὀνομάτων) leads either to the conviction that, at least in the original state of language, by nature (φύσει) forms completely agree with meanings, or to the view that this relation is fortuitous and the product of convention (νόμῳ or κατὰ συνθήκην).[12] Connected with the former position is the view that later the agreement was lost because forms were corrupted and changed. Given this view etymology helps to recover the original form and thus the true meaning of the word.

Epicurus, an exponent of the evolutionary view, distinguishes two stages, the first being that individuals felt compelled by their feelings and impressions to utter sounds in an individual way and according to their geographical situations.[13] This process is considered a natural one and

---

[9] Blank 1982, 1–4 and Ax 1991, 289–95.

[10] Research in the history of ancient linguistics received a new impetus at the end of the fifties with the publications of Fehling 1956–7 and di Benedetto 1958–9 on the analogy/anomaly controversy and the authenticity of Dionysius' *Technē* respectively, and significant progress was made from the seventies onwards. The received accounts of this history, like that of R. H. Robins 1979, are now being replaced, but a *communis opinio* has not yet been achieved. See D. J. Taylor 1987b, 177–88 and Schenkeveld 1990a.

[11] See Fehling 1965 on how the two questions get mixed up in antiquity, a confusion still virulent.

[12] Cf. M. Kraus 1987, 168–202 and Joseph 1990.

[13] *Ep. Hdt.* 75–6; Lucr. v.1041–5 and Diog. Oen. fr. 12 Smith.

Epicurus emphatically rejects the possibility of imposition by one person. Arguments against the latter view are such as 'why would one person be able to do what others could not do at the same time?' However, at a second stage Epicurus accepts the imposition of words but now as an act of consensus of the people concerned. At this stage greater accuracy is reached and new designations are introduced.

When speaking of the force of the feelings and the impressions which led to utterances Epicurus is rather vague.[14] The greater accuracy mentioned in the second stage probably refers to the replacement of deictic forms by explicit designations. The reference to different languages with their own development alludes to earlier discussions, such as in Plato's *Cratylus* 383, in which the existence of different languages with different names for one and the same notion was also used as an argument against the natural rightness of names and as a proof for the convention view. To Epicurus the geographical differences explain the existence of linguistic differences. But by speaking of 'individual feelings and impressions' and connecting these with geographical distinctions he invites the objection that it is thus impossible to translate from one language to another. This point may not have bothered him, the less so if the differences he is talking about concern those between Greek dialects.[15]

Epicurus' own account is part of the epitome of his philosophy in his *Letter to Herodotus* and has no context. Lucretius offers such a context by putting his description into the framework of a whole theory of the evolution of civilization, and Epicurus may have done the same. At any rate, his combination of a natural origin for language with a subsequent θέσει-stage is a creative reaction to older discussions.

*

Definite texts on Stoic views on the origin of language are lacking because they probably paid little attention to this question. From their view that a fully rational correspondence between word and meaning existed it may follow that they favoured a conscious invention of language. Its inventor, if any, is a king if Varro's theory on the fourth 'level' or 'step' of etymology (*gradus etymologiae*) with the Latin king (*rex Latinus*) as its name-giver (*impositor*),[16] reflects Stoic thought; but this cannot be proved. Epicurean criticism of the θέσει-view has been explained as a reaction against such a

---

[14] The same vagueness in Lucr. v.1028.
[15] Differently on these points Hossenfelder 1991b, 221–4.   [16] *LL* v.8–9.

Stoic theory but can also be seen as directed against Plato's repeated use of one law-giver.[17]

More is known of Stoic views on the relation between form and meaning. This subject is treated *in extenso* below,[18] but here a few words are in order. The Stoics assume a direct and simple mimetic relationship between the form of words and their meaning at an original stage. As one text has it, 'according to the Stoics the first sounds are imitations of the things (*pragmata*) of which the names are said'.[19] This direct relationship is best illustrated by onomatopoeic words; for there meaning and signifier coincide with each other and with their referent.[20] This interpretation is the accepted one but the text quoted above also allows an interpretation by which there is only a direct relation between form and referent. Some support for this exegesis seems to be found in the long discussion of Stoic etymology by Augustine, who distinguishes a category of words in which there is a resemblance of word to thing in *tactus*, such as *mel*, *lana*, and *vepres*. However, this statement involves a neglect of the role of meanings, which would be quite un-Stoic and it seems certain that Augustine introduces views of his own.[21] We may therefore be content with the first interpretation.

Even so, matters are problematic because according to Aulus Gellius, Chrysippus asserts that 'every word is ambiguous *by nature*, since two or more meanings can be understood from it'.[22] Because of the lack of quotation marks and other means of distinguishing between metalanguage and language Greek was very much open to ambiguity. This fact may have contributed to Chrysippus' statement on the naturalness of ambiguity but it evidently is at cross-purposes with the statement that words originally imitated the things.[23]

For non-onomatopoeic words the principle of a natural similarity is less clear since they have been gradually corrupted.[24] Already Plato refers to three modes of change in word-forms, those of adding, moving or removing a letter. After the Hellenistic period a four-stage scheme (*quadripertita*

---

[17] E.g. Lucretius v.1041–5; Diog. Oen. Fr. 12 Smith; Plato *Crat.* 388e1. See Sluiter 1990, 18–20.
[18] See below, pp. 197–213.   [19] Orig. *Cels.* 1.24.   [20] August. *Dial.* 6.
[21] August. *Dial.* 6. He probably misunderstands his source, Varro fr. 113 Goetz-Schoell (= Diomedes *Ars gramm.*, *Gramm. Lat.* 1.428, 22–8); see Sluiter 1990, 35–6.
[22] XI.12.1 and August. *Dial.* 9.
[23] Perhaps Chrysippus meant to say that every utterance can fail to achieve the correct result because the addressee misunderstands it, not that every utterance is of its nature ambiguous. Cf. Sluiter 1990, 127 and Atherton 1993, 298–310.
[24] August. *Dial.* 6. This corruption of language strongly resembles the ethical notion of διαστροφή, by which man was corrupted from a perfect rationality (D.L. VII.89). See Sluiter 1988.

ratio) is found in various departments of grammar and rhetoric, not only for etymology.[25] It is unclear whether the Stoics developed it; but some such scheme will have been used by them.

At this point etymology enters into the discussion, a method strongly favoured by the Stoics.[26] The main task of etymology is to explain for what reasons and how a word got its original form, and how this was changed – and thus to detect its true meaning.[27] The term ἐτυμολογικά is not found before Chrysippus[28] and ἐτυμολογία is to all appearances a Stoic coining, by which they indicate that the search for the reason why a particular name has been given to a particular thing is related to the search for truth.[29] In this process one detects the *similitudo* between word and meaning. However, other principles of word-formation have also been active, to wit *contrarium* (e. g. *lucus a non lucendo*) and *vicinitas*, which our source, Augustine, explains by *abusio*, figurative language, and for which he gives *piscina* (swimming pool) as a dubious example. Taken by itself this tripartite scheme looks very Stoic, for resemblance and contrariety are also known as processes in the formation of general concepts; but one should be careful in taking the whole of Augustine's chapter as truthfully representing Stoic thought.[30] Alongside this scheme the fourfold scheme of changes in words mentioned above is also applied. Application of these methods helps to bring back a particular word to a form for which the reason of its genesis can be given. Of course, the combination of these, or similar, views allows the Stoics much latitude in using etymology as a means of understanding both things and words, and one will not be surprised to find the most fantastic explanations in our texts.[31] But fantasy in this respect is not a specifically Stoic trait.

A quite different matter is the position of etymology in the whole system of Stoic dialectic and specifically its relationship to their views on correct Greek. In the genuine part of Dionysius' *Technē* etymology is one of the six tasks of the grammarian and it also plays a role in later theories on hellenism.[32] But whether etymology ever had a definite place in the Stoic system we do not know.[33]

*

[25] ἀφαίρεσις (*detractio*), πρόσθεις (*adiectio*), μετάθεσις (*transmutatio*) and ἐναλλαγή (*immutatio*). See Ax 1987 for the origins of this scheme (Plato *Crat.* 394b) and its various applications.
[26] For the relation of etymology to allegoresis see below p. 222.
[27] Varro *LL* v.2; ΣDThrax 14.23–4 and Cic. *ND* iii.62.   [28] D.L. vii.200 ἐτυμολογικά.
[29] Herbermann 1991, 356–9.   [30] Fehling 1958 on Barwick 1957.
[31] Galen, *PHP* ii.2,5–7 [= v.241K] criticizes Chrysippus' fondness for etymological explanations.
[32] Siebenborn 1976,140–6.   [33] Cf. Hülser 1987–8,746–7. Too confidently Amsler 1989, 22–3.

The relationship between form and meaning is also an object of debate when philosophers look at contemporary Greek, written texts of classical authors, like Homer and the tragedians, included. Here many discrepancies between form and meaning are to be found and Chrysippus devotes a work in four volumes to this phenomenon, *On the anomalies concerning* λέξεις. Anomaly pertains to cases such as those where words indicating privation do not have the corresponding form (e.g. πενία, 'poverty'), and also the other way round.[34] Anomaly also refers to the irregularity of one single city being designated by a plural form.[35] According to Varro[36] this theory of anomaly was wrongly transferred by Crates of Mallos to derivational and inflectional morphology when he contends that in this field arbitrariness reigns and only ordinary language (*consuetudo*, συνήθεια), not analogy, is to be followed. This, Varro says, he did in opposition to Alexandrian grammarians like Aristarchus, who favour analogy (*analogia*) that is, they detect patterns in inflection and apply these in order to decide on doubtful forms, insofar as customary language permits this.[37] Varro solves the disagreement by stating that in derivation anomaly is pre-eminent but in inflection analogy, though common parlance plays a role of its own. In books VIII–X Varro offers many instances of the anomalist position, of that of the analogists, and of his own solution, respectively. He mentions Aristarchus and Crates as the main antagonists but also refers, both in this context and elsewhere, to other Hellenistic authors. Thus, according to Varro this quarrel was rife in the period of about 200–150 BC and continued up till his own time.[38]

Apart from Varro we have no unambiguous mention of this quarrel.[39] It is wrong, therefore, to accept Varro's statement about the extent and duration of the controversy as trustworthy, and scholars should not have inferred a long and drawn out quarrel between analogists and anomalists.[40] On the basis of some disagreement between Aristarchus and Crates and using the well-known strategy of *disputare in utramque partem* Varro either invented the quarrel or, more probably, enlarged a dispute on

---

[34] These words were also discussed in Chrysippus' *On privatives* (Simp. *Cat.* 396.2–22).

[35] Ap. Dysc. *Conj.* 215, 14–22, who also mentions the use of a passive form in an active sense, e.g. μάχομαι, 'to fight', but this example looks un-Stoic, see below, p. 190.

[36] Varro *LL* IX.1 and VIII.23.

[37] The analogy, or *ratio*, has at least four terms, of which one is doubtful or unknown and can be decided upon, e.g. *amor*:*amori* = *dolor*:*dolori* (supposing that the form of this dative is doubtful).

[38] Ax 1991, 289–93.

[39] Aulus Gellius II.25 derives from Varro. Sextus *M* I.176–240 never alludes to the quarrel though attacking grammarians for defending analogy and neglecting anomaly.

[40] See the history of this interpretation in Ax 1991, 293–4.

minor matters.[41] Crates may, deliberately or inadvertently, have transferred the notion of anomaly to the domain of inflection in order to stress
the importance of common usage as compared to analogy, a factor which
was applied by some grammarians to a ridiculous extent.[42]

*

Ancient grammar is a 'word and paradigm model' based as it is on the
word as an isolable linguistic entity and on paradigms of associated
forms.[43] However, proper definitions of word as well as of phrase or sentence are lacking. The Stoics introduce the notion of αὐτοτελὴς διάνοια,
'a complete, independent thought', and this is the closest ancient linguists
come to a definition of a sentence.[44] Ancient grammar, moreover, does
not have the notion of syntactic subordination. To the Stoics a proposition like 'if it is light, it is day' is comparable to 'both it is day and it is
night'; both are a combination of two propositions which are connected
by a conjunction and function on the same level. This view becomes the
traditional one.[45] Though expressions like κατηγόρημα and πτῶσις
ὀρθή justify a syntactic interpretation of predicate and subject, the very
use of πτῶσις ὀρθή for the nominative case also prevents dissociating
subject from nominative and consequently a proper analysis of e.g. infinitive constructions. No such distinctions are made by grammarians either
nor do they develop an autonomous syntax.[46] Even so, ancient linguists
are able to describe many syntactic phenomena, albeit often in a convoluted way.

The following survey focuses on matters of phonology, morphology
and syntax insofar as they were discussed by the Stoics, the leading philosophical contributors to the development of grammar. The efforts of
grammarians will be discussed to some extent but their main contributions appear to fall outside our period.

*

The Stoics develop what we call a grammar in the context of their dialectic. We can reconstruct it from what they say both in the *topos* on
φωνή (sound, speech) and in that on σημαινόμενα (meanings). The con-

---

[41] Blank 1982, 2–4 and Ax 1991, 294–5.
[42] S.E. *M* 1.176 ff. has some amusing examples. The use of ὅμοιον, 'similar', in definitions of analogy (e.g. S.E. *M* 1.199) and its antinomy ἀνόμοιον, which looks like ἀνώμαλον (*ibid.* 236–7) as
well as the fact that the usual Greek word for 'derivation', παραγωγή, may also mean
'inflection' (Schenkeveld 1990b, 297–8), may have brought Crates to his position.
[43] Robins 1979, 25.
[44] In practice μέρος, μόριον, ὄνομα and λέξις are used for 'word' and λόγος often agrees with our
'sentence' or 'phrase'.   [45] Cf. Sluiter 1990, 137–8.   [46] Baratin 1989, 487–91.

tents of the first *topos* are mainly known from Diogenes' summary based on the τέχνη περὶ φωνῆς by Diogenes of Babylon.[47] The structure of this Stoic τέχνη is tripartite.[48] A first part considers the constituents of language: general definitions of φωνή, λέξις (*lexis*) and λόγος (*logos*) followed by the list of the letters (στοιχεῖα) and differences between *lexis* and *logos*, and concluding with a treatment of the parts of speech. A second part discusses the uses of language: right versus wrong usage, especially in prose, followed by the characteristics of poetry and a section on ambiguous use of language. The third part consists of definitions of genus, species etc. (But the position of this section here is not without problems.) For the second *topos* Diogenes is again our chief source.

Stoic phonology is the first Greek systematic theory of sound and speech,[49] though the Academy and Aristotle had imparted significant impulses.[50] Whereas to Aristotle sound was a stroke of the air, from Zeno onwards the Stoics define sound as 'air being struck', by which phrasing they express the corporeality of sound.[51] This materialism of sound, a big issue in philosophical discussions,[52] is important to the Stoics in order to underpin the differences between corporeal sound and incorporeal λεκτά (*lekta*).[53] Aristotle started from ψόφος (any sound), which he also defined as 'the proper object of perception by the sense of hearing'.[54] Diogenes of Babylon takes over the latter definition[55] but applies it to φωνή, voice. It is apparent that in this way he and other Stoics immediately focus their discussion on voice, not on sound in general, thereby giving rise to confusion between sound and voice. This mix-up was rightly criticized later on.[56]

The Stoic theory is directed towards its prime member, the *logos*. By means of a dihaeretic method based on the presence or absence of the features of scriptibility or articulacy they first narrow down voice to *lexis* (expression), as 'written, or articulated voice' and the feature of semanticity then decides whether a *lexis* is *logos* or not.[57] Zeno defines *logos* as 'meaningful voice issued from the thought'[58] and *lexis* as being scriptible.

---

[47] D.L. VII.55–62, who also cites Archedemus' treatise with the same title and Posidonius' Περὶ λέξεως εἰσαγωγή.

[48] See also Schenkeveld 1990a for the influential reconstruction of Barwick 1922, 91–2 based on the form of Latin *artes*, which is rejected here.

[49] Texts in D.L. VII.55–7 and ΣDThrax 482.5–32.   [50] See Ax 1986, 113–15 and 137–8.

[51] D.L. VIII.55.   [52] E.g. [Plu.] *Plac.* 902f–903a and ΣDThrax 482.14–19. See Ax 1986, 177–81.

[53] On λεκτά see below, pp. 198–213.   [54] *De an.* II.8 and 6, cf. *HA* I.1 and IV.9.

[55] See Ax 1986, 173 and Schenkeveld 1990b, 302 for a definition given by older Stoics.

[56] Simp. *Phys.* 425, 34–7. See also Ax 1986, 174.   [57] D.L. VII.56–7; Gal. *PHP* II.5.6–24.

[58] The addition of 'issued from the thought' is related to the discussion about the place of λόγος and the governing part of the soul (τὸ ἡγεμονικὸν μέρος τῆς ψυχῆς) in the heart, not in the brain (Gal. *PHP* II.5). The addition at the same time excludes animals and young children from having λόγος (Hülser 1987–8, 536–8).

Later, under Aristotle's influence, Diogenes of Babylon defines *lexis* as 'articulated voice which may be either meaningful (*logos*) or not'. In the latter case the standard examples are meaningless words like βλίτυρι and σκινδαψός, denoting a twang of a harp-instrument and of a kind of banjo respectively.[59] The switch from scriptibility (Zeno) to articulacy (Diogenes) as the starting point for further distinctions may be due to a wish for more exactness, as articulation is seen as the prerequisite for scriptibility. Grammarians make quadruple distinctions based on the features of scriptibility and intelligibility.[60]

Logos includes any meaningful expression, from a single word through phrases to whole texts, and these expressions are *lexeis* at the same time. Thus ἡμέρα ἐστι ('it is day') is a good example of both *lexis* and *logos*[61] since these words form a string of scriptible or articulate sounds and have a meaning as well.[62] The difference between these two important concepts is also expressed in another way: voices are uttered (προφέρειν) whereas λέγειν is expressly reserved for πράγματα (states of affairs).[63]

Both *lexis* and *logos* can be subdivided into στοιχεῖα, elements. The elements of the *lexis* are the twenty-four letters, which in Diogenes' account are grouped into seven voiced and six unvoiced. The remaining eleven letters are not mentioned here but are classified as semivoiced by Sextus.[64] Together with the unvoiced they form the group of the consonants. The Stoics may also have made a similar distinction. If this is so, they put the three aspirates theta, phi, chi, under the semivoiced, whereas in the *Technē* they are classified as unvoiced. Distinctions between voiced, semivoiced, and unvoiced sounds are known from Plato and Aristotle onwards and were further developed by students of musical metres like Aristotle's pupil, Aristoxenus of Tarentum.[65]

This Stoic theory concerns sounds, but the introduction of scriptibility suggests to scholars that the system confuses written with spoken language. Later grammatical theory may sometimes justify such a charge but generally speaking philosophers and grammarians keep written and spoken language apart and distinguish between γράμματα and στοιχεῖα as entities of graphic representation and of voice respectively.[66] Thus the Stoics speak of the elements of the *lexis*, define these as the twenty-four

---

[59] D.L. VII.57 and S.E. *M* VIII.133.   [60] See Ax 1986, 236–9 and Desbordes 1990, 104–6.
[61] The text in D.L. VII.56 is corrupt and Casaubon's restoration suggests an additional difference between a single word (λέξις) and a group of words (λόγος), a distinction known from other, non-Stoic sources. See Ax 1986, 199–200.   [62] Baratin 1991, 196.
[63] D.L. VII.57, cf. S.E. *M* VIII.80.   [64] D.L. VII.57; S.E. *M* I.100–2.
[65] Plato *Crat.* 393c; Arist. *Poet.* 20 and D.H. *Comp.* 14.
[66] Cf. the modern notions of 'graphemes' and 'phonemes'.

γράμματα but immediately notice a threefold usage of this latter word: 'The word "letter" has three meanings: (1) the element, (2) the character (written form) of that element and (3) the name, e.g. alpha.'[67] Starting from the constituent of oral voice they define the other usages in its terms. Grammarians change this perspective when they say that στοιχεῖον has three (or four) senses, namely the written character, its value (δύναμις) and its name, the fourth being the position of an element before or after another one.[68] A genuine confusion of written and oral language is therefore not a characteristic of ancient linguistic analysis,[69] but from its beginnings onwards this analysis tends to a very close connection of the two languages, a tendency caused both by the habit of reading aloud and by the fact that the primary objects of study were the written texts of classical authors.[70]

*

The elements of *logos* are the parts of speech, word classes.[71] These combine aspects of form and meaning. In fact, the verb is defined in *lekta*-terms, but *lekta* cannot be identified without words and phrases. Accordingly, the differentiation of *lekta* corresponds to that of the signifiers and so can be used by grammarians.[72] Another consequence is that Stoic 'grammar' mainly discusses what is of interest to students of logic and does not strive after completeness. On many points, e.g. the status of the copula ἐστι ('is'),[73] it is silent.

Chrysippus and Diogenes classify five parts of speech, προσηγορία, ὄνομα, ῥῆμα, σύνδεσμος and ἄρθρον and Antipater adds a sixth, μεσότης,[74] the adverb,[75] which was originally included under the verb.[76] Pronoun, participle and preposition are not seen as independent

---

[67] The insertion in D.L. vii.56 of <τὸ στοιχεῖον> is necessary and more probable than that of <καὶ ἡ τούτου δύναμις after χαρακτὴρ τοῦ στοιχείου (Barwick 1957, 54n.). Cf. Egli 1967, 27 and Desbordes 1990, 116.   [68] S.E. *M* 1.99 and ΣDThrax 317.7.

[69] See Desbordes 1987 and Sluiter 1990, 196.

[70] Apart from these distinctions the Stoics also use διάλεκτος in the senses of 'dialect' (first occurrence for this meaning) and 'national language', whereas Aristotle used it in a more general sense of 'articulated voice'.

[71] Στοιχεῖα or μέρη τοῦ λόγου D.L. vii.58 and Gal. *PHP* viii.3. Texts in *FDS* 536–93 with references to the other *topos*.   [72] A. C. Lloyd 1971, 61–3.

[73] See Nuchelmans 1973, 51 and Kerferd 1978b, 262–6.

[74] 'Proper name, appellative, verb, conjunction, article, adverb'. D.L. vii.57. The reports on the development of the whole system in D.H. (*Comp.* 2 and *Dem.* 48, cf. Quint. *Inst.* 1.18) are artificial reconstructions.

[75] Thus in Aristarchus' scholia on Homer, e.g. 1.446b. To take it as 'participle' (e.g. Forschner 1981, 70) neglects the tradition that the Stoics do not distinguish the participle as a separate class. The traditional name is later ἐπίρρημα.

[76] Stoics also call it πανδέκτης, 'all-receiver' (Charis. *Ars gram.* 247.13–3). Pinborg's suggestion (1961) that the Stoics emphasize the rational contents of interjections and put them under the adverb has no basis (Sluiter 1990, 209–11).

classes and appear under article, verb and conjunction respectively. For example, the participle is an 'inflectional form of the verb'[77] though also a species of the appellative.[78] Grammarians order these items into independent classes and increase the number of parts of speech to nine or ten, though eight becomes the standard number.[79] The Stoic series has one surprise, the inclusion of the conjunction under parts of the *logos*, for Aristotle defines his σύνδεσμος as 'non-significant'. Because, however, to the Stoics connections between states of affairs in the nature of things are real and are reflected in language by different conjunctions of implication etc., they never doubt that conjunctions have a well-defined meaning.[80] They bind together the parts of the *logos* and their meaning is to indicate the sense of this complex. Maybe a special term, 'to announce' (ἐπαγγέλλεσθαι), expresses the way this class signifies. In Diogenes' examples all conjunctions stand in front position and thus can be said to 'announce' how to take the following expressions.[81]

Apart from the adverb all Stoic parts of speech get a definition in Diogenes' account. Thus the 'article' is 'a declinable part of speech, distinguishing the genders and numbers of nouns, e.g. ὁ, ἡ, τό'. However, this article also comprises pronouns since the Stoics distinguish between 'indefinite (or non-specific) articles' (= articles proper), and 'definite (or specific) articles' embracing personal, demonstrative and anaphoric pronouns.[82] Later the latter words get a status of their own and are called ἀντωνυμίαι. To call the articles 'indefinite' looks strange but it may be significant that examples like ὁ δειπνήσας ('one who has dined') with a non-specific reference are often cited.[83]

Προσηγορία, appellative, is distinguished from ὄνομα, proper name. This differentiation is attacked by grammarians, who prefer ὄνομα to cover all nouns.[84] The main reason for this division lies in the theory of the categories, where a distinction between 'commonly qualified' and 'particularly qualified' exists.[85] The definitions are for the appellative 'a part of speech signifying a common quality' (e.g. ἄνθρωπος, 'man'; or ἵππος, 'horse'), and for the proper name 'a part of speech showing an

---

[77] ΣDThrax 356.11–12 and 518.17–32, on which see Schenkeveld 1990b, 297–8.

[78] Priscian. XI.1, 548,15–17 *appellatio reciproca*.

[79] Aristarchus uses eight classes (Ax 1991, 285), Dionysius of Halicarnassus nine (Schenkeveld 1983, 70–2).

[80] Frede 1978, 62–4; Sluiter 1990, 14. Differently e.g. Nuchelmans 1973, 70–1. Posidonius (Ap. Dysc. *Conj.* 214.4–20) challenges the view of σύνδεσμοι being non-signifying – see below, p. 209. [81] D.L. VII.71–3.

[82] Ap. Dysc. *Pron.* 5.13–19. Schenkeveld 1983, 74–6; di Benedetto 1990, 19–29.

[83] Frede 1974a, 51–67. [84] ΣDThrax 356.16–357.26 with allegedly Stoic arguments.

[85] The relationship between Stoic 'categories' and parts of speech is much debated. See Hülser 1987–8, 1008–9.

individual quality' e.g. Διογένης, Σωκράτης. The distinction is of value
in discussions about the truth-value of propositions and is related to the
use of deictic pronouns,[86] but it has little success in grammatical treatises.

Stoics distinguish at least four cases,[87] nominative (ὀρθή), genitive
(γενική), dative (δοτική) and accusative (αἰτιατική), and perhaps a fifth
case, the vocative (κλητική).[88] Whereas Aristotle takes the nominative as
the noun of which the other cases are πτώσεις,[89] to the Stoics the nominative, like Σωκράτης, 'falls' from the concept of Socrates in our mind
and is therefore a 'case'.[90] The various names of the cases are Stoic inven-
tions and become traditional.[91]

The definition of the conjunction as 'a part of speech without cases
which joins the parts of the *logos*' covers both our conjunction and our
preposition. For 'the parts of the *logos*' are not only individual words or
parts of a sentence bound together by prepositions or conjunctions but
also parts of the *logos* as an argument consisting of a complex of phrases.[92]
Prepositions are called prepositive conjunctions and the conjunctions
proper just σύνδεσμοι. Later the status of prepositions as a word class of
their own (προθέσεις) becomes secure.[93] The conjunctions[94] are classified according to their semantic value in non-simple propositions. Thus
the Stoics call εἰ ('if') a σύνδεσμος συναπτικός because it functions as a
conjunction of implication in the ἀξίωμα συνημμένον by announcing
that its second part follows consequentially upon the first part. Further
types are 'subconditional' (ἐπεί, 'since'), 'conjunctive' (καί, 'and'), 'disjunctive' (ἤτοι ... ἤ, 'either ... or'), 'causal' (διότι 'because'),[95] and 'indicating "more" or "less"' (μᾶλλον, ἧττον).[96]

*

The Stoic treatment of the verb is highly original.[97] Diogenes' definition ῥῆμα is 'a part of speech signifying a non-combined κατηγόρημα'.
This and his alternative one, 'an undeclined part of speech, signifying

---

[86] S.E. *M* VIII.96–8; D.L. VII.68–70.   [87] E.g. Ammon. *Int.* 42.30–43.24.
[88] The content of Chrysippus' *On the five cases* (D.L. VII.192) is unknown.
[89] He uses πτῶσις in other contexts for e.g. adverbs derived from adjectives.
[90] Ammon. *Int.* 42.30–43.24.
[91] The reason for the name αἰτιατική (*accusativus*) is problematic.   [92] D.L. VII.76.
[93] Ap. Dysc. *Synt.* 436.13–437.2 and *Conj.* 214.8–9 but D.H. *Comp.* 102.16–17 is still troubled by
the status of ἐπί (a conjunction or a preposition?).   [94] Compare above, p. 188.
[95] This type may have included final conjunctions; see Sluiter 1990, 154–5.
[96] D.L. VII.71–3. Ap. Dysc. *Conj.* 251.27–252.6 and 250.12–19 also mentions 'inferential' (ἄρα) and
'assumptive' (δέ γε) as conjunctions. From D.L. VII.67 and S.E. *M* VIII.70–4 one may perhaps
infer a distinction of expletive conjunctions. For the use of this theory of conjunctions in other
parts of Stoic philosophy see Brunschwig 1978b, 62–9 and Sluiter 1988, 59–62.
[97] Cf. Hülser 1987–8, 932–1007, with discussion of the various, often contradictory traditions.
Müller 1943 still is fundamental, followed by Pinborg 1975, 85–95.

something which can be attached to one or more things' have no reference to time, which to Aristotle distinguishes ῥῆμα from ὄνομα.[98] The
reason for this omission may be that the early Stoic ῥῆμα includes
adverbs.

Two texts which discuss different types of predicate suggest or imply
distinctions at the linguistic level.[99] Predicates are divided into 'upright,
active' (ὀρθόν), 'supine' or 'passive' (ὕπτιον)[100] and 'neuter'
(οὐδέτερον). This distinction is linked to that between active and passive
dispositions (διάθεσις) whereas in the case of 'neuter predicates' the verb
shows pure activity or passivity (ποίησις or πεῖσις καθαρά). These
semantic distinctions are made without attention to the form of the verb.
Because of their interest in morphology grammarians later introduce a
different ordering and call, for example, περιπατεῖ ('he walks') an 'active
verb'.

The Stoics probably discern several moods of the verb,[101] called
διάθεσις or ἔγκλισις. The indicative, optative, imperative and moods of
question, oath and suggestion are distinguished whereas neither infinitive nor subjunctive are yet seen as separate moods.[102] Originally treated
as concomitants of verbs, adverbs,[103] especially modal ones, seem to be
exploited in order to distinguish between moods of question, whereas
adverbs like μά or νή are thought to announce an oath. The various *lekta*
are connected with dispositions of the soul.[104] No text, however, states
that the production of a *lekton* results from an inclination of the soul
(ἔγκλισις ψυχῆς), a statement which would give a definite link with a
Stoic theory of moods.

Their theory of tenses (χρόνοι), a hot item in modern scholarship,[105]
has the following terms:[106]

ἐνεστώς* παρατατικός (extending present)	– present
ἐνεστώς συντελικός (completed present)	– perfect

---

[98] *Int.* 16b6.   [99] Porph. *apud* Ammon. *Int.* 44.11–45.9; D.L. vii.64 – below, p. 245.
[100] Within the class of ὕπτια the reflexive predicates have a status of their own and are called
ἀντιπεπονθότα, e.g. κείρεται, 'he cuts his hair off', because the agent includes himself in the
sphere of the action (D.L. vii.64). Probably, this predicate is interpreted as κείρεται ὑφ'
ἑαυτοῦ. Thus Müller 1943, 57.   [101] Texts in *FDS* 909–13. See Schenkeveld 1984, 333–51.
[102] D.L. vii.65–8 and Ap. Dysc. *Synt.* 43.15–18.
[103] This follows from the criticism by Stoics of Zeno's definition of the τέλος as τό
ὁμολογουμένως ζῆν without τῇ   φύσει. They call this definition an ἐλάττον ἤ
κατηγόρημα (Stob. ii.75.11–76.8). The missing πτῶσις πλάγια is governed by the adverbial
part of the κατηγόρημα.   [104] S.E. *M* viii.397; Theon *Prog.* 62.13–20 and Sen. *Ep.* 117.3.
[105] Texts in *FDS* 807–26. A survey of interpretations in Berretoni 1989, 33–8.
[106] The examples, if present, all concern indicatives, not other moods. – Traditional theory
keeps the words marked by *; for perfect and pluperfect it uses παρακείμενος and
ὑπερσυντέλικος.

παρῳχημένος παρατατικός* (extending past)	~ imperfect
παρῳχημένος συντελικός (completed past)	~ pluperfect
ἀόριστος* (undefined)	~ aorist
μέλλων* (future)	~ future

From this list with its oppositional pairs it has been inferred that the Stoics apply a tense system to one based on the notion of 'aspect'[107] or *vice versa*. However, there is no indication that next to tense the Stoics distinguish a separate category of aspect. To the Stoics time is an incorporeal continuum which can be infinitely divided. For this reason no time is wholly present inasmuch as the present consists of a part of the past and a part of the future. Past and future are parts of time and stretch out infinitely on one side but are limited by the present, which acts as a kind of joining.[108] Like Aristotle,[109] the Stoics start their division from the moment of speaking, the present,[110] and use temporal adverbs to define the relations of times, and thus of tenses, to the present time. Thus, the present tells that some action, started in the past, will continue; the imperfect that a small part has yet to be achieved.[111] The aorist, with its past sense, is made more precise by the addition of ἄρτι ('just/just now') and so becomes a perfect; the addition of πάλαι ('once') makes it a pluperfect.[112] But the perfect is not a past tense notwithstanding close links with the past,[113] for it tells about something present which has been achieved a short time ago. In all, the Stoics use only one category, χρόνος, and define tenses both in terms of the location of processes in time and in terms which structure time seen as completed or extending.[114] The latter opposition concerns both the time of an action and its progress, both of which are related to motion.

The Stoics may have led grammarians in organizing categories of mood, voice and tense – as well as gender, number and case of the *nomina* –

---

[107] Often also called *Aktionsart*, confusingly. Pohlenz 1939, 177–8 thinks of influence of the Semitic aspectual system on the analysis of the Greek verb since the early Stoics came from a Semitic milieu. Though often repeated this view is wrong, see Versteegh 1980, 349.

[108] Cf. Long and Sedley 1987, vol. I, 304–8.   [109] *Phys.* IV.10–14, esp. 13.

[110] S.E. *M* VIII.254–6.

[111] ΣDThrax 250.26–21.25; Choerob. *Can.* 11.23–13.17; Priscian. VIII.38–40 and 51–6; these texts probably go back to a work of Ap. Dysc. – See Berretoni 1989, 60 for a graphic representation of the tenses put on a continuous line.

[112] To Aristotle, *Phys.* 222a24–6, πότε ('once') indicates a time defined (ὡρισμένος) in relation to 'the now' because it is separated from it by a certain time; his examples contain an aorist and a future tense. Perhaps the Stoic term ἀόριστος contains a criticism of Aristotle. In our sources aorist and future are closely coupled.

[113] See the discussion in S.E. *M* VIII.254 of expressions with perfect tenses referring to the past.

[114] Cf. S.E. *M* x.85–100 on ἀξιώματα συντελεστικά and παρατατικά. See Berretoni 1989, 60–3.

by means of *accidentia*, 'constant attributes'. This Latin term is a translation of συμβεβηκότα and in texts on the Stoic theory of causes and effects
this word means necessary or constant consequence.[115] But it is not
found in grammatical texts as a technical term for constant attributes of
verb or noun.[116] The traditional Greek name is παρεπόμενα, a word
known from Aristotelian works in the sense of necessary consequence,
and it may well be that Stoics, too, used this term.[117]

The Stoic system is continued by grammarians although not without
changes. It is the first conscious effort to structure the description of the
Greek verb, it is original in many respects and at times looks naive.[118] But
it shaped Latin grammar and consequently those of modern languages.

*

The contribution of Hellenistic scholars to the development of Greek
grammar is difficult to ascertain because the tradition is fragmentary and
first and foremost because their task is conceived as of explaining literary
texts, especially poetry, not writing a grammar. The first to write such a
treatise is Aristarchus' pupil Dionysius Thrax but what we have under the
name of *Technē* is, apart from the first five sections, not by him.[119] He
defines γραμματική as 'the practical study of the normal usage of poets
and prose writers' and divides it into six parts, out of which the fifth one,
'a detailed account of regular patterns' would come close to what we call
grammar. The parts are in an ascending order, the final being 'a critical
assessment of poems', which is called 'the noblest part of all that the art
includes'.[120] Dionysius' forerunners, too, give thought to grammatical
matters in their explanations of Homer and other poets but not in a
systematic way. We can reconstruct, therefore, a set of rules being applied
in practice ('practical grammar'), rather than a formal grammar. Thus
Aristophanes of Byzantium has a knowledge of regular patterns in the
inflection of words, uses several technical terms and talks about the characteristics of the preposition. He also applies five different criteria (e.g.,
gender, case) to decide which is the correct form of a word but does not
prescribe a norm for the correct word.[121]

Aristarchus of Samothrace uses a system of eight parts of speech with

---

[115] Forschner 1981, 85–90.
[116] D.H. *Comp.* 132.7 and 135.4 = *Dem.* 242.20 uses τὰ συμβεβηκότα for *accidentia* in an unusually
       wide sense.   [117] Frede 1978, 67–8.
[118] E.g. in what is said about the difference between perfect and pluperfect tenses. Most scholars
       ascribe those statements to the grammarians, without much validity, however.
[119] Kemp 1991 with a survey of modern scholarship, and Schenkeveld 1995, 41–52.
[120] 'Critical assessment' (κρίσις) concerns the authenticity of texts (S.E. *M* 1.93), not their literary
       value.   [121] Ax 1991, 277–82.

their accidents and applies these and other notions to decide on syntactical differences (σχήματα) between Homeric usage and that of his own time. All this presupposes a highly developed apparatus to describe grammatical, and specifically morphological, phenomena. Aristarchus also deals with grammatical matters in their own right when defining pronouns as 'words ordered according to person' and calling the pronoun αὐτός 'subsidiary', because it is put after specific personal pronouns.[122] His pupil Dionysius Thrax shows Stoic influence by labelling several pronouns 'deictic articles' (see above), defining the verb as 'a word signifying a predicate' and separating the proper noun from the common noun.[123] His definition of γραμματική (see above) includes the term ἐμπειρία, 'practical study', against which designation later grammarians, like Asclepiades of Myrlea, protest because to them γραμματική is a τέχνη having a logical basis, not merely dependent on practical skill.[124] But Dionysius' term does not imply such a contrast.

Alongside these *artes* with their succinct presentation, longer treatises of a different character are mentioned; their general title is *On Hellenism* (i.e. correct Greek). The oldest ones apparently date from the first century BC and also from this time date their first Latin counterparts, *de sermone latino*. In these treatises matters of pronunciation, orthography, inflection and conjugation, usage of single words and syntax are discussed. Three factors guide the authors in their activities, analogy, common usage (συνήθεια) and literary tradition (*historia* or παράδοσις).[125] As we have seen, some of these subjects are also a matter of discussion among philosophers.

2: Meaning

Chrysippus described dialectic as the study of what signifies and of what is signified (D.L. VII.62): the concept of signification, or meaning, thus stands in the middle of his logical interests; and it will not surprise that semantic issues engaged Stoic attention.

> The Stoics say that three items are linked to one another: what is signified, what signifies, what obtains. What signifies is the utterance (φωνή), e.g. 'Dio'. What is signified is the object (πρᾶγμα) itself which is shown by the utterance and which we grasp when it subsists in our minds but which foreigners do not understand although they hear the utterance. What obtains (τὸ τύγχανον) is the external item, e.g. Dio himself. Of these items, two are bodies – viz. the utterance and what

---

[122] Ap. Dysc. *Pron.* 3.12–13; 62.16–17; *Synt.* 137.9–138.9. See Schenkeveld 1994, 275–8.
[123] Ap. Dysc. *Pron.* 5.13–19; ΣDThrax 160.24–161.8. In all these points the *Technē* ascribed to him differs. [124] S.E. *M* 1.57–90. See Calboli 1962, 162–9.
[125] Siebenborn 1976, 35 and ch. 4.

obtains – and one is incorporeal – namely the object signified or the say-able (λεκτόν) ... (S.E. *M* VIII.11–12)

The Stoics thus appear to offer a three-tiered account of meaning: utterances signify objects, which in turn stand in a certain relation to external items: the word 'Dio' signifies an incorporeal item, which Dio himself 'obtains'.

Aristotle had spoken of four tiers:

The items in the utterance are symbols of affections in the soul, and the written items are symbols of items in the utterance. Just as the written forms are not the same for all, so the utterances are not the same either. But the primary items of which these are signs – affections in the soul – are the same for all, and the objects of which these are likenesses are thereby the same. (*Int.* 16a3–8)

Three of Aristotle's tiers seem to match the Stoic tiers:[126] 'items in the utterance' correspond to the Stoic 'utterances'; 'affections in the soul', which the later tradition usually identified with thoughts,[127] answer to the Stoic 'objects'; and Aristotle's 'objects' match the items which in the Stoic account are said to 'obtain'.

Aristotle's pregnant remarks raised numerous questions for his follow-ers, among them the following two. First, why suppose that the 'interme-diate' items, the items between utterances and external things, are 'affections of the soul'? Here the Stoics were taken to be in disagreement with the Peripatetics; for they called their own 'intermediate' items λεκτά or 'sayables'. This first question will return after the Stoic view has been outlined. Secondly, why suppose that there are any 'intermediate' items at all? To this second question at least one early Peripatetic could find no answer,[128] and abandoned the Aristotelian view:

Epicurus and Strato the physicist allow only two items, what signifies and what obtains ... (S.E. *M* VIII.13)

Thus Strato apparently adopted a more parsimonious account. But we hear nothing more of Strato's semantic views, nor does any other Hellenistic Peripatetic seem to have interested himself in semantic issues.[129]

Sextus couples Strato with Epicurus – and here we are better informed.

*

---

[126] For the place of γράμματα in the Stoic account see e.g. D.L. VII.56.
[127] E.g. Ammon. *Int.* 17.22–6, 18.29–30; Boeth. *Int.*² 11.28–30 (from Alexander).
[128] A later answer in Alexander, *apud* Boeth. *Int.*² 40.30–41.11.
[129] Ammon. *Int.* 65.31–66.9, has been taken to show that Theophrastus too preferred parsimony (Bochenski 1947, 39–40; Graeser 1973, 60); but the text bears on a completely different topic: Gottschalk 1992.

Epicurus 'admits only two things'. Sextus' brief reference at *M* VIII.13 is repeated at *M* VIII.258 and echoed by a polemical passage in Plutarch:

> If these things subvert life, then who goes more wrong about language than you (i.e. you Epicureans), who do away entirely with the class of sayables (λεκτά), which gives substance to language, admitting only utterances (φωναί) and what obtains (τυγχάνοντα) and saying that the intermediate objects which are signified – through which learning and teaching and preconception and thought and impulse and assent come about – do not exist at all? (Plu. *Col.* 1119f)

It is not clear how much theory lay behind these jejune reports;[130] but Epicurus' view on meaning, developed or undeveloped, explicit or implicit, seems to have made do with only two sorts of item, words and things.

So much the better. For, very roughly speaking, you know what the word 'cow' means if you know that 'cow' is true of an object just in case that object is a cow (or just in case that object is an animal of such-and-such a shape).[131] In general, and still very roughly, you know what a declarative sentence, S, means when you know that S is true if and only if P; you know what a predicative expression, 'F( )', means when you know that 'F( )' is true of x if and only if Gx; and so on. An account of meaning developed along these lines will not invoke any 'intermediate' items.

Yet there are other texts which suggest that Epicurus held a modified version of the Peripatetic theory, and the chief text comes from the pen of Epicurus himself:

> First, then, Herodotus, we must grasp the items which are collected under the sounds (τὰ ὑποτεταγμένα τοῖς φθόγγοις), so that we may refer what is believed or investigated or puzzled over to them and may thus come to a judgement, lest everything be unjudged (if we offer proofs *ad infinitum*) or else we make empty sounds. For it is necessary that the primary concept (τὸ πρῶτον ἐννόημα) should be looked at in connection with each sound and should need no proof, if we are to have something to which to refer what is investigated or puzzled over and believed. (*Ep. Hdt.* 37)

Presumably 'the items which are collected under the sounds' are the meanings of the sounds; and since these items are then identified with 'primary concepts', Epicurus is saying that meaningful sounds mean concepts.

This text is supported by a parallel passage in Diogenes Laertius (x.33,

---

[130] 'There really is no such thing as Epicurean semantics': Glidden 1983b, 204.
[131] See S.E. *PH* II.25 and *M* VII.267 for the Epicurean definition of man.

where 'preconceptions' replace primary concepts); and the claim that
there can be no investigation and no inquiry without preconceptions is
ascribed to the Epicureans in several further texts.[132] Thus it seems that
the Epicureans did postulate 'intermediate' items between words and
things: where the Peripatetics placed affections of the soul, there the
Epicureans located concepts or preconceptions.[133]

But is the *Letter* really inconsistent with the reports in Sextus and
Plutarch?[134] We may usefully distinguish two questions. (1) What does
the word 'cow' mean? Or in general, what does a linguistic item L mean?
One answer might be: 'The word "cow" signifies an animal of such-and-
such a sort; and in general, L signifies some sort of thing.' (2) When I utter
the sentence 'That's a cow', how is it that I may thereby say that that is a
cow? Or in general, how, by uttering L can I thereby say something about
objects of a particular type? One (partial) answer is roughly this: 'In uttering "That's a cow" I say that that is a cow only if I have a true preconception of what a cow is, that is, only if I truly believe that cows are animals of
such-and-such a sort.' The two questions are linked; but they are not the
same question and they do not admit the same answer. The idea which
Sextus and Plutarch report is an appropriate answer to question (1). To
which question does the passage from the *Letter* address itself?

The passage is primarily concerned with epistemological problems,
and it makes (*inter alia*) two connected points. First: if you are to investigate or puzzle over anything – more generally, if you are to believe or talk
about anything – then you must have a concept of the thing in question.
This point is simple and true: if I am to wonder whether, say, the thing
over there is a cow, then I must know what a cow is; for if I have no idea of
what a cow is, no conception of a cow, then I cannot think (and I cannot
say) anything at all about cows.[135] The second point is that these concepts
must be 'primary' or 'evident'; that is to say, they must not stand in need
of 'proof'. This suggests that concepts should be construed as *propositional*
items: my concept of a cow is, or is expressed by, a proposition such as 'A

---

[132] S.E. *M* 1.57; VIII.331a; XI.21; Cic. *ND* 1.43; Clem. *Strom.* I 14.16; Plu. fr. 215f. Note also Phld. *Ir.*
XLV.1–6: the word θυμός has two senses – and it is sometimes to be taken 'in accordance with
this πρόληψις', sometimes in accordance with that. Here it would be easy to translate
πρόληψις as 'meaning'.

[133] So e.g. Long 1971d, 120–2; Sedley 1973, 20–1; Long and Sedley 1987, I.101 (further references
in Glidden 1983b, 186 n. 8). The view is summarized thus: 'πρόληψις is some sort of mental
entity to which words refer' (Long 1971d, 131 n. 33).

[134] For a developed account of the following sketch see Barnes 1996c; an alternative account in
Everson 1994b.

[135] This point is closely connected with 'Meno's paradox', and it was perhaps so connected by
Epicurus himself; at all events, Plu. fr. 215f cites the point as the Epicurean answer to the paradox.

cow is an animal of *that* shape.'¹³⁶ The suggestion is confirmed by two fragments of Book XXVIII of Epicurus *On Nature*: there the verb 'collect under' (ὑποτάττειν) reappears in a context which is clearly concerned with words and utterances, and in one of the two passages it is explicitly stated that what is 'collected under' an utterance is a belief.¹³⁷

If I am to investigate cows, or even to say that the animal over there is a cow, then I must have a preconception of a cow; and this preconception must be primary in the sense that it does not itself presuppose some further belief (a prepreconception, as it were). If there were no primary preconceptions, then there would be a regressive infinity of beliefs: an investigation requires a preconception, a preconception requires a prepreconception ... If there were no preconceptions at all, my words would be 'empty' and I would not be engaged in any investigation.

All of this bears directly on question (2); none of it bears directly on question (1) and it is not evident that it implies, indirectly, any answer to question (1). If this is so, then we may accept the evidence of Sextus and Plutarch: the Epicureans saw no need to posit any intermediate semantic items.

*

The Stoics thought more about meaning than the Peripatetics or the Epicureans cared to do; and certain texts, among them the passage in Sextus, *M* VIII.11-12, with which this section began, insinuate a rich and subtle semantic theory. But it is best to proceed modestly.¹³⁸

First, then, the Stoics distinguished between what is uttered and what is said:

> Saying and uttering are different; for what we utter are utterances (φωναί), whereas what we say are objects (πράγματα), which in fact are sayables (λεκτά).¹³⁹

Secondly, they distinguished between what is said and what is spoken about:¹⁴⁰ you may speak about Chrysippus, but you cannot say Chrysippus.

---

¹³⁶ So e.g. Striker 1974, 71–2.
¹³⁷ *PHerc.* 1479/1417, fr. 6 col. 1 5–13, at line 13; see also fr. 13 col. VI inf. 2-col VII sup. 5 (text from Sedley 1973).
¹³⁸ The issue is difficult and contested; for recent accounts see Schubert 1994, and Frede 1994. A view different from the one developed in this section is preferred below, pp. 400–2.
¹³⁹ D.L. VII.57 (the force of the last clause – ἃ δὴ καὶ λεκτὰ τυγχάνει – is obscure). Certain grammarians later used the word λεκτόν as a synonym for λέξις (S.E. *M* 1.76–8), and this usage may perhaps explain how some authorities were capable of identifying Stoic λεκτά with φωναί (e.g. Phlp. *APr.* 243.4; [Ammon.] *APr.* 68.6).
¹⁴⁰ *plurimum interest utrum illud dicas an de illo*: Sen. *Ep.* 117.13.

Chrysippus is not an 'object'; for objects lie 'between' words and the world.[141]

The Stoics called these objects λεκτά: the word was used by Chrysippus, and by Cleanthes before him;[142] but it was not a Stoic neologism. It occurs several times in fifth-century drama: there, something is λεκτόν (for someone) if it can be said or is the sort of thing to be said (by him);[143] and the word did not change its sense when the neuter adjective hardened into a noun – a λεκτόν is a 'sayable'.[144]

Sayables are, among other things, meanings.[145] Suppose, then, that you utter the Greek sentence 'Δίων περιπατεῖ': then what (if anything) that sentence means is fixed by what (if anything) you can say in uttering it. More precisely, the sentence 'Δίων περιπατεῖ' means that Dio is walking if and only if in uttering 'Δίων περιπατεῖ' you can thereby say that Dio is walking. In general:

S means that P if and only if in uttering S x can thereby say that P.

This abstract schema may serve to introduce the notion of the sayable into an account of meaning. But it only fits assertoric sentences: meanings and hence, presumably, sayables must also be associated with *non-assertoric* sentences, and with *sub-sentential components* of sentences.

The Stoics speak of sayables in connexion with non-assertoric utterances. Thus

they call certain sayables imperatival, namely those saying which we give a command (e.g.: Come hither, dear wife). (S.E. *M* VIII.71)

In uttering the sentence 'Come hither, dear wife', I thereby say something, and in saying it I give a command. But what sayable do I say? The question causes anglophones a minor embarrassment; for we standardly report what someone says by saying 'He said that . . .', and sentences of this form can only report *assertoric* sayings. A paratactic analysis will spare the blushes. The analysis invites us to rewrite 'He said that Dio was walking' as:

Dio is walking.
He said that.

---

[141] For the metaphor see e.g. Plu. *Col.* 1119f; Ammon. *Int.* 17.25–8. For the word πρᾶγμα see e.g. Nuchelmans 1973, 47–9; P. Hadot 1980.

[142] For Chrysippus see e.g. *Logika Zētēmata*, *PHerc.* 307, VIII.16; XI.23; for Cleanthes, see Clem. *Strom.* VIII.9.26.4.   [143] E.g. S. *Phil.* 633; E. *Hipp.* 875; Ar. *Av.* 422; Pherecrates fr. 157.

[144] 'Sayable' is vile; but English has nothing decent to offer.

[145] For their other employments see below, pp. 400–1. Note that some grammarians later used the word λεκτόν in the sense of 'meaning': e.g. Ap. Dysc. *Pron.* 59.1–6; *Adv.* 136.32.

– where the demonstrative pronoun 'that' may be taken to refer to what is said by the first sentence. In general, the analysis offers us the formula:

P.
He said that.

The formula is not a barbarism ('He's as honest as the day – that's what they said before he became a politician'); and non-assertoric sentences may be substituted for 'P' ('Forget all about her – that's what he said'). Thus we may report the sayable said in uttering the imperatival sentence as follows:

Come hither, dear wife.
He said that.

This indeed is more or less what the ancient texts do.

The abstract meaning schema can now be adapted; and we might choose to express the general idea thus: To know what a sentence S means is to know something of the following sort:

P.
In uttering S x can say that.

And here *any* sentence may be substituted for 'P'.

Different sentences express different kinds of sayables, and these kinds are catalogued in several sources. No catalogue contains more than eleven items, but in all some fifteen or sixteen items are mentioned.[146] The classification depended on the different kinds of thing which a speaker may do in saying a sayable, rather than (say) on any grammatical features of the sentences used to express the sayables.[147] Thus imperatival sayables are 'those saying which we give a command'; and in general, different replacements for 'φ' in the schema

P.
In saying that, x φ's.

---

[146] Ammon. *APr.* 2.5 (cf. 26.33), *Int.* 2.28, implies that the Stoics had a canonical list of ten items, five of which he identifies with the five sorts of λόγοι which the later Peripatetics recognized. Lists explicitly attributed to the Stoics: S.E. *M* VIII.72–5; D.L. VII.65–8; Ammon. *Int.* 2.9–3.6; Anon. *Proleg. Hermog. Stat.* 186.17–188.5; ΣArist. 93b20–36. (These lists differ in important respects, and there are also trifling differences in terminology and choice of example.) See also: Suda *s.v.* ἀξίωμα (an abbreviated version of D.L.); ΣAphthon. 11.661.25–662.26 (deriving from Anon. *Proleg.*). Similar lists, without reference to the Stoics: Phil. *Congr.* 148; *Agr.* 140; D.H. *Comp.* 8 (32.7–13); Theon *Prog.* 62.10–21, 87.13–90.17. Note also D.L. VII.63 (with Suda *s.v.* κατηγόρημα); Simp. *Cat.* 406.20–8. On the issues raised by the list see esp. Schenkeveld 1984; cf. Pachet 1978; Hülser 1987–8, 1114–17.

[147] D.H. *Comp.* 8 (32.7–13) says that 'we give our expressions a form appropriate to the different things we do in uttering them'; but he does not ascribe this thought to the Stoics.

will determine different kinds of sayables.[148] In this formula, 'φ' may presumably be replaced by any verb which denotes a 'speech-act', so that there will be as many kinds of sayable as there are speech-acts. But there are indefinitely many kinds of speech-act and indefinitely many possible replacements for 'φ'. Philosophical (and perhaps also rhetorical) interests will have determined which kinds of sayable came to be mentioned.

The surviving lists of sayables no doubt derive from handbooks (cf. Philo *Agr.* 140); but we know that Chrysippus discussed some of the sayables they catalogue,[149] and it is plausible to suppose that the handbooks draw ultimately on Chrysippus.

Diogenes Laertius mentions ten items in all, offering first an unadorned list and then a descriptive catalogue. The catalogue begins with (1) ἀξιώματα or assertibles, items 'saying which we make assertions, and which are either true or false'. Note that ἀξιώματα are not assertions: the sentence 'If Dio is walking, there is grain in the market' makes *one* assertion but it contains three ἀξιώματα; for the antecedent and the consequent of the conditional are each ἀξιώματα.[150] Then come (2) questions and (3) inquiries: questions demand 'Yes' or 'No' in reply, inquiries demand something discursive. Next, (4): 'an imperatival is an object saying which we command, e.g.: You, go to the streams of Inachus'. Then (5) oaths; and (6) invocations – an invocation is 'an object such that were one to say it, one would be making an invocation; e.g.: Great son of Atreus, Agamemnon, King of Men'. (7) 'Like an assertible is an object which, while having assertible expression, falls outside the class of assertibles because it is filled out by a further item or because of an alteration (πάθος); e.g.: The Parthenon is indeed beautiful; how like the sons of Priam is the shepherd.' Both these examples contain an additional particle: 'indeed (γε)' or 'how (ἄρα)'. It is not clear what 'alterations' might be pertinent.[151] The discursive catalogue ends with (8) puzzlements, which are items like questions ('Are pain and life related?') but which do not demand an answer.

Diogenes' list omits (8) but contains two items not in the catalogue:[152] (9) curses (Sextus' illustration: 'May his brains flow on the ground as the

[148] S.E. *M* VIII.71–3 uses the formula 'λεκτά of such-and-such a sort are those saying which we do so-and-so' for four of the seven types he lists; D.L. VII.66–8 uses virtually the same formula for four of his ten items.

[149] In addition to the texts discussed below note the titles in D.L. VIII.191: Περὶ προσταγμάτων (2 books), Περὶ ἐρωτήσεως (2 books), Περὶ πεύσεως (4 books).

[150] On ἀξιώματα see above, pp. 93–103.

[151] Or does 'πάθος' here mean 'emotional tone'? (So Atherton 1993, 357.) S.E. gives D.L.'s second example and says that it is 'more than an assertible': if this is his name for this class of sayable (cf. Theon *Prog.* 87.14), then presumably 'altered' assertibles were not included in it.

[152] The text of D.L. VII.66–8 is certainly corrupt in places; and it is likely that the list and the catalogue originally coincided.

wine flows from this goblet'), and (10) hypotheses or suppositions (Ammonius' illustration: 'Suppose that the earth is the centre of the sun's sphere'). To these ten items we may properly add (11) prayers, which appear in Sextus (and also in Philo). Some would subjoin (12) expositions ('Let this be a straight line'); but it is perhaps a later supplement.[153]

The Stoics were not the first philosophers to observe that there are differences among assertibles and imperativals and questions and the rest; but their analysis of these sayables was original – and unlike Aristotle, who had relegated to rhetoric or poetics the study of any items which are neither true nor false,[154] they regarded all these things as falling within the province of logic. How they treated them may be illustrated by two texts.

The first concerns oaths.[155] In the course of an argument, the details of which may be ignored, Chrysippus urged that:

> Swearers must either swear truly or swear falsely at the time at which they swear; for what they swear is either true or false, since it is in fact an assertible.

Suppose that Porsenna swears an oath by uttering the sentence 'By the nine gods, I shall not let them pass.' What he *says* is:

> By the nine gods, I shall not let them pass.

What he *swears* is:

> I shall not let them pass.

And this is an assertible (although Porsenna does not assert it), and hence it is either true or false. (In the same way, if you say:

> Do not steal,

you thereby forbid, and also order; but you do not forbid or order what you say, nor do you forbid what you order.)[156]

There are obscurities here; but it is plain that Chrysippus had reflected on the relations among sayables of different types: in particular, an oath is not an assertible, and yet it may 'contain' an assertible. The phrase 'contained assertible' is found in the *Logical Investigations*,[157] and

---

[153] Only in Ammon. and ΣArist. (Egli's addition of <καὶ ἐκθετικόν> to the list in D.L. is gratuitous). It is true that Chrysippus wrote Περὶ ὑποθέσεων and *also* Περὶ ἐκθέσεων (D.L. VII.196) – but these works are not listed in the τόπος περὶ τὰ πράγματα and probably have nothing to do with types of λεκτά.

[154] See *Int.* 16b33–17a7. The first attempts to distinguish among items of this sort were made by Protagoras and Alcidamas: D.L. IX.53–4 (cf. Arist. *Poet.* 1456b15–17).

[155] Stob. *Ecl.* 1.28.17–19; cf. J. D. G. Evans 1974. Note that (in this text at least) oaths are taken to refer to the future, i.e. to be solemn promises. [156] See Plu. *Stoic. Rep.* 1037de.

[157] x 9–10: περιειλημμένα ἀξιώ{ματα (oaths are in the offing: note]ομν[in line 8).

it is reasonable to suppose that Chrysippus had said more on the matter than our brief text preserves.

The *Logical Investigations* supply a second illustration. In columns XI–XIII of the papyrus, Chrysippus is discussing some puzzles raised by imperatives, one of which is indicated in these words:

> ... such cases too, e.g.
> Walk – otherwise sit down.
> For everything falls under the command; but it is not possible to take any predicable in its place – for no object is signified by such a thing as He is walking – otherwise sitting down.[158]

The problem is this. The sentence 'Walk – otherwise sit down' appears to express a command, and a *single* command. ('Everything falls under the command.') Now in general if a sentence 'φ*a*!' expresses a command addressed to *a*, then to the verb or verbal phrase 'φ( )' there must correspond a predicable; and if this predicable is expressed by the verbal phrase 'φ*( )', then the sentence 'φ*δ' (where 'δ' is a demonstrative pronoun) must express an 'object' and in particular an assertible. But in the case before us 'no object is signified by such a thing'.

Chrysippus eventually concludes that 'it is plausible that there *is* a predicable of the sort *to be walking – otherwise sitting down*' (XIII.19–22): there *is* an object signified by 'φ*( )', and the command is after all unproblematical. But the interesting point is not the conclusion nor even the puzzle itself; rather, it is the fact that Chrysippus' discussion was based on two semantic principles. The first principle, that to every imperatival sentence 'φ*a*!' there must correspond a predicable 'φ*( )', rests on the thought that every command is a command *to do something*, to ψ.[159] The second principle, that if 'φ*( )' expresses a predicable, then 'φ*δ' expresses an assertible, connects predicables to a particular sort of assertible. Thus commands and assertibles, two different types of sayable, are linked. The link is made by the predicable and with predicables we pass from the sentential to the subsentential level.

*

There were sayables connected with subsentential items:

> Of sayables, the Stoics say that some are self-complete (αὐτοτελῆ), others deficient (ἐλλιπῆ). Deficient are those which have an unfinished

---

[158] XII.12–19. At 15–17 I read: ... 'κατηγόρημ[α δὲ] μεταλαβεῖν οὐθ[ὲν] ἔστιν ...' Otherwise I follow the text in Hülser 1987–8, 826. For discussion see Barnes 1986b.

[159] The next puzzle to which Chrysippus turns (μετὰ δὲ ταῦτα: XIII.24) relies on the same principle (XIII.24–9).

expression, e.g.: 'writes' (γράφει) – for we go on to ask: Who? Self-complete are those which have a finished expression, e.g.: Socrates writes. (D.L. VII.63)[160]

Sayables are thus classified by appeal to the linguistic items which express them, so that a sayable is self-complete if and only if it is expressible by a finished expression.[161] But when is an expression 'finished'? The answer in the text is unsatisfactory. Having heard 'I write' (γράφω), I will not ask: Who?, and having heard 'Socrates writes', I may well ask: What? or To whom? – yet the former expression is unfinished, the latter finished.[162] Perhaps the best we can do is take the notion of a finished expression (a sentence) as primitive: a sayable is self-complete if and only if it is expressible by a sentence.

Deficient sayables are genuinely sayable (the adjective 'deficient' is not alienating), even if they were perhaps regarded as potentially 'parts' of self-complete sayables (S.E. M VIII.83), which are themselves sometimes called compound or complex.[163] Although several texts imply that there were different types of deficient sayables, no text offers a list. But it is clear that predicables, κατηγορήματα, were deficient sayables *par excellence*: there were monographs on them by Sphaerus (D.L. VII.178), Cleanthes (D.L. VII.175), Chrysippus (at least four works, one in ten books: D.L. VII.191).

Diogenes Laertius offers three distinct accounts of what a predicable is:

A predicable is (1) what is remarked of something, or (2) an object put together about some thing or some things, as Apollodorus says, or (3) a deficient sayable put together with a nominative case to generate an assertible. (D.L. VII.64)

The definitions are successively more specific; but it would be rash to infer that they are also chronologically successive. They all agree that a predicable is a sayable – an 'object (πρᾶγμα)' or something 'remarked'. In the sentence 'Socrates writes', the verb 'writes' is not itself a predicable;[164] rather, the verb expresses or signifies a predicable.[165]

---

[160] Cf. e.g. S.E. M VIII.12, 70; Phil. Agr. 140 (τέλειος/ ἀτελής). The Peripatetics and the grammarians make a similar distinction: see Nuchelmans 1973, 90–7.

[161] See ΣDThrax 514.35–515.5, 536.1–4, for the idea that parts of speech combine to 'finish' a λόγος (a view which is ascribed to 'the philosophers'). Note that the Suda, s.v. κατηγόρημα, refers to a finished *thought* (διάνοια) rather than a finished expression (cf. Varro, *apud* Gell. XVI.8.6–8; Apul. *Int.* 190.3; and e.g. Ap. Dysc. *Synt.* III.155; S.E. *PH* II.176).

[162] 'γράφω' is classified as a verb, i.e. an unfinished expression: D.L. VII.58; Suda s.v. ῥῆμα. Presumably the Stoics took it as elliptical for 'ἐγὼ γράφω'.

[163] E.g. S.E. *PH* II.108–9; M VIII.79–84; cf. the definition of 'predicable' at D.L. VII.64, cited below.

[164] The Stoics often used the infinitive form of the verb to name the predicable: see Chrysippus *Logika Zētēmata*, PHerc. 307; S.E. *PH* III.14; M IX.211; Cic. *Tusc.* IV.9.21; Sen. *Ep.* 117.3, 12. Note the infinitive in the text ascribed to Zeno at Stob. *Ecl.* I.13.1c.

[165] See the definitions of the verb, ῥῆμα, at D.L. VII.58 (with Suda s.v. ῥῆμα): see above, pp. 189–90. The second definition clearly matches the Apollodoran account of predicables.

A predicable is a deficient sayable inasmuch as it cannot be said *simpliciter*; it is a sayable inasmuch as it can be *said of* something or other. The meaning of a verb or verbal phrase is fixed by what, in uttering it, you can say of something: you understand what a verb or verbal phrase, V, means if and only if you know that anyone who utters a sentence which couples V and a name can thereby say of something that it is so-and-so. (You know the meaning of '. . . pontificates' if you know that anyone who utters a sentence of the form 'x pontificates' may thereby say of something that it pontificates.)

Definition (3) refers explicitly to assertibles; but predicables are also contained in other types of self-complete sayable. Should we suppose different predicables for different self-complete sayables? (Does the verb in 'Is Socrates writing?' signify an interrogative predicable, distinct from but no doubt closely related to the predicable signified by the verb in 'Socrates writes'?) The fragments of the *Logical Investigations* show that, for Chrysippus, one and the same predicable may feature in different sorts of self-complete sayable. And definition (3) indirectly supports this notion: a predicable is something which will make an *assertible* if put together with the right items (although it will of course generate other sayables in other surroundings).

Definition (3) also invokes a 'nominative case'. Why only the nominative? and why, indeed, a case, in the singular? The definition restricts predicables to the meanings of verbs which produce a sentence when they are concatenated with a single noun in the nominative case; and it ignores one-place verbs which take an oblique case, and many-placed verbs. Definitions (1) and (2) are not thus restrictive. According to definition (2), a predicable is 'put together about some thing or some things':[166] the plural disjunct, 'or some things', is presumably meant to add something. Now verbs take plural as well as singular subjects, and perhaps the definition intends to make it clear that predicables may be said of a plurality of items as well as of a single item.[167] But perhaps the plural was intended to meet the needs of many-placed verbs.

However that may be, the Stoics were aware of such items. Porphyry outlines what he calls 'the Stoic classification of the terms predicated in propositions'.

---

[166] Cf. Cic. *Tusc.* IV.9.21: . . . *earum rerum* (= πραγμάτων?) *quae dicuntur de quodam aut quibusdam, quae* κατηγορήματα *dialectici appellant* . . .

[167] Note that Chrysippus wrote about singular and plural expressions: D.L. VII.192; and self-complete λεκτά will presumably be either singular or plural (see e.g. S.E. *M* x.99). Chrysippus' *Logika Zētēmata*, *PHerc.* 307, refers more than once to singular and plural *predicables* (fr. 1.5–7; 1.15–20; II.21–6): see Marrone 1984.

What is predicated is predicated either of a name or of a case; and either
it is complete as predicated and self-sufficient, together with the subject,
for the generation of an assertion, or else it is deficient and needs some
addition in order to make a complete predicate. Now if it makes an assertion when predicated of a name, they call it a predicable or a concomitant
(σύμβαμα) (both words mean the same): thus 'walks' – e.g. 'Socrates
walks'. If when predicated of a case, they call it a quasi-concomitant, as
though it resembles a concomitant and is as it were a quasi-predicable:
thus 'it rues' (μεταμέλει) – e.g. 'it rues Socrates' (Σωκράτει μεταμέλει).
Again, if what is predicated of a name requires the addition of a case of
some name in order to make an assertion, it is said to be less than a predicable: thus 'loves', 'favours' – e.g. 'Plato loves' (when Dio is added to this
it makes a definite assertion, 'Plato loves Dio'). If what is predicated of a
case needs to be put together with another oblique case to make an assertion, it is said to be less than a quasi-concomitant: thus μέλει ('there is
care') e.g. Σωκράτει 'Αλκιβιάδους μέλει ('to Socrates there is care for
Alcibiades', i.e. 'Socrates cares for Alcibiades'). (Ammon. Int. 44.19–45.6)

The passage is contaminated with Peripatetic terminology, but its Stoic
credentials are not to be denied.[168]

Two intersecting distinctions are made, from which four types of deficient sayable emerge. Among (Greek) verbs, some take a noun in the nominative as their subject, while others take a noun in an oblique case. (The
Greek for 'Socrates changes his mind' is Σωκράτει μεταμέλει, where
μεταμέλει is impersonal and Σωκράτει is in the dative.) Call sayables signified by the former sort of verb *direct predicables*, those by the latter
oblique predicables. Again, some verbs make a sentence when attached to a
single noun, others require something more ('walks' needs one noun,
'loves' two). Call sayables signified by the former sort of verb *complete
predicables*, those signified by the latter *deficient predicables*. Then the
Stoics, according to Porphyry, distinguished: (1) complete direct predicables, which they called concomitants, or simply predicables; (2) complete oblique predicables or quasi-concomitants; (3) deficient direct
predicables or less-than-predicables; and (4) deficient oblique predicables
or less-than-quasi-concomitants.

They thereby saw something which Peripatetic logic missed, namely

---

[168] Similar material in: Steph. *Int.* 11.2–21; Anon. *Int.* 3.6–17; ΣLucian 128; Priscian *Inst. Gramm.*
XVII.4–5; Suda *s.v.* σύμβαμα (see Hülser 1987–8, 954–7); also Ap. Dysc. *Synt.* III.155, 187 (see
Hülser 1987–8, 946–9); *Pron.* 115.9–13. Note also the casual reference to a 'less than a predica-
ble' at Stob. *Ecl.* II.7.6a (for the text see Long and Sedley 1987, vol. II, 390); and observe that
D.L. VII.64 originally alluded to at least some of the material (the lacuna will have contained the
contrast to τὰ μὲν συμβάματα...).

the distinction between what we now call monadic and polyadic predicates. But their vision was partial and blurred. First, the distinction between complete and deficient predicables corresponds to a distinction between monadic and *dyadic* predicates and nothing suggests that the Stoics had grasped the general notion of a *poly*adic predicate. Secondly, the distinction is interlaced with another distinction which is of no logical interest: the distinction between direct and oblique predicables merely reflects an idiosyncrasy of Greek grammar. Finally, there is no evidence that any Stoic exploited the distinction in his account of inference and syllogism – the distinction remained logically inert.

But Chrysippus wrote at length on predicables; and his *Logical Investigations* shows how detailed – and how recherché – his discussions could be. In particular, he wrote *On Upright and Supine Predicables* (D.L. VII.191),[169] and this distinction is closely related to the distinctions rehearsed by Porphyry:

> Some predicables are upright, some supine, some neutral. Upright are those which are put together with one of the oblique cases to generate a predicable e.g. 'hears', 'sees', 'converses'. Supine are those put together with the passive particle e.g. 'I am heard', 'I am seen'. Neutral are those of which neither is the case: e.g. 'to think', 'to walk'. (D.L. VII.64)[170]

Little is known of the doctrine summarized here: 'the Stoics did much work in this area, but their teaching and most of their writings are now lost' (Simp. *Cat.* 334.1–3).

The terminology, allegedly taken from wrestling, was adopted by the grammarians and used for the active ('upright') and passive ('supine') moods;[171] and the Stoic distinction, although it was not primarily linguistic, presumably somehow reflects these grammatical notions. Thus neutral predicables will have answered roughly to intransitive verbs, uprights and supines to transitive verbs; and the distinction between upright and supine will have matched the linguistic distinction between active and passive. It is tempting to connect all this with the distinctions reported by Porphyry; but there is no easy way to produce a satisfying synthesis.

*

[169] The matter is alluded to in the *Logika Zētēmata*, *PHerc.* 307: fr. 3.4–18; 1.23; 11.17–21: see Marrone 1984. Note also the Περὶ συμβαμάτων (D.L. VII.192 – if von Arnim was right to emend the MS reading συναμμάτων).

[170] D.L. adds a reference to reciprocals, ἀντιπεπονθότα; but the text is uncertain, and the two other passages which refer to them are obscure (Phil. *Cher.* 79–81; Orig. *Cels.* VI.57 – neither of whom mentions the Stoics). See Hülser 1987–8, 962–3.

[171] See ΣDThrax 247.10–11; 401.1–20; 548.34–549.3.

Predicables were discussed in detail and from several points of view.[172]
And predicables are 'parts' of complete sayables. What of their other
parts? In the simple sentence 'Socrates writes' a proper name is combined
with the verb: presumably the name has a meaning. Does it signify a sayable, and is the complete sayable expressed by 'Socrates writes' composed
of two deficient sayables, one expressed by 'writes' and the other by
'Socrates'? And what of common nouns or 'appellatives' such as the word
'cow'? Or of the demonstrative pronouns ('this', 'οὗτος') which were of
such importance to Stoic logic?[173]

Predicables were said to combine with cases, πτώσεις. Cases are not
utterances, but rather objects which are signified;[174] and we should
therefore expect proper names and the rest to signify cases. Sextus speaks
of cases as the items signified by common nouns:

> By this utterance ('κύων', 'dog') is signified the case under which the
> barking animal falls . . . (S.E. M xi.29)

The utterance signifies the case, and items in the world fall under the case.
Cases stand to appellatives as predicables stand to verbs. The same view
emerges from a text in Clement:

> Cases are agreed to be incorporeal – hence the sophism is solved as fol-
> lows: 'What you say comes out of your mouth' – true; 'But you say a
> house: therefore a house comes out of your mouth' false; for we do not
> say the house, which is a body, but the case, which is incorporeal and
> which the house obtains. (Clem. Strom. viii.9.26.5)[175]

It seems reasonable to assume that proper names too signify incorporeal
cases.[176]

As for demonstrative pronouns, one passage reports that they 'signify a
reference (δεῖξις) or an anaphora' (ΣDThrax 518.39–519.3). This might

---

[172] I have not mentioned tenses, for which see above, pp. 190–3.

[173] For different views on these matters see e.g. Egli 1967, 31; Long 1971c, 104–6; Nuchelmans
1973, 57, 68 (two contradictory positions); Baldassarri 1984, 81–3.

[174] So, explicitly, ΣDThrax 230.34–6 (but he does not explicitly mention the Stoics, and in some
texts πτώσεις are said or implied to be nouns: see Atherton 1993, 279–89); see e.g. Delamarre
1980.

[175] Clement is purporting to represent a Stoic view (the sophism was propounded by Chrysippus,
D.L. vii.187, with a wagon instead of a house); and the passage from which this text is extracted
has been treated as an important document for various Stoic notions. Alas, Clement is irremediably confused.

[176] But note D.L. vii.58: 'an appellative, according to Diogenes of Babylon, is a part of speech signifying a common quality – e.g. man, horse; a name is a part of speech showing a proper quality
– e.g. Diogenes, Socrates'. Qualities are bodies. Hence either cases are not incorporeal or nouns
do not signify cases. Perhaps Diogenes of Babylon held a heterodox view? or perhaps the report
in D.L. is mistaken?

suggest that the meaning of a demonstrative is given by its reference (you understand what 'he' means in the sentence 'He is writing' if and only if you know who 'he' is being used to refer to); and then there is no case or πτῶσις intervening between the word and its referent. But elsewhere we are told that in the sayable expressed by the sentence 'οὗτος περιπατεῖ', a predicable is linked to a deictic case (πτῶσις). Hence demonstratives, like proper names and appellatives, signify incorporeal cases.

Sextus reports that proper names signify sayables: at *M* VIII.11–12 the name 'Dio' signifies a sayable which the man Dio in turn 'obtains';[177] and elsewhere he says that the Stoics

> take self-complete sayables[178] to be composite: thus 'It is day' is composed of 'day' and 'it is'. (*M* VIII.79)

He no doubt construes the word 'day' as an appellative; and he strongly suggests that both parts of the assertible 'It is day' are sayables. At *M* VIII.83 'Socrates is' is treated in the same way as 'It is day': the proper name 'Socrates' is implicitly taken to signify a sayable. Appellatives and proper names signify sayables. And since they also signify cases, cases must be a special type of sayable.

If names and the like signify sayables, then presumably they can be used to *say* something. But can words such as 'cow' and 'Dio' and 'this' be so used? No ancient text hints at an answer. A guess: you understand what an appellative, A ('cow'), means if and only if you know that anyone who utters a sentence of the form 'x is an A (a cow)' can thereby say of something that it falls into the class of Fs (that it is an animal of such and such a sort). You understand what a name, N ('Dio'), means if and only if you know that anyone who utters a sentence of the form 'x is N (Dio)' can thereby say of something that it is b (Dio). You understand what a demonstrative α ('this') means if and only if you know that anyone who utters a sentence of the form 'φδ' can thereby say of the item to which he is adverting that it is φ.

However that may be, even if words like 'this' and 'Dio' signify non-corporeal cases, they are surely also (and at the same time) used to refer to something other than a case – to this thing, to Dio himself. And in fact several texts report that external items 'obtain' (τυγχάνειν) or fall under (πίπτειν) cases: Dio and dogs fall under or obtain the cases which the words 'Dio' and 'dog' signify.[179] Although these notions are nowhere

---

[177] The text of the crucial sentence (... ἐν δὲ ἀσώματον ὥσπερ τὸ σημαινόμενον πρᾶγμα καὶ λεκτὸν ὅπερ ἀληθές τε γίνεται ἢ ψεῦδος) may be corrupt; but *M* VIII.75 takes up the same example and unmistakably implies that there is a sayable signified by 'Dio'.

[178] Text after Heintz.

explained, it is natural to suppose that an item obtains or falls under a case insofar as a word which signifies the case refers to the item.

Cases have items falling under them: does anything else? Are there items which fall under predicables? or under complete sayables? The passage at *M* VIII.11–12 has suggested a luxuriant theory: any sentence, S, signifies a self-complete sayable, Λ, which in turn may be obtained by an item in the world, I; and each significant part of S signifies a deficient sayable, which is a part of Λ, and which may be obtained by an item in the world, which in turn is a part of I.

The luxuriant theory faces some difficult questions; and the evidence for ascribing it to the Stoics is exiguous. Perhaps, then, it was only cases which enjoyed obtainers. And perhaps these obtainers are not really part of the Stoic semantic theory at all: in order to know what A, or N, means we do not need to know what A, or N, refers to except insofar as knowing that x falls into the class of Fs, or that it is b, is itself a way of knowing what A, or N, refers to.

So much for verbs and names. But there are also other parts of speech, and it is natural to wonder whether the Stoics associated incomplete sayables with such things as adverbs and connectives. In particular, we might expect the Stoics to have said something about connectives; for otherwise their semantic views will not have engaged with sentences central to their logical concerns. The evidence bearing on this issue is meagre and difficult to assess;[180] but we are least ill informed about connectives.

Connectives fall into the hospitable class of σύνδεσμοι, a class which also includes prepositions and verbal prefixes.[181] And we know that

> Posidonius, in his *On Connectives*, argues against those who say that connectives do not show anything but only bind the expression together. (Ap. Dysc. *Conj.* 214.4–6)

It is not clear who or what Posidonius[182] was attacking. Late Peripatetic texts endorse the view that only nouns and verbs have genuine signification in their own right: other linguistic items merely 'co-signify'. It is possible that this view goes back to Theophrastus, who held that nouns and verbs are the only parts of *logos*, other linguistic items being parts of *lexis* (Simp. *Cat.* 10.23–7); and perhaps Posidonius was attacking a Theophrastan theory.

---

[179] S.E. *M* VIII.12, 75 ('Dio'); XI. 29 ('dog'); cf. Clem. *Strom.* VIII.9.26.5; Plu. *Col.* 1119f. And note two controversial texts: on Simp. *Cat.* 209.10–14 see Mansfeld *apud* Hülser 1987–8, 1068–71; Stob. *Ecl.* I.12.3 (= Arius Didymus) is either corrupt or confused.   [180] See Atherton 1993, 304–10.

[181] See above, p. 189.

[182] Here, and at *Synt.*IV.65, Ap. Dysc. is surely referring to the Stoic Posidonius: Kidd 1988, II.200. Posidonius' view was accepted by Chaeremon: Ap. Dysc. *Conj.* 248.1–12.

Nor is it clear what view Posidonius himself preferred. In particular, it is not clear whether he gave an account of the meaning of connectives in terms of 'intermediate' items – whether, in other words, he thought that connectives signified sayables. Such an account is not difficult to formulate. For example: you know what 'and' means if and only if you know that anyone who utters a sentence of the form 'S and S*', where S means that P and S* means that Q, can thereby say that P and Q.

*

Why did the Stoics introduce sayables in the first place? It is often supposed that the word 'λεκτόν' was first used by Cleanthes of predicables; then extended by Chrysippus to cover self-complete sayings; and later stretched to include the meaning of any part of speech.[183] The only evidence for this pretty story comes from Clement, who remarks that 'Cleanthes and Archedemus call predicables sayables' (*Strom.* VIII.9.26.4); but Clement does not mean that Cleanthes (and Archedemus) used the word 'sayable' *exclusively* of predicables. In any event, we may still wonder why the Stoics wanted to insinuate something between words and the world, and why the items which they insinuated were sayables rather than something else.

The Stoics did not, so far as we know, argue for the existence of sayables. After all, it is evident that there are sayables; for it is evident that we can say things and sayables are simply what we can say. In a sense, then, neither the Peripatetics nor the Epicureans can have denied the existence of sayables; rather, they held that there was no need to posit sayables *in addition to* certain other items. The Stoics differed from their colleagues in according a special status to sayables. What was this status?

First, sayables figure regularly in the standard list of Stoic incorporeals: time, place, void, sayables; and a dozen texts repeat the claim that sayables have no body.[184] The point was hardly contested within the school[185] – and yet it cannot have been an obvious or a welcome truth. Not obvious, since the Stoics were notorious materialists who saw solid stuff in virtues and vices, impulses and assents (Plu. *Comm. Not.* 1084a); not welcome, since on Stoic theory only bodies can act and be acted on[186] – and sayables appear to do both. They appear to be acted upon, insofar as certain assertibles may change their truth-value and others may perish. They appear to

[183] See e.g. Hülser 1987-8, 832-3; cf. Nuchelmans 1973, 47, 71-2.
[184] The four incorporeals: e.g. S.E. *M* X.218; XI.224, 230; *M* I.28 (see e.g. Bréhier 1910). Sayables as incorporeal: e.g. S.E. *PH* VII.81; *M* VII.38; VIII.12, 69, 258, 409; IX.211; XI.224; *M* I.20, 155-6; Plu. *Comm. Not.* 1074de; D.L. VII.140 (reading τὰ λεκτά with von Arnim for ταῦτα); Sen. *Ep.* 117.13; Cleom. I.i.8.   [185] Except by Basilides: S.E. *M* VIII.258.
[186] E.g. Cic. *Acad.* II.39 (Zeno): see below, pp. 383 and 481-3.

act: proofs, which are sets of sayables, may affect us in one way or another (S.E. *M* VIII.409–10); being wise, which is a predicable, benefits us (Sen. *Ep.* 117.2–3). The Stoics conjured away these appearances. Their prestidigitations could have been avoided had they simply declared sayables to be corporeal. And there is worse: not only are sayables not corporeal – they do not even exist. A sayable is something, τι; but it does not exist, it is not ὄν (Plu. *Col.* 1116bc; *Comm. Not.* 1074d).

No text expressly tells us why the Stoics adopted these theses. In his account of the Stoic theory of concept formation Diogenes Laertius reports that 'things are also conceived of in virtue of a sort of transference (μετάβασις) – e.g. sayables and place' (VII.53). Now the fact that the *concept* of X is got by 'transference' from Y might perhaps have been taken to show that X's are essentially dependent on Y's and hence are not 'real' existents. But Diogenes Laertius does not report such an argument (nor does he indicate *what* was the base from which the concept of a sayable was transferred). Nonetheless, the Stoic theses are coherent – indeed, plausible. Of course, *there are* sayables; that is to say, people can (and do) say things. But sayables do not really *exist*: Chrysippus uttered the sentence Σοφὸς ὁ Ζήνων and thereby said that Zeno was wise; Chrysippus existed, and so did the sounds he uttered (and so, come to that, did Zeno); and there is the sayable which he said – but this is not some further item in the world, distinct from Chrysippus and his utterance.[187]

Next, how do sayables relate to utterances and to thoughts? Plainly there are unsaid sayables – there are things which we can say and which no one has said or ever will say.[188] Plainly, too, there are unthought sayables – there are things which we can say and which no one has thought or ever will think.[189] But two theses connecting sayables and thinking may plausibly be ascribed to the Stoics: every sayable is thinkable, or whatever can be said can be thought; and every sayable which is said is also thought, or whatever is being said is being thought.

In more than one text, sayables are closely allied to presentations, and hence to thoughts, in the following way:

A sayable, they say, is what subsists in accordance with a rational presentation; and a presentation is rational if what is presented in accordance with it can be set out in a λόγος. (S.E. *M* VIII.70)[190]

---

[187] 'But then the Stoic theory is barely distinguishable, ontologically speaking, from the Epicurean.' Exactly.

[188] *Pace* S.E. *M* VIII.80: 'every sayable must be said – that is how it got its name'.

[189] See Barnes 1993c; *contra* D.L. VII.43, which is muddled or corrupt; and Syr. *Met.* 105.19–30, which conveys a late misunderstanding.

[190] Cf. D.L. VII.63 (with Suda *s.v.* κατηγόρημα); S.E. *M* VIII.12.

The second sentence is difficult;[191] but what matters here is that rational presentations are to be identified with *thoughts* (D.L. VII.51). The first sentence is also difficult: I take it to mean that if something is sayable, then it corresponds to a rational presentation, its content is the content of a rational presentation; or in other words: if something is sayable, then it is thinkable – indeed, if x can say that, then x can think that.

The second thesis emerges from the following passage:

> Saying, they say, is producing an utterance which means the object which is being thought. (S.E. *M* VIII.80)

I say something at a time t if and only if at t I produce an utterance U which signifies a sayable S and in addition I am thinking S at t. Or rather, if I say S it is not merely that I utter U *while* thinking S; rather, my uttering U is in part *caused* by my thinking S. For, in the words of Diogenes of Babylon,

> it is plausible that speech (λóγος), being given significance and as it were stamped by the thoughts in the intellect, should be emitted and should extend in time for as long as the thinking and the activity of saying last.[192]

The metaphor suggests that the sentences which I utter would be senseless had I not given them my intellectual stamp; but the suggestion is false (I cannot create significance in my utterances, nor can I stamp them at will). Diogenes' argument, however, requires only the following thesis: I say S at t only if, at t, I utter U, which means S, because I am thinking S. My thinking does not endow my utterance with meaning: it ensures that its meaning is my meaning and it thereby distinguishes me from a babbler or a parrot. (According to Chrysippus, parrots and infants 'do not speak but as it were speak', *non loqui sed ut loqui*: Varro *LL* VI.56.)

One final question about the 'ontology' of sayables may be mooted: what are the identity conditions for sayables? when is S¹ the same as S²? The question arises in at least two fields in which the Stoics laboured: it arises in connection with definitions (which induce synonymy – and hence sameness of sayables); and it arises in connection with ambiguity (which points to difference of sayables). No ancient text suggests that the Stoics discussed the question of 'same-saying'.

*

---

[191] For a different translation see Kerferd 1978b, 253–4.
[192] *Apud* Gal. *PHP* v.242, where there are also similar fragments of Chrysippus: see Tieleman 1996.

The twin strengths of the Stoic theory are plain: meanings are explained in terms of saying and thus placed firmly in the public realm – no hint of the 'private thoughts' which bedevilled the history of semantics for two millennia; and at the same time, the theory is ontologically parsimonious – it does not invent entities (not even sayables, which do not exist). The weakness is this. The Stoic theory rests heavily on the notion of saying – and yet it offers no account of the identity conditions for sayables, it does not explain when you and I say the same thing.

*

Like other philosophers[193] the Stoics pay attention to ambiguities.[194] Their definition is: 'an ambiguity is an expression which signifies two or even more things, as far as expression is concerned, taken in its proper sense, and according to one and the same linguistic idiom. This expression consequently makes the plurality of meanings understood simultaneously'.[195] Diogenes' instance concerns a written text,[196] and Galen too has written expressions in mind when he refers to a list of eight types of ambiguity distinguished by 'the more refined Stoics',[197] in order to prove its inferiority to Aristotle's distinction of sophisms παρὰ τήν λέξιν:

(amphiboly which is)

(1) common to what is divided and what is non-divided (Diogenes' example);

(2) due to homonymy in single words (ἀνδρεῖος, meaning both 'manly, brave' and 'belonging to a man');

(3) due to homonymy in complex expressions (ἄνθρωπός ἐστιν), referring to the existence of either the substance (οὐσία, 'man is') or the case (πτῶσις, ' "man" is');[198]

(4) due to omission (example corrupt);[199]

---

193 From Democritus (DK 68 B26) onwards.

194 Witness Chrysippus' seven treatises on this subject (D.L. VII.193) and cf. Gell. XI.12.1. More on this in Atherton 1993.

195 D.L. VII.62. This definition thus excludes amphibolies arising from metaphorical or different local usages.

196 ΑΥΛΗΤΡΙΣΠΕΠΤΩΚΕΝ meaning either 'a flutegirl has fallen' or 'a court has fallen three times'. For centuries Greek was written without word division.

197 On Fallacies 4. A partially parallel text in Theon Prog. 81.30–83.13; cf. Quint. Inst. VII.9. Augustine Dial. 8 contains an extensive list of types of ambiguitas, which list is a blend of logical, grammatical and rhetorical doctrines but looks essentially Stoic (Ebbesen 1981, 1.38–9).

198 Thus Ebbesen 1981, 1.36 and n. 41. Differently, referring to the 'Nobody' sophism (D.L. VII.186–7), Edlow 1975, 429–30.

199 Probably: 'Of which are you?' For the middle word is omitted, e.g. 'master', 'father' (Galen's text as restored by Sedley in Long and Sedley 1987, vol. II, 230–1). Some link with the sophism in Arist. SE 179b39–180a7 seems present, pace Sedley.

(5) due to pleonasm (ἀπηγόρευσεν αὐτῷ μὴ πλεῖν, admitting of the interpretations 'he forbade him to sail' and 'he forbade him not to sail');
(6) due to uncertainty to which word a non-significant part belongs;
(7) the same but now for a signifying word;[200]
(8) amphiboly which does not show what refers to what (Δίων <ἐστι καὶ> Θέων,[201] 'Dion <is also> Theon', or *vice versa*, or 'Dion is, also Theon', meaning that both are existing).

The Stoic types of ambiguity look like a mixed bag and are probably based on the following distinctions: (A) single words (1)–(5), divided into cases of homonymy of single words, words in combination and both at the same time (1)–(3), and cases of omission and redundancy (4)–(5);[202] (B) construction of words (6)–(8).[203] The difference between types (2) and (3) will be that ἀνδρεῖος has two meanings whereas type (3) adverts to the fact that every word, in addition to its regular signification(s), is also its own name, a point stressed in reports on the sophism 'what you say goes through your mouth'.[204] Ambiguities (6) and (7) involve both joining or separating morphemes and introducing pauses in the continuous script and look therefore at an act of σύνταξις.[205] Type (8) is comparable to phrases with two accusatives in an accusative–infinitive construction which Aristotle examines[206] and in which the governing role of the constituents is unclear. Despite the presence of a syntactical aspect in types (1) and (3) they concern the ambiguity of one word only and this marks them off from types (7) and (8).

Galen deplores the absence of a type due to προσῳδία, which covers accent, breathing and quantity, but type (6) seems related to this. In all, the Aristotelian list of six types of sophisms due to linguistic features[207] has been radically rearranged by the Stoics. The main difference in approach is that Aristotle lists types of sophistical arguments whereas the Stoic classification has a much wider scope of linguistic ambiguities. Thus while Aristotle distinguishes one type based on amphiboly, the Stoics use *amphibolia* as a general term.

[200] The examples concern two epic lines; the latter line is also discussed by Arist. *SE* 166a37.
[201] Text as restored by Sedley in Long and Sedley 1987, vol. II, 230–1.
[202] These are part of the *quadripertita ratio* of *adiectio*, *detractio*, *translatio* and *mutatio* (Ax 1987), cf. above, p. 182. These categories recur in Sextus' account of the Stoic classification of inconclusive arguments (*M* VIII.429–34 and *PH* II.146–50) – and in Quintilian's list of means of disambiguation (Ebbesen 1981, I.32–3).
[203] The main distinction of types (A) and (B) is in agreement with that of Aristotle between λόγος and ὄνομα in cases of homonymy and amphiboly (*SE* 166a15–16) and that in Quint. *Inst.* VII.9.
[204] D.L. VII.187 and Clem. *Strom.* VIII.9.26.5 with the telling word πτῶσις.
[205] Cf. Desbordes 1990, 227–34.   [206] E.g. *SE* 166a22–32.
[207] *SE* 4. Homonymy, amphiboly, joining and separation of words, προσῳδία and σχῆμα τῆς λέξεως, e.g. active forms of verbs not meaning an activity.

The examples sometimes betray trivial pursuits[208] but are intended to drive home the idea that sentences may conceal ambiguity, which fact can hinder the right way of doing dialectic. Disambiguation is often very easy to achieve provided one considers the examples in their context. But most discussions of ambiguity start from isolated cases. Perhaps the Stoics said that ambiguous expressions are disambiguated by their context, for we find such statements later.[209]

This theory influences both rhetoric and grammar. The lists of Theon and Quintilian (see note 197) are rhetorical applications. Of more importance is the influence on the theory of *status* by Hermagoras[210] and the reception of ἀμφιβολία in the wide sense under the tropes. Thus grammarians adopt ἀμφιβολία under the vices of style (*vitia orationis*).[211]

*

At the end of his survey of the *topos* περὶ φωνῆς Diogenes lists short definitions of some notions, like 'definition', 'outline' and 'partition', which the Stoics use as tools of methodology. The presence of these items here is not self-evident, witness Diogenes' remark 'according to some Stoics', but they appear nowhere else.[212] The list consists of nine items[213] and after this comes ἀμφιβολία, the presence of which together with solecism etc. elsewhere[214] is less surprising. These methods are much used in ethical texts, and Chrysippus' treatises concerning definitions are put under his ethical works.[215] One understands the predicament of some Stoics where to put these in their system.[216]

Partition occurs when a generic subject matter is split up into its subheadings but does not imply that these are species; they are more like sectors of discussion.[217] In contrast with Platonic and Aristotelian dihaeretic methods the host of Stoic definitions does not look like the result of διαίρεσις.[218] Within definitions Stoics allow for looser definitions, called 'outline accounts', a term taken over from Aristotle. By means of an outline one offers initial help for discussion. The true nature

---

[208] Cf. Arist. *SE* 166a18–21 on ἐπίσταται γράμματα, 'he knows letters' and 'letters have knowledge'.   [209] Ap. Dysc. *Pron.* 52.2–8; Quint. *Inst.* vii.9.9; Aug. *Dial.* 8.

[210] Frs. 12 and 20; but the Stoic Nestor (date unknown) eliminates this *status* (ΣHermog. *Stat.* vii.1.226.13–20).   [211] Because of its obscurity. Ebbesen 1981, i.36–40.

[212] D.L. vii.60–2 cf. 44.

[213] Definition (ὅρος); outline (ὑπογραφή, a simpler kind of definition); division (διαίρεσις) and its related notions of contradivision (ἀντιδιαίρεσις) and subdivision (ὑποδιαίρεσις); genus (γένος) and species (εἶδος); concept (ἐννόημα) and partition (μερισμός). Related texts in *FDS* 622–31.   [214] D.L. vii.44. Cf. Schenkeveld 1990a, 89–96.

[215] D.L. vii.199–200.   [216] For the sake of completeness they are discussed here.

[217] Μερισμός is to grammarians the 'parsing' of words.   [218] Long and Sedley 1987, vol. i, 193.

of a subject, however, must be revealed by the true definition. Chrysippus defines it as 'a representation of a peculiar characteristic' and Antipater as 'a statement of analysis matchingly expressed'. Chrysippus' peculiar characteristic (ἴδιον) is an essential, not just a unique, feature. By 'matchingly' (ἀπαρτιζόντως) Antipater apparently means that a true definition is neither too broad nor too narrow, whereas the term 'analysis' may point to the division by genus and species.[219]

11 Rhetoric

About 160 BC the debate on the status of rhetoric started by Plato gets a new impetus,[220] which is caused by a renascence of rhetorical studies. Under the Hellenistic kings oratory loses parts only of its domain, but for unknown reasons teaching in rhetoric steeply declines until the start of the second century. The teachers of rhetoric, now called σοφισταί, have a high rating because they instruct aspiring politicians. The same goal is professed by philosophers and hence there is a revival of the philosophers' debate on the art of rhetoric.[221]

The main challenge to rhetoric is that it is not an art or expertise (τέχνη). Additional arguments are that it does not make individuals or states happy and that an orator is often constrained to defend criminals. Moreover, one can be a good orator without formal training and, conversely, many instructors of rhetoric are poor speakers. But the chief point of the attack is that rhetoric is not an organized body of knowledge,[222] so that the rhetorician is not an artist or expert.[223] Thus the debate turns on the question whether with Aristotle one accepts rhetoric as an art even though like dialectic it does not belong to a specific field of knowledge, or rejects his argument.[224]

*

---

[219] D.L. VII.60. Another definition of Antipater's, 'a statement expressed with necessary force', and explained by 'with reciprocal force inasmuch as a definition is meant to be reciprocal' (ΣDThrax 107.4-6), should be linked with Chrysippus' statement about the relation between universal propositions and definitions (S.E. *M* XI.8-11, see above, p. 113).

[220] Traditionally linked with the Athenian embassy of three philosophers to Rome in 155 BC (Cic. *De or.* II.155).

[221] See Goudriaan 1988. Critolaus, Carneades and Diogenes are mentioned in this connection (Phld. *Rhet.* books I-III; Cic. *De or.* 1.91; 96-112; Quint. *Inst.* II.17.1-4; S.E. *M* II.10-47). Discussion in Barnes 1986d with earlier studies.

[222] This definition of τέχνη is Stoic but accepted by many others, see Hülser 1987-8, 426-7.

[223] Phld. *Rhet.*, *PHerc.* 1672, II.xxviii.2-15 and S.E. *M* II.9-10.

[224] Cic. *De or.* 1.91 reports debates on this subject held in the late second century by Charmadas the Academic and the rhetorician Metrodorus; the accounts in Quintilian and Sextus probably reflect a contemporary revival of the issue (Barnes 1986d, n. 20).

After Theophrastus the Peripatos no longer, so far as we know, makes original contributions to rhetorical theory. Demetrius of Phaleron, Hieronymus of Rhodes and others write on several aspects but leave almost no trace in the tradition and Critolaus with his pupils reject rhetoric.[225] This picture agrees with the fact that Cicero and Quintilian mention these individual Peripatetics a few times only, much less often than Aristotle and Theophrastus. However, according to Quintilian 'especially the leaders of the Stoics and Peripatetics' studied rhetoric more zealously than rhetoricians, and Cicero too speaks of 'very many precepts' left by Aristotle's followers.[226] In their reconstruction of the history of rhetoric they probably follow a tradition in which recollection of Peripatetic contributions is still alive but these are mainly Aristotle's and Theophrastus'.[227]

Ancient sources stress a consistently hostile attitude of Epicureans to most rhetorical activities.[228] Now Philodemus asserts that Epicurus and his followers Metrodorus and Hermarchus accept an art of sophistic rhetoric.[229] Philodemus' thesis is that there is a τέχνη, called σοφιστική, which concerns written and impromptu speeches of an epideictic kind, but that this art is not competent in instruction in forensic and symbouleutic oratory. For these latter genres no art at all is competent. By analysis of statements of Epicurus and Metrodorus he tries to show that these 'Men' are of the same opinion, but then he interpolates his own ideas into the text of Metrodorus and misrepresents the views of the Men.[230] Epicurus did write a book on rhetoric but in this he will have urged the rejection of all types of rhetoric.

More is known about the Stoic theory of rhetoric though their contribution is now seen as less important than in previous studies.[231] Rhetoric, the 'science (ἐπιστήμη) of speaking well', is closely connected with dialectic, both being parts of 'logic'.[232] These sciences can only be practised well by the infallible wise man, who will thus play a role in society unless circumstances make this impossible.[233] The Stoics distinguish

---

[225] Wehrli 1969d, 125 with references.   [226] Quint. *Inst.* III.1.13–15; Cic. *Inv.* II.7.

[227] See Kennedy 1994a.

[228] Cic. *Fin.* I.5.14, *Tusc.* II.7; Quint. *Inst.* II.7.15 and XII.2.24; D.H. *Comp.* 24, p. 122, 8–12. See Sedley 1989a and De Lacy 1939, 88–9 for a possible explanation of this attitude.

[229] *Rhet.* I, *PHerc.* 1427, vii.9–29.

[230] Goudriaan 1989, 33–5 comparing *Rhet.* II, *PHerc.* 1672, xxii.7–20; *lib. inc.*, *PHerc.* 1015/832, vol. I. p. 283 Sudhaus; and III, *PHerc.* 1506, xl–xli Hammerstaedt. Differently now Blank 1995, 186–8.   [231] See Kroll 1940, 1081 on the tendency to ascribe much to Stoics without proof.

[232] Their main difference is that rhetoric involves continuous discourse (D.L. VII.41–2, cf. Zeno's illustration by means of a closed fist and an open hand, Cic. *Or.* 32.114 etc.), whereas dialectic though initially restricted to the form of question and answer and later having a wider reach (Long 1978c, 102–13) never loses its purely argumentative character.

[233] D.L. VII.121–2; Phld. *Rhet.* III, *PHerc.* 1506, coll. ii and vii (vol. 2.203 f. and 209 f. Sudhaus); Cic. *De or.* III.18.65 and S.E. *M* II.6.

a triad of oratorical genres and it may be indicative of their preferences
that next to forensic and symbouleutic oratory they call the third one not
epideictic (display oratory), as Aristotle did, but encomiastic.[234] The
Stoic orator will be involved in all three kinds. To some Stoics, however,
rhetoric was an expertise. Science differs from expertise inasmuch as the
former is an unchangeable disposition and the latter a tenor (ἕξις), which
admits of degrees and can be attained by not (yet) wise men. To define
rhetoric as an expertise offers hope for an aspiring Stoic orator to attain
proficiency and, at any rate, allows for more technical instruction.[235] But
some problem still remains on this point.[236]

As to the technical part of rhetoric, Diogenes gives a very short summary, which looks like traditional theory: rhetoric has three parts, forensic, symbouleutic and encomiastic. Its division is into invention, style
(φράσις), disposition (τάξις) and delivery, and a speech consists of pro-
logue, narration, the part against the adversaries and epilogue; the
absence of the traditional part of proof probably is a matter of inadvertent
omission in our source.[237] The stress on forensic speech is in accordance
with ancient teaching.

Stoic presentation is austere, without much ornament, rather argumentative and, at least to Cicero, unattractive.[238] The style of Stoic oratory is like that of their dialectic and in accordance with their ethics of the
wise man.[239] With this picture agree other pieces of information about
Chrysippus' exclusion of emotional appeal from the epilogue,[240] which
injunction derives from the Stoic abhorrence of passions, the rejection of
rhetorical devices like hyperbaton which disturb the natural word-order
the Stoics assume to exist,[241] and the report on Chrysippus' admittance
of occasional solecisms and ellipses.[242]

So a Stoic list of five virtues of speech (ἀρεταὶ λόγου) with its inclusion
of κατασκευή seems to contradict what a Stoic speaker should do.
However, in comparison with Theophrastus' canonical list this group
contains one significant addition, brevity (συντομία). Moreover, some

---

[234] D.L. VII.142.
[235] Plu. Stoic. Rep. 1047a (Chrysippus); Phld. Rhet. III, PHerc. 1506, col. viii (vol. 2.211 f. Sudhaus);
Quint. Inst. II.17.2.   [236] Atherton 1988, 420–2.
[237] Atherton 1988, 398. Similar explanation for the absence of memory among the tasks of an orator.
[238] Cic. Brut. 117–21; Parad. Stoic. 1–3; De orat. 1.50; II.157–9; III.65–7; cf. Atherton 1988, 401–5,
who, rightly, points out the biassed stance of Cicero.
[239] Thus P. Rutilius Rufus, an almost perfect Stoic, when accused of extortion refuses to employ
the usual rhetorical devices and is consequently condemned (Cic. De orat. 1.229 and Brut.
114–15).   [240] Rh. Gr. 1.454.1 Spengel; cf. Quint. Inst. VI.1.7.
[241] Theon Prog. 81.30–83.14 with Atherton's explanation (1988, 415–17).
[242] Plu. Stoic. Rep. 1047b.

definitions show a specifically Stoic approach. The five virtues are ἑλληνισμός, σαφήνεια, συντομία, πρέπον and κατασκευή while among the
vices are mentioned βαρβαρισμός and σολοικισμός.[243] Hellenism, correct Greek, is 'language faultless in its technical and non-arbitrary
usage'.[244] This definition presupposes a set of rules to be followed concerning the usage of Greek.[245] Often three criteria are mentioned, analogy, linguistic usage and literary tradition,[246] but we do not know
whether the Stoa also applies these criteria. The next three virtues stress
the link between wording and content, clarity presenting in an intelligible way what is thought, brevity containing the bare minimum required
for clarification of the subject-matter, while appropriateness is concerned
with the object in question only. The audience is not involved, as they
were in Aristotle's treatment.[247] This neglect of the audience also
explains the elevation of brevity to the Stoic list, since common rhetoric
does not require this feature in every instance. Κατασκευή, finally, is not
ornamentation in a favourable sense but avoidance of ἰδιωτισμός, vulgar-
ity or colloquialism.

All this comes down to a theory of a sober style which is applicable to
both philosophy and oratory without any, or much, difference between
the two. Nevertheless Cicero exceptionally praises Stoic orators for their
use of embellishment.[248] Chrysippus encourages attention to various
kinds of delivery[249] and, indeed, in order to be successful a Stoic orator
will not avoid every kind of ornament or emotion. But in principle he will
eschew these as mere appendages.[250]

*

Direct influence of Hellenistic philosophies on rhetorical theory is
difficult to detect: thus the existence of the important theory of στάσεις
(*status*), a contribution of Hermagoras of Temnos and other rhetoricians,
can be explained without having recourse to philosophical influence. A
more acceptable view is that rhetoricians use ideas of Aristotle and
Theophrastus but also of Isocrates, apart from what their own practice
taught them. Thus they continue the instruction begun by Aristotle and
Theophrastus of setting up themes for discussion[251] but apply these to
their own situation. Like philosophers, rhetoricians train their pupils for

---

[243] Diogenes' phrasing (VII.59) suggests more vices; in [Herodian] *De soloec.* 308.16 six vices are
mentioned, one of which is ἀκυρολογία, use of words in an improper sense. This together
with ἀσάφεια also occurs in D.H. *Lys.* 4.   [244] Cf. D.L. VII.42.   [245] Frede 1978, 39–41.
[246] Siebenborn 1976, 53–5.   [247] *Rhet.* III.7.   [248] *De fin.* III.19.
[249] Plu. *Stoic. Rep.* 1047a–b.   [250] Hence their failure as rhetoricians: thus Atherton 1988, 425–7.
[251] E.g. *Top.* 104b1–8 and 35–6.

discussing general and specific subjects. These exercises are called θέσις and ὑποθέσις respectively. A θέσις, or an undefined question (*quaestio infinita*), is 'Should one marry?' or 'Do gods exist?', but 'Should Cato marry?' is a ὑποθέσις because defined (*finita*).[252]

Some parts of Aristotle's theory of τόποι[253] recur in Hermagoras' system, albeit with a big difference. For whereas Aristotle's τόποι (places where to find arguments) are applicable to all three kinds of oratory Hermagoras focuses on judicial oratory and gives to each individual *status* there a particular list of τόποι.[254] Aristotle distinguished general τόποι, which give arguments applicable in every discipline, from specific τόποι and Hermagoras replaces this distinction by *loci communes* and *loci* belonging to a specific *status*. At the same time *loci communes* are now also called the arguments themselves, not only sources for arguments, and they may be used in every situation and serve to heighten the style of the oration.[255]

As to the theory of style, the author of *On Style* heavily leans on Aristotle's *Rhetoric* in his discussion of periodicity and prose rhythm but his theory of four styles (and their vices) is a development of Theophrastus' doctrine of *virtutes dicendi*.[256] Later rhetoricians follow suit for to them these virtues no longer have to prevail everywhere in a speech. They set those which must be present everywhere (ἑλληνισμός and σαφήνεια) apart from the others which may be present in specific circumstances and which are now split up into three types of style.[257] This system of ἀρεταί has rivals and all these find a definite form in the theory of three *genera dicendi* ('high, low and mixed or middle styles').[258]

Rhetorical handbooks offer an elaborate theory of tropes and figures, which influential scholars have claimed to be a major invention of the Stoics,[259] but this view is now being abandoned.[260] A more useful answer is that with the help of Peripatetic notions both grammarians and rhetori-

---

[252] Cic. *Or.* 45-6.

[253] Theophrastus is said to have revised the topics curriculum (Alex. *Top.* 55.24-7 and 125), Strato to have added a new τόπος (Alex. *Top.* 339.30) and according to Chrysippus (Plu. *Stoic. Rep.* 1045f) he was the last Peripatetic to pay attention to dialectic. See Ophuijsen 1994 for likely further indications. And above, p. 000.

[254] Calboli Montefusco 1991, 24-6. *Status* is the issue on which a speaker may base his attack or defence. The main *status* are those of conjecture, definition, quality and objection (Kennedy 1994b, 97-101).

[255] Calboli Montefusco 1991, 25-32. These *loci communes* become the 'common-places' in the sense of 'cliché, truism'. Another development concerns Aristotle's enthymeme, a rhetorical syllogism in which one premiss and/or the conclusion may be omitted. Alongside of this comes the full-blown argument, ἐπιχείρημα, consisting of five parts (Cic. *De inv.* 57-76).

[256] Kennedy 1989a, 196-8.   [257] D.H. *Pomp.* 239.5-240.20 and *Th.* 360.2-21.

[258] Schenkeveld 1964, ch. iii.   [259] Barwick 1957, 88-111 followed by Kennedy 1994b, 91-2.

[260] E.g. by Ax 1987 and Baratin and Desbordes 1987.

cians gradually make systems of their own.[261] Some separate evolution of these theories in the circles of grammarians and rhetoricians must be assumed, since from Cicero onwards differences in definition, classification and terminology are linked to these groups.[262]

III Poetics

In the classroom the grammarian explains classical poetry as a part of the cultural heritage. This instruction does not threaten the philosopher's status though problems still arise, for example, to what extent pupils should accept poetical wisdom, and, probably, this question is tackled in Chrysippus' treatise *On the interpretation of poems*, the subject of which belongs to the ethical department.[263]

Epicurus may well have been hostile to poetry but later Epicureans seem to have weakened this position to a certain extent. Philodemus, our main source, slashes down all theories of others and interesting ideas of his own, like inseparability of form and content, seem prompted by his wish to expose others' follies rather than to make an original contribution of his own.[264]

After Theophrastus, Praxiphanes of Mytilene advocates 'the Long Epic of organic size'[265] and Callimachus writes a treatise against his views. Praxiphanes specializes in the sort of literary criticism which came to be called γραμματική and according to Clement of Alexandria he was the first to be called γραμματικός.[266] But Peripatetic contributions to poetical theory after Theophrastus are not known.[267]

Chrysippus is credited with the wish 'to accommodate the stories of Orpheus, Musaeus, Hesiod and Homer to his own statements about the immortal gods in order that even the most ancient poets, who did not even suspect this, might be seen to have been Stoics'; but this representation is Cicero's distortion of Epicurean polemic against the Stoics,[268] and

---

[261] A first step can be seen in *PHamb.* 128, wrongly ascribed to Theophrastus (Schenkeveld 1993).
[262] Schenkeveld 1991.
[263] D.L. VII.200. Cf. Plu. *Poet. Aud.* ('How the young man should study poetry'), but it is uncertain whether Chrysippus' treatise is the main source of Plutarch's.
[264] See Innes 1989, who is more confident on this point. Philodemus' theory falls outside the scope of this survey, but see Obbink 1995.   [265] Schol. Flor. on Call. *Aitia* 1–12.
[266] *Strom.* I.16.79.4.
[267] Wehrli 1969d, 121–5. Philodemus' attack in *Po.* IV, *PHerc.* 207, concerns Aristotle's *On Poets*, not an early Peripatetic treatise, as Janko 1991 shows.
[268] Cic. *ND* I.41, which arguably derives from Phld. *Piet.*, *PHerc.* 1428, col. 6. 16–28 Henrichs (cf. Long 1992, 49–50). Philodemus just says that 'Chrysippus, like Cleanthes, tried to harmonize the things [i.e. divine names and myths transmitted by the poets] attributed to Orpheus and Musaeus, and things in Homer, Hesiod, Euripides and other poets with Stoic doctrine.'

should not be taken as proof that the Stoics are the great practitioners and defenders of the allegorical interpretation of poetry.[269] In other texts[270] they say that Homer and Hesiod included in their poems myths which give a true insight. Moreover, the great bulk of what is viewed as Stoic allegoresis consists of etymologies of names of gods because originally these names represent the way people understood the world.[271] In other words, the poems of Homer and Hesiod are like clearing houses of ancient, pre-philosophical wisdom on theology. These myths must be interpreted, but this does not imply that Chrysippus detects a gap between surface meaning and hidden sense. Zeno's statement 'that Homer wrote some things in accordance with opinion and other things in accordance with truth'[272] is not a plea for allegorical interpretation either, for it expresses the common view that Homer sometimes overlays truths with a mythical covering to flavour his style and to enchant his audience.[273] Zeno, Chrysippus and other Stoics apply much philological acumen to the text of the epics by suggesting other readings or when etymologizing; their interpretation goes along the lines of Stoic beliefs but does not imply that either the poets or the original myth-makers deliberately concealed their truths about nature in misleading myths. Others, like Heraclitus and Pseudo-Plutarch go several steps further and propagate the view that Homer was his own allegorist.[274]

Other facets of ancient poetics have been ascribed to the Stoics,[275] albeit without much foundation. Several titles of Stoic works on poetry are known[276] and their fragments mostly pertain to philological interpretation. But an interesting remark of Cleanthes shows his awareness of the power of poetic form: philosophical prose lacks the words proper to 'divine greatness', and metre, melodies and rhythms come as close as possible to the truth of theory on divinity.[277]

*

So far the harvest of philosophers' contributions to poetics is not significant. This statement would be different if more were known of the con-

---

[269] E.g. Joosen and Waszink 1950, 285–6; Pépin 1976, 125–31; Pfeiffer 1968, 237.

[270] Cic. ND II.63–72 (the account of the Stoic spokesman Balbus) and [Plu.] Plac. 879c–880d.

[271] E.g. Cornutus (first cent. AD) in his De natura deorum.   [272] D. Chr. Or. 53.4.

[273] Thus Strabo (e.g. 1.2.7–9), who holds the same view for Homer's geographical descriptions; cf. Plu. Poet. Aud. 20f., who attacks the Stoics for giving childish etymologies, not for using allegorical interpretation.   [274] Long 1992.

[275] De Lacy 1948 and (extremely liberally) Colish 1990, 58–60.

[276] Zeno wrote On Homeric Problems (in five books) and On Poetic Reading, Cleanthes On the Poet and Chrysippus On Poems, How to Interpret Poems and Against the Kritikoi (D.L. VII.4; 175; 200).

[277] Phld. Mus. IV, PHerc. 1497, col. 28; cf. Sen. Ep. 108.10 and see Asmis 1992, 400–1. For Posidonius' definition of poetry see below (p. 224).

tents of Philodemus' *On Poems* and the works of authors he attacks.[278] We now have much of book v and pieces of the other books. In book v he deals with views of several persons of whom Neoptolemus, an anonymous author (a Stoic?) and Crates of Mallos get a long discussion, and he ends with a short disputation of thirteen opinions, culled from a similar work of his teacher Zeno of Sidon. Other fragments mention a specific group of κριτικοί. On the whole, Philodemus' targets look more like grammarians and literary critics than philosophers[279] but this distinction may be too definite. From his treatment we get the impression of a continuing discussion in the Hellenistic period of the relationships between content (διάνοια) and form, especially composition and arrangement of words into lines (σύνθεσις), and its ensuing effect of sound (εὐφωνία). Thus to the κριτικοί content and choice of words are common to all poets and a poet's only means to achieve excellence is in putting together his material in an individual way, that is, through σύνθεσις and εὐφωνία. If these are good, a poem is good. To know this one needs no *logos*, for the trained ear is sufficient to make judgements.[280] Crates accepts euphony as a criterion but only insofar as it agrees with the rational principles of the poetic art; but he also says that what one judges in a poem is 'not without the thoughts, but not the thoughts themselves'.[281] The anonymous author, who is said perhaps to adhere to Stoic tenets and whose name may be Aristo,[282] also accepts euphony as very important but at the same time asks for serious meaning. Similar and other statements are found in Philodemus' doxography at the end of his fifth book.[283]

Before this part Philodemus discusses views of a Neoptolemus, who is identical with Neoptolemus of Parium, one of Horace's sources for his *Ars poetica*.[284] He distinguishes between ποίημα as the aspect which is related to style only and ποίησις which involves content, thought, plot, and characters. Together they are the εἴδη of the poetic craft, which is mastered by its third member, the poet. Philodemus opposes this theory and finds the main *differentia* in the fact that a short poem, or a part of a larger one, is ποίημα, and a large poem, like the *Iliad*, ποίησις. Probably

---

[278] See now the contributions in Obbink 1995.

[279] Praxiphanes, Demetrius of Byzantium, Neoptolemus, an anonymous author (see n. 282) and Crates of Mallos. See Isnardi Parente 1987, 97.

[280] See Schenkeveld 1968; Blank 1994 and Porter 1995.

[281] See Asmis 1992, 398 and Porter 1992, 112–14, who interprets these lines (col. 28. 26–9) as suggesting allegoresis. Though Crates calls himself κριτικός, not γραμματικός (S.E. *M* 1.79 and 248), Philodemus does not present him as belonging to the κριτικοί (*Po*. v.xxvii.7–9 Mangoni).

[282] Aristo of Chios was a pupil of Zeno. The latest discussions of Jensen's crucial supplements in col. 13.28–30, which give awkward Greek, in Isnardi Parente 1987, 1–3 (*contra*) and Asmis 1990c, 149–50 and Porter 1994 (*pro*).   [283] See Asmis 1992.

[284] *Po*. v coll. 13.32–16.28 Mangoni. See Brink 1963, 48–51; and Mangoni 1993, 53–61.

Neoptolemus' differentiation is a reaction against Callimachus' insistence on small poems displaying the poet's craft, for he claims unity for big poems also.[285] Later, Posidonius argues that ποίημα is a metrical or rhythmical way of elaborate speech (he exemplifies it by one poetic line), and ποίησις is a 'significant ποίημα that contains an imitation of things divine and human'. This difference is related to the Stoic distinction between *lexis* as diction and *logos*, meaningful diction,[286] but the addition about the particular type of *mimēsis* shows that he has epic poetry in mind in particular.[287] In this way Posidonius, too, is involved in the debate on long and short poems.

Like most Greeks (and Romans) Neoptolemus stresses both moral function and pleasing effect as aims of poetry.[288] Eratosthenes is one of the few who hold that every poet aims at entertainment (ψυχαγωγία) only[289] and though to Philodemus, too, poetry is morally neutral[290] he does not mention him. Connected with entertainment is the notion of φαντασία, visualization or presentation of images to the mind of a writer and through the text to a reader. Perhaps this theory of φαντασία in literary criticism is a Stoic contribution. Indeed, Chrysippus says that any product of human *technē* is preceded by a φαντασία of the τεχνίτης,[291] but already in Aristotle the term is there, albeit outside his *Poetics* and *Rhetoric*, as well as all the separate elements of this theory. The ensuing typology of the narration which has degrees of truthfulness as its criterion[292] may be due to Peripatetic scholarship as well.[293]

*

The relationship between Alexandrian scholarship as the art of understanding, explaining, and restoring the literary tradition and Peripatetic philosophy is a complex one. Pfeiffer favours the opinion that because of a new conception of poetry Philitas and Zenodotus initiate a new discipline.[294] At the same time he acknowledges as a second stage of the process the great debt of the Alexandrians to Aristotelian criticism, and this point should be stressed to a greater extent.[295] The scholia on Homer and the tragedians show that the Alexandrian scholars use Peripatetic stan-

---

[285] Brink 1963, 43–74; 79–150 for more (possibly) Aristotelian reminiscences in these fragments.
[286] See above, p. 186.   [287] D.L. VII.60.   [288] Phld. *Po.* v col. 16 and cf. Hor. *Ars* 333–4.
[289] Strabo I.1.10.   [290] *Po* v. col. 1–2 Mangoni.
[291] David *Prol.* 43.30–44.5, cf. Meijering 1987, 105.
[292] 'True, false and as-it-were-true stories' are distinguished by Asclepiades of Myrlea (S.E. *M* I.252–5 and 263–4).   [293] Meijering 1987, 18–25; 53 and 73–98.
[294] Pfeiffer 1968, 140, cf. 1, 67, 88, 104 etc.
[295] Pfeiffer 1968, 95; Meijering 1987, and Richardson 1994, 27–8.

dards in their criticism. The terms may change[296] but the ideas remain the same: poetry creates emotions and this effect is also achieved by a poet's arrangement of his material (οἰκονομία). Aristarchus' atheteses depend on his implicit poetics about functionality and internal consistency[297] and his defence of mythical impossibilities recalls Aristotle's views.[298]

A special case is Crates.[299] Practising in Pergamum he applies Stoic views in his own way to Homer's description of the heaven represented on the shield of Achilles[300] and thinks that Homer's cosmos is spherical in shape, which view he defends at other places too. Aristarchus often reacts against Crates' exegetic *tours de force*. In all, Crates seems to be an outsider to the mainstream of Hellenistic scholarship.[301]

---

[296] Thus μῦθος (plot) is replaced by ὑπόθεσις.   [297] See Schenkeveld 1970.

[298] Porter 1992, 73–84, also defending Aristarchan provenance of the maxim 'elucidate Homer from Homer' against Pfeiffer 1968, 225–7.   [299] Porter 1992, 85–114.

[300] *Il.* xviii.481–9.

[301] Janko 1995, 92–5 (cf. also Porter 1992, 95–114) suggests that Crates had great influence on Roman thought about poetry and language.

PART III

EPISTEMOLOGY

*

7

Introduction: the beginnings of Hellenistic epistemology

JACQUES BRUNSCHWIG

I The epistemological turn

It is generally agreed that the Hellenistic period is the great age of ancient epistemology. For a variety of reasons, many of which have nothing to do with the history of philosophy, the period is standardly deemed to start in 323 BC on the death of Alexander the Great. By a curious coincidence, two philosophers of signal and symbolic importance had connections with Alexander. The first is Aristotle, who had been tutor to the young Alexander and who died a year after his royal pupil, leaving a vast body of scientific and philosophical work which, after a period of mixed fortune, would for centuries be considered – in particular by the sceptics[1] – as a model of dogmatic thought. The second is Pyrrho, some twenty years younger than Aristotle, who accompanied Alexander on his eastern campaign: he returned from Asia in his prime, and the words and deeds which filled the rest of his long life caused him, rightly or wrongly, to be regarded for centuries as the eponymous hero of scepticism.

It is tempting – and conventional – to assert that, on Aristotle's death, philosophy saw itself driven from a happy paradise of epistemological innocence, and that the poison of doubt, spat out by the serpent of Pyrrhonism, would oblige any future philosopher who failed to succumb to it to earn his neo-dogmatic bread by the sweat of his brow. And this picture makes a pleasing diptych with the picture which is painted, with equal facility, of the state of ethics: before the geopolitical earthquake provoked by Alexander, the moral existence of the Greeks had been firmly framed by the ethical and political structures of the city-state; after the earthquake, the new Hellenistic schools could offer the shaken citizenry nothing more than recipes for individual salvation.

The widespread notion that the beginning of the Hellenistic period is

---

[1] See S.E. *PH* I.3.

marked by an 'epistemological turn' rests on considerations both philosophical and historical. From the philosophical point of view, it seems
natural to suppose that the birth of an epistemology worthy of the name –
that is to say, of systematic reflection on the possibilities and the limits of
knowledge, on its criteria and its instruments – implies the prior existence of a sceptical challenge; for there must be something to jolt us out of
the naive complacency which marked our initial forays into the field of
knowledge before we had taken stock of the intellectual means at our disposal. The gage will be thrown – and picked up – only by men who have
already lost their epistemological virginity.

From the historical point of view, it can be maintained that, before the
death of Aristotle, there were no true sceptical schools of thought in
Greece. Sceptical inclinations, sceptical arguments, even sceptical thinkers may indeed be discovered. But the inclinations coexist with opposite
inclinations; the arguments are not collected in any systematic fashion;
and the thinkers, isolated or eccentric, are peripheral figures. Again,
before various types of self-conscious and articulated scepticism made
their appearance at the beginning of the Hellenistic period, Greek thinkers, when they considered epistemological problems, took the possibility
and the actuality of knowledge for granted and concerned themselves primarily with the nature of knowledge, its origins, and its structure. (The
case of Aristotle is often presented as a paradigm.) This epistemological
optimism is of a piece with what are called the 'realist' presuppositions of
Greek thought; for, since the time of Parmenides, it was not – or not primarily – truth which raised philosophical problems: it was error.[2]

Towards the end of the fourth century, however, Greek theorizing
about knowledge seems to 'undergo some dramatic changes: new technical terms are introduced by Epicurus and the Stoic Zeno, indicating a
shift of interest from the question "What is knowledge?", given that there
is such a thing, to "Is there any knowledge?"'.[3] It is tempting to suppose
that this reorientation was the effect of a radical questioning of the very
possibility of knowledge, a questioning which first appears in the two
chief versions of Hellenistic scepticism which go back to Pyrrho and to
Arcesilaus (who was the younger by some fifty years). After these men, the
critical question became the primary question to which every philosophical school had to provide an answer. (Thus Aristocles of Messene at the
start of his critical exposition of Pyrrhonism: 'It is necessary to examine
first of all our capacity for knowledge; for if by nature we are incapable of

---

[2] See esp. Burnyeat 1982a; Denyer 1991.   [3] Striker 1990, 143.

knowing anything, then there is no need to proceed further on any other matter' (cited by Eus. *PE* XIV.18.1).)

The answer to the critical question usually took the form of a theory about the 'criterion of truth': either it was said that we have no access to truth at all, that is, that there is no such criterion; or else it was maintained that we do have one or more ways of discovering the truth, ways which must then be identified and described (this was the task to which, each in their own manner, the Epicureans and the Stoics dedicated themselves). The official stance of the sceptics was this: they suspended judgement about whether or not there is a criterion (cf. *PH* II.18). In this way the remarkable interest shown by Hellenistic philosophy in the problem of the criterion[4] may be seen as a sign of the new predominance of epistemological concerns.

This orthodox interpretation needs to be modified in various ways, both philosophically and historically. First, it is plain that the two questions which are supposed to have dominated classical epistemology and Hellenistic epistemology – the questions 'What is knowledge?' and 'How, if at all, is knowledge possible?' – are not entirely independent of each other. An answer to the first question necessarily has implications for the second. The higher the bar of knowledge is set, the more difficult it is to clear – and you can only clear it at the height at which it has been set. If we look, say, at Plato's *Theaetetus* we see that the first answer to the question 'What is knowledge?', namely the suggestion that knowledge is perception, is immediately conflated with Protagoras' thesis that 'man is the measure of all things', which excludes all objective knowledge and leaves the notion of truth with no sense outside a framework of universal relativism.[5] Again, Aristotle, discussing demonstrative knowledge rather than knowledge in general, had already shown (*APo* I.3) that if you suppose all knowledge to be demonstrative, then you must admit (as some of his contemporaries admitted) that knowledge either is impossible, insofar as it presupposes an infinite regression, or else is either circular or based on arbitrary hypotheses.[6] Before the Hellenistic period, then, it seems that philosophers were perfectly aware of the fact that any conception of what knowledge is will have implications for the possibility of human access to knowledge.

---

[4] For which see below, pp. 261–4; 316–21; 338–9.

[5] The seminal importance of the *Theaetetus* for all ancient and modern epistemology has often been stressed; see most recently and most forcefully Burnyeat 1990.

[6] Infinite regression, reciprocity (or the 'diallele'), and mere hypothesizing were invoked, much later, in the sceptical interest: they are three of the 'tropes' ascribed to Agrippa. See Barnes 1990b.

From an historical point of view, observe that the different versions of scepticism which appeared in the Hellenistic period always claimed pre-Aristotelian pedigrees. This is true of Pyrrho, who, we are told, declared himself indebted to Democritus (D.L. IX.67); it is true of Timon, who assigned a special role to Xenophanes in his *Silli*; and it is true of Arcesilaus, scholarch of the Academy, who claimed to be faithful to the tradition of Socrates and Plato.[7] These exhibitions of ancestral portraits were admittedly retrospective; and they were sometimes so contrived as to border on the absurd. Even so, and remembering that our evidence is patchy and that a large number of texts are lost, we can be sure that Hellenistic scepticism was not a creation *ex nihilo*, and that reflection on the limits and sometimes on the vanity of knowledge had occupied the Presocratics and the Sophists, not to mention Socrates himself. If it is suggested that the earlier philosophers had never faced epistemological challenges comparable to those which were to determine a central part of the agenda of the Hellenistic schools, then it is enough to invoke the seriousness with which Plato, in the *Theaetetus*, treats the threat posed by Protagorean relativism,[8] and the crucial debate on the principle of non-contradiction and the law of excluded middle which Aristotle conducts with opponents whom later Peripatetics – and some modern scholars – thought they could identify as precursors of Pyrrho or even as Pyrrho himself.[9]

*

To introduce the issues discussed in this Part it is useful to recall that the ancient authors – historians, doxographers, polemicists, philosophers (including the sceptical philosophers themselves) – found it difficult to locate scepticism on the philosophical map. For – to change the metaphor – in the farmyard of ancient philosophy there strutted many a fine dogmatic fowl and scepticism waddled about like an ugly duck.

There are many reasons why it was difficult, both historically and conceptually, to classify and categorize scepticism. First, if scepticism made its official entry in the Hellenistic period, it did so in two different intellectual contexts and in two different forms: the scepticism of Pyrrho and the scep-

---

[7] See Cic. *De Orat.* III.67; *Fin.* II.2; *Acad.* I.46; Anon. *Proleg. in Plat. Phil.* 10. On the sceptical interpretation of Plato see the discussion between Annas 1990a and Lévy 1990; and also Lévy 1992.

[8] Note, however, the important remarks in Annas and Barnes 1985, 97–8, on the difference between relativism and scepticism.

[9] See Aristocl. *apud* Eus. *PE* XIV.18.2. On Aristotle's attitude to the sceptical ideas of which he was aware see Long 1981; Berti 1981; Barnes 1987. On Pyrrho as *au fait* with Aristotle see Conche 1973, 17, 35–6; Reale 1981, 281–3, 316–21.

ticism of Arcesilaus. And since these two thinkers made a great stir and yet left nothing in writing, their views were all the more liable to be adapted and distorted by later thinkers. Pyrrho, as peripheral a figure as he was original, was deemed to have introduced a version of scepticism which was upheld for a time by his immediate pupils, in particular by Timon, and which was revived much later by a long sequence of philosophers from Aenesidemus to Sextus Empiricus, philosophers whom it is convenient to label Neopyrrhonians. A little later than Pyrrho, Arcesilaus was elected head of Plato's Academy and introduced a sceptical interpretation of the heritage of Socrates and Plato. He thus inaugurated a series of 'Academies', which developed and changed, through incessant argument with the Stoics, down to the time of Carneades and of Philo of Larissa and Antiochus. The historical and philosophical relations between the two branches of scepticism are very obscure. It seems likely that Arcesilaus had heard of Pyrrho; but ancient sources which couple the two men usually do so to mock or compromise Arcesilaos.[10] Later, the Neopyrrhonians refer to the sceptical Academy only to distance themselves from it, ascribing to the Academy a negative meta-dogmatism – which they seem to have invented for their own purposes.[11] Philosophically speaking, it is difficult to distinguish between the Neopyrrhonian and the Academic versions of scepticism, and scholars ancient and modern have offered different accounts.[12]

The dual nature of ancient scepticism was not the only reason for doxographical embarrassment. To begin with, could you speak of a sceptical *school* at all? The very idea of sceptical doctrines, on a par with the doctrines of the other philosophical schools, seemed a contradiction in terms: if a philosophical school is defined by its 'dogmas' – by the characteristic theses which it maintains and in favour of which it argues – then how could there be a school without dogmas, an antidogmatic (or rather an adogmatic) school? The problem was posed in these terms first by the sceptics themselves and then by the doxographers. Sextus[13] asks whether properly speaking scepticism is a 'sect' (αἵρεσις) at all. His answer is interestingly subtle. Instead of flatly denying that the sceptics 'belong to a sect', he distinguishes between two senses of 'αἵρεσις', a strong and a

---

[10] As did Aristo in his famous parody of Homer, on which see below, n. 72.

[11] On all this see S.E. *PH* 1.1–3, 226–35; Cic. *Acad.* 1.45; on the sense which should be given to the terms 'negative dogmatism' and 'metadogmatism' see Barnes 1992, 4252 n.54, 4254 n.72.

[12] See Gell. XI.5.1–8. Plutarch wrote an essay on the subject (Lamprias catalogue no. 64) which has not survived. See Striker 1981; Decleva Caizzi 1986.

[13] *PH* 1.16–17, the immediate source of which is certainly the same as that of a text in D.L. 1.20. (According to Glucker 1978, 176 the source is Aenesidemus; but note that the same problem about non-dogmatic schools is posed in connection with the Cynics: D.L. VI.103.)

weak. In the strong sense a sect involves 'adherence to a number of dogmas which cohere both with one another and with the phenomena', a dogma being 'an assent to something unclear': in this sense only dogmatic schools are sects. But in the weak sense a sect is

> a way of life which coheres with an account in accordance with the phenomena, the account showing how it is possible to live correctly (where "correctly" is taken not specifically with reference to virtue but more loosely) and also supplying the ability to suspend judgement. (S. E. *PH* 1.17)

and in this sense the sceptics do belong to a sect. This distinction and the fact that it is found in Sextus is enough to show how the sceptics' own reflection on their philosophical position could influence and guide the work of the doxographers: in order to write *On Sects*, Περὶ Αἱρέσεων, they needed a criterion to determine what was a sect and what was not.

The same connection between philosophical preoccupations and historical concerns can be seen in another branch of the doxographical tradition, where the material is organized not by sects but by 'successions' (διαδοχαί). Pyrrho's position in a scheme of this sort seems firmly fixed by the authors of 'Successions', who regularly set him in a line which goes back (by way of intermediaries) first to the Atomists, Leucippus and Democritus, and then to the Eleatics, Parmenides and Melissus and Zeno.

The most interesting thing about these genealogies, from our present point of view, emerges from their attempts to fit the sequence Parmenides–Democritus–Pyrrho into a larger context; for here we find hesitations and debates which show what was at stake when scepticism came to be located in the history of ancient thought. Sometimes the general schema is bipartite (Ionians and Italians);[14] the succession Parmenides–Democritus is fitted in either by positing a line Pythagoras–Xenophanes–Parmenides[15] or else by connecting Parmenides directly to the Pythagorean Ameinias.[16] In the latter case, Xenophanes finds himself isolated – perhaps as the first of the sceptics.[17] Sometimes the general schema is tripartite (Ionians, Italians, Eleatics). The Eleatic line is then presented as starting from Xenophanes, the putative teacher of Parmenides. Xenophanes stands at the interchange, with possible connections upline towards the Pythagoreans and downline towards the Eleatics. Diogenes Laertius reflects these differences inasmuch as he presents Xenophanes now as a pupil of the Pythagoreans (1.15), now as an iso-

---

[14] See D.L. I.13–15.   [15] D.L. I.15; cf. Arist. *Metaph.* A.986b21.   [16] Sotion in D.L. IX.21.
[17] Sotion in D.L. IX.20.

lated figure (ix.20), now as someone whom Parmenides 'heard but did not follow' (ix.21).

The fact that Xenophanes occupies the key position is no doubt due first of all to his sceptical inclinations which are exemplified above all in DK 21 B 34, a celebrated and much discussed fragment which, on one possible interpretation, may be seen as an exposition of the first argument in favour of scepticism.[18] But equally important is the fact that, for this very reason, he was an object of sustained attention, if not from Pyrrho himself,[19] then at least from his principal pupil Timon. Timon was certainly the first to set the new form of wisdom incarnated by his master in the context of the Greek philosophical tradition: he was concerned to scotch the idea that Pyrrho was a peripheral or even an exotic figure, and to show that several earlier philosophers could be presented as honourable if errant ancestors of Pyrrhonism. Timon's work, despite its satirical and burlesque aspects, was based on accurate knowledge. Antigonus of Carystus made use of it in his life of Pyrrho. It was taken seriously by Sotion, who wrote in detail about Timon in Book xi of his *Successions*[20] and who had devoted a whole book to the *Silli*.[21] Timon not only set Pyrrho on a pedestal: he also gave him a determinate position on the chessboard of ancient philosophy.

Let us now consider, from the epistemological angle, the section of the 'succession' which runs from Democritus to Pyrrho. Here we meet a notion often invoked by modern scholars – the notion of sceptical atomism. What it amounts to is this. A certain number of philosophers, of whom the least ill known to us are Metrodorus of Chios and Anaxarchus of Abdera, developed the atomistic physics of Democritus and at the same time watered the seeds of scepticism which they found sprouting in his epistemological nursery. But their sceptical atomism was inherently unstable and it soon separated into a non-atomistic scepticism (Pyrrho) and a non-sceptical atomism (Epicurus).

This schema implies, among other things, that Pyrrho was a thinker preoccupied by epistemological issues – indeed, that he was a sceptic whose views derived straight from Democritus.[22] In order to assess the historical and philosophical credentials of the schema let us first examine

[18] The fragment was often cited and discussed by the sceptics (see S.E. *M* vii.49, 110; viii.326; partial quotations elsewhere). Among numerous modern analyses see Fraenkel 1925, Guthrie 1962, 1.395–401, Barnes 1979, 137–43, Lesher 1978, Hussey 1990.
[19] As far as I know, no text indicates that Pyrrho had any interest in Xenophanes.
[20] See D.L. ix.110, 112, 115.   [21] See Athen. viii.336d.
[22] On Democritus' epistemology see (out of a vast literature) Guthrie 1965, ii.454–65; Barnes 1979, 559–64; MacKim 1984.

the relation between its two extreme points, Democritus and Pyrrho. Pyrrho's interest in Democritus is firmly attested: according to the evidence of his close pupil and follower, Philo of Athens, the authors whom Pyrrho quoted most frequently were Democritus and Homer. What Democritus did he quote? The text does not tell us but we may guess, on analogy with what it tells us about Homer:

> He admired him and frequently cited the line: 'As are the generations of leaves, so are the generations of men' [*Il.* vi.146]; he also compared men to wasps and flies and birds;[23] and he quoted these verses too: 'And you too, my friend, you die. Why grieve so? Patroclus is dead, a far better man than you' [*Il.* xxi.106–7]; and all the verses which seem to bear on men's instability and futility and on their childishness. (D.L. ix.67)

This invocation of Homer is utterly different from that of 'certain people' who presented Homer as 'the founder of the sceptical school' on the grounds that 'more than anyone he said different things at different times about one and the same matter and never asserted anything fixedly dogmatic' (D.L. ix.71). This absurd explanation comes at the beginning of a passage, workmanlike if somewhat muddled, in which Diogenes lists the ancestors of scepticism (ix.71–3) – and where of course we find Democritus and his 'sceptical' fragments.

It is plain that the Homer who interested Pyrrho was the observer of the human tragi-comedy and not the putative author of a sceptical epistemology. It is odds-on that there was a similar difference between the Democritus who interested Pyrrho and the Democritus whose epistemological patronage Pyrrho's later followers were to claim. Pyrrho's Democritus, we may suppose, was the laughing philosopher: not a man who theorized about knowledge but a man who contemplated a world entirely ruled by chance and necessity; not an epistemologist who despaired of finding the *truth* but a detached observer of a universe which has no *meaning*.

The line which leads from Democritus to Pyrrho does not, after all, seem to take us from one sceptical epistemology to another. And thus we should not suppose that the principal intermediaries who, in the traditional genealogy, separate and link the two thinkers will be found in their expected places. They are Metrodorus of Chios and Anaxarchus of

---

[23] Decleva Caizzi 1981a, 20 and 173, is surely right to construe the sentence in such a way that Pyrrho rather than Homer is the author of the comparisons (*pace* Hicks 1925, Russo 1978, Gigante 1983b).

Abdera, men who are in any case very different from each other; and although they are not properly speaking Hellenistic philosophers, a few lines may be devoted to them here inasmuch as they standardly feature in Pyrrho's intellectual pedigree.

*

If the label 'sceptical atomist' can be applied to anyone, then Metrodorus of Chios is probably the best candidate. We are told that, an atomist and a Democritean as far as principles went, he was independent 'in everything else' (Theophrastus *apud* Simp. *Phys.* 28.27 = *Phys. Op.* fr. 8 Diels = fr. 229 FHSG). It is not easy to determine what 'everything else' was. It seems clear that he was very interested in meteorological questions (DK 70 A 9–21). Again, in support of Democritus' theory of the infinity of worlds, he employed an original metaphor and implicitly used an interesting version of the principle of sufficient reason: 'It is absurd that a single stalk of corn should appear in a large field or a single world in the infinite void' (DK 70 A 6).

At the same time, he appears to have been a sceptic; for according to several sources he began his work *On Nature* with a shattering declaration: 'None of us knows anything not even whether we know or do not know this very thing (sc. that we do not know anything).'[24] The phrase was striking enough to win notoriety, extreme enough to be taken[25] as the inspiration for Pyrrho's extravagances, and subtle enough to have been transmitted in different forms, some of them more and some of them less complex.[26] Whatever the precise wording and the exact sense of Metrodorus' declaration, it turns on the ingenious device of combining a first order statement of ignorance ('we do not know anything') with a second order statement of ignorance the content of which is the first statement ('we do not even know this, viz. that we know nothing'). This complexity seems to intimate a scepticism which has already reached a refined level and which is trying to defend itself in advance against the

---

[24] Οὐδεὶς ἡμῶν οὐδὲν οἶδεν, οὐδ' αὐτὸ τοῦτο, πότερον οἴδαμεν ἢ οὐκ οἴδαμεν (Eus. *PE* XIV.19.8). The sentence seems to admit of two grammatically possible construals: (a) one, which my translation presupposes, takes αὐτὸ τοῦτο to refer to the initial proposition ('none of us knows anything') and to serve proleptically as object of the verbs οἴδαμεν ἢ οὐκ οἴδαμεν; (b) αὐτὸ τοῦτο could also be read as a second object of οἶδεν and taken to refer to the indirect question, πότερον οἴδαμεν ἢ οὐκ οἴδαμεν: the translation would then be: 'None of us knows anything, not even this, viz., whether we know or do not know.' But I find it difficult to construe the verbs of the indirect question without any object; hence I prefer (a).

[25] Already by Eusebius, in the context of his quotation.

[26] See esp. Cic. *Acad.* II.73; S.E. *M* VII.88; cf. DK 69 A 2; 70 A 23, A 25. See Brunschwig 1996.

charge of negative meta-dogmatism to which first order sceptical statements are liable.[27]

These reflections only sharpen the paradox: how can Metrodorus' sophisticated scepticism be reconciled with his atomistic physics and with his meteorological researches? To solve this problem some scholars have played down Metrodorus' dogmatism in physics,[28] others (more numerous) his scepticism.[29] A third solution may be suggested. It starts from asking who are 'we', to whom Metrodorus ascribes a dual ignorance. The word 'we' need not necessarily refer to all men at all times: it might refer rather to men as they are now, before they have read Metrodorus' book and before they have been convinced by the truth of the doctrines which he expounds there. From this point of view, the opening declaration, far from forbidding a dogmatic exposition of atomistic physics, might actually have been designed to underline the rational power and the scientific importance of the atomic theory.[30]

Democritean atomism is a strongly counterintuitive theory. We see colours and we hear sounds (in other words, we use the 'bastard' form of knowledge: M VII.139) not only before we have learned the truth of atomism but also long afterwards (see M VII.136–7; D.L. IX.72). In this way, then, we remain 'separated' from the truth even after we have learned atomic physics, and thus first order scepticism is true. But once we have been taught atomism, we know that we are 'separated' from the truth, we know why we are, and we know what this truth is: in this way we can overcome second order scepticism. The double form of the sceptical statement, far from making its scepticism more radical, may therefore be intended to show us our second order ignorance and to encourage us to make the necessary effort to overcome it, without thereby offering any hope of conquering first order ignorance.

Such an interpretation is speculative; but it fits well enough with the few other pieces of information which we have about Metrodorus' epistemological ideas. These pieces, it is true, seem at first sight full of contradictions. On the one hand we are told that according to Metrodorus (as according to Pythagoras, Empedocles, Parmenides, Zeno, Melissus,

---

[27] It is often supposed (e.g. Ernout and Robin 1925–8, II.226–7, Burnyeat 1978) that the form of scepticism criticized at Lucr. IV.469–73 is Metrodoran; and from this are drawn conclusions of some historical magnitude (Lucretius could not himself have chosen to attack such an antique form of scepticism and must therefore be drawing directly on Epicurus). But I do not see how one can identify Metrodorus with a sceptic against whom Lucretius *objects* that he cannot know that he knows nothing. So too Vander Waerdt 1989, 241–2 and n. 48.

[28] E.g. Nestle 1932.   [29] E.g. Brochard 1887/1923, 48.

[30] Cf. Zeller & Mondolfo 1969, 314; dal Pra 1975 (1950), 53.

Anaxagoras, Democritus, Protagoras and Plato) 'all sensations are false' (Aet. IV.9.1). On the other hand, we are told that according to him (as according to Protagoras) 'we must trust only our bodily perceptions' (Eus. *PE* XIV.2.4 and 19.8). Note that this mirrors the contradiction which pervades the doxography on Democritus in relation to his view of the 'phenomena'.[31] Note further that, in the first text, Metrodorus is placed in the company of those many philosophers who, in rejecting the senses, gave a fundamental role to imperceptible entities in their ontology (numbers, particles, atoms, Forms): no doubt he is placed among them *qua* atomist. On the other hand, in the second text Protagoras is his only companion; and here Eusebius tells us who his source was.

Aristocles, whom Eusebius quotes, said:

> Some have maintained that one should trust nothing but perception and images. According to some people, Homer himself hints at such an idea when he says that Ocean is the principle of everything, meaning that things are in a state of flux. Of those of whom we have knowledge, Metrodorus of Chios seems to have expressed the idea, although it is Protagoras of Abdera who first stated it plainly. (Eusebius *PE* XIV.20.1)

It is clear enough that Aristocles is here drawing on the first part of Plato's *Theaetetus*; for he is about to summarize its objections to Protagoras. Nonetheless, he cautiously introduces Metrodorus into the sensationalist genealogy of Plato's dialogue. Why does he do so? and why with such caution?

It is probable that he had a text of Metrodorus to hand but an obscure text, separated from its context. I think that this text has survived. Eusebius tells us (*PE* XIV.19.9) that near the beginning of his work *On Nature* Metrodorus wrote: 'All things are whatever τις may think them.' It is an enigmatic phrase which has baffled the modern commentators.[32] You need only interpret the word 'τις' in an individual sense in order to reach a Protagorean interpretation ('All things are whatever *each* may think them'). Nonetheless, Aristocles had some reason for hesitating to enlist Metrodorus in the army of the sensationalists; for Metrodorus' sentence can also be interpreted in a rationalist sense ('All things are whatever *one* can think them' that is, 'everything rational is real'). Connect this with the argument in proof of the plurality of worlds which I cited earlier and

---

[31] According to Democritus, the phenomena are 'all true' (Arist. *An.* 1.404a27; *GC* 1.315b9; *Metaph.* Γ.1009b12) or 'all false' (S.E. *M* VII.135, 369; VIII.6, 56).

[32] See Zeller & Mondolfo 1969, 314; Dumont 1988, 946; des Places 1987, 169; Alfieri 1936, ad loc; Mondolfo 1934, 305–6.

it corresponds well to the intellectual position of a tough Democritean, for whom all worlds exist which are conceptually compossible with one another and with our own – and who thus lies on the line leading from Democritus to Epicurus rather than on the line leading from Democritus to Pyrrho.[33]

According to the traditional 'succession', Anaxarchus of Abdera stands somewhere between Metrodorus and Pyrrho, whose teacher and friend he was. He was certainly a complex and an interesting character – and a philosopher of sorts.[34] But – despite a few scraps of evidence to the contrary – he seems to have been neither an atomist nor a sceptic, and he may be held to have contributed nothing to epistemology. To be sure, Sextus counts him among those who 'abolished the criterion' (*M* VII.88), and it is in this context that he ascribes to him (and also to the Cynic Monimus) a splendidly Shakespearean saying: 'they compared the things that exist (τὰ ὄντα) to scene-painting, and supposed that they were like the visions of a dreamer or a madman'. The theatrical image might well have appealed to a Democritean inclined towards scepticism; but the association with Monimus might rather suggest an interpretation of the words τὰ ὄντα ('the things that exist') in terms not of the world of nature but rather of the world of human action and human practice.

The fact is that Anaxarchus was primarily a court philosopher, whose complex attitude towards Alexander the Great has been assessed in widely differing ways. Two fragments of the only work ascribed to him, an essay *On Kingship*, show him mainly interested in the practical relations between intellectuals and the king: he claims to be a polymath (a claim hardly compatible with his supposed scepticism), and tries to show when polymathy is advantageous and when it is disadvantageous in dealings with the powerful. As to his influence on Pyrrho, it appears to have been fundamentally ethical in content and negative as well as positive.[35]

---

[33] In Lucr. v.526–8, 531–3 (cf. 1344–5), if not in the surviving works of Epicurus, we find the idea that in virtue of the principle of ἰσονομία all the rationally possible explanations of a meteorological phenomenon are true in one or other of the infinite worlds, even though it is impossible to say which of them holds in our world. Nothing allows us to ascribe to Metrodorus an anticipation of the Epicurean doctrine of multiple explanations; nonetheless, his well attested interest in meteorology, the domain *par excellence* for the doctrine, might have drawn him to the attention of the Epicureans. Perhaps they discovered in him the model for their own combination of a confident rationalism with a limited and tentative form of 'scepticism' (as in the passages of Lucr. just cited). See, along similar lines, Sedley 1976a, 136 and 156 n. 77.

[34] See Loppolo 1980b, Gigante & Dorandi 1980, Dorandi 1994c and d, Brunschwig 1994f.

[35] See the anecdotes in D.L. IX.63; and note Timon's ambivalent quatrain (fr. 58) where the ultimate source for the judgement must surely have been Pyrrho himself.

II Pyrrho

Pyrrho has much in common with Socrates – in particular, each had a unique character, and each wrote nothing. Such things lend themselves to passionate attachments, to the birth of legend, and to distortions of every kind. With regard to Pyrrho it is sometimes tempting to adopt the splendid agnosticism of a late sceptic, Theodosius, who said, logically enough, that scepticism should not be called Pyrrhonism 'since if the movements of someone else's mind cannot be grasped, we shall never know Pyrrho's state of mind, and, in ignorance of that, we shall not be able to call ourselves Pyrrhonians' (D.L. IX.70). Modern interpretations of Pyrrho's thought are numerous and deeply divided.[36] The problem which most concerns us here, and which is not at all new, is this: to what extent can we attribute to Pyrrho a sceptical epistemology more or less close to the one which was developed in his name by Aenesidemus and the Neopyrrhonians? and to what extent was Pyrrho rather – or indeed primarily – a moralist, the inventor of a new art of happiness based on impassibility and imperturbability? (Which is how he always appears in Cicero, whose texts regularly associate him with the indifferentists Aristo of Chios and Herillus of Carthage.)[37]

According to an ancient orthodoxy, promoted by the Neopyrrhonians,[38] Pyrrho was above all an epistemologist: he was a thorough-going sceptic. Modern scholars who accept this orthodoxy rely primarily on a passage in Aristocles, which is unanimously and rightly held to be crucial to the interpretation of Pyrrho's thought, and which will later be quoted in full. In spite of certain difficulties, which will be rehearsed in due time, this text has been thought to ascribe the following epistemological position to Pyrrho: 'he urged, no doubt on the basis of some of the arguments later collected by Aenesidemus, that "our perceptions and our beliefs are neither

[36] A helpful summary in Reale 1981, who catalogues no less than eight different (and unequally represented) interpretations, namely: (1) 'epistemologico-phenomenalistic' (roughly, the Neopyrrhonian interpretation, still the most widespread since Hirzel 1877–83, Natorp 1884, Zeller 1909; cf. Stough 1969, Dumont 1972, dal Pra 1950/1975, Russo 1978); (2) 'dialectico-Hegelian'; (3) 'scientistic' (Pyrrho as an empirical thinker, like the later sceptical doctors; cf. Mills Patrick 1899 and 1929); (4) 'practico-ethical' (the main rival to (1), mainly represented by Brochard 1887; cf. Robin 1944, von Fritz 1963, Ausland 1989, Hankinson 1995); (5) 'metaphysical' (Raphael 1931); (6) 'antimetaphysical-nihilist' (Conche 1973); (7) 'orientalist' (Frenkian 1958, Piantelli 1978, Flintoff 1980); (8) 'literary' (see the astonishing – and in many ways prophetic – paper by Malaparte 1929).

[37] See 69A-M Decleva Caizzi. Aristo and Herillus are peripheral Stoics: Cicero refers several times to the fact that these representatives of indifferentism – with whom he associates Pyrrho – have been discredited and forgotten (see Off. 1.6; Fin. 11.35, v.23; Tusc. v.85; De orat. 111.62).

[38] But note the cautious words of Sextus, PH 1.7.

truthful nor liars". Then "how are things?" They are unassessable and undecidable. Our attitude to them will therefore be one of indifference, and ἀφασία (*aphasia*) will follow, with tranquillity its shadow. "Is honey really sweet?" We shall not say "Yes", we shall not say "No". (Nor shall we say "Yes and No", nor even "Neither Yes nor No".) Rather, we shall say "No more sweet than not." By that formula we shall mean that we cannot say what honey is like, and our use of the formula expresses our suspension of judgement on the question . . . All we can do is say how things appear.'[39] Since the text in Aristocles derives from Pyrrho's own pupil Timon, orthodox scholars think that we shall do well to believe it.

Other scholars have denied that Pyrrho's motivation was epistemological. With individual variants and using different arguments, most of the heterodox have portrayed a Pyrrho who was primarily a moralist; and they have offered a different interpretation of the passage in Aristocles. Since this section will offer a fairly radical version of the ethical interpretation, the reader should be reminded that there are many other suggestions on the market and that the case of Pyrrho is, and is likely to remain, highly controversial.

It may be helpful to begin by looking at the evidence for Pyrrho's philosophical education. We have already seen that the distant influence of Democritus must have been that of a moralist rather than an epistemologist; and we have also seen that the direct influence of Anaxarchus was less that of a teacher of doctrine than of a model – a controversial model – of behaviour. But Anaxarchus is not the only teacher whom the tradition ascribes to Pyrrho.

At first obscure and poor, a painter of little talent,[40] Pyrrho became the pupil of 'Bryson <pupil> of Stilpo' (Alexander Polyhistor, *apud* D.L. ix.61) before becoming the pupil of Anaxarchus. This text has given rise to much discussion – not least because there may have been more than one philosopher called Bryson. The details need not concern us, but there is something philosophical at stake: the presence of Bryson ensures that Pyrrho is not solely attached to the tradition of Abdera and Democritus; in addition he is connected to the Megaric or the Dialectical tradition – and hence to Socrates. (Thus Pyrrho gains legitimacy and chronological priority over Arcesilaus, who also claimed Socrates as a forebear.) We may suppose

---

[39] Stopper 1983, 274–5.

[40] Antigonus of Carystus *ap.* D.L. ix.61–2. According to Aristocles (Eus. *PE* xiv.18.27) – if the text is construed in what I think is the correct way, given the syntax and the context (so des Places 1987) – Anaxarchus himself had been an unsuccessful painter before being converted to philosophy by reading Democritus (*pace* Decleva Caizzi 1981a, 91, and most other commentators). Why not?

either that Pyrrho was in fact taught by Bryson (of Heraclea) but that the doxography falsely made this Bryson a Megaric,[41] or else that Bryson was indeed attached in some way to the Megaric tradition and that the doxography falsely made him Pyrrho's first teacher. The second hypothesis may be supported by several considerations. The sources closest to Pyrrho – Timon and Antigonus of Carystus – are silent about Bryson. Moreover, Pyrrho's peculiar attitudes to language are not at all Socratic or dialectical: he often talked to himself; if someone with whom he was conversing left him, he continued to talk by himself; he went off on his own without saying anything to anyone; above all, he broke the first rule of the dialectical game by giving long speeches in answer to questions (D.L. IX.63–4).[42] In order to give Pyrrho's philosophical pedigree a Socratic touch, by means of the putative influence of Bryson, the doxography had to do some pretty fancy footwork.

The education of Pyrrho calls for a few words on another question which has spilt much ink: were there any eastern influences on his thought or his style of life?[43] We know that he accompanied Anaxarchus on Alexander's expedition to the east – although we know virtually nothing about his relations with Alexander. He was impressed by the criticism which 'an Indian' addressed to Anaxarchus (D.L. IX.63). And Diogenes Laertius says that, in following Anaxarchus 'everywhere', 'he made contact with the Indian gymnosophists and with the <Persian> Magi; and this appears to have been the origin of his noble manner of philosophizing, when he introduced <into Greece> the form of inapprehensibility and of suspension of judgement, according to Ascanius of Abdera'.[44] But even if we allow that there was a genuine oriental influence,[45] we must still determine whether the influence was felt on the practical or rather on the theoretical level.

On the practical level it has been maintained that Pyrrho must have borrowed from the east certain types of ascetic and 'impassive' behaviour which had no genuine precedents in the Greek world, but the oddities of

---

[41] So Döring 1972; Decleva Caizzi 1981a.

[42] ἐν ταῖς ζητήσεσιν ὑπ' οὐδενὸς κατεφρονεῖτο διὰ τὸ ἐξοδικῶς λέγειν καὶ πρὸς ἐρώτησιν ('in philosophical inquiries he was inferior to no one because he spoke continuously even in answering questions'). We must certainly reject Wilamowitz' conjecture <καὶ δι>εξοδικῶς ('because he spoke equally well in continuous discourse and in replying to questions') which does not fit the context and which takes the wit from the remark. The MSS text is retained by Robin 1944, 22 (with excellent comments) and Decleva Caizzi 1981a, 42, 94, 182.

[43] Most of the general works on Pyrrho discuss the question; see also Frenkian 1958; Piantelli 1978; Flintoff 1980; Stopper 1983.

[44] The 'gymnosophists' or naked sages were a sort of fakir – like the legendary Calanus who climbed fearlessly onto the pyre and did not flinch as he burned, much to the astonishment of Alexander and his companions (Plu. Alex. 69.7; Arr. An. VII.3).

[45] But note the doubts in Long 1974, 80.

Pyrrho's conduct have been sketched earlier and need not be rehearsed here.[46] On the theoretical level, we must admit that the probability of any deep influence of Indian thought on Pyrrho is greatly reduced by the linguistic obstacles to intellectual communication between Greeks and orientals.[47] Despite this difficulty, some scholars have thought to find a precise trace of eastern influence in the use of a fourfold argument-schema or quadrilemma. The form is often used by certain Indian philosophers to expound problems and to show by successive steps that they are insoluble. (For example, is the world (1) eternal, or (2) non-eternal, or (3) both, or (4) neither?) Did Pyrrho use the schema?

The question arises in connection with the most important surviving piece of evidence for Pyrrho's thought, namely the fragment of Aristocles (*apud* Eus. *PE* xiv.18.1–4). Here I cite only the part which is relevant to the quadrilemma. It is the statement of what you must say 'of each thing' if you are to be happy, namely: 'it no more is or is not or is and is not or neither is nor is not'.[48] This key sentence (like so many key sentences in Greek philosophy) is, alas, syntactically ambiguous; and the translation has tried to reproduce the ambiguity. In order to dissolve it, we must choose between the following two constructions:

[A] Of each thing you must say <either> [A1] 'it no more is than is not' or [A2] 'it both is and is not' or [A3] 'it neither is nor is not'.

[B] Of each thing you must not say [B1] 'it is' rather than [B2] 'it is not', nor rather than [B3] 'it both is and is not' nor rather than [B4] 'it neither is nor is not'.

The quadrilemmatic structure is found in [B], not in [A].

The choice between [A] and [B] bears on a second issue, philosophically far more significant. According to [A] we are to state the contradictory propositions [A2] and [A3], while according to [B] we are to avoid stating these same propositions [B3] and [B4]. The question of the quadrilemma thus connects with the question of whether Pyrrho wanted deliberately to pick up the challenge thrown down by Aristotle to anyone who denied the principle of non-contradiction and to show that he could perfectly well speak and think in ways which Aristotle had claimed were impossible.[49]

---

[46] Note merely that in reaction to the anecdotes which were intended to stress Pyrrho's eccentricity (Antigonus, *apud* D.L. ix.62–3), Aenesidemus maintained that he did not lack 'foresight' in practical affairs (D.L. ix.62). Certain anecdotes allow us to see how this double interpretation derived from the studied ambiguity of some of his sayings (see Brunschwig 1992).

[47] See Str. xiv.1.64.

[48] οὐ μᾶλλον ἔστιν ἢ οὐκ ἔστιν ἢ καὶ ἔστιν καὶ οὐκ ἔστιν ἢ οὔτε ἔστιν οὔτε οὐκ ἔστιν.

[49] The same problem arises at the practical level. Aristotle asks 'why does [anyone who rejects the principle] not fall into a well or over a precipice in the morning unless he thinks that it is *not* equally good and not good to do so? It is quite plain that he thinks one better and the other

Aristotle said, of anyone who rejected the principle, that 'plainly discussion with him gets nowhere since he says nothing; for [i] he does not
say thus or not thus, but rather [ii] he says at the same time both thus and
not thus, and [iii] conversely he denies both these propositions, saying
neither thus nor not thus. Otherwise there would already be something
determinate' (*Metaph*. Γ.1008a30–4). If we compare this text with the text
of Aristocles, then at first sight the comparison favours interpretation [A]:
[i] answers to [A1], [ii] to [A2] and [iii] to [A3]; it is just as if Pyrrho took
over the words which Aristotle had found absurd. But it has been argued,
in the opposite sense, that the parallelism between the two texts is in itself
suspect.[50] Moreover, the state of '*aphasia*' which, according to Timon, is
the result of the Pyrrhonian 'disposition', excludes the assertion of
contradictory conjunctions such as [A2] and [A3]: *a fortiori* it excludes the
separate assertion of each conjunct, which is implied in the assertion of
the conjunction itself.[51]

These are real difficulties for interpretation [A] (which remains the
more commonly accepted and which is grammatically the more natural).
But they do not oblige us to accept the quadrilemmatic interpretation,
[B]. Rather, they encourage us to revise interpretation [A] in such a way
that it does *not* encourage a violation of the principle of non-contradiction. Such a revision is possible enough: since [A1] does not violate the
principle, whereas [A2] and [A3] do, we could suppose that [A2] and [A3]
are intended not as expressing alternatives to [A1] but rather as 'rhetorical
variants, couched in a deliberately paradoxical form, of the οὐ μᾶλλον
formula, <and> are not to be taken literally or at their face value'.[52] Or,
and perhaps better, [A2] and [A3] may be taken as expressing a *pis aller*:
'"of each thing, do not say that it is rather than (οὐ μᾶλλον) is not"; or, *if
you insist on affirming or denying something*, "affirm both that it is and that it
is not, or deny that it is and that it is not"'.[53] In other words: do not affirm
anything rather than deny it; but if you must affirm something, then
affirm its contradictory at the same time, and if you must deny something,
then deny its contradictory at the same time.[54] Whatever the merits of
such a solution, we may at least conclude that interpretation [A] can be

worse' (*Metaph*. Γ.1008b15–19). The anecdotes about precipices and swamps, told in very similar terms by Antigonus in D.L., seem expressly designed to show that Pyrrho had meant to
demonstrate that you could live in a manner which Aristotle had declared impossible. See
Conche 1973; Reale 1981.   [50] See Stopper 1983, 272–4.
[51] This point too is made by Stopper 1983, 274.   [52] Stopper 1983, 273.
[53] Robin 1944, 14 – my italics.
[54] We might suggest that Pyrrho found himself affirming and denying for the same reason which
made him climb trees when he was chased by fierce dogs: it is hard 'wholly to divest the man'
(D.L. IX.66). But in cases of verbal weakness, the fight τῷ λόγῳ is easier – you need only add
the contradictory.

maintained without making Pyrrho into an enemy of the principle of non-contradiction. It follows that interpretation [B], with its orientalizing implications, is not mandatory.

It is now time to set down the whole of Aristocles' report. All commentators agree that it is of primary importance for understanding Pyrrho's thought.

> It is necessary to examine first of all our capacity for knowledge; for if by nature we are incapable of knowing anything, then there is no need to proceed further on any other subject. This was maintained by some people in the past whom Aristotle confuted.[55] Pyrrho of Elis is famous for having said things of this sort; but he himself left nothing in writing. His pupil Timon says that anyone who is to be happy must consider the following three items: [1*] first, what things (τὰ πράγματα) are like by nature; [2*] secondly, what our attitude towards them ought to be; [3*] finally, what will be the result for those who adopt this attitude. [1] As for the things, he (sc. Timon) says [1a] that he (sc. Pyrrho) declares them all to be equally without difference, without balance, without decision (ἐπ᾽ ἴσης ἀδιάφορα καὶ ἀστάθμητα καὶ ἀνεπίκριτα), [1b] that for this reason (διὰ τοῦτο) neither our perceptions nor our beliefs are either true or false. [2] This is why [2a] we must not trust them, but [2b] must be without belief, without inclination, without bending (ἀδοξάστους καὶ ἀκλινεῖς καὶ ἀκραδάντους), [2c] saying of each thing: it no more is than is not, or it is and it is not, or it neither is nor is not. [3] For those who adopt this attitude, Timon says, the result will be first *aphasia* and then tranquillity (ἀταραξία). (Aenesidemus says pleasure.) Such, then, are the main points of what they say. Let us now see if they are right. (Eusebius *PE* xiv.18.1-5)

The text has a complex structure. Eusebius quotes from Book viii of Aristocles' *On Philosophy* (*PE* xiv.17, title and 10). Aristocles himself is summarizing (τὰ κεφάλαια: xiv.16.5) a text taken from an unspecified work by Pyrrho's pupil, Timon, there being no texts from Pyrrho's own hand. But since he mentions Aenesidemus, he cannot have taken the whole passage directly from Timon.

Whereas the relation between Aristocles and Timon has been the subject of much discussion, there has been too little interest in the relation which the text supposes to hold between Timon and Pyrrho: what exactly (according to Aristocles) does Timon ascribe to Pyrrho?[56] We cannot answer: everything in the text. For in addition to the sentences preceded

---

[55] Aristocles must be thinking of texts such as *Metaph.* Γ.1007b20; Ι.1053a35; K.5-6.
[56] Here I summarize the ideas developed in Brunschwig 1994e; see also Bett 1994b.

by 'Timon says that . . .' we find one sentence, and only one, preceded by 'Timon says that Pyrrho declares . . .'. This is sentence [1a]; and, on syntactical grounds, it seems that we may assert that the text does not ascribe to Pyrrho what follows, namely inference [1b].[57] Presumably Timon does not ascribe the inference to Pyrrho because it is in fact his own.

The content of the inference has embarrassed the commentators. If 'things' are 'without difference, without balance, without decision', surely this is because we lack the means to differentiate and to balance and to decide them? The cognitive impotence of our perceptions and beliefs ought, it seems, to be the *cause* and not the *consequence* of these characteristics of 'things'. This is why Zeller[58] proposed to read διὰ τὸ instead of διὰ τοῦτο ('things are without difference . . . *because* our perceptions . . .'). Certainly, the inference is found in this form among the Neopyrrhonians. Nonetheless, if an 'epistemological' premiss must thus be prefixed to the 'ontological' proposition [1a], it is hard to see why or in what sense the 'nature of things' could then be the *first* point which, according to Timon, anyone seeking happiness should consider. Can we conserve the transmitted text and at the same time give a decent sense to the inference?

Some scholars have tried to do so by giving the three Pyrrhonian adjectives an 'objective' rather than a 'subjective' meaning.[59] Others have preferred an ethical meaning.[60] In fact, there is a very simple way of ensuring that the inference is not 'zany':[61] we need only suppose that, for Timon (if not also for Pyrrho) our perceptions and our beliefs are themselves 'things' (πράγματα). With this premiss understood, what holds of 'things' in general will hold also of perceptions and beliefs in particular – and we need only add that the special way in which perceptions and beliefs are 'without difference, without balance, without decision' consists in being 'neither true nor false'.[62]

If we put these different observations together, we shall conclude that it was Timon who took it on himself to subsume perceptions and beliefs under the general heading of 'things' and hence to give Pyrrho's thought

[57] It is natural to construe the sentence as consisting of two acc. + inf. clauses depending on φησίν ('Timon says (a) that Pyrrho declares . . ., and (b) that for this reason our perceptions . . .') rather than as a conjunction of a participial clause and an acc. + inf. clause, each of which depends on ἀποφαίνειν ('Timon says that Pyrrho declares (a) things to be indifferent . . . and (b) *that* for this reason our perceptions . . .').   [58] 1870, 493 n. 2; warmly endorsed by Stopper 1983, 293.

[59] See esp. Decleva Caizzi 1981a, 104, 223–7.

[60] See the references in Görler 1985, 333, and esp. Ausland 1989.

[61] As Stopper calls it: 1983, 293.

[62] On this interpretation we need not be embarrassed by the fact that, according to [1b], our perceptions and beliefs are *neither* true *nor* false: on other interpretations logic suggests that they should simply be called false.

an epistemological complexion – a complexion which it cannot originally have had, precisely because Timon found the need to introduce it. If we remove from Aristocles' text everything which derives from Timon rather than from Pyrrho, that is, at least [1b] and [2a], then the remainder has no epistemological significance. For the remainder is a three part recipe for happiness: the first part concerns 'the nature of the things' (in a sense different from the one adopted by Timon, namely: the nature of things and of states of affairs to the extent that they bear upon our acting, πράττειν, and form possible objects of positive or negative choice); the second part concerns the attitude which we ought to take to 'things' of this sort; and the third part describes the ethical gains which will accrue from this attitude. Nothing in all this, so construed, bears on the problem of our cognitive access to the world: on the contrary, everything bears on the problem of our moral attitude and of our happiness. If we ascribe to Timon rather than to Pyrrho the epistemological part of Aristocles' text, then we have confirmation of the ethical interpretation of Pyrrho's philosophy which has rivalled the dominant epistemological interpretation ever since the time of Cicero.

Let me briefly offer a second argument for the same conclusion. We have seen earlier that at the beginning of his account of Pyrrho, Diogenes Laertius draws on the unknown Ascanius of Abdera in order to find in Pyrrho's travels in the East and his meetings with the gymnosophists and the Mages the origins of the 'noble mode of philosophizing' which he introduced into Greece. This noble mode consisted in 'the form of inapprehensibility and of suspension of judgement' – that is to say, a sceptical theory of knowledge.[63] What did Diogenes (or his source) find to justify this interpretation? 'Pyrrho said that nothing is either noble or ignoble, just or unjust, and that similarly in every case nothing is in truth – rather, men do everything which they do by convention and custom; for each thing is no more this than that.' The generalizations in the text ('nothing', 'in every case', 'everything') seem at first sight to have a vast scope – indeed it is tempting to believe that they cover all possible predicates ('each thing is no more F than not-F') including even existence itself ('nothing exists in truth'). But the context invites us to limit the generalizations to ethical predicates of the sort illustrated in the text ('noble' and 'ignoble', 'just' and 'unjust'); and 'truth' is contrasted, in the context, simply with 'convention and custom' which determine the actions of men.[64]

---

[63] See above, p. 44 and n. 243.

[64] The strictly practical import of the paragraph seems to be confirmed by the next sentence: ἀκόλουθος δ' ἦν καὶ τῷ βίῳ ('he was consistent <with these declarations> in his practical life

This being so, it is easier to understand how Timon, when he decided to speak in his master's *persona*,[65] was able to endow his moral 'word of truth' with what has seemed a strangely dogmatic tone.[66] It is also easier to understand the attitude of Epicurus and of the first Stoics, who were early engaged in bloody battles with the sceptical Academy but who seem to have had no interest in attacking Pyrrhonian scepticism.[67] Pyrrho was not the first Pyrrhonian. The first Pyrrhonian was Timon, the most celebrated of Pyrrho's immediate pupils.

*

Timon played a major part in placing Pyrrho's thought in its historical and philosophical setting, and it was he, it seems, who first gave Pyrrho's ideas an epistemological complexion. Next something must be said about the epistemological aspects (such as they are) of Timon's work.

In analysing the text of Aristocles we found arguments to show that Timon had introduced into his exposition of Pyrrho's thought an epistemological motif which was not originally there. This fits well with other texts which indicate Timon's own epistemological interests. He wrote a work *On Perception* (cited by D.L. IX.105), in which he expressed an idea typical of Neopyrrhonian phenomenalism and illustrated it with an example which was to become celebrated: 'That honey is sweet, I do not affirm (οὐ τίθημι); that it seems so (φαίνεται) I allow.' The same phenomenalism is attested by a verse from the *Indalmoi* which is quoted several times:[68] 'But appearance (φαινόμενον) dominates everywhere, wherever it can reach.'

Timon also found occasion to exercise his satirical muscles in epistemological discussion. According to D.L. IX.114 'against those who claimed that the senses had value when they were confirmed by the intellect, he used constantly to cite the line: "Attagas and Numenius have joined forces"'. Attagas and Numenius, it seems, were two celebrated bandits; and whatever the precise sense of the barb, its aim was evidently to discredit the senses and the mind at the same time. It thus appears to attack a very precise epistemological position, namely a non-Epicurean version of the theory of confirmation or ἐπιμαρτύρησις.[69] It is noteworthy that

---

too'). Given the context, Dumont 1969, 720 and 1972, 176, 190–1 etc. is surely wrong to translate 'He took ordinary life as his guide' (modelled on the several Neopyrrhonian formulae of a similar form and with this sense: S.E. *M* XI.165; *PH* III.2; etc.).

[65] Cf. S.E. *M* XI.20 (= *Indalmoi* fr. 68 Diels).

[66] On this much discussed fragment see Brochard 1887 (1923), 62; Robin 1944, 31; Burnyeat 1980b (who suggests an ingenious way of silencing the dogmatic tone); Decleva Caizzi 1981a, 255–62.   [67] See Vander Waerdt 1989.   [68] D.L. IX.105; S.E. *M* VII.30; Gal. *Dig. Puls.* I.2.

[69] See below, pp. 283–5.

Timon 'constantly' engaged in epistemological discussions of this sort. Nor was he content to limit his answer to a joke. According to Sextus *M* III.2, he wrote a book *Against the Physicists* in which he seems to have treated seriously and technically certain fundamental issues in the philosophy of science: he urges us to consider first of all the question of what principles should be adopted 'by hypothesis' and without demonstration.[70]

It is interesting, too, to learn that Timon was much engaged with Arcesilaus: for the most part he attacked him;[71] but he also wrote in praise of him – presumably after Arcesilaus' death – in his *Funeral Banquet for Arcesilaus*. According to Numenius (quoted by Eus. *PE* xiv.6.5), he went so far as to recognize Arcesilaus' title to the name σκεπτικός or 'sceptic' – a report which is probably not literally correct but which may contain a kernel of truth. We may suppose that the initial animosity which Timon felt towards Arcesilaus, who belonged to his own generation, was motivated by the desire to show Pyrrho as the inaugurator of a sceptical philosophy for which Arcesilaus, although he hid in the shadow of Socrates and Plato, himself claimed authorship. Thus Timon needed to show that Arcesilaus had plagiarized Pyrrho, that he had added nothing to the scepticism which Pyrrho had invented apart from the fraudulent resources of dialectic and eristic.[72] The best – if not the most elegant – way of discounting the originality of Arcesilaus was plainly to inject, retrospectively, a suitable dose of epistemology into Pyrrho's thought; and this is precisely what Timon did. Once the operation had been performed (and once Arcesilaus was dead), Timon could afford to be magnanimous and to 'point out not the elements of disagreement but rather the elements of agreement between his own position and that of the philosopher who, throughout his life, had been his rival'.[73]

Given the ambivalent interest which Timon showed for the person and the thought of Arcesilaus, it may well seem 'plausible to assume that the Pyrrho of Timon's writings represents the doctrine Timon himself developed under Pyrrho's influence – at a time when the debate between Academic sceptics and the dogmatists was well under way and had reached considerable sophistication'.[74] Pyrrho's role in the creation of a

[70] On the hypothetical method from Aristotle to the Neopyrrhonians see above, p. 231 and n. 6.
[71] D.L. IX.115, fully confirmed by fragments 31–4 of the *Silli*.
[72] See the fragments of the *Silli* reported by D.L. IV.33 and Numen. *ap*. Eus. *PE* XIV.5.11–14 (= fr. 25 des Places). The rapid success of Timon's operation is shown by the celebrated verse of the Stoic Aristo of Chios who, parodying Homer in a very Timonian vein, described Arcesilaus as 'Plato in front, Pyrrho behind, Diodorus [Cronus, the celebrated dialectician] in the middle' (S.E. *PH* I.234; Numen. *apud* Eus. *PE* XIV.5.13).   [73] Di Marco 1989, 14.
[74] Frede 1973, 806.

sceptical theory of knowledge, then, is no more than an *ex post facto* invention; and the invention dates not from Aenesidemus in the first century BC but rather – to some degree at least – from Timon two centuries earlier.

This may help us to understand why the problem of distinguishing between Academic and Pyrrhonian scepticism, to which the ancients themselves devoted whole essays,[75] has remained unsolved and is perhaps insoluble: the two traditions were contaminated from the start. We can also understand why the ancients disagreed with one another about the continuation of Timon's school.[76] The efforts of those ancient scholars who were set on discovering gapless 'successions' only masked the fact that the success of Timon's operation was ephemeral. The lively and fertile epistemological debates during the Hellenistic period are those which match the Stoics with the Academics and the Epicureans. We must wait until Aenesidemus for the name of Pyrrho to come to the surface again. This time, it is true, it will remain afloat for centuries.

III Cyrenaic epistemology

The sceptical Academy is not the only Hellenistic school to produce an epistemology which would later attract the Neopyrrhonians: the Cyrenaics did so too.[77] Although the school is often presented in the doxography as though its sole interest were ethics,[78] so that today it is primarily known for championing a moral hedonism which is at odds on certain central points with Epicurean hedonism,[79] it in fact also advanced, probably from the second half of the fourth century, certain epistemological views. The epistemology was original and radical and strictly sceptical in tenor – at least insofar as the external world is concerned. Alas, we are ill informed on the theory and our sources are rare and for the most part hostile.

The Cyrenaics are traditionally counted among the 'minor Socratics'. Story ascribes the foundation of the school to Aristippus of Cyrene, a

---

[75] See above, n. 12.   [76] See D.L. IX.115–16.

[77] Basic texts: the complex doxography in D.L. II.65–104, which juxtaposes an account of the doctrines 'common' to the school and accounts of the various 'independent' members of the sect, and which is particularly concerned with Cyrenaic ethics and psychology; see also Aristocl. *ap.* Eus. *PE* XIV.19.1–7; Plu. *Col.* 1120b–f; S.E. *M* VII.190–200. Fragments and testimonia have been collected and edited more than once: Mannebach 1961; Giannantoni 1958, 1990. A detailed study of Cyrenaic epistemology in Tsouna McKirahan 1992 and 1998.

[78] See esp. Arist. *Metaph.* B.996a29–b1; Eus. *PE* XV.62.7–11 (it is not clear how this testimonium should be divided between Aristippus and Aristo of Chios); but the idea that the Cyrenaics were solely interested in ethics must be qualified – see D.L. II.92, and esp. S.E. *M* VII.11 (= Sen. *Ep.* 89.12).   [79] See esp. Bollack 1975; Döring 1988; Laks 1993b.

friend of Socrates and a contemporary of Plato. But it is unlikely that we should attribute to Aristippus, who was a witty and sophisticated devotee of pleasure, the philosophical elaboration of Cyrenaic hedonism,[80] let alone the peculiar epistemology of the school, which is in many respects of a piece with its psychology and its ethics. The elaboration of all this was probably the work of Aristippus the Younger, known as the Metrodidact because he had received his philosophical education from his mother, Arete, who was the daughter and pupil of the older Aristippus.

The career of the Cyrenaic school was relatively short: there are only five generations of teachers and pupils in the 'succession' at D.L. II.86, which is in any event a fabrication. But it was an active career. As well as those who kept alive the spirit of the school's founder, we hear of three philosophers who introduced innovations and ideas of their own: Hegesias, Anniceris, Theodorus. But as far as epistemology is concerned we cannot tell whether these three men held any theories of their own; and, relying on the evidence of Eusebius (*PE* xiv.18.31–2), we may assume that Cyrenaic epistemology is essentially the creation of the younger Aristippus,[81] and hence of a thinker who stands, chronologically, somewhere between Pyrrho and Epicurus.

Virtually the whole of Cyrenaic epistemology is contained in a phrase which all our sources report in almost the same words: 'feelings (πάθη) alone are apprehensible (καταληπτά)'. The language is mongrel: if it is certain that the word 'πάθος' played an important part in all aspects of Cyrenaic thought, 'καταληπτός' belongs to the epistemological vocabulary of the Stoa, and it must have been borrowed thence to express the Cyrenaic thesis either by later members of the school or else by the doxographical tradition. Eusebius perhaps preserves the wording originally used by Aristippus:[82] 'we have perception (αἴσθησις) of feelings alone'. Any account of Cyrenaic epistemology will consist in a commentary on this phrase.

First let us consider the word 'πάθος'. It belongs to the same family as the verb 'πάσχειν' ('undergo', 'suffer', 'feel'); and it denotes any effect produced on a patient by the action of an agent which affects it. The word does not in itself imply that the patient is a perceiving subject: a heated stone 'suffers' under the action of fire. Nonetheless, we may ask whether

---

[80] The cardinal text is Eus. *PE* xiv.18.31–2. But see Döring 1988.

[81] Aristocl. *ap*. Eus. *PE* xiv.19.1, ascribes the epistemological theory to 'some of the people from Cyrene'. It is hard to give a precise sense to this phrase; but it is plain that Aristocles would not have used it had he thought that the theory had been common doctrine in the school since Aristippus the Elder.   [82] So Mannebach 1961, 116.

the Cyrenaic notion of 'feeling' should be understood as a physical change or whether it denotes a subjective psychological experience or perhaps muddles these two things together.

Certain texts suggest a physical interpretation. According to the doxography 'common' to the whole school, the Cyrenaics 'posited two feelings, pain and pleasure, the one, pleasure, being a smooth movement and the other, pain, a rough movement' (D.L. II.86). The two feelings seem here to be identified with two movements, each of which is characterized in physical terms; and the identification appears to be confirmed by some of the words which the Cyrenaics used to express perceptible feelings: 'we can say infallibly . . . and irrefutably that we are whitened (λευκαινόμεθα) and that we are sweetened (γλυκαζόμεθα)' (S.E. *M* VII.191).

Some scholars have in fact cited these expressions as evidence that the Cyrenaic doctrine was not precisely delineated: for this reason (and not merely because of the paucity of our evidence) we cannot tell whether they had in mind a physical alteration (the 'whitening' of the eyes) or the subjective mode (the impression of white) in which it is sensed.[83] And yet there are arguments which favour a straightforwardly subjective interpretation:

(a) Expressions of the form 'we are whitened' are not the only ones which the Cyrenaics used to express their feelings: they also made use of some notable neologisms, such as 'to be disposed whitely (λευκαντικῶς διατιθῆναι)' (S.E. *M* VII.192). The locution is so original that we must suppose it to have been introduced precisely in order to distinguish the subjective experience from the physical change: if a stone is painted white you will surely not say that it is 'whitely disposed'.

(b) The physicalist identification of pleasure and pain with particular kinds of movement must in all probability be qualified, either by taking the terms 'smooth movement' and 'rough movement' metaphorically or else and better by distinguishing between a physical movement and its effect on subjective consciousness. A definition which is ascribed at D.L. II.85 to the elder Aristippus identifies the goal of life (*telos*) with 'smooth movement when it reaches to perception (εἰς αἴσθησιν ἀναδιδομένην)': we may infer that some physical alterations are subliminal and have no conscious effects, and that a movement gives rise to a feeling if and only if it crosses the threshold of perception. We have seen earlier, in a phrase which perhaps preserves the very words of the younger Aristippus, that the notion of perception was used precisely to describe the relation between an affected subject and the feeling.

[83] See Burnyeat 1982a, 27–8; and, with qualifications, Everson 1991b, 128–47.

(c) One of the most important consequences of the Cyrenaic theory is that feelings cannot be shared, that they are strictly private to the person whom they affect.

> Everyone grasps his own feelings. Whether a particular feeling comes to him and to his neighbour from something white neither he nor his neighbour can say, since neither receives the other's feelings. Since there are no feelings common to us all, it is rash to say that what appears thus-and-so to me also appears thus-and-so to my neighbour. Perhaps I am so composed as to be whitened by the external object which impresses me whereas someone else has perceptions so constituted as to be differently disposed. (S.E. *M* VII.196–7)

Now 'it would seem difficult to read this as anything other than an argument for the privacy, and hence the subjectivity, of experience'.[84]

The Cyrenaic concept of feeling raises a further question. How, within the class of feelings, do we characterize those which immediately concern ethics, namely pleasure and pain (the affective feelings as we may call them), and those which immediately concern epistemology, namely 'whitening' and other items of this sort (the representative feelings as we may call them)? The question must be answered in two stages.

First, affective feelings seem never to be simply affective and without any representative component. As examples of expressions of affects our texts never offer us such phrases as 'I am enjoying myself' or 'It hurts'; rather, they offer phrases such as 'I am burned' and 'I am cut' (Aristocl. *apud* Eus. *PE* XIV.19.1). Hence we must suppose that, within the very experience of pain, there is a difference in 'colour' between the pain of a burn and the pain of a cut.

Secondly, we might ask whether, if there are no purely affective feelings, there are any purely representative feelings. It is not easy to find an answer. According to the 'common' doxography in D.L. II.89–90, the Cyrenaics rejected the view, which they ascribed to Epicurus, that 'the removal of whatever causes pain' is a pleasure – a 'static' or 'catastematic' pleasure which the Epicureans identified as the supreme good. According to the Cyrenaics, the absence of pain is not pleasure nor the absence of pleasure pain. Now these two 'intermediate states (μέσαι καταστάσεις)', precisely because they are states and not movements, are unconscious: the absence of pain is 'like being asleep'.[85] If it is essential to a feeling to be

---

[84] Everson 1991b, 130.

[85] According to Clem. *Strom.* II.21.130.8, the Cyrenaics of Anniceris' persuasion 'rejected Epicurus' definition of pleasure as absence of pain, saying that that was the state of a corpse'. The analogy with sleep is not very different; and it seems that we may conclude from this text

conscious, then we must infer that there are no feelings which are neither pleasant nor painful, and hence that there are no purely representative feelings.

Is this conclusion supported by the passage in Eusebius which has already been mentioned more than once?

> Aristippus the Younger [. . .] used to say that there were three states in which we could be: one in which we are in pain, and which is like a storm at sea; a second in which we experience pleasure, and which is like a gentle swell (for pleasure is a smooth movement, like a favouring wind); and the third, intermediate, in which we feel neither pain nor pleasure, and which is like a flat calm. It is of these feelings alone, he said, that we have perception. (τούτων δὴ καὶ ἔφασκε τῶν παθῶν μόνων ἡμᾶς τὴν αἴσθησιν ἔχειν; Eusebius *PE* xiv.18.32)

The thesis expressed here differs in certain points from what we read in the doxography in Diogenes. There is no longer the contrast between *states* (without movement) and *movements* (identical with, or at least tied to, feelings). According to Aristippus our psychophysical compound may be in any of three possible states, symbolized by the three possible states of the sea;[86] and to these states there appear to correspond feelings, symbolized by the movement, violent or smooth, of the air.

But is there a conscious feeling corresponding to the intermediate state, so that there will therefore be feelings which are purely representative? Everything turns on the reference of the words 'these feelings' (τούτων τῶν παθῶν) in the final sentence of the quotation. If it refers implicitly to the feelings which accompany the *three* states which have just been described, then the answer to our question must be Yes (and the text then confirms Sextus *M* vii.199, which ascribes to the Cyrenaics the idea of a feeling 'intermediate between pleasure and pain'). But this is not the only possible interpretation. It has been suggested that the words refer right back to the beginning of the text which ascribes to the Cyrenaics in general the thesis that 'feelings alone (that is, in contrast to external objects) can be apprehended'.[87] But since our sentence certainly refers to Aristippus the younger (ἔφασκε), we might more economically and more exactly suppose that the words 'these feelings' denote only the feelings of pleasure and pain

---

that certain elements of late Cyrenaicism have been intruded into the 'common' doxography in D.L. In any event, the many items of anti-Epicurean polemic which are found there can hardly be explained in any other way.

[86] Note that in Aristippus there is only one intermediate state, whereas in D.L. ii.90 there are two, absence of pleasure and absence of pain. The Cyrenaics had presumably found it necessary to distinguish them in order to attack the Epicurean identification of catastematic pleasure with mere absence of pain.   [87] Laks 1993b, 26 n. 31.

which have just been mentioned as the items *absent* from the intermediate state.[88] It is prudent, then, not to ascribe to Aristippus the notion of a purely representative feeling: every 'whitening' is pleasant if it is gentle, painful if it is violent. And thus the Cyrenaic epistemology is not independent of their ethics.

In what sense is it, properly speaking, an epistemology at all? The basic thesis, that 'feelings alone are apprehensible', plainly implies that feelings are apprehensible. Although the proposition in this second form is extremely rare in our sources[89] and although the term 'καταληπτός' is not authentically Cyrenaic, it has nevertheless often been supposed, from antiquity onwards, that one of the great novelties of the school was to have realized, contrary to the dominant philosophical tradition, that internal states or events constitute suitable objects of knowledge and suitable contents of true propositions.[90] It seems, however, that the Cyrenaics did not care to put much emphasis on this positive side of their thesis – certainly they did not use it in order to refute any version of scepticism.

In stressing that 'feelings *alone* are apprehensible', they were primarily concerned to contrast feelings with all other things, which, unlike feelings, are not apprehensible. The inapprehensible remainder consists essentially of the causes of the feelings: 'feelings alone are apprehended and they are infallible: of the items which have produced the feelings, none is either apprehensible or infallible' (S.E. *M* vii.191). 'The feeling which comes about in us shows us nothing apart from itself' (*ibid.* 194). That the causes of feelings are inapprehensible is reflected clearly in the fact that no cause is mentioned in the sentences by which the Cyrenaics express feelings ('I am burned', 'I am whitely disposed'). Hence, no doubt, the vacillation in our sources when it comes to describing more precisely what it is that the Cyrenaics refuse to affirm. Take, say, the feeling of being burned, expressed by the sentence 'I am burned': sometimes it is said that the patient cannot distinguish the cause of his feeling from any other hot item;[91] sometimes that he can identify the cause but cannot say whether it is naturally such as to burn;[92] sometimes – and this is the minimal and

---

[88] I thank Pierre Pellegrin and Francis Wolff for drawing my attention to this possibility.

[89] It appears at D.L. ii.92, but in a suspect form and loosely anchored in the context.

[90] Cic. *Acad.* ii.142 and 20: the Cyrenaics admit no 'criterion of truth' apart from *permotiones intumae* which are apprehended by the *tactus interior* (or *tactus intumus*: ii.76). In the same vein S.E. *M* vii.191 says that according to the Cyrenaics the feelings are κριτήρια – which amounts to saying that they give us access to truth.

[91] See Aristocl. *apud* Eus. *PE* xiv.19.1: 'if they were burned or cut, they said that they knew that they experienced something but could not say whether what burned them was fire or what cut them was steel'.

[92] See Anon. *In Tht.* 65.33–9: 'That I am burned, they say, I grasp; but whether or not fire is natu-

perhaps also the most accurate version – that he cannot even say whether the cause is hot.[93]

Two further points may be made. First, if the feelings 'do not show us anything apart from themselves', then at least they do show us themselves, that is to say, they show us everything which they have, so to speak, as their internal objects. When the Cyrenaics were asked by their opponents to admit that, since they knew their own feelings, they knew much more than they were willing to say,[94] they maintained firmly that they knew nothing at all about the external cause of the feeling or of its intrinsic and objective properties; but they surely allowed that they knew all the internal characteristics of the feeling (for example, the fact that it belongs to a self, which is implied by such expressions as 'I am whitened'; its relative time and place; its sensory modality; whether it is pleasant or painful).

Secondly, the actual existence of causes external to us which produce our feelings is never doubted.[95] Not for a moment supposing that we could be the causes of our own feelings, the Cyrenaics applied a version of the principle of causality which was too weak to allow them to affirm that since they are affected F-ly the cause of the feeling must itself be F, but which was strong enough to allow them to assert that there exists a cause which produced the feeling and that this cause is capable, given the circumstances in which it acts and our own state at the time we are acted upon, of producing in us the precise effect which it does produce. We may thus describe the cause of the feeling 'I am burned' as the 'burner' of this burning.[96] In this sense it is correct to say that the Cyrenaics were no exception to the general truth that Greek thought had realist presuppositions.

In the same way, the Cyrenaics seem to have admitted without question the existence of other minds. (At any rate, our sources show no trace of any doubts on this score.) In their illustrative examples, they pass

rally such as to burn [καυστικόν], that is unclear – for if it were so, everything would be burned by it.'

93 This emerges from S.E. *M* VII.191–2 if we change the example: 'That we are whitened, they say, or sweetened, we can say infallibly . . . and irrefutably; but that what produces the feeling is white or sweet we cannot affirm. For it is likely that someone might be whitely disposed by something not white or sweetened by something not sweet.'

94 See the long list of objections made by Aristocl. *apud* Eus. *PE* XIV.19.2–7.

95 See the picturesque image in Plu. *Col.* 1120b: 'Like men in a besieged castle, they evacuate the outer areas and shut themselves up in their feelings.' One text which might lead us to suspect that the Cyrenaics had doubted the existence of these 'outer areas' is a passage at *M* VII.194 where Sextus says that 'the external object which causes the feeling perhaps exists [τάχα μέν ἐστιν ὄν] but is not apparent to us'. But it may be urged that in this text Sextus is rewriting the theory in the phenomenalist terms which are familiar to him (Tsouna McKirahan 1992, 172–4). Another text, *M* VI.53, can be still more easily explained away in terms of contextual considerations (*ibid.* 189 n. 133).   96 τὸ καῖον: Aristocl. *apud* Eus. *PE* XIV.19.1.

indifferently from singular ('I am burned') to plural ('We are burned'). They upheld an interesting version of a conventionalist theory of language;[97] but they did not ask how we know that there is anyone else to talk to or that anyone else experiences any feelings, given that these feelings are inaccessible to us – no more than they asked how and why our language functions for most of the time without a hitch. We do not know whether the Cyrenaics explicitly raised the question of other minds, nor, if they did, how they answered it.

There are at least three other problems on which we are equally ill informed. First, on which side of the border between the apprehensible and the inapprehensible are we to place our own bodies? If the feelings to which we have access are strictly mental, then the Cyrenaics must logically require that our own bodies be considered as part of the exterior world whose existence we are entitled to assume but about which we can know nothing. Thus if I suffer from toothache nothing allows me to say that it is because I have got teeth, still less that it is because my teeth are decayed. Alas, our sources present no examples in the least similar to this.

Secondly, the fact that the feeling belongs to its subject might, as we have seen, be regarded as a feature of the feeling itself. But feelings, like pleasure, last only a moment (μονόχρονον: Athen. XII.544d). Then does a Cyrenaic know that it was the same self which was burned on Monday and whitened on Tuesday? And if he knows it, how does he know it?

Thirdly, the same problem of synthetic unity arises about objects. The feelings which the Cyrenaics had in mind, to judge from their illustrative examples, always correspond to elementary qualitative impressions (white, sweet, and so on). The Epicurean Colotes ridiculed their theory by extending it to objects: 'Here are people who won't say that there is a man or a horse or a wall – they say that they are manned or horsed or walled' (Plu. *Col.* 1120d). Plutarch's only criticism of Colotes is to say that he ought to have expressed the Cyrenaic theory in terms used by the Cyrenaics themselves; but he allows that 'their theory has these implications'. In fact this is far from clear. On the contrary, it is probable that the Cyrenaics only allowed elementary feelings. But do these feelings, according to their theory, combine to make a conscious representation of an object which is both white and sweet and . . .? And if so, how? We have no way of answering these questions.

---

[97] See S.E. *M* VII.196–8: 'everyone calls things white or sweet in common; but the things have nothing white or sweet in common since each person only grasps his own feelings. . . . Thus we impose [τιθέναι] common names on objects although we have private feelings.'

With this admission of frustration – which may be the effect either of the chances of survival or of lacunae in the original theory – I end the account of Cyrenaic epistemology. Despite everything, the theory surely remains one of the most original and interesting which Hellenistic philosophy has to offer us.[98]

---

[98] This chapter has been translated by Jonathan Barnes.

8

Epicurean epistemology

ELIZABETH ASMIS

1 Canonic

The two main issues of Epicurean epistemology may be put as follows: what is the foundation of knowledge; and how is knowledge built on this foundation? There is general agreement that Epicurus proposed to rely on sensory observations as a means of knowing what is unobserved. But there is much debate on the extent to which he proposed to rely on empirical observations, on what he took to be the basic objects of observation, and on how he proposed to proceed from sensory information to the discovery of what is not perceived by the senses.

It has been argued that Epicurus proposed to use empirical observation as the only means of determining the truth or falsity of beliefs. He set out two rules of investigation at the beginning of his physics requiring that the truth and falsity of beliefs rest entirely on sensory observations. The two rules consist of a demand for empirical concepts and a demand for empirical data. The latter consist of uninterpreted, or what may be called 'raw' or 'incorrigible', acts of perception. Epicurus proposed to infer all truths about the physical world and human happiness from this incorrigible foundation.[1]

Against this interpretation, it has been held that Epicurus was not nearly as methodical in his use of empirical observations. Rather, he accepted many nonempirical claims, while proposing to support theories (much like Aristotle) by agreement with perception. Although he supposed that all perceptions are in a sense incorrigible, Epicurus singled out what are ordinarily called true perceptions as the basis for checking scientific theories. Thus he bolstered his atomic theories by adding empirical evidence, but did not propose a method for inferring physical and ethical truths solely on the basis of empirical facts.

The following discussion attempts to adjudicate between these two

---

[1] See in general Asmis 1984, and Barnes 1996a.

interpretations. Epicurus' epistemology was considered problematic, even incoherent, from its very beginning. Epicurus' followers engaged in the debate and tried to strengthen his arguments. The polemics that ensued can be confusing. Yet there is enough novelty and brilliance about the Epicurean effort to encourage the modern investigator to sort out the ancient lines of inquiry and propose a reconstruction. For regardless of their answers, Epicurus and his followers advanced epistemology enormously by the way they framed their problems. Epicurus plotted the ascent from sensory experience to knowledge of the hidden structure of the world by distinguishing, in the first place, between what is 'evident' (ἐναργές) and what is 'nonevident' (ἄδηλον). The 'evident' is known immediately by sense perception and by preconceptions based on sense perception; the 'nonevident' must be inferred. Epicurus also drew a contrast between uninterpreted sensory information and belief, between ordinary and scientific concepts, and between conjectures and scientific conclusions. In elaborating these distinctions, he elevated epistemology into a major branch of philosophy.

The sources on Epicurean epistemology extend from Epicurus himself to Sextus Empiricus and beyond. Because relatively little is preserved of Epicurus' own writings, we must often resort to later reports, some of which are quite detailed. A basic point of difference among modern interpreters concerns the reliability of these later sources.

*

Epicurus invented (so far as we know) the term 'canonic' (κανονική) to designate epistemology as a branch of philosophy. Etymologically, canonic is the science of using a 'measuring stick' or canon (κανών). It was the subject of a work by Epicurus, *Canon* (also called *On the Criterion*), which is no longer extant. Sextus Empiricus (*M* VII.22) describes Epicurean canonic as dealing with what is 'evident' and 'nonevident' and related matters. It has two components: it deals with the measures by which we obtain an immediate grasp of what is true or 'evident'; and it deals with how we use what is 'evident' as a measure of what is 'nonevident'.

In Epicurus' philosophical system, canonic takes the place of logic or dialectic as the first subject of study. It is also closely linked with physics. Whereas the Stoics classified logic as the first of three parts of philosophy, co-ordinate with physics and ethics, Epicurus joined canonic to physics as both preliminary and subordinate to it.

It was commonplace to accuse Epicurus and his followers of being ignorant of logic. Epicurus' followers retorted that the truth that others seek through logic is revealed by physics, as guided by the rules of canonic. As Torquatus, the Epicurean spokesman in Cicero's *De finibus* (1.63), puts it, 'it is by this science [that is, physics] that the meaning of words, the nature of discourse, and the relationship of consequence or conflict can be understood'. Physics attains these insights by observing 'the rule that has glided down, as it were, from heaven for the knowledge of all things'. The 'rule' is Epicurus' canon, understood as either his book or the standards it proposes.

Although we lack Epicurus' book *Canon*, there is ample evidence for his epistemology. His *Letter to Herodotus*, a summary of his physics, includes a summary of his canonic. We also have a brief survey of the *Canon* itself by Diogenes Laertius. In addition, there are numerous ancient discussions of various aspects of Epicurean canonic. They consist of both attacks and defences. Among the latter, the most important are Lucretius' explanation of sense perception in his poem *On the Nature of Things*, Philodemus' *On Signs*, and Sextus Empiricus' account of Epicurus' criterion of truth.

The *Letter to Herodotus* shows how canonic is related to physics. Epicurus presents his canonic in two stages: he prefaces his summary of his physics with a brief outline of his two rules of investigation (*Ep. Hdt.* 37–8); then he explains these rules in the course of outlining his physical system. The main part of this explanation consists in showing how the senses serve as a means of determining the truth (*Ep. Hdt.* 48–53). Epicurus also adds explanations about concepts (*Ep. Hdt.* 72) and about the formation of language (*Ep. Hdt.* 75–6). Torquatus refers to this sequence of preliminary rules and subsequent explanation when he says that 'unless the nature of things is seen, we will not be able to defend in any way the judgements of the senses' (Cic. *Fin.* 1.64).

Epicurus' initial statement of his rules is as follows:

> First, Herodotus, it is necessary to have grasped what is subordinate to our utterances, so that we may have the means to judge what is believed or sought or perplexing by referring to [what is subordinate to our utterances], and so that we will not leave everything unjudged as we go on proving to infinity, or have empty utterances. For it is necessary that the first thought in accordance with each utterance be seen and not require proof, if we are to have a referent for what is sought or perplexing and believed.

> Next, it is necessary to observe everything in accordance with the perceptions (αἰσθήσεις) and simply the present applications (ἐπιβολάς) of the mind or any of the criteria (κριτήρια), and similarly [in accordance

with] the existing feelings (πάθη), so that we may have signs (σημειωσόμεθα) for both what is waiting (προσμένον) and what is nonevident (ἄδηλον). (*Ep. Hdt.* 37–8)[2]

This preamble is followed by the announcement: 'After making these distinctions, it is now time to consider what is nonevident.' Then Epicurus begins a sequence of deductions about the universe.

In the first place, Epicurus requires thoughts associated with the words that we utter. These initial thoughts, for which Epicurus coined the term προλήψεις, 'preconceptions', do not require proof. Second, Epicurus requires observations to serve as signs of what is not observed. These observations are of two kinds: perceptions, and feelings.

By following the two rules of inquiry, the investigator arrives at truths about what cannot be observed. This intellectual journey is at the same time a process of discovery and a method of proof. To be sure, there is a psychological process by which an investigator tries out ideas gathered from a variety of sources. But the investigator does not properly make a discovery until he proves the idea by following the rules of inquiry. There is no doubt that Epicurus' physics includes claims (beginning with 'nothing comes to be from non-being', *Ep. Hdt.* 38) that he derived from the Eleatics and other philosophers. But this makes no difference to Epicurus' empiricism. If Epicurus offers an alternative, empirical argument in support of these claims, their provenance is irrelevant. What matters is that they should rest on empirical evidence, not that they should have been prompted by it.

Epicurus' initial remarks, as we have them, are very condensed and their interpretation is controversial. We will return to each main point in what follows. But it can be seen at first glance that Epicurus sets out the three 'criteria' that later authors attribute to him: preconceptions, perceptions, and feelings. Epicurus also refers to what later authors attribute to him as a fourth 'criterion', the so-called 'presentational applications of the mind'.[3] Whereas Epicurus himself seems to reserve the term κριτήριον, 'instrument of judgement', for the five senses and the mind

---

[2] πρῶτον μὲν οὖν τὰ ὑποτεταγμένα τοῖς φθόγγοις, ὦ Ἡρόδοτε, δεῖ εἰληφέναι, ὅπως ἂν τὰ δοξαζόμενα ἢ ζητούμενα ἢ ἀπορούμενα ἔχωμεν εἰς ταῦτα ἀναγαγόντες ἐπικρίνειν, καὶ μὴ ἄκριτα πάντα ἡμῖν ᾖ εἰς ἄπειρον ἀποδεικνύουσιν ἢ κενοὺς φθόγγους ἔχωμεν. ἀνάγκη γὰρ τὸ πρῶτον ἐννόημα καθ' ἕκαστον φθόγγον βλέπεσθαι καὶ μηθὲν ἀποδείξεως προσδεῖσθαι, εἴπερ ἕξομεν τὸ ζητούμενον ἢ ἀπορούμενον καὶ δοξαζόμενον ἐφ' ὃ ἀνάξομεν. εἶτα κατὰ τὰς αἰσθήσεις δεῖ πάντα τηρεῖν καὶ ἁπλῶς τὰς παρούσας ἐπιβολὰς εἴτε διανοίας εἴθ' ὅτου δήποτε τῶν κριτηρίων, ὁμοίως δὲ κατὰ τὰ ὑπάρχοντα πάθη, ὅπως ἂν καὶ τὸ προσμένον καὶ τὸ ἄδηλον ἔχωμεν οἷς σημειωσόμεθα. On the text see Asmis 1984, 83 n. 1, and Long and Sedley 1987, vol. II, 92.

[3] D.L. x.31; cf. Cic. *Acad.* II.142. As Diogenes points out, Epicurus himself groups the presentational application of the mind with perceptions and feelings in *KD* 24.

acting as a sense, later authors use the term to designate the three (or four) types of awareness.[4]

In his statement of the rules, Epicurus moves from language to preconceptions, then to observations. This order differs from the arrangement found in Diogenes' summary, which deals first with perceptions, then preconceptions, then feelings. Since preconceptions are built up from perceptions, it is reasonable to explain the latter before the former. Diogenes' order may well have been the order that Epicurus used in his *Canon*. The present chapter offers a variation on Diogenes' order: it will deal first with perceptions and feelings, then preconceptions.

II Perceptions

The proliferation of technical vocabulary in Hellenistic philosophy can be extremely confusing. The vocabulary of sense perception is particularly treacherous. A key problem is: what is an 'object of perception', αἰσθητόν? Further, what is αἴσθησις ('sense perception', 'perception'), φαντασία ('presentation' or 'impression'), and the meaning of 'true' as added to either of these terms? Amid the plethora of terms, two demand special attention: ἐπιβολή ('application', 'act of attending') and ἐνάργεια ('evidence'). This pair of terms is especially prominent in Epicurean epistemology and may be said to characterize it. Ἐπιβολή is not found as a technical epistemological term before Epicurus; and ἐνάργεια receives a new sense and importance.

The basic problem is this: can sense perception show what exists in the external world? Epicurus identifies all acts of perception as 'present' acts of sensory attention. What makes these acts a means of measuring the truth?

Epicurus explains 'applications', together with ἐνάργεια and κριτήριον, in the central epistemological section of the *Letter to Herodotus* (49–53). By the time he comes to this section, Epicurus has already established that everything in the universe is atoms and void. He now explains sensory perception. Turning first to sight and thought, he claims that very fine configurations (τύποι) of atoms, called 'images' (εἴδωλα), are continually detached from the surface of external solids, having similar shape and colour to the solid. These images form a stream that extends from the solid to the sense organ while preserving a 'sympathy' with the pulsation of atoms deep within the solid. When this stream enters the eyes or the mind, it produces a 'presentation' (φαντασία).

The mind obtains visual impressions in the same way as the sense of

---

[4] But see Striker 1974, 59–61, and 1990, 144.

sight. It has 'perceptions', therefore, just like any of the sense organs, and acts as a sensory criterion, just like the five senses. Its sensory activity includes dreams, memories, hallucinations, and so on. Elsewhere, it is called 'presentational' by contrast with the non-sensory, rational activity of the mind. In conformity with this unusual doctrine, Epicurus classifies the mind's sensory acts as a subdivision of 'perceptions' in the *Letter to Herodotus*. His followers later made a concession to standard philosophical terminology by classifying mental perceptions as a separate category, coordinate with the perceptions of the five senses. But they did not thereby alter Epicurus' theory.

Immediately after arguing that we see an external solid by means of a continuity between the presentation and the solid, Epicurus summarizes his theory of truth and falsehood:

> And whatever presentation we take hold of by an application (ἐπιβλητικῶς) of the mind or the senses, whether of shape or of concomitants, this is the shape of the solid, coming to be in accordance with successive compacting or a remnant of the image.
>
> But falsehood and error always lie in what it is additionally believed will be witnessed or not counterwitnessed and then is not witnessed <or is counterwitnessed>. For appearances that are obtained as a likeness or that happen in sleep or by some other applications of the mind or of the remaining criteria would never have a similarity with things that are called 'existent' and 'true' if they were not also things that we encounter.
>
> Error would not exist if we did not also take within ourselves some other motion that is attached, but has a distinction. In respect to this motion, if there is no witnessing or counterwitnessing, falsehood comes to be; if there is witnessing or no counterwitnessing, truth comes to be.
>
> It is necessary to hold on tight to this belief, in order that the criteria that judge in accordance with evidence may not be eliminated, and that error, by being similarly upheld, may not confuse everything. (*Ep. Hdt.* 50–2)[5]

---

[5] *Ep. Hdt.* 50–2: καὶ ἣν ἂν λάβωμεν φαντασίαν ἐπιβλητικῶς τῇ διανοίᾳ ἢ τοῖς αἰσθητηρίοις εἴτε μορφῆς εἴτε συμβεβηκότων, μορφή ἐστιν αὕτη τοῦ στερεμνίου, γινομένη κατὰ τὸ ἑξῆς πύκνωμα ἢ ἐγκατάλειμμα τοῦ εἰδώλου. τὸ δὲ ψεῦδος καὶ τὸ διημαρτημένον ἐν τῷ προσδοξαζομένῳ ἀεί ἐστιν ἐπιμαρτυρήσεσθαι ἢ μὴ ἀντιμαρτυρηθήσεσθαι, εἶτ' οὐκ ἐπιμαρτυρουμένου <ἢ ἀντιμαρτυρουμένου>. ἥ τε γὰρ ὁμοιότης τῶν φαντασμῶν οἱονεὶ ἐν εἰκόνι λαμβανομένων ἢ καθ' ὕπνους γινομένων ἢ κατ' ἄλλας τινὰς ἐπιβολὰς τῆς διανοίας ἢ τῶν λοιπῶν κριτηρίων οὐκ ἄν ποτε ὑπῆρχε τοῖς οὖσί τε καὶ ἀληθέσι προσαγορευομένοις, εἰ μὴ ἦν τινα καὶ ταῦτα πρὸς ἃ βάλλομεν. τὸ δὲ διημαρτημένον οὐκ ἂν ὑπῆρχεν, εἰ μὴ ἐλαμβάνομεν καὶ ἄλλην τινὰ κίνησιν ἐν ἡμῖν αὐτοῖς συνημμένην μὲν διάληψιν δὲ ἔχουσαν. κατὰ δὲ ταύτην, ἐὰν μὲν μὴ ἐπιμαρτυρηθῇ ἢ ἀντιμαρτυρηθῇ, τὸ ψεῦδος γίνεται. ἐὰν δὲ ἐπιμαρτυρηθῇ ἢ μὴ ἀντιμαρτυρηθῇ, τὸ ἀληθές. καὶ ταύτην οὖν σφόδρα γε δεῖ τὴν δόξαν κατέχειν, ἵνα μήτε τὰ κριτήρια ἀναιρῆται τὰ κατὰ τὰς ἐναργείας μήτε τὸ διημαρτημένον ὁμοίως βεβαιούμενον πάντα συνταράττῃ. For the text, see further Asmis 1984, 142 n.1.

Epicurus distinguishes between two kinds of 'taking': we take hold of a presentation by an 'application' of the sensory organ; and we take hold of another, inner kind of motion, which is linked to the first but distinct from it. The first type of motion is a 'present' application of a sensory organ (*Ep. Hdt.* 38). The second adds a belief to the presentation, and this belief may be true or false. There is no falsehood or error, on the other hand, in the first kind of 'taking'.

Epicurus divides the first kind of taking into two kinds: those by which we get hold of dream images or copies (such as a picture) or other resemblances to what is 'called existent and true'; and those by which we get hold of what is 'called existent and true'. Epicurus' language is circumspect and strained. While distinguishing between simulations (such as dreams) and things called 'existent and true', he excludes falsehood from the former on the ground that the simulations would not be similar unless they were also certain things 'that we encounter'.[6]

Whenever we have a perception, therefore, we need to distinguish between two kinds of activity: the perception itself, which is a present application to something encountered from outside; and the addition of a belief, which is a movement from inside ourselves. This distinction provides a foundation for knowledge. Perceptions in themselves are uncontaminated by any belief: they are 'raw' acts of cognition, presenting the world to us without any interpretation. Because they are free of belief, they serve as the means of judging the truth or falsehood of beliefs. They are the ultimate basis of judgement; for there is no further criterion by which the perceptions themselves can be judged. As the later sources explain, one perception cannot judge another, since all have equal validity; nor can one sense judge another, since each has a different object; nor can reason judge perception, since it is wholly dependent on perception.[7] Epicurus warns that one must not throw out any perception: otherwise one will throw out every instrument of judgement (*KD* 24).

The claim that there is no falsehood in perception is boldly counterintuitive. Surely we have false perceptions, and these are sometimes so similar to true perceptions as to be indistinguishable from them? Socrates had addressed this objection in Plato's *Theaetetus* (157e–158e). Against the claim that dreams and other allegedly 'false perceptions' can be so similar to allegedly true perceptions as to be indistinguishable from them, he responds, on behalf of the thesis that perception is knowledge, that all perceptions are unique experiences, occurring to different subjects at

---

[6] πρὸς ἃ βάλλομεν: this is the reading of one MS., viz. F.   [7] D.L. x.32 and Lucr. IV.482–98.

different times. There is no conflict among them; for all 'are' equally and
are equally 'true'. Epicurus holds likewise that a perception is a present
interaction between a percipient subject and a perceived object. The very
similarity between allegedly true and false perceptions provides the basis
of his argument: the similarity shows that there is in each case something
that we 'encounter'. These objects of encounter are without falsehood.

Epicurus does not actually say in his extant writings what the later
sources say, namely that 'all presentations', or 'all (sense) perceptions', or
'all objects of perception' are 'true', and that all objects of perception are
'existent' or 'real'.[8] But the later versions purport to capture Epicurus'
meaning; and indeed there is no substantive difference.

Thus Demetrius of Laconia explains that 'we call the perceptions true
by reference to the objects of perception'.[9] According to Sextus (*M* VIII.9),
Epicurus 'said that all objects of perception are true and existent (ἀληθῆ
καὶ ὄντα), for there is no difference between saying that something is true
and saying it is real (ὑπάρχον)'. Epicurus' followers also argued that the
presented object (τὸ φανταστόν) is in every case just as it appears, that is,
is something 'real'. As they put it, all presentations are not only from, but
also in accordance with, the presented object (*M* VII.203–10). This
Epicurean argument consists of an analogy between the 'primary feelings', pleasure and pain, and perceptions. Just as pleasure and pain are
necessarily from and in accordance with something real (for example,
pleasure is from and in accordance with something pleasant), so every perception necessarily corresponds to its producer, which 'is' just as it
appears.

But granted that Epicurus and his followers are agreed on the reality of
whatever is perceived, what sort of reality does this object of perception
have?[10] In *Ep. Hdt.* 50 Epicurus explains the object of perception, exemplified by the shape of a solid, as an effect produced by incoming atoms: at
the causal level, the presentation or presented object corresponds to
atoms interacting with each other. The truth of a presentation, therefore,
may be explained in two different ways, phenomenally and causally: a
presentation is true insofar as it presents something that is in reality just
as it appears; and a presentation is true insofar as it corresponds to an
impact of atoms on the sense organ. The second formulation provides the

---

[8] See frs. 247–54 Usener.   [9] *PHerc.* 1012, col. 72.3–6 Puglia 1988.

[10] A much disputed question: while most interpreters take the truth of a perception to consist in
some sort of correspondence between the presentation and its atomic stimuli (so Furley 1971,
616, C. Taylor 1980, 119–22, Everson 1990b, 173–4), Rist 1972, 19–20, proposes that what
makes a presentation true is that it is a real event, and Striker 1977, 134–5, 142, suggests that
what is true is a proposition expressing the content of a sense impression.

physical explanation for the first. For it identifies the object of perception as the effect of an arrangement of atoms coming from outside.

Epicurus' followers rely on the physical explanation when they claim that a perception is true because it is 'moved' by something, as opposed to moving itself. Diogenes Laertius (x.32) applies this explanation to allegedly illusory appearances: 'The appearances (φαντάσματα) of madmen and dreams are true, for they move [the sense or mind], and what does not exist does not move anything'. More precisely, a perception is true because it is not moved by itself and, when moved by something else, cannot add or take away anything (S.E. *M* viii.9). Hence it is 'irrational' and without memory. Sextus (*M* viii.63) identifies the mover as images which 'underlie'. Alleged misperceptions, such as Orestes' vision of the Furies, are true because they are moved by underlying images. That there are external solid Furies is a false inference added by the mind. Because a perception is no more than a response to an external stimulus, it is free of any interpretative contamination.

Clearly, this notion of perceptual truth does not agree with our ordinary notion. Ordinarily, a perception is considered true if it corresponds to an independently existing external object, not to an immediately impinging stimulus. Epicurus seems to evade the problem by redefining perceptual truth. This seems all the more reprehensible as Epicurus proposes to test all answers by reference to ordinary concepts. His followers, moreover, certainly give the impression that they deal with external reality (as ordinarily understood) when they advance the claim that all perceptions are true.

Then let us look more closely at how Epicurus explains the difference between true and false perceptions in the ordinary sense. It has generally been supposed that the first sentence of *Ep. Hdt.* 50 spells out the conditions of a 'true' (in the ordinary sense) or 'reliable' perception. Epicurus claims that the shape of the solid is produced in one of two ways: by 'successive compacting', or by a 'remnant of the image' (*Ep. Hdt.* 50). It has been held that these two methods guarantee a perception that is faithful to the external solid.[11] However, it is clear that all visual presentations, whether true or false (in the ordinary sense), are formed by these two methods.

The first way consists in the successive merging of images in the sense organ. Atoms that have entered are continually reinforced by new arrangements of atoms arriving in imperceptibly small units of time.

---

[11] So Furley 1971, 607–11; cf. 1967, 208.

The successive arrival of parts of images in the eye results in a composite image which presents a whole.[12] As Lucretius explains, we do not see the individual *images* that stream from an external thing. Instead, we see the 'thing itself' as a result of the merging of images in the sense organ:

> In this one must not wonder in the least bit why, when the images that strike the eyes cannot be seen singly, things themselves (*res ipsae*) are discerned. For also when the wind lashes us little by little and bitter cold flows, we are not in the habit of perceiving each individual particle of wind and its cold, but rather we perceive the wind as a whole, and we note blows happening on our body just as if some object were lashing it and providing a perception of its own external body. Moreover, when we strike the stone itself (*ipsum*) with the finger, we touch the outermost colour of the rock at the very surface, yet we do not perceive this by touch but instead we perceive the hardness itself (*ipsam*) deep within the rock. (Lucr. IV.256–68)

Lucretius draws an analogy between the sense of touch and the sense of sight. When we feel a cold wind blowing, we do not perceive the successively arriving particles of wind, but the wind as a whole. When we touch a rock, we do not perceive the fine surface layer with which our finger makes contact, but rather the hardness deep within the rock. Analogously, what we see is not individual images, but 'things themselves', *res ipsae*. The images are simply the means by which we obtain a perceptual grasp of the solid from which they flow.

According to Epicurus (*Ep. Hdt.* 48), the images that stream from a solid preserve 'for a long time' the arrangement they had on the surface of the solid; but their arrangement may also be disturbed. Similarly, in the case of hearing (*Ep. Hdt.* 52–3), the stream of atoms from the external source produces a perception of the source 'for the most part'; but it may also show only what is 'external' to the source.[13] In general, whenever the sensory organ is at a distance from the source of the perception, there is a perceptual stream extending from the source to the sense organ. If no disturbance occurs, the successive compacting of effluences permits a perception of the source itself. In this case, the source reaches through the perceptual stream right to the sensory organ, so that there

---

[12] In addition to Lucretius, see Aug. *Ep.* 118.30 and Alex. *de Sens.* 56–63 and *de An. Mant.* 134–6 (discussed by Asmis 1984, 128–37). The merging of εἴδωλα explains how we can see objects larger than the surface of the pupil: we do not see an object as the result of a single εἴδωλον shrinking between the object and ourselves, but as the result of a stream of εἴδωλα depositing eidolic parts in the eye.   [13] See also S.E. *M* VII.207–9; Lucr. IV.353–63.

is an immediate perceptual contact with the source itself. Otherwise, we have a perception only of what is outside the source. But this makes no difference to the veracity of the perception: whether or not the perceptual stream has become disturbed, we encounter an object that is real.

There is a further complication. Images do not always come from an external source, but may be formed spontaneously in midair, like clouds (Lucr. IV.129-42). Even when they come from an external source, moreover, the images that cause mental visions are prone to combine with each other in midair because they are especially fine (Lucr. IV.722-48). For example, a horse image may combine in midair with a man image to produce the mental vision of a centaur.[14] Although our sources mention composite streams only with reference to mental images, there is no reason why such streams should not also occur in sight, hearing and smell. In all cases, there appear to be three possibilities: a stream may form an undisturbed continuum between the percipient and an external source; a stream from an external source may be disturbed; and a stream may form spontaneously (i.e. combine) in midair.

The second way in which the perceived shape of a solid is said to be produced is by a 'remnant of the image' (*Ep. Hdt.* 50). Since atoms may remain in the sense organ for a time after they have entered, it is reasonable to suppose that an image that has been constituted in the sight or mind by successive compacting may linger so as to produce a kind of after-image. This after-image corresponds to what remains of the image. The remnant does not stay long enough to produce dreams and memories, for these are produced by newly arriving images.[15]

In the case of touch and taste, there is no external stream intervening between the sensory organ and the source. Instead, there is an immediate contact between percipient and source. Yet here too we ordinarily draw a distinction between true and false perception. Epicurus explains this distinction as well. For apart from external arrangement, there is an internal factor that determines the kind of perception; and it applies to all senses. This is the condition of the sensory organ. Even if there is no disturbance in the external stream, a derangement of the sensory organ may alter the perception.

---

[14] Lucretius points out that a single mental εἴδωλον, even though extremely fine, is able to move the mind; for the mind too is extremely fine (IV.746-8). This does not imply, as is generally supposed, that a mental presentation is due to a single εἴδωλον entering the mind. Here too the image is due to an eidolic stream, as Lucretius' explanation of moving dream images indicates (IV.794-806).   [15] See Asmis 1984, 137-9.

Basically, a sense organ takes in precisely what is commensurate with it (σύμμετρον, *Ep. Hdt.* 53, cf. 50). Its condition, therefore, determines what parts of the perceptual stream it encounters.[16] As a result, perceptions vary from one type of animal to another, from one individual to another, and from one perception to another. If the organ of taste is in a healthy condition, for example, honey tastes sweet. But if it is diseased, the taste is bitter. In the former case, atoms productive of sweet taste interact with the sense organ; in the latter, atoms that produce a bitter taste are admitted instead (Lucr. IV.658–72). When we enter a dark room, we may not be able to make out colours at first, although we can do so after a little while (Plu. *Col.* 1110c–d). The reason lies in the adjustment of the sense organ to the incoming atoms.

In receiving particles from outside, moreover, the sensory organ does not simply submit passively to the impacts. It engages in an active response called 'application' (ἐπιβολή). Epicurus refers to this contribution along with 'successive compacting' and 'remaining'; and it is essential to the formation of any presentation. How it works can best be gauged from Lucretius' defence of Epicurus' theory of mind.

The dependence of the mind on newly arriving images is a peculiarity of Epicurean psychology that provoked much criticism in antiquity. It conflicts with the well-entrenched position that, unlike the five senses, the mind has objects of its own, which it can call up whenever it likes, regardless of what happens to it from outside. Lucretius defends the Epicurean view by arguing that the mind, like any other sense organ, has an active role in perception. This sensory activity is not a self-movement, as Diogenes Laertius (x.31) makes clear, but an act of responding to incoming atoms. By an act of application, etymologically an 'onslaught' or 'thrust upon' an object, the sensory organ goes to meet what is presented to it.

Lucretius asks (IV.779–880): how can the mind straight away think of anything it likes? The answer is twofold. On the one hand, there is a vast number of images impinging upon the mind at any single perceptible time. On the other hand, the mind cannot see anything clearly unless it 'strains' to see it; it must 'have prepared itself' for what it sees. To obtain a sequence of thought, it 'prepares itself further and hopes that it will see what follows each thing, with the result that it happens' (IV.802–6). Lucretius compares the mental act of preparation to the focussing of eyes on tiny objects. Then he extends this analogy to perception in general:

---

[16] Lucr. IV.668–70, 706–21; Plu. *Col.* 1109c–1110d.

even when things are openly perceptible, if one does not pay attention, everything is 'as though separated by all time and far removed' (IV.812–13).

Sensory application, then, is the act of attention by which the sense organs (including the mind) obtain a clear awareness. This activity need not be deliberate.[17] What makes it an active response rather than passive submission is that the organ is in a state of attentiveness toward what is presented to it. Though determined by preceding atomic movements, this state in turn determines the effect of the incoming streams. Without it, there is only the vaguest awareness: nothing is clear. In other words, nothing is 'evident' (ἐναργές). This vague awareness is not sufficient to constitute a presentation.[18]

All presentations are evident; and all equally show what is true.[19] This evidence is, in Sextus' words (*M* VII.216), the 'base and foundation' of all cognition. What makes a sense organ an organ of judgement, a 'criterion', is that by making an application it always gets hold of what is 'evident'. Epicurus draws this correlation between the sense organs and evidence when he warns us not to eliminate 'the criteria that judge in accordance with evidence' (*Ep. Hdt.* 52) and urges us to pay attention to 'all the evidence that is present in accordance with each of the criteria' (*Ep. Hdt.* 82).

In sum, two factors are necessary for the production of any sense perception: a stream of atoms that impinges on the sensory organ; and a sensory organ that responds actively to this stream. In every act of perception, a presentation or 'evidence' is produced by an act of attention of the sensory organ to incoming arrangements of atoms. What is presented – the object of perception – is not an arrangement of atoms, but an effect produced by the atoms. These effects differ for each sense. In the case of sight, it is colour, along with the shape and size of colour at a remove from us. In hearing, it is sound. The sense of taste perceives flavours; the sense of smell perceives odours; and touch perceives body, as well as the contiguous shape, size, and so on, of body.[20]

We do not perceive an image, or any arrangement of atoms; nor do we perceive some sort of inner mental object. We perceive in every case some-

---

[17] As shown by Furley 1967, 208; cf. 1971, 611. But neither is ἐπιβολή an entirely passive process, as Furley proposes.

[18] As Sextus observes (*M* VII.203), Epicurus also used the term ἐνάργεια for presentation.

[19] *Pace* e.g. Bailey 1928, 242–3, 254–7.

[20] *Ep. Hdt.* 49–53; Lucr. IV.489–95. The anonymous (Philodemus?) *PHerc.* 19/698 has a detailed (though fragmentary) discussion of these objects of perception; see esp. cols. 17, 18, 22, 25, 26, and fr. 21 Scott. New edition of the papyrus in Monet 1996. For a different view of the objects of perception, see Sedley 1989b, and Long and Sedley 1987, vol. 1, 84.

thing projected outside ourselves, as existing outside us. We see a red square, or hear a shrill cry, or touch a hard body. When Orestes has a vision of a Fury, he does not see an image of a Fury or a mental image; he sees a Fury as a three-dimensional object existing outside of himself.

We must distinguish, therefore, between what we ordinarily call an object of perception and the object of perception as revealed by physical science. In redefining perceptual truth, Epicurus redefines 'object of perception'. Whereas we ordinarily take it to be an external object distinct from us, it is the convergence of an external stream on the sense organ. The organ reads off a part of this stream. If the stream comes from a particular source and the sense organ reads off what is directly 'on' the source, there is a true perception (in the ordinary sense). If the organ reads off a part outside the source or altogether detached from a particular source, there is still a truthful object of perception, even though it does not coincide with a particular source. The difference between a true and false perception (in the ordinary sense) comes down to this: does the object of perception, as redefined, coincide with what it presents as its source? If the sense is able to reach, by means of the perceptual stream, the very source it shows, there is what is ordinarily called a true object of perception; otherwise, not.

Let us now return to Epicurus' sentence on the shape of the solid (*Ep. Hdt.* 50). Epicurus mentions both the internal cause of the presentation, the application, and the external cause, an influx of images. Nothing in this causal analysis suggests that Epicurus is here singling out what is ordinarily called a 'true' perception; and the indefinite form of the sentence ('whatever presentation we take...') suggests rather that he is referring to any visual presentation of an external solid at all, whether distorted or not. As Sextus puts it, what is presented is either the colour outside the solid or the colour on the very surface of the solid. Either type of colour shows the shape of the solid.

But there remains a problem. Epicurus describes the shape of the solid as 'coming to be' in accordance with the impact of images. At the same time, he indicates that there is an external solid that has shape and colour, which may be conveyed to the percipient by means of images. Qualities such as colour and shape, sound, odour, and so on, are not just temporary qualities, existing only at the moment of perception, but more or less enduring features of the external world. Epicurus himself divides these qualities into permanent and occasional, and says that the former make up a body's 'own nature' (*Ep. Hdt.* 68–9).

How does this view square with Epicurus' physics? Physical investigation shows that there is no colour, sound, odour, flavour, or bodily texture independently of perception. There are just atoms, having shape, size, and weight, moving about in various arrangements in the void. What is presented in perception is the effect of an interaction between us and incoming atoms. Apart from perception, there is no external red sphere: the coloured three-dimensional shape that we see exists only in perceptual interaction; outside us, there are fine networks of colourless atoms that are densely arranged in the so-called 'solid' source and very thinly distributed in the perceptual stream reaching from the source to the beholder.

Now Epicurus draws a distinction between 'in relation to us' (πρὸς ἡμᾶς) and 'in itself' (καθ' αὐτό): 'in relation to us', he writes (*Ep. Pyth.* 91), the size of the sun and other heavenly bodies is just as it appears; 'in itself' it is larger or a little smaller or the same. Elsewhere, Epicurus contrasts 'in relation to us' with 'the underlying thing in itself'.[21] 'In relation to us' clearly means 'as we perceive it'. The size of the sun 'in itself', by contrast, would seem to be the underlying cause of the perception, namely the size of the distant sun. To take our perceptual stream, with the percipient at one end, the solid sun at the other, and the stream of images in between: from the point of view of the beholder, that is 'in relation to us', the size of the sun is just as it appears; the size of the sun 'in itself', on the other hand, is the size of the solid sun considered in itself, apart from the beholder.

One and the same thing, therefore, may be described in two ways: 'in relation to us', it is just as it appears; 'in itself', it is the same as it appears or different. 'In itself' the sun is tiny. It is also brightly coloured and hot. Moreover, it is a network of colour-producing and heat-producing atoms. Because this atomic source effects certain perceptual qualities – those that are perceived in a perception 'upon' the source – the external source may be said to have these qualities 'in itself'.

Epicurus thus combines a robust ontology of perceptual objects with his atomic theory. The senses always present what exists in the external world and often (though not always) present a source 'in itself'. Because they always present an immediately underlying external thing, they never lie. They also often present the object that we think (by the addition of a belief) they present. Hence physical theory not only justifies a trust in all perceptions, but also saves our ordinary beliefs about perception.

But there is still a problem. Although the senses can display an external solid without distortion, or 'in itself', they cannot tell whether their dis-

---

[21] *On nature* xi, *PHerc.* 1042, col. vb.6–8 Sedley 1976b, 34, where the contrast between κατὰ . . . τὸ ὑπο[κεί]μενον καθ' ἑα[υτὸ] and πρὸς ἡμᾶς applies to the rising and setting of the sun and moon.

play is without distortion: their judgement is necessarily 'in relation to us'. In the words of Lucretius, the senses cannot know the 'nature of things' (*naturam rerum*, IV.385). Instead, reason must discover whether the objects that appear to be moving or stationary, one or many, same or different, distant or close, straight or bent, round or square, and so on, really are so (IV.380–461, 500–6).

We return, therefore, to the question whether there is any way of singling out certain perceptions as reliable witnesses about enduring objects. At the conclusion of the *Letter to Herodotus* (82), Epicurus pairs the perceptions and feelings again:

> One must pay attention to the present feelings and perceptions, to those that are common in accordance with what is common and to those that are particular in accordance with what is particular, and to all the evidence that is present in accordance with each of the criteria of judgement.

A further distinction among perceptions is that they may be particular to an observer or common to all. This distinction depends on the assumption that there are enduring objects of perception that are the same for all. Does reliance on common perceptions, then, help us to a solid basis of inference? We will return to this possibility when we discuss preconceptions.

*

In his procedural note (*Ep. Hdt.* 38), Epicurus joins 'feelings' (πάθη) to perceptions as a basis of inference. In his survey of Epicurean canonic, Diogenes Laertius (x.35) states that there are two feelings, pleasure and pain, by which choice and avoidance are judged. This is in agreement with Epicurus' own claim that pleasure is the starting-point of choice and the measure (κανών) of all good (*Ep. Men.* 129). But this does not imply that pleasure and pain are not also a criterion of truth. For they determine action by serving as a measure of what truly is good and bad. In addition, the feelings are signs of what is nonevident in the area of psychology (*Ep. Hdt.* 63 and 68).

Epicurus does not explain feelings separately in the *Letter to Herodotus*. Their epistemological role can be inferred, however, from what he says about perceptions. The basic difference between these two measures of truth is that feelings are acts of awareness of inner states, whereas perceptions are directed at what is external to us. As a type of canon, the feelings are not simply altered conditions of the sense organ; they include an awareness of the condition. Epicurus agreed with others that every act of perception depends on an alteration of the sense organ; and this may be called a feeling. In addition to being moved, the sense organ may have a feeling of being moved; and this constitutes a criterion of truth.

At the most general level, this criterion is a feeling of pleasure or pain. Subsumed under these feelings is the whole range of bodily sensations, such as feeling sated or hungry or having a pain in the stomach, and the entire range of emotions, such as anger, sadness, or joy. Since feelings are a kind of awareness, they may be subsumed in turn, along with perceptions proper, under the general heading of 'perception', as occurs in the later sources.[22] And just like perceptions in the narrow sense, the feelings depend on an 'application' of the sense organ and are correlated with 'evidence'.[23]

As a criterion of goodness, feelings form the foundation of Epicurean ethics. In physics, the area in which feelings are most important is psychology. Epicurus signals this special role by framing his analysis of the soul in the *Letter to Herodotus* (63 and 68) with references to both perceptions and feelings. One highly controversial claim supported by reference to feelings is the claim that the mind is situated in the heart. Like the Stoics (though with a different logical apparatus), the Epicureans sought to determine the location of the mind by the 'evident' fact that the heart is where we feel fear, joy, and other emotions.[24] Since the mind is the seat of the emotions, this feeling shows that the mind is located in the heart.

III Preconceptions

In addition to perceptions and feelings, the investigator must have preconceptions (προλήψεις) at the outset of an inquiry (*Ep. Hdt.* 37–8). Preconceptions correspond to the utterances used to state a belief or problem. They must not require proof; otherwise proof would go on to infinity. Rather, they share with perceptions and feelings the property of being 'evident' and so constitute a third type of measure or canon.

Since Epicurus says very little about preconceptions, it is best to turn immediately to Diogenes Laertius (x.33):

They say that preconception is something like apprehension (κατάληψις) or correct belief (δόξα) or a conception or a general (καθολική) stored notion, that is, a memory of what has often appeared from outside, for example, 'a human being is this sort of thing'. For as soon as

---

[22] See Cic. *Fin.* 1.30–31 and 11.36.
[23] They are linked with ἐνάργεια at *PHerc.* 1251 col. 13.8–12; cf. Indelli and Tsouna 1995, 93 and 171–3.   [24] Lucr. III.141–2; Demetrius of Laconia, *PHerc.* 1012, cols. 42–7 Puglia 1988.

'human being' is spoken, an outline of a human being is thought of in accordance with the preconception, as a result of antecedent perceptions. What is first subordinate to every word, therefore, is evident.

And we would not have sought what we seek if we had not previously come to know it, for example: is the thing standing in the distance a horse or a cow? For it is necessary to have come to know at some time by preconception the shape of a horse and cow. Nor would we have named anything unless we had previously learned its form by preconception.

Diogenes adds that we would not seek anything unless we had first learnt what it is; nor would we name anything unless we had first acquired a preconception of it.[25] In conclusion, he reiterates that preconceptions are 'evident'. As attested elsewhere, a preconception is an act of 'application'.[26] Like sensory self-evidence, conceptual self-evidence consists in a 'thrust upon' something real.

In this account, which is clearly influenced by later debates with non-Epicureans, two things stand out: preconceptions are derived from sense perception;[27] and their function is to serve as points of reference for inquiry. Epicurus states the second point explicitly in his procedural note. The first is the more problematic: how soundly are Epicurus' preconceptions based on sense perception? How can they exclude an element of interpretation added to sensory information?

Diogenes offers alternative descriptions of preconception in response to positions taken by various other philosophers.[28] His basic explanation is that it is a 'memory of what has often appeared from outside'. The appearances from outside are sensory appearances 'preceding' the formation of the conception. Their repeated occurrence results in a 'memory' of a type of thing or of an individual item. For just as we associate the outline of a human being with the words 'human being', so we associate an outline of Socrates, for example, with the word 'Socrates'. We use this notion whenever we form any sort of belief about Socrates. In the case of individual human beings many perceptions result in a notion of a certain kind of shape and behaviour; and this is a 'stored, general notion' no less than the more general notion of 'human being'. Indeed, Epicurean preconceptions range in complexity from notions of simple sensory qualities, such as 'red',

---

[25] The function of preconceptions is to answer a problem put by Plato in the *Meno*: how can we inquire into anything without previously knowing it? Epicurus' solution is that we have notions derived from sense perception. Having learned by observation what a horse and a cow are, we can ask the question: is the indistinct shape seen in the distance a horse or a cow? (see above, pp. 195–6). [26] Clemens Alex. *Strom.* II.4.

[27] See Asmis 1984, 63–80; cf. Long and Sedley 1987, vol. I, 89.

[28] For difficulties in Diogenes' account, see Glidden 1985, 180–6.

'bitter', 'hot', to notions that combine a number of sensory properties, such as 'Socrates', 'human being', 'god', and 'just' (said to be 'what is communally advantageous', *KD* 36).

By attending to sensory appearances, the mind comes to pick out certain features as constituting a type. This conceptual act poses a special problem within Epicureanism: is it an interpretation added by the mind to sensory impressions? If so, it is not simply the product of outside influences and consequently requires verification by the senses. It appears that a preconception is a special kind of belief formed out of an accumulation of sensory impressions. Repeated in the mind, sensory impressions turn into a conception, which is continually reinforced and confirmed by further sensory impressions.

The self-evidence of preconceptions, then, is much more complex than that of individual sensory impressions. Another complexity concerns the existence of what is conceived. Does the object conceived exist in the peculiar Epicurean sense in which all objects of perception exist, or does it have existence 'in itself'?

The preconception about which we have most information and which therefore promises to throw most light on this question is the notion of god. It was highly controversial in antiquity and is still much debated.[29] In Epicurus' words (*Ep. Men.* 123), 'the common notion of god outlines' that god is an 'indestructible, blessed living being', and 'the gods exist, for the knowledge of them is evident'. Cicero (*ND* 1.43–4) shows that 'common' means 'common to all people', and he cites this consensus as proof of the existence of gods:

> . . . [Epicurus] saw that there are gods, because nature herself had impressed a notion of them in the minds of all. For what nation or race of men is there that does not have a certain preconception of the gods without any teaching? . . .

> Since [this] belief has not been established by some convention or custom or law and there abides a firm agreement among everyone, it must be understood that there are gods. For we have implanted, or rather inborn, notions of them; what the nature of all is agreed on must be true; therefore it must be admitted that there are gods.

Cicero draws a distinction between the natural formation of the concept and the imposition of a belief by some form of teaching, such as custom or law. The thought that there are gods is naturally implanted in everyone; it

---

[29] For a detailed discussion, see below, p. 455.

follows that there are gods. In addition, we all naturally think of the gods as 'blessed and immortal' (1.44):

> For the same nature that gave us an outline of the gods has engraved in our minds that we consider them everlasting and blessed. (1.45)

On the basis of universal natural agreement, Cicero establishes two basic claims about the gods: they exist, and they are immortal and happy.

While this account is compatible with Epicurus' views, it has been carefully adjusted to fit a conceptual framework that is shared by other philosophers. These adjustments are not without problems. Thus what makes an Epicurean preconception natural is that it has been imposed on human minds by the external environment, whereas Stoic preconceptions, for example, are rooted in human nature. The Epicurean preconception of god is produced, like any other, by repeated sensory presentations. It is the result of waking and dreaming visions of the gods, which are caused by images streaming into our minds (Lucr.v.1169–71). While Epicurean preconceptions may be called ἔμφυτοι ('in one's nature', a term translated by Cicero as *innatas*, 1.44), as Stoic preconceptions were called, the term can mislead the reader into taking it to imply an origin entirely within the human being or, worse, to mean 'innate'. Epicurean preconceptions are naturally implanted from outside; and this is what distinguishes them from customs, conventions, and laws, which are taught.

Nothing in the Epicurean account of preconceptions suggests that all preconceptions are held universally. Such a requirement would exclude preconceptions not only of individuals such as Socrates, but also of elephants, mangoes, oceans, islands, and so on. Do only common preconceptions, then, guarantee existence? All preconceptions, as Diogenes Laertius says, are 'evident'; and Epicurus appeals to 'evident' knowledge as proof of the existence of the gods. In the case of perceptions, 'evidence' guarantees a certain kind of existence, that which is 'relative to us'. Do preconceptions likewise show only existence that is 'relative to us'? Certainly preconceptions of centaurs and other fictional entities – if there are any such preconceptions – do not show objective existence. We return to the question: do common preconceptions, then, show objective existence?

There is little doubt that Cicero's Epicurean spokesman, Velleius, takes the gods to be real creatures and not just mental constructs. This is how the Academic critic, Cotta, understands his claim (1.62–4). Is Velleius' appeal to universal agreement, then, simply a premiss taken from his opponents, which he does not endorse himself? This is unlikely, since he attributes the argument to Epicurus. Indeed Epicurus appeals to the universality of the preconception in his own brief discussion. Did Epicurus, then, propose common agreement, when naturally implanted, as a guarantee of objective existence? We saw earlier that Epicurus distinguishes between common and individual perceptions and feelings in the *Letter to Herodotus* (82). Earlier in the *Letter*, Epicurus cites the 'common' perception of bodies as evidence that there are bodies.[30] He also appeals to the common feeling (common not just to humans, but to all animals) of the pleasant as good as evidence that pleasure is the supreme good (Cic. *Fin.* 1.30). Is universal experience, then, a guarantee of objective existence both for perceptions and for preconceptions?

If this were the case, one would surely expect some mention of this criterion in the later discussions on Epicurean perception. As it is, the Epicurean position is distinguished from it. Sextus points out that whereas the sceptical followers of Aenesidemus accept common (though not individual) sensory appearances as true, the Epicureans accept all sensory appearances as true (*M* viii.8–9). Neither Sextus nor any other source mentions that Epicurus singled out common perceptions as showing objective existence. Indeed, how could such an assumption fit Epicurean epistemology? It is plausible, for example, that everyone sees the sun as tiny. But Epicurus does not use this as proof that the sun is tiny 'in itself'; instead, he reasons out this conclusion by analogy with other perceptions.

In short, preconceptions pose a problem that was previously confronted in connection with perceptions: how can one bridge the gap between relative and objective existence? The most consistent strategy for Epicurus, it seems to me, would be to rely only on perceptions and preconceptions that are common. This is also historically the most plausible solution. Epicurus' confidence that we 'often' have a perception of the source suggests that, because of their great frequency, he thought that common perceptions can be taken to show objective existence. Common preconceptions, since they are based on so much higher a degree of consensus, can all the more justifiably lay claim to certainty. Common perceptions and preconceptions are not distinguished in their nature from those that are individual; they are formed in just the same way. Nonetheless, they support 'authoritative opinions'.

How, then, does the mind ascend from sensory impressions to a preconception? The content of the preconception of god is not a so-called proper object of perception, such as colour, shape, and so on, but properties inferred from such objects. Lucretius lists a sequence of beliefs: the

---

[30] *Ep. Hdt.* 39, cf. Lucr. 1.422.

first three constitute a preconception of the gods, whereas the fourth is a
false addition (v. 1169–93). The repeated appearance of human-shaped figures with exceptionally vigorous bodies, he explains, caused humans to
attribute sensation, immortality and perfect happiness to these figures.
But humans also made the enormous mistake of holding the gods responsible for the events in the heavens. The appearances, it seems, give rise
equally to true and to false beliefs. How is one to distinguish between
them? What demarcates a preconception from a false belief?

Epicurus (*Ep. Men.* 123–4) warns against attaching anything to the gods
that is 'alien' to their indestructibility and happiness. Such additions, he
says, are false suppositions, not preconceptions. Similarly he distinguishes between an evident state of affairs and an attached belief in the
case of perceptions. The difference is that in the case of preconceptions
what is evident is itself a belief, and that additional beliefs are tested
against it by their compatibility or incompatibility with it. Epicurus illustrates this test in the first of his *Kuriai Doxai*: 'What is happy and indestructible does not take trouble or make trouble for another, so that it is
subject neither to acts of anger nor to favours; for everything of this sort
belongs to weakness.' The test is an inference, which consists in taking the
evident superiority of the gods as proof that they are not given to anger or
favouritism.

How, then, do we come to think of the evident properties that constitute the preconception? It was suggested earlier that they are patterns
imprinted in the mind. This explanation requires some refinement; for
preconceptions are not simply impressions from outside, but inferences
from them. By using Cicero's distinction between natural and taught
beliefs, we obtain the conclusion that a preconception is an inferred pattern imposed naturally from outside. Reasoning is an activity produced in
the mind by means of atomic movements. To reason is to arrange images;
and this mental power is the result of images continually impinging on
the mind and establishing certain patterns within it. From the beginning,
successively arriving images are arranged automatically according to similarity and difference. This process gradually becomes an ability of the
mind to sort out images deliberately, that is, to perform acts of reasoning.

Some Epicureans indeed assimilated the formation of preconceptions
to the type of reasoning used in constructing scientific arguments. Their
position will be examined in detail later; but what they said on preconceptions is relevant here. Zeno of Sidon proposed that all valid inferences
about what is not observed are inductive inferences, obtained by passing
from carefully scrutinized observed cases to similar unobserved cases.

This method is called 'transition by similarity' (ἡ καθ' ὁμοιότητα μετάβασις). Preconceptions are one type of inference made by this method. For example, we infer that a body, insofar as it is a body, has mass and resistance, and that a human being, as human being, is a rational animal.[31]

By treating preconceptions just like scientific theories, Zeno runs the risk of obliterating the difference between initial conceptions and the theories built on them. If preconceptions are theories, they are in need of proof. In his text, Philodemus does not distinguish the testing of preconceptions from that of scientific theories. This does not mean, however, that there is no difference. What is needed is the distinction between a natural type of inference, which results in preconceptions, and a technical type, by which we prove theories. Zeno's analysis must allow this kind of difference if preconceptions are to have epistemological priority.

Let us return now to Epicurus' initial instructions. A preconception is 'subordinate' to 'utterances' (*Ep. Hdt.* 37). When linguistic sounds are uttered, the hearer has thoughts corresponding to the sounds, and these thoughts are of general features existing in the world. A preconception is also the 'first' (*Ep. Hdt.* 39, cf. D.L. x.33) thought corresponding to an utterance. This is generally, though not necessarily, the first thought that comes into a person's mind when hearing the sounds. Preconceptions are 'first' in the sense that they are epistemically prior to the beliefs that are attached to them. What makes them 'first' is that they are derived directly from sensory perceptions, with the result that they too are 'evident'.

As evident starting-points, preconceptions do not require either proof or definition.[32] Epicurus rejected the requirement for definitions: we must indeed be clear about our terms in order to have something to which we may 'look' and 'refer'; but it is never appropriate to start with a definition.[33] We may be reminded of a preconception by a brief description, such as 'god is an indestructible and blessed living being'. But this descriptive sketch merely states what we naturally think of first when we hear the word 'god'. Since we already have a distinct concept, there is no need for it to be supplied or sharpened by a definition.

If the foregoing discussion is roughly correct, Epicurus intends to base all knowledge on the phenomena of sense perception. The two points on which his method seems most problematic are the gap between relative and objective existence, and the exclusion of interpretation from both

---

[31] Phld. *Sign.* col. 34.5–11.   [32] See Asmis 1984, 39–45.

[33] See further Cic. *Fin.* ii.4; and the anonymous commentary on Plato's *Theaetetus*, col. 22.39–42 (Bastianini and Sedley 1995, 320).

perceptions and preconceptions. It remains to see how these empirical starting-points can lead to correct beliefs about what is not observed.

IV Beliefs

Equipped with preconceptions and perceptions, we may formulate problems and test beliefs. These beliefs are of two kinds: about what is 'waiting' (προσμένον),[34] and about what is 'nonevident' (ἄδηλον). The former are verified by 'witnessing' (ἐπιμαρτύρησις) and falsified by 'no witnessing' (οὐκ ἐπιμαρτύρησις). The latter are falsified by 'counterwitnessing' (ἀντιμαρτύρησις) and verified by 'no counterwitnessing' (οὐκ ἀντιμαρτύρησις).

The senses can display the things that we believe to exist. For example, upon seeing a roundish tower from a distance, we might form the belief that the tower is square. This belief is correct if is 'witnessed' by the appearance of a square tower when we come close, and false if it is 'not witnessed' in this way. The component -μαρτύρησις shows that the test of truth and falsehood lies in the first-hand reports of the senses. The square tower is an object of belief that 'awaits' verification by a present perception. Epicurus warns specifically that belief about 'what is waiting' must be distinguished from 'what is present already in perception' (*KD* 24).

Without actually using the term 'waiting' (προσμένον), Sextus gives an example in his account of Epicurean verification and falsification. His report, which is the only survey of Epicurus' theory of verification that we have, supplements Epicurus' own schematic distinctions in the *Letter to Herodotus* (50–1).

> Witnessing is an apprehension by evidence (κατάληψις δι' ἐναργείας) that what is believed is such as it was formerly believed. For example, when Plato approaches from afar, I guess and believe, by reason of the distance, that it is Plato. When he has come near, it was witnessed in addition (προσεμαρτυρήθη), when the distance was eliminated, that it is Plato, and this was witnessed (ἐπεμαρτυρήθη) by evidence (δι' ἐναργείας) itself. (S.E. *M* VII.212–13)

---

[34] The MSS are divided between the active and passive participles at *Ep. Hdt.* 38 and *KD* 24. Bollack 1975 and Long and Sedley 1987 vol. II, 91, attribute the passive form to Epicurus. Diogenes (x.34) gives some support to this interpretation by assigning the wait to the beholder: 'to wait (προσμεῖναι) and come near the tower and learn how it appears (φαίνεται) from close up'. On the other hand, the active form, insofar as it designates an object, makes a parallel with both παρόν and ἄδηλον; and the strangeness of the usage suits Epicurean terminology, as well as providing an explanation for the substitution of the less strange passive form.

'No witnessing', the 'opposite' of witnessing, is explained as follows:

> It is an impact by evidence (ὑπόπτωσις δι' ἐναργείας) that what is
> believed is not such as it was believed. For example, when someone
> is approaching from afar, we guess, by reason of the distance, that it is
> Plato, but when the distance has been eliminated, we have learned by
> evidence (δι' ἐναργείας) that it is not Plato. (S.E. *M* VII.215)

Beliefs about what is not presently observed are verified by the actual
appearance of what was previously conjectured. They are falsified, on
the other hand, by the appearance of something other than what was
believed. Presumably, the beholder makes a conjecture about an object
'in itself': he conjectures, for example, that what he sees really is Plato.
This object is the three-dimensional source of the perception. In vision,
it usually presents itself when the distance is short. A belief about
such an object is true whenever it is matched by an appearance of the
object.

But how will the beholder know that he has a presentation of the object
'in itself'? His knowledge of the object is always mediated by a presentation. As a perceiver, he cannot gauge the amount of distortion in the
atomic stream. Physical theory can tell him about distortion, but it is
based on a prior faith in perception; nor can it ever give him sufficiently
accurate knowledge about any particular perceptual stream.

Further, what is the truth value of a belief whenever there is no present
appearance that matches the belief? Epicurus' terminology seems
designed to fit the theory that objects of perception are nothing but
momentary states of the perceiver. Since such objects of perception exist
only when perceived, 'no witnessing' is a necessary and sufficient condition for the non-existence of a perceptual object. On this view, everything
that is 'waiting' to appear does not yet exist.[35]

As we have seen, however, Epicurus posits not only real momentary
objects of perception, but also enduring objects of perception. If there are
enduring objects of perception, a belief may be true even in the absence of
an appearance. Consequently, Epicurus' theory becomes a theory of verification. Even though a belief may be true, it cannot be accepted as true
unless there is a confirmatory appearance; and even though a belief may be
false, it cannot be rejected as false unless there is an appearance that
clashes with it.

Sextus' examples and explanation agree with the latter interpretation.
The observer ventures a guess that it 'is' Plato; and this belief is verified by

[35] So Asmis 1984, 190–3.

an appearance that is without distortion since it is from close up. It is falsified by an appearance that takes the place of a confirmatory appearance.
'No witnessing' must be understood not merely as the absence of a confirmatory appearance, but as the non-existence of conditions that would
produce a confirmatory appearance. Just when a confirmatory appearance
should occur, there is an appearance of something else; and this appearance turns out to be evidence of the falsity of the belief. As Sextus
explains, when the distance is eliminated there is evidence that it is not
Plato. This is precisely when a confirmatory appearance would appear if
there were an object corresponding to the belief.

Plutarch (*Col.* 1121c) faults the Epicureans for thinking that they can
escape the realm of appearances. His blustering, hypothetical Epicurean
proclaims: 'When I approach the tower and when I touch the oar, I will
declare that the oar is straight and the tower angular; but he [the sceptical
opponent] will agree to no more than the belief (δοκεῖν) and the appearance (φαίνεσθαι), even when he comes close.' Plutarch responds that the
Epicurean is in just the same position as the sceptic, without realizing it.
Since no 'presentation or perception is any more evident than another'
(*Col.* 1121d–e), he cannot pick out any particular presentation as proof of
external reality; all presentations equally show only inner conditions.

Is there any way the Epicureans can justify the move from inner conditions to outer reality? We confronted this question earlier in discussing
perceptions. The step that Epicurus proposes as a way out is the existence
of an atomic stream reaching from an external source to the observer.
Since this stream can present the source without distortion, it is possible
for an observer to have a true opinion about an external perceptual object.
Coming close to a visual object is a test of the perception, although there
is nothing about a presentation itself that makes one more reliable than
another: that is just the point of saying that all are equally evident. The
critics appear to be right that, as far as Epicurean theory goes, no amount
of testing can guarantee that a belief is true. Epicurus and his followers
seem to insist that in practice, when all are agreed on the confirmation of a
belief by a presentation, a belief can be upheld as certain or 'authoritative'
(κυρία).

*

We now turn from sensory phenomena to the hidden entities that are
investigated by physical science. By contrast with things that are 'waiting',
'nonevident' things are not expected to become evident. But they too are
known by reference to appearances. If a theory is 'counterwitnessed' by

sensory evidence, it is false; if it is 'not counterwitnessed', it is true (*Ep. Hdt.* 50–1). Again, the component *-marturēsis* shows that the ultimate test of the belief lies in the reports of the senses.

Just a little way into his physical investigations in the *Letter to Herodotus* (39), Epicurus states that one must infer (τεκμαίρεσθαι) the nonevident by calculation (λογισμός) in accordance with perception, 'as I said before'. This is a reference to the preceding note (*Ep. Hdt.* 38), in which he said that one must use sensory observations as 'signs'. The verb τεκμαίρεσθαι implies that sensory phenomena serve as conclusive signs, τεκμήρια, of what is nonevident. Whereas the phenomena serve only as plausible indicators of what will appear, they show conclusively whether a theory is true or false. The conclusion is worked out by a calculation that shows the perceptual consequences of a theory.

Whereas beliefs about perceptible things are verified by an appearance and falsified by the lack of a confirmatory appearance, beliefs about nonevident things are falsified by appearances and verified by the lack of disconfirmatory appearances. Sextus explains falsification as follows:

> Counterwitnessing (ἀντιμαρτύρησις is . . . the elimination (ἀνασκευή) of the phenomenon by the posited nonevident thing. For example, the Stoic says that there is no void, claiming something nonevident, but the phenomenon – I mean motion – must be co-eliminated by what is thus posited. For supposing there is no void, necessarily motion does not occur either . . . (S.E. *M* VIII.214)

The belief that there is no void is 'counterwitnessed' by the phenomenon of motion; for motion is eliminated by the elimination of void. The proof is constructed in this way. We conjecture: there is no void. This is a hypothesis about what is nonevident. Next we calculate: if there is no void, there is no motion. But we observe that there is motion. It follows that there is void.

In his abbreviated account at *Ep. Hdt.* 39–40, Epicurus supplies no argument in support of the conditional claim 'if there is no void, there is no motion'. Both Lucretius (1.335–9) and Sextus (*M* VII.213) indicate that he argued along these lines: if everything is packed tight with bodies, there is no place for bodies to move into; hence there can be no beginning of movement. What in turn supports this calculation? The claim 'if there is no void, there is no movement' looks suspiciously like an a priori claim borrowed from the Eleatics; and it has usually been understood as such. If Epicurus did take over an Eleatic claim, without somehow recasting it as an empirical claim, then his two initial rules do not summarize his method. If Epicurus is content to adopt a priori truths, he does not build his scientific structure entirely on a foundation of sensory phenomena.

Epicurus' followers argued vehemently that the conditional is known empirically. Epicurus himself might well have supported his apparently Eleatic claim by appealing to empirical conceptions of body, motion, and void. In constructing the conditional 'if there is no void there is no motion', he uses the preconception of 'body' as something that resists touch. This notion is derived from perception. Suppose, then, that every-thing is body: there would everywhere be resistance, so that none of the bodies could begin to move.

Epicurus uses the same method of 'counterwitnessing' to prove the first two doctrines of his physics. He supports his first claim that 'nothing comes to be from nonbeing' by arguing: if this were not the case, then everything would come to be from everything. As Lucretius (1.159–73) makes clear in his detailed proof, this consequence is in conflict with the phenomena. That we do not see everything coming from everything is an evident sign of the nonevident state of affairs 'nothing comes to be from nonbeing'.

Here is a clear example of an apparently Eleatic doctrine being verified by reference to an empirical fact. It is important to note that Epicurus proves the truth of the apparently Eleatic claim by an argument that takes the phenomena as evidently true. He does not simply add confirmation by showing an agreement with the phenomena. He establishes its truth wholly by an argument showing that it must be true if the phenomena are as they are. A critic may well doubt whether the premiss 'if something were to come from nonbeing, everything would come from everything' can be established empirically. Epicurus presumably thought he could verify it by reference to an empirical concept of coming-to-be.

Epicurus' second claim, that nothing is destroyed into nonbeing, is established in the same way by reference to the phenomena. The founda-tion of Epicurus' physics, then, rests on the method of 'counterwitness-ing'. A theory is proved by the refutation of its contradictory. But how does this fit with the method of 'no counterwitnessing', by which a theory is said to be verified? Sextus explains as follows:

No counterwitnessing (οὐκ ἀντιμαρτύρησις) is the consequence (ἀκολουθία) of the posited and believed nonevident thing upon the phe-nomenon. For example, when Epicurus says that there is void, which is nonevident, this is proved by something evident, motion. For if there is not void, there must not be motion either, since the moving body does not have a place into which it will pass because everything is full and packed. So, since there is motion, the phenomenon 'does not counter-witness' the believed nonevident thing. (S.E. *M* VII.213)

Again, Sextus' account implicitly contains a conditional. The argument may be formulated as: if there is motion, there is void; there is motion; therefore there is void. The non-evident thing, void, has the relationship of 'consequence' to the evident thing, motion. In other words, it 'follows upon' motion. This consequence defines 'no counterwitnessing'. Since the conditional is equivalent to the contrapositive 'if there is no void, there is no motion', 'no counterwitnessing' turns out to consist in the dis-proof ('counterwitnessing') of the negated hypothesis.

This restriction of 'no counterwitnessing' is surprising. One expects 'no counterwitnessing' to mean simply that there is no counterevidence against a hypothesis, not that there is evidence against its contradictory. 'Consequence' seems too strong a requirement. Why should the nonevi-dent thing 'follow upon' the phenomena rather than simply be in agree-ment with them? But if we fault Sextus' definition as being too restrictive, another difficulty looms. Mere agreement with the phenomena permits multiple alternative explanations, all equally plausible. How can multiple explanations all be true? It has been suggested that Epicurus viewed 'no counterwitnessing' simply as a test of possibility.[36] But this goes against his own statement (*Ep. Hdt.* 51) that 'no counterwitnessing' is a test of truth, as well as upsetting the symmetry of his fourfold scheme of verifica-tion and falsification.

Epicurus himself made much use of multiple explanations; and these promise to throw some light on the difficulty. He held that, whereas single explanations are required for the foundation of physics, there is no need for single explanations of all events. Multiple explanations for the events in the heavens, for example, are sufficient for our happiness. Single explanations have a 'single agreement (συμφωνία) with the phenomena'; multiple explanations have a multiple agreement (*Ep. Pyth.* 86). Epicurus repeatedly refers to this multiple agreement by saying that there is 'no counterwitnessing'. He asserts, for example, that images may be formed in various ways, none of which 'is counterwitnessed by the perceptions' (*Ep. Hdt.* 48). He defends his extensive use of multiple explanations in astronomy and meteorology by saying that all are 'in agreement with' or 'not counterwitnessed by', the phenomena (*Ep. Pyth.* 86–8, 92, 95, 98). Singling out one explanation, on the other hand, when there are several, 'conflicts' with the phenomena (*Ep. Pyth.* 96).

[36] See Striker 1974, 73–80.

Lucretius shows how there is truth in multiple explanations. He compares the observation of events in the heavens with seeing a corpse at a distance (VI.703–11). It is necessary to state all causes of death – sword, cold, illness, poison, and so on – he writes, in order to state the one cause of this particular death; similarly, for some events it is necessary to state several causes, 'of which one nonetheless is the case'. After proposing several explanations of the movements of the stars, he points out that 'it is difficult to state for certain' which of these causes applies to this world; yet he does state 'what can and does happen' in the universe as a whole and one of these events 'necessarily' occurs in this world (v.526–33). One of the multiple explanations, therefore, does apply to the specific event under investigation. All of them together apply to the general type of event under investigation. Just as each cause of death applies to some death, so each cause of stellar movement applies to some star in the universe as a whole.

Multiple explanations, therefore, are all true with respect to the general type of event; and one of the explanations is true of the specific event. Since the event to be explained is known only as a general type, all explanations are true of just what is being explained. If the investigator had more specific information (by being able to come closer, for example, as in inspecting a corpse), then the explanation might be narrowed to a single cause. What is 'persuasive' (as Epicurus puts it) about multiple explanations is that any one of them might apply, and one does apply, to the specific event under investigation. In a sense, therefore, each explanation is 'possible' rather than true. At the same time, however, each explanation is true of some specific event belonging to the general type.

If this interpretation is correct, the method of 'no counterwitnessing' is at least in part an inductive method. 'No counterwitnessing' occurs whenever there is unopposed similarity between a phenomenon and something nonevident. Yet Sextus Empiricus says nothing whatsoever about induction in his explanation of this method. How can his view of 'no counterwitnessing' as the counterwitnessing of the contradictory hypothesis be reconciled with Epicurus' use of induction? We might suppose that there are two kinds of 'no counterwitnessing': counterevidence against the contradictory hypothesis; and the lack of counterevidence against an inductive inference. Sextus mentions only the former kind. But this does not imply that his account is inaccurate. Provided that his definition of 'no counterwitnessing' as a 'consequence' of the nonevident thing upon the phenomenon can accommodate unopposed induction, his account is not even incomplete, even though he uses an example that illustrates only one type of 'no counterwitnessing'.

It will be objected that induction can never yield 'consequence': it does not 'follow upon' observed facts, no matter how numerous or how thoroughly tested, that something else, that is known to be similar in other respects, has the inferred similarity. Yet Epicurus' followers did argue just this. Drawing on his teacher Zeno, Philodemus argues in his book *On Signs* that there is 'consequence' in inductive inferences no less than in inferences by 'elimination': in both cases, the nonevident thing 'follows upon' the phenomenon. Indeed, he maintains that all truths about what is nonevident are really inductive inferences. By recasting all calculations about what is nonevident as inductions, Zeno and his associates tried to remove all shadow of a doubt that there might be some a priori truths lurking in the foundations of Epicurean science.

Before we make a final judgement, then, about Epicurus' method of inference, we must turn to his followers.

*

Philodemus' *On Signs* is a response to an attack against the Epicurean method of inductive inference, called 'method of similarity' or 'transition by similarity' (ἡ καθ' ὁμοιότητα μετάβασις).[37] The opponents claim that only the 'method of elimination (ἀνασκευή)' is valid. Philodemus responds that the method of similarity is the only valid method of inference and that it subsumes elimination.

This response was worked out by Philodemus' teacher, Zeno of Sidon, in association with other Epicureans. Only one opponent, a certain Dionysius, is named. He has customarily been identified as a Stoic.[38] But he could just as well have been an Academic. We have one other attack on Epicurean induction. It is part of a sustained attack on Epicurean theology by the Academic Cotta in Cicero's *De natura deorum* (1.87–90, 97–8). Mocking the 'very great delight' that the Epicureans take in similarity ('Isn't a dog similar to a wolf?', he asks, 1.97), Cotta makes some of the same objections that occur in Philodemus' work. In fact, there was a broad coalition of philosophers and scientists who were aligned against Epicurean induction; and Philodemus seems to be responding to all of them. He offers a revised Epicurean theory of signs that takes into account developments of the preceding two centuries, and he presents this revision in several versions: his own report of con-

---

[37] Barnes 1988c, 110–11, warns against calling the method of similarity 'induction'; but see Long's response (1988c, 140).

[38] Sedley 1982c, 240–1, defends the view that he is the Stoic Dionysius of Cyrene, a pupil of Diogenes of Babylon.

versations with Zeno; a report of Zeno's teachings by a fellow student, Bromius; a summary by the Epicurean Demetrius of Laconia, followed by a detailed attack and defence by an unidentified source who may well be Demetrius again.

A sign inference may be expressed with the help of a conditional: 'if the first, the second', where 'the first' expresses the sign, which is something evident, and 'the second' is the nonevident thing that is signified. In common with other philosophers, the Epicureans call this kind of sign 'particular' (ἴδιον, 14.7, 32.36, 33.3). Instead of signifying a multiplicity of situations and so being common (κοινόν) to what is true and false, a particular sign uniquely signifies what is the case. A particular sign, moreover, 'necessitates' the existence of the nonevident thing that it signifies (1.12–16).

A basic issue, then, is this: what makes a conditional true? Philodemus accepts that a conditional is true whenever its contrapositive is true (11.32–7). However, he insists, it does not follow from this that only the method of elimination has the necessity of a particular sign (11.37–12.1, 32.31–33.1). A conditional is true by elimination whenever the removal of the hypothetical nonevident thing, just by itself, brings about the removal of the evident thing (12.1–14, 14.11–14). Sometimes, indeed, the elimination of the consequent carries with it the elimination of the antecedent, as in the conditional 'if there is motion there is void'. But there is also another valid method, that of similarity. According to this method, a conditional is true whenever it is impossible to conceive of the first being the case and the second, which is similar, not being the case. An example is: 'If Plato is a human being, Socrates too is a human being' (12.14–31). This is true because it is inconceivable that Plato is a human being and Socrates is not; and what makes it inconceivable is the similarity between Plato and Socrates. Philodemus claims that in the second type of conditional, too, there is 'consequence' (37.9–17) of the nonevident thing upon the evident thing and a necessary 'link' (συνηρτῆσθαι, 35.5).

Philodemus (37.1–12) grants that there is sometimes a special 'interweaving' (συμπλοκή) between what is evident and what is nonevident. An example is the link between a product and its constituents. In these special cases, a sign conditional is true by elimination. Philodemus here seems to be singling out necessary causal connections. But there is also a conceptual link, which is just as necessary as the causal link. In these cases, the removal of the nonevident thing (such as Socrates' humanity) is not accompanied by the removal of the evident thing (Plato's humanity), but it is inconceivable (ἀδιανόητον) for the observed thing to exist or be of a certain sort and for the nonevident thing not to be likewise.[39]

In defence of this position, Philodemus distinguishes between two uses of the expression '(insofar) as'. The first has the form: since certain things in our experience are of a certain sort, nonevident things are also of this sort 'insofar as' the things in our experience are of this sort. An example is: since humans in our experience, insofar as they are humans, are mortal, if there are humans anywhere they are mortal (33.24–32). Here '(insofar) as' picks out the similarity (humanity) which is assumed to be common to observed and nonevident instances. Since it is always observed to be conjoined with another feature, mortality, one may draw the general conclusion that humans, '(insofar) as' humans, are mortal. This universal claim, Philodemus insists, is a conclusion that is reached by, and indeed only by, the method of similarity (17.3–8). Conceptual necessity is established empirically, by inductive inferences based on observed conjunctions.

Philodemus states the relationship between elimination and similarity in various ways. At times, he is concerned to show that the method of elimination is not the only valid method and so argues for two methods. At other times, he subordinates the method of elimination to the method of similarity. He claims that the method of similarity 'extends' entirely through the method of elimination, which is 'secured' by it (7.8–11, 8.22–9.8). He also says outright that there is just one method of sign inference, similarity; those who abolish it, abolish all inference by signs (30.33–31.1).

Along with promoting induction as the only method of knowing the truth about what is nonevident, the Epicureans attempted to strengthen it. Within their own system, they needed to set apart scientific induction from guesses about what will appear, which are verified only by an actual appearance. The Epicurean task was particularly urgent since other philosophers, joined by scientists, concluded that induction, no matter how well tested, yields no more than a good guess. Thus the Empiricist school of medicine, which originated in the third century BC, developed an intricate method for using accumulations of observations as guides to treatment, not as a means of discovering what is nonevident.[40] Whenever they did not have past observations, the Empiricists proposed to resort to 'transition by similarity', by comparing the present situation to a similar observed situation.[41] Philodemus closes his book *On Signs* with a parting shot at the physicians who use 'transition of similarity'.[42] These are surely

[39] See also 14.2–27 and 32.31–33.9.   [40] Gal. *Subf. Emp.* chapters 1–6.   [41] See below, pp. 511–12.
[42] 14.17; cf. 15.37–8, 38.6–8, and 14.23–4.

Empiricists, refusing to use the method of similarity as a means of discovering the truth.

Against this trend, Zeno and his friends argued that a careful calculation of the phenomena, called ἐπιλογισμός, produces knowledge of what is unobserved. Epicurus had distinguished 'calculation' (ἐπιλογισμός) from 'proof' (ἀπόδειξις). It is an analysis of what is evident, as opposed to a demonstration of what is nonevident. 'There is need of calculation, not proof' for example, that we associate time with days, nights, and so on (*Ep. Hdt.* 73). We must 'calculate' what our natural goal is (*Ep. Men.* 133). As well as extending the method of induction to all sign inferences, Zeno and his group extend calculation to all forms of reasoning. It turns out that the type of rational reflection used to discover what is nonevident is nothing but calculation. In short, scientific proof is nothing but a calculation about the phenomena.

Philodemus sums up the Epicurean method as 'scrutinizing [or 'going around', περιοδευόντων] the similarities by calculation' (17.32-4) and 'drawing conclusions by calculation' (23.5-6). There are three main points. One must consider many instances that are not only of the same kind but also varied (20.32-6, 33.12-13, 35.9-10). Further, one must rely not only on one's own observations, but also on the reports of others (16.35-8, 20.37-9, 32.13-21). Last, there must be no indication to the contrary (e.g. 16.38-17.2, 21.13-14). The inferences are so thoroughly tested that there is 'neither a footprint nor a glimmer' to the contrary, as Demetrius vividly puts it (29.1-4). These rules incorporate methods used by the opponents. Carneades proposed the 'scrutinized' (περιοδευομένη) presentation as the most trustworthy of three kinds of presentation.[43] The Empiricist doctors divided observations into two kinds, 'seeing for oneself' and 'inquiry'. Philodemus charges his opponents with ignoring the fact that the Epicureans rely not only on their own experience, but also on the reports of others (32.13-21).

How faithful, then, are the later Epicureans to Epicurus? Let us first consider Sextus. According to Philodemus, the truth of a belief about what is nonevident does indeed consist in a relationship of 'consequence' between what is evident and what is nonevident. Philodemus analyses this consequence differently from the way Sextus illustrates it. But since Philodemus recognizes elimination as a special type of inference, there is no conflict with Sextus' report. Sextus does not say that the whole of 'no counterwitnessing' is elimination: he merely exemplifies it by elimination.

---

[43] S.E. *M* VII.182-4; it is also called διεξοδευομένη.

Nothing in his analysis implies that he (or his source) did not know of the reformulation proposed by Zeno. Indeed, the fact that he does not define 'no counterwitnessing' as a form of elimination, but defines it instead as 'consequence', suggests that he may have been familiar with Zeno's views.

As for Epicurus, there is no evidence that he ever reformulated his argument for the void, or any other argument later said to exemplify 'elimination', as an induction. Epicurus' followers are notorious for refusing to depart from the doctrines of their master. But they showed themselves very willing to interpret these doctrines in new ways, especially in response to attacks by other philosophers.[44] It was suggested earlier that, if his methodology is to be consistent, Epicurus must reduce all calculations about what is unobserved to empirical judgements. He does not explain in his extant writings how this reduction is to be accomplished. With help from their opponents, his followers worked out what they considered to be the implications of his position. All calculations about what is unobserved, they proposed, are inductive judgements. Among these judgements are preconceptions. The Epicureans thereby restructured Epicurus' distinction between what is evident and what is nonevident. In agreement with Epicurus, they demarcated what we observe from what needs to be inferred from observations. But very differently from Epicurus, they built a transition from the one to the other by allowing sufficiently tested empirical judgements to become, in the end, judgements about what is unobserved. The sign conditional, which grounds the inference, is verified in this way entirely by empirical observations. As a result, the conclusion rests entirely on self-evident, empirical premisses.

---

[44] Cf. Sedley 1989a.

9

Stoic epistemology

MICHAEL FREDE

1 The possibility of knowledge

Stoic epistemology[1] is best understood as a response to a twofold challenge. Socrates had assumed that whether one had a good life depended on whether one had managed to acquire a certain kind of knowledge, which he identified with wisdom, in particular the knowledge of what is good and what is bad. For this reason he had devoted his life to philosophical inquiry concerning the good, the bad and related matters. Yet, for all of his efforts, even he himself did not think that he had obtained this knowledge. At the same time Socrates had made it clear that we should not content ourselves with mere belief or opinion concerning these matters, even if this belief happened to be true. One would not want to rely for the success or failure of one's life on mere opinion which at best happened to be true. Moreover, the Socratic elenchus suggested that one was not entitled to any belief which one did not hold as a matter of knowledge. For Socratic refutation seemed to rest on the fact that somebody who holds a belief as a matter of mere opinion can be made to see that he has equal reason to espouse the contradictory belief.

A century of philosophers since Socrates had done no better. Indeed, as if oblivious to Socrates' strictures against mere belief, they had rushed precipitously to produce thesis after thesis, theses often quite extravagant and often contradicting each other, and in any case all a matter of mere opinion, as closer scrutiny would reveal. The first challenge, then, was to find a way to break out of the realm of mere belief in order to arrive at true knowledge. This challenge was first taken up by the Epicureans, and it is important to see that the Stoic response is patterned on the Epicurean response. The Stoics follow the Epicureans in assuming that knowledge is made possible by the facts (i) that some of the impressions we have are by

---

[1] Main texts: Cicero *Acad.* 1.40–2; II.17–31, 143–6; Sextus *M.* VII.150–8, 227–60, 401–35. D.L. VII.49–54. Note, in addition, *PHerc.* 1020; Stobaeus *Ecl.* II.7.5; Aëtius IV.12.1–5. Literature: Watson 1966; Sandbach 1971; Striker 1974; Frede 1983; Annas 1990b.

their very nature infallibly true and thus can serve as a secure foundation for knowledge, and (ii) that one of the ways in which these impressions are foundational is that, by a natural process, they give rise to certain concepts, the so-called anticipations, in terms of which we naturally think about objects and which reliably embody certain general truths about those objects.

But as the first Stoics try to develop their own version of a theory of how, on the basis of certain privileged impressions and concepts, we might arrive at knowledge, another challenge arises in the form of Academic scepticism. The Academic sceptics, too, go back to Socrates and reflect on the moral to be drawn from Socrates' failure to attain knowledge. They, too, are scandalized by the endless proliferation of mere opinion, easily disposed of by the kind of dialectical questioning to which Socrates subjected his interlocutors. But the sceptics also question Zeno's first attempts to show how we might break out of the circle, in which opinion just breeds further opinion rather than knowledge. Zeno assumes that nature provides us with certain infallibly true impressions of things and that she also provides us with a basic set of notions or concepts which are true to things. But why should we not regard these assumptions, too, as just further opinions? Thus, almost from the start, Stoic epistemology also has to respond to the sceptic challenge.

One reason why, in the face of weighty sceptical arguments to the contrary, the Stoics continue to insist that knowledge is attainable and that it must be possible to identify how it is attainable, is this. The Stoics believe that our life depends on whether we are wise or not. They also believe that nature is provident, and hence must have arranged things in such a way that the knowledge which constitutes wisdom is humanly attainable, if it is true that a good life depends on wisdom. Hence it must be possible to identify the way in which nature has made knowledge and wisdom attainable by us. Looked at in this light, Stoic epistemology amounts to a complex hypothesis as to how nature has endowed us with the means to attain knowledge and wisdom. This hypothesis itself should be such that one can come to espouse it as a matter of knowledge precisely in the way the theory tells us that we can attain knowledge.

11 Cognition

If we think of Socrates' arguments, or – for that matter – of any kind of philosophical arguments, there is the notorious problem of how, on this basis, we are supposed to arrive at knowledge. However plausible and incontrovertible the premises may appear, as long as they represent mere belief, the conclusion, too, will represent no more than mere belief. There is no way to get from mere belief to knowledge, however cogent one's arguments may be. It is fairly clear that Zeno's first cautious move was to claim that, beside mere belief or opinion (*doxa*) and knowledge (*epistēmē*), we have to distinguish a third kind of state, namely cognition (*katalēpsis*):

> He ascribed reliability not to all impressions, but only to those which manifest, in a certain particular way, those objects which make the impressions; and such an impression, when it is perceived in itself, he called cognizable . . . And when it is already received and accepted, he called it a cognition (*comprehensio*). (Cicero *Acad.* I.41)[2]

It will turn out that cognition prominently includes, but is not restricted to, perceptual cognition. What matters here is that Zeno starts out by drawing our attention to the fact that sometimes when we believe that something is the case, for instance because we clearly perceive it to be the case, our belief is not just a matter of mere opinion. When I clearly see that the book in front of me is green, it is not a matter of mere opinion if I think that the book is green. Nor yet, however, is it a matter of knowledge. For to know that the book is green is supposed to be a matter of being in a state such that there is no argument which could persuade one that it is not the case that the book is green. But the mere fact that one clearly sees that the book is green does not suffice to rule out the possibility that one can be argued into not believing that the book is green. Hence the distinction between mere belief, cognition, and knowledge.

Given the importance Zeno attaches to this threefold distinction, it may help to reflect on what Zeno might have in mind when he talks about cognition. Suppose the book in front of me in fact is green. I clearly see that it is green and thus believe it to be green. Somebody else, too, believes it to be green. But he believes it to be green, not because he clearly sees it to be green, but because I tell him that it is green, or because he believes all books to be green (and hence does not bother to look at this book) or because of any number of other reasons. Reflecting on this 'because', one sees that there are any number of possible connections between the fact that the book is green and somebody's belief that it is green. In the case of some of these connections we are willing to say that one would not think that the book was green, unless it actually was green, that, if it were some other colour, one would think that it was of this other colour, and that one believes it to be green, precisely because it is green. We have a connection

---

[2] See also Sextus *M* VII.150–1.

of this sort when under normal conditions we clearly see a green book in front of us. In most cases, however, the connection between the fact and the belief is such that one would not be able to say that the person believed something to be the case precisely because it is the case. If, for instance, somebody believes the book to be green because he is told that it is green, the connection is too tenuous to guarantee that the person, given this connection, would not think the book to be green unless it actually was green, and that the person would think otherwise if it were of some other colour. The belief might still be true; but this would be due not to the connection specified, but to the fact that certain further conditions happen to be satisfied.

In each case the connection explains the belief. But in the first case the connection also guarantees the truth of the belief. A belief which is such that one holds the belief that something is the case precisely because it is the case, is guaranteed to be true. Hence we can call it a 'cognition'. In the second kind of case, on the other hand, the connection does not guarantee that the belief is true. Somebody who believes something to be the case just because he is told so may have a true belief; but the way he comes to have this belief, far from guaranteeing its truth, leaves open a number of possibilities that his belief may be false. In this case we talk of 'mere opinion' or 'belief'.

When Cicero turns to Zeno's innovations in logic (of which epistemology is treated as a part), he focuses on Zeno's introduction of the notion of cognition. He also reports that Zeno, to mark this new notion, introduced a new technical term, '*katalēpsis*', literally 'grasp'.[3] In having a cognition the mind is in touch with things so as to grasp them. Accordingly, Cicero renders this term and its cognates by '*comprehensio*' or '*perceptio*' and their cognates. If we remember that '*perceptio*' is used as a literal translation of '*katalēpsis*', it will be easier to avoid the rash, and wrong, assumption that all cases of cognition are cases of perception in our sense, even though cases of perceptual cognition are paradigms of cognition. That this would be wrong is clear, for instance, from the Stoic definition of science as a certain kind of body of cognitions. The Stoics surely do not mean to say that we know the theorems of a science, for instance geometry, as a matter of perceptual cognition. Indeed, they explicitly distinguish (D.L. VII.52) between perceptual and rational or intellectual cognitions. So it certainly is not part of the notion of cognition that a cognition is a perception, even if a perception is the paradigm of a cognition.

---

[3] *Acad.* 1.41; cf. *Acad.* II.17.

Cicero also renders '*katalēpsis*' by '*cognitio*', and this seems to be a particularly apt term to refer to the kind of grasp which goes beyond mere belief, and which already would amount to knowledge, if the Stoics did not further require of knowledge that one cannot be argued out of what one knows to be the case. Later times which were not particularly interested in this further requirement did in fact treat cognition as the basic form of knowledge, as we can see, for instance, in Augustine's *Contra Academicos*.

How is the introduction of the notion of 'cognition' as a third kind of epistemic state supposed to explain how we might attain knowledge? A clue is offered by the fact that both accounts of Zeno's threefold distinction, in spite of their brevity, insist that, though knowledge is available only to those who are already wise, cognition is available to sage and fool alike. So, the point of the threefold distinction is to establish that we are not in the hopeless situation of trying to arrive at true knowledge on the basis of mere opinion. Even the fool has something better to rely on than mere opinion, namely cognition. In fact, if we follow Sextus, Zeno seems to have made a more precise suggestion. Given that Sextus claims to be reporting Arcesilaus' attack on the Stoic position, the position attacked, for chronological reasons, must be Zeno's position. If this is correct, then Zeno not only introduced the threefold distinction of opinion, cognition and knowledge, as is explicitly attested by Cicero: he also went on to claim that cognition constitutes the criterion of truth (*M* VII.153). Setting aside the subtleties involved in a precise understanding of the notion of a criterion of truth,[4] it would seem that Zeno must at least have meant to say the following. We are to treat cognition as the criterion of truth in the sense that we are to believe only those things to be true of which we have cognition and to judge the truth of other things in terms of these. We in fact believe lots of things to be true. But we are not to believe them, even if they happen to be true, unless we have cognition of them. This closely accords with another Stoic view, independently attested for Zeno (Cic. *Acad.* II.77) that, if one is wise, one will have no mere opinions.

It is easy to see what would happen if we actually managed to follow this criterion of truth. All of our beliefs would be cognitions, and this very fact would turn each of these cognitions into a piece of incontrovertible knowledge. As long as we allow ourselves mere opinions, there is no guarantee that some of these opinions might not be false and that, being false, might serve as premises in a conclusive argument to the effect that something we believed to be the case was not the case, even if it is true and if we

---

[4] Cf. Striker 1974 and 1990.

as a matter of cognition believe it to be the case. This is why isolated cognitions as such are controvertible. But if we no longer entertain any mere opinions, the possibility that our cognitive grasp on a fact may be undermined by an argument to the contrary is eliminated. And with this possibility eliminated, each cognition we have will automatically turn into a piece of knowledge.

So we have the beginnings of an account of how knowledge is possible in terms of 'cognition'. But this account raises a number of questions. To begin with, we want to know whether there really are cognitions, that is to say beliefs which by their very nature, or the way they have come about, are guaranteed to be true. We also want to know how in practice we are supposed to be able to distinguish between mere opinion and cognition in such a way as to believe only those things of which we have cognition. And, finally, we want to know whether the cognitions we have will suffice to attain and to support the knowledge we are after, namely wisdom. For suppose it turned out that we only had cognition of those things which one can perceive to be the case, this would hardly suffice to attain the truly general knowledge which is involved in being wise.

It is reasonably clear that, in order to be able to address these questions, Zeno went beyond the first step of introducing the notion of cognition and of claiming that we should treat cognition as the criterion of truth. For Arcesilaus in his dispute with Zeno raised at least the first two questions. And our sources attribute to Zeno the introduction of a further crucial notion, closely associated with the notion of cognition, namely the notion of a cognitive impression; and they testify to a dispute with Arcesilaus about the appropriate definition of cognitive impressions. What is at issue in this dispute is the existence and the distinctness and distinguishability of cognitive impressions and hence of cognitions. So it is clear that Zeno began to work out a more elaborate theory to answer the questions which his doctrine of cognition raises. It is difficult to say, though, to what extent the more elaborate theory attributed in our sources to the Stoics in general can be traced back to Zeno himself. And I will not make any further attempt to trace the evolution of what came to be the standard Stoic doctrine in this matter, which, in the form it had been given by Chrysippus, was later attacked by Carneades.

III Cognitive impressions

Zeno's suggestion as to how we come to have knowledge is that we discard mere opinions and espouse only those beliefs which are cognitive, which we have as a matter of cognition. This presupposes that it is up to us what we believe and what we do not believe. And this is, indeed, the view Zeno and the Stoics take and articulate in the following way. They assume that to believe something involves two things. It involves having an impression or thought (*phantasia*), and it involves giving assent to, or accepting, this impression or thought (*sunkatathesis*).[5] The impressions, as the term indicates, are a matter of passive affection. We do not deliberately form the particular impressions we form. But whether we assent to them or not, is our doing. This is why we are responsible for our beliefs. Cognition, too, is a matter of giving assent to an impression.

Now a belief will be true or false, depending on whether the impression it is an assent to is true or false. Hence, if cognitions are true, they are true because the corresponding impressions are true. What is more, if cognitions have a privileged epistemic status due to the way they come about, such that they cannot fail to be true, then the impressions to which they are an assent must similarly have a privileged epistemic status such that they cannot fail to be true, given the way they come about. After all, the way they come about just is the way the corresponding cognition comes about, except that the cognition involves the further step of giving assent to the cognitive impression.

The Stoics call such impressions the assent to which constitutes a cognition '*phantasiai kataleptikai*', that is 'cognitive impressions'. There has been some debate about the precise force of '*kataleptikos*' in this context.[6] But if we assume that Zeno first introduced the notion of a *katalepsis* and only then the notion of a corresponding impression, the use of the term '*kataleptikos*' for the impression is no more puzzling than the parallel use of 'cognitive' in 'cognitive impression'. It signals that the impression referred to is the distinctive kind of impression involved in cognition. It might also indicate, though, that the impression is such as to enable us to grasp the corresponding fact, if we give assent to it.

However this may be, having analysed a cognition into a cognitive impression and the assent to it, the Stoics now have to show that there are cognitive impressions, that is to say that cognitive impressions form a class of impressions which in reality are distinct from the impressions involved in mere opinions. It is primarily on this that the debate between Stoics and Academics focused, from Arcesilaus down to the end of the sceptical Academy early in the first century BC. In this sense the doctrine of cognitive impressions formed the nucleus of Stoic epistemology.

---

[5] Cf. Görler 1977 and Arthur 1983.   [6] Cf. Sandbach 1971; Pohlenz 1959, vol. I, 62.

Not surprisingly, then, a good deal of the effort of the Stoics, beginning with Zeno, was devoted to the definition of cognitive impressions and to the defence of this definition.[7] Our sources attribute to the Stoics a number of formulations by means of which they try to define cognitive impressions. Closer inspection shows that all this variety reduces to a shorter and a longer version of one definition, versions which differ in that the longer version adds a further clause to the two clauses of the shorter version. According to the shorter version, an impression is cognitive if:

(i) it comes about from what is (ἀπὸ τοῦ ὑπάρχοντος), and
(ii) it is formed in exact accordance with what is.[8]

The longer version adds the further clause

(iii) (it is) such as it would not come about from what is not.[9]

Let us first consider the shorter version. The first clause raises two questions: what is the precise force of 'it comes about from . . .' and what is meant by 'what is'? A natural understanding of the phrase 'what is' is that it refers to a real object, rather than a figment of the mind, which produces an impression on us. This is how Sextus understands it at times, for instance *M* VII.249, where he is explaining the Stoic definition of a cognitive impression. And this is how many modern authors translate and understand the clause in the different texts in which it is mentioned.

But the expression 'what is' (*huparchon*) also has a technical use in Stoicism. Since the Stoics assume that only bodies exist (are *onta*), they will say for instance of the present time, though not of the past or the future, that it is *huparchon*. And similarly they will say that, whereas a false proposition merely subsists (*huphistanei*), a true proposition or fact also *huparchei*. Thus the point of the first clause would be, not that a cognitive impression has its origin in a real object, but in a fact. For the impression that A is F to be cognitive it must have its origin in the fact that A is F.

This is how Cicero at least at times understands the phrase (cf. *Acad.* II.112). This is how Sextus himself understands the expression in *M* VII.402 ff. when he reports Carneades' criticism of the third clause of the definition, thus suggesting that Carneades had already understood the phrase in this way. Here Heracles' impression that his children are those of Eurystheus is treated as an impression from what is not, though Sextus at the same time emphasizes that the impression has its origin in Heracles'

[7] Cf. Frede 1983.   [8] D.L. VII.46; Sextus *M* XI.183; cf. Cicero *Acad.* II.77.
[9] Cicero *Acad.* II.77; D.L. VII.50; Sextus *M* VII.248; *PH* II.4.

own children which stand in front of him. So there is a real thing which gives rise to the impression, namely Heracles' children; nevertheless the impression is not counted as one from what is. What is more, there is at least one passage in Sextus (*M* VIII.85-6) in which he explicitly tells us that the sense of '*huparchon*', as it is used in the definition of cognitive impressions, is precisely the sense in which (according to the Stoics) a true proposition is what is the case. Moreover the phrase occurs in all three clauses, and it would be desirable to have a uniform interpretation of it for all three clauses. But in the third clause the sense of 'real object' is much too weak, and ancient authors uniformly take the expression in the third clause to refer to what is, or rather what is not, the case.[10] Hence, on balance, we should take the reference to be to what is the case, rather than to a real object. This conclusion makes good sense in terms of our considerations concerning cognition. In the case of cognition we have the belief or the impression which we have precisely because this is the way things are. This will also explain the sense in which the impression, if it is cognitive, has come about from what is. For we can explain the 'because' in our account of cognition by specifying the connection which is such that it is because A is F that we have the impression or think that A is F. The connection might, for instance, be the one in which we stand to the fact that this object is green, if we perceive this object under normal conditions. We shall not worry that, given the Stoic notion of a cause, a fact, not being a body, cannot cause anything, whereas a real object can. For we should not rashly commit ourselves to the view that the connection to be specified has to be a simple causal connection. And, in any case, Sextus explicitly attributes to the Stoics the view that a true proposition, or what is the case, does move us to have a cognitive impression.

It is still somewhat disconcerting that the definition of cognitive impressions, given that it plays such a crucial rule, hence surely was carefully formulated and, in any case, retained throughout the history of the school, should involve this kind of ambiguity, referring either to an object or to a fact about an object. But there is a possible explanation for this ambiguity. It is crucial for the Stoic theory that children, from the time of their birth, receive impressions which the Stoics are willing to call 'cognitive', though they differ significantly from the cognitive impressions of mature human beings. Since children on the Stoic view do not have minds, they are not sensitive to facts, nor can they form impressions with propositional content. Their cognitive impressions are brought about by

[10] See Cicero *Acad.* II.77-8; 112; Sextus *M* VII.152, 252.

an object which the impression faithfully represents without having the internal articulation which would allow it to present the object as being something or other: it can represent a green book, but not a book as being green. Hence it is possible that the definition was deliberately formulated so as to cover both kinds of impressions, it being understood that it will refer to objects or the absence of them when we talk about the impressions of mindless children, but to facts or states-of-affairs which do not obtain when we talk about the impressions of rational beings.

Let us turn to the second clause. One thing which the second clause clearly requires is that the impressions be formed in accordance with the fact. It is easy to see why this would be required. If one were temporarily colour-blind in such a way as to see green things as red and red things as green, one might have the impression that the object is red precisely because the object is green. The impression would have its origins in a fact in the sense required by the first clause and thus would satisfy the first condition. But clearly this would not be a cognitive impression. Hence we require that an impression, in order to be cognitive, also be in accord with the fact which gives rise to it, in the sense that it represents A as being F, if A is F, in other words that it be true. Now this by itself trivially guarantees truth, but it does not guarantee cognitivity. We might, for instance, have an instrument which is supposed to discriminate between things which are F and things which are not F, and to signal things which are F. But the machine does not work properly and hence, instead, signals things which are not F. Moreover, we might mistakenly believe that the machine is supposed to signal things which are not F. Hence, on a certain occasion, given that it does not signal A's being F, we correctly have the impression that A is F, precisely because A is F. But this impression can hardly be said to be cognitive; for it rests on two mistakes which just happen to cancel each other out. So we would expect the further detail of the second clause to refer to a particular feature of the impression which is supposed to guarantee its cognitivity.

An impression is not completely characterized by its propositional content: there is a lot more detail to it. You may, for instance, have an impression with the propositional content that this book is green. Though the propositional content remains the same, the impression may vary considerably. It will, for instance, vary depending on whether you actually see the book or have the impression for some other reason. And when you actually see the book, the impression may still vary considerably depending on the conditions under which you see it. When, for instance, you clearly see the book from nearby, you have one kind of impression, but as you move away from the book and come to a point where you can barely make out that it is a book and that it is green, your impression, though still an impression that this book is green, surely is quite different from the one you have when you see the book clearly in front of you. All these impressions represent the same propositional content, but they differ in the way they represent it. The Stoics are evidently seeking in these further details which cognitive impressions offer a further mark of their cognitivity. To identify this further mark, we need to look at the second clause more closely.

There are two further details to the second clause which we have not exploited so far. The clause refers to the way the impression is formed by using verbs like 'seal', 'imprint', 'stamp';[11] and it insists that the impression be formed in exact or precise accord with the fact. Obviously, without a good deal of explanation not much can be made of these details. And unfortunately our main source of explanations is the passage in Sextus (*M* VII.249–52), which not only goes on the assumption that the clause demands correspondence with a real object rather than a fact, but also is at variance with the other major source of information concerning these further details, namely Cicero *Acad*. 1.42. Finally, caution seems indicated, because Sextus' account, at least as it is often read, makes an assumption which seems rather implausible, namely that the impression is in exact accord with the object by representing it with all of its features. This seems to be an incredibly strong assumption, especially given that not all of an object's features are perceptual features, and that we would not expect an auditory impression, for instance, to represent the visual features of an object.

An impression might be in accord with a fact in two ways. It might, for instance, be in accord with the fact that this book is green by being a representation of this green book. After all, the Stoics attribute cognitive impressions to children in their pre-rational state, when their impressions do not yet have propositional structure. But standardly, in the case of mature human beings, a cognitive impression will accord with the fact by representing this book and by representing it as being green. There are different ways of representing the book as being green, depending on whether one uses the common notion of green or some other notion, for instance a notion which is more articulate than the common notion. But, if we keep in mind that we are quite ready to say that we represent the book's being green in terms of the concept 'green', it is obvious that the

---

[11] Cf. D.L. VII.50; *Acad*. II.77.

main differences will depend on the way the object, rather than its being green, is represented. And, given that, we will be able after all to draw on the information supplied by Sextus in *M* VII.249–52, who assumes that a cognitive impression is characterized by its exact representation of the object; what is more, given that this information is relevant to the understanding of the second clause, we can have some confidence that Sextus is drawing on Stoic doctrine, even if he is mistaken or confused about the sense of 'what is'.

The question is: how could an impression be not only in accord with the fact but in precise accord with the fact? Let us take the impression that this (a book which I see) is green. The impression will represent this object, and it will represent it as being green. That is why it is an impression to the effect that this is green. Now the object might be represented in one's impression in more or less detail. It might, for instance, be represented in such detail that its precise colour is represented. But its representation might also involve a set of characteristic features of an object. The Stoics assume that each object has a set of characteristic and distinctive features. And these produce a characteristic look which is constituted by a set of characteristic visual features. So in the case of a visual impression an impression might be in precise accord with the fact that this is green if it represents the object in such a way as to fully and precisely capture its characteristic visual features and its colour.

On this interpretation we see the point of the verbs in the second clause of the definition to emphasize that, with a cognitive impression, the object is faithfully represented in all its characteristic and relevant detail. With a proper seal we do not expect each and every feature of the seal-ring to be captured in the seal-wax, but we do expect the characteristic and identifying features to be fully stamped in. Without this we would still have an imprint of the seal-ring, but not a seal which left no room for doubt as to its identity.

This talk about imprints and stamps should not mislead us into conceiving of an impression in the manner which Chrysippus tried to rectify when he suggested that 'impression' (*tupōsis*) should not be taken literally (D.L. VII.50). We should not assume that, for instance, in the case of perception under normal conditions the object we see will automatically produce an impression in us which, among other things, represents it with its distinctive features in the way a seal-ring will, if properly used, produce the appropriate seal. Though the Stoics do think of impressions as passive affections, this should not obscure the fact that rational impressions are formed in the mind and that the mind is involved in their formation. After all, rational impressions, impressions with a propositional content, involve the use of notions or concepts in representing something as being a certain way. They thus not only presuppose a mind which can form such impressions: they are also sensitive to the characteristics of the particular mind involved. For different minds have different notions available to them and apply the same notions in different ways, given their further beliefs. The way this is relevant here is this: if we have not learnt to discriminate a certain object, for instance a particular egg (as opposed to having learnt to discriminate a certain kind of object, for instance eggs), so as to be able to distinguish this egg from all other objects and thus also from all other eggs, we will not necessarily have a cognitive impression that this egg is green, however well developed our sensory apparatus is, and however much the other normal conditions for perception may be met. One should also note in this context that the first two clauses of the definition do not say what on certain interpretations we would expect them to say. They refrain from saying that the cognitive impression is impressed on us by the object or the fact. It rather is said to be formed in accordance with the fact. Indeed, it is formed in the mind and in some way by the mind rather than by the object. This becomes clear even from Sextus' account in *M* VII.250. Here, as elsewhere, we are told that the cognitive impression is formed artfully (*technikōs*). This does not mean that the object has an art which allows it to produce a cognitive impression of itself. It rather means that the soul or the mind has an ability to form impressions of objects which are faithful to these objects in their crucial detail. This competence or ability to discriminate can be enhanced by learning and training. As a result we can come to be able to perceptually discriminate things we originally were unable to distinguish. So rational impressions, the impressions of mature human beings, though a matter of receptivity, involve the mind and reflect the particular mind's disposition, for instance its ability to discriminate.

Sextus, in fact, seems to claim that in a cognitive impression the object is represented with all its features (*M* VII.251), if we assume that '*idiōmata*' here means 'features' or 'characteristics'. But it is difficult to see how, for instance, a visual impression could or should represent an object with all its features, for instance its olfactory characteristics. Hence in Cicero, *Acad.* 1.42, we find the more modest claim that a cognitive impression generated by means of a certain sense will represent all the features which fall within the range of what can be discriminated through this sense. But even this seems too strong. For, surely, even if we see an object under ideal conditions, we do not necessarily see all the minute visual detail we would see, for instance, if we saw it from so close up that we no longer could see the object as a whole properly, that is to say, if a normal condition on proper vision were violated. So perhaps we should not assume that Sextus means to say that the cognitive impression represents the object with all its features, but should rather understand the term '*idiōma*' which he uses in this context (*M* VII.248, 250, 251) in the sense of 'characteristic' or 'distinctive feature', rather than in the sense of 'feature' taken quite generally.

From Sextus' explanation in *M* VII.251 we can add a further requirement, which we might have guessed anyway, namely that these features themselves are to be represented precisely (*akribes*). Thus, if we think that it is part of the characteristic look of this book that it looks like a book and that it looks green, then the impression should be such as we would have if we clearly and unambiguously recognized it to be a book and to be green. With this in mind we can say that the second clause demands that a cognitive visual impression to the effect that this object is green should be such as to represent this object in a way which perfectly and unequivocally matches its characteristic look and its colour, and moreover such as to present it as being green.

When we now turn to the third clause: '(it is) such as it would not come about from what is not', it is important to briefly consider the relation between the longer and the shorter version of the definition. It is clear that the shorter version continued to be used even after the longer version had been introduced. This strongly suggests that, at least from the Stoic point of view, the third clause does not add a further restriction on what is to count as a cognitive impression, but just makes explicit a feature of all impressions which satisfy the first two conditions. In fact, the Greek of the third clause is most naturally understood in such a way that 'such' does not refer to a further feature, introduced but not specified by the third clause, but refers back to the character ascribed to cognitive impressions in the first and the second clauses, presumably more specifically to the character ascribed to cognitive impressions in the second clause. The point would be this: impressions which satisfy the first two clauses have a certain character; the third clause tells us that an impression which has this character cannot possibly have its origin in what is not. I take this to be a way of saying that an impression which has this character cannot possibly be false. This understanding of the relation between the longer and the shorter version seems to be confirmed by Sextus and by Cicero. Sextus explains that the Stoics only added the further clause in response to an Academic objection based on an assumption which the Stoics themselves do not share, namely the assumption that two objects might be exactly alike and hence indiscernible (*M* VII.252). Cicero tentatively suggests the same, adding that it was Arcesilaus who prompted Zeno to add the third clause (*Acad.* II.77). Thus the third clause is supposed to offer merely a clarification which, on the Stoic view, does not go beyond what is already stated or implied by the first two clauses.

It will help if we consider Arcesilaus' objection. It seems that Arcesilaus argued that two objects, say two eggs or two grains of sand, might be exactly alike, or at least so much alike as to be indiscernible. And, on the basis of this, he seems to have argued that the shorter definition, or at least its second clause, is guaranteed to be inadequate, since it will be satisfied by certain false impressions, but that the longer definition, though in virtue of its third clause it manages to rule out false impressions, does so only at the price of ruling out all impressions. For, however strong conditions an impression may meet, there always can be an impression exactly like it which is false, or which fails to have its origin in what is. So on the shorter version, according to Arcesilaus, cognitive impressions do not form a distinct class of impressions, and on the longer version they do not exist. This, roughly, is how Cicero presents the matter.

Unfortunately the precise way in which Arcesilaus is supposed to bring the case of possible indiscernibles to bear on the definition of cognitive impressions is far from clear. Their relevance is spelled out by Cicero *Acad.* II. 84-5, in this way. Suppose you see Cotta under ideal conditions and you form the correct impression that this is Cotta. But suppose also that, unknown to you, Cotta has an exact look-alike, Geminus. So it can happen that you actually see Geminus under ideal conditions, but, not surprisingly, you now form the false impression that this is Cotta.

There are two ways to interpret this. One is that Arcesilaus understands the 'what is' in the shorter definition to refer not to the fact, but to the object, and that he argues that, given the indiscernibility of Cotta and Geminus, the false impression that this is Cotta satisfies the first two conditions as well as the true impression that this is Geminus. For it, too, has its origin in a real object (we actually see Geminus), and it does represent this object with as much faithfulness as we wish. It nevertheless is false and hence not cognitive. In fact, the two impressions, taken by themselves, will be exactly alike, and hence each of them, including the one which is true, taken by itself, will be compatible with two mutually exclusive states of affairs. To which Zeno is supposed to answer by denying that Cotta and Geminus are indiscernible, but also by adding the further clause to make explicit that the impression that this is Cotta which we form when we see Cotta under the appropriate conditions will be unlike any impression we form when we do not see Cotta. We cannot rule out the possibility that Zeno himself originally understood his shorter definition in such a way as to invite this objection, because he still thought of the impression primarily as an imprint which an object leaves on us, such that two indiscernible objects would produce the same impression. But it also may be the case that Arcesilaus referred to pairs of indiscernibles just to challenge the second clause of the definition, because this clause was understood by the Stoics in a certain way. It seems that the Stoics assumed that, given the way a cognitive impression comes about, it represents the object with a faithfulness which an impression which does not come about in this way, and hence *a fortiori* an impression which does not have its origin in a fact, cannot possibly match. The second clause insists on this kind of faithfulness. The possibility that we are presented with a pair of indiscernibles would show that however faithful an impression is to the object, this does not rule out the possibility that it is false. Zeno's answer to this, on this interpretation, would be to deny that there are indiscernibles, but to make explicit in a third clause that the kind of faithfulness to the object attributed to cognitive impressions by the second clause is incompatible with its being false, with its failing to have its origin in a fact.

In any case, the Stoic response to the Academic claim that there are indiscernibles and that hence there might be no difference between the cognitive impression that this is Cotta which we have when we clearly see Cotta and the impression that this is Cotta when we clearly see Geminus is based on two assumptions: (i) there are no indiscernibles, and (ii) the impressions we form are sensitive to our state of mind such that, if we have learnt to discriminate Cotta, the cognitive impression which we have of Cotta cannot possibly be like the impression which we have of Geminus. The first assumption is not *ad hoc*, but supported by Stoic physics and Stoic metaphysics. The Academics will not accept it, but at least the Stoic position remains defensible. The second assumption raises a problem. Suppose one first sees Cotta under normal conditions and forms the cognitive impression that this is Cotta. But then one sees Geminus, and, because one is confused or even temporarily deranged, one forms an impression of Geminus that he is Cotta which presents Geminus precisely with the characteristic features of Cotta. The two impressions will be exactly alike, even if it is the case that Cotta and Geminus are discernible. The Academics consider more dramatic versions of this sort of case.

There is Orestes who in his madness takes Electra, though she is standing in full sight of him, to be a Fury (Sextus *M* VII.249). There is the case of Heracles who in his madness takes his children, though they are standing clearly in front of him, to be the children of Eurystheus (*M* VII.406). What is characteristic of these cases is that the perceiving subject with one exception sees the object under ideal conditions. Barring the exception, the subject should have a cognitive impression. But the subject does not have a cognitive impression, because he is temporarily deranged, and this drastically interferes with the formation of the impression in such a way as to, for instance, give Heracles the impression that these are Eurystheus' children. Now this can only be so if in his impression Heracles represents his own children with features of Eurystheus' children. But, if this is possible, it should also be possible that Heracles, precisely because of his heightened imagination in this deranged state, represents his children with precisely the distinctive features of Eurystheus' children. Hence he will have, it is argued, an impression which is indistinguishable from the impression he would have if he saw Eurystheus' children under normal conditions. But in this case his having the impression is compatible with two possible states of the world, one in which Heracles is sane and these in fact are Eurystheus' children, and one in which he is insane and what is in front of him is something else. The Stoic answer to this is that the impression, taken in itself, under normal conditions has a distinctive character which can never be matched by an impression formed by a subject in an abnormal state.

So the Stoic claim is that nothing but a fact can produce an impression which has precisely the character of a cognitive impression, that an impression of this character cannot possibly be the product of dreaming, hallucination, derangement or any other non-normal or abnormal mental state. Indeed, they claim that not even the gods can (or will) produce such an impression in us in the absence of the corresponding fact (Cic. *Acad.* II.50). Again, this is not an *ad hoc* claim, though, needless to say, it will not be accepted by the Academics. As we saw, the Stoics insist that great art is involved in the formation of cognitive impressions. They involve the mind's readiness to perform a highly delicate task which involves its complete attention and concentration. A sleeping or even sleepy mind, a deranged or intoxicated mind, will not be able to perform such a delicate task. Moreover, Stoic physics allows for the assumption that impressions bear the mark of how they have come about. We also have to take into account that the Stoics, given their belief in providence, can argue that nature, if it means us to have cognition and knowledge, can most simply arrange for this by supplying us with impressions with a distinctive character which reflects the way they come about, which, in turn, guarantees their truth.

IV Clearness, distinctness, evidence

Cicero tells us (*Acad.* 1.41) that a cognitive impression is supposed to have a distinctive way of making those things clear (*declarare*) which it presents as being the case. The question is what this distinctive character may be. As already noted, the 'such' in the third clause may refer to a further, though unspecified, feature which all cognitive impressions have and which distinguishes them from all non-cognitive impressions; or it may refer to a feature which all impressions satisfying the first two clauses have, and which the third clause claims an impression would not have unless it had its origin in a fact in such a way as to be itself guaranteed to be true. Given that the third clause is treated as merely clarificatory and redundant, and given the Greek of the third clause, we should assume that this distinctive character is not a further feature, but one already implied by the first two clauses. And since, given the Academic counter-examples, it should be an internal feature of the impression which no non-cognitive impression can match, it should be a feature implied by the second clause. If we consider D.L. VII.46 it seems fairly clear that the feature we are looking for is the clarity and distinctness of cognitive impressions, and that this feature is supposed to be crucially involved in their representing something in precise accordance with the fact. In D.L. VII.46 we first get the two clause definition of cognitive impressions. We then get a corresponding definition of a non-cognitive impression as one which does not satisfy the first clause or which, even if it satisfies the first clause, does not satisfy the second clause. And this is glossed by saying 'the one which is not clear (*tranēs*) nor distinct (*ektupos*)'. This strongly suggests that impressions are clear and distinct by being in precise accordance with the fact, and that this is the feature to which the third clause refers. This is not the place to discuss whether clarity and distinctness are two separate features, as the 'nor' might suggest. What seems to be demanded is this: the relevant features of the object which a cognitive impression represents are represented in such a way that this representation could not be the representation of some other features, and that they jointly constitute a distinctive representation of the object, that is, a representation which captures a set of jointly distinctive features of the object, for instance its distinctive look. This corresponds to the fact that a seal may be deficient in two ways: it may lack some of the features which would make it identifiable as this rather than that seal, or it may have all the features, but some not with sufficient clarity to make it identifiable as this rather than that seal. Cognitive impressions are unambiguously identifiable as impressions of the object they are an impression of, and as representations of the fact which gives rise to them. And the claim is that an impression will be clear and distinct in this way only, if it has its origin in a fact in such a way that the manner in which it comes about guarantees its truth.

Cognitive impressions are also characterized in other ways, for instance as striking or vivid (*plēktikos*, Sextus M VII.403). I shall comment on one of these characterizations, namely the claim that they are *enargēs* (cf. *ibid.*), a term rendered by Cicero as '*evidens*' or '*perspicuum*' (*Acad.* II 1.17). To understand this, we have to take into account that in Greek one can call something which clearly and exactly looks like an ox an 'obvious' or 'evident' ox. This does not commit one to the view that an evident ox actually is an ox. It might be a god taking on the appearance of an ox. But as a matter of Stoic physics the Stoics believe that nothing but Socrates can have the distinctive look of Socrates, and that nothing but an ox can have the distinctive look of an ox, that is to say the characteristic and jointly distinctive visual features of an ox. Now a visual cognitive impression of an object, being clear and distinct, will represent the object clearly with its characteristic and distinctive look. Hence such impressions themselves also are called 'evident'. For a Stoic, then, their evidence will guarantee their truth. But for an Academic evidence will not guarantee truth for the simple reason that, even if there is something which looks exactly like Socrates, it might be something else. If nothing else, for the Academics the possible indiscernibility will guarantee this.

v Assent to cognitive impressions

Now, even if we grant that we do have cognitive impressions, this will be of little help, unless we can also come to acquire a disposition in which we unfailingly give assent only to cognitive impressions. The fact that the Stoics talk of cognitive impressions as having a distinctive character and as being the criterion of truth might mislead us into thinking that on the Stoic view this, at least in principle, is rather an easy matter. Since cognitive impressions have a distinctive character, we just have to determine which of our impressions are cognitive and then give assent to them. But it is obvious that in practice this is such a difficult task that even the Stoics themselves do not claim to have achieved it. And it is clear why in principle it would be a more difficult task than at first might appear. The very fact that cognitive impressions are supposed to be criteria raises a problem. In trying to find out whether an impression is cognitive, one can check the conditions under which one has formed it. And, having satisfied oneself that it came about under normal conditions, one can conclude that it must be cognitive and hence accept it. But, though one can do this, this cannot be how the Stoics think that cognitive impressions play the role intended for them in their theory. For in this case our acceptance of them is based on the assumption that we have sufficient evidence for their cognitivity. This assumption can be questioned. And any evidence we produce in support of it can in turn be questioned. So we seem to fall into an infinite regress precisely of the kind which we tried to avoid by introducing cognitions and cognitive impressions in the first place. We also can check our impressions against our beliefs, and accept them if they seem true in the light of our beliefs. But, again, to do this is to appeal to further evidence to determine the cognitivity of our impressions. And this evidence in principle will be as questionable as the cognitivity of the impressions, and hence questioning the evidence will again lead to a regress.

Now we might assume that the Stoics think that we do not look for evidence outside the impression in question, but rather for the distinguishing mark of cognitive impressions, for something like evidence or clearness and distinctness, and that, having spotted it, we infer that the impression must be cognitive and hence true. But one may object that one can also question whether an impression in fact has this distinctive mark. In response one might be tempted to assume that the Stoics must think that we can infallibly recognize the distinguishing mark. But there is no evidence that the Stoics do believe this. And, given that there is a great deal of evidence for the Stoic doctrine concerning cognitive impressions, it would be surprising if such a crucial assumption were never referred to. It also would be, philosophically, a desperate assumption to make. And, if it had been made, it would be very difficult to explain why knowledge and wisdom are supposed to be so difficult to attain. Finally, though cognitive impressions do have a distinctive character, this should not be understood to mean that cognitive impressions bear on their face, as it were, an easily recognizable mark of their cognitivity. The distinctive character of cognitive impressions is not a feature an impression has over and above its representing a particular fact in a certain way, and thus its presence cannot be determined independently of determining whether it exhibits this manner of representation.

So the Stoics must assume that cognitive impressions, having a distinct character, are such that we can immediately recognize them as such and do not have to depend on further evidence to determine their cognitivity. In any case, the Stoic view does not seem to be that we have some mysterious ability to infallibly recognize cognitive impressions as such, and

Stoic theory does not require the postulation of such an ability. All that it requires is that we can learn to get so good at recognizing cognitive impressions that we always get it right. In each case there is the possibility that we could get it wrong, but it is not by good luck that we do not, but because our ability has been so developed that we are able to successfully deal with each case we encounter. To make this assumption is not to assume some infallible cognitive faculty.

Now, to say that we are able to recognize cognitive impressions as such can be understood in two ways. It can be understood to mean that we are able to make a correct judgement concerning the cognitivity of an impression and, on the basis of this judgement, give assent to the impression. But it also can be understood to mean that we are sensitive to the cognitivity of an impression, that there is an internal mechanism which registers and scans impressions and which is able to discriminate between cognitive and non-cognitive impressions so that, if it discriminates an impression as cognitive, we give assent without forming the judgement that the impression is cognitive. We might have a sense for cognitivity in this latter way. Nevertheless, we could assume that this sense can be developed and perfected, if we assume that it is also sensitive to our beliefs.

There is some reason to think that the Stoics at least sometimes thought along the lines of such a mechanism. They certainly must have assumed that children possess such a mechanism to sort cognitive from non-cognitive impressions. For they claim that children are endowed by nature with an impulse towards cognitions (Cic. *Fin.* III.17). It is easy to see why. According to the Stoics, it is these cognitions which give rise to the so-called natural notions or anticipations, concepts which are faithful to the distinctive character of the things which fall under them. The acquisition of a sufficient set of notions of this kind is supposed to amount to the acquisition of reason. Now the privileged epistemic status of these concepts depends on the fact that they are based on cognitive impressions or cognitions. Hence children, to acquire reason, must be able to sort cognitive from non-cognitive impressions. And to do this, they obviously cannot resort to judgement and inference, since *ex hypothesi* they do not yet have reason. And it also is clear that children accept those impressions which they sort as cognitive. Otherwise they would not have cognitions. So there is not just a primitive non-rational version of cognitive impressions in children, but also a primitive non-rational version of assent, which is supposed to follow if an impression is recognized as cognitive.

Now, as to mature rational human beings the Stoics observe that when we get a perceptual impression of something which is of interest to us, but the impression does not seem satisfactory, we, as it were, instinctively rub our eyes, move closer or further away, try to provide more light etc., that is to say try to establish normal conditions to see properly (Sextus *M* VII.259). This would suggest that there is a mechanism which not only is sensitive to the cognitivity of an impression, but also can tell on the basis of the character of the impression, in which way the impression is deficient, and which can set us in motion in the appropriate way to obtain further impressions till it receives an impression which it deems satisfactory. And assent may be no more than this acceptance as satisfactory. In any case, we here have the idea of a highly sophisticated sensitivity to the cognitivity of impressions.

Now this sensitivity is in many ways affected by beliefs. It is adequate for the rather simple impressions children have. But, as soon as we have concepts, we can form extremely complex impressions and acquire highly complex beliefs. To the extent that we learn to discriminate between different particular objects, different kinds of objects, and different features of objects, and acquire true beliefs about them, it also will be easier to learn to discriminate between the corresponding impressions; but to the extent that we also acquire false beliefs, it will be more difficult. We may fail to recognize an impression as cognitive, because it is incompatible with what we wrongly think we know for certain. Since it is the mind which forms even perceptual impressions, and since the mind in forming impressions is influenced by its state, including its beliefs, its false beliefs may make it difficult for it to form cognitive impressions. In any case, its impressions will reflect its false beliefs. So it is obvious how we can improve and perfect our sensitivity to cognitive impressions. We have to attend to our impressions, we have to eliminate our false beliefs, and we have to learn what the things we are concerned with are like and how they differ from other things, and look at our impressions carefully in the light of this. In the end we will have a reliable sense for whether an impression is cognitive and give assent to precisely those impressions which are cognitive. This is what Boethus had in mind, when he said that right reason is the criterion (D.L. VII.54). If we have a perfected reason we will have a reliable sense for which impressions are cognitive.[12]

VI The criteria

If we follow the Stoics up to this point, we have cognitive impressions and we can learn to discriminate between cognitive and non-cognitive

---

[12] Cf. Kidd 1989.

impressions in such a way as to give assent to cognitive impressions. So, having cognitions, we will be on safe ground. And having only cognitions, we will have knowledge. The question is whether and how with just this knowledge we will be able to attain wisdom. To answer this question we have to look more closely at the kinds of cognition which we have available to us.

It is clear that, if there are any cognitions at all, then perceptual cognitions will be among them. It is because we are prepared to accept that it is not a matter of mere opinion if we think that the book is green when we see it clearly in front of us, that the notion of cognition seems promising in the first place. So one class of cognitions we have available to us are perceptual cognitions. Indeed, Cicero, having reported that Zeno introduced the notion of cognition and discussed our assent to cognitive impressions, goes on to tell us that he then singled out perceptual cognitions as a class of cognitions we can rely on (*Acad.* 1.42). What is more, Zeno is supposed to have identified perceptual cognitions as a criterion.

This fits the testimony in D.L. VII.54, according to which Chrysippus claimed that perception constitutes a criterion. But it creates a problem, because it seems to conflict with other evidence. In many places we are told that according to the Stoics cognitive impressions constitute the criterion. This view is attributed to Chrysippus (D.L. VII.54). And hence Chrysippus is accused of inconsistency in sometimes claiming that cognitive impressions are the criterion and sometimes saying that perception is a criterion. What is more, Zeno also must have said that cognitions quite generally are the criterion (Sextus *M* VII.153). Now to make sense of this apparent conflict we have to assume two things, (i) that there is a shift in the use of the term 'criterion', and (ii) that in discussing knowledge and its attainability in general the Stoics talk about cognitions and cognitive impressions quite generally, whereas when they go into the details of how we attain knowledge they distinguish between perceptual cognition and anticipations, that is to say the intellectual cognitions involved in the possession of anticipatory concepts.

As to the shift in use, when Zeno introduces cognition as the criterion it is in the context of an argument to the effect that no argument based on premises which we hold to be true as a matter of mere belief will lead to knowledge. Here cognition is a criterion in the sense that it is a belief which is not held as a matter of mere opinion, and hence can be used to judge the truth of further beliefs. But when we turn to the question of how any beliefs, including cognitive beliefs, can be judged to be true or false, the answer will be 'in virtue of cognitive impressions'. This shift in the use of 'criterion' is not surprising, given that philosophers were using the term in a number of related ways. Once we take this into account, it is easy to make sense of the variety of things different Stoics according to D.L. VII.54 are prepared to call a criterion. If, for instance, we make cognition the criterion in one sense, we can also make right reason the criterion in a different use of the term.

Now, in saying that cognitive impressions or cognition or perfected or right reason are the criterion, we do not yet address the question how we attain the complex knowledge which is wisdom. In order to do this, we now distinguish different kinds of cognition. And we first single out perceptual cognition as one criterion. We do so for at least three reasons. (i) If one is willing to admit any kind of cognition, one will admit perceptual cognition. (ii) Perceptual cognition, or perceptual cognitive impressions, are supposed to be the basis on which we develop the so-called natural or common notions or anticipations which constitute a further criterion. (iii) There is an obvious parallel with Epicureanism which similarly postulates perceptions as a criterion.

We can now discuss a crucial difference between the Stoic and the Epicurean position, which might be overlooked given their striking superficial similarity. Epicureans take perceptions in the sense of sense-impressions to be criterial. This commits them to the view that all sense-impressions are true. This position the Epicureans try to defend by saying that often what we take to be a sense-impression actually is a combination of sense-impression and mere belief. So we have to learn to distinguish in our impressions what is the product of sense and what is the result of an activity of the mind, a task analogous to the task of distinguishing cognitive from non-cognitive impressions. The Stoics, by contrast, assume that there are false sense-impressions and hence distinguish sense-impressions and perceptual impressions, restricting perceptual impressions not just to true impressions, but to cognitive impressions, that is to say to impressions which are guaranteed to be true. And they also assume that, at least in the case of mature human beings, even perceptual impressions are thoughts formed in and by the mind. So, if the Stoics like the Epicureans claim that perceptions are criterial, their view, nevertheless, differs quite substantially. But perceptual cognitions obviously do not suffice for the kind of general knowledge which constitutes wisdom. And so the Stoics, again like the Epicureans, introduce a further criterion, anticipations (prolēpseis).

*

Perception will give us knowledge of particular observable facts. To gain the truly general knowledge which constitutes wisdom we will have to rely on more than perception. To this purpose the Stoics, following the Epicureans, introduce the notion of anticipations.[13] Perhaps they are called anticipations because they are concepts which provide us with an antecedent general understanding or grasp of the things which as rational beings we perceive and think about, and which even in perceiving them we represent in terms of these notions. Already Zeno, having singled out perception as a criterion, went on to explain how these privileged notions provide the principles on the basis of which reason can derive further truths (Cic. *Acad*. 1.42). We are not told that Zeno called them a criterion, but this is what Chrysippus (D.L. VII.54) and later Stoics did.

It is easy to see how this is supposed to work. The mastery of a concept involves certain assumptions about the items to which one applies the concept. Traditionally one will think of these as being captured in a definition of the kind of item falling under the concept. To say that anticipations (or common or natural notions, as they are also called) are criterial is to say that these definitions and the assumptions involved in them have the status of cognitions. They can thus serve as a criterion to judge the truth of further beliefs. Since they are truly general, we can deduce further general truths from them as principles. These theorems, having been deduced from cognitive assumptions, will themselves have the status of cognitions. In this way we arrive at whole bodies of such cognitions and thus at sciences, and in this way, ultimately, we will also arrive at that particular body of cognitions which constitutes wisdom.

Now all this depends on the premise that the assumptions involved in the use of one of these privileged criterial concepts are cognitions. Cognitions are beliefs which come about in a way which guarantees their truth. The further theorems will be cognitions, inasmuch as they have been deduced from principles which are cognitions, deduction counting as a canonical way of coming about. These principles are cognitions because they are just the assumptions one makes if one has these privileged concepts. So what remains to be shown is that these concepts, and thus the assumptions involved in them, come about in such a way that their truth is guaranteed. And the Stoics set out to show this by trying to argue that by nature we are constructed in such a way as to form these notions on the basis of cognitive impressions. (This is why they are also called natural

---

[13] Cf. Sandbach 1930; Todd 1973; Schofield 1980b.

notions.) And because human beings are so constructed, anyone who grows up in a natural environment which provides him with the normal cognitive impressions, and who is not in some other way radically deprived, will form the same notions. (Hence they are also called common notions.)

These notions, then, are supposed to owe their special epistemic status to the way they come about. What distinguishes them from other concepts, for instance technical concepts, is that natural concepts are not concepts we set out to form, shaping them to accord with our beliefs and our presumed needs. They rather come to us naturally. If one grows up in an environment with trees and camels, one will naturally end up with a notion of a tree and a notion of a camel, without having set out to form them. The reason why this seems important is that, if we set out to form a concept, this formation is sensitive to our beliefs and to our presumed interests. But we may make mistakes in the way we form a concept, our beliefs may be wrong, and we may be mistaken about our needs and interests. The formation of natural notions does not suffer from this sort of interference. Also, natural notions, at least to begin with, just capture the common content of cognitive impressions. Given the guaranteed truth of these, the corresponding natural notions are guaranteed to be faithful to the objects of which the cognitive impressions are impressions. When natural notions go beyond what we perceive, we note that their formation follows a certain simple natural pattern. If, on the basis of perception, we have the notion of a certain kind of perceptual feature, it is natural for us to form the notion of the opposite feature, even if we have never perceived it (cf. D.L. VII.53). That these patterns of formation are natural, i.e. that our mind is by nature constructed in such a way as to naturally form notions in this way, we can see from the fact that all human beings seem to form these notions.

Needless to say, Academic sceptics were not impressed by this view. But we have to keep in mind that Aristotle at the beginning of the *De interpretatione* takes a much stronger view when he claims that the affection of the soul (that is, the notion in the mind) which corresponds to a meaningful word is the same for all human beings across different languages. Similarly Plato seems to think that the way we conceive of things is at least guided by some awareness of the Platonic ideas which define the right way to think about things. So the Stoics in this regard can at least appeal to a distinguished tradition of privileging certain concepts as the ones one naturally would have.

*

However that may be, these notions are supposed to provide the starting-points or principles from which we can proceed to deduce the rest of our knowledge. And so the Stoics in their logic also set out to formulate canons for deduction, which will guarantee that the beliefs we arrive at by inference come about in the right way.

VII Conclusion

In this way the Stoics account for the possibility of knowledge and wisdom. We have only been able to consider what seem to be the crucial points of the standard Stoic doctrine. I have not, for example, discussed the Stoic theory of signs and sign-inference, or the Stoic conception of proof.[14] In conclusion I want to make some general remarks about the character of this account. Stoic epistemology standardly is characterized as 'empiricist'. This seems to be misleading. It is true that the Stoics in their reaction to wildly speculative theories about the world, involving the postulation of a host of immaterial entities, insist that the world is a world of bodies, and that our primary epistemic contact with it is through perception. It is also true that our perceptions are supposed to constitute the basis on which we form concepts. But on the Stoic theory the content of our criterial natural concepts is not at all fully determined by our perceptions. It is also determined by the natural mechanism which leads us to form, on the basis of perception, concepts like the concept of a god or the concept of the good, which go far beyond the content of our perceptions. And it is natural concepts, including these concepts, which are supposed to underwrite our general knowledge. In this sense the Stoics are rationalists, and they were regarded as such in antiquity. We have to remember here that the Stoics in the first instance try to explain how we might attain the knowledge Socrates was after. Once we keep this in mind, an empiricist approach to this kind of knowledge seems highly implausible.

One might also, given the Stoic doctrine of the criteria of truth, at first think that the Stoic account was a simple foundationalist and even infallibilist account. But it does not seem to be an infallibilist account. It claims that the wise man can manage to correctly discriminate cognitive and non-cognitive impressions. But this does not involve the postulation of some infallible cognitive ability. It is rather like Aristotle's claim that the practically wise man will always know the right thing to do. Similarly,

---

[14] Cf. Brunschwig 1980.

though the Stoic theory is foundationalist, being an account of knowledge, it is an account of the wise man's knowledge, since only he according to the Stoics has any knowledge. And this knowledge is a rather elevated kind of knowledge which involves an understanding of what is known. It certainly meets much more stringent demands than what we ordinarily call knowledge.

Finally, though the Stoics give an account of how knowledge and thus wisdom is attainable, it is an account which is very much focused on this abstract theoretical possibility. If we expect a consideration of the details of actual scientific knowledge of the kind we get in Aristotle's *Analytica posteriora*, we will be disappointed. But we have to remember, however paradoxical this may sound, that the Stoics did not think that they themselves had any knowledge of the kind whose possibility they tried to assure us of. And they seem to have taken a very dim view of our ability to understand the actual workings of nature. Even the wise man is far from omniscient.[15] Being wise for the Stoics, after all, is just a matter of knowing those things one needs to know to live well. In this too they were following Socrates, though perhaps, unlike Socrates, they assumed that this involved a basic understanding of the world, for instance of the fact that the world, down to the smallest detail, is governed by divine reason and providence.

[15] Cf. Kerferd 1978a.

10

Academic epistemology

MALCOLM SCHOFIELD

1 Introduction

Early in the Hellenistic period the Academy went sceptic.[1] Sceptic it remained until the two leading figures in the school at the beginning of the first century BC, Philo of Larissa and Antiochus of Ascalon, adopted more sanguine positions on the possibility of cognition – albeit mutually incompatible positions.[2] The philosopher who effected this change of outlook in the Academy was Arcesilaus, scholarch from c.265 BC until his death around twenty-five years later, and reputed as a dialectician whose employment of the Socratic method led him to suspend judgement about everything. He impressed the contemporary polymath Eratosthenes as one of the two leading philosophers of his time.[3] And in his assaults on the Stoic theory of cognition he established the principal focus of argument between the Stoa and the Academy for the best part of the next two hundred years.

The most notable of Arcesilaus' sceptical successors[4] was Carneades, the greatest philosopher of the second century BC. Although like Arcesilaus – and in similar emulation of Socrates – Carneades wrote nothing, his pupil Clitomachus published voluminous accounts of his arguments on issues across the whole range of philosophical inquiry; and it is principally to this source that – albeit indirectly – we owe our knowledge of a subtle system of thought.[5] In the course of his engagement with both

---

[1] The principal ancient sources for Academic epistemology are Cicero, *Academica* and Sextus Empiricus, *Adversus Mathematicos* VII. There are useful collections of the Greek and Latin texts which constitute the basic evidence for Academic views in Mette 1984 (Arcesilaus) and Mette 1985 (Carneades). General surveys: Brochard 1923, Stough 1969, dal Pra 1975.

[2] Study of the views of these philosophers lies outside the scope of the present volume. For discussion see Glucker 1978, Sedley 1981, Tarrant 1985, Barnes 1989c, Görler 1994b.

[3] Str. 1.15; the other he named was the Stoic Aristo of Chios.

[4] Lacydes, his immediate successor as scholarch, maintained the Academy in scepticism. The evidence about him (conveniently assembled in Mette 1985) is biographical and anecdotal. For an attempt to extract some philosophy from it see Hankinson 1995, 92–4.

[5] Like Socrates neither put any philosophy in writing: Plu. *Alex. Fort.* 328a; cf. D.L. 1.16, IV.32. Although Philodemus' *Academicorum historia* (*PHerc.* 1021) claims that a pupil of Arcesilaus

Stoicism and Epicureanism Carneades worked out for the first time in Greek philosophy an alternative non-foundationalist epistemology, sometimes misleadingly dubbed 'probabilism' in modern discussions of his views – although whether Arcesilaus or Carneades *had* any views of their own, or were simply dialecticians intent on undermining the positions of others, is a disputed question.

II Arcesilaus: the problem of interpretation

It has proved difficult to come to terms with the complexities of the evidence about Arcesilaus' stance in epistemology.[6] Some of the more general characterizations of his philosophical position in the sources portray him as a proto-Pyrrhonist. 'Arcesilaus', says Diogenes Laertius (IV.28), 'was the first to suspend his assertions owing to the contrarieties of arguments.' Sextus Empiricus sees a very close affinity between Arcesilaus' philosophy and his own Pyrrhonism:

> He is not found making assertions about the reality or unreality of anything, nor does he prefer one thing to another in point of convincingness or lack of convincingness, but he suspends judgment about everything. And he says that the aim is suspension of judgment (*epochē*), which, we said, is accompanied by tranquillity. (S.E. *PH* 1.232; translation Annas and Barnes)

Although Sextus goes on to accuse him nonetheless of exhibiting unPyrrhonist signs of dogmatism, he is more willing to see a genuine sceptic in Arcesilaus than he is in the case of any other Academic.

On this reading of Arcesilaus, what leads him and his interlocutors to *epochē* is the realization that there is as much to be said on one side of the issue debated in an argument as on the other. Other texts, however, repre-

Footnote 5 (*cont.*)
called Pythodorus made a written record of his discussions (*Acad. hist.* xx.43–4), most of the philosophical arguments ascribed to him in the sources derive from accounts which relate his views to Carneades', and may well depend on an oral tradition transmitted through Carneades. For Clitomachus' literary activity: D.L.IV.67; Cic. *Acad.* II.16. But a rival account of Carneades' philosophy was espoused by another pupil, Metrodorus, whose version was for a time espoused by Philo of Larissa: *Acad. hist.* xxvi.4–11; cf. Cic. *Acad.* II.16, 78. And unClitomachean 'dogmatist' interpretation has certainly left its mark e.g. on Sextus Empiricus' presentation of Carneades' epistemology: see nn. 36, 72 below.

[6] One dispute – prominent in the literature and pursued further in this chapter – is whether Arcesilaus argues solely *ad hominem* or adopts scepticism *in propria persona*. For versions of the first view see Couissin 1929, Striker 1981, Frede 1984; for versions of the second Ioppolo 1986, Maconi 1988, Bett 1989, Hankinson 1995, ch. v. The suggestion in some sources (e.g. S.E. *PH* 1.234, Numen. in Eus. *PE* xiv.6.6, Aug. *Acad.* III.38) that Arcesilaus was an esoteric Platonic dogmatist is generally and rightly rejected nowadays: see e.g. Glucker 1978, 296–306, Lévy 1978.

sent Arcesilaan *epochē* not as the outcome of weighing equally balanced trains of reasoning, but as the conclusion of *one* particular line of reasoning, namely his attack on the Stoic theory of the cognitive impression. This polemic is in fact the best attested piece of philosophizing attributed to Arcesilaus.[7] The sources give no indication that he regarded its conclusion as one to be balanced against the Stoic viewpoint. Rather the opposite: they suggest that he took *epochē* to be a more reasonable position than Stoic commitment to the cognitive impression. So there is a problem of reconciling the evidence about his arguments against the Stoics with his proto-Pyrrhonist appeal to contrarieties of arguments.

There is also a problem about evaluating those anti-Stoic arguments in themselves. Is their conclusion – that the wise person will suspend judgement or assent – represented as something to which Arcesilaus himself subscribes? Or is it meant to work solely *ad hominem*, as the outcome of a dialectical manoeuvre designed to corner the Stoics into admitting that on their own principles, together with premises they cannot reasonably deny, *epochē* is the only tenable posture where questions requiring judgement or assent are concerned? It might be argued in favour of this second alternative that a dialectical interpretation fits neatly with the evidence of Arcesilaus' proto-Pyrrhonism, yielding the following story about his overall stance: if attacks on the doctrine of the cognitive impression convince the Stoics of the need for *epochē*, that is their affair. If the production of opposing arguments that are equally convincing or unconvincing convinces others of it, that is *their* affair. Arcesilaus need not take a view himself on whether either or both of these routes to *epochē* is reasonable, even if he employs a general argumentative strategy of getting people to draw the conclusion that there is a need for *epochē*, and even if he finds himself taking the second-order view that it is a good thing that people should conclude that there is such a need – as Sextus (*PH* 1.233) suggests he did.

The dialectical interpretation can also appeal to Arcesilaus' well-attested revival of the Socratic method.[8] In the Socratic elenchus it is in the first instance the interlocutor, not Socrates, who is brought to an acknowledgement of ignorance, perplexity (*aporia*), and numbness 'in both soul and mouth' (*Men.* 80a–b). Again, in the fullest surviving report of Arcesilaus' argument against the cognitive impression, Sextus emphasizes the *ad hominem* status of the reasoning. Arcesilaus' first move was to prove that there *are* no cognitive impressions, that is, no impressions

---

[7] It is the centrepiece of the presentation of Arcesilaus' philosophy in both Sextus (*M* VII.150–8) and Cicero (*Acad.* 1.43–6, II.59–60, 76–8).   [8] See Cic. *Fin.* II.2, *ND* I.11.

which satisfy the Stoics' definition of cognitive impression. He famously offered 'many and varied considerations' for 'why no true impression is to be found of such a kind that it could not turn out to be false' (*M* VII.154).[9] If this is so, then 'it will follow, according to the Stoics too, that the wise person refrains from judgement' (*M* VII.155). The conclusion is argued as follows:

> Given that everything is incognitive, owing to the non-existence of the Stoic criterion, then if the wise person assents, the wise person will hold opinions. For given that nothing is cognitive, if he assents to anything, he will assent to the incognitive, and assent to the incognitive is opinion. So if the wise person is among those who assent, the wise person will be among those who hold opinions. But the wise person is certainly not among those who hold opinions (for they [sc. the Stoics] claim this to be a mark of folly and a cause of wrongdoing). Therefore the wise person is not among those who assent. And if this is so, he will have to withhold assent about everything. But to withhold assent is no different from suspending judgement. Therefore the wise person will suspend judgement about everything. (S.E. *M* VII.156–7)

This star example of Arcesilaus' dialectic is plainly designed to make a sceptic of his Stoic interlocutor, not (or not in the first instance) to explain how he comes to a position of *epochē* himself.

So it is not in doubt that Arcesilaus sometimes argued *ad hominem*. The question is whether the whole of his philosophical activity was conceived as a dialectical enterprise in which argument proceeded *always* and *exclusively* from the principles of some opponent, or at any rate from premises with which such an opponent could be persuaded to agree.[10] The evidence we have been reviewing already gives reason to answer: No. Arcesilaus' claim that the Stoics 'too' must agree to the rationality of *epochē* suggests an attempt to recommend that position to all and sundry, as one that *even* the Stoics – the most deeply entrenched dogmatists – ought to see that they are committed to accepting.[11] And his assault on

---

[9] Sextus gives no details; but this kind of argument remained the standard weapon used by Academics against the Stoics, and the sorts of example they used are recorded at length by both Sextus and Cicero: see section VI below.

[10] The 'many and varied considerations' (S.E. *M* VII.154) by which Arcesilaus sought to show that there were no impressions which satisfied the Stoic definition of a cognitive impression were plainly *not* derived from Stoic principles alone; and the Academics' success in getting the Stoics to agree to them was limited. See further section VI below.

[11] Sextus' καί could be read not as 'too' but as 'even' or 'actually' (Maconi 1988, 241 n. 32). But it is not obvious that these renderings make the implications of the text any different. Maconi also notes (ibid. 244) that Cicero clearly takes Arcesilaus to be himself committed to both the premises and the conclusion of the anti-Stoic argument recorded by Sextus: see *Acad.* II.67,77.

the cognitive impression is most obviously construed as designed to show principally that the Stoics are *wrong*, rather than that they ought to accept that they are wrong. Moreover the bulk of the rest of the evidence portrays Arcesilaus as holding a definite position for which he presented on his own account a variety of arguments, as the next two sections of this chapter will document.

III Arcesilaus' position

The main thesis to which Arcesilaus is said to have subscribed is the claim that nothing is known for certain, or more precisely that there is no such thing as what the Stoics called cognition. Two brief quotations will illustrate the centrality of this thesis in his thought, as well as giving some idea of its probable motivation. Cicero tells us:

> Arcesilaus was the first who from various of Plato's books and from Socratic discourses seized with the greatest force the moral: nothing which the mind or the senses can grasp is certain. (Cic. *De Orat.* III.67)

Numenius is one of several authors who confirms that Zeno's doctrine of cognition was the principal target,[12] although his colourful interpretation of the controversy in terms of competition for public status is more idiosyncratic:

> Seeing that Zeno was a rival in the art and a credible challenger, Arcesilaus launched without hesitation an attempt to demolish the arguments which were being produced by him. . . . And observing that the cognitive impression, that doctrine which he [sc. Zeno] was the first to discover, was highly regarded in Athens – both it and its name – he used every possible resource against it. (Eus. *PE* xiv.6.12–13)

It is readily intelligible how someone steeped in the writings of Plato (as Arcesilaus doubtless was) might be aghast both at Zeno's doctrine of the cognitive impression and more generally at the Stoics' attempt to appropriate Socrates, and indeed elements of Plato's own thought.[13] In part we should suppose such a response to have been a function of incompatible philosophical styles. The aporetic manner and agnostic outcome of Socratic questioning, as exhibited in many of Plato's Socratic dialogues,

---

[12] This is notably the explicit focus of Cicero's account of Arcesilaus: see e.g. *Acad.* I.44, II.16, 66, 76–7. So also Lact. *Inst.* VI.7 (no doubt dependent on Cicero). Sextus (*M* VII.150–8) speaks generally of the Stoics as the target, but chronological considerations alone make Zeno far the likeliest author of the views he represents Arcesilaus as attacking.

[13] On Stoic appropriation of Socrates see e.g. Schofield 1984, Long 1988b; and for Platonic elements in Stoicism e.g. Krämer 1971, 108–31.

are far removed in spirit from Zeno's insistence that everyone has cognitive impressions which can form the basis of knowledge or understanding (*epistēmē*). And we know that Arcesilaus associated himself quite specifically with Socrates' disavowal of knowledge:

> So Arcesilaus was in the practice of denying that anything could be known, not even the one thing Socrates had left for himself – the knowledge that he knew nothing. (Cic. *Acad.* 1.45)

There is also scope for the suspicion that some of his particular objections to the doctrine of the cognitive impression may owe something to arguments Plato had developed in the dialogues, although the case cannot be put more strongly than that. For example, people who have what Zeno calls cognitions must on Stoic premises be either wise or foolish. But if they are wise, said Arcesilaus, cognition (*katalēpsis*) for them must simply be the same thing as knowledge or understanding (*epistēmē*); if they are foolish, it is merely opinion (*doxa*). The reasoning he presented is not recorded by our source (Sextus Empiricus, *M* VII.153), but the outcome is reinstatement of the familiar Platonic dichotomy of epistemic states. Again, Sextus informs us that Arcesilaus attempted to rebut Zeno's thesis that cognition is assent to a cognitive impression: 'assent relates not to impression but to *logos* (for assents are to propositions)' (*M* VII.154). The point at issue between them is not clear from this brief report. One plausible interpretation takes Arcesilaus to be re-using Plato's argument in the *Theaetetus* against the idea that truth is accessible to perception: if perceptions are passive affections (as on Stoic theory they seem to be conceived), they cannot be true or false, and cannot therefore be proper objects of assent – truth and falsehood will have to be the domain of the propositions which are expressed in reasoning *about* perceptions (cf. *Tht.* 184–6).[14]

It is often suggested that if Arcesilaus represented his scepticism as something consistent with or derived from a reading of Plato, then the reading he offered must have been at best selective and at worst implausible and disingenuous.[15] But his critique of Zeno's theory of cognition is at least along the sorts of lines one might have expected of Plato himself.

---

[14] So Ioppolo 1990. Other treatments of Arcesilaus' Platonic inheritance: von Staden 1978, Glucker 1978, 31–47, Ioppolo 1986, 40–9, Annas 1992c. A useful summary in Görler 1994b, 821–4.

[15] Whether Plato was in some sense a sceptic (in which case Arcesilaus' 'New Academy' might not be new after all) was already debated in antiquity: see e.g. Cic. *Acad.*1 and 46, S.E. *PH* 1.221–5. Modern literature exploring the case for seeing him in this light includes Woodruff 1986, Annas 1992c, Frede 1992.

Nor is there any sign that he rejected Plato's *conception* of what systematic knowledge or understanding (*epistēmē*) consists in. If he thought it humanly unattainable, he could appeal to the *Phaedo* to support the view that in this life we must content ourselves with a cautious and painstaking method of hypothesis. Indeed the witness of philosophical authorities is just what Arcesilaus did invoke in confirmation of his position.[16] Plutarch alleges that 'the sophists of his time accused him of rubbing off his doctrines about suspension of judgement and non-cognition on Socrates, Plato, Parmenides and Heraclitus, who did not need them, whereas it was in fact as if he was acknowledging his indebtedness to some famous men and trying to claim confirmation from them' (*Col.* 1121e–1122a).

Given that attack on the Stoic doctrine of cognitive impressions was one route to *epochē*, how did it relate to the other which is attested for Arcesilaus: suspension of assent owing to contrarieties of arguments? There is one passage in our sources which indicates an answer to this question. After remarking that Arcesilaus went beyond even Socrates in what he said about the impossibility of knowledge, Cicero continues:

> Such was the extent of the obscurity in which everything lurked, on his assessment, and there was nothing which could be discerned or understood. For these reasons, he said, no one should maintain or assert anything or give it the acceptance of assent, but he should always curb his rashness and restrain it from every slip – for it would be extraordinary rashness to accept something either false or incognitive, and nothing was more regrettable than for assent and acceptance to run ahead of cognition and grasp. His practice was consistent with this theory: by arguing against everyone's opinions he drew most people away from their own, so that when reasons of equal weight were found on opposite sides on the same subject, it might be easier to withhold assent from either side. They call this Academy new, though I think it is old if we count Plato as one of the old Academy. In his books nothing is asserted and there is much argument pro and contra, everything is investigated and nothing is stated as certain. (*Acad.* 1.45–6; translation after Long and Sedley)

According to Cicero Arcesilaus' argumentation against the Stoic cognitive impression provided the *theoretical* basis for *epochē*: the production of equally balanced contrary arguments on philosophical subjects was the way he attempted to *implement* the theory in practice – in order to

---

[16] Arcesilaus' citation of authorities is a feature of his philosophizing particularly difficult to explain on a purely dialectical reading of his arguments in epistemology.

encourage people actually to suspend assent. In other words, on Cicero's interpretation his proto-Pyrrhonism is not the core of his philosophy, but the application of some non-Pyrrhonist theorizing.

As described by Cicero Arcesilaus' practice is characterized by a certain complexity. It is suggested that (i) he regularly argued against people, (ii) so as to get them used to being weaned from opinion, so that (iii) when reasons of equal weight were discovered they would find it easier to withhold assent from *either* side. Other texts associate (i) with Arcesilaus' revival of the Socratic elenchus;[17] and the rationale supplied by (ii) is a familiar rationale of the elenchus. (iii) is not nowadays seen as its ulterior motive. This is where Arcesilaus appears to innovate, although Cicero is right to point out that argument *pro* and *contra* is a feature of Platonic dialogues, as, for example, in the considerations advanced in the last part of the *Meno* for and against the view that virtue is teachable, or in the antinomies worked out in *Lysis* and (on a grand formal scale) *Parmenides*.[18] It is not hard to see how Arcesilaus might think of (iii) as no less Socratic than (ii). For if with him we interpret the elenchus as inspired by the conviction that nothing can be known, we shall expect Socrates in conducting it to be trying not only to purge his interlocutors of unfounded opinion, but to help them develop a frame of mind in which they refrain altogether from opinion, and therefore assent, with regard to *any* theoretical questions. For it is not just that people happen to be wedded to their own unjustified opinions. If they assent to any theoretical proposition at all, they will inevitably succumb to any unjustifiable opinion.[19]

Sextus claimed that Arcesilaus made *epochē* 'the aim' (*telos*), and in particular that he said *particular* suspensions of judgement were good and *particular* assents bad. Cicero's evidence suggests an interest on his part in the intellectual habituation of his interlocutors which makes sense of this stress on particular cases. As with the Socratic elenchus, the underlying aim will have been ethical as well as intellectual: the false conceit of knowledge is regarded as morally debilitating, and philosophy must bend all efforts to do away with it.[20]

---

[17] See Cic. *Fin.* II.2, *ND* I.11.

[18] Arcesilaus is sometimes thought to have borrowed from Aristotle the practice of arguing either side of the case (e.g. Weische 1961, Krämer 1971, 14-58); but Cicero stresses the differences between Aristotle's and Arcesilaus' uses of the method (*Fin.* v.10).

[19] For further discussion of how far Arcesilaus' use of the elenchus may be regarded as Socratic in spirit see Annas 1992c, Shields 1994.

[20] Modern scholarship has found Sextus' assertion that Arcesilaus made *epochē* the *telos* hard to evaluate: see e.g. Sedley 1983a, Ioppolo 1986, 34-40, 157-65, Annas 1988b. No doubt it was not his express 'doctrine', but if the account of his philosophical strategy at *Acad.* 1.45 is correct his argumentative practice was systematically designed to induce *epochē*. (Sextus' reminder that

Arcesilaus' contemporary, the maverick Stoic Aristo of Chios,[21] is credited with adapting Homer's description of the Chimaera to characterize his philosophical make-up (D.L. IV.33):[22]

Plato in front, Pyrrho behind, Diodorus in the middle.

'That is', as David Sedley aptly comments, 'behind his formal pose as Plato's heir in the Academy lay Pyrrho's philosophy, while Diodorus' dialectical technique held the heterogeneous creatures together.'[23] Aristo's quip is not easy to evaluate. It gives no intimation of any Socratic inspiration for Arcesilaus' thought, so strongly emphasized by Cicero, our main (although much later) authority on the motivation of his scepticism. No other source elaborates on debts to Pyrrho or Diodorus. In default of further evidence, we are in no position to adjudicate on whether any similarities with Pyrrho and Diodorus were superficial or, as Aristo presumably meant to suggest, constituted evidence that Arcesilaus was an eclectic intellectual parasite – or, as is a priori more plausible, represented real influences which he absorbed and made his own.

IV Two objections to Arcesilaus

In conclusion it is appropriate to consider two objections to Arcesilaus' position, one theoretical, one practical. The theoretical objection complains that if Arcesilaus is interpreted as claiming on his own account that nothing can be known and consequently that it is wise to refrain from assertion on all matters, then he refutes himself. To be sure, he explicitly denied that he *knew* that nothing could be known. But on his own principles, if he does not know it, he should not assert it at all.[24]

Three main strategies for dealing with this difficulty deserve consideration. The first is to propose that we should after all prefer the dialectical interpretation of Arcesilaus, which makes all his arguments nothing but *ad hominem* manoeuvres against opponents. But while this way out would

---

according to Pyrrhonism *epochē* is accompanied by tranquillity is gratuitous – there is no evidence of Academic interest in tranquillity, nor does Sextus mean to suggest the contrary.)

[21] See Long 1986a for the argument that philosophical debate with Aristo formed a significant part of Arcesilaus' philosophical activity.

[22] Similar jibes carrying the same philosophical point were made by Timon of Phlius, in lines also reported at D.L. IV.33 (cf. Numen. in Eus. *PE* XIV.5.12–14, 6.4–6).

[23] Sedley 1983a, 15. He finds more truth in the imputation of dependence on Pyrrho than is allowed by Long and Sedley 1987, 1.446.

[24] The ancient text in which this line of objection is pressed against Arcesilaus in particular is Lact. *Inst.* VI.10–15, probably drawing on a lost section of Cicero's *Academica*. The discussions about the epistemological status of the Academic position Cicero records in surviving passages relate to debates dating to the second century BC: see *Acad.* II.28–9, 109–10.

dispose of the problem, the fact remains that it runs counter to the great body of ancient evidence about Arcesilaus. A second strategy would be to credit him with one or other of the subtle devices deployed by later sceptics, Academic as well as Pyrrhonist, for qualifying their own sceptical claims. For example, Arcesilaus might have represented his position on the impossibility of knowledge not as something he asserted, but simply as the way things appeared to him. This suggestion runs the danger of anachronism: sceptic self-qualification was very likely the outcome of later debate. Moreover Sextus implies that so far as he was aware, Arcesilaus did *not* enter disclaimers of this sort, for example, in his evaluations of particular assents or suspensions of judgement (*PH* 1.233). It might be better to suppose that Arcesilaus conceived his own position in Platonic fashion as a *hypothesis*, i.e. as a theory advanced for consideration as the best explanation we have of human cognitive performance. If this solution seems unduly speculative, one might finally and glumly conclude, in default of any evidence to the contrary, that he *had* no position on the status of his own position.

The other and principal ancient objection pressed against Arcesilaus was the charge of *apraxia*, 'inability to act'.[25] If wholly rational persons never assent, how are they to act? The Stoics made this question their major counter-weapon against the Academic critique of the cognitive impression throughout the Hellenistic period, and it was also levelled against Arcesilaus by the Epicurean Colotes. From Plutarch we have details of an Academic answer to it. It consists in an explanation of action as the outcome of impression and impulse alone, without the additional need – insisted on by the Stoics – for assent. This is usually interpreted as an *ad hominem* stratagem, not a theory the Academics advanced on their own account. However that may be, Plutarch does not expressly ascribe it to Arcesilaus. Conceivably it is the work of Carneades or Clitomachus.[26]

The defence against the *apraxia* criticism which *is* attested for Arcesilaus is recorded by Sextus:

Arcesilaus says that one who suspends judgement about everything will regulate choice and avoidance and actions in general by 'the reasonable'

[25] On Academic defences against arguments of this kind see Striker 1980, Bett 1989.
[26] See Plu. *Col.* 1120c, 1121e–1122f. The main reason why the Academic rebuttal of the charge of *apraxia* reported at 1122b–d is usually attributed to Arcesilaus is simply that it is introduced in the context of Colotes' attack on his position (for supplementary considerations see Striker 1980, 65 n. 29). But Plutarch probably implies that it was a reply to *Stoic* criticism (1122a–b), as its exploitation of Stoic conceptual apparatus confirms; and elsewhere he suggests that such Stoic criticism belonged mainly to a later phase of debate, being principally the work of Chrysippus and Antipater (*Stoic. Rep.* 1057a). Against Arcesilaan authorship see e.g. Mette 1984, 92 n. 1, Lévy 1993, 266–8; also below, p.333 n. 39.

(*eulogon*); and that by proceeding in accordance with this criterion he will act rightly and successfully – for (1) happiness is acquired through prudence, and (2) prudence resides in right and successful actions, and (3) right and successful action is whatever when done has a reasonable justification: therefore one who attends to the reasonable will act rightly and successfully and be happy. (S.E. *M* VII.158)

The status of Arcesilaus' theory is hotly debated. The notion of 'the reasonable' (*to eulogon*) was one Zeno employed, and Arcesilaus' premiss (3) predicates of 'right and successful action' (*katorthōma*) Zeno's definition of an *appropriate* action (*kathēkon*) as 'whatever when/if done has a reasonable justification'.[27] Since premisses (1) and (2) are also Stoic, it seems likely that Arcesilaus is replying to the Stoic challenge by exploiting theses and concepts central to the Stoics' own ethics.[28] This has inevitably suggested to some scholars that Arcesilaus' argument is meant to function only as *ad hominem* dialectic against the Stoa: 'He did not teach the doctrine of the *eulogon*; that was a thesis he derived from Stoicism in order to attack and wound it in its weakest part. He behaved as a nihilist, a fifth columnist inside the Stoa.'[29]

The suggestion labours under a difficulty. Arcesilaus' argument was conceived as a *defence* in the face of Stoic criticism. It will only work as a simultaneous counter-attack provided that the Stoics abandon their standard account of right and successful action (*katorthōma*) as 'appropriate action which possesses all the measures' (Stob. *Ecl.* II.93.14–15 [= *SVF* III.500]), or more simply as a 'perfect appropriate action' (Stob. *Ecl.* II.85.18–20 [= *SVF* III.494]). For as things stand, the Stoics would insist that following the course that is 'reasonable' will not guarantee that one performs a *perfect* appropriate action, even if it will prove to be *true* of any such action that it was a or the reasonable thing to do. But Sextus records no reasons Arcesilaus put forward as to why the Stoics should give up their ordinary definition of *katorthōma*.[30] It might therefore seem better to accept that Arcesilaus is replying rather more directly on his own account to the Stoic challenge to show how action is compatible with *epochē*. Yet it then becomes hard to understand why he should have opted for just the Stoic-sounding rationale he is represented as advancing, and why there is no obvious trace of its being adopted or adapted by any other Academic sceptic.[31]

---

[27] D.L. VII.107, Stob. II.85.13–15. No account survives of how the Stoics would have defined 'reasonable' in this context; nor does it appear that Arcesilaus sought to supply the omission.

[28] So Couissin 1929, Bett 1989, 62–9; *contra* Ioppolo 1986, 120–34.

[29] Couissin 1929, 38; cf. Striker 1980, 63–6.   [30] Cf. Maconi 1988, 247–52, Bett 1989, 62–9.

[31] But see n. 66 below.

On either interpretation there is a further difficulty. How will those who regulate their conduct by 'the reasonable' thereby avoid assent? Someone who says of the course of action *A* he proposes to adopt: '*A* is the reasonable thing to do' does not claim or imply that he is opting for *A* on the basis of cognition. But nor is he suspending judgement about it or the reasonableness of pursuing it. Compare the Stoic Sphaerus, who when tricked into taking wax pomegranates for real ones, and charged with assenting to something false, replied: 'I didn't assent to the proposition that they are pomegranates, but to the proposition that it is reasonable to think they are pomegranates' (D.L. VII.177). Perhaps Arcesilaus thought that doing something because it is the reasonable course to follow was like entertaining a hypothesis about some theoretical matter: reliance on what is reasonable similarly requires only a working assumption about what should be done, not an assent or a judgement about truth. If so, his proposal turns not (as Sextus suggests) on the idea of the reasonable, but on the unexpressed notion of a working assumption.

v Carneades on opinion and assent

'I agree with Clitomachus', says Cicero (*Acad.* II.108), 'when he writes that it was a labour of Herculean proportions Carneades went through in dragging from our minds that wild and savage monster assent – i.e. opinion and rashness.' Not every Academic would have wanted to describe Carneades' achievement in these terms. Cicero elsewhere makes a contrast between Arcesilaus and Carneades.[32] Arcesilaus argued against the Stoic cognitive impression (1) that there is no true impression such that there could not be a false impression indistinguishable from it. From this he further argued (2) that in that case if the wise person assents, what he will be holding is an opinion – since cognition is impossible. And he held (3) that it is necessary for the wise person not to hold opinions, and so not to assent. But Carneades appeared to allow (contrary to (3)) that sometimes the wise man *will* assent, and so will hold an opinion:

> This [sc. (1)] is the one argument which has held the field [sc. within the Academy] down to the present day.[33] For the thesis: 'The wise person will assent to nothing' [i.e. (3)] had nothing to do with this dispute[34]

---

[32] See *Acad.* II.59, 66–7, 76–8.

[33] So the Loeb translates *haec est una contentio quae adhuc permanserit*. Long and Sedley 1987, 1, 243 have: 'This is the one controversial issue which has lasted up to the present.' But that makes Cicero claim something false and apparently inconsistent with what immediately follows.

[34] Cicero overstates the case, perhaps because he wants to indicate that the *apraxia* argument is the principal context for a discussion of (3) (so Striker 1980, 75). He has in mind the sound point

[i.e. over the possibility of cognition]. For it was permitted for the wise person to grasp nothing cognitively but yet hold an opinion – a thesis Carneades is said to have accepted, although for my part, trusting Clitomachus rather than Philo or Metrodorus, I think that this was not so much something he accepted as something he put forward in debate. (Cic. *Acad.* II.78)

Carneades and the Academy in general agreed with Arcesilaus in arguing against the cognitive impression. But as Cicero here records, it became a matter of controversy among Carneades' heirs what conclusions he was prepared to derive from that generally agreed position. And according to the interpretation of Philo and Metrodorus he took a different line on (3) from Arcesilaus: the wise person *might* sometimes hold an opinion. On their view any Herculean labour ascribed to Carneades must have had an outcome other than the wholesale extrusion of assent from the mind.

The conflict in the assessment of Carneades' treatment of opinion attested by Cicero is easily explained. Once again the crux is a choice between a dialectical reading of a position and one which attributes to its author views that are in some sense his own. If Clitomachus is right,[35] Carneades will have varied Arcesilaus' anti-Stoic dialectic by saying in effect: given (1) and (2), *either* the wise person will never assent to anything (as in (3)) *or* – supposing he does assent – he will sometimes hold opinions. The point would be to insist that the Stoics are confronted with a dilemma. If they regard the option of *epochē* with horror, as forcing them into Arcesilaus' camp, then they can of course allow that the wise person will sometimes assent, but at the heavy price of having to agree to exactly what Arcesilaus supposed their Stoic principles would never permit them to accept: that the wise person will sometimes hold mere opinions.

The alternative interpretation of Carneades advocated by Philo and Metrodorus is amplified a little by Catulus, the Philonian speaker in *Academica* Book II, in the closing lines of the dialogue:

I am coming round to my father's view, which he used to say was Carneades' in fact. I think nothing can be grasped cognitively. Yet I also

---

that (3) does not follow from (1) directly, only from the conjunction of (1) and (2). At II.68 he makes it quite clear that the existence of controversy over (3) *presupposes* that a case for (1) – and for its consequence that cognition is impossible – has been made.

[35] Most modern scholarship supposes with Cicero that he is: see e.g. Long and Sedley 1987, I, 448–9, 455–6, following Couissin 1929, 45–6. For arguments in favour of this verdict see e.g. Bett 1989, 70 n. 24. Note in particular that according to Cicero Carneades only *sometimes* pursued the second option, of granting that the wise person sometimes assents (*Acad.* II.67): which strongly supports the view that this was a dialectical ploy.

think that the wise person will assent to what is not grasped cognitively, i.e. he will hold opinions – but in such a way that he understands he is holding opinions and knows that there is nothing which can be grasped cognitively. (*Acad.* II.148)

This tantalizingly brief construal of Carneades' stance in epistemology does a little to explain what on the Philonian view holding an opinion would add up to for a wise person. A number of Hellenistic attempts to characterize opinion are recorded, but the one that seems to shape Catulus' formulation is the Stoic conception of it as 'yielding to an incognitive impression' (Plu. *Stoic. Rep.* 1056f). His way of removing anything objectionable from opinion so conceived is to suppose it may involve a second-order mental attitude: the wise person does not just hold an opinion, but is also aware *that* it is merely an opinion and not something cognitively grasped. What he is presumably assuming is that the reason for *avoiding* opinion is because it is ordinarily accompanied, as Socrates so often pointed out, by the false conceit of knowledge: not merely do people holding opinions believe (truly or falsely) that *p*, but they falsely believe that they know that *p* – falsely, because there is nothing that *can* be grasped cognitively. Catulus' wise person is not infected by the false conceit of knowledge. Although he believes that *p*, he does so well aware that he does not *know* that *p*. Therefore he is free of what is debilitating about opinion. So construed, the Philonian interpretation of why Carneades said that the wise person will sometimes hold an opinion differs from the Clitomachean in two fundamental respects. First, it takes him to have accepted the claim himself. It was not just something he propounded as one horn of a dilemma for the Stoics. Second, it attributes to him a sanitized notion of opinion, such that a perfectly rational person need not seek to avoid holding opinions.

Did Clitomachus represent his dialectical Carneades as holding no views of his own of any kind on this issue of opinion and assent?[36] Far from it. Here are two pieces of evidence which favour the opposite conclusion. First, the passage about Carneades' Herculean labour quoted at the beginning of this section. If it was a great achievement to 'drag from our minds that wild and savage monster assent' (*Acad.* II.108), Clitomachus is very likely supposing that Carneades himself assumed that

---

[36] Much modern discussion of Carneades denies him any such views on this or any matter: so e.g. Couissin 1929, 50–1, Striker 1980, 82–3 (*contra* e.g. Bett 1989, 76–90). Many of the texts which portray him as having views of his own derive from sources that have an axe to grind (e.g. Numen. in Eus. *PE* xiv.8.1–10, S.E. *PH* 1.226–31, *M* vii.159–84 (where he perhaps follows Antiochus: so Sedley 1992a, 44–55)). But Clitomachus' evidence that he did needs more careful attention (however note also Clitomachus' remark, conceivably made with a specific reference to ethics, that he could never understand what was 'approved' (*probaretur*) by Carneades: *Acad.* ii.139).

the wise person will refrain from assent. His implication will be that that
assumption motivated much of Carneades' philosophical activity – as on
our account it did Arcesilaus' before him. Second is some information
about a distinction between two meanings of the thesis that 'the wise person will refrain from assent' which Cicero reports a few pages earlier
on.[37] The report makes most readily intelligible sense if Clitomachus
took the thesis to be one which represented Carneades' own position. For
the distinction Clitomachus drew between different ways of taking it
indicates a concern on his part to rebut the charge of *apraxia* ('inability to
act') levelled against the Academy: a response which is difficult to interpret unless Academics did in some sense themselves advocate the view
that the wise person will not assent.

Cicero's account of the two meanings is unfortunately compressed, and
probably at one or two points textually corrupt. But there seems to be a
contrast between refraining from *judgement*, which the wise person will
always do, and refraining from *saying* 'Yes' or 'No' to a question, where his
position will be more nuanced. Here the wise man *will* say 'Yes' or 'No',
but without thereby expressing a judgement, that is, without meaning
that he takes something to be true or false. He will simply be signalling
that he is 'following' or 'going along with' an impression which he finds
persuasive in one direction or another.[38] The contrast is a perfectly general
one, not restricted to questions relating to how a person is to act. However
Cicero suggests that the idea of 'following' an impression without forming
a judgement was for Clitomachus particularly relevant to the problem of
how someone who refrains from assent 'nonetheless does move and does
act' (*Acad.* II.104): the wise man 'goes along with' those impressions by
which he is roused to action. When Plutarch gives his account of the
Academic rejoinder to the charge of *apraxia*, he may well be reproducing a
more detailed version of this response by Clitomachus to the problem:[39]

---

[37] Clitomachus' distinction is discussed by Frede 1984, Bett 1990.

[38] Cf. S.E. *PH* 1.230: 'Carneades and Clitomachus say that they go along with things – and that
some things are persuasive or convincing (*pithanon*) – with an intense (*sphodrās*) inclination.'
'Intense inclination' would no doubt be the natural and appropriate response to 'the intensity
of its appearing true' which is a feature of convincing impressions, according to Carneades (S.E.
M VII.171). Sextus implies that Arcesilaus was closer to Pyrrhonism than Carneades because he
did not rank impressions according to whether they were more or less deserving of conviction:
PH 1.232. An unsafe inference: Arcesilaus did not work with the conceptual apparatus of the
pithanon at all.

[39] Note particularly the correspondence between Clitomachus' talk of 'impressions by which we
are aroused to action' (*Acad.* II.104) and the account of impulse as 'aroused by that [sc.the move-
ment] of impression' in Plutarch's report. The role of nature implied in the report perhaps finds
an echo in Clitomachus' claim that it is 'contrary to nature that nothing should be acceptable
(*probabile*)' (*Acad.* II.99). For discussion of the philosophical content of Plutarch's text see
Striker 1980, 66–9.

The soul has three movements – impression, impulse and assent. The movement of impression we could not remove, even if we wanted to; rather, as soon as we encounter things, we get an impression and are affected by them. The movement of impulse, when aroused by that of impression, moves a person actively towards appropriate objects, since a kind of turn of the scale and inclination occur in the commanding-faculty. So those who suspend judgement about everything do not remove this movement either, but make use of the impulse which leads them naturally towards what appears appropriate. What, then, is the only thing they avoid? That only in which falsehood and deception are engendered – opining and precipitately assenting, which is yielding to the appearance out of weakness and involves nothing useful. For action requires two things: an impression of something appropriate, and an impulse towards the appropriate object that has appeared; neither of these is in conflict with suspension of judgement. For the argument keeps us away from opinion, not from impulse or impression. So whenever something appropriate has appeared, no opinion is needed to get us moving and proceeding towards it; the impulse arrives immediately, since it is the soul's process and movement. (Plu. *Col.* 1122b–d; translation Long and Sedley)

VI Carneades on the impossibility of knowledge

Why on Clitomachus' view did Carneades conclude in the first place that the wise person should refrain from assent? Just as with Arcesilaus, the answer lies in his rejection of the Stoic cognitive impression. Cicero stresses that the whole question of whether the wise man assents or holds opinions becomes a problem precisely because (as the Academics argue) nothing can be cognitively grasped: 'if I succeed in proving that nothing can be cognitively grasped, you must admit that the wise man will never assent' (*Acad.* II.78).[40] And Clitomachus' differentiation between two sorts of assent is worked out in the light of the claim that impressions differ in persuasiveness even though they have no mark of truth and certainty peculiar to themselves and found nowhere else (*Acad.* II.103).

It was not just the Stoic cognitive impression that Carneades attacked. In the most general and comprehensive account of Carneades' epistemology preserved in our sources his entire position is represented as founded on rejection of *any* infallible criterion of truth. 'On the subject of the crite-

---

[40] Cf. *Acad.* II.59, 68, and see p. 334 n. 34 above.

rion', says Sextus (*M* VII.159), 'Carneades marshalled arguments not only against the Stoics but also against all previous philosophers.' Two particular arguments are summarized, the first very briefly. This consisted in showing that there *is* no such criterion as philosophers claim – not reason, not sensation, not impression, not anything: 'for all of these alike deceive us' (S.E. *M* VII.159). *How* exactly Carneades showed this Sextus does not record, nor just what he meant by 'criterion' in this context.[41] Perhaps his contention amounted to the claim that we have no psychological faculty such that every use of it which appears to result in our grasping thereby some true state of affairs as 'evident' actually does give us thereby a grasp of just that state of affairs as 'evident'. In what sense would such a claim constitute an attack 'aimed at all of them [sc. previous philosophers] jointly'? Probably only because Carneades supposed that the different candidates for criterial faculty he considered effectively included every basis for cognition so far proposed by philosophers.

The second Carneadean argument recorded by Sextus is reported in greater detail (S.E. *M* VII.160–5). Carneades started by supposing for the sake of argument that (1) there *is* after all some criterion. But if so (2) our ability to grasp what is evident must be a function of how what is evident affects us as we employ some criterial faculty (as assumed in (1)). And once it is accepted that (3) an affection (in this instance an impression) is one thing and the evident state of affairs it is taken to reveal another, the possibility has also to be accepted that (4) some impressions which appear to reveal what is evident are deceptive – the match is imperfect. Therefore (5) not every impression can be a criterion of truth, but (if any) only the true impression. But (6) there is no true impression of such a kind that it could not turn out false, so the supposed criterion will turn out to consist in an impression which spans true and false. (7) Such an impression is not cognitive, and cannot therefore be a criterion. Therefore (8) no impression is criterial. But in that case (9) reason cannot be a criterion either, since reason derives from impression. Therefore (10) neither irrational sensation nor reason is a criterion. (10) does not formally contradict (1); but (8) to (10) between them eliminate the favoured candidates for what the criterion hypothesized in (1) might be.

Sextus is not explicit about which philosophers are the target of this complex sequence of reasoning. There is much to be said for the view that Epicurus is the principal opponent in view. Two features of the argument

---

[41] On the notion of a criterion in Hellenistic philosophy see Striker 1974, Brunschwig 1988b, Striker 1990.

in particular support this interpretation. First, most space and effort are devoted to proving (5), which hits at the Epicureans, who believed that *all* impressions are true – there is no such thing as a false impression. (5) is something the Stoics, by contrast, take for granted; and indeed in recommending (2) by the argument that sensation cannot register or reveal anything unless it is altered by what it registers or reveals, Carneades follows the Stoics, and borrows from Chrysippus in particular the idea first that such an alteration is what an impression is, and second that impressions are like light in simultaneously revealing themselves and something external to them.[42] Secondly, in formulating the conclusion of the whole argument in the terms in which (10) is couched he rounds off the proof in a way calculated once more to address a specifically Epicurean position. The articulation of (10) as a disjunction between irrational sensation and reason corresponds to the Epicurean conception of the division of labour between perception and reason, not the Stoic – for the Stoics insist that cognitive impressions are *rational* impressions.[43] Of course steps (6) and (7) of the argument are standardly reported as anti-Stoic manoeuvres in our accounts of Academic scepticism. But Carneades' point here is doubtless that once Epicureans are persuaded to accept (5), the only way they can sustain belief in a criterion of truth is in effect to accept the Stoic doctrine of the cognitive impression – which succumbs to the considerations advanced in (6) and (7).

Sextus' evidence that Carneades argued about knowledge and the criterion of truth over a broader front than Arcesilaus is indirectly confirmed by what Cicero tells us of 'the Academy's' approach to the topic. 'The Academics', he says (*Acad.* II.40), 'embody their entire case in the reasoning of a single argument.' The argument he goes on to set out turns out to be a portmanteau proof, designed to demolish with a single sequence of strokes the epistemologies of Stoics and Epicureans alike. It is impossible to decide whether the idea of such an all-purpose demonstration was Carneades' own or something his concern to deal comprehensively with other schools inspired his pupils to attempt. Here is the argument, which has obvious affinities with the proof recorded by Sextus we have just been examining:

> (1) Of impressions, some are true, some false. (2) A false impression is not cognitive. But (3) every true impression is such that a false one just like it can also occur. And (4) where impressions are such that there is no difference between them, it cannot turn out that some of them are cogni-

[42] Cf. *SVF* II 54.
[43] So Long and Sedley 1987, II, 453. The Epicurean view: D.L. x.31–2; the Stoic: D.L. VII.51.

tive but others not. Therefore (5) no impression is cognitive. (Cic. *Acad.* II.40)

Cicero comments as follows:

Of the premises which they adopt in order to reach their conclusion, they take two to be conceded to them, since no one raises an objection. These are, first, (2) that false impressions are not cognitive; and second, (4) that when impressions do not differ at all it is impossible that some of them should be cognitive, others not. But the other premises they defend with a long and wide-ranging disquisition. Here again there are two of them: first, (1) that of impressions some are true, others false; second, (3) that every impression arising from something true is such that it could also arise from something false. (*Acad.* II.41; both translations by Long and Sedley)

The 'long and wide-ranging disquisition' needed to defend (1) presupposes principally Epicurean opponents;[44] (3), on the other hand, is as noted above the Academics' classic anti-Stoic move. Some indication of the sorts of consideration that were adduced in support of (1) is given in *Acad.* II.79–83, where Cicero runs through a battery of now familiar sceptical arguments[45] questioning the reliability of the senses: they represent the sun as a foot in diameter and an oar in water as bent; their scope is limited and species-relative; etc. As expected Epicurus is mentioned as the chief proponent of the 'credulous' view that 'the senses never lie' (ibid. 82). By contrast the Academics worked out what they had to say on (3) by attacking the Stoic definition of the cognitive impression. Both Arcesilaus and Carneades took as their specific target the third clause of the definition: which provided that a cognitive impression is 'of such a kind as could not arise from what is not'.[46]

Two main lines of objection were developed by the Academics in this context, both aimed at showing that there are false impressions indistinguishable from the true impressions which satisfy the other two clauses of the Stoic definition, namely that they arise from what is, and are stamped and impressed exactly in accordance with what is. They are referred to in our sources as arguments from 'indiscernibility', *aparallaxia*. Falling under the first of the two were appeals to the experience of dreamers, those suffering from hallucinations, etc. Such persons are moved by their impressions in just the same way as people normally respond to the sorts of

---

[44] As is explicitly remarked at *Acad.* II.83; cf. 101.
[45] Cicero tells us they were *communes loci*, stock arguments, in his own day: *Acad.* II.80.
[46] Arcesilaus: S.E. *M* VII.154, Cic. *Acad.* II.76–8; Carneades: S.E. *M* VII.401–11.

impression the Stoics believe to be cognitive. The second and perhaps subsidiary type of *aparallaxia* argument focused on cases where even healthy persons in full possession of their senses find it impossible to tell two things apart – two twins, two eggs, two applications of the same seal.[47]

Sextus' report of the arguments derived from dreaming and the like makes their logical structure transparent. What they are intended to establish is that there are false impressions indistinguishable from true impressions inasmuch as they are equally evident and striking. This conclusion is taken to follow from the fact that e.g. hallucinations move those who experience them to the same *behaviour* as supposedly cognitive impressions move those who experience them:

> Just as in normal states too we believe and assent to very clear appearances, behaving towards Dion, for instance, as Dion and towards Theon as Theon, so too in madness some people have a similar experience. When Heracles was deranged, he got an impression from his own children as though they were those of Eurystheus, and he attached the consequential action to this impression – killing his enemy's children: which [sc. killing the children] was what he did. If then impressions are cognitive in so far as they induce us to assent and to attach to them the consequential action, since false impressions are plainly of this kind too, we must say that incognitive ones are indiscernible from the cognitive. (S.E. *M* vii.404–5; translation after Long and Sedley)

Similarly dreamers get the same pleasure or feel the same terror at what they are experiencing as waking persons do, for example, when quenching their thirst or running screaming from a wild animal (S.E. *M* vii.403). Here the claim that dreaming behaviour is identical with waking behaviour seems harder to sustain: the Academics must be arguing that there is the same *impulse* and accordingly the same assent, and that these constitute identical behaviour.

So on Sextus' account the Academics do not claim that there is any direct way of establishing the nature of dreaming or hallucinatory experience. They make a proposal about what it *must* be like – namely (in the cases discussed) 'evident' and 'striking' – on the basis of inference. Cicero's treatment of the dispute between the Stoa and the Academy over this issue does not present the Academics' line of reasoning with the same clarity.[48] Nonetheless his evidence can be interpreted as consistent with

---

[47] These arguments are discussed from the Stoic point of view in chapter 9. Cf. also Frede 1983, Annas 1990b, Striker 1990. Arguments from dreaming etc. are given pride of place in Cic. *Acad.* 11.47–58, S.E. *M* vii.401–11, although the case of twins etc. gets more prominence at Cic. *Acad.* 11.83–90.   [48] See Cic. *Acad.* 11.51–4, 88–90.

Sextus'. He suggests that the Academics' key point was that so far as the assent of the mind is concerned, there is no difference between the false impressions experienced by dreamers and the insane and the true impressions of sane wakeful persons (*Acad.* II.90). So when he represents them as stressing that 'what we are asking is what these things [sc. dreams, hallucinations, etc.] looked like at the time' (*Acad.* II.88; cf. 52), this should be seen as a way of putting the challenge: if there is the same assent, must we not suppose that the impressions which prompt the assent are equally evident and striking when they occur?

The reply of the Stoicizing Antiochus as documented by Cicero may be interpreted as resisting the Academic argument so construed at two points in particular. First, he stressed that when dreamers wake or the insane recover they dismiss their dreaming or hallucinatory impressions as feeble and insubstantial (*Acad.* II.51). Here Antiochus can be read as capitalizing on the inferential nature of our understanding of such experiences (conceded by the Academics). His rejoinder in effect says: the self-conscious judgement of those who recover their normal senses provides a sounder basis for deciding how evident and striking their abnormal impressions were than the appeal to assent proposed by the Academics. Second, Antiochus disputed that dreamers or the insane *do* assent to their impressions in the same way as waking or sane persons. For example, he appealed to the similar phenomenon of inebriation:

> Even men acting under the influence of wine do not act with the same kind of approval as when they are sober. They waver, they hesitate, they sometimes pull themselves back. They give a feebler assent to their impressions. And when they have slept it off they realize how insubstantial those impressions were. (Cic. *Acad.* II.52)[49]

But in reminding us[50] of how the mad Heracles transfixed his own sons with his arrows when in the grip of hallucination the Academics had the better of the argument on both points. Perhaps a single example (such as Heracles' insanity) where assent to a false impression is best explained by its being as evident and striking as any true impression is not sufficient to make their case, but the ball ends up in the Stoic court.[51]

---

[49] See also S.E. *M* VII.247.   [50] Cic. *Acad.* II.89, S.E. *M* VII.405.

[51] Carneades' articulation of the dreaming and hallucination examples in terms of 'evident and striking' impressions (as Sextus represents him) suggests that he was directing his argument specifically against the position of the 'younger Stoics' (*M* VII.253), for whom the cognitive impression is not the criterion of truth unconditionally, but only when it has 'no impediment'. For 'this impression, *being evident and striking*, all but seizes us by the hair, they say, and pulls us to assent, needing nothing else to achieve this effect or to establish its difference from other impressions' (*M* VII.257).

The other principal problem for the cognitive impression developed by the Academics is described by Sextus as 'proving indiscernibility with respect to stamp and impress' (*M* VII.408).[52] It focused principally on the powers of discrimination of the wise. Even a wise person is unable to say infallibly which of two exactly similar eggs he is being shown; and he will 'get a false impression, albeit one from what is, and imprinted and stamped exactly in accordance with what is, if he has an impression of Castor as though it is of Polydeuces' (ibid. 410) – which since identical twins are coins from a single mint he very well might.

The Stoics' reply to this objection has already been explained in an earlier chapter. The Academics were unmoved by their rejoinders. Against the Stoic appeal to the metaphysical principle that no two individuals – not even two grains of sand – are qualitatively identical, they pitted Democritean metaphysics. Democritus held that some whole worlds 'completely and absolutely match each other in every detail, so that there is no difference between them whatever' (Cic. *Acad.* II.55). Why should not the same be true of individuals within one and the same world? But the Academics believed the more important issue concerned the wise person's powers of discrimination.[53] If someone has impressions of two individuals which satisfy the first two clauses of the Stoic definition but which he cannot successfully tell apart – even if (for the sake of argument) we grant that they *do* differ – then it follows according to the Academics that neither is 'of such a kind as could not arise from what is not'.

In order to see why they think this we need to notice an interesting assumption they are making about the third condition of the Stoic definition: if an impression is to count as being of such a kind as could not arise from what is not, the person who has it must be able to make discriminations which reflect the fact that it is of that kind. Someone whose impression of Castor was such as could not arise from Polydeuces must be able to tell that it could not – and his impression would therefore have to carry a 'mark' (*nota*) giving him that ability (Cic. *Acad.* II.84). It seems that the Stoics came to agree with this characterization of their position.[54]

The dispute about twins and eggs seems inconclusive. The Academics rightly insist that if they could produce cases of impressions the Stoics

<hr/>

[52] Cicero's discussion is fuller and richer: *Acad.* II.54–8, 84–6.

[53] See Cic. *Acad.* II.40, 57; cf. S.E. *M* VII.409–10.

[54] According to Sextus (*M* VII.252) the Stoics hold that a cognitive impression has a 'peculiarity' (*idiōma*; translated by Cicero as *nota*) which enables the person who experiences it to fasten on the objective *differentia* in things in a 'craftsmanlike way' (*technikōs*). This notion was evidently taken over by Antiochus: see e.g. *Acad.* II.33–6, 58.

would have to count as cognitive, but which even a wise person could not distinguish, then on reasonable assumptions about the nature of the Stoic theory its idea of a cognitive impression would be fatally undermined. The Stoics simply deny that there are any such cases. If a wise man could not discriminate between his impressions of eggs or twins, those impressions are not cognitive and he would be right to withhold assent. Perhaps that means that the Stoics are requiring a higher standard of *exactness* in cognitive impressions than might have been supposed. But if the higher standard makes its demands felt as stringent only in exceptional cases it is not clear that nature turns out to be less generous and providential in its *general* supply of reliable information.[55]

The Academics deployed many other *aparallaxia* arguments against the cognitive impression than the two examined in detail here. The whole critique was launched, according to Cicero, with more a priori considerations (*Acad.* II.47–8). For example, there was appeal to the likelihood that just as exactly the same state of shivering can be brought on either by internal imagining or by external threat, so exactly the same impression of the mind can be caused either by the imagination (as in dreams or madness) or by external causes. Another line of reasoning was given a soritical form. If some false impressions are persuasive, why not those that approximate very closely to true ones? And if these, why not those capable of being distinguished from true ones only with extreme difficulty? And if these, why not those which are no different from them at all? The critique was apparently rounded off with proofs that nothing could be cognitively grasped by reason or inference any more than by the senses.[56] Thus the Academics attacked the view that reason, for example, as employed in dialectic could discriminate between true and false. This seems to have been the context in which they used paradoxes like the Sorites and the Liar against the Stoics. Even a wise person cannot tell the difference between a cognitive impression that some number n is few and a non-cognitive impression that some other number $n+1$ is few.[57]

VII Carneades' 'probabilism'

Is the conclusion that nothing can be grasped cognitively itself something grasped cognitively? Arcesilaus said: No. Carneades conducted a debate on the question – no longer fully capable of reconstruction – with his

---

[55] For further discussion of the issues raised in this paragraph see above, pp. 306–11; also Annas 1990b.   [56] *Acad.* II.42; cf. 91–8.
[57] See *Acad.* II.91–8; cf. S.E. *M* VII.415–21. For discussion see Barnes 1982b, Burnyeat 1982b.

Stoic contemporary Antipater.[58] He too said: No. Cicero suggests a way in which a Carneadean might wish to elaborate on that answer. It is to say that the wise person has the impression that nothing can be grasped 'in just the same way as he has those other impressions that are acceptable but not cognitively grasped' (*Acad.* II.110). That is, his acceptance of the second-order proposition that nothing can be cognitively grasped is a matter of 'going along with' or 'following' without assent the acceptable impression that this is the case, just as his acceptance of first-order propositions consists simply in 'following' without assent the corresponding acceptable impressions.

In proposing this solution to the problem of the Academics' own stance, Cicero draws on Carneades' highly developed theory of impressions in general and 'acceptable' (*probabilia*) or 'convincing' (or 'persuasive': Greek *pithana*) impressions in particular. He has earlier informed us that the Academics began their exposition of their epistemology 'by constructing a sort of expertise concerning what we are calling "impressions", defining their power and their kinds, including among them the kind that can be cognized and grasped' (*Acad.* II.40). 'Their account', he adds, 'is as full as that given by the Stoics.' Sextus ascribes just such a detailed scheme to Carneades by name.[59]

The schema is most conveniently presented by a diagram:

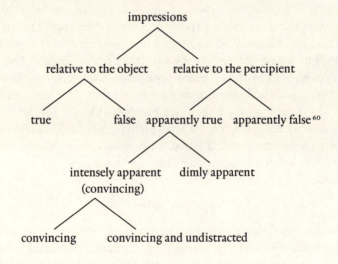

[58] See *Acad.* II.28, 109; discussion in Burnyeat 1997.
[59] See *M* VII.166–75. The diagram below does not attempt to capture all the distinctions Carneades drew.
[60] Carneades called the apparently true impression an 'appearance' (*emphasis*: following Stoic usage, D.L. VII.51), the apparently false an 'anti-appearance' (*apemphasis*), as being *un*persuasive and *un*convincing: *M* VII.169. Cicero seems to be rendering *emphasis* as *species* at *Acad.* II.58.

There is more to say about the last line of the right-hand division, since Carneades also spoke of impressions which were 'convincing and thoroughly examined'. But for the moment we may note the broad resemblance between the division as a whole and the Stoic classification of impressions, which was elaborated by permutations of the categories of the convincing and the unconvincing, the true and the false.[61] The key feature of Carneades' scheme is the fundamental distinction between truth and falsehood, which obtain with respect to the relation between impressions and the things or facts they purport to represent, and *apparent* truth and falsehood, which are merely functions of the way impressions seem to those who experience them. For Carneades there always remains an epistemological as well as a logical gap between the two sorts of assessments of impressions – they concern utterly different relations in which impressions stand.

That basic distinction is what Carneades exploits in his argument against Epicurean epistemology. As section VI of this chapter demonstrated, his chief complaint against Epicurus is effectively that he confuses what the Epicureans call 'evidence' (*enargeia*), which as properly understood is apparent truth, with truth. His further inference that *no* impression can be a criterion was derived, as we saw, from the consideration – fundamental to his critique of the Stoa – that for any true impression there can be an indiscernible false impression: which led him to say that the supposed criterion is merely an apparently true impression which 'spans [literally: 'is common to'] both true and false', and so is no criterion at all.[62] That formula recurs in Carneades' discussion of his classificatory scheme. It represents one of three ways of taking 'convincing' or 'persuasive': sometimes when we call an impression convincing or persuasive we mean to imply that it is true, sometimes that it is false, sometimes that it might be either. And Carneades comments that 'might be either' or 'spanning true and false' is what fits the supposed criterion of truth (S.E. *M* VII.173–5).

But Carneades also put his schema to more constructive work. Sextus claims that in some sense he *accepted* that convincing impressions 'spanning true and false' *were* after all the criterion of truth.[63] One way of construing

---

[61] Cf. S.E. *M* VII.242–52.   [62] See *M* VII.164; cf. Cic. *Acad.* II.33–4.

[63] See *M* VII.166; cf. 173–5. Sextus implies that Carneades took this position (as the Pyrrhonists did too: *PH* I.21–4, *M* VII.29–30) out of concern for 'the conduct of life and the attainment of happiness' – i.e. to meet the *apraxia* argument. Antiochus likewise claimed that the Academics made the *pithanon* their criterion, although 'both in the conduct of life and in inquiry and discussion' (*Acad.* II.32; cf. S.E. *M* VII.435–8). But while Clitomachus agrees in making 'following the *pithanon*' the Academic response to the charge of *apraxia* (Cic. *Acad.* II.104), he says nothing about its being the criterion of truth. It seems likely that it was Philo of Larissa (probably the target of the critique launched at *Acad.* II.32: see e.g. Sedley 1983a, 26) who first construed the *pithanon* as Carneades' *own* criterion.

this apparent *volte face* is to see it in terms of controversy with the Stoics. On this view what Carneades is saying is: *your* criterion of truth is simply misdescribed by you. The kind of impression you take to be the criterion is not a *cognitive* impression (there is no such thing), but a particularly striking form of apparently true impression which might be true or false. So either the kind of impression you identify as cognitive is not a criterion (because *not* in fact cognitive), or – if you insist that it *does* work as a criterion – what your position really reduces to is the view that *convincing* impressions are the criterion.

But Carneades was not simply showing something about Stoic epistemology and its collapse into a form of 'probabilism', even if the specific evidence of Carneadean endorsement of a 'criterion' is best interpreted as belonging to a dialectical context of that sort. On Clitomachus' presentation of the topic too, it was Carneades' own position that the wise person 'will make use of whatever impression acceptable in appearance he encounters, if nothing presents itself contrary to the acceptability of that impression, and his whole plan of life will be governed in this manner' (Cic. *Acad*. II.99).[64] Otherwise the *apraxia* argument against the Academy would succeed. If there were no acceptable or convincing impressions life would indeed be impossible, because there would be nothing that could incline us (rightly or wrongly) to one course of action rather than another. As will have been clear from the discussion in section v, this position is not in conflict with the Academic view that the wise man does not assent. The point is rather that he does not *need* assent or a criterion to live his life: 'following' convincing impressions without assent will suffice.

Carneades had a good deal to say about what 'following' convincing impressions involved.[65] It would often be a more active and critical business than talk of 'following' initially suggests. If there is time and the matter at issue sufficiently important, the wise person will put his impression through a series of checks – presumably because he is by hypothesis a perfectly rational person, and this is the rational thing to do.[66] The checking procedures described are compared to the cross-questioning of witnesses in court or to the scrutiny of candidates for political or judicial office; or

---

[64] At *Acad*. II.99–101 Cicero says he is drawing on the first volume of Clitomachus' four-book work on *epochē*. II.99 continues by *contrasting* Carneades' wise person with 'the person whom your school [sc. the Stoicizing Antiochus] bring on stage as the wise man'.

[65] See *M* VII.176–89, *PH* I.227–9; cf. *Acad*. II.35–6.

[66] That this is conceived as a *rational* procedure is argued e.g. by Bett 1989, 76–90; note that the outcome of the fullest testing is said to 'make the judgement most perfect' (*M* VII.181). On this interpretation Carneades' prescription of proper method may be construed as an elaboration of Arcesilaus' recommendation to follow what is rational (*eulogon*, *M* VII.158), and not simply as a description of *actual* practice in ordinary life – to which however it is compared (*M* VII.184).

again to the use by doctors of the examination of a syndrome of symptoms, for 'an impression never stands in isolation, but one depends on another like links in a chain' (S.E. *M* VII.176). An impression which passes such tests 'undistracted' (*aperispastos*) becomes more convincing, even though the possibility that it is in fact false can never be excluded. All Sextus' examples actually involve cases which *fail* examination: e.g. something which on a quick look leaves us convinced that it is a snake 'appears as a rope in virtue of an impression that is convincing *and* scrutinized' (*PH* 1.228).[67]

So much is clear about the theory. Accounts of its details given by our sources are confused and confusing. Cicero operates with a single contrast between acceptable impressions and impressions that are acceptable and 'not impeded' (*quae non impediatur*, *Acad.* 11.33:[68] his rendering of *aperispastos*, 'undistracted'). But Sextus thinks Carneades had a tripartite scheme: as well as satisfying himself that an impression is 'undistracted' or 'unimpeded' by the outcome of his checking, the rational person will want to ensure that it is 'thoroughly examined' (*diexhōdeumenē* or *perihōdeumenē*). Hence a convincing impression can become not only (at a second stage) more convincing, but (at a third stage) even more convincing. Unfortunately in the two versions of the theory he presents Sextus gives contradictory identifications of the second and third stages he introduces, and on both occasions other aspects of his treatment are also unsatisfactory.[69]

A better if necessarily conjectural interpretation takes Carneades to be envisaging not two possible *stages* in an inquiry into an impression, but simply two *sorts of testing*.[70] One focuses on its compatibility with other associated impressions, and may be taken as what Cicero's expression 'looking around' (*circumspectio*, *Acad.* 11.36) refers to. Here what will have been important is the *content* of the impressions examined. The analogy of a syndrome of medical symptoms seems appropriate to this form of scrutiny. The other kind of test focuses on the *background circumstances* involved: when the person having the impression had it, how far he was from the object represented in it, what condition his sensory equipment was in, how long he had to look or hear, etc. This is perhaps what Cicero means by talking of 'elaborate consideration' (*accurata consideratio*, ibid.),

---

[67] The version of this example in *M* VII.187–8 claims that after his tests the person following the method 'assents to the fact that it is false that the body presented to him is a snake'. This is one of several places where the account in *M* VII forgets that Carneades' wise person *refrains* from assent, i.e. judging that something is true, and simply 'goes along with' his convincing impressions.   [68] Cf. e.g. *Acad.* 11.99, 101, 104.   [69] Cf. e.g. Mutschmann 1911b.
[70] The following interpretation is due to Allen 1994.

and what corresponds to the analogy of cross-examination of witnesses or candidates.[71] Contrary to what Sextus implies, one might expect that in testing a convincing impression both these forms of scrutiny would be employed simultaneously. And it would be when an impression survives the application of the two together that it would count as 'undistracted' or 'unimpeded' by possible counter-evidence.

Partly because Cicero translated the Greek *pithanon*, 'convincing', into Latin as *probabile*, acceptable, the theory described above has often been construed as a form of probabilism. Denying as he does that we can ever conduct either our lives or our theoretical inquiries on the basis of knowledge, Carneades is seen as proposing that we should take probability as our guide – that is, we should work out what has more chances of being true than not, and let that govern our thoughts and actions. Little in the evidence supports this reading of the theory.[72] Cicero's choice of *probabile* is designed to connect with use of the verb *probare*, 'accept' or 'approve', as applied to the wise person's 'acceptance' of convincing impressions without assent. The process of testing by which such impressions are to be examined is certainly conceived as a *rational* procedure. But it is entirely focused on ensuring that the impressions on which we place reliance in important matters are internally consistent and not suspect on account of some abnormality in the circumstances in which they are experienced. It is not articulated as a form of calculation of the likelihood that they are actually true. No doubt an impression which fails some element of the scrutiny might seem less likely to be true, but that is not how Carneades puts the point. He says that what then happens is that some other impression drags or distracts us away from conviction.

VIII Conclusion

The framework of Carneades' thought is entirely Hellenistic: the major presences in his philosophizing are Epicurus, Chrysippus and Arcesilaus. We get no sense, as we do with Arcesilaus, of someone standing on the shoulders of Socrates and Plato. But like Arcesilaus Carneades rejected

---

[71] Allen 1994, 98–9, suggests that *circumspectio* may correspond to *perihōdeumenē phantasia*, *accurata consideratio* to *diexhōdeumenē phantasia*.

[72] But Sextus makes Carneades say that we should not distrust the impression 'which tells the truth for the most part [sc. that which spans true and false]: for both judgements and actions, as it turns out, are regulated by what holds for the most part' (*M* VII.175). 'As it turns out' suggests that this is not an account of a *calculation* we make in our response to a convincing impression. This may be another point at which the dogmatist assumptions of Sextus' source are showing through: see p. 336 n. 36 and p. 349 n. 67.

principally Stoic claims about knowledge. Like him, he shared the general Hellenistic hostility to assertion based on mere opinion. And like him he tried to show that it was possible nonetheless to do philosophy and to live one's life in accordance with reason. What Carneades offers is a model of rationality – testing convincing impressions and then 'following' them without assent to their truth provided they survive the scrutiny – which constitutes an ingenious and attractive alternative to the foundationalist epistemologies which prevailed in the other schools.[73] Whether the idea of a rationality without the commitments of assertion is a coherent notion remains a matter for debate.[74]

---

[73] He suggested that on Stoic premisses reason destroyed itself like Penelope undoing her web (Cic. *Acad.* II.95) or the octopus devouring its own tentacles (Plu. *Comm. Not.* 1059e, Stob. II.2.20): discussion by Burnyeat 1976, 62–5.

[74] For a sceptical exploration of this question see Burnyeat 1980a; cf. Bett 1989.

PART IV

PHYSICS AND METAPHYSICS

*

11

Hellenistic physics and metaphysics

DAVID SEDLEY

I Introduction

The Stoics are leading champions of the continuum, the Epicureans its leading opponents. Any such division of Hellenistic schools into continuists and discontinuists provides a useful skeleton, but one which needs careful fleshing out.

The Stoic world – like the Aristotelian world before it – is a continuum both materially and structurally: materially because it contains no void gaps, structurally because it is infinitely divisible, or divisible at any point. The Epicurean world is discontinuous in both ways: materially to the extent that it consists of bodies separated by void gaps, structurally both because those bodies are themselves unbreakable ('atoms') and because at a still lower level there is an absolute unit of magnitude not capable of analysis into parts (the 'minimum').

In case such a characterization should suggest that the material and structural continua are inseparably united, it is important to appreciate that this was by no means assumed by the contemporaries and immediate forerunners of Epicurus and Zeno. Strato of Lampsacus, head of the Peripatos during the later part of their careers, viewed the world as materially discontinuous, thanks to the existence of minute interstitial pockets of void, but as structurally continuous. If, as seems probable, he gave matter a particulate structure, this was in order to account for change, mixture and the like, and his particles were in no obvious sense indivisible. The same can probably be said of the puzzling theory of 'dissoluble lumps' (ἄναρμοι ὄγκοι) proposed by the Platonist Heraclides of Pontus in the mid or late fourth century BC.[1] Diodorus Cronus, on the contrary,

---

[1] This assumes that the findings of Vallance 1990, 1–43 on the meaning of ἄναρμοι ὄγκοι in Asclepiades (see below, p. 605) hold good for Heraclides too. But the matter is controversial: for a partly different reading see Gottschalk 1980, 37–57. Weakly particulate theories of matter probably retained considerable currency in the Hellenistic medical schools, but had little impact on philosophical discussions.

postulated material continuity but structural discontinuity.[2] Since Diodorus' theory is an integral part of the background to Epicurus' atomism, we shall turn to it first.

II Diodorus Cronus[3]

Although Diodorus is sometimes credited with a *bona fide* physical theory of elements[4] – that of 'minimal and partless bodies' – there is no evidence that he had any broader interest in physics and cosmology, and it looks rather as if the theory of minima was ancillary to his well-known four arguments against motion, to which we shall turn shortly.

The background to Diodorus' thesis lies in Plato's *Parmenides* and Aristotle, *Phys.* VI. At *Parm.* 138d–e it emerges that what is partless cannot move, since it could never be in transition to a new place, that is, part in and part out. Aristotle develops this difficulty in *Phys.* VI.10,[5] observing that partless items could be endowed with motion only on the unacceptable supposition that time consists of discrete instants, so that in each successive instant the partless item could occupy a different place, without there being any intervening time during which the transition occurs: thus it would (unacceptably, Aristotle suggests) be true to say of it that it 'has moved', but never that it 'is moving'.

Now when Aristotle speaks of a 'partless' item, he tends to have in mind a geometrical point, or a temporal instant, things which have no extension at all. His main concern is to show that these cannot be constitutive parts of, respectively, magnitudes and periods of time. That something might be partless yet extended is not a possibility Aristotle feels the need to confront explicitly, since he regards it as a mathematical nonsense (*Cael.* 303a2–4). It is doubtful whether the early atomists Leucippus and Democritus had made any such strong claims. But Aristotle's contemporary Xenocrates, in the Academy, was developing such a theory – the doctrine of 'indivisible lines' – and we even have a Peripatetic response to it in the pseudo-Aristotelian treatise *On indivisible lines*. Diodorus, however, probably Xenocrates' junior, propounded the earliest indivisibilist thesis for which we can reconstruct a plausible theoretical context.

Diodorus postulates ultimate constituents of the world which he names 'minimal and partless bodies' (ἐλάχιστα καὶ ἀμερῆ σώματα),

---

[2] So too perhaps Xenocrates, at least according to Aët. 1.13.3, 1.17.3, in addition to the testimony for his theory of 'indivisible lines': Xenocrates frr. 123–51 Isnardi.

[3] Texts: *SSR* II F 8–17. Discussion: Sedley 1977, Denyer 1981a, Sorabji 1983, 16–21, 369–71, Montoneri 1984, 126–40, Döring 1992, M. J. White 1992, 259–69.   [4] *SSR* II F 8–10.

[5] Cf. below, p. 377.

perhaps adding 'minimal' precisely in order to specify, with Aristotle's discussions in mind, that they are partless *yet extended* – not mere extensionless points, but vanishingly small dots of magnitude, of which larger magnitudes are composed in a sort of granular structure. He attributes a similarly granular structure to place too.[6]

How he defended the existence of these minima is not explicitly recorded. But there can be little doubt that the paradoxes of divisibility propounded in the fifth century BC by Zeno of Elea are their ultimate inspiration. In particular, Zeno had argued that movement is impossible through an infinitely divisible continuum, since it would involve passing, in sequence, an infinite series of discrete points; and also that an infinitely divisible magnitude, being the sum of its infinitely many parts, would have to be of infinite size (29 A 25, B 1 DK). According to Aristotle, it was Zeno's dichotomy paradox (a name applicable to both these arguments) that first inspired some thinkers to introduce 'atomic magnitudes' (Arist. *Phys.* VI.187a1–3). Given Diodorus' manifest Zenonian heritage, and Epicurus' appeal to the same Zenonian paradoxes for his own theory of minima,[7] it is hard to doubt that they form at least part of the background to his theory of minima. But there is also, recorded by Sextus Empiricus, one specific argument for spatial minima which may come from Diodorus:[8]

> If something is moving, it is moving now. If it is moving now, it is moving in the present time. If it is moving in the present time, it turns out that it is moving in a partless time. For if the present time is divided into parts, it will be absolutely divided into the past and future, and in this way it will no longer be present.
>
> If something is moving in a partless time, it is passing through places indivisible into parts. If it is passing through places indivisible into parts, it is not moving. For when it is in the first partless place, it is not moving, since it is still in the first partless place. And when it is in the second partless place, again it is not moving, but *has* moved. Therefore it is not the case that something is moving. (S.E. *M* x.119–20)

The concluding inference about motion will be discussed further shortly. Our present concern is with the argument from the partlessness of the present to the existence of partless places. The present must be a partless

---

[6] It is better to avoid the term 'atomism', despite its frequent use in connection with Diodorus in modern discussions, since when we come to Epicurus (below p. 374) we will have to maintain a clear distinction between atoms and minima. The term 'atom' is not attributed to Diodorus in the ancient sources.   [7] See below, pp. 374–5.

[8] As argued by Sorabji 1983, 19–21 and Denyer 1981a – even though Sextus himself at *M* x.142–3 appears not to know that its appeal to temporal minima is Diodorean. *Contra*, see Döring 1992, 115.

time, it is argued, because any separable parts of it would be hived off into the past or future. This partless time is presumably conceived as an irreducibly short period of time, not a durationless instant, if the following argument is to be intelligible. For Diodorus goes on to argue that in a partless time a moving object must traverse a partless place, i.e. a minimal unit of extension. (That a partless place is conceived by Diodorus as having extension is effectively confirmed at S.E. *M* x.86, where it is said to 'contain' a partless body.) And that could hardly be done in no time at all.

How does this inference from partless times to partless places work? The text leaves us to reconstruct it for ourselves. Within a single partless time, he may mean, it will be impossible to distinguish two or more separate sub-distances traversed in sequence by the moving object, since these would have to be traversed one by one in separate sub-times, and a partless time can contain no sub-times. We must conclude that either (a) the distance traversed in a partless time contains no sub-distances, or (b) it contains sub-distances which the moving object does not traverse or occupy at all, despite traversing the whole. Of these, (b) sounds sufficiently absurd to commend (a) as the more acceptable conclusion. And (a) entails that there are partless units of extension.

Thus Diodorus' thesis includes partless times, partless places, and partless bodies. The partless bodies are clearly minimal three-dimensional units, and since they are said to 'fill' the partless places (S.E. *M* x.86), these latter must also be extended in three dimensions. How does he conceive of 'place'? In the discussion of Diodorus' paradox at S.E. *M* x.95, his anonymous critics take a thing's place to be the body which surrounds it, e.g. the air round a person or the jar containing a liquid. But the discussion there is of macroscopic objects, and it is hard to see how Diodorus could have applied any such notion of place to that containing a partless body, since then its place would turn out to be identical with, or to include, the sum of all the partless bodies adjacent to it. If so, its place could not reasonably be called partless. And since the surrounding partless bodies might well be moving with it (if they jointly with it constituted a single solid object), Diodorus would have to abandon his analysis of a minimum's motion as transition *from* place *to* place.[9] We must therefore take it instead that the partless place which a minimum 'fills' is a three-dimensional stretch of space coextensive with it.[10]

---

[9] Analogous objections would apply to an Aristotelian-type view of place as the inner *surface* of the containing body.

[10] This implication will be important later, in connection with the origins of Epicurus' notion of space, p. 367.

Diodorus' objection to the idea of motion is that although we can say that a partless body is now in this partless place, P_1, now in a neighbouring partless place, P_2, it is at no time in transition between P_1 and P_2. The reason is that there can be no 'third place',[11] that is, one between P_1 and P_2. It could with equal propriety have been added that the partless body cannot be partly in P_1, partly in P_2, for the obvious reason that what is partless cannot be 'partly' in anything.

Diodorus' conclusion is not an absolute outlawing of motion, but the thesis that all motion is staccato. At the lowest level, that of an individual partless body, motion consists of a series of states of rest: it is now in P_1, now in P_2, now in P_3. As Diodorus puts it, following the lead of Aristotle, *Phys.* VI.10, it is true to say of a partless body 'It has moved', but never true to say 'It is moving'. Diodorus differs from Aristotle in regarding this paradoxical outcome as a perfectly correct account. He argues at some length for a thesis in tense logic,[12] that a proposition may be true in the past tense without ever having been true in the present tense (S.E. *M* x.97–101). I may truly say of two married men 'These men have married' without its ever having been true to say of them 'These men are marrying'.[13]

The aim of this staccato thesis is to accommodate the evident fact of motion:

> Therefore it is not moving. But it stands to reason that it *has* moved. For what was previously observed in this place is now observed in a different place – which would not have happened if it had not moved. (S.E. *M* x.86)

Diodorus must be picturing the world as follows. Space is analysable into innumerable juxtaposed partless granules. Every one of these is occupied by a partless body – for Diodorus explicitly denies the existence of void (S.E. *M* VIII.333). This absence of gaps might appear to leave no room for motion to take place. Yet there is nothing to stop a partless body from occupying different places at different times, provided that each of those places is simultaneously vacated by the partless body which occupied it at the preceding partless time. In the simplest case, two partless bodies could just swap places between one partless time and the next: since there was no intervening time, there is no question to be asked about how they manoeuvred round each other in order to get there. In a more complex and more plausible case, a cluster of partless bodies, constituting, say, a

---

[11] *M* x.143. The point is never made very clear, and it is curiously absent from the first formulation of the paradox at *M* x.86.

[12] A thesis Aristotle had never actually denied, and indeed had endorsed on other occasions, e.g. *Metaph.* B.1002a28–b11.

[13] Diodorus' 'clearer' example, S.E. *M* x.100–1, is altogether baffling.

stone, will occupy a succession of such positions in successive times, the
partless bodies of the surrounding matter (e.g. air or water) simultaneously redistributing themselves round it. Thus the visual impression of
motion is created, in a world which – in a gesture towards Eleatic thought
– is in fact a long series of static arrangements. A familiar twentieth-century comparison is the apparent movement of figures on video screen,
conveyed by a series of static patterns composed of individual pixels.

What is less clear is how, in such a world, different stuffs can be
differentiated. The Epicurean atomists are able to distinguish stuffs by the
different shape, size and spacing of their constituent atoms, but Diodorus
is denied that luxury, if his particles are all irreducibly small and crammed
up against each other. One possible solution is to suppose that they are
partless units of irreducibly different stuffs – e.g. water, earth and iron –
each with its own ineliminable properties. But there is no real evidence
even that Diodorus pronounced on the question, and we must be wary of
seeking a cosmological theory in what is primarily meant as a conceptual
analysis of body, motion and space.

This last point can be amplified by considering Diodorus' philosophical lineage. The Dialectical school, of which he was a leading member,[14]
almost certainly considered itself Socratic, being an offshoot from the
Megarian school, founded by the Socratic philosopher Euclides of
Megara. The Megarians themselves clearly made Socratic ethics their philosophical keynote, and above all the thesis of the unity of goodness. But
the Dialectical school was concerned with forms and methods of argument, and in view of its chosen title it seems a good guess that the school
considered the special emphasis on dialectical virtuosity to be Socrates'
true legacy. 'The greatest good for man', says Socrates in Plato's *Apology*
(38a), 'is to hold discussions every day about virtue and about the other
things about which you hear me conversing [*dialegomenou*, cognate with
'dialectic'] and examining myself and others, and the unexamined life is
not worth living for man . . .' Hence we need not be entirely surprised that
the school's title 'Dialectical' was taken as expressing its *ethical* orientation (D.L. 1.18). But if so, why does Diodorus add a distinctively Eleatic
dimension, emulating Zeno of Elea even to the extent of propounding his
own four paradoxes of motion, just as Zeno had done?[15] Perhaps on the

---

[14] Cf. p. 47, n. 105.

[15] It is sometimes supposed that the Eleatic denial of change was already part of the Megarian
tradition, on the strength of Aristotle, *Metaph.* Θ.3. But there the abolition of change is presented by Aristotle as an absurd and unwelcome implication of the Megarians' modal theory,
not as their own doctrine.

authority of Plato's *Parmenides*, where Socrates is portrayed as himself inviting and receiving a long lesson in what is, in effect, Zenonian dialectic. (We have already noted that Diodorus' arguments about the motion of the 'partless' have their origin in the *Parmenides*.) This might well have been read as an indication that if Socratic dialectic was to become a true science it must learn from Eleatic argumentation.

If this is on the right lines, we should take very seriously Sextus' ascription to Diodorus of mere 'hypotheses' about partless entities. Sextus uses the term 'hypothesis' three times for philosophical theses attributed to Diodorus (*M* x.85, 100, 111) – including that of partless entities – yet barely at all elsewhere for those of other philosophers.[16] Significantly, investigating the consequences of a hypothesis is the hallmark of dialectic as advocated in the *Parmenides*. By contrast, the denial of (present) motion is described by Sextus not as Diodorus' hypothesis, but as 'his own doctrine'.[17] The picture which thus begins to emerge from Sextus is of Diodorus advocating, as his own Eleatic doctrine, the denial of (present) motion, and basing it on four arguments, two of which start from the hypothesis of partless entities.[18] (For his second argument based on partless entities, see S.E. *M* x.113–17.)

For the other two arguments against motion attributed to Diodorus make no use of the partlessness assumption at all. The better known of these is dilemmatic in form:

> If something is moving, it is moving either in the place where it is, or in the place where it is not. But neither is it moving in the place where it is (for it is at rest in it), nor in the place where it is not (for it is not in it). Therefore it is not the case that something is moving. (S.E. *M* x.87)[19]

Why can it not be moving in the place where it is? The text quoted may seem to say that this is because to be in one place *is* to be stationary. But that would just collapse this argument into Diodorus' remaining, and much weaker, paradox, 'What is moving is immediately in a place; but what is in a place is not moving: therefore what is moving is not moving' (*M* x.112). (This has little plausibility unless the reference is taken to be to being in one place over some period of time, and that would in turn

---

[16] *M* vii.396 seems to be a solitary exception.

[17] *M* x.86, οἰκεῖον δόγμα. That the reference is to the denial of motion, not to the theory of minima, is shown by Döring 1992, 110.

[18] For the debate as to whether Diodorus' thesis of minima was merely a 'hypothesis', as distinct from his own physical tenet, cf. Giannantoni 1990, iv 79–80.

[19] Cf. *PH* ii.242, iii.71. The argument was well known as Diodorus', and should not be assimilated to Zeno's arrow, despite the lead given at D.L. ix.72. The dilemmatic form of the argument is characteristic of Diodorus, cf. *M* x.347.

require some further defence, such as the postulation of partless times.)
The more satisfactory answer, which can be indirectly recovered,[20] is that
the object cannot move in the place where it is because it completely fills
that place, thus leaving itself no room for manoeuvre.

III Epicurean physics

1. Introduction[21]

Epicurus, like Diodorus, has a thesis to propound about a set of ultimate
indivisibles. But this time we are dealing with a complete physical system,
and Epicurus' method is to develop it in linear fashion from a foundational series of principles, or 'elements'.[22] The following order of topics
was that of the opening books (roughly books I–X) of his great work *On
Nature*. We can reconstruct it from the surviving epitome, his *Letter to
Herodotus* (*Ep. Hdt.*) and amplify it further from parallel passages in
Lucretius' poem. Chapter references from the *Letter to Herodotus* are
added in brackets:

(a) The ultimate constituents of the 'all' must be permanent (38–9).
(b) The ultimate constituents of the 'all' are bodies and space (39–40).
(c) Other contenders for the role turn out not to exist independently of
    bodies and space (40).
(d) The ultimate bodies are atomic (40–1).
(e) Both body and space are infinite in extent (41–2).
(f) The range of atomic shapes is finite, the number of exemplars of each
    is infinite (42–3).
(g) The everlasting motion of atoms (43–4).
(h) The infinity of worlds (45).
(i) Perception (46–53).
(j) The properties and sizes of atoms (54–6).
(k) The ultimate structure of atoms – minima (56–9).
(l) Atomic motion, simple and in compounds (60–2).
(m) Soul (63–8).
(n) The metaphysical status of secondary properties (68–73).

Here it might be said that (a)–(c) map out the universe with very broad
brushstrokes. (d)–(h) draw in some basic dimensions: the limits, or
absence thereof, on size, shape and number. (i) explains perception to pre-

---

[20] From Sextus' discussion at *M* x.93 and 108–10, and from 86, even though this last is meant to be
about partless bodies.
[21] Main texts: Ep. *Ep. Hdt.* as cited directly below, and frr. 266–92 Usener, Lucr. I–IV.
[22] For this term (στοιχεῖα, στοιχειώματα), see Clay 1973, esp. 258–71.

pare the ground for (j). (j) distinguishes the primary properties, which atoms cannot lack, from perceptible properties. (k) takes the analysis of atoms to its most primitive level. (l) explains how atomic compounds function. (m) investigates the most advanced atomic compound. (n) stands back and reflects on the metaphysical implications of the foregoing.

While this may risk overschematizing Epicurus' exposition, we will in what follows see repeated signs of the scrupulous linear ordering of his demonstrations, so arranged as to presuppose nothing which is yet to be proved.

2. Conservation

Having set out his empiricist criteria of truth (*Ep. Hdt.* 37-8),[23] Epicurus opens his physical exposition with a set of laws which underline the permanence of the world's constituents – thus, as it were, underwriting the omnitemporality of the truths which will follow: 'Nothing comes into being out of what is not. For in that case everything would come into being out of everything, with no need for seeds' (*Ep. Hdt.* 38).

The argument for this is expanded by Lucretius (1.149–214). Everything that comes into being must be compounded out of things which pre-exist. If instead there were absolute generation from nothing, there would be no possible physical constraints on generation. Accordingly 'everything would come into being out of everything', that is, without restriction as to attendant circumstances. These circumstances are listed by Lucretius as location, season, timespan, sources of nutrition, and maximum size, all of which are seen in natural processes to be closely circumscribed. Fish are not born on dry land, apples don't grow on peach trees, and nothing grows without nutrition. Epicurus, followed by Lucretius, sums up these regularities by referring to the role of seeds in biology, no doubt on the ground that the growth of a seed to maturity encapsulates all these constraints. We must take it that comparable constraints are meant to apply to inorganic generation (processes of manufacture, etc.), but no examples are given.[24]

Confusion may be caused by the fact that Lucretius, throughout this set of arguments, exploits the double meaning of 'seeds', i.e. biological seeds and also atoms, in order to imply a dependence of natural regularity on the atomic composition of things,[25] appealing for example to the fact

[23] See above, pp. 262-4.   [24] See also below, pp. 498-503.
[25] 'Seeds' are biological at 160, 'atoms' at 176, 185, 221; indeterminate at 169, 189. That 'seeds' can mean 'atoms' Lucretius has already forewarned us at 59.

that plants can grow only when and where the right 'seeds of things' flow together to generate them. It is of the utmost importance to see that this, like other covert references to atoms in the same passage,[26] is a rhetorical device on Lucretius' part, quite alien to Epicurus' own more severe methodology. Several more steps have yet to be accomplished before the existence of atoms can be established. Epicurus' own reference to 'seeds' (above) is to be taken at face value, as an appeal to biological regularity.[27]

Epicurus continues as follows: 'Also, if that which disappears were destroyed into what is not, all things would have perished, for lack of that into which they dissolved' (*Ep. Hdt.* 39). Lucretius once again amplifies, adding two further arguments (1.217-24, 238-49): if there were literal annihilation, destruction would be an instantaneous process, and all things, however composed, would be destroyed with equal ease. Both arguments rely on the firmly empirical premiss that destruction is visibly a gradual process, requiring the application of an appropriate force to disintegrate cohesive parcels of matter.

Here then we have the first two laws of conservation: there is no literal generation from nothing or annihilation. The two principles are as old as philosophy. They underlie the insistence of the sixth-century BC Milesian philosophers on an everlasting primary stuff. They were defended on idiosyncratic logical grounds by the anti-empiricist Parmenides in the fifth century, and the former of them was invoked as a self-evident truth by his follower Melissus. Many Greek philosophers regarded them as conceptually indubitable laws. Against this background, what is remarkable about Epicurus' defence of them is its determinedly empirical tone. Although appeals to what is conceivable will play a part in some of his later arguments, his pointed empiricism on this opening issue sets a clear keynote for his style of physical speculation. It confirms his seriousness about the empiricist criteria of truth with which he prefaces his exposition.

Looking ahead, we may feel that this empiricism has at least one unfortunate limitation, namely its restriction to processes of *corporeal* change. The laws of conservation are meant to apply equally to space (or 'void'), the second constituent of the 'all' alongside body (see next section). But in practice none of the arguments given by Lucretius applies to it, and Epicurus' eventual success in convincing us of the permanence of space will depend on independent considerations, especially its intrinsic incapacity to be causally affected (explicitly at Lucr. III.811-13).

---

[26] *Genitalia corpora, materies, corpora prima, primordia rerum.*
[27] As a matter of fact, 'seeds' in Greek lacks the sense of 'primary particles' conferred on it in Lucretius' Latin.

The same issue must be borne in mind when we turn to the following proof:

> Moreover, the all was always such as it is now, and always will be. For there is nothing into which it changes, and[28] there is nothing over and above the all which could pass into it and produce the change. (Ep. *Ep. Hdt.* 39)

The basic claim here is, not of course that the universe does not change at all, but that the sum total (the 'all') of what there is does not change. To understand the grounds for this, we must look at a more explicit formulation, used by Lucretius at a later stage:

> ... the sum of sums is everlasting, and there is no place outside for things to disperse into, nor bodies which might fall into it and break it up by the strength of their impact. (Lucr. III.816–18)[29]

Here the argument is clear: the universe cannot be disrupted through subtraction or addition of *bodies*, since there is no space outside it for bodies to move into, and no bodies outside to enter it. In contrast, Epicurus' scrupulousness in avoiding mention of body and space, whose role as ultimate components has yet to be established, typifies his strict linear methodology.

A critic might ask whether the argument is intelligible without covert assumption of these notions of body and space. For example, wouldn't the same argument be baffling if used to establish the permanence of non-spatial entities like Platonic Forms? To mount a defence of Epicurus' procedure, one must re-emphasize the empiricist criteria of truth with which he prefaces his physical exposition. In that light, the mapping out of the universe into body and space, which will now follow, can be seen less as the introduction of some brand new entities than as the whittling down of an already familiar empirical universe to its most elementary components.

To sum up, we have now seen Epicurus outlaw any change in the basic composition of the universe, whether by generation of new entities, by annihilation of existing entities, by removal of parts, or by importation of new parts. As we proceed, it will become clear that he also holds the basic existing items to be absolutely unchangeable qualitatively: if they could change, then the regularities of nature would be seen to change with them. Lucretius, at least, objects to qualitative change at the basic level on the grounds that this is tantamount to destruction of the old plus generation

---

[28] The two successive uses of γάρ ('for') give two co-ordinate reasons for what is stated in the first sentence: see Brunschwig 1977, 128.   [29] See also II.304–7 and v.361–3.

of the new (I.670-1, 792-3, II.753-4, III.519-20). The point is that qualitative change in a compound, e.g. wood becoming fire, can be due to mere redistribution of enduring components, but qualitative change in something irreducibly simple must be an intrinsic change in what the thing itself is. The Epicureans' real objection to that is that it would conflict with the perceived stability of nature – an objection we will not encounter until we reach the arguments for atoms. For now, we can simply note that this is one kind of possible change in what the universe consists of which none of their arguments, as reported so far, has ruled out of court.

3. Body and space

Moreover, the all is bodies and void. That bodies exist is universally witnessed by sensation itself, in accordance with which it is necessary to judge by reason that which is non-evident, as I said above. And if place, which we call 'void', 'room', and 'intangible substance', did not exist, bodies would not have anywhere to be or to move through, as they are observed to move. (Ep. *Ep. Hdt.* 39–40)

That bodies exist is presented here as inseparably bound up with the empiricist criteria of truth. The claim, however, is not just that they exist, but that they exist *per se* or as independent substances,[30] that is, they are not parasitic on, or reducible to, something more fundamental. Might not bodies themselves be further analysable, for example (to adapt an Aristotelian view of the elements) into combinations of sensible properties like hot, cold, wet and dry? No explicit Epicurean defence against this possibility is recorded. But their clear position is that a property like heat is only intelligible as the hotness *of some body*,[31] and that the only items in the world perceived as being free of such dependence are bodies and space. Bodies, given their ability to move, simply are the most obviously independent items in our experience. And that in turn makes it inescapable that the spaces which they vacate as they move must exist independently of *them*.

A further point to bear in mind is that 'bodies' here is being left as a completely unrefined notion, beyond the inescapable fact that they at least include phenomenal bodies. No talk of atoms has yet been allowed to intrude: before atoms can be made intelligible, we need the notion of empty space.[32]

---

[30] This is more explicit in the expanded version given at Lucr. 1.419–48. See below, pp. 369–71.

[31] Cf. below, pp. 380–2.

[32] The interpretation of space defended here (including the readings of the Epicurus and Lucretius texts) is largely that in Sedley 1982a.

Epicurus may seem to conflate, even to confuse, two different kinds of space, namely 'void' and 'place'. Void is empty, whereas place, in ancient usage, is always *something*'s place, i.e. an occupied location, and hence not void. When Epicurus lists four interchangeable terms – 'place' (τόπος), 'void' (κενόν), 'room' (χώρα) and 'intangible substance' (ἀναφὴς φύσις, lit. 'intangible nature') – and adds that the thing in question is needed to provide bodies with somewhere *to be*, as well as with movement, the impression is strengthened that he is failing to maintain a distinction between full and empty space.

We may speculate on the motives of this conflation. In his critique of void in *Phys.* IV.8, Aristotle had raised the question what happens to a stretch of void when a body enters it, supplying the problematic answer that it will have to remain and become coextensive with the body. But how, we may wonder, can it still be 'void'? Epicurus, if he worried about the same question, could hardly respond with the countersuggestion that the void is displaced, or ceases to exist: void cannot be displaced, since it cannot be acted upon at all;[33] and to allow it to cease to exist would contravene the laws of conservation already established. His solution is to accept that void can indeed be occupied by body without ceasing to exist. It does so, however, not *qua* void, but *qua* space. His generic name for space is, we are told (S.E. *M* x.2), 'intangible substance'. This is what we might call geometrical space, or container space – a three-dimensional extension which persists whether occupied or unoccupied by body. When it is occupied, it is called 'place'; when unoccupied, 'void'; and when bodies are moving through it, 'room' (χώρα, etymologically linked with χωρεῖν, 'to go'). But according to Epicurus, these are inessential differences, of little more than linguistic interest (Aët. x.20.2), and as a result he makes a point of shifting indifferently between them in his own usage.

Such a conception was not entirely new. Aristotle had already described the notion of geometrical space in order to reject it (*Phys.* IV.4), and we have seen that Diodorus must have operated with some such notion of 'place'.[34] However, neither Aristotle nor Diodorus allowed the possibility that a place could come to be empty, and it was left for Epicurus to work out and defend the formal relation of identity between place and void.

The hallmark of this entity – space, as we may from now on call it for our own convenience – is that it is three-dimensionally extended yet non-resistant (hence 'intangible') – properties which are entirely unaffected by

---

[33] See below, pp. 367–8.   [34] Above, p. 358.

the presence, absence or passage of bodies. That hallmark is the basis for the formal proof that the 'all' is exhaustively analysable into body and space (Lucr. 1.430–9). If something has its own independent existence, it is argued, it must have some volume. If a thing with volume is resistant, it is body. If non-resistant, it is space. Therefore all existing things are either body or space.

This still leaves Epicurus the task of proving that some space is empty – that there is 'void' in the strict sense. Absolute vacuum was a conception which few of Epicurus' predecessors had thought coherent, the primary exception being the early atomists. In his own day its coherence was generally accepted.[35] But it remained in dispute whether there is in fact any vacuum within the cosmos, the Stoics in particular championing the view that there is not.

Against those earlier thinkers who had held vacuum to be an incoherent notion (for example, because it allegedly requires the existence of the non-existent), or those, like the Stoics, who exclude void altogether from the cosmos, the Epicureans offer an experiment.[36] Take two flat-edged objects, juxtapose them, then pull them apart. However fast the air may rush in to fill the gap thus created, it cannot fill the whole of it in no time at all. Therefore a temporary vacuum must be created.

The arguments for the actual existence of vacuum in the world are also empirical. The phenomena of motion, permeation, and relative weight are only explicable if one supposes there to be void gaps within or between bodies (Lucr. 1.329–69). Lucretius cites and counters a favourite response of the continuists (1.370–84), that motion can occur even in a plenum by redistribution, in the way that water redistributes itself round a fish as it swims. Lucretius' reply is that even here there must be void: otherwise the fish could not move forward until the water in front had moved behind it, and the water could not move behind the fish until the fish had already moved – a literal *impasse*. Clearly this reply is inadequate, since it fails to allow for *simultaneous* redistribution. (If valid, it would prove too much, e.g. that a wheel cannot rotate, since each segment must wait for the segment in front to move first.) But the real nub of the disagreement lies elsewhere. Lucretius is here already anticipating one thesis of atomism, namely that body *per se* is completely rigid. For in a world of rigid bodies without gaps redistribution would indeed seem either impossible or at least massively complex. The continuist opponents – who include

---

[35] At least by the Stoics (below, pp. 395–7) and by the Peripatetic Strato (above, p. 355).
[36] Lucr. 1.384–97, an argument which, despite its presentation by Lucretius, must have been designed to show that vacuum can be created, not that it already exists in nature.

Aristotle and, in due course, the Stoics – assume infinitely divisible matter, which could in principle be fluid through and through, and hence yielding. We can see in this disagreement the effects of Epicurus' dichotomy between body and space: since, as we have learnt, body's resistance and space's non-resistance are their defining characteristics *par excellence*, body *per se* is treated as absolutely resistant, *space* as absolutely non-resistant. Intermediate states, such as softness and fluidity, will be attributed to the presence of void gaps within compound bodies.

We may end this section by considering Epicurus' exhaustive division of 'the all' into body and space. Since space is not just vacuum but can be coextensive with body, we should not see Epicurus' division as a horizontal mapping out of the world into two co-ordinate elements, one negative one positive, comparable to the division of a monochrome computer-screen into black and white pixels. In the Epicurean world, compound objects are made exclusively of body, and neither space nor, more specifically, vacuum is ever considered a second constituent or element alongside it. Rather, space is analogous to the computer screen itself. It stands in the background, providing bodies with location, with the gaps between them, and with room to move. Body and space are the only two ultimate components of the 'all' in the sense that they alone have *independent* existence. Everything else, we shall learn next, is parasitic for its existence on body and space. But space itself is not parasitic on body, because it continues to exist even when no body is present.

4. Elimination of other per se existents

At *Ep. Hdt.* 40, Epicurus simply adds:

> Beyond these [i.e. body and space], nothing can even be thought of, either by imagination or by analogy with what is imagined, as completely substantial things and not as the things which we call accidents and properties of these.

At the corresponding point in Lucretius (1.445–82) we receive a fuller account. Apart from body and space, all other things designated by their own names will turn out to exist not *per se* but as properties of body and void. He lists four such pretenders. The first two are inseparable properties and accidental properties. These, which we will examine more carefully later,[37] are introduced here simply as properties which are, respectively, essential and inessential to a thing's continued existence. The thing to which they belong is itself a *per se* (= independent) existent

---

[37] Below, pp. 380–2.

(body as such, or such and such a kind of body, or void), and the point made is that its properties, whether inseparable or separable, are parasitic on it for their own being, that is, they do not exist as further *per se* entities. It may be wondered why the distinction between inseparable and accidental properties need have been introduced at all at this stage. One reason is no doubt that it was needed for repeated use over the coming sections, especially in analysing the primary properties of atoms and those acquired by compounds – even though in our very brief surviving epitome few explicit traces survive.[38] Epicurus may also, in the original discussion, have wanted the opportunity to make the important distinction that the separability of a property – such as that of slavery from a human being, as contrasted with the inseparability of tangibility from body – is the ability of the property's bearer to survive without the property, with no implication at all that the property can survive without the bearer. At least, there can be no doubt that the central message is that for *all* properties, whether inseparable or accidental, sensible or (as in Lucretius' example 'freedom') abstract, to exist just is to belong to some *per se* entity. This states – though in its surviving form it does not argue – a crucial anti-Platonic point. For it was Plato's most characteristic doctrine that numerous properties exist primarily *per se* and only secondarily by belonging to spatio-temporal subjects.

The third pretender to *per se* existence is time. But unlike space, time proves to be parasitic for its existence on bodies:

> Time, likewise, does not exist *per se*: it is from things themselves that our perception arises of what has happened in the past, what is present, and further what is to follow it next. It should not be conceded that anyone perceives time *per se* in separation from things' motion and quiet rest.
> (Lucr. 1.459–63)

The Epicurean Demetrius of Laconia (*c.* 100 BC)[39] explains that time is parasitic on the motion and rest of bodies, and that *measured* time depends in particular on the motion of the sun. Motion and rest are themselves accidental properties of bodies, so time is, according to Demetrius' interpretation of Epicurus, an 'accident of accidents' of bodies.[40]

Finally, Lucretius adds a most curious fourth pretender: facts about the past (1.464–82), such as the (presumed) fact that the Greeks defeated the

---

[38] Accidental properties occur in the account of soul at *Ep. Hdt.* 64 and 67.

[39] Reported at S.E. *M* x.219–27. He appears to be giving a formal analysis of Ep. *Ep. Hdt.* 72–3.

[40] 'Accident' of accidents presumably because, although it is an inseparable property of all motion that it takes time, it is accidental that any individual motion takes the particular time that it does.

Trojans. It is clear enough why these pose a difficulty for the Epicureans. Such facts surely do have continuing existence, in at least as strong a sense as that in which an abstract property like freedom exists. How then can we explain the anomaly that, whereas freedom only continues to exist so long as at least one currently existing *per se* thing is free, the fact that the Greeks defeated the Trojans continues to be a fact even though none of the *per se* things of which it is true – Agamemnon, Priam etc. – still exists? Since there is no one around for it to be a property of, it seems to follow that it itself exists *per se*, that is, independently of the bodies of which it is true.

That is the challenge, and the first Epicurean answer is that there *is* still something for such facts to be properties of, namely the world. Let us call this the geographical answer. The fact that there was a Trojan War survives as an accidental property of the world, or more specifically of places like Troy and Mycenae.[41] Lucretius then adds an even simpler solution: you can if you like call the fact an accidental property of body and space. For (he seems to mean) the body of which the participants were composed, and the space in which they acted, must, as we know by now from the laws of conservation, still exist. We may call this the metaphysical answer.

The attractiveness of the geographical answer is that if I point at the site of Troy and say 'The Greeks razed this city to the ground', I am indeed talking about a property of an existing thing. Historical facts live on *in their present effects*[42] (perhaps another such present effect is the *Iliad*). If the Epicureans were uneasy with this solution, and felt impelled to add the metaphysical answer, that may be because of a worry that truths about the past would otherwise be erased when the present world ceased to exist. Thereafter, only the indestructible body and space would be available as their bearers.[43] The disadvantage of this resort – albeit not a fatal one – is that the disposition of body in the universe at large could not plausibly have its causal history written on it in any way comparable to the site of Troy, and, much worse, space could not have *any* causal history written on it, being in the Epicureans' own view totally incapable of being acted upon.

---

[41] Lucr. 1.469–70, 'the world, . . . actual places'.

[42] Note the analogy with the Epicurean position on truths about the future: these exist only if *causes* sufficient to bring them about already exist now.

[43] Lucr. 1.471–82 may appear to deny facts about the past independent existence merely on the ground that they could not have occurred if there *had not been* body and space. But (a) that would fail to address the stated issue of their *present* existence, and (b) it would invite the retort that in that case body lacks independent existence because it could not exist without space to be in.

5. Atoms

Only now does Epicurus turn to his proof that body is atomic.

> Of bodies, some are compounds, others the things from which the compounds have been made. These latter are atomic [lit. 'uncuttable'] and unalterable – if all things are not going to be destroyed into the non-existent but be strong enough to survive the dissolution of the compounds – full in nature, and incapable of dissolution at any point or in any way. The primary entities, then, must be atomic kinds of bodies. (Ep. *Ep. Hdt.* 40-1)

Epicurus starts from the undeniable empirical fact that there are compound bodies. If there are compounds, it follows that there must be components.[44] Epicurus' language here implies an active notion of components: not merely items which a compound consists of, but items which have *come together* to constitute it and which will separate when it is destroyed. Given this expectation, it follows in Epicurus' view that there are ultimate components which do not themselves have components. If they did, real destruction would be the compound's separation into those. And if they too had components, and so on *ad infinitum*, a thing's destruction would be pulverization into sizeless bits, i.e. into nothing. That would immediately contravene the second law of conservation, 'Nothing is destroyed into nothing'.[45] Hence the components of body must be particles which have not been compounded out of, and cannot be fragmented into, anything smaller. And those are, in a word, 'atoms'.

How could bodies be breakable at some points but not at others? The atomist answer is that bodies can be broken apart along void gaps between their constituents, but not elsewhere. And in that case what makes an atom atomic can only be that it contains no void gaps at all. Accordingly the binary mapping out of the universe into bodies and (partly empty) space[46] itself grounds the further refinement that at the lowest level of analysis body is atomic – incapable of further fragmentation.[47]

Finally (Lucr. 1.584-98) this result is confirmed, in the view of the Epicureans, by the observed regularities of nature, which seem to survive all individual processes of disintegration.[48] Only if all such processes yield matter with absolutely fixed properties can we begin to see how, when

---

[44] Lucr. 1.483-4 undermines the force of this implicit inference by reversing the order: 'Some bodies are primary particles, others are composed of a collection of primary particles.'
[45] See further Lucr. 1.540-64.   [46] See above, pp. 366-9.   [47] See further Lucr. 1.503-39.
[48] See Long 1977.

recombined, it should carry on just as before. That means that the ultimate components must be inherently unchangeable. This the atoms undoubtedly are. The same cannot be said for the stuffs other philosophers offer as elementary – for example, earth, air, fire and water.[49]

6. Infinity

The infinity of time is not treated as requiring separate proof. Time, we have seen, exists so long as there are moving bodies, and the demonstration of the permanent nature of what there is can thus with retrospect be seen to have established that past and future time are infinite.[50]

What has now to be explicitly (*Ep. Hdt.* 41–2) added is that the two independent existents in the universe, body and space, are themselves infinite in extent. Epicurus' arguments to this effect are discussed elsewhere in this volume.[51] Another aspect of infinity then follows. The number of atomic types in the universe, although it must be unimaginably large in order to account for the full diversity of phenomena, is finite; but there are infinitely many tokens of each type (*Ep. Hdt.* 42–3). The reason for considering the number of atomic types finite is as follows (cf. Lucr. 11.478–531). (i) Within a finite size range only a finite number of atomic shapes can be found; so (ii) if there were infinitely many different atomic shapes, (iii) there would be an infinite range of atomic sizes.

(iii) is held to be incredible partly because it would mean 'expanding atoms to absolute infinity in their sizes' (*Ep. Hdt.* 43). What does this mean? If the conclusion were (as Lucretius takes it to be, 11.481–2) that some atoms would be infinitely large, that would indeed be an objectionable consequence, since the motions and collisions of such atoms would surely be beyond comprehension. But in fact Epicurus seems only entitled to the conclusion that for any given size there would be atoms which exceeded it, and it is not immediately clear why that need be objectionable. He does later explicitly deny that there could conceivably be atoms large enough to see (*Ep. Hdt.* 55–6), but the grounds are left obscure.[52]

---

[49] Lucr. 1.665–89, 753–62, 782–829, 847–58.

[50] Lucr. 1.233, already appeals to the infinity of past time in his proof of the second law of conservation, 'Nothing is destroyed into nothing': otherwise *in the infinity of past time* all matter would have been used up. Since they have already proved that nothing absolutely comes into being, the Epicureans are indeed by now entitled to the premiss that there has always been something in existence. It is enough that they should be careful not to imply anything about the metaphysical status of time at this early stage.   [51] See below, p. 419.

[52] Lucretius' discussion of the same point, referred to at 11.498–9, is unfortunately missing from the text. Of course, such an atom could not be seen in the normal way, see above, pp. 264–9, since it could not give off *eidōla*; but it could appear as a black patch, obscuring whatever was behind it. The empirical absence of large atoms, which Epicurus mentions, could be attributed to the sorting of different grades of atom in cosmogony, with the large ones sinking far down below us.

The more intriguing question is how Epicurus justifies (i). In the fuller
and more explicit treatment given by Lucretius (II.483–96), the argument
relies on the theory that any atom is analysable into a set of minimal magnitudes. There is only a finite series of arrangements into which any given
set of these minima can be placed. Here the unstated premiss is that two
adjacent minima cannot have their relative position varied by a distance of
less than one whole minimum, there being no such distance. A useful
analogy is with a sheet of graph paper on which you make shapes by filling
in whole squares, taken to be the smallest units in the design:[53] on a single
sheet of graph paper, there will be a finite number of possible shapes, since
the positions of adjacent squares relative to each other cannot be indefinitely varied.

Lucretius has by this stage already introduced the theory of minima,
whereas Epicurus at the equivalent point in his exposition has not. This
may explain why Epicurus' own statement of (i) offers no comparable
argument. How he justified (i) in the corresponding full exposition in *On
Nature* is a matter for speculation. He may have simply referred forward,
saying that the point would only be demonstrable once infinite division
had been ruled out. That would explain why a scholiast adds to the statement of (i) at *Ep. Hdt.* 42–3 the gloss, 'For nor, he says later, does division
go on to infinity.'

7. *Minima*[54]

Epicurus starts by making the first clear distinction in ancient thought
between (i) things which are physically indivisible, and (ii) things so small
that there *is* nothing smaller, which modern scholarship sometimes calls
theoretically, conceptually or mathematically indivisible, but which in
ancient usage are called either 'minimal' (ἐλάχιστα) or 'partless' (ἀμερῆ).
Not only, he says (*Ep. Hdt.* 56), (i) can things not be 'cut' to infinity (and
here we must remember that atoms are literally 'uncuttables'), as proved
earlier, 'but also (ii) we must not consider that in finite bodies there is *traversal* to infinity, not even through smaller and smaller parts'.

Traversal here means moving along a magnitude part by part, the
assumption being that by so doing you pass every one of its parts in
sequence. If it contained infinitely many parts – even, he says, parts
ordered in a convergent series like 1/2, 1/4, 1/8 . . . – you could never com-

---

[53] Furley 1967, 41–3.
[54] Texts: Ep. *Ep. Hdt.* 56–9; Lucr. 1.599–634. Comment: Mau 1954a, Vlastos 1965, Furley 1967,
Krämer 1971, Sedley 1976b, Sorabji 1983, Long and Sedley 1987, vol. 1, 39–44; M. J. White
1992, 269–80; Purinton 1994.

plete the traversal. This in effect re-applies the old dichotomy paradox of Zeno of Elea[55] which, according to Aristotle, had stimulated the original fifth-century atomic theory, and which seems to have been subsequently invoked in defence of mathematical indivisibles by Xenocrates. Epicurus adds the further Zenonian objections that a magnitude consisting of infinitely many parts would itself be infinite (deriving from Zeno fr. B1 DK), and that by thinking your way along such a magnitude bit by bit you would, impossibly, 'reach infinity in thought', count to infinity.[56]

By showing that a finite body cannot contain an infinite number of parts, Epicurus considers that he has established the existence of an absolutely smallest portion of body. Henceforward he feels entitled to refer to this as 'the minimum in the atom': clearly it cannot be larger than an atom, or it would not be a minimum, so it must be either an entire atom or part of one. (Why it cannot in fact be an entire atom we will learn later.)

Aristotle in *Physics* VI had mounted an attack on the idea that partless entities could ever be constituent parts of magnitudes.[57] One ground was the difficulty of seeing how two adjacent partless items could be in contact. Not part to part, in the sense edge to edge, since being partless they could not have distinct parts. And not whole to whole either, or they would be coincident, not adjacent. Therefore partless entities could never combine to compose a larger magnitude. This argument gained some currency in the Hellenistic age. Whether it passed through the hands of Diodorus is not known, but it was used by the Stoics in defence of continuum theory (Plu. *Comm. Not.* 1080e), and in the present passage we find Epicurus offering an ingenious reply to it.

To this end, Epicurus offers an analogy. Compare a minimum, the smallest magnitude there is, to 'the minimum in sensation', the smallest magnitude you can see. This must be perceived as partless, since any part of it would be below your visual threshold. If you place a set of these visible minima side by side, they will build up a larger visible magnitude. Yet the interrelation between them as you see it is neither part-to-part contact (you cannot see their parts), nor complete coextensivity. How then do they combine? 'In their own special way' is the most Epicurus ventures on the matter. Moreover, he adds, any larger visible magnitude will prove to consist of an exact number of visible minima. This last inference seems a sound one: when you have divided a visible magnitude up into visible

[55] See above, p. 357.
[56] See [Arist.] *Lin. Insec.* 968a19–22 for the attribution of a similar argument to Zeno, whether historical or not. For a fourth Epicurean argument in the same vein, see Lucr. 1.615–22.
[57] Cf. p. 356 above.

minima, there cannot be a fraction of a visible minimum left over, since any such fraction would be invisibly small.

Therefore real minima, those 'in the atom', can after all be so arranged in relation to each other as to constitute an atom. The analogy shows, at the very least, that Aristotle's list of the ways in which juxtaposition can occur is not exhaustive – we can actually *see* it happening in a third way – and that his argument against the combination of real minima into larger magnitudes therefore fails. Some have further inferred that Epicurus must think of these real minima, the ones 'in the atom', as being 'conceptually' indivisible, with conceiving taken to be itself a kind of mental seeing analogous to literal seeing. But this is an overinterpretation of the analogy. 'Conceptual' or 'theoretical' indivisibility is a purely modern import to the debate. The status of Epicurus' minima is an objective one, as the smallest magnitudes there are, and contains no epistemological component.

Epicurus now specifies one further lesson that the analogy can teach us, and one that it cannot. What we are entitled to infer is that real minima, analogously to their visible counterparts, are exact submultiples of all larger magnitudes. The reason is clear: when a magnitude has been analysed into component minima, there could not be *part* of a minimum left over. Now this, as Epicurus is well aware, is a radical proposal which undercuts the basis of conventional geometry. Mathematicians had long known that geometrical figures contain incommensurable lengths, most notoriously the side and diagonal of a square. According to the Epicurean theory, there can be no incommensurable lengths, since all have a common submultiple. It follows that geometry is dealing with impossible figures: the world can contain no perfect squares.

That Epicurus drew and accepted this consequence is likely, since he is said to have persuaded his leading pupil Polyaenus, formerly a distinguished mathematician, to reject geometry as false.[58] It may be more accurate to say that Polyaenus challenged the basis of geometry, while leaving open the technical possibility that an Epicurean rescue of it could be launched. There are two grounds for this. First, although some later Epicureans continued to reject conventional geometry, others did apparently practise it,[59] and since Polyaenus had authoritative standing in the school as one of the four founding fathers they could not have done so if he had unambiguously outlawed it. Second, Polyaenus wrote a mathematical work called *Aporiai*, 'Puzzles', and that these were interpretable as

---

[58] On the Epicureans and geometry see below, pp. 587–90.   [59] Evidence in Sedley 1976b.

soluble puzzles is shown by the surviving fragments of reply to them by the late second-century BC Epicurean Demetrius of Laconia, *Reply to Polyaenus' Puzzles* (Πρὸς τὰς Πολυαίνου Ἀπορίας).[60]

Finally Epicurus draws the limits of the analogy. Although minima are the components of larger magnitudes, they differ from visible minima in not being *movable* components. That is, no minimum is a discrete component which can be detached and relocated. Or, to put it another way, no atom is constituted by a single minimum.

Why not? Lucretius (1.599–608) argues that minima, or 'extremities', are in their very nature parts of larger magnitudes. But while it is true that the Epicureans do consider the extremities of magnitudes to be three-dimensional minima rather than points or two-dimensional surfaces, it is equally clear that not all minima are extremities, since most will be located somewhere inside atoms. It is hard to see, therefore, how they can be functionally relegated to the status of mere edges, and denied the power of discrete existence on that score. Epicurus' own comment, though brief, puts emphasis on the impossibility of minima having the power of independent motion. And this sounds more promising, since it pointedly recalls an argument of Aristotle's in *Phys.* VI, a book which seems either directly or indirectly to have influenced the Hellenistic debate on minima from Diodorus on.[61] In chapter 10, Aristotle argues that something partless (he is thinking of a geometrical point) could never be in motion, other than incidentally to the motion of a larger body: it could never, in its own right, be in transition from one place to another, since only something with parts can be in the process of crossing any given boundary. If Epicurus accepts this reasoning, it provides just the right rationale for his view that minima can only move by courtesy of the motions of the atoms they help to compose, while the atoms themselves, to be mobile, must have parts.

The reason why the analogy with visible minima breaks down here will no doubt be the following. A discrete visible minimum – say a vanishingly small falling speck of dust – might have been supposed never to be in the process of transition, for just the same reasons as apply to actual minima. But that surmise does not correspond to visible fact. The series of distinct locations which it occupies constitute a smooth continuous *visible* transition. And an important methodological point, emphasized by Epicurus in a similar context soon after (*Ep. Hdt.* 62), is that, where the visible pattern of motion is disanalogous to what reason shows must

[60] Angeli and Dorandi 1987.   [61] Cf. above, pp. 356, 359.

obtain at the microscopic level, we must say that the fault lies in the analogical inference, and not – contrary to the most basic tenet of Epicurean
canonic – that the appearance is false.

*

We now encounter a small complication. In *Physics* VI.10 Aristotle's objection to the motion of partless items takes the form of a disjunction: *either*
(i) they will only move incidentally to the motion of a larger body, *or* (ii)
they will move in staccato fashion, so that you can only say 'It has moved',
never 'It is moving'. The latter Aristotle takes to be impossible, especially
since it would, so he claims, require time to consist of discrete 'nows',
with each location occupied in a successive 'now'. We have seen that
Diodorus decided to opt for the second horn of Aristotle's dilemma,
defending both the staccato theory of motion and all the consequences
imputed to it. And while Epicurus in the *Letter to Herodotus*, as we have
now seen, appears to choose the first horn of the dilemma, and shows no
sign of a staccato theory of motion, there is also evidence for his school's
accepting the latter. Simplicius reports:

> That this obstacle which Aristotle has formulated is itself not entirely
> beyond belief is shown by the fact that, despite his having formulated it
> and produced his solution, the Epicureans, who came along later, said
> that this is precisely how motion does occur. For they say that motion,
> magnitude and time have partless constituents, and that over the whole
> magnitude composed of partless constituents the moving object moves,
> but that at each of the partless magnitudes contained in it it does not
> move but *has* moved; for if it were laid down that the object moving over
> the whole magnitude moves over these too, they would turn out to be
> divisible. (Simp. *Phys.* 934.23–30)

If this is to be believed, we must take it that at some date after the composition (perhaps *c.* 306 BC) of the *Letter to Herodotus* either Epicurus or followers of his concluded that choosing the first horn of the Aristotelian
dilemma did not save them from its second horn.[62] The influence of
Diodorus looks evident here. Diodorus had not only adopted the second
horn, but had defended it as logically respectable.[63] And he had drawn
attention to the need for space, along with body, to be analysed into minima. Once this latter point was accepted, it must have become evident that
the staccato analysis was inevitable. Even if minima were safely ensconced
within larger bodies, the atoms, each atom would as a whole have to move

---

[62] On the date of the *Letter to Herodotus* see Sedley 1976b, 45–6, n. 73.   [63] Cf. above, p. 359.

one spatial minimum at a time, so that its motion could not but be staccato. It fits in with this that, although the *Letter to Herodotus* contains no theory of time minima,[64] such a theory did eventually become school doctrine.[65] Here again the positive influence of Diodorus may be discerned.

Aristotle had also argued (*Phys.* VI.2) that differences of speed depend on the infinite divisibility of time and magnitude. Compared with the time taken by the slower of two objects to move a given distance, there must always be a shorter time which the faster object will take. And for any distance covered by the faster object in a given time, there must always be a smaller distance which the slower object will cover in the same time. This would become impossible if time or magnitude were only finitely divisible. Although it is not known whether Diodorus took account of this argument, it too seems to have filtered through eventually to the Epicureans, since Simplicius (*Phys.* 938.17-22) reports that they accepted both it and its consequence, that there are no real differences of speed. This time, however, it was a welcome confirmation of what was already school doctrine. In the *Letter to Herodotus* (61-2) Epicurus had already argued that at the atomic level all speed is equal, but on the quite independent ground that, since they move in a vacuum, there is no obstructive medium to enforce differences of speed.[66]

8. Properties[67]

Atoms have only the ineliminable properties of all body: resistance, size, shape and weight. That they lack the perceptible properties – colour, flavour etc. – is argued on three main grounds. (i) These are not ineliminable from the conception of body, as any blind person will confirm in the case of colour (Lucr. II.739-47). (ii) Such properties are inherently unstable, whereas atoms were postulated as something totally unchangeable underlying all change (Ep. *Ep.Hdt.* 54). (iii) The atomic theory gains in explanatory power if we suppose that perceptible properties are generated only out of arrangements of atoms: for instance, if the sea were blue because it consisted of blue atoms, it would become harder to explain why its surface, when ruffled, becomes white (Lucr. II.757-87).

This last point, the explanatory elegance of the atomic theory, is elaborated at some length by Lucretius (e.g. I.814-29, II.381-477). Just as the

---

[64] The διὰ λόγου θεωρητοί χρόνοι of *Ep. Hdt.* 47 and 62 have sometimes been thought to be minima, but the phrase implies only that they are microscopically small, and nothing in the contexts requires that they should be partless.   [65] Long and Sedley 1987, vol. II, 46.

[66] See below, p. 421.

[67] Texts: Ep. *Ep. Hdt.* 54-5, 68-73, Lucr. I.449-82, II.381-990. Bibliography: Sedley 1988.

small number of letters in the alphabet can be rearranged to make an indefinite number of words, so too the same atoms can be rearranged to produce quite different macroscopic properties. And those phenomenal properties can comfortably be explained by the type and arrangement of the underlying atoms. For example, the differing fluidity and powers of penetration witnessed in light, fire, water and oil are attributable to the varying size and smoothness of their constituent atoms. Bitter tastes correspond to jagged atoms, pleasant tastes to rounded ones, each having a different effect on the tongue. Colours are taken to have an analogous explanation, in the types and arrangements of the atoms making up the 'images' (εἴδωλα) travelling from the external object to the eye.[68]

*

It would be a tempting, but mistaken, inference that, for Epicurus as for Democritus before him, colours and other perceptible properties are nothing more than atomic configurations. That reductionist move is never made by any Epicurean, and it is ruled out by what Epicurus says about the status of such properties (*Ep. Hdt.* 68–71; cf. Lucr. 1.449–58, S.E. *M* x.219–27): that they are real, yet have no existence at the microscopic level.

Properties come in two types. Generically they are just called 'properties' (συμβεβηκότα), but specifically they divide up into 'permanent accompaniments' (τὰ ἀίδιον παρακολουθοῦντα, in Lucretius' Latin *coniuncta*) and 'accidents' (συμπτώματα, in Lucretius *eventa*). They are distinguished as, respectively, ineliminable and eliminable properties of the items they are said to belong to. Importantly, those items are not confined either to the level of atoms and void, or to that of macroscopic body. Although in a causal context Epicureanism privileges the atomic over the phenomenal, since it is normally atomic change that causes phenomenal change and not vice versa,[69] metaphysically it shows no sign of imposing any such disparity. A permanent property may be located purely at the level of atoms, as unbreakability is. Or it may belong ineliminably to a phenomenal object or stuff – as heat does to fire, though not to the atoms which constitute fire, atoms being neither hot nor cold. Or it may belong equally at both levels, in the way that resistance belongs to all bodies, both atomic and phenomenal.

Epicurus first introduced these properties in order to discount them as *per se* existents.[70] But when he reverts to the topic much later in the *Letter*

---

[68] See above, pp. 273–4.   [69] For a possible exception see pp. 523–4.   [70] See above, pp. 369–70.

to Herodotus (68–71), having in the mean time established a physical account of both atomic and phenomenal properties, his purpose is to re-assess their ontological status (along with that of time, 72–3) in more pos-itive terms.

With regard to permanent properties, he steers a careful course (68–9). (i) They do not exist *per se*. (ii) Nor are they non-existent. (iii) They are not separate incorporeal items which have come to belong to some body. (iv) They are not its constituent parts, in the way that atoms are. (v) The body's nature does nevertheless in a way consist of them. Here (i) recurs to the earlier proof that only bodies and space exist *per se*; (ii) rejects a sceptical reductionist position, often attributed to Democritus, that nothing but atoms and void is real, all the contents of experience being merely some arbitrary or conventional construction placed upon them by human minds and sense organs; (iii) denies, either specifically or *inter alia*, the Platonic theory of separated Forms;[71] (iv) could conceivably be tar-geted at a Stoic theory of qualities,[72] although it would be a little surpris-ing to find an Epicurean response to Stoicism at so early a date; and (v) alone gives Epicurus' own position – that permanent properties are a thing's constituents, but in the non-material sense that they are the (con-ceptual or logical?) constituents of its nature. We might here think of Epicurus' own characterizations of man as 'such and such a form, plus animation' (S.E. *M* vii.267), and of body as a combination of size, shape, resistance and weight (S.E. *M* x.240).

He then turns to accidental properties (*Ep. Hdt.* 70–1). These (i) have no existence at the microscopic level; (ii) are not incorporeal; (iii) lack the nature that the whole body has; (iv) are not non-existent; (v) do not exist *per se*; (vi) are in reality just as they present themselves to our perceptions. Here (i) and (iv) are especially important. Atoms have no properties except permanent ones, so that accidents, including all sensible proper-ties, must exist only at the macroscopic level. A thing's colour, then, although caused by its atomic configuration, is not a property that belongs to it at the atomic level. Yet, where Democritus might well have concluded directly that colour is unreal, Epicurus declines to make that move, in line with his general refusal to privilege the atomic ontologically over the macroscopic. If then they are real, what sort of reality do they have? Not (v) as *per se* existents, since they are evidently parasitic on the bodies they belong to; therefore not (ii) as incorporeals either, since that

---

[71] For Epicurus' term here, ἕτερος ('other'), used of the separateness of Platonic Forms, see espe-cially Plato *Phd.* 74a–c.   [72] See below, pp. 402–3.

term is properly only applied to *per se* existents, with void the sole true claimant to it (*Ep. Hdt.* 67). All that he can tell us positively is (vi) that the way we experience them coincides with their true nature, and that perception actually 'makes' their individual character (ἰδιότης). We might take this to mean that redness, for example, is not even in theory analysable into anything altogether mind-independent, whether an atomic structure or anything else – that what we experience as redness is, irreducibly, what redness actually is.[73]

It is hard to go further on the basis of this difficult and highly condensed text. But one general implication should be clear. Epicurus has a split-level ontology. The properties of atoms are of special importance to natural philosophers, because of their explanatory role. But atomic structures are not the only real structures. The macroscopic world which we experience from birth as pleasant and painful, and on which all our valuations are consequently focused, has just as much claim to reality.

A matching ontological point is made by Polystratus, third head of the Epicurean school. Many properties of things, including values, are relative to a given observer, and not the same for everybody. There was a familiar sceptical inference that they are therefore not part of the objective nature of things at all. Polystratus (*De Contemptu* 23–6) replies that some relative items, such as the nourishing and the fatal, have too obvious a causal efficacy to be thought unreal (if you think hemlock is not 'really' fatal for humans, try swallowing some). While relative items are undoubtedly different from absolute ones, he adds, that in itself gives us no more reason to argue from the reality of absolutes to the unreality of relatives than from the reality of relatives to the unreality of absolutes.

IV Stoic physics and metaphysics[74]

1. Introduction

Unlike the case of Epicurean physics, for Stoic physics we do not have any text which *argues* for the theory from first principles. But the presentation of it, at least, did follow some such sequence, as is clear from Diogenes Laertius' report (VII.132) that they divided physics into the following sequence of topics: bodies, principles, elements, gods, limits, place and void.

---

[73] Plutarch reports Epicurus (fr. 30 Usener) as saying that colours, although caused by atomic configurations, are 'relative to vision'. However, it is unclear how such accidents as motion (cf. p. 370 above) could be relativized in any comparable way.

[74] General studies: Sambursky 1959, Hunt 1976, Hahm 1977, Lapidge 1978.

The sequence corresponds to that in which the topics will be treated below, and it forms a highly appropriate order of exposition, although for the purposes of the present volume 'gods' will be taken separately.[75] Very much as in Epicureanism, the opening topics map out the cosmos, as it were, whereas what will then follow tackles the range of metaphysical questions which this world-picture can give rise to – the status of time, predicates, universals and so on.

2. *Bodies*[76]

This opening heading introduces the primary furniture of the world. Only bodies 'are'. So strong is the Stoics' commitment to their view of the world as an interactive whole that only items with the power to interact are deemed to constitute it, and these are in turn identified with bodies.

This thesis had been put on the map by the 'Giants', often called the 'materialists', whom Plato opposes to the 'Gods' or idealists in the *Sophist*. The Giants initially insist on confining being to bodies. But they are persuaded to reconsider, once it has been pointed out to them that they seem to be outlawing justice and other virtues and vices from 'being', along with the souls in which these qualities inhere – for surely none of these things can be corporeal. Plato suggests that this will lead them to substitute a new hallmark of being in place of corporeality, namely the capacity to act or be acted upon.

The Stoic response is a bold one. It is to recombine the Giants' original and their revised criterion of being. It is bodies, and bodies alone, that have the capacity to act or be acted upon (S.E. *M* VIII.263). Body is defined as 'what has threefold extension along with resistance' (cf. [Gal.] *Qual. Incorp.* 19.483.13–16K),[77] and it is argued that only something of that nature could be a party to causal interaction. If the soul interacts with the body, Cleanthes argued (Nemes. 21.6–9) – as it does when it responds to the body's sufferings, or when its shame makes the body blush – it must itself be corporeal. And since not only our souls but also their moral qualities, such as justice, have the capacity to act upon our bodies, the Stoics infer that they too must be corporeal. The same will apply to the world as a whole: its wisdom and other moral qualities are its primary governing features.

Hence being can after all, and must, be limited to bodies. Bodies alone, that is, interact to constitute a world. Other items, such as space and

---

[75] See below, ch. 13.
[76] Texts: *SVF* II 357–68. Comment: Goldschmidt 1979, Brunschwig 1988a.
[77] Cf. also the Epicurean analysis of body above, p. 381.

time,[78] can at best provide the background against which the world operates. In themselves they are causally inert.

The answer to the further question of *how* souls and their moral qualities can be corporeal will emerge piecemeal in what follows. In outline, it is that virtue is identical with a soul in a certain condition; and that the soul itself is *pneuma*, which, as well as being intrinsically active and intelligent, also has corporeality, thanks to which it can act upon the body.[79]

This last point is important to bear in mind. Although all that makes a body a body is its solidity, it cannot be inferred that body in itself possesses no properties other than material properties of bulk, weight, position in space etc. That way lies extreme materialism, the strategy of reducing such non-material properties as life and intelligence to *purely* material entities – entities, e.g. atoms, which have material properties *and no others*. The Stoics are far from being materialists in any such sense. In their world, body is alive and intelligent all the way down. It needs its interactive powers simply in order that the dictates of intelligence can be put into practical effect, but those powers do not exhaust its properties. Just how it comes to possess life and intelligence as irreducible properties we will learn in the next section.

3. The principles[80]

At the lowest level of analysis, the world is a combination of two ultimate and indestructible bodily principles (ἀρχαί), matter and god. These are never found in actual separation, but they must nevertheless be separated in thought if we are to understand the causal relations underlying processes of change.[81] Body, we have seen, is characterized by the power to act *or* be acted upon. The most overt causal processes (cf. Sen. *Ep*. 65.3–4) are those in which one discrete body is seen to act upon another, each having some capacity to play an active and a passive role. But change at the most fundamental level is to be sought within a single discrete body, whether an individual organism or the world as a whole, and there too we must ask what is acting upon what (Sen. *Ep*. 2, 23–4; cf. S.E. *M* IX.75–6, quoted below). The answer (cf. Sen. *Ep*. 65.2) is that the immanent principle god, defined by its power to act, is acting upon the principle matter, defined by its power to be acted upon. In any physical process a portion of matter, the essentially passive and formless locus of change, is altered by god, the intelligent creative force which imbues it

---

[78] Cf. below, pp. 395–400.   [79] See below, pp. 387–9 and 562–72.
[80] Texts: *SVF* II 299–328. Comment: Graeser 1975, Sandbach 1989 (1975) 71–5, Hahm 1977, 29–56, Todd 1978, Lapidge 1973 and 1978.   [81] See below, pp. 435–6, 481–3.

through and through and endows it with whatever properties it may have.

There are obvious analogies with Aristotelian form and matter, especially if one (controversially) attributes to Aristotle a theory of prime matter. For Stoic matter certainly is prime, in the sense that it is viewed as being in itself totally without qualities – 'unqualified substance' (ἄποιος οὐσία, D.L. VII.134). But the Aristotelian analogy is of limited value. First, the Stoic principles are themselves corporeal,[82] and owe to this their power to interact. (Body is defined as that which has the capacity to act *or* be acted upon, thus carefully allowing god and matter, each of which has just one of these two capacities, still to count as bodies.) Second, and in keeping with this, god is never identified with the *form* present in the matter (e.g. with its shape or colour), but imbues the matter as the intelligent craftsman of that form. He is immanent in the matter, not *qua* its form, but because, all causation being by bodily contact, his causal capacities would be drastically threatened if he were transcendent in the manner of the Aristotelian god.

Surprisingly it is Plato, not Aristotle, who stands in the immediate background. Far from being an outright rejection of Platonism, the Stoic twin principles were almost certainly seen as a development or interpretation of it. It is the Platonic, not the Aristotelian, god who is viewed as a creative causal agent. And by Zeno's day there was a current reading of the *Timaeus*, accepted by Theophrastus (*ap.* Simp. *Phys.* 26.5–15), according to which Plato posits two 'principles', (a) 'matter,' and (b) 'a moving cause which he connects with the power of god'. 'Matter' here is simply a technical rendering of the 'receptacle' posited by Plato as the matrix on which form is imposed by god. The identification of god with an *immanent* causal principle may look like a curious way of reading the *Timaeus*. They probably had in mind not Plato's divine craftsman (often regarded by ancient interpreters as a fiction), but the world soul, which at 34b is said to extend throughout the world and to make it, as a whole, a god. What Stoicism adds is the need for this causal principle to be corporeal – and even that, as we have seen has an origin in Platonic debate.[83]

Also more Platonic than Aristotelian in spirit is the Stoic argument for the ultimacy of god as causal agent, reported by Sextus:

---

[82] D.L. VII.134: σώματα εἶναι τὰς ἀρχάς, repeated in the *Suda* with the controversial variant reading ἀσωμάτους. For the corporeality of the principles, cf. Calcidius 293. They are never listed among the Stoic incorporeals (below, pp. 395–402), and if they were incorporeal they would lack 'being', contrary to the regular designation of matter as οὐσία, 'substance', literally 'being'. See below, p. 407.   [83] Above, p. 383.

The substance of what exists, they say, since it is without any motion from itself and shapeless, needs to be set in motion and shaped by some cause. For this reason, when we look at a very beautiful bronze we want to know the artist (since in itself the matter is in an immobile condition), so when we see the matter of the universe moving and possessing form and structure we might reasonably inquire into the cause which moves and shapes it into many forms. It is not convincing that this is anything other than a power which pervades it, just as soul pervades us. Now this power is either self-moving or moved by some other power. But if it is moved by another power, this second power will not be capable of being moved unless it is moved by a third power, which is absurd. So there exists a power which in itself is self-moving, and this must be divine and everlasting. For either it will be in motion from eternity, or from a definite time. But it will not be in motion from a definite time; for there will be no cause of its motion from a definite time. So, then, the power which moves matter and guides it in due order into generations and changes is everlasting. So this power would be god. (S.E. *M* ix.75–6)

This argument explains that, being both creative and everlasting from all eternity, the active principle is naturally to be identified with 'god'. And in doing so it presents it as a kind of immanent self-mover. This looks back to Plato's thesis in the *Phaedrus* (245–6) and *Laws* (896–9) that all motion must originate in *self*-moving soul, rather than to Aristotle's doctrine of god as a transcendent *un*moved mover.

The twin principles are the only items in the Stoic universe which have permanent being, surviving as they do even through the periods of 'conflagration' which punctuate distinct world-phases.[84] Change is their realignment in relation to each other, not their creation or destruction, even in part (e.g. D.L. vii.134, Ar. Did. *ap*. Stob. 1.132.27ff.). To this extent they play the role fulfilled in Epicureanism by atoms and void, and which in early Presocratic cosmologies had been fulfilled by the primeval underlying stuff (air, fire, etc.) held to survive all change. This probably accounts for the Stoics' choice of the term 'principles' (ἀρχαί), standardly used to designate these Presocratic substrates. In fact, their adoption of 'god' as an immanent bodily principle which is nevertheless divine looks very much like a conscious reversion to Presocratic cosmology, and in particular to Heraclitus, on whose thought Stoic physics draws at many points.[85]

[84] See below, p. 434–9.   [85] Long 1975–6.

4. Active and passive elements[86]

In listing four elements – earth, air, fire and water – the Stoics place themselves in a tradition which by their day included Empedocles, Plato and
Aristotle. But they are closer to these latter two to the extent that, like
them, they do not regard the elements as absolutely primary ingredients
of the world, but as themselves further analysable downwards to an even
more fundamental level, at which they are finally resolved into the two
principles matter and god (pp. 384–6 above). The value of the elements is
that – unlike the irreducibly primitive matter and god, theoretical constructs whose explanatory role is purely general – they represent the stratification of the world, from earth at the centre to fire at the periphery, and
its main processes of climatic and other change, at a level at which they
can be directly observed. The details of these processes, along with the
special cosmic role of fire, will be considered separately below.[87] For now,
it is important to bear in mind just that the elements are generated out of
matter and god, that they are the stuff of which all more complex substances are composed, and that they have some capacity for intertransfor-
mation:

> In the beginning all by himself he turned the entire substance through
> air into water. Just as the sperm is enveloped in the seminal fluid, so god,
> who is the seminal principle (σπερματικὸς λόγος) of the world, stays
> behind as such in the moisture, making matter serviceable to himself for
> the successive stages of creation. He then creates first of all the four ele-
> ments: fire, water, air, earth. (D.L. VII.135–6)

The Stoics analyse all causal processes as involving one body acting upon
another.[88] Hence when, as most often, causal analyses are focused on the
elements, the Stoic practice is to distinguish them functionally into active
elements, with a causal role analogous to that of 'god' at the primary level,
and passive elements, with a primarily material role. Like the 'principles',
the passive elements are held to be entirely permeated by one or both
active ones. All this applies equally to individual organisms, to the world
at large, itself regarded as a living and intelligent organism, and to discrete
inorganic entities: all owe both their cohesion and their qualities, vital
and other, to the active elements.

As for which elements are active, Stoicism seems to embody two
different traditions. One, perhaps the earlier of the two and developed

---

[86] Texts: *SVF* II 412–62. Comment: Verbeke 1945, Solmsen 1961, Hahm 1977 and 1985.
[87] See below, p. 440.   [88] See below, pp. 481–3.

especially by Zeno's colleague and successor Cleanthes, echoes Heraclitus
in selecting fire as the governing element. Fire is thought of not just as a
destructive force – the variety which the Stoics call 'uncraftsmanlike fire',
πῦρ ἄτεχνον. It also takes the form of 'craftsmanlike fire' (πῦρ τεχνικόν), embodying the creative forces of warmth and light which are seen
to be basic to life, and especially associated with the rarefied fiery stuff of
the heavens, 'aether'. Since the world as a whole is considered a living
thing, fire can account for its creation, its vital properties, and its eventual
periodic destruction.[89] Consequently one guise in which Stoicism from
an early date represents god, or nature, is as 'intelligent, a craftsmanlike
fire which proceeds methodically in making the world, embracing all the
seminal principles in accordance with which individual things are fated to
come about' (Aët. 1.7.33).

The second tradition which Stoicism incorporates picks out *pneuma*,
literally 'breath', as the active and creative presence in matter. Its origin
lies largely in a medical tradition which located the basis of human vitality
in a kind of warm breath, thus reflecting the obvious indispensability of
both breathing and warmth to life. Related ideas were also to be found in
Aristotle's theory of inborn *pneuma* (the causal relation of the Aristotelian
to the medical theory is controversial); but probably the primary influence on the Stoic theory came from the doctor Praxagoras of Cos,[90] a contemporary of Zeno, who was later cited as an authority by Chrysippus. He
developed the thesis that, while the veins contain blood, it is *pneuma* that
flows through the arteries and transmits motion from the heart to the
limbs.

On the Stoic analysis, *pneuma* is an amalgam of the two active elements,
fire and air. Some sources allow in addition that either one of these on its
own may count as *pneuma*,[91] but it remains probable that when *pneuma* is
acting as soul it is considered to involve both elements. The sources for
Zeno himself vary between making fire and *pneuma* the stuff of the soul.
As we shall see shortly, the difference between the two accounts is mainly
one of emphasis.

At all events, during the third century BC the vital powers of *pneuma*
became more and more central to medical thought, especially when the
nerves were discovered and taken to be the channels of *pneuma*.[92] By the
time we get to Chrysippus, fire has receded as a vital principle, and *pneuma*

[89] See below, pp. 434–41.   [90] See further, below, pp. 600–2.
[91] See Gal. *CC* 1, and Sorabji 1988, 85–9. But for psychic *pneuma* as an amalgam of the two (both
    warmth and breath being integral to animate life), cf. *SVF* I 135, II 786–7; Cic. *Tusc.* 1.42.
[92] See Solmsen 1961, and see below, p. 601.

has become the vehicle of divine 'reason' (λόγος)[93] in matter, not just in animals but throughout the world. Since *pneuma* consists of the two active elements, fire and air, it follows that the matter which it imbues and informs consists of the other two elements, earth and water (e.g. Nemes. 52.18–19), which henceforth take on at the level of elements the same passive material role which pure 'matter' occupies at the primary level. In cosmic terms, this will be typified by the way in which air, light and warmth, from above, act upon and vitalize combinations of the inert stuffs water and earth, to produce organisms. That such processes can be so successfully creative is due to the divine reason which characterizes all *pneuma*, while their regularity can be attributed to the 'seminal principles' which god embodies – presumably principles for repeatable organic generation.

Since its fiery component is hot and rarefied while its airy component is relatively cold and dense, *pneuma* is found in varying degrees of rarefaction, according to the mixture. At its most rarefied, it is soul – and since this is identical with its most fiery form, there is ultimately little difference between the early Stoic association of life and intelligence with fire, in the tradition of Heraclitus, and the alternative, medically inspired emphasis on *pneuma*, favoured by Chrysippus.

Below the level of soul, the powers of *pneuma* can be traced further down the natural scale. Plants too have a life force which gives them cohesion, endurance and their individual qualities; and this is *pneuma* in its lesser guise of 'nature' (φύσις) – the state of vegetative, as distinct from animate, life. Finally, even a lifeless object, such as a stone or log, has coextensive with it a *pneuma* which unifies and shapes it, and this is called its 'state' or 'tenor' (ἕξις).[94]

What differentiates these three kinds of *pneuma* from each other, and accounts for every variation even within each class, is the varying tension between its outward and inward motions, a tension which in turn apparently depends on the proportions of air and fire. The fire in the *pneuma* has a naturally centrifugal motion, rarefying the object and having primary responsibility for its qualities. Meanwhile, the air has a centripetal tendency, which contributes in particular the object's solidity and cohesion. Whereas 'soul', and to a lesser extent 'nature', have special associations with fire and heat (e.g. Cic. *ND* 11.23–5), 'state' (ἕξις) is more closely linked with air (Plu. *Stoic. Rep.* 1053f–1054b), and this difference of emphasis may reflect the fact that what is prominent in the former type of case is vital

---

[93] See below, pp. 440–1.   [94] See below, pp. 563–4.

qualities (most fully realized in the very pure aetherial fire of the heavens), while the primary feature of a 'state' is cohesion as a single object. But nothing has the latter feature to the total exclusion of the former. To the extent that the world as a whole is a living and intelligent organism, the fiery element permeates it even down to individual rocks – which have a role in it analogous to that of bones in individual organisms (cf. D.L. VII.139, Philo *Leg.* II.22–3).

5. The continuum[95]

Both at the primary and at the elemental level, we have seen, a material substrate is entirely permeated by a second body, an active and intelligent one. How can this be? According to atomism mixture at the lowest level of analysis is simply the juxtaposition of discrete particles of two or more types. In Stoic eyes mere external contact could never constitute the intimate causal link between god and the matter which makes the world an inherently and ideally intelligent being. The active body must permeate the passive body 'through and through':

> According to Chrysippus . . ., blendings (κράσεις) occur through and through, and not by surface contact and juxtaposition. For a little wine cast into the sea will coextend with it for a while, and will then be blended with it. (D.L. VII.151)

According to Plutarch (*Comm. Not.* 1078b–e), Chrysippus took this to the extreme of insisting that a single drop of wine could permeate the whole sea, indeed the whole world. And he reports that Arcesilaus had already mounted an Academic attack on the same doctrine of through-and-through blending, asking rhetorically whether, if a severed leg putrefied in the sea and was blended into it, an entire naval battle might not then take place 'in the leg'. Chrysippus' uncompromising response suggests that the paradox was one that he not only considered indispensable to Stoic physics, but also relished.

The developed Stoic theory distinguishes three grades of mixture (Alex. *Mixt.* 216.14–218.6). 'Juxtaposition' conforms to the atomist model described above, and is exemplified by mixed grains. 'Blending' involves total interpenetration, but the ingredients retain their own distinctive properties, as is witnessed by the fact that they can at least in theory be separated again. Finally there is 'fusion' (σύγχυσις), a kind of interpenetration in which the ingredients irreversibly lose their distinctive proper-

---

[95] Texts: *SVF* II 463–91. Comment: Samfrom 1959, Hahm 1972, Cherniss 1976, 810–33, Sorabji 1983, M. J. White 1992, 284–326.

ties and a new stuff is generated. Of these it is 'blending' that correctly describes the relation of *pneuma* to the material substrate. The point is illustrated by two examples. In so far as *pneuma* is fire, it can be compared to the ('uncraftsmanlike') fire which is seen to permeate a red-hot piece of iron: the fire is present throughout the iron, but each keeps its own nature, as is evident when they are separated again – that is, when the fire spreads from it, or when the iron cools. And soul, itself a kind of *pneuma*, can be seen to permeate the entire body, yet to retain its own distinctly 'psychic' properties (during incarnation and also, most Stoics would add, after eventual separation from the body).[96]

One evident paradox of the Stoic theory is that two bodies are required to occupy all of the same space simultaneously. Examples like that of the red-hot iron no doubt help to make this less shocking. A lump of matter will normally be spatially coextensive with the properties it possesses, and the theory of blending is, in a way, just a physicalized version of this evident truth.

A weightier problem, however, is how total blending is to be analysed in terms of mathematical division, an issue implicit in the following sequence of topics reported by Diogenes Laertius (VII.150–1): 'Division is to infinity, or "infinite" according to Chrysippus (for there is not some infinity which the division reaches, it is just unceasing). And blendings, also, are through and through.' Clearly in an Epicurean world, in which there is an absolutely smallest magnitude,[97] no mixture could be other than by juxtaposition of discrete portions. Conversely, in the Stoic world there must be no smallest magnitude, or through-and-through blending will be similarly ruled out. That may be why the non-existence of a smallest magnitude – of a 'limit' in the Epicurean sense – is among the topics which Stoic physics addressed directly after 'Elements', under the heading 'Limits'.

Introducing this topic, Plutarch starts with some Epicurean-inspired challenges to the Stoics (*Comm. Not.* 1078e–1079b), including: (a) How can a magnitude fail to have an extremity which is the first part of it? (b) How can one magnitude exceed another, if both have the same number of parts, viz. infinitely many (cf. Lucr. 1.615–22)? He reports an answer to the second challenge in what purport to be Chrysippus' own words:

> When asked if we have parts, and how many, and of what and how many parts *they* consist, we will operate a distinction. With regard to the inexact question we will reply that we consist of a head, trunk and limbs – for

---

[96] See below, pp. 560–2.   [97] Cf. pp. 374–9 above.

that was all that the problem put to us amounted to. But if they extend their questioning to the *ultimate* parts, we must not, he says, assume any such things, but must say neither of what parts we consist, nor, likewise, of how many, either infinite or finite. (Plu. *Comm. Not.* 1079b–c)

Here Chrysippus shrewdly rejects as misconceived the very project of analysing a magnitude into its ultimate parts. A magnitude may be infinitely divisible, but, as we saw earlier, it does not follow that there is an actual infinity of ultimate parts of which it consists.[98] Nor for that matter does it have any determinate number of parts. There is simply no non-arbitrary answer to the question how many parts it contains. He thus rejects the Epicurean presupposition that a thing's size is a function of the ultimate number of parts it has.

Sextus Empiricus (*M* x.139–42) urges against the Stoic continuum a closely related paradox, also invoked by the Epicureans. This is the old argument of Zeno of Elea according to which an infinitely divisible continuum makes motion impossible, because for any distance you set out to traverse there will be an infinite number of sub-distances that you have to traverse first. Hence no sub-distance is the first, and motion cannot begin. Slightly earlier (*M*. x.123–30) Sextus has dismissed as hopeless what looks like the Stoics' reply to this paradox: that the moving object 'completes a divisible distance as a whole in one and the same time'.

What does this mean? Not, obviously, that the journey takes no time at all; nor, even worse, that the object reaches its destination without passing through the intervening space.[99] To see what it might mean, we should start by bearing in mind once again Chrysippus' axiom that a magnitude, although infinitely divisible, does not contain an actual infinity of parts, the demarcation of its 'parts' being a purely arbitrary matter. It will follow that *any* sub-distance adjacent to the starting line might claim to be the 'first' part of the distance to be traversed. That, however, is not yet enough, since it leaves it entirely undetermined which motion will be the first, and invites the challenge that any motion chosen will contain smaller parts whose demarcation is no more arbitrary than its own.

What we need is a non-arbitrary way of choosing the first motion in the series. And this seems to be provided by another Stoic thesis, that mathematical limits 'subsist in mere thought' (Procl. *Eucl.* 1.89.15–18): they are thought constructs, or idealizations. It follows that on a runner's journey there are only as many dividing points as anyone analysing it marks off in thought. At some point the analyst will find himself incapable of isolating

---

[98] Cf. Stob. 1.142.2–6 (assigned by Diels to Aëtius 1.16).   [99] Cf. p. 358 above on Diodorus.

further dividing points, and at that stage he will be left with a first motion which, though divisible, is undivided. And this first motion will have to be thought of as accomplished *legato*, all in one go, not in discrete stages. That may be all that is meant by 'in one and the same time'.

We have here also an answer to the former of Plutarch's two challenges, how a magnitude can fail to have an extremity which is the first part of it. The challenge exploits the Epicurean idea of a body's limit as an irreducibly small part of it: unless you could start with such a limit, then work along the body by means of further minimal parts of it, you would never succeed in traversing it, even in thought. The Stoic theory of motion, we have seen, offers an alternative account of what constitutes the first part of the magnitude. And Plutarch records (*Comm. Not.* 1080e) a related Stoic distinction, one that had eluded Aristotle as well as the Epicureans: that the limit or edge of a body is not itself a part of it at all.

Stoic interest in limits goes further. But there is little sign of an interest in the properties of pure mathematical entities, and instead concern seems to be focused on the material continuum. This is well illustrated by a geometrical problem (*Comm. Not.* 1079e ff.) which exercised Chrysippus, and which appears to arise only in connection with physical solids, as distinct from abstract geometrical ones. The early atomist Democritus had asked what happens if you slice a cone along a plane parallel to its base. Are the resulting upper and lower faces equal or unequal in size? If they are equal, the cone is not tapering towards its apex, and must be a cylinder. But if the two adjacent faces are unequal, the cone's side will turn out to be stepped and irregular.

Democritus' own motivation in raising the puzzle is unknown. But Chrysippus takes it very seriously in its own right. His solution, as reported by Plutarch, is that the lower surface is 'larger but not exceeding', or alternatively that the two surfaces are 'neither equal nor unequal'. These expressions seem more successful in conveying Chrysippus' puzzlement than in revealing any chosen theoretical position. They reflect the fact that as you run your finger down the reconstituted cone you will feel it widening at the original plane of intersection (hence 'larger') but will not feel a projecting ridge (hence the lower plane is 'not exceeding'). Whether these terms were meant to be translatable into the language of mathematics, and if so whether the distinction was a coherent one, is a matter of controversy.[100] Be that as it may, he does at least seem to accept that we are dealing with two distinct though adjacent surfaces, one of

---

[100] See especially M. J. White 1992, 301–14 for speculation.

them higher than the other in the cone – and this confirms that he treats it as a physical cone, since if it were a purely geometrical construct the two 'surfaces' could hardly fail to be, mathematically speaking, one and the same plane. It is the physical world, not pure geometry, that offers the puzzling phenomenon of adjacent but non-coincidental planes. This is confirmation, if any were needed, that Chrysippus' interests in the problems of the continuum are geared to the understanding of the physical world, and not of abstract mathematical entities – a reminder of the intimate link between his defence of infinite divisibility and the Stoic theory of mixture.

This consideration brings us to the borderline of the two kinds of continuum distinguished above[101] – the structural continuum, divisible without end, with which we have been concerned in this section, and the material continuum, unpunctuated by void gaps. The Epicureans reject the material continuum on the ground that without void gaps motion is ruled out. The Stoics' response – although direct documentation for it is sparse – relies on the structural continuum. The division of matter need not yield ultimate rigid particles like Epicurean atoms. Since body is infinitely divisible a stuff like air can be conceived as fluid *all the way down*, in which case motion can comfortably take place by the redistribution of body within the plenum that is the world.

*

We move finally to the temporal continuum,[102] which appears to have been treated on a par with its spatial counterparts: 'Chrysippus said that bodies are divided to infinity, and likewise things comparable to bodies, such as surface, line, place, void and time' (Stob. 1.142.2–6).[103] Diodorus, whose anti-continuist theories have been lurking in the background throughout this section, had argued that the present is a 'partless' stretch of time, on the ground that if divisible it would be exhaustively divided into past and future, and thus vanish without trace.[104] This assumes that the present has duration, discounting from the outset the alternative, Aristotelian idea of the present as a durationless instant, a mere boundary between past and future. That idea, which seems not to have been seriously revived until relatively late in the Hellenistic age, threatens to generate the paradoxical consequences that no change can take place in the present, and that the present, far from being a privileged part of time, is

---

[101] See pp. 355–6.   [102] The following remarks are heavily indebted to Schofield 1988.
[103] Cf. Ar. Did. *ap.* Stob. 1.106.11–13, where Chrysippus compares the infinity of time to that of void.   [104] See above, pp. 357–8.

not a part of time at all.[105] (The Stoics, we have already seen, recognized that limits are not parts.)

Chrysippus' position is reported as follows by Arius Didymus:

> He says most clearly that no time is wholly present. For since continuous things are infinitely divisible, on the basis of this division every time too is infinitely divisible. Consequently no time is present exactly, but it is broadly said to be so. (Arius Didymus *ap*. Stob. 1.105.13–18 = fr. 26)

To this Plutarch adds the information that in his work *On parts* Chrysippus said that 'of the present time, part is future and part is past' (*Comm. Not.* 1081f). Although any present temporal duration contains past and future elements, the infinite divisibility of time is Chrysippus' guarantee that no process of peeling away the past and future elements from the present need pare it down to a Diodorean partless 'now' or to a mere temporal boundary. One can use the term 'now' with varying degrees of 'broadness' – this week, today, this morning, the duration of this conversation, etc. – and, with each narrowing, some past and future parts of the present are stripped away. But no amount of such narrowing will yield an altogether durationless instant.

If the Stoics need theoretical justification for following the trend and excluding a present instant from their account of time, we need only bear in mind their thesis that limits are mere thought-constructs or idealizations. Although this doctrine is not recorded explicitly other than with regard to the limits of bodies, their consciously parallel treatment of the temporal and spatial continua virtually guarantees that temporal limits, i.e. instants, were subjected to the same constraint.

6. The incorporeals[106]

Only bodies have 'being'. That, we have seen, is because only bodies play an interactive part in the world-process. Nevertheless, Stoic ontology standardly acknowledges four incorporeals, which will in this section be considered in the following order: place, void, time, and the *lekton* (e.g. S.E. *M* x.218).

The basis of Epicurean physics is the assignment of independent existence not only to body but also to an incorporeal, space. Stoic physics goes much of the way with Epicureanism on this point, but there are .

---

[105] The latter is used by Plutarch (*Comm. Not.* 1081e) against the second-century BC Stoic Archedemus, who revived the punctual view of the present, perhaps under pressure from Academic attacks of the kind echoed by Plutarch in the same chapter.

[106] Texts: *SVF* II 166–71, 501–21, *FDS* 699–708. Comment: Bréhier 1910, Goldschmidt 1979, Brunschwig 1988a, Schofield 1988, Algra 1993 and 1995.

some subtle differences too. The common ground includes the tripartition, invoked by both schools, of the genus space into 'place' (τόπος),
'void' (κενόν), and 'room' (χώρα). Greek has no ready-made term corresponding to 'space'. Where the Epicureans invent one, 'intangible substance', the Stoics, as the following definitions will make clear, content
themselves with the generic description 'that which is able to be occupied by what-is'. The genus is divided into its three species as follows.

First, Chrysippus defines place as '(i) that which is occupied throughout by what-is; or (ii) that which is able to be occupied by what-is, and is
occupied throughout, whether by something or by somethings (εἴτε ὑπό
τινος <εἴτε> ὑπό τινων)' (Ar. Did. ap. Stob. 1.161.8–11). Here (ii) is just a
more articulated statement of (i), the first clause giving place its genus –
roughly, space –, the second its differentia, namely that its capacity to be
occupied must be being exercised, and the third adding that the 'being',
i.e. body, which occupies it may be comprised of one or more discrete
individuals.[107] Put non-technically, a place is a fully occupied portion of
space, whether occupied by a single entity or by a collection of entities.

It must be borne in mind that the Stoic world is a plenum, containing
no void gaps, but that it is surrounded by an infinite void, into a part of
which it expands during its periodic conflagrations.[108] It is with this periodic expansion in mind that void is defined as 'that which is able to be
occupied by what is, but which is not occupied' (S.E. M x.3). So far we
have a close correspondence with the Epicurean use of the same terms. It
is with the third, 'room' that the picture becomes less simple.

In Epicurean terminology 'room' is space which is neither simply occupied nor simply unoccupied, but which has body passing through it.
Chrysippus defines it enigmatically as 'either (i) the larger thing able to be
occupied by what-is, and like a larger container of a body, or (ii) that
which is roomy enough for (χωροῦν) a larger body' (Ar. Did., apud Stob.
1. 161.8–11). 'Larger' here seems to mean larger than the body as whose
location it is being considered. There seems no reason why, on this conception of 'room',[109] 'Trafalgar Square' should not be the right answer to
the question 'Where is Nelson's Column?', despite the fact that the

---

[107] For this technical sense of 'something', τι, see below, pp. 410–11.   [108] See below, pp. 441–2.
[109] Likewise Aët. 1.20.1, 'that which is partly occupied'. The only truly anomalous definition is the
alternative which Sextus now adds (M x.4; cf. PH III.124): 'Some have said that room is the place
of the larger body, so that it differs from place in that place does not indicate the size of the contained body – even if it contains a tiny body it is none the less called a place – whereas 'room'
indicates that the size of the body in it is considerable.' The explanation seems simple: these
interpreters have misunderstood Chrysippus' definition of room as a 'larger' container to mean
that it is large *compared with other containers*.

remainder of Trafalgar Square is occupied by other bodies.[110] To this extent the Stoics may simply be trying to do justice to everyday broad notions of location, which rarely require the precision implied by their formal definition of place. Another motive is no doubt to meet an Epicurean challenge: Epicurean 'room' is the space that leaves atoms free to move, and the Stoics will want to show that, even in their own voidless world where motion requires no 'room' in the Epicurean sense, the term itself has a proper significance.[111] These two considerations can help explain the relative neglect of 'room' in their formal ontology. For it never appears, alongside place and void, on their standard list of four incorporeals.

Why, conversely, do place and void find their way onto this list? No formal argument survives, but we can get help from the following comment of the later Stoic cosmologist Cleomedes:

> So void must have a kind of subsistence (ὑπόστασις). The notion of it is very simple, since it is incorporeal and intangible, neither has shape nor takes on shape, neither is acted upon in any respect nor acts, but is simply able to receive body. (Cleom. *Cael.* 8.10–14)

'Subsistence' is the technical ontological status of the incorporeals, one which falls short of actual 'being'. Void earns this status by its potential role, as receptor of body, in objective processes of change. It is an integral part of the structure of the universe – of what the Stoics call 'the all', the combination of the world and the surrounding void. But it is not a body, precisely because it lacks the defining mark of body, the power to act or be acted upon.

And if void is so classified, the same must inevitably apply to place. Void, when body moves into it, becomes that body's place, but could hardly be thought thereby to become a body. The Stoics were admittedly prepared to go to considerable lengths to reduce supposed incorporeals to bodies – virtue, for example, being the soul, itself corporeal, in a certain

[110] The definition can quite well allow the combination of the world's place with all or some of the surrounding void to count as a special case of χώρα, namely the world's χώρα (cf. Chrysippus *ap.* Plu. *Stoic. Rep.* 1054c). But we should not infer that, at least for Chrysippus, the term *means* 'space' in this all-embracing sense, since Arius Didymus *ap.* Stob. 1.11–13 reports Chrysippus thus: 'If ever, of that which is able to be occupied by what-is, part is occupied but part not, the whole will be neither void nor place, but something else *which has no name.*' So this kind of composite portion of space would not, as such, be classified as χώρα, despite as a matter of fact being the world's χώρα. However, some other Stoics may have given χώρα this precise sense; cf. S.E. *M* x.3, and Algra 1995, 263–81.

[111] Hence the rival etymology proposed (see above). Epicurean χώρα is that through which bodies 'roam' (χωρεῖν) – see above p. 367. Stoic χώρα is that which 'is roomy enough for' (χωρεῖν again) a larger body than the one in it.

state. But the price of so reductive a treatment of place would have been unacceptably high. If an object's place were identical with that body viewed in a certain way, it would become hard to give any account of motion – of a place being vacated by one body and entered by another.

Next among the incorporeals we come to time. In the previous section we learned something of the structure of time, as a continuum in which the present is an extended part along with past and future. An asymmetry must now be added. According to Chrysippus:

> . . . only present time is real (ὑπάρχειν); past and future time subsist (ὑφεστάναι), but by no means are they real, just as only predicates which belong as properties (συμβεβηκότα) are real – for example, walking is real for me when I walk, unreal when I lie or sit. (Ar. Did. *ap*. Stob. 1.106.18–23 = fr. 26)

Officially speaking, 'subsistence' is the metaphysical status that time as a whole, or any portion of it, possesses in virtue of being an incorporeal. The point of Chrysippus' remark is not to elevate the present above the status of an incorporeal, but to make it a special kind of incorporeal. The comparison with predicates like 'walking' offers some illumination. They too, for reasons we will encounter shortly, are incorporeals. They gain their subsistent status from their availability to become truly predicable of bodies, their capacity to be instantiated in them: that, we might say informally, is why there *is such a thing as* walking – why walking 'subsists' – whether or not anyone is actually walking at the moment. The fullest realization of the predicate is when it does become instantiated in a body. But this does not in any way affect the kind of thing it is – namely a subsistent incorporeal. Likewise the present has a special status. It too is 'real' (ὑπάρχει), so that it can for example provide the content of cognitive impressions.[112] But like past and future it remains a subsistent incorporeal.

Why is time an incorporeal? Puzzlingly, the Stoics seem happy to analyse portions of time as bodies: days and nights are identified with, for example, the world's atmosphere in a certain state, and similar corporealization is then allowed to spread to other portions of time, including seasons and years (Plu. *Comm. Not.* 1084c–d). Then given their general programme of corporealization, why do they not simply content themselves with this analysis?

We may guess that days and years are regarded as bodies when viewed as items with a causal history: this week has exhausted me, the year's

---

[112] For the cognitive impression and its definition as ἀπὸ ὑπάρχοντος, see above, p. 302.

length is governed by the sun's movement in the ecliptic, etc. There is, however, a guise in which time's role is non-causal, but rather to provide parameters – that is, under Chrysippus' formal definition of time as 'the dimension (διάστημα) of the world's motion' (Simp. *Cat.* 350.15–16).[113] There are important similarities here to Plato's *Timaeus*, where time is likewise viewed from the top downwards, as a measure of cosmic regularity, of the repeated and mathematically precise motions in the heavens. These were widely believed to operate in a cycle of many millennia known as the Great Year, which for the Stoics was also the length of each world phase, between successive conflagrations.[114] Since Chrysippus insists that time is infinite in both directions (Ar. Did. *ap.* Stob. 1.106.12), he must think of it as the entire series of such ages, although individual times will include its components, such as months, days, and parts of days.

Now the world is a body, and so is its motion, being simply the world moving. Yet the Stoics hold that time, properly defined as the dimension of that motion, is not itself a body. We must speculate why not. The regularity of a body's motion presupposes fixed spatial and temporal intervals through which it takes place. If either of those intervals were identical with the moving body itself, viewed in a certain way, they might say, its motion would be left altogether without objective coordinates. It is, then, anything but surprising that the Stoics should treat not only the spatial intervals – or 'places' – but also the temporal intervals as subsisting independently of the moving bodies which pass through them. And that consideration already points to the incorporeality of time.[115]

If this is the right story, it implies that time is not, in the manner of Plato's *Timaeus*, totally parasitic on the motions of the heavens. Its function is to measure change, and above all the regular change in the heavens, just as void's function is to receive body. In both cases that function is even built into the definition. But it by no means follows that either space

---

[113] Cf. Cleom. II.5.92–101 Todd, where two corporeal senses of 'month' are distinguished from two incorporeal senses, one of which is as a χρονικὸν διάστημα.

[114] See below, pp. 434–9.

[115] That we might not be able to *specify* those intervals other than in terms of cosmic motions should constitute no obstacle to this interpretation. Cf. *lekta* (below, p. 401), which subsist independently of language as the rational structure onto which language is mapped, yet can themselves only be specified by means of that language. Nor need the description of time as 'accompanying' (παρακολουθοῦν, Ar. Did. *ap.* Stob. 1.106.7) the world's motion make it parasitic on that motion, any more than the definition of a *lekton* as 'subsisting in correspondence with' a rational impression makes it parasitic on that impression for its subsistence (cf. the description of place as 'subsisting in correspondence with bodies' at *SVF* II 507, an authentic-sounding Stoic phrase despite the doubts raised by Algra 1993, 499 n. 57; cf. also Plato *Men.* 75b, where shape is defined as what always accompanies colour, again with no implication of dependence).

or time has a reality totally derived from that of the bodies travelling though it.[116] Rather, they are presupposed as the background to motion, the dimensions through which the moving bodies must pass in order to move at all.

So far, then, we have seen that place, void and time are all classed as incorporeals because they provide the dimensions within which bodily movement can occur, and must therefore themselves be independent of body.[117] The remaining item on the list of incorporeals is the *lekton*, literally 'sayable' or 'thing said' (from λέγειν, 'to say'), but better left untranslated. It is treated in more detail elsewhere in this volume.[118] Our task at present is to account for its inclusion in the list of incorporeals.

Plato in the *Sophist* (261–2) distinguishes two linguistic tasks: naming, which is to pick out a subject, and 'saying' (λέγειν), which is, roughly, to attach a predicate to that subject. This is probably the background to the Stoic *lekton*, which seems to have originally meant, as distinct from a subject, the sort of thing that you can say (λέγειν) about a subject.[119] As in Plato, it is typically expressed by a verb like 'walks'. The earliest attested use of the term is one attributed to Cleanthes, in the context of causal theory.[120] Causation is the action of one body upon another, say a knife upon flesh. But what the knife brings about in the flesh is not a further body, the cut flesh, since the flesh was there all along. It brings about an incorporeal *lekton*, namely the predicate 'is cut' which comes to be truly predicable of that body. Thus in a causal context, what can be said of a body is a distinct, incorporeal item, without which the causal process could not be rationally analysed.

A closely comparable use of the *lekton* is in the Stoic account of wishing. Wishes are not for bodies, but for the incorporeal predicates which we want to belong to us.[121] Here too, similar reasoning can be conjectured: if I want to be happy, my wish is not for my happiness, which is my (corporeal) soul in a certain state; my soul already exists, and the addition I desire is not a further body, but for something to be true of my soul which is not true now, namely that it 'is happy'. There is reason to regard this as another very early Stoic use of the *lekton*, since it was apparently drawn from the work of the Stoics' immediate precursors in logic, the Dialectical school.[122]

---

[116] Likewise the very name *lekton*, 'sayable', specifies its linguistic function, although especially in their causal role *lekta* subsist even when not being 'said'.

[117] For a less homogenizing interpretation, see Algra 1993.   [118] See above, pp. 197–213.

[119] Plato's distinction between naming and saying is preserved in Seneca's account of the *lekton* at *Ep.* 117.13.   [120] Clem. *Strom.* VIII.9.26.3–4, with the important observations of Frede 1977.

[121] Stob. II.97.15–98.6.   [122] As argued by Brunschwig 1990b, 391.

Stoic logic applied the same analysis to the predicates which are expressed by verbs within complete grammatical sentences. Since predicates only serve a full linguistic function when a subject for them is also named, the notion of a 'complete *lekton*' is used to mark off such cases. Hence a sentence like 'Dion walks' turns out to express an incorporeal complete *lekton* – despite the fact that the name 'Dion', taken by itself, does not express anything incorporeal at all.[123] This is the road leading to a highly characteristic Stoic view, that the propositions with which logic concerns itself are not sentences but the incorporeal *lekta* expressed by declarative sentences.

Place, void and time have proved to have some sort of mind-independent reality. Can the same be said for *lekta*? The original causal role of *lekta* strongly suggests that it can, since causal processes presumably go on in the same way whether or not anyone is there to analyse them. It is true that the *lekton* is defined as 'that which subsists in correspondence with a rational impression' (e.g. D.L. VII.63), which could be taken to make it parasitic on the thought processes of rational beings. But the definition need mean no more than that a *lekton* is a formal structure onto which rational thoughts, like the sentences into which they can be translated, must be mapped. We may compare what we have learnt of space – an objective dimension onto which the motions of bodies are to be mapped, but not altogether parasitic on those motions for its reality. The analogy must not be pushed too far, since the *lekton* differs from the other three incorporeals in not being any kind of mathematically analysable extension. But if rationality is as much an intrinsic feature of the Stoic world as dimensionality, we should not resist the implication that there are objective parameters against which its rational structures can be measured.[124]

It would be tidy to leave the subject there, but there is one annoying loose end left. Should mathematical limits not constitute a fifth incorporeal? 'Chrysippus said that bodies are divided to infinity, and likewise things comparable to bodies, such as surface, line, place, void and time' (Stob. 1.142.2–6). This might well seem to locate surfaces and lines in the class of incorporeals; and the inference that limits are incorporeals is indeed drawn not only by the unfriendly Plutarch (*Comm. Not.* 1080e), but even, with regard to surfaces, by the late Stoic cosmologist Cleomedes

---

[123] For this view, see Long 1971c, Long and Sedley 1987, vol. I, 195–202. Contra, see above, pp. 207–8.

[124] Cf. D.L. VII.53, 'Somethings (τινά: see below, pp. 410–11) are also conceived by transition (μετάβασις), e.g. *lekta* and place.' Whatever this obscure process may be, it seems that *lekta* and place are conceived in the same way. This would be surprising if *lekta* were actually generated by thought while place was discovered by it.

(1.1.139–42 Todd). In the previous section, on the other hand, we saw how the Stoics drew certain advantages from the thesis that points, instants and other limits are pure idealizations, lacking in mind-independent reality. Taking that consideration along with the immediately foregoing conclusion, we can conjecture that the Stoic list of incorporeals is designed to include only those items which, albeit not bodies, are an ineliminable part of the world's objective structure.

7. Qualities[125]

We have now learnt how far the Stoics are prepared to go in modifying their determinedly corporealist programme. The agenda, we saw earlier,[126] was set by Plato, who had doubted whether even the most committed materialist could hold that souls, and their virtues and vices, are bodies. Here the Stoics are quite confident that they can allay Plato's doubts.

That the soul itself is corporeal follows from its being a specially attuned portion of *pneuma*.[127] What must now be emphasized is that every quality (ποιότης) that a thing has is likewise a portion of its *pneuma*, or its *pneuma* in a certain state. Hence the *pneuma* that constitutes your soul also constitutes your individual psychic qualities, including your virtues or vices. Without being corporeal, how could these mental qualities so evidently have causal efficacy on the movements of your body?

A thing's *pneuma*, in its role as its 'state' (ἕξις), is also what makes it cohere as a single entity, or as what is technically called a 'whole' (ὅλον) and 'unified' (ἡνωμένον).[128] Since a quality is a single portion of *pneuma*, it follows that only a whole can have a quality. And there are two main kinds of whole: (i) discrete entities like animals, plants and stones, and (ii) the entire world. Any collection of discrete items, like an army or a forest, or any composite artefact like a ship, is discounted. Since these have no unifying *pneuma*, they have no quality. That is not to say that they cannot be 'qualified' in this or that way: the army may be fanatical, the ship unseaworthy. But these are qualifications which fail to correspond to an intrinsic 'quality', in the technical sense of that term (Simp. *Cat.* 214.24–37). Analogously (S.E. *M* IX.332), while the world is a unified whole – it is in fact called 'the Whole' – the universe is not, since the world and the surrounding void do not jointly constitute a pneumatically cohering entity: it is simply called 'the All', the sum total of things.

---

[125] Texts: *SVF* II 76–98, *FDS* 831–65. Comment: Rieth 1933, 22–9, 55–69, Sedley 1982b, Long and Sedley 1987, vol. I, 166–76, Brunschwig 1988a.   [126] Above, p. 383.
[127] See below, pp. 562–72.   [128] See p. 482 (with n.9) on cohesive or containing causes.

Even where there is a single *pneuma*, not every qualification corresponds to a 'quality' (Simp. *Cat.* 212.12–213.1). On a broad enough sense of 'qualified', even temporary activities like running are qualifications, as are habitual activities like gluttony. But qualities, properly understood, are long-term dispositional states, which persist even when the corresponding activity is prevented. Thus the paradigmatic Stoic cases of quality are virtues and vices, the transition from vice to virtue being rare and difficult, and virtue, once acquired, hard if not impossible to lose. In fact the Stoics' central concern with the status of virtues and vices may be one factor that explains their preference for the stricter notion of quality. Another may be their search for an inalienable quality unique to each individual. It is to this latter that we now turn.

*

The type of quality we have been considering so far has been that of the 'commonly qualified individual' (κοινῶς ποιός), as typically signified by a common noun or adjective like 'man' or 'wise'. But an equally important type, with a history of its own, is that of the 'peculiarly qualified individual' (ἰδίως ποιός), as typically expressed by a proper name like 'Dion'. This is an individual viewed in the light of whatever characteristic makes him that person and no other. The Stoic thesis is that such unique qualities exist, and that they are lifelong. For once we can trace the theory's origin and motivation in some detail.

Its impetus came from the Growing Argument (αὐξανόμενος λόγος), a puzzle whose author was agreed to be the fifth-century BC Sicilian dramatist Epicharmus. Take any number, and alter it by a small addition or subtraction. You cannot say that the number has grown or shrunk: rather, it has been replaced by a new number. Now apply the same thought to yourself. If the particles of matter which jointly constitute you have a single particle added, that is no longer you but a new set of particles. In which case not only are our identities constantly changing, but we cannot ever grow: since every new particle added creates a new individual, there is no enduring individual who can be said to have done the growing.

We learn from Plutarch (*Comm. Not.* 1083a–1084a) that the Academics propounded a version of this against the Stoics, and that the Stoic (almost certainly Chrysippean) response was to analyse an individual at two distinct levels: (i) a 'substance', a standard Stoic term for matter, and (ii) a 'peculiarly qualified individual'.[129] Viewed as (i) a lump of matter, you

---

[129] The text is defective here, but other sources support the supplement ἰδίως ποιός.

cannot be said to grow, and for exactly the reasons given by the Growing Argument. Your matter comes and goes, and in itself retains no enduring identity. But viewed as individuated by the peculiar quality that makes you the person you are, you do have enduring identity: and it is that peculiar individual who can be correctly said to grow.

What is the relation of you the peculiarly qualified individual to you the lump of matter? Not one of simple identity, or the two of you would have identical histories. Not that of two distinct individuals either, as Plutarch maliciously tries to infer. The lump of matter is a *part* of you the qualified individual (Ar. Did. *ap.* Stob.1.179.2–3), since it constitutes you jointly with your qualities.[130] And a part, according to the Stoics, is neither identical with the whole nor different from it.[131]

From what we have now seen, it follows that your sustained self-identity over your lifetime depends on your retaining your peculiar quality from birth to death (Simp. *de An.* 217.36–218.2). What could such a quality be? While there is a little evidence that it may have been assumed to be a unique blend of common qualities (Dexippus *Cat.* 30.20–6), it is extremely hard to see how any suitable such combination could plausibly be thought lifelong. It is perhaps better to say that the Stoics were confident, on their own metaphysical grounds and perhaps also intuitively, that there must be such a quality; it was left for twentieth-century biochemistry to tell us what it is – the individual's genetic code.

One reason for the Stoics' confidence is epistemological. Their defence of the cognitive impression also relies in part on the doctrine that every individual is qualitatively unique.[132] Academic attacks on cognitive certainty had centred on the challenge that for every true impression there might be an indiscernible false one. The Stoics' uniqueness thesis thus not only serves the metaphysical role we have seen, but also comes to the aid of their epistemology by ensuring that every individual can in principle be recognized on the basis of an intrinsic and inalienable property – the role which in the twentieth century has in certain contexts come to be filled by fingerprints. In attempting to turn the tables on their Academic opponents, the Stoics alleged that their indiscernibility challenge amounted to 'forcing a single qualified individual to occupy two substances' (Plu. *Comm. Not.* 1077c) – the alleged metaphysical absurdity of locating one and the same individual in two separate bodies.

*

---

[130] Retaining the MSS reading τὴν οὐσίαν at 179.3.
[131] S.E. *M* IX.336. The distinction originates from Plato *Parm.* 146b. See also Barnes 1988b, 262–5.
[132] See pp. 300–13, esp. 308–10.

Whether or not a peculiar quality is analysable as a set of common qualities, the question arises how the different common qualities are related to each other within a single individual. Iamblichus offers the following clues:

> How are the soul's faculties distinguished? Some of them, according to the Stoics, by a difference in the underlying bodies. For they say that a sequence of different portions of *pneuma* extends from the commanding-faculty, some to the eyes, others to the ears and others to other sense-organs. Other faculties are differentiated by a peculiarity of quality in regard to the same substrate. Just as an apple possesses in the same body sweetness and fragrance, so too the commanding-faculty combines in the same body impression, assent, impulse, reason. (Iambl. *De an. ap.* Stob. 1.368.12–20)

What Iamblichus applies to soul faculties can equally well be applied to other kinds of pneumatic state, including qualities. The soul itself permeates the whole body, although with some concentration in the commanding-faculty (ἡγεμονικόν), located in the chest. Some qualities, such as strength and good eyesight, will be located in the *pneuma* linking the commanding-faculty to the appropriate limbs and organs. But each mental quality is concentrated in the commanding-faculty itself, so that for example all the virtues become materially coextensive there. This fits in with the fact that Chrysippus, who wrote at length to establish that each virtue is a distinct quality (Gal. *PHP* vii.1.12–15), nevertheless considered them all to be states of the intellect, inseparable because they are sciences with their main theorems in common.[133] He can hardly have failed to locate them together in the very same portion of *pneuma*. Any lingering puzzlement as to why coextensive qualities do not erase each other he would have blamed on physical naivety – just as on another occasion he warned for similar reasons against too literal a reading of Zeno's 'wax imprint' account of mental impressions, substituting the more subtle but still physical analogy of a single portion of air simultaneously carrying multiple sounds (S.E. *M* vii.228–31).

Two or more common qualities, then, can coexist in the same portion of matter. It seems equally clear that two or more peculiar qualities cannot – not in the sense that I might not have two or more unique qualities, but in the sense that the same piece of matter cannot simultaneously have the distinguishing qualities of two or more different individuals, for example (to use the standard Stoic example) be both Dion and Theon simultaneously. Chrysippus is reported to have considered the following puzzle.[134]

---

[133] See pp. 717–18.   [134] Philo *Aet.* 48; interpretation in Sedley 1982b.

Take an individual, Dion, and give the name Theon to that portion of him
which includes everything except one foot. Then amputate the foot. Dion
and Theon now threaten to be two individuals occupying precisely the
same material substance at the same time. Since that is impossible, we
must ask which one of them has perished. Chrysippus' answer is: Theon.
Why is Dion the survivor? Apparently because the survivor is visibly
someone whose foot has just been amputated, and that can only be Dion:
Theon cannot have lost a foot he never had.

The puzzle confirms Chrysippus' own commitment to the principle
that two peculiarly qualified individuals cannot occupy one and the
same substance – common ground in the debate between Stoics
and Academics.[135] But another of its premisses hardly looks Stoic.
Chrysippus can surely not have accepted that Dion and Theon even start
out as distinct individuals. They are related as whole to part. Only the foot
differentiates them, and it cannot have been or contained Dion's peculiar
quality, since he turns out to survive its loss. The premiss looks more like
one dialectically assigned to the Academics, whose Growing Argument
does implicitly make whole and part into distinct individuals, at least to
the extent that, as we have seen, it takes every material addition to generate a new individual. Significantly, Chrysippus' discussion is said to have
been in his work *On the Growing Argument*. We may speculate that his aim
was to turn the Growing Argument against the Academics by concocting
an instance in which material diminution, far from terminating someone's identity, is actually a condition of enduring identity: the undimin-
ished Theon perishes, while it is the diminished Dion who survives.

8. The four genera[136]

In reporting the Stoics' solution to the Growing Argument, Plutarch
(*Comm. Not.* 1083a-1084a) mocks their analysis of each individual into two
distinct items, substance and quality. He adds that in fact the Stoics make
each of us not just two but four things, but that two are quite enough to
bring out the absurdity. What are the four things? There is no doubt that
he is referring to the doctrine which modern convention has dubbed
that of the four Stoic 'categories', although there is no reason to think that
they used that term or that, as its use implies, they compared their theory
to Aristotle's category theory. It was debated whether Aristotle's theory

---

[135] Despite Plutarch's attempts to show that the Stoics contravene it in their conflagration doctrine, *Comm. Not.* 1077c–e.
[136] Texts: *SVF* II 369–404, *FDS* 827–73. Literature: Rieth 1933, esp. 55–91, A. C. Lloyd 1971, Long
and Sedley 1987, vol. I, 166–79, Mignucci 1988, Rist 1969b.

was linguistic or ontological in orientation, and Athenodorus (first century BC), the only Stoic whose views on it are recorded,[137] argued that it was linguistic, whereas one thing that is relatively uncontroversial about the Stoic theory is that it is ontological. Our sources report it as a classification of 'genera' (γένη) of being, although there is no evidence that even this term was the Stoics' own. Plutarch passes on one more salient feature of the theory: each individual is four things, that is, each individual can be viewed under all four aspects.

The four genera are: object (ὑποκείμενον), qualified (ποιόν), disposed in a certain way (πως ἔχον), and relatively disposed in a certain way (πρὸς τί πως ἔχον). The first two we have already met in the previous section. Any being can be thought of (ignoring its distinctive qualities) merely as an object, something out there, and as such it is treated simply as a discrete lump of matter, which in Stoic usage is most commonly called 'substance'.[138] It can also be thought of as an object possessing a set of qualities, both common and peculiar. Plutarch's evidence showed how that distinction probably evolved largely in response to the Academic Growing Argument.

We must now consider the physics underlying the distinction between quality and 'substance'. Qualities are portions of *pneuma*, consisting of one or both of the active elements fire and air, in relation to which the role of substance is taken by one or both of the passive elements earth and water. At this level of analysis, matter is not totally undifferentiated in a way comparable to prime matter, since earth and water have their own distinctive properties – they are dry and wet respectively, and both have a centripetal motion. But it falls to *pneuma* to endow them not only, in the case of living things, with vital properties, but even with the basic cohesion which makes anything a single entity. Thus from the point of view of Stoic metaphysics, which is very much a metaphysics of discrete singular entities, elemental substance does count as undifferentiated, and its role is firmly material.

The 'object', then, may well be the discrete mass of passive elements in which qualities are found. But the Stoics' usage is flexible on this point, and we hear of them varying the use of the term both downwards, to real prime matter, and upwards to commonly qualified stuffs, like bronze, or even to peculiarly qualified individuals, which in turn serve as the bearers

---

[137] Simp. *Cat.* 18.26–19.7, 62.25–7, 128.5–8. He also, far from comparing the Aristotelian ten with the Stoic four, argued that ten was too *few*.

[138] Cf. Plutarch (*Comm. Not.* 1083a–1084a) where substance (οὐσία) is quite clearly what the Stoics call the first of the four genera.

of further qualities (Porphyry, quoted by Simp. *Cat.* 48.11–16). This points to a cardinal feature of the Stoic theory of genera: that an item does not belong absolutely to only one genus. The feature can now be illustrated by turning to the third genus.

> Truth is a body. For it is knowledge (ἐπιστήμη) capable of stating everything true; and knowledge is the commanding faculty (ἡγεμονικόν) disposed in a certain way, just as the fist is the hand disposed in a certain way; and the commanding-faculty is a body. (S.E. *PH* II.81)

This is a typical manoeuvre of Stoic corporealism, using the third genus to re-analyse an apparent incorporeal as a body. In so far as the commanding-faculty is thought of as already qualified, and therefore as belonging to the second genus, a further differentiation of it such as knowledge is placed in the third genus, being the commanding-faculty 'disposed in a certain way'. Now one kind of knowledge is virtue, and Chrysippus placed the virtues in the *second* genus, arguing that each was a distinct quality. Do we then have a contradiction? Not at all. Relative to the commanding-faculty virtue stands in the third genus, while relative to the body it stands in the second. Likewise, we may take it, the human body stands in the first genus, substrate, relative to mental qualities, but in the second genus, qualified, relative to its constituent earth and water.

Use of the third genus in Stoic corporealist analyses is extremely widespread. It is not always instantly recognizable, because the generic formula 'disposed in a certain way' will often be replaced by a specific description of that disposition. For instance, a word is corporeal because any sound is 'air struck in a certain way' (D.L. VII.55),[139] and winter is 'the air above the earth cooled because of the distancing of the sun' (D.L. VII. 151).

The fourth genus, 'relatively disposed in a certain way', is explained in a complex passage from Simplicius.[140] Items thus classed are not merely relative (πρός τι, as opposed to καθ' αὑτά, *per se*).[141] The sweet is relative, since to be sweet involves having such and such an effect on a per-

---

[139] See *FDS* 479–87 for the use of this formula in defence of Stoic corporealism.

[140] *Cat.* 165.32–166.29, a text very thoroughly examined by Mignucci 1988. In reply to Mignucci's doubts about the attributability to Chrysippus of this genus, at least as described by Simplicius, it may be observed that Plutarch (*Comm. Not.* 1083a–1084a) indirectly associates all four genera with Chrysippus, that Chrysippus' debate with Aristo (below) contrasts the second with the fourth genus in a way which matches Simplicius' analysis well, and that the Chrysippean fragment at Plu. *Stoic. Rep.* 1054e-f, discussed below, also seems to use the fourth genus as described by Simplicius.

[141] This familiar categorial distinction between *per se* and relative, of Platonist origin, is used by the Stoics, as by the Epicureans and Academics (p. 382 above), but it is not itself part of the four-genera scheme.

ceiver, but it is also an internal qualitative state of the item thus described, which remains sweet whether or not it is being tasted. So a merely relative property like this is 'differentiated' (κατὰ διαφοράν), that is, intrinsically characterized, and can comfortably belong in the second genus, 'qualified'. The fourth genus is reserved for items whose very being depends on a relation, so that a change in their relata is sufficient to terminate their existence, even if the items undergo no internal change at all: perhaps 'property', for example, since my property can cease to be property if, although it remains intact, I die or relinquish it. For the Stoics Simplicius records the examples 'on the right' and 'father'.

The most celebrated context in which this genus was put to work was the debate between Aristo and Chrysippus about the Unity of the Virtues.[142] Aristo considered virtue to be a single state of psychic health, with its so-called species – justice, courage etc. – differentiated merely by the circumstances in which it was placed, as if, he said, one were to call vision 'blackseeing' and 'whiteseeing' according to its current objects. Whether or not Aristo used the technical designation 'relatively disposed in a certain way', Chrysippus certainly took him to be placing the species of virtue in this fourth genus, and criticized him accordingly, defending instead his own view that each virtue is a distinct qualitative state of the soul.

Chrysippus also used the fourth genus to make a point about whole-part relations (Plu. *Stoic. Rep.* 1054e–f).[143] A whole is complete, but its parts are not, 'because they are disposed in certain ways relative to the whole'. The characterization of a part can change purely due to an intrinsic change elsewhere in the whole. My finger, while intrinsically unchanged, can become an invalid's finger if I break my leg. But the reverse cannot occur: any intrinsic change in the part is *ipso facto* an intrinsic change in the whole as well: I could not stand in any merely external relation to my leg or finger. The same applies to that ultimate whole, the world, which alone is totally self-contained, with none of its characterizations depending on an external relation. Under some characterization everything else, including us, is what it is through its external relation to the rest of the world – a thought fundamental to Stoic ethics. Being a father is just one example of a fourth-genus relationship which imposes moral obligations. Citizenship, both local and cosmic might well count as another.[144]

---

[142] See p. 718.   [143] On Stoic treatments of part-whole relations in general, see Barnes 1988b.
[144] Cf. Epict. *Ench.*30.

We can thus see reasons for accepting Plutarch's report that, for the Stoics, 'each of us is four things'. You are not just (1) a lump of matter, but have (2) psychic qualities which characterize you, both as a human being and as the unique individual you are; (3) further dispositions of those qualities, which represent your individual mental states; and finally (4) certain extrinsic relations to the world, which are necessary to complete the picture of what, and who, you are.

9. 'Something' and 'not-something'[145]

The Stoic world includes both bodies and incorporeals. Bodies 'are'. Incorporeals lack being, but do at least 'subsist' – indicating perhaps that they are proper objects of discourse and part of the background against which the interaction of bodies is to be understood.[146] Bodies and incorporeals, which jointly constitute the 'all',[147] form a single domain of discourse. Consequently it becomes natural for the Stoics to make them joint members of a single supreme genus, broader even than being. Possibly taking a lead from Plato,[148] they christen this class the 'something' (τό τι). Given its utter generality, what characteristics could it possibly have to entitle it to be considered a unified class? A plausible answer seems available from the sources. Even the class of 'somethings' has a membership requirement that still manages to exclude one class of item, namely universals, which are relegated to the separate class of 'not-somethings' (οὔτινα).[149] In short, 'something' is a designation limited to *individuals*.

The Stoics have a formal demonstration of this. Take a universal like the species Man, and let it substitute for the term 'something', or its masculine form 'someone' (τις), in a syllogism:

> If someone is in Athens, he is not in Megara.
> But Man is in Athens.
> Therefore Man is not in Megara.[150]

---

[145] Texts: *SVF* I 65, II 329–35, *FDS* 315–21. Comment: Sedley 1985, Brunschwig 1988a.

[146] A third term, which perhaps straddles the first two, is 'to be real' (ὑπάρχειν). Either a body or an incorporeal may 'be real' simply by obtaining in the world. Cf. p. 398 above on the present time as 'being real', and on the cognitive impression as ἀπὸ ὑπάρχοντος etc., probably referring to a complete state of affairs rather than a body as such. For differing views on Stoic ὑπάρχειν, cf. P. Hadot 1969, Goldschmidt 1972, Schubert 1994.   [147] See above, pp. 397, 402.

[148] Despite the doubts of Brunschwig 1988a, 62–3, the Platonist Severus does seem to have read Plato *Tim.* 27d6–28a1 (with indefinite τι instead of interrogative τί) as making 'something' Plato's own supreme genus: see Procl. *Tim.* I.227.15–17. This may reflect a Stoic reading of the same passage.

[149] See Brunschwig 1988a, 31–3 for the suggestion of other possible 'not-somethings' – the 'all', and fictional entities. At ib. 56–7 he argues that the Stoic inclusion of fictional items in the 'something' class reported at Sen. *Ep.* 58.15 is non-standard. However, it might also be questioned whether they could be thought to pass the 'not-something' test, on which see immediately below.   [150] Simp. *Cat.* 105.9–16.

The syllogism's invalidity evidently arises from allowing a species, Man, to count as a 'someone'. The implication is that such a species is 'not-someone'. To make this lesson unambiguous, the argument was known as the 'Not-someone (οὔτις) argument'.

The lesson has a particular anti-Platonic point to make, for Platonic Forms were regarded by the Stoics as false pretenders to the status of individuals:

> (Zeno's doctrine) They say that concepts (ἐννοήματα) are neither somethings nor qualified, but figments (φαντάσματα) of the soul which are quasi-somethings and quasi-qualified. These, they say, are what the old philosophers called Ideas. For the Ideas are of the things which are classified under the concepts, such as men, horses, and in general all the animals and other things of which they say that there are Ideas. The Stoic philosophers say that the Ideas are unreal, and that what we 'participate in' are the concepts, while what we 'bear' (τυγχάνειν) are those cases which they call 'appellatives'. (Stob. 1.136.21–137.6)

This compressed but important text is perhaps less a dismissal of Platonic Forms than an attempt to recategorize them in Stoic terms. The universal Man is no part of the actual furniture of this or any other world, as the Platonists wanted him to be. He is a 'concept', the intensional object of a mental act of conceptualization on our part, and as such a mere 'figment' of our thought. Nevertheless, he is indispensable. As the final sentence says, we can be said to belong to ('participate in') the species, and it is in virtue of that membership that we are describable by the common noun 'man'.

Moreover, the primary Stoic dialectical activities, definition and division, were regarded as having these fictional concepts as their objects. When you define Man, or divide Animal into Man, Horse etc., these are not individual men and horses, they are the corresponding concepts, or species. Then doesn't the Not-someone argument show that, as such, they are to be excluded from rational discourse? Fortunately not, because statements about them can be easily translated into logically impeccable talk about 'somethings'. Thus the definition 'Man is a rational mortal animal' is given the same logical force as 'If something is a man, that thing is a rational mortal animal', and likewise the division 'Of existing things some are good, some bad, some intermediate' is translatable as 'If some things (or 'somethings': τινα) are existent, they are either good or bad or indifferent' (S.E. *M* xi.8–11). The important Stoic lesson here is, not to abandon all talk of universals, but to be aware that when you talk about them you are using a convenient fiction, whose truth content is represented by generalized conditionals ranging over all individuals.

12

Cosmology

DAVID FURLEY

1 Introduction: the fourth-century legacy

By the time of the death of Aristotle, there was some measure of agreement among educated Greeks about the nature of the cosmos. The word cosmos itself soon acquired a canonical meaning. Aristotle used it in its wider sense to mean 'good order' or 'elegance', but in the context of the study of the natural world he used it as a synonym for *ouranos*, thinking particularly of the heavens and their orderly movements. But the word was defined by the Stoic Chrysippus as a 'system of heaven and earth and the natures contained in these' (Ar. Did. fr. 31 *ap*. Stob. 1.184.8–10), and this is a definition that reappears, sometimes with small variations, fairly frequently. It is repeated by the Peripatetic author of the treatise *On the Cosmos* attributed to Aristotle (391b9). The Epicurean definition was not significantly different (Ep. *Ep. Pyth.* 88).

From the start this definition marks a difference between the classical use of the word and our own in the twentieth century. The ancient use of the word leaves open the possibility that the cosmos in which we live is only a part of the universe. A cosmos is a limited system, bounded on its periphery by the heavens: what lay beyond the heavens of our cosmos, if anything, was open to debate. This chapter will therefore be careful to preserve the distinction between the cosmos and the universe.

Aristotle had already provided arguments to show that the earth does not move and occupies a position at the centre of the cosmos (*Cael.* 11.14). These two propositions were almost universally agreed upon; the observed movements of the heavens were therefore interpreted as real movements. An exception with regard to the earth was Aristarchus of Samos, who theorized that the sun was the centre, on which see below.[1]

It was quite generally agreed, too, that the orbits of the heavenly bodies were circular, and that the shape of the heavens as a whole was spherical.

---

[1] See below, p. 596.

The great astronomers of the fourth century, Eudoxus and Callippus, had worked out a model of concentric spheres, each inner one having poles located in the one next to it on the outside. The outermost sphere rotated on its axis once a day. The inner spheres rotated on their own axes, the poles of which moved in circular orbits around the axis of the next outer sphere, in which they were fixed. The observed motions of the stars, planets, and moon were explained on the assumptions that the stars were fixed to the outermost sphere, and the other heavenly bodies to the inner spheres. Aristotle had adopted this model for his cosmology (*Cael.* I–II and *Metaph.* Λ). Not all of the Hellenistic cosmologists adopted the model of concentric spheres, but there was general agreement that the stars mark the spherical outer boundary of our cosmos.

This left a wide area in which controversy was possible. In fact the classical period bequeathed not one orthodox cosmology but two opposed theories, and since both of them reappear, with variations, in the Hellenistic period, something must be said about both.

Before Plato and Aristotle there was Democritus, writing in the last decades of the fifth century, and his atomic theory of the natural world. Plato wrote the *Timaeus*, in which he adopted positions that were systematically opposed to Democritus on most issues, although he never mentioned Democritus; a generation later again Aristotle worked out a theory that rejected all the important cosmological theses of Democriteanism. It is worth setting out the points of difference in summary form, before looking at the way in which the Hellenistic thinkers adapted them.

Democritus held that our world is one among an infinite number of worlds, past, present, and future, in an infinite universe; Plato and Aristotle took our cosmos to be all that there is or was or will be. Democritus believed our cosmos to have had a beginning in time, and to be ultimately perishable: it is a mortal compound, no more stable, ultimately, than the mortal creatures that inhabit it; Plato and Aristotle both believed that our cosmos will remain eternally the same, although Plato wrote about the creation of the cosmos, whereas Aristotle denied that it had any beginning.

Democritus held that gods had no part in the organization and maintenance of the physical world-order. Plato and Aristotle both gave gods a part to play, although they differed widely from each other about the manner of it. In the *Timaeus* – a dialogue of immense influence in later history – Plato tells a story of the creation of the cosmos by a Craftsman God and a team of subordinate gods. He works out the process of creation in detail: first the making of the heavens, which are the soul of the world, then the construction of the world's body, beginning with the four elements and working up to the complexity of the human body. Throughout, Plato stresses that the Craftsman aims at the greatest possible beauty of design, given that perfection is impeded by the recalcitrance of matter. Some of Plato's immediate pupils took Plato's creation story to be no more than an explanatory device; but it could not be doubted, because of what he wrote elsewhere (especially in *Laws* x), that he regarded the heavens as divine beings. Aristotle took Plato's creation story literally, and expressed his disagreement with it. In his view the heavens and the whole cosmic order are without beginning or end in time. Like Plato, he did not doubt that the heavenly bodies are divine beings, ensouled and alive; and he made their eternal revolutions – and through their influence also the eternal cycles of change in the terrestrial region – dependent on a single divine Mover. The divinity of the heavens and the absolute difference between the heavens and the earthly region are common to the cosmologies of Plato and Aristotle.

Democritus explained the cosmos and its contents as being compounded of indivisible, indestructible, and unchanging atoms, and void space; Aristotle at least – Plato's position was more complicated – argued that there is no void space in the universe, that matter is continuous in the cosmos, and that on earth and in the surrounding atmosphere matter constantly changes its qualities, although it preserves its quantity. Democritus held that the heavens are made of the same kind of matter as the earth; Aristotle posited a special matter for the heavens, endowed with a natural circular motion. Democritus explained the characteristics of compound bodies, including living things, as outcomes of their material components; Aristotle insisted on the priority of form over matter.

In the Hellenistic period the school of Plato turned away from cosmology to mathematics and metaphysics, and later to epistemology. Aristotle's own successors, or some of them at least, took up some of the problems of his *Physics* and *De Caelo*, and discussed the cosmological questions raised in his *Metaphysics*. The achievements of Theophrastus were most striking in the special sciences, but something must be said about his short piece on *Metaphysics*, and about his views on two subjects of particular relevance to cosmology – place, and the fifth element.

It may be the case that his *Metaphysics* is not strictly 'Hellenistic' at all. The text takes a notably critical attitude to several of Aristotle's theses, and consequently is often spoken of as something that postdates Aristotle's own major works. But there is something to be said for the view that it was written during the period of the formation of Aristotle's treatises: perhaps it records Theophrastus' contributions to the discussion within the Peripatos before Theophrastus took over the headship of the school after Aristotle's death.[2] However that may be, Theophrastus argues for a position that in some ways anticipates Stoicism. He is much concerned with the question of the unity of the cosmos. That is to say, he raises doubts about Aristotle's heavenly spheres, made of a different element from the sublunary world contained by the spheres, and about the modes in which such bodies can act as causes of sublunary interactions, as Aristotle's theory requires them to do. The tone of voice is questioning, rather than critical or dogmatic: in his *Metaphysics* Theophrastus does not put forward an articulated alternative theory.

As we shall see in the next two sections, the question of the existence of void space was of the utmost importance in Hellenistic cosmology. Aristotle denied its existence, largely basing his argument on his analysis of the concept of place. Theophrastus raises objections to Aristotle's notion that the place occupied by a body is to be identified as the interior *surface* of the body that surrounds it. We have a reliable record, in a verbatim quotation from Theophrastus by Simplicius (*Phys.* 639.13–22), that Theophrastus developed instead a theory of place as *order* (τάξις), deriving the idea from the natural relative positions of the parts of an organism.[3] Once Aristotle's identification of place as a surrounding surface is dropped, and once other concepts of place (such as place as a three-dimensional extension) become more prominent, the way lies open to the possibility of an *empty* place; at any rate other grounds than mere incompatibility with Aristotle's conception of place must be found if that possibility is to be denied.

Theophrastus devoted a comparatively lengthy portion of his *Metaphysics* to the subject of causation, and particularly to the range of the final cause in natural processes.[4] He is troubled by the generality of Aristotle's remark that 'nature does nothing at random', and debates whether some natural processes can be explained wholly in terms of matter in motion – as Aristotle himself proposed in his more cautious moments.

Theophrastus' successor Strato of Lampsacus also interested himself in the two problems of space and teleology.[5] Like Theophrastus, he appears

---

[2] See Laks and Most 1993a for discussion of this point.

[3] Simp. *Phys.* 604.5–11. Different interpretations of this fragment and of Theophrastus' position have been given by Sorabji 1988, 192–204, and Algra 1992, 146–65 and 1995, 237–48.

[4] Especially 10a21–b25. See Lennox 1985.   [5] Texts: Wehrli 1969a, Gottschalk 1965.

to have been critical of Aristotle's conception of place as a surrounding surface – he defined it instead as the volume contained by the interior surface of the surrounding body – but the scanty surviving evidence suggests that he nevertheless continued to deny the existence of the kind of void space believed in by the Epicureans and the Stoics. What he did allow was a concept of 'microvoid', as it may be called – imperceptibly small interstices of empty space in the texture of material bodies. This thesis was used to explain phenomena such as compression, and the penetration of light and heat through apparently solid bodies.[6] It was the basis for the mechanics adopted by Hero of Alexandria in his *Pneumatica*, but was irrelevant, for different reasons, both to Epicurean and to Stoic physics. There is solid evidence that Strato rejected the purposive teleology of Plato's *Timaeus* and Stoic pantheism, substituting nature itself as a satisfactory ultimate cause of natural processes, but it is not clear that he went all the way with Democritus and other Atomists in this regard.[7]

What was Theophrastus' position concerning Aristotle's fifth element? It has been argued that he did indeed drop the fifth element, and so removed the radical dualism of heaven and earth from the Peripatetic system.[8] A case can be made for thinking that he worked out alternative means of dealing with the consequent problems of durability and circularity. But the evidence is contradictory, and I believe the balance tells the other way.

First, the evidence for Theophrastus' retention of the dualism. There is a direct statement that he did so in a passage quoted from the Platonist Taurus by Philoponus (*Aet. Mund.* 13.15). We do not know the context from which Taurus took this, and it might be part of a dialectical passage in which Theophrastus was mentioning arguments to which he did not subscribe. More compelling is a quotation from Simp. *Phys.* 20.17, which implies that Theophrastus drew a distinction between the element of the heavens, where locomotion is the only form of change, and the sublunary elements, which are perishable.

A passage from Theophrastus' *Metaphysics* (10a10–19) rules out the possibility that the heavens are composed of elements whose natural motions are up or down; in that case, it would be necessary to explain why the heavens move in circular orbits. Theophrastus claims that their move-

[6] Strato fr. 65a Wehrli. See Gottschalk 1965, and Furley 1989b (1985).
[7] Strato frr. 32–7. Plutarch (*Col.* 1115b) claims that he made nature subordinate to chance, and that τὸ αὐτόματον is the source of natural motions. But Cicero (*Acad.* 11.32) *contrasts* his idea of natural motions with Democritus' conception of the motion of atoms in the void.
[8] See Steinmetz 1964, 158–68, and Gottschalk 1967.

ment needs no explanation, and that must be because circular motion is natural to them, as it is not natural to the earthly elements.[9]

If Theophrastus remains an orthodox Aristotelian in his view of the fifth element, he nevertheless appears to be more concerned than Aristotle was with the question of the unity of the cosmos.[10] He complains (*Metaph.* 5b19–26) that in Aristotle's scheme the movements of the sublunary world are a mere accidental effect of the rotation of the heavens. His own answer appears to be based on a new distinction between heat and fire. There are difficulties in supposing that the sun is composed of fire, and that its life-giving energy comes from a fiery nature: fire needs fuel, but the sun does not; fire consumes things, but the sun does not. But Theophrastus holds, in opposition to Aristotle, that heat is of the essence of the sun, and is involved in its actuality (*entelecheia*). The actuality of the sun corresponds to a receptiveness in the sublunary world; so there is an essential, not accidental, connection between the sun's heat and its motions and the cycles of change in the sublunary world.[11] To summarize the position of Theophrastus, it was a concern of his that Aristotle's world picture was too dualistic: the connection between the heavens and the sublunary world seemed too much a matter of chance. One of the moves he proposed to overcome this was to claim that the heat of the sun is not an accident but part of its essence, and hence that the action of this heat on the sublunary world was part of the sun's essential nature.

Theophrastus' successor Strato did away with the fifth element (fr. 84), but the surviving fragments do not reveal his arguments for this shift.

The really important cosmological theories of the Hellenistic period were the work of Epicurus and the Stoics.[12] There is much that is new in both of them, but it is nevertheless a striking fact that these two major schools differed from each other in very much the same way as Democritus differed from Plato and Aristotle. Epicurus adopted Democritean Atomism; the Stoic school followed Plato and Aristotle. Neither of them

[9] Is this claim inconsistent with the view that the motion of the heavens comes about through desire? Perhaps it is the *form* of their motion that is in question here. They move, because of desire to emulate the life of the Unmoved Mover; they move *in circles*, because that is part of their essence. On the other hand, it appears to be movement itself, rather than a particular form of movement, that is of their essence. Then we must take it that their desire is itself an expression of their essence, not a cause apart from their essence.

[10] Although I disagree with Steinmetz 1964 about Theophrastus' view of the fifth element, I find much of importance in his analysis of Theophrastus' theories about the connections between heaven and earth.   [11] See Simp. *Phys.* 1236.1–10.

[12] That is, if we confine our investigation to *physical* cosmological theories, and disregard for the moment the important developments in Hellenistic *mathematical* astronomy, on which see below, pp. 595–9.

followed slavishly or pedantically: there were considerable differences of emphasis, and even substantial modifications.[13] But the general outlines are unmistakeable.

II The Epicureans

1. The goal of Epicurean cosmology[14]

If we were in no way troubled [wrote Epicurus] by our suspicions about what's in the sky, and about death – that it may be something to us – and furthermore by our failure to understand the limits of pains and desires, then we would have no need of natural science (phusiologia). (KD 11 ap. D.L. x.142)

The same three themes are repeated, at much greater length, by Lucretius: the evils of religious fear in I.80–101, II.1090–104, V.1218–40, VI.379–1094; of fear of death in III.830–1094; of unlimited desires in II.1–61, IV.1037–1287, VI.1–42; and in many shorter passages.

Epicurean cosmology is offered to humanity for its comfort and reassurance. It is important both to grasp this, and not to make too much of it. There have been those who aimed to dismiss Epicureanism as a serious attempt to understand the natural world, on the ground that Epicurus was not a disinterested seeker after truth. But the arguments with which he defended his theories were as good as he could make them; he tackled the propositions of the Timaeus and the Physics,[15] and endeavoured to show that they were wrong and he was right. What matters is whether his arguments were good or not, rather than his psychological motivation for producing them.[16]

But KD 11 should serve to remind us, nevertheless, of the strong and tight connection that was felt to exist between the structure of the natural world and the life of man. This connection was not ignored or denied by Plato and Aristotle: the morality of the Republic is manifestly in tune with the cosmology of the Timaeus, and no one can overlook the influence of

[13] There are texts that suggest that Epicurus seized opportunities for denying his heritage from Democritus, but these have been explained as critical divergence rather than outright refusal to acknowledge any debt. See Sedley 1976a and Huby 1978.

[14] The main texts are Epicurus' Letter to Herodotus (Ep. Hdt.) and Letter to Pythocles (Ep. Pyth.), both preserved in Diogenes Laertius x, and Lucretius De Rerum Natura.

[15] There is little doubt that Epicurus knew the Timaeus: there is a critique of the theory of the four elements as set out in Tim. in PHerc. 1148, identified as containing portions of Epicurus' On Nature xiv (the evidence is discussed by Schmid 1936). There is perhaps more doubt about his knowledge of Aristotle's extant works; see Sandbach 1985, 4–6; for an argument in favour of his knowledge of the Physics see Furley 1967, 18.

[16] Nussbaum 1986 excellently describes the status of Epicurean philosophy as psychotherapy. See now her fuller discussion of the whole issue in Hellenistic philosophy in Nussbaum 1994.

Aristotle's philosophy of nature on the *Nicomachean Ethics*. But the connection becomes even more marked in the Hellenistic period: Epicurean hedonism is hardly separable from Epicurean atomism, and the Stoic Wise Man could hardly be imagined in detachment from the optimistic providentialism of Stoic cosmology. In studying cosmology in this period, it is always necessary to take account of the relation between cosmological theory and morality.

2. *Infinitely numerous atoms in an infinite void*

We have two primary sources for Epicurean cosmology: a brief summary in Epicurus' own *Letter to Herodotus*, and a much fuller account in Lucretius' poem *De rerum natura*, especially the fifth book.[17] Both begin, almost in the manner of a geometrical textbook, with a series of basic propositions of the theory.[18] The most basic of them, which concern the existence of atoms and void and the various shapes of the atoms, have been treated elsewhere in this volume.[19] We shall here concentrate on the more strictly cosmological tenets of the infinite number of the atoms and of the infinite extent of the universe.

The argument for the infinity of the universe is that anything finite has a limit, and a limit is discerned by contrast with something else. Since there *is* nothing other than the universe (this clause is missing from Epicurus' text, but is supplied explicitly by Lucretius), the universe has no limit and consequently must be infinite (*Ep. Hdt.* 41; Lucr. 1.1007). Lucretius adds arguments that are lacking in Epicurus' sparse summary, including an argument borrowed from the old Pythagorean Archytas (see Eudemus *ap.* Simp. *Phys.* 467.25–6): if the universe has a boundary, then imagine yourself situated at the boundary, and ask what happens if you try to thrust a hand beyond the boundary (Lucretius substitutes a javelin for the hand). If the hand goes beyond the boundary, then there is something, namely space, beyond; if not, then there must be something beyond to prevent it. In any case there is something beyond the putative limit of the universe, and since this argument applies to every such limit, the universe is infinite.

In the infinite universe, both matter and space are infinite (*Ep. Hdt.* 42; Lucr. 1.1008–51). If matter were finite but void infinite, there would be no opportunity for atoms to collide and form compounds. If matter were

---

[17] It cannot be assumed without argument that Lucretius follows Epicurus without philosophical theses or arguments of his own. But my own view is that he is a remarkably close follower. See Furley 1989a (1966), Clay 1983a, ch.1, and Sedley 1998. For a contrary view J. Schmidt 1990.
[18] See further Clay 1983a, ch. 4 'The philosophical armature'.   [19] See above, pp. 366–9, 372.

infinite but void finite, there would be no room for the matter. The total of the whole, bodies plus void, remains immutable.[20]

3. The motions of atoms

Epicureans asserted that all atoms have a natural tendency to move downwards.[21] We can observe that every perceptible object that has weight moves downwards when its fall is unimpeded, and there is no reason to deny this same tendency to atoms. Aristotle's theory of the natural upward motion of fire and air is rejected, and a defence of that rejection is supplied at Lucr. 11.184–215. A plank of wood held forcibly under water and then released rises rapidly to the surface, although we know that it is heavy and falls downwards if it is unsupported in air. All atoms are made of the same material, and are naturally thought of as having the same tendency as each other. Observation of the plank of wood in water shows that pressure of some kind can account for the rise of heavy things, and this analogy enables us to understand how some atoms can rise, through the pressure of air, even though they are heavy.

But what does 'downwards' mean? Aristotle had argued that it meant towards the centre of the universe, but the infinite universe of the Epicureans had no centre. Epicurean metaphysics allowed for no forces acting on the atoms except by collision: there was no room for a theory of attraction at a distance. So it was not possible to adopt the idea later put forward by Stoics, that matter was attracted to its own centre, so that downward motion could be regarded as the manifestation of this attraction towards the centre of the cosmic mass. Epicurus and his followers were left, as it seemed, with no option but to take up the assumptions of the builder who uses a plumb-line, that all falling bodies fall in parallel lines at right angles to the earth's surface – this is why the earth's surface is generally speaking flat.

Plutarch says that Epicurus took 'up' and 'down' to be related not to the cosmos but to the universe at large. He writes sarcastically of Epicurus as 'moving all his atoms to the places below our feet – as if either the void has feet or the infinite allows any distinction of down and up in it' (*Def. Or.* 425d). According to Plutarch again, Chrysippus and other Stoics objected to Epicurus that his theory broke down on the impossibility of distin-

---

[20] See Brunschwig 1977 for an analysis of the argument.

[21] This may be a point in which Epicurus differed from Democritus. I have argued that Democritus held this view too (Furley 1989c, ch. 7 (1976) and ch. 8 (1983)). But the point remains controversial. A different view of Democritus' theory is defended at length in O'Brien 1981.

guishing directions in the infinite (*Stoic. Rep.* 1054b). But this is not a valid objection. Epicurus' strategy was extraordinarily simple: he just observed that the plumb-line establishes a direction as a matter of fact, and he asserted that all lines of fall, however far away from this plumb-line in any direction, are parallel to it.[22]

The flat earth was a commonplace of the fifth century and earlier, but after Plato and Aristotle it became hard to accept. Lucretius does his best with it, by poking fun at the idea, which he took to be entailed by the geocentric theory, of creatures walking upside-down on the other side of the world, like the images we see reflected in water. They must see the sun when we see the stars; and their days are our nights (Lucr. 1.1058–67).

It is hard to know what degree of obstinacy and obscurantism, if any, was required to maintain this reactionary position at the end of the fourth century BC. Aristotle's argument for the sphericity of the earth had largely depended on his own centrifocal theory of the natural motions of the elements (*Cael.* II.14.297a8–b23), and we have seen that the Epicureans rejected that theory. But Aristotle already knew of astronomical reasons for believing the earth to be spherical, particularly the observation that as one moves on a north–south line, different stars appear in the zenith (*Cael.* II.14.297b23–298b20). This could be explained by the Epicureans only on the assumption that the stars are rather close to the earth: the effect is like that of walking across a room under a painted ceiling. Other astronomical arguments, such as the shape of the earth's shadow on the moon during an eclipse, could be accounted for by a disk-shaped earth as well as by a sphere.

Given, then, that atoms are endowed with a natural tendency to fall downwards through the void, and that 'downwards' means in parallel straight lines, it appears that some extra assumption is needed to explain how it comes about that atoms form compounds. One might suppose that collisions could occur by virtue of differences of speed among the falling atoms; but that is ruled out a priori (*Ep. Hdt.* 61; Lucr. II.225–42). The reason given by Epicurus is that differences of speed could be explained only by differences of resistance of the medium through which motion takes place. But the void offers no resistance whatever; hence there is no reason why any atom should fall faster or slower than any other. All of them move at a speed described in the phrase 'as quick as thought'. Neither differences of weight or size nor differences in direction of motion will

---

[22] For a clear analysis of *Ep. Hdt.* 60, in which Epicurus explains his conception of 'up' and 'down', see Konstan 1972.

affect the speed of motion of atoms, so long as they move through pure void, without collisions (*Ep. Hdt.* 61).[23]

That is not to say that *compounds* cannot move at different speeds. All variations of speed are possible, between the two limiting cases of the speed of motion of individual atoms, 'as quick as thought', on the one hand, and rest on the other. In a compound, atoms are to be thought of as moving, individually, at standard atomic speed without intermission, but remaining always within the boundaries of the compound. That is a statement that needs qualification, because some atoms escape from the boundaries to form the *eidōla* ('images') postulated by Epicurean theory to explain perception.[24] Approximately, however, a stable compound is one in which the component atoms move backwards and forwards, up and down and side to side, colliding with each other, within the same space. The compound itself moves when the algebraic sum, so to speak, of the motions of the individual atoms has some positive value in one direction or another. The limit of speed is reached when all the component atoms are moving in the same direction – a state of affairs achieved only by thunderbolts, apparently (Lucr. VI.323–51).

But if differences of speed cannot account for collisions between atoms, what can? Of course, granted that there *are* collisions, they can explain further collisions: once atoms are moving in all directions, they will continue to collide with each other, although perhaps not indefinitely. However, given that atoms naturally move downwards in parallel straight lines at a constant and equal speed, there appears to be no reason why this uniform and regulated march should not continue uninterrupted to infinity. To deal with this difficulty, the Epicureans introduced their most famous physical thesis – the swerve of atoms (*parenklisis* in Greek, *clinamen* in Latin).[25]

There is no mention of this doctrine in the extant fragments of Epicurus himself. This is puzzling. Some have argued that it was introduced for the first time by later Epicureans, before the first century BC when it is attested certainly for the first time, particularly in the passage of Lucretius which we shall examine in the next paragraph. Others (includ-

---

[23] I have argued that Epicurus was influenced in the formation of this theory by Aristotle's discussion of speed of motion in *Phys.* VI, 232b20–233a12. Aristotle showed that differences of speed imply infinite divisibility. Epicurus (I believe) held that neither body nor void is divisible to infinity. So motion is always a matter of 'jerks' – of total change from one place to another without any process of transition. So much is asserted explicitly about Epicurus by Them. *Phys.* 184.9 and Simp. *Phys.* 934.24. See Furley 1967, 111–30. The question of the range of Epicurus' atomism (whether it was confined to 'body' or extended also to space and time) is discussed by Vlastos 1965, and by Mau 1954a and 1973.   [24] See above, p. 264.

[25] Recent treatments of the swerve include Furley 1967 and Englert 1987; see below, pp. 501–2.

ing the present writer) believe that it is an accident that it is missing from the extant fragments, or that it was developed relatively late in Epicurus' career. It is significant that ancient writers had no hesitation in attributing it to Epicurus himself.

The swerve served two purposes in the Epicurean system: to explain the possibility of collisions between atoms, and to account, in some way, for the voluntary motions of animals, including humans. The latter purpose will be examined in another chapter of this book;[26] we can limit ourselves now to the cosmological context. It is worth quoting some lines of Lucretius, our best source for the doctrine:

> On our present subject there is this, too, that I want you to know: when bodies move straight downwards through the void by their own weight, at some uncertain time and in uncertain places they shift aside a little in space, so much that you can say their bearing is changed. If they were not used to swerve, all would fall downwards, like rain drops, through the bottomless void; no meeting would be brought about, no blow would be set up for the elements; and so nature would have created nothing.

> It must be that bodies swerve a little – but not more than the least bit, lest you think we are inventing oblique motions, refuted by the facts. For we see this to be obvious and manifest, that weights, by themselves, cannot move obliquely when they fall from above, as you can see. But that nothing at all swerves from the straight path – who is it that can see so much as that? (Lucr. II.216–24, 243–50)

The only other surviving Epicurean text that mentions the swerve is the inscription of Diogenes of Oenoanda, who contrasts Epicurus with Democritus: Democritus failed to 'discover' the swerve, he says (fr. 54 col. III Smith). It is noticed at Aët. 1.23.4, by Plutarch *An. Procr.* 1015c, and with some relish by Cicero, who found in it a good target for scorn. It is a 'childish fiction', he said, and ineffectual too, because the atoms might all swerve together and so might still never collide. Moreover there is no bigger disgrace for a 'physicist' than saying that something happens without a cause (*Fin.* 1.19).

Among modern writers there is no agreement even about the basic mechanics of the swerve, so to speak. Do all atoms swerve, or only some of them? Presumably all of them may do so, since otherwise there would be an unaccountable difference in kind between the swervers and the non-swervers. But how often do swerves take place? Opinions differ widely; the answer depends largely on one's interpretation of the swerve's role in

---

[26] See below pp. 522–6 and 553–7.

voluntary motion. Does an atom, when it swerves from the straight downward path, take up a straight motion at an oblique angle to the vertical? Or does it swerve momentarily like a car changing lanes on a motorway? Each answer has its advocates.[27] Some things are clear. The swerve of an atom has no cause in events previous to its occurrence; it is in principle unpredictable and random. Moreover in its cosmological role it is not to be thought of as the beginning of the world, or of any world. We are not to think of an uninterrupted downward rain of atoms that is at some moment for the first time disturbed by the occurrence of a swerve: rather, atoms have fallen, swerved, and collided for all eternity.

4. The origin of the world

The *Letter to Herodotus* is a summary of the principles of Epicurean physics and cosmology; as such, it remains at a certain level of generality. Almost ostentatiously, as if to make a point, Epicurus describes what worlds, in the plural, are like, and how they come into existence and pass away again from various causes, without saying anything about our world in particular. One of the strangest features is his suggestion that worlds may be of various shapes – 'some spherical, some egg-shaped, others of different shapes, but they do not have *every* shape' (*Ep. Hdt.* 74).

What is emphasized first is that worlds have an origin and an end, like all other compounds. They are 'produced from their particular conglomerations'[28] – a phrase probably meant to have a biological tone: the verb is one that is used in biology to mean 'secrete', and the noun is a vague word that can be used to denote a mass of tissue. The idea is that all things have their appropriate 'seeds';[29] and there are some seeds in the infinite universe whose proper product is a cosmos.

The statement that worlds do not come in every conceivable shape is contradicted by another passage written by Epicurus himself, which contains more detailed information about the origin of the worlds:

> A world is a perimeter of sky containing stars and earth and all the phenomena, having separation from the infinite, and ending in a limit that is either rare or dense – on the destruction of which all the contents will be confounded – ending in a limit that either rotates or is at rest, having a perimeter that is round, or triangular, or any shape at all – all are possible, since none of the phenomena in our world offers counter-evidence to show that any ultimate boundary is unintelligible.
> That such worlds are infinite in number is something that can be con-

---

[27] Englert 1987, ch. 2; Asmis 1984, 279–80; Sedley 1983b, 25–6.
[28] *Ep. Hdt.* 73: ἐκ συστροφῶν ἰδίων ἀποκεκριμένων.   [29] See above, pp. 363–6.

ceived, and that such a world can come into being both inside a world and in an inter-world, as we call the interval between worlds, in a region of much void (but not in a great, pure void, as some say); [it happens] when certain appropriate seeds flow from one world or inter-world or from more than one, little by little making additions, articulations, relocations to another place, if it so happens, and irrigations drawn from suitable sources, up to the point of perfection and stability, so long as the established foundations are able to accept increment of material.

It is not true that all that is needed is that a mass of material be formed, or a vortex, in a void space in which a world can come into being, as is supposed, by necessity, and that it grow until it crashes against another, as one of those who are called 'physicists' says. That is in conflict with the phenomena. (*Ep. Pyth.* 88–90)

This badly written text presents many problems and is disappointingly vague, but there are some characteristic features of Epicurean cosmology that stand out clearly enough.[30] The last two paragraphs contain some polemics, probably against Democritus, since 'necessity' was often associated particularly with his cosmological theories.[31] Evidently the earlier and later theories agreed that a considerable void space was required for the formation of a cosmos. This reflects an ancient notion in Greek cosmology, that our world is something like a big cave hollowed out in a mass of surrounding material. Between the earth and the outer shell of the world, where the heavenly bodies are located, it was supposed that there is a vast space, loosely filled with air and aether. Epicurus accepts much of this notion, but holds that the space between earth and the heavens is relatively small, as we shall see below,[32] and insists that the existence of a suitable space, and a mass of matter whirling in a vortex, is not in itself enough to explain the birth of a cosmos. Several other conditions are necessary. There must be *suitable* materials; this echoes what was written in *Ep. Pyth.*, quoted above – like anything else, a cosmos needs the right seeds if it is to grow. Secondly it requires 'irrigations'. This is an extraordinary word to find in this context. It must be supposed that Epicurus wanted to emphasize his biological model for the growth of a cosmos: after the formation of the seed, further material of the right type is needed, just as a seed needs watering. Thirdly, the world does not grow for ever until there is no room left between itself and other worlds: all living things have a right and proper size. After they attain this, as Lucretius explains (Lucr. II.1122–74), it becomes harder for them to assimilate the material necessary to sustain

---

[30] Recent discussion: Mansfeld 1994a, who finds it less confused.   [31] See D.L. IX 44.
[32] See below, n. 41.

life, they lose more than they take in from the environment, and ultimately they succumb to 'blows from without' (line 1140). These are the phenomena mentioned in the last line as being in conflict with the idea that the world grows until it collides with another one.

The cosmology of Epicurus is a mechanistic one, in the sense that it uses nothing but matter and motion as ultimate factors in explaining the natural world, but it nevertheless offers biological analogies to support physical hypotheses. The 'world-animal' of Plato's *Timaeus* has not wholly been killed off. The worlds of Epicurus are born, absorb nourishment, and die.

How Epicurus envisaged the very first steps in the formation of a cosmos is unfortunately obscure. The standard model for explaining the sorting of matter into kinds, used by Anaxagoras, Empedocles, and Democritus, was the vortex.[33] They thought of whirlwinds, and their effects on objects of different shapes, sizes and weights caught up in them: large and heavy things tended to collect in the middle, light and small things to rise and disperse. In very broad terms, this offered the right kind of pattern for a world consisting of earth and water, surrounded by a circular canopy of lighter air and the fiery matter of the heavens. But the vortex is mentioned by Epicurus only in a critical context, when he rejects the theory of Democritus in *Ep. Pyth.* 90, quoted above. It is possible that all he meant here was that the vortex and the other factors mentioned were not in themselves sufficient causes for the formation of a cosmos, and that he left open the possibility that a vortex is one of the necessary causes. Later in the same Letter (93), he refers to the possibility of a vortex motion surviving 'from the beginning' in the motions of the sun and moon, and the beginning referred to is presumably the origin of the cosmos. Lucretius speaks merely of 'a fresh storm and an assembled mass' (Lucr. v.436); out of this came a sorting of like-to-like so as to form the great world masses of earth and sea and the heavens. He offers the further explanation that the original mass, consisting of all sizes and shapes of atoms, was originally in such a state of discord that the atoms could not 'produce motions that harmonized among themselves' (445), and so separated out by kinds into different regions of space. There is no mention of a vortex.[34] Perhaps a circular vortex was posited as the cause of the sorting of material at the birth of our cosmos, but the possibility was left open that other mechanisms sorted the material for others – triangular ones, for instance!

[33] DK 59 A 88, 31 B 35, 68 A 67 and 69.
[34] Lucr. v.432–48. The manuscripts preserve the lines in an order that most editors believe to be unacceptable. I am not sure that they are right, but the issue does not affect the present point.

The theory that our world is one of an infinite number, coexisting in the present as well as in the past and the future, is taken over from Democritus.[35] The idea may possibly have been even earlier: some attribute it to Anaximander,[36] but it probably originated with the fifth-century atomists. It is one of the major differences between the Epicureans and others in the Hellenistic period, given splendidly rhetorical treatment by Lucretius in the peroration to his second book (II.1023–1104): what possible reason could there be for the formation of a single cosmos, when everywhere in the infinite universe there is a supply of atoms similar to those that compose our world, performing similar motions and colliding in similar ways? What other compound is unique? The idea was singled out particularly for ridicule by later Christian critics of Epicurus.

5. The formation of the heavens: Epicurean astronomy

Neither *Ep. Pyth.* nor Lucr. v is clear and full on the subject of the first stages in the birth of our cosmos, but together they offer a reasonably consistent description of a cosmogony, even if much is left unexplained. It is particularly disappointing that there is no explicit account of the different roles played by weight, collision, and the swerve of atoms in the cosmogonical process.

The first stage was the settling down of the heavy and interlocked bodies of earth, which 'assembled in the middle and occupied the lowest positions' (Lucr. v.450–1). But what is the reference of 'middle' and 'lowest'? The cosmos itself, with its boundary, was not yet formed. The only available reference point mentioned so far by Lucretius is the 'fresh storm and assembled mass' of atoms (line 436); from *Ep. Pyth.* 89 we can add that this mass has occupied a large void space in the infinite expanse of atoms-and-void in the universe; so the middle may equally be regarded as the middle of this space.

Although the cosmos is not yet formed, this mass has a determinate lowest point, since the downward direction is determined for the universe as a whole by the free fall of heavy bodies, as we have seen above. The picture, then, is of a region of the universe in which a particular, identifiable mass of atoms, all of them of course having a natural tendency to fall downwards, attained something like a stationary position in

[35] See Hipp. *Ref.* 1.13.2. Democritus' follower Metrodorus of Chios said it was as absurd that a single ear of corn should grow in a wide plain as that a single cosmos should grow in the infinite (Aët. 1.5.6).

[36] Simp. *Phys.* 1121.5 ff. For a critical examination of the evidence, see Kirk 1955.

the universe because of constant collisions among themselves. As the collisions proceeded in this region, the heavier and bulkier atoms settled downwards, thus squeezing outwards and upwards the smaller and lighter ones. First, says Lucretius, came the 'fire-bearing aether', and fire – much like the mist that rises from pools and streams, and sometimes from the earth itself, in the morning. Having risen upward, the aether spread all round the mass to form a kind of fence (*saepsit*, 470; the whole passage is v.449–94).[37]

A difficult problem then arose about the position of the earth in the cosmos. It is acknowledged that the earth is surrounded on all sides and above and below by air and the fiery aether of the heavens. What prevents the earth, which is heavy, from falling to the bottom of the cosmic mass? This is an ancient problem: it troubled the first Greek philosophers of nature, the sixth-century Milesians.[38] Lucretius presents the Epicurean answer (v.534–63). In essence, it claims that the earth is in organic unity with the rest of the cosmos: it is to be thought of not as an alien body imposed on a bed of air, but as an integral part of a compound in which a part is heavier than others. He proposes an analogy with the human body: we do not feel the weight of our head resting on our neck, although we do feel the weight of an alien load when we carry it. Soul atoms are exceedingly fine and light, and serve to lighten and support the weight of the limbs: similarly air and aether, linked to the earth, serve to keep it from plunging downwards through space.

After the formation of the aetherial fence around the earth, the sun and moon began to grow, being intermediate in weight.[39] The sun, after its formation, assists the process of separation of different kinds within the cosmos by 'sweating' the moisture out of the earth to form the oceans.

In *Ep. Pyth.* there now follows a strangely worded section:

> The size of the sun and the remaining heavenly bodies is just as big as it appears, when considered in relation to us; but considered by itself it is either bigger than the body as seen or a little smaller or just as big. For just so fires around us, when observed from a distance, are observed according to perception. (*Ep. Pyth.* 92)

---

[37] By *aether* Lucretius means the fiery material of the heavenly regions. The word does not, of course, carry the load of theory – eternal circular motion, and difference from the sublunary elements – that accompanies it in Aristotle's cosmology.

[38] See Furley 1989c, 14–26 and for a contrary view Bodnár 1992.

[39] The *Letter to Pythocles* 90, as preserved in the manuscripts, appears to give a different account, in that the sun and moon and stars are said to have an independent origin, not described, and later to be incorporated into the cosmos. Editors insert a negative, and take the sentence to be a denial of an opponent's theory.

There is only one sun in our world, and it has only one size. So the curious contrast between its size 'considered in relation to us' and 'considered by itself' presumably means no more than that we have to infer its size from its apparent size; the first sentence, then, means no more than 'we can all agree on how big the sun looks to us.' The analogy with fires is supposed to show that the effects of distance are less great in the case of the sun than in the case of objects that shed no light; distant lights still stand out brilliantly, even though they are relatively small. When we see a mountain in the distance, it is so small that it can be blocked from sight by the extent of a hand; yet we know, from a close look, that it is enormous. In the case of the sun, the effect is not the same, because the sun is a light, and lights behave differently.

It is not clear why Epicurus wanted to insist that the sun is not so very large after all, but one can guess at a reason why he wanted it to be not so very distant. An astronomical argument for the thesis that the earth is spherical, used by Eratosthenes to calculate the earth's circumference but possibly known much earlier, depended on taking the sun's rays at different latitudes on the earth's surface to be parallel to each other.[40] On a flat earth theory, which Epicurus wanted to maintain, in order to support his theory of motion, as we have seen, the different angles of the sun's elevation observed at the same time at different latitudes can be accounted for only if the sun is relatively close to the earth, so that its rays at different earthly latitudes cannot be taken as parallel.[41]

How do the heavenly bodies move? Epicurus abandoned the elaborate theory of concentric spheres worked out by Eudoxus and Callippus in the fourth century and canonized by Aristotle. He substituted a collection of suggested mechanisms. Perhaps the whole heaven is blown round by currents of air, as a water wheel is turned by the current of the river; perhaps the heaven itself is at rest, and the stars are blown about by internal or external air currents; perhaps they are drawn by the need for nourishment (these suggestions are in Lucr. v.509–32, less fully in *Ep. Pyth.* 92–3).

Two critical comments are needed here. First, it is at this point in the cosmology that Epicurus' practical goal becomes most obvious. The point of his astronomical theory is to show how the formation and the motions

[40] Eratosthenes' method is described by Cleomedes 1.7. Translated (with other relevant passages) in Cohen and Drabkin 1966, 149–53.

[41] Given the same figures attributed to Eratosthenes, the sun would have to be only about 39,579 stades from the earth (less than 5000 miles). I am grateful to Alan Bowen for this calculation. There is a brilliant discussion of the astronomical controversy between the successors of Eudoxus at Cyzicus and the Epicureans at Lampsacus (both towns on the south shore of the Hellespont) in Sedley 1976b. For the size of the sun see Barnes 1989a.

of the heavens can plausibly be explained without postulating divine agencies. The exact nature of the explanation is much less important than the possibility of such an explanation. So the principle of the *Canonic*, that in the case of non-evident things we are to take as true whatever is not 'counter-witnessed', is invoked here to justify the provision of multiple explanations for single phenomena.[42] Secondly, although Epicurean astronomy is plainly disastrous in that it ignores the achievements of scientific astronomy (he speaks of 'the slavish contrivances of the astronomers', probably referring to astronomical instruments, *Ep. Pyth.* 93), and makes prediction virtually impossible (who can predict how the wind will blow next?), it has one outstanding merit to which full weight must be given. It does not require special laws of motion for the heavens, as Aristotelian cosmology does. There is no dualism in the Epicurean theory: circular motion is explained as the outcome of the rectilinear motion of currents of air, and the material of the heavens is no different from the material that composes the earth and the things between heaven and earth.

This is not the place for a detailed exposition of the rest of Epicurean astronomy, as set out in *Ep. Pyth.* and Lucr. v.592–771. The principles of the explanations offered are similar to those we have seen. Perhaps night is to be explained by the movement of the sun beneath the earth's surface; perhaps by the temporary exhaustion of the sun's fire (Lucr. v.650–5). Perhaps the phases of the moon are explained by reflection of the sun's light, perhaps by the interference of another, unseen body; perhaps the moon is a turning ball, with one side light and the other dark, perhaps there is even a new and different moon every day (Lucr. v.705–50). It is noteworthy that although Epicurus stresses frequently, in *Ep. Pyth.*, his use of the principle that we can accept whatever is not 'counter-witnessed', he makes no attempt to collect together his multiple explanations into those which are consistent with each other and those which are not.[43] For example, if night is to be explained by the extinguishing of the sun's light, then the moon's light cannot be explained as a reflection of the sun. There are other examples.

As has already been said, one of the weaknesses of this astronomy was its failure to account for the predictability of the motions of the heavenly bodies – for long recognized as their outstanding characteristic. Lucretius (v.666–79) attempts to bolster up the theory in this respect in an interesting way. His remarks apply to the succession of night and day, but they

---

[42] See above, pp. 285–90, for this principle.

[43] See Wasserstein 1978. On multiple explanation (already a feature of Theophrastus' *Meteorology*) see Mansfeld 1994a and see below, pp. 505–7.

apply to other subjects equally well. He simply lists a number of examples of regularity, obvious to everyone, drawn from nature: the growth and fall of blossom on trees, the loss of a child's first teeth, the first growth of a beard, seasonal changes in the weather. The causes are always the same, and so the phenomena occur with regular timing.

6. The development of the cosmos

The Demiurge of Plato's *Timaeus* filled the created cosmos with its animal, vegetable, and mineral contents by making copies from pre-existent Forms. Aristotle's cosmos was an eternal system, containing natural kinds that had existed for ever and would exist for ever without change. The Epicurean atomists were committed to the vast enterprise of showing how the natural kinds that we see exemplified around us might have originated, out of simpler elements, in a cosmos in which there was previously no such thing. It is an enterprise that still to a large extent defeats twentieth-century cosmologists.

The fundamental problem was to show how accidental collisions of atoms could plausibly be thought to produce our orderly world, stocked with well adapted creatures. Cicero articulated the problem in a critique of atomism in *Fin.* 1.20: 'How will this stormy concourse of atoms ever be able to produce the ordered beauty of the cosmos?'

The Epicurean answer rests on three claims. The first is that given infinite time and an infinite supply of atoms moving and colliding with each other, it is to be expected that eventually they will produce everything that they *can* produce:

> For sure, not by design did the prime elements of things place themselves each in its order with thoughtful mind, nor fix among themselves what movements they should make. But since many prime elements of things, in many ways, driven by collisions now from infinite time past and moved by their own weight, have been used to move, to conjoin in all ways and to essay all the things that by their union with one another they can create, so it comes about that through a vast age of wandering, by attempting every kind of gathering and of motion, at last those meet which, suddenly connecting, often become the origins of great things – of earth, sea, sky, and the race of living beings. (Lucr. v.419–31)[44]

The second is the principle of the survival of the fit, borrowed from Empedocles. The earth, after its first formation, produced out of itself

---

[44] This is a principle so important to Lucretius that he repeats various elements of it in other places – I.1021–37, II.1058–65, v.187–94.

first vegetation, then a motley variety of animal life. Again Lucretius is the
source:

> And many monsters too the earth then tried to make, compounded of
> wonderful faces and limbs, androgynous, not one nor the other, remote
> from both, sometimes footless, or it might be without hands, mouthless
> and dumb, faceless and blind, single bodies with limbs interlocked, so
> that they could do nothing, go nowhere, escape no harm, gather no
> needful things. More monsters of this kind grew from earth – in vain,
> since nature denied them increase. They could not reach the coveted
> flower of age, nor find food nor couple in the work of Venus. (Lucr.
> v.837–48)

Only the well adapted survive: hence we can understand why the present
population of the earth can be described in the teleological terms of Plato
or Aristotle.

The third principle, which is implicit in the texts rather than expressly
formulated, is that the same causes produce the same effects. Thus once
the progenitors of a species are formed, able 'to couple in the work of
Venus', we can understand how the reproduction of the species continues
true to type. There is no evolution of species in Epicurean theory.

Lucretius' fifth book continues with a wonderfully imaginative
description of the development of human civilization. It is based on
Epicurus' own theory, baldly summarized in *Ep. Hdt.* 75–6: 'One is to
assume that nature itself was instructed and constrained as to many and
various facts, and that reasoning later sharpened up and added further discoveries to the lessons passed on by nature, in some matters more quickly
and in some more slowly.' The interaction between the natural environment and human reason brings about a gradual adaptation of social organization; in a magnificently imaginative account Lucretius traces its course
in government, communication, warfare, religion, agriculture and the
arts.[45]

III The early Stoics

1. *Sources and background*[46]

It is lamentable that the cosmological literature of the early Stoics – like
the rest of their work – has survived only in inadequate fragments. There

---

[45] See also Kenney 1972.

[46] The sources for early Stoic cosmology are scattered and late. Cicero's *De natura deorum* 2 contains an elaborate defence of Stoic theology, which necessarily includes much cosmological
information. Cleomedes' *Caelestia* (so-called in the latest Teubner edition by R.B.Todd; for-

is nothing in the field of Stoicism to compare with Lucretius' great
Epicurean poem, hardly even consecutive texts of the length and importance of the surviving *Letters* of Epicurus. Epicurus may be counted as
lucky: the *Letters* depended for their survival on the continuing popularity
of Diogenes Laertius' work, and Lucretius survived because admiration
for his Latin epic outweighed disagreement with his philosophy.[47]

Stoicism had influential supporters among thinking people in the
Hellenistic and Roman world. Writers such as Plutarch in the first century AD[48] and Diogenes Laertius in the third[49] were able at least to give
the names of a large number of books, but the texts themselves are now
lost to us. Zeno's *On the Whole* (one has to translate it thus, because there
is a distinction to be made between the universe (τὸ πᾶν) and the Whole
(τὸ ὅλον), a synonym for the cosmos); Cleanthes' *On Time*, *On Zeno's
Physiologia*, *Against Democritus*, and *Against Aristarchus*; Chrysippus'
Physics, *On the Cosmos*, *On Substance*, *On Motion*, *On the Void*; Antipater's *On
the Cosmos* – all these are lost.[50]

Stoic cosmology is known to us mainly through doxographers, who as
a rule were not interested in the reasoning with which the philosophers
defended their doctrines, and through the works of opponents of the
Stoics, who were generally not as concerned as they should have been to
give a fair account of Stoic arguments. As a result, although we know the
doctrines at least in outline, we know too little about the context within
which they were framed. It is obvious that the Stoics were opposed to the
Epicureans, but we have little in the way of argument against Epicurean
positions. It is obvious that the Stoics were in agreement with Plato and
Aristotle in much of their philosophizing about the natural world, but
there is little agreement about the extent to which their work was actually
influenced by reading Plato or Aristotle.[51]

Like Plato and Aristotle, the Stoics held that the cosmos in which we
live is the only one in the universe. It is spherical in shape, with the stars,
planets, sun, and moon moving in circular paths once daily around the
earth, which is stationary at the centre. Their cosmos, like Aristotle's, is a
corporeal continuum, with no void space inside it, and matter itself is

---

merly *De motu circulari*; see Todd 1985) is a summary of Stoic views about the heavens written
about the first century AD. Diogenes Laertius book VII reviews Zeno at length, Cleanthes and
Chrysippus more briefly. The standard collection of fragments is *SVF*.

[47] On the letters see above, p. 5.   [48] See Glucker 1988.   [49] See Mansfeld 1986.

[50] There is an extensive reconstruction of Stoic cosmology in Hahm 1977. See also Lapidge 1978.

[51] See Sandbach 1985, for a sceptical account of their relationship with Aristotle, with some
detailed criticism of earlier work on the subject. In general, the result of this monograph is to
show that Aristotelian influence is not conclusively proven. Often it still remains a plausible
hypothesis. For a more positive view, see Hahm 1991.

continuous, not atomic. The cosmos is teleologically organized, not the result of random processes of matter in motion. This much is enough to place the Stoics squarely in the same camp with Platonists and Aristotelians, against the atomists. But differences arise at once, and they are of great significance.

2. *The birth and death of the cosmos*

One major difference is that whereas Aristotle believed our cosmos to be everlasting, the Stoics held that it has a birth, and a death by conflagration (*ekpurōsis*), followed by a rebirth, and so on for ever.[52] Both Aristotle and the Stoics believed that our cosmos is unique, but the Stoics added that it has a limited lifespan which is endlessly repeated. Sometimes the surviving reports of Stoic doctrine distinguish between κόσμος and διακόσμησις – that is, between the ordered world and its ordering. This marks an important distinction, but the word κόσμος is sometimes also used as equivalent to διακόσμησις.[53] It must be noted that *ekpurōsis* was rejected by some prominent later Stoics. Boethus of Sidon rejected it on the ground (among others) that God would have nothing to do during the time of the conflagration (Philo *Aet.* 17). Panaetius also rejected it (fr. 64–6 and 68 Van Straaten), believing the cosmos to be everlasting. When the present cosmos perishes, it will not pass out of existence altogether, to be replaced by an entirely new one. The same material persists: the *order* changes. So although in a sense the Stoics and Epicureans were in agreement that our world will come to an end, the Epicurean theory of the birth and death of quite different worlds was of a different sort altogether from the Stoic theory.

Plato in the *Timaeus* had combined the similes of biology and the crafts in describing the origin of the cosmos – leaving posterity to doubt whether either of the similes was to be taken literally. The Stoics chose the biological model, but used it in a way that was almost mystical. An account given by Diogenes Laertius will serve as a starting point:

> Now in the beginning, God, being all by himself, turns the whole of substance by way of air into water; and just as the seed is contained in the sperm, so God, being the seed-formula (σπερματικὸς λόγος) of the cosmos, is deposited as such in the moisture, making matter well adapted for the generation of things in succession. So he generates first the four elements, fire, water, air, and earth. These things are described by Zeno

in his *On the Whole*, and by Chrysippus in the first book of his *Physics*. (D.L. VII.136)

Whereas Plato described a Craftsman God working on a material to make the cosmos, which then took on its own life, Zeno takes God to be identical with the cosmos in its initial state (about which we shall say more shortly). God is the principle of life. At first there is nothing else: then God creates a difference within himself, such that as the principle of life he is 'contained' in moisture. This is the living 'sperm' which produces the cosmos according to the 'formula' of which it is the bearer; God is the σπερματικὸς λόγος. God is at the same time material fire, and providential intelligence.

It is as if the Stoics deliberately combined numerous elements from earlier theories. The emphasis on fire recalls Heraclitus, although there is much disagreement among scholars about the nature of Heraclitus' own doctrines (some of the important testimonia about Heraclitus actually come from Stoic sources, so that it is difficult to separate what is genuinely Heraclitean from Stoic interpretation). The cosmogonic role of a transcendental divine intelligence recalls Anaxagoras, as well as Plato, and the embryological model of the seed goes back at least so far, if not even to Thales and Anaximander themselves, the founders of the Greek cosmological tradition. The careful analysis of the sperm into a moist vehicle and an active 'formula' or λόγος is found also in Aristotle's *GA*.

In more general terms, this duality is described as 'the active' and 'the passive' (τὸ ποιοῦν, τὸ πάσχον), and these are called the first principles (ἀρχαί) of physics. There is much hesitation in the texts as to whether they are to be regarded as being themselves 'bodies'. One rather dubious text declares them to be incorporeal.[54] This makes things easier, in a sense, because they are no more than aspects of the single substance of which the universe consists at the time of the conflagration. On the other hand, the cosmogonic seed apparently consists of an active ingredient that is warm and a passive ingredient that is moist, and under this description the first principles seem to be more like two different kinds of body, thoroughly mixed. Since the Stoics adopted a theory of through-and-through mixture,[55] it would seem to be perfectly possible for them to regard the two first principles as being corporeal, and this is said explicitly in some of the surviving texts: Aristocles contrasts Zeno with Plato in this

---

[54] D.L. VII.134, incorporating the Suda's reading ἀσωμάτους, followed by von Arnim. See Todd 1978 and Kidd 1988, 105–6.   [55] See above, pp. 390–1.

respect (Aristocles *apud* Eus. *PE* xv.15.14.1). Indeed, corporeality follows
directly from the nature of these two principles as acted and being acted
upon, because the Stoics held that nothing can act or be acted upon unless
it is a body (Cic. *Acad.* 1.39).

The decision to view the cosmos as a living creature may be regarded as
the foundation of Stoic cosmology. We can guess at the reasons that made
it an attractive picture. Like living organisms, the cosmos is a material
body endowed with an immanent power of motion. It consists of
different parts, which collaborate towards the stable functioning of the
whole, each part performing its own work. The relation of the parts to
each other and to the whole exhibits a kind of fitness, not always obvious
in detail indeed, but unmistakeable in the large picture. This sense of fitness suggests rationality: it is an easy inference that the cosmos itself is
possessed of reason, and since reason is a property confined to living creatures, this again suggests that the cosmos is a living being.

The cosmos is permeated by Reason (λόγος): this is the most distinctive claim of the Stoics, with ramifications into every field of their
thought. It is far more than the epistemological claim that it is possible to
understand the workings of the cosmos rationally. It amounts in fact to a
very large metaphysical theory. Being thoroughgoing materialists, they
had to give a corporeal form to the *logos*. Since nothing less than divine
power could move and control something so vast as the cosmos, they
identified the *logos* with God. And as we have seen in the passage quoted
above, they assumed that the *logos* itself was something that can have no
origin itself, but must be the origin of everything else.

It may be that the notion of 'seed-formula' (σπερματικὸς λόγος)
saved or prevented the early Stoics from working out a detailed cosmogony in the manner of Book 5 of Lucretius' poem. The surviving reports
tell us very little about their cosmogonical ideas, beyond the generation
of the four elements. The first change is from fire through air into moisture: part of the moisture is compacted into earth, and part goes the
other way, from air to fire (D.L. vii.142). Diogenes adds that the subject
of cosmogony is treated in Zeno's *On the Whole*, Chrysippus' *Physics* 1,
Cleanthes, and Antipater's *On the Cosmos* 10, but no more details are
given. A more detailed account of Cleanthes' theory comes from Arius
Didymus:

> Cleanthes says something like the following. When the universe has
> been totally inflamed, the middle of it subsides first, and successive parts
> are quenched throughout the whole. When the universe has become
> thoroughly moistened, the last of the fire, when the middle clashes with

it, <causes it to> turn[s] again into its opposite.[56] When this turning takes place, he says it grows upwards, and begins to set the whole in order (διακοσμεῖν). During the operation of this everlasting cosmic cycle, the tension in the substance of the whole does not cease. For just as all the parts of a single individual grow from seeds at the due times, so do the parts of the whole cosmos, namely, animals and plants, grow at the due times. And just as certain formulae (λόγοι) of the parts are assembled and mixed in the seed and are again separated when the parts grow, so it happens that all things come into being from one, and one thing is compounded from all, as the cycle proceeds in its set and fitting way. (Ar. Did. fr. 38 *ap*. Stob. *Ecl.* 1.153.7–22)

As these reports (inadequate though they are) make clear, it was a crucial thesis of the theory that when the cosmos is periodically consumed by fire and becomes a single fiery mass, the seed-formula is preserved intact. That is the point of Cleanthes' insistence that 'the tension in the substance of the whole does not cease'. It does not become formless or chaotic: it retains the unifying 'tension' which is the vehicle or cause of qualitative distinctions in Stoic physics.[57] The seed-formula for the cosmos as a whole, and for each one of the natural kinds specifically, is present from the beginning; the formula is eternal, the generative force is immanent. So there is no need, as there is in the atomic theory, for an account of the gradual emergence of more complex forms from simple elements.

The end of the world – or more exactly, of the present phase of the world – comes about through conflagration; the technical term is ἐκπύρωσις. Again, little detailed description or defence of the doctrine survives. The standard argument is presumably that outlined in D.L. VII.141: in the case of ordinary perceptible objects, if the parts are destroyed, so is the whole – and the parts of the cosmos are destructible.

This theory follows a long tradition, stretching back into mythology, which told of the periodic destruction of the world either by fire (the myth of Phaethon) or by flood (the myth of Deucalion). The tradition was mentioned in Plato's *Timaeus* (22d–e), and this is enough in itself to account for its being known to the early Stoics. The great flood is mentioned rather more frequently than the great fire – for example, by Plato in the *Laws* (677a, 682bc), and by Aristotle in his dialogue *On Philosophy* (fr. 8, from Aristocles quoted by Philoponus), if this is a genuine report. The old tradition was mainly concerned with the destruction, or partial

---

[56] I adopt von Arnim's emendation (*SVF* I, p.111n): τρέπεσθαι . . . <ποιεῖν>. It should be the moistened centre, rather than the last of the fire, that turns into its opposite at this stage.

[57] See above, pp. 387–90.

destruction, of mankind, and its subsequent regeneration from the survivors. The Stoics turned it into a rather precise physical doctrine, claiming that the entire corporeal substance of the universe is turned into fire.

They had reasons for preferring fire to flood. It was a thesis of Stoic physics that the heavenly bodies, and especially the sun, consumed fuel in the form of 'exhalations' from the world below them (Aët. II.20.4). If parts of the sublunary cosmos were thus assimilated by the fiery sun, it was reasonable to assume that the same might happen to the whole cosmos in due course. In fact, this doctrine is explicitly attributed to Zeno of Citium by the Platonist Alexander of Lycopolis, writing at the beginning of the third century AD:[58]

> Everything which burns and has something to burn will burn it completely; now the sun is a fire and will it not burn what it has? From this he [i.e. Zeno] concluded, as he supposed, that the all will be totally destroyed by conflagration. (Alex. Lyc. *Contra Manichaei opiniones* 19.4–6)

But quite apart from this argument, the Stoics could hardly do other than choose a fiery rather than a watery end for the life of the cosmos. The end of the cosmos was to be the beginning, the seed, of the next phase: the active power in the seed was heat, rather than moisture.[59] In Stoic theory, this heat was identified with God; living creatures (including the whole cosmos) thus contain an innate providential agency which accounts for their well adapted structures and capacities.

But why, we may ask, did the Stoics adopt a cyclical theory of destruction and rebirth at all? Why could they not follow the path of Plato, who held that God would not destroy his own creation, or of Aristotle, who held that the cosmos is eternally the same, without beginning or end? We can make some reasonable guesses. It must be observed first that Aristotle was the exception in Greek cosmology: from the myths of Hesiod through all the rest of the earlier history of natural philosophy, there was speculation about the origin of the world. It was less universally agreed that the world would come to an end: Lucretius treats this as a surprising thesis. All the same, many previous philosophers did theorize that our world would come to an end. Even if we dismiss the precedent of Heraclitus as being too controversial, Empedocles was certainly interpreted as holding a cyclical theory by Aristotle, who was probably correct in outline, although he may have got some of the details wrong (*Phys.* VIII.1, 250b25).

---

[58] See Mansfeld 1979, 146–9, Long and Sedley 1987, vol. I, 276.
[59] See below, on 'designing fire'.

We have already noted a physical reason for positing that the world order will come to an end in conflagration: fires consume fuel, and it is to be expected that the sun will burn up everything in time. A different reason – or perhaps the same reason expressed in different language – is also reported. God is a living being, composed of body and soul, and his soul is always growing: so there will come a time when he becomes nothing but soul. If one thinks of the seed-formula in this way, it can be seen not as the death of the cosmos, but as its fullest life.[60]

The cyclical theory is connected with the astronomical idea of the Great Year. The ordinary year is determined by the position of the sun relative to the earth; a year has elapsed when the sun and the earth return to the same relative position. Astronomers speculated about the length of time that elapses between two moments at which the sun, moon, and five known planets were all in the same relative position (Plato *Tim.* 39d). This period, of which different estimates were made, was the Great Year. It appears that the period between one conflagration and the next was supposed to be one Great Year (Nemes. 38).

This could hardly be otherwise, if the Stoics were to claim, as they did, that events in one world were precisely repeated in the next. Socrates will defend himself against Meletus and Anytus with the same words, and will be condemned by the same jury, every time the cosmic wheel turns full circle. One does not have to accept that the stars exercise a causal influence on the affairs of men: it is enough that the exact description of an event must include all its features, including the position of the sun, moon, and planets when it occurs, so that if it is to be exactly repeated these features of it must be the same. The notion that all events are exactly repeated in each successive cosmic period was thought very striking, particularly by opponents of Stoicism.[61]

The reasons for adopting this bizarre theory are not reported by our sources. They must lie in the Stoic theory of causation, coupled with the premiss that divine Providence organizes the cosmos for the best. For if this world is the best, succeeding worlds could differ from it only at the cost of being worse, and no reason could be given for the existence of a worse world. So each cosmos must be exactly the same as the last one.

---

[60] See the quotations from Chrysippus' *On Providence* in Plu. *Stoic. Rep.* 1052c, and Mansfeld 1981.

[61] See for example the Aristotelian commentator Alexander (*APr.* 180.33–6); the Christians Lactantius (*Inst.* VII.23) and Origen (*Cels.* IV.68); the Platonist Nemesius (111.14–112.6). Barnes 1978 traces the sources of the doctrine of exact repetition to the Stoic deterministic view of causation. On the whole subject of endless repetition, see Sorabji 1980a, 65–6, and 1983, 183–90.

3. *Fire*, pneuma *and tension*

Zeno created the concept of 'designing fire' (πῦρ τεχνικόν). There are two kinds of fire: one is the ordinary fire that consumes fuel and assimilates it; the other is creative, being identified with the warmth that creates and maintains life. It is also the substance of the stars (Ar. Did. fr. 33 *apud* Stob. 1.213.15–27).

The notion of an innate heat in animals is familiar from earlier biology. Zeno extended it to the heavenly bodies, presumably because of the life-giving heat of the sun. But since the characteristic of designing fire is to burn without consuming what it burns, how can this be consistent with the notion, mentioned above, that the sun and the other heavenly bodies consume fuel by turning it into their own substance? This seems to be another case, like that of the first principles, mentioned above, where a distinction of aspect becomes, in some contexts, a distinction between two kinds of being. 'Designing fire' is, properly speaking, fire in its capacity of generative heat, the active substance in the cosmic seed. It is localized, in the later life of the cosmos, in the sun and the other heavenly bodies, and in its localized form it behaves as other fires in consuming fuel, while also imparting life to the sublunary world.

Cleanthes took up and developed the importance of fire and its localization in the sun; his ideas are described at some length in Cicero *ND* II.23–5. But Chrysippus appears to have given the doctrine a new form, with the concept of *pneuma* or breath. This, too, had an earlier history, especially in Aristotle's biological works, and Zeno had identified it with the psyche in animals (*SVF* I 135–8, 140). In non-philosophical contexts, the word can mean either 'breath' or 'breeze' – the noun is from the verb 'to blow'. (Latin *spiritus* and English 'spirit' are later translations.) Chrysippus made a cosmic principle out of it, and it became one of the most characteristic Stoic ideas.

It is a mixture of hot and cold, fire and air, and it pervades the entire universe, down to its smallest parts: the Stoics developed a new concept of 'through-and-through mixing' (κρᾶσις δι᾽ ὅλου)[62] to describe the total union of *pneuma* with the rest of the substance in the world. By mixing with the whole world it exercises control over everything. It is the vehicle of (perhaps more strictly, it is identical with) God's providence.

As the active ingredient in all things in the world, *pneuma* is responsible for the 'tension' that holds all the world and everything in it together. The guiding idea in this doctrine is that there is a difference between an iden-

[62] See above, pp. 390–1.

tifiable thing and a formless heap of matter. It is most obvious, of course, in a living being, but even a lake or a rock has a principle of unity that differentiates it from a mere quantity of water or mineral deposit. The Stoics said that inanimate things were held together by their 'holding-power' (ἕξις),[63] plants by their *nature* (φύσις) and animals by their *soul* (ψυχή), and each was identical with the *pneuma* that permeated them and held them in tension. In one graphic description, it is '*pneuma* that turns back towards itself. It begins to extend itself from the centre towards the extremities, and having made contact with the outer surfaces it bends back again until it returns to the same place from which it first set out.'[64] This theory has important implications for the theory of natural motion, as Aristotle would call it – in modern terms, gravitation. But that deserves a section to itself.

4. Void and infinity

The Stoics, like Aristotle, held that there is no void space within the cosmos: matter fills the whole region within the exterior spherical boundary within any interstices (e.g. Aët. 1.18.5, IV.19.4). This decision probably arose from the need to preserve the unifying tension imparted to the whole by *pneuma*. Void intervals would interrupt and endanger the unity.[65] On the other hand, they differed from Aristotle in positing a void space stretching in all directions outside the boundary of the cosmos, and some of their reasoning is preserved in this case.

> If all of substance is actually dissolved into fire, as the most refined philosophers of nature believe, it must occupy a place thousands of times as big, like solid bodies that are vaporized into smoke. Now the place occupied by the substance that vaporizes in the conflagration is now void, since no body occupies it. Even if someone objects that there *is* no conflagration, that does not establish that there is no void. For if we only imagine that substance vaporizes and expands – and there is nothing that can get in the way of such expansion – it would be void space into which, in our imagination, it would move when it expanded; for of course what is now occupied by it is void space that is filled. (Cleom. 1.1.43–54 Todd)

This quotation is clear enough. Simplicius reports that the Stoics also used a form of the argument borrowed from Archytas by the Epicureans.

---

[63] I borrow this translation of ἕξις from Sorabji 1988. Others use 'tenor' (Long and Sedley), 'habitude' (Cherniss), or 'state'.

[64] Philo in *SVF* II 458, in Long and Sedley's translation. Sambursky 1959, ch. 2 drew analogies between this description of the 'tensional motion' of the *pneuma* and modern notions of wave motion and fields of force.   [65] This is confirmed by D.L. VII.140.

If there is no void outside the cosmos, what would happen if someone stood on the edge of the cosmos and stretched out his hand?[66] The argument as attributed to Archytas, however, is used to prove that the universe is infinite, rather than that there is void space.

Granted that the cosmos is finite, it would presumably require only a finite space for its expansion in *ekpurōsis*. So it requires further argument to prove that the extracosmic void space is infinite. An argument of sorts is offered by Cleomedes (1.1.106–9 Todd). It does not follow that void could be infinite only if body were infinite; the notion of body itself contains the idea of its being limited, but the conception of void has no such limit. Whatever is limited is limited by something else, as for example in the cosmos aether[67] is limited by air on one side and void on the other, air is limited by aether on one side and water on the other, and so on. But the only thing other than void is body. But there could not be any body outside the void, since the cosmos (it is assumed) contains all the body that there is. Hence the void must be unlimited. Thus Aristotle's claim (*Phys.* iv.8, 208a11–14) that the notion of limitedness does not require the presence of something external to the limited body is rejected on the ground that in the cases we are familiar with there *is* always an external something.[68]

The thesis that there is infinite void space outside the cosmos carries an extremely important corollary. No sense can now be made of the notion of the centre of the *universe*. The centre would have to be picked out either by being equidistant from the boundary of the universe everywhere, or by some distinction of quality within it. But if the universe has no boundary, the first cannot apply, and the second is ruled out because there can be no qualitative distinction between any point in the void and any other. Hence Aristotle's dynamic theory, which uses the centre of the universe as its focal point, must be rejected: the focal point must be the centre of the cosmos itself. I have not found the first clause argued in the Stoic fragments, but the second, according to Plutarch, was frequently argued by Chrysippus in his writings (*Stoic. Rep.* 1054e).[69]

---

[66] See above, p. 419.

[67] The Stoics used the name 'aether' for the kind of fire that is found in the heavens: it is not the same as Aristotelian aether, which is an element distinct from the four elements below the moon.

[68] See also Stob. 1.161. This argues that the void is infinite in its own nature. Posidonius asserted that the extracosmic void is not infinite but just large enough to accommodate the expanded cosmos in *ekpurōsis* (fr. 97 EK). See now the discussion of the evidence by Algra 1993.

[69] Note that Cherniss' Loeb translation is extremely misleading here, since he uses the word 'universe' to refer to the cosmos.

5. Gravity and the motion of the heavens

Unfortunately the texts on this subject are more than usually confused and contradictory. To understand the position it is necessary to go back briefly to Plato and Aristotle.

Plato in the *Timaeus* accounted for the phenomena of gravitation by a theory of the tendency of like to join up with its like (like-to-like). The mass of earth is located at the centre: any piece of earth that is unnaturally elevated from contact with the main mass tends to move towards that mass, and this tendency is what we perceive as 'heaviness' (weight) and accounts for the fall of heavy objects to the ground. The mass of fire is located in the heavens, and a portion of fire trapped near the earth's surface tends to rise towards the main mass, and so is perceived by us as 'light'. If we were located in the heavens, we should think of fire as being 'heavy', because it tends to 'fall' towards us, and earth as light. What gives the elements the tendency to move and thus sort themselves by kinds is the pressure upon them exerted by the outermost sphere of the heavens.[70]

Aristotle objected that this gave no reason for the position of earth, rather than fire, at the centre. His own scheme took it as a datum of nature that the earth is naturally at the centre of the universe, fire at the periphery bordering on the sphere that carries the moon, water and air at intermediate stations. Displaced portions of each element tend to move, if not prevented, to their natural place.

As we have seen, the Stoics were unable to follow Aristotle without any change, because they had forfeited the right to speak of a centre of the universe.[71] The most interesting text is from Arius Didymus:

From Zeno. With regard to all the things in the cosmos composed with a holding power of their own, their parts have motion towards the centre of the whole,[72] and this includes the cosmos itself. So it is right to say that all the parts of the cosmos have motion towards the centre of the

[70] See *Tim.* 58a–c, 80b–c. Plato denies that there is any such thing as 'attraction'.

[71] It is extraordinary that Chrysippus apparently contradicted himself on this subject. According to Plutarch (*Stoic. Rep.* 1054b–c) he 'often' said that the infinite has no centre or other co-ordinates, and castigated the Epicurean theory of the downward motion of the atoms on this ground. But elsewhere, in the fourth book *On Possibilities* (Περι δυνατῶν) he said that one of the reasons for the indestructibility of the cosmos is its position at the centre of the universe. One can only hope that in *On Possibilities* he was dealing in a dialectical way with the theories of others (and Plutarch was treating him unfairly). For detailed discussion of this passage, see Hahm 1977, Appendix v, pp. 260–6; Algra 1988, 160–7 and 1995, 336–9; Wolff 1988. Their cosmos must account for its own dynamics.

[72] I take 'the whole' to mean the whole of each individual thing, not the whole cosmos, as in Long and Sedley 1987, vol. I, 296.

cosmos, and especially those that have weight. The cause is the same for the stationary position of the cosmos in infinite void, and likewise that of the earth in the cosmos; for it [sc. the earth] is equally poised around the centre [sc. of the cosmos]. It is not the case that body has weight in all cases: air and fire are weightless. These too tend towards the centre of the whole sphere of the cosmos, but they form a mass towards its circumference, since they are naturally upwardly mobile by virtue of having no weight. In similar fashion they claim that the cosmos itself has no weight since its whole composition is from elements that have weight and others that are weightless. They believe that the whole earth has weight in its own right, but by virtue of its position, since it occupies the middle space and bodies of this kind have motion towards the centre, it stays in its place. (Ar. Did. fr. 23 *ap*. Stob. 1.166.4–27)

Even this text, although it is one of the clearest on the subject, has some points of great difficulty. Let us take the simplest points first.

The things that have a 'holding power of their own' are the things that are not arbitrary collections but unified objects. The expression 'holding power', as we have seen, is used to refer to the unifying principle of inanimate bodies, whereas plants properly have 'nature' and animals 'soul'. 'Holding power' is here used to denote the minimal level of unification, and no distinction is intended between the inanimate and animate. We learn in this first sentence, then, that all unified physical bodies have an internal dynamic system such that the parts are drawn towards the centre. Since the cosmos is itself a unified physical body, its parts obey the same law. That this was a thesis of Stoic cosmology is confirmed quite explicitly by Cicero (*ND* II.115) and it occurs as part of an explicitly anti-Aristotelian argument in Cleomedes (1.1.5).

The thesis entails the rejection of Aristotelian dynamics. There is no sense in which fire in Aristotle's system, being naturally light, can be said to be drawn towards the centre; the reason why it does not fly outwards for ever away from the centre is that there is no place beyond the sphere of the fixed stars for it to go, and it is in any case held in by the outer 'shell' of aether.

So fire and air in the Stoic system should not be described as 'light' in the strict sense. But they must be distinguished from earth and water, and so the term 'weightless' is applied to them. In our text they are also described as 'naturally upwardly mobile'. This sounds like an inconsistent remnant of the Aristotelian system, but we can save the consistency if we supply the qualification 'in the presence of the heavy elements'. In themselves, air and fire have no tendency to move in any direction, but in the context of our cosmos their negative property of weightlessness, contrasted with the weight of earth and water, gives them upward motion – but only, of course, until they have cleared the boundaries of earth and water. Then the fact that *all* bodies tend towards the centre reasserts itself. So the Stoics have an answer to the Epicurean objection to Aristotelian dynamics, that if there is an extracosmic void (a point on which Epicureans and Stoics agreed), fire and air would fly out into space for ever (Lucr. 1.1101 ff.) and the cosmos would be destroyed. The Stoics reply that fire and air stay as near to the centre of the cosmos as they can get. Arius Didymus' testimony on this part of the theory is confirmed by the Peripatetic commentators Alexander (Simp. *Phys.* 671.1) and Themistius (*Phys.* 130.12).

The explanation of why the earth as a whole remains immobile in the cosmos without falling through space – the problem that had troubled Greek cosmology since the time of Thales himself – is supplied by the same theory. Weight means a tendency to move towards the centre: but the earth *is* at the centre, and so its weight gives it no tendency to move. It would be better to say that the earth as a whole has no weight, rather than that it has weight 'in itself', but does not move because of its position. Perhaps that was rejected because of its apparently paradoxical nature: how could the earth as a whole lack weight if all of its parts had weight? That there was much uncertainty about how to express this part of the theory is shown by a passage from Achilles' introduction to Aratus' *Phainomena* (*Isag.* IV), which attributes to Chrysippus the idea that the earth is held in place in the cosmos by the equal pressure of air all round it, just as a millet seed can be held suspended in the middle of a balloon, or so it is alleged.

There is a bigger problem about the explanation of why the cosmos as a whole does not move in the void. In the first place, since the void has no co-ordinates and no qualitative differences, no sense can be given to the distinction between uniform motion and rest; but that is a thought that had to wait a long time for its articulation. The Stoics had an argument to prove that the cosmos is in fact stationary: if it were falling downwards, then rain would not be able to catch up and fall to earth (Achilles *Isag.* IX). This same passage adds the right explanation: all the parts of the cosmos tend to move towards the centre, and so it has no tendency to move in any direction.

In several testimonia, air and fire are said to be *light* (not just 'upwardly mobile') in Stoic theory (Aët. II.25.5; Philo *QG* 1.64 and *Prov.*; Alex. *Mixt.* 218.3). If 'light' means 'having a natural tendency to move away from the centre', as it does in Aristotelian theory, then this appears to be inconsistent with the thesis that all parts of the cosmos have a natural tendency towards its centre.

In spite of the inconsistencies in the testimonia, we should hold on to the well-documented thesis that all parts of the cosmos have a tendency to move towards its own centre. Plutarch quotes the words of Chrysippus himself, from the second book of his *On Motion*:

> Since the whole has tension and motion in the same direction, and the parts have this motion too from the nature of body, it is plausible that for all bodies the primary natural motion is towards the centre of the cosmos – for the cosmos which is thus in motion towards itself, and for its parts inasmuch as they are parts. (Plu. *Stoic. Rep.* 1054f)

The centre of the cosmos is not located at any point identifiable independently of the cosmos; the focus of motion is the centre of the material sphere, wherever that may be located in the infinite void. It appears, therefore, that this statement is equivalent to saying that all the matter in the cosmos tends to move towards its own centre: in other words, we have something very close to a theory of *gravity*. If that is what it is, it is the first such statement in history. The Atomists had claimed that atoms have weight, and weight is a tendency to fall downwards in parallel straight lines; Plato had held a theory of like-to-like sorting; Aristotle introduced the idea of motion towards natural places in the universe.

But is the Stoic theory in fact equivalent to saying that there is a force of attraction in matter itself? There are important qualifications to be made: the first sentence of the Arius Didymus passage quoted above limits the application to bodies 'composed with a holding-power of their own'. This needs to be investigated further. As we have already noted, Stoic theory held that there is a *pneuma* running through the whole world which is responsible for the nature of each thing – or rather, for the holding-power, nature, or soul of each thing according to whether it is inanimate or a plant or an animal. Perhaps, then, we must regard the *pneuma* as a causal agent that is to be distinguished from matter as such. In that case we may not say that there is a force of gravitational attraction between matter as such, but only that there is a force in unified bodies, including the cosmos, that holds them together.

This qualification, however, tends to lose all of its meaning on further examination. The *pneuma* that runs through everything is itself identical with the qualities of that thing, according to the Stoics. Hence, to say that a thing is pervaded by *pneuma* which draws the parts of it towards its centre is the same as to say that its parts are of their own nature attracted to the centre: the *pneuma* is the nature.

It is important to note, however, that the 'centre' in question is not necessarily the geometric centre of the unified body. In the case of the cosmos as a whole, the centre towards which all things are attracted is in fact the geometric centre, because the cosmos is a sphere. But the theory of *pneuma* is drawn from biological models. *Pneuma* is what permeates the body of an animal or plant, of whatever shape, and holds all the parts together so as to constitute a single organism. The notion is applied to inanimate objects such as pieces of metal or rocks by analogy. The cosmos as a whole is conceived to be a single living organism, with a soul of its own. If the divine *pneuma* which permeates the whole of the material sphere and keeps all the parts together draws them towards the geometric centre of the sphere, that is something almost accidental, and not an essential property of the attractive force inherent in the matter.

We have some idea now of how the Stoics described and accounted for the unforced motions of the elements in the region of the earth. But centripetal motion in the geocentric cosmos could not by itself explain the motion of the heavenly bodies. If the earth stands still, as they assumed, then the heavens go round in circles. In early Greek speculation this circular movement was held to be a survival from the original vortex from which the cosmos was formed. Aristotle found it necessary to posit a special element, endowed with the natural property of circular motion, to account for it. What was the Stoic solution?

It is clear that they did not take up Aristotle's fifth element. The Stoics were more impressed than Aristotle was with the importance of the *heat* of the sun. Later Peripatetics found this a great problem with Aristotle's theory: if the sun was separated from the element of fire by lunar spheres of non-fiery aether, how were they to explain the sun's heat, and its effects on the earth? The Stoics accepted heat as the predominant characteristic of the sun, and declared that the element of the heavens is predominantly fire. They called it 'aether', but they meant something quite different from what the Peripatetics meant. They drew parallels between the life-giving heat of the sun, and the heat that is a sign of life in animals. It was another indication that the cosmos as a whole is a living being.

A few of the fragments suggest that the Stoics followed Aristotle in assuming a *natural* circular motion in the heavens, even though they rejected the idea of a special element endowed with this motion; but this is probably wrong.[73] The disappointing truth is that they fell back upon the mythical notion that the heavenly bodies are living beings who *choose* to move in circles. Cleomedes distinguishes between the movement of the fixed stars, which he explains only by saying that it is 'providential, for the maintenance and durability of the whole', and the movement of the 'wanderers', which is due to choice (1.2.1–9 Todd). The teleological description of the whole is often repeated in the fragments: the cosmos is 'girdled' by the sphere of the stars, which protects it and holds it together. The animistic imagery is sometimes carried to great lengths: there is even a theory, attributed to Cleanthes, that the solstices are due to the fact that the sun needs food, his food comes from the ocean, and so he turns back when he reaches the northern and southern limits of the ocean (Macr. *Sat.* I 32.2; cf. Cic. *ND* III.37). The conclusion is inescapable that although the Stoics came quite close to a theory of gravity, they were nowhere near to seeing its application to the motions of the heavenly bodies.

6. *Teleology, providence and fate*

It is useful to distinguish two kinds of teleology, which we will for the present designate 'Platonic' and 'Aristotelian'. These terms beg some questions that are important in some contexts, but not here. Plato, in the *Timaeus*, asserted that the cosmos was produced by a Maker, whose purpose was to make it as good as it could be, given certain limitations imposed by the materials with which he was to work. Aristotle asserted that nature works for ends or goals, but that this activity is immanent in the natural world rather than chosen and imposed upon it by an external agent. If we ask which of these two models was followed by the Stoics, we have to answer: 'Both at once'. The Stoic view is that God is the maker of the world, and made it to be as good as possible; but this God is at the same time immanent in the world – indeed is sometimes said to be identical with the world. All three of these cosmologies take the view that the world is as it is in order to satisfy the design of the creator-God (in the case of Plato and the Stoics) or to fulfill its own coherent form (in the case of Aristotle). They are worlds apart from the accidental cosmogony of the Epicureans.

The Stoics, indeed, are the most whole-hearted in their embrace of the teleological description of the world. The classic text on the subject is the

---

[73] Aët. I.12.4 attributes to the Stoics the thesis that earthly light moves in straight lines, while heavenly light moves circumferentially. But that is ridiculous, if taken literally: if the sun's light moved around the circumference, it would never reach the earth.

long and lyrical speech put into the mouth of a Stoic spokesman by Cicero in *ND* II.98–153. He explains that seeds are implanted in the fruits of trees and plants both to supply food for man, and to replenish the stock each year. Animals are divided into male and female, and supplied with reproductive organs and sexual desires. Cicero's spokesman runs systematically through the parts of the cosmos in this vein, beginning with the four elements, then describing the order of the heavens, the seasons, the adaptation of plants to their environment, and the devices used by animals for protection and getting food. Much of the detailed biology in this section comes from Aristotle's *History of Animals*. But the section concludes with a much stronger emphasis than we find in Aristotle on the place of man at the top of the whole tree.[74] It is asserted that the whole structure of the earth, and all of the vegetable and animal kingdom, are for the sake of man and the gods, who surpass all the rest of creation by virtue of their possession of reason (Cic. *ND* II.133).

All of this belongs to theology, rather than to science or philosophy of nature. Its successor is the work known to all the students of Divinity in the nineteenth century as 'Paley's Evidences' – more exactly, *Natural Theology, or Evidences of the Existence and Attributes of the Deity collected from the Appearances of Nature*, by William Paley (1802). Whereas the school of Aristotle studied the natural world, and especially zoology, with a view to understanding more about plants and animals, their structure and mode of life, the philosophers of the Stoa seem to have studied it for reassurance about the rationality of the god or gods who had power over the cosmos. We find no 'History of Animals', 'Parts of Animals', 'Generation of Animals', and such like in the catalogues of the books of Zeno, Cleanthes, and Chrysippus. Not until Posidonius in the first century BC do we find evidence of a serious interest in the natural world for its own sake, and then it is largely concentrated on astronomy, meteorology, and geography.

So far in this section we have spoken about the transcendent aspect of Stoic theology: the providence of God is regarded as something presiding over the course of the world from a superior position, deciding what is best, and bringing it about. But we must not forget that this picture is to a considerable extent metaphorical in the Stoic system. God is not transcendent, but immanent. The providence of God is another way of describing the course of nature itself. 'The cosmos is a living being, rational, ensouled,

---

[74] Aristotle wrote that plants are for the sake of animals, and animals for the sake of man, in a brief passage of the *Politics* (1.8.1256b15–22).

thinking.' This is asserted by Chrysippus in the first book of *On Providence*, Apollodorus in his *Natural Philosophy*, and by Posidonius (D.L. VII.142).

The early Stoics described God as 'the ἀρχή of all things, the purest form of body, penetrating through all things as Providence' (Hipp. *Philos.* 21.1), as the soul or mind of the cosmos (Aët. 1.7.23), as the fiery *pneuma* that pervades the cosmos (Aug. *Acad.* III.17.38), sometimes as the aether in the heavens (Cic. *ND* I.36), sometimes as being found in the meanest parts of the natural world (Clem. *Protr.* 58).

This doctrine of the total interpenetration of the physical cosmos by God served to unify the notion of providence with that of fate. Providence did its work in the natural world through natural causation. The Peripatetic commentator Alexander describes the doctrine this way:

> They (sc. the Stoics) say that this world is a unity which includes all existing things in itself and is governed by a living, rational, intelligent nature. This government of existing things in the world is an everlasting one that proceeds in a linked and ordered sequence. The things that happen first are causes for those that happen after them. In this way they are all bound together with each other; neither does anything happen in the world such that something else does not unconditionally follow upon it and is attached to it as cause, nor again can any of the following events be detached from the preceding events so as not to follow from one of them as if bound together with it. Every event has its consequent which is by necessity linked to it as cause, and every event has something before it to which it is linked as cause. Nothing in the world exists or comes to be without a cause, because nothing in the world is detached and separated from all the things that preceded it. For the cosmos would be torn apart and divided, and would no longer remain a unity for ever, governed by a single ordering and economy, if a causeless motion were introduced; and that would be introduced if it were not the case that all existing things and events have antecedent causes, upon which they follow of necessity [. . .] The very fate, the nature, and the reason, in accordance with which the whole is governed – this they say is God, and it is in all the things that exist and come to pass, and it thus makes use of the proper nature of all the things that exist for the economy of the whole. (Alex. *Fat.* 191.30–192.28)

Thus the idea of a rigid physical determinism is introduced into cosmology, perhaps for the first time. It is certainly very different from Plato's theory, according to which reason is opposed to necessity, and the proper nature of physical matter is regarded as a hindrance, in some respects, to the best providential ordering of the cosmos: Plato's necessity, embodied in matter, has to be persuaded by reason to come to order. It is also different from Aristotle, who was prepared to allow a certain degree of indeterminacy in his physical system. The new Stoic theory posed new problems – especially the problem of reconciling human action and morality with strict physical determinism. But that problem is discussed elsewhere in this history.[75]

[75] See below, pp. 526–541, esp. pp. 531–4.

13

Theology

JAAP MANSFELD

1 Philosophical theology

Though theology[1] without some form of religion to prompt it would be an odd phenomenon, it is by no means the same thing as religion. Theology, or at least philosophical theology, is a rational enterprise or at any rate an attempt to rationalize the irrational. Rationalist forms of reflection concerning the gods, or the divine, are part of Greek philosophy from its very beginning. On the one hand, the primary principle or principles were often said to be divine or provided with divine attributes, while on the other traditional views of the gods were criticized and other proposals formulated.[2] But the first philosopher to elevate theology (at least in principle) to the status of *a* part of philosophy was Aristotle, who at *Metaph*. E 1.1026a19 affirms that there are 'three theoretical disciplines: mathematics, physics, theology'. Before Aristotle, Plato had argued that those who write about the gods should follow certain 'models' (*Rep.* 379a6). According to this prescription, a god is good and so not the cause of evil but only of what is good,[3] and he does not change but always remains the same. The sharp contrast with the gods of traditional Greek religion, who assume different shapes at will and may not only favour human beings but also deceive and harm them, is very deliberate.

Divinities which conform to this ideal play a decisive part in Plato's and Aristotle's cosmologies. According to Plato's *Timaeus* we live in the best of all possible worlds because it has been constructed by a Divine Craftsman and his help-mates. According to Aristotle all regular events and processes in the world are ultimately dependent on the unmoved, self-centred and divine First Mover described in *Metaph.* Λ. Theophrastus expresses this general idea as follows:[4]

---

[1] For the history of the word *theologia* see Kattenbusch 1930, Festugière 1949, 598–605.
[2] Overview of preplatonic philosophical theology in Babut 1974, 15–57.
[3] Cf. e.g. *Phdr.* 247a, *Tim.* 29d; for precedent in Xenophanes see below, n. 92.
[4] Trans. Daiber 1992, 270. Epicurus knew this treatise, see Mansfeld 1992b, 1994a.

It is not correct (to say) that God should be the cause of disorder in the world; nay, (He is) the cause of its arrangement and order. And that is why we ascribe its arrangement and order to God [. . .] and the disorder of the world to the nature of the world. (*Met.* 14.14–17)

The reactions of the Epicureans and Stoics to these doctrines were different, but reactions they were. In the present chapter I am only marginally concerned with the part played by the gods, or God, in Stoic cosmology or in the context of the Stoic concept of fate,[5] though some attention has to be given to the fact that in the Epicurean cosmology the gods play no part whatever.[6] I shall concentrate on three ingredients of Hellenistic theology which together form a sort of triptych: (1) the issues of the existence and attributes of the gods, (2) the questions of divine providence and theodicy, or the relation between the gods and the world and humans, and (3) problems regarding our knowledge of the divine. This division is to some extent artificial because in our sources these issues may be blended, although they are also presented as distinct themes. Aëtius devotes separate chapters to the question of the origin of the concept of the gods (1.6) and that of their existence and nature (1.7).[7] Such a bipartition is also a feature of Sextus' account; first the origin of the concept (*M* IX.14–48), then the question of existence (*M* IX.49–194). This sequence, first the genesis of the concept and then existence and attributes, is interesting. Cicero's Stoic spokesman too uses distinctions of this nature;[8] for the origin of the concept see e.g. *ND* II.4–15, for existence (including a number of attributes) e.g. *ND* II.16–44. But his Academic opponent argues that such distinctions may to some extent be overruled (*ND* III.17–18). They are indeed impossible to maintain in certain arguments, as we shall see.

The existence of the gods was a traditional problem, because courageous spirits had doubted or even denied that there are gods, or that they care about humans. The first prominent so-called atheists we hear of are Democritus' contemporaries Prodicus of Cos and Diagoras of Melos, and Theodorus of Cyrene who was brought to trial in Athens in the years just before Epicurus settled there.[9] Even earlier the agnostic sophist Protagoras had formulated the following statement at the beginning of his *On Gods*:[10]

As to the gods, I cannot know either that they are or are not, or how they are as to their shape-and-character [*idea*], for many [i.e. various] are the

---

[5] See above, pp. 384–6 and 434–9, and below, pp. 527–41.   [6] See below, pp. 463–4.
[7] On Aët. 1.7 see Runia 1996b.   [8] Mansfeld 1990a, 3193–6, 3207–8.
[9] Texts: Winiarczyk 1981; for Prodicus see below, n. 93. See further Fahr 1969, 85–101, Winiarczyk 1984, 1990; Winiarczyk 1992 overlooks the evidence in Epicurus, for which see below, n. 15.   [10] Mansfeld 1981, 39–43.

obstacles to knowledge: things are obscure [*adēlotes*] and man's life is short. (*ap*. D.L. ix.51)

In this lapidary sentence we already encounter a threefold problem: knowledge of the gods, their existence and their attributes.

Xenophon took up the challenge; at *Mem.* 1.1.4 he has Socrates formulate a series of arguments in favour of divine existence and providence, and of cosmic design. Plato did so as well. A particularly important passage is the beginning of the preamble concerned with the gods and providence of *Leg.* x, where he provides an overview of his opponents' positions. These men either (a) hold that there are no gods or (b) that, if there are, (b^1) they do not care about humans or, (b^2) if they care, (b^{2i}) that they are easily persuaded to change their mind by sacrifice and prayer (*Leg.* x.885b). Plato disagreed. That Aristotle is aware of this issue is clear from *APo.* ii.1.89b33, where the question-type concerned with being *simpliciter* is exemplified by the question 'whether the god exists'. In his view this question takes precedence over those concerning the nature and attributes of the entity involved.[11] As Simplicius reports, Aristotle had formulated an argument for the existence of God in his now lost work *On Philosophy*. This type of proof, later known as *e gradibus entium* ('according to the degrees of being') or as the 'existential argument from the degrees of perfection', was taken up by the Stoics:[12]

> According to a generally valid rule, where there is a better, there is also a best. Since, then, among existing things one is better than another, there must be something that is best, which will be the divine. (Simp. *Cael.* 289.2–4)

Though the available evidence does not permit us to say to what extent the Hellenistic philosophers were influenced by Aristotle's school treatises,[13] scholars believe that his so-called exoteric works were in circulation. The references to and summaries of Aristotelian views and tenets given at Cic. *ND* 1.107 and ii.95–6, for instance, are generally thought to derive from the *On Philosophy* which is cited at 1.33.

ii Existence and attributes

Because they wished to counter the negative positions advocated by the so-called atheists, Epicurus as well as Zeno and his followers were obliged

[11] Mansfeld 1990a, 3198, 1992c, 70–6.
[12] Cf. Verbeke 1949, 186. On superlatives in Plato's theology see Runia 1992.
[13] Sandbach 1985, but the matter is far from being settled.

to formulate arguments in support of the existence of the gods. In the *On Nature* Epicurus mentioned the opponents by name according to Philodemus:[14]

> Epicurus charges those who eliminate the divine from among the things that exist with total lunacy; e.g. in book twelve he criticizes Prodicus and Diagoras and Critias and others . . . [15] (Phld. *De Piet.* 519–27 Obbink)

His tersely formulated main argument in favour of their existence stands Protagoras' on its head:

> For there are gods, since the knowledge of them is self-evident[16] (*enargēs . . . gnōsis*). (Ep. *Ep. Men.* 124)

'Self-evident' or 'vivid' knowledge according to Epicurus is only possible of what is real. But further proofs of the existence of the gods, such as were formulated by the Stoics, are not provided. No direct and unambiguous textual evidence survives which explains this epistemic process.[17] What we do have is a short account of the god as a living being (*zōion*)[18] based on the 'common notion' (*koinē noēsis*) or 'preconception' (*prolēpsis*),[19] which also furnishes us with his essential attributes, that is to say blessedness and indestructibility:

> First of all, acknowledging that the god is a living being that is indestructible and blessed, even as the common notion of 'the god' indicates, do not connect with him anything alien to his indestructibility or inappropriate to his blessedness. Nay, hold about him everything that is capable of maintaining his blessedness along with his indestructibility.[20] For there are gods, since the knowledge of them is self-evident. But such as the many believe them to be they are not, for they do not maintain them consistently with the way they acknowledge them. Impious is not he who eliminates the gods of the many but he who connects the views of the many with the gods. For the assertions of the many concerning gods are not preconceptions but false beliefs. (Ep. *Ep. Men.* 123–4)

---

[14] Text: Obbink 1996, 142–3.

[15] Long and Sedley 1987, vol. II, 151 argue that Epicurus criticized those 'who were held to have explained the gods as calculated human fictions'. This is correct for Critias but not for Diagoras and only in part for Prodicus. The atheism of Diagoras and Protagoras is criticized Diog. Oen. fr. 16 Smith.

[16] For the history of the term see Zanker 1981, who argues that literary critics borrowed it from the Epicureans. At D.H. *Lys.* 7, *enargeia* is the stylistic effect which turns the listener into an eye-witness. [17] See above, pp. 276–83.

[18] Mansfeld 1993, 175–80. Obbink 1996, 11 n. 5 argues that *Ep. Men.* 123 proves that this is 'how we are instructed to *think* [his italics] of the gods as existing': the obvious reply is that we have to do this because they exist. [19] Schofield 1980b, 291–4.

[20] Paraphrased (without Epicurus' name) at Porph. *Marc.* 17.

We must add *KD* 1:

> What is blessed and indestructible knows no trouble itself nor causes
> trouble to any other, so that it is never constrained by fits of anger, or by
> favours; for everything of this kind (is) only in the weak. (D.L. x.139)

We see that these passages do not seem to specify the manner of existence of the gods, and that they tell us nothing about their shape or
appearance, or their habitat (supposing they do have one). Later sources
tell us that Epicurus believed the gods to have the same shape as humans.
The primary evidence is the difficult scholion to *KD* 1, which cites
'another passage' by Epicurus and so should be accepted.[21] Cic. *ND*
1.46–9 on the one hand appeals to preconception, and on the other
argues (i) that human shape is the most beautiful and (ii) that you cannot
have blessedness without virtue and virtue without the rationality
which is only found in the *Gestalt* of man. These arguments, however,
may be a later development. Furthermore, in later sources the gods are
said to dwell in the so-called *metakosmia* or *intermundia*, the 'empty
spaces between worlds'.[22] Lucr. v.146–55[23] affirms that the dwelling-
places of the gods are not anywhere inside the cosmos.[24] Their abodes
must be entirely different from ours, just as their fine-textured bodies
are different from our bodies. He promises that he will expound this
matter in more detail, but unfortunately did not make good his promise.
Cic. *ND* 1.49 tells us that 'the nature of the gods is such that it is perceived not by the senses but by the mind' because they have neither the
solidity nor the individuality of the objects around us. One specific thesis is however attributed to Hermarchus, cited at Philodemus *On Gods*,
PHerc. 152/7, col. 13.20–41:[25] the gods breathe and are not mute but
converse with each other,[26] since felicity is incompatible with lack of
conversation. He is even said to have provided an argument: the gods are
living beings, and the notion of a living being entails that of breathing,
just as that of a fish that of water and of a bird that of wings; breathing,
we may infer, is a 'permanent property' of the gods. Philodemus col.
4.8–13 adds that their language is Greek. He also tells us, col. 10.25–30,

---

[21] Cf. Aët. 1.7.34, and see below, n. 115 and text thereto.

[22] Cic. *ND* 1.18, *Div.* 11.40, Quint. *Inst.* vii.3.5, Hipp. *Ref.* 1.22.3.

[23] Cf. 11.646–51 (ending with a quotation of part of *KD* 1), iii.18–24. For the differences between
Lucretius' and Epicurus' views see Dionigi 1976, 120–3.

[24] Cf. Atticus fr. 3.75–81 des Places, with the comments of Obbink 1996, 8 n. 1.

[25] Text: Herm. fr. 32 Longo Auricchio 1988; comments *ib.* 128–37. The edition of Phld. *On Gods*
by Diels 1916–17 is unreliable; I quote only passages which have been newly edited.

[26] S.E. *M* ix.178 (which may go back to Carneades) seems to attribute the idea that the god is gifted
with speech to Epicurus.

that the Epicureans not only accept the existence of the gods of the Panhellenes but say that there are even more. But we are unable to determine to what extent the ideas found in our later sources may be traced back to Hermarchus and Epicurus.[27]

Cicero and Sextus have preserved a whole battery of Stoic proofs in syllogistic form which are concerned with the existence, attributes and identification of the gods or God.[28] This very form inspires confidence as to their historical reliability; what we have must be rather close to what Zeno and his successors wrote, as is also clear from the fact that revised versions of individual premisses were proposed. The Stoics held that such arguments were needed to *prove* existence and providence: some by resemblance, some by analogy, some by transposition, and some *e contrario* (compare the account of concept-formation at D.L. vii.52). Whether they work is another thing entirely.[29]

We may start with a syllogism by Zeno[30] pertaining to existence; appealing to worship he argued as follows:

> The gods one may honour on good grounds (*eulogōs*);[31] but those who do not exist one may not honour on good grounds; so the gods exist. (S.E. *M* ix.133)

Just as the city honours real persons by erecting statues, publishing decrees, giving them citizenship, naming days after them and so on,[32] so men honour the gods by erecting statues, building temples, performing religious rites, holding festivals, composing and reciting hymns and so forth. Zeno's argument was understandably criticized by opponents.[33] Diogenes of Seleucia tried to make it less vulnerable. Using a traditional interpretative ploy, i.e. bringing what he supposed to be its implicit meaning out into the open, he formulated the second premiss as follows:

> but those who are not of such a nature as to exist one may not honour on good grounds. (S.E. *M* ix.134)

---

[27] Long and Sedley 1987, vol. i,147–9 argue that they may not. For the interpretation of Epicurus by his followers see Erler 1992a and b, 1993. For Philodemus' star-gods see below, n. 58, for permanent properties see above, pp. 379–82.

[28] Full treatment in Dragona-Monachou 1976, 41–129. For Stoic syllogistic see pp. 121–5.

[29] Schofield 1980b, 305–7.   [30] On Zeno's syllogisms see Schofield 1983.

[31] The *logos*-element in *eulogōs* should not be pressed, *pace* Dragona-Monachou 1976, 47–9.

[32] For a list of 'wise men' honoured by cities see Alcidamas *ap*. Arist. *Rhet*. ii.23.1398b10–20. Elis made Pyrrho a high priest and on his account gave exemption from taxation to all philosophers, and Athens honoured him with citizenship (D.L. ix.64, 65). For the *hēmera epōnumos* ('day celebrating a person') see Plu. *Praec. Ger. Reip*. 820d, D.L. ii.14–15. Zeno himself is said to have been honoured by an Athenian decree (D.L. vii.10–12) in which what we may call the 'good grounds' are formulated.

[33] The argument contra cited by Sextus replaces the gods by the Stoic Wise Man.

Sextus explains that the gods may be put on a par with atoms. The concept of an atom includes that it is imperishable and ungenerated, so if they existed at any time they do so now. In its revised form the second premiss is by some scholars believed to anticipate the ontological argument, made famous by Anselm of Canterbury, according to which God's essence entails his existence.[34]

Another syllogism (or rather set of similar syllogisms) by Zeno is clearly dependent on Aristotle's argument from the degrees of perfection, but also is a form of what came to be called the *via eminentiae*, that is to say the argument that the attributes of the divinity are perfect:

> What is rational is better than what is not rational; nothing is better than the cosmos; so the cosmos is rational.

> The same holds in regard of what is intelligent, and also in regard of what partakes of being animate. (Cic. *ND* II.21 and S.E. *M* IX.104)

Cicero adds that it follows that the world is God. It is self-evident that that than which there is nothing better must be the best of what is available. That the best there is will be God is already the conclusion of Aristotle's argument. That it is the world which is the best there is, however, is simply presupposed in Zeno's second premiss. In fact, we do not have his proof that there is nothing which is better than the world though, as we shall see, one by Chrysippus is extant. Zeno is here concerned not so much with the existence of the gods, or God, as with proving the attributes of the *cosmos*: animate, intelligent, rational.[35] The argument concerning the existence of the divine is implicit; if what possesses these attributes is the best there is, it can only be divine. This issue becomes clearer if we compare Zeno's arguments with those of Cleanthes.[36] The existential argument from worship may be interpreted as concerned with the human conceptions of God. But these conceptions do not yet provide a correct picture of the divine; they have to be revised and amplified.

Zeno's arguments show how Stoic theology is an essential ingredient of Stoic natural philosophy, and conversely, and it is perhaps no accident that he did not write a separate treatise dealing with theology. Nevertheless, our sources present these syllogisms (and two others still to be quoted) as arguments in favour of the existence of the god(s). The Dialectician Alexinus refuted Zeno by pointing out that what is poetical is better than what is not poetical, so the cosmos is a poet too, etc. Later

---

[34] E.g. Dragona-Monachou 1976, 46, Dumont 1982, Hankinson 1995, 241. Brunschwig 1994d, with useful references to the literature, argues contra.

[35] Cf. Long 1990, 282. For the history of the idea of the cosmic God see Festugière 1949, 75–340, 375–424.   [36] Below, p. 459.

Stoic exegetes defended Zeno's position by insisting that 'better' means 'absolutely better'. Archilochus is a better poet than Socrates but not a better person (S.E. *M* IX.108–10).[37]

That the cosmos is sentient and rational was proved by Zeno through two other syllogisms as well. These argue by analogy (according to a version of what came to be called the *via analogiae*) and similarity, i.e. from the part to the whole.[38] The first is as follows:

> No part of anything that lacks sensation can be sentient; but parts of the cosmos are sentient; so the cosmos does not lack sensation. (S.E. *M* IX.85, Cic. *ND* II.22)

The second runs (S.E. *M* IX.101, with a slightly different version at Cic. *ND* II.22):

> What emits a rational seed (*sperma logikon*)[39] is itself rational; the cosmos emits a rational seed; so the cosmos is rational.

It is interesting to note that in our sources no version of the cosmological argument from design is attributed to Zeno, that is to say the argument proving God's existence from the regularity to be observed in the heavens and in natural processes in general, the technical formula for which is *sensus dei ex operibus suis*.

Cleanthes too worked out a version of an existential argument from the degrees of perfection, combining it with that from the part to the whole. This is too long to quote in full; it begins as follows:

> If one thing is better than another, there will be a *best* thing; if one soul is better than another, there will be a best soul. And if one living being is better than another, there will be a best living being, for such matters are not of such a nature as to proceed to infinity. (S.E. *M* IX.88)

Cleanthes next shows that some living beings are better than others but that not even man is the best, for he is a weak and mostly evil creature. Accordingly,

> What is perfect and best will be better than man and fully possess all the virtues and be immune to evil, and this will not be different from God. So God exists. (S.E. *M* IX.88)

Cleanthes naturally must have agreed with Zeno's proofs. His own argument is concerned with stipulating in addition and by analogy that the god has all the virtues, that is to say wisdom, courage, temperance and justice

---

[37] Cf. Cic. *ND* III.22–3, where however Alexinus' name is not mentioned and the counter-argument is omitted.   [38] Precedent at Xen. *Mem.* 1.4.8, noted by Cic. *ND* II.18 and S.E. *M* IX.92–5.
[39] See above, p. 436.

as well as all those that are subordinate to these cardinal virtues. Cleanthes, in short, explicitly integrates theology and ethics.

Chrysippus used the argument from the degrees of perfection as well, combining it with the already traditional argument from design:

> If there is anything in nature that man's mind and human reason, strength and power cannot bring about, that which brings it about is certainly better than man; now the phenomena in the heavens and what exhibits everlasting regularity cannot be brought about by man; therefore that by which they are brought about is better than man – what other name is there for this than 'god'? (Cic. *ND* II.16)

Interestingly enough, Chrysippus here does not argue from the 'better' to the 'best'.[40] Following the view of Cleanthes which is attested at Cic. *ND* II.15, Chrysippus also appeals to design according to Cic. *ND* II.17, where the order and arrangement of the cosmos are said to be analogous to that of a beautiful human dwelling.

Another Chrysippean argument, a complex one paraphrased by Cicero, begins by offering a justification of the premiss assumed by Zeno, viz. that there is nothing that is better than the cosmos:

> Just as a shield-case is designed for a shield and a sheath for a sword, so everything else except the cosmos is designed for the sake of some other thing. [. . .] But the cosmos is entirely perfect, because it contains all things and there is nothing which is not within it.[41] (Cic. *ND* II.37–8)

Chrysippus radicalizes the argument from teleology and design,[42] already found at Xen. *Mem.* 1.4.5–6, which is also a major feature of Plato's *Timaeus*.[43] We may compare the argument that 'the cosmos alone is self-sufficient' quoted from *On Providence* (hereafter *De Prov.*) 1 at Plu. *Stoic. Rep.* 1052d. The emphasis on the fact that the teleological series must have a stop will be indebted to Cleanthes. The proof reported by Cicero continues by arguing from perfection to rationality (as in Zeno) and virtue (as in Cleanthes):

> How then can it lack what is the best? But there is nothing better than intelligence and reason, which the cosmos therefore cannot lack.

---

[40] It seems to be implied in the first part of the argument that follows at II.16: 'if there are no gods, then what in the nature of things can be better than man? For reason, than which there is nothing better, is in man.'

[41] That there is no matter outside the cosmos was already argued by Plato *Tim.* 32c–33b, Arist. *Cael.* II.9.278b21–a11, and Arist.(?) *ap.* Philo *Aet.* 21.

[42] For Chrysippus' teleology cf. e.g. the report at Plu. fr. 193 Sandb. *apud* Porph. *Abst.* III 20 and the quotations from the *On Nature* at Plu. *Stoic. Rep.* 1044c–d.

[43] Cf. Arist. fr. 10 R³ *ap.* S.E. *M* IX.22.

[. . .] That which is best in the cosmos as a whole must be present in what is perfect and self-sufficient; but nothing is more perfect than the cosmos, nothing better than virtue; therefore the cosmos has its own and proper virtue. [. . .] Therefore it is wise, and consequently divine.[44] (Cic. *ND* II.38-9)

Information concerning the detailed theological doctrines of Zeno, Cleanthes, Chrysippus and Diogenes of Seleucia is to be found in the parallel accounts at Cic. *ND* 1.36-41 and Phld. *De Piet.*, *PHerc.* 1428, cols. 1-10.8.[45] These presumably derive from an earlier Epicurean survey which is critical of Stoic theology, but its contents agree with what is reported in unprejudiced sources.[46] The early Stoic scholarchs provided allegorical interpretations of the commonly accepted gods;[47] more specifically, they declared that the heavens and heavenly bodies are what the traditional names really represent, as other philosophers had done before them.[48] Zeno argued that the cosmos taken as a whole is God, and declared that the parts of the cosmos, especially the aether and the heavenly bodies, are gods. Cleanthes, who composed his famous *Hymn* and wrote an *On Gods* (D.L. VII.175), declared the aether and the mind and soul of the cosmos and the heavenly bodies to be God and gods. The titles of two treatises by Chrysippus are cited which deal with theological themes: a work *On Gods* in at least three books (e.g. Plu. *Stoic. Rep.* 1052b), and a treatise *De Prov.* in at least four (Gell. VII.1-2).[49] Theological topics were also treated by Chrysippus in other works. It is worthwhile to quote part of Philodemus' detailed description of his theology:[50]

Chrysippus, who traces everything back to Zeus, says in book one of his *On Gods* that Zeus is the Reason which administers all things and the Soul of the All, and that all things by participation therein [are in various ways alive . . .],[51] even the stones, which is why he is called *Zēna* ('Life'), and (he is called) *Dia* ('Through') because he is the Cause and Master of all things. The Cosmos itself is animate, and the Regent Part and Soul of the Whole is God; the argument valid in respect of Zeus also holds for the Common Nature of all things and Destiny and Necessity. And Lawfulness and Right and Concord and Peace and Love and so on

---

[44] Cf. Cic. *Acad.* II.119. The questions concerned with the fact that it is a living being, rational, reasonable and a god were treated in Chrysippus *On Nature* v, *ap.* Phld. *De Piet.*, *PHerc.* 1428, cols. 7.31-8.4 (for the text see next n.); see Schofield 1991, 75-6.

[45] Text: Henrichs 1974, with German trans. which I have not followed in all respects; note that cols. 1-3 (on Zeno and Cleanthes) are mostly too damaged to be intelligible.

[46] E.g. D.L. VII.147-9.   [47] Cf. Cic. *ND* III.63; survey in Pépin 1976, 125-31.

[48] E.g. [Plato] *Epin.* 980a-988e, Arist. *Cael.* I.3.270b5-12 and at Cic. *ND* II.41, 44.

[49] For the contents Gercke 1885 is still useful.   [50] Text: Henrichs 1974.

[51] Several lines are missing.

are the same thing. And there are no male or female gods, just as there are no (male or female) cities or virtues, but they are merely given male and female names though they are the same, as for instance Mooness and Moon. And Ares pertains to war and either side in battle, and Hephaestus is fire, and Cronus is the stream of what flows, Rhea the earth, Zeus the aether – others say this is Apollo – and Demeter the earth or rather the *pneuma* in the earth. And it is infantile to describe and form gods with human shape,[52] just as (infantile as to believe in) cities and rivers and places and passions (with human shape). And Zeus is the air surrounding the earth, and the dark (air) is Hades, that in the earth and sea Poseidon. The other gods he combines with such inanimate things in the same way. And he believes the Sun and Moon and the other heavenly bodies to be gods, and the Law too. And he also affirms that humans change into gods. In book two [sc. of the same treatise] he, like Cleanthes, attempts to accommodate what is ascribed to Orpheus and Musaeus and what is in Homer and Hesiod[53] and Euripides and the other poets to their [sc. the Stoics'] doctrines. (Phld. *De Piet.* cols. 4.12–8.13)

Near the end of his overview Philodemus prefers to ignore the fact that the Stoic theology is pantheistic, the gods being parts, or rather manifestations, of the supreme ruling divinity who pervades the whole cosmos,[54] though at the beginning of his report the pantheistic colouring is clearly visible. It is also well brought out by Diogenes Laertius:

The god [. . .] so to speak is the father of all things, both in general and as to the part of him which pervades all things, which is called by many appellations according to its powers. [. . .] He is given the name Zeus insofar as he is the cause of life or is present in all that is alive, Athena because his regent part extends to the aether, Hera because (it extends) to the air, and Hephaestus because (it extends) to the technical fire, and Poseidon because (it extends) to the wet, and Demeter because (it extends) to the earth.[55] In the same way the other appellations have been given with regard to a particular affinity. (D.L. VII.147)

III The gods, the world and men

The views of the Epicureans and the Stoics on the relation between the gods and the world and men are radically opposed to each other.

---

[52] Against the Epicureans rather than popular religion.
[53] Zeno already allegorized Hesiod, e.g. Cic. *ND* 1.36; *Schol. Hes. Theog.* 30.6–8 Greg. (text at *SVF* 1.100 not good).   [54] See above, pp. 448–51.
[55] Cf. Phld. *De Piet.* col. 8.28–33 Henrichs, citing the *On Athena* of Diogenes of Seleucia.

Nevertheless they share a common purpose in that they both strive to liberate us from fear.

Epicurus wrote at least two theological treatises (lost): *On Gods* and *On Holiness* (D.L. x.27, cf. Cic. *ND* 1.115);[56] he also spoke of the divine in other works. In the Epicurean system the gods play a dual role. They are important in the context of ethics, their blessedness and immortality in fact being the paradigm of what may be attained by mortal men, whereas their role in the context of Epicurean natural philosophy is entirely different from that attributed to them by other philosophers. Epicurus' primary aim is to establish that the gods cannot, consistently with their blessed state, be in any way involved in what happens in nature, let alone in what happens to humans. Hence the positioning of the formulation of the nature of the gods, according to which blessedness is incompatible with having to worry about mundane matters, as the very first of the *KD*,[57] and the careful placement of theological statements at the beginning and end of the ethical *Letter to Menoeceus*, in a sort of ring-composition (123–4, partly quoted above, and 143–5). What is said about the gods in the *Letter to Herodotus* occupies a less conspicuous position. Still, at *Ep. Hdt.* 76–7 Epicurus forcefully argues that it is excluded that what is 'blessed and indestructible' can be the cause of celestial and meteorological phenomena. At *Ep. Hdt.* 81, again, he emphatically rejects the belief that the heavenly bodies are 'blessed and indestructible', that is to say divine,[58] and are capable of 'intentions', 'actions' and of being 'causes' of what happens in a world. This false view of the gods is singled out as one of the two main sources of anxiety among men. In the *Letter to Pythocles* the gods are present only insofar as they are consistently absent, that is to say are removed from the cosmos. The regularity of the orbits of the heavenly bodies is not to be explained by their divine nature: the gods are blessed and free from labour (*Ep. Pyth.* 97, cf. 113 and 115). All celestial and meteorological phenomena can be explained by means of (pluralities of) natural causes; there is nothing in nature that is intentional.[59] Epicurus here extends the argument of Theophrastus' *Meteorology* concerning the de-divinization of the meteorological phenomena to those in the heavens.[60] The argument in favour of the divinity of the heavenly bodies based on their vast size is

---

[56] The former is cited Phld. *De piet.* 189–90, 753–4, 1043–4, and 1261–2, the latter *ib.* 206–7, 362–4, and 1266–7 Obbink. See further below, pp. 472–4.

[57] Versions of *KD* 1 have this prominent position in other accounts too (Lucr. 1.44–9, Cic. *ND* 1.45), and it is the first maxim to be quoted in the *Gnom. Vat.* and at Diog. Oen. fr. 29.111 Smith.

[58] Philodemus' star-gods (*On Gods* III, *PHerc.* 152/157, cols.8–20), for which see Woodward 1989 with text at 33–6, are an innovation.   [59] See below, p. 499.

[60] Mansfeld 1992b, 324–7. See above, p. 453.

countered by Epicurus' statement that the sun is as big as it appears to be, or a bit bigger or smaller (*Ep. Pyth.* 91, with scholion).[61] Similarly, the observation at *Ep. Pyth.* 89 and *Ep. Hdt.* 74 (with scholion) that a heaven, or cosmos, need not be spherical but may equally well be triangular or egg-shaped is directed against the argument of Plato and Aristotle in favour of the divinity of the heaven based on its sphericity.[62]

Accordingly, Epicurus' theology is relevant to both physics and ethics, and he does not have to bother about justifying the ways of the gods to men. His gods cannot be held responsible for cosmological or moral evil. Providence is a myth (Plu. *Def. Or.* 420b, *Non Posse* 1101c). Epicurus' cosmos is godless (*atheos*). Nevertheless he is not an atheist (*atheos*) himself, although in antiquity he was occasionally accused of being one, or at least of being a crypto-atheist.[63] In the Epicurean ethics *hēdonē* ('enjoyment', 'happiness', 'satisfaction') is the highest good. Concentrating on the blessed state of the gods and on the causes for this blessedness, among which is the fact that they are not involved in what goes on in the cosmos, will help us in achieving happiness and detachment ourselves. Because we need not, indeed cannot reasonably, be afraid of the gods, one major obstacle on the road to happiness has been removed. But there is no short cut. The insight that this anxiety is obsolete is a corollary of one's familiarizing oneself with the correct explanations of the phenomena of nature. For all that, the Epicurean is in a position to participate in traditional acts of worship provided he does so while concentrating on the correct conception of the divinity.[64] In the same state of mind he attends the religious ceremonies in honour of Epicurus, the members of his family, and of other prominent early Epicureans.[65] As a matter of fact, Epicurus was venerated by his followers as the great liberator (Lucr. 1.66–79), and even, paradoxically but presumably metaphorically, as a god (see the fragments of the *Letter to Colotes* at Plu. *Col.* 1117c–d, cf. *Ep. Men.* 135; Lucr. v.8–12), though Lucretius (of course) states that he is dead (v.1042, vi.7), i.e. is not an immortal.

The Stoic view of the relation between the gods and the cosmos and men is strongly opposed to the Epicurean. This is brought out very well by the rider Antipater[66] shrewdly added to the Epicurean preconception of the divinity and by his similar appeal to the *enarges*:

---

[61] Barnes 1989a, 40–1. Cf. also Demetrius of Laconia *PHerc* 1013, for which see Romeo 1979.

[62] Mansfeld 1994a, 39–40.

[63] E.g. Cic. *ND* 1.85, Plu. *Non Posse* 1102c–d; see Obbink 1989, 1996, 13–17.

[64] See Lucr. II.655–60, D.L. x.120, and *POxy.* 215, an early Epicurean text newly ed. with trans. and comm. by Obbink 1992; cf. further Obbink 1984, Festugière 1985, 77–9, Obbink 1996, 10–11. [65] Clay 1986, Obbink 1996, 9–10, 389–458.

[66] Stoic definitions similar to Antipater's quoted at Orig. *Sel. in Ps.*, *PG* 12, 1055E–56A (not in *SVF*).

Antipater of Tarsus in his *On Gods* writes word for word as follows: 'To introduce the whole doctrine we shall briefly formulate the self-evident apprehension (*enargeia*)[67] which we have of God: our concept of God is that of a blessed and indestructible being which is beneficent towards men. [. . .] Indeed, all men hold them to be indestructible.' (Plu. *Stoic. Rep.* 1051e–f)

Though we have no verbatim quotation from Chrysippus, Plu. *Stoic. Rep.* 1051d–e testifies that he strongly opposed Epicurus, and others who abolish providence, by appealing to the common concept[68] which necessarily includes the attribute of beneficence. Irrational fear of the gods is therefore groundless. What is more, poverty, disease, death and other unpleasant conditions or events are not really evils in the Stoic view but indifferents, and fear is one of the four cardinal affections that have to be eliminated.[69]

In his chapter 'On fate and the excellent order of events' Stobaeus lists the tenets of a number of philosophers, including Zeno.[70] The passage merits some confidence because a book-title is given:

Zeno the Stoic in his *On Nature* (says Fate is) the force which moves matter in the same respect and in the same way;[71] it makes no difference to call this Providence (*pronoia*) and Nature. (Stob. *Ecl.* 1.5.15)

We do not have any proofs for the attribution of *pronoia* to the gods which are ascribed to early Stoics by name. But numerous anonymous Stoic arguments (including several in dialectical form) are to be found at Cic. *ND* II.73–167 and in various places in Philo *Prov.*[72] As our starting point we may perhaps take the fact that Cleanthes and Chrysippus declare God to be in possession of all the virtues. Now *pronoia* according to the rather late evidence of [Andron.] *De Virt.* 3.2 (confirmed at Cic. *De Inv.* II.160) is a sub-species of wisdom; it is defined as a 'condition which is capable of bringing things about in a methodical way[73] in respect of the future, so that actions will be performed the way they should'. This is a bit surprising as a definition of a human virtue. Zeno is claimed to have said that Nature, an 'artistic Fire', brings all things about 'in a methodical way' (Cic. *ND* II.57). The definition of human *pronoia* will have been derived

---

[67] Cf. Ep. *Ep. Men.* 124, quoted above, p. 455.
[68] Literally 'the concepts we have'; cf. below, n. 102. He also annexed the Epicurean preconception, see Schofield 1980b, 293–8.
[69] See Mansfeld 1992b, 334–5, and see below, pp. 690–705.   [70] Text also at Aët. 1.27.5.
[71] See Mansfeld 1979, 163–5.   [72] Comments: Dragona-Monachou 1976, 131–59.
[73] Text in Glibert-Thirry 1987, but ὁδοποιεῖσθαι should be emended to ὁδῷ ποιεῖσθαι; for parallels see Mansfeld 1983b, 60–3.

from that of its divine counterpart; it was observed above that Zeno believed Fate, Nature and Providence to be identical. One may therefore credit the early Stoics too with the view that the attribution to the divinity of providence, or providential care and foresight, follows from the proofs concerning the existence of the gods and the full-blown rationality of the perfect and divine cosmos, as Cicero indeed argues at *ND* II.76–9.

Philo *Prov.* I. 2–4 has preserved an interesting dialectical dialogue, which culminates in an argument from the part to the whole, that is, from foresight in humans to providence in the cosmos.[74] Arguments from design and purpose are not only used to prove the existence of God, but also his demiurgic activity and loving care for the world and humans, in short his *pronoia* (Cic. *ND* II.87–162, in often boring detail; Philo *Prov.* I.33 and 42–5, II.62–8). Epicurean arguments against this view are found at Lucr. II.167–83 and V.156–99. Though some of these may have originally been aimed by Epicurus against Plato (especially the *Tim.*),[75] the emphasis on the idea that the world was fashioned for the sake of men – a polemical exaggeration of a prominent Stoic doctrine[76] – suggests that they were adapted to embrace other creationists who believed in providence.

At V.199 Lucretius famously says that the world is 'blameworthy' (*tanta stat praedita culpa*). The Epicureans do not need a theodicy, that is to say do not have to find a way of reconciling cosmological and moral evil with divine providence or with the conviction that the best of all possible worlds has been created by a wise and virtuous god. But the Stoics, like Heraclitus[77] and Plato before them, are obliged to justify the existence of evil, or even to explain it away. We may begin with what Cleanthes has to say on moral evil. His *Hymn* is too long to be quoted in full, but we may reproduce its most significant part. Addressing Zeus, who 'with his law steers all things', he writes (lines 3–15):

> This whole cosmos, as it turns around the earth, obeys you wherever you direct it, and is willingly dominated by you. [. . .] For no event occurs on earth or in the aetherial heavens or in the sea, God, without your permission, except what bad men do in their own stupidity. But you know how to make properly fitting what is out of line and to order what is out of order. (Stob. *Ecl.* I.1.12)

---

[74] Cf. Philo *Prov.* I.24–8, Cic. *ND* II.79.

[75] Though Furley 1989a, 200–3 argues that lost works of Aristotle are the main target.

[76] Cf. Cic. *ND* I.23 (*hominum causa*), *Acad.* II.120, Gell. VII.1.1. At *ND* II.130–3 Cicero's Stoic spokesman argues that the world has been made for the sake of men and gods, but what is useful for men comes first. See also *ND* II.154–62.

[77] Cleanthes wrote an *Interpretations of Heraclitus* in four books (D.L. VII.174, cf. IX.15). One such exegesis survives at Ar. Did. fr. 39 *ap.* Eus. *PE* XV.20.2, which however may be from the *On Zeno's Physics* (D.L. VII.174).

The first verses quoted summarize the Stoic doctrine of fate and providence. But even what is morally evil has its place in the order of things and
so, in the ultimate reckoning, is part of the divine plan.[78]

Gell. VII.1 provides excerpts from Chrysippus' *De Prov.* in which he
argues against those who deny the existence of evil. Echoing Plato (*Tht.*
176a) he points out that good and evil are contraries and that neither can
exist without the other.[79] Echoing Heraclitus (as *ap.* Clem. *Strom.*
IV.iii.10.1) he points out that justice is only known because of the existence of unjust acts, and goes on to point out that this holds for all the
opposites: truth and falsehood, good and evil, happiness and unhappiness, pleasure and pain,[80] virtue and vice. Cosmological, or physical, evil
(which is only bad in the popular sense of the word) may also be explained
away. That people fall ill, or have skulls that are fragile,[81] is not a primary
ingredient of the divine plan but only an unavoidable side-effect (*kata
parakolouthēsin*) of the best possible arrangement of things. Even harmful
and unpleasant animals have their uses; in his *On Nature* V (cited Plu. *Stoic.
Rep.* 1044d), for instance, he points out that bed-bugs wake us up and
mice make us attentive in putting things carefully away. Faced with the
hoary question why good and virtuous people suffer he explains, in his *On
Substance* III (quoted Plu. *Stoic. Rep.* 1051c), that some things may be overlooked, just as a certain amount of wheat may get lost in well-managed
households. Alternatively, such unfortunate events and even natural disasters may serve the good of the whole (quotation from *On Gods* II at Plu.
Stoic. Rep. 1050e).[82]

From a quite obvious and indeed common point of view the end of the
ordered cosmos in which we live will be a major disaster. Some philosophers argued that the world will never end. According to Plato *Tim.* 41ab
the Demiurge, because good, will never unmake what he has made. In a
lost work cited by Philo (*Aet.* 10–11) Aristotle accused those who deny that
the world is ungenerated and indestructible of 'horrible atheism'.
Another Peripatetic argument preserved by Philo *Aet.* 39–43, which may
also derive from Aristotle, states that a Divine Craftsman would have only
two reasons for destroying his handiwork, namely either to cease from
making a world or to construct another. Both motifs are incompatible
with his perfect nature. We only need to look at the second of these.

---

[78] Cf. Heracl. at *Schol. vet. Il.* Δ 4; Long 1975–6, 145–8, Inwood 1985, 76. For moral evil see below,
pp. 690–7.
[79] Cf. the quotations from *On Justice* I at Plu. *Stoic. Rep.* 1051a–b, from *On Nature* II at Plu. *Stoic.
Rep.* 1050e–f (cf. *Comm. Not.* 1065a), and from an unidentified work at Plu. *Comm. Not.* 1065d.
[80] Explicit reference to Plato *Phd.* 60b at Gell. VII.1.6.   [81] Cf. already Plato *Tim.* 75c.
[82] Cf. *On Gods* III at *Stoic. Rep.* 1049a–b.

Another world would either be worse or equal or better. To make a worse world would entail that God had changed[83] for the worse, to make an equal one is to labour in vain, and making a better one would entail that God was less good the previous time. But according to the ineluctable laws of Stoic physics the world as we know it cannot but end in total conflagration (*ekpurōsis*), and then of necessity must start all over again.[84] Eternal recurrence of the same, for according to Zeno Socrates will again be accused by Anytus and Meletus (Tat. *Adv. Graec.* 5). The Stoics therefore had to counter the theological arguments of Plato and Aristotle.

Chrysippus' position is relatively well known.[85] The fact that part of our information derives (again) from the *De Prov.* is no accident, because at first glance *ekpurōsis* seems incompatible with divine *pronoia*. It has to be justified, just as the end of the world is justified in Christian theology. Chrysippus makes his escape by using the word *kosmos* both for the organized world of experience and for the condition of things during total conflagration.[86] Accordingly the *kosmos* is eternal. In *De Prov.* 1 he argued that 'the cosmos does not die' (quoted Plu. *Stoic. Rep.* 1052c), affirmed that during *ekpurōsis* Zeus withdraws into *pronoia* whereupon both together are thoroughly mingled with the aether (paraphrased Plu. *Comm. Not.* 1077e), and stated that 'when the cosmos is wholly fiery it is *ipso facto* its own soul and regent part' (quoted Plu. *Stoic. Rep.* 1053b). It would appear that at this stage *pronoia* is the most prominent divine virtue, for it is the only one to be mentioned (but it should be recalled that according to Stoic theory the presence of one virtue entails that of all the others). At the very least, this homogeneous cosmic state is not inferior to that of the differentiated world we know,[87] and our sources describe the transformation which brings it about in positive terms (e.g. Plu. *Comm. Not.* 1075d, on Cleanthes). Chrysippus admitted that, with the exception of Zeus, the gods, e.g. the sun and the moon, are subject to generation and destruction (quotation from *On Gods* III at Plu. *Stoic. Rep.* 1052a).[88] Opponents saw this as contradicting the common concept of what constitutes a god, but Chrysippus held that eternal recurrence neutralizes this objection. Antipater's formula quoted above may seem to deviate from Chrysippus' view,[89] but Plutarch, who gleefully con-

---

[83] Cf. Arist. *ap.* Simp. *Cael.* 289.4–14.
[84] Mansfeld 1979, 144–56, Long 1985, 14–21, see above, pp. 436–41.
[85] Mansfeld 1979, 174–83, Long 1985, 22–5.
[86] *Ap.* Plu. *Stoic. Rep.* 1053b; Philo *Aet.* 9 cites this as the standard Stoic view.
[87] At Mansfeld 1979, 177–8 I have argued that it is superior; rejected by Long 1985, 25.
[88] Cf. Plu. *Comm. Not.* 1075a–e, which includes a reference to Cleanthes.
[89] Argued by Long 1990, 286–7.

structs this disagreement, is notoriously selective in his reportage and may well have omitted qualifications which failed to suit his polemical purpose.

Paradoxically, *pronoia* is most prominently present when it is no longer, and not yet, engaged in the construction and administration of our world. These are indeed the 'mysteries of philosophy'.[90] What Chrysippus could have said, and indeed may have said, is that you cannot have construction without de-construction, and conversely, and hence that both are equally part of the providential arrangement of things. One understands why *pronoia* is said to remain during total conflagration, for if it were to disappear there would be no eternally recurring replicas of the organized cosmos, and on purely physical grounds the condition of total conflagration cannot last forever.

Chrysippus attached such value to theology that he declared it to be the crowning part of physics and stipulated that it is the last part of philosophy to be taught. In his *On Lives* IV, quoted Plu. *Stoic. Rep.* 1035a–b, he calls theological instruction an 'initiation' (*teletē*). This is confirmed at *Etym. Magn.* under *teletē*, and something similar is already attested for Cleanthes, who allegedly said that the gods are 'mystical shapes' (thus Epiph. *Adv. Haer.* III.2.9).[91]

IV Knowledge of God

Religion was a fact of life, as it still is. Alternative views as to what the gods, or God, are and what they do or do not do had been proposed by philosophers, most prominently by Xenophanes.[92] In the days of the great Sophists, as we have seen, doubts about the legitimacy of the traditional belief that the gods exist had been formulated. In some cases explanations of the origin of religion were provided: the gods as the deification of useful things in life such as bread, water and wine,[93] or as invented by politicians who sought to impose law and order and fooled people into believing in a watching deity.[94] Democritus argued that traditional religion arose out of fear and wonder; thunder, lightning, thunderbolts, comets and the eclipses of sun and moon (which had always been interpreted as signs of divine anger) frightened men into believing

---

[90] See immediately below.   [91] Mansfeld 1979, 134–6.
[92] Fragments quoted Clem. *Strom.* v.14.109, S.E. *M* IX.144 and 193, Simp. *Phys.* 23.11–12 and 20.
[93] Prodicus at Cic. *ND* I.118; Phld. *De Piet.*, *PHerc.* 1428, fr. 19; S.E. *M* IX.18; cf. Henrichs 1975, 107–15. For Persaeus and Cleanthes see below, n. 104 and text thereto.
[94] Critias at S.E. *M* IX.54; see Döring 1978.

that these phenomena were caused by gods (*ap.* S.E. *M* IX.24).[95] Such religious beliefs indeed were very powerful, and continued to be so. Democritus did not deny that the gods exist but derived the origin of our awareness of them in a more scientific way from the perception[96] of images which are big and strong but (as he said) in the end not indestructible; these foretell the future and speak (S.E. *M* IX.19).[97] Aristotle in a lost work provided, or cited, two explanations (S.E. *M* IX.20–2). On the one hand, he adduced the inspired psychic states which occur during dreams and the prophecies pronounced by the dying, when the soul is being separated from the body. Arguing by analogy and, as it would seem, applying the argument from the degrees of perfection without being aware they did, men conceived the existence of a divine being, similar to the soul and of all the most capable of knowledge. He also appealed to the argument from design first formulated by Xenophon,[98] adding that men concluded from the regularity of the motions of the heavenly bodies[99] that these must have been caused by a god. At *Metaph.* Λ.8.1074a38–b14 he combines two earlier views and argues that the mythological accretions to the insight that the heavenly bodies are divine were added in the past by persons who wished to impose law and order.

We need only concern ourselves with explanations that do not appeal to pragmatic motives. The first thing that needs pointing out is that an explanation of the origin of a notion is by no means the same thing as acquiescence in its validity. A correct notion may still have to be established.[100] To account for the historical origin of religious beliefs Epicurus too appealed to what occurs during sleep (S.E. *M* IX.25, cf. Phld. *De piet.* 225–31 Obbink), though *Gnom. Vat.* 24 states that dreams 'have no divine nature nor any divinatory force'. He even adduced the human fears of meteorological and celestial phenomena and the false belief that the heavenly bodies are divine.[101] These explanations are also set out at Lucr. v.1161–93.

As to the Stoics, Cic. *ND* II.13–15 lists no less than four grounds for

---

[95] The seasons too were sent from above (Democr. *ap.* Phld. *De Piet.*, *PHerc.* 1428, fr. 16; see Henrichs 1975, 96–106). The Democr. fr. quoted at Clem. *Protr.* 68.5 seems to affirm that clever people had capitalized on these impressions.

[96] In dreams, as it would appear; cf. Diog. Oen. fr. 9.VI.3–13 Smith (text heavily restored).

[97] At fr. 10 IV.10–V.6 Smith, Diogenes argues against Democritus that images cannot speak etc. Long and Sedley 1987, vol. I, 145 affirm this means that Democritus was wrong because he attributed vital powers to the images which *are* his gods. But the further point seems to be that he was mistaken in stating that though alive the gods are nothing but images.

[98] Above, p. 454.   [99] Anticipated at Plato *Crat.* 397c–d.

[100] For the Stoics see Schofield 1980b, 298–300.   [101] Above, p. 463.

the 'formation in men's minds of notions of the gods' provided by Cleanthes.[102] The first resembles Democritus' view and Aristotle's report, and appeals to foreknowledge of future events.[103] The second, a revision of a Sophistic argument, points at the benefits derived from our excellent climate, the fertility of the earth and the abundance of other useful things.[104] The third, echoing another suggestion of Democritus (and Epicurus), points at the fears inspired by thunderbolts and other meteorological phenomena and by earthquakes and so on. The fourth and 'most important', building on arguments of Democritus, Xenophon and Aristotle, appeals to the regular motion of the heavens and the distinction, utility, beauty and order of the sun, the moon and the other heavenly bodies. As in Aristotle, this is capped by an argument from analogy. Just as somebody, upon entering a house or gymnasium and observing that things are organized in an orderly way, will have to infer that there is someone in control, so, observing the perfect order which obtains in the vast cosmos, one cannot but infer that its grand natural motions and processes are governed by a Mind.

Cleanthes' explanations do not all operate on the same level. His fourth and most important may also serve as a proof of the existence of the divine, and shows that proofs regarding existence and speculations concerning the origin of the notion may overlap. The first and second need working over if they are to result in an appropriate concept. Foreknowledge has to be linked to fate, and the abundance of beneficent things must be incorporated in a teleological world-picture. According to a Stoic view cited at Aët. IV.11, in some cases the notions that arise naturally have to be developed by further instruction and attention.[105]

Cleanthes' third explanation, from fear, describes one among the several spontaneous sources of the notion of the gods, but this does not entail that he believed it to be capable of leading to a correct concept of what the gods really are and do. Quite the reverse. Knowledge of God and the gods according to the Stoics is provided by such proofs and arguments concerning their existence, identity, attributes and *pronoia* as have been studied in the previous section. As their point of departure these proofs must avail themselves of natural notions that already hint at the true state of

[102] Cf. the appeal to common notions at *ND* II.5 and 12 (see also III.8), Plu. *Stoic. Rep.* 1051e (Antipater); see further Boyancé 1962, 46–8, Schian 1973, 142–3, Schofield 1980b, 301–2. Extended version of such an inventory at Aët. (pseudo-Plutarch) I.6.10.

[103] Zeno said that divination is a *technē* (D.L. VII.149); Cleanthes and Chrysippus expanded the subject (Cic. *De Div.* I.6).

[104] Cf. Cic. *ND* I.38 on Persaeus, and Phld. *De Piet.*, *PHerc.* 1428, cols. 2.28–3.8 Henrichs on Persaeus' endorsement of Prodicus.   [105] Cf. D.L. VII.52.

affairs. Fear has to be abolished and to be replaced by admiration and acceptance. We have seen above that Antipater, who presumably was anticipated by Chrysippus, began his account of theology with the preconception. We may safely believe that he went on to add the required proofs and qualifications.

According to Epicurus, on the other hand, we may be certain that the gods exist because our preconception of them as blessed and indestructible living beings already provides knowledge that is clear and therefore certain.[106] This preconception has to be distinguished from the muddled notions men derive from what happens when they are asleep, or construct e.g. in regard to cosmic phenomena. These wrong and even disastrous notions come into being because, or when, men are incapable of sticking to the preconception and add further attributes which are incompatible with it. It is the task of the philosopher to point the way back to the correct preconception.

If, however, one wishes to find out what causes this pure, or purifiable, preconception the evidence, unfortunately, is of a derivative kind; we have to make do with testimonies such as the difficult abstracts from Epicurus in Philodemus' *De Pietate*,[107] the cryptic abstract from 'another passage' of Epicurus in the scholion to *KD* 1, the baffling report of Cic. *ND* 1.49-50 (text in crucial places uncertain), passages in Lucretius, e.g. VI.76-7 (cf. also Aët. 1.7.34), and the heavily restored theological works of Philodemus, who like Cicero may reflect later developments and present an *Epicurus interpretatus*. Lucr. VI.76-7 speaks of 'images (*simulacra*) reporting the divine shape which are transferred from the holy body to the minds of men'. Images are also mentioned in the Ciceronian passage (*imagines*) and in the scholion (*eidōla*). Cic. *ND* 1.49 tells us that 'the gods are discerned not by the senses but by the mind',[108] and that 'our mind, by focusing and concentrating with the keenest feelings of pleasure on these images, is capable of understanding a nature which is both blessed and eternal'.

But according to Cicero's text as transmitted[109] the 'infinite shape of

---

[106] See above, pp. 455-6.

[107] Above, n. 56; for Philodemus' references to other early Epicurean writings see Obbink 1996, 662.

[108] The mind functions as a sense-organ. I refrain from discussing at appropriate length the difficult formula *similitudine et transitione perceptis* ('perceived by similitude and transition') which is about how the divine images are discerned. The images are 'perceived' (*perceptis*), i.e. we are aware of them in a way that is analogous to our immediate awareness of the data of sense-perception.

[109] At *ND* 1.49 *species* ('shape') and *ad deos* ('towards the gods') are difficult; *series* ('series') and *ad nos* ('towards us') have been conjectured. Scholars as a rule accept either or both of these emendations, though *species* is protected by the sloppy repetition at *ND* 1.105.

most similar images arises from the innumerable atoms and streams towards the gods', not 'towards us', as some prefer to write. This admits of two interpretations.[110] The first and traditional one is that an uninterrupted supply of images flows to the gods out there and so ensures their indestructibility.[111] Perhaps we then have to assume that our mind, by a further effort, does not only focus on the images that enter it (the fact that the gods *are* perceived by it has been mentioned previously) but also thinks of the images out there, that is to say contemplates the conditions which guarantee the gods' blessedness and immortality and so confirm our preconception.[112] But it is hard to understand how the images out there are formed in the first place, or what the very word 'images' represents. The second, proposed by an influential nineteenth-century German historian of materialist thought (one of the heroes of young Nietzsche),[113] is that there are no gods out there and that subtle human images which are continuously coming towards us in fact stream 'towards the gods', that is to say produce these in our minds. This view makes the gods imaginary living beings, ideals, 'thought-constructs' formed by the transformation of the concept of a happy and long-lived human being into that of an immortal and blessed creature.[114] To know the gods is to create them, and conversely. The crabbed scholion to *KD* 1 can be interpreted accordingly, and may then be translated as follows:[115]

> Elsewhere he says that the gods are seen by reason, some (οἱ μέν) numerically distinct, others (οἱ δέ) with formal unity, resulting from the continuous influx of similar images to the same place, (and) human in form. (D.L. x.139)

---

[110] Bibliography of the dispute at Woodward 1989, 29–30 n. 2.

[111] E.g. Lemke 1973, 22–41, 77–98.   [112] Mansfeld 1993, 190–201.

[113] Lange 1974 (repr.), 79–80, dismissed by Zeller 1909, 451 n. 2 as flying in the face of all our ancient sources.

[114] The best argument in favour is that of Long and Sedley 1987, vol. I, 144–9; cf. also Obbink 1989, 201. I argue contra at Mansfeld 1993. To be sure, S.E. *M.* IX.43–7 attributes this explanation to the Epicureans themselves – esp. 45, 'the notion that the god is eternal and indestructible and perfectly happy was formed by way of transference (*metabasis*) from men' – but this is said to be their reply to an objection, so may be a mere dialectical ploy. *Metabasis* in this sense derives from the Stoic theory of concept-formation (D.L. VII.53); it is a favourite term of Sextus.

[115] Quoted from Long and Sedley 1987, vol. I, 143, interpretation ibid. 148; I have replaced their 'in other works' by 'elsewhere' because ἐν ἄλλοις does not necessarily refer to more than one work or even a single passage (scholia jargon, but see already Arist. *Metaph.* 1009b19, *De An.* 427a24, *Polit.* 1338a27, also e.g. [Plu.] *Cons.* 104b, 104c, 116f, 118a, and Stob. 1.156.15, probably from Ar. Did., where what follows pertains to *Phys.* bk. 4 and the first definition, not entirely literal, = 212a20). Thinking of what we have in the other Epicurean scholia in Diogenes I do not believe this phrase is a verbatim quote; it is a compressed abstract, at best only echoing Epicurus' words. One may also translate '. . . in one way (οἱ μέν) as existing individually, in another (οἱ δέ) as (existing) with formal unity' etc. Cf. Mansfeld 1993, 203–6, with references to earlier literature; to the examples cited there for μέν and δέ in this sense add Arist. *Phys.* IV.13.222a18–19. Obbink 1996, 303 argues that the scholium is confused.

On this view, the 'same place' would have to be the human mind, not the gods themselves. The numerically distinct gods are deified persons, the others mere corporeal concepts. The main difficulty of this exegesis is that a thought-*construct* which *integrates* blessedness and indestructibility is different from the preconception advocated by Epicurus which includes these attributes from the start. Cicero's text states that *the gods* are perceived, not (modified) human images. Epicurus moreover affirms that the gods are 'living beings' (*zōia*), and appears to have argued that they are somewhere outside the cosmos;[116] our corporeal concepts, of course, are here. According to the text of Philodemus as restored, he described the gods as 'unified entities' (*henotētes*), consisting of ingredients that are 'identical' as well as of ingredients that are 'similar'.[117] Obbink argues at length that these passages prove the gods to be concepts, but the physical processes of continuous concept-formation as described by him[118] are equally valid for the continuous formation of gods out there, provided the hypothesized idealization performed by the mind be discounted. In the present context, however, I prefer not to argue in favour of either interpretation.

*

The problem already formulated by ancient critics, viz. that a being composed of atoms should *ipso facto* be destructible (e.g. Cicero's Academic at *ND* 1.68),[119] retains its virulence on both interpretations. The solution proposed by Philodemus in his theological treatises, namely that the nature of the gods is capable of warding off destruction,[120] is a form of special pleading. It reminds one of Molière's doctor-to-be, who attributes the somniferous effects of opium to its 'sleep-inducing virtue which lulls the senses'. The argument from *isonomia* ('equal distribution') attributed to Epicurus at Cic. *ND* 1.50, according to which the causes of conservation (in this case the infinite streams of images towards the gods out there) are not less infinite than those of destruction, also seems to have been invented *pour le besoin de la cause*.[121] But it is at any rate clear that in later Epicureanism the mode of existence of the gods is inextricably bound up

[116] Above, n. 24.   [117] *De Piet.* 205–19, 320–37 347–64 Obbink.
[118] Obbink 1996, 4–12, 296–7, 321–32, and elsewhere.
[119] Arguments contra cited from Metrodorus at Phld. *De Piet.* 63–70, 189–201 Obbink.
[120] Similar views attributed to Epicurus at Phld. *De Piet.* 100–4, 181–9 Obbink. Lucr. III.819–23 argues that the human soul lacks such a special power.
[121] At *ND* 1.109 it is considered to be fundamental to the Epicurean theory though easy to refute. It is accepted by Kleve 1979 but rejected by Long and Sedley 1987, vol. II, 149, who argue that its use is inconsistent with the apparently exhaustive list of the conditions for indestructibility at Lucr. III.806–23.

with the ways in which our knowledge of and ideas about them are thought to be achieved.

v Academic views and criticisms

Cicero *ND* III.29–52 and Sextus *M* IX.138–90 have preserved a series of Academic theological arguments. Both mention Carneades' name[122] and ascribe arguments to him. We may safely attribute to the great Carneades the points these two sources have in common, or which in either of these are explicitly said to be his. We should however take into account that the arguments concerning the divine attributes were probably abridged by Cicero and expanded by Sextus, or rather in the tradition he depends on, and that Cicero seems to provide a blow-up of the sorites arguments. Cicero presents the sceptical counter-proofs as aimed against the Stoics (cf. *ND* I.4, II.162, where the Stoics are said to be Carneades' favourite opponents), Sextus as aimed against the Dogmatists in general.

Carneades refutes conclusions, not premisses. One of his lines of attack is to undermine the tenet, held and argued by Stoics as well as Epicureans, that the gods are living beings (Cic. *ND* II.29–34, S.E. *M* IX.138–43). To this purpose he deploys a whole array of counter-proofs which can be only partly summarized here. God is corporeal according to both Epicureans and Stoics, but nothing that is corporeal can be immortal. Focusing upon the Stoic doctrine (Cic. *ND* III.29–31 and 34), Carneades argues that the divine body must consist either of one element (water, air, fire, earth) or a combination of these. But these elements are divisible and perishable. It has been argued that the point about the destructibility of God does not hold water against the early Stoics, who claim that the gods disappear into fire when the world comes to an end.[123] But Carneades' argument is still pertinent to Chrysippus' undying divine cosmos which consists of fire only.[124] Furthermore, to be a living being is to be sentient (as the Stoics had forcefully argued), but to be sentient entails to be pleased by some things and displeased by others.[125] To be displeased entails being changed for the worse or even to suffer and so, ultimately, to be perishable (Cic. *ND* III.32–4, S.E. *M* IX.139–47).[126] But this is at odds with the notion of God.[127] A third argument is aimed against the Stoic proofs that the god

---

[122] Cic. *ND* III.29,44; S.E. *M* IX.140, 181, 190. On the differences of treatment in Cicero and Sextus see Couissin 1941; overview of the arguments in Hankinson 1995, 242–4.

[123] Long 1990, 283–7, who suggests that Carneades' contemporary Antipater is the butt of the attack.   [124] Above, p. 468.   [125] Cf. Arist. *De An.* 2.413b21–4.

[126] See Long 1990, 283.

[127] As Plato and Aristotle had already argued, see above, p. 452, p. 467.

is rational and has all the virtues (Cic. *ND* III.38-9; S.E. *M* IX.152-77, at far greater length). Carneades cleverly exploits the Stoic definitions of the virtues. Practical wisdom (*prudentia*, *phronēsis*), for instance, is 'knowledge of things good, evil and indifferent' (Cic. *ND* III.38, S.E. *M* IX.162). But why should God have to choose between good and evil (Cicero)? What is more, knowledge of indifferents entails knowledge of suffering, but to know this one must have experienced it, and to suffer is to change and in the end to be perishable (S.E. *M* IX.163-4). If the Dogmatist (in fact, the Epicurean) answer is that God only knows happiness (*hēdonē*), the Academic reply is that (Epicurean) happiness is absence of suffering and so presupposes it (S.E. *M* IX.165-6). Similar arguments are developed in respect of the other virtues.

God cannot be proved to be rational either, for reason is used to argue from the known to the obscure, but nothing can be hidden from God (Cic. *ND* III.38, cf. S.E. *M* IX.169 and 171). Carneades presumably made short shrift of the Epicurean preconception; the Academic at Cic. *ND* 1.62-3, however, attacks his Epicurean opponent's appeal to the common conception of mankind by pointing out that we do not know all the nations, and by recalling the famous atheists of the past. An interesting argument found at Cic. *ND* III.20-1, not attributed to Carneades but perhaps deriving from an anonymous Dialectician from whom the Academics borrowed it (it comes just before, and resembles, those from the part to the whole at III.23 which derive from Alexinus)[128] reduces the Stoic arguments from the degrees of perfection to absurdity. What precisely is the meaning of 'better' in 'nothing better than'? 'More beautiful' or 'more useful' may be acceptable equivalents, but 'rational' is not. Nothing is superior to Rome, but this does not make the city rational or sentient. Furthermore, on the Stoic line of reasoning an ant, because sentient, should be rated 'better' than a city.

Sextus tells us that the sorites, or step-by-step, arguments[129] were recorded by Carneades' pupil Clitomachus (*M* IX.182; at IX.190 he says that he has cited only a few). These were aimed against the Stoic arguments in favour of pantheism, that is to say their revisionary interpretation of traditional religion (Cic. *ND* III.44),[130] and perhaps, by implication, against the argument from design. A typical example runs as follows:

---

[128] Cf. above, n. 37.   [129] For this type of paradox see above, pp. 170-6.
[130] See the quotations from Philodemus and Diogenes Laertius above, pp. 461-2, and Burnyeat 1982b, 326-33.

If Zeus is a god his brother, [the sea-God] Poseidon too will be a god, and if Poseidon is a god, the [great river] Achelous too will be a god. If the Achelous, then also the Nile, and if the Nile, then every river, and if every river, then streams as well will be gods, and if streams, then torrents. <But torrents are not gods>,[131] and streams are not, so Zeus is not a god either. (S.E. *M* IX.182–3)

Beginning with Zeus and continuing step after step, one arrives at something which is no longer held to be divine. Retracing one's steps, one is forced to admit that the starting-point is not divine either.

We may end by pointing out that Carneades' purpose, as that of the Academics and sceptics in general, is only to show that the dogmatist *arguments* in favour of the existence, attributes and so on of the gods are not valid. We cannot have *knowledge* of the gods. In fact, the Academics (just as, subsequently, the Neopyrrhonists)[132] see no harm in following the custom of the land and acting in accordance with traditional religious beliefs. Philosophical theology is what they reject. The early Pyrrhonist Timon was not afraid of applying religious terminology to the master himself. Pyrrho is apostrophized by him as someone who lives 'always without worrying (*aphrontistôs*) and immutably in the same way'.[133] This language fits a divine being; one understands why Epicurus is said to have been curious about Pyrrho,[134] for Epicurus' exemplary gods and wise men also live without worries. Immutability, as we have seen, is a traditional attribute in philosophical theology, but it acquires a different sense when applied to a mortal man. Timon continues by stating 'you alone lead the way for men in the manner of the god who revolves around the earth . . .' (viz., the sun). In another fragment (S.E. *M* XI.20), Pyrrho is introduced as holding that it 'appears to' him that the 'nature of the divine and the good consists in what makes human life as equable as possible'. This is difficult because hard to square with rigorous scepticism, and its meaning is disputed.[135] Perhaps one may say that, though Pyrrho (or Timon) will refuse to commit himself as to the real nature of the divine and the good and therefore only says what appears to him, what appears to him is a way of life which is an expression of the divine and the good. These words, then, are being used in their everyday sense, just as the god revolving around the earth is that of popular religion. The Academics and

---

[131] A few words seem to be missing.   [132] E.g. Cic. *ND* I.61, III.5, and *Div.* II.148; S.E. *M* IX.4.

[133] Pyrrho T 61A (l.3) Decl. as reconstructed from D.L.IX.64 and S.E. *M* I.305 and XI.1.

[134] D.L. IX.64; yet according to D.L. x.8 he called him names.

[135] See Decleva Caizzi 1981a, 255–62, and Bett 1994a, who implausibly argues that the speaker is Timon who expresses views that are mistaken.

Pyrrhonists are religious conservatives, while the Stoics transformed the traditional religion and proposed interesting improvements. The Epicureans, as we have seen, rejected most parts of traditional religion and proposed a revised version of what remained, though they recommended participation in traditional acts of worship. The average citizen would have found it hard to distinguish between Epicurean, Stoic and Academic or Pyrrhonist participants in the religious rites. The differences were in their heads.

14

Explanation and causation

R. J. HANKINSON

1 Background

Our principal topic will be the views of the Stoics and Epicureans, and the various sceptical attempts to undermine their pretensions to explanatory understanding. Much of this is the history of polemic and dispute; but we may at the outset identify certain points of contact shared by all or most of the adversaries.

Most importantly, the Hellenistic causal theorists were materialists. And whatever materialism may be taken to amount to, most of them agree that causing is essentially corporeal: causal power is transmitted by bodily contact. Sextus notes that 'some [sc. of the Dogmatists] say that body is what can act and be acted upon' (S.E. *PH* III.38; cf. *M* IX.366), thus defining corporeality in terms of causal efficacy. Congruently, the Hellenistic period sees the emergence of the notion that, properly so called, a cause is something active.[1] Plato had defined *aition* ('cause') quite generally as 'that because of which (δι' ὅ) something comes to be' (*Crat.* 413a); and Aristotle's four 'causes' (*aitia*: *Phys.* II.3) include the material from which something is made, its structure, and its purpose, as well as whatever it is which made it. By contrast, for Seneca a cause is *id quod facit*, 'that which actually does or produces something' (*Ep.* 65.4); he objects to the 'crowd of causes' associated with the Platonists and the Peripatetics; design, purpose, and goal drop out of the causal vocabulary. Not that they disappear altogether; but for something to be a cause, an *aition*, now implies more than merely that it is an irreducible feature of a complete account or explanation of something, as it was for Aristotle. This fact is emphasized by the proliferation of terms in our period for causal efficiency.[2] Although Sextus remarks that 'some say that cause is corporeal, others that it is incorporeal' (S.E. *PH* III.14), he is presumably in the second case referring

[1] See Frede 1980, 217–21, for a discussion of this development.
[2] Cf. Barnes 1983a, 191 n. 20: and Barnes' list is not exhaustive.

to Plato and the Pythagoreans (cf. *M* IX.364); and he continues: 'in general it would appear that in their [i.e. the Dogmatists'] view a cause is that because of whose action (δι' ὃ ἐνεργοῦν) an effect comes about'. The addition of the word for action, ἐνεργοῦν, to Plato's more inclusive definition is what makes all the difference here.

Given this Hellenistic emphasis on the active nature of *aitia*, I shall generally render *aition* and *aitia* as 'cause', although in some cases 'explanation' and 'reason' are preferable. Both *aition* and *aitia* derive ultimately from the adjective *aitios*, 'responsible'. The concept of responsibility was for the Greeks as broad as its modern English counterpart, a fact which in itself accounts for Aristotle's inclusion of a range of distinct explanatory factors under the term's spreading umbrella. The Stoic restriction of the extension of the term, then, amounts to limiting its range to that of causal responsibility.

Nor are *aition* and *aitia* systematically distinguished. Stobaeus (reporting the views of Arius Didymus)[3] indeed says that Chrysippus used the former to refer to the object doing the causing, while the latter was reserved for an account of the *aition*, and that suggests that *aitia* more properly refers to explanations rather than causes, where an explanation is propositional in form. But this Chrysippean distinction is not universally or even generally observed.[4] Even so, it is important to distinguish cause from explanation; while even in Aristotle's catholic usage, *aition* rarely means 'explanation' as such (a much better, if clumsier, translation would be 'explanatory factor'). Causes, at least in this narrow sense, are properly to be considered extensionally: if we simply want to advert to whatever it is that is as a matter of fact responsible for something, it doesn't matter how we do so. But if we wish to draw attention to what it is in virtue of which it has the effect that it has (and hence, at least provisionally, to explain that effect), we need to pick it out in a particular way. In Aristotle's terminology, Polycleitus may be the 'incidental' cause of the sculpture, since Polycleitus is the name of its sculptor: but the proper *aition* is 'a sculptor', or 'the art of sculpture', since it is reference to that which explains the outcome.[5] Causal contexts are referentially transparent; explanatory ones are opaque. The Hellenistic theorists were concerned with both explanation and cause: but one side effect of the concentration on active production (as well as the belief that causes are corporeal) is a tendency to stress the extensional, causal talk at the expense of its intensional, explanatory cousin.

---

[3] Quoted below, section III.
[4] The two terms are later said to be synonymous: [Gal.] *Syn. Puls* VIII.458.
[5] See section VII below.

There is also widespread agreement in our period concerning the universality of causation. Galen even goes so far as to treat propositions like 'nothing occurs without a cause' and 'nothing comes to be from nothing' as metaphysical axioms whose certainty is a priori.[6] None the less, there is a crucial exception to this. It is important to distinguish

(T1) every event has a cause,

from

(T2) every event has an effect.

(T1) and (T2) are obviously logically distinct; and their conjunction may be taken to express the Law of Universal Causation. They are, however, compatible with general indeterminacy. Only if they are strengthened to

(T1*) every event has a specific cause

and

(T2*) every event has a specific effect

do we approach determinism.[7] The Stoics did indeed adopt (T1*) and (T2*). The Epicureans, on the other hand, rejected even (T1); and their reasons for so doing are central to this and to the following chapter.

II Stoic materialism

The basic structure of the Stoics' physical picture of the world is dealt with more extensively elsewhere.[8] Their fundamental physical (as opposed to metaphysical) distinction is that between the Active and the Passive principles. Sextus again takes this to be a point of widespread agreement: 'it is agreed by most that of principles (*archai*) some are material and some efficient' (S.E. *PH* III.1); thus he remarks the similarity between Aristotle's view and that adopted by the Stoics. However, such an apparent concinnity disguises a fundamental démarche taken in Stoic theory. The active and the passive are, for them, both material, the active principle being assimilated to the lighter, more dynamic elements of air and fire, while the grosser water and earth form the passive substrate. In particular it is the

---

[6] Gal. *MM* x.36–7; see Hankinson 1991, 19–20 and notes ad loc. Strictly speaking, of course, Galen lies outside the ambit of this *History*; but he is an invaluable source for the Hellenistic debates, as well as an acute critic and analyst of them.

[7] By 'specific cause' here I mean to rule out the possibility, left open by (T1), that two events entirely similar in type might yet be brought about by distinct causes, and similarly for effects, and (T2).   [8] See above, pp. 382–411, 432–51.

highly volatile compound of air and fire (its precise structure is unclear) known as *pneuma* which is responsible not merely for the intelligence of the universe but also for its material cohesion. All material objects are permeated by *pneuma* in a state of dynamic tension which holds them together.

The actual mechanics of this are obscure. What matters is that, as Galen puts it, the Stoics invoke not only causes of becoming; they introduce causes of being as well (*Adv. Jul.* XVIIIA.278–9). These causes they labelled *aitia sunektika*, or 'containing causes',[9] and are initially at least conceived quite literally as holding things together. And this permeation is total – solid bodies do not have interstices filled with *pneuma* like reinforcing bars in concrete: rather the entire substance is a complete intermixture. Galen explains:

> If after they had been mixed these ingredients (*pneuma*, water, and earth) were all to remain in their original state, that would imply that their minute parts had simply been juxtaposed and not that they had been totally intermingled. But this is just what Empedocles thought. For he used to hold the view that natural bodies are produced not by an intermixture of the four elements but by their combination and for this reason on this point his theory coincides with that of Epicurus and Democritus, whereas neither the Stoic philosophers nor Aristotle talked of juxtaposition. (Gal. *CC* 5.2–3)

Galen proceeds to attack the view that there must be a containing cause of absolutely everything. Although he does not explicitly say so (his direct target is Stoic-influenced doctors), the notion is probably Stoic; and Galen finds it incoherent:

> If every single existent thing requires a containing cause without which it cannot exist, that cause, as it is an existent, must inevitably have another containing cause itself which must in turn have yet another – and so on *ad infinitum*. (Gal. *CC* 6.3; cf. *Plen.* VII.524–8)

Materialism generates the regress. If

(1) every cause is corporeal

and

(2) every corporeal thing requires some further distinct containing cause of its existence,

---

[9] This is the standard English translation of the term, and as such I retain it. It is not very satisfactory; 'cohesive causes' might be better in the case of causes of being. Long and Sedley 1987, vol.I, 492 prefer 'sustaining causes', which at least has the merit of making sense in English – however I fear that it purveys the wrong impression as to their role.

then if anything is to exist at all, there must be an infinite number of causally-dependent, hierarchically organized bodies. That supposition is, if not incoherent, at the very least ontologically extravagant, and (one might also think) explanatorily null. The Stoics may however deny that (2) holds universally, by making *pneuma*, although corporeal, self-cohesive. But in that case they need to hold (absurdly, in Galen's opinion) that the grosser elements are somehow held together by the lighter and more volatile ones.

Clearly the Stoic account as we have it is lacunose – but it is not obviously incoherent. The heavy elements (in particular earth) hold together on Galen's view simply because that is what it is to be solid: 'the fact that they (i.e. rocks and metals) are solid depends on this very quality, namely their self-coherence' (*CC* 6.5). But there is no logical reason why one should not treat solidity as a derived instead of a basic attribute, to be explained in terms of some further properties (as indeed it is in modern physical chemistry). Consequently the requirement that persisting objects need causes of that persistence does not conflict with the notion that a cause is essentially something active. In order to prevent solid objects like cups and tables simply disintegrating into an amorphous pile of matter a constant active tension of the *pneuma* is required; thus objects really are constantly being caused to be the way they are, and these containing causes, although intimately intermixed with the materials themselves, are none the less separable from them.[10]

III The Stoic analysis of causation

Of more moment, however, is the Stoics' conception of the proper analysis of causation. The founder of the school, Zeno

> says that a cause is 'that because of which (δι' ὅ)' while that of which it is a cause is an attribute; and that the cause is a body, while that of which it is a cause is a predicate. He says that it is impossible that the cause be present yet that of which it is the cause not belong. This thesis has the following force. A cause is that because of which something occurs, as, for example, it is because of prudence that being prudent occurs, because of soul that being alive occurs . . . Chrysippus says that a cause is 'that because of which'; and that the cause is an existent or a body . . . He says that an explanation (*aitia*) is the statement of a cause, or the statement of a cause *qua* cause. (Arius Didymus *ap.* Stob. 1.138.14–139.4)

---

[10] In this sense Frede 1980, 243 is right to describe containing causes as 'the Stoic analogue to Aristotle's formal cause'.

Zeno asserts a metaphysico–semantic thesis: the proper form of a causal statement is

(3) x causes F,

where x names an object and F an attribute. (3) is obviously deficient: Sextus allows us to refine it:

> The Stoics say that every cause is a body which becomes a cause to a body of something incorporeal. For instance the scalpel, a body, becomes the cause to the flesh, a body, of the incorporeal predicate 'being cut'. (S.E. *M* IX.211)

thus (3) may be expanded to

(3*) x causes y to be F;

the causal relation is triadic, linking two bodies and an incorporeal attribute: it involves one object effecting a change in the condition of some other object, the first being the active efficient principle, the second the passive material.

The Arius Didymus passage expresses the thesis of causal sufficiency:

(4) if x is the cause of y's being F, then whenever x is present, y will be F.

That thesis requires further analysis. At first sight, Arius Didymus appears to attribute to Zeno the view that causes and effects must be simultaneous; but that was certainly not (at least in complete generality) the canonical Stoic view. Causes can be causes of processes, and processes take time. Moreover, the condition of being present is not entirely lucid: must the cause be in contact with the affected body? Near to it? Linked to it by some physical connection? The Stoics' position on this will become clearer as we proceed.

Arius Didymus' intimation that, for Zeno, cause and effect must in some sense be contemporary might suggest that he was primarily concerned here with *aitia sunektika*, operating continuously to preserve things' structures; and his examples are consistent with that. But clearly (4) is not restricted to the domain of conserving causes. Sextus again:

> The majority of them hold that of the causes some are containing (*sunektika*), some co-operative (*sunaitia*), and some auxiliary (*sunerga*); and that causes are containing if, when they are present the effect is present, when they are removed the effect is removed, and when they are decreased the effect is decreased (thus they say that the application of the noose is the

cause of the strangling); and that a co-operative cause is one which contributes a force equal to that of its fellow cause to the occurrence of the effect (thus they say that each of the oxen drawing the plough is a co-operative cause of the drawing of the plough); and that an auxiliary cause is one which contributes a slight force to the easy production of the effect, as for instance when two men are lifting a heavy weight with difficulty, a third appears to lighten it. (S.E. *PH* III.15)

Although different (and mutually inconsistent) accounts of these relations survive,[11] the basic idea is simple enough. *Sunaitia*, as defined in Sextus and elsewhere,[12] do not resemble their Platonic homonyms (*Tim.* 46c–e). Two[13] *sunaitia* are the co-operative causes for an effect when they each supply some causal power to it. Sextus stipulates that they contribute an equal force to the outcome: but this seems theoretically unnecessary, and rigorously applied would enormously restrict the applicability of the notion. A *sunergon* is characterized as that which contributes to an outcome, but is not its primary cause, in that it is not counterfactually necessary for it. Here too the texts sometimes conflict:[14] but a *sunergon* apparently reinforces an existing *aition sunektikon*, whereas two or more *sunaitia* co-operate to bring about an effect which each individually could not achieve, and thus collectively amount to an *aition sunektikon*. This is Clement's testimony:

Whereas the auxiliary cause aids the containing cause, so as to intensify what comes about through the latter, the co-operative cause does not correspond to the same conception, since a co-operative cause may exist where there is no containing cause. For the co-operative cause is conceived along with another which is itself equally incapable of producing the effect on its own, since they are causes co-operatively. The difference between the co-operative cause and the auxiliary cause lies in the fact that the co-operative cause produces the effect along with another cause which is not independently producing it, whereas the auxiliary cause, in creating the effect not independently but by adding to another, is acting as auxiliary to the very cause which is

---

[11] Clem. *Strom.* VIII.9.25 mentions αἴτια προκαταρκτικά, συνεκτικά, συνεργά, and αἴτια ὧν οὐκ ἄνευ, or prerequisite causes (cf. Plato *Phd.* 99b); at 9.32 he substitutes συναίτια for αἴτια ὧν οὐκ ἄνευ. It is clear that Clement's distinctions are not systematic, and συναίτια and αἴτια ὧν οὐκ ἄνευ cannot be synonymous, given the normal definition of what it is to be a *sunaition*. See however below, n. 16. [12] See [Gal.] *Int.* XIV.691–2, [Gal.] *Def. Med.* XIX.393.

[13] Or more: Sextus deals only with the simplest case, but it is readily generalizable to cover any number of co-operative causes.

[14] [Gal.] *Def. Med.* XIX.393 implies that a *sunergon* can bring about an effect on its own; but that is surely aberrant.

independently creating the effect, so that the effect is intensified.[15]
(Clem.[16] *Strom.* VIII.9.33)

Sextus' notion of containing causation is one that involves functional dependence, which represents a further strengthening of (4); *aitia sunektika* are not only co-temporal with their effects – they are co-variant with them as well.[17] Moreover it extends the ambit of containing causation beyond the domain of conservation into that of genuine causal efficacy, as Galen recommends (*Adv. Jul.* XVIIIA 278). Compare this with the fact that all the examples attributed to Zeno by Arius Didymus are cases of conservation: the soul's presence in the body keeps it alive; the prudence in a man's soul makes him prudent.[18]

Thus we may infer that the concept of containing causation was extended beyond the explanation of persistent states to cover events and processes.[19] In the process it became apparent that, if the thesis of causal sufficiency represented by (4) was to be retained it needed further refinement, since in many cases there is clearly no one individual item (on any commonsensical metaphysics of individuation at least) which is exclusively responsible for a given effect, as the example of the oxen ploughing shows. Thus, while it was considered important to be able to retain (4) in some form, the requirement that there need be a unique cause is dropped, provided that there is some collection of items which meets both the sufficiency and contemporaneity conditions.

---

[15] [Gal.] *Int.* XIV.692 allows that *sunaitia* are sometimes individually sufficient for their effects, and glances interestingly, if briefly, at the notion of causal over-determination: this seems to be an off-case, albeit an interesting one. Even so, details of the relations between and proper characterizations of the triad of causes remain obscure, and it is possible that there was some overlap between the categories of *sunaitia* and *sunerga*; Frede 1980 presents a clear reconstruction of how the classifications may have evolved.

[16] Clement of Alexandria is a relatively late writer (second century AD) but probably earlier than Diogenes Laertius; a word is in order to justify using him as a source for the distinctions of our period (see above, p. 481, n.6). Suffice it to say that it seems to me highly plausible that the technical senses he distinguishes were already deployed by the Stoa of Chrysippus: see the discussion of Cic. *Fat.* 41 below.   [17] Cf. [Gal.] *Def. Med.* XIX.393; and see Hankinson 1987a, 84–5.

[18] It is the canonical form of causal sentences given by (3) that is responsible for the Stoic view that virtues are corporeal: they must be if they are going actually to do anything, and only things which do things are causes (see p. 479). Here too we may see the Stoics' containing cause as analogous to Aristotle's formal cause (n. 10 above).

[19] Cf. [Gal.] *Syn. Puls.* VIII.458: 'it is necessary to remember how we said we were speaking of the containing cause not in the strict sense but using the term loosely. For no one before the Stoics either spoke of or admitted the existence of the containing cause in the strict sense. And what have even before our time been spoken of as containing have been causes of something's coming to be, not of existence'.

IV Antecedent causes

Here the Stoic analysis runs into difficulties. All sorts of ordinary, everyday cause will fail to satisfy the strict conditions on containing causation. We ordinarily think that causes can precede their effects, and so did the Greeks: not all causes satisfy (4). In fact,[20] we operate with two quite distinct and irreducible notions of cause-as-preceding and cause-as-contemporary. They are not incompatible; but metaphysical sophistication is needed to unite them in a coherent account of the causal structure of the world:

> Some of them, however, have said that things present can be causes of things future as well, as antecedents (*prokatarktika*), as for instance protracted exposure to the sun of fever. But some reject this since the cause is relative, and relative to the effect, and hence cannot precede it as cause. (S.E. *PH* 1.16)

Sextus does not tell us who these people are – and crucially does not indicate whether the latter group are Stoics too, or opponents from other schools.[21] But however that may be, the notion of antecedent causes, *aitia prokatarktika*, is clearly Stoic: Chrysippus exploits it to rescue human freedom from the clutches of an all-embracing fate.[22] In the analysis of the notion itself, however, one must range a little further than texts which can be securely ascribed to the Stoics, since, as Sextus' example suggests, the concept was particularly applicable to medical contexts. Galen wrote a short text *On Antecedent Causes* (*CP*) in which his purpose was to rehabilitate the concept against the attacks of Erasistratus and others.

Since an antecedent cause precedes its effect, it also precedes its containing cause. Clement writes:

> When antecedent causes are removed the effect remains, whereas a containing cause is one during whose presence the effect remains and on whose removal the effect is removed. The containing cause is called synonymously the perfect (*autoteles*) cause since it is self-sufficiently productive of the effect. (Clem. *Strom.* VIII.9.33)

This distinction goes back at least to Chrysippus. In a famous illustration[23] Chrysippus compares the mechanism of human action with that of

---

[20] See e.g. R. Taylor 1975.

[21] The sceptics were to make great play with the relational nature of causing, arguing that this fact rendered all causal talk incoherent: S.E. *PH* III.25–8; but that is beyond the ambit of this discussion. See however Barnes 1983a.   [22] See below, p. 529.

[23] Reported in Cic. *Fat.* 42–3, and Gell. VII.2.10.

a rolling drum. An external push is required to set it in motion, analogous to the perceptual impression which initiates human movement; but for it actually to roll, it must itself be (at least approximately) cylindrical. It is this fact of its internal constitution that accounts for its ability to roll (and which is analogous to human dispositions).

The initial impulse is an event, while the cylinder's 'rollability' (*volubilitas*) is a persisting condition. The impulse is external to the cylinder, while its rollability is internal to it. And antecedent causes are universally defined as being external to the things of which they are causes (cf. Cic. *Fat.* 24).[24]

Cicero reports Chrysippus' account:

> 'Some causes', he says, 'are perfect (*perfectae*) and principal (*principales*), others are auxiliary (*adiuvantes*) and proximate (*proximae*). Hence when we say that everything takes place by fate from antecedent causes, we should not be taken to mean by perfect and principal causes, but by auxiliary and proximate causes.' Accordingly he counters the argument which I have just set out as follows: 'if all things come about by fate it does follow that all things come about from prior (*antepositae*) causes, but not from principal and perfect but from auxiliary and proximate causes'. (Cic. *Fat.* 41)

Cicero is generally a careful translator of technical Greek terms into Latin; but it is difficult to extract coherent correspondences from Cicero's text. Most obviously, he apparently groups auxiliary and proximate causes together, while they are explicitly distinguished from the 'perfect and principal' causes which must at least include *aitia sunektika*.[25] Yet at *Fat.* 44, admittedly *in propria persona*, Cicero refers to 'proxima illa et continens causa', where *continens* surely stands for *sunektikon*.[26] It seems that the Greek *aition proseches* is the most likely original for the Latin *causa proxima*;[27] and Galen (*Caus. Puls.* IX.107) insists that there is no difference between *proseches* and *sunektikon*. However that identification may be, it quite clearly delivers precisely the wrong sense here, since Cicero must be referring to antecedent causes. Moreover, Erasistratus (*ap.* Gal. *CP*

---

[24] Although the precise sense in which they are to be external is difficult, see Hankinson 1987a, 92–7.

[25] *Perfecta* presumably renders *autoteles*; the case is less clear with *principalis*, see below, p. 489.

[26] Or *sunechon*; but there is no determinable difference between the two: see Hankinson 1987a, 81 n. 6.

[27] Frede 1980, 241, lists *proseches*, *proēgoumenon*, and *prokatarktikon* as the possible Greek originals behind Cicero's *proxima*; and he plumps for *prokatarktikon* as the most likely candidate. But we have little evidence for Chrysippus' actual terminology, apart from Plu. *Stoic. Rep.* 1056b; that text talks of Chrysippus' incoherent views regarding *aitia autotelē* and *prokatarktika* – but it does not explicitly attribute the use of that terminology to him.

xiv.174) apparently used *aition proseches* to pick out what was genuinely the cause of some outcome, as opposed to merely being a causally relevant antecedent,[28] and such causes were for him proximate in our sense: immediately contiguous to the effect in question. The basic feature of an *aition proseches*, then, is its proximity to its effect. But that need not make it a containing cause; more is needed to assimilate *aitia proseche* to *aitia sunektika*: and Chrysippus makes no such assimilation. Cicero, perhaps confused by later theorizing, disastrously identifies proximate with containing causes in *Fat.* 44.

More significant is the question of whether each member of Cicero's two pairs of terms picks out a different item in the causal analysis, or whether they are merely synonyms. Does a perfect cause differ from a principal cause? Are proximate and auxiliary causes distinct items?[29] '*Principalis*' may well render '*kuriōtaton*', which sometimes modifies '*aition*', although not apparently with any technical sense. Thus it would simply reinforce '*perfecta*'. However, it is possible that Cicero's '*principalis*' may translate *proēgoumenon*. Many texts refer to *aitia proēgoumena*, or preceding causes; but none of them appear to be authentically Stoic, or at least early Stoic, and the distinction is most frequently to be found in medical contexts.

Alexander of Aphrodisias uses the term in his *de Fato*, in his refutation of the Stoic doctrine; and he appears to waver between the senses 'preceding' and 'primary'.[30] If the latter sense is intended here, then it will be indistinguishable from 'perfecta'. If, however, it were to mean 'preceding', then, given that *aitia autotelē* are synonymous with *aitia sunektika*, and the latter are contemporaneous with their effects, there must be a distinction between the two terms. But Alexander is not particularly helpful. His target is the Stoic notion of chance: he holds that ordinary people describe events as being chance or fortuitous 'when they supervene on the *aitia proēgoumena* of other things'. Here *proēgoumenon* naturally translates as 'principal' or 'primary'.[31] A little later on, Alexander challenges his Stoic opponents to say how it can be that anything is a matter of chance if this common intuition about chance is correct, and yet 'everything that is or comes to be does so of necessity from certain prior and preceding causes'. Here the notion of precedence seems to be important in addition

---

[28] Gal. *CP* xiv.174–6; see also *MM* x.97–9; and Hankinson 1991, 179.

[29] A further possibility is that they have the same reference but differ in sense: one designation denoting the time, the other the nature, of the cause.

[30] Alex. *Fat.* 172.17ff., 173.13ff.; see Sharples 1983, 132–3.

[31] Indeed, as a synonym for what Alexander elsewhere calls '*per se* causes': *Fat.* 172.17ff.

to that of primacy – and one suspects that Alexander is deliberately mis-reading his opponents' position for his own polemical ends.

The evidence so far, then, is indeterminate, both as to the possible Greek original for Cicero's *principalis* and as to what it might have meant. However, if it does render *proēgoumenon*, and if *proēgoumenon* does not mean 'primary' (and hence does not simply reinforce *perfecta*), what might it mean? Here evidence from the medical schools becomes important.

v The concept of preceding causes

Whatever the truth about Stoic usage, there is an amply attested medical concept of the *aition proēgoumenon*. Galen again:

> As for Athenaeus of Attaleia, he founded the medical school known as the Pneumatists. It suits his doctrine to speak of a containing cause in ill-ness since he bases himself upon the Stoics and he was a pupil and disci-ple of Posidonius . . . Athenaeus' three types are as follows: the first consists of containing causes, the second of preceding causes, and the third of the matter of procatarctic [i.e. antecedent] causes: for they call everything external to the body which harms it and produces disease in it thus. If what is produced in the body belongs to the class of what causes disease, then, while it has not actually brought the disease about, it is called the preceding cause. Alterations are produced in the natural *pneuma* by these [i.e. preceding] causes together with those which are external [i.e. antecedent causes], and with the body moistened or desic-cated, chilled or heated, these are said to be the containing causes of dis-eases. (*CC* 2.1–4)

The physiology and pathology here need not concern us; what matters is the tripartite scheme of causes the passage introduces, and the close rela-tions it adduces between the Stoic Posidonius and the physician Athenaeus, the first century BC founder of the Pneumatists. Here a clear distinction emerges between antecedent *aitia prokatarktika* and *aitia proēgoumenon*. Frede writes:[32] 'if I understand the distinction correctly, the *prokatarktikon* is the external antecedent cause, the *proēgoumenon* an internal disposition brought about by the *prokatarktikon* which in turn activates the *sunektikon*'. This understanding is confirmed, for medical contexts at least, by a number of passages;[33] and the ascription to Athenaeus is reinforced by [Galen] *Def. Med.* XIX.392. Elsewhere Galen gives the following example:

[32] Frede 1980, 242.   [33] E.g. Gal. *MM* x.65–7; *Praes. Puls.* IX.386.

Suppose that as the result of a chill falling from the outside the skin is tightened, and as a result of this tightening the usual exhalation from the pores is checked, and since it is checked it builds up, and thus a fever takes hold as a result of which the function (*chreia*) of the pulses is altered, and as a result of this the pulses are altered too: in this case the antecedent cause is the externally incident chill, while all the rest up to the alteration of the function of the pulses are preceding causes. So through the mediation of the preceding causes the antecedent cause alters the function of the pulses, which is one of the containing causes, and thus affects the pulses themselves. (*Caus. Puls.* IX.2–3)

There are some obscurities here. It is not clear, for instance, how the alteration of the pulses' function can itself be a cause on all fours with the others; but for all that, the broad lines of Frede's interpretation seem vindicated. However, such distinctions are not universal in the medical schools,[34] and Galen himself does not employ them consistently. It appears that they were the province of a specialized type of medical theory, one originated by Athenaeus[35] – and if that is right, further doubt still is cast upon their Stoic credentials.

Yet Athenaeus had Stoic connections: the issue cannot so easily be settled. And as Frede notes, the distinction between an external occasioning force and the internal disposition upon which it operates seems tailor-made to fit the psychological theory which Chrysippus is expounding. So let us return to Chrysippus' text.

VI Dispositions and powers

On the assumption that *perfecta* and *principalis* really do advert to different features of the causal structure of things, the distinction may be cashed out as follows. Take the cylinder. Even at rest it possesses its rollability – a dispositional property that derives directly from its structure. When it receives a shove (and when other necessary conditions are met) that potentiality becomes actualized. It is obviously useful to distinguish between such dispositions and their actualizations, no less so in the case of human psychology, which is Chrysippus' main concern.

It is thus tempting to conclude that, congruently with the medical evidence, Chrysippus used *aition proēgoumenon* to refer to the persistent dispositional conditions of an agent in virtue of which a particular external occasion would have a particular result. Only if I have a weakness for

---

[34] See Hankinson 1987a, 87–92.
[35] Such is the view of Hankinson 1987a; and see Wellmann 1895.

sticky cakes will the sight of a danish pastry arouse in me the desire to consume it, and set in train a sequence of events towards that end. 'Of causes', Clement writes,

> Some are antecedent (*prokatarktika*), some containing (*sunektika*), some auxiliary (*sunerga*), some prerequisite (*hōn ouk aneu*). Antecedent are those causes which primarily provide the impulse towards the coming to be of something, as beauty is to those intemperate in love; for when it is seen by them it conditions the erotic disposition, but not however in such a way as to necessitate it. (Clem. *Strom.* VIII.9.25)

Clement pretty clearly reports a Stoic view here (albeit possibly a late version): even when the disposition has been primed by a suitable stimulus, action in accordance with that disposition will not necessarily result. The agent must assent to the impulse which the disposition, in concert with the impression, gives him.[36] This suggests that human action requires a more complex account. We might have thought, given Chrysippus' example, that there were really only two internal states: the persisting disposition, and the disposition in a state of actuality, stirred up by some suitable impression. Cashing out the metaphor of the drum, its rollability corresponds to the first condition, and its actually rolling to the second. But that conflicts with the medical evidence, where the *proēgoumenon* appears to be an internal actualized condition. However, if we read Clement in the manner suggested, the *aition proēgoumenon* will be the internal disposition in a state of actualization waiting for some further input before the causal activity gets under way. This is, however, difficult to square with Chrysippus' illustration, since nothing in it appears to correspond to the extra input that assent to the action-guiding content of the aroused disposition is supposed to provide.

Perhaps Chrysippus' example was badly chosen; perhaps he thought that the additional stage of assent was irrelevant to the matter at issue; or perhaps Chrysippus' theorizing was of an earlier and less developed kind. Of these possibilities the third seems the most probable. And all of this speculation only makes sense if one assumes that 'perfecta' and 'principalis' in Cicero's text really do pick out distinct items.

Let us now consider his other pair, *adiuvans* and *proxima*. *Adiuvans* suggests *sunergon*.[37] We have already treated the possible meanings of *prox-*

---

[36] For a very detailed and clear reconstruction of the details of the philosophical psychology behind this early Stoic position, see Inwood 1985 and below, pp. 560–84.

[37] Frede 1980, 239–40, allows that *adiuvans* might render *sunaition* (although not in its standard Hellenistic sense – it would rather correspond to the *sunaitia* of *Tim.* 46c–e): but he takes it to be clear that the reference here is to *sunerga*.

ima. Now, if *perfecta* and *principalis* are to have different senses, one would expect the second pair similarly to pick out different things; and of course there is ample later evidence for such a separation of denotation. Supposing that *proxima* at the very least denotes *prokatarktikon* and *adiuvans* denotes *sunergon*, we are left to determine what Chrysippus intended by the distinction.

Frede assumes that the two are effective synonyms, and then asks 'how an antecedent cause can be conceived of as a *sunergon*, if a *sunergon* is the kind of item which helps to bring about the effect by making it easier'.[38] He is working with the hypothesis that there are two distinct classificatory triads, that of (A) *autoteles*, *sunaition*, and *sunergon* on the one hand, and (B) *sunektikon*, *proēgoumenon*, and *prokatarktikon* on the other. Things are not quite as clear-cut as that (*sunaitia* and *sunektika* frequently appear in the same contexts); although significantly Galen never makes use of (A) at all. None the less, even if Frede is broadly right, the triads can hardly cover the same ground. (A) makes distinctions within the category of contemporaneous causing; (B), by contrast, involves temporal considerations. The two triads were no doubt separately conceived to fulfil distinct roles.

Thus Frede's attempt to find a way in which *aitia prokatarktika* might seem to be at least a member of the class of *sunerga* seems misguided. However, if we suppose Cicero's Chrysippus not merely to be offering synonyms with his *adiuvans* and *proxima*, then his thought may be as follows. In the case of the cylinder, what is required to set it in motion is a *causa proxima*, an *aition prokatarktikon*. This is categorially quite distinct from whatever it is internal to the cylinder which is responsible for its rolling, something explicitly characterized by Cicero as a *vis*, a force. As Frede notes,[39] one must not imagine the Stoics simply to be saying that only suitably-shaped things can roll. Of course they are saying that – but there is more to it. The cylinder, having been started, continues to roll by its own force and nature (*suapte vi et natura*). That is, there is something internal to it which is actually doing the moving.[40]

This is not merely adventitious: on the contrary, it marks a vitally important feature of the ancient concept of causation in general, one

---

[38] Frede 1980, 240–1.   [39] Frede 1980, 236.

[40] This aspect of the theory is clearly visible in Gellius' account: "'just as", he says, "if you push a stone cylinder on steeply sloping ground you have produced the cause and beginning of its forward motion, but soon it rolls forward not because you are making it do so, but because such are its form and smooth-rolling shape'" (Gell. VII.2.10). Only by building a great deal into the notion of form here do we get anything like Cicero's version – but I suspect that is due to Gellius' own misunderstanding of the nature of the argument.

which differentiates, from any modern notion, and one which is very widely shared, perhaps even by the mechanistically-minded Epicureans. Thus the *aition prokatarktikon* sets the cylinder off, but after that it is its own internal force that keeps it going. Even so, I might give it an additional shove to help it on its way – then I would be assisting a process already undertaken; I would be acting as a *sunergon*, since the extra push is neither necessary for the continued roll, nor is it part of the internal process which is keeping the rolling going. Thus, although antecedent and auxiliary causes are distinct, they share the crucial feature of externality to the process in question.

If this is right, there is some philosophical point to Chrysippus' distinguishing between each member in his two pairs; and that fact in turn lends some support to the hypothesis canvassed above concerning the distinction between the *causa perfecta* and the *causa principalis*; both are internal to the object in question – but only the former is in itself sufficient to bring about the effect, being the actualized state of the latter. Thus the original Chrysippean distinction does not precisely parallel that to be found in the later medical tradition, or the view reconstructed from Clement. It is, however, intelligible.

The suggestion, then, is this. Chrysippus had already distinguished between the internal proclivity to action, and that proclivity in its galvanized state, and he perhaps also called them respectively the *aition proēgoumenon* and *autoteles*. This distinction was taken over and refined, both by later Stoics interested in making room for assent in their action theory, and by doctors wishing to distinguish between different stages of an internal pathogenic process. Secondly he distinguished between initial triggers to the disposition which set up a perfect cause, and later assistance to it; here too, in a modified form, his distinctions were to become adopted and canonized by later theorists. This is speculation: but at least it makes sense of the evidence, and answers to the concerns that motivated Chrysippus in the first place.

VII Causes and conditions

But what exactly is an internal cause? Cicero writes:

> They [sc. the Stoics] say that there is a difference between whether a thing is of such a kind that something cannot be brought about without it, or such that something must necessarily be brought about by it. None of the causes mentioned therefore [namely a set of remote prerequisite conditions] is really a cause, since none by its own force brings about

that of which it is said to be the cause; nor is that which is a condition of a thing's being brought about a cause, but that which is such that when it is present that of which it is the cause necessarily is brought about. (Cic. *Fat.* 36)

The distinction between real causes and mere prerequisites is found in Plato (indeed the Hippocratics);[41] and Galen, too, talks of causal prerequisites.[42] The intuitive idea involved here is clear enough: some things seem to contribute directly to an outcome, while others merely allow that contribution to be made. Cicero clearly distinguishes here between necessary and sufficient conditions of an outcome – but this distinction cannot capture the notion of causal efficacy at issue (no version of it can – this is an important fact about the concept of causation, and one to which many recent accounts do violence).[43]

The terminology of causes *per se* and causes *per accidens* (*kata sumbebēkos*) is Aristotelian (*Phys.* 11.3.195a33–b3), although Galen's distinction is not the same as Aristotle's. For Aristotle it is largely a matter of explanatory function. What distinguishes a cause *per se* from a cause *per accidens* is that, while they both refer to the same item, it is only the former that serves to pick it out by the precise description under which it is a cause of the object in question. Hence the Peripatetic distinction relates more to explanation than to causation.[44]

Clement (not to mention Galen and the Stoics) has something else in mind:

I know that many say that that which does not hinder is a cause as well. But we say against them that the conception of cause involves doing, being active, and performing. In this respect at least that which does not hinder is inactive. (Clem. *Strom.* 1.17.83)

The original Stoic notion of the cause as active lies behind this. The necessary conditions which permit that action are not properly to be called causes at all. In a more relaxed vein, Galen will allow that you can call

---

[41] Clement makes the same distinction, although his example is puzzling: 'all of the causes can be exhibited in order in the case of the pupil. The father is the antecedent cause of learning, the teacher the containing cause, the pupil's nature the auxiliary cause, while the time reserves the place of the prerequisite' (Clem. *Strom.* viii.9.25).

[42] He mentions place, and an unimpeded intervening space, as being prerequisites to the production of an artefact: *CP* vii.76–90. He also calls them 'incidental causes', by contrast with those items that 'contribute of their own nature to something's coming to be' which may be called indifferently 'causes from their own nature', or 'causes properly so called', or 'causes in virtue of themselves' (76).

[43] I do not mean to suggest that causes might not be either necessary or sufficient in the circumstances for their effects – they may well be. But necessity and/or sufficiency in the circumstances cannot constitute an analysis of the causal relation.   [44] See above, section 1.

them causes if you like, as long as you are aware that they are merely factors incidental to the production of the outcome.[45] Clement wavers: here
he appears to side with the Stoics, but elsewhere he allows, for example,
that the flesh is a cause to the knife of cutting as well as the knife's being a
cause to the flesh of being cut.[46] What matters is the Stoic insistence on
the primacy of agency.[47]

But this is not the whole story. It is not just that, properly so called, the
sequence of causation is a stream of activity. That activity is conditioned
by the internal properties and states of the objects which are causes. And
this brings us back to a set of earlier issues, which connect intimately with
the theme of the next chapter. If Fate is, as the Stoics say, an uninterrupted
sequence of causes,[48] then, given that causes are uniquely paired one-to-
one with effects,[49] it is difficult to resist a determinist conclusion; and the
Stoics did not resist it. But if determinism is true, and hence the way in
which events unfold is ultimately determined from all eternity, then what
is to justify our singling out agents as responsible for what they do? The
basic Stoic answer is that agents do what they do as a result of their own
internal structure. The fact that we are the way we are, have the characters
and dispositions that we have, causally explains (at least in part) why we
do what we do: it is in this sense that our actions are up to us (*eph' hēmin*.[50]
Cicero reinforces this:

> 'Cause' is not to be understood in such a way as to make what precedes a
> thing the cause of that thing, but what precedes it effectively: the cause
> of my playing ball was not my going down to the campus, nor did
> Hecuba's giving birth to Alexander make her the cause of the death of
> Trojans, nor was Tyndareus the cause of Agamemnon's death because he
> was the father of Clytemnestra. (Cic. *Fat.* 34)

Cicero quotes from Ennius' adaptation of Euripides' *Medea* 1–8: would
that trees had never been felled on Pelion to build the Argo. But such causal antecedents, although (in the circumstances at least) necessary conditions of Medea's falling in love with Jason, her jealousy, and her eventual

---

[45] Galen here follows his syncretist tendencies, borrowing something – although not a precise terminology – from the Peripatetics.

[46] Clem. *Strom.* VIII.9.30. Clement is making a semantic distinction: 'causes are not causes *of* each
other but *to* each other ... thus the stones in a vault are the causes to each other, of the predicate
"remaining", but not of each other'. The point is important if you want, as the Stoics do, to
insist on the categorial distinction between cause and effect (the one corporeal, the other not),
and yet still preserve the notion of a sequence of causes. This will be of relevance later on.

[47] It is this that allows Seneca, in spite of the terminological proliferation we have examined, to
contrast the unity of the Stoic position with the 'crowd of causes' offered by the Peripatetics
and others: *Ep.* 55.11.   [48] D.L. VII.149; Aët. 1.27.3, 28.4.

[49] The distinction between (T1), (T2), and (T1*), (T2*) is relevant here.   [50] See below, pp. 531–4.

filicide, do not really cause these outcomes.[51] It is the agents' being the way they are that causes them to act in the way they do, although of course their actually acting thus is itself co-determined by events external to them. Once again the basic distinctions between a disposition primed to behave in a certain way, and the occasions for its behaviour, are called into play.

VIII Causes and time

We have seen how the Stoics, and those influenced by them, attempted to answer to two basic intuitions about causes, namely that there is a sense of 'cause' in which causes are contemporary with their effects, a sense captured by proposition (4); but secondly that, if the causal structure of the world is one that unfolds diachronically, in some (distinct) sense causes had better precede their effects. Sextus, naturally, holds that you can't have it both ways, and concludes that for this reason the whole notion of causing, at least on the Dogmatists' analysis, is incoherent (*PH* III.25–30). That conclusion is hasty and unwarranted. But temporal considerations are important. If causes are sufficient (in the circumstances) for their effects, as any determinist must hold, then why does causing take time? Why is it not the case that the whole causal history of the world is collapsed into an instant? Such worries are profound – and while there is no direct evidence that the Stoics puzzled over them, it seems that their idea that the basic causal forces are internal properties is well adapted to cope with it (as is Aristotle's concept of the gradual realization of form). Time is, as it were, built directly into the fundamental concepts involved. Processes, and not atomic events, are taken to be ontologically primary. Events are merely the three-dimensional slices through a four-dimensional continuum. It is significant that the ancient texts rarely (Epicurean atomic collisions apart) deal with instantaneous events at all. Rather the elements are processes and states; processes tend towards states, and states are the natural outcome of processes (such is the Aristotelian view). This ontology has the advantage of resisting the temptation to temporal collapse.

Some indirect evidence for it is to be found in disputes concerning the proper semantic analysis of causal language:

> The sun, or the sun's heat, is the cause of the wax being melted or the melting of the wax. For even on this they are in dispute, some saying that

---

[51] Clement makes a similar point at *Strom.* VIII.9.27: all of the preceding events are chance causes, and hence not real causes, of Medea's crime.

causes are causes of nouns like 'the melting', others of predicates like 'being melted'. (S.E. *PH* III.14)

Clement echoes the point:

Some are causes of predicates, e.g. 'is cut' whose inflection is 'being cut', others of propositions, e.g. 'a ship is built', whose inflection this time is 'a ship's being built'. (Clem. *Strom.* VIII.9.26)

The predicate-expressions are clearly suited to the denotation of states ('the wax's being melted'), while the noun-phrases naturally advert to processes. There is of course nothing incoherent in adopting both modes of expression.[52]

This suggests a model of the universe's causal structure in which individuals (conceived as broadly Aristotelian substances) lead existences which causally intersect with each other at spatio-temporal nodes; these intersections are the antecedent causes in virtue of which the substances' dispositional structures are roused into actuality and the processes which are the basic causal constituents of the world get under way.[53]

IX The Epicureans and causal explanation

Crucial to what has gone before is the notion, already present in Aristotle (and perhaps to be found in Plato's ever-moving soul: *Phdr.* 245c–246a), that processes require continuous immanent causes to keep them going. It is well known that the Greeks lacked a systematic concept of inertia,[54] the idea that a process will just continue linearly once begun until something intervenes to stop or alter it. This lack explains Chrysippus' invocation of the internal force of the cylinder that propels it, and indeed the general notion of the containing cause. Indeed the drive to provide causal explanations of such continuities rather than simply referring them to some conservation law is one of the principal divergences between ancient and modern patterns of explanation.

The atomists might appear to run counter to this general tendency. After all, they systematically reduce their explanatory resources to a small stock of primitive concepts, principal among them being the motion and interaction of the atoms, and their solidity, resistivity, and non-interpenetrability. Everything in the macroscopic world is to be explained as the

---

[52] Diodorus Cronus' celebrated argument against motion (see above, pp. 356–62) only attacks the concept of the process.

[53] This will take on additional significance in the debate over human freedom: see below, pp. 529–31.   [54] See Duhot 1989.

outcome of such atomic collisions and intertwinings. Everything is, then, the result of such random (in the sense of unplanned) interactions. The challenge of Epicurean physics and cosmology is to be able to produce a convincing account of the complexity of the cosmos, and crucially of its apparent order, on the basis of such a limited range of explanatory concepts.

First of all, Epicurus accepts the basic causal principles of conservation that underlie Stoic physics, since total annihilation and creation *ex nihilo* are impossible. Hence there must always have been a universe (not, for the Epicureans, identical with our cosmos, which is but one of many); and the eternity of the universe is itself a reason for thinking that nothing can be destroyed, since, in the infinite totality of past time, if it could have been it would have been.[55]

The *nil ex nihilo* principle (cf. Lucr. 1.150 ff.) may be construed in two distinct ways:

(5) nothing can be created without previously existing matter,

and

(6) nothing can occur without a cause.

It is clear that the Epicureans are concerned primarily with (5); indeed they reject (6) (which is simply the contrapositive of (T1) above) in its full generality. Their opponents were not slow, however, to accuse them of inconsistency on this score. In the following, Alexander reports Stoic arguments presumably directed against the Epicureans:

> Nothing in the world exists or happens causelessly, because nothing is independent of or insulated from everything that has happened before. For the world would be wrenched apart and divided, and no longer remain a unity, for ever governed in accordance with a single ordering and management, if an uncaused process were introduced. And an uncaused motion would be introduced, were everything that exists or happens not to have some preceding causes from which it necessarily follows. For something to happen causelessly is, they say, both similar to and as impossible as something coming to be out of what is not. (Alex. *Fat.* 192.7 ff.)

The last sentence clearly asserts that the considerations which support (5) equally support (6) – and there is something in that, even if one is inclined to think they support neither.

---

[55] See above, pp. 363–6.

The basic atomist ontology of atoms and the void needs no rehearsal here – suffice it to say that the Epicurean project consists precisely in the attempt to show that all other properties of things are either derivative of or emergent upon the basic properties of the ontological primaries.[56] Nor is it necessary here to assess the success of their programme: its structure is what matters. In the first place, the project is an extraordinarily bold one; and the ingenuity with which Lucretius, our most complete source, attempts to carry it out is testimony to the seriousness with which the Epicureans viewed it.

None the less, it runs into severe, perhaps insuperable difficulties. A fundamental problem for Epicurean physics and cosmology is that of explaining how the world can exhibit such a high degree of order and regularity if it is merely, as the atomists have it, the chance outcome of random atomic collisions. Given that the only explanatory tools at their disposal are the reboundings and intertwinings of the atoms as they bump together during their endless fall through infinite space, it becomes very hard to see how such limited machinery could explain the generation of a world such as ours, much less explain its extraordinary degree of stability. One of the standard reasons for thinking that there are causes (i.e. regular causes) at all is the observed regularity of natural production:

> That cause exists is plausible; for how could there come to be increase, decrease, generation, destruction, in general change, each of the physical and mental outcomes, the ordering of the whole universe and everything else except by reason of some cause? . . . Moreover, if cause were non-existent, everything would have been produced by everything at random; thus horses might have been born of flies, and elephants of ants. (S.E. *PH* III.17–18)

And Lucretius echoes this view (1.159–73). The Epicurean response is to posit the existence of 'seeds' (Ep. *Ep. Hdt.* 39) conceived of as resistant molecules of organized atoms that can act as templates for the organization around them of a copy of the same kind. Of course, they are right to think that they need something of the sort – but their own atomistic physics is woefully inadequate to provide an answer in detail as to how it is supposed to work. The atomists tend to argue first for the inescapability of the atomic hypothesis, and then having established that for the need for seeds on their model. But that inference is only as good as its first step; and the atomists' arguments for their fundamental physical principles are fragile.[57]

---

[56] See above, pp. 380–3, 550–3.   [57] However see above, p. 000.

The atomists have long been praised for adumbrating modern scientific styles of explanation, and for seeing that one may reductively explain macro-properties as being emergent upon quite distinct micro-structures. But in fact the Epicureans could not emancipate themselves from the tendency to conceptualize the micro-properties as being similar in type to their phenomenal macroscopic counterparts: 'things that seem hard and stiff must be made up of deeply indented and hooked atoms' (Lucr. II.444–5); while fluids are composed of smooth rounded atoms.[58]

If we allow the Epicureans their atomic primary qualities of weight, size, resistance, and shape, what use can they make of them? First of all, atomic weight is taken to be a hypothesis necessary to explain atomic motion (Ep. *Ep. Hdt.* 61; Lucr. II.83–5, 216–18). The atoms have a continuous nisus to move in a particular direction ('downwards'), moreover one which does not vary from atom to atom (Lucr. II.225–42). It is not, therefore, a function of weight, contrary to Aristotle's view; and this direction is not given by the centre of the cosmos (the Epicurean cosmos, being infinite, has no centre), but rather is a set of rectilinear parallel trajectories. Solidity and shape of course account for their rebounding in a determinate manner after collisions, and for their intertwining:

> The atoms move continuously and for ever, some separating a great distance from each other, others keeping up their vibration on the spot whenever they happen to get trapped by their interlinking, or imprisoned atoms which link up. For the nature of the void brings this about by separating each atom off by itself, since it is unable to lend them any support; and their own solidity causes them as a result of their knocking together to vibrate back, to whatever distance their interlinking allows them to recoil from the knock. There is no beginning to this because atoms and the void are eternal. (Ep. *Ep. Hdt.* 43–4; cf. Lucr. II.80–124)

That last sentence suggests an economical answer to an obvious question: how did the cosmic buzz of interacting atoms ever get started? It didn't: it's always been like this. Nevertheless, later testimony uniformly attributes to Epicurus a doctrine which is supposed precisely, among other things, to show how collisions could get started: the notorious swerve. Lucretius writes:

> When bodies are being borne down by their own weight straight through the void, at quite uncertain times they veer a little from their

---

[58] They do however allow that colour is a purely emergent property (Lucr. II.737–841), as are heat and cold (842–64); and no one in their right mind would assume that there are laughing atoms (973–9).

course, just enough to be called a change of motion. If they did not have this swerve, everything would be falling downwards like raindrops through the depths of the void, and collisions and impacts among the primary bodies would never have arisen, with the result that nature would never have created anything. (Lucr. II.218–24)

The swerve clearly violates (6); and as such was the object of much ancient scorn. The fact that Democritus apparently saw no need of it, and its absence from the epitome of physical doctrines in *Ep. Hdt.*, perhaps suggests that it is a late edition to the Epicurean physical armoury – and it is a plausible assumption that it owes more to Epicurus' determination to rescue human freedom from the clutches of universal determinism than to any perceived lacuna in the cosmological story. But that is a matter for the next chapter.

Epicurus' innovation was derided as being ad hoc, explanatorily null, and a violation of an intuitively secure a priori principle. Whatever Epicurus' reasons for introducing the minimal swerve, and whatever its explanatory shortcomings, we may at least commend him for refusing to be imprisoned within a straitjacket of a prior-ism. The modern, quantum-mechanical overtones of the doctrine are to a large extent adventitious – but at least Epicurus saw that the question of whether every event has a cause must, in the last resort, be an empirical one (for a suitably weak sense of 'empirical').

For all that, Epicurean causal explanation seems unimpeachably materialistic in its structure. The ultimate constituents of the world, bumping and jostling in the void, are to explain not only macroscopic events (which are ontologically parasitic upon bodies: Lucr. 1.64–81), but also macroscopic properties. The Epicureans too think that all causing is corporeal; and the function of the void in physical explanation is precisely to provide a prerequisite cause, or necessary condition, of causal interaction (there could be no motion without void, for example: Lucr. 1.370–83). Still, it is important to realize that the engine for Epicurean action is, as it was for the Stoics, a set of internal properties in constant activity. It is the weight of the atoms that makes them fall and keeps them falling. There is no more hint of any concept of inertia in Epicurus than anywhere else in Greek physics.

Indeed, Lucretius does not conceptualize the physics of atomic collision as involving analogues to our familiar notions of mass, momentum, and so on. It is not that there will be a transfer of kinetic energy and vector from one object to another in proportion to their relative masses and velocities. Rather the striking of the one by the other actualizes the internal potentiality for motion along a particular vector that the other possesses. Two passages suggest this. In the first, Lucretius is accounting for the unimaginable speed with which the filmy *simulacra* ('images') given off from the surface of objects can traverse distances as a result of 'a very slight initial impetus far behind them which launched them and propels them' (Lucr. IV.193–4). In the second, he describes how the motion of the tiny, volatile atoms that make up the mind can bootstrap their way up to produce animal movement; such a fact need occasion no surprise, Lucretius thinks, when we reflect that the wind may drive a ship (IV.886–91, 898–906). If this is right, then Epicurus too preserves (contrary to the usual exegesis) much of the underlying conceptual structure we have already seen at work in the Stoics. The atoms move essentially under their own steam, less like the clattering billiard-balls of modern mechanistic analogy than runners in a relay-race, primed to take off at a touch.

x Teleology and mechanism

For all that, one huge divergence between the atomists and their opponents remains: their utter rejection of purposive explanation, at least in the realm of cosmology. For Epicurus, the formation of the cosmos is the chance result of random atomic events ('chance' here in a sense quite compatible with determinism, although of course Epicurus was no determinist: the swerve need play no role here at all). Sooner or later, somewhere or other in the temporally and spatially infinite universe, a particular sequence of atomic events will occur that results in the agglomeration of a world, and all that it contains. There is no call for the Stoic–Platonic hypothesis of a benevolent divine organizer, or for the Aristotelian notion of the explanatory primacy of macroscopic form and its nisus towards actualization. Everything, the Epicureans think, can be explained on the basis of the principles briefly reviewed above:

> One mistake . . . is that of supposing that . . . the eyes have been created in order that we might see; that it is in order that we might take lengthy strides that the knees and hips can be flexed above their base of feet . . . and hands supplied on either side as servants in order that we could perform whatever acts were needed for living. All other explanations of this type which they offer are back to front, products of distorted reasoning. For nothing has been engendered in our body in order that we might be able to use it. It is the fact of its being engendered that creates its use.
> (Lucr. IV.23–35)

'They' are primarily, no doubt, the Stoics – although such creationist teleologies are also Platonic. And, albeit in a more naturalistic vein, Aristotle took Anaxagoras to task precisely for getting, as he saw it, the direction of explanation the wrong way round: Anaxagoras thought humans were intelligent because they had hands; on the contrary, says Aristotle, nature gives the appropriate tools to those fittest to use them (*Part. An.* IV.10.687a7–23). The Epicureans side with Anaxagoras: structure determines function, not vice versa. Lucretius goes on to hold (IV.836–57) that all bodily organs antedate their uses – in this they are quite distinct from artefacts, which are specifically designed with some purpose in mind.

Equally, the Epicureans reject out of hand the idea that the world is the product of divine intelligence, and in particular the view that it was created for the benefit of human beings (Lucr. v.156–69). Their gods are far too busy enjoying a life of untroubled blessedness to worry about creating a cosmos simply for human beings to flourish in it (Ep. *Ep. Hdt.* 76–8). Here their principal opponents are again the Stoics, who held that God pervaded and permeated the entire world in the form of *pneuma*, effectively its containing cause (*SVF* II 526, 1027, 1077, etc.).[59] Furthermore, they held that everything in the world served some rational end, much of it being directly for the benefit of human beings – thus notoriously Chrysippus thought bed-bugs beneficial, since they prevent us from idling in bed (*SVF* II 1163; cf. 1152). The Stoics' strategy was to develop a version of the argument from design in order to defend the concept of a creator-god:

> Suppose someone were to bring to Scythia or Britain the orrery recently built by our friend Posidonius which . . . brings about in the sun, the moon, and the five planets effects identical to those brought about day by day and night by night in the heavens. Who in those foreign lands would doubt that the sphere was a product of reason? And yet these people hesitate as to whether the world, from which all things come into being, is itself the product of some kind of accident or necessity or of a divine mind's reason. And they rate Archimedes' achievement in imitating the revolutions of the heavenly sphere higher than nature's in creating them – and that when the original is a vastly more brilliant creation than the copy. (Cic. *ND* II.88)

And the Stoics ridiculed what they took to be the enormous improbability of the Epicurean story:

---

[59] See above, p. 482.

Does it not deserve amazement on my part that there should be anyone who can persuade himself that certain solid and indivisible bodies travel through the force of their own weight and that by an accidental combination of those bodies a world of the utmost splendour and beauty is created? I do not see why a person who supposes this can happen does not also believe it possible that if countless exemplars of the twenty-one letters . . . were thrown into a container and shaken out onto the ground, they might form a readable copy of the Annals of Ennius. I'm not sure that luck could manage this even to the extent of a single line. (Cic. *ND* II.93)

Of course, the Epicureans were careful to stress the infinity of space and time, and the inevitability in a suitably long run of all conceivable arrangements of atoms being realized; but there is no doubt that it requires both a great confidence in the explanatory power of materialism as well as explanatory tools well beyond anything the Epicureans developed to make such an explanation of the persistence and regularity of the world plausible. And of course even now, when we have both the confidence born of successful physical science and the tools, the argument from design dies hard.[60]

XI   The limits of explanation: multiple explanations

For all their confidence in the explanatory power of atomic physics, the Epicureans did not believe that they could offer definitive explanations for every phenomenon; nor did they feel they needed to. For they took extremely seriously the general Hellenistic conception of the philosophical primacy of ethics, construed as the science of the good life. The Epicureans were not, officially at least, interested in physics, or science, for its own sake. Atomism is commended as the path to happiness:

We hold that to arrive at accurate knowledge of the cause of the most important things is the business of natural science, and that happiness depends on this. (Ep. *Ep. Hdt.* 78)

Given this point of view, it is unsurprising that the Epicureans were untroubled by what they took to be the impossibility of offering certain, precise, and incontrovertible explanations for a wide range of phenomena

---

[60] Elsewhere I argue that, given the conceptual and evidential resources available to ancient scientists, some form of directed teleology was indeed the most rational available hypothesis to adopt: see Hankinson 1988a, 1989. For the argument from design see above, pp. 448–51, 464–9.

(principally meteorological and seismic). They considered (or at least gave the impression of so doing) that atomism was sufficiently well entrenched for it to be certain that phenomena like lightning, thunder, and earthquakes could be explained along atomist lines, and that the ultimate truth about their structure and aetiology would be atomic – but they did not much mind what that truth was in our own world, as long as a possible explanation fitted the data of experience. It was enough to realize that earthquakes were not the result of some malevolent deity in order for irrational human fears concerning them to be banished. Or so they pretended to think:

> There are also a number of things of which it is not enough to name one cause, but rather many causes, one of which will however be the actual one – just as if you were to see at a distance the dead body of a man, it would be appropriate to list all the causes of death, so as to include the specific cause of his death. For you would not be able to establish that he died by the sword, from cold, from disease, or by poison; yet we know that something of the sort must have happened to him. And similarly in many other matters we are in a position to say the same. (Lucr. VI.703–11)

Epicurus, although holding that on the basic facts of physics 'we must recognize . . . no plurality of causes or contingency' (*Ep. Hdt.* 78), none the less continues

> But when we come to subjects for special inquiry, there is nothing in the knowledge of risings and settings and solstices and eclipses and things of this kind that contributes to happiness . . . hence if we discover more than one cause that may account for them . . . we need not think our account falls short in accuracy, so far as is necessary to keep us tranquil and content. (*Ep. Hdt.* 79–80)

The form, then, of an Epicurean 'explanation' of such phenomena will be disjunctive: x occurs because either E_1 or E_2 or . . . E_n. At most one of the E's will actually be the real explanation; but if the account is good enough, one of them must be in some world at some time – and that is enough. Epicurus devoted his *Letter to Pythocles* to the consideration of 'celestial and meteorological phenomena', *ta meteōra*. Reiterating the view that the purpose of physical explanation is to allay fears, Epicurus writes:

> We do not seek to wrest by force what is impossible, nor to understand all matters equally well, nor make our treatment always as clear as when we deal with human life or explain the general principles of physics, for example that everything consists of bodies and intangible nature, or that

the ultimate elements of things are indivisible, or any other proposition which admits only one explanation of the phenomena to be possible. But this is not the case with the things up there (*ta meteōra*): these admit a multiplicity of causes of their coming to be and explanations of their nature consonant with perception. For we must not do science by way of empty assumptions and arbitrary fiat, but as the phenomena demand. (*Ep. Pyth.* 85–7)

All explanation starts with the appearances, the phenomena: in some cases only one explanation is consonant with the sum total of empirical evidence. In that case, the evidence entails the explanation. But in many other matters, things are not so clear-cut: any number of mutually inconsistent explanations account for the phenomena. In the latter cases, we must rest content with disjunctive explanation.[61]

Epicurus' rejection of a priori 'certainties' (reinforced in the immediately succeeding paragraphs) is refreshing. Nevertheless he will no doubt seem excessively sanguine in his belief that there are any cases of uniquely entailed explanations, a belief which is the target of the second of the Pyrrhonist Aenesidemus' eight modes against the aetiologists.[62] In this sense, Epicurus was only partly an empiricist, and only some of the time.

XII The limits of explanation: empiricism

For a more full-blooded empirical attitude to the business of causation and explanation, we need to turn to the medical schools, indeed principally to the school known as the Empiricists.[63] But it is perhaps appropriate to begin with a fragment of another, earlier doctor, Diocles of Carystus:

(1) Those who think that one should state a cause in every case do not appear to understand first that it is not always necessary to do so from a practical point of view, and second that many things which exist are somehow by their nature akin to principles, so that they cannot be given a causal account. (2) Furthermore, they sometimes err in assuming what is

---

[61] For actual examples of the multiple explanation strategy, see *Ep. Pyth.* 92–3 (heavenly motions: Lucr. v.509–33); 94–6 (the phases, illumination, and face of the moon, eclipses: Lucr. v.705–70); 99–104 (clouds, rain, thunder, lightning: Lucr. vi.96–534); and 105–6 (earthquakes: Lucr. vi.535–607). On precedents in Theophrastus (and Aristotle) and multiple causation itself see Mansfeld 1992b and 1994a.

[62] Aenesidemus is, unfortunately, beyond the remit of this study; the eight modes are of particular interest, and seem to be directed particularly against Epicurean notions of explanation. The second mode shows that frequently when there is an abundance of ways of assigning an explanation to what is under investigation, some of them account for it in one way only (S.E. *PH* 1.181).   [63] See below, pp. 511, 606–8.

unknown, disputed, and implausible, thinking that they have adequately given the cause. (3) You should disregard people who aetiologize in this manner, and who think that one should state a cause for everything; (4) you should rather rely upon things which have been excogitated over a long period on the basis of experience (*empeiria*); (5) and you should seek a cause for contingent things when that is likely to make what you say about them more understandable and more believable. (Diocles fr. 112 W)

Diocles was a rough contemporary of Aristotle's (and hence just about falls within the scope of this study): and this, the *Große Methodenfragment*,[64] seems to betray Aristotle's influence.[65] At the beginning of *Posterior Analytics*, Aristotle stresses that first principles, the *archai* or axioms of a science, cannot be proved or demonstrated, and hence cannot be given an explanation (*APo.* 1.2.71b26–33; 3.72b19–25) – indeed, explanation has got to terminate somewhere (cf. *Metaph.* Γ 4.1006a6–9) in prior and unexplainable premisses in order to avoid infinite regress or circularity (*APo.* 1.3).

But Diocles' concerns are not merely theoretical. Rather he holds it to be of no practical use to try and aetiologize everything: for ordinary medical purposes explanation must stop somewhere. Neither does he say that the things to be left unexplained actually are first principles, only that they are akin to them – and his point may be that some things must be accepted for pragmatic reasons as basic, even if they may not in fact be so. Diocles may well be the first explicitly to point out the pitfalls of explanatory dogmatism, while echoing the anti-theoretical empiricism of the Hippocratic treatise *On Ancient Medicine*; he even goes so far as to suggest that aetiologizing serves a purely rhetorical function.

Erasistratus apparently went further still, refusing to allow that antecedent causes were genuine causes on the grounds that they were not sufficient for their effects. Galen devotes much of *CP* to refuting his 'sophism' to the effect that if something really is a cause of something else, it should invariably produce it: but antecedent causes, being at best necessary conditions of the outcomes to which they are antecedent, cannot meet this criterion.

It was universally allowed that the alleged antecedent causes of fever (overheating, chilling, excessive eating, drinking, and sexual indulgence, to name but a few) were not invariably correlated with their effects: in the example Galen cites on Erasistratus' behalf (*CP* II.11), of a multitude of

---

[64] So labelled by Wellmann 1901.

[65] Indeed, he has sometimes been portrayed as a straightforward Aristotelian; but this is certainly wrong, as Frede among others has noted (Waltzer and Frede 1985, xxviii).

people watching the same theatrical performance on a sweltering afternoon (and hence *ex hypothesi* subjected to the same causal influences), only
four suffer at all and of them only one goes on to develop a full-blown
fever – hence, Erasistratus infers, the excessive heat cannot be implicated
in the disease: the vast majority were unaffected. Galen accuses
Erasistratus and his followers of captiousness:

> Thus the sophists find reasons for their arguments that attempt to show
> that, even if on some occasion these things [sc. antecedent heat, cold,
> etc.] harm weak bodies, not even then can they properly be called causes.
> For if indeed they do act because of their own internal nature, and this
> action derives from themselves, then they must be seen to have an effect
> at all times. (Gal. *CP* I.9–10; cf. Celsus *Med. Pr.* 54)

Later, Galen quotes Erasistratus directly:

> Most people, both now and in the past, have sought the causes of fevers,
> trying to ascertain and learn from the sick whether the illness has its ori-
> gin in being chilled or exhausted or repletion, or some other cause of this
> kind; but this kind of inquiry into the causes of diseases yields results
> neither true nor useful. For if cold were a cause of fever, then those who
> have been chilled the more should suffer the greater fever. But this is not
> what happens: rather there are some who have faced extreme danger
> from freezing, and who when rescued have remained unaffected by fever
> ... [while] many people who experience far worse exhaustion and reple-
> tion than that which coincides with fever in some others yet escape the
> illness. (Erasistratus, in Gal. *CP* VIII.102–3; cf. XI.141–4; XIII.166–8)

Unsurprisingly, Sextus makes use of similar arguments (*M* IX.242–3).
Thus Erasistratus apparently denies causal status to anything which fails
to meet these stringent requirements.

It is not, however, clear whether this amounts to much more than a terminological injunction: reserve the term 'cause' for the real (i.e. proximate and determining) cause of the event in question, a position clearly
not equivalent to the view that no event, unless constantly conjoined with
some other, can have any causal relevance to it. Galen does indeed try to
pin the latter on Erasistratus (and such would be the natural interpretation of Celsus' brief notice); but he also accuses him of indulging in verbal
quibbles, and of treating as substantial mere verbal disagreements. At all
events, it is by no means apparent that Erasistratus did indeed deny all
causal relevance to non-necessitating antecedents (although for all that
Galen may of course be right that he was confused and inconsistent on
this score).

In fact he is said to have allowed that over-eating and exhaustion are implicated in the triggering of disease, although he apparently refused to grant them the title of causes.[66] At all events, Galen (*CP* XIV.174) attributes to him an aetiology of disease in which excessive ingestion of food (a standard Galenic antecedent cause) brings about *plēthōra*, which in turn results in the compression of blood at the valves between vein and artery, which then forces blood through the valves into the arteries (where, on Erasistratean pathology, it should not normally be), which generates fever. Only the last stage (the preternatural transfusion of blood) is actually called a 'cause' – but it is hard to see how Erasistratus could have denied the causal import of the earlier steps in the process, even if he had wanted to.

On the other hand, the passages quoted above seem to be substantial in import: heat and cold cannot be causal factors, because they do not determine their outcomes. And Erasistratus may have wished to distinguish between the relations that held (whatever they might be) in the overheating case, and the sequence of events sketched above that are consequent upon over-eating; in the latter case it seems plausible to think that the sequence will play out to its pathological conclusion unless something or someone intervenes to prevent it. But even that is not true for the former case – no intervention is necessary at all to prevent most of the theatregoers coming down with fever: the causal connection, then, (if any) between the afternoon sun and the evening fever is far more etiolated. Erasistratus may have a substantial point after all.

But even so, Galen counters by maintaining that the overheating can still be a cause of the fever in a particular case: it is part of the set of conditions which, along with the patient's particular susceptibilities (which must be specified in a non-circular manner if the account is to have any substance to it), jointly account for his illness. Of course, it is not the sole cause of the fever, which accounts for the fact that not everyone succumbs: some people are more constitutionally prone to it than others (*CP* VIII.100; X.126; XIII.167).

Herophilus, Erasistratus' great contemporary, is equally worried about causal explanation: and he appears to have inherited a Dioclean circumspection about the matter. Unlike Erasistratus, who seems only to have attacked the notion of causal antecedence (Gal. *CP* XIII.164), Herophilus'

---

[66] Garofalo 1988, 30 holds that Erasistratus called them 'origins' (*archai*) of disease: *Ven. Sect. Er. Rom.* XI.236–7; *Ven. Sect. Er.* XI.155; but it seems rather that Erasistratus reserved the term *archē* for the condition of *plēthōra*, or congestion of the veins, which is consequent upon them. See further Garofalo 1988, 29–31.

interests were more general. Two fragments exhibit his aetiological caution:

> Whether or not there is a cause is by nature undiscoverable; but in my opinion I believe I am chilled, warmed and filled with food and drink. (Herophilus, in Gal. *CP* XVI.198)

> Some, such as Herophilus, accept causes 'on the basis of a hypothesis'. (Gal. *CP* XIII.162)

The interpretation of these fragments is controversial:[67] but I take Herophilus to be accepting causal explanations not because they are in any objective sense probable, but rather because they offer a heuristically useful and rationally satisfying model for the physical and physiological world.

The (indirect) heirs to this tradition were the Empiricist doctors.[68] Unlike their opponents the Rationalists, who attempted to provide some theoretical underpinning for their practice, Empiricists held that medicine consisted simply of repeated observations of what worked and what didn't in repeated, relevantly similar conditions. Personal experience could be supplemented, subject to some fairly rigorous controls, by an appeal to the writings of others, and (or so at least some allowed) by appeal to a type of analogical reasoning, the so-called 'transition to the similar'.

In matters concerning explanation, they were quite prepared to take account of antecedent causes (Gal. *SI* 1 73), e.g. the bite of a mad dog in the case of rabies (*SI* 1 88). The Empiricist notes that past cases of bites where the dog was mad differed from those in which the dog seemed sane and required different treatment.[69] By contrast, Rationalist doctors will construct a theory explaining the connection between the dog's mental state and the patient's physical condition in terms of how the dog's bite can alter his internal constitution (which, being intrinsically unobservable, plays no role in Empiricist theory). Essentially the Empiricists build up, on the basis of suitably supplemented experience, a picture of which phenomena tend to be associated with which. They have no interest in the deep reasons (if any) why they do so. Insofar as they refer to causes they do so in a non-theoretical proto-Humean fashion, rigorously avoiding any talk of occult powers.

---

[67] See von Staden 1989, ad loc.; Hankinson 1990a.

[68] For accounts of the rise and development of the Empiricist school of medicine, see Frede 1987b, 1988, 1990, and Matthen 1988a.

[69] Their practice thus contrasts sharply, or at least so Galen alleges, with that of the Methodical school, who simply treat such bites as cases of wounds and bandage them up (*SI* 1 88–9). For the Methodists and their attitude to causes, see Frede 1982; and Lloyd 1983, 188–200.

Here we must confront an anomaly. Galen remarks that Empiricists 'do not hesitate to ask for the so-called antecedent cause' (*SI* I 74; cf. *Med. Exp.* 24; Celsus *Med. Pr.* 27); yet in *CP* he claims that the Empiricists 'doubt whether there are causes or not' (XIII.162), while later writing that

> Even those doctors from the Empirical school, who above all others proclaim things in accordance with common sense, were so overcome by the sophism as to be moved to doubt concerning antecedent causes. (Gal. *CP* XIII.170)[70]

The apparent inconsistency evaporates with an understanding of the sense in which the Empiricist accepts antecedent causes. He does so not on the basis of any causal theory of how the dog's bite induces rabies: he simply knows that rabies follows bites of that sort. That is simply to observe an empirical connection, not to postulate some arcane underlying productive mechanism, as the Rationalist does. Rationalist and Empiricist, then, do not disagree about the evident facts; rather they part company on their proper interpretation. Thus an Empiricist accepts antecedent causes as signs while rejecting any account of how they might operate.

Moreover, according to Galen (*SI* I 72–3), good Rationalists and good Empiricists generally agree about diagnosis and therapy. They differ in that the Rationalist is 'led by the nature of the matter', and believes that a theory of things' underlying physical structures and interactions explains why the therapies work. The Empiricist has no such pretensions: his explanations are epistemic rather than metaphysical in nature. Thus he can account for his adoption of a certain practice and what gives him (limited) confidence in it; but he will be quite agnostic about the structure of reality, if any, in virtue of which his procedures work.[71]

---

[70] For a full discussion, see Hankinson 1987b. The 'sophism' is Erasistratus' argument against non-sufficient causes (above, p. 509).

[71] See Matthen 1988a, for a development of the view that the fundamental distinction between Empiricist and Dogmatist is ontological.

15

Determinism and indeterminism

R. J. HANKINSON

1 The origins of the question

The notion of universal causation was ubiquitous in later antiquity; to loosen those ties threatened the irruption of chaos. How could the evident continuity and regularity of the world survive the intervention of casual elements into its structure? Still, there is a clear distinction, one exploited by the Epicureans, between the assertion of a universal principle of causation and any determinism. It is one thing to accept that every event is caused, quite another to believe that the nature and sequence of all events is rigidly fixed for all eternity. The latter belief forms the core of any determinism – and it is its prima-facie implausibility, along with what are taken to be its unacceptable consequences (for human freedom, for the concept of responsibility), that lays it open to attack.

The origins of the problem in the Greek world were not, however, metaphysical. The Sophistic movement of the late fifth century BC was particularly interested in new forms of forensic argument, especially defence argument. Gorgias' *Helen* is a case in point: Helen of Troy is innocent of adultery, he argues, because she did what she did either under physical compulsion, or under the influence of love, or at the whim of some god, or persuaded by arguments. In none of these eventualities can she be held responsible for her actions, since in all of them she is compelled by some external force; the list is exhaustive; hence she is not responsible for what she did. Gorgias' rhetorical exercise is not serious philosophy, but it raises serious philosophical points. If our actions are indeed conditioned by factors that lie outside our control, how can we reasonably be held responsible for what we do? Society is, indeed, to blame: Gorgias is the Ur-progenitor of hard determinism.

Aristotle saw the problem with characteristic clarity. At the beginning of Book III of his *Nicomachean Ethics*, he wrote:

> Since ethical virtue is concerned with emotions and actions, and those which are voluntary are praised or blamed, while those which are invol-

untary receive pardon and sometimes pity as well, students of ethical virtue must presumably determine the limits of the voluntary and the
involuntary . . . Actions are regarded as involuntary when performed
under compulsion or through ignorance. (*EN* III.1.1109b30–1110a1)

And he was well aware of the dangers that attended any attempt to miti-
gate responsibility by blaming factors outside the agent's control:

> If it were argued that pleasurable and admirable things have a compul-
> sive effect (because they bring external pressure to bear on us), it would
> make all acts compulsory, since every act of every agent is done for the
> sake of such objects . . . It is absurd for the agent to lay blame on the
> external factors and not upon himself for falling easy prey to them, and
> to attribute his fine acts to himself, but his disgraceful ones to the attrac-
> tions of pleasure. It seems reasonable, then, that an act is compulsory
> only when its originating cause is external, and receives no contribution
> from the person under compulsion. (*EN* III.1.1110b9–17)

Aristotle holds that we are responsible for what we do just in case the origin of the action is within us (he has a rather literal notion of coercion); if
we contribute at all to it, then we are responsible for it. It is, fundamentally, in virtue of the state of our characters that we are praised or blamed;
and it is insofar as we act on the basis of choice, or after deliberation, that
we are morally responsible for what we do. When we make a choice, we
choose to perform or refrain from performing some action – that choice is
up to us, the outcome of our desires, beliefs, and deliberations. We desire
a particular end, and deliberate about and select means to that end;
actions of this sort are performed in accordance with choice and are thus
voluntary: 'therefore virtue is 'up to us' (*eph' hēmin*)' (*EN* III.5.1113b3–6).
Helen may have been persuaded by arguments – but it was she who was so
persuaded: Penelope did not succumb. Or she may have been swept away
by powerful emotions and desires – but she shouldn't have been: so much
the worse for her morals. Aristotle may accept Gorgias' disjunction of
alternatives as exhaustive – he can still resist the conclusion that Helen's
action was not her fault.

Aristotle starts from the obvious fact of moral life that we do hold people, including ourselves, responsible for what they do; otherwise we could
not legitimately praise or blame them. But if praise and blame are legitimate, some things must be up to us (*eph' hēmin*). He is not blind to the
difficulties of the picture he tries to develop. We are responsible for our
actions insofar as they derive from our choices, made in line with our preferences – and hence derivatively because they are the products of our char-

acters. It is because I am weak-willed that I eat another danish pastry when you, exercising self-control, refrain from so doing. But as Aristotle clearly saw, it is only if we are further responsible for our states of character themselves that we can be held to account in any strong sense for actions performed as a result of them. He scouts a possible objection:

> Everyone aims at what seems to him to be good, but over this appearance he has no control. How the end appears to each individual depends on the nature of his character, whatever this may be. So if the individual is in a way responsible for his state of character he will also be in a way responsible for his view of what is good; but if he is not responsible for the former, then no wrongdoer is responsible for doing wrong. (*EN* III.5.1114a31–b4)

Perhaps virtuousness is simply a matter of natural endowment, or proper upbringing – but neither of these seem to be in any obvious sense up to the individual in question. The problem is occasioned by the transitivity of responsibility. Suppose some individual I's action A is reasonably pinned on his character C – nevertheless, if we can trace responsibility for C to some set of factors F, where F are outside I's control, then F, and not I, are truly responsible for A. That argument has a certain plausibility to it, and it re-opens Helen's defence.

Central to Aristotle's account (and many others) of human responsibility is the notion of choice. We are free, and hence responsible, just insofar as we can choose to do what we do. If it can be shown that this choice is a chimaera, then human freedom may turn out to be equally illusory. And one way of going about doing that is by arguing for determinism. If the entire course of the universe is ineluctably mapped out in advance, its unfolding being merely the working out of an inevitable fate, there seems little room for genuine human agency at all. Rather we are all puppets of the ultimate causal forces of the universe, and our autonomy is mere illusion.

That inference, from the ineluctability of fate to the impossibility of human freedom, has been deployed by determinist and indeterminist alike, although from different directions. The unthinkability of human bondage has frequently formed the basis of an argument to indeterminism via a *modus tollens* of that implication – that strategy was pursued by the Epicureans. Conversely, the rationally compelling nature of the argument for universal causation has sometimes pushed people in the other direction: Gorgias is only the first of many. Others, most famously Hume, have tried to reconcile some concept of human freedom with determinism. That was Chrysippus' line. But first of all another source for the debate merits brief consideration.

11 Logic and contingency

In another famous passage (*Int.* 9), Aristotle discusses the question of whether singular propositions about the future have determinate truth values.[1] Suppose it is fine today; surely then it was true yesterday to say that it would be fine today – and the proposition 'it will be fine tomorrow' was true yesterday. More than that: it was true 10,000 years ago, indeed it has been true since the dawn of time. But if it is now true (let us say) that there will (to use Aristotle's famous example) be a sea-battle tomorrow, surely it is now unavoidable that there will be such a battle? And similarly with the most contingent-seeming propositions:

> Consequently it is necessary that either the affirmation or the denial [of a certain proposition] be true. Nothing then will either be or come to be by chance or contingently . . . everything will be of necessity and not contingent (*Int.* 9.18a6–8)

and

> these and other bizarre consequences follow, if at least we assume that of every affirmation and denial . . . of contradictory opposites one must be true and the other false: there can be no contingency in things that come to be, and everything that is and comes to be does so of necessity. (*Int.* 9.18b26–31)

However, Aristotle goes on to reject this as being plainly inconsistent with our experience that human deliberation is a source of events (*Int.* 9.19a7).

Aristotle's argument rests in part on the thesis that

(T1) the past is necessary.

What's done cannot be undone: and if we gloss 'necessary' as 'fixed, unalterable', then (T1) is attractive. It is surely one of the fundamental temporal distinctions that future events, unlike past ones, can be affected and altered by what is done now. But if that is right, it seems reasonable to think, as Aristotle apparently did, that the status of propositions about the future should be different from that of propositions about the past,

---

[1] At least, this is the most usual interpretation of what he is doing; a rival account was urged by G. E. M. Anscombe (Anscombe 1956), to the effect that what was at issue was not future *truth* but future *necessity*.

and not merely for epistemic reasons (not merely, that is, because in the nature of things we can know less about the future than the past). The past is determinate, hence propositions about it are necessarily true. The future is not, and so utterances referring to it must at best be contingently true if they are true at all.[2]

That argument is seductive – it seduced Epicurus. But it is won at the price of abandoning the semantic principle of bivalence, at least in its most general form. And there is something to be said for bivalence, most obviously that it seems guaranteed by the logic of negation. Surely, if a proposition makes sense it must be either true or false? And in any case, are we not merely dealing with differently-tensed and indexed versions of the same proposition in the case of today's fine weather? It seems at best arbitrary to say that, even if it is fine today, yesterday's accurate weather-forecaster wasn't telling the truth. But if he was, then it was already going to be fine today yesterday – and that, at least for Aristotle, entails multiple absurdities. That sequence of argument is perhaps confused – but its confusions are not trivial (it took a Carneades to expose them), and they still have the power to perplex.

On the basis of (T1), and the further (also Aristotelian) thesis that

(T2) an impossibility cannot follow from a possibility,

Diodorus Cronus attempted to do away with contingency altogether by way of his celebrated Master argument (11.1).[3] Whatever its precise form there is no doubt that it was of enormous influence on succeeding generations of philosophers, and its move from logic to metaphysics appears to have been widely accepted as valid.

III The Hellenistic response

The Epicureans countered by holding that the principle of bivalence failed for future contingents: they were neither true nor false prior to their being actualized, and hence *a fortiori* were not either necessarily true or impossible (Cic. *Fat.* 21). Furthermore, the apparatus of the swerve is introduced explicitly, Cicero says, to provide a physical, indeterminist

---

[2] This is inadequately crude as it stands – no indeterminist need think that *all* propositions about the future are undetermined: 'in 100 years I shall be dead' seems about as necessary (causally speaking) as anything else. For Aristotle, there are certain truths about natural kinds which are dictated by the structure of the kind itself – these can be given a future tense, but they are no less settled for all that. Yet there are indefinitely many things about my death which are, on this view, undetermined at the present time. Its date, its place, its mode, and so on.

[3] See above, pp. 88–92.

basis for the rejection of bivalence which is taken to be a necessary concomitant of the maintenance of human freedom:

> Epicurus introduced this theory [i.e. of the swerve] because of his fear
> lest, if the atom was always carried along by its natural and necessary
> gravity, no freedom would be left for us, since the mind will move under
> compulsion from the atoms. (Cic. *Fat.* 23)[4]

But the Epicureans' attempt to rescue freedom along with contingency
has its price. They must reject bivalence; and they are forced to compromise the clean lines of their physical theory by introducing the minimal
atomic swerve. Chrysippus and the Stoics, on the other hand, accepted
bivalence, since they could not see how a proposition could fail to be
either true or false – and as a result they felt themselves forced to accept a
version of determinism. Both Epicureans and Stoics, then, accept the following theses:

(T3) if truths are timeless (or eternal), then if a proposition p is true at any
time, p is true at all times;

and

(T4) if p is true at all times, then p is necessary (in the sense of its being
determined).

The Stoics accepted the timelessness of truth,[5] and hence the determination of all truths; the Epicureans discountenanced the determination of
all truths, and hence rejected their timelessness, as well as bivalence. But
rejecting bivalence is a tricky business. After all, surely even if Caesar
might have escaped death at the hands of the conspirators, the claim that
he will not be murdered is actually false whenever uttered prior to the
Ides of March. If Teiresias or Elijah had said, centuries earlier, 'Caesar will
be murdered on the Ides of March', they would have been telling the
truth. One does not even need anything as strong as (T1) to do the trick
here: past truth alone will do. On the other hand, the Stoics have a difficult

---

[4] This translation (and subsequent ones) follows those of Long and Sedley 1987, vol. 1, 102–7. For
the swerve also see above, pp. 501–2.

[5] I should note here that I do *not* mean to imply that for the Stoics the proper unit of fundamental
semantic appraisal was a timeless proposition construed in the manner of contemporary classical logic. See above, pp. 95–6. On the contrary, the Stoics, in common with other ancient
semanticists, held that non-indexed sentences were the basic truth-bearers, and hence that
'propositions' such as 'it is fine' may change their truth-value. But that is irrelevant to the point
at issue, which is whether or not an indexed 'proposition' ('it is [tenseless] fine at spatio-temporal region *S*') is such as to be always true if true at all – the Stoics hold that it is: and in *that*
sense their propositions are timeless.

time of it explaining how truths can be determined without being (in some sense) necessary.

It is one of the great achievements of the Academic sceptic Carneades to see that this dilemma is not forced upon us. We may distinguish[6] between Causal Determinism (CD: the thesis that each event is the ineluctable product of antecedent causes); Logical Determinism (LD: if an event is going to happen it is already true that it will happen); and Epistemic Determinism (ED: if it is known that an event will happen, then that event cannot fail to occur).[7] The Stoics rely on the view that if a future proposition is now true there must be some truth-maker for it in the world now: it must already be true that it is unavoidable. But as Carneades showed, that is a mistake. LD does not entail CD. For any future contingent proposition, either it or its contradictory is true. But it is not true necessarily in virtue of anything in the world now; rather it will be made true by the event as it turns out:

> The truth of propositions like 'Cato will come into the Senate' is brought about by contingent causes, not by causes bound up in nature and the world. And yet that something will come about, when true, is as immutable as the truth that something has come about. (Cic. Fat. 28)

If it is now true that I shall die at sea, then nothing I can now do will alter that truth. But does that mean I am fated to die at sea? No: because it is only true that I shall die at sea if as a matter of fact I now do nothing to prevent it, and as a matter of fact act in such a way that eventually leads to my maritime death. If I prevent my own watery demise, then it will never have been true that I was going to die at sea. The assimilation of LD to CD rests on a straightforward mistake; CD entails LD – but not vice versa, as both Stoics and Epicureans believed. As regards ED, Carneades holds that it entails CD (and hence LD); and so, if CD is false, ED must be too:

> That is why Carneades used to say that not even Apollo could tell the future apart from things whose causes were embodied in nature in such a way as to render their coming about necessary. For by inspecting what could even the god himself tell that Marcellus . . . would die at sea? This was something that was true from eternity but did not have causes working to bring it about. (Cic. Fat. 32–3)

That is, I think, a mistake: it is logically possible that one might know that some future event will occur, and yet it need not be the case that the event

---

[6] With Long and Sedley 1987, vol. 1, 466.

[7] Sorabji (1980a) discusses these categories (although not under these names) and the relations that hold between them, see especially chs. 1–3; also see Sorabji 1980b.

is causally determined at the time of knowledge. Perhaps one can simply see the map of time laid out before one, as it were; perhaps the fact of the later event actually causes (or is part of the cause of) my current knowledge of it, even though it has not yet occurred and is not yet causally determined. And theologians have argued that God may know how we are going to choose, and hence whether we are doomed to damnation or are saved, without that entailing that our choices are unfree, even for a non-compatibilist sense of freedom.

But even if such possibilities are logically open, they are exotic suppositions, and nothing in our experience gives us any reason to suppose that they are true. Furthermore, it seems clearly to be the case that if ED holds then the future events which are within its grip are in some sense already fixed, and if they have already been fixed it surely does follow that nothing can now be done to prevent them. This does not, perhaps, entail that they are causally determined; but it does entail that they are determined, and that fact alone may be enough to undermine any robust notion of freedom. Here is Carneades' argument, as reported by Cicero:

> (1) If all things come about through antecedent causes, all things come about through the interconnection in a natural chain. (2) If that is so, all things are the product of necessity. (3) If that is true, nothing is in our power. (4) But there is something in our power. (5) But if all things come about through fate, all things come about through antecedent causes. (6) Therefore it is not the case that whatever happens happens through fate. (Cic. *Fat.* 31)

The Stoics accept (5) and (1); they reject (2), but Carneades is surely right, as we have seen, to see that they are committed to it at least in a sense strong enough to cast doubt on the view that human agents are anything more than instrumental causes of their actions, and hence (3) will follow, at least for a strong sense of 'in our power'. (4) is simply a bald assertion: no argument is offered for it. Perhaps, like Dr Johnson, Carneades relies on the view that 'all experience is for it'; perhaps he simply takes the Stoics to be committed to it. At all events, (4), along with the other premisses, clearly entails (6).

Here we should turn to another Carneadean argument from Cicero's *De fato*. In order to counter arguments like that of (1)–(6) above, the Epicureans felt it necessary to introduce the atomic swerve, a sudden, unpredictable, uncaused quantum movement in atomic motion, in order to account, among other things, for human freedom (IV.3).[8] Carneades

---

[8] 'Quantum' is more than mere metaphor here; the evidence suggests that the swerve involves the minimal possible divergence from the atom's previous trajectory.

pointed out that the swerve was superfluous to the Epicureans' requirements:

> A more penetrating line was taken by Carneades, who showed that the Epicureans could defend their case without this fictitious swerve. For since they taught that a certain voluntary motion of the mind was possible, a defence of that doctrine was preferable to introducing the swerve, especially as they could not discover its cause. And by defending it they could easily stand up to Chrysippus. For by conceding that there is no motion without a cause, they would not be conceding that all events were the results of antecedent causes. For our volition has no external antecedent causes. (Cic. *Fat.* 23)

If we say someone acts without a cause, Carneades continues, we mean only without external causes: their volitions still cause their actions. But their volitions are not themselves caused. Hence the Epicureans can avoid uncaused events (at least if volitions are not events), with all the problems that they entail, and still reject universal determinism, and hence support freedom. Carneades holds that the Epicureans can admit the truth of

(7) no event occurs causelessly

and so avoid 'incurring the scorn of the natural philosophers' (Cic. *Fat.* 25),[9] and yet still hold that actions are events and are caused, since

(8) actions are caused by the will;

but the volitions themselves are not caused, at least not by anything external to us. This line of argument requires that either the volitions themselves, or what causes them, are not themselves events (if events must have antecedent, and hence independent, causes); 'pure acts of the will', or something of the sort, are supposed in some sense to be self-caused, brought about by their own internal nature, in just the same way as atoms fall (on the Epicurean account) because of their intrinsic weight.

There are obscurities in this doctrine, and it will convince no Humean, wedded to the necessary distinctness of cause and effect. And there are difficulties with reconciling the notion of the human will as a sort of self-starting mechanism with the evident fact, noted by Chrysippus, that external influences are at the very least necessary conditions of our having acts of the will at all.[10] The following argument suggests itself: if autonomy involves having control over one's actions, then the will of the autonomous agent must be sufficient for those actions. But that conflicts with

---

[9] See above, p. 502.   [10] See below, pp. 531–4 and 577–80.

the admission that externals are necessary conditions for the action (except on the absurd supposition that the act of will is itself a sufficient condition for the presence of external conditions). However, given the notion of causation canvassed in the previous chapter, this need not be the problem it appears to be; when the external object impinges, it sets the process in motion – but it is the volition itself that keeps it going. This will be developed later on.

iv The Epicurean position

So much for the logical argument designed to show that the principle of bivalence entails determinism. Even if that argument fails, there is still work to be done for the anti-determinist. The grip of the principle that every event must have a cause was a strong one – and provided that the principle is interpreted strongly such that every event has a specific cause,[11] determinism, with all that it entails, seems unavoidable. Causation will become assimilated to necessitation.[12] Certainly there is reason to believe that Aristotle did not think of his causes as invariably necessitating: if A is only for the most part causally correlated with B, none the less there is nothing amiss in saying that A causes B, although it does not necessitate it: for to say that A necessitated B, it would have to be the case that A-type events were invariably followed by B-type events. But even if that is the case, it still leaves wide open the question of whether events (considered as individual tokens, and not under some particular generic and allegedly explanatory description) are uniquely determined by antecedent circumstances – and here the evidence is far more equivocal.

So if you think that universal causation entails determinism, while determinism is incompatible with human freedom, yet you also think that human freedom is an incontrovertible datum of ordinary experience, then you will be bound to deny universal causation. And that is precisely the path Epicurus and his followers took. Carneades, as Cic. *Fat.* 23 above demonstrates, clearly thought that the Epicureans solved nothing simply by introducing unpredictable swerves – randomness is not the form of human freedom; and such views have frequently surfaced in the succeeding debate. If my actions are detached from the fetters of necessity at the expense of making them simply random, it is hard to see what concept of

---

[11] See above, p. 481 (T1*).
[12] There have been modern attempts to deny the link between the two, and equally some modern commentators, notably Sorabji 1980a and 1980b, wish to ascribe such a denial to the ancients.

freedom can be embodied thereby. We surely do not think of ourselves being free just insofar as we are loose cannons, firing uncontrollably. Indeed, an influential concept of human freedom, one endorsed in different ways by the Stoics, the early Christians, and Galen, has it precisely that human freedom involves self-control, and hence regularity in behaviour. Moreover, even if volitions may be thought of as possessing causal efficacy which is in some way independent of, or at least not reducible to, the sum of the atomic motions, it is not clear why the atoms should need to be able to swerve: all that is necessary is that acts of the will can deflect them from their normal trajectories, as Carneades saw.

However, Epicurus may not have thought the swerve to be constitutive of human freedom. Recently, David Sedley has argued[13] that the function of the swerve is simply to allow for acts of volition: that every swerve is of its nature uncaused, is an unjustified inference of Epicureanism's opponents. Rather, the atoms' ability to be deflected allows volition a toehold into causal efficacy, since the will can now actually affect the mechanical course of atomic events.[14] To say (in the case of volitions at least) that the atoms swerve is simply to say that their motions are not exhaustively determined by the force, momentum, shape and velocity of the atoms themselves, that is by their intrinsic, essential properties. This is not of course to say that all the swerves are caused by volitions – just that there is available, as it were, a set of alternative trajectories into which the atoms can be forced by acts of the will; the will can then take advantage of the causal elasticity so permitted, and, within limits at least, mould events in its image.

This interpretation at least avoids the reduction of freedom to randomness. But it is highly controversial;[15] and it is clear neither whether Epicurus actually held it, nor if he did how it was to be developed. Sedley bases his case upon a papyrus fragment of the *On Nature*, in which Epicurus discusses the proper attitude to take towards those who squander their natural gifts:

> The nature of their atoms has contributed nothing to some of their behaviour, and degrees of behaviour, and character, but it is their developments which themselves possess all or most of the responsibility for certain things. It is a result of that nature that some of their atoms move with disordered motions, but it is not on the atoms <that responsibility should be placed>. Thus when a development occurs which takes on

[13] Sedley 1983b and 1988; see also the brief account in Long and Sedley 1987, vol. 1, 107–12; it is assessed and criticized in Laursen 1988.
[14] See Long and Sedley 1987, vol.1, 110–12. [15] See the criticisms of Everson, pp. 553–7.

some distinctness from the atoms in a differential way – not in the way which is like viewing from a different distance – he acquires responsibility which proceeds from himself. Then he immediately transmits this to the primary substances. (Ep. *Nat.* xxv, [34] 21–2 Arr.[2])

That passage is obscure, and its readings are disputed.[16] But Epicurus does appear to make a distinction between the ordinary, bottom-up causality of atomic motion and the way in which the individual's settled disposition must be conceived of as operating: it is not, so he suggests, merely one of scale or perspective (this is presumably the point of the aside about viewing from a distance). Rather (if this account is correct), he appears to envisage a new level of causal power emerging above the microscopic level, whose activity is in some way autonomous, and can even feed back into the workings of that micro-level.

Yet, as far as we know, if Epicurus did adopt such a two-level causal position, he made no attempt to elaborate upon it; furthermore, the passage may be read in such a way as not to involve the emergence at the macroscopic level of new causal forces. Epicurus may simply be denying the inference from the fact that the individual is composed of atoms with their own laws of working to the claim that it is the atoms themselves, and not the individual, who is responsible for that individual's actions. The target of the passage would then be not physicalism (or reductionism) as such, but rather physicalist determinism.[17]

Even so, it is quite unclear how, even on that view, Epicurus' thought is supposed to be developed here, and there is no real indication (although given the fragmentary nature of the sources, such remarks should be handled with care) that Epicurus did develop it. Perhaps he felt that a simple outline was enough to establish its possibility, and hence preferability to an utterly deterministic view of mind and action of the type he ascribes to Democritus and his followers, and which he takes to be absolutely rationally unacceptable. In a relatively well-preserved fragment (*Nat.* xxv, [34] 26–30 Arr.[2]), Epicurus takes his Democritean opponents to task for not seeing the self-refuting nature of the thesis of determinism: they 'debate this very question on the assumption that their opponent is himself responsible for talking nonsense'. And if the opponent alleges that this behaviour is itself necessitated, then he will be forced into a regress.

Once again, the exact nature of Epicurus' complaint is difficult to establish – he does not appear to think that regress is itself vicious, merely that in some sense the fact of it renders the determinist's stance empty. The

---

[16] As is its location in *On Nature*, see below, p. 532, n. 30.   [17] See below, pp. 529–31.

point seems to be that even the determinist relies on the persuasiveness of his arguments – that is, they are supposed to supply reasons why his opponent should modify his views. But one can only act upon reasons if one can act, that is, if one is free (if there is, in Epicurus' language, some 'auxiliary element or impulse within us': *Nat.* xxv, [34] 29 Arr.²) – hence the determinist's position is pragmatically at least self-stultifying. That argument is not convincing (no committed determinist will find it too difficult to evade) – but it is subtle.¹⁸

There is, however, a less subtle but still important general line of criticism to be examined. It is put most succinctly in one of the collections of Epicurean sayings:

> The man who says that all events are necessitated has no ground for criticizing the man who says that not all events are necessitated, since according to him it too is necessitated. (Ep. *Sent.Vat.* 40)

Universal determinism, so it is said (and has been repeated innumerable times since) makes the practices of praise and blame, reward and punishment, ethically null. We shall return to the Stoic response to this later.

Lucretius leaves us with no doubt that it is the apparent undeniability of the real existence of independent volitions which pushes the Epicureans to take the line they do;

> Furthermore, if all motion is always linked, and new motion arises out of old in a fixed order, and atoms do not by their swerve make some beginning of motion to break the decrees of fate, so that cause should not follow cause from infinity, from where does free volition exist for animals throughout the world? From where, I ask, comes this volition wrested away from the fates, through which we proceed wherever each of us is led by his pleasure and likewise swerve off our motions at no fixed time or fixed region of space, but wherever the mind carries us? For without a doubt it is volition that gives these things beginnings for each of us, and it is from volition that motions are spread through the limbs . . . Nor is it the same when we move forward impelled by a blow through another person's great strength . . . For then it is plain that all the matter of the whole body moves and is driven against our wish, while volition reined it back through the limbs . . . So in the seeds too you must admit . . . that there is another cause of motion besides impact and weight, from which this power [i.e. volition] is born in us, since we see that nothing can come to be out of nothing . . . That the mind should not itself possess an internal necessity in all its behaviour, and be overcome, and as it were forced

---

¹⁸ See once again below, pp. 529–31.

to suffer and be acted upon – that is brought about by a tiny swerve of the atoms at no fixed place or time. (Lucr. II.251–93)

Lucretius apparently invokes volition to avoid the complete linearity of causal behaviour, to explain interruptions in motion, irregularities of behaviour, and so on. It is indeed an evident fact of animal behaviour that animals do not react in the same way to stimuli as inanimate objects. Kick a stone in Johnsonian fashion and, even if you fail to refute Berkeley thus, at the expense of a certain foreseeable discomfort you may none the less propel it a certain distance – and the trajectory it follows will be determinate, and in principle predictable on the basis of familiar physical laws. Kick a puma, on the other hand, and the outcome is a good deal less certain, both in terms of puma-trajectory and of your own subsequent discomfort. Animals quite clearly do, as Aristotle put it, have an internal principle of motion that stones do not.

But it is one thing to point out that fact – quite another to refute determinism on its basis, and it is far from clear whether it calls for anything resembling an atomic swerve. Lucretius seems to think that because animals swerve 'at no fixed place or time', i.e. not in response to crude mechanical laws, so too must the atoms. But that involves a gross fallacy, one moreover that the atomists' own insistence on the possibility of emergence should have warned them against. In short, nothing Lucretius says in this passage seems to require the swerve, or indeed to militate against any but the crassest determinisms.

v The Stoic response to the Master argument: fate and necessity

The Stoics too were perplexed by Diodorus' argument – and while they wished to reject the conclusion (that all truths are eternal and necessary), they were apparently unsure as to how to do so. Cleanthes, Zeno's immediate successor, seems to have rejected (T1);[19] Chrysippus his successor, on the other hand, denied (T2) (Cic. *Div.* 1.14).[20] At all events they found it deeply troubling – and something had to be wrong with it.

This may appear puzzling. The Stoics, after all, are partisans of a universal causality. Numerous texts attest to their belief in an all-embracing ineluctable fate, which they identify variously with the will of Zeus, Zeus

---

[19] See above, p. 516.
[20] Chrysippus' adoption of this fairly desperate manoeuvre need not detain us: his defence of it turns on a peculiarity of Stoic semantics; see Sorabji 1980b, 263.

himself, the *Logos* of the world, and so on. Furthermore, several texts ascribe to Chrysippus belief in the necessity of fate:

> Chrysippus . . . said that there was no difference between what was necessitated and fate, saying that fate was an eternal, continuous, and ordered movement. (*SVF* II 916; cf. 926)

Fate is described as a chain (or rope) of causes (*SVF* II 915, 917, 920, etc.), unravelling in an ineluctably determined manner; and as Sorabji writes 'the Stoics had a battery of other words for the inevitability which they applied to this all-embracing fate'.[21] Finally, Chrysippus is expressly said to have composed the first book of his *On Fate* in order to show 'that everything is encompassed by necessity and fate' (Diogenianus *ap.* Eus. *PE* VI.8.1). How do they manage what Sorabji calls their 'retreat from necessity'?

First of all, note that Chrysippus says that things are necessitated by fate, not that they are themselves necessary. This is not as trivial as it seems. We need here briefly to examine the Stoic treatment of the modal concepts of necessity and possibility, whose proper interpretation was already a matter of philosophical dispute among Diodorus' circle. Diodorus held that necessity was a matter of eternal truth;[22] the Stoics' view was apparently more generous:

> A proposition is possible which admits of being true, there being no external factor to prevent its being true . . . Necessary is that which, being true, does not admit of being false, or if it does so admit is prevented from being false by external factors. (D.L. VII.75)

The interpretation of the definitions given here is a matter of scholarly controversy (and the examples offered by Diogenes Laertius are not very illuminating).[23] The notion of 'admitting of' is murky; and the precise role of the second clause in each definition, referring to 'external factors' is a matter of dispute.

None the less, on the most reasonable interpretation it appears that the Stoics are prepared to treat as necessary those things which simply as a matter of fact have turned out to be true, and whose truth is now unassailable (that fits in well with Chrysippus' acceptance of (T1), the first premiss of the Master argument). That last sentence may be misleading –

---

[21] Sorabji 1980b, 261–2; cf. *SVF* II 202, 528, 913–14, 917–18, 923–4, etc.

[22] This is a little loose, but it will do: the actual definition he offers is 'that which, being true, will not be false' (Boethius *Int.* 2, p. 234 Meiser). But he is clearly *committed* to eternal truth by the Master argument.

[23] See most clearly Frede 1974a, 107–17; also Bobzien 1986, Mignucci 1978, and see above, pp. 118–20.

for the Stoics, there will always be a causal explanation as to why things have turned out thus and so – there is no such thing as simply turning out true. It is tempting to try to interpret this on the basis of the time of the preventing. A statement that we would normally consider contingent will only be necessary for the Stoics if there is as a matter of actual fact some causal factor operative at the time to prevent its failing to be true.

If this is right, the Stoics can evade an obvious objection: if your definition of necessity holds, then anything that will as a matter of fact turn out true must be necessary, not for logical reasons, but because, given the iron-clad necessity of the unfolding of fate, there are reasons in the world now (in the form of the total nexus of its causal processes) why things will turn out thus. Determinism should, after all, be temporally indifferent. But, the Stoics will reply, consider what it is to be a cause, or at least a perfect cause.[24] If A is a perfect cause of B, A is actually acting to bring B about. In this sense, there are no perfect causes of future events (crucially causal perfection is not simply a matter of causal necessity and sufficiency in a Davidsonian fashion).

This yields two distinct types of modality. The first one might label 'species possibility'. In this case some predicate P is possibly applicable to an individual of natural kind K just in case K's can, other things being equal, be P's. Thus Philo of Megara apparently held that a piece of wood at the bottom of the ocean could be burnt, just because wood is naturally flammable. But secondly there is what might be called actual possibility, according to which the submerged wood is not now flammable because of actually obtaining circumstances. The Stoics, on this view, restrict non-actual species-possibilities to future cases; but they do none the less admit some of them. The Stoics buy Philo's account in forward-looking cases only; otherwise the actual prevention condition in their modal definitions kicks in.

If this is right, it is false to say that the only type of possibility available to the Stoics is epistemic. Consider an example of Aristotle's: a new cloak might perish as a result of ordinary wear, or it might be cut. For the Stoics, *sub specie aeternitatis* there is only one thing that can happen to it – the unravelling of fate will see to that. However, there is nothing now in the world that prevents either outcome, for no causally efficient state of affairs is now making it the case that it will (or will not) be cut. There is thus a point to Chrysippus' insistence that fate is an ineluctable chain of antecedent causes.

[24] On the notion of a 'perfect' cause, see above, pp. 488–90.

VI The Chrysippean notion of fate: soft determinism

Cicero reports that

> Between the two views held by the old philosophers, one being that of
> those who held that everything takes place by fate in the sense that fate
> exercises the force of necessity – the view of Democritus, Heraclitus,
> Empedocles, and Aristotle, the other that of those who said that the
> movements of the mind are voluntary and not at all controlled by fate,
> Chrysippus stands as an honorary arbiter and wished to strike a mean
> between the two; though he leans rather towards those who hold that
> mind is free from all necessity of motion . . . none the less he slips into
> such difficulties that against his will he lends support to the necessity of
> fate. (Cic. *Fat.* 39)

Cicero has Chrysippus impaled on the horns of a dilemma. On the one
hand reluctant to abandon proposition (4) above,[25] he nevertheless
wishes to affirm universal causal determinism. To drive a wedge between
the two positions, he attempts to disengage assent, *sunkatathesis*, from the
grip of fate. Since

> those old philosophers who used to say that everything takes place by
> fate held that assent is given by force and necessity. But those who dis-
> agreed with them released assent from fate and denied that if assent were
> tied to fate it would be possible to disentangle it from necessity. They
> argued as follows: if (9) all things occur by fate, all things occur by an
> antecedent cause; (10) and if desire is caused, those things which follow
> desire are also caused; therefore (11) assent is also caused. But (12) if the
> cause of the desire is not situated within us, even desire itself is not in our
> power; (13) and if this is so, those things which are caused by desire do
> not rest with us. Thus it follows (14) that neither assent nor action are in
> our power. Hence (15) there is no justice in either praise or blame, hon-
> ours or punishments. (Cic. *Fat.* 40)

We have seen the bulk of this argument elsewhere. It has (for the anti-
determinist) the form of a multiple *modus tollens*: deny (15), and you are
committed to denying the antecedent of (9). By contrast, a hard determinist will take the truth of (9) to entail (15), and the emptiness of conventional morality. Chrysippus tries to avoid either conclusion, impugning
the argument's validity by distinguishing antecedent causes from internal
causes, as we saw in the last chapter.[26]

---

[25] See p. 520.   [26] See above, pp. 490–4.

Chrysippus does not deny that there are antecedent causes of our desires, and hence (since such causes are transitive) of our assents to them: 'assent cannot take place unless prompted by a sense-impression' (Cic. *Fat.* 42). But antecedent causes are not of themselves determining. They determine only in conjunction with other factors, the internal states and conditions they operate upon: and these causes are not transitive in form. Thus our assents are caused, but not determined. Chrysippus accepts (11) in a sense – and equally in a sense he accepts (12): but he holds that they equivocate on the notion of cause at play in each of them. In no sense of 'cause' for which (11) is true will the antecedent of (12) follow; hence the argument fails.

But this is immediately puzzling: while elsewhere it is indeed confirmed that Chrysippus identifies fate with antecedent causes (Cic. *Top.* 59; cf. [Plu.] *Fat.* 574d). However, Plutarch (*Stoic. Rep.* 1056b–c) complains that if Chrysippus does make fate merely the antecedent, and not the perfect cause of right action and thought, he will contradict himself, since the antecedent cause is supposedly weaker than the perfect, yet nothing is more powerful than the will of Zeus (with which Chrysippus wants to identify fate). Furthermore, fate is supposed to be unconquerable, ineluctable, and unavoidable.

Sorabji distinguishes three ways in which Chrysippus' argument may be taken.[27] According to the first (to which he inclines), Chrysippus is trying to avoid the necessitation of assent – but it is, as Sorabji admits, hard to see how the argument could begin to show this with any generality. The second view has Chrysippus making a point about moral responsibility rather than necessity – if our actions derive partially from something internal to us, then we are responsible for them.[28] But then it is hard to see how the argument goes; for, as we have noted, Aristotle was already well aware that to show that our dispositions and so on are responsible for our actions in this sense will still not establish any genuine responsibility. Finally, it might be that Chrysippus wants to deny not necessity as such, but the necessity of fate.[29] This accords well with Cicero's language, and with the view that fate is a sequence of external causes.

If this is right, then there will be no relaxation of the fetters of necessity – but fate in and of itself will not be the sole producer and determiner of that necessity. Even so, it is hard to see how the Stoics could have thought

---

[27] Sorabji 1980b.   [28] Donini 1974–5.
[29] Sorabji 1980b, 274, attributes this interpretation to Frede.

of fate on its own, if it is simply the sequence of antecedent causes, as being determining – for antecedent causes do not themselves determine. It is only when they are combined with the potentials contained within things in temporal and causal sequences that the determination of events arises at all. However, there will be another sense in which fate is determining: given the structure of natural potentialities which obtains in the world, plus various contingent (contingent in a relaxed sense: nothing turns on the notion here) facts about their physical and spatial relationships, then their entire history of interaction will be plottable by a Laplacean super-scientist – their impingement upon one another being precisely the play of antecedent causes. Thus, looking backward, we can say that fate necessitated the outcome of every event given that spatio-temporal structure.

We can still give a perfectly clear and coherent sense to the claim that things might have turned out otherwise: they might, indeed would, have done so had that structure, *per* (causal) *impossibile*, been different. If it had been you rather than I who was tempted by that extra helping of zabaione, the pudding would have remained virtuously on the plate. And the truth-makers for these counterfactuals of possibility will be real-world situations that are relevantly similar in all important aspects (last week you were offered a second helping of zabaione, but virtuously declined). Hence possibility does not collapse into necessity; and nor does it become merely epistemic in form.

Thus Plutarch's charge of self-contradiction also fails. Considered simply *qua* collection of antecedent causes, fate is not all-powerful; but there is a perfectly clear real-world sense in which, given the way things are, things could not turn out differently given that set of causes. The will of Zeus really is ineluctable.

VII Fate and responsibility: *confatalia* and the *eph' hēmin*

One may still ask where this leaves the concept of responsibility. We may allow Chrysippus the distinction between internal and external causes – we may even admit that, in some metaphysical sense, the inner causes really are the causes that keep the system going. But even if that shows that in some sense the things we do are *eph' hēmin*, 'up to us', in that it is the structure of our individual desires and beliefs and so on which causally determines how we react individually to stimuli (as in the zabaione case), is that sense strong enough to justify the ascription of praise and blame?

While my gourmandise is evidently responsible for my custardly *akrasia* (and equally your self-control conditions your restraint under the same circumstances), am I responsible for the state of my dispositions?

This is of course Aristotle's problem: only if I am responsible for the development of my states of character can I be held responsible for the excesses of that character. Aristotle thought, and Epicurus appears to have echoed him here,[30] that there was a stage in the development of our characters, before the dispositions hardened into *hexeis*, where they were sufficiently elastic for us to be able to influence which way they went. We become good, on the Aristotelian model, by performing good actions, by making them a part of our make-up (*EN* II.2.1104a11–4.1105b18). But while that process is under way we are genuinely free to choose either the straight-and-narrow or the primrose path. So, while it may be true of the old reprobate that he genuinely cannot now refrain from vice, the young blade he was thirty years ago could have done so. There is a window of opportunity, as it were, in the development of our characters when that development is up to us.

This is not easy to make sense of; when I 'freely' choose vice over virtue, why assume that my choice is somehow free of the constraints which later condition my vicious life-style? The fashionable distinction between first- and second-order desires does no work here (was not my second-order choice to develop a vicious disposition itself the result of existing traits of character, or external pressures?). Moreover, Aristotle stresses the importance of a proper upbringing in developing a good character – but that is surely definitionally outside the control of the individual properly brought up.

Suffice it to say here that the mere fact that the agent's desires, beliefs, etc. play an instrumental role in causing his actions does nothing to support the view that what he does is up to him in any strong sense. It does show that such actions are attributable to him – it is he who does them, in a sense in which those 'actions' of someone physically compelled by main force are not. That Humean response will deflect the Epicurean accusation that anyone who espouses this kind of determinism can make no sense of the notion of coercion (although the subtler point that there is no

---

[30] *Nat.* xxv, [34] 26 Arr.[2]: 'from the very outset we always have seeds directing us some towards these, some towards those, some towards these and those, actions and thoughts and characters, in greater and smaller numbers. Consequently that which we wish to develop – characteristics of this or that kind – is at first absolutely up to us; and the things which of necessity flow in through our passages from that which surrounds us are at one stage up to us and dependent upon beliefs of our own making.' Quite what Epicurus' account is here is difficult to determine – but the overall tenor of his developmental view is unmistakeable.

morally relevant difference between coercion and voluntary action may of course still be defensible).[31] But the thornier problem remains of explaining how ascription of responsibility is to be justified if everything that happens is indeed necessitated by fate, even if an individual's actual dispositions are part of the causal nexus that determines those outcomes. The Stoics held that we were responsible for what we did because our natures were such as to determine how we chose – our natures, that is, are partially (and for evaluative purposes relevantly) causally responsible for our making the decisions we make, and hence our decisions are 'up to us'.[32] But the rejoinder is obvious:

> If they assign impulse as being up to us on the grounds that we have it by nature, what is to stop us from saying that burning is up to fire since fire burns by nature? (Nemes. 106.7–9)

The Stoics seem to have thought that, the more convoluted the internal causal process leading from impression to action in an individual, the more attributable to that individual becomes the action. But it is hard to see how a mere increase in complexity can deliver the required result, at least if responsibility, like causation, is taken to be transitive.[33]

Hard determinism would be an option – but as Sorabji stresses, it was not one much canvassed in antiquity.[34] There is a famous story about Zeno:

> He was once beating a slave for stealing, and when the latter said 'I was fated to steal', he replied 'and to be flogged'. (D.L. VII.23)

But, as Sorabji says, while compatible with a hard determinist stance this by no means entails it: and it is clearly intended rather to illustrate the Stoic doctrine of 'co-fated events' (*confatalia*).

A standard objection to Stoic determinism was that known as the 'lazy argument', the *argos logos*; if everything is preordained since time began, what is the point of my making any interventions in the world at all? Cicero again:

---

[31] It is worth pointing out that such a response can also make room for a notion of coercion richer and more interesting than simply that of main force – an action (handing over money to an armed robber, for instance) is coerced in this sense just in case the agents' desires are not directly involved in their coming to be in a situation in which their freedom of action (i.e. the set of options over which their desires can range) is curtailed by the actions of another (in this case the robber offering the alternatives of 'your money or your life'). I owe these points to numerous discussions with my wife, Jennifer Greene.

[32] See e.g. Alex. *Fat.* 181.3–182.20; 205.24–206.2.

[33] Of course, one may deny that responsibility is, in the appropriate sense, thoroughly transitive – complex systems will, on this view, take on 'a life of their own', and serve as an appropriate locus for evaluation – but it is one thing to *state* this position – quite another to *argue* for it.

[34] Sorabji 1980b, 280–2. An exception is Galen: see Hankinson 1992, which deals in greater detail with the issues of causation, determination, and responsibility.

They pose it [i.e. the lazy argument] thus: 'if it is your fate to recover from illness, you will recover, regardless of whether or not you call the doctor. Similarly if it is your fate not to recover . . . you will not recover whether or not you call the doctor. And one or the other is your fate. Therefore it is pointless to call the doctor.' (Cic. *Fat.* 28–9)

The lazy argument confounds determinism with what one might call Islamic fatalism, the notion that no matter what you do a particular fate is in store for you. By contrast genuine determinists must reject this – they should (and the Stoics did) say that whatever we do is predetermined, including our reaction to the lazy argument. Here is Chrysippus' response:

Some events in the world are simple, some complex. 'Socrates will die on such and such a day' is simple: his day of dying is fixed, regardless of what he may or may not do. But if a fate is of the form 'Oedipus will be born to Laius', it will not be possible to add 'regardless of whether or not Laius has intercourse with a woman'. For the event is complex and co-fated (*confatale*). He [i.e. Chrysippus] uses this term because what is fated is both that Laius will have intercourse with his wife and that by her he will beget an Oedipus . . . All fallacies of this sort are refuted in the same way. 'You will recover regardless of whether or not you call the doctor' is fallacious. For it is just as much fated for you to call the doctor as for you to recover. (Cic. *Fat.* 30)

Elsewhere, Chrysippus employed a different, pointed example – even if it is fated for Hegesarchus to win the bout without taking a punch, it would still certainly be absurd to expect him to fight with a dropped guard on the grounds that he was so fated (*SVF* II 998). In general, the doctrine of *confatalia* has it that if some event E is fated, then so are all the necessary conditions of E. Thus I eat the zabaione because I am greedy – I am fated not only to eat it, but to be greedy too. And my being greedy explains why I eat it. My actions are not robbed of point simply because in one sense at least I could not do otherwise. Persistent acratics can still try to mend their ways in a thoroughly determined universe; and they may still succeed through their own efforts (although of course the fact that they make the effort is determined too). But whether or not they do so will be determined by causes remote from their own control.

VIII Divination and fate

Whether or not the universe is determinist in character is, as we saw earlier,[35] logically distinct from the question of whether that future can be

---

[35] See p. 519 above.

known – but if one assumes, as the ancients in general did, that the future can be known only if there are determinate causes of it knowable in the present, then the possibility of large scale accurate forecasting of the future will seem to depend on that future's being determined. The Stoics, by and large (Panaetius was an exception) believed in divination; and they found that belief comfortingly compatible with their determinism. Indeed their views of the relations between the two were sometimes charged with circularity:

> Chrysippus gives this demonstration to us, proving each one by way of the other. For he wants to establish that everything comes to be according to fate on the grounds of divination, while that divination exists he is able to show by no other means than by assuming that everything comes about according to fate. (Diogenianus *ap*. Eus. *PE* IV.3.2)

The circularity is not, however, vicious; and our text confuses explanation with support. The (supposedly) empirical fact of divinatory success supports the hypothesis of determinism (indeed perhaps on their, mistaken, view it entails it); conversely, the deterministic hypothesis explains divination, or at any rate is part of its explanation.

Of course, the mere fact that the universe is deterministic would be no guarantee that its future course would be patent to the miserable human intelligence. Perhaps it is just vastly too complex for that. In that case, it will help to have a benevolent deity who is au fait with those complexities – but that there is such a deity is a feature of Stoic theology. Thus it would be good for us if we could know the future; the gods (or God) can tell us what it will be like; they have concern for us; hence they will tell us (cf. Cic. *Div*. I.101-2; *ND* II.161-8). Of course, that argument is vulnerable at every turn – and the Stoics' ancient critics exploited that vulnerability (cf. Carneades, in Cic. *ND* I.4; Favorinus *ap*. Gell. XIV.1-36).[36] But for all that, the Stoics have a consistent set of at least mutually supportive doctrines in theology and metaphysics.

The ins and outs of the debate on divination are beyond the scope of this chapter.[37] But one feature of the dispute is of importance. The Stoics defined divination as 'the foretelling of events that come about by chance' (Cic. *Div*. II.13-15, 26): but in the Stoic universe there is no room for chance. Indeed, the Stoics' stubborn refusal to admit that there is such a thing as genuine chance forms the core of the Peripatetic attack on Stoic determinism.[38] Cicero indeed attempts to convict the Stoics of a formal

[36] On the Stoics and divination in general see Hankinson 1988b, and Long 1982a.

[37] Arguments both for and against may be found in Cic. *Div*.; and S.E. *M* v is a compendium of arguments, many probably Carneadean in origin, against divination.

[38] To be found principally in Alex. *Fat*.; I do not deal with the Peripatetic views in detail in their own right, since it is not certain that they were developed in the period covered by this volume. None the less, they are of much intrinsic interest, see Sharples 1983.

self-contradiction on this score. The future cannot be predicted if it is the result of chance, since if we can know an event is going to occur, it is not now possible that it will not occur; hence it cannot be a chance event. Furthermore, Cicero argues, the only basis for any such knowledge would have to be causal – the event in question follows in a lawlike manner from known initial conditions. But in that case too, it cannot be chance. But the Stoics have no difficulty with this, for they specifically define chance epistemically as 'a cause obscure to human understanding'.[39] To describe an event as a matter of chance is to say that it was not predictable by us on the basis of known causal laws and initial conditions. Of course, that is quite compatible with the idea of its being causally predictable by some super-intelligence; and hence of such events being foreshadowed for us in some other manner (by the cleft in an ox-liver, for instance).

What is at issue here is the nature of the divinatory sign. Sign-theory and its ramifications are fully treated elsewhere in this volume.[40] But crudely the issue is this. In the case of a certain type of sign, the so-called indicative sign, the sign-event is such that it is more than materially tied to that which it signifies. The sign is a sign in virtue of a determinate causal relationship which holds between it and what it signifies (further conditions also need to be fulfilled – but they need not concern us). By contrast, a commemorative sign merely serves to call to mind that of which it is a signifier: there may be, but crucially need not be, any causal connection between the two.

This distinction lies behind Chrysippus' famous attempt to evade the unpalatable implications of treating divinatory 'theorems' as conditionals in the Stoic sense. If

(T5) whoever is born at the rising of the Dog-star will not die at sea

is such a theorem, and Fabius was born at that time, then

(16) if Fabius was born at the rising of the Dog-star, Fabius will not die at sea

looks as though it is a sound conditional, a simple substitution instance of (T5). But, given the Stoics' own account of its truth-conditions,[41] for (16) to be sound there must be a connection of relevance (it is tempting to say causal relevance) between antecedent and consequent – the consequent is true in virtue of the antecedent's truth. But (16) does not appear to satisfy that condition, since Fabius' being born at that time does not seem to be a

---

[39] Alex. *Fat.* 172.12, 173.13, 174.1; *SVF* II 965–71.
[40] See above, pp. 286–94 and below, pp. 611–3.   [41] See above, pp. 106–8.

cause of his avoiding a watery grave. Hence Chrysippus reformulated such propositions as negated conjunctions:

(16*) it is not the case both that Fabius is born at the rising of the Dog-star and that he dies at sea.

Cicero, who reports this (*Fat.* 15), also ridicules it – why cannot doctors and geometricians simply do the same with their own theorems:

> What is there that cannot be carried over in that sort of way from the form of a necessary consequence to that of a negated conjunction? (Cic. *Fat.* 16)

But he misses the point, which is that such reformulations carry no commitment to there being any necessary relationship between the two component propositions (or perhaps more accurately if there is a necessary relation between them it is derivative, not direct). This does not imply that there can be no causal relation between them (they may, for example, be collateral effects of some more remote cause), although for reasons briefly canvassed earlier it does not seem that there need be. Thus, Cicero's jocularity notwithstanding, Chrysippus is making a serious point with his plea for reformulation.

IX Soft determinism

None of the Stoics wished to invoke their determinism to exonerate the wrong-doer; indeed, their stern morality lays great store by the individual's own efforts at self-improvement and moral progress. But the suspicion still remains that, for all Chrysippus' attempts to find a middle way between hard determinism and the causal chaos of the Epicurean swerve, there is something missing in the determinist's universe, namely the justification for punishment and reward – the sense in which things are, for them, *eph' hēmin* is not strong enough to bear the weight of moral evaluation. To be sure, the determinist can explain why they occur; perhaps he can even do so in terms of their beneficial effects (by developing an evolutionary theory of them, for instance). Crimes may still be punished *pour encourager les autres*; deterrence works, indeed perhaps works best, in a determinist cosmos. Furthermore, a determinist is not debarred by his views from attempting to reform a criminal, or from protecting society from him. But the notion of desert seems to be in bad order – and the ancients were not prepared readily to abandon it. Let us conclude by examining some texts which bear upon the issue.

The Stoics adduce a number of arguments in order to defend their thesis of the compatibility of moral judgement with their form of determinism. First of all they argue that, since such judgements arise of necessity out of the natural order, they must themselves be natural – it is part of our natures to praise and blame. Man is rational, mortal – and censorious:

> They [i.e. the Stoics] suppose that everything naturally constituted is such as it is in accordance with fate, 'natural' being the same thing as 'in accordance with fate', and they add 'consequently it will be in accordance with fate that animals have perceptions and impulses. And some animals will be merely active, while others will perform rational actions. And some will do wrong, while others will do right actions. For these are natural to them. But so long as wrong and right actions remain, and their natures and qualities are not removed, there also remain commendations and censures, punishments and honours. For such are the sequence and order to which they are subject.' (Alex. *Fat.* 205.24–206.2; cf. 207.5–21)

Right and wrong actions are just as much written into the causal sequence of things as anything else; and so, consequently, are their consequences. Zeno's slave has no right to complain. This raises some immediate questions. Alexander himself asks pertinently how the concepts of right and wrong can retain any content in the Stoic universe. It is precisely because, he avers, the actions which invite moral appraisal are up to us in the sense of not being externally compelled that we can meaningfully label them right or wrong. But such a position is not open to the Stoics, since whatever they say, all actions are compelled (Alex. *Fat.* 206.2–207.3).

Alexander effectively challenges the Stoics to show not merely how such institutions might be explained, but how they can retain their moral value. The Stoics can, he allows, give a natural history of their genesis – but to give a natural historical explanation is precisely to explain them away, to show how they can have the appearance of content without actually possessing any: but that is hard, and not soft, determinism.

The Stoics cannot, I think, avoid accepting some shift in the content of these moral notions. It is a further question how damaging that shift need be, and whether it need empty them of all recognizable evaluative content. The following is a sketch only of what the Stoics need to say on the issue (whether they actually did or not is a further question). They borrow from Aristotle the notion of natural hierarchy of functions; and like him they interpret this in a teleological fashion (the differences between Aristotelian and Stoic teleology need not detain us). Different animals do different things: and what they do uniquely or best is their proper or definitive function. It is their nature for them to act thus; and hence it is right for them to do so. Man censures; hence it is right for man to be censorious.

It is not difficult, however, to see where that argument is vulnerable. First of all, the Stoics can be accused of an equivocation on the notion of rightness here. Perhaps 'right' just means 'fitting' or 'appropriate'; in that sense it is clearly right for a carving-knife to slice meat, and wrong to use it to slice flesh. And, at a stretch, you might censure people who do so for misusing their tools. But it would be absurd to censure the knife itself, since its capacity is merely instrumental; and yet it is difficult to see how, in the Stoic cosmos, human beings have any morally richer role simply in virtue of their structural complexity.

But the Stoics have a further line of defence. Divine providence sees that the world is a hierarchy not merely of functions but of good ones. But if that is the case, surely we can view the gradual approximation of the world to a perfect condition as being itself a good thing. Thus there is a further sense over and above their mere functionality why it is good that knives cut, or men blame: it is part of the benevolent, providential ordering of things; God has made things as good (compatible with the material restraints imposed upon him: Epict. *Diss.* 1.1.7–12, following Plato *Tim.* 29e–30b; 75a–c) as they could possibly be.[42] But the Stoics notoriously held that everything that occurred was good (see e.g. Marc. Aurel. IV.10, 23, 26; cf. II.3; and cf. Chrysippus' attitude to bed-bugs);[43] consequently, it is not a mere fact that we praise and blame – it is good that we do so; praise and blame are part of the causal working of the best of all possible worlds. But if that is right, how can the Stoics differentiate between good and bad actions? Since the world is as good as it could be (sc. at this particular time), and since its evolution is towards a state of perfection, and since every event that occurs within it is part of and contributes towards that evolution, every event must be good.

The Stoics are in some sense committed, I believe, to that. But they are not debarred thereby from developing a non-trivial conception of the relative rightness and wrongness of individual actions and events which relies on the distinction between temporally-indexed and timeless judgements of worth. Let us consider some action that would be considered wrong, both conventionally and by the Stoics (for the Stoics notoriously do not subscribe to a conventional morality: S.E. *PH* III.200–1, 205–6,

---

[42] The limitations on creative possibility supplied by material recalcitrance common to the Platonic, Stoic, and Galenic view of providential creation allows them to sidestep some of the notorious difficulties associated with maintaining that ours is the best of all possible worlds: see Hankinson 1989.   [43] See above, pp. 467, 504.

etc.): premeditated murder, for example. A murder is an event, and hence datable. Suppose x kills y at spatio-temporal region s. We may consider the action either as (a) a murder *tout court*, or as (b) a murder-at-s. Other things being equal, murder is wrong; hence *sub specie* (a) we condemn it; however viewed *sub specie* (b), it is an event conducive towards the perfection of the world, and hence we can welcome it, not because it is an action of the type that it is (that is still reprehensible), but simply because it is so conducive. We can even add a little further flesh to that: the truth-maker for the claim that the action is wrong is the fact that when the world attains its most developed condition there will no (a)-type acts, which allows us to evaluate (b) the way we do.

Thus the Stoics can rescue a non-trivial sense in which actions can be genuinely evaluated. But of course it is one thing to evaluate the act – quite another to evaluate the agent as being responsible. Here, I think, the opponents of the Stoics can make out their case. As a Stoic, I can think that you are a frightful bore; I can wish it were otherwise; and I can look forward to the blessed day when the world will contain only interesting people. But it seems unfair to hold you any more responsible for that than you are for your basic physical nature.

x Fate and moral progress

Finally I turn to the issue of how the Stoic view of moral progress relates to their determinism. Earlier I distinguished determinism of the Stoic type from fatalism, the view that no matter what you do, your fate is bound to be thus and so. The Stoics do, however, appear at times to stray close to a position that resembles at least a limited fatalism. This is most apparent in their famous comparison of human fate to a dog tied behind a cart – it can choose to go willingly along, or it can choose to resist: but either way the end result is the same (Hipp. *Ref.* 1.21). That appears to suggest that, contrary to the burden of the argument so far, the Stoics conceive of human beings as having a sort of Humean liberty of spontaneity. They cannot choose how things will be; but they can choose, and apparently in some strong sense, whether or not to like it. Thus human choices are in a sense genuine – but they are causally insulated from the working of the world.

But if what has gone before is even remotely correct, that cannot be right. The dog and cart image is not a particularly happy one, precisely because it does have these fatalistic overtones: none the less it can be interpreted consistently with a non-fatalist view of the structure of causation.

The point is primarily, I think, about our attitude to our projects. The Stoics held that, until we actually arrive at the condition of the sage, in which we will simply never make mistakes, every expression of projected action should be hedged with a mental rider, a 'reservation (*huphexairesis*)' to the effect 'God willing'. I should want to do things only on condition that they will as a matter of fact take place (and hence by definition are part of the unravelling of fate). What the Stoic aims to do is to bring his own impulses and desires as closely as possible into harmony with the way things are actually going to go; he will not strive for the impossible. Now that can be interpreted fatalistically, if one assumes that the way things are going to go is fixed independently of human decisions and desires. But it does not require such an interpretation; and all that we have seen of the Stoic position so far tells against it. As I approach moral perfection, the extent to which my desires will be frustrated will diminish. In the perfect world there will be no such frustrations at all. And the Stoics hold that the world is evolving towards such perfection. Of course its evolution is determined – and part of that evolution is driven by human desires and their frustrations. But, as we have seen, we can make sense of the claim that it is good that there are such frustrations even though frustrations are not good. That position is coherent, and non-fatalistic (it does not assert that things would have been the same whatever decisions were made). Whether there is anything else to be said for it is, however, another matter.

16

Epicurean psychology

STEPHEN EVERSON

1 Introduction

In an age which has produced much agonizing over how to reconcile the
life of the mind with a materialist physics, we are likely to feel an immediate affinity with an earlier theorist who combined the project of explaining human psychology with a commitment to the claim that 'the totality
of things is bodies and void' (*Ep. Hdt.* 39). In common with the vast majority of modern psychologists and philosophers of mind, Epicurus was
committed to atomistic materialism – and indeed, unlike that of most
modern psychologists and philosophers, his commitment actually
extended to arguing for the truth of that position. It was not a thesis
which he accepted merely on authority. Like that of Aristotle in the generation before him, Epicurus' psychology needs to be seen as part of an
attempt to provide a complete natural philosophy. At least part of what he
has to say about the *psuchē* is directly intended to show that his atomic
theory is capable of explaining such complex natural phenomena as perception, thought and action.[1] All of what he has to say is intended to be
consistent with that physical theory.

This, however, places fewer constraints on what will count as a successful theory of the relation between the mental and the physical than is
sometimes supposed. We are perhaps apt to be over-impressed by
Epicurus' espousal of atomism and to assume that, just by accepting the
thesis that all material objects are divisible into atomic parts, he took on
the task of showing that all the properties of material objects can be

---

[1] I leave *psuchē* (plural: *psuchai*) transliterated: there is no satisfactory English translation,
although 'soul' has come close to being orthodox. In its widest sense, it is that which is responsible for life – so, in Aristotle, even plants have *psuchai*. Although this wide usage is preserved in
some Epicurean texts (thus Diogenes of Oenoanda states that the *psuchē* 'provides nature with
the reason for the (presence or) absence of life' (fr. 37 Smith)), Epicurus' interest is more
restricted than Aristotle's, focusing on those living creatures which are capable of sensation or
perception. For the general Hellenistic restriction of the activities of the *psuchē*, see Annas
1992a, 8–10.

reduced to the states and movements of those parts. It is important to recognize from the start that such reductionism is not forced on Epicurus by his commitment to atomism – which is a thesis about the nature of matter and not a metaphysical thesis about the nature of substances and their properties. The acceptance of an atomic physics provides no greater pressure to identify substances with their matter or to reduce all properties to the properties of matter than does the acceptance of the claim that matter is continuous. It may turn out that Epicurus did make reductionist claims of this sort but he was certainly under no atomist obligation to do so.

Determining what relation Epicurus does in fact take to obtain between mental events and physical events is not, as will become apparent, a straightforward matter. Before pursuing this in more detail, however, it is necessary to put some basic theses of Epicurean psychology into play.

II The *psuchē*

In the *Letter to Herodotus*, his own summary of his philosophy of natural science, Epicurus deals with the *psuchē* once he has outlined the nature of atomic motion. He begins his account with a re-affirmation of materialism:

> The next thing to see – referring it to the perceptions and affections, since that will provide the strongest confirmation – is that the *psuchē* is a fine-structured body diffused through the whole aggregate [i.e. the animal's whole body], most strongly resembling wind with a certain blending of heat, and resembling wind in some respects but heat in others. But there is that part which differs greatly also from wind and heat themselves in its fineness of structure, a fact which makes it the more liable to co-affection with the rest of the aggregate. (*Ep. Hdt.* 63)

For Epicurus, as for Aristotle, 'bodies' (*sōmata*) are individual substances[2] and so to say that the *psuchē* is *a* body is to make a stronger claim than is required simply to maintain materialism – since that would require no more than the thesis that all living things are bodies. Both Aristotle and Epicurus accept that claim but whereas Aristotle describes the *psuchē* as the 'form' or essence of the living body – so that to say what something's

---

[2] In *Ep. Hdt.* 68–71 he distinguishes between 'permanent attributes' and those which are accidental and twice specifies that the term for the substance itself – 'the whole' – is 'body'. See also above, pp. 379–82.

psuchē is is to say what it is to be that kind of thing – Epicurus places the *psuchē* as an *individuated part* of the body. Like the other bodily parts, such as hearts and livers, the *psuchē* is spatially identifiable and has a distinctive material constitution.[3]

Epicurus' discussion of the *psuchē* takes up only five and a half sections (63–8) of the *Ep. Hdt.* and there is no attempt there to provide a full précis of his psychological theory. In particular, perhaps, little if anything is made of the distinction, apparently drawn elsewhere by Epicurus, between a rational and an irrational part of the *psuchē*.[4] In our fullest and most detailed report of Epicurean psychology, Book III of *De Rerum Natura*, Lucretius distinguishes these parts at the very beginning of his discussion, saying that he will make clear 'the nature of mind (*animus*) and spirit (*anima*)' (III.31–6). At III.94–7, he says that the *animus* is also called the *mens* and is itself a genuine part of the body. The relation between the two parts of the *psuchē* is discussed further at III.136ff:

> My next point is that the mind and the spirit are firmly interlinked and constitute a single nature, but that the deliberative element which we call the mind is, as it were, the chief, and holds sway throughout the body. It is firmly located in the central part of the chest. For that is where fear and dread leap up, and where joys caress us: therefore it is where the mind is. The remaining part of the spirit,[5] which is distributed throughout the body, obeys the mind and moves at its beck and call. (Lucr. III.136–44)

The spirit is thus that part of the *psuchē* which is responsible for producing movement in the body and for making it capable of sensation.

Nevertheless, although the *animus* and the *anima* are distinguishable as parts of the *psuchē*, together they form a unified part of the body – they have, as Lucretius says, a 'single nature'. This unitary nature is emphasized not only in relation to its two parts but also to its constituent atoms. Aëtius provides a succinct report of the Epicurean account of the material constitution of the *psuchē*:

> Epicurus [said that the *psuchē* is] a blend (*krama*) consisting of four things, of which one kind is fire-like, one air-like, one wind-like, while

---

[3] The point is confirmed by Lucr. III.94–7, where he says that the mind (*animus*) is as much a part of the body as are the hands, feet and eyes.

[4] The *Ep. Hdt.* as it is preserved in Diogenes Laertius x, contains an interpolation in 66 which points this out: 'Epicurus says in other works that . . . one part of it, which is dispersed through the rest of the body, is irrational and the other, which is rational, is in the chest, as is evident from fears and joys.'

[5] '*cetera pars animae*': '*anima*' is used both as a term to denote the *psuchē* as a whole and as a term denoting just the irrational part, the *anima* proper (see Lucr. III.421–4).

the fourth is something which lacks a name. This last he made the one responsible for perception. (Aët. IV.3.11)[6]

Whilst these different kinds of atoms are all present in the *psuchē*, however, what allows the *psuchē* to function is the fact that they make up a particular blend which has its own distinctive nature:

> The primary particles of the elements so interpenetrate each other in their motions that no one element can be distinguished and no capacity spatially separated, but they exist as multiple powers of a single body ... Heat, air and the unseen force of wind when mixed form a single nature, along with that mobile power which transmits the beginning of motion from itself to them, the origin of sense-bearing motions through the flesh. (Lucr. III.262-5; 269-72)

The *psuchē*, then, is made of a certain blend of atoms, and, as such, possesses properties lacking in things which do not consist of this particular blend.[7] It is, for instance, capable of maintaining life in a living body, of forming beliefs and of deciding how to act.

The *psuchē* and the body are mutually dependent. One of Epicurus' most cherished doctrines is that the *psuchē* dies with the rest of the body and much attention is paid to establishing this claim. When the *psuchē* ceases to be contained within the body, its constituent atoms dissipate rapidly:

> We must grasp too that the *psuchē* has the major share of responsibility for sensation. On the other hand, it would not be in possession of this if it were not contained in some way by the rest of the aggregate ... Moreover, when the whole aggregate disintegrates the *psuchē* is dispersed and no longer has the same powers, or its motions. Hence it does not possess sensation either. For it is impossible to think of it perceiving while not in this organism, or moving with these motions when what contains it and surrounds it are not of the same kind as those in which it now has these motions. (*Ep. Hdt.* 63; 65-6)

When released from the body, the atoms of the *psuchē* disperse even more rapidly than do those of liquids, or of cloud or smoke (Lucr. III.434-9). The body too will not survive separation from the *psuchē*, although its disintegration is not as immediate as that of the *psuchē*. The *psuchē* is

---

[6] We should not worry that Epicurus makes no mention of air (or air-like) atoms in *Ep. Hdt.* 63, as if he were there committed to the presence of only three types of atom rather than the four reported by Aëtius and Lucretius. In fact, he does not mention any of the *psuchē*'s constituent atoms at all: it is the blend which we should take to resemble wind mixed with heat.

[7] For further discussion of the Epicurean notion of a 'blend' (*krama*), see Kerferd 1971, 89-91. The composition of the *psuchē* is discussed in Annas 1991, 93-5 and 1992a, 137-43.

contained by the whole body, and is itself the body's guardian and cause of its survival; for they cling together with common roots, and manifestly they cannot be torn asunder without destruction. (Lucr. III.323–6)

Not only the two parts of the *psuchē*, but also the *psuchē* and the body form an individual substance: 'since conjunction is necessary to their existence, so also theirs must be a joint nature' (III.347–8). In the *Against Colotes*, Plutarch reports the Epicureans as claiming that a human is made from two things – a body of a certain sort and a *psuchē* (1118d). It is thus the living body, of which the *psuchē* is a part, which is the animal and not the *psuchē* by itself.[8] Lucretius stresses that sensation is an affection which is common to the mind and the body (III.335–6): the presence of the *psuchē* makes the whole body able to enjoy sensation (III.350–69). All of the body has powers it would not have if it did not contain the *psuchē*. As Diogenes of Oenoanda puts it,

It is true that the number of its [i.e. the *psuchē*'s] constituent atoms ... does not equal that of the body; yet it girdles the whole man and, while being itself confined, binds him in its turn, just as the minutest quantity of acid juice binds a huge quantity of milk. (Fr. 37 Smith)[9]

III Physicalism and materialism

With these basic doctrines in place, we can turn to consider Epicurus' status as a materialist and physicalist. Clearly, given his claim that the *psuchē* is a body, there can be no quarrel with applying either of these labels to him, since they are sufficiently vague to apply to almost any philosopher who is not a Cartesian dualist. For such labelling to do any work, however, these terms need to be made precise: they need to be defined when they are employed if they are to further rather than to hinder understanding. Let us say that someone is a materialist if he accepts that all individual substances are composed of matter. On this definition, Epicurus clearly

---

[8] Although see Annas 1991, 92–3, and 1992a, 149–51, for the claim that Epicurus sometimes identifies the person with the rational part of the *psuchē* rather than the living body as a whole, including the *psuchē*. Her principal evidence for this, however, is D.L. x.137, where Epicurus is reported as saying that the pains of the *psuchē* are worse than those of the body because 'the flesh is storm-tossed only in the present, but the *psuchē* in past, present and future'. Annas is quite right to find that the contrast expressed here as that between the *psuchē* and the body is properly that between the rational part of the *psuchē* and the irrational part together with the body. This in itself does not show, however, that Epicurus identifies the person with the rational part of the *psuchē* – any more than it would had Epicurus claimed that ear-ache is more painful than indigestion.   [9] Translation M. F. Smith.

qualifies as a materialist. (This is consistent with his acceptance of the existence of void, since there are in his system no individual substances which are constituted of void.)

'Physicalism' is more difficult to define, if only because it is more frequently, and more variously, used. Clearly, for the application of the term to a theory of the mind to have any point, the theory must give some sort of priority to the physical over the mental – but different physicalist theories may attribute different sorts of priority. So, one type of physicalism is simply an analogue of materialism and holds that all events are physical – that is, they satisfy physical descriptions. This sort of physicalism gives ontological priority to the physical: it maintains that every mental event is identical with some physical event. Alternatively, one can still maintain a physicalist account of the mental whilst denying that mental events are identical with physical events if one accords a causal or explanatory priority to the physical over the mental.

Explanatory physicalism need not, of course, exclude ontological physicalism: someone who accepts the latter is very likely to accept, in McDowell's words, that 'under their physical descriptions, all events are susceptible of total explanations, of the kind paradigmatically afforded by physics, in terms of physical laws and other physically described events'.[10] Explanatory physicalism does not require ontological physicalism, however. Whilst McDowell's characterization of physicalism allows that all events have physical descriptions, it can be modified to accommodate an abandonment of that identity claim. If one accepts that all events are either physical events or are non-causally determined by physical events, then one can maintain that even those events which are not physical can still be explained by reference to physical laws and other, physically described, events.[11] In this case, however, the total explanation would also require reference to specifications of which mental events are determined by which physical events. On such an account, the physical is given

---

[10] McDowell 1980, 128. See McDowell 1985, section 7, for a rejection of ontological physicalism.

[11] Some have found the notion of non-causal determination obscure. What I have in mind is the sort of dependency of the mental on the physical which, following Davidson 1980, 214, is called 'supervenience' – so that, if one set of properties supervene on another, two objects cannot be identical in respect of the latter whilst differing in respect of the former and an object cannot alter in respect of the former without altering in respect of the latter. Thus, if, for instance, we take liquidity to supervene on molecular structure, two substances could not differ in respect of liquidity without differing in molecular structure and a substance could not change in respect of its liquidity without an alteration in its molecular structure. (The example is from Heil 1992, ch. 3.) Thus, although the molecular structure determines the liquidity, we should not say that the structure and the liquidity stand in a causal relation. See, however, Charles 1992 for an important tightening-up of the notion of supervenience.

explanatory priority over the mental, since whilst any mental state or change will be explicable by reference to physical states or changes, the corollary will not be true.

It will be noted that these characterizations of physicalism have not sought to explicate the notion of the physical itself. In fact, that notion is considerably less determinate than is often supposed in discussions of the relation between mental and non-mental events.[12] Whilst mental events can be taken to be those which involve intentionality or consciousness, there are no similar criterial features of physical properties and events. Until we have a complete physics, we do not know which predicates will be required for physical explanations – and so some principle is needed for discriminating physical from non-physical properties. We cannot, however, take physical predicates to be just those which are such as to feature in basic science, since if it turns out that mental properties are not reducible to some other kind of property (and neither ontological nor explanatory physicalism requires the reducibility of the mental), this would mean that mental predicates would feature in basic science and so themselves count as physical predicates. This would hardly be a victory for physicalism.

The problem is that whilst one can ask perfectly good and determinate questions about, say, the relation between the physiological and the chemical, or between the atomic and the sub-atomic, there is no determinate set of 'physical' properties or events such that one can usefully explore the relations between those properties and other sorts. Fortunately, for our present purposes, we do not need to come up with a definition of physical properties and events which will serve to distinguish these from all other sorts of property and event. The present issue is not whether all properties can be reduced or explained in terms of some basic set of properties but just how mental states and events are related to putatively *more* basic states and events. Thus, I shall take it that a description counts as a physical description if it can be satisfied by something which does not satisfy any mental description. The goal of physicalism, then, would be to show either (in the case of ontological physicalism) that one can describe all events without making use of mental descriptions or (for explanatory physicalism) that all events can be explained in non-mental terms – terms, that is, which will be used, more generally, for the description and explanation of non-mental events.

A physicalist theory of the mind, then, can be said to be one which gives

---

[12] See Crane and Mellor 1990.

either or both of ontological and explanatory priority to the physical over the mental. Now, materialism does not by itself require physicalism. One can be a monist about substances, accepting that every substance is a material substance, without being a monist about events. Epicurus' commitment in *Ep. Hdt.* 63 is to materialism not to physicalism, and it is worth noting that the general materialist claim in *Ep. Hdt.* 39 that everything is bodies and void should not be taken to suggest a desire to reduce the behaviour of substances to the behaviour of their atomic parts. His claim is not that only *atoms* and void exist but that only *bodies* and void exist – and, as we have seen, the *psuchē*, for instance, is itself a body. Indeed, Epicurus' argument for his materialist claim requires that the bodies in question are not atoms:

> Moreover, the totality of things is bodies and void. That bodies exist is universally witnessed by perception itself, in accordance with which it is necessary to judge by reason that which is non-evident. (*Ep. Hdt.* 39)

Since we cannot perceive the atoms which constitute solid objects, the bodies referred to here must be those which are constituted by atoms and not the atoms themselves. Epicurus is thus not restricting his ontology to atoms and void but to material objects (which will include atoms) and void.[13]

This is important, since although Epicurus certainly rejects the teleological explanation of the nature of a substance's parts by reference to the nature and activities of the substance,[14] this does not mean that he thinks that the behaviour of a substance can be described simply by making reference to the behaviour of its parts.[15] It remains open to him to accept that certain systems of atoms cannot be understood other than as *systems* of atoms and that their behaviour is not describable merely as the conglomeration of the behaviour of their constitutive atoms (although, again, this is consistent with his thinking that the behaviour of the system can be explained by reference to the interaction of its parts). Atomism is a thesis about the nature of the material constitution of things, it is not a thesis about the nature of the things which have material constitutions. Consistently with his materialism, Epicurus can allow that living bodies

---

[13] The point is made by Sedley 1988, 303.

[14] 'Nothing has been engendered in our body in order that we might be able to use it. It is the fact of its being engendered that creates its use. Seeing did not exist before the lights of the eyes were engendered, nor was there pleading with words before the tongue was created' (Lucr. IV.834–7).

[15] To put it in more Aristotelian terms (which are not Epicurus'): just because Epicurus denies the place of a substance's form in final explanation, he does not have to seek to expunge formal explanation in favour of material explanation.

have properties and act and be acted on in ways which other systems of atoms cannot and that such states and events are not identical with, nor simply sets of, states and events of their constituent atoms.

IV Epicurean physicalism

Whilst Epicurus' psychological materialism may not itself commit him to physicalism, it is less obvious that his arguments for the material nature of the *psuchē* do not presuppose it. For the claim that the *psuchē* is a 'fine-structured body diffused through the whole aggregate' (*Ep. Hdt.* 63) is, after all, a highly theoretical one – despite Epicurus' assurance that it is supported by our perceptions and affections (*pathē*). Certainly, the details of his account are not given in experience. What, then, are the arguments for it? That the *psuchē* has a material constitution is taken to follow from the fact that it can act and be acted upon:

> It is impossible to think of the incorporeal *per se* except as void. And void can neither act nor be acted upon, but merely provides bodies with motion through itself. Consequently, those who say that the *psuchē* is incorporeal are talking nonsense. For if it were like that it would be unable to act or be acted upon in any way, whereas as a matter of fact both these accidental properties are self-evidently discriminable in the *psuchē*. (*Ep. Hdt.* 67)

We know from experience that psychological states can be both causes and effects: that, for instance, my hand's moving towards the cigarette is caused by my desire to smoke and my fear is caused by the sight of the spider. What is changed and what produces change in these cases – the *psuchē* – must be material since only what is material can be an agent or patient of change. Now, this by itself does not imply that the changes which the relevant substances undergo are changes which involve the movement of atoms. What underpins the principle that agents and patients must be material may just be that agency requires contact and that for two things to be in contact, they must both be material.[16] Unless mental causation required atomic changes, however, it would be difficult to see what could motivate this requirement – and when Epicurus turns to argue that the *psuchē* has the particular constitution it does, it becomes apparent that he subscribes to some kind of physicalist theory of mental activity.[17]

So, Lucretius cites, for instance, the quickness of the mind as evidence

---

[16] Lucretius, in arguing for the corporeality of the *psuchē*, makes the point that the sort of changes which it effects – the movement of the limbs, for instance – require contact (Lucr. III.161–7).

[17] On Epicurus and causal explanation in general, see above, pp. 498–503.

that the *animus* is 'exceedingly delicate and is constituted by exceedingly minute particles' (III.179–80):

> Nothing is seen to be done so swiftly as the mind determines it to be done and initiates; therefore the mind rouses itself more quickly than any of the things whose nature is seen plain before our eyes. But that which is so readily moved must consist of seeds exceedingly rounded and exceedingly minute, that they may be moved when touched by a small moving power. (Lucr. III.182–8)

Lucretius moves from a datum of experience – that the mind produces its effects more rapidly than any non-psychological cause produces its effect – and argues that this shows that the atoms of the *psuchē* are smaller and rounder than any other atoms. This rests on the general principle that the smaller and rounder an atom is the more easily it is affected: 'so, insofar as bodies are extremely small and smooth, they enjoy mobility; but, alternatively, whatever is found to be heavier and rougher, is that much the more stable' (III.199–202).[18] Thus, since the mind is tremendously mobile, its atoms must be very small and round.

This argument only goes through, however, if mental change requires change at the atomic level – if mental changes could occur without changes to the atoms of the *psuchē*, there would be no need for the atoms of the *psuchē* to be able to move at the speed with which an intention, say, leads to action. This does not show that Epicurus accepts that my currently having a desire, for instance, is identical with the atoms of my *psuchē* having a certain arrangement but it does suggest strongly that Epicurus accepts that atomic change determines mental change. He must accept that any mental change requires an atomic change – otherwise the demand that the *psuchē*'s atoms are the most mobile atoms would be unsupported – and, unless he takes it that a substance's atomic changes determine its mental changes, he would seem to be committed to an unmotivated parallelism between mental and atomic changes.

Lucretius' elucidation of how the *psuchē* initiates action at IV.877ff. confirms that atomic causation indeed underpins mental causation:

> Now I shall tell you . . . how it comes about that we can take steps forward when we want to, how we have the power to move our limbs, and what it is that habitually thrusts forward this great bulk that is our body. First, let me say, images (*simulacra*) of walking impinge on our mind and

---

[18] This is supported by a comparison of volatility of water with that of honey and the ease with which poppy seeds are blown around by wind with the stability enjoyed by stones. Water and poppy seeds are constituted by smaller and rounder atoms than are honey and stones.

strike it, as I explained earlier.[19] It is after this that volition occurs. For no one ever embarks upon any action before the mind first previews what it wishes to do, and for whatever it is that it previews there exists an image of that thing. So when the mind stirs itself to want to go forwards, it immediately strikes all the power of the spirit distributed all over the body throughout all the limbs and frame: it is easily done because the spirit is firmly interlinked with it. Then the spirit in turn strikes the body, and thus gradually the whole bulk is pushed forward and moved.
(Lucr. IV.877–91)

Action (generally) involves the movement of our limbs. The explanation of action, then, must show how the limbs are moved and this requires reference to physical causation. The *animus strikes* the *anima* which in turn strikes the body thus causing it to move.

What we are given here is an explanation of action in which both atomic and mental terminology is employed. The *animus* obtains an image of what is intended and there is then a volition: this gives rise to movement in the *anima* which causes movement in the limbs. Now, it might seem that this is quite consistent with a theory in which autonomous mental events (the reception of the image and the volition) cause atomic events (the movement of the spirit and the limbs) without any underlying atomic causation. There is, however, strong reason to doubt the putative autonomy of the mental here. The 'images' are indeed images in that they are pictures of what they represent – but they are also structures of very fine atoms. The solid objects around us are constantly emitting films of very fine and very quick-moving atoms whose arrangement is determined by the shape of the object from which they come.[20] In order to perceive an object – or even to think of it – one needs to receive an image of it. The ability to be affected by these is itself a sign of the *psuchē*'s being constituted by very small atoms since if it were not, it could not be moved by the tiny atoms which make up the image (Lucr. III.425–30). This, then, posits an *atomic* change in the case of the reception of images: the atoms of the *psuchē* have to be sufficiently small to be moved by the atoms coming in from outside. Whilst in the case of perception, it is the *anima* which is initially affected, in the case of thought, it seems that it is the *animus* itself (see Lucr. IV.745–8). Thus, in both perception and thought, the relevant part of the *psuchē* needs to undergo atomic change if it is to receive the required image. Mental change cannot occur without atomic change.

---

[19] Lucr. IV.722–75. Epicurus' term is *eidōla*.

[20] See *Ep. Hdt.* 46; 47; 49; and Lucr. IV.722–75. Epicurus' theory of perception is discussed in Striker 1977, C. C. W. Taylor 1980, Asmis 1984, chs. 6–7, Everson 1990b and Annas 1992a, ch. 7.

Lucretius also explains the onset of emotions in terms of the effective predominance of the different kinds of atom in the *animus*:

> The *animus* also has that kind of heat which it takes on when it boils with anger and the eyes shine with a fiercer flame; it has plenty of cold wind, the companion of fear, which excites fright in the limbs and rouses the frame; and it has that state of the still air which is found in a tranquil chest and in a calm face. (Lucr. III.288–93)[21]

In none of these examples does Lucretius explicitly *identify* the emotion with the material state, but it is at least clear that he takes those atomic states to be constantly associated with their respective emotions. More particularly, it seems that the explanation for the effects of the emotion will make reference to the accompanying material state – it is the cold, the 'companion' of fear, which excites the limbs. Now, neither Epicurus nor Lucretius provides any general specification of the precise relation between mental events and atomic events but the view which is suggested by this is one in which, whilst there are not mental–atomic identities, nevertheless mental events are determined by what happens to the atoms which make up the *psuchē*. That the *animus* is hot, say, is sufficient for anger and, since anger is always accompanied by this material state, it is also necessary. The anger is not an effect of the heating but rather at least supervenes upon it and may be identical with it.[22] Even if this does not make mental states or events identical with atomic states or events (although this is still open to Epicurus), it nevertheless offers a firmly physicalist account of the mind, since a person's mental states are determined by the states of his atoms and atomic change is required for mental change. If this is Epicurus' view, then he would not allow that an animal could have had the same atomic but a different mental history.

v Voluntary action

Unless Epicurus accepted at least a physicalism according to which atomic change is explanatorily prior to mental change, he would not be able to draw the conclusions he does about the material constitution of the *psuchē*. It would be unfortunate, then, if, when he comes to defend

---

[21] He goes on to explain the possession of different emotional dispositions in terms of different material constitutions of the *psuchai* of different species (III.294–306). Epicurus, it seems, agrees with the Aristotelian thesis that the material basis of anger involves boiling, although whereas Aristotle takes it to be the blood around the heart which boils, Epicurus, in taking the *psuchē* to be a body, can attribute the boiling to the *psuchē* itself.

[22] For the relation of supervenience, see above, n. 11.

human responsibility against a certain kind of determinism, he were to have renounced physicalism – yet this is just what some have taken him to have done in *On Nature* Book 25.[23] So, David Sedley has argued that the account of mental states presented there is that of 'radically emergent properties'; properties which emerge given a certain degree of material complexity. So, 'matter can, [Epicurus] holds, acquire entirely new, non-physical properties, not governed by the laws of physics'.[24] Although mental states fall outside the laws governing the behaviour of atoms, they are not causally inert but can actually bring about changes at the atomic level. On this interpretation, Epicurus turns out to hold a decidedly non-physicalist view of the mental. Not only are mental states and events not to be identified with atomic states and events but they have a causal power which is independent of the atoms of which the person is constituted. The mental is not even supervenient on the atomic – so that an animal can undergo mental change without needing to undergo atomic change and two animals could share all relevant atomic properties but differ mentally.[25]

Fortunately, whilst Epicurus is certainly concerned in these fragments to validate our preconception (*prolēpsis*) that we are responsible for our actions, it is far from obvious that he seeks to achieve this through any denial of physicalism.[26] What encourages the view that Epicurus denies physicalism in *On Nature* Book 25 is that he draws a contrast between a person's atomic constitution and what he calls 'developments' which happen to the person. We are responsible for actions when they come about because of such developments:

> These (developments) are therefore a main target of our attacks and criticisms, because we ... behave in accordance with the original, disturbing nature, as is the case with animals as a whole. For the nature of the atoms

[23] See above, pp. 523–4. We have a series of papyrus fragments (*PHerc.* 697, 1056, 1191) which deal with voluntariness and responsibility and which come from Epicurus' *On Nature*. Sedley 1974 argued that the book was either 5, 25, or 35 and Laursen 1987 has managed to read the title of *PHerc.* 697 so that it says 'Epicurus on Nature 25'. Readings of these texts are given in Arrighetti 1973 (Arr.²) in section [34] – and I will use this numbering for reference here. Laursen 1987 also argued that three further papyri should be taken to come from this book: *PHerc.* 419, 1420 and 1634. See now Laursen 1995.

[24] Sedley 1988, 322–3. See also his 1983b and Long and Sedley 1987, vol. I, 109–10.

[25] Cf. Long and Sedley 1987, vol. I, 110. That this is still consistent with taking Epicurus to be a materialist only shows how little that position commits one to. Long and Sedley themselves note that 'the familiar "materialist" label is beginning to fit Epicurus less neatly' – but it is not entirely clear what materialism is intended to amount to here.

[26] Indeed, because of the difficulties involved both in reading and in interpreting these texts, it cannot be said that anything is obvious in them. Given this, there is in any case some reason to hesitate before using them to build interpretations which are not already secured by other, more tractable, texts.

never did help them in any way to (perform) certain acts or to (develop) certain dimensions of acts and dispositions, but the developments themselves were fully or for the most part responsible for these particulars ... Consequently, whenever something develops which takes on some distinction among the atoms in a differential way which is not like that from another distance, it/he acquires the cause out of it/himself;[27] then it/he gives it on immediately until it comes to the first natures and in some way makes all of it one.[28] (Ep. *Nat.* xxv, [34] 21–2 Arr.²)

One thing should be obvious from the translation here and this is that the text is not one which is easily construed either in detail or even in terms of its general line of argument. Epicurus is addressing someone who seeks to excuse bad behaviour by explaining it as the result of atomic causation. Epicurus' response is to distinguish between behaviour which is to be explained by reference to someone's atomic nature and behaviour which is brought about by 'developments' which occur, or have occurred, to that person.

It is tempting to find in Epicurus' talk of such developments the postulation of non-atomic properties or events – 'emergent' properties which are neither identical with nor determined by the states of a person's constituent atoms but which nevertheless produce effects on those atoms. The threat to responsibility posed by atomic determinism would thus be averted since there would be events which were themselves 'not governed by the laws of physics'[29] – such as volitions – but which are able to initiate the movements of atoms. When behaviour is caused by these events, then it would be behaviour for which the agent is responsible and which is done freely. On this reading, Epicurus' solution depends upon leaving mental events and states undetermined by atomic events since, if they were atomically determined they would thereby be brought within the laws of physics and the determinist's case would not be met. The physicalism assumed in the *Ep. Hdt.* could only be maintained at the cost of denying human responsibility – and that would violate our *prolēpseis*.[30]

Such a reading of the passage from *On Nature* Book 25 is not forced on us, however, and if it can be read in such a way that it does not deny physicalism, this would clearly be preferable. One point which can immediately be noted is that Epicurus is concerned in these texts not with

---

[27] It is not obvious what the subject of the sentence is. Long and Sedley understand it as the agent, but this is doubted by Laursen 1988, 14–15.

[28] The translation is adapted from that given in Laursen 1988, with some help from that given in Annas 1993b, 56–7. Long and Sedley's translation is given as their 20B1–5. See above, pp. 523–4.

[29] See Sedley 1988, 322.   [30] *Prolēpseis* are one of the criteria of truth according to Epicurus.

freedom as such but rather with responsibility: his aim here is to show that we are accountable for our actions and not that our actions are undetermined. The determinism he is attacking is one which seeks to deny moral responsibility by claiming that human actions are really only the result of *atomic* causation. Epicurus can attack this argument without having to take on determinist claims more generally. Indeed, when Epicurus was concerned to deny determinism as such, he seems to have done so by postulating indeterminacy precisely at the atomic and not the psychological level. Thus, according to Cicero,

> Epicurus thinks that the necessity of fate is avoided by the swerve of atoms . . . That this swerve occurs without a cause he is forced to admit in practice even if not in so many words . . . Epicurus' reason for introducing this theory was his fear that, if the atom's motion was always the result of natural and necessary weight, we would have no freedom, since the mind would be moved in whatever way it was compelled by the motion of atoms. (Cic. *Fat.* 22–3)

It is quite clear from this report that Epicurus accepted that unless there were indeterminacy at the atomic level, psychological states and events would be determined by atomic motion. If it were Epicurean doctrine that determinism was false because mental events have a causal power which is independent of atomic causation, then Cicero's report would be seriously misleading.[31]

Rather than seeing Epicurus' argument in the fragments of *On Nature* 25 as directed against the position that all events are determined, one should rather take it as denying the more specific claim that the explanation of action should properly only make reference to events described in terms of the movement of atoms. In a second, and even more difficult, fragment from *On Nature* 25, Epicurus seems to maintain that it is sufficient to defeat his determinist opponent to show that what is explained is human action and that such behaviour is caused by the psychological states of the agent rather than (just) by the movements of the agent's constituent atoms:

> For this sort of account is self-refuting, and can never prove that everything is of the kind called 'necessitated'; but he debates this very ques-

---

[31] Cicero, of course, is a somewhat hostile critic but his report is confirmed by Lucr. ii.251–60, where again the claim is made that unless there is a type of atomic motion which 'breaks the decrees of fate', then there will not be free volition. If mental events were neither supervenient on, nor identical with, atomic events but were nevertheless able to produce atomic effects, there would be no need to introduce the swerve. For fuller discussion of the role of the swerve, see above, pp. 522–6.

tion on the assumption that his opponent is responsible for talking nonsense. And even if he goes on to infinity saying that this action of his is in turn necessitated, always appealing to arguments, he is not taking it [sc. his thesis] into account so long as he goes on imputing to himself the responsibility for having reasoned correctly and to his opponent that for having reasoned incorrectly. But unless he were to stop attributing his action to himself and to pin it on necessity instead, he would not even be ... (Ep. *Nat.* xxv, [34] 28 Arr.[2])

The determinist, who claims that everything is 'necessitated', is inconsistent if he judges his opponent for, as he sees it, reasoning incorrectly. This would require that the opponent is responsible for the reasoning and so would be inconsistent with his denial of human responsibility. His opponent, however, has no trouble in this respect, since he is precisely maintaining that agents are responsible for their actions. There is no reason to take the responsibility in question here to be other than causal (and hence moral) responsibility and, if this is right, then a 'necessitated' event is not just any event which is causally determined but an event which is determined by atomic motion *rather than* by an agent's volition.[32]

Read in this way, these texts need present no straightforward difficulty for Epicurean physicalism.[33] Epicurus would not be denying that mental events are determined by atomic events nor asserting that there can be mental causation in the absence of atomic causation. Rather, he would be emphasizing that one cannot understand the behaviour of certain systems of atoms – i.e. humans – without describing it as the behaviour of a *system* – i.e. of the person – and so as having psychological causes. In any case of psychological causation, there will be events at the atomic level without which the psychological events would not occur, but a proper explanation cannot be given unless it makes reference to the psychological events – and these latter events are not identical with any of the atomic events. The mental is ineliminable but it is not causally autonomous.[34]

---

[32] Later in the passage, Epicurus seems to say that if the determinist were to call an event 'necessitated' in virtue of its being brought about by the agent then he would be changing the meaning of the word – see *Nat.* xxv, [34] 29 Arr.[2]

[33] The reading also removes the need to determine the precise contrast between the developments and the constitution of the atoms. As Annas notes (1993b, 58), the constitution could be understood either as the animal's original constitution – i.e. that with which it is born – or to 'the constitution, on each occasion, prior to the information received from the environment'. Her paper provides a much fuller discussion of these issues than is possible here.

[34] The shortness of this discussion obviously belies both the importance and the difficulty of these texts. Detailed discussion of Long and Sedley's interpretation can be found in Laursen 1988 and there is further discussion in Annas 1991, 1992a and 1993b.

VI Conclusion

Epicurus' arguments for his claims about the atomic constitution of the *psuchē* require a physicalism about mental events. His arguments against the denial of responsibility to humans require that mental events be cited in the causal explanation of certain actions. What needs to be shown is what the relation between mental and atomic events is if mental events can act as causes without being causally autonomous. Earlier, I drew a distinction between what I called 'ontological physicalism' and 'explanatory physicalism': according to the first, mental events are a species of physical event and themselves satisfy physical descriptions. Explanatory physicalism, in contrast, does not require that mental events should be identical with physical events – merely that all events should be explicable by reference to physical events. Thus, even if one denied, say, that the action of my raising my arm (a mental event) were identical with my arm's rising or any other physical event (or set of physical events), one could still maintain that the action can be explained by reference to certain physical events – those on which it supervenes. The problem for a theorist who maintains this sort of account, however, is in securing the place of mental events within the causal scheme. For if all events are either physical events or supervene on physical events and all physical events have physical events as causes (if they are caused at all), then the only events which will enter into causal explanations will be physical events. Although mental events will be determined by physical events (the physical history of the world could not have been the same and the mental history different), this will be a non-causal determination. Even a complete causal explanation of every event which has occurred would have no place for mental events. The only way to secure a place for mental events within causal explanation would be to allow gaps in the causal chain of physical events – gaps which would be filled by mental events. This would be to give up physicalism.

For a theorist such as Aristotle, who maintains the teleological claim that the relevant physical events happen in order to instantiate the mental events which they constitute, there may be a way round this problem.[35] This sort of teleological claim, however, is explicitly rejected by Epicurus and there is no sign of his having attempted to fill the gap it would leave in accommodating the mental within the causal scheme of things. In the light of this, we have reason to find in Epicurus not merely an explanatory but also an ontological physicalism. The events studied by the Epicurean

---

[35] See Everson 1994b, *ad fin.*, for a brief discussion of this possibility.

psychologist would then be a species of the events susceptible to physical
enquiry. Mental events are not causally inert since they are identical with
atomic events and these are not causally inert. Although it would be possible to provide a causal explanation of any event merely by reference to its
physical causes, one would not understand the behaviour of people *as* the
behaviour of responsible agents (which we know they are) without making
use of the mental descriptions which certain physical events satisfy.[36]

[36] I have benefited from the comments of Hugh Johnstone on an earlier version of this section.

17

Stoic psychology

A. A. LONG

1 Introduction

As the previous chapter has shown, Epicurean psychology is physicalist in ways that have some affinity to contemporary use of that explanatory model. The Stoic theory is harder to characterize though no less intriguing so far as scientific and philosophical issues are concerned. Modern western thinkers are likely to find the Stoics to be considerably more sophisticated than the Epicureans in analysing the faculties and subjective content of the mind but less plausible than their rivals in accounting for the mind's ontological foundations. By way of introduction, we may note some striking similarities and differences between the two theories.

Like the Epicureans, the Stoics identify the principle of sentient life with a corporeal *psuchē*.[1] In both theories the *psuchē* is distributed throughout the limbs and organs of the animal, whether human or non-human. Like the Epicureans again, they draw a sharp distinction between the human mind (which they call 'thought' or the 'governing part' of the *psuchē*), located in the heart,[2] and the rest of the *psuchē* (the 'spirit' in Lucretius' Epicurean terminology), situated in all the other parts of the body. Ignoring differences of detail concerning the relation between the mind and the rest of the *psuchē*, we have something broadly analogous in both theories to the modern allocation of functions to the brain and the central nervous system respectively.

The physical constituency of the Stoic *psuchē*, together with its functional division into governing and instrumental parts, differentiates it sharply from the psychology of Aristotle as well as Plato. However, the Stoics' similarity in these respects to Epicurus should not be over-emphasized. Epicurus, as I understand him, takes mental capacity to be a supervenient property of the atomic aggregate which constitutes human

---

[1] For a selection and brief discussion of the basic texts, see Long and Sedley 1987, vol. 1, 313–23; for further treatment, see Annas 1992a, 37–70.   [2] See below, p. 567.

and non-human animals as the living bodies that they are. Atoms as such are lifeless bodies. In Stoicism by contrast, life and mind are not properties that supervene on physical principles which are inanimate themselves. Taken as a whole, the world at its most basic level of existence, according to the Stoics, is an intelligent organism. The world's 'active principle', also called God, is irreducibly physical *and* mental. The Stoic God is not a body primarily and a mind secondarily. It is his nature to be an intelligent body.[3]

The term that will get us on this track in approaching the Stoic theory of mind is vitalism. They identify the entire *psuchē*, of which the 'governing part' in humans is mind, with *pneuma*. This gaseous substance permeates all the world's grosser 'matter' (Alex. *Mixt.* 216. 14–17).[4] Since *pneuma*, viewed universally, is identical to God, the intelligent life of God is omnipresent throughout the world (D.L. VII.137–8). This does not mean that *pneuma* confers an individual life or mind on every part of the world where it is present. The *psuchē* is *pneuma* that has a special kind of constituency or 'tension'. This particular *pneuma* begins its life at the birth of the animal. Yet unlike the Epicurean *psuchē*, the Stoic animating principle, at least in the case of humans, is a living being in its own identity as *psuchē* (Stob. II.65.1–2). Although it permeates and acts in conjunction with the organic parts of the body, the mental life that the Stoic *psuchē* facilitates to the whole organism is its own property. In human beings, as distinct from other animals, the pneumatic *psuchē* withdraws from the body at death and survives on its own for a time.

The Stoics have left us little to show what this means and how it is possible.[5] It looks partly like a vestige of Platonism, and comparison with Plato is appropriate for other reasons. While literally corporeal, unlike the Platonic *psuchē*, psychic *pneuma* resembles the world soul of Plato's *Timaeus* (34b) in being 'extended' throughout the entire organism. There is no part of a human or non-human animal's frame that is impervious to its *psuchē*, a point the Stoics illustrated by adducing the way heat can totally interpenetrate a lump of iron (Alex. *Mixt.* 218.1–2). Unlike Epicurean atoms, which are discrete and impenetrable, psychic *pneuma* is literally continuous with the body's matter. Translated into

---

[3] For texts that justify these assertions see D.L. VII.134–6, Aët. 1.7.33, Plu. *Stoic. Rep.* 1052c–d (Zeus or God as the soul of the world); see above, p. 384 and p. 435.   [4] See above, p. 391.

[5] For evidence and discussion of the post-mortem existence of the human *psuchē*, see Hoven 1971. Only the *psuchē* of the wise survives fully intact, up to the end of the world; see Sedley 1992b, 149, who is no doubt right in suggesting that what enables the disembodied *psuchē* of the wise to persist is its perfected rationality which, viewed purely physically, is the strong coherence of its *pneuma*.

Latin as *spiritus*, and influencing the early fathers of the Church, Stoic *pneuma* contributed to the concepts of a spiritual body and the spirit as distinct from the body. Like Plato (and with support from Heraclitus and Plato's Socrates) the Stoics tend to identify a human being with *psuchē*, or at least with the principle's 'governing part'. They trade on this doctrine when they seek to justify the indifference of everything that concerns the body so far as human excellence is concerned.

These general points show that the Stoics have a model of the *psuchē* which is scarcely detachable from the goals of their philosophy as a whole. What they are looking for is a theory that fits their intuitions about *pneuma* physics (which is also the mind-directed structure of the world) and the special faculties human beings have been providentially given as the means of living well in such a world. Their theory of the mind is designed to show not merely what our mental faculties are or how they function but what they are for – to contribute to the rational life of the world, of which our life is a part, by doing everything we can to perfect our nature as rational beings. This amounts to saying that our normative nature as human beings is grounded in our minds as distinct from our bodies.

Given their conception of the mind as the essential bearer of human identity, we can expect the Stoics to advance a theory which emphasizes the unity or potential unity of all mental functioning. The way in fact that they do this was perhaps their greatest contribution to the philosophy of mind. What should be clear, from these preliminary remarks, is that at least three strands are combined in their theory – physicalism that is functionally similar to that of Epicurus, vitalism or pantheism, and an ethical affinity to Platonic dualism. The challenge for a modern interpreter is to keep a proper perspective on all of these strands while, at the same time, remaining sensitive to Stoic contributions which are fruitful irrespective of their role in any general theory of the mind.

11 The physical structure of the *psuchē* and its location in the body

Our evidence for Stoic psychology during the school's creative phase is extremely uneven in its range and detail. For many of the more technical concepts we are dependent on brief and scattered references by compilers or philosophers who were not Stoics. However, on certain matters we are unusually well informed. Thanks to extensive quotations by Galen in his work *On the Doctrines of Plato and Hippocrates* (*PHP*) we can read excerpts of what Chrysippus wrote in two of his lost works, *On the Soul* and *On*

Emotions.[6] Another first-hand source is Hierocles.[7] Though this Stoic philosopher wrote during the second century AD, his systematic remarks on the *psuchē* cohere well with our more summary evidence for earlier Stoicism. What can be gleaned directly from Chrysippus and Hierocles naturally requires supplementation from other material. There is every reason, however, to give their words pride of place.

*

At the beginning of his work entitled *Foundations of Ethics* Hierocles explains how the life of an animal begins at birth when *phusis*, the vegetative principle governing a foetus, is transformed into *psuchē*:

> In the early stages [of a foetus's life] the 'nature' (*phusis*) is *pneuma* of a rather dense kind and considerably distant from *psuchē*; but later, when it is close to birth, it becomes more refined. . . So when it passes outside, it is adequate for the surrounding [air], with the result that, having been hardened thereby, it is capable of changing into *psuchē*. For just as the *pneuma* in stones is immediately kindled by a blow, on account of its readiness for this change, so the *phusis* of a foetus, once it has ripened, does not hesitate to change into *psuchē* on meeting the surrounding [air]. So whatever issues from the womb is at once an animal. (*El. Eth.* col. 1.15–28; cf. Chrysippus, *ap.* Plu. *Stoic. Rep.* 1052f)

The Stoic *psuchē* is the vital principle of animal *as distinct from* plant life. Its basic functions, as Hierocles indicates a few lines later, are sensation (*aisthēsis*) and impulse (*hormē*). Of this pair, sensation is primary, a point emphasized in Stoic descriptions of the *psuchē* as 'sentient exhalation' (*aisthētikē anathumiasis*).[8] Some Greek philosophers, notably Aristotle, had attributed *psuchē* to plants as well as animals.[9] In Aristotelian theory, there is psychic continuity between animals and plants in respect to metabolism and reproduction. Although most Stoics accept reproductive capacity as a part of the *psuchē*, none of them assigns it a part specifically responsible for metabolism.[10] Hierocles, it is true, says that the foetal

---

[6] References are to De Lacy 1984.

[7] For reference to Hierocles I draw on Bastianini and Long 1992a, for an afterthought on which see Bastianini and Long 1992b. Citations in the form col. 1. 21 etc. refer to the column and line numbers of the papyrus.

[8] This account of the *psuchē* goes back to Zeno, and was interpreted by Cleanthes as a mark of the founder's affinity to Heraclitus; cf. Eus. *PE* xv.20.2, and Long 1975–6, 151–2.

[9] Cf. Aristotle *de An.* 11.4.415b23–416b29. Plato does so too in *Tim.* 77b, but the plant *psuchē* has little bearing on Plato's psychology elsewhere.

[10] Panaetius was exceptional in assigning reproduction to 'nature' (Nemes. 212.6–8). This presumably means that he went a step further than his predecessors in narrowing the functions of specifically psychic, i.e. mental, life. See Tieleman 1996, 99.

phusis changes into *psuchē* at birth, but we should not take this to mean that the newly emerging *psuchē* simply inherits the pre-existing work of metabolism.[11] Evidence from elsewhere shows that the Stoics normally attribute this function after birth to vegetative *pneuma* as distinct from psychic *pneuma* (cf. *SVF* II 458, 714, 716). A third kind of *pneuma*, called *hektikon* (*SVF* II 716) and manifested in minerals (as Hierocles observes), is responsible for the coherence of bones and sinews. The three kinds of *pneuma* must be assumed to co-operate in constituting an animal's total coherence and vital functioning. Indeed, we should probably suppose that the heart is the primary location of vegetative as well as psychic *pneuma*. However, the Stoics' main interest is not in details of physiology but in the functions of the *psuchē* as the principle of specifically sentient life.

To translate *pneuma* as breath would misrepresent its highly theoretical nature and peculiar dynamics. Yet, as Hierocles shows, the Stoics have recourse to breath in its everyday sense when they identify the beginning of psychic life with a new-born creature's first inhalation. Blood too has a vital role to play in maintaining the pneumatic nature of the *psuchē*. As we shall see shortly, Chrysippus went to great lengths to defend the heart as the location of the 'governing part' of the *psuchē*. Breath, blood, heart – these make an essential contribution to metabolism and to the 'nourishment' of the *psuchē*, but it is neither identical with them nor supervenient on them.[12] The psychic *pneuma* is an independent physical principle with causal powers intrinsic to itself. What the *psuchē* bestows on an animal, in standard Stoic theory, is not vital capacity in its widest extension but the capacity to behave on the basis of sensation and impulse.

This is a capacity, according to the Stoics, with which human beings as well as other animals, are fully endowed at birth. In the human case, however, the *psuchē* gradually develops the additional capacity of reason (*logos*; Orig. *Princ.* III.1.2–3; D.L. VII.86). It is the presence of reason that

---

[11] For a detailed defence of this point, see Long 1982b, 42–6, and more briefly Annas 1992a, 54. The matter is further explored by Tieleman 1996, esp. 95–9. In a passage of Calcidius (220), purporting to cite Chrysippus, nutrition and growth are included among powers that the parts of the *psuchē* (which are not specified) provide to the body. If this text, which seems to be without parallel, is accurate, we may take Chrysippus to be invoking a broader sense of *psuchē* than that which he generally used; see S.E. *M* VII.234 for a Stoic distinction between *psuchē*, as 'governing part' (i.e. mind), and *psuchē* as 'that which sustains the whole compound', with discussion by Long 1982b, 40–1.

[12] For the complex relation between heart and *psuchē*, see Long 1982b, 43–9, and Tieleman 1996, 67–87. At least one Stoic, Diogenes of Babylon, argued that the governing part of the *psuchē* must be located in the heart because the heart is what first draws in nutriment and *pneuma* (Galen *PHP* II.8.40). This attests to an intimate tie between the *psuchē* and the nutritive principle, but it stops short of identifying them.

differentiates human or divine *psuchē* from that of non-human animals. Another way of making the Stoics' point is that humans and God have minds but animals do not. Taken strictly, the Stoic theory of mind is a theory about what it means to have a rational *psuchē*.

Before exploring this point, the concept of *psuchē* as it pertains to all animals merits further examination. This is because the Stoics characteristically elucidate the human *psuchē* by considering the way rationality modifies the capacities our species shares with other animals. Once again, we may adduce Hierocles: he provides the fullest account of how any *psuchē* interacts with the body whose *psuchē* it is.[13]

> Since (1) an animal [including human beings] is a composite of body and *psuchē*, and (2) both of these are tangible and impressible and, of course, subject to resistance, and also (3) blended through and through, and (4) one of them is a sensory faculty which itself undergoes movement in the way we have indicated, it is evident that an animal perceives itself continuously. For by stretching out and relaxing, the *psuchē* makes an impact on all the body's parts, since it is blended with them all, and in making an impact it receives an impact in response. For the body, just like the *psuchē*, reacts to pressure; and the effect is a state of their joint pressure upon, and resistance to, each other. From the outermost parts turning inward, the effect travels. . . to the governing part in the chest, with the result that there occurs a grasp both of all the body's parts and those of the *psuchē*. This is equivalent to the animal's perceiving itself. (*El. Eth.* col. 4. 38–53)

In this fascinating passage Hierocles is summarizing a 'theoretical' argument he has been developing, to prove that animals 'perceive themselves continuously from the moment of birth'.[14] His account is impressively consistent in its physicalism. The interaction of the body and the *psuchē* is supported by two premisses [numbered (2) to (3) above] which pertain with equal validity to all 'unified bodies' including minerals and plants.[15] Their structure, just like that of all animals, is due to the 'through and through blending' of *pneuma* with grosser material. Psychic *pneuma* functions like all other *pneuma* by 'stretching and relaxing', which is Hierocles' description of what the Stoics call 'tensional motion' (*tonikē kinēsis*; cf. Alex. *Mant.* 131.5). Because it is inherently dynamic, psychic

---

[13] For more summary accounts, see Alex. *Mixt.* 216.25–217.2, Nemes. 78.7–79.2.

[14] 'Self-perception' is the foundation of an animal's self-preserving disposition, its *oikeiōsis* to itself (D.L. VII.85, Cic. *Fin.* III.16); cf. Bastianini and Long 1992a, 381–5 and Long 1993b, 93–104.

[15] For the concept of 'unified bodies', see *SVF* II 366–8 with discussion by Long 1982b, 36–41, and Annas 1992a, 50–1.

pneuma 'makes an impact' on the bodily frame, and because it is corporeal itself it is affected by any way in which it is impacted by the bodily frame.

Psychic *pneuma* differs from other *pneuma* not in its basic mode of blending with grosser bodily structures, but by the 'tension' (one is tempted to say 'wave-length') of its motion.[16] The special tension of psychic *pneuma* is reported in Hierocles' fourth premiss, where it is identified as 'a sensory faculty'. If we may fantasize briefly, an expert in *pneuma* physics should be capable, in principle, of identifying psychic *pneuma*, and therefore its sentient power, by measuring its 'tensional motion'. The effect of this 'through and through' blending of psychic *pneuma* with an animal's body is an interaction (the Greek is *pathos*, which I translate by 'effect') that becomes 'self-perception' when it is transmitted to the 'governing part' of the *psuchē*.

The power of the *psuchē* to govern the whole animal is its constant and dynamic contact with *all* the animal's parts. Hierocles' 'empirical' support for self-perception is drawn mainly from what we would call muscular and reflex activity – for instance a stag's use of its legs, rather than its antlers, as its best means of self-defence (*El. Eth.* col.2.46–3.2). The stag's impulse to avoid danger by flight requires us to suppose that the stag's *psuchē* stretches itself into the animal's legs, which are then caused to move and transmit the sensation of running back to the *psuchē*. However, in the section immediately following our extract Hierocles argues that self-perception is at work during every moment of an animal's life including even the times when it is asleep (*El. Eth.* col. 4.54–5.30). Self-perception is not only an animal's capacity to *be aware of* its psychosomatic condition; it is also an animal's continuous disposition to monitor itself without necessarily registering any specific sensation.

Later, too, Hierocles argues that 'the sentient principle' (i.e., psychic *pneuma*), like the pneumatic principles controlling plants and minerals, is self-activating by its very nature (*El. Eth.* col. 6, 10–22). Psychic *pneuma*, then, though it confers sentience on an animal's body, is a sentient power intrinsically, by virtue of the kind of *pneuma* that it is. Here we witness the vitalist strand of the Stoic theory, which I alluded to in my introduction. The independent existence of the *psuchē* as a substance in its own right is also presupposed by its 'through and through' blending with the body; for in that kind of mixture the constituents, though interpenetrating completely, retain their own identities and are, at least theoretically, separable from one another (Alex. *Mixt.* 216.25–217.2).[17]

*

[16] For diversity of 'tension', see Annas 1992a, 51–4.   [17] See above, p. 390.

Having now established the basic properties of psychic *pneuma*, let us turn to an excerpt of what Chrysippus said about the *psuchē* in his *Peri psuchēs* ('On the Soul'). Galen, our source for the passage, reports that in the first half of his first book Chrysippus dealt with the 'substance' of the *psuchē* (*PHP* III.1.16). Galen does not say what this involved. It is a fair conjecture that Chrysippus began by surveying the views of earlier thinkers, and then presented reasons for such basic Stoic doctrines as the corporeal substance of the *psuchē* (Nemes. 78.7–79.2, 81.6–10) and the identification of this with *pneuma*. In the second half of the book, Galen says, Chrysippus dealt with the 'governing part', and attempted to establish its location in the heart. Chrysippus began this project as follows:

> The *psuchē* is *pneuma* integral to our nature, extending continuously throughout the entire body as long as the regular breath of life is present in the body. Of the parts of the *psuchē* which are assigned to each segment of the body, the one that extends to the throat is voice; that to the eyes, sight; that to the ears, hearing; that to the nostrils, smell; that to the tongue, taste; that to the entire flesh, touch; and that which extends to the genital organs, since it has a different principle, is seminal. The heart is the location of the part where all these meet, which is the governing part of the *psuchē*. That is our doctrine. But while there is agreement about the other parts, people disagree about the governing part of the *psuchē* and have different theories about its location. Some say it is in the region of the chest, others in the head. They also disagree among themselves about where it is located in the head or the chest. Plato, who said that the *psuchē* has three parts, placed the rational part in the head, the spirited part in the region of the chest and the appetitive part in the region of the navel. Thus the place [of the *psuchē*] seems to elude us since we have neither a clear perception of it, as we had with the others, nor indications from which its location might be deduced. Otherwise there would not have been so much disagreement among physicians and philosophers. (Gal. *PHP* III.1.10–15)[18]

It is clear from this passage that Chrysippus does not anticipate disagreement over his general model of the *psuchē* – its pneumatic nature, the identification of its parts, and their centring in a 'governing part'. Important in explaining his procedure, including his focus on the governing part's location, is the Stoics' indebtedness to contemporary medicine and also (less directly perhaps) to Peripatetic theory.[19] By the time of

---

[18] For detailed discussion of this passage, with important comments on Chrysippus' dialectical approach (recalling Aristotle's methodology), see Mansfeld 1989c, esp. 311–14, 334–42 and 1990a, 3167–77.   [19] For detailed discussion, see Annas 1992a, 17–33.

Chrysippus there was general agreement among physicians that at least some of the body's vital functions are due to *pneuma*, conceived as a warm, vaporous substance transmitted through the arteries. Aristotle, though he did not identify the *psuchē* with *pneuma*, drew on the concept, especially for explaining the transmission of psychic activity into purposive bodily movement. The later Peripatetic Strato held that *pneuma* is spread throughout the body and has a 'governing part' in the head. Among Hellenistic physicians the use made of *pneuma* was complicated by Herophilus' and Erasistratus' remarkable discoveries concerning the nerves. They succeeded in isolating the nerves from the cardio-vascular system and connecting them with the brain. But instead of abandoning the concept of *pneuma*, Erasistratus took the nerves to be channels containing *pneuma* responsible for sensory and motor functions.[20] He distinguished this *pneuma*, issuing from the head, from the *pneuma* responsible for metabolism, which he centred in the heart. (One should compare the Stoics' distinction between psychic and vegetative *pneuma*.)

Chrysippus, Galen reports, disclaimed any knowledge of anatomy (*PHP* 1.6.13). In this respect we may liken him to a modern philosopher who lacks expertise in evaluating the findings of neuro-physiologists. Herophilus and Erasistratus were making their spectacular discoveries during his lifetime. Chrysippus can scarcely be faulted for not appropriating their radical findings, of which he seems to have been well aware.[21] Instead, he pinned his faith on an earlier Hellenistic physician, Praxagoras. This man, not recognizing the independent function of the nerves, treated them as if they were the endings of the arteries. In the light of his mistaken physiology, Praxagoras had every reason to opt for the heart rather than the head as the principal location of psychic *pneuma*.

Galen reports that Chrysippus cited Praxagoras against those who thought that the nerves originate from the head (*PHP* 1.7.1). The theorists referred to no doubt include Herophilus and Erasistratus.[22] Chrysippus had his own reasons, to which we shall come, for preferring the heart to the head as the organ in which the *psuchē* is centred. In drawing on

---

[20] Herophilus' position on the nerves is less clear. He may have regarded them as quasi sinews for manipulating the muscles; see Mansfeld 1992d, 140.

[21] If we may believe Galen (*PHP* 11.5.71), Chrysippus did not ignore the theory that the head is the source of the nerves. He argued that even if that theory is true, it does not prove that the head, rather than the heart, is the starting-point of psychic activity; see Mansfeld 1992d, 140-1, who shows how Chrysippus could defend himself for rejecting the nerves as channels for the *pneuma*, and see Tieleman 1996, 51-2.

[22] Note, however, that the Hippocratic author of the treatise *On the Sacred Disease* (17) had already identified the brain as the source of emotions and mental activity. Aristotle on the other hand, just like Chrysippus, put these in the heart.

Praxagoras for his physiology, Chrysippus was able to develop a theory of the *psuchē* that is highly economical (since it explains all life functions by *pneuma*) and has the further advantage of identifying a single organ, the heart, as an animal's vital centre. The philosophy of mind that he developed on the basis of this physiology is not seriously vitiated by its errors over the brain and the nerves. Chrysippus' most interesting contributions could fit a brain-centred model of mind just as well as a cardiovascular one.

It would be a mistake to take Chrysippus and other Stoics to be merely synthesizing pre-existing concepts of *pneuma*. As the divine 'active principle' of the world in its entirety, Stoic *pneuma* has a thoroughly distinctive nature. What is important is to recognize Chrysippus' concern that his psychology should be as accommodating as possible to established scientific precedents. Another mark of his intellectual responsibility is his admission (in the passage cited) that the location of the 'governing part' is not only controversial but impossible to determine by 'clear perception'. Chrysippus recognizes that he will have to work hard in order to make a convincing case in favour of the heart. Since the matter was contested by experts, he advances a number of theoretical and empirical considerations, and supplements these by looking to support from ordinary language use, etymology and the statements of poets, especially Homer.

Galen, writing four centuries later, would have us believe that Chrysippus made heavy weather of a hopeless task.[23] Expert as he was concerning the nervous system, Galen knew that the intellect was centred in the brain. However, Galen divided the *psuchē* into the three parts and distinct bodily locations Chrysippus mentions above as Plato's doctrine. Although Chrysippus was wrong in opting for the heart as the seat of the 'governing part', he intuited a truth that Galen missed in assigning appetency and emotion to parts of the *psuchē* spatially as well as ontologically distinct from reason.[24] What Chrysippus was adamant to prove in his work *On the Psuchē* was not only a thesis about the location of the 'governing part'. This question is chiefly important to Chrysippus because of the bearing he takes it to have on the nature of that crucial part.[25] In his view,

[23] Tieleman 1996 should be consulted for a thorough study of Chrysippus' methodology, and for a convincing defence of it against much of Galen's polemic.

[24] Galen's psychology is much inferior to that of Chrysippus in accounting for the causal connection of thought and desire to action; see Mansfeld 1992d, who points out, 143, that in the Arabic abstract of a lost work Galen expresses indifference as to whether the three independent principles are called 'separate souls' or 'parts' of one soul or 'three different faculties' of the 'same essence'.

[25] For the doxographic tradition concerning the question of the mind's location, see Mansfeld 1990a, 3092–106.

and that of most Stoics who followed him, the 'governing part' is responsible for everything that a Platonist like Galen distributes between distinct parts identified as reason, spirit and appetency.

The Stoics' unification of all mental functions in the single 'governing part' is their most far-reaching contribution to ancient psychology. Before pursuing its details, we should consider the principal strategy they use in support of uniting what a Platonist would keep apart. Chrysippus, as we have seen, admits that perception is insufficient to settle the question of where the 'governing part' is located in the body. He finds it 'reasonable', however, to infer that: 'Since anger arises here [in the heart], the other desires are here too, and indeed the remaining emotions and deliberations and such-like things' (Gal. *PHP* iii.5.2). Common opinion too tells in favour of the heart as the region of the body where the emotions are felt:

> I think that people in general are led to this belief because they are conscious, as it were, of their mental feelings taking place in the area of the chest and especially in the location of the heart – the sort of feelings especially associated with grief and fear and anger and passion. (Gal. *PHP* ii.7.8)

Not only introspective experience but also the Greek language, as in expressions like 'his heart boiled with anger', point to that region of the body as the seat of the emotions. Against Platonists, who admit this point, but assign separate locations to reason, spirit and appetency, Chrysippus and other Stoics advance an argument to show that their inference about the mind's location in the heart is not a *petitio principii*, but a thesis that can be justified by considerations to do with reason as manifested in spoken language.

> It is reasonable that the destination of meanings and the source of discourse (*logos*) is the governing part of the *psuchē*. For the source of discourse is not different from the source of thought, nor again is the source of voice different from that of discourse, nor (to state the whole point simply) is the source of voice different from the governing part of the *psuchē*. For the entire source from which discourse issues must be where reasoning occurs and thinking and the preparation of language, as I said. But these latter plainly occur in the region of the heart since both voice and discourse issue forth from the heart through the windpipe. It is also plausible in addition that the place to which language conveys meaning should be where it acquires meaning and that words should come from there in the way described. (Gal. *PHP* ii.5.15–20)

This argument, which I cite in the version of Chrysippus, had been already adumbrated by Zeno, and was further elaborated by Diogenes of Babylon, who took over the headship of the Stoa from Chrysippus.[26] Galen is predictably scornful concerning the linkage made between the windpipe and the heart. The interest of the argument is not this egregious error, but the ties it assumes between language, reason and thought. For the Stoics, as for many philosophers, the decisive mark of mind is rationality as manifested in linguistic capacity. They were the only Greek philosophers who specified voice as a distinct part of the *psuchē*.

From the thesis that all mental functions are centred in the heart, it does not immediately follow either that they are all functions of the single 'governing part' of the *psuchē* or that the 'governing' part of the human *psuchē* is exclusively a rational faculty. The *psuchē* including the mind might, in principle, have a unitary centre but distinct faculties, rational and irrational, with functions corresponding to those in the Platonic model. This alternative was adopted by the dissident Stoic, Posidonius.[27] Orthodox Stoics, at least as early as Chrysippus, insist on two much stronger claims: first, the 'governing part' of the human *psuchē* is a rational faculty, through and through; and second, its uniform rationality is quite compatible with, or rather, is the explanation for its being the locus of emotion and appetency. An interpretation of these radical positions will concern us in the later part of the chapter. For the present, it will be best to conclude treatment of the mind's relation to the body.

Chrysippus, as we have seen, specifies eight 'parts' of the *psuchē*, which include the centrally located 'governing part'. In a doxographical testimony (Aët. IV.21.1–4), the seven subordinate parts (i.e., the five senses, reproduction and voice) are described as 'growing out from the governing part and stretching out into the body like the tentacles of an octopus', an effective image for the tensile workings of psychic *pneuma*. In another vivid image, reported by Calcidius as a statement by Chrysippus, the relation of the 'governing part' to the other parts is likened to a spider's control of its web:

> Just as a spider in the middle of a web holds all the beginnings of its threads with its feet, in order to observe at once when any tiny creature enters the trap from any region – so the governing part of the *psuchē*, situated in the midst of the heart, keeps hold on the beginnings of the

---

[26] Galen cites the other two versions in the same context of *PHP*; see Tieleman 1996, 42–3. For a detailed discussion of their bearing on the Stoic philosophy of language, see Ax 1986, 145–51.

[27] See the commentary of Kidd 1988 on Posidon. fr. 142 E.–K.

senses, in order to be immediately cognizant of anything they report. (Calcid. *In Tim.* 220)

The spider image, though it fits psychic *pneuma* less well than the octopus, shows how close the Stoics are to a model of mental functioning akin to the brain and nervous system. Their 'governing part' is both the controlling principle of the entire *psuchē* and also the part where everything that happens to the body and other parts of the *psuchē* is registered and interpreted. Because it is the seat and faculty of all awareness, the 'governing part' tends to be construed as the entire *psuchē*[28] and its subordinate parts as merely the instruments of its activity. The Stoics' conception of the 'governing part' centralizes and co-ordinates psychic life to an extent that is without parallel in the rest of Greek philosophy.[29] This 'mind', as we may call it from now on, constitutes not only the perceiving, feeling, thinking and wanting of human beings but all that they do, as intentional agents. Chrysippus even identified the act of walking with the 'governing part' (Sen. *Ep.* 113.23).

III Rationality and the faculties of the mind

We have next to consider how the Stoics analyse and justify the unitary rationality of the mind or 'governing part' of human beings. In approaching this large question, we need to start by recalling the psychic faculties common to all animals.[30]

As I noted at the beginning of the previous section, the powers that the *psuchē* confers on every animal include sensation (*aisthēsis*) and impulse (*hormē*). The standard name for the 'faculty' responsible for sensation is *phantasia*. A particular *phantasia* is a mental impression or representation, defined as 'an event occurring in the *psuchē*, which reveals itself and its cause' (Aët. IV.12.1). Such 'impressions' (as I shall call them here), are 'alterations' (D.L. VII.50) of the 'governing part'. At their simplest and most basic, they are caused by the impact on the sense-organs of something external to them. The psychic *pneuma* in these organs transmits the sensory properties of the external object to the 'governing part', where the effect is registered as an impression of something white or cold and so forth.

The mechanics of such sensory processes are poorly attested. What first needs to be emphasized, in approaching the concept of *phantasia*, is its teleological relation to the other basic faculty, impulse:

---

[28] See n. 11 above.   [29] For further comments along these lines, see Annas 1992a, 61–4.
[30] For detailed discussion of the mind's 'faculties', see Inwood 1985, 18–41.

The animal is superior to the non-animal in two respects, impression and impulse. An impression is formed by the approach of an external object which strikes the mind through sensation. Impulse, the close relation of impression, is formed by the tonic power of the mind. By stretching impulse out through sensation, the mind grasps the object and goes towards it, eager to seize and reach it. (Phil. *Leg*. 1.30)

Philo of Alexandria, the author of this passage, uses the term 'mind' (*nous*) where a Stoic, in a context about animals in general, would write 'governing part'. Apart from this detail, we can regard his remarks as a reliably succinct account of the way the Stoics take impression and impulse to co-operate, as stimulus and response, in maintaining an animal's life.[31] Endowed as they are with 'self-perception' (recall the second excerpt from Hierocles), all animals are predisposed to observe and pursue things conducive to their natures, and to observe and avoid everything harmful.[32]

Impression and impulse are not spatially distinct 'parts' of the *psuchē*, like vision or voice. They are distinct 'faculties' of the single 'governing part'. What this means is that, unlike vision for instance, which has its own specific *pneuma* that is limited to the facilitation of seeing, the 'governing part' contains plural powers in virtue of its own constitutive *pneuma*. It can do different things – receive impressions *and* react positively or negatively to them – without altering or fragmenting its identity.

In the human case, the mind is described as having two further 'faculties' or 'qualities' besides impression and impulse. These are assent (*sunkatathesis*) and reason (*logos*). Iamblichus, an important source on all this (*ap*. Stob. 1.368.12–20), says: 'Just as an apple possesses in the same body sweetness and fragrance, so too the mind combines in the same body [i.e. the mind's *pneuma*] impression, assent, impulse and reason.' The point of the apple analogy is presumably twofold – to undercut any suggestion of spatial separation between the mind's faculties and to insist that they do not function autonomously but only as interdependent manifestations of its own operation.

This account of the mind's faculties tells strongly in favour of the mind's unity. What does it imply about the way the mind works? How do the Stoics distribute responsibility between the four faculties? Are their functions sufficiently commodious and flexible to comprehend everything that we might incorporate under the concepts of perception, mem-

[31] For a full treatment concerning 'impulse', see Inwood 1985, ch. 3, 'The psychology of action'.
[32] See n. 14 above.

ory, imagination, thought, belief, knowledge, desire, emotion, volition and so forth? What is their point in specifying assent as a distinct faculty of the mind? How should we construe the status of reason, especially its relation to the other three faculties? These are the principal questions to which I now turn.

*

Once again, continuity and difference between human and non-human animals is a decisive step in the argument. The Stoics are curiously ambivalent in their assessment of non-human animals. They insist, as we have seen, that non-human animals lack anything that can be properly called a mind. Yet, their elucidation of the mind, like their starting-point in ethics, is strongly influenced by presumptions about faculties common to all animals. One of their favourite strategies is to invoke a *scala naturae*:

> Nature, they say, is no different in regard to plants and animals at the time when it directs animals as well as plants without impulse and sensation, and in us certain processes of a vegetative kind take place. But since animals have the additional faculty of impulse, through the use of which they go in search of what is appropriate to them, what is natural for them is to be administered in accordance with their impulse. And since reason, by way of a more perfect management, has been bestowed on rational beings, to live correctly in accordance with reason comes to be natural for them. For reason supervenes as the craftsman of impulse. (D.L. VII.86)

Reason is not a faculty simply additional to and co-ordinate with impulse and sensation (the powers common to any *psuchē*). The Stoics treat reason as the determining faculty of the human *psuchē*. It so influences the other mental faculties that, instead of remaining non-rational (as they are in other animals), they too become rational. What is mere impulse in the purely animal *psuchē* becomes volition, 'rational impulse', in the human mind – 'impulse crafted by reason'. Reason similarly has the effect of making *every* human impression (*phantasia*) 'rational' – making it a 'thought' (D.L. VII.50). As for assent, though we have yet to explore the details, its link with rationality is evident from its function – the capacity to endorse or reject propositions (Stob. II.88.2–6). Since only rational animals can entertain and respond to propositions, we should take assent to be strictly a faculty peculiar to mind. Other animals, though they are credited with assent by some sources, can have it in only a weak sense at best – what is sometimes described as 'yielding' (*eixis*).[33]

The upshot of these findings is that our sources are correct, but misleading, when they say that the mind or 'governing part' of the human *psuchē* has the four faculties, impression, assent, impulse, reason. The Stoics' model of the mind would be better rendered by saying that there are three mental faculties – rational impression, rational impulse, and rational assent. Reason is not something over and above the other three. It is the mind in its entirety. Hence reason (*logos*), mind (*nous*), and thought (*dianoia*) are all terms that refer to the distinctive nature of a human being's *psuchē*.

We now have a preliminary response to some of the questions I posed concerning the relationship between mental faculties. What we need next to consider is the effectiveness of these faculties in accounting for the mental events I previously enumerated – perception, memory, imagination, thought, belief, knowledge, volition, desire, emotion, and so forth. In addition, we shall need to ask how the Stoics can respond to the frequent objection that, in unifying the mind as a purely rational faculty, they are unable to explain irrational behaviour of human beings.

The first point to emphasize is the vast scope they assign to the faculty of *phantasia*. Although I am adopting 'impression' as my translation of this term, other possible translations will help in its elucidation. These include representation, appearance, and, with qualifications, awareness. To *be having* a *phantasia* of something is to have something perceptual or non-perceptual present to the mind. However, although anything of which one is conscious will involve a *phantasia*, the term also covers memories and concepts which are latent and therefore not things of which one is presently conscious (Plu. *Comm. Not.* 1084f–1085a). Instead of drawing a basic distinction, as Aristotle and Plato do, between sensation or perception (*aisthēsis*) and thought, the Stoics subsume both sets of mental events under *phantasia*. This amounts to saying that the mind is capable of having both perceptual thoughts or impressions, and non-perceptual thoughts or impressions. Although only the former are directly mediated by the senses, they are the primary source of the concepts or impressions we present to ourselves in non-perceptual thought (Aët. IV.11.1–4).

---

[33] On the question of animal assent, see Long 1982b, 50, and Inwood 1985, 72–91. Animals are 'active', but they are not 'agents' (Alex. *Fat.* 205.28). The content of their *phantasia* is 'non-conceptual' (Aët. IV.11).

Nothing is attested about why the Stoics treat *phantasia* in this completely general way. Their empiricism must surely have contributed. If perceptual experience precedes and subsequently helps to shape non-perceptual thought, it is plausible to suppose that what both experiences share – awareness of something with conceptual content – is far more significant than the ways in which they differ with respect to the circumstances causing them. However that may be, the Stoics' readiness to admit perception as a species of thought is an enormous advance in the philosophy of mind. It frees them from the Platonic error, to which Aristotle too is partly liable, of supposing that reason and interpretation are disengaged from, or not fully engaged in, the activities of sense-perception. Perceptual impressions, according to the Stoics, range from simple recognition of sensory properties to categorical judgements about complex objects. Since *phantasia* is the generic faculty of perceptual and non-perceptual thought, there is no need to regard perceptual impressions as 'irrational' material for something else – the intellect – to process. They are fully rational activities of the unitary mind (as Strato advocated too, Plu. *Soll.* 961a).

The faculty of *phantasia* embraces perception, abstract thought, imagination, memory and latent concepts.[34] Not only that. Because a *phantasia* 'reveals *itself* and its cause', it is both informative (reveals what it is an impression of) and informative in a self-revealing way. What this almost certainly means is that occurrent impressions generally (which is not to say invariably) involve reflexive awareness; they make the person subject to them conscious of having the perceptual or non-perceptual experience corresponding to their content. Earlier Greek philosophers go some way towards recognizing apperception and consciousness as properties of the mind. It is the Stoics, however, who were the first to identify consciousness explicitly as a decisive property of mental life. According to Hierocles, the first impression or perception any animal experiences is that of 'itself' (*El. Eth.* col. 6, 20–2). What this self can amount to, in the case of non-human animals, is a question too complex to discuss in detail here.[35] Minimally, however, the concept of self-perception implies some kind of reflexive awareness – some kind of recognition of the body in pain or pleasure as *belonging to* that which is feeling the pain or pleasure.

---

[34] Sometimes a distinction is drawn between a particular *phantasia*, an impression generated by something objective, and a *phantasma* or mere 'figment' (Aët. IV.12.1–5). But although imagination (*phantastikon*) is thereby marked out as something distinctive, the faculty of *phantasia* must be responsible for imagination as well as all other representations.

[35] For an exploration of animal 'self-perception', see Bastianini and Long 1992a, 385–90, Long 1993b.

In the case of human beings, thanks to Epictetus (second century AD), we can say a lot more. In his way of formulating Stoicism, the principal task facing human beings is to learn 'how to use one's impressions correctly' and 'to attend to their use'.[36] Drawing a contrast with non-human animals, Epictetus indicates that 'attending to an impression' signifies not simply going along with it but focusing on it, interpreting it, asking what it tells one not only about objective reality but about oneself. The problem with someone like Medea, he argues, is a problem to do with her impressions (Epict. *Diss.* 1.28.7–9). She sees herself simply as a desperately wronged wife – that is the way things 'appear' to her, and she accepts it, identifies with it. As the remedy for such self-identification, Epictetus urges:

> Do not be carried away by the intensity of an impression, but say: 'Wait a moment for me, impression; let me see who you are and what you are about; let me test you.' And next, do not let it lead you on by depicting the consequences. Otherwise, it will take possession of you and take you wherever it wants to. What you should do, rather, is to oppose to it a fair and noble impression and discard this sordid one. (*Diss.* II.18.24–6)

Passages such as this one show that impressions furnish not only the content of thought and action; they also help to constitute the thinker and agent, the self in other words. Marcus Aurelius makes this point, when he says: 'Your mind will be just like the repetition of your impressions; for the *psuchē* is coloured by its impressions' (*Med.* v.16). But there is more to the Stoic self, and to Stoic interest in reflexive consciousness, than the faculty of impression on its own delivers. As Epictetus points out, where Medea went wrong was in 'assenting' to a particular impression of her situation. What is the faculty of assent, and why do the Stoics, uniquely among Greek philosophers, introduce it?

The term *sunkatathesis*, translated by assent, is derived from a verb (συγκατατίθεσθαι) which was used in everyday Greek to signify 'go along with', 'vote for' or 'commit oneself to'. Impressions taken on their own are merely thought contents. Only some of them represent matters that are veridical, and of these, only *kataleptic* impressions represent veridical matters in ways that are indubitable.[37] The function of assent is to evaluate impressions, to adjudicate on the truth-value of their propositional content, to decide whether or not they represent something one

---

[36] See Epict. *Diss.* I.1.7, II.1.4, II.22.29, IV.6.34. 'Attend to' translates παρακολουθεῖν (I.6.13). Stoic usage no doubt influenced the Neoplatonists, who use the word with the reflexive pronoun to denote 'being self-conscious'.   [37] See p. 300.

has good reason to endorse as one's judgement of the way things are. This description of assent shows why it is sometimes treated as the very hall-mark of rationality.[38]

Knowledge and belief in Stoicism are functions of the way people assent to their impressions.[39] In cases where assent is fully justified (because the impression is *kataleptic*), the cognitive state is a genuine grasp (*katalēpsis*) of the truth represented in the impression, a grasp which becomes 'irrefutable knowledge' (*epistēmē*) if further conditions are satis-fied (Stob. II.73.19–74.3). Belief (*doxa*) is a weaker cognitive state, result-ing from any kind of assent. It straddles truth and falsehood, and even when true it lacks the grounding of the assent involved in irrefutable knowledge.

We are to think of assent, like *phantasia*, as both a faculty of the mind and a name for the particular activities of the faculty. In the former sense, assent constitutes a disposition in terms of which a mind can be assessed both with respect to its cognitive powers and with respect to its moral character. Once again, Epictetus is particularly informative:

> Man, you have a capacity for decision (*prohairesis*) which is by nature unconstrained and unimpeded. . . I will prove this to you first under the heading of assent. Can anyone prevent you from inclining to what is true? No one can. Can anyone compel you to accept what is false? No one at all. Don't you see that in this region you have a capacity for decision that is unconstrained, unimpeded and unobstructed? (*Diss*. 1.17.21–3)

> The heading of assent deals with things that are plausible and alluring. For just as Socrates used to say that the unexamined life is not worth liv-ing, so we should not accept an unexamined impression, but should say: 'Wait, let me see who you are and where you are coming from.' (*Diss*. III.12.14–15; cf. II.18.24–6 cited above)

Epictetus, as is his wont, combines psychology with ethics, but the appropriateness of his doing so is evident when we turn to the last three properties of mind on which I want to examine the Stoics – volition, desire and emotion. From what I have already said about basic animal psychology, we know that the behaviour of non-human animals is caused by the conjunct operation of their impressions and their impulses. As the response to an attractive or repellent impression, impulse is the psychic movement that issues in purposive behaviour. In the human case, the sit-

---

[38] Cf. Orig. *Princ*. III.1.3 where 'reason' is said to 'pass judgements on impressions'. The text is dis-cussed in detail by Inwood 1985, 78–81.

[39] Or more strictly, perhaps, the way they assent to the propositions or *lekta* that are 'subsistent' on impressions; see Long and Sedley 1987, vol. I, 240.

uation is immensely more complex because of rationality and, in particular, the operation of assent.

We might expect that assent would intervene following both an impression *and* an impulse. That, after all, is the way people including the ancient Greeks typically see the relation between desire, decision and action: these mental events seem to occur in the order I have just given. A person experiences an impulse or desire; the person decides whether to endorse the desire; if the decision is affirmative, an action consistent with the desire follows. The Stoics go some way towards accepting this account. They acknowledge that some of our impressions are *hormetic*, which means that these impressions are a *prima facie* stimulus to action.[40] But *hormetic* impressions, though they will be a causal factor of action if we assent to them, are not activities of *hormē*, the faculty of impulse. Mediating between such impressions and any actual impulse is the faculty of assent. The Stoics' point is that, while *hormetic* impressions precede assent, impulses are *outcomes* of assent, or even, as one source states the matter, impulses *are* acts of assent.[41]

According to this account of action, there is a confluence between decision (assent) and desire (impulse). What precedes an assent is not, strictly speaking, an impulse. The mind entertains the thought of something desirable, but it is the mind's assent to this thought which activates and even constitutes the desire or impulse. If the mind declines to assent, the faculty of impulse remains inactive. Action ensues on desire and decision, as in the standard model, but the desire is conditioned by the decision.

Three interesting consequences follow: first, decision procedure is not construed as adjudicating on or between actual desires but as deciding whether to permit the thought of something attractive to become a desire. Secondly, since there can be no gap between decision and desire, what one decides on *is* inevitably what one desires. Short of external constraint or a change of mind, there can be no desires that fail to give rise to action. The place that ordinary language would assign to such desires is filled by attractive thoughts that do not become impulses to action because they are not given assent. The third consequence is the clarity the model provides for showing how decisions can result in actions. An

---

[40] Stob. II.86.17–87.6. Inwood 1985, 56–86, is the first scholar to bring out the significance of *hormetic* impressions.

[41] Stob. II.88.2–6. In this brief testimony, 'propositions' are said to be the objects of assent, but impulse is directed at 'predicates'. This interesting refinement is too complex to be examined here. For discussions of it, see Long 1976, Inwood 1985, 60–6, Annas 1992a, 93–102. There is also a big question to ask about how the corporeal mind can be cognizant of 'incorporeal *lekta*'. I have explored this briefly in Long 1982b, 51–3 and Long 1991a, 118–20.

impulse is a decision (act of assent). But it is also, quite literally, 'a movement of the *psuchē* towards something' (Stob. 11.86.19), a stretch of psychic *pneuma*, activating the limbs in the direction of the mind's objective.[42] The confluence of assent and impulse gives the Stoics something like a concept of the will, but one which, thanks to their physicalism, lacks the mystery often attached to that concept.[43]

Volition and desire – these properties of the mind, it should now be clear, are at the forefront of the Stoics' interests. They make 'assent' rather than 'impression' the 'principal' cause of an action.[44] Because assent is 'in our power', in the sense that it depends on nothing outside the mind, human agents are held fully responsible both for what they do, and also, as we have seen, for what they desire. But there is more, of course, to desire than we have considered thus far. In ordinary language, desire is an emotion as well as being the volitional element of action. Where do the emotions fit in the Stoics' philosophy of mind?[45]

*

It goes without saying that the ideal Stoic life is totally free of every emotion that could disturb a perfectly rational state of mind. To put this another way, the Stoic sage is subject neither to passionate pleasure and passionate desire, nor to distress and fear. His rational disposition is completely equable. This paragon, however, is someone no actual human being has been known to instantiate more than approximately. The Stoics need to show what emotions are, in the lives of ordinary mortals, and how the Stoic model of mind can explain their occurrence.

Their approach to these issues trades heavily, though not exclusively, on the four faculties of the mind. According to the standard account, the emotions are a species of 'impulse', one which is 'excessive and disobedient to the dictates of reason, or a movement of the *psuchē* which is irrational and contrary to nature' (Stob. 11.88.8–10). Since, as we have seen, all impulses involve 'assent', that faculty is also operative. We already know too that assent has the function of attending to and evaluating 'impressions'. The outcome of any act of assent is a cognitive state. This state, at its weakest, is a mere 'belief', and at its weakest and worst, a 'false belief'. In addition to being defined as 'excessive and irrational impulses', emo-

---

[42] The faculty of impulse can also generate 'repulsion', a movement of the *psuchē* away from something (Stob. 11.87.5–6).

[43] For stimulating treatments of Stoic ideas of the will, see Mansfeld 1992d, and Kahn 1988.

[44] See pp. 494, 703 and 717.

[45] For further discussion of the Stoic treatment of emotions, see below, p. 699. They are also treated, from the perspective of mind, by Annas 1992a, 103–20.

tions are 'false beliefs'. Distress, for instance, is defined as 'a fresh [to which we can add false] belief that something bad is present' (Andronicus *Pass.* 1). Thus, in characterizing the emotions in the ways just mentioned, the Stoics accommodate them to their basic model of action: an impression, followed by assent/impulse, which ensues in an action.

What differentiates an emotional from a non-emotional action, on the evidence thus far, is not the intrusion of an element of the mind other than reason – what a Platonist, for instance, assigns to the so-called 'spirited' part of the *psuchē*. An emotional action is like any other action in its three causal components. What makes it distinctive is the 'excess and irrationality' of its impulse, a failing which must also apply to the agent's assent to the badness or goodness represented in the impression. (We should recall Epictetus' warnings against letting assent act precipitately.) The Stoics construe 'irrationality' not as the intervention of an 'irrational' faculty (since there is none), but as error of judgement, reasoning that goes wrong. A comment by Plutarch gives one of the clearest statements of their view:

> Some people [meaning the Stoics] say that emotion is no different from reason, and that there is no dissension and conflict between the two, but a turning of the single reason in both directions, which we do not notice owing to the sharpness and speed of the change.[46] We do not perceive that the natural instrument of appetition and regret, or anger and fear, is the same part of the *psuchē*, which is moved by pleasure towards wrong, and while moving recovers itself. For appetition and anger and fear and all such things are bad opinions and judgements. They do not arise in the region of only one part of the *psuchē*. They are the whole 'commanding part's' inclinations, yieldings, assents, impulses, and quite generally activities which change rapidly, just like children's fights, whose fury and intensity are volatile and transient, owing to their weakness. (Plu. *Virt. Mor.* 446f–447a)

What we have here is a brilliant revision of the standard belief in a divided self. The mind is not composite, as Plato had famously inferred because it can be simultaneously attracted to and repelled by the same object. That premiss is false. The experiences which make it seem plausible are actually successive, a sequence of very rapid changes of the mind in its entirety. Apparent conflict of desires, apparent conflict between reason and passion – these are the unitary mind's oscillation between pro and

---

[46] For 'turning' (*tropē*), cf. D.L. VII.158 and discussion by Mansfeld 1992d, 116 n.17, who comments on the contraction and dilation of the *pneuma* that the use of the term implies.

contra judgements. Reason is fully at work throughout, so the emotions are not due to something other than reason. They are errors of reasoning, reason that goes wrong, false judgements of what is valuable or harmful.

The Stoics, accordingly, take themselves to be entitled to attribute 'irrationality' to a rational *psuchē* which is reasoning 'badly'. This is entirely coherent. Someone who plays a musical instrument badly is playing unmusically, but the performance is still a musical one. Yet, the Stoics' recourse to this point is insufficient to distinguish the irrationality characteristic of emotions from faulty reasoning quite generally. Some further differentia is needed. The obvious candidate is the 'excess' of the impulses that constitute emotions. Here is Chrysippus' elucidation of the issue from his work *On Emotions*:

> First of all, we should bear in mind that a rational animal follows reason naturally, and acts in accordance with reason as if that were its guide. Often, however, it moves towards and away from certain things in a different way, pushed to excess in disobedience to reason. Both definitions [i.e. the definitions of emotions as 'irrational' and as 'excessive impulses'] refer to this movement: the movement contrary to nature which occurs irrationally in this way, and the excess in impulses ... For this irrationality must be taken to mean 'disobedient to reason' and 'reason turned aside'; with reference to this movement we even speak in ordinary language of people 'being pushed' and 'moved irrationally', without reason and judgement. What we mean by these expressions is not as though a person moves in error and overlooking something that accords with reason, but we refer chiefly to the movement outlined by the expressions, since it is not a rational animal's nature to move in *this* way but in accordance with reason. ... This also explains the expression 'excess of the impulse', since people overstep the proper and natural proportion of their impulses. My meaning can be made more intelligible in this way. In the case of walking in accordance with impulse, the movement of a person's legs is not excessive but commensurate with the impulse, so that it is possible to stop or change when one wants to. But when people run in accordance with their impulse [to walk], this sort of thing no longer happens. The movement of their legs exceeds their impulse, so that they are carried away and unable to change obediently as soon as they have started. Something similar, I think, takes place with impulses, owing to their going beyond the rational proportion. The result is that when someone has the impulse he is not obedient to reason. The excess in running is called 'contrary to the impulse', but the excess in the impulse is called 'contrary to reason'. For the proportion of a natural impulse is what accords with reason and goes only so far as reason thinks right. (Gal. *PHP* IV.2.10–18; see also p. 702 below)

The subtlety of this passage is ample testimony to the loss we have suffered from the disappearance of every complete work by Chrysippus. His argument depends on four principal points. First, when Chrysippus refers to reason, he is using the term normatively, with reference to the reasoning that it is natural for a rational animal to employ. Secondly, he makes room for ordinary language expressions, like 'acting without reason and judgement', by taking them to pick out something distinctive of 'emotional movements': they manifest 'disobedience' to reason in its normative sense. Thirdly, he elucidates the 'excess' of an impulse by an analogy or proportion: as someone with the impulse to walk exceeds that impulse if he runs, so someone who has reasoned that x is to be pursued or avoided has an excessive impulse if he pursues or avoids x to a degree that is incommensurate with normative reasoning. Chrysippus' fourth point is that emotions are 'movements'. They have their own momentum, and thus they exceed the impulses compatible with normative reasoning. Physically speaking, emotions are extreme expansions or contractions of the mind's *pneuma*. Either way, they manifest a 'governing part' that lacks the degree of pneumatic 'tension' constitutive of sound reason – the strong personality Chrysippus called 'sinewy', playing upon the word *neurōdes*, 'tendon-like'.[47]

This account of the emotions raises many questions. Its principal strength, in my opinion, is its recognition that emotions are not simply 'animal' forces that sometimes intrude on the rational mind. Only rational animals, according to the Stoics, can be subject to the irrationality of emotions. That is because, as they see things, emotions include concepts, cognitive states, propositional attitudes. Emotions are malfunctions of reason, and especially reason as deployed in impulse or action. They are manifestations of a mind whose wants and aversions can be likened to a machine that is running too fast or too slow to perform its function effectively.[48] Perhaps the chief weakness of the Stoics' position is its apparent refusal to allow the mind to contain hidden motive forces. Unlike Plato for instance, they seem to have had no sympathy for anything that today we would call the unconscious.

---

[47] See Mansfeld 1992d, 115–18, for Chrysippus' liking to draw a parallel between physical strength and strength of mind (will), with further comments by Sedley 1992b, 150–2.

[48] The Stoics were notorious for treating correctness of reason, and the virtue that it constitutes, as an all or nothing matter. One fault is enough to wreck the harmony that marks a perfectly rational disposition. For an exploration of this, with reference to musical harmony as their favoured model, see Long 1991b.

IV Concluding remarks

The Stoics' account of mental faculties is striking in its economy. Taking the mind to be rational through and through, they undertake to show that mental life can be fully explicated by reference to just three basic faculties – impression, assent and impulse. In treating these faculties as functions of reason, they are also treating them as functions of language. Human beings resemble other animals in being subject to impressions and impulses, but because we humans are language animals the way we represent the world to ourselves has the structure of propositional thought. In later philosophical traditions, language capacity and a special kind of consciousness are frequently regarded as primary characteristics of mind. It was perhaps because the Stoics emphasize both of these characteristics so strongly that their philosophy of mind is also a philosophy of the self. What interests them chiefly about the mind is its being the centre of individual agency, the locus of subjectivity, the vehicle of intentionality and moral identity.

We know enough about the Stoic theory of mind to see that it is a challenging contribution. That holds good irrespective of any bearing it may have on contemporary debate about the mind's ontological status. I happen to think that such affinities as there are between Stoics and moderns on this issue are largely superficial.[49] The ancient context of the Stoic theory is remote from Descartes' mind/body legacy, concerns about reductionism or antireductionism, emergent properties and so forth. We can admit all this, and also acknowledge the provisionality of anything we think we know about the mind. The Stoic concept of psychic *pneuma* points to a confluence of the physical and the mental we are still struggling to articulate. Their reasoning about the mind's location in the body, though they got the answer wrong, helped them to unify the locus of everything we call mental. What they made of that unity is something that will bear thinking about long after the dust has settled on controversies about the mind's relation to the findings of molecular biology.

---

[49] This is not to say that interpretation of the Stoics cannot be enhanced by consulting modern theorists, especially Davidson 1982 and Searle 1992. I am also aware that more could be said concerning the mind's relation to the body (more on this in Long 1982b) and the bearing that psychic *pneuma* has on the Stoics' construal of mental states.

18

Philosophy, science and medicine

GIUSEPPE CAMBIANO

1 Philosophy and mathematics

The relationship between philosophy and mathematics appears to be less close in the Hellenistic age than in previous centuries. The mathematicians proceeded with their work without any explicit adhesion to philosophical doctrines or any reply to the theoretical and epistemological problems raised by the Epicureans and the sceptics when dealing with mathematics. In the fifth century AD the Neo-platonist Proclus saw Euclid as a Platonist, because his *Elements* concluded with the construction of regular polyhedrons, the basis of the cosmic structure outlined by Plato in the *Timaeus* (*Eucl.* 68.20–3; 70.22–71.5). But there is no proof that Euclid meant to direct the whole of his writing towards the creation of a cosmology.

Another level on which Proclus tried to show Euclidean geometry's dependence on philosophy was the formal structure of the *Elements*. This was based on the distinction between a small number of principles, assumed at the outset without demonstration and listed in the first book as definitions, common notions and postulates, and a body of propositions reached deductively starting from the principles. Proclus highlighted a correspondence between this structure and the theory of science formulated by Aristotle, particularly in the *Posterior Analytics*, and also between Euclid's principles and those mentioned by Aristotle (*Eucl.* 76.6–77.2). It is in fact possible to make out some parallelism: for example, Aristotle includes among the principles used by mathematicians Euclid's third common notion, which is that if equals are subtracted from equals, the remainders will be equal (*APo.* 76a41). But we cannot speak of an absolute coincidence in the terminology used to classify the kinds of principle, or in the techniques of deduction of propositions from principles, theorized by Aristotle and employed by Euclid. In Euclid valid argumentative forms are used which are not easily reduced to Aristotelian schemata of categorical inference or even hypothetical inference, which was discussed subsequently especially by the Stoics.[1] The partial parallels between Aristotle and Euclid can be explained by reference to a shared tradition. The axiomatic–deductive form was not invented by Euclid, but was already used in two works from the second half of the fourth century BC: the treatise on spherical astronomy *On Risings and Settings* by Autolycus of Pitane, and the third book of *Harmonics* by Aristotle's pupil Aristoxenus of Tarentum. Ancient sources record other authors of *Elements* prior to Euclid, some prior to Aristotle as well, such as Leo and Theudius of Magnesia in the fourth century and Hippocrates of Chios, who lived in the second half of the fifth century BC (Procl. *Eucl.* 66.7–67.16).

In post-Euclidean mathematics there is no indication of a precise distinction between kinds of principle. The terminology by which they are defined is not fixed in Archimedes nor in Apollonius of Perge. But the *Elements* became the model by which to organize and expound the results of geometrical research. The model was also used in an astronomical context by Euclid himself in the *Phainomena* and by Aristarchus of Samos in his surviving work *On the Size and Distances of the Sun and Moon*. This does not mean that the mathematicians did not make use of other heuristic techniques. These included, especially in the resolution of problems concerning squaring and cubing, ample use of analytical techniques, usually consisting of the reduction of so far unknown propositions and figures to ones already known. Plato and Aristotle were interested in these techniques, but so far as we know the philosophers of the Hellenistic age displayed no such interest in them. Archimedes, in his writing on theorems of mechanics, conceives discovery as the attainment of knowledge or a true conclusion by deduction from premises which have also been drawn from mechanics, and distinguishes it from proper demonstration using geometrical principles. In describing the relationship between discovery and demonstration he uses terms and considerations which display an air of familiarity with the vocabulary and themes of contemporary philosophies, particularly Aristotelianism and Stoicism. But this does not mean that Archimedes was principally guided by philosophical concerns or logical theory, nor that his position can be equated with a specific philosophical point of view.[2]

---

[1] On the question of principles, see von Fritz 1971 (1955), 335–429; Szabó 1960 and 1969; Knorr 1976; Mueller 1981; on the techniques of deduction see Mueller 1974, Barnes 1990a and the section on logic in this volume.

[2] On the analytical method in mathematics and philosophy see Robinson 1969, 1–15; Hintikka and Remes 1974; Knorr 1986, important also for Archimedes (on whom see Dijksterhuis 1987 and Cambiano 1992).

The later mathematicians did not question the Euclidean model. They sometimes gave alternative demonstrations of specific theorems or different definitions of geometric entities, as is documented in Proclus' commentary on Euclid and in the work *On the Definition of Geometrical Terms* by Hero. One could suppose from this that they were aware of the problematic nature of certain Euclidean definitions, but not that they doubted the validity of the axiomatic–deductive structure of geometrical knowledge. The problem concerned only the good order of propositions within this structure: must certain propositions be assumed as principles without demonstration, or can they be demonstrated? But this does not lead to a discussion of the validity of assuming axioms in general. Radical critics of geometry came instead from the philosophical side, especially the Epicureans and sceptics. This was not entirely new: in the fifth century BC Protagoras had already noted a difficulty in assuming that the tangent touched the circle only at one point (Arist. *Metaph.* B.2.998a2–4). In the fourth century BC, the rejection of the *mathēmata* ('arts and sciences') by the Cynics and Cyrenaics had also included mathematics in the specific sense.

II Epicureanism and mathematics

The Epicurean critics of geometry also had its exploitation by the Platonic Academy in their sights.[3] Before opening his own school in Athens, Epicurus taught at Lampsacus, where he may have begun an argument – continued by especially Polyaenus – with Eudoxus' pupils working at Cyzicus. According to Cicero (*Acad.* II.106) Polyaenus, who started as a mathematician, became attached to Epicureanism and came to hold the view that 'all geometry is false'. From the title and what little remains of a work by Demetrius Laco, *On the Aporiai of Polyaenus*, one can infer that *Aporiai* was the title of a work by him or at any rate that Polyaenus had raised problems with regard to geometry. It is likely that his target was the geometry of Eudoxus and his pupils, not yet that of Euclid; and that the nub of the difficulties concerned the incompatibility of geometry with the Epicurean doctrine of minima. This seems to be confirmed by the fact that Philonides, in the second century BC, had produced geometrical explications of Epicurus' doctrine of minima. Epicurus considered that

---

[3] The evidence for Polyaenus, Philonides and Demetrius Laco is collected and commented on respectively in Tepedino Guerra 1991; Gallo 1980, 23–166 (dealing with a biography of Philonides contained in *PHerc.* 1044) and Angeli and Dorandi 1987. On ancient critics of geometry see also Apelt 1891, 253–86. On the Epicureans see Sedley 1976b, also for the controversial interpretation of the significance of the title of Demetrius' work, and above, pp. 374–9.

the idea of the infinite divisibility of magnitudes was contrary to experience and to the doctrine of the existence of a minimum unit of magnitude, theoretically not divisible any further.

Aristotle (*Metaph.* A 9.992a20–2) attributed to Plato the doctrine of the existence of uncuttable lines, that is to say of units of longitude which are theoretically indivisible. The tract *On Indivisible Lines*, of Peripatetic origin, sets out a battery of arguments against this theory which probably was widely held in the Academy. It is indeed the opposite of Aristotle's view, according to whom the continuum cannot be composed of indivisibles and mathematics falls apart if the concept of minimal quantities is introduced (*Cael.* 1.5.271b9–11). The Epicurean theory of minima is opposed to this Aristotelian conception as well, but it is less easy to determine whether it was incompatible with the practice of ancient geometers. Euclid did not actually explain his own view of continuity. The so-called method of exhaustion, introduced by Eudoxus and later developed by Euclid and Archimedes, required the use of a principle of bisection (Eucl. *El.* x prop. 1), which seemed to admit the possibility of infinite division. On the other hand Archimedes, in his work *Method for Theorems in Mechanics*, assumes that a geometric figure, plane or solid, is a collection of constituent parts, respectively lines and surfaces. But he does not say whether their number is finite or infinite. One cannot rule out the possibility that he thought of them as indivisible minimal bodies. In any case he did not tackle clearly the question of continuity and indivisibility which also occupied the philosophers.

The alternative views adopted by philosophers on the problem of continuity translated into different attitudes towards geometry. Unlike the Epicureans, the Stoics allowed for the infinite divisibility of bodies, not in the sense that they were composed of an infinite number of parts, but in the sense that there was no limit to division. This coincided with their interpretation of bodies as continuous collections of parts. They therefore had no difficulty in recognizing the scientific status of geometry.[4]

There is no evidence of Epicurean attempts to strengthen their doctrine of minima by developing an alternative, finite geometry. None can be extracted from the fact that Philonides and Protarchus, mentioned with approval by mathematicians like Apollonius of Perge and Hypsicles, author of Book xiv of the *Elements* (Apoll. Perg. 1.192.5–11; Eucl. v.2.1–4.4), may be the same as the similarly-named exponents of the

---

[4] On the theory of minima and on the problem of infinite divisibility in philosophy and mathematics see Furley 1967, 1–158; Knorr 1982; M. J. White 1992, 193–251 and above, pp. 374–9. On the Stoic definition of geometry see Mansfeld 1983a, 7 and Tarrant 1984.

Epicurean school, since it is not possible to determine whether, at the time Apollonius and Hypsicles mention them, they had already become attached to Epicureanism. What is certain is that the doctrine of minima and the related problem of infinite divisibility continued to be central to the writings of Demetrius Laco, incompletely preserved on papyrus, both the one about or against Polyaenus' *aporiai* and another entitled *On Geometry*. In the latter (coll. x–xiv) he puts forward the problem of whether it is possible to bisect a given rectilinear angle and a given finite straight line – Euclid's propositions 9 and 10 from *El.* i are cited, with the relevant figures. But the text offers no information about the course of Demetrius' discussion. It would seem to support criticism designed to show, with supporting citations, that Euclid, using the principle of bisection, allowed the infinite divisibility of magnitudes and thereby remained entangled in the *aporiai* this caused. But the papyrus does not suggest that it led Demetrius to draw the conclusion that the whole of geometry was false. One should remember that Apollonius of Perge had given a solution to the problem of bisecting a straight line which was different from that of Euclid (Procl. *Eucl.* 279.16–280.9), but there is no sign of this solution in Demetrius.

The criticisms of geometry advanced by another Epicurean and a contemporary of Demetrius, Zeno of Sidon, strike a different note.[5] These are recorded by Proclus in a review of arguments against Euclidean geometry (*Eucl.* 199.3–200.3; 214.15–218.11). He mentions Epicureans who 'propose only to discredit the principles of geometry' and differentiates these from others who 'admit the principles but deny that the propositions coming after the principles can be demonstrated, unless they grant something that is not contained in the principles'. This was the path taken by Zeno of Sidon, which the Stoic Posidonius argued against. Zeno tried to demonstrate his own view on the basis of Euclid's first proposition, concerning the construction of the equilateral triangle. According to Zeno, if one does not make the further concession that two straight lines cannot have common segments, one cannot demonstrate that the triangle constructed following Euclid's procedure is equilateral. Zeno showed that, in the problem in question, if one assumes the existence of a common segment one reaches an absurd conclusion: one must therefore assume no common segment. This means that even if one accepts the axioms assumed by

[5] Cf. the edition of Angeli and Colaizzo 1979. On Zeno and Posidonius see also Bréhier 1914 (1955, 117–30). Vlastos 1966 has interpreted Zeno's criticism of geometry as constructive; corrections to and arguments against this are in Sedley 1976b, Mueller 1982 and Kidd 1988, 205–14.

Euclid, they do not form a complete system. Zeno's discussion has been interpreted as a purely methodological criticism, intended to perfect the collection of Euclidean axioms. He will have argued not for the falsity of Euclidean axioms or the non-demonstrability of the theorems which derived from them, but for their demonstrability so long as they introduced additional axioms. This interpretation contrasts with Proclus' declaration, according to which so many people made objections to the Euclidean solution of the construction of the equilateral triangle, including Zeno, that it seemed to him to 'refute the whole of geometry' (214.17). If this were true, the admission of the validity of Euclidean axioms was only a dialectical concession to the opposition, so as to provide further arguments against geometry. Zeno replied to Posidonius' counter-objections by showing that even in this case it was necessary to assume further premisses. In his opinion the incompleteness of the collection of axioms in Euclidean geometry was therefore a chronic malady which irremediably struck down the whole structure of geometry and definitely prevented it from being treated as a science.[6]

III Scepticism and geometry

Besides the Epicureans and Zeno, Proclus noted other opponents of geometry, who 'do away with all knowledge, like enemy troops destroying the crops of a foreign country, in this case a country that has produced philosophy' (199.6–9). Proclus called them *ephektikoi*, 'those who withhold assent', a term usually used to define the sceptics; it is not certain whether Proclus refers to Pyrrhonists only or also includes the sceptical Academics. Their criticism of geometry differed from that of the Epicureans, who did not regard the rejection of geometry as a special case of that of knowledge in general. The major surviving account of sceptic criticism of geometry is Sextus Empiricus *M* III, dating some centuries after the Hellenistic age but possibly preserving much earlier material, especially if the overall organization of the arguments against geometry can be placed, though with difficulty, in a period preceding the modes of the Neopyrrhonists Aenesidemus and Agrippa.

The aim of *M* I–VI was to show that grammar, rhetoric, geometry, arith-

---

[6] The problem of the completeness of the system of axioms was also noted by ancient geometers, as suggested by the fact that the source which produced the *Elements* knew of ten common notions, possibly added as a sort of sequel to the original three. In another case, referred to by Proclus (*Eucl.* 322.4–14), the Epicureans reproached Euclid not for incompleteness, but for useless enthusiasm for demonstrating what was obvious even to a fool, such as how in every triangle any two given sides will be longer than the third.

metic, astrology and music were not really arts, since they had no object. In *M* III this aim is pursued by way of two blocks of direct argument against the procedure of the geometers (and others) of 'taking hypotheses as principles' and, subsequently, against the contents of the geometers' principal assumptions. For Sextus hypothesizing axioms as points of departure for demonstration was quite simply assertion, without sustaining arguments. If what is hypothesized is true, there is no need to hypothesize it; if it is not true, there is still no need; so hypothesizing is pointless either way. Furthermore, certain arguments conclude, albeit in different ways, that if one hypothesis is acceptable, any hypothesis is acceptable and there is no way of deciding which hypothesis is necessary or most suitable to be chosen.[7] A hypothesis and its opposite are equal, and if one argues in favour of one or the other one has abandoned the procedure of hypothesis. Sextus' arguments are backed up by the fourth mode of Agrippa (D.L. IX.89; S.E. *PH* 1.168), but the fact that he states that he wants to use against the mathematicians what the early Pyrrhonist Timon, in his writings against the physicists, had done regarding the problem of whether anything should be assumed by way of a hypothesis (*M* III.2), does not rule out the possibility that his arguments were at least partly an extension to geometry of criticisms already formulated long ago.

However, Sextus does not stop at this methodological criticism, but goes on to show the falsity, inconsistency and unacceptability of the principal assumptions in the geometers' theories. His fire is trained first on the definitions of point, line, surface and body, and then on derived notions such as straight lines and angles.[8] Many of the arguments put forward by Sextus aim to show that the objects of which geometers speak not only have nothing corresponding on a sensible level but cannot even be objects of thought. At their root is the presupposition that concepts can be formed and thought only on the basis of the data of sense-experience. Sextus mentions a series of ways in which concepts can originate *via* 'transition' (*metabasis*) from things evident to the senses: by resemblance or composition or proportionality according to growth or diminution (III.40–2). In none of these ways, claims Sextus, can a line as 'length without size' (the geometers' definition) be conceived, nor can one think of it by mentally reducing the size of a length. In that case, he argues, even if one arrived at length without size, one would also end up with something

[7] *M* III.7–17 and parallel passages in *PH* 1.173–4 and *M* VIII.369–78; see Barnes 1990b, 90–113.
[8] *M* III.18, 92. The section III.19–91, with parallels in *M* IX.367–436, opposes the definitions of primitive notions, while 94–107 opposes derived ones. See especially Mueller 1982, 69–95; cf. also Freytag 1995; Berryman 1998.

which no longer had length (III.51–6). A second kind of argument used by Sextus gets a purchase on the relationships between geometrical objects of dimension n and others of dimension $n-1$, e.g. between lines and points, or between surfaces and lines. In such cases Sextus assumes that a line is composed of points as a surface is of lines, and that points and lines are limits of lines and surfaces respectively. The difficulties arise from the fact that the limit is interpreted as an extremity or part of something, and therefore, since it also has a dimension, to take it away from something reduces the size of the thing itself. A variation is the thesis that objects of dimension n are generated by flowing (*rhusis*) from objects of dimension $n-1$, e.g. a line flowing from a point or a surface from a line. One objection amongst several to this thesis is that the point, considered incorporeal by geometers, cannot generate anything. Furthermore, if one thinks of flowing as an extension from one place to another, the point is no longer without parts but formed of many parts, contrasting with the geometrical definition of a point.

At whom was Sextus aiming his refutations? Some of the definitions criticized correspond to those found in Euclid's *Elements*, while others crop up in the definitions listed by Hero (Eucl. *El.* I deff. 2, 4, 5; Hero IV.14.10–18.6; 20.12–22; 22.14–21). But in arguing against the mathematicians he sometimes makes assumptions which they would find difficult to accept. For example, the assumption that a line consists of a collection or sum of points contradicts Euclid's first postulate, which requires the ability to draw straight lines connecting every point. Faced with a refutation based on this assumption, a geometer would have difficulty in getting himself to feel beaten.

It is not implausible that Sextus also had other targets. Philo of Alexandria refers to a doctrine which takes the treatment of the definitions of scientific principles as relevant to philosophy. It is philosophy which defines a point as something which has no parts, a line as length without size and a solid as something with three dimensions. Starting with these definitions, geometry discovered other notions, such as the isosceles and scalene, the circle, the polygon and other figures.[9] Presumably the philosophers who claimed a monopoly on definitions of scientific principles were mostly Stoics. A series of definitions of points, lines, surfaces and bodies is attributed in D.L. VII.135 to the Stoics, with explicit reference to the work *On Physics* by the Stoic Apollodorus of

---

[9] Phil. *Congr.* 146–7 (where he uses the same term θεμέλιος, 'foundation', as Sextus *M* III.10, 12; v.50; VIII.373). From the parallel at Cic. *De Or.* 1.187–9 one can assume that this theory had been advanced prior to the first century BC.

Seleucia, pupil of Diogenes of Babylon. Here, as in Sextus about five centuries later, definitions of the same entities crop up again, conceived in terms of the notion of limits. But a serious concern with the problem of these definitions is already found in Plato, the early Academy, and Aristotle.[10] In particular, definitions in terms of 'limits' and in terms of flowing were already widely known. One can therefore suppose that in attacking the definitions of fundamental geometrical entities Sextus and his ultimate sources were at the same time accusing also the dogmatic philosophers, who assumed responsibility for these definitions.

The problem of the conceivability of geometrical entities also predates Sextus. He mentions an example adapted from Aristotle in support of thinking of the line as length without size: the fact that we understand the length of a wall without reference to its size is proof that it can be thought of in this way. The cogency of the argument is based on the supposition that what occurs and works on an experiential level is transferable by analogy to the level of thought. Sextus concurs with this supposition, but makes the objection that we do not think of the wall as not having *any* size, but only without the size that particular wall actually has.[11] This line of argument and Aristotle's wall example were later used by the mathematician Apollonius of Perge. He used the fact that we can perceive the line which separates light from shadow (Procl. *Eucl.* 100.5–19; Hero IV.16.5–16) to confirm at the sensible level that we can think of a line as length without size. Possibly Apollonius was in this way trying to reply to the objections of earlier philosophers. The Epicureans and in particular the Stoics had listed a series of possible ways of conceiving intelligible entities (D.L. VII.52–3, X.32). Sextus took up these same methods, but put them to anti-dogmatic work with a view to showing that we cannot think of geometrical entities in the way they are defined by mathematicians and philosophers.

He was convinced that, with the principles destroyed, the theorems (*theorēmata*) which followed from them would also prove inconsistent: since it had no objects on which to base its existence, geometry could not be an art. Nevertheless he dedicated the last section of MIII (108–16) to showing that 'even if we disregard the principles, geometry can neither

---

[10] See for example Plato *Men.* 75d–76a; Arist. *Top.* VI.4.141b15–22; *Metaph.* N.3.1090b5–7; *An.* I.4.409a4. Authors of works entitled ὅροι are the Stoics Sphaerus (D.L. VII.178), Antipater (D.L. VII.60) and Chrysippus himself (see D.L. VII.199, under the title Ὅρων (τῶν) κατὰ τὰς ἄλλας τέχνας, but in a collection of ethical writings). On the question of the ontological status of mathematical entities according to the Stoics, see Mansfeld 1978, 158–67.

[11] *M* III.57–9; see also *M* IX.412–13. This theory does not appear in extant Aristotelian texts; the definition of a line as length without size is discussed at *Top.* VI.6.143b11–32.

construct nor demonstrate any theorem' (III.93). As well as theorems in the technical sense, he was speaking of problems and operations such as bisecting a given straight line or dividing a circle into equal parts. In these cases too the difficulties arose from considering the relationships between objects of different dimensions. As an example Sextus assumes that a straight line consists of nine points. Its bisection would therefore result in two unequal segments or the bisection of a central point. But the latter would be impossible, since the geometers define a point as having no dimensions. Sextus' last section shows formal parallels with the argument attributed by Proclus to Zeno of Sidon. In both cases an attempt is made to show that, even if the axioms are conceded, what follows from them is groundless. It should, however, be noted that Sextus makes no attempt to demonstrate the incompleteness of the collection of axioms. We certainly find indication of Epicurean arguments being used in Sextus' texts. One should remember that Demetrius Laco had also discussed the problem of bisecting the straight line. Sextus himself mentions an Epicurean objection to the idea of the revolution of a straight line (III.98).

But it would be restrictive to suppose that the anti-geometric argumentative arsenal used by Sextus was confined to Epicureanism.[12] In particular, one should not underrate the possible influence of material from the sceptical Academy, as well as from Pyrrhonism. A passage of Cicero's seems to confirm that even in Academic circles the definitions of point, line and surface were discussed, 'the mathematical principles, which must be conceded if any progress (*progredi*) is to be made' (*Acad.* II.116). This involves the distinction we have already met in Zeno of Sidon and Sextus between principles and what follows from them.[13] Sources attribute to Arcesilaus study in mathematics first with Autolycus of Pitane and subsequently at Athens with Hipponicus (D.L. IV.29, 32). The axiomatic–deductive structure is used by Autolycus and it could be that Arcesilaus learnt its characteristics from him, even if there is no sign that he attacked the basics of geometry. But Galen explicitly says of Carneades that he threw into doubt Euclid's first common notion that 'magnitudes which are equal to each other are all equal'. Carneades' arguments, preserved in the writings of followers of his, were still available at the time, but Galen does not report them (*Opt. Doct.* 2 1 45 K). Sextus does not discuss this axiom; in general, he does not discuss Euclid's common notions

---

[12] On the question of Sextus' Epicurean sources, in particular Zeno and Demetrius, see Angeli and Colaizzo 1979, 124–5; Gigante 1981, 210–14; Fowler 1984, 253–4.
[13] Cicero's *progredi* corresponds to Sextus' προκόπτειν (*M* III.18, 21; VIII.369) and προβαίνειν (III.65).

or his postulates, but only his definitions. One should compare this, however, with Apollonius of Perge's position, who before Carneades' time
had demonstrated Euclid's first axiom by using the idea of 'occupying
the same space' as a definition of equality (Procl. *Eucl.* 194.9-195.22).
Apollonius' reason for devising this demonstration is not known. Proclus
charges Apollonius with wanting to demonstrate an obvious thing by way
of something obscure and controversial, i.e. space. If Carneades was aware
that Apollonius had demonstrated this axiom, he might have considered
it a confirmation of its non-self-evident character, or of the existence of a
disagreement among the geometers themselves. The debate over the content of geometrical definitions must have developed before Carneades
anyway: Sextus mentions Eratosthenes as responding to objections
against the idea of the line, supporting the thesis that a point does not
occupy space, but produces a line by flowing (*M* III.28).

IV Philosophy, astronomy and astrology

Eratosthenes was the focus of contact between the world of the philosophers in Athens and the scientists in Alexandria. He lived in Athens at the
time when Aristo of Chios and Arcesilaus were active there, and was subsequently invited by Ptolemy Euergetes to Alexandria, where he was head
of the library. Archimedes dedicated his *Method for Theorems in Mechanics*
to him, characterizing him as a student of philosophy and someone able to
appreciate mathematics (II.428.18-24). The author of a work entitled
Platonicus, he recognized in the idea of proportion the link between the
different mathematical disciplines, probably by developing suggestions
from the *Republic* and the *Timaeus*.[14] His most famous scientific achievement was the measuring of the circumference of the earth. But in uniting
philosophical interests and the technical investigations of astronomy,
Eratosthenes is an exception. The dominant tendency implied a distinction in competences between astronomers and philosophers. The problems of measuring dimensions and distances of celestial bodies and the
construction of geometrical models of planetary movements, reproduced
by mechanical devices since the time of Eudoxus and subsequently by
Archimedes, were reserved for astronomers.

Epicurus' view regarding the division of responsibilities also represents
an exception, but of a different kind from the case of Eratosthenes.
Epicurus rejected the use of orreries, because they did not allow people to

[14] Theon Sm. 82.22-83.7; 107.15-24; Procl. *Eucl.* 43.22-3. See Solmsen 1942.

formulate in their minds a faithful reproduction of the phenomena that needed explaining. They were actually set up with the idea of determining the intrinsic properties of celestial bodies, which to us would appear to be characterized only by accidental properties. The verification of optical illusions raised doubts about the possibility of making accurate measurement of such phenomena from a position of terrestrial observation. In particular, the dimensions of the sun, which 'is just as it appears to us, but in itself is greater or smaller or as it appears', could not precisely be determined. The impossibility of determining precise measurements left open the entire gamut of possibilities and fed into the more general Epicurean objection to the pretexts of 'vain astronomy' of establishing a single cause for celestial phenomena. The analogy with terrestrial fires, which did not appear smaller even when at a distance, served to support the supposition that this also held true for the sun. The objective of these Epicurean considerations was probably to eliminate fears raised by the belief, shared by the Platonic Academy as the *Epinomis* (983a) confirms, that the celestial bodies appeared small but in reality were not. Epicurus' battle with mathematical astronomy was one chapter in a more general struggle which he fought against superstitious fears and those philosophies which justified or encouraged them.[15]

The Stoics on the other hand saw the regularity of the movements of the celestial bodies, demonstrated by the astronomers, as confirmation of the divine order of the universe and the power of the stars over what happened on earth. Convinced that the sun was the directing principle of the cosmos and revolved round the earth to take nourishment from its humid exhalations, Cleanthes firmly opposed Aristarchus of Samos, judged guilty of impiety for having put forward the theory that the earth revolved around the sun, which he represented as immobile at the centre of the orbit (Plu. *Fac. Lun.* 922f–923a; *Quaest. Conv.* 1006c). Perhaps Cleanthes thought that the positions of the celestial bodies in Aristarchus' model would no longer help to sustain Stoic cosmology, such as the doctrine of cycles and conflagration. This was tied to the completion of the great year, determined by the return of the sun, the moon and the planets to the same relative position. Aratus of Soli echoed Cleanthes' *Hymn to Zeus* to celebrate the divine rule of the world also expressed in the action of the stars, in his 1154-hexameter poem entitled *Phainomena*. As a true Hellenistic learned poet he furnished a detailed description of the constel-

---

[15] Ep. *Ep. Pyth.* 86, 91, 93, 113–14; Lucr. v.564–91 and Demetr. Lac. *PHerc.* 1013 (on the dimensions of the sun). See Sedley 1976b, Romeo 1979, Barnes 1989a and above pp. 418, 463, 505–7.

lations, and recounted their mythical origins. But as to its strictly astronomical content Aratus' poem is limited to the reproduction of a similarly entitled treatise by Eudoxus. Its last part concerns meteorological predictions, and is founded on the assumption that our world is full of signs sent by the gods to indicate the best time to sow or sail, but makes no reference to the drawing up of horoscopes. Yet it was exactly the astrological use of astronomy which became the debating point among philosophers, especially between the Stoics and the Academic sceptics.

The technical articulation of astrology is tied to the development of complex procedures of observation and calculation. These were developed thanks to the wide-ranging gathering of numerical data collected from observations, which was undertaken by Hipparchus of Nicea and others. Hipparchus seems to have displayed a certain interest in Stoicism. He criticized, how is not clear, the calculus of combinatorial logic of the conjunction of propositions made by Chrysippus (Plu. *Stoic. Rep.* 1047c–e; *Quaest. Conv.* 732f), while he shared with the Stoics the doctrine of weight as a propensity towards rest and as the capacity of bodies to resist movement (Simp. *Cael.* 264.25–266.3), as distinct from the notion of weight as the tendency to move downwards and to the centre, proposed by Aristotle.[16] This does not mean that Hipparchus was an adherent of Stoicism, nor that Stoicism or any other philosophy exerted a direct influence on the development of mathematical astronomy. Later sources associate Hipparchus with astrology, but it is difficult to assess their reliability. In fact, in his only surviving work, a commentary on Aratus, Hipparchus severely criticizes the astronomical part of the poem but says nothing about the last section, which deals with meteorological forecasts.[17] The earliest example known to us of a horoscope appears in the first century BC, but the possibility of drawing up horoscopes relies on data and calculations made in the second century BC by Hipparchus and later by Hypsicles in his work *On Ascension*. Horoscopes differ from simple predictions of the manner of one's death based on the date of one's birth, since they require the determination of the planetary positions within the signs of the zodiac at the point of birth, and therefore use tables which supply degrees and measurements to determine these positions. Euclid's *Phenomena* contains theories about the rise and fall of zodiacal signs, but does not give numerical data. In this context it seems more credible to

---

[16] On the Stoic theory of weight and gravity see pp. 443–8.
[17] On the possible connections of Hipparchus' doctrine of weight with Stoic theories see Wolff 1988; on his astronomical investigations see Neugebauer 1975, in particular vol. I, 277–8, 331–2 for the problems of astrology; on Aratus' commentary see Franco Repellini 1985.

assume that astrology took off in the Greek world in the second, rather than in the third century BC.[18]

The battle which from this point on took place among philosophers who were for or against astrology was absorbed into the wider argument about divination and divine providence. The philosophical support for astrology as a valid form of divination found in it a confirmation of determinism and cosmic harmony. This was the way the Stoics went; they were opposed by the Academic sceptics, in particular Carneades, who in his polemic against divination and the possibility of predicting the future may have included a consideration of astrology. But not all Stoics defended astrology to the end. Diogenes of Seleucia thought it was limited to the prediction of individual dispositions, not of particular events (Cic. *Div.* II.90). This restriction must have been drawn from the counter-example of twins, mentioned by Carneades in order to show that individuals born at the same time could have different lives and deaths. Panaetius added that he doubted the existence of a capacity for divination and, alone among Stoics according to Cicero (*Div.* 1.6; II.88), rejected astrological predictions. Cicero specifically mentions Panaetius as the source of the arguments against astrology put forward in his work *On Divination* (II.87–97). These are followed by other arguments in II.97–9, which may have their source in Carneades. The second book of Cicero's work contains material opposing astrology, which could have come from either the Academy or Panaetius. But the first book does not put forward arguments in favour of astrology. From this one can presume that the Stoics adopted only general formulations or that it was enough for them to recognize the existence of astrological and divinatory predictions in general without examining the reasons for them. As an indication of the validity of astrological knowledge, the Stoic spokesman in Cicero's work limits himself to examples from ancient tradition: the Chaldeans recorded their observations over the course of thousands of centuries. This affirmation is brutally rubbished in the second book: there is no evidence of this practice of recording and if it had existed it would not have come to an end.[19]

Another source concerned with the arguments against astrology is S.E. *M* v, where two levels of objection to astrology are distinguished: the first opposes it in principle and the second concerns the effects which should follow from the configuration of signs and planets at the moment of birth. The first objections are epistemological and methodological and are

---

[18] In support of the second century BC, see Neugebauer 1975, vol. II, 607–13 and Long 1982a; in support of bringing it back to the time of Chrysippus see Ioppolo 1985a. On astrology see also Bouché-Leclercq 1899 and, on the problems connected with divination and determinism, see above, pp. 534–7.   [19] Cic. *Div.* 1.2; 1.36–7; 1.111; II.97. See also S.E. *M* v.103–5.

directed towards showing the impossibility of constructing a horoscope, since it is impossible to observe and to record accurately and simultaneously the precise moment of birth and the astral configuration which goes with it. This more technical aspect is missing from Cicero's text, which is limited to pointing out that astrologers' observations depend on 'that most unreliable of senses', sight (*Div.* II.91).

The objections put forward by Cicero are instead directed at destroying or putting into doubt the general assumption of astrology, that is, that individual events necessarily depend on the influence exerted by the stars at the time of one's birth. But, says Cicero, it is difficult to believe that the differences in the distances of the planets from the earth are irrelevant, or that an influence could not come even from an almost infinite distance. Furthermore, the consequences produced by the influence of the stars must be unchangeable. But physical malformations present at birth can be corrected, by surgery for example. His final objection comes from the fact that the position of the planets and zodiacal signs at a particular moment vary according to the place of observation. The general conclusion from this first series of arguments, which Cicero claimed to have drawn from Panaetius, is that people born at the same time have different fates. Other arguments follow which show close parallels with Sextus' second section, regarding the outcome of the supposed causal activity of the stars.[20] The first two are presented in the form of a rhetorical interrogation, which comes to a necessarily negative response; the one starts from the point of view of the moment of death, the other from that of the moment of birth. Those who die in the same battle have the same destiny: should one conclude that they were all born at the same time? Alternatively, many people are born at the same moment: would they all have become a Homer? Two other arguments establish the arbitrariness of confining the influence of the stars to the destiny of human individuals, taking it as absurd that the destiny of animals and inanimate objects should also be determined by the stars. The arsenal of arguments for and against astrology increased after the Hellenistic era, when other astronomers dedicated to astrology, such as Ptolemy, entered into the discussion.

v Anatomy and philosophical questions

Links between philosophy and medicine are recorded in the fifth and fourth centuries BC, but there is no complete surviving medical text from

---

[20] The first set of arguments is laid out in *Div.* II.91–5; the second in II.97–9 with parallels, but not in the same order, in S.E. *M* v.88–94 and Favorinus in Gell. XIV.1.26–31.

the Hellenistic age earlier than the commentary on Hippocrates' *On Joints*, written in the first century BC by the Empiricist physician Apollonius of Citium. Most of our information on Hellenistic medicine comes from works written in the Imperial age, like the *De Medicina* of Celsus, who worked in the first century BC; the so-called *Anonymus Londinensis*, a papyrus which probably dates from the second century AD, belonging at least partly to a doxographical tradition originating with Aristotle and concluding with a section on the development of physiological doctrines from Herophilus to the first century AD; the work on *Women's Illnesses* by Soranus, a doctor belonging to the Methodist school of thought and active in the first half of the second century AD, as well as the author of a work on acute and chronic diseases, translated and reworked into Latin by Caelius Aurelianus (fifth century AD); and above all various works by Galen, especially *De Sectis ad Ingredientes* (*SI*), *De Placitis Hippocratis et Platonis* (*PHP*), *De Naturalibus Facultatibus* (*Nat. Fac.*), *De Usu Partium* (*UP*) and *De Methodo Medendi* (*MM*), and writings attributed to him erroneously such as *Introductio sive medicus* (*Int.*), the *Definitiones medicae* (*def. Med.*) and *De optima secta* (*Opt. Sect.*). It was above all Galen who established connections between the doctrines espoused by doctors in the Hellenistic age and philosophical views previous to or contemporary with these, but it is not always easy to determine whether these are actual historical links or affiliations devised by Galen himself or his sources.

A conspicuous novelty in Hellenistic medicine was the systematic use of anatomical dissection of human bodies, even if only for a brief period – the first half of the third century BC – and possibly only in Alexandria. According to Celsus this would have applied to the vivisection of criminals, which were put at the disposal of Herophilus of Chalcedon and Erasistratus of Ceos by the rulers of Alexandria.[21] The use of dissection led to problems which also attracted the attention of philosophers, like the explanation of voluntary and involuntary movements and the anatomical position of the principle which directs psychic activity. In *De Motu Animalium* Aristotle, in order to explain the transmission of voluntary movements produced by intellect and appetition, had recourse to the notion of the *pneuma* as a vehicle for them.

A learned doctor from the end of the fourth century, Praxagoras of Cos, had recognized the heart as the central organ of psychic and vital functions, but had distinguished between veins and arteries and shown the

---

[21] Cels. *Prooem.* 23–4; see also Tert. *An.* 10.4 and 25.5. There are doubts about the evidence of Celsus raised in Fraser 1969, but in opposition to these see Lloyd 1975 and von Staden 1989, 139–53. In general see also Edelstein 1932 and Kudlien 1969.

canals in the latter through which the *pneuma* carried its functions: the heart was the organ which helped to distribute to the body blood through the veins and *pneuma* through the arteries.[22] The dissection practised by Alexandrian doctors allowed the identification of relevant functions originating in the brain. Thanks to this Herophilus was able to observe the ventricles of the brain and to show in one of these the site of the central psychic organ and, in general, the origin of nerves in the brain, divided into sensory and motor nerves. Erasistratus also proceeded along this path, advancing the theory that the brain's ventricles contained *pneuma*, which was transmitted to the nerves; he called this kind of *pneuma* psychic to distinguish it from vital *pneuma*, present in the heart and arteries (it is not clear on what grounds).[23] In both cases, however, they were kept going by air taken in from outside by respiration; but in our documentation on Herophilus and Erasistratus there is no trace of the inborn *pneuma* of which Aristotle had spoken. It was instead the Stoics who took up this Aristotelian notion and gave support to the theory that the heart was the central organ of psychic functions.

According to Galen, Chrysippus maintained that the left ventricle of the heart contained psychic *pneuma*, while Erasistratus thought it contained vital *pneuma*. This disagreement was connected with the fact that while Chrysippus thought that there was only one origin for the nerves and veins, that is the heart, Erasistratus distinguished between the brain, the origin of the nerves, and the heart which was the origin both of the veins, which contained only blood, and of the arteries, which contained only vital *pneuma*.[24] It is perhaps not clear whether the contrast between Chrysippus and Erasistratus was emphasized by Galen or reflects an argument taken directly from Chrysippus. A verbatim quotation by Galen (*PHP* III.1, v 287–9K, pp. 200–2 De Lacy) from the first book of Chrysippus' *On the soul* shows that he knew a doxographical scheme which contrasted the different theses which, in a medical and philosophical context, placed the commanding principle (*hēgēmonikon*) of the soul in the chest or in the head or in a specific part of these parts of the body. Chrysippus does not name the supporters of the various theories, apart from Plato; parallel passages in other authors fill this gap and explicitly

---

[22] For what follows see also above, pp. 567–72.

[23] On the question of the nerves see Solmsen 1961 and Vegetti 1993; on Herophilus in particular see von Staden 1989, 247–59; on the theory of respiration see Furley and Wilkie 1984; on the vascular system see Harris 1973.

[24] Gal. *PHP* 1.6, v 185K; 11.8, v 281K, and also *Diff. Puls.* VIII 759K and *Foet. Form.* 4, IV 674K. On the Stoic concept of *pneuma* in cosmology and psychology see above, pp. 440–1 and 562–72; on psychology see Annas 1992a and Tieleman 1996.

mention Erasistratus. One cannot therefore rule out that Chrysippus knew Erasistratus' view, if only by way of doxography, even if there is no evidence that he had read Erasistratus.[25] He supported Praxagoras' theory not because he considered him a better anatomist, but because his tenet was in agreement with the conclusions of non-anatomical arguments which Chrysippus thought cogent and decisive.[26] The question of the location of the directive principle of the soul continued to be debated among philosophers, with opinion clearly favouring the heart and not for anatomical reasons. This is the position, following Chrysippus' line, of Diogenes of Babylon, author of a work entitled *On the Regent Part of the Soul*. Epicurus, starting from analysis of the passions, came to the same conclusion, though he did not share the Stoic theory of the unity of the soul: he placed it in the chest, and his school seems to have devoted some energy to supporting him on this point.[27]

Was the structure of organs and their connections, brought to light by dissection, enough on its own to explain their functions? This question had already troubled Aristotle, and we learn from Cicero (*Fin.* III.18) that even among doctors there was a dispute about the function of individual parts. Erasistrateans contemporary with Galen praised their founder for having followed Theophrastus and the Peripatetic philosophers.[28] Galen thought the Peripatetic connection counterfeit, made up by the Erasistrateans with the aim of ennobling their own sect by inferring a doctrinal affinity with Aristotelian tradition. He felt that Erasistratus and the Peripatetics had only one idea in common, namely that nature did nothing pointlessly. This was, however, a purely verbal agreement, since in practice Erasistratus destroyed this claim through his explanation of the functioning of the individual organs. He only referred to their mechanical movements, such as the opening and closing of the cardiac valves in relation to the working of the heart (*PHP* VI.6, V 549–50K, p. 396 De Lacy) or the epiglottis, which by closing prevented the mixing of air breathed in with ingested food and drink (Plu. *Quaest. Conv.* 698a–d). In the case of the epiglottis and also of the spleen, it is interesting that

---

[25] See Mansfeld 1989c and 1990a.

[26] See also Gal. *PHP* I.7, V 189K, and see the quotation from Chrysippus' *Physical questions* at Plu. *Stoic. Rep.* 1047c on his caution about questions which for their solution require *empeiria* and *historia*, like those of the epiglottis. On Chrysippus' methodology see Tieleman 1996, 147–255.

[27] On Diogenes see *SVF* III Diog. 27–39, and Tieleman 1996, 66–106. On Epicurus see D.L. x.66; Lucr. III.138–42; Demetr. Lac. *PHerc.* 1012, col. 46–7 Puglia.

[28] *Nat. Fac.* II.4, II 88–93K; *Art. Sang.* 7, IV 729K. One cannot eliminate the possibility that those to whom D.L. v.57 attributes the information, credible to him, that Erasistratus had been Theophrastus' pupil were Erasistrateans. See also S.E. *M* I.258. On the relationship between Erasistratus and Aristotle see Lonie 1964; Scarborough 1985; see now Von Staden 1997.

Erasistratus' view was similar to that of Aristotle, who did not consider such organs useful in themselves, even if nature could make advantageous use of them, and had consequently suggested that a teleological explanation should not be sought in all cases.[29]

Galen, however, made no comment about this agreement with Aristotle, just as he was silent in his *Procatarctic Causes* about the absence in Erasistratus of his supposed teleology. On the other hand, he records (*PHP* VII.3, V 602–4K, pp. 440–2 De Lacy; cf. *UP* VIII.13, III 673–4K) a quotation from Erasistratus, from which it appears that the great complexity of the anatomical structure of the human brain depends on the superiority of human thought over that of animals. Galen was a shade embarrassed, especially in *Natural Faculties* and *The Use of Parts*, in discussing the relationships between anatomy and physiology according to Erasistratus. He was unable to place Erasistratus among either the supporters or the opponents of the teleological interpretation of nature, and therefore adopted a strategy similar to that used by Plato in the *Phaedo* regarding Anaxagoras: Erasistratus had sung the praises of a nature which did nothing without a purpose and exhibited a providential concern for living things. But when it came to explaining the function and use of individual parts of the body, he failed to come up with a teleological explanation.[30]

Galen interpreted this as an explicit denial of the presence of a final cause in nature; perhaps however Erasistratus simply avoided the larger issue and limited himself to a general appreciation of the well-ordered structure of the organs. It is useful to recall that according to Plutarch (*Am. Prol.* 495c) Erasistratus had declared that 'nature has no trumpery (*rhōpikon*) about her'; but this is not the same as suggesting that 'nature does nothing without a purpose'. Perhaps Erasistratus conceived nature not in terms of intentionality but in those of a good disposition of the complex of organs, which is not incompatible with his mechanistic explanations of various physiological processes, such as digestion, the secretion of bile and urine, the flow of blood, and respiration. In these cases, as in the problem of why when an artery, which contains only *pneuma*, is seen to emit blood and not *pneuma* when punctured, Erasistratus made use of the notion of 'following into what is empty' (πρὸς τὸ κενούμενον ἀκολουθία), which implies that there is never

---

[29] Arist. *PA* III.670b31–3 on the spleen, together with IV.677a15–19; on the epiglottis, *PA* III.664b 20–665a26 and *Resp.* 476a23–b12 (see Repici 1990).

[30] There are numerous passages to this effect in Galen: see for example *UP* V.5, III 364–5K; *Nat. Fac.* II.2, II 78K; II 3, II.81 and 87K; *At. Bil.* 7, V 131–2K; *Ven. Sect. Er.* XI 158K, where the term προνοητική appears again; there is no proof that this term was used by Erasistratus himself, under the influence of the Stoa, *pace* Pohlenz 1967, I 336. See Lloyd 1991b.

anything actually in a state of emptiness. It is probable, judging from a quotation in Galen (*Nat. Fac.* II.6, II 99K), that Erasistratus recognized the difference between massed empty space, which he rejected, and dispersed void, which he was not concerned with. Both concepts were found useful by Hero, whose source is identified as Strato of Lampsacus, but there is no proof of a direct derivation of Erasistratus' theory from Strato's, even though the latter had sojourned in Alexandria.[31]

VI   Medical knowledge and experience

Medicine in the ancient world did not constitute a unified field of knowledge, founded on the acceptance of common assumptions, theories and methods, but was criss-crossed with other theories, often radical ones, about the character of medical knowledge and the roads leading to it. A common weakness at the therapeutic level helped to accentuate competition among doctors at the theoretical level and prompted them to adopt and elaborate upon doctrines and techniques which originally were employed in a philosophical context. In their turn the doctors proceeded to put together their own arguments which could be transferred to the arena of philosophical discussions, with the consequence that on specific questions, especially epistemic ones, the boundaries of medicine and philosophy remained fluid, even if, because of the lack of evidence, it is almost always impossible to identify the exact direction of these flows and currents between philosophy and medicine.[32]

A key moment in the epistemological discussions began when some doctors, perhaps as early as the second half of the third century BC, defined themselves as Empiricists in opposition to other doctors, designated collectively under the general label of Rationalists.[33] The Empiricists counted among the Rationalists all those who made the basis of medical knowledge a theory regarding the nature of the human body, its structure and functions, its normal or pathological states and the causes which produced them. The task of elaborating these theories was given to reason, which was capable of inferring, from what was visible, the existence of

---

[31] On the question of empty space see Furley 1985, Vallance 1990, 63–78, Algra 1995, 53–69 and Sedley in this volume.

[32] See Edelstein 1952 and Frede 1986a.

[33] The earliest evidence for the existence of the name 'Empiricist' dates to the end of the second or the beginning of the first century BC, in *PHerc.* 1012, where in col. 23 Puglia, Demetrius of Laconia mentions Apollonius the Empiricist; the text of col. 58 Puglia appears to claim that all sensations are false, which is of course not easily compatible with medical Empiricism. However, the attribution of this section to Apollonius, by Gigante 1981, 173, is conjectural, and seems also unlikely.

theoretically unobservable entities. This general characterization overlooked the often radical differences among the various doctors who could
be characterized as Rationalists, but was found to be an economical and
useful device particularly for purposes of controversy. We are told that the
Empiricist Serapion of Alexandria, mentioned in various texts as the
founder of the Empiricist school, whose *floruit* can be placed around 225
BC, had written a work entitled *Against the sects*. If this information is reliable it is not unlikely that he will have made use of the mostly polemical
literature *On sects*, also widespread in philosophical circles from the time
of Hippobotus.[34]

The most important sources for Empiricist medicine are the preface to
Celsus' *de Medicina* and three works by Galen: *An Outline of Empiricism* preserved in Latin translation, *On Medical Experience*, surviving only in Arabic
apart from two short sections in Greek, and *On Sects for the Beginners*.[35]
These works presuppose the existence of three schools among doctors,
named respectively Rationalists, Empiricists and Methodists, who are
presented as being at odds among themselves over how to get to know and
to practise the correct treatment of illnesses. Unlike the first two, the
Methodist tendency was formed and established only in the first century
AD, thanks principally to the work of Thessalos, a contemporary of Nero.
For the Methodists medical practice could be learned in a short time and
required only the recognition of three generalities or recurrent common
features (κοινότητες): all illnesses were in fact forms of constriction, dilation or both.

The theory worked out by Asclepiades of Bithynia, who lived between
the second and the early first century BC, is perhaps based on this conception, although he is usually placed among the Rationalist doctors and connected with the tradition of philosophical atomism. Indeed, according to
Asclepiades the body was composed of invisible corpuscles and pores, and
illnesses were caused by the obstruction of such pores or an excessive flow
through them.[36] But in contrast to Asclepiades the Methodists did not
consider the state of constriction or dilation to be hidden, unobservable
and inferable only by reason. These conditions were actually directly
observable, although their recognition (contrary to the opinion of the
Empiricists) did not require experience or repeated observations. These

---

[34] See Cael. Aurel. *Acut. Morb.* 11.6.32; Gal. *Lib. Prop.* XIX 38K and *Subf. Emp.* 11, p. 86.1–9. See
above, pp. 19–23.
[35] The second is translated by R. Walzer and the other two by M. Frede in Walzer and Frede 1985.
The documentation on the Empiricists is collected in Deichgräber 1965 (1930); on Celsus see
Mudry 1982. In general on Empiricist doctors, as well as Deichgräber, see Edelstein 1933,
Marelli 1981, Viano 1981 and especially Frede 1987b, 1988 and 1990.   [36] See Vallance 1990.

pathological states, as soon as they were observed, immediately furnished an indication of the means by which they could be cured, namely constriction by means of dilation and conversely, just as hunger immediately indicates a need for food (S.E. *PH* 1.238–40). The accounts of Hellenistic medicine supplied by texts from the Imperial age, therefore, reflect in an advanced stage discussions and polemics which had gone on among those belonging to these three schools about the origins, characteristics and scope of medical knowledge. It is accordingly not always easy to retrace the original physiognomy of the Empiricist school, still less to identify its precise relationship with previous or contemporary philosophies.

The general theory that medical knowledge is acquired only through experience can be attributed to the early Empiricists. Medicine was a collection of theorems, i.e. direct personal observations (*autopsia*) of whatever proved beneficial or harmful to sick people not just once, but repeatedly. These observations were not deliberate but – for the most part – casual or improvised and, according to the Empiricists, one could not raise in advance the issue of the relevance of what was to be observed. Rationalist doctors would object that only reason allowed one to decide what should be observed, but this objection focuses upon the notion of intentional observation, which according to the Empiricists is not equally relevant. For them, what was important was not the reason why remedies are successful, but the fact that they have been successful. Past experience informed them of this. But the observations of one individual were not on their own enough to constitute medical experience; it took the accumulated experience of numerous individuals over the course of time. For this, an essential ingredient of medical knowledge was *historia*, the collection of facts recorded by other people from their own observations.

Later on, the problem of evaluating the reliability of these accounts may have been put to the Empiricists: among their criteria they list agreement among however many people had written about a particular thing or event, as long as it was something observable. Galen (*Subf. Emp.* 8, p. 68.8–13) uses the example, also found in the Epicurean Philodemus (*Sign.* col. 32.13–21), of Crete, Sicily and Sardinia, which even those who had not visited them considered to be islands, since those who did have direct experience of them agreed in calling them islands. According to Celsus (*Prooem.* 17 and 36), the Empiricists, following the Hippocratic treatise *On the Places in Man* (VI 342 L), thought that all remedies had been discovered and that there could be no new kinds of illness. This was a subject discussed again in the Imperial age in a non-medical context (Plu. *Quaest. Conv.* VIII.9).

There seems to be a contrast between this conviction about the definitive acquisition of medical knowledge and a third ingredient of the craft of medicine, 'the transition to the similar', attributed in the sources to the Empiricists. This referred to a situation in which one is fighting against a disease which has not previously been observed, or one which is known but in a place in which treatment is not known to be definitely effective. In such cases, treatment shown to be beneficial for a particular organ or disease is appropriate to a similar organ or disease, as is a remedy similar to one already tried out, but still related to the same illness. The 'transition to the similar' involves a conscious and intentional extension of experience already acquired to cases not yet studied, and has heuristic overtones, not immediately reconcilable with the purely receptive character of the original notion of experience. It was actually introduced later on by the Empiricists, but the titles of works by Serapion and Glaucias of Tarentum (a little after Serapion), respectively the *Per tria sermo* ('Account of the Three') and the *Tripod*, mentioned by Galen (*Subf. Emp.* 11, p. 83.22–3), could lead one to attribute this third element of medical skill to early Empiricists.

In the second century AD, however, Menodotus maintained that Serapion had not thought of the transition to the similar as a third constituent part of medicine, but only made use of it, while the Pyrrhonist Cassius sought to show that he had not even used it at all (*Subf. Emp.* 4, p. 49.23–31). Because the ancient sources fail to provide indubitable information, it is difficult to determine with certainty whether Serapion had already worked out the concept of the transition to the similar in an articulate way, though this cannot be excluded insofar as Glaucias is concerned.

The early Empiricists' theory of experience was not created out of thin air: it had predecessors in areas which were not only medical, such as the Hippocratic treatise *On Ancient Medicine*, but also non-medical, such as the historians who indicated sight and hearing as the basic channels by which information was recorded, or philosophers like Plato and Aristotle who had already taken note of the connections between perception, memory and experience.[37] In antiquity Empirical medicine and sceptical philosophy were already put on a par because both contended that one should suspend judgement about the things that are obscure, and concentrate on the *phainomena* instead. Yet it does not follow that the Empiricists raised

---

[37] See for example Plato *Grg.* 448c, 501a; *Rep.* 516c–d; Arist. *Metaph.* A.980a27–981b2; *APo.* 99b36–100a9; D.L. x.33 for Epicurus and Aët. iv.11 for the Stoics.

doubts about the reliability of the perceptions, or even denied this reliability by employing arguments which would show that perceptions are relative. The problems about whether the senses were deceptive or whether what appeared was as it appeared or whether it was possible to distinguish between true or false observations do not seem to have been among the concerns of the Empiricists, who gave credence to their own perceptions and, under certain conditions, also trusted those of others. Nor did they seem to share with the Academics and Pyrrhonists (Cic. *ND* 1.62; S.E. *PH* 1.88–9, II.45) the refusal to consider favourably any argument based on the consensus of everyone or the majority. In fact, they considered that the same thing or event or sequence of events could be observed in the same way by different observers even when separated by time or space. It was actually the Rationalist doctors who formulated sceptic arguments against the Empiricists' theory of experience, by asking how it was possible to know that one illness is always the same as another, and that what one individual sees is the same as what another sees, or by using sorites arguments to show that it was impossible for the Empiricists to determine the number of observations necessary to make a theorem of medical practice acceptable.[38]

VII Medical disputes and philosophical arguments

Medical doctrines considered Rationalist often introduced entities and states which were unobservable, not only occasionally but by their very nature. A typical case was that presented by Erasistratus, who had assumed the existence of *pneuma* in the arteries, of a flow of blood from the veins into the arteries in pathological situations through small canals called *anastomōseis*, and of the so-called *triplokia*, that is, the structure of veins, arteries and nerves as constituted by the interlacing of these three kinds of vessel, introduced so as to explain how the nerves could be nourished. Erasistratus had also conducted experiments with the aim of proving the occurrence of events which were not directly observed.[39] For the Empiricists it was a matter of combating the pretensions involved in inferring what was unobservable and attributing to reason a role in the acquisition of medical knowledge. In this respect their view turned out to have an affinity with that of the sceptic philosophers.

---

[38] Gal. *Med. Exp.* 4 and 7. See Barnes 1982b, Burnyeat 1982b.
[39] See Gal. *Art. Sang.* VI 708–9K; *UP* VII.8, III 537–8K; *Nat. Fac.* II.6, II 95–6K; Anon. Lond. XXI.23–33 and XXXIII.43–51. On experiments see Lloyd 1964 and von Staden 1975.

An attempt to connect the Empiricist physicians with the Pyrrhonist school by inserting them into the succession that begins with Pyrrho appears in D.L. IX.115-16, but probably is an elaborate construction by later Pyrrhonists.[40] The information in D.L. IX.109 that Timon taught medicine to his son Xanthus and made him his heir has led to the hypothesis that Timon also was a doctor. This does not entail that Xanthus succeeded Timon as head of a school; in fact Xanthus is not mentioned in the Pyrrhonist succession and Diogenes reports the view of Menodotus, according to whom Timon had no successors at all. Galen (*Subf. Emp.* 1, p. 43.2-3), in his turn, also names Timon among the founders to whom the Empiricists might have traced their movement, and presents Menodotus as a Dogmatist who did not hesitate to make assertions, unlike Pyrrho, who was praised by Menodotus nevertheless. The attitude of a true Empiricist towards medicine is compared in Galen's text to that of a Pyrrho towards life (11, pp. 82.20-83.2 and pp. 84.31-85.3). On the other hand, Sextus Empiricus links Empiricist medicine with Academic philosophy, which dogmatically claims that things cannot be understood, unlike the true sceptic who suspends judgement (*PH* 1.236-41; cf. *M* VIII.191). These discussions on the relationship of Empiricist medicine with Academic scepticism or with (Neo-)Pyrrhonism assume that a distinction between these two schools had already been worked out. Therefore it probably dates to a subsequent stage in the rebirth of Pyrrhonism, and to the work of Aenesidemus in the first century BC.[41]

To the Empiricists even anatomy, as a means of conducting intentional observations in artificial conditions, seemed completely untrustworthy. They rejected vivisection, calling it a useless cruelty since in fact it coincided with the dissection of a corpse and did not supply any further information. The dissection of corpses, in its turn, produced alterations in the object of observation, and it was therefore impossible to maintain that the body's internal parts, once they had been artificially exposed, remained in the same condition as before. This objection came up again in the context of the Academic argument in support of the unknowability of things, as Cicero shows (*Acad.* II.122). Moreover, the Empiricists refused to accept the hypothesis that systematic anatomical inquiry leads to knowledge. Such knowledge could not in fact be superior to that resulting from casual

---

[40] See above, p. 46.

[41] Edelstein 1933 has drawn attention to the Academy as an outlet for scepticism in the Hellenistic age and therefore as an appropriate target of confrontation for Empiricist medicine; on the affinity with the Academics in the presentation of the Empiricists in Celsus see Mudry 1990. For the relationship with Pyrrhonism see Decleva Caizzi 1986 and especially 1992a.

observation of the configuration, the location and the order of internal parts, when these were uncovered in the bodies of wounded gladiators, soldiers, or travellers attacked by bandits.[42] But one should not forget that Herophilus had been cautious about the knowledge furnished by anatomical descriptions: this was a necessary point of departure, but not sufficient to develop a theory regarding the functions of bodily parts. According to Galen (*Foet. Form.* IV 678–9K), Herophilus thought it necessary to integrate anatomical observation, but this integration was supplied by other appearances (*phainomena*) rather than by theory (*logos*) or the appeal to theoretically unobservable entities. This was perhaps his basic methodological precept: 'Let the appearances be described first even if they are not primary.'[43]

Even before the Empiricists, Herophilus had criticized the concept of cause through the following kind of argument: if there is a cause, it must be A or B or C; but neither A nor B nor C; therefore cause does not exist. Such arguments are mentioned by Galen (*CP* 13.162–4 and 16.197–204) and they reappear, in the same order, with expanded demonstrations of why neither A nor B nor C in Sextus (*M* IX.207, 210, 227–36); here they are attributed to anonymous *aporētikoi* ('problem-seekers'). This has led to the suggestion that Herophilus drew on sceptic arguments, but it has been rightly observed that sceptical arguments about causality are not attested for Aenesidemus' predecessors; it is therefore wise to assume a medical origin for them. This does not entail that the disjunctive form was invented by Herophilus, for this is already found in earlier philosophers, e.g. Gorgias in the *Helen*, or Zeno of Elea's or Diodorus Cronus' arguments against motion. An anecdote (S.E. *PH* II.245) recounts that Diodorus, having dislocated an arm, went to Herophilus for a cure, but was told: 'Your shoulder has been put out either in the place where it was or where it was not; but it was put out neither where it was nor where it was not; therefore it has not been put out.' There is, of course, no proof of the accuracy of this tale, which nevertheless is not a banal repetition of Diodorus' argument against motion, in which the verbs used are in the present tense. The use of verbs in the perfect and imperfect tenses in the anecdote seems intentionally designed to attack the possibility, acknowledged by Diodorus, of stating that something has moved in the past (S.E. *M* X.85–101).[44]

---

[42] Cels. *Prooem.* 40–4; Tert. *An.* 10.4; Gal. *AA* II 288K; [Gal.] *Def. Med.* XIX 357K.
[43] Anon. Lond. XXI.18–23; Gal. *MM* II 5, X 107K. Kudlien 1964 puts Herophilus with the sceptics, while von Staden 1989, 117–24 emphasizes his Aristotelian background. See also Tieleman 1996, 22–3, Hankinson 1990, 213–15.   [44] See above, pp. 356–60.

Even Erasistratus, a doctor inclined to allow for theoretically unobservable entities, had conducted a destructive campaign against the notion of cause. The superfluity of blood which poured out from the veins and arteries was seen by him as the sole cause of diseases, on the basis of the assumption that something can have the status of a cause only if it unfailingly produces the same effect.[45] This argument also has parallels in philosophical contexts, as in the definition of cause given by the Stoic Zeno (Stob. 1.138.14–22) and in S.E. *M* IX.237–48, but in the present case there is no need to assume a non-medical origin. It is indeed possible that Erasistratus developed the kind of argument which can be found in the Hippocratic treatise *On Ancient Medicine* (xx.5–6), where it is stated that if cheese were harmful to human nature, it would affect all men and not only some of them.

The Erasistratean conception of causality is incompatible with the acceptance of antecedent or procatarctic causes, which do not always produce illness. The Empiricists accept procatarctic causes, which Celsus (*Prooem.* 18 and 27) calls *evidentes*, and considered them to be components of the syndrome as causes of this nature (Gal. *MM* x 244K; *Comp. Med. Loc.* XII.527K). The appearance of these in the syndrome led to connecting them with the notion of signs. To identify an illness, according to the Empiricists, it was not enough to point out the salience of a single sign: the ailment is the collection or the coincidence of many symptoms, which present themselves as connected among themselves and occur in the same order in repeated observations. The name of an illness is only a label or a compendious expression invented for a syndrome in a teaching context (Gal. *MM* x 460K; *Loc. Aff.* VIII 14K; *Subf. Emp.* 6, pp. 56.12–58.27). This does not mean that one should record everything that presents itself to observation, nor that one should choose by reason what it is appropriate to observe; only unintentional repeated observations permit the narrowing down of details, ascertaining the frequency and the order in which they occur, and the distinction between signs common to most complaints and signs unique to this one (Gal. *Hipp. Off. Med.* XVIIIB 644K; *Opt. Sect.* I 135–6K).

This distinction between common and specific signs is noted by Cicero (*Acad.* II.34) and one finds connections with that between indicative and commemorative signs in Sextus (*M* VIII.200–2), in the sense that the indicative signs are signs of a single and identical thing, while the commemorative

---

[45] Gal. *Ven. Sect. Er.* XI 153–4K; *Art. Sang.* IV 715K; *CP* 1.9–10, 8.102–4 and 13.166–7; Cels. *Prooem.* 54. On the problem of causality in philosophy and medicine see Barnes 1990c, 2614–17, 2649–89, as well as Hankinson 1987b and 1990; see also above, pp. 508–9.

ones can belong to many different things and are therefore not real signs. But in the view of the Empiricists both common and specific signs came under what Sextus called commemorative signs, the only kind of sign which they recognized and for which [Gal.] *Def. Med.* xix 396K preserves the definition they had given it. What remains controversial is the question of the origin of the distinction between indicative and commemorative signs: is it medical or philosophical?[46] One cannot rule out the idea that the two notions were developed independently in different environments, and were only linked later. The reportage in Sextus (*M* viii.141–298; *PH* ii.97–133) connects them, but the references to Aenesidemus (*M* viii.215–16 and 234; cf. D.L. ix.96–7) show that he was attacking the sign in general. Nor are there definite traces of a discussion of the sign by the Empiricists in terms of propositions and conditionals, as is the case in Sextus' treatment.[47]

In turning their attention to the notion of signs, the Empiricist physicians did not necessarily need to draw on the heritage of philosophical arguments. In the texts cited by Diogenes Laertius and Sextus there are connections between signs and the domain of obscure things (*adēla*) and their relationship with the three dimensions of time. In both of these concerns the Empiricist doctors had behind them an established medical tradition, aware of the diagnostic and prognostic function of signs, as appears for example in the Hippocratic treatises *Prognostic* and *Epidemics* i. The contrast between obvious and obscure things, i.e. the internal and inaccessible parts of the body, is already found in *Ancient Medicine* and *On the Art*. The latter work (11–12) shows signs to be the means thought out by medicine to allow for the knowledge of things not directly perceivable, and mentions procedures intended to stimulate artificial manifestations of symptoms by which to formulate inferences about the pathological situation. An Empiricist physician could not have welcomed this programme, which points directly to the indicative sign. On the other hand, the connection of signs with time was at the centre of attention for Praxagoras, who had differentiated between concomitant signs and those which emerged during the course of an illness.[48] According to the Empiricists Rationalist doctors transformed signs into causes and the

---

[46] The attribution of this to the Dialecticians, in particular to the Megaric Philo, is maintained in Ebert 1991. See also Burnyeat 1982c, 212–14 and especially Glidden 1983a, also for a discussion of the preceding literature; see further Allen 1993 and Hankinson 1995, 225–36.

[47] For the opposite theory see Matthen 1988a, 109–13.

[48] Gal. *Hipp. Aph.* xviii A 56K and xviii B 390K, as well as Steckerl 1958, 27–9. See also the agreement between Herophilus and the Empiricists in the use of the triple-timed inference from signs (τρίχρονος σημείωσις) (Gal. *Plen.* 8, vii 554–5K).

temporal sequence into a logical connection, established not empirically but by the use of reason. They felt that one could not infer that what came before in time was the cause of what followed: in this sense the so-called procatarctic or antecedent signs were more properly signs, that is, events which one could see occurring repeatedly before other events. The connection between before and after in the sign relation was therefore properly established in the memory only as a recollection of repeated observations: at their centre was a conjunction of events in accordance with temporal co-ordinates, not with logical connections in the form of a conditional. It was memory which allowed the accumulation of observations of oneself and of other people, and the possibility of recalling them as a guide for treatment (Gal. *Subf. Emp.* 6, p. 58.11–21): memory could perform functions like the formulation of empirical generalizations, recognition in what was observed of something which had been observed before, diagnosis and prognosis through signs, which the Rationalists had attributed to reason. In this way the theory of the Empiricist physicians, even if it shows parallels with concepts and doctrines found in Aristotle or Epicurus, followed its own path.[49]

[49] On this point Frede 1990 is important.

PART V

ETHICS AND POLITICS

*

19

The Socratic legacy

A. A. LONG

1 Introduction

From the perspective of 100 BC the history of ethics in the Hellenistic period is dominated by Stoicism and Epicureanism. The sceptical Academy had also made a significant contribution by criticizing the Stoics and by classifying alternative theories of the *summum bonum*,[1] but in the Peripatos social philosophy, though it remained alive, was scarcely vigorous. When Epicurus and Zeno first established their schools at Athens, these developments could not have been foreseen. At that time the Academy was still the centre of doctrinal Platonism, and Theophrastus at the Peripatos included ethics among the numerous subjects on which he wrote and lectured. Many other philosophers were also stimulating reflection on the foundations of happiness and attracting followers – Cynics, Cyrenaics, Menedemus, Stilpo, Pyrrho. Ethics was a hotly debated subject around the year 300 BC.

That fact helps to explain why Epicurus and Zeno were rapidly able to acquire an audience. Yet there was no reason to predict that the schools they founded would soon become the main ethical options. Why did those schools achieve such a dominating position? With hindsight it can be seen that they offered an informed choice between two radically different ways for persons to orient themselves. Antithetical though they are in cosmology, theology, attitude to politics and evaluation of virtue relative to pleasure, Stoicism and Epicureanism closely resemble one another in being comprehensive philosophies of life. Both their mutual exclusiveness and their comprehensiveness are factors that help to explain the remarkable success both philosophies achieved.[2] These, of course, are also retrospective judgements. There is no evidence either that Zeno was primarily inspired by opposition to Epicurus or that Epicurus gave serious attention

---

[1] For Academic criticism of Stoic ethics, cf. Long and Sedley 1987, ch. 64, which includes Carneades' classification of alternative ethical theories (Cic. *Fin*. v.16–20), and ch. 69.
[2] For detailed treatment of these two factors, see Long 1993a, 138–42, 154–6.

to his younger rival. For understanding where both philosophers start from, we need to review the limits of agreement and disagreement to be found in philosophical ethics as it already existed. That kind of survey is essential in order to approach such questions as the novelty or special character of Hellenistic ethics, its relation to the impulses inaugurated by Socrates and his followers, and the proposal, which is often made, that Stoicism and Epicureanism were peculiarly suitable for persons living in the Hellenistic world.

11 The Socratic presence in Greek ethics

The concept of a Socratic tradition in ethics goes back to the Hellenistic historians of philosophy (cf. D.L. 1.13–20). It derives from their practice of identifying 'founders' of intellectual movements, and of tracing lines of 'succession' from the founder to the latest representative of a 'school'. From an historical point of view this procedure is much too contrived and uniform. However, the 'succession' writers, if only accidentally, identified the fact that Plato and other followers of Socrates were primarily responsible for establishing most of the ethical concepts and issues which were familiar to and explored by thinkers as distant from Socrates in time as Zeno, Epicurus, and the second generation of Peripatetics headed by Theophrastus. The concepts include happiness (*eudaimonia*) as the ultimate objective of all action (*telos*),[3] the identification of this objective with the acquisition of good(s), and the relation of both of these primary concepts to the following – excellence or virtue (*aretē*), rationality, desire or volition, emotion, pleasure, justice, friendship, and the distinction between soul (*psuchē*) and body. Socrates' name could also be associated with such issues as the inter-relation of the virtues (especially wisdom, courage, justice and moderation), the relation of the virtues to knowledge, the supreme importance of wisdom or *phronēsis*, the value of pleasure relative to virtue, the criteria for utility, the distinction between intrinsic and instrumental goods, the relation of happiness and virtue to social and familial obligations. These concepts and issues are as central and vital to Hellenistic ethics as they had been in their original Socratic contexts.

The strongest and most diffused element in this Socratic tradition is the notion that it is the task of philosophy to establish rational foundations

---

[3] Although Plato's Socrates does not emphasize the concept of *telos* in Aristotle's manner, it is first adumbrated in the Platonic corpus; cf. *Grg.* 499e, *Symp.* 205a–d. For *telos* in the evidence for Cyrenaic ethics, cf. D.L. 11.87–8, 97–8.

for an individual's happiness.[4] On this point nearly all philosophers were agreed, however much they differed in their doctrines concerning the content of happiness and the scope of philosophy itself. On the broadest construal of philosophy, by Aristotle and Theophrastus, scientific study for its own sake is an essential element of happiness. The Cynics, by extreme contrast, restrict philosophy to a practice for training persons so as to reduce their needs and desires to a minimal 'natural' level. In Stoicism and Epicureanism philosophy includes more than ethics, but the official justification for other studies is their utility for the conduct of life (cf. Epicurus *Ep. Men.* 122, *KD* 11–12; and for Stoicism, *SVF* II 35 and Cicero *Off.* I.13–19).

This Socratic tradition is sufficiently unitary to facilitate dialogue and comparison between the alternative ethical theories. However, the formal unity of the conceptual framework coincides with enormous differences – not only, as has been noted, over the scope of philosophy but also over its style of presentation, social role, organization, and urgency or radicalism as an art of life. For understanding the Socratic legacy to Hellenistic ethics, we need to distinguish between Socrates' generic influence, as transmitted by his followers, and ethical theories which are modelled directly on interpretations of the life and persona of Socrates. It is the second of these which will particularly concern us in this chapter. How it adds to and differs from the first kind of influence can best be clarified by reference to Aristotle.

From our modern perspective, it is Aristotle who did the most to formalize ethics along the lines first charted by Socrates, or rather, Plato's Socrates. Yet, as a moral philosopher Aristotle was far more directly indebted to Plato than to anything he himself admitted to be Socratic. On the few occasions when Aristotle discusses a thesis he attributes to Socrates, it is largely to criticize.[5] He scarcely hints at the moral significance of Socrates' life, or his paradigmatic role. As for Aristotle's successors, some of them were notorious for spreading scandalous stories about Socrates' personal conduct. We can probably conclude from this that the Peripatos, at the time of Zeno and Epicurus, wished to distance itself from any official affiliation to Socrates. In what survives of Theophrastus' ethics, there is almost complete silence about him.

Many explanations for the calumny and the silence suggest themselves. Cynics, and possibly Cyrenaics too, were publicizing Socrates' reputed

---

[4] On Socratic eudaimonism, cf. Vlastos 1991, 200–32. For discussion of it as the common property of Plato, Aristotle, Epicurus and the Stoics, cf. Long 1988a, 79–83.

[5] This point and those that immediately follow are more fully developed in Long 1988b, 154–5.

aversion to scientific speculation. That could not have gone down well
with the Peripatetics. Another factor to reckon with is rivalry between the
Peripatetics and those philosophers who wanted to be perceived as
Socrates' heirs. Still more important, probably, is the general tenor of
Peripatetic ethics. Although Aristotle's ethical treatises are a marvellous
analytical achievement and in some respects far from conventional, they
take much of their material from the values and practices that were common currency among the elite of Athenian society. Aristotle also had a
much more hard-headed view of what ethics can do to assure a person's
happiness than is typically to be found in the theories that preceded and
followed him. Such realism is still more evident in the fragmentary
remains of the ethics of Theophrastus. In addition to making happiness
vulnerable to misfortune, he acknowledged that chance could warp character and that virtue could be lost.[6]

Whether or not Epicurus and the earliest Stoics had immediate access
to Peripatetic literature on ethics, we can assume that they had a general
familiarity with such points as have just been outlined.[7] Those points
facilitate a contrast, not only with Stoicism and Epicureanism, but also
with some of the other ethical options available at the time when Epicurus
and Zeno began to teach. These include the Cynics, Cyrenaics and
Pyrrho. The first of these movements had a decisive influence on Stoicism;
the second, probably more negatively than positively, on Epicurus, who
also confessed to admiration for Pyrrho's lifestyle (D.L. IX.64). Even
though some Epicureans (but not perhaps Epicurus himself) were critical
of Socrates, he was a precursor of Epicurus in his devoted band of followers and the paradigm he afforded of someone perfected in his own practices.[8] The Hellenistic philosophers trade heavily on the concept of a
'wise man', which had already been foreshadowed by the hagiography of
Socrates.[9] Equally Socratic and non-Aristotelian is their depreciation of
conventional values such as wealth or public renown, and their specification of happiness in terms of freedom, tranquillity and autonomy. These
common factors are the final promise of philosophies which arrive at their
shared agenda by different routes and involve different assessments of

[6] Cf. F 495–9, 462–3, 465 in Fortenbaugh 1992b.

[7] See Long 1968; cf. Irwin 1986. But Sandbach 1985 argues against influence on Stoic ethics from
Aristotle's treatises. I argue a similar thesis against influence from Theophrastus in Long 1997.

[8] For Epicurean hostility to Socrates, see Kleve 1983. In Long 1988b, 156, I suggest that
Epicurean attacks on Socrates may 'be seen, at least in part, as a means of undercutting the most
obvious alternative (i.e. non-Epicurean) models of the philosophical life – Socrates as interpreted by Stoics and Academics'.

[9] For evidence on the *sophos* (early Pyrrhonism, Epicureanism, Stoicism, Academic scepticism),
cf. the references cited in Long and Sedley 1987, vol. I, 512 s.v. 'wise man'.

particular values. However, it clearly makes sense to distinguish them all from the more conservative ethics of Aristotle and Theophrastus.

The 'wise man' has a history in Greece that predates philosophy. In its Hellenistic usages, adumbrated already by the Cynics and Cyrenaics (cf. D.L. II.93-9, VI.72), the 'wise man' becomes a technical term for the paradigm of ethical understanding *and* every other positive attribute of a specific philosophy. It is this second condition which distinguishes the Socratic and Hellenistic philosophers' 'wise man' from the *phronimos* to whom Aristotle in his ethics frequently appeals as the standard of rationality. Unlike Aristotle, those philosophers most directly influenced by Socrates were radical in their approach to convention – hence such distinctive figures as Diogenes, Aristippus, and also the utopianism of Plato himself. The once fashionable treatment of Hellenistic ethics as a panacea for contemporary unhappiness failed to indicate that it is Aristotelian ethics which looks anomalous from a third century BC perspective on the Greek philosophical tradition. Aristotle's respect for many of the things traditionally valued in Greek social and political life made his ethics ill-suited to the more cosmopolitan realities of the Hellenistic world. But it would probably be a mistake to suppose that Zeno and Epicurus had highly original insights into these cultural data, which they made central to their ethics. The truth seems to be rather that the ethical theories which most shaped their thinking – those deriving from philosophers who had associated with Socrates (and from Democritus too, in the case of Epicurus) – were already less dependent on gender, class and ethnic identity than an outlook such as Aristotle's.[10]

Our Socrates is predominantly Plato's, but for persons of the age of Zeno and Epicurus Plato was only one of Socrates' renowned associates. The others include Antisthenes, Aristippus and Xenophon. Antisthenes and Aristippus are shadowy figures, but important for their formative influence on Cynicism and Cyrenaicism respectively. Xenophon, though less of a philosopher than either, was widely read for his record and defence of Socrates. Indeed, the biographical tradition on the Stoic Zeno refers to Xenophon's *Memorabilia* of Socrates as his introduction to philosophy (D.L. VII.2-3; cf. VII.31-2). That anecdote may well be apocryphal, but it rings true to the central role some Stoics accorded to Socrates as an authority in ethics.

To his immediate circle Socrates had been a paradigm of the excellence

---

[10] For affinities between Democritus and Socratic ethics, cf. Kahn 1985, esp. 6-10, 26-9. For the common ground between Plato's and Xenophon's Socrates, cf. Morrison 1987.

he investigated. The strangeness of his life and the tragedy of his death were challenges to inquiry. No less provoking were divergences in the interpretation of his role and attitudes by those who had known him. Was Socrates a hedonist, or an enemy of pleasure? Did he intend his profession of ignorance to be taken seriously? Where did he stand on political involvement? On such questions the Socratic literature gave ambiguous responses. Yet it was unanimous in regarding Socrates as the model of how a philosopher should conduct himself.

In the various representations of Socrates by those associates who wrote about him common features are not hard to find. What Plato emphasizes, and what most forcefully impressed Xenophon, Antisthenes or even Aristippus, is Socrates' advocacy and practice of 'caring for' oneself, for one's autonomy and rational integrity. (Although Aristippus' hedonism may seem antithetical to Socrates' moral concerns, it is quite compatible with a commitment to rational integrity and autonomy.) This 'technology of the self', as Michel Foucault has well described it, was Socrates' great challenge to popular morality.[11] There justice had largely been seen as obedience to divine or human rules. Prosperity or happiness (*eudaimonia*) was vaguely believed to depend upon the gods' approval of such obedience, but because happiness primarily signified good fortune its connection with justice was a piece of piety scarcely justified by experience. What probably struck Socrates' followers as most remarkable about him was his radically internalist conception of happiness, what Plato calls 'the health of the soul', and its detachment from conventional ideas of good fortune. Both Plato and Xenophon stress Socrates' mastery over the appetites that trouble ordinary people, and which typically motivate unethical conduct. If that characterization strikes us today as banal, we should reflect that Greek literature prior to Socrates offers nothing comparable. That no doubt explains why Xenophon says:

> Socrates was the most self-controlled of all men over sex and bodily appetite, the most resilient in relation to winter and summer and all exertions, and so trained for needing moderate amounts that he was satisfied when he had only little. (*Mem.* II.1.1)

A Socrates of this kind is presupposed, *mutatis mutandis*, by Antisthenes and the Cynics on the one hand, and the Aristippean/Cyrenaic school on the other. What distinguishes these interpretations from one another is their over-emphasizing certain Socratic traits at the expense of others.

---

[11] Cf. Foucault 1988.

What the interpretations agree on, as they also agree with Xenophon and Plato, is that a Socratic lifestyle is one in which a person is maximally self-sufficient, in control of his or her own life, and uses reason as the instrument of satisfying the conditions for happiness.[12] The essential point is captured by the following anecdote concerning the Megarian philosopher Stilpo. He had lost his property in an Athenian attack on his homeland. When the general Demetrius offered to restore it to him, Stilpo responded: 'I have lost nothing that belonged to me since no one has removed my education, and I still have my reason and understanding' (D.L. II.115).

III Antisthenes and Diogenes – Cynic ethics

Of all the routes by which Socrates' philosophy was transmitted to the Hellenistic world, that followed by the Cynics was the most startling and, in some respects, the most influential.[13] Crates is described as 'a man like the Socrates of Xenophon's *Memorabilia*' (D.L. VII.2–3). This observation occurs in the biography of Zeno. The Stoics can be assumed to have readily propagated such stories, determined as they were to connect their founder with Socrates.[14] Hence they publicized the philosophical succession: Socrates, Antisthenes, Diogenes, Crates, Zeno. In the Stoic canon of quasi-sages Socrates and Diogenes form an ubiquitous duo (cf. e.g. Epict. *Diss.* II.13.24, II.16.35).

In contrast with the Stoics, Epicurus specifically denied that the wise man would 'practise Cynicism' (D.L. x.119). Yet the principles an Epicurean should adopt concerning satisfaction of desires, attitudes to society, self-sufficiency and freedom have much in common with Cynic precepts. This affinity is most clearly seen in the satirical tone of Epicurean maxims, many of which call attention to the 'vanity' of conventional human motivations (cf. Epicurus *KD* 15, 21, 29, 30; *Sent. Vat.* 21, 25, 33, 46, 65). Cynic tendencies are still more evident in our accounts of the philosophies of two of Epicurus' rivals, the Cyrenaics Theodorus and Hegesias (D.L. II.94, 99). There are also pronounced Cynic elements in

---

[12] For an elaboration of this point, see Long 1993a, 140–6.

[13] Book VI of Diogenes Laertius' *Lives* is devoted to the Cynics. An extensive collection of testimonia is available in *SSR* v. For Antisthenes see also Decleva Caizzi 1966.

[14] See Long 1988b, 150–71, esp. 151–4, 161–2. Some later Stoics, especially the Pergamene librarian Athenodorus, tried to play down the Cynic influences on early Stoicism, to avoid contaminating the founders of the Stoa with Cynic 'shamelessness'. These contrasting attitudes to the Cynics have left their mark on Diogenes' life of Zeno: cf. Mansfeld 1986, 347–51 and Hahm 1992, 4088–105.

Timon's Pyrrhonian critique of the philosophical tradition.[15] Whether their official acknowledgement of the Cynics was positive or negative, the new Hellenistic schools recognized that Cynicism was an ethical movement which anticipated and adumbrated some of their own leading concerns.

An informed appreciation of this point is rendered difficult for many reasons. First, our reliable evidence for the earliest Cynics is sparse and difficult to evaluate. Secondly, it would be false to the nature of the Cynic movement to abstract a *purely* theoretical set of notions from the Cynics' deliberately bizarre styles of behaviour and literary expression. Thirdly, Cynic principles of action, to the extent that they can be formally stated, are likely to appear jejune when considered alongside the more sophisticated ethics of Stoics and Epicureans. In view of such difficulties one may be tempted to agree with Hegel that: 'There is nothing particular to say of the Cynics, for they possess but little philosophy, and they did not bring what they had into a scientific system.'[16]

The temptation should be resisted. Cynicism was built on systematic philosophical foundations, which may be articulated as follows:

1 Happiness is living in agreement with nature.

2 Happiness is something available to any person willing to engage in sufficient physical and mental training.

3 The essence of happiness is self-mastery, which manifests itself in the ability to live happily under even highly adverse circumstances.

4 Self-mastery is equivalent to, or entails, a virtuous character.

5 The happy person, as so conceived, is the only person who is truly wise, kingly and free.

6 Things conventionally deemed necessary for happiness such as wealth, fame and political power have no value in nature.

7 Prime impediments to happiness are false judgements of value together with the emotional disturbances and weakness of character which arise from these false judgements.

Collectively, these propositions constitute the account of eudaimonism which had paramount appeal in Hellenistic philosophy. An Epicurean or a Pyrrhonian sceptic, unlike a Stoic, would not accept all of them. But there was no disagreement on the connections drawn between happiness and

---

[15] Timon's Cynic leanings have been explored in detail: cf. Long 1978a, and Brancacci 1981.
[16] *Lectures on the History of Philosophy* 1.479 (Haldane-Simson translation).

self-mastery, training, rejection of mere convention as a foundation for values, and virtuous character. Hellenistic philosophers shared a general interest in completely internalizing happiness; their project was to make happiness depend essentially on the agent's character and beliefs, and thus to minimize or discount its dependence on external contingencies. The Epicurean, as well as the Stoic wise man, is happy on the rack – a thought known independently to Aristotle, who found it outrageous (*EN* VII.14.1153b19).

Antisthenes, presented in the doxographical tradition as founder of the Cynic movement, may never have met Diogenes of Sinope (active in the mid-fourth century BC), who was the first authentic Cynic.[17] Even so, Antisthenes' writings and his interpretation of Socrates were probably the most potent influences on Diogenes' philosophical development. In a passage from Xenophon's *Symposium* (4.34–44) Antisthenes defends the claim that, though penniless, he prides himself on his wealth. He observes people who are conventionally wealthy yet pathologically unsatisfied by their possessions. As for himself, he has sufficient to satisfy all his basic bodily needs and, not being choosy, he can always find a willing woman if he wants sex. For enjoyment, instead of buying luxuries he draws on his soul's resources. Anticipating Epicurus, he says that it is more pleasurable to satisfy the appetite when genuinely hungry or thirsty than when not in need. Such frugality promotes honesty and contentment.

This passage fits well with two theses elsewhere attributed to Antisthenes: 'Virtue pertains to actions and does not need copious theories (*logoi*) or lessons'; and 'Virtue is sufficient for happiness, since happiness needs nothing else except Socratic strength' (D.L. VI.11). The anecdotal material concerning Diogenes is evidence for his consistent attempt to play the role of 'Socrates gone mad' (as Plato is reputed to have called him, D.L. VI.54) and to make himself into a public exhibition of Antisthenes' recommended self-sufficiency. Characteristic examples are his masturbating in public, living in a wine-jar, sleeping rough, walking on snow barefoot, trying to eat raw meat.[18] However, most of the anecdotes are concerned not with what Diogenes did but with what he said.

---

[17] Diogenes Laertius credits Antisthenes with basically the same Stoicizing ethical doctrines as the Cynics (cf. VI.10–13 with VI.103–5). There must be some oversimplification here, probably at Antisthenes' expense. What is clear is that the early Stoics found Antisthenes and Diogenes sufficiently close to their own ethical viewpoint to welcome them as links for connecting themselves with Socrates.

[18] Mansfeld 1988b, 163, suggests that Diogenes' exhibitionism undercuts his professed independence and calls into question his moral seriousness. But the sober Chrysippus cited Diogenes' conduct with approval (Plu. *Stoic. Rep.* 1044b).

His philosophical significance rests on his efforts to 'deface the currency', as the Cynic slogan puts it.

> Asked where one might see good men in Greece, he said: 'Men nowhere, but boys in Sparta' (D.L. vi.27). When captured and put up for sale, he was asked what he knew how to do, and answered, 'rule over men', and he told the herald to announce, 'Does anyone want to buy a master for himself?' (D.L. vi.29). Seeing temple officials arresting someone who had stolen a bowl belonging to the treasurers, he said: 'The big thieves are arresting the little thief' (D.L. vi.45). Asked which beast has the worst bite, he said: 'Of wild ones, the sycophant, and of tame ones the flatterer' (D.L. vi.51).

Such aphorisms as these have at least three things in common – black humour, paradox and ethical seriousness. They accept the ordinary connotations of words, and insist that their conventional denotations are misapplied or need to be inverted. A genuine man must be hardier and better trained than a Spartan warrior; a real master must be someone with total command over himself and the moral authority to tell others how to behave; theft is committed by state officials no less than common criminals. These sentiments are a powerful challenge to unreflective views on the relation between language and ethical judgement. Diogenes sought to deface the currency of convention (*nomos*) and to substitute for it values grounded in a 'rational' understanding of 'nature' (*phusis*). The conventions he wanted to dislodge by his discourse and behaviour were ones he regarded as irrational prejudice and as inimical to the satisfaction of natural needs. He accepted the nickname 'dog' (*kuōn*) as a symbol of his 'shamelessness' (*anaideia*). *Aidōs*, the opposite quality, was hallowed in tradition as a necessary condition of civilized life. As such, it served as a sanction both against anti-social conduct in the strong ethical sense, and also as the grounds of 'decency' in daily life. In the latter sense, *aidōs* covered manners rather than morals – the socially acceptable behaviour of men and women in matters of dress, styles of eating, conversing, sex and so forth.

As publicized by Diogenes, Cynic 'shamelessness' is contemptuous of *aidōs* largely in this second sense. The anecdotes and aphorisms of Diogenes include caustic criticism of thieves and profligates. He is said to have reproached various people for behaving unethically with the words, 'Are you not ashamed . . .?' (D.L. vi.65). The positive counterpart of Cynic 'shamelessness' is summed up in the catch-word *parrhēsia*, 'frankness'. Having reduced all valid norms to those dictated by nature, the Cynic is liberated from bourgeois inhibitions and social practices. These are merely conventional, as is shown by the great variety of different people's customs (D.L. VI.73). Equipped with a rough cloak, a wallet and a stick (the beggar's standard accoutrements), the Cynic adopts a lifestyle which symbolizes his independence from the values that enslave most people. Triumphing, as he claimed to do, over all adversities (as conventionally conceived, D.L. VI.38), Diogenes compared himself with Heracles, slayer of monsters (D.L. VI.71).[19] Because he alone has command over himself, the Cynic is the only genuine ruler.[20] The diffusion of this hyperbolical language is evident from the Stoics' practice of restricting such terms as 'king' and 'free' to their wise man.[21]

Though simple and minimalist in its needs, the Cynic life demands constant training and exertion. This requirement offers perhaps the most promising explanation of the connections Diogenes seems to have intuited between nature, happiness, virtue, rationality, self-mastery and internal and external freedom. Discussion of this point depends largely on the following passage from the biography by Diogenes Laertius.

He [sc. Diogenes] used to say that training is of two kinds, mental and bodily. The latter refers to the acquisition in continuous exercise of mental impressions [*phantasiai*], which provide easy access to virtuous deeds. The one kind of training is incomplete without the other, since good condition and strength are no less included in the appropriate things that concern the mind as in those that concern the body. He used to provide evidence of the fact that from exercise virtue is easily acquired. Thus in the case of manual and other crafts we observe craftsmen achieving extraordinary dexterity by practice; similarly we observe the extent to which flautists and athletes excel in their respective fields by continuous exertion. We realize that if they had transferred their training to the mind as well, they would not have toiled unprofitably and unproductively. He used to say that nothing at all in life can succeed without training, and that training can prevail over anything. Therefore instead of useless toils people should choose ones that are natural and thus live happily, whereas in fact they are unhappy as a result of folly. In fact the actual despising of pleasure is thoroughly pleasurable when it has become habitual. Just as those accustomed to live pleasurably find it disagreeable to pass to the opposite, so those whose training has been the converse derive more pleasure from despising actual pleasures. (D.L. VI.70–1)

[19] For Antisthenes' and Cynic sanctification of Heracles, see Hoeistad 1948, 22–73.
[20] For this tradition and its background, see Hoeistad 1948, passim; for the Stoics, cf. e.g. D.L. VII.122. Even if the encounters between Diogenes and Alexander the Great are spurious, they became the favourite Cynic illustration of the superiority of ethical to political kingship.
[21] Cynics and Stoics could invoke the precedent of Socrates: cf. Xen. *Mem.* I.1.16, where Socrates authorizes 'slavish' as the characteristic of people who are ignorant of morality, and Plato *Grg.* 521d, where Socrates claims to be perhaps the only Athenian expert in politics.

Although some of the language and thought of this passage are probably anachronistic, so far as Diogenes himself is concerned, its main tenor coheres with the anecdotal evidence and with what seems plausible in a philosopher whose principal antecedents were Socratic.[22] (It is Socrates who pioneered the usage of craft analogies in moral philosophy.) The passage also tallies well with the kind of education Diogenes is said to have given the sons of Xeniades (D.L. VI.30–1): sufficient physical training to promote 'a good condition' as distinct from athletic bodies, memorizing literature, the habit of looking after themselves without servants, contentment with a minimal diet, plain and simple dress.

If Diogenes is now beginning to sound too much like Rugby's Dr Arnold, a quick reminder of his public masturbation and eating of raw flesh will rapidly dispel the impression. But underlying his radical exhibitionism is a unitary philosophy, unsystematic in formulation though this doubtless was. That body and soul are mutually related and affect each other's good or bad condition is a thought which has ample Socratic backing. Yet the emphasis on bodily hardiness is distinctively Cynic. It obviously fits the notion that one will be happier the less dependent one is on external circumstances, but apparently more is involved: a good physical condition helps to promote a steady flow of 'mental impressions which provide easy access to virtuous deeds'. What could this mean?

If Diogenes had a theory (as distinct from an unarticulated concept) of virtue, that is not revealed in our record. Yet the Stoics would not have endorsed much of Cynicism if the Cynic life in accordance with nature was seriously at odds with their own ethics. Indeed the Stoic Apollodorus (second century BC) recommended Cynicism as 'a short cut to virtue' (D.L. VII.121), that is, virtue as the Stoics themselves understood it. Perhaps this memorable expression can help. Cynicism presumably gets you to virtue quickly because, if you can actually live the Cynic life – if you can master your passions, restrict your needs and interests solely to what your rational nature requires, treat no contingencies as capable of disturbing your strength of mind – you have acquired or come close to acquiring a virtuous character, as the Stoics conceived of this. And you have done so without spending years of study in logic, physics and ethics.

More problematic, it may seem, is the relation supposed to obtain between 'training' and living in accordance with nature. Training involves deliberate practice, the shaping of what may (or may not) be 'nat-

---

[22] Goulet-Cazé 1986, 210–13 argues that the passage is *heavily* contaminated with Stoicism. The contrary position of Dudley 1937, 216–20, and Hoeistad 1948, 38–47, is more convincing.

urally' given. Probably the best rejoinder available to Diogenes would invoke animal behaviour, which became a favourite Cynic device for illustrating the superiority of the natural to the conventional. The notion that humans have something to learn from animals does not imply, as has been supposed, that Diogenes wished to reduce human nature to that of beasts.[23] Against this interpretation, it is sufficient to invoke his maxim, 'reason or a hangman's rope' (D.L. vi.24). Diogenes' ethical theory and practice only make sense on the assumption that human nature is rational, and that reason can and should be deployed to remove the impediments of irrational convention. At the same time, he evidently insisted that human beings *are* animals, and as such share many properties with beasts. Civilized and conventional humanity, he probably reasoned, has lost sight of this fact. Animals, living in their natural way, fend effectively for their needs and have no needs that they cannot fulfil. They are trained by nature, as it were. But human nature, which is essentially rational, requires deliberate training in order to attain the self-sufficiency that is the appropriate condition of every animal.

Diogenes has sometimes been characterized as a cultural primitivist, who advocated renunciation of all social life and 'roaming about in solitude'. That designation fits neither the evidence for his career nor the influence of Cynicism on Hellenistic thought. Diogenes appears to have been a well educated man who enjoyed argument with other philosophers, and earned the respect of many citizens. His way-out lifestyle had a philosophical purpose, as his contemporaries seem to have realized. In addition, he is credited with the composition of a large number of writings (D.L. vi.80). Some of these were almost certainly genuine, especially his *Republic*, a work cited by several Stoic philosophers.[24] His agenda was not the abandonment of all forms of social organization but a radical critique of the conventions of the Greek *polis*.

iv Crates and the literary transmission of Cynicism

Diogenes probably had no pupils in the sense of persons he trained to be his official followers. But whether through personal contact, hearsay or writing, he succeeded in establishing his own lifestyle as an ethical practice

---

[23] This seems to be the view of Niehues Pröbsting 1979, 77, 139.

[24] The key text concerning the authenticity of Diogenes' *Republic* is Philodemus *De Stoicis* cols. 15–20 (= *SSR* v b 126). For discussion see Mansfeld 1986, 348–51, Schofield 1991, 9–10; cf. also, on Diogenes' literary activity, Goulet-Cazé 1986, 85–90.

which others could imitate. Those who did so, like Crates of Thebes, were consequently called Cynics. In the last years of the fourth century BC the influence of Cynicism, or at least of its ethical principles, was much more widely diffused than would be apparent from a tally of those who bore this description. Because Cynicism was not a formal school with a codified body of doctrine some of its characteristic precepts and attitudes could be readily appropriated by philosophers of other persuasions.[25]

However Crates came to know of Cynicism, his life and surviving writings are entirely consonant with Diogenes' ethical principles as reconstructed above.[26] The chief difference between Crates and Diogenes lies in their external circumstances. Diogenes may well have suffered exile and slavery; he vaunted his indifference to his misfortunes (D.L. VI.38), which no doubt contributed to his appeal. Crates was a citizen of Thebes and a wealthy landowner. We are entitled to doubt the nice story that he turned to philosophy after seeing the beggar king Telephus in a tragedy (D.L. VI.87), but the story probably has its basis in a remarkable fact: Crates sold his lands and gave away the proceeds to his fellow-citizens.

If Crates' renunciation of wealth was a deliberate assumption of Cynic poverty, his practice in regard to sex was no less radical. The second thing for which he is renowned was his relationship with his wife Hipparchia. In the face of all Greek convention, but in line with the views of Diogenes (D.L. VI.72), the relationship of Crates and Hipparchia was apparently based on nothing except mutual consent (D.L. VI.96). Flouting parental approval and the normal criteria of wealth and status, Hipparchia is said to have fallen in love with Crates and his life and discourses. Scandalmongers gave prurient accounts of public sexual intercourse between the pair. More interesting, and probably closer to truth, is the tradition that Hipparchia was a liberated woman who shared Crates' philosophical interests and did not differ in her public behaviour from her husband. On the conventional view of a Greek woman's proper place, that will have counted as a shocking example of sexual exhibitionism. Criticism of convention in regard to wealth and sex had been among Diogenes' prime objectives. The Stoic Zeno's respect for Crates and the 'memoirs of Crates' (D.L. VII.4) that he wrote are reason enough to believe that Crates consistently acted upon his Cynic principles.[27]

[25] Two philosophers who manifest this diffused influence are the Megarian Stilpo, linked to Crates in the testimonia (cf. Döring 1972, 46–55), and Menedemus of Eretria, said to have once been called 'dog' by his fellow countrymen (D.L. II.140).

[26] Diogenes Laertius gives his account of Crates at VI.85–98; further testimonia in *SSR* V H.

[27] The Cynic imprint on early Stoic literary activity is very strong: books of *chreiai* or anecdotes are attributed to Aristo (D.L. VII.163), Persaeus (D.L. VII.36) and Cleanthes (D.L. VII.175). Other

Crates' life should be regarded as a contribution to Hellenistic ethics, just like the lives of Socrates and Diogenes. He also publicized his Cynicism by writing satirical verse. The surviving lines in a variety of metres include parody of archaic poetry. This device can be interpreted as one of Crates' contributions to 'defacing the currency', and was directly imitated by the Pyrrhonist Timon.[28] In a famous hymn to the Muses, the Athenian statesman Solon had prayed that he might enjoy prosperity and a good reputation from all men. Crates (*SSR* v H 84) substitutes 'constant fodder for my belly'. Where Solon wished that he be 'sweet to my friends and bitter to my foes', Crates writes: 'helpful, not sweet, to my friends'. Instead of desiring, as Solon had done, 'justly acquired possessions', Crates likens these to the wealth of a beetle or an ant; he asks simply for 'a share in justice and wealth that is harmless, easy to transport, easy to acquire, and valuable for virtue'.

The opening of his most famous poem (D.L. VI.85) begins by parodying the Homeric description of Crete (*Od.* XVIII.172–3):

> There is a city Pera [punning on the word for the beggar's wallet] in the midst of wine-dark mist [punning on the Cynic catchword *tuphos* = the 'trumpery' of conventional values] fair and fertile, thoroughly squalid, possessing nothing, into which no fool sails, no parasite or lecher who delights in a whore's backside; but it bears thyme and garlic, figs and loaves, which are no cause for its inhabitants to war with one another, nor do they take up arms for profit or for fame.

Another verse worth citing here is this:

> I don't have one country as my refuge, nor a single roof, but every land has a city and house ready to entertain me. (D.L. VI.98)

Crates stamped his mark on the Cynic tradition not just through poetry but also through records of his remarks. Many of these set the scene for what later became stock Cynic themes – the indifference of exile, the necessity, for happiness, of freedom from passion. One surviving item has more theoretical interest.

Crates argued that a happy life cannot be based upon a preponderance of pleasures (*SSR* v H 44). He sought to prove this by running through all stages of life from infancy to old age: 'at every stage, one who reflects will find pains are considerably more numerous than pleasures'. As formulated,

---

Cynic-sounding titles include 'Memorabilia on vain opinion' (Aristo, D.L. VII.163), 'On training' (Herillus, D.L. VII.166), a work in two books with the same title for Dionysius of Heraclea (D.L. VII.167), and much else besides.

[28] For examples of Timon's parodies, see Long 1978a, 75–7.

this argument is scarcely a searching attack on hedonism. Crates may have developed it more subtly than it is transmitted. In any case, he probably had a philosophical target in view as well as, perhaps, a popular conception of happiness. If so, the best candidate is Cyrenaic hedonism (see below). That an attack like Crates' went home is virtually proved by the odd attempts of the later Cyrenaics to modify their hedonism. One of them, Hegesias, even denied the possibility of happiness, on grounds similar to those found in Crates' refutation of hedonism, and nominated absence of pain as the ethical goal (D.L. 11.94–5). It was left to Epicurus to disarm the force of Crates' criticism by identifying the ethical goal and limit of pleasure with absence of pain (*Ep. Men.* 128, 131). Thus he could agree that pleasurable sensations, as construed by the Cyrenaics, might not predominate over pains, without conceding that tranquillity (freedom from pain in body and mind) was similarly at risk.

Crates emerges as a Cynic who remained faithful to Diogenes' principles. By disseminating those principles in attractive and satirical verse, he helped to promote Cynicism as a popular brand of ethics. A generation or so after Crates, Bion of Borysthenes (D.L.iv.46–54) was composing Cynic sermons ('diatribes') that blended moralizing with sarcasm. The Cynic became a familiar figure of Hellenistic culture, contributing to literature and appearing in it as a stock character. If the simplicity and extremity of Cynicism were its undoing, so far as creative philosophy is concerned, they also help to account for its significance in Hellenistic ethics. The Cynics had succeeded in showing that many conventional values were vulnerable to critical scrutiny. They had dramatized the capacity of reason to challenge the customary dependence of happiness on external circumstances. Thus they transmitted to Hellenistic philosophy the notion of a 'wise man', who is autonomous and unaffected by the passions that trouble less fortified characters. These were radical contributions to Greek ethics, and capable of being fruitfully developed quite independently of the Cynic's way-out life-style and hyperbolical discourse.

v   Aristippus and Cyrenaic hedonism

In the classical tradition Epicurus' name has become virtually synonymous with hedonist, but in Carneades' famous 'division' of the possible ends of life that position is accorded to Aristippus of Cyrene, hereafter Aristippus Senior (Cic. *Fin.* v.20; cf. 11.35). As an associate of Socrates and contemporary of Plato, Aristippus Senior must have been a hundred years or so older than Epicurus. What gave him the status of honorary

Hellenistic philosopher was his position, or believed position, as the founder of the Cyrenaic school or schools.[29]

A number of Cyrenaic philosophers were active in the years from about 330 to 270 BC. Aristippus the Younger, a grandson of the Socratic philosopher, had probably developed his own brand of hedonism some years before Epicurus began his professional career. To the next generation, as contemporaries of Epicurus, we can date three further Cyrenaic philosophers, Anniceris, Theodorus and Hegesias. The differences between them individually, and between them collectively and Epicurus, show that all four philosophers offered rival interpretations of hedonism. In the event, Epicurus' version won out, as it deserved to do. By the middle of the third century BC Cyrenaic philosophy was obsolete. It had succeeded, however, in provoking opposition from the early Epicureans, while the doctrines of Anniceris, Hegesias and Theodorus, in their turn, include features that are clear responses to Epicureanism.[30] We can assume that controversy between these schools was much livelier than our meagre record of Cyrenaic philosophy makes explicit. Of the nine philosophical sects distinguished by the doxographer Hippobotus (writing in about 200 BC), no fewer than three refer to Cyrenaics – the Annicerians, the Theodoreans and the Cyrenaics as such (D.L. 1.19; cf. 11.85). The remaining six are the Megarian, Eretrian, Epicurean, Zenonian or Stoic, Old Academic and Peripatetic. The followers of Hegesias were also counted as a distinct school.

What impulse to Cyrenaic philosophy was given by Aristippus Senior? In *Mem.* 11.1.1–34, Xenophon presents a conversation between him and Socrates. The latter finds Aristippus 'too unrestrained' in reference to sensual desires. To encourage him and his like to practise 'self-control' (*enkrateia*), Socrates tries to persuade Aristippus that the life of a ruler, which requires self-control, is superior to that of a subject. Aristippus, however, insists that there is a third option, a life neither of rule nor of slavery but of 'freedom, which is the best route to happiness' (11.1.11). He declines the ruler's life as too burdensome: 'I assign myself to the class of those who want to live in the easiest and pleasantest way' (11.1.9). As to

---

[29] Diogenes Laertius' account of Aristippus and the Cyrenaics: 11.65–104; further testimonia in *SSR* IV.

[30] For the Epicurean Colotes' presumed but anonymous attack on Cyrenaic epistemology, cf. Plu. *Col.* 1120c–1121c. It is widely and rightly assumed that Epicurus formulated some of his ethical doctrines in deliberate opposition to the Cyrenaics: cf. D.L. x.136–7, with Giannantoni 1958, 102–5 (includes bibliography). As to the latest Cyrenaics, including Anniceris, I think that some of their doctrines involve more direct reaction to Epicureanism than Laks 1993b seems prepared to allow.

the life of a subject, or 'slavery', Aristippus has a policy for avoiding that too: 'I do not confine myself to a nationality, but I am an alien everywhere' (11.1.13).[31] Xenophon's Socrates tries to persuade Aristippus that he would do better to emulate Heracles, and choose the hard road of Virtue instead of the easy path to happiness promised by Vice. From this we can infer Aristippus' fame in his lifetime as a highly successful hedonist, or as someone who 'always made the best of circumstances; for he derived pleasure from what was available, and did not laboriously pursue enjoyment of things not present' (D.L. 11.66). He was perceived as someone for whom happiness consists in the freedom to enjoy pleasurable sensations without surrendering autonomy and rationality. It is this latter element, the maintenance of self-mastery, which primarily connects Aristippus Senior with Socrates.[32] He was famous for saying about his girl-friend Lais – 'I have Lais, but I am not had by her.'[33]

Cyrenaic hedonism is best construed as a theoretical defence of this lifestyle. As formulated by Aristippus the Younger, the effective founder of the school (Eus. *PE* xiv.18.31–2), what constitutes the goal of life is the bodily pleasure of the moment.[34] Construed as a movement or as a mental state (*pathos*) supervening on movement, pleasure is limited to its experienced duration. A 'pleasure' which is merely remembered or merely anticipated does not count (D.L. 11.89), or rather it has either ceased to exist as an actual pleasure or does not yet do so. The ethical goal, then, is not happiness, in its traditional construal as a long-term state (*eudaimonia*, D.L. 11.87–8). This focus upon the unconditional enjoyment of momentary, and especially bodily, pleasures fits what is attested concerning the physicalist and subjectivist tendencies of Cyrenaic philosophy.[35] Since all that securely exists for someone is what he is currently experiencing, immediate feelings are the only guide to what is genuinely valuable.

For justifying their hedonism, the Cyrenaics relied on an argument (probably a commonplace at the time) that 'from childhood onward, without taking thought, we have an affiliation for pleasure'.[36] The sup-

---

[31] The last remark might be read as an anticipation of Cynic cosmopolitanism, as perhaps it was by Theodorus, 'who said the world was his country' (D.L. 11.99). But Aristippus' itinerant life is the more probable basis of Xenophon's statement; cf. Classen 1958, 188.

[32] For further discussion of Aristippus' Socratic identity, cf. Döring 1988, esp. 5–6, 62–70.

[33] See testimonia collected as *SSR* iv a 96.

[34] As a working hypothesis, I assume that the main body of Cyrenaic doctrine in D.L. 11.86–93 derives from Aristippus the Younger and not from his grandfather. However, the account is also contaminated with developments initiated by the later Cyrenaics, especially Anniceris, who are discussed in D.L. 11.93–103. See Döring 1988 and Laks 1993b.   [35] See chapter 7.

[36] D.L. 11.88. A more elaborated version of the argument, in reference to all animals, is attributed by Aristotle to Eudoxus, *EN* x.2.1172b9–15.

posed strength of the argument (and also its obvious weakness) is the instinctual nature of this behaviour. Epicurus adopted the argument too, but in general his hedonism is in striking contrast to that of the Cyrenaics. For him absence of pain *is* pleasure, static pleasure is superior to kinetic, mental pleasure is preferable to pleasure of the body. Above all, the happy Epicurean life is strongly constituted by pleasures of anticipation and recollection. Epicurus also sought to combine hedonism with careful attention to the values Socratic philosophers other than the Cyrenaics had assigned to rationality, ethical virtue and a long-term plan of life. The Cyrenaics are interesting precisely because they acknowledged that such values must be subordinate at best in an ethical theory emphasizing the pleasure of the moment.

A Cyrenaic will be an intelligent user of immediate sources of pleasure; he will respect other values only as prudence dictates (D.L. II.91). Yet, as Epicurus clearly saw, so simple an ethical theory is highly vulnerable. For Cyrenaicism as so formulated to be at all plausible, immediate pleasures need to be more accessible than human experience commonly finds them to be. In addition, many people want more from their lives than instant gratification. The latest Cyrenaics, who were contemporary with Epicurus, modified the account that has just been given in several respects:

> Those of the Cyrenaic succession called Annicerians assigned no definite end for the whole of life, but said that there is a particular end for each action – the pleasure which results from it. These Cyrenaics utterly excluded the defining mark of Epicurean pleasure, i.e. the removal of pain, calling it the state of a corpse. For, in their view, we take joy not only in pleasures, but also in company and public distinction. Epicurus, on the other hand, thinks that all the soul's joy depends on the prior condition of the flesh.[37] (*SSR* IV G 4)

The rejection of a 'definite end for the whole of life' will have helped Anniceris to emphasize his difference from Epicurus. In his view, Epicurus' attempt to found lasting happiness on pleasure was a cheat: Epicurus could only make this thesis sound at all plausible by conflating pleasure with absence of pain, and by such expedients as claiming mental pleasures and pains to be better or worse respectively than bodily ones. In defending the latter doctrine (D.L. IX.137), Epicurus argued that bodily pleasure or pain is a thing only of the present, in contrast with the soul's

---

[37] For statements by Epicurus which seem to justify Anniceris' final gibe, cf. *KD* 18, Cic. *Tusc.* III.41–2, Athen. 546f.

involvement in the past and the future. It was probably Anniceris and his followers who made a point of reversing Epicurus' order of priorities for body and soul (D.L. 11.90). At the same time, however, Anniceris is attested (above) as extending the scope of enjoyment to include social life and public acclaim.[38]

Anniceris' hedonism is an intelligible development of earlier Cyrenaicism in response to the ethics of Epicurus.[39] The special doctrines of Theodorus and Hegesias, to which we now turn, manifest further attempts to retain vestiges of their Aristippean legacy, while diverging sharply from Anniceris as well as from Epicurus.

Aristippus Senior had served as the paradigm of a life that was both autonomous and effortlessly successful in turning circumstances into sources of bodily enjoyment. The second of these characteristics had become the distinctive mark of the Cyrenaic school, but for understanding its latest developments, it is essential to focus upon the first as well, treating it as both a Socratic trait and as the ethical disposition which all Hellenistic philosophies in their different ways took to be the hallmark of the wise man. In the case of Theodorus and Hegesias, we witness a further movement away from Aristippus' sensualist hedonism towards a philosophy which has much in common with the Cynic interpretation of Socratic ethics. Theodorus and Hegesias, however, continue to differ from the Cynics in the value they assign to a hedonistic interpretation of self-interest.

Theodorus is described as a pupil both of Aristippus the Younger and of Anniceris. Both of these reports may be correct, since Theodorus was probably about the same age as Anniceris, and slightly older than Epicurus. As influences on his philosophy, the Cynics appear to have been as important as his Cyrenaic mentors. Theodorus in turn was a teacher of the Cynic Bion of Borysthenes, whose career has strong resemblances to his own.[40] No later than the year 307, Theodorus was banished from Athens for writing a book *On the gods*, in which he totally denied the gods' existence.[41] For this he became notorious as one of the few declared atheists of antiquity. Not surprisingly, he was credited with influencing Epicurus (D.L. 11 97), whose theology was regularly criticized for its athe-

---

[38] Contra Döring 1988, 55, Anniceris is orthodox in this view: cf. Laks 1993b, 39–49.

[39] Note too the Cyrenaic wise man's immunity from envy, erotic passion and superstition (D.L. 11.91). Despite its attribution to the Cyrenaics in general, this testimony reads like an attempt by Anniceris to bring the Cyrenaic wise man into line with his Epicurean counterpart.

[40] For Theodorus' Cynic leanings and his teaching of Bion, see Kindstrand 1976, 11, 68–70.

[41] For the evidence on Theodorus' atheism, see *SSR* iv h 14–24, and for the date of his exile from Athens, cf. Kindstrand 1976, 5.

istic implications.[42] Even if there is no truth in this report, the exile of Theodorus may well have served as a warning to Epicurus about how not to formulate his own account of the gods.

Theodorus went much further than Anniceris had done in modifying Aristippean hedonism. Anniceris had admitted some conventionally valued practices as sources of gratification additional to bodily pleasure. Theodorus had no use for conventional morality, on the grounds that the only sanction against theft, adultery and sacrilege was the worthless prejudice of popular opinion; circumstances could justify such actions (D.L. II.99). Yet he was not, as this might imply, a moral sceptic. Earlier Cyrenaics had granted only instrumental goodness to prudence (*phronēsis*, D.L. II.91). Theodorus said that prudence *and* justice were 'goods', and that the first of these was the foundation of 'joy': joy was the supreme desirable and distress the supreme undesirable (D.L. II.98). These statements, even if they do not upgrade prudence to a *per se* good, certainly emphasize its primacy to a degree that is Epicurean (cf. *Ep. Men.* 132) rather than Cyrenaic. By grounding joy in prudence – i.e., the wise character of the agent – he presumably thought he could offer an ethical theory which would compete successfully with the other Hellenistic options, while retaining an appeal of its own in its emphasis on the wise man's autonomy and self-sufficiency. Still more remarkable in a Cyrenaic, Theodorus relegated bodily pleasure and pain to a status intermediate between the good states of character, prudence and justice, and their bad opposites.[43] In what we should read as opposition to Anniceris (cf. D.L. II.96) he did away with friendship and patriotism on grounds that make use of the Cynic distinction between wise and foolish. Genuine, as distinct from purely utilitarian, friendships do not exist between fools, and wise men have no need of friends. As for patriotism, it would not be reasonable for a wise man to give up his life for the sake of fools.

Hegesias, the final Cyrenaic we have to consider, can similarly be interpreted as moving towards a position which could claim some of the attractions of the other Hellenistic schools. Taking a cue from the Cynics, he claimed that circumstances – for example, poverty, wealth, freedom, slavery – are utterly indifferent as the measure of pleasure or pain (D.L. II.93–6). In a manner that anticipates the sceptical modes of

---

[42] See chapter 13.

[43] What did Theodorus mean by justice? If D.L. II.93 is any guide (general Cyrenaic doxography), he agreed with Epicurus that the virtuous man will be deterred from doing anything unacceptable by punishments and public opinion: i.e., his view of justice was probably entirely prudential.

Aenesidemus, he supported this thesis by rejecting any causal connection between pleasure or pain and the nature of their sources.[44] A wise man acts purely out of self-interest. Since the senses are no objective criterion of truth, he always does 'what *appears* reasonable'. This last presumably means 'what appears reasonable to promote his interests', where interests are specified by pleasures and the avoidance of pains. Hegesias agreed with Anniceris in taking these pleasures and pains to be mental *and* bodily; he did not adopt Theodorus' extreme position of judging bodily pleasures and pains to be indifferent. Like Theodorus, however, he rejected conventional morality, even denying the existence of gratitude, friendship and beneficence, on the grounds that these are misleading names for purely self-interested action.

Sceptical though he was about any objective discrimination between circumstances as sources of pleasure or pain, Hegesias actually agreed with Crates that happiness on hedonist foundations is completely impossible. He reached this gloomy conclusion by arguing that suffering is endemic to body and soul, and that fortune frequently frustrates one's hopes. Instead of considering other possible sources of happiness, Hegesias seems to have insisted that, despite its disappointing outcome, hedonism remains the only feasible ethical viewpoint. Accordingly, to be consistent with his negative position on happiness, he formulated his ethical goal not as pleasure but as 'living without bodily or mental pain'.

Anniceris had caustically labelled 'absence of pain' the state of a corpse, thereby indicating his total rejection of the value Epicureans made supreme. That a fellow Cyrenaic, albeit a rival exponent, should agree with Epicurus on this point must have been 'the kiss of death' to Aristippus' hedonism. I use this colloquialism in order to allude to an alleged consequence of Hegesias' philosophy, which earned him notoriety equal to that of Theodorus' atheism. It is reported thus by Cicero:

> Death removes us from bad things, not from goods, if we are looking for the truth [about death]. This very point was treated in such detail by the Cyrenaic Hegesias that he is said to have been forbidden by King Ptolemy to lecture on the subject because many of his audience later committed suicide. (Cic. *Tusc.* 1.83)

Hegesias represents an extraordinary reversal of the original impulses of Cyrenaic philosophy. After being interestingly formulated by Aristippus

---

[44] 'It is because of scarcity or rarity or surplus that people differ in what they find pleasurable or the reverse' (D.L. 11.94). Cf. Aenesidemus' ninth mode, 'frequency or scarcity', as reported by S.E. *PH* 1.141–4.

the Younger, the school fell apart in the doctrinal disarray manifested by Anniceris, Theodorus and Hegesias. Each of these philosophers, as we have seen, tried to retain a distinctive version of hedonism in the face of Epicureanism. It is attractive to suppose that part of Epicurus' success was due to the necessity of meeting Cyrenaic challenges and of developing a hedonistic ethics which would prove, as indeed it did, to be incomparably more sophisticated and comprehensive than all its rivals.

VI Socratic ethics and Hellenistic scepticism

Rational control over emotions and external circumstances, criticism of conventional ethics, inner freedom, independence of judgement, tranquillity, the guidance of prudence or wisdom – these are the elements of Socrates' ethical legacy which left their mark on the Cyrenaics as well as on the Cynics, on the Epicureans as well as on the Stoics. However, there was another aspect or interpretation of Socrates which none of these schools, doctrinal as they were, had any interest in appropriating or countenancing – Socrates' disavowal of knowledge. Only Plato among those of Socrates' disciples who wrote about him emphasized this aspect, and even Plato never presented Socrates as someone who denied or doubted that knowledge is accessible to human beings. Whether we interpret Socrates' disavowal of knowledge as a dialectical device, or as a complex irony, or as a confession of human limitations, the identification of him as a full-fledged sceptic almost certainly originated in the post-Platonic Academy of Arcesilaus (c.316–241 BC). On the evidence of Cicero, Arcesilaus made it his business to replace doctrinal Platonism with the practice of refuting every thesis he was offered; and he invoked Socrates as the authority for his negative dialectic (*Acad.* 1.44–5). [45]

From Arcesilaus, whose stance was one of 'suspending judgement about everything', substantive ethical doctrines are not to be expected. Socrates was important to him primarily as someone he could adduce as a precedent for his own sceptical objectives. None the less, there is also an ethical dimension to Arcesilaus' scepticism, and in this too we may clearly trace Socrates' legacy. The Platonic Socrates had made it his principal mission to expose the self-deception of those who thought that they knew things when they did not. Arcesilaus, starting from the unSocratic position that nothing can be known (Cic. *Acad.* 1.45), drew the conclusion that

[45] Evidence on Arcesilaus: in Mette 1984, Long and Sedley 1987, ch.68. Reasons for regarding him as the discoverer or inventor of the sceptical Socrates are developed in Long 1988b, 156–60. See also Long 1986a, 440–1.

wisdom consists in refraining from opinion, or, to put it in ethical terms, that complete suspension of judgement is 'the right and honourable' characteristic of a wise man (Cic. *Acad.* II.77). Even if the language is Cicero's, and even if Arcesilaus developed this position only in the context of arguing against the Stoics' theory of knowledge, Arcesilaus' ruthless opposition to 'opining' has the ring of historical truth. The Stoics and the Epicureans, confident though they were in attributing knowledge to their wise man, were no less insistent on stigmatizing opinion, or 'empty opinion', as the condition that accounts for unhappiness and emotional disturbance.

In the eyes of doctrinal philosophers opinion was a weak cognitive state, unjustifiable when scrutinized and typically identified not only by its falsity but also by its damaging ethical consequences. Standard examples, which go back to Socrates of course, are the opinions that death is an evil and that happiness depends on material success. Stoics and Epicureans thought they could show why such opinions are false, and what the truth is about death, and so forth. To a Hellenistic sceptic the problem about opinions is not simply their liability to be false but their never being justifiable, irrespective of their content or their ethical implications. We should live without opinions, and commit ourselves to nothing. That posture was adopted not only by Arcesilaus, but also by Pyrrho one or two generations earlier. In Pyrrho, however, rigorous scepticism has a psychological benefit, which Arcesilaus did not apparently specify: it leads to tranquillity.

Pyrrho is a bridge-figure, old enough to have accompanied Alexander the Great to India, but looking forward, in his influence, to the new movements in Hellenistic thought.[46] Some Greek historians of philosophy tried to fit him into the succession of philosophers who were directly Socratic. Although that is probably incorrect, he can appropriately be related to the Socratic legacy.

Like Socrates, Pyrrho wrote nothing, so we are dependent for the little that is known about him on his publicist, Timon of Phlius, and an unreliable biographical tradition. Pyrrho's chief ethical importance consists in connections he is said to have drawn between happiness, epistemology and nature (objective reality). He urged that happiness depends upon how

---

[46] Diogenes Laertius presents his account of Pyrrho in Book IX.61–108. For further texts and discussion see Decleva Caizzi 1981a, Long and Sedley 1987, chs. 1 and 2; I here substantially repeat what I wrote in my contributions to L. C. Becker 1992a, 469–70 and L. C. Becker 1992b, 24–5. Passages relating to the epistemological basis of Pyrrho's ethics are quoted and discussed above, pp. 241–9. A highly original interpretation of Pyrrho's ethics, connecting it with theories of the Stoic Aristo, is given by Ausland 1989.

we dispose ourselves to nature. However, nature is completely unknowable, and therefore the attitude we should take towards it is one of complete suspension of judgement. Thereby we shall attain happiness in the form of tranquillity.[47]

Timon characterizes Pyrrho himself as someone who had fully achieved this state. Pyrrho does not accept that anything is good or bad by nature. He achieves serenity precisely by committing himself to nothing. This radical attitude liberates him from fear and desire. He governs his life by what he takes to be mere 'appearance', unconcerned about what if anything it is an appearance of. Whether someone can in fact live a life of radical scepticism became an issue that was soon to be debated between Stoics and Academics. Pyrrho's importance for Hellenistic ethics consists in his raising the question at the beginning of the period. In his concern to undermine baseless opinions and unjustified emotional reactions, he anticipates the Stoics and Epicureans. His supreme evaluation of tranquillity also foreshadows their ethical ideals.

Important though these connections are, Pyrrho's greatest significance for Hellenistic ethics lies in his linking that field of inquiry to philosophy of nature and epistemology. Like Plato, and to a more limited extent Aristotle, but unlike Socrates and the Cynics, Pyrrho held that ethics cannot be isolated from an understanding of how the physical world impinges upon us. Although he interpreted that understanding in wholly negative terms, he set an agenda which other philosophers, dissatisfied with scepticism, could use positively. That point was taken by the Stoics and the Epicureans. They insisted that knowledge is possible, and that what we can know about the way the world is structured bears directly upon our own good, and upon how we should dispose ourselves to the world. Thus their ethical ideals, though importantly similar to one or other of the Socratic options, were given a comprehensive philosophical grounding far more ambitious than anything available in the Socratic legacy itself.

[47] See especially fr.53 Decleva Caizzi (= Euseb.*Praep.Ev*. XIV.18.1–5).

20

Epicurean ethics

MICHAEL ERLER AND MALCOLM SCHOFIELD

1 Introduction[1]

On a goblet found in Boscoreale two philosophers are depicted as skeletons: Zeno the Stoic, and Epicurus. According to the inscription on the goblet they are engaged in discussion as to whether pleasure is the goal of all actions (*telos*).[2] It is clear from Zeno's attitude that he is eagerly trying to persuade Epicurus. Epicurus is depicted in a rather more casual pose. His attention is concentrated less on the person opposite him than on a piece of cake lying on a table in front of him. This scene encapsulates the popular image of the two schools in a mixture of true insight and false understanding. The contrasting attitudes of the two philosophers in fact symbolize a fundamental distinction between Stoa and Garden: Zeno's tense bearing is appropriate as a representation of the Stoic school, whilst the casual pose suited the Epicureans. The Epicureans believed it was folly to dwell in the mind on evils which might possibly occur or have already occurred. In their view this leads to aggravation of our distress. Alleviation will result if as well as taking our minds off what troubles us (*avocatio a cogitanda molestia*) we give our attention to what brings pleasure (*revocatio ad contemplandas voluptates*) (Cic. *Tusc.* III.32–3). But it is equally interesting to consider the misconception of Epicurean ethics which is suggested by the scene on the goblet. Epicurus allows himself to be distracted by a piece of cake; he is thus presented as honouring physical pleasures. As if to confirm this interpretation, at his feet a piglet is depicted, reminiscent of Horace's ironic description of himself as 'a true hog of Epicurus' herd' (Hor. *Ep.* 1.4.16).

---

[1] The principal ancient sources for Epicurean ethics are: Diogenes Laertius x, which contains Epicurus' *Letter to Menoeceus* and *Key Doctrines* (*Kuriai Doxai*) as well as doxographical material; Cicero *De Finibus* I and II; Lucretius, *De Rerum Natura* (although of course physics is its principal focus). The *Sententiae Vaticanae* ascribed to Epicurus are available e.g. in von der Mühll 1922 or Bailey 1926. Much further material is provided by Usener 1887 (hereafter Us.), especially nos. 396–607. Also important are the anti-Epicurean writings of Plutarch, the ethical treatises of Philodemus, and the fragments of Diogenes of Oenoanda.

[2] Dunbabin 1986, especially 224; Zanker 1995, 200 with plate 109.

Thus the goblet portrays Epicurus in a manner that reflects the popular understanding. He was regarded as the representative of a hedonism which owed allegiance to the stomach rather than the mind. This misinterpretation of Epicurean ethics has a long history, which can be traced back even as far as Epicurus' own circle.[3] Timocrates, one of his pupils, later deserted the cause and re-examined his teacher critically. When he did so he inveighed against the exaltation of pleasure and accused Epicurus of excess. With him began a tradition which not only continued through antiquity but evolved throughout the Middle Ages and the Renaissance right up to the modern period, and at times has even influenced scholarly analysis of Epicurus' ethics.[4]

To some extent Epicurus himself can be held responsible for such polemics. Aphorisms like the following almost invite an interpretation of his ethics as a philosophy advocating gross physical pleasure: 'The beginning and root of all good is the stomach's pleasure' (Athen. 546f).[5] When taken out of their original context, it was easy to misconstrue remarks of this kind. It should of course be borne in mind that such statements were intended to provoke, and probably had a role in counter-polemic. In the *Letter to Menoeceus*, Epicurus comments on misinterpretations of his views:

Neither drinking-parties nor continual revelry nor the enjoyment of boys and girls, or fish and all that a lavish table can offer, can provide a life of pleasure – only sober reason. (Epic. *Ep. Men.* 132)

Epicurus in fact extols a kind of asceticism, a reduction in the number and scope of our desires dictated by reason. In his school his students competed fiercely over who led the most modest lifestyle. Many adversaries of Epicurus are perfectly well aware of the distinction between Epicurus' true opinions and the image of excessive indulgence. Thus later philosophers and scholars like Valla or Gassendi quite rightly acquit Epicurus when he is accused of vulgar hedonism. Nietzsche made a particularly apt appraisal:

A little garden, some figs, a piece of cheese, plus three or four good friends – that was the sum of Epicurus' extravagance.[6]

---

[3] See Schmid 1962, 774ff.; Jones 1989, 94ff.

[4] For early polemic against Epicurus, see Sedley 1976a; for the history of Epicureanism in the Middle Ages and thereafter, see Hossenfelder 1991a, 140ff., Jones 1989, 117ff.

[5] Cf. Sedley 1976a, 132.

[6] Nietzsche's remark: *Human, All Too Human*, vol.II part 2, no. 192. On Lucretius' interpretation of the reduction of desires (with comments on Porphyry's use of Epicurus) see Schmid 1978; also Nussbaum 1994, chs. 5 and 7.

11 Ethics within the philosophy of Epicurus

In common with other Hellenistic schools, Epicureanism advocates the good life or *eudaimonia* as the goal of all actions. What is distinctive in its position becomes apparent in the concrete form of the good we are thereby to achieve: pleasure, construed as quiet of mind (*ataraxia*) and the absence of bodily pain (*aponia*). If the precepts formulated in his ethics are heeded, then Epicurus promises that man can lead a divine life on earth:

> Then practise these things and all that belongs with them to yourself day and night, and to someone like yourself. Then you will never be disturbed waking or dreaming, and you will live amongst men like a god. (Epic. *Ep. Men.* 135)

In common again with what other Hellenistic schools thought, Epicurus sees in philosophy an art of living, and lays emphasis on its function as an activity 'which through arguments and discussions brings about a life of happiness' (S.E. *M* xi.169). He offers not only a general methodology but also practical advice for dealing with widely varying conditions of life on earth, as well as a foundational ethical theory.

Keeping his eyes fixed on the goal, Epicurus eliminated everything which he considered superfluous to its attainment. This included not only cultural values but also the sciences and arts. 'Hoist your sail', he told Pythocles, 'and flee from every form of *paideia*' (D.L. x.5). All of it he rejected in the belief that such studies are not necessary to reach that state of happiness in which men can scarcely be distinguished from the gods. Epicurus thought the only thing needed to make someone an Epicurean was knowledge and acceptance of his basic teachings, as these are summarized in the *Tetrapharmakos*. In this way it is possible even for ordinary people to attain to *eudaimonia* without previous *paideia*.[7]

Despising external circumstances, as something which cannot be mastered,[8] goes hand in hand with the belief that man can control his inner attitude. Diogenes of Oenoanda, an Epicurean from Imperial times, gives classic expression to this view in his inscription:

> The key to happiness is the inner attitude (*diathesis*) of which we ourselves are masters. A military campaign is an arduous affair and is under the control of others; an orator's life consists of agitation and anxiety as to whether he will manage to convince. So why do we pursue such things over which others exert power? (Diog. Oen. fr. 112 Smith)

[7] See Gigante 1981, Dihle 1986b.
[8] But Epicurus rejects the notion of fate, as a philosophers' fiction: see e.g. *Ep. Men.* 133–4.

The state of happiness to which man aspires is attained by eliminating illusions about the gods; by achieving the correct attitude towards death; and by confining desires to goals that are within easy reach. These principles are formulated in the so-called *Tetrapharmakos*:

> God presents no fears, death no cause for alarm; it is easy to procure what is good; it is also easy to endure what is evil. (Phld. *Ad Cont.*, *PHerc.* 1005, col. 4.9–14)[9]

The first two of these basic maxims, reproduced in longer versions as *KD* 1 and 2, point us to something of crucial importance in the whole Epicurean approach to philosophy. For these are principles which can be established only by physics, not by ethical inquiry narrowly conceived. It is Epicurus' mechanistic philosophy of nature which eliminates from explanation of the phenomena divine providence or indeed any kind of divine involvement in the world or in human affairs. We are then left with a preconception (*prolēpsis*) of gods, purified of false popular beliefs, as blessed imperishable beings whose nature is not subject to the weakness from which anger and favour originate.[10] Similarly, what should arm us against the fear of death is Epicurus' demonstration of the nature of the soul as nothing but a particular kind of atom distributed throughout the body during its life, but dispersed when we die. The terrors of hell are therefore nothing to us, since physics tells us that matter which is dispersed has no feeling.[11] So ethics needs physics in order to get these things in proper perspective.[12] But Epicurus goes further: the whole point of doing physics in the first place is to release us from fears without which happiness, the goal of life determined by ethical inquiry, cannot be attained:

> There is no way to dispel being afraid about matters of supreme importance if someone does not know what the nature of the universe is, but is anxious about some of the things retailed in myths. Hence without natural philosophy it is impossible to secure the purity of our pleasures. (*KD* 12)

---

[9] Greek text available in Angeli 1988a, 173.

[10] Cf. *Ep. Men.* 123–4; on the πρόληψις of gods see e.g. Manuwald 1972, Glidden 1985.

[11] The fullest exposition of this thesis is presented by Lucretius in *De Rerum Natura* III; cf. Kerferd 1971.

[12] Although the Epicureans had things to say in the context of physics about the atomic basis of pleasure and pain (cf. e.g. Lucr. II.963–6, IV.622–32), they appear never to appeal to it in ethical writings when presenting ideas about the nature of these πάθη, contrary to what the interpretations of some scholars (e.g. Rist 1972, 102; Glidden 1980) would lead one to expect. For discussion of their general view of the relation of the mind and the body see above, chapter 16.

Were we not upset by the worries that celestial phenomena and death might matter to us, and also by failure to appreciate the limits of pains and desires, we would have no need for natural philosophy. (*KD* 11)

And as Torquatus is made to say in the *De Finibus* (Cic. *Fin.* 1.64), if and only if we practise philosophy will we acquire courage to face the fear of death, steadfastness to resist religious dread, peace of mind because it removes ignorance of what is unseen, and moderation thanks to its explanation of the nature and species of desire (this like *KD* 11 indicates that the second pair of maxims in the *Tetrapharmakos*, stated in more detail as *KD* 3 and 4, in the end depend on understanding nature – human, not now cosmic, nature).

'*Tetrapharmakos*' means 'fourfold remedy'; and Epicureanism often characterizes philosophy as a therapy. In one collection of Epicurean sayings we find the remark:

We must not pretend to philosophize – we must *really* philosophize: for what we need is not to think we are in health, but actually to *be* in health. (Epic. *Sent.Vat.* 54)

And Porphyry cites the Epicurean aphorism, reminiscent of Pythagorean teaching:

Empty is that philosopher's discourse which offers therapy for no human passion. Just as there is no use in medical expertise if it does not expel the sicknesses of bodies, so there is no use in philosophy if it does not expel the passion of the soul. (Porph. *Marc.* 31)

Philosophy as therapy and the philosopher as a doctor of the soul: the analogy is familiar from Democritus and Plato. Yet in Epicurus' case it is carried through with particular thoroughness. His teaching is a sort of medicine and his writings a kind of prescription. Philologically exact readings and interpretations of these texts form an integral part of their therapeutic ethics for Epicureans.[13]

Anyone who successfully experiences an Epicurean therapy and frees himself from the erroneous views that lead mankind astray can be counted a wise man. He is self-sufficient and for this reason not a burden to others. For him the promise of Epicurus has been fulfilled, that a state of virtually divine bliss can be attained on earth. The gods experience no difficulties themselves, nor cause others any.[14] Epicurus was himself evi-

---

[13] See further Erler 1993.
[14] So *KD* 1; this formulation finds a remarkable echo in *Sent. Vat.* 79: 'The person who has achieved *ataraxia* causes no disturbance to himself or to another'.

dently convinced that he had achieved this condition. This is suggested in a letter to his mother, which Diogenes of Oenoanda immortalized in the inscription on his monument:[15]

> For these things to which I aspire are not trivial. It is a question of things which make my condition resemble that of the gods and which prove to me as a human being that, despite mortality, I do not take second place to that nature which is immortal and blessed. For whilst I am alive, I have pleasure to the same degree as the gods. (Diog. Oen. fr. 125-6 Smith)

Thus Epicurus' life itself is offered as evidence for the truth of his theory. His pupils are therefore required to practise imitation, and they honour their master, almost as in a cult, in that they constantly behave as if he were a witness of their actions.[16]

III Philosophical background

Already before Epicurus, poets and philosophers tried to answer the question of how much significance should be attributed to pleasure in human life. Like Heracles at the crossroads, man must weigh up whether to prefer pleasure or virtue.[17] From Democritus in particular came several lines of thought which were helpful in laying the theoretical foundations of hedonism as we find it in Epicurus.[18] The debate between Epicureanism and the rival hedonistic theories of contemporary Cyrenaics has already been introduced in the previous chapter.[19] Finally, we must also take account of the possible influence of Academic and Peripatetic doctrine. When Epicurus awarded pleasure the rank of ultimate good, and pain that of ultimate evil, he completed the last stage of a transformation of the older ethics of virtue (*aretē*) as prowess on a public stage into a concern with *eudaimonia* interpreted in terms of subjective experience: a transformation that may with hindsight be perceived as mediated by the fierce and unresolved debate over the role of pleasure in which Plato, Aristotle and the Academy engaged.

Both Plato and Aristotle accept that pleasure can be seen as an ingredient in the human good. Plato advocates a mixed life, in which pleasure and reason are combined. In Plato's ranking of goods understanding is certainly accorded a higher position. In his view pleasure belongs to the

---

[15] See M. F. Smith 1993, 555-8 for doubts about Epicurus' authorship; like Clay 1990, 2451-2, he gives a positive verdict.   [16] See Clay 1986 (and cf. p. 674 below).

[17] Cf. Xen. *Mem.* II.1.21-34.

[18] Gosling and Taylor 1982, ch. 2, discuss the Democritean material.

[19] See pp. 632-9 above; further discussion below, pp. 652, 654-7.

realm of becoming. Because everything that comes into being has a purpose, pleasure cannot in itself be a *telos*.[20] The value of pleasure has to be assessed against yardsticks such as purity or measure which are not intrinsic to it. Like Plato Aristotle argues against pure hedonism, as expounded, for example, by Eudoxus of Cnidos, a contemporary of his in the Academy.[21] But he too extracts from hedonism something positive. For example, in his treatment of the topic in Book VII of the *Nicomachean Ethics* he finds the essence of pleasure in the unimpeded activity (*energeia*) of a natural condition (*hexis*) of soul (*EN* 1153a14–15). In line with the status he gives to human intellectual activity, the pleasure associated with it is accorded the highest value. Both Plato and Aristotle accordingly hold complex and nuanced views of pleasure, with positive as well as negative aspects. This is a standpoint which Epicurus rejects. For him every pleasure is, *qua* pleasure, inherently good, and pain, *qua* pain, inherently evil.

Here, then, is the backdrop for our presentation of the main elements and characteristics of Epicurus' teaching. It is a hotly debated question how far Epicurus developed his doctrine through conscious engagement with his predecessors by direct reference to their works. Epicurus himself stresses repeatedly the originality of his position and denies ever having had teachers. Already in antiquity his own assertion of independence stood in opposition to others' accusations that he was dependent on predecessors, indeed guilty of plagiarism. If Epicurus does add anything original to what he borrows, in Cicero's view he simply makes it worse.[22] We may ignore the exaggerations of the warring parties, but that Epicurus knew his hedonism owed something to his reading of e.g. Democritus and Plato, as well as to debate with Aristippus the Younger, is hard to doubt. It would be particularly interesting and useful to know in this context whether Epicurus had access to the works of Aristotle other than his dialogues.[23]

IV Pleasure and the foundation of ethics

For Epicurus as for philosophers of other schools, the ultimate goal of all actions is to attain human *eudaimonia*. Starting from the conviction that

---

[20] Cf. Plato *Rep.* 581c–588a, *Phlb.* 53c–55a, 65a–67b.

[21] Cf. Arist. *EN* x.1172b9–1173a13, with discussion e.g. by Merlan 1960, 30 ff., Gosling and Taylor 1982, ch. 14, and Krämer 1983, 73ff.

[22] Cf. e.g. Cic. *ND* 1.72, *Fin.* 1.17; S.E. *M* 1.3; Eus. *PE* xiv.20.14.

[23] Cf. Phld. *Ad Cont.* (*PHerc.* 1005) fr. 111 Angeli, with discussion in Angeli 1988a, 233–40. See also Sandbach 1985, 4ff. The question of Epicurus' originality is bound up with the nature of his relationship with his teachers Praxiphanes and Nausiphanes. A brief general survey of the background to his hedonism: Rist 1974.

all men strive after happiness, Epicurus, like others, saw happiness as a good. Epicurus equates this good unequivocally with pleasure[24] and correspondingly identifies the greatest evil with the greatest pain. Thus it is fundamental to his ethics to regard pleasure as something valuable in itself. Furthermore Epicurus maintains a connection between the elimination of all pain and the degree of pleasure attained. In his view there is no third state, no so to speak neutral state, between the two poles of pain and pleasure. Accordingly freedom from physical pain (*aponia*) and freedom from mental disturbance (*ataraxia*) constitute the ultimate goal of all actions for Epicurus. He sums up his position as follows:

> We declare pleasure to be the beginning and end of the blessed life; for we have recognized pleasure as the first and natural good, and from this we start in every choice and avoidance, and this we make our goal, using feeling as the canon by which we judge every good. (Epic. *Ep. Men.* 128)

In support of his viewpoint Epicurus alludes here to observations which every person can make about himself and others: all humans strive by nature after pleasure because it is good, and avoid pain because it is bad. For his principal thesis, however, he relies on appeal to 'feeling' (*pathos*) or – as other passages indicate – 'sensation' (*aisthēsis*). He does not consider it necessary to present *argument* in proof of the identity of pleasure and good, because he takes sensation and feeling to be the criteria of truth: on his view all good and evil are immediately accessible to sensation. In Cicero's *De Finibus*, the Epicurean Torquatus comments in his account of Epicurus' thesis that the same self-evidence attaches to the equation of the highest good with the highest pleasure as attaches to the facts that snow is white, fire is hot, and honey is sweet. No intricate line of reasoning is necessary here (*Fin.* I.30).[25]

Given the basic principles of his epistemology, Epicurus' position makes sense. Yet it became enveloped in controversy. The conjunction of Epicurus' claim that what he states is evident with his refusal to provide any proof of it was found particularly provocative. At any rate, some of his followers clearly tried to find an argumentative basis for the thesis that pleasure is the good despite Epicurus' stance on the matter. For example, his observation (reported by Diogenes Laertius) that as soon as they are born, animals find satisfaction in pleasure but are upset by pain, is there described as a 'proof' (*apodeixis*) of the thesis that pleasure is the goal

---

[24] But for complications see below, p. 665 with n. 58.
[25] Cf. also *Fin.* II.36, III.3. On *pathē* as the criteria of choice and avoidance see Gosling and Taylor 1982, ch. 20.

(D.L. x.137). This 'cradle' argument, as it has become convenient to call it, is not contained in the parts of Epicurus' writings that survive. However there is good reason to think it goes back to him. In the version preserved by Cicero it is made clear enough what status Epicurus accorded to it. It is presented not as a direct, independent proof that pleasure is good, pain bad, but merely as a reason for thinking that our adult desire for pleasure and aversion to pain must be something natural to us, not the consequence of exposure to the corruptions of upbringing or society.[26]

Cicero's presentation of Epicurus' position continues with reports of some specific attempts by later Epicureans to palliate his insistence on the self-evidence of the goodness of pleasure and the badness of pain (*Fin.* 1.31). One group held that it was not sufficient to appeal to the judgement of sensation: reason too needs to be invoked. And they found a way of resorting to reason here which they evidently took to be entirely compatible with Epicurus' eschewal of proofs. They claimed that it is as if our minds are naturally endowed with a conception (*quasi naturalis atque insita notio*; Greek *prolēpsis*, 'preconception') of the desirability of having pleasure and not having pain. Whether this was the manner in which Epicureans standardly conceived of preconceptions is doubtful: they were the outcome of experience, not innate ideas – although the *quasi* carefully avoids saying otherwise. It was certainly orthodox to treat them as criteria comparable with feelings and sensations in directly guaranteeing the truth of what they enunciate. The attempt to find in our reason a criterion of the truth of Epicurus' thesis about pleasure and pain was presumably an attempt to forestall or rebut the criticism that only reason could judge whether pleasure is good or bad.[27]

There follows an interesting reference to a further group, to which Torquatus is made to declare his allegiance:

> Others again, with whom I too am in agreement, believe that we should not be too self-confident about our case. After all, a great many philosophers give all manner of grounds for *not* counting pleasure amongst goods nor pain amongst evils. Accordingly, we think one should treat the question of pleasure and pain with a clear line of reasoning, in-depth discussion, and carefully considered arguments.

Perhaps these Epicureans are not disagreeing with Epicurus about the self-evidence of the goodness of pleasure and badness of pain, but

---

[26] See Brunschwig 1986, with the doubts of Sedley 1996.

[27] For further discussion see Brunschwig 1986, 122–3. *Prolēpsis* as criterion of truth: D.L. x.31. Empirical basis: D.L.x.33. A passage which does – problematically – treat *prolēpseis* as innate: Cic. *ND* 1.43–4. Rebuttal of criticism: Cic. *Fin.* 11.36–7.

only questioning its adequacy as a defence in philosophical debate.[28] Unfortunately Cicero gives no example of the lines of thought they had in mind. But traces of a discussion of the correct interpretation of Epicurus' assertion that his fundamental thesis needs no proof survive in a papyrus text of Demetrius Laco (second century BC). Its poor state of preservation makes reconstruction of the course of Demetrius' argument a matter largely for conjecture. But the very existence of such reasoning deserves attention, and confirms Cicero's story of developments in attitudes to Epicurus' position adopted by later Epicureans.[29]

v Pleasure as the goal

Our feelings and sensations tell us that pleasure is good and pain bad. But how do we know that the pleasure which we should accordingly seek as our goal in life is freedom from physical pain and mental disturbance? Epicurus does not appear to have claimed that that too was evident, disclosed immediately by the senses. What is required for proper understanding of the goal is thought: not proof, but reflection on the nature of desire: 'surely directed consideration' of our desires (*Ep. Men.* 128); 'sober reasoning searching out the causes of every choice and avoidance, and driving out the opinions through which enormous tumult takes possession of our souls' (*Ep. Men.* 132). We have seen that the basis of this reflection must be supplied by natural philosophy, since study of the nature and species of desire belongs to inquiry into human nature. But Epicurus makes it mostly the job of practical wisdom (*phronēsis*), and goes so far as to say that its importance makes it a more precious thing even than philosophy (*Ep. Men.* 132). There is an analogy here with our knowledge of the physical world. Sense perception is the criterion of truth: everything it tells us is true, and there is no other basis for knowledge of the world. But for the interpretation of its reports, and for understanding why we must posit as the fundamental realities atoms and void, even though they are not apparent to the senses, we must employ reason, albeit under the methodological constraints of *epimarturēsis* and *ouk antimarturēsis* imposed by application of the criterion.[30]

Epicurus explains that the result of the reflection he enjoins will be to discover that every choice we make, whether positive or negative, is really

[28] Cf. Asmis 1984, 36–9.
[29] Demetrius of Laconia, *PHerc.* 1012, col. 51–2; cf. Puglia 1980 and 1988, 272–80. If Sedley 1989a is correct, Demetrius will have regarded his contribution as exegesis of Epicurus, not innovation.   [30] For the analogy cf. Gosling and Taylor 1982, 405.

motivated by concern for health of the body and tranquillity of soul.[31] Of
course, we sometimes *think* that we want something different from this;
and even when we recognize that these are our real objects, we often have
mistaken ideas of how to achieve them. Hence the need to 'drive out opinions'. More will be said about this and about Epicurus' analysis of desire in
the next section. For the moment we must focus on the doctrine that constitutes its outcome, which is stated as follows:

> It is for the sake of this that we do all things: so that we may not be in
> pain nor suffer disturbance. When once we have this come about, all the
> storm of the soul abates, seeing that the living creature cannot then go as
> if in search of something it lacks, or of anything else by which the good of
> the soul and the body will be fulfilled. For it is then that we have need of
> pleasure, when we are in pain because of the absence of pleasure. When
> we are not in pain, we no longer have the need for pleasure. (Epic. *Ep.
> Men.* 128)

With the image of the storm in the soul Epicurus takes up a simile used
also by the Cyrenaics.[32] As was indicated in an earlier chapter,[33] the
grandson of Aristippus the Socratic, the younger Aristippus, also compared pain with a rough sea. But he worked out the comparison further:
pleasure is the sea with a gentle swell, and there is a middle condition
between pleasure and pain which is equivalent to a dead calm (Eus. *PE*
XIV.18.31–2 = *SSR* IV B 5). To the Cyrenaics' way of thinking, Epicurus
simply conflates two conditions – pleasure and absence of pain – which
need to be kept distinct (cf. e.g. D.L. II.89–90, X.136), as of course Plato
had insisted before them: *Rep.* 583c–584a, *Phlb.* 42c–44a. The charge that
in making the conflation he flouts common usage and the facts of nature is
pressed for pages on end in the critique of Epicurean ethics contained in
Book II of Cicero's *De Finibus*, where Epicurus is taken as effectively introducing *absence of pain* as his own private meaning for 'pleasure' (*Fin.*
II.6–19). The critique continues with complaints of self-contradiction: in
his account of the *summum bonum* as freedom from pain and disturbance,
Epicurus says that he cannot conceive of the good except in terms of sensory pleasures, that is, precisely the kinds of pleasure recognized as such by
Aristippus (*Fin.* II.20–30); the cradle argument is intended to support
Epicurus' account of the *summum bonum* as 'katastematic' pleasure, but
the pleasures enjoyed by new-born animals have to be construed as
'kinetic' (*Fin.* II.31–2).[34]

---

[31] Thus in modern parlance he propounds a version of psychological hedonism; cf. Striker 1993,
   6 n. 1.   [32] The image is discussed in Clay 1972.   [33] See p. 255 above.
[34] On the pleasures of infants see e.g. Rist 1972, 103–6; Brunschwig 1986, 126–8.

The suggestion that he simply collapses the idea of pleasure into that of absence of pain would have been firmly rejected by Epicurus. It is certainly the Epicurean view that if we are conscious of how we are feeling at all, we are always aware either of pleasure or of pain (*Fin.* 1.38). But the formula 'in pain because of the absence of pleasure' (*Ep. Men.* 128, quoted above) runs the danger of tautology if there is no more to pleasure than absence of pain. Moreover the delight we feel in *aponia* and *ataraxia* really does satisfy requirements which might reasonably be expected to be met by something counting as a pleasure. And from this the Epicureans devised an argument for reckoning *aponia* and *ataraxia* as pleasures themselves, even though they do not meet those same requirements:

> The pleasure we pursue is not just that which by a certain attractiveness moves our physical being, and is perceived by the senses with a particular kind of gratification. We hold the greatest pleasure to be that which is perceived once all pain has been removed. For when we have pain removed from us, we delight in that very emancipation and in the absence of all distress. But everything in which we delight is a pleasure, just as everything which upsets us is a pain. So the complete removal of pain has rightly been named pleasure. (Cic. *Fin.* 1.37)

The pleasure which is the *summum bonum* is not the mere negation of a sensory state. It consists in a perception accompanied by a kind of delight or enjoyment, namely one that has the absence of pain or distress and emancipation from them as its intentional object. But absence of pain would not give us this delight unless it were itself pleasurable.[35]

Although the 'greatest pleasure' identified in this text is different from the physical pleasures of sensory gratification, it is intimately connected with them. A verbatim extract from Epicurus' *On the Goal* translated by Cicero in the *Tusculan Disputations* indicates one way in which this is so:[36]

> For my part I cannot conceive of the good [i.e. the *summum bonum*] if I take away the pleasures felt in taste and sexual experience and listening to music, and those which beauty causes the eyes to experience as agreeable motions, and any other pleasures produced in a person as a whole *via* any of the senses. It certainly cannot be said that joy of the mind is the only thing that is good. For as I understand it, the mind will experience

---

[35] For fuller discussion of this argument to prove *aponia* and *ataraxia* pleasures see Purinton 1993, 283–7. But his interpretation differs from that given here, which construes as pleasures both the delight we feel and the absence of pain or anxiety which causes delight, although pleasures in different senses (cf. D.L. x.136 quoted below).

[36] Fuller discussion of this important text e.g. in Rist 1972, 108–9, Gosling and Taylor 1982, 367–73, Purinton 1993, 309–14 (with 298–9). Cf. Lucr. 11.17–19, Phld. *De Epicuro*, *PHerc.* 1232, col. 18 Tepedino (cf. Tepedino Guerra 1987, 85–8 and 1994, 24).

joy when it has expectation of all the things I just mentioned – i.e. when it expects that one's physical being will have those pleasures without pain. (Cic. *Tusc.* III.41)

Freedom from pain is in the broadest terms the focus of the joy or delight which strictly speaking constitutes the *summum bonum*. But unlike the body, which is tied to the present, the mind also looks forward and back, and many of its pleasures will be those of memory and especially of expectation. This is not the only way in which sensory pleasures are accommodated within Epicurus' conception of the greatest pleasure. As *KD* 18 puts it, 'in the flesh pleasure is not increased when once pain due to need has been removed, but is only varied'. We cannot improve on the enjoyment we take in having slaked our thirst with water (so e.g. *Ep. Men.* 131), but sensory pleasures associated with natural desire (e.g. the pleasure of drinking an exquisite dessert wine) will if wished introduce some variety into it.

As we have seen, the anti-Epicurean second book of *De Finibus* makes polemical use of a distinction Epicurus apparently invented between *kinetic* (*en kinēsei, kata kinēsin*; Latin *in motu*) and *katastematic* (Latin *in stabilitate, stabiles*) pleasures (*Fin.* II.31–2; cf. also II.9–10, 16, 75). Modern scholarship finds the distinction obscure.[37] It does not occur in the *Letter to Menoeceus* or the *Kuriai Doxai*; and interpretation of the one quotation from Epicurus' own writings which appears to exploit it is controverted. There is particular disagreement on the range of pleasures which fall within the kinetic class, and over the philosophical provenance of the actual idea of a kinetic pleasure. Are we to think primarily of the discussions in Plato and Aristotle of whether there are pleasures of process, e.g. of the restoration of the body from conditions of deprivation to its natural state?[38] Or does Epicurus borrow the notion of kinetic pleasure from Aristippus, who is reported to have insisted that both pleasure and pain are 'motions' (D.L. II.86, 89; *SSR* IV B 5)?[39]

The ancient sources consistently represent Cyrenaic hedonism as the intellectual context appropriate to understanding Epicurus' distinction. He is said to have derived the starting points for his exposition of the goal of life from the Cyrenaics (*SSR* IV A 173). The suggestion is that he agreed with Aristippus in recognizing a pleasure 'in motion', but argued that this was only one sort of pleasure, to be contrasted with another not acknowl-

---

[37] It is the subject of a large literature; see e.g. Diano 1935, Merlan 1960, Rist 1972, App. D, Gosling and Taylor 1982, ch. 19, Purinton 1993.
[38] See e.g. Gosling and Taylor 1982, 373–5.   [39] So e.g. Purinton 1993, 304–5.

edged by the Cyrenaics, namely the so-called katastematic pleasures of *aponia* and *ataraxia* (D.L. x.136). The Cyrenaics in turn are said to have disagreed with Epicurus' claim that the removal of pain is a pleasure (D.L. II.89). Although there is evidence of an attempt to charge Epicurus with plagiarizing Aristippus' teaching (D.L. x.4), this is not the general theme of the reports; and it is after all probable that the ideas of two contemporary schools of hedonists should owe more to debate with each other than to study of texts written in an earlier period. Moreover, the pleasures of 'variation' which Cicero firmly identifies as kinetic (*Fin.* II.10) clearly have nothing to do with processes of restoration; nor do those pleasures of the senses without which Epicurus says he cannot conceive the good, e.g. the pleasant motions which beauty causes the eyes to experience (Us. 67). In criticizing the Epicureans Plutarch takes it for granted that their conception of sensory pleasure is primarily of a 'smooth and gentle motion', i.e. precisely as it is defined by the Cyrenaics – although he plainly has Epicurean, not Cyrenaic, texts in mind (Plu. *Non Posse* 1087e, *Col.* 1122e).

In comparison with the numerous passages which speak of the pleasures of the senses as gentle and agreeable motions, there are very few which focus on pleasures like slaking one's thirst or filling the belly, despite the importance Epicurus attached to the cry of the flesh to be relieved of hunger and thirst and cold (*Sent. Vat.* 33). The emphasis is usually on the stable condition of *aponia* in the body which is the outcome of the process. Cicero once claims that on the Epicurean account the pleasure of quenching thirst is kinetic (Cic. *Fin.* II.9). But this is an isolated text whose interpretation is fiercely contested. It is not easy to reconcile with the other evidence, including the explanation of kinetic pleasure as variation Cicero goes on at once to give (*Fin.* II.10).[40] On the other hand, in a context which alludes to pleasures of the stomach Plutarch appears to cite an Epicurean description of pleasure as: 'a delightful motion through the flesh which is transmitted upward, resulting in a particular pleasure and joy of the soul' (Plu. *Non Posse* 1087b). This looks like an attempt on the part of the Epicureans to formulate an account of kinetic pleasure which will cover both gentle variations of *aponia* and the satisfaction of acute bodily needs. Perhaps Epicurus himself never indicated how he would classify pleasures of restoration of the body's natural state: understandably, if the main thrust of the distinction between kinetic and katastematic pleasures was to insist that there is another form of pleasure beside kinetic pleasure understood as Aristippus had defined it.

[40] Cf. e.g. Long and Sedley 1987, II.125 against Diano 1935, 260ff.

Our best clue to how that other kind of pleasure was conceived by Epicurus is supplied by another extract from *On the Goal* cited by ancient authors:

> The well-balanced state (*katastēma*) of the flesh and reliable expectation about it [sc. the flesh] hold the greatest and most secure joy for those who are capable of an appraisal. (Plu. *Non Posse* 1089d)

If we apply the principle enunciated at *Fin.* 1.37 (see p. 653 above), according to which everything that gives us joy is a pleasure, it will follow that this well-balanced state of the body is itself a pleasure: indeed, the greatest pleasure, since it gives the greatest joy. The specification of such pleasure as katastematic is accordingly to be understood as echoing the word '*katastēma*', as it is employed in the proposition just quoted. It will emphasize that the hallmark of this kind of pleasure is simply that it is a stable condition, as Cicero's translations *stabilis* and *in stabilitate* show he appreciated. When the body is in such a *katastēma*, it is entirely free of pain: hence the designation of *aponia* as katastematic pleasure. We must suppose that *ataraxia*, the katastematic pleasure of the soul, is achieved when it attains an analogous condition of stable psychic harmony.[41]

What matters most for Epicurean ethics in the end is not katastematic pleasure itself, but the joy and delight it gives us. For joy and delight are forms of awareness, or *pathē*, as katastematic pleasure is not. Presumably it is this that leads Epicurus to make them *kinetic* pleasures, as in the contrast he draws in a famous fragment of *On Choices*:[42]

> Freedom from disturbance and absence of pain are katastematic pleasures; but joy and delight are regarded as kinetic activities. (D.L. x.136)

From one point of view, therefore, Epicurus' disagreement with Aristippus is much less than he makes it appear, since the greatest pleasure remains strictly speaking a kinetic pleasure, namely our delight in *aponia* and *ataraxia*.[43] The Cyrenaics certainly acknowledged the existence of

---

[41] Epicurus' conceptions of a *katastēma* and of katastematic pleasure may well derive somehow or other from the idea found in the Aristotelian corpus (*EN* 1153a 2–6, *MM* 1205b20ff.) that one of the kinds of pleasure we feel occurs when our nature is *settled or composed* (φύσεως καθεστ-ηκυίας): Aristotle has in mind pleasures of sight and hearing. Epicurus' innovation is to make the settled state of our nature *itself* a pleasure, which may then be varied by such 'kinetic' pleasures. Others see the origin of Epicurus' kinetic pleasures in Aristotle's contrasted type of pleasure – the pleasure connected with the *replenishment* of our nature (φύσεως καθισταμένης): so e.g. Gosling and Taylor 1982, 373–5. The epithet 'well-balanced' (εὐσταθές) is probably inspired by its use in defining the ideal condition of the soul in Democritus' ethics (D.L. IX.45; DK 68 B 191).

[42] 'Activities' translates the reading ἐνέργειαι adopted by Long and Sedley 1987, II.124–5.

[43] Compare Aristotle's differentiation in *EN* x of the pleasure we take in an activity from the activity itself – as its perfection or 'bloom' (*EN* 1174b2–1175a3).

mental as well as bodily pleasures (D.L. 11.89–90). So the issue could be construed as narrowing to the question whether physical (so the Cyrenaics) or mental pleasures (so the Epicureans) are greater, which is indeed the way Diogenes Laertius eventually articulates it (x.137), perhaps reflecting debate on the point between the two schools (cf. 11.90).

Why, then, did Epicurus insist on the odd notion of a katastematic pleasure, and on standardly expressing his view of the good in negative terms, as the absence of pain or disturbance? These otherwise puzzling decisions have the great merit of indicating clearly where the centre of gravity of Epicurean hedonism is located, and where its fundamental philosophical allegiances lie. Epicurus plainly accepts that hedonism constitutes the correct framework within which a conception of the good life must be worked out. And the pleasures and pains of the body remain its focus, as his interpreters and critics alike never tire of emphasizing. But hedonism has to be adapted from its crude Cyrenaic form to accommodate an outlook hospitable to the imperturbable self-sufficiency of the Pyrrhonian wise man and to Democritus' emphasis on balance and aversion to 'large motions' in the soul – and as if by anticipation to Epicurus' own certainty that the pleasures of conversation he recalled on his deathbed outweighed excruciating physical pain (D.L. x.22).[44] The superficial unobviousness of the attractions of *aponia* and *ataraxia* serves to reinforce Epicurus' assurance that only sober reasoning about the nature of desire will bring us to appreciate that stability is what we really want.

vi Desire and the limits of life

Epicurus' analysis of desires turns on an assessment of human nature and its needs. This emerges from the brief summary given in the *Letter to Menoeceus*:

> We must reckon that some desires are natural and others empty, and of the natural some are necessary, others natural only; but of the necessary some are necessary for happiness, others for the body's freedom from disturbance, and others for life itself. (Epic. *Ep. Men.* 127)

To judge from the writings of Plato and Aristotle distinctions between pleasures or desires that are natural and those that are not, or again between necessary and non-necessary ones, were commonplace in Greek

---

[44] For Pyrrho see e.g. D.L. IX.63–5, where reference is made to Epicurus' admiration for him; also pp. 640–1 above. The principal relevant Democritean text is DK 68 B191.

philosophy.[45] The two distinctions were generally taken as giving an identical outcome: the fundamental forms of hunger, thirst, sexual and other physical appetites were seen as having the same basis, setting them apart from all other desires.[46] Epicurus registered dissent from this common assessment on a number of counts. Thus on his view desire for food and clothing is necessary as well as natural, desire for sex merely natural (Usener 456). More importantly, whereas the philosophical tradition restricted natural or necessary desires to the bodily appetites, and regarded the corresponding forms of satisfaction as the lowest kinds of pleasure, Epicurus regards natural desires as the *only* ones a prudent person will seek habitually to satisfy (*Ep. Men.* 129–32). And while these of course include bodily appetites as pre-eminent examples, we may infer that he counts the wish for *ataraxia* as natural and necessary too. This is indicated by the correction to the undifferentiated use of 'necessary' he issues in spelling out the various things necessary desires may be necessary for, and particularly in distinguishing the genus 'necessary for happiness' from the species 'necessary for the body's freedom from disturbance'.[47] The tradition would have regarded the desire for happiness, when properly conceived, as altogether other and better than a natural appetite.

If Epicurus makes the importance of satisfying bodily appetites so much greater than earlier philosophy would have acknowledged, how does he avoid the commitment to a profligate lifestyle with which his critics charged him? The answer has to turn on what the object of bodily desires is taken to be. A much quoted maxim indicates what this is in the cases Epicurus regards as fundamental for ethics:

> The flesh cries out not to be hungry, not to be thirsty, not to be cold. If someone is in these states and expects to remain so, he would rival even Zeus in happiness. (*Sent.Vat.* 33)

The basic bodily desire is for freedom from pain or discomfort: no recipe here for self-indulgence. We might agree, but ask: is it not natural after

---

[45] Cf. Plato *Rep.* 558d–559c (necessary vs. non-necessary); Arist. *EN* 1118b8–27 (natural vs. non-natural).

[46] For example Plato makes the desire to eat (i) 'up to the point of health and good condition' or (ii) food itself (559a11–b1) necessary, but (i′) that which goes beyond that point or (ii′) seeks foods of particular sorts non-necessary. Aristotle's division between natural and non-natural desires exploits criterion (ii) vs. (ii′); and the scholium on *EN* 1118b8 [= Us. 456] suggests that it may have been used by Epicurus to differentiate natural and necessary desires from those that are neither natural nor necessary. Most of our other evidence indicates that criterion (i) vs. (i′) was in Epicurus' eyes more fundamental for determining which desires are necessary. See further Annas 1993a, 188–200.   [47] See further Hossenfelder 1991a, 89–90.

satisfying hunger to want to eat either more (as the glutton does) or more interestingly (like the gourmet)? And if it is, has Epicurus sufficient argument *against* self-indulgence?

At this point we are disadvantaged by the absence in the sources of any explanation of how the Epicureans conceived and defended their conception of nature as it is invoked in this context. What the evidence does indicate is a strong appeal to a principle of natural equilibrium, namely between what nature – i.e. the natural world at large – provides and what it is natural for us to want:

> The wealth demanded by nature [sc. human nature] both has its bounds and is easy to procure; but that demanded by empty opinions goes off into infinity. (*KD* 15)

One aphorism is a prayer of thanksgiving to Nature:

> Thanks be to blessed Nature, because she has made what is necessary easy to procure, but what is hard to procure not necessary. (Stob. *Flor.* XVII.23)

This principle of equilibrium is used by Epicureanism as a working criterion to distinguish what are natural desires from what are not. Thus bread and water are easy to come by, but a luxurious diet, whether the emphasis is on quantity or variety, is not (*Ep. Men.* 130–2).[48] Indeed the desire for more will be insatiable if unchecked:

> Insatiable is not the stomach, as the many say, but false opinion about the stomach's boundless need to be filled. (*Sent. Vat.* 59)

The objects of sexual appetite are not difficult to attain – nor to do without: which indicates that such desire is natural but not necessary (Cic. *Tusc.* v.93; Plu. *De bruta ratione uti* 989b [= Usener 456]). We might think this view of sex was contradicted by experience of the pangs of love. But Epicurus explains how phenomena of this sort are to be understood:

> Wherever intense seriousness is present in those natural desires which do not lead to pain if they are unfulfilled, these come about because of empty opinion; and it is not because of their own nature that they are not relaxed, but because of the empty opinion of the person. (*KD* 30)

What causes stress is not failure to satisfy sexual appetite, but the human beliefs which infect such appetites, whether satisfied or not, with unnatural intensity: for example the belief that my happiness depends on

---

[48] The scholium on *KD* 29 is probably therefore incorrect when it makes the desire for pleasures of variety, e.g. expensive foods, natural (although not necessary).

reciprocation of affection by the person I am in love with, which is an 'empty opinion' because it embodies a false conception of happiness and of how to achieve it.[49] This is presumably the general fault that runs through all unnatural desire. It is perhaps significant that *KD* 30 attributes it to the person or human being (*anthrōpos*). The animal (*zōion*) within us will be content with provision for our natural needs (cf. *Ep. Men.* 128).

Epicurus holds that grasp of the principle of natural equilibrium will liberate us from unnatural desire:

> He who knows the limits of life knows how easy it is to procure that which removes pain due to need and that which makes the whole of life complete. So he does not want any dealings involving competition. (*KD* 21)

Understanding of the principle is here presented as a function of knowledge of the limits of life in general, i.e. of the parameters laid down by the axioms of the *Tetrapharmakos* (*KD* 20; cf. 1–4). The use of the term 'limits' reminds us that while the things which are the object of natural desire are easily procured, they are also bounded (*KD* 15), or as we might more readily say, not boundless. Epicurus develops this cardinal thesis in many sayings devoted to exposition of the doctrine of the limits (*perata*) or bounds (*horoi*) of the extent of pleasure, in the first instance in *KD* 3:

> The bound of the magnitude of pleasures is the removal of all pain. Wherever pleasure is present, as long as it is there, pain or distress or their combination is absent.

On other occasions he speaks of 'the goal and limit of the flesh' (*KD* 20), and says that 'in the flesh pleasure is not increased when once the pain due to want is removed' (*KD* 18). This has the effect of locating the question of magnitude of physical pleasures firmly within the context of the natural needs of the body: its desire not to be cold or hungry or thirsty. Given that account of bodily appetite, the only obvious basis for measuring quantity of bodily pleasure is assessment of the degree of satisfaction of bodily need.[50] The luxury of the rich man's table may look to the *mind*

---

[49] See further Nussbaum 1994, ch. 5. As she notes (Nussbaum 1986, 35 n. 5) Lucretius supplies much of our evidence for the contrast between natural sexual desire and *erōs*, defined by Epicurus as 'an intense desire for intercourse, along with madness and anguish' (Us. 483). Annas 1993a, 193 n. 29, proposes that natural sexual desire is not merely natural but necessary. But necessary for what? Does the flesh here cry out not to be . . .? What pain do we suffer if sexual desire goes unsatisfied?

[50] It does not follow that satisfaction of desire is simply what a pleasure is for the Epicureans (the theory of Mitsis 1988a, ch. 1).

as though it offers greater pleasures than the poor man's bread and water, but for the flesh – or from the point of view of the flesh – there can be nothing *more* pleasurable than having its cry for an end to misery fully answered: anything further can – again, from its point of view – only be variation, i.e. qualitative differentiation. And as will by now be abundantly clear, it is the perspective of the flesh and its natural and necessary desires which should dominate our pursuit of the good. Once we abandon it, we run the risk of succumbing to false ideas of how happiness can be achieved.

Nature's prescription for happiness is effectively a recipe for self-sufficiency. Enjoyment of the pleasures of luxury is not prohibited: but we must be liberated from craving for them and so from fear of being unable to have them (*Ep. Men.* 131). Self-sufficiency is to be regarded not as a regime of self-denial, but as freedom (*Sent. Vat.* 77) and as riches:

> He who follows nature and not empty opinions is self-sufficient in all things. For relative to what is sufficient for nature every possession is riches, but relative to unbounded desires even the greatest riches are not riches but poverty.[51] (Usener 202)

Although satisfaction of the natural and necessary desires of the flesh must be our aim, we need a broader perspective than the flesh can itself supply if we are to be effective in this pursuit of what Epicurus often calls 'the goal of nature'. Bodily sensation and desire are a matter of what we feel *now*: 'the flesh is storm-tossed only in the present' (D.L. x.137). It is the mind which is equipped to plan for an optimal balance of pleasure and pain, by virtue of its grasp of time (cf. D.L. x.137, Cic. *Fin.* 1.55) and its understanding of the limits of pain as well as pleasure:

> Pain does not last continuously in the flesh: when acute it is there for a very short time, while the pain which just exceeds the pleasure in the flesh does not persist for many days. Chronic illnesses contain a predominance of pleasure in the flesh over pain. (*KD* 4)

Here Epicurus is thinking primarily of the unavoidable pains of illness. But as well as assuaging anxiety about these and making room for realistic pleasures of anticipation, the knowledge enshrined in *KD* 4 makes it rational to undergo voluntarily such things as surgery or painful exercise in order to enjoy the pleasures of a healthy body. Epicurus accordingly advocates employment of a hedonistic calculus, specified in terms strikingly reminiscent of Plato's *Protagoras*:

---

[51] The end of this text is lacunose. Bignone's conjecture πλοῦτος ἀλλὰ πενία is translated here.

We do not choose every pleasure, but there are times when we pass over many pleasures, when their outcome is a greater quantity of discomfort for us. And we regard many pains as better than pleasures, when endurance of the pains over a long period is followed by greater pleasure for us. Every pleasure, then, because of its natural affinity, is something good, yet not every pleasure is choiceworthy: just as every pain is something bad, but not every pain is always of a nature to be avoided. However, it is appropriate to judge all these things by comparative measurement and by survey of advantages and disadvantages. For at certain times we treat the good as bad and conversely the bad as good. (*Ep. Men.* 129–30)

One of Epicurus' most difficult sayings contrasts the attitude to death the mind should adopt with one representing somehow or other the perspective of the flesh:

The flesh takes the limits of pleasure as unlimited, and unlimited time brings it [sc. unlimited pleasure] about. But the mind, making its appraisal of the goal and limit of the flesh, and dispersing fears about the time to come, brings about the complete life, and we no longer need the unlimited time [sc. demanded by the flesh]. It neither shuns pleasure nor – when circumstances bring about our departure from life – does it approach the end supposing it is in any way falling short of the best life. (*KD* 20)

Since the flesh is capable only of present sensation, and naturally desires only to be free from immediate pain, Epicurus cannot mean that the flesh actually perceives pleasure as unlimited or wants it to be unlimited: that would be to assimilate its perspective to that of empty opinion. He must be arguing in counterfactual terms: if *per impossibile* the flesh were to be able to look into the future, what would be its recipe for a *life* in which fulfilment is achieved? It could conceive such fulfilment only in terms of an infinite sequence of pleasures. But an infinite sequence of pleasures is obviously a human impossibility, since it would require infinite time. So not merely does the perspective of the flesh as a matter of fact give no basis for a conception of the good or complete life. Even if we imagined it enriched with a grasp of time, it could still yield no feasible conception of a happy life. To achieve that we need to employ our minds, first to understand what the limits of pleasure in the flesh really are (cf. *KD* 3), and then to appreciate the nature of death (cf. *KD* 2). By 'taking away the yearning for immortality' (*Ep. Men.* 124) this will bring us freedom from anxiety (*ataraxia*). And the achievement of *ataraxia* is all someone needs to register his life as complete, i.e. as needing nothing further to make it ideal. The person who is in this state of mind will neither ascetically abstain from further pleasure, but nor if death is upon him will he feel deprived of something which might have made his life better.

It is sometimes suggested that Epicurus' treatment of fear of death is too narrowly focused.[52] The argument that death is nothing to us is based on the thesis that it is not bad for us when present, because only pain is bad and a dead person can feel nothing at all (*Ep. Men.* 124). If we accept and thoroughly digest this thesis we shall lose our fear, for example, of what may happen to our dead bodies (Lucr. III.870-93), or of punishment in an underworld (Lucr. III.966-1023) - and also the distress of anticipation itself, which is now deprived of its foundation:

> So one who says he fears death, not because it will hurt when it is here, but because it hurts when it is to be, talks nonsense: what causes no distress when it is present hurts in the expectation only on account of empty opinion. (Epic. *Ep. Men.* 125)

But what if our fear at the thought of death is caused not by apprehension that something bad will or may befall us, but by belief that we will be deprived of good things we *might* have enjoyed or gone on enjoying (cf. Plu. *Non Posse* 1106a-1107c)? Such a belief would be particularly upsetting if the goods in question were conceived as forms of pleasure or enjoyment needed to make our lives in some important sense complete. A fear of this kind is not adequately dealt with by the argument that in death we *actually* experience nothing at all.

We know that Lucretius thought about such cases:[53]

> 'No more for you the welcome of a joyful home and a good wife. No more will your children run to snatch the first kiss, and move your heart with unspoken delight. No more will you be able to protect the success of your affairs and your dependants. Unhappy man', they say, 'robbed by a single hateful day of all those rewards of life.' (Lucr. III.894-9)

A saying such as *KD* 20 suggests that Epicurus himself had also reflected on them, even if he does not engage with the problem they present in his principal argument against fear of death. His response seems to have involved a further application of the notion of limits of pleasure. For 'the appraisal of the goal and limit of the flesh' and the treatment of fears which according to *KD* 20 (cf. also *KD* 21) bring about the complete life are said in *KD* 18 to produce the limit of pleasure in the *mind*. The surviving

---

[52] Epicurean views on death have been much discussed. See e.g. Furley 1986, Rosenbaum 1986, 1990, Annas 1993a, 342-50, Nussbaum 1994, ch. 6.
[53] As did Philodemus: see *On Death* IV, col. 12.2-14.14.

evidence does not explicate this version of the limit idea further. But very likely Epicurus regarded the basic form of the mind's natural desire for happiness as analogous with the body's: the mind, we might say, cries out not to be anxious or distressed, particularly by pain and fear. Now philosophy shows that nature is such as to make pain tolerable and fear groundless. And it thus produces the limit of mental pleasure. That limit is accordingly conceived in distinctly Stoical terms. The flesh demands not to be in pain, but the mind is content if it *understands* that pain is tolerable and pleasure easy to procure.[54]

It is not hard to see why someone who has achieved such contentment should be thought to have a life that is complete. For he will be unruffled whatever circumstances may bring. He will never be in the position of being upset because he has failed in some project or is suffering bodily pain or enjoying few sensory pleasures. He may possess little that is good in his life, but there is no good he needs to supply contentment: his poverty is great wealth (cf. *Sent. Vat.* 25). This flexibility means that his life lacks nothing to make it the best possible – ideally adapted to the constraints imposed by nature. Of course, it is conceivable that at some given moment within it he might have been enjoying more pleasure than in fact he is. But that does not show that his *life* might have been better: for a life is to be conceived from the ethical point of view not as a set or sum of moments or episodes, but as the implementation of a strategy for living.[55] A similar argument suffices for the analogous likelihood that at some moment *after his death* he might have enjoyed 'the rewards of life'. Well he might; but given Epicurus' conception of life as life-plan that does nothing to support the view that the life he actually lives is – in the sense we have defined – incomplete, nor *a fortiori* to make it rational for him to fear death on that account.

Given this interpretation of what it is for life to be complete we can make sense of Epicurus' avowal of his own happiness as he lay in agony on his death-bed (D.L. x.22), or again of his dictum:

> Unlimited time and limited time contain equal pleasure, if one measures its limits by reasoning. (*KD* 19)

Here as in *KD* 20 Epicurus must mean that the pleasure of contentment afforded by his perfect life strategy would not be increased if death were to be abolished and the time available for its implementation infinite: con-

---

[54] See Hossenfelder 1988 for the claim that Epicurus 'would have preferred to be a Stoic'.

[55] This conception of a life is the one involved in the notion of the choice of lives which is familiar in e.g. Aristotle as well as the subject of substantial treatises by leading Hellenistic philosophers, Epicurus included (D.L. x.28).

tentment is something complete. Cicero asks (*Fin.* 11.88) how having pleasure go on for a longer time can fail to be more desirable if the longer pain continues the more miserable we become (cf. *KD* 4), and if the blessedness of the gods is associated with their imperishability (cf. *KD* 1). This is to misunderstand Epicurus' view both of the duration of pleasure and of the complete life.[56] Plutarch quotes from a letter in which he summons one Anaxarchus to 'continuous pleasures' (*Col.* 1117a) by taking up Epicureanism: this presupposes that sustained is preferable to brief pleasure. If one life contains more and longer episodes of pleasure than another does, there is an obvious sense in which it contains more pleasure and is *ceteris paribus* more desirable.[57]

The complete life, then, is self-sufficient in that it is invulnerable to fortune. The powerlessness of chance is a constant topic of Epicurean literature. It is the theme which dominates the close of the *Letter to Menoeceus* (D.L. x.133–5), and the subject of many Epicurean aphorisms. Metrodorus, a member of Epicurus' immediate circle, is credited with this saying:

> Fortune, I have made advance preparations against you, and barred the passage against every secret entry you try to make. We shall not give ourselves up as captives to you or to any other circumstance. But when necessity leads us out, we shall spit upon life (*to zēn*) and upon those who emptily plaster themselves in it, and we shall depart from it with a noble song of triumph, crying out at the end: 'We have had a good life (εὖ ἡμῖν βεβίωσθαι).' (*Sent. Vat.* 47)

And a briefer and quieter remark advises:

> He who least needs tomorrow will go with greatest pleasure to meet tomorrow. (Plu. *Tranq. An.* 474c)

Such a person may not be in that 'well-balanced state of the flesh' accompanied by 'reliable expectation about it' which suffices for *aponia* or for 'the greatest and most secure delight' in *aponia* (Plu. *Non Posse* 1089d). He may very well have fallen short of the limit of pleasure in the flesh, as does the man who moans and wails in the torture chamber, or as did Epicurus himself on his deathbed; and like them he may have nothing but death or – so far as the body is concerned – more pain to look forward to. But happiness is possible in both cases (D.L. x.118, 22).[58] That must be because

---

[56] For difficulties scholars have found in Cicero's interpretation see e.g. Mitsis 1988a, 23–6.

[57] Hence the recommendation to adopt a hedonistic calculus: cf. Purinton 1993, 315–18.

[58] It seems to follow that for Epicurus the idea of the good or *summum bonum* is quite distinct from the notion of happiness: the good is a condition in which a person feels pleasure and no pain, whereas happiness is an attribute of his life as a whole, achievable even if the good is not attained (although if it *is* achieved he will rival Zeus in happiness, *Sent. Vat.* 33; cf. D.L. x.121, where such happiness is contrasted with a lesser sort).

the limit of pleasure in the *mind* can be attained by someone in such a position, enabling him to face the next day with greatest pleasure on account of the *ataraxia* brought by the operation of the *Tetrapharmakos*.

The Epicurean theory of desire and the limits of pleasure therefore has a shape very similar to the Stoic theory of appropriate action. Appropriate action will initially be focused on 'the primary things in accordance with nature', and above all on what promotes preservation of our animal constitution: compare Epicurus on the natural and necessary desires of the flesh. But perfect appropriate action requires a strategy of life ultimately indifferent, like *ataraxia*, to the actual achievement of naturally desirable objectives. As with Epicureanism, the perfection of the strategy is what happiness and the best life depend upon.

VII Virtue and friendship

The role of virtue in Epicurean ethics[59] is very different from the place it holds in Stoicism. Cleanthes is said to have portrayed Epicurean hedonism as seating pleasure on a throne and surrounding her with servants – the virtues. They urge prudence upon her, with the assurance: 'We virtues were born to be your slaves: we have no other business' (Cic. *Fin.* 11.69). Epicurus himself is recorded as saying:

> We should prize the honourable and the virtues and those sorts of things if they bring about pleasure. If they do not bring it about, we should bid them goodbye. (Athen. *Deipn.* 546f)

Since pleasure is the good, the only legitimate function of virtues is to furnish means to that end; and according to Epicurus we shall attain it if and only if we practise the virtues. They derive from practical wisdom, which teaches that 'it is impossible to live pleasurably without living in accordance with practical wisdom or what is honourable or just' or vice versa. The reason is that 'the virtues have grown together with living pleasurably, and living pleasurably is inseparable from them' (*Ep. Men.* 132): which sounds like a closer relation than that of means to end.

This set of ideas is worked out in more detail in the exposition of Epicurean ethics presented in Book I of *De Finibus*. Indeed, the topic of virtue looms much larger in the Epicurean books of *De Finibus* than in what survives of Epicurus' own writings, no doubt because this was a subject on which critics intent on portraying the Epicureans as subvert-

---

[59] For fuller discussion see Annas 1993a, 334–42.

ers of morality had fastened, provoking response and counter-response. In any event, Torquatus is made to take each virtue in turn, and show how properly conceived it fits within the ethical scheme explained in sections 4–6 above (*Fin.* 1.42–54). He stresses for example how for the Epicureans wisdom enables us to distinguish empty from necessary and natural desires (1.43–5), while temperance supplies the tenacity needed to apply the restraint often called for by the hedonistic calculus: it is desirable not because it renounces pleasures, but because it procures greater ones (1.47–8). The person who makes light of death and takes the view of pain recommended in the *Tetrapharmakos* is on that account (and on that account only) courageous (1.49). The case of courage deserves a further comment, since it suggests a reason for the shifting formulations Epicurus employs in describing the relation of the virtues to pleasure. Courage is worthwhile only if harnessed to the goal: the pleasure of *ataraxia*. But once we understand what is involved in *ataraxia*, we will see that being courageous simply *is* facing pain and death without anxiety.

Justice (*dikaiosunē*) is the virtue on which – besides practical wisdom – Epicurus apparently had most to say.[60] It is logically dependent on the prior notion of justice as a principle of association (*to dikaion*), explained in terms of the mutual advantage of neither harming nor being harmed, as implemented in a social contract. Epicurus calls this *natural* justice because it is designed to satisfy our natural desire for security, which is evidently a form of the desire for *ataraxia*. The associated virtue is simply the disposition to abide by the contract: valuable in the first instance because of the security, benefiting the agent as much as others, to which the contract is directed. (No one who has absorbed the *Tetrapharmakos* is likely to want to harm others, but the contract is still a protection against less enlightened persons.) But *dikaiosunē* has an incidental value also. For the unjust man, who is ready to break the contract when he thinks he can get away with doing so, is never free from fear of discovery and punishment (*KD* 31–5). So the just man has the further advantage of liberation from that kind of second-order anxiety:

The just person is maximally unanxious, the unjust full of enormous anxiety. (*KD* 17)

Friendship is an even more important means to happiness than the virtues in general or justice in particular:

---

[60] See Vander Waerdt 1987, Mitsis 1988a, ch. 2, Annas 1993a, 293–302. These discussions find Epicurus' view of justice more complex than is suggested by the account offered here. Epicurus' theory of the social contract is explained more fully below, pp. 000–00.

Of all the things wisdom prepares for the blessedness of life as a whole, much the greatest is the possession of friendship. (*KD* 27)

Its value lies in the first instance in the security it affords, as a number of other sayings of Epicurus indicate, although the fullest account is once again in Book 1 of *De Finibus*. A life without friends risks the sorts of assaults from other people that one cannot easily guard against – and labours under the fear of such assault. Reason therefore advises the formation of friendships to reduce the risk and to increase confidence in the face of it. But a friendless life is also lonely, and so reason also has in view the pleasures which intimate association will generate: both enjoyment in the present and pleasures of anticipation (*Fin.* 1.66–7).

The motivation of friendship is therefore self-interested; and while we may be concerned for our friends' pleasure as well as our own, it is the latter which is in itself more desirable to us (*Fin.* 1.66). At this point in the theory Epicurus seems to have introduced a subtle development which later Epicureans found hard to explain or justify. It is a response to the thought that friendship will not work unless we love our friends as much as ourselves. The means to pleasure and security will be ineffective unless themselves treated as an end.[61] So although our friends' pleasure and wellbeing are not intrinsically as important to us as our own, we must love them as though they were. And the only way someone can do that is actually to feel the same towards his friend as he does towards himself (*Fin.* 1.67–8). This means being prepared to take risks and suffer pains and even die on a friend's behalf. Hence the theory is made to yield reason to treat friends altruistically. Nor was this mere theory for Epicurus. Some of his most eloquent sayings about friendship have an emotional charge powered by something more than self-interest:

Friendship dances round the world announcing to us all that we should wake up and celebrate blessedness. (*Sent. Vat.* 52)

A noble person is much occupied with wisdom and friendship: of these one is a mortal, the other an immortal good. (*Sent. Vat.* 78)

Moreover Epicurus' ideal of a community of friends, realized in the society of the Garden (*Fin.* 1.65), is described in terms which suggest full identification with the concerns of others (*KD* 40, quoted below, p. 756).

Epicurus' attempt to extract altruism from a basically self-interested

---

[61] This thought is explicitly voiced in one of Epicurus' sayings, provided the text is emended: 'All friendship is choiceworthy (αἱρετή) for its own sake, but it takes its origin from benefit' (*Sent. Vat.* 23). The MS. text (ἀρετή) is defended in Long 1986b, 305b, but Usener's conjecture makes for a much more intelligible thesis.

conception of friendship is a philosophical manoeuvre now familiar in the writings of modern utilitarians. His version of it seems to embody a contradiction: I both do and do not care for my friend as much as I do for myself. Cicero records two different Epicurean attempts to negotiate the difficulties. One consisted in a diachronic solution. Friendship begins from a hedonistic motive, but that is replaced by altruistic concern if the friendship blossoms (*Fin.* 1.69). As Cicero comments, part two of this suggestion effectively posits a moral basis for action not rooted in desire for pleasure or expectation of it – which threatens the whole foundation of Epicurean ethics (*Fin.* 11.82). The other proposal was that the wise make a *contract* to love their friends as much as themselves (*Fin.* 1.70). Although the utilitarian rationale of the contract is not spelled out, it is evidently assumed, and is accordingly an idea more in tune with the basis of Epicurean ethics. Moreover it gives a clearer (if not more plausible) account of the mechanism effecting the altruistic turn. Yet the mechanism of the contract looks more appropriate for what Aristotle would call advantage friendships than for the morally impressive friendships Epicurus seems to have in mind. And it does not remove the contradiction apparently inherent in his theory.[62]

VIII Practice

Epicurus' work in four books entitled *On Lives* (D.L. x.28) was evidently one of his most important ethical writings (cf. D.L. x.30). From the surviving information about it and from our knowledge of the genre we can infer that it advised the reader on what choices of life were and were not appropriate given that pleasure is the goal. Book 1 condemned participation in politics, Book 11 the Cynic way of life (D.L. x.119). The sources attribute no major positive prescription to *On Lives*. But there can be little doubt that it will have recommended the quiet life of 'withdrawal from the many' (*KD* 14) in company with friends (*KD* 27–8): 'live unknown' (*lathe biōsas*: cf. Plu. *An Recte* 1128a–1129b) was one of the Epicureans' most notorious slogans, summing up in two words the way the key decision should go. For the Epicureans' advice on more specific practical choices we have to rely on a hotch-potch of evidence, and notably on a disorganized scissors-and-paste compilation reproduced by Diogenes Laertius (x.117–20). This includes the barest summaries of their stances

---

[62] For further discussion see Rist 1972, ch. 7, 1980, Long 1986b, Mitsis 1988a, ch. 3, Annas 1993a, 236–44.

inter alia on sexual relations and marriage (negative),[63] treatment of slaves (humane), behaviour at a symposium (restrained), music and poetry (the wise man will discuss but not write it), and making money (he will do so only from imparting his wisdom, when hard up). Presentation and selection of topics seem to be shaped at least partly by the doxographer's desire to set up an opposition between Stoic and Epicurean positions on issues which were to become standard fare for Hellenistic practical ethics, although it is clear from the pages of Philodemus that Epicureans did indeed attack, for example, the views of Diogenes of Babylon on music and the symposium.

To judge from references and allusions in later classical literature, it was not detailed *praeceptio* of this kind which made a significant impact on the thought and behaviour of those receptive to philosophy, but the treatment of the fundamentals of the good life presented in the *Letter to Menoeceus* and in collections of sayings such as the *Key Doctrines* or the *Vatican Sentences*. We would have guessed that the *Key Doctrines* were designed to be memorized and absorbed into the intellectual and emotional bloodstream. The guess is confirmed by the specific instructions given at the beginning and end of each of Epicurus' surviving letters, enjoining the addressees to learn by heart the compendia of doctrines they contain, so as to achieve *ataraxia*. The *Letter to Menoeceus* concludes with some words already quoted:

> Practise these things and all that belongs with them to yourself night and day, and to someone like yourself, and you will never be disturbed either awake or in your dreams, but you will live like a god among men. For quite unlike a mortal animal is a man who lives among immortal goods.
> (*Ep. Men.* 135)

Practise must here mean simultaneously verbal repetition and the attempt to put Epicurus' teaching into effect. The last page of the *Letter*, for example, recapitulates the *Tetrapharmakos*: Menoeceus will need to run through its main points in his mind over and over again, so that as they become his settled convictions they will drive out the deeply rooted empty opinions which fuel fear of pain and death.[64]

---

[63] Cf. Chilton 1960, which successfully defends the emendation καὶ μηδὲ γαμήσειν at D.L. x.119.

[64] Cf. the remark (*Sent. Vat.* 41): 'We must simultaneously laugh and philosophize and run our households and attend to the rest of our family affairs and never cease voicing the sayings of the true philosophy.' For further discussion of memorization in Epicurean theory and practice see Rabbow 1954, especially 127ff., 336ff., Hadot 1969a and 1969b, 54ff., Clay 1972, Angeli 1986, Erler and Ungern-Sternberg 1987, Capasso 1988a and 1988b.

Epicurus' advice that Menoeceus should rehearse these and similar doctrines with someone like himself as well as on his own introduces the only reference to friendship in the entire *Letter*. It is significant that the reference takes this form. Friendship is not one more item of teaching to be absorbed. Rather it constitutes the framework within which the amendment of a person's life required by Epicurean ethics is to be worked through. Evidence that Epicurean communities conceived themselves as societies of friends having this among other functions is supplied by Philodemus' treatise *On frank speaking* (*PHerc.* 1471). This work explores the question of how a philosopher should correct the moral faults of a student. As Martha Nussbaum comments, Philodemus 'represents himself as giving a picture of the way things go in a well-functioning Epicurean community'. The title page indicates that as elsewhere in Philodemus the material derives largely from lectures of Zeno of Sidon, i.e. from the latter part of the second century BC.[65]

The fragmentary preservation of the text makes the argument of *On frank speaking* often hard or impossible to determine, but the broad shape of the work is reasonably clear. First comes a section (fr. 1–35) advising on the general strategy to be adopted by the teacher or 'leader' (*kathēgētēs, kathēgoumenos*); then one (fr. 36–52) on the frankness he should expect of the pupil or 'person being prepared' (*kataskeuazomenos*); and finally (fr. 53 onwards) a much longer part which takes up a sequence of particular practical problems that may confront or trouble the teacher. The relationship envisaged between pupil and teacher is captured in a passage which dissuades students from listening to those who

> inflame [sc. those they criticize] when they themselves are guilty of the same things, and do not love them or know how to correct them or indeed have any chance of persuading persons who are much superior to themselves, instead of to someone who is purged and cherishes and is superior and knows how to apply therapy. (fr. 44)

Philodemus expects three things of the leader. He must be purged of the faults he criticizes in others, and so be their moral superior. He has to have the practical knowledge requisite for correction or therapy. And he will speak to his pupils with the sort of love that a parent has for its child. These attributes will enable him to avoid 'inflaming' the diseased condition of

---

[65] For the text one still has to rely on the 1914 Teubner edition of A. Olivieri; but see the recent studies of Gigante 1975, 1983a, 55ff., Nussbaum 1986, 1994, ch. 4 (quotation from 1986, p. 37).

the patient. Instead he effects the purge he himself has already undergone. Other passages also stress that in doing so he is motivated by goodwill and sympathy. What he says should be received in a similar spirit as helpful and beneficial.[66]

The friendship between the two parties is what makes frankness on both sides appropriate. At one point Philodemus comments that

> we could demonstrate by a comparative appraisal that, although many fine things result from friendship, none is so important as having someone to whom it is possible to speak one's heart and listen when he speaks his. (fr. 28)

Different cases call for different approaches. The leader will look for the right moment (col. 17b), not taking up every fault, even including quite serious ones, but he will view them with sympathy (fr. 79), bearing in mind that he is dealing with young people (fr. 52) who are apt to throw over the traces (fr. 71). He will accordingly prefer to adopt a varied and gentle critical register or 'technique of friendship' (*philotechnia*, fr. 68), including elements of praise, encouragement (fr. 68), laughter (fr. 23) and 'irony – which pleases but bites into everyone pretty well' (fr. 26). But sometimes he will have to be just frank (fr. 10) and resort to a sharpness which may be misconstrued as abuse (fr. 60). For

> with those who are more robust than the delicate and those who need more attention he increases the pressure, while with those robust people who will hardly change course if they are shouted at he will use the harsh form of frankness. (fr. 7)

The pupil will then have to take what is said as an enema or other strong medicine like wormwood (col. 2b) or hellebore (tab. 12, M), again and again if that is necessary to achieve the purge (fr. 63–4). Philodemus' *On anger* (PHerc. 182), which likewise resorts to the medical analogy, even refers to surgery (col. 44.22). For his part the person being prepared is expected to declare his faults to the leader (fr. 49), encouraged in this by 'seeing that we [sc. the leaders] are accusers of ourselves also when we go completely astray' (fr. 51). It is also legitimate for fellow pupils to draw such faults to the leader's attention:

> He [sc. the leader] will not think someone who desires his friend to receive correction an informer, when he is no such thing, but rather a person who loves his friend. (fr. 50)

[66] Cf. fr. 25 and 43, and col. 17b. For sympathy as an ingredient of friendship see *Sent. Vat.* 66.

What the pupil wants, after all, is a cure, and to get it he needs to hand himself over to the leader as his 'saviour' (*sōtēr*) for therapy (fr. 40). He should not then object if well-wishers mention to his physician symptoms he is not aware of himself or may foolishly be trying to ignore.

How much of this theory of the therapeutic relationship between philosopher and student goes back to Epicurus and his immediate circle is impossible to tell. What is clear is that the theory was legitimated by appeal to the authority of Epicurus and the other *kathēgemones*:[67]

> And now to the common thread and the cardinal point: we shall be obeying Epicurus, in accordance with whom we have chosen to live. (fr. 45)

> To sum up, the wise man speaks frankly to his friends as did Epicurus and Metrodorus. (fr. 15)

Frankness of speech is not a subject on which Epicurus has anything to say in what survives of his writings.[68] But his school did possess copies of the large number of letters he sent his friends, pupils and relatives. From the fragments of these, together with other information about them, it is clear that Epicurus wrote to his correspondents in tones of great personal concern and often urgency. At key points *On frank speaking* is probably relying on particular passages in them where Epicurus either took correspondents to task (fr. 6) or indicated his approval of their openness about their shortcomings:

> Heraclides is praised because he supposed the criticisms he would incur as a result of what was going to come to light were less important than the benefit he would get from them, and so informed Epicurus of his mistakes. (fr. 49)

The text becomes lacunose at this juncture, but refers to Polyaenus (one of the *kathēgemones*), probably as having earned credit for mentioning someone else's bad attitude to Epicurus.[69]

It is not surprising that scholars have found here anticipations of the Catholic confessional or Freudian analysis.[70] Seneca will supply us with

---

[67] On the καθηγεμόνες – the founding fathers of Epicureanism – see Longo Aurrichio 1978, and on the supreme authority of Epicurus himself Sedley 1989a, Erler 1993. N.B. Sen. *Ep.* 33.4: *omnia . . . unius ductu et auspiciis dicta sunt.*

[68] One use of the term παρρησία at *Sent. Vat.* 29, where frank speaking is contrasted with conforming to popular opinion in the hope of winning praise.

[69] Further references to letters of Epicurus at fr. 9, 72. For details of a collection of letters of Polyaenus designed to illustrate his humanity, and preserved in the Herculaneum library (Anon. *PHerc.* 176; see Tepedino Guerra 1991, fr. 4, 5, 15, 41; and Sedley 1989a, 105).

[70] Confessional: Sudhaus 1911; cf. also Schmid 1962, 740–7. Psychiatry: Nussbaum 1994, 134–5.

an appropriately sombre conclusion, for he ascribes to Epicurus the saying:

Do everything as though Epicurus were watching you. *Ep.* 25.5[71]

---

[71] Cf. Cic. *Fin.* v. 3, where Atticus says: 'I could not forget Epicurus even if I wanted to, since our people put his likeness not only in pictures but on drinking-cups and rings'; see further Frischer 1982 on the role of sculpture and other images in Epicureanism. The 'penitential' dimension of Epicurean ethics is a particular interest of Seneca's: see besides *Ep.* 25.4–6, *Ep.* 11.8, 28.9, 97.15, with discussion in Schmid 1957, 301–14; 1962, 740–7.

21

Stoic ethics

BRAD INWOOD (I–VII) AND
PIERLUIGI DONINI (VIII–XI)

I Foundations and first principles[1]

Stoic ethics starts from foundations and first principles which are more explicit than those of most ancient ethical systems.[2] Chrysippus announced in his *Propositions in Physics* that 'there is no other or more fitting way to tackle the theory of good and bad things, the virtues, and happiness than on the basis of nature as a whole and the administration of the cosmos' (Plu. *Stoic. Rep.* 1035c). This explicit statement about starting points puts the emphasis on nature in the cosmic sense, i.e. the nature of the entire providentially governed cosmos; but elsewhere Chrysippus turns to a more inclusive sense of nature: when he says 'Where should I begin from and what should I take as the starting point for the appropriate and as the raw material for virtue, if I skip over nature and what accords with nature?' (Plu. *Comm. Not.*1069e), it is clear that the nature in question is not just cosmic. Crucial ethical concepts also find their roots in the nature of humans and in theories about what accords with human nature.

The central importance of human nature clearly goes back to the

---

[1] The principal sources for early Stoic ethics are the doxographical summaries in Stobaeus (thought to be based on an earlier work by Arius Didymus) and in Book VII of Diogenes Laertius, and the connected discussion in Cicero's *De Finibus* III. Important information also comes from other works of Cicero, Alexander of Aphrodisias, Plutarch's moral essays, Seneca's philosophical works, Epictetus, Marcus Aurelius, and a wealth of scattered sources. Galen's *On the opinions of Plato and Hippocrates* (*PHP*) is of exceptional importance for the Stoic theory of the passions. The doxographical accounts are of most value for their expository framework and relatively exact technical terminology, though often they mute any sense of the philosophical issue which lies behind the theories. The polemical treatments of our non-Stoic sources can be very helpful in setting a philosophical context – though it is not clear that Plutarch, Alexander, or Galen have in view the very philosophical issues which animated Chrysippus or Zeno centuries earlier. Later Stoics present quite different problems; Seneca, Epictetus, and Marcus Aurelius all tell us something about their predecessors, but they also develop Stoicism in new directions. It is a delicate and ultimately uncertain task to make the necessary distinctions.

[2] Another exception is Epicureanism, whose first principles emerge with great clarity from our sources. It is perhaps no accident that the Stoic tradition began shortly after Epicureanism and in the same city.

founder of the school. In the list of titles given by Diogenes Laertius (VII.4) we find a treatise *On the life according to nature* and one *On impulse*, also titled *On human nature*. But we have no record of an *On goals* or *On virtue*; indeed, the main evidence given for Zeno's views on the *telos* is the work *On human nature* (D.L. VII.87). Whatever the rôle of human as opposed to cosmic nature in Zeno's thinking, it is striking that the major ethical treatises (aside from the *Republic*) suggest a strong interest in the former. A similar interest in human nature is also suggested for Zeno by the position taken by Cleanthes on the *telos*: as reported by Diogenes Laertius (VII.89), he 'no longer' included particular nature in the formulation of the *telos*. The obvious implication of this is that Zeno did include it.[3]

Both human and cosmic nature serve as the foundations and first principles of Stoic ethics. Although it might seem natural for us to wonder how these two focuses of ethical theory can be made to cohere, the Stoics had no such worries. Nothing is more characteristic of the school, from the beginnings in the late fourth century to the end of antiquity, than the thesis that human and cosmic nature are related as part to whole.[4] As humans, we have natures which grow out of the nature of the whole cosmos; and when, in considering the foundations of their ethics, we see the early Stoics moving with comfort and confidence from the one to the other (and often even leaving it unclear which sense of nature they are concerned with in a particular argument), we might as well refrain from the obvious criticisms. The thesis that human and cosmic nature are related as part to whole is only occasionally argued for, but never doubted. And without this fixed point, no consideration of the foundations of Stoic ethics is possible.

Since Stoic physics is handled elsewhere in this volume, the cosmic sense of nature must be subordinated, somewhat artificially, in this chapter.[5] Hence it is best to begin from the starting points of human nature, at birth and shortly after, before turning to the whole of which we are parts. Only then is it appropriate to discuss the *telos* and the good.

---

[3] See Striker 1991, 3–5.
[4] The Stoics, most notably Zeno, argued specifically that the cosmos has many attributes possessed by humans, in particular rationality and sense perception: S.E. *M* IX.104–10. Similarly Cic. *ND* II.22 presents a Stoic argument from the attributes of the parts (animals) to those of the whole (the cosmos). Seneca (*Ep.* 92.30) is explicit that men are 'parts' as well as 'allies' of God. See Schofield 1983.
[5] For representative statements of opposing views on the relevance of cosmology to Stoic ethics, see Long 1988a (stressing, as I would, the indispensable role of cosmological theses) and Annas 1988a (de-emphasizing it). Annas 1993a, ch. 5, also argues that cosmological nature is of subordinate importance in Stoic ethics; for critical response see Inwood 1995. See also Striker 1991, Engberg-Pedersen 1990, ch. 2, and N. P. White 1985.

11 *Oikeiōsis* and primary impulse

The Stoic view that virtue is somehow naturally ingrained in human beings, and that virtuous behaviour is at least a part of our natural function as rational animals, is one of the basic positions they share with Peripatetic and Platonic ethics. This view contrasts with the instrumental conception of virtue held by the Epicureans, who believed that our natural affiliation is to pleasure (in the sense of 'freedom from pain'). One (though only one) Epicurean argument for hedonism was based on the alleged observation that even new-born animals (including humans) display affiliation to pleasure; the importance of this claim lay in the fact that such an affiliation obviously predates and so is independent of any influence from education and culture. The Stoic response[6] is expressed not just in a counter-argument, but in a general theory of human development which is tied to the technical term *oikeiōsis*, first attested in Stoic contexts, and probably a typical Stoic neologism, though there is no evidence that it was coined by Zeno.

The word *oikeiōsis* is a nominal form of the verb *oikeiousthai*, 'to make familiar, make one's own, introduce'. The verb in turn derives from an adjective *oikeios*, which often has the sense of 'one's own, properly belonging to someone'. The verb's overtones of affection are quite strong, and it is often used of family members and intimate friends.[7] *Oikeiōsis* is a difficult term even to translate; I will use 'affiliation', though most attempts to capture its sense have been unsatisfactory.[8] As for the associated theory, there are other influences to reckon with, such as the Peripatetic account of *oikeiotēs* or natural adaptedness apparently developed by Theophrastus on the basis of Aristotelian ethics.[9] But the

---

[6] It was Pohlenz 1940 who established that the Stoic theory of *oikeiōsis* is most plausibly regarded as a response to such Epicurean claims. See also Brunschwig 1986.

[7] The ultimate origin is from *oikos*, 'house(hold)', which reinforces the sense of possession often found in the derivative expressions.

[8] Long and Sedley 1987, 1.489, use 'appropriate' (which I use here for *kathēkon*, see below) and 'appropriation'; Inwood 1985, ch. 6, uses 'orientation'; Striker 1983, 145 paraphrases 'recognition and appreciation of something as belonging to one' and then transliterates, which is also the solution adopted by Pembroke 1971, whose work is still the standard introduction to the topic. Kerferd 1972 emphasizes the sense of 'belonging' and gives an admirably detailed discussion of the development of the term; see too Görgemanns 1983, Forschner 1981, 144–5.

[9] See Görgemanns 1983, 166–8 and Kerferd 1972; also Striker 1983 and Forschner 1981, ch. 9. Theophrastus' views: Porph. *Abst.* 3.25.1–4 (fr. 531 in Fortenbaugh *et al.* 1992b). The originality of the Stoic contribution as against Theophrastean claims was established by Pohlenz 1940 and Brink 1956; Philippson 1932 is still worth attention. Of recent authors Giusta 1964–7 is virtually alone in retaining significant aspects of the alternative view developed by Dirlmeier 1937 and von Arnim 1926.

Epicurean view seems to have been the principal catalyst for the early Stoic theory of *oikeiōsis*.[10]

If human nature is a foundation for ethics, then, as the Epicureans saw, the importance of neonatal behaviour is that it is a clear and uncorrupted illustration of that nature. The challenge for the Stoics in rebutting the Epicurean claims came from the fact that it is difficult to hold that newborns are committed to virtue. Of course, the Stoics did not have to retain the Epicurean view that all animals have the same natural neonatal tendencies. They could have held that human animals are different in this respect. But even so there is no readily observable commitment to anything like virtue in newborn humans. As it turns out, they did choose to retain the view that human newborns are relevantly similar to other newborn animals. Our principal sources for the Stoic theory of *oikeiōsis* agree that the object of the first affiliation of humans is self-preservation, and that this is the case for all animals. Hence, there is nothing distinctive about humans at this stage of life.

*

The most important piece of evidence is in Diogenes Laertius, near the beginning of his general doxography of Stoic ethics (cf. Cic. *Fin.* III.16–17):[11]

> They say that the first impulse an animal has is to self-preservation, because nature affiliated it [thus] from the beginning, as Chrysippus says in book one of *On goals*, maintaining that the first affiliation for each animal is to its own constitution and the awareness of it. For it is not reasonable [for nature] to make the animal alienated from itself, nor, having created it, to make it neither alienated from nor affiliated to itself. Therefore, the only remaining claim is that having constituted the animal [nature] affiliated it to itself. For in this way it can repel harmful things and pursue congenial things. They assert that the claim which some people make, viz. that the first impulse of animals is to pleasure, is false. For, they say, pleasure, if it comes into the matter at all, is a by-product which supervenes when nature all by itself has sought out and attained those things which are suited to its constitution. It is like the condition of thriving animals and plants in top condition. And nature, they say, is no different in the case of plants than it is for animals, since it

---

[10] This is most plausible for *oikeiōsis* as applied to the explanation of the human affiliation to virtue; Epicurean claims seem less germane to the more difficult question of the relationship between self-regarding and other-regarding virtues (for which see below, p.680, and ch. 22).

[11] I assume throughout (contra e.g. Engberg-Pedersen 1990) that the account in D.L. VII and that in *Fin.* III should be treated as complementary.

governs them [sc. plants] too, though without impulse and perception, and in us too some things occur in a plant-like way. Since impulse is superadded to [the life of] animals, and they use it to pursue congenial things, for them the natural is determined by what accords with impulse. And since reason has been given to rational animals as a more complete form of governance, for them the rational life turns out, correctly, to be according to nature. (D.L. VII.85–6)

As an anti-hedonistic move this might do.[12] But there is so far little to help the Stoics with their positive claim that our commitment to virtue is grounded in human nature. Indeed, if their theorizing about human psychological development stopped here, it would do little more than explain the obvious and regrettable commitment of people to selfish, self-preserving egoism. The challenge for Stoics is to show convincingly that the commitment of normal, healthy moral agents to virtue is rooted in and explained by this neonatal affiliation to self-preservation. That this point is not made by way of a conventional 'argument' seems clear.[13] But the set of claims advanced to meet this theoretical challenge is an important part of the foundations of Stoic ethics and reveals how closely those foundations are tied to moral psychology.

The key to this part of Stoic ethics lies in the notion of a person's 'constitution'. We have met the notion already in the text of Diogenes Laertius quoted above; it also appears in Cicero's treatment of this topic (*Fin.* III.16 ff.). In these texts 'constitution' seems to refer to the person, the compound of body and soul which constitutes the identifiable individual. It is most natural to think of it as the Stoic counterpart of what we would call the 'self'.[14] One's constitution has both general and individual features,[15] but is still one's own self, the self to whose preservation one is committed from birth on. The notion of a constitution enables the Stoics to articulate the object of one's primal attachment; to refer to nothing more specific than the self provides no encouragement to analyse what makes it up.

In an important letter (*Ep.* 121) Seneca supplies the rest of the theory. The constitution is said to change as the person grows up. Whereas it

---

[12] But there are few knock-down arguments against the Epicurean proposals in Stoic texts (cf. Brunschwig 1986). Even the Stoic allegation that our preference for pleasure is merely 'supervenient' looks like counter-assertion. At best it shows that a determined anti-hedonist could give a coherent account of the same phenomena as the Epicureans claimed.

[13] See Striker 1983, who infers that *oikeiōsis* was 'probably not the foundation of Stoic ethics' (p. 165). But explicit argument is not the only way to recommend a philosophical position: cf. Inwood 1984, which deals with the later but doctrinally conservative Stoic Hierocles.

[14] It is probably the early Stoic antecedent of the *personae* as developed by Panaetius. See Gill 1988.

[15] Corresponding to 'commonly' and 'peculiarly qualified' individuals (see pp. 402–6).

might be odd to say that the child and the adult have different selves, it is relatively straightforward to say that they are differently constituted, that is, have different constitutions. It is the notion of the evolving constitution which enables the Stoics to develop the claim that one's primal affiliation to oneself can be both stable and dynamic: it is always directed to one's constitution, but that constitution itself develops. Since it is defined as the 'commanding faculty in a certain relation to the body' (*Ep*.121.10), it seems evident that changes in the commanding faculty will be the most important (but not the only) factor in development of the affiliation to self. Thus when the commanding faculty becomes rational, the affiliation to oneself remains unchanged; but the object of our attachment is now intrinsically rational, and that makes an enormous difference to the ethics built upon such an attachment.

The gap to be bridged by Stoic naturalism was between primal self-love and the commitment to virtue. The concept of the self as a naturally evolving constitution has carried us most of the way across the chasm; the space left to be covered is short, but crucial. How are we to get from our commitment to rationality to a commitment to virtue – in particular to those virtues which are fundamentally other-regarding (for an egoistic attachment to self can easily ground such virtues as prudence and self-control)? Justice is the most interesting test case for Stoic naturalism.

There are three considerations which the Stoics relied on (implicitly or explicitly) to get them across this final gap, to reconcile our apparently natural egoism with other-regarding virtues. First, they held (and argued at some length) that in some sense the virtues are 'one' (see below). Whether Stoics believe with Aristo that all the virtues are identical, only the name varying, or that they are distinct but mutually entailing,[16] the unity thesis ought to help them here. For if prudence is rooted in rational self-love, so must be justice. The work of justifying such a connection might then be done not in the naturalistic framework of a theory of *oikeiōsis*, where it is open to direct challenge by Epicureans (among others), but rather in the context of the analysis of virtue itself. Second, the Stoics could point to features of the adult constitution which clearly support the claim that other-regarding behaviour is 'natural' to humans, just as natural as it is to other animals. A text of Plutarch (*Stoic. Rep.* 1038bc) shows at least that adult animals have a natural tendency to nurture their young.[17] So too do most other animals, especially the social animals.

---

[16] On this debate see Schofield 1984. See also below, pp. 707, 717–19.
[17] This issue is explored at length in Blundell 1990.

Hence man *qua* animal and not just *qua* rational has a teleologically explicable and naturally grounded commitment to others. The social nature of the human species is evident, so that such adaptively successful behaviour is an essential part of our nature. Once that is established, all one needs to do is to generalize that commitment on the basis of rational considerations, i.e., those which apply uniformly to all relevantly similar cases. Nature makes all animals love their offspring as members of their own species; so too with humans. We love our children as humans, for their distinctively human capabilities. We love them for their rationality, potential though it may be. And with the consistency given to us by reason we must eventually come to see (as the later Stoic Hierocles hopes and urges, and as some Academics doubt) that our commitment must then be to all rational animals equally; for it is precisely in virtue of their rationality that they are valuable.[18]

This brings us to an anticipation of what must be dealt with later, the substantive content of reason itself as something characterized by consistency (in at least two senses: internal coherence and similar treatment of relevantly similar matters). The good, according to the Stoics, is 'virtue and what participates in virtue' (D.L. VII.94); it is also defined as 'what is complete [or perfect: *teleion*] according to nature for a rational being *qua* rational'. Since rationality brings with it a rich notion of consistency, consistency will be a component of the Stoic conception of the good, and so also of virtue. As we have already seen, rationality as such will give the Stoics what they need to include other-regarding virtues as grounded in self-love, though only because they presuppose a notion of rationality which is not instrumental and colourless, but substantive.

The third line of consideration which the Stoics could rely on to span the distance between egoistic rationalism and the foundation of other-regarding virtues is also suggested by the passage of Plutarch we are considering. Chrysippus seems to have grouped together our affiliations to ourselves, our parts, and our offspring. It might well be argued that the attachment to our parts is a natural extension of our attachment to our constitution. We could hardly be inclined to preserve our selves without being inclined to preserve our component parts. And, on a view of reproductive biology not utterly foreign to Greek philosophy, our offspring are at least in origin parts of their parents. Hence parental love is partial self-love; and as those parts grow to autonomy, we continue to love them.

---

[18] Relevant texts of Hierocles (Stob. IV.671.7-673.11) and an anonymous Academic (Anon. *In Tht.* 5.18-6.31) are conveniently available in Long and Sedley 1987, ch.57, G and H. For further discussion see below, pp. 762-4.

Once again, the Stoics find in their theory of human nature what they need to ground other-regarding virtues.

There is, of course, a serious residual problem: sometimes there might appear to be conflicts between other-regarding virtuous actions and self-regarding virtuous actions. The Stoics are committed – with whatever degree of plausibility – to regarding such cases as merely apparent conflicts;[19] this follows from even the weakest version of the thesis of the unity of virtues (see below, pp. 717–19).

III Cosmic nature and human nature

The Stoics were not content to ground their ethics in facts about human nature considered on its own. Nature as a whole, that is, the rational and providential structure of the world, also lies behind the norms and principles which define human perfection. That this is so emerges at many points from a reading of the fragmentary remains of Stoic ethics. Consider, for example, the text from Diogenes Laertius quoted above, p. 678. In it, we are told not just that animals are affiliated to the preservation of their own constitutions, but that they were made that way by nature. Nature endowed humans with this affiliation because it would not have been reasonable (εἰκός, *eikos*) for her not to do so, in view of the fact that she made them. Only a negligent or non-providential nature could make animals and then abandon them to the world with no internalized drive for self-preservation.[20] But it is a basic tenet of Stoic cosmology (shared with Plato and Aristotle)[21] that nature and/or God is neither negligent nor non-providential. And it is just that tenet of cosmology which is used to prove that animals have by nature the foundations of ethical behaviour built into them from birth onwards.

More general features of cosmology are relevant to the foundations of ethics. The world is a single whole, permeated by divine rationality. That rationality is concentrated in certain parts of the world, such as the fiery

---

[19] This view is defended at length by Cicero in the *De Officiis*.

[20] The idea of animals being created by a rational and providential agent is common in Greek speculation. One thinks of the Great Myth of Plato's *Protagoras* and the creator god of the *Timaeus*. Xenophon's providential deity (*Mem.* 1.4) and Aristotle's nature which does nothing in vain are also relevant.

[21] Sandbach 1985 argues against knowledge of Aristotle's esoteric works on the part of the earlier Stoics. But while Theophrastus lived these books were surely available to a philosopher of Zeno's inquisitive temperament. Hence, despite the relative lack of direct references (attributable to the state of our sources), Aristotle's esoteric treatises may reasonably be treated as relevant background for (and even as influences on) early Stoicism. For an earlier and still useful view, see Long 1968, Rist 1969a, ch. 1.

heavenly bodies (the commanding faculty of the cosmos[22]) and the human soul. All of the distinct components of the world are parts of it, but they are arranged on a rank-ordered scale ranging from the simplest to the most complex kinds of objects, from inert earth and stones, through plants and brute beasts, to humans. We humans are more than mere parts of the whole; we are privileged parts, parts which unlike any others share in the distinctive attributes of the whole. Hence humans, as the best parts of the whole, are in a position to collaborate with the rationality of all nature; we are, as Seneca says (*Ep.* 92.30: see above, p. 676 n. 4), not just parts, but also 'allies' of nature. In view of our privileged role and shared nature, humans will naturally find their perfection and fulfilment not just in rational behaviour, but in behaviour as a member of a community of gods and men.[23]

This cosmological perspective on ethics is relevant in many ways. Our role as collaborators or allies will certainly affect the treatment which Stoics give to the question of determinism and the possibility of morally responsible action. And the Stoics will also hold that humans can learn important things about human behaviour from the observation of nature as a whole. But most important of all, this cosmological perspective gives the Stoics good reasons for emulating the world's rationality, orderliness, and structured interdependence. For after all, we are parts which share a nature with the whole, i.e. the world. Such a whole is more complete than we are, just because it is a whole. And since our goal as humans is to complete ourselves, to achieve the fulfilment of our nature in the attainment of our *telos*, we do so most effectively by imitating the relevant features of the world. These external reference points underpin the Stoic conception of what is natural to humans; they take ethical foundations beyond what one might learn by mere observation of humans as humans, and certainly far beyond what an Epicurean might find by application of the criterion of feelings (*pathē*). They also provide a way for ethical naturalism to transcend the typically Aristotelian appeal to what is 'always or for the most part' – which for Aristotle is an indication of what is natural.

But the Stoics often fly in the face of broad human consensus about values, and in so doing they reject Aristotelian criteria in ethics[24] just as much as they reject the Epicurean ethical criteria, feelings. Plato does so too, of course, but by transcending the world of nature for an otherworldly grounding in a distinct divine and noetic realm. The Stoics go

---

[22] See ch. 12.   [23] See ch. 22.
[24] Though they are willing to argue dialectically; see Brunschwig 1991.

beyond the naturalism of Aristotle and Epicurus (and common sense) but do so without abandoning naturalism in a Platonic way. Their transcendental naturalism is possible because of their readiness to see human life as a dependent part of the rational whole.

iv The goal of life

Since Aristotle at least and throughout the Hellenistic period the concept of the goal of life (the *telos*) was central to ethical theory.[25] 'Goal' is not a particularly happy translation, since it fails to connote completeness and culmination, which are important aspects of the concept. But it does have the advantage of emphasizing the fact that the *telos* is the unified object of all human striving. The goal of life for Stoics has two aspects, formal and substantive. Formally, the concept of goal meets the criteria which Aristotle set out in Book I of the *Nicomachean Ethics*,[26] including the designation of the goal as that 'for the sake of which everything is done' and what 'is itself done for the sake of nothing else' (Stob. ii.77.16–17). In addition to being the ultimate object of striving, always being chosen for its own sake, it is also complete, self-sufficient, and most worth choosing (in the sense that any other good added to it could not make it more worth choosing). On this level most Hellenistic schools would agree in their description of it. But in substance the Stoic goal differs from that laid down by any other school, and that difference was apparent in all the formulations which they gave, from the founder Zeno onwards.

Let us look at some of these formulations. First, in a text of Arius Didymus quoted by Stobaeus:

Zeno defined the goal thus: 'living in agreement'. This means living according to a single and consonant rational principle, since those who live in conflict are unhappy. Those who came after him made further distinctions and expressed it thus: 'living in agreement with nature', supposing that Zeno's formulation was an incomplete predicate.[27] For Cleanthes, who first inherited [the leadership of] his school, added 'with nature' and defined it thus: 'the goal is living in agreement with nature'. Chrysippus wanted to make this clearer and expressed it in this way: 'to live according to experience of the things which happen by nature'.[28]

---

[25] Compare the treatments in Striker 1991, 1–13, Engberg-Pedersen 1990, ch. 1.

[26] Cf. Irwin 1986, 206 ff., summarizing part of *EN* 1.7.

[27] D.L. vii.87 states: 'Zeno first, in his book *On the Nature of Man*, said that the goal was to live in agreement with nature, which is to live according to virtue.' Probably Zeno gave both the longer and shorter formulae and the followers mentioned by Stobaeus reacted against the short version.

[28] Information repeated at D.L. vii.87, where it is attributed to Book i of *On goals*. Note also D.L.

And Diogenes: 'to be reasonable in the selection and rejection of natural things'. And Archedemus: 'to live completing all the appropriate acts'.[29] And Antipater: 'to live invariably selecting natural things and rejecting unnatural things'.[30] He often defined it thus as well: 'invariably and unswervingly to do everything in one's power for the attainment of the principal natural things'. (Stob. II.75.11–76.15)

A bit later we read that Zeno, Cleanthes and Chrysippus defined happiness as 'a smooth flow of life' (II.77.21). Diogenes Laertius reports on the connection of these general views to virtue and to cosmology:

> Thus Zeno first, in his book *On the Nature of Man*, said that the goal was to live in agreement with nature, which is to live according to virtue. For nature leads us to virtue. And similarly Cleanthes in *On Pleasure* and Posidonius and Hecaton in their books *On the Goal*. Again, 'to live according to virtue' is equivalent to living according to the experience of events which occur by nature, as Chrysippus says in book one of his *On Goals*. For our natures are parts of the nature of the universe. Therefore the goal becomes 'to live consistently with nature', i.e., according to one's own nature and that of the universe, doing nothing which is forbidden by the common law, which is right reason, penetrating all things, being the same as Zeus who is the leader of the administration of things. And this itself is the virtue of the happy man and a smooth flow of life, whenever all things are done according to the harmony of the divinity in each of us with the will of the administrator of the universe. (D.L. VII.87–8)

It is evident that whatever the differences in detail, the thrust of all of these formulations of the goal of life is essentially the same.[31] A life in complete accordance with nature in the relevant senses (human nature

---

VII.89: 'by nature, in consistency with which we must live, Chrysippus understands both the common and, specifically, human nature. Cleanthes only includes the common, and not the individual, as the nature with which one must be consistent.' This difference in emphasis between Cleanthes and Chrysippus is not surprising.

[29] Information repeated at D.L. VII.88.

[30] More literally, the 'things in accordance with nature' and 'contrary to nature' respectively. These are things like health, prosperity, etc. and their opposites and are roughly equivalent to the 'preferred' and 'dispreferred' indifferents discussed below. See also the discussion of selection below.

[31] Clearly so for Zeno, Cleanthes and Chrysippus, but also for the apparently different formulations from the second century BC; cf. also Panaetius' definition: 'to live according to the starting points given to us by nature' (Clem. *Strom.* II.21 (p. 183 Stählin) = fr. 96 van Straaten). A similar story for the apparently divergent views of Posidonius (Galen *PHP* v.6.3–29 = fr. 187 Kidd). Discussion: Kidd 1971, Long 1967, Soreth 1968, Striker 1986, and Striker 1991, 24–35. The view of Aristo of Chios, that the goal consists in a life of indifference to everything except virtue and vice (not a word about nature), is significantly different, and is reported elsewhere (D.L. VII.160, in his biographical entry). See Striker 1991, 14–24, Ioppolo 1980a, ch. 5.

and cosmic nature) is the one thing which humans are made to live for. Such a life will be consistent, smoothly harmonious, virtuous, and happy; it will be the full expression of a flourishing human life and will be characterized by the performance of actions which are reasonable when judged by the standard of nature. Hence the 'things according to nature' will be an important part of our focus in life.[32] These naturally preferred things are what Chrysippus called 'the raw material of virtue' (Plu. *Comm. Not.* 1069e), and it is unlikely that he was departing from the substance of Zeno's views when he took this view.[33] The agent will also live, as Chrysippus says, 'according to experience of the things which happen by nature', and here it is probably cosmic nature and the determined events of the natural world which he has most in mind. Nature thus plays the roles of standard and guide for human actions in two senses: the 'things according to nature' are reasonable as objects of choice for human beings just because our human nature is what it is; but the larger plan of nature is the ultimate framework and constraint for all of our particular and local choices. Human and cosmic nature both matter.

When later heads of the school developed their formulations of the goal they attempted to bring out more clearly the role of 'things according to nature' as central objects of choice in the life of virtue; they did so, in part, as a response to serious criticisms of early formulations by Carneades. This development culminated in the position taken by Antipater, and though it is generally agreed that these later thinkers did not yield on the central thesis of Stoic ethics (that virtue is sufficient for happiness; or, as Antipater put it more Platonically, that only the morally fine is good),[34] views have differed on how fruitful the debate was. Long regards it as a kind of 'cold war' and maintains that the Stoic position was 'ambiguous and liable to self-contradiction'.[35] Striker, by contrast, rethinks Antipater's formulation from the point of view of the Stoic thesis that virtue is a kind of craft or art (*technē*) of living[36] and concludes (correctly, in my view) that the debate with Carneades led to substantial progress: the earlier Stoic theory is sharpened and strengthened by his polemical exchange with the greatest dialectician of the day.[37]

[32] Though as Long 1967, 62 points out, Zeno did not mention them explicitly in his formulations of the goal of life.
[33] If Zeno did not hold roughly the view which Chrysippus apparently attributed to him, we would have to regard him as being, in essence, still in agreement with his early Cynic 'teachers'. But as Rist 1977, esp. 171–2, points out, we have good reason to reject that view.
[34] See *SVF* III Antipater 56, with Rieth 1934, 15.   [35] Long 1967, 89.
[36] To be exact, a stochastic craft, the paradigm example of which was archery, which figures prominently in our sources for the debate, not just Plutarch (*Comm. Not.* 1071bc) but also Cicero (*Fin.* III.22).   [37] Striker 1986.

The Stoic goal is the one thing in reference to which we are to live. It has often been thought implausible to hold that there is any single thing which can serve as *the* reference point for life. Hence the debate about inclusive and dominant goals of life in Aristotle.[38] But if the goal is a life according to nature and nature is understood as a unified phenomenon, then it is easier to understand the characterization of the goal as a single point of reference. If we live by nature then there really is just one standard to which we look: pleasure, honour, wisdom, all the other potentially conflicting values of life for an Aristotelian man, these are all set firmly in a subordinate role. A single criterion co-ordinates our attitude with respect to all of them.

*

This leaves, of course, many problems about what exactly is natural in any given set of circumstances, problems with which the Stoics struggled in their works *On appropriate actions*. Moreover, one might think that the duality of human and cosmic nature threatens this tight unity. On the latter point, however, the Stoics would not agree. For human nature is regarded as a part of cosmic nature, and consistency with human nature is in effect a necessary condition for consistency with cosmic nature;[39] and since cosmic nature is rational, it follows that living with an eye to cosmic nature will itself be a sure guide to human perfection too.

v The good

In the *Meno* (77b–78b) Plato shows Socrates arguing with Meno to the conclusion that all men desire the good, or at least the apparent good, what they believe to be good for themselves. It is convenient that Meno is slow to be convinced, for it gives Socrates the opportunity to justify this crucial claim in clear and direct terms: people pursue the good because it is good for them, provides them with benefit; the bad is understood as the source of harm for the agent. Once that is explained, the claim seems obviously true. It is made elsewhere in Plato too, and it became a basic Platonic and Aristotelian doctrine. The same kind of argument also lies behind the common Socratic claim that no one does wrong (or makes mistakes) willingly.[40]

[38] For this terminology see Hardie 1965, 1968; recent summary discussion in Kenny 1992, 6–7.
[39] See Inwood 1985, 105–11.
[40] See for example *Apol.* 25d–26a, where Socrates rejects the suggestion that he might corrupt his associates willingly, on the grounds that if he did so he would be running the risk of suffering great personal harm – which no one would do. Hence, any damage Socrates does to his companions must be unintended.

The assumptions which underlie such Socratic reasoning are fundamental to Stoic ethics.[41] For the Stoics 'good' is the source of genuine benefit to the agent. In Stobaeus II.69.16–70.7 the word 'good' is said to have many senses; the primary sense 'which plays a role like that of a source [for the other senses]' is: that from which or by whom it results that one is benefited. Diogenes Laertius VII.94 gives a similar account. Good is in general 'some benefit', and more particularly is either the same thing or 'what is not other than benefit'.

In line with the Socratic tradition, the Stoics held that the only genuine benefit is virtue; and the benefit it provides is primarily to the agent himself. Hence good is described as virtue and what participates in virtue, namely, virtuous people and actions done in accordance with virtue (see S.E. *M* XI.22–6). The Socratic concentration on 'care of the soul' also lies behind this approach to the good.[42] Socrates claimed that he urged the Athenians to work for 'the best possible state of their souls' (Plato *Apol.* 29e, 30b), and such excellence he regarded as virtue.

Greek philosophical ethics consistently held that moral virtue is an excellence of the soul (the word *aretē* is ambiguous between these two meanings). But despite that, it is not a trivial analytical truth that moral virtue is an excellence; the case of Thrasymachus in *Republic* 1 shows clearly that in the fourth century BC excellence of the soul could be conceptualized in completely amoral terms. Philosophical defence of the thesis was called for and duly offered by Plato and Aristotle. In the *Republic* it is argued that a particular virtue, justice, is the excellent state of the soul because it is analogous to health in the body. In the *Crito* it is claimed, and in the *Gorgias* argued for, that it is better for an agent to be wronged than to do wrong. Aristotle (in both versions of the *Ethics*) attempts to connect moral and intellectual virtue to human excellence through arguments based on a conception of the function of the human organism.

The Stoics are heirs to all of this. Hence, they provide another description of the good (D.L. VII.95): it is 'what is complete according to nature for a rational being *qua* rational' (cf. Cic. *Fin.* III.33). To bring one's rational soul to a condition of completeness or perfection, to make it a superb example of its kind, is just to take care that it be in the best possible state.[43] Diogenes Laertius goes on to note that 'virtue is such a condition'.

---

[41] The importance of Socratic influence in Hellenistic thought has been discussed by Long 1988b. See ch. 19, this volume.

[42] Socratic rather than Platonic: nothing in Stoic ethics resonates with the impersonal and transcendental good of Plato's *Republic*.

[43] On the connection between man's rational nature and the cosmic nature (which is also rational), see Sen. *Ep.* 124.14, Cic. *Fin.* III.21.

The absence here of any argument designed to prove that moral virtue is such a perfection shows only that this work has been done elsewhere. What matters now is the conception of good as a state of perfection in accordance with one's rational nature. This is indeed 'benefit' for the agent.[44]

The good is a state of perfection (it is *teleion*) in the rational agent. As such, it is intimately related to the concept of the 'goal' (*telos*) of life. The Stoics held that the good, i.e. virtue and associated states, is the key to achieving the goal, i.e. happiness. One is often uncertain about the best way of rendering the concept of perfection or completeness (*to teleion*) into English; in view of its connection with the goal of life one might do well to entertain yet another translation of *teleion*. 'Goal-like' or 'connected with the goal' capture aspects of the term which 'perfect' and 'complete' miss. The good, then, is rooted in nature just as the goal is. But goodness is natural to humans in another sense too. The *notion* (*ennoia*) of good is said to be natural to man. The point is put most bluntly at D.L. VII.53: 'we acquire the notion of something just and good naturally'. The naturalness of the concept means that it is natural and normal for humans to develop the concept in the course of their experience.

There are also Socratic roots for the view that from the ordinary and rather banal concept of 'advantage' we can move to the concept of genuine advantage. Socrates' exhortation in the *Apology* (see esp. 30ab) to change one's normal priorities, so that bodily wellbeing and wealth are seen as secondary to virtue, suggests an argument of this sort. His audience accepts that health and wealth are beneficial; Socrates' exhortation to them relies on that, and claims that care of the soul provides an even greater benefit. Such reasoning also turns up in Stoic sources. The concept of good comes to us naturally in that it grows out of analogical reflection on other values (Cic. *Fin.* III.33–4, Sen. *Ep.* 120) in accordance with common conceptions and consistently with ordinary life (Plu. *Stoic. Rep.* 1041e, S.E. *M* XI.22). Reflection on those values and on the experiences of human life is said to lead naturally to an awareness of the good and its relationship to the goal of life; particular emphasis is put on the natural attraction for rational beings of a sense of orderliness and planning (*Fin.* III.21).

A number of distinct appeals to experience are combined in the various claims that our concept of good is natural. The Stoics held, apparently, that

---

[44] See also S.E. *M* XI.22, where the beneficial nature of the good is said to be in line with the common conceptions. Whatever is meant by common conceptions, this is clearly a Socratic commonplace.

when we reflect on the full range of values we will simply come to see that virtue holds a special place. They also claim that careful consideration of genuine benefit will lead us to their understanding of the good. And finally, the appeal of order to a rational being like man also plays a crucial role.

VI Values, actions and choice

Stoic ethics is fundamentally agent-centred. This is only to be expected, in view of the tradition they inherited. Since Socrates, mainstream Greek philosophical ethics had focused primarily on the care of the soul, the effort to make one's soul as good as possible. The central place of agents coheres with their role in the evaluative scheme used by the Stoics. But evaluation is only one function of ethical writing, and the Stoics put at least as much emphasis on argument and persuasion aimed at moral improvement, and on providing guidance for the difficult business of engaging in rational choice. As we shall see, the Stoic theory of how such choices are made plays an integral role in their educative scheme. For one of the most important paths to the improvement of the agent's character is through the quality of the moral choices he makes. Like Plato and Aristotle, the Stoics too think of agents as making moral progress by exercising their capacity for rational choice in a way which leads to virtue.

Insofar as they wished not just to judge agents but to guide and change them, an approach which goes beyond the starkly evaluative point of view was needed. To convince an agent to change his actions or thoughts one must begin from a starting point already held by that agent. Typically that will involve a concern with things outside the agent himself. For the immediate focus of concern for an agent is typically the intentional objects of his actions, both things and states of affairs. These must be the starting point for reasoning with a moral agent about moral improvement, even if they do not themselves determine the central doctrines of Stoic ethics.

This double focus is characteristic of Stoic ethical thought, and in considering Stoic ethics it will be necessary to move back and forth between what we might call the evaluative and the educative frames of reference. We shall see that some of the paradoxes and alleged confusion in Stoic ethics are a product of this double frame of reference. But let us begin with a consideration of the moral life, a life of choices about actions, from the agent's point of view.

*

Every moral agent is working towards living a life according to nature. His own nature and that of the world in which he lives (the only kind of world in which his own nature could possibly exist) are such that if he should succeed in this aim his life will be a life of virtue. Such an agent faces, as any human must, a series of choices; no coherent life is possible without choosing to act. But each action has considerable intentional content, and so is 'about' something, some object or state of affairs in the world.

The Stoic theory of good, bad, and indifferent things concerns such objects and states of affairs.[45] The English term 'things' is of course a bit misleading here: it may suggest concrete individual objects. The Greek terms, however, do not entail that. The neuter plural form of an adjective serves to pick out a wide range of entities and types of entities, grouped together as objects of human concern. The part of Stoic theory which deals with such objects is designed to help the moral agent make those choices which promote progress towards the final goal of a life according to nature, by clarifying the character of those entities.

There are discussions about good things and bad things in all of our main doxographical sources; and much of our other evidence on Stoic ethics also concerns this theme. But if we put ourselves in the place of the typical moral agent, the theory of indifferent things is far more pressing. After all, good is restricted to virtue and what 'participates' in virtue, and bad to vice and what 'participates' in vice;[46] and the ordinary moral agent does not yet have access to virtue; and vice is (according to the Stoics) the state in which ordinary people live at all times, a state to which the only alternative is perfection. Hence it can hardly be an immediately relevant object of choice for most people. The claim which lies behind this understanding of goodness, that such a good is the only genuine 'benefit', expresses the motivational hold that goodness has over the agent. But until the agent has made considerable philosophical and moral progress (*prokopē*), such an abstract claim can do little to affect his choices and moral reasoning. What it can do is to keep him focused on the ultimate goal of his enterprise and to remind him of the provisional character of any interim and partial successes.

Most actions and moral choices deal directly with things which would be called indifferent; this becomes apparent when a typical list of indifferent

---

[45] This classificatory scheme is made the opening theme of Stobaeus' Stoic doxography (II.57.18–58.4), and underlies parts of the organization of Cicero's and Diogenes Laertius' presentations. Its centrality for Chrysippus is confirmed by the fragment from Plu. *Stoic. Rep.* 1035c quoted at the beginning of this chapter.   [46] D.L. VII.94; Stob. II.57.20–58.4.

things is set out: life and death, health and illness, pleasure and discomfort, good looks and ugliness, physical strength and weakness, wealth and poverty, good and bad reputation, high and low birth (D.L. VII.102), and also natural ability, skill, even moral progress itself and their opposites (D.L. VII.106), etc. With a generous interpretation of the '*et cetera*', it is fair to say that such things constitute the explicit and immediate objects of most human concern and striving. That they are of considerable importance in the eyes of the Stoics is clear from their description of them as 'those things which stimulate pursuit or avoidance' [*hormē, aphormē*], in contrast to utterly insignificant things such as whether the number of hairs on one's head is odd or even, or the precise position of one's finger when it is extended (D.L. VII.104–5). Moreover, if such trivialities are set aside, then what is left can be divided into 'preferred' and 'dispreferred' things, and these can be described as having positive or negative value (D.L. VII.105).[47]

Things which are not good or bad are indifferent, but as Stobaeus notes at one point, 'indifferent' is a relative concept (II.80.8–9).[48] What makes a difference or is indifferent can only be understood with respect to something else. 'Indifferent' here is a matter of not making a difference to the goal of life. The indifferents are described not just as things which lie between good and bad, being neither, but also as things which make no contribution to a happy or unhappy life.[49]

Despite this, indifferents (at least those which are preferred or dispreferred) are of fundamental importance to the moral agent. This importance is reinforced by their close connection to the concept of nature, a connection rooted in the fundamental teleological fact of *oikeiōsis*.[50] While they may not make a difference to the goal of life, they do matter greatly for the so-called natural life. When discussing the concept of value, Diogenes Laertius sums this up neatly:

> They say that one sort of value is a contribution to the life in agreement, and this applies to every good; but another sort [of value] is an intermediate potential or usefulness which contributes to the life according to nature, as much as to say, just that [value] which wealth and health bring forward for [promoting] the life according to nature. (D.L. VII.105)

The natural life as understood here is evidently a life of the sort which is naturally worthwhile for a human, which is teleologically adapted for the

---

[47] See further Ausland 1989, 380–90, whose discussion is excessively concerned with supposed parallelisms with Pyrrhonian 'theory'.   [48] Cf. *SVF* III 145.

[49] Stob. II.79.16–17; 80.9–13. That happiness is the reference point for 'indifference' should not be surprising; the goal is 'that to which everything else is referred'.

[50] Cf. Inwood 1985, ch. 6; and see further Plu. *Comm. Not.* 1060c.

human organism and which provides a justifiable satisfaction for the human agent. But it is not a life characterized by agreement with nature in any larger sense.

Preferred indifferents are clearly 'according to nature' and dispreferred things 'contrary to nature'.[51] So important are such things that Chrysippus can say, 'as long as the consequences are unclear to me, I always cling to what is better suited to getting what is according to nature. For God himself made me such as to select these things' (Epict. *Diss.* 11.6.9).

The moral agent spends a good part of his time dealing with the preferred things, making decisions and choices among them. The challenge for Stoic moral theory and practice, then, is not to motivate moral agents to pay attention to such things nor even to put a positive value on the preferred things; people will do that on their own. Rather, it is to induce them to do so in the way which will bring them closer to virtue. This is an important point to stress, since some schools (notably Cynicism, Pythagoreanism, and possibly some ascetic brands of Platonism) and even some members of the Stoic school (notably Aristo of Chios), aimed to pry people loose from their normal attachment to naturally preferred things. We will deal below with the challenge to the mainstream Stoic approach from within, but it is worth noting first that on this point the school in general was true to its policy of respecting 'common conceptions'. Indeed, Chrysippus allows the occasional use of ordinary terminology for preferred indifferents, calling them 'goods' as long as the real sense is clear. This exposes him to criticism and misguided ridicule at the hands of Plutarch (*Stoic. Rep.* 1048a), and indeed led to charges of incoherence.

Because they relied heavily on common-sensical ideas about what is important to a moral agent, the Stoics had to be explicit in their arguments for the difference between what is preferred and what is actually good. Hence in Diogenes' doxographical summary we are told (VII.102–3) that indifferents are those things which are neither good nor bad, and this class is immediately described further as the set of things which 'neither benefit nor harm' the moral agent. The basis for this position is that good has a distinctive property (*idion*), namely to benefit and not harm, a property which operates as certainly and as necessarily as the calorific property

---

[51] Stob. II.79.20–82.19, esp. 80.4–13 and 81.3–4; D.L. VII.105–7. See too Inwood 1985, 197–200. Though the school in general agreed that pleasure is indifferent (except in the sense of a *pathos*), there was considerable controversy about whether to count it as preferred. See e.g. Cic. *Fin.* III.117, S.E. *M* XI.73.

of the hot.[52] The argument is completed by the premiss that indifferent things like wealth and health benefit moral agents no more (*ou mallon*) than harm them. This is a Socratic argument in origin, though one which became widespread. It is supplemented in Diogenes by a second Socratic claim, that something cannot be good if it is capable of being used well or badly; this too is turned into an argument by a second premiss, viz. that health and wealth can be used well or badly.[53]

The emphasis of these arguments is on the difference between preferred things and good things, which is central from a moral–pedagogical point of view, especially for a school which gave great weight to our natural preference for what might be called the 'good' things in life and chose nevertheless to distinguish them sharply from genuine goods. Other arguments, of less distinguished pedigree, were also used. Thus we read in Clement (*Strom.* IV.5 [= *SVF* III 150]) that bodily health and disease are indifferent because they do not cause vice or virtue in the soul. And Seneca in *Ep.* 87 gives a list of the characteristic properties of goodness: that it does make people good, that it cannot come to evil and contemptible men, that it does not come from what is bad, that the pursuit of it does not lead us into evils. Hence any prima facie desirable thing which contradicts these characteristics cannot be good, and must be regarded at best as a preferred indifferent. The list of preferred things generated here includes the results of luck, wealth and riches.[54] Similarly (*Ep.* 85.30) pain and poverty are rescued from being bad on the grounds that they lack the characteristic feature of bad things, which is that they do real harm to the moral agent.[55]

How do the indifferents feature in the reasoning of a moral agent? The quotation from Chrysippus above gives us some clue. They are generally the object of an agent's efforts and activities, although the value of pursuing preferred things can be overridden if 'the consequences' become clear and indicate otherwise. The meaning of this reference to consequences is not immediately obvious, but most likely it contains at least an allusion to the longer-term benefits or disadvantages to be had from a particular action.[56] It could be that the pursuit of wealth in a given case will turn out

[52] This is apparently based on a 'Socratic' argument. See *Rep.* 1.335 b–d.
[53] Cf. Plato *Grg.* 467–8, *Euthd.* 278–82, *Men.* 87–9, Xen. *Mem.* IV.6.8.
[54] Alexander of Aphrodisias (*SVF* III 152) has a very similar argument to exclude wealth from being good. The major premiss is: what comes to be through bad is not good.
[55] The argument in Alex. *Ethical Problems* 1 (= *SVF* III 165) to the effect that life itself is not a good is probably Stoic, and betrays its Socratic origins both in its use of an analogy with a craft (navigation) and in its contrast between living and living well.
[56] Inwood 1985, 120–1 argues that the consequences mentioned here also contain a reference to the providentially ordered and determined plan of events in the world. Hence, any decision to

to impair other interests, such as the preservation of one's health or the development of virtue. There are also unusual circumstances to take account of, which might suggest that in the concrete case before him the agent should pass up the chance to choose a preferred thing.[57] And it is perfectly possible that two preferred things might be incompatible in the case at hand: it is easy to imagine that a preferred activity of soul, such as developing one of the crafts which 'can make an extensive contribution to the life according to nature' (Stob. II.81.3–4), might be incompatible with a bodily good such as increasing one's physical strength – every hour spent in the gym is one less hour spent in learned reflection. In such a case the choice would be clear, though perhaps not easy.[58] The importance of making such choices among indifferents is, presumably, part of the reason for specifying the distinction between intrinsic (δι' αὐτά) and indirect (δι' ἕτερα) indifferents.[59] Most important of all, some indifferents will tend to promote the acquisition of virtue and some will (at least sometimes) tend to hinder it; keeping in mind the ultimate importance of the good will aid with such choices.

Clearly there is a need for a general plan or method to help the moral agent to balance such considerations, the sort of thing referred to as a 'method of selection'.[60] Part of such a method would consist in the specification of preferred and dispreferred things; part would overlap with or even consist in the parainetic activity to be discussed below and would be reflected in the casuistry for which later Stoics eventually become famous – perhaps one should say 'notorious'.

One important observation which emerges from this way of looking at the indifferents is that the theory and the recommendations it makes to agents as an aid in their moral choices operate on the level of general truths. For example, it is generally the case that health is preferable to

---

pursue a preferred thing has to be provisional until one finds out whether attaining it is fated to happen or not.

[57] See N. P. White 1978, though his discussion deals with actions. On actions see below, but the point is also valid for things and states of affairs.

[58] Preferred psychic attributes are more important than bodily because of the soul's rôle in living a life according to nature (Stob. II.81.19–82.4). This relative valuation is traditional and unproblematic: see e.g. Plato *Prt.* 313 on the relative importance of body and soul. But it is characteristically Stoic to ground it in the central importance of life according to nature.

[59] D.L. VII.107; Stob. II.72.19–25; see too *SVF* III 133–5. See also Stob. II.82.11–83.9 for two further distinctions, between primary natural things and those which are derivatively natural (κατὰ μετοχήν) and between καθ' αὐτά and ποιητικά natural things. These distinctions would all prove useful in a deliberative setting.

[60] ὁδόν τινα ἐκλεκτικήν: Stob. II.73.14. The reference here is to a much narrower method, one which helps the agent to choose from among the generally useful crafts those which will aid in the development of virtue. But that the Stoics recognized the general need should be clear. I would suggest that the art of living (τέχνη τοῦ βίου) is in part such a method.

sickness, but (as the debate with Aristo highlighted) it is sometimes the case that sickness is preferable.[61] From the occasional or even fairly frequent preferability of something classed as dispreferred an important lesson can be learned.[62] For we can use it to confirm that the theory of indifferents operates on the level of types not tokens; this is shown by the way Aristo uses it to impugn the usefulness of the mainstream theory.

As Sextus reports it, Aristo's attack starts from the claim that on the normal Stoic theory to call a thing 'preferred' is the same as deeming it to be 'good'. The reason for this claim is revealing: there is in general no difference among those things intermediate between virtue and vice; there is no natural or necessary (*M* xi.65) link between preferred things and choosing them in a specific case, nor between dispreferred things and rejecting them in a specific case. The coupling of 'natural' and 'necessary' is the instructive point. A mainstream Stoic would have no hesitation about there being a natural connection between preferred status and choice. But for him 'natural' would not *mean* 'necessary'; as we have seen, something good or bad would be so both naturally and necessarily, because it has a fixed property peculiar to itself.

When Aristo conflates 'natural' and 'necessary' important changes ensue. If a natural connection between the preferability of *x* and the choosing of *x* must mean that one necessarily chooses it in all circumstances, then the natural preferability of *x* must be rejected. This is what Aristo does, denying that anything is naturally preferable except the good. But a mainstream Stoic does not accept that interpretation of 'natural'. As Chrysippus would say, things are naturally preferable if choosing them is rooted (by God) in our nature in such a way that if the consequences are unclear (as seems to be the normal case) one chooses them. Aristo's insistence on a necessary connection between the natural and preferred status of something and choosing it betrays a determination to make moral recommendations about concrete token-actions rather than types, or at best about types every token of which necessarily has the attribute 'good'; for only a class of actions or intentional objects of action every member of which is to be chosen can be described as worth choosing in this strong sense. And both Aristo and the mainstream Stoic would

---

[61] S.E. *M* xi.64–7. On Aristo, see Ioppolo 1980a and more recently Ausland 1989, 381–9, Striker 1991, 14–24.

[62] See too the argument about indifferents in D.L. vii.103: Hecaton says that pleasure is not a good because there are some shameful pleasures. Clearly the pleasures which are shameful are more specific than the generalized pleasure which is indifferent. So when pleasure is said to be indifferent the Stoics are talking about a type – only types all tokens of which are good can be called good.

agree that only actions with 'good' or 'virtue' as the relevant part of their intentional content would meet this standard.

Mainstream Stoics did not insist on the necessary connection which Aristo demanded and were prepared to talk about natural preferability (preferred status) without insisting that it represent a class every token member of which is worth choosing.[63] Perhaps Aristo's view that there was nothing intermediate between good and bad was motivated by a concern to avoid granting any ontological standing to a mere generalization. After all, every token action was agreed to be either good or bad, so why court the kind of criticism such a view might attract from Arcesilaus?[64] But even while pointing out the difference between his stance and that of the school in general we should stress what they share. When we move from the level of types or general classes to the level of individual objects and situations the mainstream view and that of Aristo tend to converge. Though the mainstream Stoic would assert and Aristo would deny that good health is something preferred, they would both agree that in a given individual case, with all relevant factors specified and known by the moral agent, the virtuous person would have but one correct choice, and that the wrong choice would indicate that the agent was not virtuous.[65]

*

Choosing what to do on particular occasions is central to the life of any moral agent. We must accordingly conclude the present section by laying some groundwork for the discussion to be pursued in later sections. Several central concepts bear on the question of choice. First and most general[66] is the notion of the appropriate[67] (*kathēkon*). The appropriate is something, usually a possible action, which is natural to the animal in the sense that it would normally enhance its normal and healthy way of life. Hence it would be a fit object of pursuit. The standard definition of the appropriate is 'that which, when done, admits of a reasonable justification', something which makes sense in terms of the nature of the

---

[63] See below on the two kinds of 'choice' recognized by Stoic theory: choice proper (of the good) and selection.

[64] Note that Arcesilaus treated *katalēpsis* in just this way (see S.E. *M* VII.153). He argued that every token *katalēpsis* either occurred in a sage (in which case it should be called knowledge) or in a fool (in which case it should be called opinion); consequently the general term *katalēpsis* is a mere name with no correlate in the real world. Aristo's position is safe from such an attack, while the general Stoic position is not.

[65] Though the right choice would not prove that he was virtuous; see below on appropriate acts.

[66] As Arius Didymus (Stob. II.85.15–17) notes, the 'appropriate' pertains to animals too, 'since even they act in accord with their own nature'. At D.L. VII.107 it is noted that even plants have something appropriate to them.

[67] Long and Sedley translate 'proper function'. See their discussion: 1987, I.365.

animal in question. Impressions of 'the immediately appropriate' are
what stimulate the impulse to action (Stob. 11.86.17–18). A special case of
the appropriate which is relevant to humans is the morally right action
(*katorthōma*), sometimes defined as a 'perfect appropriate action', one
which 'has all the numbers'.[68] It is an action which has the completeness
and self-contained quality which accompanies virtue and the happy life.

Evidently the same action can be both appropriate and morally right;
deciding what is appropriate in the circumstances of action is a necessary
but not sufficient condition for morally right action. The additional factors needed to ensure virtuous action (and so happiness) can only be
described in the context of an account of Stoic views on moral education.
But an important paraphrase of Chrysippus' views establishes that the
crucial additional factor turns on stability of character: 'he who has made
the greatest possible progress carries out in every respect all the appropriate actions and omits none. But his life is not yet happy; happiness comes
to him when these intermediate actions acquire the stability which comes
with character and take on a certain fixity which is all their own' (Stob.
v.906.18–907.5 = *SVF* III 510; see also below p. 726).

Another important contrast is that between selection and choice.[69] In
Stoic philosophy of mind, every human action represents a kind of decision, since it can only be an action if it is the result of an assent to the
impression that the thing in question should in fact be done. And the
assent is given to actions under descriptions, as one might say today. As far
as we can tell from the fragmentary remains of early Stoic technical terminology, the two most important kinds of action were labelled 'selection'
(*eklogē*) and 'choice' (*hairesis*). The former picked out actions aimed at
what is natural or appropriate to the agent in the circumstances; the latter
describes actions aimed at under the description 'good', actions which the
agent decides on not just because they are appropriate but because they
embody the good (i.e. moral virtue or what partakes in it). Thus any
'choice' in the technical sense is also a selection of some appropriate
action, an assent to what is fitting for that agent in the circumstances; but
it also entails an unconditional commitment to the course of action just
because it embodies the good, the central and unconditionally natural
value which motivates every rational animal. Moral education will involve
not just the cultivation of habits which conduce to correct selection, but

---

[68] See Cic. *Fin.* III.24, Stob. II.85.18–20, 93.14–16. This obscure phrase is normally interpreted to
mean that the action covers all necessary and relevant aspects and answers to all natural and
rational requirements. For a novel interpretation in terms of musical metaphor see Long 1991b.
[69] See Inwood 1985, 201–15, 238–40.

also those which guide the agent to such selections as embodiments of the good.

VII Passions[70]

Assent and practical decision are central to Stoic ethics. But as we shall see, most agents fail to use their rationality properly. The summary in Diogenes Laertius catches this well: 'from falsehoods there arises in the mind corruption; this is the source of many passions, and they are responsible for instability' (VII.110). Having imperfectly developed rational souls, people make mistakes, commit themselves to false propositions, and so further corrupt their own reason. The most evident result of such psychological weakness is the occurrence of passions (*pathē*).

A passion is a mental or emotional event produced by an excessive impulse (*pleonazousa hormē*); it is an 'irrational and unnatural motion of the soul' (D.L. VII.110). It is variously described by early Stoics either as being a result of a mistaken opinion (about the relevant subject matter) or as itself being such a mistaken opinion. Zeno is typically associated with the former view and Chrysippus with the latter. But despite all the controversy there is not much to choose between these two versions of the theory.[71] In the context of Stoic philosophy of mind, the distinction comes down to a matter of emphasis, not substance. What distinguishes the Stoic theory most clearly is the conviction that passions are causally dependent on intellectual mistakes about values, that in principle one eliminates passions and the underlying psychological instability by correcting one's beliefs.[72] This stands in marked contrast to the general approach taken by Plato, Aristotle, and their followers in later antiquity, though it bears a marked kinship with the intellectualism of Socrates in earlier Platonic dialogues, especially the *Protagoras*.

A consequence of this approach to rationality and moral error is that the Stoics must take what seemed to many in antiquity a rather strange stance on the issue of weak will (*akrasia*): they do not explain erratic or unstable behaviour and moral error as the result of an undisciplined power in the soul which disturbs the proper function of reason. In cases of weak will, people are not wrestling with irrational forces inside themselves; they are merely muddled in their moral decisions. Their inconsistent behaviour is a result of rapidly shifting and unstable moral

---

[70] See Lloyd 1978a, Frede 1986b, Striker 1991, 61–72, Nussbaum 1987.
[71] See Inwood 1985, 130–1.   [72] Nussbaum 1987; Inwood 1985, ch. 5.

decisions.[73] This kind of instability is, of course, just what one would expect if the agent is committed to conflicting principles.

The Stoics divided the passions into four groups, each of which is indicated by a general term: fear (*phobos*), desire (*epithumia*), pain (*lupē*), pleasure (*hēdonē*).[74] Fear and desire are the primary types; they are concerned with the apparent good and the apparent bad in the future, as objects of striving or avoidance. The other two types also deal with the apparent good and bad, but in a reactive way. Desire is what we feel about what we believe to be good, do not have, and might be able to get;[75] pleasure is what we feel about what we believe to be good and believe we have.[76] Conversely for fear and pain.[77] It is because people are wrong about these values that their reactions are excessive and inappropriate.

*

Organized under each of these four types of passion are many specific passions. The summary in Stobaeus captures the spirit of this project of classification:

> Under desire are subsumed such [passions] as these: anger and its forms (spiritedness and irascibility and wrath and rancour and bitterness and such things), vehement sexual desire and longing and yearning and love of pleasure and love of wealth and love of reputation and similar things. Under pleasure are mean-spirited satisfaction, contentment, charms, and similar things. Under fear are hesitation, agony, shock, shame, panic, superstition, fright, and dread. Under pain are envy, grudging, resentment, pity, grief, heavy-heartedness, distress, sorrow, anguish, and vexation. (Stob. II.90.19–91.9)

The fine distinctions are of course specifically appropriate to Greek culture.[78] But the nature of the attempt should be clear. A comprehensive range of wrong or counterproductive affective states are grouped compactly in a scheme which displays the importance of mistaken beliefs about central moral values. The educative goal of improving men's characters is dramatically shaped by the role assigned to false belief.

A passion is, like an action, a reaction to an impression; the way things

---

[73] Plu. *Virt. Mor.* 446f–447a. See too Inwood 1985, 132–9; Gill 1983, Gosling 1987.

[74] D.L. VII.110; Stob. *Ecl.* II.88.12–21.   [75] Hence it is described as an ἄλογος ὄρεξις.

[76] It is described as an ἄλογος ἔπαρσις. The term ἔπαρσις indicates both a feeling of 'uplift' (a reasonable attempt to capture metaphorically the affective reaction which partially constitutes pleasure), and a physical expansion of the material stuff of the soul.

[77] ἄλογος ἔκκλισις, συστολή respectively.

[78] The Peripatetics likewise engaged in detailed classification of virtues and vices: witness not only Aristotle's own ethical writings, but e.g. the later pseudo-Aristotelian *Virtues and Vices*. The short treatise *On Passions* attributed to Andronicus of Rhodes (closely linked to *Virtues and Vices*), is a valuable source of information for the Stoic theory of the passions.

look to the agent gives him his starting point. And also like an action, a passion cannot occur unless the agent gives his assent to the way things look and to the notion that a certain course of action is reasonable. Hence in the fuller descriptions of the beliefs which trigger episodes of passion considerable complexity is apparent:[79]

> They say, then, that desire is a striving which is disobedient to reason; its cause is believing that a good is approaching, and that when it is here we shall do well by it; this opinion itself <that it really is worth striving for> has a <fresh> [power] to stimulate erratic motion. Fear is an avoidance disobedient to reason, and its cause is believing that a bad thing is approaching; this opinion that it really is worth avoiding has a 'fresh' [power] to stimulate motion. Pain is a contraction of the soul disobedient to reason, and its cause is believing that a 'fresh' bad thing is present, for which it is appropriate to <suffer contraction [in the soul]. Pleasure is an elation of the soul disobedient to reason, and its cause is believing that a fresh good thing is present, for which it is appropriate to> suffer uplift [in the soul]. (Stob. II.90.7–18)

In a passion the agent judges that his affective response is appropriate to himself and the situation. And of course that will be false. When the thing we believe to be good is not really good, then uplift is not the rationally defensible (hence appropriate) reaction. Of course, if the thing present to us really were good and were recognized as such, then uplift in the soul would be appropriate: but then, we would not have a passion (*pathos*), but a good affective response (*eupatheia*), in this case joy (*chara*).[80]

An important aspect of the nature of passion is the 'freshness' mentioned in this extract. It is that factor in the experience of an event or state of affairs which evokes the contraction or uplift.[81] It may fade with time; or it may persist incomprehensibly. The freshness is closely connected to the judgement that contraction or uplift is appropriate. Hence one may cease to experience the uplift or contraction characteristic of a passion if the freshness fades. But the false opinion about what is good and bad may well remain in the soul, a crucial component in the unstable character of the non-virtuous man.[82]

Arguably the most disturbing and destructive aspect of a passion is the

---

[79] The supplements to this text indicated by diamond brackets are relatively uncontroversial.

[80] Cautious avoidance (εὐλάβεια) is the correct counterpart to fear; 'wish' (βούλησις) to desire. There seems to be no virtuous counterpart to pain; if there were one, it would have to be the appropriate response to the presence to a virtuous agent of something genuinely bad, i.e., vice. And that just does not happen. On εὐπάθειαι see further Inwood 1985, 173–5.

[81] Stob. II.89.2–3; cf. Cic. *Tusc.* III.74–5. More detail at Inwood 1985, 146–55.

[82] The Stoics routinely compared the underlying unstable character traits to bodily diseases or weaknesses (the comparison goes back at least to Plato (*Rep.* IV)). See Kidd 1983.

accompanying sense of being out of control. When strongly committed to an affective stance or course of action on the basis of a mistaken belief that its object is good or bad, it is natural that this commitment take on a feeling of irreversibility. The comparison of a man in the grip of a passion to runaway motion turns up in the doxographical survey,[83] but goes back to Chrysippus himself. We owe to Galen's polemical verbosity the important quotation which outlines Chrysippus' view:[84]

> The excess of the impulse was also spoken of in terms of this, because they overstep the boundary of impulses which is proper to themselves and natural. What I say would be made easier to understand by means of the following examples. In walking according to impulse the movement of the legs is not excessive, but is in a sense coextensive with the impulse, so that it can come to a standstill when he [sc. the walker] wishes, or change direction. But in the case of those who are running according to impulse, this sort of thing is no longer the case, but the movement of the legs exceeds the impulse so that it is carried away and does not change direction obediently in this way as soon as they start to do so. I think something similar to these movements [of the legs] occurs in the impulses because of the overstepping of the symmetry which is according to reason, so that whenever one has an impulse he is not obedient with respect to it, the excess being said to be beyond the impulse in the case of the running and beyond reason in the case of impulse. For the symmetry of natural impulse is that according to reason and is as far as reason deems proper. There since the overstepping is according to this [standard] and in this way, the impulse is said to be excessive and an unnatural and irrational movement of the soul. (Gal. *PHP* iv.2.14–18 [= *SVF* iii 462])

However we understand the reason whose bounds are overstepped,[85] it is clear that the sense of being out of control is aptly figured by the comparison to a runner. Someone who is running has a momentum which makes his bodily motions not immediately subject to control. No one, when running, can stop 'on a dime'. Similarly in a passion: no one in the grip of a passion, committed to feelings or activities driven by mistaken evaluative judgements, can instantly regain his composure, equanimity and self-control when he wishes. We are left trembling in fright for a while after we recognize that what shocked us is not really harmful. We are left with a sense of empty longing even after we accept that the death of an aged loved one was a blessing and not a tragedy. The psychological inertia of

---

[83] Stob. ii.89.6–9 This is a curious text, speaking of a disobedient horse. It is arguably in conflict with the monism of conventional Stoicism.   [84] See ch. 17, pp. 582–3.

[85] Probably normative right reason is in question.

erroneous value judgements is so great that the best cure is to avoid such erroneous judgements to begin with. And that is the task of moral education.

The underlying error is not that one cares about things at all; for many of the things which provoke passions are indeed worth caring about. Serious physical harm may not be a bad thing, but it is certainly dispreferred. The passion 'fear' ensues when one reacts to the prospect of such harm as though it were in fact bad. But what is the proper form of reaction? Not, surely, complete equanimity. The Stoics did not expect men to stand around inertly while things contrary to nature threatened.[86] Avoidance and even concern about such a prospect was perfectly in order, providing it was kept within the proper, rational and natural boundaries Chrysippus recognized. The way to do that was evidently by a form of emotional management characterized by a moral stance dubbed 'reservation' (*hupexhairesis*).[87] As several later Stoics make clear,[88] reservation involved making a tentative or conditional commitment to a course of action in the world. We might desire health, but only if it turns out to be fated for us. If serious obstacles arise to our efforts, then it is a sign that we should accept the illness which comes our way.[89] Our pursuit or avoidance of things which are merely preferred is protected by this conditional commitment. The uncontrollable inertia which sweeps us into a passion is the result of approaching actions and feelings which are indifferent to the goal of life as though they were crucial to it (as the good or the bad would be). Turbulence in life is the result of uncontrolled and unregulated engagement, not of engagement in any form. In regard to such things one should act, as Epictetus says, 'lightly, reservedly, and gently' (*Ench*. 2). That is the secret of the smooth flow of life, true *apatheia*.

Finally, one further aspect of the Stoic theory of the passions demands notice, though it will be difficult to determine with confidence what the earliest Stoics thought about it.[90] The existence and importance of affective reactions which are not subject to the rational control of assent is hard to deny. It is common to experience fearful or startled reactions which we cannot anticipate or repress, which we suffer even before our rational faculties can react. A sudden loud noise startles us, even though we might immediately deny our assent to the notion that something

[86] Compare the doctrine of *confatalia*. See p. 534.   [87] Inwood 1985, 165–73.
[88] E.g. Sen. *Tranq. An*. 13.2–3, *Ben*. IV.34.4, Marc. Aur. VI.50, Stob. II.115.5–9, Epict. *Ench*. 2.
[89] Compare the remarks of Chrysippus quoted at Epict. *Diss*. II.6.9–10; above p. 693.
[90] Further discussion and bibliography: Inwood 1985, 175–81, Inwood 1993.

frightful is occurring. What is the nature of such reactions (called *propatheiai* or 'preliminary passions' by the tradition)?

That the early Stoics were concerned with the question seems clear. Epictetus held that such reactions did occur in our souls, and Aulus Gellius maintains that his view is consistent with that of Zeno and Chrysippus:

> Impressions in the mind, with which the intellect of man is struck as soon as the appearance of something which happens reaches the mind, are not voluntary or subject to one's control; but by a force of their own they press themselves on men to be acknowledged. But the assents . . . by which the same impressions are acknowledged are voluntary and occur under human control. Therefore, when some frightening sound from the sky or a collapsing building or the sudden announcement of some danger or something else of the sort occurs, it is inevitable that even a wise man's soul be moved for a short while and be contracted and grow pale, not because he has formed an opinion of anything bad, but because of certain rapid and unreflective movements which forestall the proper function of the intellect and reason. Soon, though, the wise man withholds his assent . . . from such impressions . . . but he rejects and refuses them and judges that there is nothing in them to be feared. And they say that the difference between the mind of the wise man and that of the fool is that the fool thinks that the violent and harsh impressions which first strike his mind really are as they seem; and he also confirms with his own assent these initial reactions, just as though they really were to be feared, and he 'adds to the initial reactions a further opinion' (for the Stoics use this word [*prosepidoxazei*] when they discuss the matter). The wise man, however, when he has been affected briefly and in a limited fashion in his colour and expression, does not assent but retains the condition and strength of the opinion which he always had about such presentations, as things not at all worthy of being feared which try to frighten us with a false show and empty dread. (Gell. XIX.1.14–20)

An important passage of Seneca's *De Ira* (1.16.7) attributes a similar view to Zeno: 'for, as Zeno says, there remains even in the soul of the wise man, even when his wound has healed, a scar. Therefore he will feel certain hints and shadows of passions, but passions themselves he will not have.' The views Seneca adopts in Book II of the same treatise are somewhat more problematic.[91]

If such views really were those of the early Stoics, they provide an interesting and important complement to their theory of the passions. We are given a picture of the rational soul which is, even at its highest and most

---

[91] Discussed in Inwood 1993.

rational development, vulnerable to transient disturbances. No one, not even the wise man, is immune to some form of upset. What distinguishes the wise man from the rest of us is the 'condition and strength of the opinion which he always had about such impressions'. The wise man has firm convictions about the difference between things which matter for human happiness (the good and the bad, virtue and vice) and things which do not; while remaining humanly vulnerable to the temptations and assaults of the external world, he stands uncorrupted by them.[92] The passionless wise man is not someone who never feels. But he remains clear-headed about what he feels, distinguishing what makes a difference to happiness from what does not. By keeping this difference firmly in view, he prevents the transient upsets of life from gaining the momentum which would turn them into passions.

VIII Moral education and the problem of the passions

This chapter has touched frequently on the importance the Stoics attached to moral development and teaching. They needed a theory, or at least a motivated conception, of the person and ways of influencing the formation of character. The Stoic conception appears to be conditioned by more general presuppositions about anthropology and psychology accepted in the school. One might put the point schematically by saying that the ancient Stoics recognized the triad of explanatory factors found in previous philosophy from Protagoras to Aristotle:[93] nature, habit, reason or teaching. But they restructured this triad in an original way. This is particularly obvious with habit, and is a consequence of their new way of conceiving of the human soul. Where there is no psychic part or function totally detached from reason, it is impossible to speak of *ēthos* as the conditioning of the irrational by means of repeated processes of habituation as distinct from straightforward cognitive processes, that is teaching or the transmission of knowledge directed towards the formation of opinions. Only later representatives of the school, who abandoned orthodox Stoic psychology by making room for parts or functions of the soul that were irrational *per se* (because distinct from reason), returned to uninhibited talk of *ēthos* and habituation.[94]

---

[92] Compare D.L. VII.89.

[93] DK 80 B 3; Arist. *EN* x.9.1179b20–31. The classic triad is directly attributed to the Stoics in *SVF* III 214.

[94] For example cf. Posidonius in Gal. *PHP* IV.7.7–8 (V 417–18K) and Kidd 1971a, 205–6.

The Stoics did not ignore the importance of exercise and training in the field of virtue. But they preferred to speak of *askēsis* or *sungymnasia*[95] rather than *ēthos*: as if the traditional term appeared to them too closely tied to a mistaken conception of man and his psychic constitution. And it is perhaps not insignificant (unless this is merely owing to gaps in our information) that they preferred to speak of 'habit' in descriptions of the origin of vice[96] or, at the most, in connection with *prokopē*, progress towards virtue, rather than in contexts that directly describe virtue and how it is acquired. Plutarch (*Stoic. Rep.* 1043c–d) states that Chrysippus spoke at one point of

> those who have made some progress by having been engaged in a certain kind of discipline and habituation, for example at the courts of Leuco and Idanthyrsus. (trans. Cherniss)

One could therefore say that the mechanical repetition of actions and psychic reactions suggested by the traditional concept of *ēthos* pushed the Stoics towards use of the term in cases of at least relative imperfection, inertia or passivity of reason. Even in the case of development of bad habits or in that of *prokopē*, *ēthos* could be intended to carry a different sense from that familiar in the Platonic or Aristotelian tradition: not habit in the irrational part of the soul, but the formation of correct or incorrect opinions about good or evil.[97] The Christian author Clement (*Strom.* VII.3.19) can assert with supreme confidence that *ēthos* is the origin not of virtue but only of vice, an ingenuous but understandable simplification of the Stoic view.

The other two factors inherited from the tradition, nature and reason (taken as seat of understanding and subject of moral development), were also subjected to revision. In one sense of the word, nature was still considered as the innate endowments that make every individual different from every other. The importance of these endowments had been recognized from the early days of the school, as is shown by the evidence for Cleanthes and Chrysippus.[98] In another sense, more notable because it was tied to general assumptions of Stoic philosophy, nature and reason could not be contrasted and were not really different, since reason was rooted in nature as principle of man and the cosmos. Thus Seneca explains that 'nature has made us capable of receiving teaching; it has given us a

[95] *Askēsis* in *SVF* I 370, II 35, III 278; *sungymnasia* III.214. Cf. also the definitions of *technē* in I 73, II 93, 95. [96] E.g. Sen. *Ep.* 75.11–13, 85.15, 95.36. On moral progress see below, pp. 724–31.

[97] Note the insistence upon terms such as *opinio* and *sententia* in contexts relevant to the origin of vice, in which the acquisition of bad attitudes is implicit: e.g. *SVF* III 229; Cic. *Tusc.* III.2–3.

[98] Gell. VII.2, with Long 1971b, 187 and 197 n. 48.

reason which is imperfect, but which can be brought to a state of perfection' (*Ep.* 49.11). One could ask whether this reason, still imperfect when we are infants (this is a fact on which other sources insist),[99] should not be included among the natural gifts mentioned above: this would reinforce the argument for identifying nature and reason; and whether, when they speak of 'natural tendencies towards virtue',[100] the older Stoics in fact meant anything more than the innate predisposition which all men possess to develop rationality within themselves.

Evidence[101] relating to a dispute about the unity of virtue between Aristo and contemporary Stoics (almost certainly Cleanthes and perhaps also Zeno; less probably Chrysippus[102]) seems to point towards this conclusion. From the fact (admitted even by his opponents) that there is only one natural excellence (*euphuia*), presupposed by all the virtues, Aristo thought we should conclude that it could develop only into a single virtue. The idea of a single natural excellence was apparently prevalent among Zeno's closest disciples; this makes sense if one considers that the original state of the ruling part of the mind was compared by the Stoics in our source to easily-fashioned wax, naturally disposed to receive any representation.[103] The text seems thus to imply an original state of mind which could be the embryo of a rationality developed and differentiated into a variety of concepts as much as into different virtues. The idea of differentiation between natural endowments perhaps originated only as a consequence of the dispute initiated by Aristo about the unity of virtue;[104] it first appears fully detailed in Panaetius, with his theory of four *personae*. According to Cicero's account (*Off.* 1.107–10) these are the 'roles', the 'parts' which everyone is called upon to play in life:

> It should also be understood that nature has endowed us with two roles, as it were. One of these is universal, from the fact that we all share in reason and that status which raises us above the beasts; this is the source of all rectitude and propriety and the basis of the rational discovery of our proper functions. The second role is the one which has been specifically assigned to individuals. Just as there are great bodily differences between people . . . so too there are still greater mental divergences . . . To the above-mentioned two roles a third is appended, which some chance or circumstance imposes: and a fourth as well, which we take upon ourselves by our own decision. (trans. Long and Sedley)

[99] E.g. Sen. *Ep.* 120.3; Cic. *Leg.* 1.27.   [100] Stob. II.65.8.   [101] Anon. *In Tht.* XI.12–40.
[102] Schofield 1984, 91.
[103] A probable reading of the papyrus is *phantasia*: Luschnat 1958, 200 n. 4.
[104] Cf. below, p. 718. On Panaetius' theory of the four *personae* see Rist 1969a, 187; De Lacy 1977, 163–72 and Long and Sedley 1987, I.427.

So, according to Panaetius, every man would have a primary role assigned by the reason common to all humankind, and a secondary one established for him by inclinations specific to his own physical, temperamental and intellectual nature. A third role is assigned by external circumstances: he can be born in noble or lowly conditions, he can become a military leader or a magistrate. Finally, everyone has a role which he himself chooses for his life by a personal decision. Panaetius exhorts everyone to follow his own inclinations, as long as they are not vicious. But this can be done only by taking account of the requirements of the rational nature common to humanity: these remain the limits and the foundation of every other role. One thing always remains clear: that, according to the Stoics, nature initially endows men with enough to orientate them towards goodness and virtue, but not to lead them there; Seneca therefore says (*Ep.* 124.13) that we should attribute the acquisition of virtue to the care which man takes of himself rather than to nature.

Why should natural tendencies not be capable of leading man towards virtue on their own? Why is there a need to introduce teaching? The Stoics' reply to this question is more radical than the one an Aristotelian would give – the latter would probably say that nature can sketch many things in outline but cannot bring them to completion on its own: art, education, teaching are nothing more than an imitation and prolongation of nature, and complete the process which it began.[105] For a Stoic, recourse to education is necessary because in everyone natural tendencies are perverted and distorted right from infancy. This perversion[106] shows every sign of being inevitable. A passage in Cicero, certainly influenced by Stoicism, reproduces the principal points of the Stoic position:

> When we come into the light of day . . . we find ourselves immersed in a corrupt atmosphere and a sea of mistaken opinions. It seems as if we drink in error with our nurse's milk. When we are restored to our parents and handed over to teachers, we are drenched with various species of error . . . We should add also the poets, whom we have to read, listen to, commit to heart, and thus impress deeply in our minds. When we add in also popular opinion, in the role of chief instructor, with the whole mob rushing from all sides to agree on vice, then we are completely corrupted by false opinions and we are alienated from nature. (*Tusc.* III.2–3)

Above all there is the irresistible persuasion exercised upon the human mind by presentations (*phantasiai*), e.g. the first the child is aware of upon

---

[105] For example, see *Protrepticus* fr. B 13 Düring.
[106] *Diastrophē, diastrephesthai*: SVF III 228–36. On this whole topic see Kerferd 1978a, Nussbaum 1987, 162 n. 65a, and Nussbaum 1994, 389 n. 68.

emerging from the womb: brought roughly from a warm, damp environment to the colder air outside, a newborn child has a painful sensation,
which the obstetricians try to relieve by bathing in warm water, thereby
reproducing the pleasant pre-natal environment.[107] From this point the
child begins to form the incorrect opinion that what is pleasant is good,
and what is painful should be avoided as a bad thing. Then the processes
of socialization to which every child is subjected aggravate the situation:
the hopes for his material prosperity he hears coming from his nurses or
parents; distorted values transmitted to him by current teaching, especially through reading the poets; the inculcation of objectives held in popular esteem – riches, honour, power, fame. The future adult cannot help
making errors of judgement, which in their turn give rise to passions and
vices.

This explanation of the origin of vice raises a number of problems. For
example, it suggests a negative image of socializing processes, which
seems difficult to reconcile with the idea that the social community is also
something natural. But at least it has the merit of clarifying why education and teaching are truly indispensable and why *everyone* without exception is a victim of bad influences (even the wise person, before he becomes
such, will have to be freed from the influence of presentations and popular
opinions).[108]

*

Before Panaetius' time the Stoics seem therefore to have concentrated
almost exclusively on the formation of rationality and thereby on the
ways moral conceptions are transmitted. This latter problem was discussed by the first generation of Zeno's pupils: we have a record[109] of a
controversy which divided Cleanthes and Aristo as well as other figures
who cannot easily be identified. Under discussion were the merits and
efficacy of what the Latin source, Seneca, identifies by the terms *decreta*
and *praecepta*, i.e. 'doctrines' and 'precepts'. Doctrines were propositions
of a general character about ethics and philosophy in general, for example, the definition of the goal of life, the doctrine of good and
indifferents, the concept of justice (Sen. *Ep.* 94.2, 7–8,11). Precepts were

---

[107] The insistence in *SVF* III 229 on pre-natal experiences seems reliable: cf. Cic. *Tusc.* III.2 and the
requirements detailed by Chrysippus concerning the qualities needed for wet-nurses in Quint.
Inst. 1.1.4, 10.32. Vegetti 1989, 239 makes some interesting points about Agatinus the doctor.

[108] Note also the language used in other texts, e.g. Zeno in Sen. *De Ira* 1.16.7 *vulnus sanatum* and Cic.
Tusc. III.83 *morsus relinquetur*. Chrysippus in Plu. *Stoic. Rep.* 1039d is also significant.

[109] From Sen. *Ep.* 94 and 95. For the unnamed people who dissented both from Cleanthes and
Aristo, see Ioppolo 1980a, 132.

rules or recommendations on behaviour relevant to individuals or classes of individual, taking the form of injunctions or prohibitions: do this, don't do that (*Ep.* 94.11). But while there were those who used only precepts in moral education, Aristo wanted to do without them and rely solely on doctrines in teaching ethics. He was convinced[110] that anyone who knew the general doctrines would know how to resolve any particular case for himself, by reducing it to the principles which defined it. According to him, precepts stated *what* one should do, but not *why*; but to advise on a course of behaviour without explaining its foundations would leave the person to whom the precept was addressed in ignorance, while the advice would be superfluous for anyone who already possessed a general knowledge of the good. What teaching should do, therefore, was to remove false opinions and substitute for them correct doctrines concerning life and happiness. It is likely that Aristo's pedagogical radicalism was tied to his rebuttal of the doctrine of levels of preferability among the indifferents.[111] If among things that are neither good (like virtue) nor bad (like vice) none is preferable to any other, it is no longer necessary to spell out a lot of rules to distinguish between particular objectives and situations.[112]

Opposing Aristo, Cleanthes maintained the utility of specific advice and rules of behaviour: on condition, however, that the rules should be tied to the general considerations which established them (Sen. *Ep.* 94.4), i.e. to *decreta*. Since in the division of ethics taken up by Chrysippus and his successors (in D.L. VII.84) one of the regular topics to crop up is exhortation and dissuasion, it is clear that Cleanthes defended what already had or at least would become the dominant position of the school: the rules expressed in the 'precepts' would remain the norms of practical orientation to be adopted by those who were on the way to moral perfection, and who would carry out appropriate, if not virtuous, actions.[113] As Seneca explains in *Ep.* 95.12 and 63–4:

Note that no one . . . will properly perform what he should do unless he has acquired the system of being able to execute all the measures of proper functions in every matter. These will not be secured by someone who has received precepts for the matter in hand but not for everything . . . It is doctrines which fortify, which protect our safety and tranquillity, which embrace the whole of life and, at the same time, the whole nature of things . . . When we advise someone to treat a friend just like himself,

---

[110] His view can, with care, be deduced from Sen. *Ep.* 94.2–17.
[111] See also Steinmetz 1994, 560–1; on Aristo, see Boys-Stones 1996.
[112] See pp. 696–7.   [113] Sen. *Ep.* 94.33, 37; below, section x.

or to think that an enemy can become a friend . . . we add the words 'it is just and honourable'. But what is just and honourable is comprised by the system of our doctrines. This system, therefore, is the necessary condition of those precepts. But let us unite precepts and doctrines. Without a root, in fact, branches are useless, and the roots themselves are aided by what they generate. (trans. Long and Sedley)

The hypothesis on which Cleanthes and his followers worked seems therefore to have been that anyone who, in his actions, stuck to the rules contained in the system of precepts would eventually also have assimilated and comprehended the basic doctrines which justified the rules and were the object of the most theoretical part of the teaching. It does not seem that they would have recognized any reason to limit this teaching only to general ethical propositions. Aristo excluded logic and physics from philosophy,[114] but for Cleanthes, Chrysippus and their followers the fundamental doctrines of ethics were closely connected with the Stoic conception of the world and with the rational character of discourse in general. Seneca, who in *Ep.* 95 defends a position close to Cleanthes', connects the precepts relating to the cult of the gods with the knowledge of nature and the operations of the divinity, that is, questions of theology and physics.[115] Logic and physics must therefore form part of the full range of the teaching of *decreta* relating to virtue and the practical life; this explains why these two disciplines could themselves be considered 'virtues' alongside the traditional ones such as wisdom, justice, etc. (Cic. *Fin.* III.72–3; D.L. VII.46).

The aim of moral education would therefore, according to the Stoics, have been attained when there is established in the mind a complex of correct opinions, perfectly mutually coherent and coinciding with the propositions of right reason and accordingly with the will of Zeus.[116] But there is a threat to any such conception of education, dominated by emphasis on cognitive processes: passion, interpreted as incorrect opinion.[117] Since passion could no longer be confined to a non-logical part of the soul, as in the psychological model familiar in the Platonic-Aristotelian tradition, it posed a major threat to consistency of opinion and therefore of life. Teaching how to achieve freedom from passions was thus one of the Stoic's most important duties, and one of the most urgent

---

[114] *SVF* I 352–7.

[115] Sen. *Ep.* 95.47–50, cf. Kidd 1971, 158. Cf. also Chrysippus on the place of physics in the curriculum: Plu. *Stoic. Rep.* 1035c. On the whole topic see also Inwood 1995, 657–60 (against Annas 1993a, 163–5).

[116] Cf. Chrysippus in D.L. VII.88 (quoted above, p. 685), with Inwood 1985, 106–8.

[117] Or as the *consequence* of an incorrect opinion, cf. above, p. 699.

intellectual challenges that he was called upon to meet from the explanatory resources of his philosophy.

If we were to believe their ancient critics, the Stoics were not up to the
task at all, and dedicated little time to the problem of curing passions (Cic.
Tusc. IV.9). But such judgements betray incomprehension or polemical
exaggeration, since we know that to his three books *On passions*
Chrysippus added one specifically devoted to therapy (Gal. *Loc. Aff.* III.1,
VIII 138K). Again, the fussiness in defining and identifying the passions
with which Cicero reproaches the Stoics (*Tusc.* IV.9) can be explained as
the first stage of therapy itself. The Stoics dwell on the analogy between
bodily illness and passion, construing it as a pathological deviation from a
normal psychic state – and therefore as a disease, or the onset of a disease,
of the soul.

> Just as when the blood is in a bad state, or there is an overflow of phlegm
> or bile, diseases and illnesses take a hold in the body, so the disturbance
> of false opinions and the war they wage among themselves rob the soul of
> health and trouble it with morbid conditions. The passions give rise in
> the first instance to diseases (which the Stoics call in Greek *nosēmata*) . . .
> then illnesses, called by the Stoics *arrhōstēmata* in Greek . . . Here the
> Stoics and above all Chrysippus spend too much effort on setting up the
> comparison between diseases of the body and diseases of the soul. (Cic.
> *Tusc.* IV.23)[118]

If one adds to this analogy the reduction of a passionate deed to an error of
judgement, one can see that an accurate description of the phenomenon
was already felt by the Stoics to be the first thing to be tackled when performing therapy. However, it is more difficult to reconstruct from these
details the way the medical analogy was applied to the course run by a passion: the three stages of psychic pathology which the sources record[119]
are not entirely clear in themselves or in relation to each other.

So far as the treatment of passions is concerned, the Stoics seem to have
identified two basic methods: prevention, i.e., stopping passions from
arising; and actual therapy, i.e., treating a symptom which has already
appeared.[120] As one would expect, the first method – certainly in its practical effects the surest and most trustworthy – is also less interesting: it

---

[118] Cf. Gal. *PHP* v.4 (v 454–8K). In defence of the Stoic position: Vegetti 1989, 233 and Nussbaum
1994, chs. 1 and 9.

[119] Cic. *Tusc.* IV.23, 27; Stob. II.93.1–13. In Cicero's terminology the three stages are *proclivitas, mor-
bus, aegrotatio*; the hint of a later, Posidonian, origin can be detected especially in the first: cf.
Kidd 1983. See also I. Hadot 1969a, 143–5; Nussbaum 1987, 160–1.

[120] Sen. *De Ira* II.18, cf. *Ep.* 94.13 (Aristo?). In Cic. *Tusc.* III–IV the distinction is implicit, though
never stated. On the whole topic, see I. Hadot 1969a and Nussbaum 1994, chs. 9–12.

consisted basically in prophylactic acquisition of a range of knowledge about the world and of a mental attitude which would in fact coincide in the end with perfect wisdom. As Cicero *Tusc.* III.30 says, it is certain that whoever 'has understood and fully considered human affairs', or 'is not upset by anything that happens', or 'does not think of anything before it happens that it cannot happen' will not fall prey to passion; but to say this is merely to say that in order to avoid passions one must first become a wise person. The fact that particular expedients and pieces of prudent advice, relevant to different situations and passions,[121] were prescribed does not change the basic impression: prevention always operates within the limits and according to the methods of moral teaching outlined above. As Cicero, in *Tusc.* IV.57, goes on to observe, the risk is one of being irrelevant in practice, since the bulk of humanity consists of fools who are already prey to passions. The real conceptual difficulty, and the most important problem for practical operation of the doctrine, therefore lay in the possibility of finding treatment for active passions. Here it seems that within the school Chrysippus' position represents an advance on Cleanthes', since it provides a better explanation and a more profound analysis of what treatment might be.[122]

If passion is in some way connected with wrong judgement, it seems quite an easy thing to say: change the judgement and you thereby put an end to the passion. If, say, it were a case of *lupē*, i.e. pain on account of the presence of some (supposed) bad things, it seemed logical to Cleanthes to suggest that the therapy should consist simply in showing that it had nothing to do with anything really bad. But Chrysippus realized that such consolation was no use at all: it was inappropriate and risked compromising any possibility of a cure. And Cicero, in *Tusc.* III.77, objects that if one teaches someone in distress that the only thing that is really bad is something morally shameful, the patient will be freed not from his distress but from his folly; assuming that the teaching works, he will in fact become wise. The sheer improbability of this outcome shows the unreliability of the suggested treatment. Over Cleanthes Chrysippus seems to have had the advantage of seeing how to use the Stoic analysis of the psychic processes which constitute a passion in a more sophisticated way.

Earlier in this chapter[123] stress was laid on the complexity of the Stoic analysis of passion. For example, in a case of pain, the associated belief is expressed not simply by the proposition 'This is something bad', but is

---

[121] E.g. Sen. *De Ira* II.18.2.   [122] Cf. Cic. *Tusc.* III.76–7, with Donini 1995b.
[123] Cf. above, p. 701.

made up of the two propositions: (1) 'This is something bad' and (2) 'It is right that I should be affected by it'. Moreover, according to Chrysippus a passion has its own temporal rhythm. What happens is that either (A) in time the impulse in the soul of the person affected which corresponds to proposition (2) weakens: consequently (2) becomes ineffective, but belief in (1) remains intact; or (B) both (1) and (2) remain, but 'the consequences' diminish, that is, in the case hypothesized the contraction of the *pneuma* and probably also the exterior manifestations of the pain, weeping and wailing.[124] Chrysippus may be referring to this second case (B) when he observes that it is the moment when the inflammation of a passion abates (Gal. *PHP* IV.7.27, V 422K) which is the right time to begin treatment, and that only then is there hope that reasoning – on the part of someone offering consolation or advice – will 'insinuate itself and, so to speak, find a place to reveal the irrationality of the passion'. Thus Chrysippus avoided Cleanthes' naïveté: 'revealing the irrationality of the passion' meant to him merely attacking proposition (2). Refutation of this proposition must start from convictions held by the interlocutor needing consolation, whatever they may be; it will involve showing that it is inappropriate and inconsistent to abandon oneself to the passions (the procedure is in accordance with general Stoic principle: when it is a matter of persuasion, the wise man will start from opinions to which his interlocutor is already committed).[125] Only after having obtained results here will Chrysippus eventually attack proposition (1), bringing into play the correct notion, as the Stoics believed, that only what is morally evil is bad.

IX Virtue and wisdom

Our discussion of the cure of the passions can supply premises for an account of the specifically Stoic idea of virtue as well. Let us suppose that therapy or teaching reached a successful conclusion, that is, eliminated in the soul of the person who was not yet virtuous all propositions and judgements which constituted the basis for passionate reactions and incorrect actions; and let us suppose that, in place of incorrect judgements about certain things, teaching has resulted in stable and correct opinions in the soul about indifferents. It is clear that the person would

---

[124] See Gal. *PHP* IV.7.12–17 (V 419–20K) with Long and Sedley 1987, I.421; I have added the reference to exterior manifestations on the basis of the mention of weeping which ceases.

[125] On this whole subject see Donini 1995b. On the practice of starting from opinions to which one's interlocutor is already committed, see Nussbaum 1994, 320–4; an example from Seneca is discussed in Donini 1995a, 197–204.

then possess a complex of propositions and judgements which are perfectly consistent with each other and with right reason, coinciding with
the law of cosmic nature and the will of Zeus.[126] It therefore does not
seem accidental that one definition of virtue used by the Stoics stated that
it was a 'consistent disposition' (D.L. VII.89), and another definition
spoke of 'perfect reason' (Sen. *Ep.* 31.8; Plu. *Virt. Mor.* 441c); another definition, which refers to 'the (soul's) governing part in a particular disposition' (S.E. *M* XI.22), probably also alludes to the state of complete
consistency which is dominant in the virtuous man. Only virtue possesses
the characteristics of the *telos* which the Stoics defined, from Zeno
onwards, in terms of rational consistency.

Rational consistency is either perfect or non-existent: a collection of
propositions is either totally consistent or is utterly inconsistent, even if it
is only because of a single incongruous element. That is why the Stoics
could maintain (D.L. VII.127) that there are no degrees of virtue, and that a
man is either perfectly virtuous, or not virtuous at all (and therefore foolish or mad). This concept is in fact contained in another idea employed in
the first of the definitions quoted above: 'disposition' (*diathesis*)[127] is actually the technical term Stoicism used to define a state which does not admit
within itself variations of degree. The image of a line, to which Diogenes
Laertius resorts, makes the same point: a line cannot be more or less
straight – either it is straight or it is not. Certain famous Stoic paradoxes
concerning virtue have the same explanation: for example, the movement
from vice to virtue is instantaneous (Plu. *Virt. Prof.* 75c), so much so that
the subject of the change may not notice it.[128] But the non-existence of
degrees of virtue did not lead the Stoics to put all good actions on the same
level; the content and material objective of the action can make a difference
to its importance and suitability for praise, as Chrysippus recognizes:[129]

For, although deeds done in accordance with the virtues are congenial,
even among these there are those that are <not> cited as examples, such
as courageously extending one's finger and continently abstaining
from an old crone with one foot in the grave and hearing without pre-
cipitate assent that three is exactly four; one who undertakes to praise

---

[126] See the commentary on Chrysippus' definition of *telos* in D.L. VII.88 (quoted above, p. 685).

[127] Other complications and incongruities in Stoic terminology are explained in Long and Sedley
1987, I.376. See also Luschnat 1958, 192–9; Forschner 1981, 174–6.

[128] Plu. *Comm. Not.* 1062b, a paradox much discussed in the literature. Sedley's explanation 1977,
94–5 is preferable to Rist 1969a, 90–1. See also Forschner 1981, 175; Decleva Caizzi and Funghi
1988, 120.

[129] But Cic. *Fin.* III.48 proposes another way of recognizing differences in action; cf. Wright 1991,
159 n.200 and also Tsekourakis 1974, 37.

and eulogize people by means of such examples gives evidence of a kind of insipidity. (Plu. *Stoic. Rep.* 1038f; cf. 1039a, trans. Cherniss)

Rational consistency and the absence of degrees are therefore typical characteristics of virtue in Stoic philosophy. But obviously this was an inheritance from a long tradition of reflection developed out of Socrates' ideas through Plato and Aristotle. Aristotle had already emphasized (*EN* II.4.1105a32) firm stability and constancy as distinctive characteristics of newly-acquired virtue; stability, unshakeable steadiness and constancy were undoubtedly features of Stoic virtue (Sen. *Ep.* 120.10–11; Plu. *Virt. Mor.* 441c) – only the Stoics seem to offer a better justification for making them so than Aristotle does, since stability and firmness typically belong to knowledge (*epistēmē*; cf. *SVF* II 90–5). Unlike Aristotle who disputed it, the Stoics accepted the identification of virtue and knowledge which derived from Socrates[130] (there was however a problem regarding the effective inalienability of virtue; according to some (D.L. VII.127), exceptional conditions like delirium and intoxication could cause the loss of a virtuous disposition). Also deriving from Socrates and Plato comes the idea retained by the Stoics that virtue was something eminently advantageous to its owner;[131] but in this case, too, they did not limit themselves to repeating what others had already said. The cosmic and theological foundation of their ethics, stressed in preceding sections, and the conviction that virtue should coincide with a form of rationality such that all propositions were brought to a state of perfect mutual compatibility: all this permitted them to assert that human and divine virtue are the same (*SVF* III 245–52) and, along the same lines, that human virtue is advantageous to divinity itself (Plu. *Comm. Not.* 1076a) just as divine goodness always benefits a virtuous person.

The idea that virtue represents the natural completion or perfection (*teleiōsis*) of every being is more in line with Aristotelian ethics:[132] particularly when this idea is accompanied by another, that natural perfection coincides with the good of every being, and this in turn with the completion of its own function. As Seneca puts it:

What is best in man? Reason: with this he precedes the animals and follows the gods. Therefore perfect reason is man's peculiar good, the rest he shares with animals and plants . . . what is the peculiar characteristic of a man? Reason – which when right and perfect makes the full sum of human happiness. Therefore if every thing, when it has perfected its own good, is

---

[130] Plu. *Virt. Mor.* 441b; Stob. II.63.6. By contrast, see Arist. *EN* VI.13.1144b28–30.
[131] S.E. *M* XI.22; cf. above, p.688.   [132] D.L. VII.90, 94; cf. Arist. *Metaph.* Δ.1021b20–33.

praiseworthy and has reached the end of its own nature, and man's own good is reason, if he has perfected reason, he is praiseworthy and has attained the end of his nature. (Sen. *Ep*. 76.10, trans. Long and Sedley)

But there remain significant differences from the Aristotelian tradition:[133] the Stoics completely disagreed with the idea that virtue as a disposition was a potentiality whose corresponding actualization represented its perfect realization. Stoic disposition already implies activity: as Seneca says elsewhere (*Ep*. 113.10) virtue, where it exists, 'acts' or does something in such a way that action is totally independent of material and external conditions which might impede its realization. Cicero illustrates this point well:

> Whatever takes its start from wisdom must be immediately perfect in all its parts. For in it is situated what we call 'desirable'. Just as it is wrong to betray one's country, to show violence to one's parents . . . actions which consist in bringing about certain results, so even without any result it is wrong to fear, to show grief, or to be in a state of concupiscence. As the latter are wrong not in their after-effects and consequences, but immediately in their first steps, so those things which take their start from virtue are to be judged right from their first undertaking and not by their accomplishment. (Cic. *Fin*. III.32, trans. Long and Sedley)

It is important to understand what the Stoics meant by 'first undertaking'. A man 'undertakes' an action (x) when he decides: in Stoic terms, when he *assents*[134] to the statement '(x) is the right thing to do'. So from the moment when the agent assents to such a proposition the virtuous act is already perfect, even if in external reality there remain insuperable obstacles which prevent its effective completion. So the Stoic doctrine of virtue culminates in an exaltation of moral intention.

*

From the non-existence of levels of virtue it follows logically that for all the Stoics from Zeno onwards humanity should be divided into just two moral categories, the virtuous (or 'wise men') and the corrupt (or 'fools', 'madmen').[135] So the absolutely complete form of virtue is wisdom, and the wise man is someone who has all the virtues (Stob. *Ecl*. II.65.12–14). To possess all virtues means above all to possess the four primary virtues which are the same as in Socratic and Platonic tradition: wisdom (or prudence), temperance (or moderation), courage and justice (*Ecl*.

---

[133] See Forschner 1981, 176–8.   [134] See Inwood 1985, 95–101.
[135] Stob. II.99.3–106.20. Cf. also II.65.7.

II.60.9–11). These virtues are, moreover, inseparable from each other (*Ecl.* II.63.8): anyone who has one of them has all of them, and there can be no man who is just without also being wise, moderate and courageous. This thesis is likewise no novelty in the history of moral doctrines.[136]

Instead, novelties emerge in the way in which Stoicism justifies the two theses of the plurality and inseparability of virtues, between which a tension could arise if one or the other were stressed. There was in fact argument on this problem among the immediate disciples of Zeno, and between them and Chrysippus. The dispute probably arose from an ambiguity in the language used by Zeno when speaking about virtues. He certainly allowed that there were many virtues (Plu. *Stoic. Rep.* 1034c); but since he defined the other three primary virtues with reference to wisdom he seemed to reduce them all to the latter as a single fundamental virtue. Aristo interpreted him in this way. He recognized a single state of virtue, 'health', and held that it was differentiated only according to the circumstances in which it operated. He called it moderation, for example, when it involved putting desires and pleasures in order, or justice when it concerned relations with other men, etc.:

> Aristo of Chios also made virtue essentially one thing, which he called 'health'. It was by relativity that he made the virtues in a way different and plural, just as if someone wanted to call our vision 'white-seeing' when it apprehended white things, 'black-seeing' when it apprehended black things, and so on . . . Zeno of Citium also in a way seems to be drifting in this direction when he defines prudence in matters requiring distribution as justice, in matters requiring choice as moderation, and in matters requiring endurance as courage. (Plu. *Virt. Mor.* 440f–441a, trans. Long and Sedley)

This analogy[137] with vision seems to imply a criticism of the linguistic currency of virtue names. Cleanthes may have put forward a view like Aristo's (Plu. *Stoic. Rep.* 1034d), but Chrysippus reacted against it. According to Plutarch's account in *Virt. Mor.* 441a–b, he explained that Zeno had given the impression of thinking in terms of a single virtue simply because in his definitions of the primary virtues he had used the word 'wisdom' as equivalent to 'knowledge'; so the unifying element of the virtues would not itself have been one of those virtues, but that structure of mind, i.e. knowledge (*epistēmē*), which was the basis shared by the many virtues. Individual virtues, then, were according to Chrysippus

---

[136] Cf. e.g. Arist. *EN* VI.13.1144b32. See also Schofield 1984.
[137] That is, if the analogy of seeing is truly Aristo's and not Plutarch's: cf. Schofield 1984, 89. On Aristo's view, see also Ioppolo 1980a, 208–38.

effectively different, because they were qualitatively differentiated: corresponding, that is, to different permanent qualifications of soul.

With the situation thus clarified, Chrysippus could proceed to a further diversification of virtues by introducing a long series of virtues subordinate to each of the cardinal ones: for example, under wisdom are included judiciousness (*euboulia*), resourcefulness (*eumēchania*) and others; under moderation, continence (*enkrateia*), endurance (*karteria*), etc. (Stob. *Ecl.* II.60.9–62.6; D.L. VII.92). He thereby attracted the accusation referred to by Plutarch of having uselessly introduced a 'swarm' of virtues and of having deliberately put in danger the other ingredient of Zeno's thesis, that of the basic unity of virtue. He put right this difficulty by proposing the idea (Stob. *Ecl.* II.63.6–25) that, as forms of knowledge, virtues contained the total sum of theoretical perspectives and common rules of conduct, but each approached this sum from a different angle. So every virtue would consider as its own primary province the rules and principles which corresponded to its particular field of application; but it would also take into consideration, secondarily, all the rules and principles that are the primary concern of each of the other virtues. In this way an act of courage could be seen primarily as such, but also imply, secondarily, the theorems of all the other virtues; and it would follow that anyone who acted according to one virtue would in fact act in conformity with all of them:

> They say that the virtues imply one another not only in that he who has one has all, but also in that he who performs any act in accordance with one performs it in accordance with all. For they say that neither is a man perfect if he does not have all the virtues nor is an action perfect which is not done in accordance with all the virtues. (Plu. *Stoic. Rep.* 1046ef, trans. Schofield 1984)

The solution which Chrysippus gave in these terms constituted the basis of the Stoic view up to Panaetius, since the source (Stob. *Ecl.* II.63.26–7) from which the information about Panaetius comes introduces his explanation as an illustration[138] of the common view of the school. So even Panaetius, though introducing a distinction between two basic types of virtue, practical and theoretical (D.L. VII.92), saw the four cardinal virtues as mutually connected. But in conformity with his own theory of *personae*, he identified them differently from Chrysippus, referring to their roots in the natural tendencies of every individual.[139]

*

[138] Note the use of γάρ in Stob. II.63.25. On Chrysippus' view see Schofield 1984.
[139] Cic. *Off.* I.11–18. Cf. Rist 1969a, 192 and above, p. 707. See also Kidd 1971, 160–2.

The Socratic influence on Stoic doctrine is utterly clear from what has been said above: virtue is considered as a summation of forms of knowledge and theoretical perspectives; or as an art which has as its object the whole of human existence (Stob. II.67.1). The individual virtues are also defined as forms of knowledge, and each of the vices contrasted with them as kinds of ignorance (Stob. II.59.4–60.8). But all this presented another problem: what exactly does the wise man, in possession of all the virtues, 'know'? Since he possesses the theoretical perspectives and rules relevant to each virtue, and since he is also familiar with the logical and physical doctrines[140] which form the principles of ethics, it would be tempting to say that the wise man knows everything. While it is true that the Stoic wise man would know everything he needed to know, one should beware of evidence[141] which would attribute a kind of omniscience to him: these are either rhetorical exaggerations or completely unreliable. That the wise man could not literally know everything follows from his ability, acknowledged by the Stoics, to suspend judgement in cases of doubt (S.E. M VII.416, PH II.253). That, in particular, he could not know the 'whole of eternity' – as Cicero would have it – and therefore the future, follows from the fact that he is credited with the ability always to act on the basis 'of an impulse, but with reservation', an important concept to which I shall return later. It is true that there are a couple of texts (Stob. Ecl. II.114.16; Cic. Div. II.129) which present the wise man as the only good diviner;[142] but these must be interpreted in the light both of the notion of 'impulse with reservation' and of what Stobaeus states elsewhere regarding the wise man's knowledge of the arts:

> Only the wise man is a good diviner and poet and orator and dialectician[143] and critic; but not every wise man is like this, since some of them still need to acquire some theoretical principles. (Stob. Ecl. II.67.13–16)

This is like saying that only the wise man could have the ability correctly to perform each of the skills mentioned, but not all wise men effectively possess all the technical knowledge required for the effective performance of each skill.[144] This shows that ignorance even of many notions

---

[140] Cf. above, section VIII, regarding *decreta*; also Plu. *Stoic. Rep.* 1035c–d.

[141] Especially Cic. *Tusc.* IV.37; also *SVF* II 131, p. 41.12, on which see Kerferd 1978a, 128, with respect to the entire question.

[142] The account of Inwood 1985, 119–20, should be preferred to Forschner 1981, 208–11, N. P. White 1990, 57 n. 38.

[143] 'Dialectic' must be meant in the strictly technical sense, possibly its original Stoic meaning of 'the science of correct discussion, with arguments in the form of question and answer' (D.L. VII.2), not 'the science of things which are true, false and neither true nor false' (ibid.). On the evolution of the Stoic concept of dialectic see Long 1978c.

[144] Dio Chrysostom 71.5 (= *SVF* III 562) shows the Stoic point of view rather well.

relevant to individual skills does not in any way prevent a man from being wise. Moreover, if he always acts with caution, this implies that no man has ever possessed all the technical knowledge necessary to perform divination.

From this it follows that the wise man knows all that is necessary for virtue, and only that. It is not merely formal characteristics that make wisdom what it is. It must be in possession of substantive truths, as has already been made clear: the principles and rules of ethics, the principles of logic and of physics. But all this would be connected in the mind of the wise man within a complex of notions and propositions which were perfectly consistent. One might also say that the wise man knows the truth and not simply what is true (S.E. *M* VII.38–44); truth is a system of absolutely consistent propositions, while what is true is also accessible to fools, each of whom can state at least some true propositions. The truth which the wise man understands is rich in content; but it is in the end 'truth' above all on account of its complete rationality and systematic coherence, not because it is a box or a filing cabinet of all possible notions. His wholesale adaptability to all situations in life would depend, in the end, more on the formal characteristics of knowledge (rationality, firmness, system and consistency) and not on the impossibility of a capacity for being in possession of all notions. It is also likely that we should understand in this sense the Stoic thesis we have already mentioned (above, p. 716), which states that virtue is the same for a (wise) man as for a god. This is true precisely inasmuch as in both rationality is tied to consistency, while it remains obvious that the contents of the divine mind are much richer than those accessible to any human (Cic. *Div.* 1.127). And perhaps it would not be wrong to say that the knowledge attributed to the wise man by the Stoics was a metaphor for their own philosophy, or what they wanted it to be: an infallible ability to direct a man on any occasion in life, thanks to the exercise of rationality in accordance with correct logical principles, and to a systematic, consistent general vision of the world; not an encyclopaedia of universal knowledge.

So it is easy to see that not all the elements of the description which the Stoics gave of the wise man need be understood literally, as common sense might interpret them. The theses which state that only the wise man attains happiness and self-sufficiency (D.L. VII.127–8; Cic. *Fin.* III.26) must definitely be taken literally, and are anyway logically connected to the doctrines of the end and the good. But many other attributes of the wise man should be interpreted as metaphors which make sense if put into the general context of Stoic philosophy: otherwise they

flout linguistic usage.[145] So only the wise man is handsome (Cic. *Fin.*
III.75; Philo *QG* IV.99) because perfect harmony and symmetry of parts
rule only in his mind: this definitely alludes to the consistency of propositions which constitutes perfect rationality and, probably, also to the
full harmony between impulses and reason possessed by the wise man.
Only the wise man is rich (*SVF* III 593–600) because only he does not lack
anything which nature desires, nor any of the things which are really
good. Only the wise man is free (Cic. *Fin.* III.75; *SVF* III 597), not because
he can act or wish things according to his whim: in the Stoic universe,
completely predetermined, the wise man has not even the ability to
'make a significant change in his moral character'.[146] Rather, the wise
man's freedom is that of the man who is completely liberated from domination by the passions (Cic. *Fin.* III.75), and can get all he desires because
nothing which befalls him can hinder or destroy his constant impulse
towards good. This thoroughgoing internalization of the notion of freedom is probably the only solution possible within the general framework
of Stoic determinism.

Such a picture of the wise man could easily appear hyperbolic. It is
likely that the Stoics themselves understood this risk.[147] So it seems that
they made a realistic concession to good sense when they admitted that a
wise man was nowhere to be found, and that maybe only one or two ever
existed in the whole of human history[148] (with the final corollary that
none of them considered himself or his teachers wise: Plu. *Stoic. Rep.*
1048e). As Alexander reports:

> According to them . . . of men the greatest number are bad, or rather
> there are one or two whom they speak of as having become good men as
> in a fable, a sort of incredible creature as it were and contrary to nature
> and rarer than the Ethiopian phoenix; and the others are all wicked.
> (Alex. *Fat.* 199.14–18, trans R.W. Sharples)

Yet the descriptions of the wise man's behaviour give the impression of
referring to observable situations; moreover, Diogenes Laertius (VII.91)
could say that it was 'evident' that bad men could become good. I think
that the picture of the wise man, with its apparent incongruities, can only
be understood in connection with the protreptic and pedagogical aspect

---

[145] Cf. also Alexander's criticisms in *SVF* III 594–5.   [146] Inwood 1985, 109.

[147] Cf. the fragment from Chrysippus' *On Justice* quoted at Plu. *Stoic. Rep.* 1041f (assuming that it
deals with the wise man, as von Arnim supposed: *SVF* III 545); in any case, see also Cic. *Parad.* 4.

[148] S.E. *M* IX.133; Alex. *Fat.* 199.16–18; also Diogenianus in *SVF* III 668. Aristo may have allowed for
the existence of many wise men: Ioppolo 1980a, 117. On the fundamental optimism of the Stoic
conception, which depicts wisdom as a goal 'possible, at least on a theoretical level, for everyone', cf. Decleva Caizzi and Funghi 1988, 120–3.

of all Stoic moral teaching (emphasized above, and to be clarified further in this section and the next). For the moment, I would suggest that the Stoics, who did not admit the existence of non-corporeal objects functioning as normative criteria of actions, like the Platonic ideas of values, felt the need to indicate a sort of bodily and visible ethical norm, in which the moral values put forward in their philosophy were clearly embodied. This norm would be sufficiently high and demanding to depict a paradigm of excellence which could not be improved upon: if it could, it would cease to function as a criterion. But at the same time it needed to appear as a paradigm for the general run of mankind. Otherwise there was the risk that protreptic discourse would lose credibility, when its aim was to indicate precise and attractive objectives for human existence. That problem is common to all Hellenistic schools, just as is the solution, the figure of the wise man who exemplifies the norm.

One feature of the Stoic wise man also deserves particular mention. As previously stated, the wise man is totally free from passions. The ideal of the suppression of passions (*SVF* I 207, III 447–8) remained, throughout all antiquity, one of the most famous features of Stoic ethics; usually (e.g. Cic. *Acad.* 1.38; Sen. *Ep.* 116.1) it was seen in opposition to the ideal of the Peripatetics, which limited itself to the moderation of passions. The Stoic insistence on their abolition is, however, logical: if the passions were tied to or the same as incorrect judgements, full consistency of individual reason and its full adjustment to right reason would necessarily require the elimination of any error of judgement. Now among the passions to be excised from the mind explicit mention is made (*SVF* III 450–3) of pity – the wise man should not be lustful or dejected or anxious, but nor should he be compassionate. He should not be moved by any individual case and he should not excuse the guilty from their rightful punishment.[149] Perhaps no aspect of Stoic morality has been as unpopular as this one ever since antiquity: hence the disagreeable image of the wise man as a rigid, stern person, not open to any emotion. Recent research[150] has countered this image effectively, by emphasizing that the Stoic wise man had – at least in normal everyday situations – exactly the same impulses of attraction and repulsion as all humanity. But the attribution of normal human impulses to the wise man requires the Stoics to offer an appropriate clarification of the doctrine of *eupatheiai*, mentioned above (p. 701). This

---

[149] Stob. II.95.24, probably an argument against Aristotle and his concept of equity; see also D.L. VII.123 and Rist 1978c, 267–9.

[150] Particularly Rist 1969a, Frede 1986b, Nussbaum 1987, but see Nussbaum 1994, 429–38. Cf. also pp. 703–5 above.

doctrine actually introduces no qualifications to the doctrine recommending the total elimination of passions, nor is there any reason to think of good emotions as something different from the balanced impulses of a perfectly rational agent.

The picture of the fool[151] presents a mirror image of that of the wise man. If virtue fulfilled in the wise man has all the consistency of knowledge, vice is characterized as incoherent and ignorant disorder (Cic. *Tusc.* IV.29; Stob. *Ecl.* II.59.11–60.5, 106.13). Furthermore, fools are utterly unhappy (Plu. *Stoic. Rep.* 1048e) and it is impossible for them to perform any correct action (Plu. *Stoic. Rep.* 1037d); just as every virtuous action of the wise man implied all the virtues, everything done by fools implied all the vices (Stob. *Ecl.* II.67.2). Obviously this should not be understood as meaning that Achilles was the same as a coward (this example is in Sen. *Ben.* IV.27); not everyone is naturally prone to all vices, but a person has them all if he is a fool, because the inconsistency and ignorance which are the essence of vice make their presence felt as soon as there occurs in the soul a single judgement at odds with the perfect harmony of reason. This also explains, finally, why from the Stoic point of view all sins were equal (*SVF* III 524–43); because all of them equally are consequences of a false judgement (Stob. *Ecl.* II.107.8) and any false judgement equally destroys the harmonious consistency of reason. If a pilot wrecks a ship loaded with straw, this is no less serious than if it had been loaded with gold (Cic. *Fin.* IV.76, *Parad.* 20); certainly there is a difference in the material content of the loss, but none in the unskilfulness of the pilot. And if there is no difference in sins or errors, the misery or unhappiness of someone who has approached very close to virtue will be the same as that of the criminal who is an enormous distance from them (Cic. *Fin.* IV.21): he will always have 'all' evils, in the sense that only one of them is enough to render him unhappy (Stob. *Ecl.* II.100.13).

x Moral progress

It is time to stop and reflect. If we were to take the opposition between the wise man and fools literally, we would come up against not just hyperboles and paradoxes, but actual aporias that would endanger the consistency of Stoic philosophy. This is precisely the conclusion reached by certain opponents of Stoicism, like the great Aristotelian Alexander of Aphrodisias and the Platonist Plutarch. The Aristotelian commenta-

---

[151] See Sandbach 1989 (1975), 43–5.

tor notes (*Fat.* 199.14–22) that, if it were true that only virtue and vice are respectively good and bad and that the greater part of mankind is wicked, then we must inevitably conclude that man is indeed the lowliest of all creatures. It is true that other creatures are incapable of virtue; but also – in compensation – free of vice, the very thing which makes man unhappy. The conclusion Alexander suggests is much more explicit in Plutarch, according to whom Stoic morality clashed with teleology and its doctrines of providence and a divine rationality which governs the world:

> The wise man does not exist and has never existed in any part of the world, but there are myriads of truly unhappy men in Zeus' republic, under a rule which implies the best management. What can be more repugnant to common sense than when, with Zeus governing in the best possible way, we men find ourselves in the worst possible state? (Plu. *Comm. Not.* 1076b)

But we should beware of the risk of reading Stoic doctrine in the same way as its prejudiced and ill-disposed critics. That their reading was incorrect is shown by a series of explanations which always accompany Stoic descriptions of vice and fools; the arguments of the Platonists and the Aristotelians did not take these into account. It is true that all sins are *equal*, but not that they are therefore the *same*: they are qualitatively different depending on the external cause which is the object of the agent's judgement, and which has a greater or lesser value or importance according to the differences which exist among *morally* intermediate objects (or indifferent objects: Stob. *Ecl.* II.106.21–6, from which it appears that the opponents' criticism treats all Stoics as if they agreed with Aristo). Nor are all sins, though equal, also *equally tolerable*: Zeno (Cic. *Fin.* IV.56) showed that some were absolutely intolerable, whereas others could not be. One consequence of this seems to be that not all sins were equally *punishable*.[152] And even if it is true that all fools are equally foolish, there are in fact profound differences in the things they do, inasmuch as some derive from a hardened, completely incurable character and others do not (Stob. *Ecl.* II.113.21–3). So there are effectively degrees of greater or lesser nearness to virtues and to wisdom:[153] this is explicitly recognized by Chrysippus (*SVF* III 510: the text is about happiness – which is distinguished from the limit of moral progress – but of course the sole condition of happiness is virtue):

---

[152] Cf. Rist's argument, 1969a, 82.
[153] On this topic see Inwood 1985, 208–9; Decleva Caizzi and Funghi 1988, 107–8.

Chrysippus says: 'He who has made the greatest possible progress carries out in every respect all the appropriate actions and omits none. But his life is not yet happy; happiness comes to him when these intermediate actions acquire the stability which comes with character and take on a certain fixity which is all their own'. (Stob. v. 906.18–907.5).

But degrees of nearness to virtue had already been fairly clearly acknowledged by Zeno (Plu. *Virt. Prof.* 82f). Obviously anyone who comes close to virtue remains constantly immersed in vice, just as anybody in water drowns even if he is only just under its surface, as much as if he were at the bottom of the sea (Cic. *Fin.* iii.48) – yet he can be more or less distant from the water's surface, therefore nearer to or farther from salvation and, to drop the metaphor, virtue.

If we take account of the clear recognition of the existence of degrees of nearness to virtue, it is also clear that the radical dichotomy between fools and wise men should be understood differently from the Stoics' critics. The distinction was strenuously maintained since it seemed to be perfectly logical: it made virtue a *diathesis*, so anyone who did not have it was inevitably non-virtuous, i.e. foolish, mad, corrupt. But while logically indisputable, it did not have the status of an objective description of the human condition: rather, it probably had a normative value and a pedagogical and protreptic meaning. It does not seem that the Stoics really had the implausible conviction that the whole of humanity had been and continued to be constituted of individuals who were radically and identically evil, as Alexander and Plutarch would have it. The objective description of the human condition did not, from the Stoic point of view, lie in the dichotomy between fools and wise men, but in the doctrine of degrees of nearness to virtue: the doctrine of moral progress and levels of *kathēkon* (or proper function, which will be examined later). So if it was the case that there actually existed men who were more or less far from virtue and only rarely, or never at all, men in which not so much as a glimmer of awareness or respect for good was evident (this was the optimistic assumption of the Stoics, according to Cic. *Fin.* iii.36–8), then the insistence found in the sources on the radical dichotomy acquires another significance: which would have to be the one already indicated in connection with the hyperbolic descriptions of the wise man. There was a limit and a norm for morality, which was the wise man; to insist on the idea (logically unexceptionable) that anyone who did not yet fit that norm was not a wise man, no matter how close he was, would take on a protreptic significance. And there was perhaps some rhetorical and pedagogical efficacy in applying a single name to all the non-wise, i.e. fools, without reference to how much they deviated from the norm. Implicit in this posture is an invitation to the non-wise to persevere in their efforts and seek to improve themselves further, without ever lapsing into complacency over results already achieved.

So what is perhaps debatable about the idea is not its consistency with general assumptions of Stoic philosophy, with teleology and providentialism: there is no difficulty with this, and one could even suggest a way out of the aporia mentioned above in section VIII. If the objective description of humanity does not lie in the wise/foolish division, but in the theory of degrees of nearness to virtue, then there is no need to think that the hypothesis of *diastrophē* also implies something negative in all kinds of social association. Every human community is simply imperfect and more or less distant from the norm: this is merely to be realistic. What is questionable is the effectiveness of an educational strategy which continues to repeat, even to those who had willingly lived all their lives seeking to become better, the message: you have achieved nothing. Considerations of this kind may have led Panaetius to abandon reference to the figure of the wise man as the behavioural norm[154] and to show some appreciation for human beings in whom there appeared some approximation, albeit distant, to virtue (Cic. *Off.* 1.46, III.13, 15). Yet perhaps the method of the older Stoics was effective. Even after Panaetius the image of the wise man retained its life (witness Seneca's *De constantia sapientis*); and between Zeno and Marcus Aurelius there was no philosophy with a greater capacity to act as a guide to the conscience than Stoicism. One writer[155] has rightly noted that the Stoic attitude survives in the sense of sin experienced by Christian saints convinced they were the worst of sinners. It is characteristic of consciences which are morally elevated to have a vivid awareness of human imperfection – and their own personal shortcomings.

*

Different degrees of progressive approximation to virtue are in effect acknowledged in the sources. The criteria by which the stages of progress were distinguished might differ,[156] but, in the most significant and informative text, there are five. These distinctions must ultimately be due to Chrysippus,[157] although as given here by Cicero they probably represent

---

[154] The common assessment of Panaetius: cf. e.g. Sen. *Ep.* 116.5. See also Tsekourakis 1974, 42.
[155] Rist 1969a, 91. [156] Compare Sen. *Ep.* 75.8 with Cic. *Fin.* III.20 (quoted below).
[157] Stobaeus (*SVF* III 510) (quoted above, p. 726) attributes to him a distinction between (iv) and (v) which seems to accord perfectly with Cicero's. But beyond level (i), of which he must necessarily have taken account, Chrysippus will have allowed for an intermediary stage between (i) and (iv), the most advanced level: at least four stages in all.

formulations by successors of his such as Diogenes of Babylon and Antipater:

> The first (i) appropriate action (this is my term for *kathēkon*) is to preserve oneself in one's natural constitution; the second (ii) is to seize hold of the things that accord with nature and to banish their opposites. Once this procedure of selection and rejection has been discovered, the next consequence (iii) is selection exercised with appropriate action; then, (iv) such selection performed continuously; finally, (v) selection which is absolutely consistent and in full accordance with nature. At this point, for the first time, that which can truly be called good begins to be present in a man and understood. (Cic. *Fin.* III.20, trans. after Long and Sedley)

Implicit in this text is almost everything of importance which the Stoics had to say about appropriate actions,[158] the activities which articulate the development of morality. What is most notable is that they were rooted in the impulse towards self-preservation innate in all living beings, extending even to animals. So continuity is established between the highest level of man's mental and moral development – (v) in Cicero's text – and the basic self-preservation mechanisms of the living being. Appropriate actions typically assume, as their content and point of reference, 'things that accord with nature': these – the primary object of immediate aspiration (not yet sustained by rational choice) – continue to be the content and point of reference of gradually more elaborate and conscious choices made by the human subject in the later stages of his development. The naturalness of the exercise of appropriate actions is highlighted by the general Stoic definitions of *kathēkonta* (Stob. II.85.14; D.L. VII.107), which speak of them as 'activities that conform to constitutions in accord with nature', or as 'consequentiality in life', that is conformity with the existence that is natural for each living species. But we know[159] that in the human species natural constitution and naturalness are not defined statically once and for all; in the evolution of every normally endowed individual the emergence of reason profoundly transforms his natural constitution. As a result, the evolution of which only humanity is capable also allows the definition of appropriate actions as 'that which, when done, permits a reasonable justification'.[160]

In Cicero's account, the emergence of reason must apparently occur between stages (ii) and (iii); this obviously refers to a 'common' rational-

---

[158] Mentioned already, p. 697 and n. 67 above, where variant English versions of *kathēkon* are indicated.   [159] Cf. above, pp. 679–80 and Long 1974, 187–92. See also Reesor 1989, 83–91.

[160] Stob. II.85.14–15; D.L. VII.107. The translation and interpretation of the term *eulogos* are problematic. See in particular Forschner 1981, 187–92, and also Tsekourakis 1974, 26–30.

ity, clearly distinct from that state of perfection which the Stoics used to refer to by the expression 'right reason'. There should therefore be no possibility of confusion in the lower levels of moral development – (ii) to (iv) – between the consequentiality which is manifest in the exercise of appropriate actions and perfect rational consistency, which constitutes the goal of existence and which Cicero mentions in his description of (v). Consequentiality of action is simply the adaptation of the agent's practical behaviour to the requirements of nature; it is not defined by also taking into consideration the interior dispositions which affect the subject. Nevertheless, the distinction and transition between (iv) and (v) are quite difficult to illustrate – and it is perhaps in this difficulty that certain ancient and modern misrepresentations of Stoic doctrine have their origin.

The decisive point for understanding the issue is to notice that both in Cicero and – even more clearly – in the formulation attributed to Chrysippus, what differentiates (v) from (iv) is not the addition of some further behaviour or activities which previously (before stage (v)) were unknown by or inaccessible to the agent: in stage (iv) he already does everything that he continues to do in (v). But both texts indicate – in a remarkably similar way – that the difference between the two stages is exclusively qualitative. All behaviours remain the same, but somebody who has reached (v), the greatest good and happiness, does just the same things that he did when he was at stage (iv), but does them in a completely different way, with a disposition of absolute firmness and perfect consistency[161] (it is notable that neither Chrysippus nor his followers put forward the question of *intention* here: the intention to do good would be recognized by the Stoics in one who was still a long way from virtue but was making efforts to get there). So there is excellent textual evidence for the tendency, widespread in modern scholarship,[162] to distinguish virtuous behaviour from the behaviour of one who only acts in an appropriate way, not on the basis of *what* is done, but on the basis of *how* and *why* it is done. Thus one can perceive the reason why the Stoics had to include virtuous action in the scale of appropriate actions as the highest level, (v), only distinguishing it as 'perfect appropriate action' (*kathēkon teleion*) or 'right action' (the technical term here is *katorthōma*) from appropriate but not yet virtuous actions, which were called 'intermediate' (as in the

---

[161] Cf. also Sen. *Ep.* 95.39–40, 57 which shows this aspect clearly.

[162] Something of a *communis opinio*: cf. e.g. Nebel 1935, 441–2; Long and Sedley 1987, 1.365–7. Two exceptions: Kidd 1978c; Engberg-Pedersen 1990, 128–30, whose interpretations however are hard to reconcile with Cic. *Fin.* III.20 and *SVF* III 510.

Chrysippus text, already mentioned several times). The coincidence in exterior behaviours justified the inclusion in one category of two grades of conduct which were so different from the point of view of moral evaluation.

Some texts (like Stob. II.97.3 and Cic. *Fin.* III.58–9) seem to imply or explicitly affirm the existence of appropriate actions which would occupy an intermediate place between virtuous and vicious actions. They can be reconciled with the thesis according to which everything a non-virtuous man – i.e. a fool – would do is an error and a vice if we allow that they refer to *types*, to general classes of action which are not in themselves or by definition distinctively vicious or distinctively virtuous: for example, walking, asking questions or replying (these are Stobaeus' examples in the passage cited); while every *particular case* of such a type would be necessarily, in its actual realization, either virtuous behaviour or an example of vice. Walking thus counts as a virtuous action if one can attach to it the qualification that it is done wisely; but all cases in which someone who walks is a fool count as examples of error. But there is a further point to be added here: the rooting of appropriate actions in nature, together with the constant reference to things which accord with nature, gives us a way of defining behaviours which are distinctively and in themselves 'contrary to appropriate actions':

> Appropriate actions are ones which reason dictates our doing, such as honouring parents, brothers and country, spending time with friends; contrary to appropriate actions are ones which reason dictates our not doing, such as neglecting parents, not caring about brothers, not treating friends sympathetically, not acting patriotically, etc. (D.L. VII.108)

In conclusion, it appears that human behaviours are differentiated in Stoic descriptions much more finely than may be suggested by the radical dichotomy between vice and virtue, fools and wise men, right action and error. There is a scale of vicious actions. The basic level consists of actions done 'against the *kathēkon*', which are errors both from the point of view of the agent's interior disposition and given the objective of the action which is performed. An intermediate position – but still within the area of vice – is occupied by 'intermediate' appropriate actions: these are still errors from the formal point of view which is concerned with the agent's disposition, but can be differentiated by their gradual and ever closer approximation to virtue. Above absolute vice and intermediate functions stand perfect appropriate actions, i.e. the *katorthōmata*, the right actions befitting virtue, described as 'appropriate actions having in full all measures'.[163]

*

As is suggested by the texts of Cicero and Chrysippus previously cited, and as is implied by the fact that there is no difference in visible behaviours between those who perform appropriate actions and those who are virtuous, practising *kathēkonta* is the best way to try to become virtuous. The objective coincidence in behaviours between appropriate actions and virtue therefore shows that Stoicism did not think to propose two different moralities, one for the wise man and an inferior one[164] accessible to fools with good intentions. And this also explains why Panaetius, at least to the extent that it is his teaching which is preserved in Cicero's *De officiis*, could base his analysis of different appropriate actions by referring each of them to one of the four primary virtues: in each case he started from the relevant final reference point. That Panaetius was not keen to accept the figure of the wise man as an explicit criterion of moral actions is well documented, but it can be explained by reasons[165] other than a weakening of the traditional theoretical framework.

Once again, however, Stoic virtue was not exactly the same as Aristotle's ethical virtue.[166] We have seen that the performance of appropriate actions is not enough to lead to virtue if not accompanied by growing acquisition of knowledge. Here the instruments and contents of Stoic teaching, divided into the two categories of 'precepts' and 'doctrines', come into play. The view which prevailed in the school[167] was that the one had as much importance as the other in promoting the maturation of the person who was seeking to attain virtue, the so-called *prokoptōn* or *proficiens*. Roughly speaking, the precepts told a person what to do or to avoid in certain typical situations, while the doctrines explained the interconnection of the rules contributing to the attainment of a rational mode of existence in full accord with nature.

The Stoics were certainly not sparing in articulating rules, warnings, exhortations and advice: Cicero's *De officiis*, many of Seneca's letters and

---

[163] Stob. II.93.14, a passage already commented upon above p. 698.

[164] Contra e.g. Cic. *Off.* III.15: appropriate actions as '*quasi secunda quaedam honesta*', 'a kind of secondary morality'.   [165] Suggested above, p. 727.

[166] See above, section VIII. Aristotle's conception of ethical virtue requires acting on one's own wits (*EN* VI.13.1144a13-20), and therefore entails *phronêsis*. But it is always a property of the irrational soul conditioned by habituation.

[167] For antecedent controversies see above, pp. 696-7, 709-11.

his treatise *De beneficiis* can still give an idea of the extreme detail to which they resorted in analysing possible situations and suggesting models of behaviour. But (as some Stoics must have been aware)[168] no body of rules could ever be formulated with such particularity as to fit exactly all the infinitely varied situations in which humans find themselves. The impossibility of arriving at a complete set of rules was logically tied to the impossibility of omniscience, even for a wise man: if such a set were to be attainable, the wise man would certainly have known it; and if there were rules for every situation, the doctrines would be rendered useless. One could therefore establish different rules for a series of typical situations. For example, rules for anyone who married a woman who had not been married before or for anyone who had to marry a widow, as is envisaged in Sen. *Ep.* 94.15. But it would have been easier (and would be even easier nowadays) to imagine almost infinite variations on each of these two situations, and to object that one could never define as many rules as there were different situations[169] in which anyone who was about to marry could find himself:

> We cannot embrace all kinds of case, even if each demands its own set of precepts . . . and I would add that the precepts of wisdom must be definite and certain; things which cannot be defined are outside the sphere of wisdom. (Sen. *Ep.* 94.15-16)

So despite the rules which the *prokoptōn* would have known and assimilated, a situation would sooner or later occur in which he would have to make a decision without a precise criterion of behaviour, and rely instead on as much rational consistency as he had reached at that time thanks to his grasp of the doctrines. But was this not tantamount to leaving very dangerous areas of uncertainty open to the *prokoptōn*? According to what Cicero reports (*Off.* 1.9, III.7) Panaetius had in his writing on appropriate actions separated out three possible objects of deliberation: (1) whether an action is correct or base; (2) whether it is useful; (3) how to judge in cases where correct action *seems*[170] to be in conflict with expediency. It seems obvious that a pretty moderate knowledge of the principal Stoic doctrines could help to resolve those cases which fell into the first two categories. Knowledge that virtue and vice are contradictory opposites, that the good is what is useful or something not different from what is useful,

---

[168] Cf. Sen. *Ep.* 94.15-16 (Aristo?) and also 51, 95.5.

[169] Here Stoicism seems very close to Aristotle; see for example *EN* II.9, especially 1109a24-30, 1109b 14-23.

[170] An important qualification: only virtue can be 'advantageous'; there can be no genuine conflict with what is useful. Cf. Cic. *Off.* 1.9, III.7.

and that virtue, virtuous actions and virtuous men satisfy this description; that only through virtue is it possible to achieve happiness: these are ideas which aid the resolution of those cases of uncertainty that fall under (1) and (2). But the real problem must have been posed by the third category, and in fact Cicero (*Off.* III.7–10) says that Panaetius never wrote the study he had promised. Some scholars suppose[171] he did not write it because he was put off by the difficulty of the problem.

It is difficult to say why Panaetius abandoned his project. But we should not think the Stoics never had any suggestions to make regarding cases of conflict between interests and values. What is doubtful is whether they reached any clean decision. For example, as to the basic notion of 'appropriate actions' a distinction was introduced between 'appropriate actions regardless of circumstances' and 'appropriate actions dependent on circumstances':[172]

> Some appropriate actions do not depend on circumstances, but others do. The following do not depend on circumstances, looking after one's health, and one's sense organs, and such like. Appropriate actions which do depend on circumstances are mutilating oneself and disposing of one's property. And so analogously with actions which are contrary to appropriate action. (D.L. VII.108–9, trans. after Long and Sedley)

This is tantamount to saying[173] that taking care of one's health is something generally appropriate without there being any need to specify the circumstances in which it is so; while self-mutilation is in no way an appropriate action (and is indeed contrary to the natural impulse of self-preservation), but could become appropriate in certain specific circumstances. It is true that the problem would then become one of specifying the circumstances in which self-mutilation becomes appropriate, and that it is impossible to establish these in their totality in advance: the rules would not state the right moment, the how and the why, or up to what point (Sen. *Ep.* 95.5). What can be acknowledged is an attempt on the part of the Stoics to delineate criteria for the resolution of such conflicts.

Some have already been mentioned, for example, the superiority of spiritual values over material interests and the different distinctions which one can make among the indifferents.[174] One important criterion, mentioned by Cicero (*Fin.* III.64), ruled that the common interest should be put before personal advantage; but even the reference to general interests had

---

[171] See Striker 1991, 47.   [172] Cf. N. P. White 1978.
[173] Cf. Engberg-Pedersen 1990, 137–8 and Boys-Stones 1996, 85–6.
[174] Cf. above, pp. 692, 695. On conflicting values, see also Striker 1991, 44–50.

its ambiguities, which could have been exploited by unsympathetic critics of Stoicism.[175] However, even if one has to admit that the Stoics were in no position to specify rules or criteria that could resolve the issue in any situation of conflict whatever, one can nevertheless concede that the inter-action of their precepts with the teaching of basic doctrines equipped humanity reasonably well for most normal situations in life, and helped the *prokoptōn* to take decisions which corresponded to appropriate actions. In one important text (*Diss.* II.6.9)[176] where Epictetus quotes or para-phrases Chrysippus, the suggested rule ('always cling to what is better suited to getting that which accords with nature') is immediately justified by appealing to the place of human choice in the providential scheme of cosmic nature – or of divine will, which is the same thing: 'for God himself made me such as to select these things'. Anyone who knows the rule and its cosmic and teleological foundation; anyone who, moreover, takes account of the limiting clause with which Chrysippus introduces the rule ('as long as the consequences are unclear to me': an allusion to the deterministic framework within which future developments are pre-ordained, but also usually unknown to the agent, even to a wise man); anyone who knows all this will also know that Stoic philosophy authorizes him, in normal circumstances, to follow his own personal interests, to defend and to pro-mote his own wellbeing.

So Stoicism was never a philosophy of sacrifice and self-denial. That explains its success among the Roman aristocracy, a class not consisting solely of generous benefactors. Chrysippus even more explicitly (Cic. *Off.* III.42) authorizes participation in competition for material gain, and also guarantees the lawfulness of private property (Cic. *Fin.* III.67). The only conditions which he imposed were those which demanded honest compe-tition – which would nowadays seem rather imprecise and compatible with a completely *laissez-faire* attitude, not acceptable to supporters of public intervention in cases of social and economic conflict. Here it would have been opportune to supply a solution to the disagreement possible between legal obligations and moral requirements, a disagreement which the Stoics apparently recognized rather clearly, as witness the debate (probably invented by Cicero) between Diogenes of Babylon and Antipater.[177] Such a solution seems not to have been found. Yet it would be wrong to accuse Stoicism of not measuring up to such difficulties; and the conditions stipulated by Chrysippus in the Cicero passage must sim-

---

175 On this subject see Inwood 1984, 182–3, Atkins 1990, 275–7 and also below, p. 765.
176 See above, p. 693.
177 See Cic. *Off.* III.50–7, 91–2., with Annas 1989a. See also below, p. 765.

ply have led to the limiting clause specified in the Epictetus text: 'as long as the consequences are unclear'.

*

The Stoics were not the first philosophers to tackle the problem of the moral permissibility of suicide. Plato was in principle against it,[178] though not without some ambiguities which could be exploited to support exceptions; but the Cynics had permitted it, though they did not accord the matter much importance. Nor does it seem that even the Stoics paid much attention to it; the glorification of suicide as the supreme and perhaps only act of freedom on man's part is a peculiarity of Seneca,[179] which has no parallel in the previous tradition. But the case of suicide is nonetheless important for the interpretation of Stoic moral thought, since the difficulties encountered in trying to establish rules suitable for all occasions are particularly evident here.

There is some agreement among the sources in attributing to the Stoics the recognition that 'sometimes' (Cic. *Fin.* III.60; Stob. II.110.9) it could be an appropriate action for a man to take his own life; but there is also a certain reticence, at least in some formulations,[180] to admit that such a possibility is also valid for the non-wise. In the text where there is the most explicit recognition of the permissibility of suicide even for the non-wise a formal rule is proposed which is to decide in what situations it becomes acceptable for everyone to abandon life:

When a man has a preponderance of the things in accordance with nature, the appropriate action for him is remaining alive; when he has or foresees a preponderance of their opposites, the appropriate action is to depart from life. This clearly shows that it is sometimes an appropriate action both for the wise man to depart from life, although he is happy, and for a fool to remain alive, although he is wretched . . . The primary natural things, whether favourable or adverse, fall under the wise man's decision and choice, forming as it were the material of wisdom. Therefore, the reason for remaining in and departing from life is to be measured by those things . . . even for fools, who are wretched, remaining alive is plainly the appropriate action if they have a preponderance of

---

[178] *Phd.* 61c–62c, *Leg.* 873c–d. On the Cynics, see D.L. VI.24, 86 and on the whole subject, Rist 1969a, 233–55 and Cooper 1989.

[179] For example, see *De Ira* III.15.3–4, *Prov.* 6.7, *Ep.* 77.14–15. On Seneca, see Griffin 1986 and Nussbaum 1994, 435–7.

[180] D.L. VII.130 speaks of the wise man; discussion by Rist 1969a, 239–42, Sandbach 1989 (1975), 49n. In the sources (especially *SVF* III 764–8) justifiable suicide is constantly qualified by the adjective *eulogos*, which is also applied to the reasonableness of appropriate actions, not just those performed by the wise man.

the things we call in accordance with nature. (Cic. *Fin.* III.60–1, trans. Long and Sedley)

So, it would seem, both the wise man and the fool had well-founded reasons to commit suicide, if they found that they were undergoing intolerable suffering from an incurable illness (D.L. VII.130) or extreme poverty (*SVF* III 768). In such conditions, it might seem sensible to grant to the non-wise also that the appropriate action would be to take their own lives. What is disputable,[181] perhaps, is whether such a utilitarian calculus of gains and losses, to be computed before making a decision, is congruent with the basic assumptions of Stoicism. But there is no reason to think that the rule recorded by Cicero[182] constituted the sum total of Stoic opinion about the problem: other accounts clearly mention the rationality of a suicide motivated by altruistic considerations (D.L. VII.130) or by the desire to avoid immoral actions which might be imposed upon the subject by force (*SVF* III 768). All this may perhaps indicate that in the course of Stoic history there were variations in the method of confronting and evaluating the problem; but it certainly shows that there was no *one* Stoic rule, single and precise, for settling the question. It seems more likely that the (different) conditions mentioned in the sources were meant only as examples of typical situations whose relevance to actual cases was to be decided by the agent.

XI Determinism and ethics: impulse with reservation

We have seen that under conditions normal for human beings, who are usually unaware of what the future will bring, Stoicism authorizes every agent to seek to follow 'things in accord with nature', and this is because it is God who has made men inclined towards this kind of choice. But the failures which very often follow the choices show that it was not really in accord with divine will that the objective should be reached. Besides, Chrysippus himself, according to the text of Epictetus we have several times relied on, continues his line of reasoning as follows:

> But if I knew it were my destiny to fall ill now, my impulse would directly turn itself towards it; and my foot, if it had the intelligence, would have the impulse to cover itself with mud. (Epict. *Diss.* II.6.9)[183]

---

[181] And discussed in Long and Sedley 1987, I.428 (but see, contra, Cooper 1989, 27–9).

[182] Corroborated by Plutarch; see e.g. *Stoic. Rep.* 1042c–d, *Comm. Not.* 1063d.

[183] On the meaning of the last phrase, see Sandbach 1989 (1975), 36. Voelke 1973, 71–2, compares *Diss.* II.10.5–6.

But the fact is that nobody who feels well knows that he is destined to fall ill now; so any sensible person tries to stay healthy. On the other hand, Chrysippus himself had stated, in commenting on his definition of the *telos*, that virtue and happiness occur when all actions are performed in such a way as to keep the *daimōn* located within a man (the soul, or its ruling part) in line with the divine will which governs the All (D.L. VII.88). How is it therefore possible to keep in line with the divine will, as required by Chrysippus, when with everything – or almost everything – that one does it is unknown whether it corresponds to that will? Because the moral duty imposed on the agent must not turn out impossible or contradictory, Chrysippus and Stoicism needed to be able to show a method of selection which would respect both the human inclination to follow things which conform to nature, and the divine will on which the attainment of those objects depended. And this had to be achieved without attributing special capacities for divination[184] either to the common man or to the wise man. This apparently impossible task was performed in Stoicism by the idea of 'impulse with reservation', which Stobaeus describes thus:

> They say that nothing happens to the good man which is contrary to his inclination (*orexis*) or his impulse or his intention, on account of the fact that he does everything of this kind with a reservation (*hupexhairesis*), and nothing which he would not want can happen unexpectedly. (Stob. II.115.5–9)

The concept is further clarified by Seneca:

> The wise man sets about every action with reservation: 'if nothing happens which might stop him'. For this reason we say that he always succeeds and that nothing unexpected happens to him: because within himself he considers the possibility that something will get in the way and prevent what he is proposing to do. (Sen. *Ben.* IV.34.4)

So if a person[185] acts for the sake of things which conform to nature, but always with the interior reservation that he does what he does subject to conformity with divine and natural order, and with the presumption that the outcome could also be adverse, he is in a position to control the impulses which move him to act, staying within the limits of reason and avoiding surrender to the excessive and rebellious impulses which are the

---

[184] Or without advising constant recourse to diviners, which is not suggested by any of the sources. The Stoics did, however, admit the fallibility of human prediction: Cic. *Div.* 1.124–5.

[185] Both Stobaeus and Seneca talk of the wise man, but it is evident that he serves as a model for all humanity. See also the continuation of the argument in Sen. *Ben.* IV.35.

passions. Impulse with reservation is precisely the opposite of 'excessive' impulse which Stoic philosophy defines as passion; and it is the instrument whereby the assent given to propositions which commit the agent to a future course of action remains consistent with rational cosmic design – which might already have established that such an action would not be completed, or not have the outcome expected by the agent. In this way the agent could try to obtain the results he wanted while maintaining harmony with the general order of the cosmos. It was as if everyone were to act repeating to himself the words of Cleanthes:

> Lead me, Zeus and Destiny, wherever you have ordained for me. For I shall follow unflinching. But if I become bad and unwilling, I shall follow none the less. (Epict. *Ench.* 53, trans. Long and Sedley)

The problem under discussion seems to have been the only one which in the eyes of the Stoics required an ethical treatment related to their general deterministic physics and teleology. What would probably seem to us an obvious problem – the question of autonomy and human responsibility – must have remained unrecognized by them as a real or legitimate issue, since not one of the three manuals of Stoic ethics which have survived from ancient times in a nearly complete form take the slightest notice of it. The Stoics agreed to discuss it only in order to respond to the arguments of their opponents, who were at first principally the Academics, then, in Roman times, the Peripatetics and the Platonists; but they did not give it space in their ethical expositions. Moreover, it seems they began to take it into consideration only from Chrysippus onwards: there is no compelling evidence of a clear assessment of the problem by Zeno and Cleanthes.[186]

The objections put forward against Stoicism are, essentially, three in number. It was asserted that in a fully deterministic universe, as the Stoics conceived it, (1) human initiative and action became useless, because things would happen as they had to happen; (2) that nothing remained 'in man's power', nothing was 'dependent on him' any more; and (3) that responsibility and blame, punishments and rewards, condemnations and commendations would no longer make any sense. Most of the Stoic responses to these objections were closely tied to the conception of causality unique to the school, and have been examined in another part of this volume (see pp. 526–40).

[186] So Long and Sedley 1987, I.392. But see the story about Zeno in D.L. VII.23.

22

Social and political thought

MALCOLM SCHOFIELD

I Introduction

Hellenistic political philosophy has had a bad press.[1] In lectures published in 1983 the distinguished and influential ancient historian Moses
Finley gave it as his view that Plato and Aristotle 'were the first genuine
political theorists of antiquity, and the last'. For only they attempted 'a
complete and coherent account' of the ideal society 'grounded in systematic metaphysics, epistemology, psychology and ethics'.[2] Some thirty
years earlier, in what remains an eminently serviceable general account of
Greek political thought, T. A. Sinclair wrote as follows:[3]

> Looking back over the political thought of the third century BC one can-
> not help being struck with its barrenness. This is of course due in part to
> the decline in the *polis* and in part to the loss of contemporary writings
> on the subject. But it is also due to the refusal or inability to relate polit-
> ical thinking to the material conditions in which men lived. Epicurus
> and Chrysippus did their best to help men to face life cheerfully, but the
> men whom they helped were the few, who had sufficient education to
> understand their message and sufficient leisure for lessons in philosophy.

Finley and Sinclair are only echoing a long entrenched judgement which
finds a classic formulation in the third volume of Zeller's great history of
Greek philosophy, first published in 1852. For Zeller the Hellenistic
period found the Greeks coping with a deterioration in their external
circumstances, and particularly with loss of political self-determination as
the monarchies of Alexander's successors eclipsed the city-state, by with-
drawing into the inner world of self-consciousness. Philosophy facilitated
and responded to this development by turning away from theory to practical concerns and by divorcing morals from politics.[4] Zeller's story was
not original with him. It is a simplified version of the relevant parts of

---

[1] Best comprehensive study: Aalders 1975; useful collection of texts in E. Barker 1956.
[2] Finley 1983, 124.   [3] Sinclair 1951, 261.   [4] Zeller 1909, 12–26.

Hegel's rich and powerful dialectical philosophy of history and history of philosophy, according to which the characteristic philosophies of the Hellenistic era, and Stoicism in particular, express the alienation of political impotence, and indeed the transition from *Sittlichkeit* and the oneness of man with community to *Moralität* and the emergence of the *individual* moral agent.

This complex of fact, pseudo-fact and interpretation is what in one version or another sustains the prevailing climate of opinion about Hellenistic political and social thought. Many of its elements will not stand careful scrutiny, as will become clear as this chapter progresses. But the only real hope of displacing it is to construct a convincing alternative picture.

II An overview

One cause of the impression that political philosophy in the Hellenistic period was in decline is, as Sinclair suggests, the simple fact that most of what was written is now lost. Often we have nothing but the title of a treatise, or information about one or two details in a work which may throw little or no light on its general character. Yet the volume of writings on political themes in the Stoa and the Lyceum, at any rate, was evidently considerable. A rapid survey may be the best way to make the point.

Plutarch begins his essay on Stoic self-contradictions with the charge that although the leading early Stoics wrote a great deal on themes in political philosophy – 'form of government (*politeia*), being ruled and ruling, judging, using oratory' – none of them took up the responsibilities of political life (*Stoic. Rep.* 1033 bc). He could also have mentioned titles such as *On Law* (attested for Zeno, Chrysippus and Sphaerus), *On City and Law* (Chrysippus), *On Concord* (Chrysippus: a work which evidently used the pseudo-Platonic *Cleitophon* to elaborate Zeno's ideas), *On Laws* and *The Statesman* (Cleanthes), and *On Kingship* (Cleanthes, Persaeus, Sphaerus). Zeno's associate Persaeus wrote a critique of Plato's *Laws* in seven books and a *Spartan Constitution*, and Stoic preoccupation with Sparta was sustained in the next generation by Sphaerus (adviser to Cleomenes III) in his *On Lycurgus and Socrates*, in three books, and *On the Spartan Constitution*.[5] But it would hardly have suited Plutarch's purposes to refer to Persaeus and Sphaerus, whose role as court philosophers was well known.

---

[5] Evidence on titles: Zeno, D.L. VII.4; Persaeus, D.L. VII.36; Cleanthes, D.L. VII.175; Sphaerus, D.L. VII.178; Chrysippus, Plu. *Stoic. Rep.* 1037f, Marc. *Inst.* 1.11.25 [*On Law*], Athen. 267b [*On Concord*], Phld. *Stoic* (*PHerc.* 155 and 339, col. 15.26–7) [*On City and Law*]. Contrary views on the extent of Stoic influence on Spartan politics of the third century BC are offered e.g. by Tigerstedt 1974 (sceptical) and Erskine 1990 (sanguine).

The Spartan orientation of much of this writing reminds us that the most famous advocate in antiquity of a Lycurgan or mixed constitution, represented as the original Spartan model, was a thinker of the early Hellenistic period, Aristotle's pupil Dicaearchus, author, for example, of a *Constitution of the Spartans* as well as the *Tripoliticus*, the work which probably contained the principal statement of his position.[6] Among other Peripatetics it is a safe conjecture that no philosopher in antiquity wrote more extensively on political themes than Theophrastus. We hear of treatises on, for example, politics (in six books), political customs (in four), politics for critical moments (also in four), and a collection of laws in twenty-four books, as well as shorter works on e.g. tyranny, kingship and the best constitution. His student Demetrius of Phaleron, who became a leading figure in Athenian politics, also wrote a great deal on the subject. Until the Lyceum sank into relative obscurity after Strato, himself the author of *On Kingship* and *On Lives*, politics was evidently an absorbing interest of the school both in theory and in practice.[7]

Cicero in writing to his Epicurean friend Atticus refers at one point to a notorious disagreement between Dicaearchus and Theophrastus on whether the active or the contemplative life is to be preferred (*Att.* II.16.3). This dispute indicates something of the intellectual climate in which Epicurus wrote a treatise in four books on the choice of lives (*On Lives*). The information that the Cynic way of life was rejected in this work gives a clue to another element in the background to it (shared with Zeno's *Republic*). Epicurus' advocacy of the 'quiet' life in *On Lives* was in turn a target of Chrysippus' *On Lives*, likewise in four books, which envisaged an active, public mode of existence for the wise man. But in Epicurus' extant writings the leading political ideas are those relating to law and justice. And of all the writings of Chrysippus which fall within the scope of this chapter, probably none was more important to the author or to posterity than a sequence of treatises on justice, a topic which from the Sophists and Plato onwards was at the heart of Greek philosophical thought about the *polis* and society.[8]

---

[6] The *Tripoliticus* (Cic. *Att.* XIII.32, Athen. 141a–c) is in fact often taken to be the same work as the *Constitution* (Suda *s.v.* Dicaearchus). For discussion see e.g. Rawson 1969, 82–3. Dicaearchus' position: Phot. *Bibl.* 37. Standard modern work on ancient theories of the mixed constitution: Aalders 1968.

[7] Evidence on titles: Theophrastus, D.L. v.42–50; Strato, D.L. v.59–60; Demetrius, D.L. v.80–1. Cf. Cic. *Leg.* III.14.

[8] Epicurus *On Lives*: D.L. x.28,119; Chrysippus *On Lives*: four books, Plu. *Stoic. Rep.* 1043a; advocates political activity, D.L. VII.121; rejection of Epicurean view, Plu. *Stoic. Rep.* 1033d. A general study of the genre: Joly 1956. Chrysippus' writings on justice; Plu. *Stoic. Rep.* 1040a–1041e; other references collected in *SVF* III p.195.

III On kingship

Treatises *On Kingship* have been mentioned more than once among the titles listed in section II. Given the dominance of monarchies in the Hellenistic world, and the elaborate ideology of kingship associated with them, the likely contents of works bearing this title have been the focus of considerable speculation. Speculation it has had to be, since no extant example of the genre has survived from the period covered by this volume. There are extracts preserved in Stobaeus from a number of treatises ascribed to Pythagorean authors which have sometimes been regarded as Hellenistic productions, notably writings on kingship attributed to Diotogenes, Ecphantus, and Sthenidas. But the most authoritative research on this and similar pseudonymous material indicates a middle Platonist milieu and a date around the turn of the first and second centuries AD.[9]

Our best evidence for the character of Hellenistic kingship treatises comes from two documents, one dating from the second century BC, probably its first half, but sometimes put as late as 100 BC, the other at least thirty years after that. The earlier is a curious account of how the Greek translation of the Pentateuch was made, purporting to have been composed by a Greek official called Aristeas from the court of Ptolemy Philadelphus (283–246 BC), and known as the *Letter of Aristeas*. The section of the book which concerns us (sections 187–294) explains that each of the seventy-two wise translators was asked in turn a different question by Ptolemy. It sets out all the questions together with the answers they received. Much of the material concerns the proper conduct of kingship in particular or government in general. There is nothing much in the way of argument, and the sequence of topics seems largely haphazard. Despite some theological emphases reflecting the author's Judaism, it is generally agreed that he draws on Greek, and therefore presumably mostly earlier Hellenistic, sources, although the question–answer format is probably his own contribution.[10] The other document is preserved in a fragmentary condition among the Herculaneum papyri: an essay by Philodemus, dedicated to his patron L. Calpurnius Piso, entitled *On the Good King according to Homer* (*PHerc.* 1507). As the title indicates, Philodemus illustrates from Homer the qualities and behaviour proper to a king. The themes he

---

[9] Ideology of kingship: see e.g Sinclair 1951, ch.XIV, Walbank 1984 (with further bibliography); Pythagorean treatises: Stob. *Ecl.* IV.6.22, 7.64 (Ecphantus), 7.61–2 (Diotogenes), 7.63 (Sthenidas), also available in Thesleff 1965; the most authoritative research: Delatte 1942, supplemented by Burkert 1972, Centrone 1990, Squilloni 1991 (contra e.g. Thesleff 1961, 1972).   [10] See further Murray 1967, Fraser 1972, I.696–703, II.970–82.

chooses no doubt reflect the emphases of earlier Hellenistic writing on kingship, even if the Homeric variations are his own.[11]

These two writings tell the reader what is the function of a king and how fundamental virtue and *self*-rule are to all his behaviour, and they pronounce on many specific spheres of regal conduct or interest: worship of the gods, choice and use of friends, treatment of the citizens, warfare, leisure, daily life, decision making, legislation. The king must rule justly and promote peace, and in particular he must exhibit such qualities as humanity (*philanthrōpia*), forbearance (*epieikeia*) and gentleness (*prāotēs*, *hēmerotēs*), widely attested elsewhere as key ingredients in the ideology of Hellenistic rulers fostered both by them and their subjects. This is all reminiscent of the advice which fills most of the pages of for example, Isocrates' *To Nicocles*. Like Isocrates, Aristeas and Philodemus are offering the sort of edification characteristic of the later 'mirror of princes'. *To Nicocles* is not a work of theory: no more are the *Letter* and *On the Good King*. In particular, they resemble Isocrates' treatise in offering no theoretical discussion of the different forms of government and their comparative merits, nor any defence of kingship as the best constitution.[12]

Despite the hazards of argument from silence, it seems not unlikely that many of the treatises *On Kingship* ascribed to Hellenistic philosophers (Epicurus among them: D.L. x.28) were of this same character. Our almost total absence of information about their contents itself suggests that a Stoic or Epicurean work on kingship was not the place to look for major or distinctive statements on issues of philosophical importance, but only for variations on stock themes inherited from *To Nicocles* and similar writings.[13] This conjecture is reinforced if as seems likely some at least of the Hellenistic *On Kingship* treatises were addressed to monarchs, as Philodemus' treatise was dedicated to a leading Roman senator: Persaeus spent much of his life at the court of Antigonus Gonatas in Macedon, and Sphaerus acted as adviser to Cleomenes III of Sparta.[14] There is in fact no

---

[11] See further Murray 1965, Dorandi 1982a, Gigante 1995, ch.4.

[12] Nor is concern that a king observe the law (something *Letter* 279 certainly enjoins) given prominence, although this is a key theme of the treatment of Egyptian kingship by the very early Hellenistic savant Hecataeus of Abdera, summarized in the history of Diodorus Siculus (especially 1.69–71). See further Murray 1970. The idea of the king as *nomos empsuchos*, 'living law', is not found until later, principally in the pseudo-Pythagorean literature.

[13] The evidence for early Stoicism contains surprisingly little discussion of any kind about kingship. Erskine 1990, ch. 3, can even argue (wrongly) that Stoic thought 'inclined towards democracy'. For Epicureanism see Fowler 1989, 129–33, who convincingly rebuts attempts to interpret the school as favouring monarchy.

[14] 'Demetrius of Phalerum advised King Ptolemy to read the books dealing with kingship and leadership: the advice their friends don't like to give kings is written in these books' (ps.-Plu. *Apophthegm.*189d).

good evidence that either Epicurus or the early Stoics *anywhere* took a
stand on the comparative merits of the different constitutions or on the
claims of kingship (such claims as are advanced, e.g. in Hdt. III.82 or Isoc.
Nicocles 14–26 [a companion piece to *To Nicocles*], and a little after our
period in Cic. *Rep.* 1.56–64). One notorious text admittedly makes
Stoicism favour a *mixed* constitution (D.L. VII.131) along the same lines as
Polybius or Cicero; and it might appear tempting to connect this with the
attention Persaeus and Sphaerus devoted to the Spartan constitution. But
if as is likely their thinking was governed by the principles of Zeno's
Republic, Sparta will have impressed them more by the concord, freedom
and security which allegedly flowed from the virtue fostered by equal
property and communal living arrangements (cf. Plb. VI.48.2–3, with
Athen. 561c).[15] If the Stoics did come to favour the idea of the mixed constitution, this development should be dated to the time of the revisionist
Panaetius.[16] In any event, neither they nor the Epicureans appear to have
supplied Hellenistic monarchs with a philosophical defence of the institution of kingship.

IV Polybius on the growth and decline of constitutions

The longest essay in political theory to survive more or less intact from the
Hellenistic period is preserved in the extensive remains of Book VI of
Polybius' *Histories*.[17] Polybius was no philosopher himself. But he draws
on a variety of philosophical sources, some still identifiable, some not, to
produce a striking exercise in constitutional analysis. The analysis has two
main components: first the idea that constitutions flourish and then decay
according to a natural cyclical pattern; second the notion that a mixed
constitution, such as at Sparta or in contemporary Rome (i.e. the mid-sec-
ond century BC), has the strength to resist decline much longer than any
other. Polybius is interested here in the *polis*, not in huge Hellenistic king-
doms; it seems scarcely an accident that his focus is the one major contemporary state that was a republic, not a monarchy. The surviving parts of
Book VI do not contain material in which he worked out the details of the
application of his cyclical scheme to the special case of Rome. But there

---

[15] Cf. e.g. Griffin 1976, 203–4.

[16] This conjecture has become the standard modern view: see e.g. Aalders 1975, 100–2, Long and
Sedley 1987, vol. II, 429. Cf. Cic. *Fin.* IV.79.

[17] Detailed analysis by Walbank 1957, 635–63 (cf. also Walbank 1972, ch.5); subsequent discussion of sources by Cole 1964 and 1967; a good brief account of the theoretical content by
Aalders 1975, 105–12; a full and persuasive treatment by Trompf 1979, ch. 1.

can be no doubt that the point of introducing and expounding the scheme was principally to explain the durability of Rome's success as the dominant power in the Mediterranean world, particularly by comparison with Sparta and Carthage, another city which had (or had had) a mixed constitution according to his account.[18] And it is not difficult to divine at least the broad outlines of the cyclical version of Roman history that Polybius must have had in mind.

We should start where Polybius himself begins, with classification of constitutional forms. A key claim of his is that the popular tripartite division – kingship, aristocracy, democracy – is a mistake (vi.3.5–12). These are neither the only forms nor the best. The best is the mixed or Lycurgan constitution: conceived along Dicaearchan lines as a blend of kingship (represented at Rome by the consuls), aristocracy (the senate) and democracy (the *populus*). And there are also what Aristotle would have called deviations corresponding to each of the simple forms:

> It is by no means every monarchy which we should call straight off *kingship*, but only that which is voluntarily accepted, and governed by rational judgement rather than fear and force. Nor again should every oligarchy be considered *aristocracy*, but that which is presided over, on the basis of a selection, by the justest and wisest men. Similarly we should not count as *democracy* a system of government *(sustēma)* in which the whole populace has authority to do whatever it wishes and proposes: but where it is traditional and customary to reverence the gods, honour parents, respect older people, and obey the laws – when in systems of government of that sort the decision of the majority prevails, this we should call *democracy*.[19] (Plb. vi.4.2–5)

Polybius illustrates his idea of a cycle by specifying a typical pattern of 'revolution' *(anakuklōsis)* into which he fits the growth and decline of each of the unmixed forms of good constitution.[20] Kingship is born from monarchy and declines into its deviant form, tyranny, which supplies the conditions for the rise of aristocracy, destined in its turn to degenerate into oligarchy. From oligarchy democracy will in due course emerge and then in due course change into mob rule, creating once again the conditions for monarchy.

---

[18] See especially vi.9.10–14; cf. vi.48–57 for the comparisons with Sparta and Carthage.

[19] Notice the systematic coupling of moral with strictly constitutional provisions: the twin criteria of consent and rational rule in the case of kingship, the requirement that an aristocracy be elected, and the insistence that for a democracy popular sovereignty is not enough – as indeed Aristotle thought, although he made concern for the common good, not control by a moral majority, the extra desideratum.

[20] vi.4.7–9.9. Cf. Ryffel 1949, Walbank 1957, 643–8, Trompf 1979, ch. 1.

'This', says Polybius (VI.9.10) 'is the cycle of constitutions, this is the dispensation of nature by which constitutions change and are transformed and once again return to themselves.' As in Polybius' Greek, I have employed biological metaphors to articulate the theory. But he grounds it in what he claims is a quite general law of nature. *Everything* is subject to natural and necessary decay into its opposite, or more specifically 'into the bad condition that is proprietary to it and follows upon it naturally' (VI.10.2). This is true not just of biological organisms but of iron and timber, subject as these are respectively to rust and to inbred pests (VI.10.3).[21] The most interesting feature of Polybius' political theory is his identification of a specific kind of natural necessity governing the flourishing and corruption of constitutional forms. He works out his explanation in terms of social psychology.[22] The general pattern is as follows. A good constitution comes into being when, compelled by fear of a common danger, humans use their intelligence and experience in disciplined co-operation to achieve communal security. But over a period security breeds complacency, which brings about a collective amnesia and indiscipline that encourages indulgence of individual passions and appetites and excesses in behaviour – and ultimately ensures despotic rule of one sort or another, whether by a tyrant or a junta or a mob. Polybius applies this scheme to each in turn of the three episodes which constitute his example of a typical cycle (kingship/tyranny; aristocracy/oligarchy; democracy/mob rule), with appropriate variations in the details.

There is much here that is reminiscent of earlier political philosophy. The general notion of 'change of constitutions' (*metabolē politeiōn*) is, as Polybius himself suggests, familiar from Plato's *Republic*, as is the decision to couch explanations of such change in psychological terms. We may also be reminded of Herodotus: as well as a verbal echo at the very end of Book VI,[23] the categories in which degeneration is explained – luxury, *hubris*, and consequent envy and hatred – are the same as Herodotus himself employed in constitutional analysis (III.80–2). But as we shall see in section v, it is evidently Epicureanism which suggests to Polybius his focus on communal danger and security, and the idea of articulating changing responses to them in terms principally of *social* psychology. Also Epicurean in many key features is the account he gives of the origins of civilization and the conversion of monarchy into kingship.[24]

---

[21] But corrupt conditions are not themselves subject to this law of corruption, for which cf. Plato *Rep.* x.608e–609a.   [22] See Hahm 1995.

[23] Freedom and democracy, he says sarcastically, have 'the fairest name of all' (57.9): cf. Hdt. III.80.6.

[24] But while Epicureans apparently believed that monarchy was the original form of rule (Lucr.

This part of the *anakuklōsis* story (VI.5.4–6.12) has more subtlety and intellectual content than the later phases. Its epistemological status is constantly stressed: Polybius is offering us a *probable* account, derived to begin with from analogy with animal behaviour.[25] Monarchy is the original form of rule, and represents an assertion of strength by the leader of the pack, which herds together owing to natural weakness. It evolves into kingship only when society is established and men are able to reflect rationally – something that distinguishes them from other animals – on each other's behaviour. They note with displeasure acts of ingratitude and recognize that in future they may themselves be victims of such conduct. This is the origin of the concept of justice: men acquire a sense of appropriate action (*kathēkon*).[26] Similarly, when they observe someone conspicuous in defence of the community, they conceive of the noble and the shameful: the one is imitated because it is advantageous, the other avoided because it is not. When a monarch governs his own conduct in accordance with the noble and the just so conceived, it is no longer fear of force but an approving recognition of his rational judgement which leads men to support and maintain his rule. Monarchy thereby graduates insensibly into kingship.

How is the mixed constitution of the Roman republic to be fitted into Polybius' story of the rise and fall of constitutions? Reflection on the limited scope of the law of nature to which his story appeals will suggest an answer. What that law states is simply that everything is necessarily corrupted into an opposite condition. There is no similar necessity attaching to the transition *from* a corrupt condition. Consider in particular the form of constitution one might expect to follow the overthrow of a tyrant. The leaders of the uprising which achieves it will doubtless play a dominant role in the next phase of political activity. But a pure form of aristocracy is not the only conceivable outcome, even if – as Polybius' paradigm indicated – it is the typical sequel. Another possibility is a mixed constitution, with democratic and regal as well as aristocratic features. And it appears that according to Polybius this is just what did follow the downfall of the Tarquins at Rome.[27]

Polybius' description of Lycurgus' comparable constitution at Sparta

v.1105–12), they saw the next stage as the invention of law under the influence of 'wise men': see the extracts from Hermarchus presented in section v (echoed at Lucr. v.1143–50).

[25] The emphasis on probability contrasts with the necessity of the natural law of corruption to which Polybius appeals elsewhere. Clearly that law cannot be used to explain the *rise* of kingship.

[26] An isolated echo of Stoic ethics.

[27] Cf. Trompf 1979, ch. 1. The main reason for ascribing this view to Polybius, other than its concinnity with the surviving fragments of Book VI, is that Cicero offers just such a version of Roman history in *Rep.* II.

reveals further reflection on the paradoxical dependence of security upon fear. The superiority of a mixed constitution derives from its institution-alization of fear: Polybius is apparently the inventor of the notion of a Machiavellian[28] internal 'balance' of fear:

> Lycurgus . . . did not make his constitution simple and uniform, but col-lected together all the virtues and distinctive characteristics of the best systems of government, so that no element should grow beyond what it ought and be perverted into its congenital vices. His aim was that, the force of each element being pulled back by another, none of them should tip the scales anywhere, still less pull the balance down a long way, but the system of government should remain for a long time in equipoise and equilibrium according to the principle of counteraction.[29] Kingship would be prevented from arrogance by fear of the populace, which was to be given a sufficient share in the constitution. The populace in turn would not venture to treat the kings with contempt from fear of the elders, who being chosen on the basis of selection on merit would all of them be sure to incline always to justice. Thus the part consisting of those who because of adherence to traditional customs were in danger of being diminished would always become greater and weightier, because of the inclination and gravitation of the elders. In consequence by draw-ing up his constitution in this way he preserved liberty for the Spartans for the longest period we have knowledge of. (Plb. VI.10.6–11)

Lycurgus is portrayed as a thinker who reasoned all this out on his own, and was then able – in undisclosed circumstances – to put his ideas into practice. The Romans achieved the same goal (cf. VI.18) 'not by reason, but by many struggles and troubles, always choosing the better solution as a result of the teaching of their reverses' (VI.10.14). The outcome is 'the finest of the constitutions of our time'. Polybius makes clear (even if he is diplomatic enough not to state outright) that it will in time inevitably dis-integrate in corruption. His own work is designed to furnish the analyti-cal basis on which observers may construct their prognostications (VI.3.1–4, 4.11–13, 57.4–10).

v Epicureanism on security

In the absence of any surviving treatise on political themes from Epicurus' own pen, we are obliged to search through his fragments and those of other early Epicureans, but especially the sayings and extracts collected in

---

[28] Cf. Machiavelli *Discorsi* I.1–7.
[29] Reading ἀντιπαθίας (Walbank) in place of ἀντιπλοίας MSS.

the *Kuriai Doxai*, for evidence of his views.[30] Readers have formed contrary impressions of the message which they contain. For many the keynote is Epicurus' advice that the life free from disturbance and anxiety is best pursued away from political activity and its temptations. In recent years some scholars have given more weight to the high positive evaluation in Epicureanism of the notion of a law-governed political community; and Epicurus' contractarian theory of justice has attracted particular attention.[31] But there is a further concept Epicurus deploys in his treatment of both these themes which supplies the clue to the motivation of all his social and political thinking: *security* (*asphaleia*), together with its verb equivalent *being confident* (*tharrein*).[32]

To get a first sense of the way reference to security works in the relevant texts we may begin with three remarks which between them cover the basic range of Epicurean concern with society. The first is quoted by Plutarch from the end of a book by Colotes:

> Those who put in order laws and customs and established kingship and government in cities brought life into a state of much security and tranquillity and banished turmoil. If anyone gets rid of these things, we shall live the life of the beasts, and one man on meeting another will practically devour him. (Plu. *Col.* 1124d)

But social security is not enough, as Epicurus himself insists at *KD* 13:

> There is no benefit in creating security with respect to men if things up above and things beneath the earth and generally things in the infinite cause apprehension.

Freeing men's minds from fear of death and the gods is of much greater importance than the achievement of security *vis-à-vis* other humans, as is to be inferred from the prominence accorded to the need for a proper view of the gods and the afterlife at the beginning of the *Letter to Menoeceus* and again the *Kuriai Doxai*. None the less personal fears and social security are closely connected subjects; the sort of thinking appropriate to the one is also apposite to the other:

---

[30] No use is made here of Lucretius v.925–1157. Its treatment of the origins and growth of civilization undoubtedly exploits authentic Epicurean material (with 1120–30 compare *KD* 7; with 1151–7 *KD* 35). But some of its key ideas are hard to square with e.g. Hermarchus', as when it attributes the two main phases of community-building to the softening (1011–23) and the exhaustion (1143–50) of human nature. Lucretius' interest in technology probably derives from non-Epicurean sources (cf. Cole 1967); and a distinctively Lucretian vantage-point can also be shown to be in evidence (cf. Furley 1978). See further Manuwald 1980, Schiesaro 1990.

[31] Major studies: Philippson 1910 (which already demonstrates that Epicurus had a political philosophy), Müller 1972, Goldschmidt 1977, Long 1986b, Mitsis 1988a, Alberti 1995.

[32] A study specifically devoted to Epicurus' concept of social security is Barigazzi 1983.

The same judgement that makes us confident on account of there being nothing terrible that lasts for ever, or even for long, also makes us perceive how security within these very determinations is especially perfected by friendship.[33] (*KD* 28)

This observation is not wholly perspicuous. The idea is perhaps that the same policy which inspires the imperative: 'Find a way to minimize the grounds of fear and anxiety', enables us to find in friendship a way to maximize the chances of pleasure and tranquillity. The personal and social dimensions of the policy are two sides of one coin.

'Security with respect to men' (*KD* 13) is an expression which in one variant or another recurs a number of times in the *Kuriai Doxai*. Thus *KD* 6 talks of the goal of 'being confident from men', which must be a derivative of 'security from men' (*KD* 7, 14: 'from' is plainly defensive), and is to be compared with 'being very confident from neighbours' (*KD* 40). It is 'security from men' that Colotes probably has chiefly in mind when he praises the work of the original law-givers. But we should not forget that the need for security against wild animals is made an important element in the account of the origins of law offered by Epicurus' successor Hermarchus.[34] Hermarchus is worth quoting *in extenso*, since the extract from him on this subject quoted by Porphyry is not only the longest early text on Epicurean social and political thought that we possess, but also affords an excellent insight into the central place of the concept of security within it.

*

An account of the structure of the key passage (Porph. *Abst.* 1.10–11) will provide a convenient framework for discussion of its treatment of security as the motivation, first for the formation of society in the first place, and then for the introduction of law subsequently:

> (1) In determining what we should and should not do, the first legislators had good reason for not prohibiting the destruction of any of the other animals [sc. apart from man]. For in their case advantage resulted from the opposite action. For self-preservation would not have been possible if men did not attempt to defend themselves [sc. against the animals] by virtue of a joint livelihood with each other.

---

[33] Reading φιλίᾳ (von der Muehll) for φιλίας (MSS) and κατειδέναι (Bollack) for κατεῖναι (MSS).

[34] Extracted from his *Against Empedocles*: see further Longo Auricchio 1988, Obbink 1988 (also Vander Waerdt 1988).

Section (1) is clear enough. It tells us that the first law givers did not forbid the killing of other animals (as they did homicide), since only by defending themselves against the beasts could men survive. The clause translated 'by virtue of a joint livelihood with one another' is a participial phrase which appears to suggest that a necessary means to self-defence was adoption of a communal form of human life. This theme will be pursued further in what follows.

> (2) Some of the finer minds of that time remembered distinctly that they themselves refrained from killing [sc. other men] on account of its usefulness for self-preservation (*sotēria*); and they produced in the rest a memory of what resulted [sc. from refraining from homicide] in their joint livelihood with each other, in order that by keeping their hands off their own kind they might safeguard the community, which contributed to the individual preservation of each person. Existing as a separate community and doing no harm to those gathered into the same place was useful not only for the expulsion of animals of other species but also against humans who turned up intent on harm.

What bearing does section (2) have on the main thesis of section (1)? It provides a first quick indication of how the desire for laws arose in the first place, and as such is a natural sequel not just to section (1) in our text but to the whole treatment of law in general and the law against homicide in particular summarized by Porphyry in the immediately preceding pages. Some of the 'finer minds' at the time of the initial institution of laws got people in general to remember something that had tended to become forgotten about the basis of society, namely that not killing one's neighbours is to one's *own* advantage, since that way the community will be best placed to defend itself against the animals and against hostile humans beyond its limits. This achievement of the 'finer minds' indicates the complexity of the Epicurean theory of social security. Security against wild animals and hostile human neighbours is the primary goal. But the community needed to promote it in turn requires a solidarity of purpose among fellow-citizens which is premissed on security against any hostile intentions *they* may have: hence in due course the introduction of law. Epicurus' 'security from men' presumably covers both neighbours and citizens. What social security consists in – to return to Hermarchus – is 'the individual preservation of each person', and his 'absence of fear', as section (3) will explain.

> (3) For a time, then, men for this reason kept their hands off their own kind – as many of them as entered into the same sharing of necessities and

provided services for each of the two purposes mentioned above. But as time went on, and interbreeding had forged ahead, and animals of other species had been extruded, and the scattering [of men apart from each other was a thing of long past],[35] some undertook a rational appraisal, not merely non-rational memory, of what was advantageous in their livelihood from each other. Consequently they tried to impose more secure restraints on those who were ready to kill each other and were weakening the capacity for defence because of their forgetfulness of the past. In trying to do this they introduced the legislation which still remains in force today among cities and peoples. The masses complied with their legislators voluntarily, as a result of having by now acquired more of a perception of what was advantageous in their collecting together with one another. For their absence of fear was promoted equally by the merciless killing of everything harmful and the preservation of every means to its destruction. Consequently, with good reason, one of the types of killing we have mentioned was forbidden, the other permitted.

Section (3) gives a fuller (although still sketchy) genetic account of the origin of law. A number of stages are identified. *First* is a period – doubtless beginning with the initial formation of societies – in which people refrained from homicide for the reason identified in (2). Other evidence suggests that this conduct was probably represented by Epicureans as a *natural* although rational response by primitive man to his surroundings.[36] The fear of animals and of attacks from other humans will have resulted in the spontaneous formation of communities for defensive purposes; and likewise a spontaneous mutual regard will have grown naturally among their members in these pressing circumstances. *Then* comes a period when 'forgetfulness of the past' sets in. The reasons for this are briefly and indeed cryptically expressed. They are apparently three in number: (a) interbreeding – presumably with members of other communities, diminishing the fear of other men beyond the limits of one's own community; (b) wild animals have been extruded – wolves, lions, etc. no longer dare to live near human settlements, attacks by them upon members of the community are infrequent, and so doubtless they are not so

---

[35] There are some obscurities in the text at this point. 'Interbreeding' translates τῆς δι' ἀλλήλων γενέσεως, otherwise rendered '[increase in] population' (Long and Sedley): an odd phrase either way, with the decision associated with the issue of whether fear of attack is regarded as blunted by kinship relations with potential enemies or by strength in numbers. Before or after 'the scattering' (τῆς παρασπάρσεως) some words must have dropped out: the supplement suggested here assumes that Hermarchus is envisaging a period before civilization when men had lived in scattered settlements (σποράδην, Plato *Prt.* 322ab, D.S. 1.8.1).

[36] Thus we may extrapolate from the general theory of human development and discovery sketched in Ep. *Hdt.* 75 and there applied to the example of language (*ibid.* 75–6; cf. Lucr. v.1028–90).

greatly feared either; (c) the pattern of scattered settlements which preceded the formation of communities is so distant in time as to recede from the memory. The consequence is a slackening of the commitment to the mutual interests of the community and in particular greater readiness to kill other members of it, so weakening its defensive capacity.

Finally, the intelligentsia, perceiving the dangers of this situation, make a rational appraisal of the advantages of community as represented in section (2), reinforcing and sharpening through reasoning a natural impulse dulled by the causes listed above. They succeed in getting most other members of the community to require a keener sense of these advantages, even though immediate fear of external attack is no less diminished. But the focus of Hermarchus' account is their invention of law, and with it a system of punishment for those unable to perceive the mutual benefits of community or unwilling to accept the constraints on behaviour which such a perception dictates. What is achieved by the introduction of laws, and above all by the law against homicide, is a formalized substitute for perception of mutual advantage and consequential self-restraint. Fear of the penalties attached to non-compliance likewise represents an efficacious alternative to the fear of the loss of common advantage which would be the outcome of rational appraisal. For Hermarchus the first legislators are evidently cultural heroes comparable with Epicurus himself, since law and its observance constitute a system of social security analogous to the prophylactic against fear of death and the gods provided by Epicurus' philosophy for the individual.

Hermarchus says nothing about justice in the passage we have been discussing. From the *Key Doctrines* 31–8 it becomes clear that Epicurus himself envisaged an intimate relation between law and justice. For justice is focused on mutual advantage, particularly that to be gained from an agreement to refrain from harm to others in the community provided they in their turn refrain from harming oneself:

> Nature's justice is a token[37] of advantage relating to not harming one another and not being harmed. (*KD* 31)

The predicate *just* appears to be applied primarily to laws, conceived as devised for mutual advantage. A law which achieves this purpose 'has the

---

[37] The Greek expression translated as 'token' is σύμβολον. It is sometimes taken to be equivalent to συνθήκη (*KD* 32 and 33), and translated 'pledge' etc. accordingly. But it is just *conduct* and the associated personal virtue of justice (δικαιοσύνη) which consists in or depends upon abiding by an agreement. Epicurus here means that when we call some outcome or arrangement 'just' (he uses the adjective δίκαιον) we simply have in mind the advantage that is secured when people refrain from mutual harm (cf. e.g. *KD* 36).

nature of the just' (*KD* 38) and 'fits the preconception' of the just (*KD* 38). It may achieve it at one time or place without doing so at others. Where and when it does not the law ceases to count as just.

The reference just made to agreement indicates a contractual basis to both justice (conceived now as a characteristic of persons) and law. A little later in the extract from Hermarchus preserved by Porphyry we learn that it is impossible to make contracts with other animals because they lack the rationality requisite for association of law: even if the *invention* of law is the work of intellectuals, its acceptance and observance depend on the mutual agreement of those who accept and observe it. And that agreement is what justice or fair conduct (*dikaiosunē*), as Epicurus explicates it, consists in:

> Justice was never anything *per se*, but something arising in people's joint livelihood with one another, in whatever places and whenever there is a contract about not harming or being harmed. (*KD* 33)

Epicurus strikes a palpably deflationary tone in his maxims on justice. Not merely is their focus mutual advantage. Justice is presented as nothing but a function of advantage. The implication is that philosophers like Plato who discuss justice as though it were an eternally valid independent ideal are pursuing a phantom. Epicurus' remarks about injustice have the same flavour:

> Injustice is not *per se* bad, but in the fear that arises from the suspicion that one will not escape the attention of those who have been given the authority to punish such things. (*KD* 34)

> No one who secretly infringes any of the terms of a contract people have made with one another relating to not harming and not being harmed can have the assurance that he will escape detection, even if he does so thousands and thousands of times. Right up to his death it is unclear whether he will in fact escape. (*KD* 35)

The free rider's problem is not infringement of an absolute standard nor even the likelihood of punishment, but the same affliction which Epicureanism constantly addresses: fear (*KD* 34), lack of assurance (*KD* 35), disturbance of mind (*KD* 17).

*

How close is Epicurus' conception of a contract not to harm others, provided they do not harm oneself, to the sort of sophistic theory of Hobbeist character developed in Glaucon's speech in Plato *Rep.* 358e–360e? It is sometimes represented that whereas Glaucon's theory makes man naturally aggressive, accepting the contract *faute de mieux*, Epicureanism makes him naturally oriented towards security, and so welcoming the contract as a means to his true goal. The wise man will certainly so orient himself (Usener 530):

> The laws exist for the sake of the wise, not that they may not do wrong, but that they may not suffer it.

But others will not, whether from a desire to make a pre-emptive strike or out of false conceptions of the good, as is indicated e.g. by Colotes' reference to the bestial life men would be reduced to if law and government were abolished (Plu. *Col.* 1124d, quoted above).[38]

Membership of a law-governed community provides protection against some basic threats to life and happiness. Epicurus suggests two further social strategies designed to reinforce the consequent sense of confidence. The first is indicated in *KD* 14:

> While security from men comes about to some degree by virtue of the power of expulsion, and through easy attainment [of necessities], the purest form of security comes about from tranquillity and withdrawal from the many.[39]

In the first part of this maxim Epicurus seems to refer to two of the fundamental features of communities identified by Hermarchus: they exist for defence and for 'the sharing of necessities'. The latter part introduces the famous Epicurean injunction to 'live unknown' (Plu. *An Recte* 1128a–1129b) and take no part in political life, as a dangerous business founded on a false view of how security is to be attained. This theme is frequently heard in the surviving evidence, as at *KD* 7:

> Some have wanted to become famous and respected, thinking that this way they would achieve security from men. If, then, the life of such persons is secure, they attain nature's good. But if it is not secure, they do not possess what – in line with what is natural – they desired in the first place.[40]

The second policy recommended by Epicurus complements the first. A private life, avoiding public notice, is not to be a life of solitude. We need

---

[38] Further discussion e.g. by Long and Sedley 1987, vol. I, 134–5, Mitsis 1988a, 79–97 *contra* e.g. Denyer 1983. For other questions relating to the justice of the wise man see Vander Waerdt 1987, Annas 1993a, 293–302.

[39] Reading with Arrighetti δυνάμει τε ἐξοριστικῇ καὶ εὐπορίᾳ εἰλικρινεστάτῃ: text problematic.

[40] There are a number of texts where Epicureans allow or appear to allow participation in politics in various circumstances: e.g. Plu. *Tranq. An.* 465f, Cic. *Rep.* 1.10, Sen. *De Otio* 3.2, D.L. x.121. A good brief discussion in Fowler 1989, 126–30.

friends: for the benefits friends perform, but much more for 'the assurance of their help' (*Sent. Vat.* 34). Whereas life would otherwise be 'full of
dangers and fear', the formation of friendship 'strengthens the mind' (Cic.
Fin. 1.66). Without friendship we are unable 'to hold on to a joy in life
which is steady and lasting' (*Fin.* 1.67). But although the prospect of security is what makes it rational to acquire friends, friendship would not be
friendship unless we loved our friends as much as we love ourselves
(*Fin.* 1.67–8): which may mean taking risks (*Sent. Vat.* 28) and suffering
pain (Plu. *Col.* 1111b) and even dying (D.L. x.121) on their behalf.
Utilitarianism requires us to be non-utilitarian.[41] The *Kuriai Doxai* ends
with a remark which is generally taken to sum up Epicurus' view of
friendship – and which will serve as a summary of his social philosophy:

> As many as had the power of acquiring being very confident from neigh-
> bours, these also lived in this way most pleasurably with each other [sc.
> being confident from each other, i.e. in relation to each other], having
> the firmest of pledges; and after having the fullest sense of identity with
> each other, they did not grieve over someone's untimely death as if it
> called for commiseration. (*KD* 40)

vi Zeno's *Republic*

If Epicurean social and political thought has clear affinities with the theories of the fifth-century Sophists, Stoic political philosophy begins in
implicit dialogue with Plato's *Republic*, as will emerge from consideration
of the longest single passage concerned with Zeno's *Republic* which survives.[42] The text in question is not a straightforward piece of doxography,
but an account of those elements in the work to which a sceptic called
Cassius objected:

> But there are some, including Cassius the Sceptic and his followers, who
> attack Zeno on many points. They say first (1), that at the beginning of
> the *Republic* he proves general education useless; second (2), that he says
> that all who are not good men are personal and public enemies, slaves,

---

[41] So interpreted Epicurus will intuitively have hit upon a paradoxical insight now associated
with rational choice theory: see e.g. Elster 1983 and 1984. If so, his thinking was too sophisticated for his successors, who developed associationist (*Fin.*III.69) and contractarian (*ibid.*70)
explanations of why we love our friends for their own sake. For more on the Epicurean theory
of friendship see above, pp. 667–9, and Bollack 1969, Mitsis 1988a, ch. 3, Annas 1993a, 236–44;
on its practice in Epicurean communities see e.g. Festugière 1985, ch.III, Frischer 1982, chs. I
and II, Clay 1983b.

[42] On Stoic political thought see in general Erskine 1990, Schofield 1991. Both have chapters
specifically devoted to Zeno's *Republic*, on which see also Baldry 1959, Dawson 1992, ch.4.
There is much discussion pertinent to Hellenistic Stoicism in Griffin 1976.

estranged from each other, parents from children, brothers from brothers, kin from kin, when – in the *Republic*, once again – he makes the good alone citizens and friends and kin and free (the result is that, on Stoic premisses, parents and children are at enmity: for they are not wise); (3) that he lays down the doctrine, likewise in the *Republic*, that women should be held in common, and (4) (in the 200s) that neither temples nor law-courts nor gymnasia should be built in cities; (5) that on coinage he writes as follows, that 'it must not be thought that coinage should be introduced for purposes of exchange or for travelling abroad'. And he requires (6) that both men and women should wear the same dress and that no part of the body should be hidden away. That the *Republic* is the work of Zeno Chrysippus also says, in his *On Republic*. And (7) he has discussed erotic topics at the beginning of the work entitled *The Art of Love* but also writes much the same in *Conversations*.

These are the sorts of things one finds in Cassius, but also in Isidorus the Pergamene rhetorician, who adds that the passages criticized among the Stoics were cut out of the books by Athenodorus the Stoic, who was in charge of the library at Pergamum, and that afterwards they were set in opposition, after Athenodorus had been caught and charged. So much on the passages of Zeno which have been judged spurious.[43] (D.L. VII.32–4)

The very title of Zeno's work proclaims a Platonic pedigree; and all of the specific provisions (1) to (6) of the treatise reported here correspond to something in Plato's *Republic*. This is obvious in the case of numbers (3) and (5). (4) reminds us of how Plato predicts that there will be no litigation among the guardians (464de; cf. Ar. *Ec.* 655 ff.), and other evidence (Phld. *On the Stoics*, PHerc. 155 and 339, col. 19.17–22) indicates that the coyly phrased rule in (6) about parts of the body was connected with gymnastic festivals at which both sexes performed naked.

(1) and (2) are the items of greatest interest. Education and the redefinition of kinship and family relations are central Platonic preoccupations. Zeno's position on both is more radical than Plato's and presumably for similar reasons in each case. Plato's *Republic* transforms the family by making it coextensive with the community of guardians, and offers this as the recipe for harmony in the city. Zeno likewise recognizes no family but the community as a whole, but for him this provision merely removes an obstacle to harmony. The key to friendship and true kinship is moral virtue and its precondition wisdom: only the morally virtuous are capable of proper social relationships. Of course, Plato had

---

[43] On problems of text and translation see Schofield 1991, 3–8.

posited virtue and in particular wisdom among his guardians, and certainly in his claims about their social cohesion assumes that their moral and intellectual education has been efficacious (cf. 416bc). So virtue as well as proper institutions figures indispensably in his account also. The difference in emphasis, however, is unmistakable. Plato makes a heavy strategic investment in social stratification in the city as a whole and a regulated communism for the guardians in order to achieve his objective of concord. Zeno relies much more on the moral perfection of the individual. This difference is presumably reflected also in their provisions on education. Plato advocates a thorough overhaul of the ordinary education system, with censorship of poetry, reforms of music and gymnastics, and the introduction of higher as well as elementary mathematics. Zeno thinks that the only education we need is an education for moral simplicity, and no doubt rejects studies such as music and geometry as the Cynics did (D.L. VI.104).

Comparison of Zeno's proposals with Plato's suggests the message: think less about institutions and structures, whether of society or of education; think more about moral virtue and its acquisition. When we consider texts other than the passage on Cassius the Sceptic, it becomes apparent that this detectable shift of focus is more than that: a repudiation of the key mechanism of Plato's communism in favour of Cynicism. The texts I refer to are those dealing with sexual relations, which seems to have been a theme given central prominence by Zeno – who in so doing only follows the tradition of communist theorizing from Herodotus' account of the Agathyrsoi through Aristophanes and Plato down to Diogenes of Sinope. Indeed, such is the preoccupation of the communist tradition with sexual relations that no writer of a communist *Republic* could avoid having his proposals about them read as an advertisement of his entire manifesto and of the direction his thought in general would be taking. The evidence suggests that Zeno for his part met his readers' expectations by making proposals on love and sex the cornerstone of his theory.[44] And his principal doctrine was in stark contradiction to Plato's social regimentation: there should be no rules governing sexual relations – mate with any woman at all (D.L. VII.131), as the Cynics advise (D.L. VI.72). In other works he went further: do not avoid incest; have sex with any teenager you like, male or female, whether you have an established attachment to the person or not (S.E. *M* XI.190, *PH* III.245). This is pure Cynicism.

---

[44] See further Schofield 1991, ch.2.

Zeno had begun his philosophical career at the feet of the Cynic Crates. And it is clear that his *Republic* was perceived by many of its early readers, Stoics included, as Cynic in its teaching. Diogenes Laertius records the witticism that the book was written on the dog's tail. Chrysippus in his *On Republic* – evidently written as a defence or reaffirmation of Zeno's *Republic* – seems to have emphasized its Cynic features: for example, permissibility of incest, uselessness of weapons (a doctrine not explicitly attested for Zeno, but attributed by Chrysippus himself to the *Republic* of Diogenes of Sinope, the original Cynic). And the polemic *On the Stoics* by Cicero's Epicurean contemporary Philodemus takes as its focus attempts by other Stoics (some of them at least of his own time) to explain away the indecencies or apparent indecencies of Zeno's treatise: e.g. that it was flawed juvenile work, not the real Zeno; that it was real Zeno all right, but Stoics want to be thought of as Socratics, not Zenonians; that the teaching of the *Republic* is in fact impeccable – although its line on sexual intercourse needs explanation; and (for our purposes most pertinently) that Diogenes never really wrote the *Republic* attributed to *him* – and hence (presumably) that he never held any doctrines for Zeno to borrow.[45]

Just as the Cynic assault on convention complements an ideal of natural self-sufficiency, which other texts tell us is to be achieved by laborious effort (*ponos*) as exemplified by the Cynic hero Heracles (D.L. VI.2, 11, 104–5), so Zeno's rejection of rules governing sexual intercourse seems to have been complemented by a conviction that the only real good, and the only thing relevant to happiness, is virtue. Sexual taboos can be abandoned because at the end of the day it is quite *indifferent* who has sex with whom – indifferent, that is, to happiness (S.E. *PH* I.160, III.200; Orig. *Cels.* IV.45). Thus in its abandonment of Plato's trust in laws and institutions controlling the key matter of sexual relations, Zeno's recipe for the good life has to rely much more than does even Plato on moral education, i.e. an education which will produce moral virtue.

Where Zeno appears to have diverged from the Cynics is in the attention which he like Plato gives to the promotion of the political ideals of friendship and concord. This is closely bound up with education for moral virtue, as the following texts suggest:

[45] Dog's tail: D.L. VII.4; Cynic features in Chrysippus: D.L. VII.131, 188, S.E. *M* XI.192 [=*PH* III.246], Plu. *Stoic. Rep.* 1044b–e, Phld. *Stoic.*, *PHerc.* 155 and 339, col. 15.31–16.1; Philodemus' polemic: Phld. *Stoic.*, *PHerc.* 155 and 339, col. 9.2–15.20 (see further Dorandi 1982b). Cynic doxography, however, is often itself Stoicized: Mansfeld 1986 (also Goulet-Cazé 1982, 1986, Schofield 1991, App. H). General treatments of Cynic 'political' thought: Dawson 1992, ch.3, Moles 1995.

> The wise man will love those young persons who by their appearance manifest a natural endowment for virtue, as Zeno says in the *Republic* and Chrysippus in the first book of *On Lives* and Apollodorus in his *Ethics*. (D.L. VII.129)

> Pontianus [one of Athenaeus' *dramatis personae*] said that Zeno of Citium took love to be a god who brings about friendship and freedom, and again concord, but nothing else. That is why in the *Republic* he said that Love is god, there as a helper in furthering the safety of the city. (Athen. 561c)

Love here is, of course, not sex, although in keeping intimate personal relationships at the centre of his account Zeno sustains the focus characteristic of the communist tradition in general and of Cynicism in particular. What he has in mind is the sublimated passion of a mature person for the young resulting in concern for their moral wellbeing, to which Plato gives canonical expression in the *Symposium* and the *Phaedrus*. Plato was thinking of homosexual attachments between males, and so very likely was Zeno. It is unclear whether he managed to reconcile this element in his proposals with the principle of the community of women (D.L. VII.131) and the thesis that the same virtue belongs to a man and a woman (D.L. VII.175, Phld. *Piet.*, *PHerc.* 1428, col. 5.8-11 Henrichs). Zeno's own distinctive contribution is to find in love so conceived the dynamic not just of the moral education of individual citizens but of friendship and concord in the community at large. Presumably his idea is that if the wise man's concern for his beloved's wellbeing is reciprocated and bears moral fruit, the other too will attain wisdom and virtue, and love will be consummated as friendship (cf. D.L. VII.130). Replicate friendships throughout the society, and you then have the basis for general concord:

> They leave friendship something found among only the wise. For only among these is concord about the affairs of life to be found. Concord is knowledge of common goods. (Stob. *Ecl.* II.108.15-18)

Friendship and concord depend simply on the concern for each other shared by the good and wise. Virtue is what matters, not institutional structures.[46]

VII Justice, *oikeiōsis* and the cosmic city

The main emphases of subsequent Stoic social and political philosophy were rather different, to judge from the surviving evidence. As we have

---

[46] On the Stoic conception of friendship see Fraisse 1974, 348-73.

noted, Chrysippus' *On Republic* reiterated many of Zeno's themes; and his advocacy elsewhere of the doctrine of the cosmic city represented an influential development of Zeno's basic conception of a community of the good and wise. But he also wrote several treatises on subjects such as law and justice (cf. n. 8 above), and it is his handling of these themes which is ultimately responsible for the shape of the exposition of Stoic political thought in our main source, Cicero's *de Finibus* III.62 ff. The key idea in his (and indeed perhaps already Zeno's) account of the motivation to justice – the notion of *oikeiōsis* – was one he harped upon constantly, according to Plutarch. It is therefore no surprise that the doxographical account of the Stoics' political and social theory which Cicero is presumably exploiting in the passage starts with *oikeiōsis*.[47]

Although the word *oikeiōsis* is difficult to translate adequately, it is not hard to formulate the core thesis of the Stoic theory. They held that man is not motivated solely by self-interest, but has a natural impulse to *identify with* other humans, perceiving them as related to himself, and being concerned for them on that account. *Fin.* III.62–3 gives some indication of how they argued for this thesis. All social animals – such as ants, bees and storks – exhibit altruistic behaviour. Hence conduct of this kind on the part of humans, who are the most variously and ambitiously sociable of all animals, must be natural to them. And so, for example, 'it is in agreement with human nature that men should want to undertake and carry out public duties of state, and in order to live in accordance with nature, take a wife and want children by her' (III.68). Marriage and the production of children are seen as social or political obligations: that is, obligations incumbent on men as naturally social, and therefore willingly undertaken by them.

This conception of altruism as inherent in human nature is what underlies a great deal of Stoic discussion of the conduct of the wise person, and especially their conviction that he will play a role – or rather one or more of a variety of roles – on the public stage (although the theatrical metaphor itself, pervasive in Epictetus, may not antedate Panaetius). It must suffice to quote from Arius Didymus' doxographical summary of Stoic ethics:

> Following on these points is the thesis that the wise man takes part in politics, and especially so in the sorts of political societies [or, constitutions] which show some progress towards being perfect political societies; also

---

[47] On *oikeiōsis* in general see above pp. 677–82. Its social form is discussed in the classic study of Pembroke 1971, and e.g. by Blundell 1990, Engberg-Pedersen 1990, Striker 1991, 35–61, Annas 1993a, 262–76, Schofield 1995.

the theses that he legislates and that he educates people, and again that it is appropriate for the morally good to compose writings which can benefit those who encounter the writings; also the thesis that he descends both to marriage and to having children, both for himself and for his country, and endures struggles and death for it, if it is a moderate regime. (Stob. *Ecl.* II.94.8–20)

Behind the compressed formulations of this report lies ultimately Chrysippus' large treatise *On Lives*. We know that this work identified three preferred lives for the rational person: kingship, or living (and indeed going on campaign) with a king, no doubt as his adviser; the political life, taken again as including marriage and procreation; and the life devoted to knowledge. Our sources, mostly unfriendly to Stoicism, tell us rather more about a secondary issue: Chrysippus evidently went on to argue that there were accordingly three preferred modes of making money or providing for oneself – namely from kingship or association with a king; from politics and one's friends in high places; and from teaching (which generated the puzzle of whether Chrysippus was recommending becoming a Sophist or not).[48]

We may assume that in *On Lives* Chrysippus was tackling the old question: is the active or the quiet life to be preferred? We know that in the fourth book he characterized the quiet or leisured life disparagingly as really just a life devoted to pleasure, and gave some of its advocates (doubtless principally Epicureans) the credit of acknowledging this, but gave others (very likely the Peripatetics) a black mark for failing to do so (Plu. *Stoic. Rep.* 1033c–e). The implication is that the true pursuit of *philosophy* is to be located elsewhere, i.e. as one form of the active life. Indeed it is as if Chrysippus is saying: 'Choose the active life, but don't conceive it in monolithic terms. In particular don't contrast the active with the contemplative life, since the wise man acts out his social nature and contributes to the public advantage by his philosophical and scientific writing and teaching.'[49]

What in men and other animals *explains* natural altruism? Its causal origin lies in parental identification with offspring. This phenomenon might have been regarded as self-evidently natural, but the Stoics made an argument from probability: nature would not have equipped animals for

---

[48] Large treatise *On Lives*: Plu. *Stoic. Rep.* 1043a. Our sources: Plu. *Stoic. Rep.* 1043b–e, D.L. VII.188–9, Stob. II.109.10–110.8. For discussion see Schofield 1991, 18–20, 119–27.

[49] Cf. D.L. VII.130: of the three lives – contemplative, practical, rational – the third is to be chosen, as naturally embracing both contemplation and action. For further discussion on the whole theme in Stoicism down to Seneca see Griffin 1976, ch. 10.

reproduction, but then left them without concern for the wellbeing and nurture of their offspring (III.62). The Stoics must then be assuming that if this one form of altruism is natural to us, there is reason to suppose that other forms of it, too, are expressions of human nature.

If humans are naturally altruistic, why do not more of us promote each other's interests more often and more consistently than we actually do? The Stoics found no difficulty in attributing this failure to the corruption of human nature by the social environment (D.L. VII.89). So their conception of human nature has a strongly normative cast; and their accounts of the impulse to identify with others are expressed in terms of what we *should* do. Nonetheless the appeal to nature is intended as an explanation of the most salient *fact* about humans, that they are social animals – *politika zōia*, as the Stoics put it (Marc. *Inst.* 1.11.25, Stob. II.59.6, 75.7–8), exploiting the Aristotelian expression – and as such given to altruistic behaviour.

Fin. III.62–3 does not make it clear exactly how the particular form of sociability constituted by *oikeiōsis*, namely a natural disposition to identify with others and their interests, is to be conceived as the origin of *justice* (cf. Plu. *Stoic. Rep.* 1038b; Porph. *Abst.* III.19). In other texts reflecting Hellenistic Stoicism the connection appears to be worked out differently in different places. This suggests that certainly Zeno and perhaps Chrysippus too had been somewhat inexplicit on the issue. Stoics of the second century BC seem to have tried to tell a more determinate story. Thus it was probably Antipater who interpreted the principle that no man ought to commit injustice against any other as the idea that no one should commit violence against another, and who derived this idea from natural *oikeiōsis*: if nature tells every man that he ought to treat the interests of any other man, just because he is a man, as not alien from himself, that precludes violating those interests (*Off.* III.28; cf. *Fin.* III.63, *Leg.* 1.33). Panaetius apparently took a rather different tack. For him the virtue associated with *oikeiōsis* and natural sociability is focused on the preservation of human association and bonding as such, and justice conceived as 'assigning to each his own due' (as in the official Stoic definition) or as refraining from harming anyone is treated simply as a particular application of the more fundamental and more general obligation to maintain human society (*Off.* 1.11–20).[50]

One particularly important stimulus inducing Stoics of this period to work out the theory of justice with some care was evidently supplied by

---

[50] On Antipater and Panaetius see further Striker 1991, 35–50, 58–9, Schofield 1995, 195–205.

the criticisms of the Academic Carneades, here as in other areas of philosophy. Justice was the topic on which Carneades gave his famous pair of contradictory lectures on the occasion of the Athenian embassy to Rome in 155 BC; and no doubt he deployed similar lines of thought on many occasions. A key difficulty he raised occurs in different guises in different texts. Cicero (as reported in Lact. *Inst.* v.16) presents it as an attempt to drive a wedge between wisdom and justice. There was an explicit political point:[51] Rome won her empire by pursuing her advantage regardless of the injustice involved. And there were some memorable examples:

> If a good man has a runaway slave or a house that is insanitary and disease-ridden, and if on this account he announces that he is selling: should he confess that the slave he is selling is a runaway or the house disease-ridden, or should he conceal this from the buyer? If he confesses, he is certainly a good man, because he is not practising deceit; but he will nonetheless be judged a fool, because he will sell either at a low price or not at all. If he conceals, he will certainly be wise, because he looks after his interests; but the same person will be wicked, because he is practising deceit.

Other examples also are introduced to make the same point, notably the instance of the shipwrecked traveller in the water who gets the opportunity to dislodge someone else from a plank that floats past: if he pushes him off, he behaves unjustly (committing an act of violence against another); if he does not, he is a fool (sparing another's life at the expense of his own). The anonymous commentary on the *Theaetetus* (col. 5.18–6.31) alludes to this same example in an argument ascribed to 'the Academics'. Here it figures as one limb of a dilemma for *oikeiōsis* theory. Either *oikeiōsis* relative to others is of the same intensity as *oikeiōsis* to oneself: in which case justice is preserved, but at the cost of psychological implausibility. Or it is weaker: in which case the shipwreck example supplies an instance where, if *oikeiōsis* is the mainspring of a person's behaviour, identification with self will conflict with identification with others, and win out over it. On this alternative, all that identifying with others can generate is *philan-thrōpia*, kindly feeling towards other people, nothing as strong as a source of real commitments, which is what justice is.[52]

The Stoics disagreed among themselves about how best to meet such

---

[51] Perhaps to be related to the object of the Athenian embassy, which was to overturn a fine imposed for aggression against Oropus.

[52] A text and translation of the relevant passage from the *Theaetetus* commentary is conveniently available in Long and Sedley 1987, vol. I, 350, ll.348–9. See also Bastianini and Sedley 1995, 227–562.

difficulties. Cicero records what he presents as a debate between Diogenes of Babylon and Antipater on the subject (*Off.* III.51–7). Both apparently aimed to remove the grounds for alleging a conflict between justice and the pursuit of one's interest. In the case of the sale of goods, Diogenes held that it would not be unjust of the vendor to remain silent about the defects of the house or the slave, and so to pursue self-interest. He argued that it is one thing to conceal, another to be silent. Silence would be tantamount to concealment only if it was the vendor's responsibility to ensure that the buyer knew everything it might be in his interest to know. But the buyer is a free agent, and the responsibility is primarily his. Justice conceived as looking after another's interest seems to reduce here to refraining from deliberately harming his interest. To Antipater's way of thinking, justice imposed greater demands than this, and in the example given would require the seller to confess. But he seems to have suggested that properly understood the common interest coincides with one's own advantage or should be made to coincide with it. How he argued for the suggestion is not disclosed. It would presumably imply that for a quite different reason there is no real conflict between justice and self-interest. The problem of how to deal with such a conflict or apparent conflict continued to exercise the school. Panaetius made it the subject of the third and final division of discussion of appropriate action, but notoriously never wrote the treatise he promised about it (Cic. *Off.* 1.9, III.7). Among his pupils, Posidonius claimed it was the most important topic in all philosophy, but had little to say about it (*Off.* III.8); on the other hand Hecaton's *On Appropriate Actions* tackled all the puzzle cases in its sixth book, and appears to have defended a subtle form of utilitarianism (*Off.* III.89–90).

One issue which these debates threw up was the legitimacy of private property. Cicero makes Diogenes suggest that the logical consequence of Antipater's assimilation of common and individual interest is that there is nothing which is properly speaking a person's own due (this would mean that justice as conceived in the standard Stoic definition is an empty concept, although Cicero does not point this out). Should we therefore not buy and sell, but simply give things away (*Off.* III.53)? *Fin.* III.68 seems to offer a response to this line of attack. It exploits an analogy. The theatre is in common ownership, but the seat a person occupies is quite properly called his seat. So the fact that we inhabit a common city or universe does not preclude its being just that each of us have his own. *Off.* 1.21, presumably due to Panaetius, defends the same doctrine in different terms. Things are not private but common by nature. But something may legitimately become someone's own by virtue of long occupation, force of conquest, a contract, a lottery, etc.; and anyone else trying to appropriate it will be violating 'the justice of human association'.[53]

When the Stoics talked of justice as something natural, it was not only human nature that they had in mind. Plutarch quotes Chrysippus as writing in his *On the Gods*:

> It is not possible to discover any other source of justice nor any other origin than from Zeus and from universal nature. For from here everything of this sort must have its source, if we are going to have anything to say about good and evil. (Plu. *Stoic. Rep.* 1035c)

This thesis underpins Chrysippus' further claim (D.L. VII.128) that justice exists by nature not by posit; that is, that what counts as just and unjust is something to which there is an objectively correct answer irrespective of the positive law of particular states or communities. The mediating idea which connects the objectivity of justice (and its naturalness in that sense) with universal nature is *reason*. Chrysippus holds that the just and the unjust are determined by law, and law he understands not as any human convention, but as right reason applied to the practical end of moral injunction and prohibition (e.g. Plu. *Stoic Rep.* 1037f, Stob. II.96.10–12, 102.4–6). Right reason in an individual is in harmony with universal nature, insofar as universal nature simply *is* reason at work, prescribing the proper order of the universe (D.L. VII.88). It is therefore only to be expected that our reason should be directive: divine reason is directive; and we can only have been equipped with reason so that it may direct us. It is equally to be expected that when our reason has acquired proper understanding we will be in a position to know what under its direction we should and should not do. This is presumably one ground for calling it 'law': the role it plays in our lives is an internalized version of the function which in any particular state is usually performed by the external positive law.

Cicero sets out the Stoic derivation of justice from law in a passage near the beginning of *De legibus*:

> It has been the view, correct or not, of some very learned men, that we should begin with law [sc. in seeking the principles of justice] – given

---

[53] For Carneades' puzzles about justice and the Stoic responses see Pohlenz 1934, Annas 1989a, Striker 1991, 44–61. On property: Erskine 1990, ch. 5. These disputes have sometimes been seen as bearing on or even influenced by contemporaneous issues in Roman public life and intellectual debate. Such possibilities are the subject of a huge bibliography: see e.g. Behrends 1977, Erskine 1990, chs. 7 and 8 (sanguine), Strasburger 1965 and 1966, Jocelyn 1976/7, Rawson 1985, ch. 4 (sceptical). Atkins 1990 casts doubt on whether we have a sufficient basis to reconstruct the ideas of Panaetius, often taken to be the key figure in developing Stoicism in a more practical mode.

only that law is, as they define it, (1) the highest reason implanted in nature, which commands what ought to be done and forbids the opposite. This same reason, when it is firmly fixed and fully developed in the human mind, is law. And so they think that law is (2) practical wisdom, which has precisely that function, to command right conduct and prohibit wrongdoing. They reckon that the Greek word for it comes from (3) granting to each his own [*nomos* = law; *nemō* = grant, distribute]; I believe our word comes from choosing [*lex* = law; *lego* = choose]. As they make fairness the job of the law, we make choice its function – though each is a special property of the law. If what they say is right, as I think it mostly is, then the origin of justice is to be found in law. For it is (1) a natural power, (2) the mind and reason of the man of practical wisdom, (3) the standard of justice and injustice. (Cic. *Leg.* 1.18–19)

Assume (1) that law is prescriptive reason in nature. Then in a man (2) it will be practical wisdom (since prescription is the function of practical wisdom). But from (2) we can infer that (3) it will be the standard of justice and injustice, since that standard is fairness, as *oikeiōsis* leads us to appreciate, and fairness is the hallmark of the judgements of practical wisdom. In this sense the principle of justice is derived from law.[54]

Oikeiōsis theory shows how the impulse to justice is a function of a general human and indeed animal motivation. But appeal to universal nature supplies what is in the end more fundamental: explanation of the role of moral imperatives in the entire scheme of things. This explanation belongs to the Stoic theory of providence, according to which the universe is designed as the common home and city of gods and men, who form a just community as the only beings partaking in reason, which is natural law (cf. Cic. *ND* II.154; Arius Didymus [*SVF* II 528]). Some of the crucial moves are set out in a syllogistic chain of reasoning:

> Since nothing is better than reason, and this exists in both man and god, man's first association with god is in reason. But those who have reason in common also have right reason in common. Since that is law, we men must also be reckoned to be associated with the gods in law. But further, those who have law in common have justice in common. But those who have these things in common must be held to belong to the same state. (Cic. *Leg.* 1.23)

Here we re-establish contact with Zeno's city of the virtuous and wise. If Zeno assumes mutual knowledge and physical proximity among his

---

[54] The idea of natural law is sometimes taken to imply a code of moral rules (e.g. Striker 1987). But although *kathēkonta* seem to form a system, the fact that they do is not connected in the sources with natural law: whose range of connotations is as indicated above.

citizens, the assumption is now tacitly dropped, as is his preoccupation with love and sex. Otherwise there is a striking resemblance with the community specified in Cicero's text. The cosmic city, too, as the reference to *right* reason indicates, is a community whose only criterion of membership is virtue and wisdom. It is indeed the *only* true city. The Stoics define a city as a morally admirable group or organization of humans which is administered by law (Clem. *Strom.* iv.26; D. Chr. *Or.* 36.20). But the only group of persons that is governed by law properly understood, i.e. interpreted not as positive law but as right reason at work, are those who consistently heed right reason, i.e. the virtuous and wise. Nor is Zeno's conception of concord and friendship as the bonds uniting his city forgotten. As Plutarch puts it:

> If a single sage anywhere at all extends his finger prudently, all the sages throughout the inhabited world are benefited. This is the job they assign to friendship; this is how, by the beneficial acts common to the sages, the virtues are brought to fulfilment.[55] (Plu. *Comm. Not.* 1086f)

It has sometimes been supposed that what Stoicism advocated was a world state: a political system in which the unity of all mankind would find expression. In a notorious passage (*Alex. Virt.* 329a–f) Plutarch connected the ideas of Zeno's *Republic* with the exploits of Alexander the Great. Alexander's success in bringing under his own supreme authority Greeks and barbarians scattered over a vast extent of territory, and his attempts to obliterate cultural differences between them, were represented as Stoic philosophy put into practice. The evidence adduced in this and the previous sub-section will have indicated why Plutarch's story must be rejected as an account of Stoicism, quite apart from doubts historians may entertain about its reliability with regard to Alexander.[56] As developed by Chrysippus, the ideal city of Zeno's *Republic* is indeed in a sense a universal community, whose citizens are (as Diogenes the Cynic claimed of himself: D.L. vi.63) *kosmopolitai*. However, it is universal not in that it includes all mankind, but because it is made up of gods and sages wherever they may be: not a wider community, but a wholly different sort of 'community'. When Chrysippus uses words like 'city' and 'law', he intends a radical transformation of their meaning, robbing them of anything ordinarily recognizable as political content. In short, political vocabulary is depoliticized.

---

[55] On justice, the cosmic city and universal nature see further Long 1983b, Schofield 1991, chs. 3 and 4, Schofield 1995.

[56] For discussion of Alexander and the unity of mankind, see e.g. Tarn 1933, contradicted by Badian 1958; a good brief study is Baldry 1965, ch. iv. On the Plutarch text see also Schofield 1991, App. A.

VIII Retrospect

The major ideas about politics and society introduced in this chapter are rich, varied and ingenious. Finley, whose verdict was quoted at the beginning of section I, failed to perceive their intimate connection with theories about the natural world, especially the nature of human psychology, and the foundations of ethics. It is true that even the Stoics, the most original and fertile thinkers of the period in this field, owe much to philosophical predecessors and to dialectical engagement with them, but that is hardly a defect. Neither they nor the Epicureans have anything to say for example, about the comparative merits of democracy and aristocracy. Their preoccupation is rather with the basic rationale of society, and the roles of law, justice and utility within it. That does not mean that they are not really political theorists at all, but merely that as such they resemble Grotius, Hobbes and Locke more than Plato and Aristotle, although of course these concerns are not absent from the *Republic* and the *Politics*.

Epicureanism undoubtedly advocates quietism, and out of a fundamental preoccupation with what is the best strategy for individuals to follow in pursuit of their own interests. But the conceptual framework within which the argument for quietism is worked out was the one by now traditional in Greek political thought: Epicurus is thinking of a largely self-sufficient community restricted in size; and he and Hermarchus conceive it in terms of the contractualist versions of how society originates and functions which had been advocated particularly in the Sophistic literature of the second half of the fifth century BC. The Epicurean analysis operates throughout at a high level of abstraction. There is no indication whatever that Epicurus and his circle had begun to reflect seriously on new Hellenistic forms of political organization, or on their effects on the powers of city-states and their citizens – any more than had Polybius, who borrows so heavily from Epicureanism.

If *all* the Hellenistic philosophies had advocated abstention from political life, it might nonetheless have been plausible to postulate a new Zeitgeist not yet captured in philosophical formulae, but dictating philosophical positions all the same. In fact the most radical philosophical critique of the city-state – by Diogenes the Cynic – predates the Hellenistic age; and although later Cynics, the dissident Stoic Aristo and some Cyrenaic philosophers are found repeating it in one form or another around the beginning of the period,[57] and urging men to follow nature and consider themselves only citizens of the world, voices like theirs fall

---

[57] It is significant that this is the time when the most Cynicizing Stoic writing on the *polis* – Zeno's *Republic* – was composed.

largely silent as time goes on. Indeed the Cynic poet Cercidas (late third century BC) was to become heavily involved in the politics of his own city Megalopolis. As was noted above (pp. 623, 741), Epicurus for his part dissociated himself from Cynicism. The earliest trace of Cynic cosmopolitanism in Epicurean texts comes in a fragment of Diogenes of Oenoanda (second century AD).[58]

For the most part the major philosophical schools appear to have been as committed to endorsing political activity of a conventional kind as they ever were. The neatest and most celebrated illustration of their recognition of such political responsibilities is supplied by the choice of the heads of the Academy (Carneades), the Stoa (Diogenes of Babylon) and the Peripatos (Critolaus) to represent the Athenians as their ambassadors on a visit to Rome in 155 BC. So far from exhibiting signs of deracination, Chrysippus goes out of his way to emphasize the depths of the immersion of the wise man in the world immediately about him: whether he opts for the court or politics or teaching, he will be making money; and he will 'practise oratory and engage in politics as though wealth were a real good, and reputation and health too' (Plu. Stoic. Rep. 1034b). This sounds like a reproof to Plato for promoting too idealistic a conception of political and indeed philosophical activity. Chrysippus' interest in life at court and his assumption that conventional city-state politics involves using the good offices of one's friends to line one's pockets indicate a response to the changed political circumstances of Hellenistic times. Otherwise what is most striking about his account of the political life is just how thoroughly traditional it is.

What was novel in Stoicism was its conception of the ideal community of perfectly rational persons, all subject to the same internalized natural law of reason, and sharing with the gods in the only true city. Chrysippus' allegiance to this theory did not prevent him from making the sage engagé. But in the discussions of the leading Stoics of the early Roman empire – Seneca, Epictetus, Marcus Aurelius – the claims of citizenship of the universe come to dwarf those of the existing societies in which we find ourselves: the cosmic perspective increasingly overshadows the vantage point of ordinary life. It is important for understanding the political thought of the Hellenistic age that this is a later development.[59]

[58] Diog. Oen. fr.30 Smith; the key passage is reproduced by Long and Sedley 1987, ch.22P.
[59] Seneca manhandles the lex Chrysippi, which says that the wise man will engage in politics unless something impedes him, to mean effectively the same as Epicurus' prohibition on such activity except in emergency: existing states are too corrupt or unwilling to profit from his influence, or his own authority or ability or state of health is inadequate for the task (De Otio 3; cf.8).

Epilogue

MICHAEL FREDE

The schools which dominated the philosophy of the Hellenistic age did not disintegrate or disappear with the end of the Hellenistic era, but for the most part continued to exist well into Imperial times. This certainly is true of the two schools which came into existence only at the beginning of the Hellenistic period, and which in their very origin have a distinctive Hellenistic character, the Stoa and Epicurus' Garden. We can produce a long list of distinguished Stoic philosophers stretching well into the third century AD: a list that includes Seneca, Epictetus, and Marcus Aurelius. The Epicureans are less conspicuous in Imperial times, but, again, the list is fairly long, including e.g. Diogenes of Oenoanda in the second century AD. The generalization is also true of the two older schools. Indeed the Peripatos, which had lost some of its prominence and influence in Hellenistic times, saw a revival in the Empire, largely by returning to Aristotle, but without entirely shedding the Hellenistic heritage.

More complicated is the case of Plato's Academy. The debate in philosophy in Hellenistic times was crucially shaped by the fact that the Academy under Arcesilaus turned sceptical, and by the dominance of scepticism in the school until the time of Philo of Larissa and Antiochus early in the first century BC, when Platonism re-emerged. So here there was a break of continuity at the end of the Hellenistic era. But it was not a complete break. There continued to be philosophers, like Favorinus of Arelate, who saw themselves as in the tradition of Arcesilaus and Carneades. There were Platonists, like Plutarch, who did not think that the Academic philosophers from Arcesilaus to Philo had betrayed the tradition of Socrates and Plato: they thought of themselves as continuing a Platonic tradition which involved scepticism. And there was Aenesidemus, originally an Academic philosopher, who revived the radical scepticism of Arcesilaus, not in the school of Plato, but under the banner of Pyrrho. Pyrrhonism survived into the third century AD, finding then an exponent in Sextus Empiricus. So there is a good deal of continuity between Hellenistic philosophy and the philosophy of the Empire at least into the third century AD.

Hence it would be appropriate to conclude a history of Hellenistic philosophy with a brief account of the afterlife of the Hellenistic schools in Imperial times. First, however, it is worth asking whether Hellenistic philosophy is best understood as the philosophy of what ancient historians call the Hellenistic period, which is defined by the death of Alexander the Great in 323 BC and the end of Ptolemaic Egypt in 31 BC. There is no reason to suppose that philosophy has so little autonomy that its development is tied closely to political history. And closer consideration of the reasons one might, or does, give for thinking that Hellenistic philosophy comes to an end around 30 BC shows them to be inadequate. Indeed, pursuing them rather leads one to a date towards the end of the second century BC.

This is not a matter of tedious and superficial periodization. It is rather a matter of seeing philosophers of the past in their proper historical context. This volume is based on the assumption that Hellenistic philosophy came to an end by about 100 BC, and that philosophers like Posidonius, Philo, Antiochus, Aenesidemus, though still belonging to the Hellenistic era, are better considered in the context of later philosophy. This assumption needs some justification. Our justification will involve showing that towards the end of the second century BC something begins which comes to shape the course of philosophy well into Imperial times. At the same time we shall also come to understand better the fate of the Hellenistic schools or movements in post-Hellenistic times.

What, then, are the reasons one might propose for saying that – on the contrary – it is roughly the year 30 BC which marks a turning point in the history of philosophy? It seems that there are three developments which one could associate with that date. There is, first, the renascence of Aristotelianism. There is, second, the revival of Platonism. One might think that these two movements soon came to dominate philosophy, whereas Stoicism and Epicureanism, though they continued to exist, became insignificant in relation to Platonism and Aristotelianism, and no longer determined, nor even significantly shaped, the course of the history of philosophy. There is, third, the demise of Academic scepticism. Let us look at each of these developments in turn.

*

Usually the revival of Aristotelianism is associated with Andronicus of Rhodes. It is often thought that Andronicus produced a scholarly edition of Aristotle's works, making Aristotle's esoteric writings widely available for the first time, and so providing the basis for the renascence of

Aristotelianism late in the first century BC. There is one plausible line of argument according to which this editorial work must have taken place some time between 40 and 20 BC. If it did, 30 BC would look like a plausible date for the revival of Aristotelianism, and thus for the end of Hellenistic philosophy.

But on the whole the evidence points to a much earlier date for the revival of Aristotelianism.[1] To begin with, the evidence concerning Andronicus is far from clear. It allows for the assumption, actually espoused by some, that Andronicus' editorial work falls into the first half of the first century BC. Nor is it entirely clear what precisely Andronicus did. He evidently did edit some works of Aristotle. Perhaps he even produced an edition of Aristotelian writings from which, in the course of time, the Corpus Aristotelicum evolved. But, though he played an important role in the transmission of Aristotle's school-treatises, it is more than doubtful that he played the prominent role in the revival of Aristotelianism which has come to be attributed to him.

One has to doubt this for the following reasons:

(i) Andronicus may have helped the revival by producing better texts and texts which were more easily available, but there is no reason to think that these texts, or at least the bulk of them, had not been available before Andronicus.

(ii) Andronicus was certainly not the first to take an interest in Aristotle's esoteric writings and their text. We see this when we follow the famous story of the fate of 'the books of Aristotle and Theophrastus', which, bequeathed to Neleus, ended up in a cellar in Skepsis.[2] Whatever the truth behind this much discussed story may be, this much is clear: the books were acquired by Apellicon some time around 100 BC and thus came back to Athens. But after the capture of Athens in the Mithridatic war Sulla took them to Rome and they became part of his library. There a distinguished Greek grammarian, Tyrannio, gained access to these manuscripts. Tyrannio had copies of at least some of the Aristotelian texts made, and these copies were used by Andronicus. Hence, given a certain interpretation of the story of the cellar of Skepsis, the idea could easily arise that it was only through Andronicus' edition that Aristotle's esoteric writings became available to the learned world.

But there are some further, uncontroversial, details which suggest that Andronicus' role was much more modest. Apellicon was not just someone of dubious wealth and political association (a partisan of Athenion

---

[1] Cf. Moraux 1973, 45 ff., esp. 57.   [2] Cf. Strabo XIII.1.54; Plu. *Sulla* 26.

who had driven Athens into the war). He also had studied Peripatetic philosophy (it was then that he bought the Aristotelian manuscripts) and
professed to be a Peripatetic. We would be inclined not to take this particularly seriously. But we have to take note of the fact that Apellicon was
serious enough in his interest in Aristotle to write at least one book about
him. Hence it is not surprising to hear that he concerned himself with
editing Aristotelian writings.[3] Since we have no reason to suppose that
Apellicon was a great scholar, we have to suspect that it was the manuscripts he had bought which prompted him to get involved in editing; and
so they obviously contributed something to the knowledge of Aristotle's
texts people had at the time. However this may be, with Apellicon we
have a Peripatetic who at least as early as the 90s of the first century BC
took an interest in Aristotle's esoteric writings and concerned himself
with editing them. Similarly it is clear that Tyrannio, perhaps as early as
the 60s, also produced editions, however inadequate they may have been.
Thus it is clear, even from our very limited evidence, that Andronicus had
forerunners in the Peripatetic school with an interest in Aristotle's text at
least as early as the beginning of the century.

(iii) There is evidence that by the middle of the first century BC the revival of Aristotelianism based on a study of Aristotle's writings was already
well under way. For Aristo's work on Aristotle's *Categories* and his *Analytics*
would seem to belong to the first half of the century, if it is true that he was
born around 110 BC. It has also been suggested, rather plausibly, that
Aristo's and Cratippus' conversion to Peripateticism is only intelligible if
we assume that by the middle of the first century the revival of
Aristotelianism had gained enough momentum to attract two of the major
students of Antiochus.[4] If we look at the evidence provided by the
Aristotelian commentators, the study of Aristotle's writings in the second
part of the first century already seems to have been so widespread and so
intensive that it is difficult to believe that it was only Andronicus around
30 BC or even 50 BC who laid the basis for this activity. It rather looks as if
Andronicus himself were only part, though perhaps an important part, of
a tradition which goes back at least to the beginning of the first century BC.

In fact, we can trace the sources for the revival of Aristotelianism, if not
the revival itself, still further back. One of our most important sources
concerning the fate of Aristotle's books is a fragment of Posidonius, preserved in Athenaeus (3 a–b). Evidently Posidonius took an interest in the

---

[3] Cf. Aristocles ap. Euseb. *Praep.Ev.* xv.2.13; Strabo XIII.1.54.
[4] See Phld. *Acad. Hist.* col. 35.11–16, with Moraux 1973, 57.

matter. And no less evidently he took a strong interest in Aristotle's philosophy, so much so that Strabo in a famous passage (11.3.8) calls him 'Aristotelizing'. Aristotle was clearly some kind of authority for him, and at times he seems to be willing to side with Aristotle against his own school. But in this respect Posidonius hardly differs from his teacher Panaetius. Cicero tells us (*Fin.* IV.79) that Panaetius constantly mentioned Aristotle, and according to the *Index Stoicorum* (Phld. *Stoic. Hist.* (col. 61.3–7), he was very philaristotelian and quite ready to sacrifice a Stoic dogma in favour of an Aristotelian doctrine. Thus he rejected the Stoic doctrine of conflagration and espoused the Aristotelian assumption that the world is eternal (D.L. VII.142).

More will be said about this in a moment. For now it may suffice to note that already in Panaetius' time Aristotle seems to have acquired the status of an authority, whose thought and whose very words must be studied carefully. Moreover, he acquired this status regardless of school-boundaries. In the first century BC, certainly in the second half of the century, we find that not only Peripatetics but also Stoics like Athenodorus or Platonists like Eudorus comment on details of Aristotle's text.[5] Stoics as early as the second and the beginning of the first century BC were willing to modify their position in the light of Aristotle's remarks. Thus Sosigenes followed Aristotle in the theory of mixture (Alex. *Mixt.* 216, 9 ff.). Given that this attitude towards Aristotle was taking shape as early as the end of the second century BC, it is not surprising that Aristotle's own school, the Peripatos, should return to a study of Aristotle's more technical writings, which for the most part must have been available in some form all along.

All this strongly suggests that the renewal of Aristotelianism was not due to Andronicus' edition of Aristotelian texts, but to a renewed interest in Aristotle and his writings, even the text of his writings, which then also led to Andronicus' work. It seems clear enough that the rise of Aristotelianism is not a phenomenon of the second part of the first century BC, but can be traced back to the end of the second century BC.

Though there was a revival of Aristotelianism, we should be hesitant to believe that it became dominant almost immediately. There is, first of all, a distinction to be made between interest in Aristotle which was very considerable, and espousal of some form of Aristotelianism, which was much rarer. For the first century BC we have significant, but not overwhelming, figures like Aristo, Andronicus of Rhodes, Boethus of Sidon, Xenarchus,

---

[5] For Athenodorus see Simp. *Cat.* 62, 25 et passim; for Eudorus cf. Alex. *Metaph.* 59, 1 ff.

and a number of lesser lights. But then there seems to be a lull. We know of rather few Peripatetics in the first century AD, Nicolaus of Damascus, Alexander of Aegae, and Sotion, for instance. We have to wait until the second century to see in Peripateticism a dominant force represented by figures like Aspasius, Adrastus, Herminus, Aristocles, Sosigenes, and above all Alexander of Aphrodisias.

*

The picture for Platonism is not all that different. The first person to claim that he was trying to revive the doctrine of Plato and to restore the school of Plato to its true tradition, betrayed by Arcesilaus and his sceptical successors, was Antiochus. But the picture of Plato's doctrine which he developed is one heavily coloured by Stoicism. Already in antiquity he was characterized as being more of a Stoic than a member of the Academy.[6] Nevertheless he gained some following for his enterprise of restoring the philosophy of Plato. These new Platonists, however, quickly corrected his Stoicizing conception of Platonism. They did so by emphasizing the highly abstract and speculative elements in Plato which are associated with Pythagoreanism. That said, it remained for some time a matter of debate among them how far Stoicism was true to Platonism, just as it also remained a matter of debate whether the tradition of the school from Arcesilaus to Philo had constituted an aberration. But whichever position one took on these questions, Platonism was set on its path. In the second part of the first century BC we encounter its first important exponent in Eudorus. Early in the next century, though the details are unclear and controversial, we see Thrasyllus concern himself with Plato's text, perhaps even producing an edition. Soon there will be commentaries on Platonic texts, though one may doubt whether the Anonymous Commentary on the *Theaetetus* is as early as the middle of the first century AD.

This admittedly is a very rough sketch, but it suffices to show that around the year 30 BC we witness a development which had started long before, not later than Antiochus' break with the sceptical Academy around 90 BC. But Antiochus' move, with its simultaneous turn to Plato and the Old Academy (and indeed towards Aristotle and the early Peripatos and, to some extent, the early Stoa), can itself be seen as the natural result of developments which had set in earlier, rather than as a new beginning. We will return to Antiochus' abandonment of scepticism

[6] S.E. *PH* 1.235; cf. Phot. *Bibl.* 170 a 14–17.

later. His decision to turn to Plato and the Old Academy clearly had something to do with the fact that already in the later part of the second century BC Plato began to command respect across school boundaries, in a way similar to Aristotle, but apparently more so. Here again it is Panaetius who is the first philosopher recorded as venerating Plato in a way even the ancients found noteworthy. Cicero can talk in this way of Panaetius (*Tusc.* 1.79): 'Shall we, then, give credence to Panaetius on a point on which he disagrees with his Plato? He constantly calls him divine, the most wise, the most pious, the flower of philosophers, and yet this one view of his, concerning the immortality of the soul, he does not accept.' Other sources, too, talk of his admiration for Plato and his willingness to abandon Stoic dogma in favour of Platonic doctrine.[7] He even took some interest in Plato's text, since we are told in an epigram that he declared the *Phaedo* to be spurious.[8]

So Antiochus may have been the first student of the later Academy to declare a return to Plato's doctrine, but he certainly was not the first philosopher to insist on a sympathetic consideration of Plato's views. In this he was preceded by Panaetius, and it is striking that Panaetius had similarly advocated a return to the Old Academy, the early Peripatos, and, to some extent, the early Stoa. For Cicero says about Panaetius (*Fin.* IV.79): 'He always talks about Plato, Aristotle, Xenocrates, Theophrastus, Dicaearchus, as one can see from his own writings.' Similarly Panaetius is said to have commended Crantor (Cic. *Acad.* II.135). If we assume that he held the early Stoics in esteem, it seems that he had already singled out the very group of philosophers on whom Antiochus later wanted to base his reconstruction of the true Platonic philosophy.

A little after Panaetius, but before Antiochus, Posidonius is another philosopher who shows considerable interest in, and admiration for, Plato. As Galen puts it (*PHP* IV.7): 'He admires the man and calls him divine, and thus he also advocates his doctrines concerning the affections of the soul and those concerning the powers of the soul.' One may doubt whether Galen understood Posidonius' theory of the affections of the soul. For there is a systematic ambiguity in our evidence concerning Posidonius' position on a number of related questions like the division of the soul and the nature of the good. Depending on one's interpretation he turns out either an orthodox Stoic or else someone who leans in crucial matters towards a position more like Plato's or Aristotle's. But whether we share Galen's interpretation of Posidonius or not, there is no reason to

---

[7] Cic. *Fin.* IV.79; Phld. *Stoic. Hist.* col. 61.2–6.   [8] *AP* IX.358; cf. also Elias *Cat.* 133.18–23.

doubt his testimony as to Posidonius' admiration for Plato. Moreover, Posidonius obviously studied Plato's *Timaeus* and discussed certain passages of the text in writing. This does not mean that he wrote a commentary on the dialogue, but it does suggest that he may have treated of certain questions in the dialogue in a monograph, in the way Plutarch did later.[9]

Thus, if we follow the suggestion that the end of Hellenistic philosophy and the beginning of a new period is marked by the revival of Platonism, it too leads us not to a date around 30 BC, but back instead to Antiochus around 90 BC and indeed beyond Antiochus to the end of the second century BC. But though there was a revival of Platonism, it did not immediately constitute a major force. In fact it grew in importance remarkably slowly. In the first century BC figures like Antiochus, Eudorus, Dercylides, and, at the turn of the century, Thrasyllus were Platonists of one sort or another. But then there is a gap in the first half of the first century AD. It is obvious from Philo of Alexandria's writings, or even from Seneca (e.g. *Ep.*58), that there was a good deal of Platonism in these decades, yet we cannot associate it with particular names. This is hardly an accident, just as it is hardly an accident that we know of a Peripatetic teacher of Nero, Alexander of Aegae, and a Stoic teacher, Chaeremon, but no Platonist is mentioned.[10] When we come to the second part of the first century AD, we finally get major figures such as Ammonius and Plutarch. But it is only in the second century AD that there are a good number of well-known Platonists like Gaius, Calvisius Taurus, Albinus, Numenius, Maximus, Atticus, Harpocration.

So, as in the case of Aristotelianism, it seems that Platonism becomes a major and perhaps even a dominant force only with the second century AD. Hence the vague picture that with the end of the Hellenistic era Stoicism and Epicureanism are replaced by Aristotelianism and Platonism as the major forces in philosophy is certainly not correct, as far as the ascendance of the new movements is concerned.

*

But that picture is also based on a prejudicial view at least as far as Stoicism, if not also Epicureanism, is concerned. It seems that Stoicism remained the dominant movement well into the second century AD. We

---

[9] It is important to note that this new admiration for Plato is by no means restricted to the Stoa. Around the turn of the first century BC the medical theorist Asclepiades of Bithynia, in a dispute with the Empiricists, refers to Plato, as if his views had a certain generally accepted weight and authority (cf. Gal. *Med. Exp.* p.94 Walzer).   [10] Cf. Suda, s.v. Alexandros Aigaios.

can produce a very long list of Stoic philosophers of some significance extending from Posidonius continuously into the second century AD.

There are some relatively simple facts which tend to make us overlook the continued vitality of Stoicism in post-Hellenistic times. To begin with, no Stoic had the chance to gain the reputation of having crucially contributed to the revival of Aristotelianism like Andronicus, or to the revival of Platonism like Antiochus. If they were Stoics, it had to be Stoic doctrine that they were helping to develop.

The usual view is that this is precisely what they failed to do in Imperial times. This impression is due to primarily two factors. It is, first, due to the fact that the tradition has only transmitted certain Stoic texts, primarily Seneca, Epictetus, and Marcus Aurelius, which then tend to be regarded as representative of Stoic philosophy in this period. Second, these very texts show, what we also know from other sources, that Stoics in Imperial times were very much concerned with the practice of philosophy in actual life, emphatically discouraging the thought that the mere study of philosophical books and the intellectual exercise of discussing theoretical puzzles would by themselves produce theoretical insight and practical wisdom. What is more, a considerable effort was made to address the needs of those who had no technical philosophical training, nor planned to acquire one. It is a mistake, though, to infer from these practical concerns that the Stoics had developed an anti-theoretical bias or had come to think of philosophical theory as unimportant, or that Stoicism had degenerated into some vague popular philosophy. Let us look at these two factors in some more detail.

Our traditional picture of the Stoa in Imperial times has been shaped by Seneca, Epictetus, and Marcus Aurelius. A tradition dominated by Platonism and then Christianity found their writings worth preserving, not because of their contribution to technical philosophy, but for their moral appeal across school boundaries, an appeal which they were designed to achieve, and which they retained even in modern times into this century. To understand this better one has to take into account the following phenomenon. For the most part Platonists thought of themselves as recovering and reconstructing the true philosophy which had been Plato's. The idea was not to identify by the appropriate means what historically had been Plato's position, but to recover the philosophical truth of which Plato had been the last adequate representative. Since what was at issue was true philosophy, rather than historical fact, a Platonist was free in reconstructing it to draw liberally on the advances made by the Stoics. And this all the more so, since the commonly accepted view was that Stoicism had developed out of Platonism, and originally owed its basic motivations and insights to Platonism. So whatever was regarded as true in Stoicism could be appropriated as being part of the common heritage and would not be seen as specifically Stoic. A paradoxical consequence was that philosophers like Plotinus might be massively influenced by Stoicism and nevertheless take a hostile position towards Stoicism, identifying as Stoic only those elements which could not be assimilated into their own way of thinking. But this means that once Stoic theory had been assimilated to the extent that it seemed useful, Stoic theoretical treatises could be discarded. There was no need or incentive to preserve them, once Stoicism had died out as a theoretical force, given that what was theoretically useful had been salvaged. That Seneca, Epictetus, and Marcus Aurelius escaped this fate is due to a variety of factors, for example Seneca's presumed connection with St Paul and Marcus Aurelius' status as Emperor, but primarily to the fact that their writings were perceived as satisfying a practical moral need.

It would be a mistake to infer from the preservation of these authors that they are representative of Stoic philosophical literature in Imperial times in general, or that the Stoics had given up on philosophical theory. Unfortunately the account of Stoic philosophy in Diogenes Laertius does not extend very far into the Imperial age in the writers it takes into account, but (for example) Athenodorus, presumably Augustus' teacher (Strabo xiv.5.14), is referred to in the sections on logic, physics, and ethics (D.L. vii.68, 121, 149); apparently the same Athenodorus also wrote about Aristotle's *Categories* and is repeatedly referred to by Simplicius, but also by Porphyry.[11] Crinis seems to have been a standard author in logic (cf. d.l. vii.62, 68, 71, 76). Cornutus, too, is not just the author of an extant *Theology of the Greeks*, but wrote also on Aristotle's *Categories*. This work was thought to be important enough to be referred to repeatedly by Porphyry and by Simplicius in their commentaries. But he also had an interest in abstract metaphysical and rather technical questions, as shown by the fact that he wrote a treatise *Peri hektōn* ('On things to be had'), of which, unfortunately, only the title is preserved on a papyrus (*P. Oxy.* 52.12–13). What it was about, we can still gather from Simplicius' commentary on the *Categories* (163.31 ff.; 209.11 ff.). Even when we come to the second century AD, the fragmentary remains of Hierocles or the testimonies concerning Philopator show that the Stoa remained a serious theoretical force. It is clear that after Panaetius there was a good deal of

---

[11] Simp. *Cat.* 18, 28; 62, 25; 128, 7; 159, 32; 187, 28; Porph. *Cat.* 59, 10; 86, 22.

reflection on the notion of a person, of which we get a glimpse in Seneca and in Epictetus. It is clear, as we again see from Epictetus, that discussion concerning freedom, the will, responsibility and fate had moved on in the direction of a notion of a free will, and that the Stoics actively responded to corresponding developments in Platonism and Aristotelianism. The way Alexander, at the end of the second century AD, discusses the Stoic position in his *On fate*, cannot be understood entirely in terms of classical Stoicism, and does not at all give the impression that this is a topic to which the Stoics have long stopped contributing.

The fact that we find some of the theoretical developments in Stoicism dating to this period not particularly congenial to our philosophical interests should not make us overlook the fact that such developments took place. There is a method of allegorical interpretation based on a theory of interpretation which Porphyry traces back to the Stoics Cornutus and Chaeremon in the time of Nero (cf. Euseb. *H. E.* VI.19.3), which would be taken over and developed by Platonists such as Porphyry, and Church Fathers such as Origen. There is the development of the ideal of an ascetic life which we find, for example, in Seneca's teacher Attalus, or, again, in Chaeremon, and which would later be taken over by Platonists, but may also have had an influence on monasticism. There is an extended interest in magic, demons, and various forms of divination, including astrology, based on the theory of cosmic sympathy, represented, e.g., by Chaeremon, and subsequently in Platonism.

So Stoicism in the first century AD, far from having degenerated into more or less popular sermonizing, was still a driving force in philosophical theory. In particular it seems that Stoicism remained vital because it addressed problems of ever growing importance within the culture of the early Empire, questions concerning God and divine providence, the gods, the soul, its fate, the ineluctability of its fate. It is these questions which, according to Seneca, are central to Stoic physics. This is not the impression we get when we study Chrysippus. If we ask ourselves how this shift in emphasis came about, it again seems that we are led back to Posidonius and the end of the second century BC. It seems to have been mainly Posidonius who reoriented Stoicism in such a way that it could respond to new interests and needs.

One might, finally, associate a date of roughly 30 BC or 50 BC with the collapse of Academic scepticism. Now, as already indicated, this issue is more complex, and, indeed, to some extent a matter of controversy. For it does not seem to me that Philo even in his so-called 'Roman books' altogether abandoned scepticism. He himself at least could see this new position as one which had never been challenged in the Academy, and he continued to insist that Arcesilaus and Carneades did not constitute a break in the tradition of the school. Admittedly he now claimed that naturally we do know things, but, it seems, he continued to insist that we may be wrong in any particular case in which we think we know, since there is no such thing as an impression of how things are which guarantees its own truth. In any case there continued to be Academic sceptics like Favorinus of Arelate. And not all Platonists adopted Antiochus' view that Arcesilaus had fallen away from the tradition of Plato, though many like Numenius did. Plutarch, for one, did not.

More important for our present concerns is that it was already in the 90s and early 80s of the first century BC that Antiochus abandoned scepticism and Philo moved to the position of the Roman books. But this move was just the last leg of a longer journey which Philo had started out on years before as a student of Clitomachus. That was the time when he came to disagree with Clitomachus on the proper interpretation of Carneades' position. He came to take the view that belief can be justified, though never to such an extent as to constitute certain knowledge. This position he found difficult to defend. It caused Antiochus to break with scepticism, and he himself revised it. But all this started after Carneades' death towards the end of the second century BC, when Academics like Clitomachus and Metrodorus began to disagree about the correct understanding of Carneades' position. So again we are led back to the end of the second century BC as the point at which philosophy begins to develop in directions which will then characterize it around 30 BC and beyond.

*

Hence it seems that attempts to see the end of the Hellenistic era as marking an end of a period in the history of philosophy too do not succeed. More interestingly, in each case we are led back to the end of the second century BC, indeed to the same group of philosophers, which prominently includes Panaetius and Posidonius. What is more, if we look at this more closely there seems to emerge at just this point in time a certain pattern which comes to shape the philosophy of the first century BC and, beyond it, the philosophy of the early Empire. Perhaps the first thing to note is that it is two Stoics who show an interest in Plato and Aristotle which, as we saw, even the ancients found remarkable. This is interesting and significant in three regards.

First, Hellenistic philosophy had arisen out of a reaction to classical philosophy, with its turn to theory and its tendency to abstract speculation about postulated entities far removed, if not isolated, from experience. Epicurus went out of his way to deny that he had any teachers or predecessors, and adopted a position which on various points has affinities with ancient empiricism. He quite definitely did not want to be seen as having any connection with the schools of Plato or Aristotle. Of the four writings which Diogenes Laertius (x.25) ascribes to Epicurus' successor Hermarchus one is entitled *Against Plato* and another *Against Aristotle*. Indeed, when the Academy turned sceptical, this is plausibly seen as a revolt against what was regarded as a betrayal of the Socratic tradition of the school. Socrates had insisted on asking questions about how we should live, and on relentless examination of answers to these questions. The speculations of Speusippus or Xenocrates were hardly in the spirit of Socrates, and – in any case – certainly would not withstand dialectical examination. The Peripatos of Strato and his successors adopted a conspicuously deflationary metaphysics, if it did not abandon this interest altogether. And similarly the Stoics were out to reject Platonic ideas or Aristotelian forms or anything of the kind, and to concern themselves with the question what could serve as a reliable basis for solid knowledge as opposed to empty speculation. Both Zeno and Chrysippus also wrote against Plato.

So when Panaetius and Posidonius returned to Plato as a possible source for the truth, this in a way undermined the original motivation for Hellenistic philosophy, to the extent that it had arisen in reaction to Plato and Aristotle and their immediate followers. And correspondingly the picture of the Stoa changed. It was not just Antiochus who could point out, with some justice, that Stoicism had its origin in the Academy. This became a generally accepted view, even among Stoics, though there were then significant disagreements about the precise relation. Similarly it could now be argued, as it was by Philo and by Plutarch, that Arcesilaus was in the tradition of Plato. In short, instead of stress on a break, it was continuity with classical philosophy that came to be emphasized.

Second, it is remarkable that Panaetius, Posidonius and others not only take Plato and Aristotle seriously as philosophers; they regard them as authorities. Indeed, as we have already noted, Panaetius is said by Cicero to call Plato 'divine' constantly, and Galen tells us that Posidonius calls Plato 'divine'. It is clear that this is a reflection of a much larger cultural development, the beginning of Classicism, and – beyond that – a reflection of a more comprehensive cultural pessimism, dreaming of an original state of innocence, of uncorrupted morals, of piety, of perhaps inspired wisdom, somehow still represented by Plato, 'the divine, the most wise, the most pious, the Homer of philosophers', as Panaetius put it according to Cicero. This view involved a severe sense of discomfort with, if not condemnation of, the Hellenistic era as a period of decline, both in general and in philosophy. Hence the sense that one had to go back to the ancients, in the first instance to Plato and Aristotle, but also to Pythagoras and perhaps further back still, to Homer, Hesiod, Pherecydes, the wisdom of the ancients, if not the wisdom of the ancient nations, to look for the traces of the wisdom of an uncorrupted mankind.

Needless to say, this is a complex matter. I can here address just one aspect of it, and that only in passing. To return to the ancients, and in particular to Plato and Aristotle, involves studying their texts again. This, to begin with, has the consequence that their texts have to be made available in new editions. This in turn raises questions concerning the authenticity of transmitted writings, but also about the order in which they are to be arranged. Introductions to and compendia of Plato's or Aristotle's philosophy had to be written. One started to write monographs on specific questions in a certain text, perhaps from a special point of view, for example to explain specifically mathematical questions. Commentaries began to be written. They were written at different levels. For to treat Plato and Aristotle as authorities meant that if one at first sight did not understand them or disagreed with them, it would be worthwhile to study the text more closely and gain a deeper understanding of it. This was also the reason why reliable texts had to be prepared, to make sure that one really was studying the master's word. And the greater Plato's or Aristotle's authority was held to be, the more the study of philosophy at any level turned into a study of these texts, and writing philosophy more and more came to take the form of commentary. Correspondingly such commentary was concerned less and less to identify what the author actually may have wanted to say, and more and more to expound the truth suggested by the text. Thus we come to a point at which Origen can criticize Celsus, a Platonist of the second part of the second century, for treating Plato's text like Scripture.

All this, as far as Plato and Aristotle are concerned, is well documented. What perhaps is worth emphasizing is that it was not just Platonists and Aristotelians who studied and commented on Plato or Aristotle respectively.[12] We have already noted that the Stoics Athenodorus and Cornutus commented on Aristotle's *Categories*, whatever form this may have taken. Moreover, it is worth mentioning, though the evidence we

---

[12] Platonists later in antiquity came to write commentaries on Aristotle.

have is sparser, that the older Stoics were to some extent accorded a similar treatment. The Stoa had a problem in that it could not trace itself back to classical times. It could emphasize its Socratic heritage and point to its origin in Plato's Academy. Antiochus had been willing to regard the early Stoics' position as evidence for the true Platonic doctrine. And, especially as time went by, it became easier to count Zeno and Chrysippus among the ancients as opposed to the 'younger' or modern philosophers.

In any event, early in the first century BC we find Athenodorus, a Stoic and a librarian at Pergamum, producing editions of works of Zeno's, which he saw fit to expurgate. At roughly the same time Apollonius of Tyre drew up biographical sketches of the various Stoic philosophers from Zeno onwards, including lists of their writings (Strabo XVI.2.24). Perhaps the reference to Apollonius' *On Zeno* in Diogenes Laertius VII.6 is to a section of this compilation. Stoics also wrote commentaries on their school-texts. Thus we learn that an Aristocles of Lampsacus wrote a commentary in four books on Chrysippus' *How we say and think each thing*.[13] Indeed, Epictetus talks as if, when one had difficulties understanding a text by Chrysippus, one could resort to a commentary on it (*Diss.* I.17.16–18). It is also clear from repeated remarks in Epictetus that in the Stoa, too, studying and teaching philosophy largely involved the study of authoritative texts. Thus at *Diss.* III.21.6–7 he complains about philosophers who advertise themselves to students saying 'Come and listen to my scholia', boasting 'I will interpret Chrysippus' writings for you like nobody else, I will resolve all the unclarities about what he is saying, and here and there I will add the drift of Antipater's and Archedemus' position.' It is this kind of practice which must already have been widespread in philosophy quite generally early in the first century AD to allow Seneca to complain: 'What once was philosophy has been turned into philology' (*Ep.* 108.23), a remark echoed by Plotinus' characterization of Longinus as a philologist rather than a philosopher (Porph. *Plot.*14. 19–20).

Thus what is noteworthy about the way Panaetius and Posidonius turn to Plato and Aristotle is that, first, it signals a reaction against and an abandonment of the outlook typical of Hellenistic philosophy, and, second, it signals a regard for the classical philosophers as authoritative. But, what also is striking about it, is, third, the crossing of school boundaries, the willingness to let oneself be influenced by or even accept views characteristic of a different school. In this Panaetius and Posidonius foreshadow another characteristic of later philosophy, its eclecticism.

[13] Suda s.v. Aristocles.

*

Eclecticism too is much too complex a phenomenon to be addressed here at all adequately. For instance, in one way it has its source in the assumption that there are authorities. It is because Plato or Aristotle is an authority that his words have to be heeded, whether or not you are a Platonist or an Aristotelian. In another way eclecticism has its source in an anti-authoritative stance. It is because you do not acknowledge any particular authority inherent in the position of your school or the founders of your school that you feel free to choose on a particular point between the positions of different schools. Galen, who is one of the few philosophers in antiquity actually to characterize himself as eclectic, espouses eclecticism out of just such an anti-authoritative attitude, following a tradition going back to Academic scepticism, as we can see from Cicero's *Academica*.[14]

Given the complexity of the matter, I will here focus on one particular aspect, namely the question how the different schools handled the problem of authority across school boundaries, and the patterns of eclecticism which emerged from this. One thing to note here right from the outset is that Epicureanism seems to have been largely excluded from this eclectic exchange. Epicurus was an authority to his followers, and even outsiders would comment on the faithfulness of the Epicureans to the views of their founder.[15] But Epicurus for Epicureans was the only authority, and he was not regarded as authoritative by anybody else. The differences between Epicureanism and the other schools were too fundamental to make partial or selective assimilations possible. If Seneca sometimes appears surprisingly accommodating to Epicureanism, we have to keep in mind the 'pastoral' character of much of his writing. If one tries to win others for the good life, or even the good life conceived of by the Stoics, it will often be opportune not to insist on, or even to minimize, the disagreements concerning very fundamental, but hence also quite abstract and theoretical tenets, especially if the persons addressed have Epicurean sympathies, as is the case with Lucilius (*Ep.* 23.9). After all, the other three Dogmatic schools did have a common heritage which divided them from the Epicureans: they all derived somehow from Socrates and Plato, whereas Epicurus had made a point of not following any venerable tradition, let alone one which connected him with Plato.

Increasingly the authority was Plato, and so we should look first at the attitude which the two non-Platonic schools other than the Epicureans

---

[14] Cf. Gal. *Lib.Prop.* xix.13K = p. 95 Marquard; *Aff.Dig.*, *CMG* v.4.1, p.1.28.
[15] Numenius *apud* Euseb. *Praep.Ev.* xiv.5.3.

took towards Plato and Platonism. There had been a long tradition of admiration for Plato in the Peripatos, no doubt inspired by Aristotle himself, and revealed, e.g., in Clearchus' *Encomium Platonis*.[16] There were certain limits set by the fact that Aristotle himself criticized Plato. And so there was a tradition among the Peripatetics, exemplified foremost by Alexander of Aphrodisias, which insisted on these obvious differences. But it seems that there was little polemic against Plato or Platonism. Peripatetics like Andronicus had no qualms in espousing an old Academic doctrine ascribed to Plato, even where there was a rival Aristotelian doctrine: in his case the doctrine of two, as opposed to ten, categories, absolutes and relatives. It is clear from Atticus' remarks that in the second century AD there was a tendency among Peripatetics to regard themselves as the allies of Platonism.[17] This is borne out by the case of Aristocles of Messene who talks of 'Plato's Peripatos' (Euseb. *Praep.Ev.* xv.2.1), and also says (*Praep.Ev.* xi.3.1): 'If there ever was a true and perfect philosopher, it was Plato' – surely a somewhat surprising remark from a Peripatetic. What is more, if Panaetius had talked of Plato as the Homer of philosophers, Aristocles wrote 'Who is better, Homer or Plato?'[18]

As to the Stoics, the tone, it seems, was set by Panaetius' and Posidonius' positive attitude towards Plato. Seneca expresses himself in striking terms when he criticizes philosophers who proudly talk in a manner which has nothing to do with their own life (*Ep.* 108.38). They say things which they have not made their own: 'Plato has said this, Zeno said it, Chrysippus said it, and so did Posidonius and so did a great host of fellow Stoics, large in number and of such reputation.' Here Plato appears at the head of the Stoic cohort. Such friendly sentiments must have been encouraged by a tendency in the Stoa in the first century AD towards asceticism, often associated with Pythagoras and exemplified by Attalus, Chaeremon and the Sextii, who were Stoics, but preferred to be called Pythagoreans. There were strong common interests, for instance in demonology and magic, and there were very few fundamental differences, easily identifiable and primarily concerning the transcendence of God and the intellect. Some issues were less clearcut: thus the classical Stoic doctrine of the complete rationality of the soul was at least undermined by Posidonius' innovations, if not, as Galen thought, jettisoned by him altogether. It became possible for Porphyry to call a late Stoic, Trypho, 'a Stoic and a Platonist' (*Plot.* 17.3).

The Platonists were less accommodating. They, after all, were the guardians of the heritage of the most authoritative philosopher. His

---

[16] D.L. iii.2; cf. Ath. 393a.   [17] Euseb. *Praep.Ev.* xv.4.6–19; 5.3.   [18] Cf. Suda s.v. Aristocles.

status was invulnerable to challenge except by Pythagoras, who had left no writings. To begin with, the Platonist attitude towards Stoicism was positive, even if critical. Philo, who had taken the position that Academic scepticism was perfectly compatible with philosophical beliefs, was heavily influenced by Stoicism in his positive views. Antiochus – to judge from Cicero's *Academica* – took the view that the Stoics differed from the Academy largely in terminology. He himself was said to have introduced into the Academy Stoic views on a large scale, so that he appeared rather like a Stoic fighting Stoics (cf. S.E. *PH* 1.235). He also had been, we have to remember, a student of Mnesarchus, who had succeeded Panaetius.[19] If we assume that Mnesarchus, like Panaetius and Posidonius, admired Plato, it is even easier to see why Antiochus would study with Mnesarchus and take such a positive view of the Stoa. Even Antiochus insisted, though, that where the Stoa had deviated from Old Academic doctrine, it had done so for the worse.

Antiochus' stoicizing picture of Plato, as noted, provoked a reaction which emphasized the 'Pythagorean' elements in Plato, a reaction we first find in Eudorus. But if we look at Eudorus' division of philosophy and in particular of ethics, as preserved in Stobaeus (ii.42.7–45.6), it is so indebted to Stoicism that it is only intelligible against a Stoic background; indeed it is so faithful to it that it can itself help us to reconstruct the Stoic position on the parts of ethics. Later Platonists thought of the Stoa as having developed out of the Academy, but also noted critically the divergences which had given rise to the split, or even focused on the differences. Calvisius Taurus wrote against the Stoics. Plutarch wrote a book *De Stoicorum Repugnantiis* in which he tried to show that wherever the Stoics deviated from Platonic doctrine they fell into contradiction, as if held captive by the truth. Numenius insisted on the claim that the Stoics had abandoned the true Platonic philosophy. And Plotinus is highly critical of Stoicism.

But this last case points to an important phenomenon. Porphyry, who was very scholarly and had an extensive knowledge both of Aristotle and of the Stoics, observed that Plotinus, though highly critical of Aristotle and the Stoa, had actually absorbed a great deal both of Stoicism and of Aristotelianism (*Plot.* 14.4–7). Moderatus of Gades, as Porphyry noted elsewhere, had already described what he took to be a similar phenomenon (*VP* 53). Moderatus complained that Plato, Aristotle, and their students, with minor modifications, appropriated for themselves those

---

[19] Numenius *apud* Euseb. *Praep.Ev.* xiv.9.3, Phld. *Stoic. Hist.* col. 51.4.

Pythagorean doctrines which suited them, pretending that there was nothing particularly Pythagorean about them, thus attributing to the Pythagoreans only those views they found objectionable or even ridiculous. We may find this diagnosis mistaken in the case of Pythagoreanism, but it does seem that the Stoics in our period often were the victims of a similar attitude, for instance on the part of Numenius or Plotinus. And this was made easier by the view that, after all, the Stoa was an off-shoot of the Academy, a fact unduly obscured by Stoic innovations in terminology. Hence what was regarded as good about Stoicism could be regarded as not specifically Stoic, but as part of the common Academic heritage.

Aristotle, being a classical philosopher and nearer to Plato, had a better standing among the Platonists than Zeno and the Stoics. Antiochus had apparently minimized differences in their views. But Calvisius Taurus wrote a treatise on the differences between Plato and Aristotle.[20] Numenius rejects the view that Aristotle still somehow preserves the true doctrine.[21] He notes that Cephisodorus is supposed to have attacked Aristotle's theory of ideas, but thinks that this only shows that Cephisodorus never read Aristotle and mistook him for a Platonist.[22] Apparently it was a point that needed to be made, especially in light of the fact that some Peripatetics like Aristocles were minimizing the differences. For Atticus again tried to show that Plato and Aristotle were in basic disagreement.[23] And this certainly was the view Plotinus took.

*

Given on the one hand Aristotle's own criticism of Plato, and given, on the other hand, the fact that Aristotle in his mature thought seems to have been motivated by considerations rather similar to Plato's, and that in the debate with early Stoicism there are large areas in which Aristotle seems to be lined up with Plato against the Stoics (for instance on the parts and the affections of the soul, on goods and the good life, and on the existence of immaterial objects), one understands the ambivalence. Porphyry wrote both a treatise on the agreement of Plato and Aristotle, and a treatise on the disagreement between Plato and Aristotle.[24] And it seems to be in good part due to Porphyry's influence that a somewhat unstable compromise was found, which allowed Platonists to look upon Aristotle as an authority on logic and physics, who wrote sometimes for an audience not yet introduced to the higher realms of reality, as in his *Categories*.

[20] Cf. Suda s.v. Taurus.   [21] Numenius *apud* Euseb. *Praep.Ev.* xiv.5.8.
[22] Numenius *apud* Euseb. *Praep.Ev.* xiv.6.9.   [23] Cf. Euseb. *Praep.Ev.* xi.1.2; xv.4.6 ff.; 5.3.
[24] Cf. Suda s.v. Porphyrios; Elias *Porph.* 39.6–8.

It remains to consider the attitude of Stoics and Aristotelians to each other. Some of the relevant facts already have been mentioned, in particular Panaetius' and especially Posidonius' positive view of Aristotle. It seems, though, that on the whole the interests of the two schools developed in different directions, and that where they overlapped, as on the question of fate and determinism or in logic, there was dispute. Aristotle never was accorded the place of honour given to Plato. Peripatetics could not avoid being influenced by Stoicism, in that they had to address the questions raised by the Hellenistic Stoa and had inherited the largely Stoic Hellenistic philosophical vocabulary and conceptual framework. But they had no reason to treat the Stoics as anything but opponents who failed to agree with Aristotle and the truth on some fundamental issues in logic, physics, metaphysics, and ethics.

These, then, are some of the most important and characteristic traits of philosophy in the first two centuries AD which can be traced back directly to the end of the second century BC, by considering Panaetius, Posidonius, and their contemporaries like Philo. But there is yet more of relevance for the future evolution of philosophy to be learned from considering the stances of these thinkers.

*

It seems that Sulla's conquest of Athens in 87 BC had a devastating effect on philosophy in Athens. Not only did Sulla take Aristotle's library to Rome. Philo, the head of the Academy, had already left Athens for Rome. It seems that the Academy physically suffered very considerable damage and actually ceased to exist as an institution. Similarly the Lyceum seems to have suffered. Andronicus of Rhodes is the last scholarch of the Peripatos we know of, and, as we saw, he too went to Rome. For all we know, the Peripatos as an institution had come to an end, too. These are dramatic changes, but they were foreshadowed by earlier events.

It is characteristic of Hellenistic philosophy (i.e. from roughly 300 BC to about 125 BC) that it is essentially an Athenian affair. There were quite literally four schools in Athens. Somebody who really wanted to be a philosopher came to Athens and studied in these schools. And somebody who became a good philosopher almost invariably stayed in Athens. More likely than not the most distinguished representative of a school at some point became scholarch. Epicurus and Zeno came to Athens and stayed. Right from the time of their first successors there were attempts to persuade major philosophers to leave Athens to live at court. But they failed. Thus Zeno was invited to join Antigonus, but he sent Persaeus instead (D.L. vii.6–9). When Ptolemy asked Cleanthes to come to Alexandria, he refused; so did Chrysippus, hence Sphaerus went (D.L. vii.185; cf. 177).

This is all the more remarkable given that few of the leading figures were themselves Athenians. Zeno, Herillus, Chrysippus, and Clitomachus were not even of Greek origin. It seems that if one was serious about philosophy as a theoretical enterprise, there really was no alternative to going to Athens. Athens itself managed to retain considerable political significance and enough economic vitality to support a fairly sizeable philosophical community. Indeed, on the whole it seems to have welcomed its philosophers. When in 155 BC Athens sent an embassy to Rome, this very fact indicated that times were changing. Athens had been pressed into a treaty with Rome which it violated, for which violation Rome demanded an exorbitant fine. Athens by now saw no alternative to sending an embassy to Rome to plead for a reduction or a cancellation of the fine. The embassy consisted of three scholarchs, the Academic Carneades, the Stoic Diogenes of Babylon, and the Peripatetic Critolaus. This is not only, on any count, a group of highly distinguished philosophers. No less important is that they clearly had no rivals anywhere else, nobody even faintly comparable.

But when we come to the latter part of the century, the situation has radically changed. Here, again, Panaetius and Posidonius are exemplary. Of course, Panaetius had been a student of Diogenes of Babylon and of Antipater in Athens. But he does leave Athens, at least for about fifteen years, to return only around 129 to succeed Antipater. Equally significant is that in the meantime he goes to Rome, associates with the circle around P. Cornelius Scipio Aemilianus, and so achieves contact with the rising power of Rome. From now on many major Greek philosophers will go to Rome for extended periods of time, or even stay there for good. Rome from the first century BC onwards, until at least well into the third century AD, becomes a major philosophical centre. But to come back to Panaetius. Panaetius in the end still does return to Athens to become scholarch. But Posidonius not only leaves Athens; he sets up a school elsewhere in Rhodes. Antiochus goes to Alexandria with some of his followers, and there all of a sudden seems to be a lot of philosophical activity in Alexandria in the first century BC. By the time we get to the latter half of the century, a major philosopher more likely than not is not to be found in Athens, but in Rome or Alexandria or Rhodes or elsewhere. Athens definitely has lost its monopoly. It will be a long time before it again exercises a leading role in philosophy with the rise of the Platonist School of Athens. It is indicative of this state of affairs that

Cicero in the late 40s tries to persuade the Areopagus to induce the Peripatetic Cratippus to stay in Athens (Plu. *Cic.* 24). Romans might still send their sons to Athens to study philosophy, as does Cicero. But this was hardly a reflection of the quality of philosophy on offer at Athens at this point. In this regard they would have been better served staying at Rome.

The consequences of this are easy to see. The diffusion of philosophers and the emergence of a variety of centres of philosophical study encouraged a proliferation of philosophical positions, fostered separate and independent developments, and undermined the unity of the position of a school. There could now be a variety of Stoicisms, Platonisms, or Aristotelianisms. This goes some way to explain the absence of clear contours in the history of the philosophy done in the period from 125 BC to 250 AD. To know the position of Chrysippus is roughly speaking to know the position of the Stoa of his time. But to know the position of Posidonius or Mnesarchus or Cornutus is only to know what some Stoics in their day thought.

This effect is amplified by the fate of the Athenian schools. As institutions these schools lost their importance and seem to have gone out of existence. There was no scholarch to define the philosophical position of the school. It was no longer relatively clear what the position of a school was on a particular question at a particular time, or even what it was to be a Stoic, or a Peripatetic. Schools now became movements of thought, fairly vaguely defined. Philosophers of rather different views could claim to be Stoics or Peripatetics.

To some extent it was arbitrary how somebody was classified. Lucian in the *Eunuchus* gives us a picture of the competition for the successor to a chair of Peripatetic philosophy in Athens established by Marcus Aurelius. The competitors tried to show that they were well versed in Aristotelianism, but also that they themselves were partisans of Aristotle and his doctrines (ch. 2). There would have been little point in this if it had been clear anyway who counted as a Peripatetic and what one could expect of such a person. Obviously there was the fear that somebody might claim to be a Peripatetic without being one, or without being an orthodox one. There was also something like the reverse. Historians distinguish the school of the Sextii; but Seneca (*Ep.* 64.2) tells us that the elder Sextius, though he denied it, really was a Stoic, and that seems to be right.

While other authors too of this period are difficult to classify, like Favorinus of Arelate or Lucianus, still others, like Galen refuse to be regarded as members of any school or movement.[25] This vagueness and indefiniteness about what it is to belong to a certain school must have reinforced greatly the process by which the founders of a school turned into authorities and their writings became authoritative texts that to some extent defined the school. What came to unify a school more and more was the special status the schools accorded to their respective founder or founders. At the beginning of the period it still had been possible for a Peripatetic to take issue with Aristotle, even though Aristotle was an authority. Thus Andronicus does not accept Aristotle's doctrine of categories, and Xenarchus writes against Aristotle's assumption of a fifth element.[26] But it seems that in the course of time the explication and defence of Plato's or Aristotle's views became more and more important.

*

One thing which we set out to explain was the fate of the Hellenistic schools in the post-Hellenistic era. What characterizes the philosophy of late antiquity from the second part of the third century AD onwards is the fact that philosophers invariably espouse one form of Platonism or other: Aristotelianism, Stoicism, Epicureanism, and scepticism are no longer active movements. Needless to say, the reasons for this are manifold. But the main reason surely is that only some form of Platonism satisfied the way people in late antiquity looked at the world: the demand for a transcendent God, the belief in a vast realm of spiritual beings, an otherworldly view of life and the belief in an afterlife. In particular, with the rise and eventual domination of Christianity, and, given the form Christian dogma had taken (in good part under the influence of Platonism) by the time it became dominant, there was no longer any place for Stoicism, Epicureanism or Aristotelianism. Even Hellenism or paganism and the attempts to revive paganism were inspired by Platonism. Later in the third century AD a Peripatetic like Anatolius of Laodicea could still become bishop (cf. Euseb. *HE* VII.32.6 ff.), but by the fourth or fifth century this would have been quite difficult, given for instance Aristotle's belief in the eternity of the world, not to mention the suspicion that his logic inspired heresies like Arianism.

Some remarks by Longinus quoted by Porphyry in his *Life of Plotinus* (ch. 20) seem to give us a fairly representative view of the state of

---

[25] *Lib.Prop.* XIX.13K = p. 95 Marquard; *Aff.Dig.*, *CMG* v.4.1, p.1.28 f.
[26] Simp. *Cat.* 63.22 ff., *Cael.* 25.22 ff.

philosophy in Plotinus' time. The remarks come from the dedicatory epistle to Longinus' book *On the end*. Longinus complains that in his youth (he was born around 210 AD) there still were many philosophers of some distinction, whereas now there is hardly anybody left, except for Plotinus and Amelius who are much more philosophical than their contemporaries or even the philosophers of Longinus' youth. These philosophers of the recent past Longinus divides into two groups: those who tried to contribute to philosophy by their writings, and those who focused on teaching, though they may have left some occasional piece of writing (*Plot.* 20.25–9). Among the former he lists the Platonists Euclides, Democritus and Proclinus, but also Plotinus and Amelius, the Stoics Themistocles, Phoebion, Annius, and Medius, and the Peripatetic Heliodorus (*Plot.* 20.29–36). Among the latter he counts the Platonists Ammonius and Origen, Theodotus and Eubulus, the Stoics Herminus, Lysimachus, Athenaeus, and Musonius, and the Peripatetics Ammonius and Ptolemaeus (*Plot.* 20.36–57). So there are nine Platonists, eight Stoics, three Peripatetics, and no Epicurean, though this perhaps just reflects Longinus' bias.

Of these twenty philosophers Longinus thinks that two are outstanding, the Platonists Plotinus and Amelius. We will question his judgement concerning Amelius. But if we lower our standards somewhat, we will be able to say that the four philosophers on the list who have a secure place of considerable significance in the history of philosophy are all Platonists: Ammonius, Origen, Plotinus and Amelius. Indeed of the nine Platonists, all but one or two, Proclinus and Theodotus, are known or even well known to us from elsewhere. Of the eight Stoics four are only mentioned here; there is the faint possibility that Themistocles and Phoebion are each mentioned once elsewhere, though not because of their doctrine; there is the strong possibility that Lysimachus is the Lysimachus already mentioned by Porphyry (*Plot.* 3.43) as the teacher of Amelius. This leaves us with Medius as the only Stoic on the list of whom we do have definite, though insignificant, knowledge about his philosophical position from elsewhere (Procl. *Rep.* 1.234.1ff.). Of the three Peripatetics Heliodorus is otherwise unknown, Ammonius seems to be mentioned by Philostratus in the *Lives of Sophists* (II.27), and Ptolemaeus has been plausibly identified with the Peripatetic mentioned by Sextus Empiricus (*M* 1.60 and 72) as denying that grammar is a matter of empirical knowledge, as Dionysius Thrax had claimed.

Apart from the Platonists we thus know only Medius for some definite philosophical view, and this is the traditional Stoic view that the soul has eight parts. The impression we get is very much reinforced by Longinus' comments on these men. As to the Peripatetics, Heliodorus, according to Longinus, did indeed try to contribute to philosophy by writing, but he merely reworked the lectures (perhaps commentaries) of earlier Peripatetics; Ptolemaeus and in particular Ammonius were extremely learned (Porph. *Plot*. 20.49 and 51), but only left poems and rhetorical show-pieces, no technical works. Of the Stoics Phoebion was more concerned with style than with intellectual substance (*Plot*. 20.63–5), and in any case the Stoics who did write wrote comments on small historical questions concerning old Stoic authors, and tried to compose treatises on the same topics as their predecessors. There is no originality. There are no new problems. And this was the state of philosophy in Longinus' youth, which, he thought, had dramatically deteriorated, in that there were few philosophers left. As far as Aristotelianism or Stoicism is concerned, given our evidence, he certainly seems to be right.

So why were the old schools rapidly disappearing, if they had not already disappeared? Scepticism ran counter to the spirit of the times. Pyrrhonism all along seems to have been represented not so much by philosophers, as by Empiricist doctors, men like Menodotus, Theodas, or Sextus Empiricus. It certainly did not find public favour. Marcus Aurelius provided professorships for the four traditional schools, but not for the Pyrrhonists. Larger communities like Smyrna would have or even fund representatives of the four schools, but not of Pyrrhonism. If Pyrrhonists were aggressive, they would attack the spreading idea that the salvation of the soul required knowledge of things beyond ordinary experience or, failing that, at least unwarranted belief or faith as a first, perhaps necessary, step to knowledge. If they were conservative, they would continue in the simple beliefs and customs of their ancestors, which similarly were deemed inadequate.

Epicureanism suffered for similar reasons. Origen was mistaken in identifying Celsus, the author of an attack on Christianity, as an Epicurean. But what helped to make the identification seem plausible was that this sort of attack was precisely what might be expected from an Epicurean; and as Origen knew, there was an Epicurean called Celsus who could well have been the author of an attack on Christianity.[27] For Celsus the Epicurean had written against magic, and Lucian evidently dedicated his *Alexander* to him because he took Celsus to share his views on wonder-workers like Alexander, a student of Apollonius of Tyana who was glo-

---

[27] Orig. *Cels*. 1.68; cf. Lucian *Alex*. 25, 43, 61. Evidence on magic: *Alex*. 21.

rified by Philostratus as a holy man and a great worker of miracles, and later often compared to Jesus. For given the Epicurean view of nature, such wonder-workers could not but be charlatans, deceiving the credulous in their ignorance of the workings of nature. From the very beginning Epicureanism had aimed at freeing people from what it took to be superstitious beliefs about the interference of gods and about the afterlife. Epicureans rejected them as irrational and in conflict with a proper understanding of reality. This concern was still passionately expressed by Lucretius. But such views now damaged the attraction of Epicureanism. An understanding of reality which left no room for the supernatural was regarded as radically inadequate at a time when the influence of superior powers and their interference with the regular course of events seemed so palpable to everybody.

To some extent even Aristotelianism, with its rather sober and theoretical view of things, suffered from the fact that it did not accommodate common belief concerning God, providence, the afterlife. It also suffered from the fact that Aristotle, once accorded a carefully circumscribed authority, could be and was integrated into a Platonist view of the world. He could be seen as the master logician, as opposed to the Platonic dialectician; as the philosopher of the physical world, as opposed to the higher realms of reality; as the philosopher who had recognized the Divine Intellect, but failed to recognize God, the First Principle.

Stoicism, on the other hand, especially in the form it had received from Posidonius, was well equipped to accommodate popular belief in magic, astrology, other forms of divination, demons, the afterlife of the soul and the divine origin of at least part of it, or divine providence. It provided the basis for social criticism, it gave concrete moral advice which seemed to appeal to people, it offered attractive ways of life and justifications for them. But in the end it suffered from the fact that it was only of Hellenistic origin. What was appealing about it had been absorbed by Platonism. And it lacked what only Platonism could offer, the belief that this life is not the real life, that this world is not the real world, and that God is not part of this world. Ultimately people were not prepared to live with the idea that everything is corrupt, but that this makes good sense from a global point of view, when there was so little realistic hope that things would be radically different, even though one struggled to purify one's heart and to help others on the way. Chrysippus had said that one drowned just below the surface as much as if one was stuck at the bottom of the sea. But when he said this there was the hope, one would have thought, of emerging above the surface. The Stoics had had five centuries to try, without success. It is not surprising that it came to be thought that Stoicism had not lived up to its promise, and that something else was needed. It was in this way that the future came to belong to Platonism and then to Christianity.

Appendix
Synopsis of the principal events and schools
TIZIANO DORANDI

Year BC	Academy	Lyceum	Stoa	Kepos	Pyrrhonists	Minor Socratics
c. 412–03						Birth of Diogenes of Sinope
c. 408	Birth of Speusippus					
396/5	Birth of Xenocrates					
372/1–371/0		Birth of Theophrastus				
c. 368/5						Birth of Crates of Thebes
367 or 361	Xenocrates accompanies Plato to Sicily					
361/0	Heraclides heads the Academy					
365–360						
c. 360					Birth of Pyrrho	Birth of Stilpo
c. 360–280						Aristotle of Cyrene
c. 350–250						Antipater of Cyrene
ante 348						Birth of Euphantus
348/7		Theophrastus at Assos				
345/4						Birth of Menedemus of Eretria
342/1				Birth of Epicurus		
340–330		Birth of Strato				
340–250						Theodorus the Atheist
c. 339						Birth of Alexinus
339/8	Death of Speusippus; Xenocrates becomes scholarch					
337/6		Aristotle in Lyceum				
334/3			Birth of Zeno			
334–334					Pyrrho and Anaxarchus in Asia with Alexander	

Date					
331/0		Birth of Cleanthes	Birth of Metrodorus; Epicurus begins philosophical studies		
328/7			Birth of Idomeneus and Hermarchus		
c. 325			Birth of Pythocles	Birth of Timon	
c. 324					Death of Diogenes of Sinope
c. 324–321			Epicurus ephebe		
323–321					
322	Xenocrates' mission to Antipater				
322/1	Death of Aristotle; Theophrastus becomes scholarch				
c. 320			Birth of Colotes; Epicurus in Colophon		*floruit* of Dionysius of Chalcedon and Euphantus
320–311					
320–300					
317–307	Demetrius of Phalerum governor of Athens				
316/5	Birth of Arcesilaus				
315–284					*floruit* of Diodorus Cronus
314/13	Death of Xenocrates; Polemo becomes scholarch				
311/10–307/6			Epicurus teaches at Mytilene and at Lampsacus		
c. 310					Philo's study with Diodorus Cronus
307/6		Birth of Persaeus			

Year BC	Academy	Lyceum	Stoa	Kepos	Pyrrhonists	Minor Socratics
307/6 or 305/4				Epicurus founds the Garden in Athens		
c. 306–301				Idomeneus is court dignitary at Lampsacus		
c. 301				Idomeneus converts to Epicureanism		
301/0				Epicurus writes book XIV of the *peri physeōs*		
300/299				Epicurus writes book XV of the *peri physeōs*		
300/299 or 299/8		Birth of Lyco		Epicurus writes book XXVIII of the *peri physeōs*		
296/5				Apostasy of Timocrates; Death of Polyaenus		
c. 290						*floruit* of Hegesias
290–280						
288/7–287/6		Death of Theophrastus; Strato becomes scholarch				
288–285						Death of Crates of Thebes
c. 285			Birth of Sphaerus			
c. 284						Death of Diodorus Cronus
c. 280			Birth of Chrysippus			Death of Stilpo
c. 280–275				Death of Metrodorus		*floruit* of Panthoides
280–276						
278/7						
276/5	Death of Crantor					
275–273	Birth of Eratosthenes					
275–270					Death of Pyrrho	
c. 270					Timon in Athens	
271/0				Death of Epicurus		
270/69	Death of Polemo; Crates becomes scholarch					

Date						
270/69–269/8		Death of Strato; Lyco becomes scholarch				
268–264	Death of Crates; Arcesilaus becomes scholarch					
267/6				Hermarchus opposes Alexinus		
c. 265			Sphaerus goes to Athens			Death of Alexinus
262/1			Death of Zeno; Cleanthes becomes scholarch			
261/0						Death of Menedemus of Eretria
260–255		floruit of Prytanis; Birth of Aristo of Ceos	floruit of Persaeus			
c. 250				Death of Hermarchus; Polystratus becomes scholarch; Birth of Basilides(?)		floruit of Aristotle the Dialectician and of Artemidorus
243			Death of Persaeus			
241/0	Death of Arcesilaus; Lacydes becomes scholarch					
c. 240			Sphaerus in Sparta			
c. 235			Birth of Diogenes of Seleucia		Death of Timon	
c. 230			Death of Cleanthes; Aristocreon at Athens			
230/29		Prytanis' mission to Antigonus Doson				
229–209		Death of Lyco; Aristo becomes scholarch				
225						
226/5 or 225/4	Lacydes resigns as scholarch; Telecles and Euander succeed him					
c. 222			Sphaerus in Egypt with Cleomenes III			

Year BC	Academy	Lyceum	Stoa	Kepos	Pyrrhonists	Minor Socratics
219/8				Death of Polystratus; Dionysius of Lamptrai becomes scholarch		
214/3	Birth of Carneades of Cyrene the Elder					
208–204			Death of Chrysippus			
206/5	Death of Lacydes					
205/4				Death of Dionysius; Basilides becomes scholarch		
187/6	Birth of Clitomachus					
185/4	Death of Moschion					
185–180			Birth of Panaetius			
c. 175				Death of Basilides; Thespis (?) becomes scholarch; Apollodorus becomes scholarch		
?						
174/3	Death of Eubulus of Ephesus and of Eubulus of Erythrae					
c. 170	Death of Agamestor		Birth of Mnesarchus and Dardanus			
168/7			Panaetius studies with Crates of Mallos			
post 168/7						
167/6	Death of Telecles; Carneades the Elder becomes scholarch					
166/5	Death of Apollonius					
163/2	Clitomachus in Athens					
ante 155			Panaetius becomes hierothytes of Poseidon Hippios at Lindos			
155	Carneades' mission to Rome	Critolaus' mission to Rome	Diogenes' mission to Rome			
post 155			Panaetius studies with Diogenes in Athens			

Date			
154/3	Birth of Philo; Clitomachus begins his studies with Carneades the Elder		
c. 150			Birth of Zeno of Sidon and of Demetrius Laco
150–140		Death of Diogenes	
150–120			*floruit* of Protarchus of Bargylia
149/8		Panaetius is *hieropoios* in Athens; Panaetius meets Scipio	
post 146	Death of Eubulus		
143/2	Charmadas, aged 22, goes to Athens		
142/1	Clitomachus retires in the Palladium		
140/39		Panaetius in the East with Scipio	
140–138			Birth of Phaedrus
138		Panaetius travels between Rome and Athens	
c. 138–120			
137/6	Carneades the Elder retires as scholarch; succeeded by Carneades the Younger		
131/0	Death of Carneades the Younger; succeeded by Crates of Tarsus; Birth of Antiochus of Ascalon; Philo goes to Athens		
c. 130		Death of Antipater of Tarsus; Panaetius becomes scholarch	
130/29	Death of Carneades the Elder; Clitomachus in the Academy		

Year BC	Academy	Lyceum	Stoa	Kepos	Pyrrhonists	Minor Socratics
127/6	Death of Crates; Clitomachus becomes scholarch					
120/19	Death of Boethus of Marathon					
119/8				Phaedrus is ephebe		
c. 118		Death of Critolaus				
110/9	Death of Clitomachus; Philo becomes scholarch		Death of Panaetius			
c. 100	Antiochus' conversion					
c. 90	Philo in Rome			Zeno becomes scholarch		
post 88	Antiochus goes to Alexandria in Egypt		Death of Mnesarchus and Dardanus	Phaedrus in Rome		
c. 87–84	Death of Philo					
84/3	Antiochus in Athens					
79	Death of Antiochus					
c. 68						

Editions of sources and fragments

Collections of fragments of various authors

von Arnim, J. (1903–05) *Stoicorum Veterum Fragmenta*, 3 vols. (Leipzig); vol. 4, indexes by Adler, M. (Leipzig 1924) [abbreviation: *SVF*]

Giannantoni, G. (1990) *Socratis et Socraticorum Reliquiae*, 4 vols. (Naples) [abbreviation: *SSR*]

Hülser, K.-H. (1987–88) *Die Fragmente zur Dialektik der Stoiker*, 4 vols. (Stuttgart) [abbreviation: *FDS*]

Series of editions of individual authors

▪ Editions of many Greek and Latin authors are available in the following series:

Bibliotheca Scriptorum Graecorum et Latinorum Teubneriana, B.G. Teubner: Leipzig & Stuttgart [abbreviation: Teubner]

Scriptorum Classicorum Bibliotheca Oxoniensis [= Oxford Classical Texts], Clarendon Press: Oxford [abbreviation: OCT]

Collection des Universités de France, publiée sous le patronage de l'Association de Guillaume Budé, Les Belles Lettres: Paris (Greek or Latin text with facing French translation) [abbreviation: Budé]

The Loeb Classical Library, Harvard University Press and W. Heinemann, Cambridge Mass. & London (Greek or Latin text with facing English translation) [abbreviation: Loeb]

In general critical editions in the Teubner and Oxford series are recommended, although many in the Budé and Loeb series, especially in the last quarter century, are also valuable. The particular suggestions in the list which follows are designed to guide the reader to editions which are regarded as standard or as particularly useful for the student of Hellenistic philosophy, or which authors of this History have recommended.

▪ Standard editions of a number of the authors and works mentioned below are to be found in the following series:

Commentaria in Aristotelem Graeca, Prussian Academy series [abbreviation: *CAG*]

Corpus Christianorum, Series Latina [abbreviation: *CCSL*]

Corpus Medicorum Graecorum, Berlin Academy series [abbreviation: *CMG*]

Corpus Medicorum Latinorum, Berlin Academy series [abbreviation: *CML*]

Corpus Scriptorum Ecclesiasticorum Latinorum [abbreviation: *CSEL*]

Die griechischen christlichen Schriftsteller der ersten drei ahrhunderte [abbreviation: *GCS*]

Sources Chrétiennes [abbreviation *SC*]

Editions of (works or fragments of) individual authors

ACHILLES

Introductio in Aratum
Maass, E. (1898) *Commentariorum in Aratum reliquiae* (Berlin, reprint 1958)

AËTIUS

Placita
Reconstruction in Diels, H. (1879) *Doxographi Graeci* (Berlin)

ALCINOUS

Didaskalikos
Whittaker, J. & Louis, P. (Budé,1990) *Alcinoos: Enseignement des doctrines de Platon* (Paris)

ALEXANDER OF APHRODISIAS

In Aristotelis Analyticorum Priorum librum I commentarium
Hayduck, M. (1891), in *CAG*, vol. II.1 (Berlin)
De Anima libri Mantissa
Bruns, I. (1887), in *CAG*, Supplementum Aristotelicum, vol. II.1 (Berlin)
In librum De Sensu commentarium
Westland, P. (1901), in *CAG*, vol. III.1 (Berlin)
In Aristotelis Metaphysica commentarium
Hayduck, M. (1891), in *CAG*, vol. I (Berlin)
De Fato
Sharples, R.W. (1983) *Alexander of Aphrodisias on Fate* (London)
De Mixtione
Todd, R.B. (1976) *Alexander of Aphrodisias on Stoic Physics* (Leiden)

AMMONIUS

In Aristotelis De Interpretatione commentarium
Busse, A. (1897), in *CAG*, vol. IV.5 (Berlin)

[ANDRONICUS]

De Passionibus
Glibert-Thirry, A. (1977) *Pseudo-Andronicus de Rhodes 'ΠΕΡΙ ΠΑΘΩΝ'* (Leiden)

ANONYMUS IN THEAETETUM

Bastianini, G. & Sedley, D.N. (1995), in *Corpus dei Papiri Filosofici Greci e Latini*, pt. III: Commentari (Florence)

ANONYMUS IN SOPHISTICOS ELENCHOS

Hayduck, M. (1884), in *CAG*, vol. XXIII.4 (Berlin)

ANONYMUS LONDINENSIS

Diels, H. (1893) *Anonymi Londinensis ex Aristotelis Iatricis Menoniis et aliis medicis eclogae*, in *CAG*, Suppl. Arist., vol. III.1 (Berlin)

APOLLONIUS DYSCOLUS

De Pronominibus
De Adverbiis
De Conjunctionibus

Schneider, R. (1878), in *Grammatici Graeci*, vol. II.1 (Leipzig)
De Syntaxi
Schneider, R. (1910), in *Grammatici Graeci*, vol.II.2 (Stuttgart)

APOLLONIUS OF PERGA

Conica
Heiberg, J.L. (Teubner, 1891, 1893) *Apollonii Pergaei Quae Graece exstant cum commentariis antiquis* (Stuttgart, reprint 1974) [Books 1-4, fragments]
Toomer, G.J. (1990) *Apollonius: Conics, books V to VII*: the Arabic translation of the lost Greek original in the version of the Banu Musa (New York)

APULEIUS

Apologia
Helm, R. (Teubner, 1912) *Apulei Opera* 2.1 (Leipzig)
De Deo Socratis
De Dogmate Platonis
ΠΕΡΙ ΕΡΜΗΝΕΙΑΣ
Moreschini, C. (Teubner, 1991) *Apulei Opera* (Stuttgart & Leipzig)

ARCHIMEDES

Heiberg, J.L. (Teubner, 1910–15) *Opera omnia cum commentario Eutocii*, 4 vols. (Leipzig, reprint 1972)
Mugler. C. (Budé, 1970–2) *Archimède*, 4 vols. (Paris)

ARIUS DIDYMUS

Fragments in Diels, H. (1879) *Doxographi Graeci* (Berlin)

ATHENAEUS

Deipnosophistae
Kaibel, G. (Teubner, 1887–90) *Athenaei Naucratitae Deipnosophistarum libri xv*, 3 vols. (Leipzig, reprint 1965–6)

AUGUSTINE

De Dialectica
Pinborg, J. (1975) *Augustine, de dialectica*, ed. J.P. with translation, introduction and notes by B. Darrell Jackson (Dordrecht)
Epistulae
Goldbacher, A. (1895–1911) *S. Aureli Augustini Hippionensis Epistulae*, 4 vols., in *CSEL* 34 (double volume), 44, 57 (Vienna & Leipzig)
Contra Academicos
Green, W.M. (1970), in *S. Aurelii Augustini Contra academicos, De beata vita, De ordine*, pt.II.2, *CCSL* 29 (Turnholt)
De Civitate Dei
Dombart, B. & Kalb, A. (1955), in *S. Aurelii Augustini De civitate Dei*, pt.xiv, 2 vols., *CCSL* 47–8 (Turnholt)

AULUS GELLIUS

Noctes Atticae
Marshall, P.K. (OCT, 1968) *Aulus Gellius: Noctes Atticae* (Oxford)

BOETHIUS

In Ciceronis Topica
Orelli, J.C. & Baiter, J.G. (1837), in *M.Tulli Ciceronis opera quae supersunt*, vol. v.1
　　(Zürich)
Stump, E. (1988) *Boethius's In Ciceronis Topica* (Ithaca & London) [translation only]
De Hypotheticis Syllogismis
Obertello, L. (1969) *A.M.Severino Boezio: De hypotheticis syllogismis* (Brescia)
De Interpretatione
Minio-Paluello, L. (1965) *De Interpretatione vel Periermenias: Translatio Boethii*, in
　　Aristoteles Latinus ɪɪ.1–2 (Bruges & Paris) 1–38

CAELIUS AURELIANUS

Acutae Passiones (=Acut. Morb.)
Drabkin, I.E. (1950) *Caelius Aurelianus: On acute diseases and On chronic diseases*
　　(Chicago)
Bendz, G. (1990) *Caelius Aurelianus: Akute Krankheiten Buch I–III, Chronische Krankheiten
　　Buch I–II*, *CML* vɪ.1, pt.1 (Berlin)

CALCIDIUS

In Timaeum
Waszink, J.H. (1962) *Timaeus a Calcidio translatus commentarioque instructus* (London
　　second revised edn, Leiden 1976)

CARNEISCUS

Capasso, M. (1988) *Carneisco: Il secondo libro del Filista*, La scuola di Epicuro 10 (Naples)

CASSIODORUS

Institutiones
Mynors, R.A.B. (1937) *Cassiodori senatoris institutiones* (Oxford)

CELSUS

Medicina (including *Prooemium*)
Marx, F. (1915) *Cornelii Celsi quae supersunt*, *CML* ɪ (Berlin)

CENSORINUS

De Die Natali
Sallmann, N. (Teubner, 1983) *Censorini De die natali liber ad Q. Caerellium* (Leipzig)

CHARISIUS

Ars Grammatica
Barwick, K. (Teubner, 1964², revised F.Kühnert) *Artis grammaticae libri V* (Leipzig)

CICERO

Academica
Plasberg, O. (Teubner, 1922) *M. Tullius Cicero: Academicorum reliquiae cum Lucullo*
　　(Stuttgart, reprint 1961, 1980)
Reid, J.S. (1885) *Cicero: Academica* (London)
De Divinatione
De Fato
Timaeus
Giomini, R. (Teubner, 1975) *M. Tullius Cicero: De divinatione, De fato, Timaeus* (Leipzig)
Pease, A.S. (1920–3) *M. Tulli Ciceronis De Divinatione*, 2 vols. (Urbana, Ill., reprint
　　Darmstadt 1963)

Yon, A. (Budé, 1933) *Cicéron: Traité du destin* (Paris)

Sharples, R.W. (1991) *Cicero: On Fate & Boethius: The Consolation of Philosophy IV.5–7, V* (Warminster)

De Finibus

Schiche, T. (Teubner, 1915) *M. Tullius Cicero: De finibus bonorum et malorum libri quinque* (Leipzig, reprint 1961)

Reynolds, L.D. (OCT, 1998) *M.T. Ciceronis: De finibus bonorum et malorum*

De Legibus

Ziegler, K. (1950) *De legibus* (Heidelberg, revised edn, W. Görler, Freiburg im Breslau & Würzburg 1979)

De Natura Deorum

Plasberg, O. & Ax, W. (Teubner, 1933²) *M. Tullius Cicero: De natura deorum* (Stuttgart, reprint 1968, 1980)

Pease, A.S. (1920–3) *M. Tulli Ciceronis De Natura Deorum*, 2 vols. (Cambridge, Mass., Darmstadt 1968, 1977)

De Officiis

Winterbottom, M. (OCT, 1994) *M. Tulli Ciceronis: De officiis* (Oxford)

De Oratore

Kumaniecki, K. (Teubner, 1969) *M. Tullius Cicero: De oratore* (Leipzig)

Paradoxa Stoicorum

Molager, L. (Budé, 1971) *Cicéron: Les paradoxes des Stoïciens* (Paris)

De Republica

Ziegler, K. (Teubner, 1960) *M. Tullius Cicero: De re publica* (Leipzig, reprint 1969)

Topica

Wilkins, A.S. (OCT, 1903) *M. Tulli Ciceronis: Rhetorica vol.2 – Brutus, Orator, De optimo genere oratorum, Partitiones oratoriae, Topica* (Oxford, reprint 1957)

Tusculan Disputations

Dougan, T.W. & Henry, R.M. (1905–34²) *Tusculanarum disputationum libri V* (Cambridge)

Pohlenz, M. (Teubner, 1918) *M. Tullius Cicero: Tusculanae disputationes* (Stuttgart, reprint 1976)

CLEMENT OF ALEXANDRIA

Protrepticus

Stählin, O. (1905) Clemens Alexandrinus vol. I: *Protrepticus und Paedagogus*, GCS 12 (Berlin, 3rd edn by Fruchtel, L. & Treu, U. 1972)

Stromateis

Stählin, O. (1906) Clemens Alexandrinus vol. II: *Stromata Buch I–IV*, GCS 15 (Leipzig & Berlin, 4th edn by Fruchtel, L. & Treu, U. 1985)

Stählin, O. (1909) Clemens Alexandrinus vol. III: *Stromata Buch VII und VIII – Excerpta ex Theodoto – Eclogae propheticae – Quis dives salvetur – Fragmente*, GCS 17 (Leipzig & Berlin, 2nd edn by Fruchtel, L. & Treu, U. 1963)

CLEOMEDES

Caelestia

Todd, R. B. (Teubner, 1990) *Cleomedis Caelestia* (METEORA) (Leipzig)

DAVID

Prolegomena Philosophiae

Busse, A. (1904), in *CAG*, vol. XVIII.2 (Berlin)

DEMETRIUS OF LACONIA

Aporiai

Puglia, E. (1988) *Demetrio Lacone: Aporie testuali ed esegetiche in Epicuro (PHerc. 1497)* La scuola di Epicuro 8 (Naples)

De Dis

De Falco, V. (1923) *L'epicureo Demetrio Lacone* (Naples) 65–80

Renna, E. (1982) 'Nuove letture nel P.Herc. 1055 (libro incerto di Demetrio Lacone)', *Cronache Ercolanesi* 12, 43–9

De Poematis

Romeo, C. (1988) *Demetrio Lacone, La Poesia (PHerc. 188 e 1014)*, La scuola di Epicuro 9 (Naples)

DEXIPPUS

In Aristotelis Categorias commentaria

Busse, A. (1888), in *CAG*, vol. IV.2 (Berlin)

DIO CHRYSOSTOMUS

Orationes

Budé, G. de (Teubner, 1916–19) *Dionis Chrysostomi Orationes*, 2. vols. (Leipzig)

DIOGENES LAERTIUS

Vitae Philosophorum

Long, H.S. (OCT, 1964) *Diogenis Laertii Vitae philosophorum*, 2 vols. (Oxford)

DIOGENES OF OENOANDA

Smith, M.F. (1993) *Diogenes of Oinoanda, The Epicurean Inscription*, La Scuola di Epicuro, Suppl.1 (Naples)

DIOMEDES

Ars Grammatica

Keil, H. (1857) *Diomedis Artis grammaticae libri III*, in Grammatici Latini, vol. I (Leipzig)

DIONYSIUS OF HALICARNASSUS

De Compositione Verborum
De Demosthene
De Lysia
Epistula ad Pompeium Geminum
De Thucydide

Usener, H. & Radermacher, L. (Teubner, 1899–1929) *Dionysii Halicarnassei quae exstant*, vols. V & VI (Leipzig, repr. Stuttgart 1965)

Aujac, G. (Budé, 1978–92) *Denys d'Halicarnasse: Opuscules Rhétoriques*, 5 vols. (Paris)

ELIAS

In Porphyrii Isagogen commentaria
In Aristotelis Categorias commentaria

Busse, A. (1900), in *CAG*, vol. XVIII.1 (Berlin)

EPICTETUS

Dissertationes
Enchiridion

Schenkl, H. (Teubner, 1916) *Epicteti Dissertationes ad Arriani Digestae* (Stuttgart, reprint 1965)

Boter, G. (1999) *The* Enchiridion *of Epictetus and its Three Christian Adaptations*, Transmission and Critical Editions (Leiden)

EPICURUS

Epistulae
Fragments
Kyriai Doxai
Sententiae Vaticanae
Usener, H. (1887) *Epicurea* (Stuttgart, reprint 1966)
Von der Muehll, P. (1923) *Epicurus. Epistulae tres et ratae sententiae* (Leipzig)
Arrighetti, A. (1973²) *Epicuro: Opere* (Florence)
On Nature
Leone, G. (1984) 'Epicuro, *Della natura*, libro xiv', *Cronache Ercolanesi* 14, 17–107
Millot, C. (1977) 'Epicure de la nature livre xiv', *Cronache Ercolanesi* 7, 9–39
Sedley, D. (1973) 'Epicurus, *On nature* book xxviii', *Cronache Ercolanesi* 3, 5–83

EPIPHANIUS

Adversus Haereses (= *Panarion*)
Holl, K. (1915–33) Epiphanius, Bände 1–3: *Ancoratus und Panarion*, *GCS* 25, 31, 37
  (Leipzig)

ETYMOLOGICUM MAGNUM

Gaisford, T. (1848) *Etymologicon magnum* (Oxford)

EUCLID

Elements
Heiberg, J.L. (Teubner, 1969–77², revised E.S. Stamatis) *Euclidis Elementa* (& *scholia*), 6
  vols. (Leipzig)

EUDEMUS OF RHODES

Fragments in Wehrli, F. (1969²) *Eudemos von Rhodos*, Die Schule des Aristoteles, vol.
  viii (Basle & Stuttgart)

EUSEBIUS

Historia Ecclesiastica
Bardy, G. (1952–8) *Eusèbe de Césarée: Histoire ecclésiastique*, 3 vols., *SC* 31, 41, 55
  (Paris)
Praeparatio Evangelica
Mras, K. & Des Places, E. (1982–3²) *Eusebius: Werke*, vol. 8.1–2, *Die Praeparatio*
  Evangelica, *GCS* 43.1–2 (Berlin)
Des Places, E. (1974–91) *Eusèbe de Césarée: La préparation évangélique*, 9 vols., *SC* 206,
  215, 228, 262, 266, 292, 307, 338, 369 (Paris)

GALEN

Opera Omnia
Kühn, C.G. (1821–33) *Claudii Galeni Opera Omnia*, 20 vols. (Hildesheim, reprint 1965)
  [abbreviation: K]
Scripta Minora
Marquardt, J., Mueller, I. & Helmreich, G. (Teubner, 1884–93) *Claudii Galeni*
  Pergameni Scripta Minora, 3 vols. (Amsterdam, reprint 1967) [abbreviation: Scr.Min.]
Adversus Julianum / Adversus ea quae a Juliano in Hippocratis aphorismos enuntiata sunt
  libellus (K xviiiA)
Wenkebach, E. (1951), in *CMG* v.10.3 (Berlin) 33–70

De propriorum animi cuiuslibet affectuum dignotione et curatione (K v, Scr. Min. 1)
de Boer, W. (1937), in *CMG* v.4.1.1 (Berlin) 3–37
De Atra Bile (K v)
de Boer, W. (1937), in *CMG* v.4.1.1 (Berlin) 71–93
De Causis Contentivis
Lyons, M.C. (1969), in *CMG* Supp.Or. 11 [Arabic version] (Berlin) 50–73
Kollesch, J., Nickel, D. & Strohmaier, G. (1969), in *CMG* Supp.Or. 11 [Latin version] (Berlin) 131–41
De Causis Procatarcticis
Bardong, K. (1937), in *CMG* Supp. 11 [Latin version] (Leipzig & Berlin)
Institutio Logica
Kalbfleisch, K. (Teubner, 1896) *Galenus: Institutio logica* (Leipzig); reprinted with introd., transl. and comm. in Ramirez Trejo, A. & Otero, M. H. *Galeno: Iniciación a la dialectica*, Bibliotheca scriptorum graecorum et romanorum mexicana (Mexico 1982)
De Libris Propriis (K xix)
Müller, I. von (Teubner, 1891), in *Galenus: Scripta minora*, vol. 11 (Amsterdam, reprint 1967) 91–124
De Experientia Medica
Walzer, R. (1944) *Galen: On Medical Experience* (London)
De Naturalibus Facultatibus (K 11)
Helmreich, G. (Teubner, 1884) *Claudii Galeni Pergameni Scripta minora*, vol. 111 (Amsterdam, reprint 1967) 101–257
De animi cuiuslibet peccatorum dignotione et curatione (K v; Scr. Min. 1)
de Boer, W. (1937), in *CMG* v.4.1.1 (Berlin) 41–68
De Placitis Hippocratis et Platonis (K v)
De Lacy, P. (1984), in *CMG* v.4.1.2, 3 vols. (Berlin)
De Sectis Ingredientibus (K 1)
Helmreich, G. (Teubner, 1884) *Claudii Galeni Pergameni Scripta minora*, vol. 111 (Amsterdam, reprint 1967) 1–32
Subfiguratio Empirica
Deichgräber, K. (1930), in *Die griechische Empirikerschule* (Berlin & Zürich, reprint 1965) 42–90
De Usu Partium (K 111–iv)
Helmreich, G. (Teubner, 1907–9) *Galeni De usu partium libri xvii*, 2 vols. (Amsterdam, reprint 1968)

[GALEN]

Quod qualitates incorporeae sint
Westenberger, J. (1906) *Galeni qui fertur de qualitatibus incorporeis libellus* (diss. Marburg) 1–19

GREGORIUS THAUMATURGUS

In Origenem Oratio Panegyrica
Crouzel, H. (1969) *Grégoire le Thaumaturge: Remerciement à Origène suivi de la lettre d'Origène à Grégoire*, *SC* 148 (Paris) 94–182

HERMARCHUS

Longo Auricchio, F. (1988) *Ermarco: Frammenti*, La Scuola di Epicuro 6 (Naples)

HEROPHILUS

von Staden, H. (1989) *Herophilus: The Art of Medicine in Early Alexandria* (Cambridge)

HIEROCLES

Elementa Ethica

Bastianini, G. & Long, A.A. (1992), in *Corpus dei Papiri Filosofici Greci e Latini*, pt.1
vol.1**: Autori Noti (Florence)

HIPPOLYTUS

Philosophumena (=Refutatio omnium haeresium)

Marcovich, M. (1986) *Hippolytus: Refutatio omnium haeresium*, Patristische Texte und
Studien 25 (Berlin & New York)

Wendland, P. (1916) *Hippolytus Werke Bd. III: Refutatio omnium haeresium*, GCS 26
(Berlin, reprint Hildesheim & New York 1977)

IDOMENEUS

Angeli, A. (1981) 'I frammenti di Idomeneo di Lampsaco', *Cronache Ercolanesi* 11,
41–101

LACTANTIUS

Institutiones Divinae

Perrin, M. (1987) *Lactance: Epitomé des Institutions Divines, SC* 335 (Paris)

LUCIAN

Symposium
Verae Historiae

Macleod, M.D. (OCT, 1972) *Luciani Opera*, vol. I (Oxford)

Vitarum Auctio
Alexander

Macleod, M.D. (OCT, 1974) *Luciani Opera*, vol. II (Oxford)

LUCRETIUS

De Rerum Natura

Bailey, C. (1947) *Titi Lucreti Cari: De Rerum Natura, libri sex*, 3 vols. (Oxford, reprint 1963)

LYCO

Fragments in Wehrli, F. (1968²) *Lykon und Ariston von Keos*, Die Schule des Aristoteles,
vol. VI (Basle)

MACROBIUS

Saturnalia

Willis, J. (Teubner, 1970) *Ambrosii Theodosii Macrobii I: Saturnalia* (Leipzig)

MARCUS AURELIUS

Meditations

Farquharson, A.S.L. (1944) *The Meditations of the Emperor Marcus Antoninus*, 2 vols.
(Oxford)

Dalfen, J. (Teubner, 1979) *Marci Aurelii Antonini: Ad se ipsum libri XII* (Leipzig)

MARTIANUS CAPELLA

Willis, J. (Teubner, 1985) *Martianus Capella* (Leipzig)

METRODORUS

Koerte, A. (1890) 'Metrodori Epicurei fragmenta', *Jahrbücher für Classische Philologie*, Suppl. 17, 531–97

NEMESIUS

De Natura Hominis
Morani, M. (Teubner, 1987) *Nemesius: De natura hominis* (Leipzig)

NUMENIUS

Des Places, E. (Budé, 1973) *Numenius: Fragments* (Paris)

ORIGEN

Contra Celsum
Borret, M. (1967–76) *Origène: Contre Celse*, 5 vols., *SC* 132, 136, 147, 150, 227 (Paris)
De principiis
Görgemanns, H. & Karpp, H. (1976) *Origenes: Vier Bücher von den Prinzipien* (Darmstadt)

PANAETIUS

Straaten, M. van (1962³) *Panaetii Rhodii Fragmenta* (Leiden)
Alesse, F. (1997) *Panezio di Rodi: Testimonianze* (Naples)

PHILO OF ALEXANDRIA

Cohn, L., Wendland, P., & Reiter, S. (1896–1915) *Philonis Alexandrini Opera quae supersunt*, 6 vols. (Berlin, reprint 1962)

PHILODEMUS[1]

Academicorum Historia
Dorandi, T. (1991) *Filodemo: Storia dei Filosofi – Platone e l'Academia*, La Scuola di Epicuro 12 (Naples)
Ad Contubernales
Angeli, A. (1988) *Filodemo: Agli amici di scuola*, La scuola di Epicuro 7 (Naples)
De Bono Rege
Dorandi, T. (1982) *Filodemo: Il buon rege secondo Omero*, La scuola di Epicuro 3 (Naples)
De Dis
Diels, H. (1916) *Philodemos über die Götter, Erstes Buch* (Berlin)
Diels, H. (1917) *Philodemos über die Götter, Drittes Buch* (Berlin)
De Ira
Indelli, G. (1988) *Filodemo: L'ira*, La Scuola di Epicuro 5 (Naples)
De Libertate Dicendi
Olivieri, A. (Teubner, 1914) *Philodemi* περὶ παρρησίας *libellus* (Leipzig)
De Morte
Kuiper, T. (1925) *Philodemus Over den Dood* (Amsterdam)
Gigante, M. (1983²) *Ricerche Philodemee* (Naples) 115–234
De Musica
Kemke, I. (Teubner, 1884) *Philodemi De Musica librorum quae extant* (Leipzig)

---

[1] Information on editions of other writings of Philodemus (not all listed here) is conveniently available in Gigante (1995).

Rispoli, G.M. (1969) 'Il primo libro del περὶ μουσικῆς di Filodemo', in Sbordone, F., ed. *Ricerche sui Papiri Ercolanesi* (Naples) 1.225–86

Neubecker, A.J. (1986) *Philodemus Über die Musik, IV.Buch*, La scuola di Epicuro 4 (Naples)

Delattre, D. (1991) 'Philodème, *De la musique*: Livre IV, colonnes 40* à 109*', *Cronache Ercolanesi* 19, 49–144

De Oeconomia

Jensen, C. (Teubner, 1907) *Philodemi* περὶ οἰκονομίας (Leipzig)

De Pietate

Obbink, D. (1996–) *Philodemus: On Piety*, 2 vols. (1 published) (Oxford)

De Rhetoricis

Sudhaus, S. (Teubner, 1892–6) *Philodemi volumina rhetorica*, 2 vols. & suppl. (Leipzig)

Longo Auricchio, F. (1977) Φιλοδήμου περὶ ῥητορικῆς *libri primi et secundi*, Ricerche sui Papiri Ercolanesi (Naples)

Hammerstaedt, J. (1992) 'Der Schlussteil von Philodems drittem Buch über Rhetorik', *Cronache Ercolanesi* 22, 9–118

De Signis

De Lacy, P.H. & E.A. (1978²) *Philodemus: On Methods of Inference*, La Scuola di Epicuro 1 (Naples)

De Stoicis

Dorandi, T. (1982) 'Filodemo, Gli Stoici (P.Herc. 155 e 39)', *Cronache Ercolanesi* 12, 91–133

Stoicorum Historia

Dorandi, T. (1994) *Filodemo: Storia dei filosofi – La Stoà da Zenone a Panezio* (Leiden)

De Vitiis

Jensen, C. (Teubner, 1911) *Philodemus* περὶ κακιῶν *liber decimus* (Leipzig)

[PHILODEMUS]

Ethica Comparetti

Indelli, G. & Tsouna-McKirahan, V. (1995) *[Philodemus]: On Choices and Avoidances*, La scuola di Epicuro 15 (Naples)

PHILOPONUS

In Aristotelis Analytica priora commentaria

Wallies, M. (1905), in *CAG*, vol. XIII.2 (Berlin)

In Aristotelis Categorias commentarium

Busse, A. (1898), in *CAG*, vol. XIII.1 (Berlin)

De Aeternitate Mundi

Rabe, H. (Teubner, 1899) *Johannes Philoponus: De aeternitate mundi contra Proclum* (Hildesheim, reprint 1963)

PHILOSTRATUS

Vitae Sophistarum

Kayser, C.L. (Teubner, 1871) *Flavii Philostrati Opera*, vol. II (Hildesheim, reprint 1964) 1–127

PHOTIUS

Bibliotheca

Henry, R. (Budé, 1959–91) *Photius: Bibliothèque*, 9 vols (Paris)

PLUTARCH

AA.VV. (Teubner, 1959–78) *Plutarchi Moralia* (Leipzig)
De Communibus Notitiis
De Stoicorum Repugnantiis
Cherniss, H. (Loeb, 1976), in *Plutarch's Moralia*, vol. XIII.2 (Cambridge, Mass. &
London)
Adversus Colotem
Non Posse Suaviter Vivi Secundum Epicurum
Einarson, B. & De Lacy, P.H. (Loeb, 1967), in *Plutarch's Moralia*, vol. XIV (Cambridge,
Mass. & London)

[PLUTARCH]

Placita Philosophorum
Mau, J. (1991) *Plutrachi Moralia*, vol. V2.1 (Leipzig)

POLYAENUS

Tepedino Guerra, A. (1988) *Polieno: Frammenti*, La scuola di Epicuro 11 (Naples)

POLYBIUS

Histories
Buettner-Wobst, T. (1889–1905) *Polybii historiae*, 4 vols. (Leipzig, reprint 1962–67)

POLYSTRATUS

De Irrationali Contemptu
Indelli, G. (1978) *Polistrato: Sul disprezzo irrazionale delle opinioni popolari*, La Scuola di
Epicuro 2 (Naples)

PORPHYRY

De Abstinentia
Bouffartigue, J., Patillon, M. & Segonds, A.P. (Budé, 1977–95) *Porphyre: De l'Abstinence*,
3 vols. (Paris)
Ad Marcellam
Pötscher, W. (1969) *Porphyrios:* πρὸς Μαρκέλλαν (Leiden)
Des Places, E. (Budé, 1982), in *Porphyre: vie de Pythagore, Lettre à Marcella* (Paris)
In Aristotelis Categorias commentarium
Busse, A. (1897), in *CAG*, vol. IV.1 (Berlin)
Vita Plotini
AA. VV. (1992) *Porphyre: La Vie de Plotin, II*: Etudes d'introduction, texte grec et
traduction française, commentaire, notes complémentaires, bibliographie, Histoire
des doctrines de l'antiquité classique 16 (Paris)
Vita Pythagorae
Nauck, A. (Teubner, 1886), in *Porphyrii philosophi platonici opuscula selecta* (Hildesheim,
reprint 1977) 17–52
Des Places, E. (Budé, 1982), in *Porphyre: vie de Pythagore, Lettre à Marcella* (Paris)
Fragments
Smith, A. (Teubner, 1993) *Porphyrius: Fragmenta* (Stuttgart & Leipzig)

POSIDONIUS

Edelstein, L. & Kidd, I. G. (1988²) *Posidonius: Vol. I, The Fragments*, Cambridge Classical
Texts and Commentaries 13 (Cambridge)

Kidd, I. G. (1988) *Posidonius, II: The Commentary*, Cambridge Classical Texts and
  Commentaries 14A & B (Cambridge)

PRISCIAN
Institutiones Grammaticae
Hertz, M. (1855–9) *Prisciani Institutionum Grammaticarum libri XVIII*, 2 vols., in
  Grammatici Latini 2 & 3 (Leipzig)

PROCLUS
In primum Euclidis Elementorum librum commentarii
Friedlein, G. (Teubner, 1873) *Procli Diadochi In primum Euclidis elementorum librum
  commentarii* (Leipzig, reprint Hildesheim 1967, 1992)
In Platonis Rempublicam commentarii
Kroll, G. (Teubner, 1899–1901) *Procli Diadochi In Platonis Rem Publicam commentarii*, 2
  vols. (Amsterdam, reprint 1965)
In Platonis Timaeum commentaria
Diehl, E. (Teubner, 1903–1906) *Procli Diadochi In Platonis Timaeum commentaria*, 3 vols.
  (Amsterdam, reprint 1965)
Theologia Platonica
Saffrey, H. D. & Westerink, L. G. (1968–) *Proclus: Théologie Platonicienne*, 5 vols. to date
  (books 1–5) (Paris)

PYRRHO
Fragments in Decleva Caizzi, F. (1981) *Pirrone: Testimonianze* (Naples)

QUINTILIAN
Institutiones Oratoriae
Radermacher, L. (Teubner, 1959–71², revised V. Buchheit) *M. Fabii Quintiliani
  Institutiones Oratoriae libri XII* (Leipzig)
Winterbottom, M. (OCT, 1970) *M. Fabii Quintiliani Institutiones Oratoriae* (Oxford)

SCHOLIA ON DIONYSIUS THRAX
Hilgard, A. (1901) *Scholia in Dionysii Thracis Artem Grammaticam*, Grammatici Graeci
  vol. 1.3 (Hildesheim, reprint 1979)

SENECA
Epistulae Morales
Reynolds, L.D. (OCT, 1965) *L. Annaei Senecae ad Lucilium Epistulae Morales*, 2 vols. (Oxford)
Dialogi
Reynolds, L.D. (OCT, 1977) *L. Annaei Senecae Dialogorum libri duodecim* (Oxford)

SEXTUS EMPIRICUS
Adversus Mathematicos
Mutschmann, H. & Mau, J. (Teubner,1955–61) *Sexti Empirici Opera*, vols. II & III
  (Leipzig)
Pyrrhonei Hypotyposes
Mutschmann, H. & Mau, J. (Teubner, 1954–62) *Sexti Empirici Opera*, vol. I (Leipzig)

SIMPLICIUS
In Aristotelis De Caelo commentaria
Heiberg, J.L. (1894), in *CAG*, vol. VII (Berlin)

In Aristotelis Categorias commentarium
Kalbfleisch, K. (1907), in *CAG*, vol. VIII (Berlin)
In Libros Aristotelis De Anima commentaria
Hayduck, M. (1882), in *CAG*, vol. XI (Berlin)
In Aristotelis Physica commentaria
Diels, H. (1882–95), in *CAG* vols. IX & X (Berlin)

SOTION

Fragments in Wehrli, F. (1969²) *Sotion*, Die Schule des Aristoteles, suppl.vol.2 (Basle &
  Stuttgart)

STEPHANUS

In Librum Aristotelis De Interpretatione commentarium
Hayduck, M. (1885), in *CAG* vol. XVIII.3 (Berlin)

STOBAEUS

Eclogae
Wachsmuth, C. (1884) *Ioannis Stobaei Anthologii libri duo priores qui inscribi solent Eclogae*
  physicae et ethicae, 2 vols. (Berlin, reprint Zürich 1974)
Florilegium
Hense, O. (1894–1923) *Ioannis Stobaei Anthologium*, Bol. 3. *Liber III*, Bol. 4–5, *Liber IV;*
  Appendix, indicem auctorum in tertio et quarto libro laudatorum continens (Berlin, reprint
  Zürich 1974)

STRABO

Geography
Meineke, A. (Teubner, 1852–3) *Strabonis Geographica*, 3 vols. (Leipzig, reprint 1915–25)
Aujac, G, Lasserre, F. & Baladié, R. (Budé, 1966–) *Strabon: Géographie*, 9 vols. to date
  (books 1–12) (Paris)
Aly, W., revised by Kirsten, E. & Lapp, F. (1968–72) *Strabonis Geographica*, books 1–6, 2
  vols. (Bonn)

STRATO

Fragments in Wehrli, F. (1969²) *Straton von Lampsakos*, Die Schule des Aristoteles, vol. v
  (Basle & Stuttgart)
See also Gottschalk, H.B. (1965) *Strato of Lampsacus: some texts* (Leeds)

SUDA

Adler, A. (1928–38) *Suidae Lexicon*, Lexicographi Graeci, vols. I–V (Stuttgart, reprint
  1971)

SYRIANUS

In Aristotelis Metaphysica commentaria
Kroll, G. (1902), in *CAG*, vol.VI.1 (Berlin)

TATIAN

Adversus Graecos
Whittaker, M. (1982) *Tatian: Oratio ad Graecos and fragments* (Oxford)

TERTULLIAN

De Anima
Waszink, J. H. (1947) *Tertullianus: De Anima* (Amsterdam)

THEMISTIUS

Orationes
Schenkl, H., revised by Downey, G. & Norman, A.F. (Teubner, 1965–74) Themistii
Orationes quae supersunt, 3 vols. (Leipzig)
In Aristotelis Physica paraphrasis
Schenkl, H. (1900), in *CAG*, vol.v.2 (Berlin)

THEON OF ALEXANDRIA

Progymnasmata
Spengel, L. (1854), in *Rhetores Graeci*, vol. 2 (Frankfurt, reprint 1966) 59–130

THEON OF SMYRNA

Expositio Rerum Mathematicarum
Hiller, E. (Teubner, 1878) *Theonis Smyrnaei philosophi platonici Expositio rerum
mathematicarum ad legendum Platonem utilium* (Leipzig)

THEOPHRASTUS

Fragments in Fortenbaugh, W. W., Huby, P. M., Sharples, R. W. & Gutas, D. (1992)
Theophrastus of Eresus: Sources for his Life, Writings, Thought and Influence, 2 vols.
(Leiden)

TIMON OF PHLIUS

Fragments in Lloyd-Jones, H. & Parsons, P. (1981) *Supplementum Hellenisticum* (Berlin)
368–95

VARRO

De Lingua Latina
Goetz, G. & Schoell, F. (1910) *M. Terenti Varronis De Lingua Latina quae supersunt*
(Leipzig)
Saturae Menippeae
Astbury, R. (Teubner, 1985) *M. Terenti Varronis Saturarum Menippearum Fragmenta*
(Leipzig)

XENOCRATES

Fragments in Isnardi Parente, M. (1982) *Senocrate & Ermodoro: Frammenti*, La scuola di
Platone 3 (Naples)

ZENO OF SIDON

Angeli, A. & Colaizzo, M. (1979) 'I frammenti di Zenone Sidonio', *Cronache Ercolanesi*
9, 47–113

Abbreviations

This list contains the abbreviations used in this volume to refer to ancient authors and their works, and to collections of fragments. In the case of authors of a single work references, as a rule, are by author's name only. For modern editions of the most important works, see the the List of Editions elsewhere in this volume.

Achilles	
Isag.	*Introductio in Aratum*
Aët.	Aëtius *Placita*
Alcin.	Alcinous *Didaskalikos*
Alex.	Alexander of Aphrodias
APr.	*In Aristotelis Analyticorum priorum librum I commentarium*
Mant.	*De anima libri Mantissa*
de Sens.	*In librum De sensu commentarium*
Fat.	*De fato*
Metaph.	*In Aristotelis Metaphysica commentarium*
Mixt.	*De mixtione*
SE	*In Aristotelis Sophisticos elenchos commentarium*
Top.	*In Aristotelis Topicorum libros octo commentaria*
Ammon.	Ammonius
Int.	*In Aristotelis De interpretatione commentarius*
[Ammon.]	Pseudo-Ammonius
APr.	*In Analytica Priora Commentarius*
[Andronic.]	Pseudo-Andronicus
Pass.	*De passionibus*
Anon.	
In Tht.	*Anonymi commentarius in Platonis Theaetetum*
Anon.	
In SE	*Anonymi in Aristotelis In Sophisticos elenchos paraphrasis*
Anon.	
Int.	*Anonymi in Aristotelis De interpretatione commentaria*
Anon. Lond.	Anonymus Londinensis
Anon.	
Proleg. in Plat. Phil.	*Prolegomena in Platonis Philosophiam*
Anon.	
Proleg. Hermog. Stat.	*Prolegomena in Hermogenis De statibus*

Ap. Dysc.	Apollonius Dyscolus
Adv.	*De adverbiis*
Conj.	*De conjunctionibus*
Pron.	*De pronominibus*
Synt.	*De syntaxi*
Apoll. Perg.	Apollonius of Perge *Conica*
Apul.	Apuleius
Int.	*De Interpretatione*
Ar. Did.	Arius Didymus
Arist.	Aristoteles
de An.	*De Anima*
Phys.	*Physica*
EN	*Ethica Nicomachea*
Int.	*De Interpretatione*
Metaph.	*Metaphysica*
Rhet.	*Rhetorica*
Cael.	*De Caelo*
Polit.	*Politica*
[Arist.]	Pseudo-Aristoteles
Lin. Insec.	*De lineis insecabilibus*
Mund.	*De Mundo*
Arr.	Arrianus
An.	*Anabasis*
Athenaeus	*Deipnosophistae*
Aug.	Augustinus
Dial.	*De dialectica*
Ep.	*Epistulae*
Acad.	*Contra academicos*
CD	*De civitate dei*
Boeth.	Boethius
Cic. Top.	*In Ciceronis Topica*
Hypp. Syll.	*De hypotheticis syllogismis*
Int.	*De Interpretatione*
Cael. Aurel.	Caelius Aurelianus
Acut.	
Morb.	*De acutis morbi=Celerum sive acutarum passionum libri*
Calcid.	Calcidius
In Tim.	*In Timaeum*
Cassiod.	Cassiodorus
Inst.	*Institutiones*
Cels.	Celsus
Med.	*De medicina*
Cens.	Censorinus *De die natali*
Charis.	Charisius
Ars gram.	*Ars Grammatica*

Choerob.	Choeroboscus
Can.	*Prolegomena et scholia in Theodosii Alexandrini canones isagogicos de flexione nominum et verborum*
Cicero	
Ac.	*Academica*
Div.	*De divinatione*
Fat.	*De fato*
Fin.	*De finibus*
Leg.	*De legibus*
ND	*De natura deorum*
Off.	*De officiis*
De orat.	*De oratore*
Parad.	*Paradoxa Stoicorum*
Rep.	*De republica*
Tim.	*Timaeus*
Top.	*Topica*
Tusc.	*Tusculanae disputationes*
[Cic.]	Pseudo-Cicero
Rhet. Her.	*Rhetorica ad Herennium*
Clem.	Clemens Alexandrinus
Protr.	*Protrepticus*
Strom.	*Stromateis*
Cleom.	Cleomedes
Cael.	*Caelestia*
D. Chr.	Dio Chrysostomus
Or.	*Orationes*
D.H.	Dionysius Halicarnassensis
Comp.	*De compositione verborum*
Dem.	*De Demosthene*
Lys.	*De Lysia*
Pomp.	*Epistula ad Pompeium Geminum*
Th.	*De Thucydide*
D.L.	Diogenes Laërtius
David	
Prol.	*Prolegomena philosophiae*
Demetr. Lac.	Demetrius of Laconia
Dexipp.	Dexippus
Cat.	*In Aristotelis Categorias commentarium*
Diog. Oen.	Diogenes of Oenoanda
Elias	
APr.	*In Aristotelis Analytica priora commentaria*
Cat.	*In Aristotelis Categorias commentaria*
Porph.	*In Porphyrii Isagogen commentaria*

Epic.	Epicurus
Ep. Hdt.	*Epistula ad Herodotum*
Ep. Men.	*Epistula ad Menoeceum*
Ep. Pyth.	*Epistula ad Pythoclem*
KD	*Kyriai doxai*
Sent. Vat.	*Sententiae Vaticanae*
Fr.	*Fragmenta*
Epict.	Epictetus
Diss.	*Dissertationes*
Ench.	*Enchiridion*
Epiph.	Epiphanius
Adv. Haer.	*Adversus haereses (=Panarion)*
Etym. Magn.	*Etymologicum Magnum*
Euc.	Euclides
El.	*Elementa*
Eudem.	Eudemus
Eus.	Eusebius
HE	*Historia ecclesiastica*
PE	*Praeparatio evangelica*

FDS	K.-H. Hülser (ed.), *Fragmente zur Dialektik der Stoiker*, 4 vols., Stuttgart 1987–1988

Gal.	Galenus
AA	*De anatomicis administrationibus*
Adv. Jul.	*Adversus Julianum*
Aff. Dig.	*De propriorum animi cuiuslibet affectuum dignotione et curatione*
Art. Sang.	*An in arteriis natura sanguis contineatur*
At. Bil.	*De atra bile*
Caus. Puls.	*De causis pulsuum*
CC	*De causis contentivis*
Comp. Med. Loc.	*De compositione medicamentorum secundum locos*
CP	*De causis procatarcticis*
Diff. Puls.	*De differentiis pulsuum*
Dig. Puls.	*De dignoscendis pulsibus*
Foet. Form.	*De foetuum formatione*
Hipp. Aph.	*In Hippocratis Aphorismos*
Hipp. Off. Med.	*In Hippocratis De officina medici*
Inst. Log.	*Institutio logica*
Lib. Prop.	*De libris propriis*
Loc. Aff.	*De locis affectis*
Med. Exp	*De experientia medica*
MM	*De methodo medendi*
Nat. Fac.	*De naturalibus facultatibus*
Pecc. Dig.	*De animi cuiuslibet peccatorum dignotione et curatione*
PHP	*De placitis Hippocratis et Platonis*

Plen.	*De plenitudine*
Praes. Puls.	*De praesagitione ex pulsibus*
SI	*De sectis ingredientibus*
Soph.	*De sophismatis*
Subf. Empir.	*Subfiguratio empirica*
Syn. Puls.	*Synopsis librorum suorum de pulsibus*
UP	*De usu Partium*
Ven. Sect. Er.	*De venae sectione adversus Erasistratum*
Ven. Sect. Er. Rom.	*De venae sectione adversus Erasistrateos Romae Degentes*

[Gal.]   Pseudo-Galenus

Opt. Sect.	*De optima secta ad Thrasybulum liber*
Def. Med.	*Definitiones medicae*
Int.	*Introductio seu medicus*
Qual. Incorp.	*Quod qualitates incorporeae sint*

Gell.   Aulus Gellius *Noctes Atticae*

Greg. Thaum. Gregorius Thaumaturgus

     Or. Pan.   *In Origenem oratio panegyrica*

[Hesych.]   Pseudo-Hesychius

     Vita Arist.   *Vita Aristotelis*

Hierocl.   Hierocles

     El. Eth.   *Elementa ethica*

Hipp.   Hippolytus

Ref.	*Refutatio omnium haeresium*
Philos.	*Philosophumena* (=Book I of *Ref.*)

Hippob.   Hippobotus (*ap.* D. L.)

Hor.   Horatius

     Ars   *Ars poetica*

Lact.   Lactantius

     Inst.   *Institutiones divinae*

Luc.   Lucianus

Symp.	*Symposium*
Vit. Auc.	*Vitarum auctio*
Alex.	*Alexander*

[Luc.]   Pseudo-Lucianus

     Macr.   *Macrobii*

Lucr.   Lucretius *De rerum natura*

Macr.   Macrobius

     Sat.   *Saturnalia*

Marc.   Aelius Marcianus *Institutiones*

Marc. Aurel. Marcus Aurelius *Meditationes* (=*Ad se ipsum libri XII*)

Nemes.   Nemesius

     Nat. Hom.   *De natura hominis*

Numen.   Numenius

Orig.	Origenes
Cels.	*Contra Celsum*
Princ.	*De principiis*
Sel. in Ps.	*Selecta in psalmos*

Phil.	Philo
Agr.	*De agricultura*
Aet.	*De aeternitate mundi*
Cher.	*De Cherubim*
Congr.	*De congressu eruditionis gratia*
Prov.	*De providentia*
Leg.	*Legum allegoriae*
QG	*Quaestiones et solutiones in Genesim*
Phld.	Philodemus
Ad Cont.	*Ad contubernales*
Mus.	*De musica*
De piet.	*De pietate*
Rhet.	*De rhetorica*
Sign.	*De signis*
Stoic.	*De Stoicis*
Stoic. Hist.	*De Stoicorum Historia* (= *Index Stoicorum*)
Acad. Hist.	*Academicorum Historia* (= *Index Academicorum*)
Philostratus	
VS	*Vitae sophistarum*
Phlp.	Philoponus
APr.	*In Aristotelis Analytica priora commentaria*
Cat.	*In Aristotelis Categorias commentarium*
Aet. Mund.	*De aeternitate mundi*
Phot.	Photius
Bibl.	*Bibliotheca*
Plato	
Tim.	*Timaeus*
Crat.	*Cratylus*
Phd.	*Phaedo*
Phdr.	*Phaedrus*
[Plato]	
Epin.	*Epinomis*
Plu.	Plutarchus
Col.	*Adversus Colotem*
Alex.	*Alexander*
Alex. Virt.	*De Alexandri Magni fortuna aut virtute*
Am. Prol.	*De amore prolis*
An Recte	*An recte dictum sit latenter esse vivendum*
An. Procr.	*De animae procreatione in Timaeo*
Comm. Not.	*De communibus notitiis adversus Stoicos*
Def. Or.	*De defectu oraculorum*
De E	*De E apud Delphos*

Fac. Lun.	*De facie quae in orbe lunae apparet*
Fr.	*Fragmenta*
Gryll.	*Gryllus*
Mar.	*Marius*
Non Posse	*Non posse suaviter vivi secundum Epicurum*
Poet. Aud.	*Quomodo adolescens poetas audire debeat*
Praec. Ger. Reip.	*Praecepta gerendae reipublicae*
Quaest. Conv.	*Quaestiones convivales*
Stoic. Rep.	*De Stoicorum repugnantiis*
Soll.	*De sollertia animalium*
Sull.	*Sulla*
Tranq. An.	*De tranquillitate animae*
Virt. Mor.	*De virtute morali*
Virt. Prof.	*Quomodo quis suos in virtute sentiat profectus*
[Plu.]	Pseudo-Plutarchus
Plac.	*Placita philosophorum*
Fat.	*De Fato*
Plb.	Polybius *Historiae*
Porph.	Porphyrius
Abst	*De abstinentia*
Cat.	*In Aristotelis Categorias commentarium*
Fr.	*Fragmenta*
Marc.	*Ad Marcellam*
Plot.	*Vita Plotini*
VP	*Vita Pythagorae*
Posidon.	Posidonius
Priscian.	Priscianus
Inst. Gramm.	*Institutiones Grammaticae*
Procl.	Proclus
Eucl.	*In primum Euclidis elementorum librum commentarii*
Rep.	*In Platonis Rempublicam commentarii*
Tim.	*In Platonis Timaeum commentaria*
TP	*Theologia platonica*
Quint.	Quintilianus
Inst.	*Institutiones oratoriae*
ΣAphthon.	Scholia on Aphthonius
ΣArist. *Top.*	Scholia on Aristotelis *Topica*
ΣDThrax	Scholia on Dionysius Thrax
Sen.	Seneca
Ben.	*De beneficiis*
Ep.	*Epistulae*
Tranq. An.	*De tranquillitate animae*
S.E.	Sextus Empiricus
M	*Adversus mathematicos*
PH	*Pyrrhonei hypotyposes*

Simp.	Simplicius
Cael.	*In Aristotelis De caelo commentaria*
Cat.	*In Aristotelis Categorias commentarium*
de An.	*In libros Aristotelis De anima commentaria*
Ph.	*In Aristotelis Physica commentaria*
SSR	G. Giannantoni (ed.), *Socratis et Socraticorum Reliquiae*, 4 vols., Naples 1990
Steph.	Stephanus
Int.	*In librum Aristotelis De interpretatione commentarium*
Stob.	Stobaeus
Ecl.	*Eclogae*
Flor.	*Florilegium*
Syr.	Syrianus
Metaph.	*In Aristotelis Metaphysica commentaria*
SVF	J. Von Arnim (ed.), *Stoicorum veterum fragmenta*, 3 vols., Leipzig 1903–1905; vol. 4, indexes by M. Adler, Leipzig 1924

Tat.	Tatianus
Adv. Graec.	*Adversus Graecos = Oratio ad Graecos*
Tert.	Tertullianus
An.	*De anima*
Them.	Themistius
Or.	*Orationes*
Phys.	*In Aristotelis Physica paraphrasis*
Theon	Theon of Alexandria
Prog.	*Progymnasmata*
Theon Sm.	Theon of Smyrna *Expositio rerum mathematicarum ad legendum Platonem utilium*
Thphr.	Theophrastus

Us.	H. Usener, *Epicurea*, Leipzig 1887 (repr. Stuttgart 1966)

Val.	Max. Valerius Maximus
Varro	
LL	*De lingua latina*
Sat. Men.	*Saturae Menippeae*

Xenocr.	Xenocrates
Xen.	Xenophon
Mem.	*Memorabilia*

Bibliography

Journal abbreviations are as in *L'Année Philologique*

AA. VV. (1983) ΣΥΖΗΤΗΣΙΣ – *Studi sull'epicureismo greco e romano offerti a Marcello Gigante*, 2 vols. (Naples)

Aalders, G. J. D. (1968) *Die Theorie der gemischten Verfassung im Altertum* (Amsterdam)

Aalders, G. J. D. (1975) *Political Thought in Hellenistic Times* (Amsterdam)

Ackrill, J. L. (1963) *Aristotle's 'Categories' and 'De Interpretatione'*, Clarendon Aristotle Series (Oxford; repr. w. corr. 1966)

Ackroyd, P. R. (1970) 'The Old Testament in the making', in Ackroyd & Evans (1970) 67–113

Ackroyd, P. R. & Evans, C. F., edd. (1970) *The Cambridge History of the Bible*, vol. 1: From the Beginnings to Jerome (Cambridge)

Alberti, A., ed. (1990) *Logica, mente e persona*: Studi sulla filosofia antica (Florence)

Alberti, A. (1995) 'The Epicurean theory of law and justice', in Laks & Schofield (1995) 161–90

Alfieri, V. E. (1936) *Gli Atomisti — Frammenti e testimonianze* (Bari)

Algra, K. A. (1988) 'The early Stoics on the immobility and coherence of the cosmos', *Phronesis* 33, 155–80

Algra, K. A. (1992) ' "Place", in context: on Theophrastus fr. 21 and 22 Wimmer', in Fortenbaugh *et al.* (1992) 141–65

Algra, K. A. (1993) 'Posidonius' conception of the extra-cosmic void: the evidence and the arguments', *Mnemosyne* 46, 473–505

Algra, K. A. (1995) *Concepts of Space in Greek Thought*, PhA 65 (Leiden)

Algra, K. A. (1997) 'Chrysippus, Carneades, Cicero: The ethical *divisiones* in Cicero's *Lucullus*', in Inwood & Mansfeld (1997) 107–40

Algra, K. A., Horst, P. W. van der & Runia, D. T., edd. (1996) *Polyhistor*: Studies in the History and Historiography of Greek Philosophy Presented to Jaap Mansfeld on his 60th Birthday, PhA 72 (Leiden)

Algra, K. A., Koenen, M. H. & Schrijvers, P. H., edd. (1997) *Lucretius and his Intellectual Background* (Amsterdam)

Allen, J. (1993) 'Pyrrhonism and medical empiricism: Sextus Empiricus on evidence and inference', in Haase, W., ed., *ANRW* II 37.1, 646–90

Allen, J. (1994) 'Academic probabilism and Stoic epistemology', *CQ* 44, 85–113

Alpers, K. (1968) 'Epikurs Geburtstag', *MH* 25, 48–51

Amsler, M. (1989) *Etymology and Grammatical Discourse in Late Antiquity and the Early Middle Ages* (Amsterdam)

Angeli, A. (1981) 'I frammenti di Idomeneo di Lampsaco', *CErc* 11, 41–101

Angeli, A. (1986) '*Compendi, eklogai, tetrapharmakos*: due capitoli di dissenso nell'Epicureismo', *CErc* 16, 53–66

Angeli, A., ed. (1988a) Filodemo: *Agli amici di scuola (PHerc. 1005)*, La scuola di Epicuro 7 (Naples)

Angeli, A. (1988b) 'La scuola epicurea di Lampsaco nel *PHerc.* 176 (Fr. 5 Coll. I, IV, VIII–XXIII)', *CErc* 18, 27–51

Angeli, A. (1993) 'Frammenti di lettere di Epicuro nei papiri d'Ercolano', *CErc* 23, 11–27

Angeli, A. & Colaizzo, M. (1979) 'I frammenti di Zenone Sidonio', *CErc* 9, 47–133

Angeli, A. & Dorandi, T. (1987) 'Il pensiero matematico di Demetrio Lacone', *CErc* 17, 89–103

Annas, J. E. (1977) 'Plato and Aristotle on friendship and altruism', *Mind* 86, 532–54

Annas, J. E. (1980a) 'Aristotle on pleasure and goodness', in Rorty, A. O., ed., *Essays on Aristotle's Ethics* (Berkeley) 285–99

Annas, J. E. (1980b) 'Truth and knowledge', in Schofield *et al.* (1980a) 84–104

Annas, J. E. (1986) 'Doing without objective values: ancient and modern strategies', in Schofield & Striker (1986a) 3–29

Annas, J. E. (1987) 'Epicurus on pleasure and happiness', *Philosophical Topics* 15, 5–21

Annas, J. E. (1988a) 'Naturalism in Greek ethics: Aristotle and after', in Cleary & Shartin (1988) 149–71

Annas, J.E. (1988b) 'The heirs of Socrates', *Phronesis* 33, 100–12

Annas, J.E. (1989a) 'Cicero on Stoic moral philosophy and private property', in Griffin & Barnes (1989) 151–73

Annas, J. (1989b) 'Epicurean emotions', *GRBS* 30, 145–64

Annas, J. E. (1990a) 'Platon le sceptique', *RMM* 95, 267–91

Annas, J. E. (1990b) 'Stoic epistemology', in Everson (1990a) 184–203

Annas, J. E. (1991) 'Epicurus' philosophy of mind', in Everson (1991a) 84–101

Annas, J. E. (1992a) *Hellenistic Philosophy of Mind*, Hellenistic culture and society 8 (Berkeley)

Annas, J. E. (1992b) 'Sextus Empiricus and the Peripatetics', *Elenchos* 13, 201–32

Annas, J. E. (1992c) 'Plato the Sceptic', *OSAP* suppl. vol., 43–72

Annas, J. E. (1993a) *The Morality of Happiness* (New York/Oxford)

Annas, J. E. (1993b) 'Epicurus on agency', in Brunschwig & Nussbaum (1993) 53–71

Annas, J. E. & Barnes, J. (1985) *The Modes of Scepticism*: Ancient Texts and Modern Interpretations (Cambridge)

Annas, J. E. & Barnes, J., trans. (1994) Sextus Empiricus: *Outlines of Scepticism* (Cambridge)

Anscombe, G. E. M. (1956) 'Aristotle and the sea battle', *Mind* 65; repr. in *The Collected Philosophical Papers of G. E. M. Anscombe*, vol. I: From Parmenides to Wittgenstein (Oxford 1981) 44–55

Anton, J. P. & Preuss, A., edd. (1983) *Essays in Ancient Greek Philosophy*, vol. II (Albany)

Antoniadis, E. (1916) *Aristipp und die Kyrenaiker* (Göttingen)

Apelt, O. (1891) *Beiträge zur Geschichte der griechischen Philosophie* (Leipzig)

Appuhn, Ch., ed. (1952) Cicéron: *De la divination – Du destin – Académiques* (Paris)

Arnim, J. von, ed. (1903–24) *Stoicorum Veterum Fragmenta*, Bd. I–III; Bd. IV, indices by Adler, M. (Leipzig, later repr.)

Arnim, J. von (1926) 'Arius Didymus' Abriß der peripatetischen Ethik', *SAWW*, phil.-
hist. Kl. 204.3

Arrighetti, G., ed. (1973) Epicuro: *Opere*, 2nd edn, Biblioteca di cultura filosofica 41
(Turin)

Arrighetti, G. (1978) 'Philia e physiologia: i fondamenti dell'amicizia epicurea', *MD* 1,
49-63

Arrighetti, G. (1980) 'Aporie aristoteliche ed etica epicurea', *MD* 5, 9-26

Arrighetti, G. (1984) 'Devoir et plaisir chez Epicure', in Harmatta, J., ed. *Proceedings of
the VIIth Congress of the International Federation of the Societies of Classical Studies*
(Budapest) 385-91

Arrighetti, G. (1987) *Poeti, eruditi e biografi*, Momenti della riflessione dei Greci sulla
letteratura, Biblioteca di studi antichi 52 (Pisa)

Arrighetti, G. (1994) 'Riflessione sulla letteratura e biografia presso i Greci', in
Montanari (1994)

Arthur, E. P. (1983) 'Stoic analysis of the mind's reactions to presentations', *Hermes* III
1983, 69-78

Asmis, E. (1984) *Epicurus' Scientific Method*, Cornell studies in classical philology 42
(Ithaca/London)

Asmis, E. (1990a) 'Free action and the swerve', *OSAP* 8, 275-91

Asmis, E. (1990b) 'Philodemus' Epicureanism', in Haase, W., ed., *ANRW* II 36. 4
(Berlin/New York) 2369-406

Asmis, E. (1990c) 'The poetic theory of the Stoic "Aristo"', *Apeiron* 23, 147-201

Asmis, E. (1992) 'An Epicurean survey of poetic theories (Philodemus *On Poems* 5, cols.
26-36)', *CQ* 42, 395-415

Asmis, E. (1995) 'Epicurean Semiotics', in: Manetti (1995) 155-85.

Astin, A. E. (1967) *Scipio Aemilianus* (Oxford)

Atherton, C. (1988) 'Hand over fist: the failure of Stoic rhetoric', *CQ* 38, 392-427

Atherton, C. (1993) *The Stoics on Ambiguity* (Cambridge)

Atkins, E. M. (1990) '"Domina et regina virtutum": justice and *societas* in the *De
Officiis*', *Phronesis* 35, 258-89

Aubenque, P. (1980) *Concepts et Catégories dans la Pensée Antique* (Paris)

Aune, D. E (1987) *The New Testament in its Literary Environment*, Library of Early
Christianity 8 (Philadelphia)

Ausland, H. W. (1989) 'On the moral origin of the Pyrrhonian philosophy', *Elenchos* 10,
359-434

Avotins, I. (1983) 'On some Epicurean and Lucretian arguments for the infinity of the
universe', *CQ* 33, 421-7

Ax, W. (1986) *Laut, Stimme und Sprache*: Studien zu drei Grundbegriffen der antiken
Sprachtheorie, Hypomnemata 84 (Göttingen)

Ax, W. (1987) 'Quadripertita ratio: Bemerkungen zur Geschichte eines aktuellen
Kategoriensystem', in Taylor (1987a) 17-40

Ax, W. (1991) 'Sprache als Gegenstand der alexandrinischen und pergamenischen
Philologie', in Schmitter (1991) 275-301

Babut, D. (1969) *Plutarque et le Stoïcisme*, Publications de l'Université de Lyon (Paris)

Babut, D. (1974) *La Religion des Philosophes Grecs, de Thales aux Stoiciens* (Paris)

Badawi, A. (1971) *Commentaires sur Aristote perdus en grec et autres épîtres* (Beirut)

Badawi, A. (1987 (1968)) *La Transmission de la Philosophie Grecque au Monde Arabe*, Etudes de philosophie medievale 56 (Paris)

Badian, E. (1958) 'Alexander the Great and the unity of mankind', *Historia* 7, 425-44

Bailey, C. (1926) *Epicurus. The Extant Remains* (Oxford)

Bailey, C. (1928) *The Greek Atomists and Epicurus* (Oxford, various repr.)

Baldassarri, M. (1984) *Introduzione alla Logica Stoica*, La logica stoica: testimonianze e frammenti (Como)

Baldry, H. C. (1959) 'Zeno's ideal state', *JHS* 79, 3-15

Baldry, H. C. (1965) *The Unity of Mankind in Greek Thought* (Cambridge)

Baratin, M. (1989) *La Naissance de la Syntaxe à Rome* (Paris)

Baratin, M. (1991) 'Aperçu de la linguistique stoïcienne', in Schmitter (1991) 193-216

Baratin, M. & Desbordes, F. (1987) 'La "troisième partie" de l'ars grammatica', in Taylor (1987a) 41-66

Barigazzi, A. (1969) 'Epicure et le scepticisme', *Actes du VIIIe Congrès de l'Association Guillaume Budé* (Paris) 286-93

Barigazzi, A. (1983) 'Sul concetto epicureo della sicurezza esterna', in AA. VV. (1983) 73-92

Barker, A. (1989) *Greek Musical Writings*, vol. II: Harmonic and Acoustic Theory (Cambridge)

Barker, E. (1956) *From Alexander to Constantine*. Passages and Documents Illustrating the History of Social and Political Ideas, 336 BC-AD 337 (Oxford)

Barnes, J. (1978) 'La doctrine du retour éternel', in Brunschwig (1978a) 3-20

Barnes, J. (1979) *The Presocratic Philosophers*, 2 vols. (London/New York; repr. 1982 in one vol.)

Barnes, J. (1980) 'Proof destroyed', in Schofield *et al.* (1980a) 161-81

Barnes, J. (1982b) 'Medicine, experience and logic', in Barnes, J. *et al.* (1982a) 24-68

Barnes, J. (1982c) 'The beliefs of a Pyrrhonist', *PCPS* 28, 1-28, also in *Elenchos* 4 (1983) 5-43

Barnes, J. (1983a) 'Ancient skepticism and causation', in Burnyeat (1983) 149-203

Barnes, J. (1983b) 'Terms and sentences', *PBA* 69, 279-326

Barnes, J. (1985) 'Theophrastus and hypothetical syllogistic', in Wiesner (1985-87) I, 557-76, also in Fortenbaugh *et al.* (1985) 125-41

Barnes, J. (1986a) 'Peripatetic negations', *OSAP* 4, 201-14

Barnes, J. (1986b) 'The *Logical Investigations* of Chrysippus', *Wissenschaftskolleg Jahrbuch* 1984/5 (Berlin) 19-29

Barnes, J. (1986c) 'Diogene Laerzio e il Pirronismo', in Giannantoni (1986a) 383-427

Barnes, J. (1986d) 'Is rhetoric an art?', *Darg Newsletter* II.2, 2-22

Barnes, J. (1987) 'An Aristotelian way with Scepticism', in Matthen (1987) 51-76

Barnes, J. (1988b) 'Bits and pieces', in Barnes & Mignucci (1988a) 223-94

Barnes, J. (1988c) 'Epicurean signs', *OSAP* suppl. vol., 91-134

Barnes, J. (1989a) 'The size of the sun in antiquity', *ACD* 25, 29-41

Barnes, J. (1989b) (rev. Hülser 1987, vols. II-IV) *CR* 39, 263-4

Barnes, J. (1989c) 'Antiochus of Ascalon', in Griffin & Barnes (1989) 51-96

Barnes, J. (1990a) 'Logical form and logical matter', in Alberti (1990) 7-119

Barnes, J. (1990b) *The Toils of Scepticism* (Cambridge)

Barnes, J. (1990c) 'Pyrrhonism, belief and causation. Observations on the Scepticism

of Sextus Empiricus', in Haase, W., ed., *ANRW* II 36.4 (Berlin/New York)
   2608–95

Barnes, J. (1991) 'Enseigner la Vertu?', *RPh* 116, 571–89

Barnes, J. (1992) 'Diogenes Laertius IX 61–116: The philosophy of Pyrrhonism', in
   Haase, W., ed., *ANRW* II 36.6 (Berlin/New York) 4241–301

Barnes, J. (1993a) '"A third kind of syllogism": Galen and the logic of relations', in
   Sharples (1993) 172–94

Barnes, J. (1993b) 'Meaning, saying and thinking', in Döring & Ebert (1993) 47–61

Barnes, J. (1993c) (rev. Ebert 1991) *CR* 43, 304–6

Barnes, J. (1993d) 'Galen and the utility of logic', in Kollesch & Nickel (1993) 33–52

Barnes, J. (1996a) 'Epicurus: meaning and thinking', in Giannantoni & Gigante (1996),
   vol. I, 197–220

Barnes, J. (1996b) 'The catalogue of Chrysippus' logical works', in Algra *et al.* (1996)
   169–84

Barnes, J. (1996c) 'Grammar on Aristotle's terms', in Frede & Striker (1996)

Barnes, J. (1997) 'Logic in *Academica* I and the *Lucullus*', in Inwood & Mansfeld (1997)
   140–60

Barnes, J., Brunschwig, J., Burnyeat, M. & Schofield, M., edd. (1982a) *Science and
   Speculation*: Studies in Hellenistic Theory and Practice (Cambridge/Paris)

Barnes, J. & Mignucci, M., edd. (1988a) *Matter and Metaphysics*. Fourth Symposium
   Hellenisticum, Elenchos 14 (Naples)

Barnes, J., Bobzien, S., Flannery, K. & Ierodiakonou, K. (1991) *Alexander of Aphrodisias,
   On Aristotle* Prior Analytics *1.1–7* (London)

Barwick, K. (1922) *Remmius Palaemon und die römische* ars grammatica, Philologus
   Suppl. 15, H. 2 (Leipzig; repr. Hildesheim 1967)

Barwick, K. (1957) *Probleme der stoischen Sprachlehre und Rhetorik*, Abh. Sächsischen
   Akad. der Wiss. zu Leipzig, Philol.-hist. Kl. Bd. 49.3 (Berlin)

Bastianini, G. & Long, A. A., edd. (1992a) *Hierocles*, in *Corpus dei papiri filosofici greci e
   latini*, vol. I, 1** (Florence) 268–451

Bastianini, G. & Long, A. A., edd. (1992b) 'Dopo la nuova edizione degli *Elementi di
   etica* di Ierocle Stoico (PBerol 9780v)', in *Studi su Codici e Papiri Filosofici. Platone,
   Aristotele, Ierocle* (Florence) 221–47

Bastianini, G. & Sedley, D. N. (1995) 'Commentarium in Platonis *Theaetetum*', in
   Corpus dei papiri filosofici greci e latini, vol. III (Florence) 227–562

Becker, L. C., ed. (1992a) *Encyclopedia of Ethics*, 2 vols. (New York)

Becker, L. C., ed. (1992b) *A History of Western Ethics* (New York)

Becker, O., ed. (1957a) *Zwei Untersuchungen zur antiken Logik*, Klassisch-philologische
   Studien 17 (Wiesbaden)

Becker, O. (1957b) 'Über die vier "Themata" der stoischen Logik', in Becker (1957a) 27–49

Becker, O. (1960) 'Zur Rekonstruktion des "kyrieuon logos" des Diodoros Kronos', in
   Derbolav, J. & Nicolin, F., edd., *Erkenntnis und Verantwortung*, FS Theodor Litt
   (Dusseldorf) 250–63

Behrends, O. (1977) 'Les "veteres" et la nouvelle jurisprudence à la fin de la
   République', *RD* 55, 7–33

Benedetto, V. di (1958/9) 'Dionisio Trace e la *Techne* a lui attribuita', *ASNP* II 27,
   169–210; 28, 87–118

Benedetto, V. di (1990) 'At the origins of Greek grammar', *Glotta* 68, 19–39

Berger, K. (1984) 'Hellenistische Gattungen im Neuen Testament', in Haase, W., ed., *ANRW* II 25.2 (Berlin/New York) 1031–432

Bernard, P. (1984) 'Le philosophe Anaxarque et le roi Nicocréon de Salamine', *JS* 3–49

Bernheim, E. (1908) *Lehrbuch der historischen Methode und der Geschichtsphilosophie*, mit Nachweis der wichtigsten Quellen und Hilfsmittel zum Studium der Geschichte, 5th and 6th edn, 2 vols. (Leipzig)

Berrettoni, P. (1989) 'An idol of the school: the aspectual theory of the Stoics', *Rivista di linguistica* 1, 33–68

Berryman, S. (1998) 'Euclid and the Sceptic: a paper on vision, doubt, geometry, light and drunkenness', *Phronesis* 43, 176–96

Berti, E. (1981) 'La critica allo scetticismo nel IV libro della *Metafisica*', in Giannantoni (1981a) I, 61–79

Bett, R. (1989) 'Carneades' *pithanon*: a reappraisal of its role and status', *OSAP* 7, 59–94

Bett, R. (1990) 'Carneades' distinction between assent and approval', *The Monist* 73, 3–20

Bett, R. (1994a) 'What did Pyrrho think about "the nature of the divine and the good"?', *Phronesis* 39, 303–37

Bett, R. (1994b) 'Aristocles on Timon on Pyrrho: The text, its logic, and its credibility', *OSAP* 12, 137–81

Bichler, R. (1983) '*Hellenismus*', Geschichte und Problematik eines Epochenbegriffs (Darmstadt)

Bicknell, P. (1982) 'Melissus' way of seeming ?', *Phronesis* 27, 194–201

Bignone, E. (1936) *L'Aristotele Perduto e la Formazione Filosofica di Epicuro*, 2 vols. (Florence, 2nd enlarged edn by Alfieri, V. E. 1972)

Blank, D. L. (1982) *Ancient Philosophy and Grammar: The Syntax of Apollonius Dyscolus* (Chico. Cal.)

Blank, D. L. (1994) 'Diogenes of Babylon and the κριτικοί in Philodemus: a preliminary suggestion', *CErc* 24 (1994) 55–62

Blank, D. L. (1995) 'Philodemus on the technicity of rhetoric', in Obbink (1995) 178–88

Blomqvist, J. (1974) 'Die skeptika des Sextus Empiricus', *GB* 2, 7–14

Blum, L. A. (1980) *Friendship, Altruism and Morality* (London)

Blundell, M. W. (1990) 'Parental nature and Stoic Οἰκείωσις', *AncPhil* 10, 221–42

Bobzien, S. (1986) *Die stoische Modallogik*, Epistemata, Reihe Philosophie 32 (Würzburg)

Bobzien, S. (1993) 'Chrysippus' modal logic and its relation to Philo and Diodorus', in Döring & Ebert (1993) 63–84

Bobzien, S. (1996) 'Stoic syllogistic', *OSAP* 14, 133–92

Bobzien, S. (1997a) 'Stoic conceptions of freedom and their relation to ethics', in Sorabji, R., ed., *Aristotle and After*, BICS Suppl., 71–89

Bobzien, S. (1997b) 'The Stoics on hypothesis and hypothetical arguments', *Phronesis* 42, 299–312

Bobzien, S. (1998) *Determinism and Freedom in Stoic Philosophy* (Oxford)

Bobzien, S. (1999) 'Chrysippus' Theory of causes', in Ierodiakonou (1999) 196–242

Bochenski, I. (1947) *La logique de Théophraste*, Collectanea Friburgensia, N.S. 32 (Fribourg)

Bodnár, I. (1992) 'Anaximander on the stability of the earth', *Phronesis* 37, 336–42

Bollack, J., (1969) 'Les maximes de l'amitié', in *Actes du VIIIe Congrès Guillaume Budé* (Paris) 221–36

Bollack, J., ed. (1975) *La pensée du plaisir* – Epicure: *textes moraux, commentaires* (Paris)

Bollack, J. & Laks, A., edd. (1976) *Etudes sur l'épicurisme antique*, Cahiers de Philologie 1 (Lille)

Bouché-Leclercq, A. (1899) *L'astrologie grecque* (Paris)

Boulluec, A. Le (1982) 'Exégèse et polémique antignostique chez Irénée et Clément d'Alexandrie: l'exemple du centon', in Livingstone, E. A., ed., *Studia Patristica* vol. xvii.2 (Oxford/New York) 707–13

Boulluec, A. Le (1994) 'Clément d'Alexandrie', in Goulet (1989–94) ii, 426–31

Boyancé, P. (1936) 'Les méthodes de l'histoire littéraire. Cicéron et son œuvre philosophique', *REL* 14, 288–309; repr. in id. (1970) *Etudes sur l'humanisme cicéronien*, Collection Latomus 21 (Brussels) 199–221

Boyancé, P. (1962) 'Les preuves stoïciennes de l'existence des dieux d'après Cicéron', *Hermes* 90, 46–71

Boyancé, P. (1967) (rev. Giusta 1964) *Latomus* 26, 246–9

Boys-Stones, G. (1996) 'The ἐπελευστική δύναμις in Aristo's psychology of action', *Phronesis* 41, 75–94

Brancacci, A. (1981) 'La filosofia di Pirrone e le sue relazioni con il cinismo', in Giannantoni (1981a) i, 211–42

Bréhier, E. (1910) *La Théorie des Incorporels dans l'Ancien Stoïcisme* (Paris; repr. 1962)

Bréhier, E. (1914) 'Posidonius d'Apamée théoricien de la géométrie', *REG* 27, 44–58; repr. in Bréhier (1955) *Etudes de philosophie antique* (Paris) 117–30

Brent, A. (1993) 'Diogenes Laertius and the apostolic succession', *JEH* 44, 367–89

Brent, A. (1995) *Hippolytus and the Roman Church in the Third Century*: Communities in Tension before the Emergence of a Monarch-Bishop, VChr suppl. 31 (Leiden)

Brink, C. O. (1940) 'Peripatos', in *Pauly Wissowa, Realencyclopädie* Suppl. 7, cols. 899–949

Brink, C. O. (1956) 'Theophrastus and Zeno on nature in moral theory', *Phronesis* 1, 123–45

Brink, C. O. (1963) *Horace on Poetry*, vol. i: Prolegomena to the Literary Epistles (Cambridge and later repr.)

Brochard, V. (1887) *Les sceptiques grecs* (Paris; 2nd edn 1923)

Brunschwig, J. (1977) 'L'argument d'Epicure sur l'immutabilité du tout', in *Permanence de la philosophie: mélanges offerts à Joseph Moreau* (Neuchâtel) 127–50; repr. in Brunschwig (1995) 15–42

Brunschwig, J., ed. (1978a) *Les Stoïciens et leur logique*. Actes du colloque de Chantilly, 18–22 septembre 1976, Bibliothèque d'histoire de la philosophie (Paris)

Brunschwig, J. (1978b) 'Le modèle conjonctif', in Brunschwig (1978a) 58–86; repr. in Brunschwig (1995) 161–87

Brunschwig, J. (1980) 'Proof defined', in Schofield *et al.* (1980a) 125–60

Brunschwig, J. (1984) 'Remarques sur la théorie stoïcienne du nom propre', *HEL* 6, 3–19; repr. in Brunschwig (1995) 115–39

Brunschwig, J. (1986) 'The cradle argument in Epicureanism and Stoicism', in Schofield & Striker (1986a) 113–44

Brunschwig, J. (1988a) 'La théorie stoïcienne du genre suprême et l'ontologie platonicienne', in Barnes & Mignucci (1988a) 19–127

Brunschwig, J. (1988b) 'Sextus Empiricus on the *kritērion*', in Dillon & Long (1988) 145–75, repr. in Brunschwig (1994a) 224–43

Brunschwig, J. (1990a) 'Le titre des *Indalmoi* de Timon: d'Ulysse à Pyrrhon', *Recherches sur la philosophie et le langage* 12, 83–98; repr. in Brunschwig (1995) 271–87

Brunschwig, J. (1990b) 'Sur une façon stoïcienne de ne pas être', *RThPh* 122, 389–403; repr. in Brunschwig (1995) 251–68

Brunschwig, J. (1991) 'On a book-title by Chrysippus: on the fact that the ancients admitted dialectic along with demonstrations', *OSAP* suppl. vol., 81–95

Brunschwig, J. (1992) 'Pyrrhon et Philista', in Goulet-Cazé, M.-O., Madec, G., O'Brien, D., edd., ΣΟΦΙΗΣ ΜΑΙΗΤΟΡΕΣ, *"Chercheurs de sagesse"*, Hommage à Jean Pépin (Paris) 133–46

Brunschwig, J., ed. (1994a) *Papers in Hellenistic Philosophy* (Cambridge)

Brunschwig, J. (1994b) 'Remarks on the classification of simple propositions in Hellenistic logics', in Brunschwig (1994a) 57–71

Brunschwig, J. (1994c) 'The conjunctive model', in Brunschwig (1994a) 72–91

Brunschwig, J. (1994d) 'Did Diogenes of Babylon invent the ontological argument?', in Brunschwig (1994a) 170–89

Brunschwig, J. (1994e) 'Once again on Eusebius on Aristocles on Timon on Pyrrho', in Brunschwig (1994a) 190–211

Brunschwig, J. (1994f) 'The Anaxarchus case: an essay on survival', *PBA* 81, 59–88

Brunschwig, J. (1995) *Etudes sur les Philosophes Hellénistiques*: epicurisme, stoïcisme, scepticisme (Paris)

Brunschwig, J. (1996) 'Le fragment DK 70 B 1 de Métrodore de Chio', in Algra *et al.* (1996) 21–40

Brunschwig, J. & Nussbaum, M. C., edd. (1993) *Passions and Perceptions*: Proceedings of the Fifth Symposium Hellenisticum, Studies in Hellenistic Philosophy of Mind (Cambridge)

Brunt, P. A. (1980) 'On historical fragments and epitomes', *Classical Quarterly* 30, 477–94

Burkert, W. (1972) 'Zur geistesgeschichtlichen Einordnung einiger Pseudopythagorica', in *Pseudepigrapha* 1, Fondation Hardt 18 (Vandœuvres/Geneva) 25–55

Burkert, W., Gemelli Marciano, L., Matelli, E. & Orelli, L., edd. (1998) *Fragmentsammlungen philosophischer Texte der Antike – Le raccolte dei frammenti di filosofi antichi*, Aporemata 3 (Göttingen)

Burnyeat, M. (1976) 'Protagoras and self-refutation in later Greek philosophy', *PhR* 85, 44–69

Burnyeat, M. F. (1978) 'The upside-down back-to-front sceptic of Lucretius IV 472', *Philologus* 122, 197–206

Burnyeat, M. F. (1980a (1983)) 'Can the sceptic live his scepticism?', in Schofield *et al.* (1980a) 20–53; repr. in Burnyeat (1983) 117–48

Burnyeat, M. F. (1980b) 'Tranquillity without a stop: Timon, frag. 68', *CQ* 30, 86–93

Burnyeat, M. F. (1981) 'Aristotle on understanding knowledge', in Berti, E., ed., *Aristotle on Science*—The 'Posterior Analytics', Studia Aristotelica 9 (Padua) 97–139

Burnyeat, M. F. (1982a) 'Idealism and Greek philosophy: what Descartes saw and Berkeley missed', *PhR* 91, 3–40

Burnyeat, M. F. (1982b) 'Gods and heaps', in Schofield & Nussbaum (1982) 315–38

Burnyeat, M. F. (1982c) 'The origins of non-deductive inference', in Barnes *et al.* (1982a) 193–238

Burnyeat, M. F., ed. (1983) *The Skeptical Tradition*, Major Thinkers Series 3 (Berkeley)

Burnyeat, M. F. (1984) 'The sceptic in his place and time', in Rorty *et al.* (1984) 225–54

Burnyeat, M. F. (1990) *The Theaetetus of Plato* (Indianapolis/Cambridge)

Burnyeat, M. F. (1997) 'Antipater and self-refutation: elusive arguments in Cicero's *Academica*', in Inwood & Mansfeld (1997) 277–311

Burridge, R. A. (1992) *What are the Gospels?* A Comparison with Graeco-Roman Biography (Cambridge)

Caizzi, *see* Decleva Caizzi

Calboli Montefusco, L. (1991) 'Die Topik in der Argumentation', in Ueding (1991) 21–34

Calboli, G. (1962) *Studi grammaticali*, vol. 1 (Bologna)

Cambiano, G. (1977) 'Il problema dell'esistenza di una scuola Megarica', in Giannantoni, G., ed., *Scuole socratiche minori e filosofia ellenistica* (Bologna) 25–53

Cambiano, G. (1992) 'Scoperta e dimostrazione in Archimede', in Dollo, C., ed., *Archimede*, Mito Tradizione Scienza (Florence) 21–41

Cameron, A. (1993) *The Greek Anthology from Meleager to Planudes* (Oxford)

Cameron, H. D. (1987) 'The upside-down cladogram: problems in manuscript affiliation', in Hoenigswald & Wiener (1987) 227–42

Cancik, H. (1984b) 'Die Gattung Evangelium. Das Evangelium des Markus im Rahmen der antiken Historiographie', in Cancik, H., d. (1984a) *Markus-Philologie* (Tübingen) 85–113

Canfora, L. (1993) *Vita di Lucrezio* (Palermo)

Capasso, M. (1980) 'Note laerziane', *Elenchos* 1, 161–3

Capasso, M. (1981) 'I *Problemi di filologia filosofica* di Mario Untersteiner', *Elenchos* 2, 375–404

Capasso, M. (1982) 'Polistrato uditore di Epicuro?', *CErc* 12, 5–12

Capasso, M. (1987) *Comunità senza rivolta*, quattro saggi sull'epicureismo, Saggi Bibliopolis 26 (Naples)

Capasso, M., ed. (1988a) Carneisco: *Il Secondo libro del Filista (PHerc. 1027)* (Naples)

Capasso, M. (1988b) 'Gli epicurei e il potere della memoria (*PHerc.* 1041 e 1040)', in Mandilaras, B. G. *et al.*, edd., *Proceedings of the XVIIIth International Congress of Papyrology* 1 (Athens) 257–70

Capasso, M. (1989) 'Primo supplemento al Catalogo dei papiri Ercolanesi', *CErc* 19, 193–264

Casanova, A., ed. (1984) *I frammenti di Diogene d'Enoanda*, Studi e testi 6 (Florence)

Casertano, G. (1983) *Il piacere, l'amore e la morte nelle dottrine dei presocratici I: Il piacere e il desiderio* (Naples)

Cavallo, G. (1983) *Libri scritture scribi a Ercolano*, CErc, suppl. 1 (Naples)

Cavallo, G. (1984) 'I rotoli di Ercolano come prodotti scritti. Quattro riflessioni', *Scrittura e Civiltà* 8, 5–30

Cavallo, G. (1989) 'Libro e cultura scritta', in Momigliano, A. & Schiavone, A., edd., *Storia di Roma*, vol. 4, Caratteri e morfologia (Turin) 694–734

Cavallo, G. (1994) 'Discorsi sul libro', in Cambiano, G., Canfora, L. & Lanza, D., *Lo spazio letterario della Grecia antica* vol. 1, *La produzione e la circolazione del testo*, T. 3, *I Greci e Roma* (Rome) 613–39

Centrone, B. (1990) *Pseudopythagorica Ethica*, i trattati morali di Archita,
　　Metopo,Teage, Eurifamo, Elenchos 17 (Naples)
Chadwick, H. (1959) *The Sentences of Sextus*. A Contribution to the History of Early
　　Christian Ethics (Cambridge)
Charles, D. (1992) 'Supervenience, composition and physicalism', in Charles, D. &
　　Lennon, K., edd., *Reduction, Explanation and Realism* (Oxford) 265–96
Cherniss, H. F. (1976) Plutarch's *Moralia XIII, part ii*, LCL (Cambridge, Mass./London)
Chilton, C. W. (1960) 'Did Epicurus approve of marriage? A study of Diogenes Laertius
　　x, 119', *Phronesis* 5, 71–74
Chilton, C. W. (1971) Diogenes of Oenoanda: *The Fragments*. A Translation and
　　Commentary (London/New York/Toronto)
Cichorius, C. (1908) 'Panaitios und die attische Stoikerinschrift', *RhM* 63, 197–223
Classen, C. J. (1958) 'Aristippos', *Hermes* 86, 182–92
Classen, C. J., ed. (1983) R. Philippson, *Studien zu Epikur und den Epikureern*, Olms
　　Studien 17 (Hildesheim)
Classen, C. J. (1992) 'L'esposizione dei Sofisti e della Sofistica in Sesto Empirico',
　　Elenchos 13, 57–79
Clay, D. (1972) 'Epicurus' *Kuria doxa* xvii', *GRBS* 13, 59–66
Clay, D. (1973) 'Epicurus' last will and testament', *AGPh* 55, 252–80
Clay, D. (1983a) *Lucretius and Epicurus* (Ithaca, New York/London)
Clay, D. (1983b) 'Individual and community in the first generation of the Epicurean
　　school', in AA. VV. (1983) 255–79
Clay, D. (1986) 'The cults of Epicurus', *CErc* 16, 11–28
Clay, D. (1990) 'The philosophical inscription of Diogenes of Oenoanda: New
　　discoveries 1969–1983', in Haase, W., ed., *ANRW* II 36. 4 (Berlin/New York)
　　2445–559
Cleary, J. J. & Shartin, D. C., edd. (1988) *Boston Area Colloquium in Ancient Philosophy*,
　　vol. iv (Lanham)
Cleary, J. J. & Wians, W. C., edd. (1992) *Boston Area Colloquium in Ancient Philosophy*,
　　vol. vii (Lanham)
Cohen, M. R. & Drabkin, I. E., edd. (1966) *A Source Book in Greek Science* (Cambridge,
　　Mass.; 1st edn New York 1948)
Cole, T. (1964) 'The sources and composition of Polybius vi', *Historia* 13, 440–86
Cole, T. (1967) *Democritus and the Sources of Greek Anthropology* (Cleveland)
Colish, M. L. (1990) *The Stoic Tradition from Antiquity to the Early Middle Ages* i: Stoicism
　　in the Classical Latin Literature, Studies in the history of Christian thought 34,
　　2nd impr. (Leiden, first edn 1985)
Conche, M. (1973) *Pyrrhon ou l'apparence* (Villers-sur-Mer)
Conche, M. (1984) 'Métrodore de Chio', in Huisman, D., ed., *Dictionnaire des
　　philosophes* (Paris) 1821
Cooper, J. (1989) 'Greek philosophers on euthanasia and suicide', in Brody, B. A., ed.
　　(1989) *Suicide and Euthanasia*: Historical and Contemporary Themes, Philosophy
　　and Medicine 35 (Dordrecht) 9–38
Corcoran, J., ed. (1974a) *Ancient Logic and its Modern Interpretation* (Dordrecht/Boston)
Corcoran, J. (1974b) 'Remarks on Stoic deduction', in Corcoran (1974a) 169–81
Corssen, P. (1878) *De Posidonio Rhodio M. Tulli Ciceronis in libro I. Tusc. disp. et in
　　Somnio Scipionis auctore* (Bonn)

Cortassa, G. (1989) 'Un'ipotesi sulla formazione del corpus di Sesto Empirico: La ricerca sulla tarda antichità', in Garzya, A., ed., *Metodologie della ricerca sulla tarda antichità*, Atti del primo convegno dell' associazione di studi tardoantichi (Naples) 297–307

Couissin, P. (1929) 'Le stoïcisme de la Nouvelle Académie', *Revue d'Histoire de la Philosophie Générale de la Civilisation* 3, 241–76. Cited in the English version (1983) 'The Stoicism of the New Academy', in Burnyeat (1983) 31–63

Couissin, P. (1941) 'Les sorites de Carnéade contre le polythéisme', *REG* 54, 43–57

Crane, T. & Mellor, D. H. (1990) 'There is no question of physicalism', *Mind* 99, 185–206

Crivelli, P. (1994) 'Indefinite propositions and anaphora in Stoic logic', *Phronesis* 39, 187–206

Croissant, J. (1984) 'Autour de la quatrième formule d'implication dans Sextus Empiricus', *RPhA* 2.1, 73–120

Crönert, W. (1906) *Kolotes und Menedemos*, Studien zur Palaeographie und Papyruskunde 6 (Leipzig; repr. Amsterdam 1965)

Crouzel, H., ed. (1969) Grégoire le Thaumaturge: *Remerciement à Origène*, suivi de la lettre d'Origène à Grégoire, SC 148 (Paris)

Daiber, H., ed. (1980) *Aetius Arabus. Die Vorsokratiker in arabischer Überlieferung*, Veröffentlichungen der Orientalischen Kommission, Akademie der Wissenschaften und der Literatur in Mainz 33 (Wiesbaden)

Daiber, H. (1992) 'The *Meteorology* of Theophrastus in Syriac and Arabic translation', in Fortenbaugh & Gutas (1992) 166–293

dal Pra, see: Pra, dal

Davidson, D. (1980) 'Mental events', in id., *Essays on Actions and Events* (Oxford; repr. 1985) 207–28

Davidson, D. (1982) *Actions and Events* (Oxford)

Dawson, D. (1992) *Cities of the Gods*: Communist Utopias in Greek Thought (New York/Oxford)

De Lacy, Ph. (1939) 'The Epicurean analysis of language', *AJPh* 60, 85–92

De Lacy, Ph. (1948) 'Stoic views of poetry', *AJPh* 69, 241–71

De Lacy, Ph. (1958) 'Oὐ μᾶλλον and the antecedents of ancient Scepticism', *Phronesis* 3, 59–71; repr. in Anton, J. P. & Kostas, G. L., edd. (1971) *Essays in Ancient Greek Philosophy* (Albany) 593–606

De Lacy, Ph. (1977) 'The four Stoic personae', *ICS* 2, 163–72

De Lacy, Ph., ed. (1984) Galen: *On the Doctrines of Hippocrates and Plato*, first part: books I–V, Corpus Medicorum Graecorum v 4, 1, 2, ed. 3 (Berlin, first edn 1978)

De Lacy, Ph. H. & De Lacy, E. A. (1978) Philodemus: *On Methods of Inference*, Rev. ed., La Scuola di Epicuro 1 (Naples)

De Mauro, see: Mauro, de

De Witt, N. W. (1936) 'Organization and procedure in Epicurean groups', *CPh* 31, 205–11

De Witt, N. W. (1954) *Epicurus and his Philosophy* (Minneapolis)

Decleva Caizzi, F. (1966) *Antisthenis Fragmenta* (Varese/Milan)

Decleva Caizzi, F., ed. (1981a) Pirrone: *Testimonianze*, Elenchos 5 (Naples)

Decleva Caizzi, F. (1981b) 'Prolegomena ad una raccolta delle fonti relative a Pirrone di Elide', in Giannantoni (1981a) I, 93–128

Decleva Caizzi, F. (1984) 'Pirrone e Democrito: Gli atomi: un "mito" ?', *Elenchos* 5,
5–23, also published as 'Démocrite, l'école d'Abdère et le premier pyrrhonisme',
Proceedings of the 1st International Congress on Democritus, vol. B, 139–56

Decleva Caizzi, F. (1986) 'Pirroniani ed accademici nel III secolo a.C.', in Flashar &
Gigon (1986) 147–78

Decleva Caizzi, F. (1988) 'La "materia scorrevole" — Sulle tracce di un dibattito
perduto', in Barnes & Mignucci (1988a) 425–70

Decleva Caizzi, F. (1992a) 'Aenesidemus and the Academy', *CQ* 42, 176–89

Decleva Caizzi, F. (1992b) 'Sesto e gli Scettici', *Elenchos* 13, 277–327

Decleva Caizzi, F. & Funghi, M. S. (1988) 'Un testo sul concetto stoico di progresso
morale (PMilVogliano inv. 1241)', in *Aristoxenica, Menandrea, Fragmenta
philosophica*. Studi e testi per il Corpus dei papiri filosofici greci e latini 3
(Florence) 85–124

Deichgräber, K. (1930 (repr. w. add. 1965)) *Die Griechische Empirikerschule*. Sammlung
der Fragmente und Darstellung der Lehre (Berlin/Zürich)

Deichgräber, K. (1937) 'Persaios (1)', in *Pauly Wissowa, Realencyclopädie* 19.1, cols.
926–31

Delamarre, A. J.-L. (1980) 'La notion de ΠΤΩΣΙΣ chez Aristote et les Stoïciens', in
Aubenque (1980) 321–45

Delatte, L., ed. (1942) *Les Traités de la Royauté d'Ecphante, Diotogène et Sténidas*
(Liège/Paris)

Denniston, J. (1934) *The Greek Particles* (Oxford; 2nd edn 1950, various repr.)

Denyer, N. C. (1981a) 'The atomism of Diodorus Cronus', *Prudentia* 13, 33–45

Denyer, N. C. (1981b) 'Time and modality in Diodorus Cronus', *Theoria* 47, 31–53

Denyer, N. C. (1983) 'The origins of justice', in AA. VV. (1983) 133–52

Denyer, N. C. (1988) 'Stoicism and token reflexivity', in Barnes & Mignucci (1988a)
375–96

Denyer, N. C. (1991) *Language, Thought and Falsehood in Ancient Greek Philosophy*
(London/New York)

des Places, *see*: Places, des

Desbordes, B. A. (1990) *Introduction à Diogène Laërce*, Exposition de
l'Altertumswissenschaft servant de préliminaires critiques à une lecture de
l'oeuvre, 2 vols. (Utrecht)

Desbordes, F. (1987) 'Elementa. Remarques sur le rôle de l'écriture dans la linguistique
antique', *Cahiers de philosophie ancienne* 5, 339–55

Desbordes, F. (1990) *Idées Romaines sur l'Ecriture* (Lille)

Deuse, W. (1993) 'Celsus im Prooemium von "De medicina": Römische Aneignung
griechischer Wissenschaft', in Haase, W., ed., *ANRW* II 37.1 (Berlin/New York)
819–41

di Benedetto; di Marco; di Gregorio, see: Benedetto, etc.

Diano, C. (1935) 'Note epicuree', *SIFC* 12, 61–86, 237–89

Diano, C. (1974) 'La psicologia d'Epicuro e la teoria delle passioni', in C. Diano, *Scritti
epicurei* (Florence) 129–280

Diels, H. (1879) *Doxographi Graeci* (Berlin, later repr.)

Diels, H., ed. (1893) Anonymi Londinensis *Ex Aristotelis Iatricis Menoniis et aliis medicis
Eclogae*, Commentaria in Aristotelem Graeca, suppl. Arist. 3.1 (Berlin)

Diels, H. (1894) 'Aus dem Leben des Cynikers Diogenes', *AGPh* 7, 313–16

Diels, H., ed. (1901) *Poetarum Philosophorum Fragmenta* (Berlin)

Diels, H., ed. (1903) *Die Fragmente der Vorsokratiker* (Berlin, numerous rev. edns.)

Diels, H., ed. (1916/17) *Philodemos über die Götter*, Erstes und drittes Buch, Abh. der königlich Preussischen Akad. der Wiss. 1915.7/1916.4 and 6, philos.-hist. Klasse (Berlin)

Dihle, A. (1970) *Studien zur Griechischen Biographie*, 2nd edn, NAWG 3. F. Nr. 37 (Göttingen)

Dihle, A. (1986a) *Die Entstehung der Historischen Biographie*, SAHW, Philos.-hist. Kl. 1986.3 (Heidelberg [1987])

Dihle, A. (1986b) 'Philosophie-Fachwissenschaft-Allgemeinbildung', in Flashar & Gigon (1986) 185–223

Dijksterhuis, E. J. (1987) *Archimedes*, 2nd edn (Princeton)

Dillon, J. (1983; 1990) 'What happened to Plato's Garden?', *Hermathena* 133, 51–9; repr. in Dillon (1990) study 1

Dillon, J. M. (1990) *The Golden Chain*: Studies in the Development of Platonism and Christianity, CSS 333 (Aldershot)

Dillon, J. M. & Long, A. A., edd. (1988) *The Question of 'Eclecticism'. Studies in Later Greek Philosophy*, Hellenistic Culture and Society 3 (Berkeley/Los Angeles; repr. 1996)

Dionigi, I (1976) 'Lucr. 6, 1198–1203 e P. Oxy. 215 col. I 7–24: L'epicureismo e la venerazione degli dei', *SIFC* 48, 118–39

Dirlmeier, F. (1937) *Die Oikeiosis-Lehre Theophrasts*, Philologus, Suppl. 30, H. 1 (Leipzig)

Dobbs, B. J. T. (1985) 'Newton and Stoicism', in Epp (1985) 109–23

Donini, P. L. (1974–5) 'Fato e volontà umana in Crisippo', *AAT* 109, 187–230

Donini, P. L. (1995a) 'Pathos nello stoicismo romano', *Elenchos* 16, 193–216

Donini, P. L. (1995b) 'Struttura delle passioni e del vizio e loro cura in Crisippo', *Elenchos* 16, 305–29

Dorandi, T., ed. (1982a) Filodemo: *Il buon re secondo Omero*, La scuola di Epicuro 3 (Naples)

Dorandi, T. (1982b) 'Filodemo, Gli Stoici (*PHerc.* 155 e 339)', *CErc* 12, 91–133

Dorandi, T., ed. (1990a) 'Filodemo: gli orientamenti della ricerca attuale', in Haase, W., ed., *ANRW* II 36.4 (Berlin/New York) 2328–68

Dorandi, T. (1990b) 'Filodemo storico del pensiero antico', in Haase, W., ed., *ANRW* II 36.4 (Berlin/New York) 2407–23

Dorandi, T. (1990c) 'Gli arconti nei papiri ercolanesi', *ZPE* 84, 121–38

Dorandi, T. (1991a) 'Figure femminili della filosofia antica', in De Martino, F., ed., *Rose della Pieria* (Bari) 261–78

Dorandi, T., ed. (1991b) Filodemo: *Storia dei Filosofi [.]: Platone e l'Academia (PHerc. 1021 e 164)*, La Scuola di Epicuro 12 (Naples)

Dorandi, T. (1991c) *Ricerche sulla Cronologia dei Filosofi Ellenistici*, Beiträge zur Altertumskunde 19 (Stuttgart)

Dorandi, T. (1991d) 'Den Autoren über die Schulter geschaut: Arbeitsweise und Autographie bei den antiken Schriftstellern', *ZPE* 87, 11–33

Dorandi, T. (1992a) 'Considerazioni sull'*index locupletior* di Diogene Laerzio', *Prometheus* 18, 121–6

Dorandi, T. (1992b) 'Il quarto libro delle "Vite" di Diogene Laerzio', in Haase, W., ed., *ANRW* II 36.5 (Berlin/New York) 3761–92

Dorandi, T. (1993) 'Estratti dal III libro di Diogene Laerzio in un codice di Vienna (cod. phil. gr. 314)', *SCO* 43, 63–70

Dorandi, T. (1994a) Filodemo: *Storia dei filosofi: La Stoà da Zenone a Panezio (PHerc. 1018)*, PhA 60 (Leiden)

Dorandi, T. (1994b) 'Bryson d'Achaïe', in Goulet (1989–94) II, 142

Dorandi, T. (1994c) 'I frammenti di Anassarco di Abdera', *Atti e Memorie dell' Accademia Toscana di Scienze e Lettere La Colombaria* 69 N.S. 45, 11–59

Dorandi, T. (1994d) 'De Zénon d'Elée à Anaxarque', in Jerphagnon et al. (1994) 27–37

Dorandi, T. (1995a) 'Prolegomena per una edizione dei frammenti di Antigono di Caristo. III', *ZPE* 106, 61–90

Dorandi, T. (1995b) 'La "Villa dei Papiri" a Ercolano e la sua biblioteca', *CPh* 168–82

Döring, K., ed. (1972) *Die Megariker* – Kommentierte Sammlung der Testimonien (Amsterdam)

Döring, K. (1978) 'Antike Theorien über die staatspolitische Notwendigkeit der Götterfurcht', *A & A* 24, 43–56

Döring, K. (1987) *Historia Philosopha*, Grundzüge der antiken Philosophiegeschichtsschreibung (Freiburg i.Br./Würzburg)

Döring, K. (1988) *Der Sokratesschüler Aristipp und die Kyrenaiker*, AAWM, Geistes- und Sozialwiss. Klasse 1988.1 (Mainz)

Döring, K. (1989) 'Gab es eine Dialektische Schule ?', *Phronesis* 34, 293–310

Döring, K. (1992) 'Die sog. kleinen Sokratiker und ihre Schulen bei Sextus Empiricus', *Elenchos* 13, 81–118

Döring, K. & Ebert, T., edd. (1993) *Dialektiker und Stoiker. Zur Logik der Stoa und ihrer Vorläufer*, Philosophie der Antike 1 (Stuttgart)

Dorival, G. (1992) 'L'apport d'Origène pour la connaissance de la philosophie grecque', in Daly, R. J., ed. (1992) *Origeniana quinta*, BETL 105 (Leuven) 189–216

Dörrie, H. (1970) 'Chrysippos (14)', in *Pauly Wissowa, Realencyclopädie* Suppl. 12, cols. 148–55

Dörrie, H. & Baltes, M. (1993) *Der Platonismus in der Antike: Grundlagen – System – Entwicklung* III: Der Platonismus im 2. und 3. Jahrhundert nach Christus (Stuttgart/Bad Canstatt)

Dörrie, H. & Baltes, M. (1996) *Der Platonismus in der Antike* IV (Stuttgart/Bad Cannstatt)

Douglas, A. E. (1995) 'Form and content in the *Tusculan Disputations*', in Powell (1995a) 197–218

Dragona-Monachou, M. (1976) *The Stoic Arguments for the Existence and the Providence of the Gods* (Athens)

Dudley, D. R. (1937) *A History of Cynicism from Diogenes to the 6th Century A.D.* (London; repr. 1976)

Duhot, J.-J. (1989) *La conception stoïcienne de la causalité* (Paris)

Dumont, J.-P. (1969) 'Pyrrhon et le scepticisme ancien', in Parain, B., ed., *Histoire de la philosophie* (Paris) vol. 1: *Orient, Antiquité, Moyen Age*, 717–23

Dumont, J.-P. (1972) *Le Scepticisme et le Phénomène* — Essai sur la signification et les origines du pyrrhonisme (2nd edn Paris, 1985)

Dumont, J.-P. (1982) 'Diogène de Babylone et la preuve ontologique', *RPh* 107, 389–95

Dumont, J.-P. (1983) 'Diogène de Babylone et la déesse Raison. La Métis des stoïciens', *BAGB* 260–78

Dumont, J.-P., ed. (1988) *Les Présocratiques*, Bibliothèque de la Pléiade 345 (Paris)

Dunbabin, K. M. D. (1986) '*Sic erimus cuncti* . . . The Skeleton in Graeco-Roman Art', *JDAI* 101, 185–255

Düring, I., ed. (1932) Porphyrios *Kommentar zur Harmonielehre des Ptolemaios* (Göteborg)

Dyck, A. R. (1996) *A Commentary on Cicero, De Officiis* (Ann Arbor)

Ebbesen, S. (1981) *Commentators and Commentaries on Aristotle's Sophistici Elenchi, A Study of Post-Aristotelian Ancient and Medieval Writings on Fallacies*, 3 vols. (Leiden)

Ebert, T. (1987) 'The origin of the Stoic theory of signs in Sextus Empiricus', *OSAP* 5, 83–126

Ebert, T. (1991) *Dialektiker und frühe Stoiker bei Sextus Empiricus*, Hypomnemata 95 (Göttingen)

Edelstein, L. (1932) 'Die Geschichte der Sektion in der Antike', *Quellen und Studien zur Geschichte der Naturwissenschaften und der Medizin* 3, 50–106 (100–56); Engl. transl. in Temkin & Temkin (1967) 247–301

Edelstein, L. (1933) 'Empirie und Skepsis in der Lehre der griechischen Empirikerschule', *Quellen und Studien zur Geschichte der Naturwissenschaften und der Medizin* 3, 45–53 (253–61); Engl. transl. in Temkin & Temkin (1967) 195–203

Edelstein, L. (1952) 'The relation of ancient philosophy to medicine', *BHM* 26, 299–316; repr. in Temkin & Temkin (1967) 349–66

Edelstein, L. & Kidd, I. G., edd. (1972) Posidonius, I: *The Fragments*, Classical Texts and Commentaries 13 (Cambridge; 2nd ed. 1989)

Edlow, R. Blair, 1975, 'The Stoics on ambiguity', *JHPh* 13, 423–36

Effe, B. (1970) *Studien zur Kosmologie und Theologie der aristotelischen Schrift "Über die Philosophie"*, Zetemata 50 (Munich)

Egli, U. (1967) *Zur stoischen Dialektik* (Basle)

Egli, U. (1981) Das Dioklesfragment bei Diogenes Laertios, Sonderforschungsbereich 99 Linguistik 55 (Konstanz)

Einarson, B. & De Lacy, P. H., edd. (1967) Plutarch's *Moralia*, vol. xiv, LCL (London/Cambridge, Mass.)

Elster, J. (1983) *Sour Grapes*: studies in the subversion of rationality (Cambridge)

Elster, J. (1984) *Ulysses and the Sirens*: studies in rationality and irrationality (rev. edn, Cambridge; Paris)

Engberg-Pedersen, T. (1990) *The Stoic Theory of Oikeiosis*, moral development and social interaction in early Stoic philosophy, Studies in Hellenistic civilization 2 (Aarhus)

Englert, W. G. (1987) *Epicurus on the Swerve and Voluntary Action*, American Classical Studies 16 (Atlanta)

Epp, R. E., ed. (1985) *Spindel Conference 1984: Recovering the Stoics*. Southern Journal of Philosophy 23, Suppl. (Memphis)

Erler, M. (1991) ΈΠΙΤΗΔΕΥΕΙΝ ΑΣΑΦΕΙΑΝ. Zu Philodem Πρὸς τοὺς [ἑταίρους] (*PHerc.* 1005) col. xvi Angeli', *CErc* 21, 83–8

Erler, M. (1992a) 'Orthodoxie und Anpassung. Philodem, ein Panaitis des Kepos?', *MH* 49, 171–200

Erler, M. (1992b) 'Cicero und "unorthodoxer" Epikureismus', *Anregung* 38, 307–22

Erler, M. (1993) 'Philologia medicans. Wie die Epikureer die Texte ihres Meisters lasen', in Kullmann, W. & Althoff, J., edd., *Vermittlung und Tradierung von Wissen in der griechischen Kultur* (Tübingen) 281–303

Erler, M. (1994) '1. Epikur; 2. Die Schule Epikurs; 3. Lukrez', in Flashar (1994) 29–490

Erler, M. (1997a) 'Römische Philosophie', in Graf, F., ed., *Einleitung in die lateinische Philologie* (Stuttgart/Leipzig) 537–98

Erler, M. (1997b) 'Physics as therapy. Meditative elements in Lucretius' *De rerum natura*', in Algra *et al.* (1997) 79–92

Erler, M. & Ungern-Sternberg, J. v. (1987) 'Κακὸν γυναῖκες. Griechisches zu der Rede des Metellus Macedonius *De prole augenda*', *MH* 44, 254–6

Ernout, A. & Robin, L. (1925–8) Lucrèce: *De Rerum Natura. Commentaire exégétique et critique*, 3 vols. (Paris)

Erskine, A. (1990) *The Hellenistic Stoa, Political Thought and Action* (London)

Evans, C. F. (1970) 'The New Testament in the making', in Ackroyd & Evans (1970a) 232–84

Evans, J. D. G. (1974) 'The Old Stoa on the truth-value of oaths', *PCPhS* 20, 43–7

Everson, S., ed. (1990a) *Epistemology*, Companions to Ancient Thought 1 (Cambridge)

Everson, S. (1990b) 'Epicurus on the truth of the senses', in Everson (1990a) 161–83

Everson, S., ed. (1991a) *Psychology*, Companions to Ancient Thought 2 (Cambridge)

Everson, S. (1991b) 'The objective appearance of Pyrrhonism', in Everson (1991a) 121–47

Everson, S. (1994a) *Language*, Companions to Ancient Thought 3 (Cambridge)

Everson, S. (1994b) 'Epicurus on mind and language', in Everson (1994a) 74–108

Everson, S. (1994c) 'Aristotle's theory of the mind', in Barnes, J., ed., *The Cambridge Companion to Aristotle* (Cambridge)

Fahr, W. (1969) "ΘΕΟΥΣ ΝΟΜΙΖΕΙΝ", Zum Problem der Anfänge des Atheismus bei den Griechen, Spudasmata 26 (Hildesheim/New York)

Farrington, B. (1939) *Science and Politics in the Ancient World* (London, 2nd edn 1965)

Fehling, D. (1956/7; 1958) 'Varro und die grammatische Lehre von der Analogie und der Flexion', *Glotta* 35, 214–70; 36, 48–100

Fehling, D. (1958) (rev. Barwick 1957) *GGA* 212, 161–73

Fehling, D. (1965) 'Zwei Untersuchungen zur griechischen Sprachphilosophie', *RhM* 108, 212–29

Fehling, D. (1979) (rev. Siebenborn 1976) *Gnomon* 51, 488–90

Ferrari, G. A. (1981) 'L'immagine dell'equilibrio', in Giannantoni (1981a) I, 337–70

Ferraria, L. & Santese, G. (1981) 'Bibliografia sullo Scetticismo antico (1880–1978)', in Giannantoni (1981a) II, 753–850

Ferrary, J. L. (1988) *Philhellénisme et Impérialisme*, Aspects idéologiques de la conquête romaine du monde hellénistique, de la seconde guerre de Macédoine à la guerre contre Mithridate (Rome)

Festa, N. (1935) *I frammenti degli stoici antichi*, vol. 2 (Bari; repr. Hildesheim/New York 1971)

Festugière, A.-J. (1949) *La révélation d'Hermès Trismégiste*, II: Le Dieu cosmique (Paris, later repr.)

Festugière, A.-J. (1985) *Epicure et ses dieux*, 3rd edn (Paris, 1st edn, 1946)

Fillion-Lahille, J. (1984) *Le De ira de Sénèque et la philosophie stoïcienne des passions*, Etudes et commentaires 94 (Paris)

Finley, M. I. (1968) 'Diogenes the Cynic', in id., ed., *Aspects of Antiquity*: Discoveries and Controversies (London)

Finley, M. I. (1983) *Politics in the Ancient World* (Cambridge)

Flashar, H., ed. (1983) *Grundriß der Geschichte der Philosophie. Die Philosophie der Antike*, Band 3: Ältere Akademie-Aristoteles-Peripatos (Basle/Stuttgart)

Flashar, H., ed. (1994) *Grundriß der Geschichte der Philosophie. Die Philosophie der Antike*, Band 4: Die hellenistische Philosophie (Basle/Stuttgart)

Flashar, H. & Gigon, O., edd. (1986) *Aspects de la philosophie hellénistique*, Fondation Hardt 32 (Vandœuvres/Geneva)

Flintoff, E. (1980) 'Pyrrho and India', *Phronesis* 25, 88–108

Foraboschi, D. (1984) 'Filodemo, Sull'economia', in *Atti del XVII Congresso Internazionale di papirologia* (Naples) vol. 2, 537–42

Forschner, M. (1981) *Die Stoische Ethik*: über den Zusammenhang von Natur-, Sprach- u. Moralphilosophie im altstoischen System (Stuttgart; repr. Darmstadt 1995)

Forschner, M. (1982) 'Epikurs Theorie des Glücks', *ZPhF* 36, 179–88

Fortenbaugh, W. W., ed. (1983) *On Stoic and Peripatetic Ethics*. The Work of Arius Didymus, RUSCH 1 (New Brunswick/London)

Fortenbaugh, W. W., Huby, P. M. & Long A. A., edd. (1985) *Theophrastus of Eresus*: On his Life and Work, RUSCH 2 (New Brunswick/Oxford)

Fortenbaugh, W. W. & Sharples, R. W., edd. (1988) *Theophrastean Studies*: On Natural Science, Physics and Metaphysics, Ethics, Religion, and Rhetoric, RUSCH 3 (New Brunswick/Oxford)

Fortenbaugh, W. W. & Steinmetz, P., edd. (1989) *Cicero's Knowledge of the Peripatos*, RUSCH 4 (New Brunswick/London)

Fortenbaugh, W. W. & Gutas, D., edd. (1992a) *Theophrastus*: His Psychological, Doxographical and Scientific Writings, RUSCH 5 (New Brunswick/London)

Fortenbaugh, W. W., Huby, P. M., Sharples, R. W. & Gutas, D., edd. (1992b) *Theophrastus of Eresus*: Sources for his Life, Writings, Thought, and Influence, 2 vols., Philosophia Antiqua 54.1–2 (Leiden)

Fortenbaugh, W. W. & Mirhady, D. C., edd. (1994) *Peripatetic Rhetoric after Aristotle*, RUSCH 6 (New Brunswick/London)

Foucault, M. (1988) 'Technologies of the self', in Martin, L. H., Gutman, H. & Hutton, P. H., edd., *Technologies of the Self*: a Seminar with Michel Foucault (Amherst) 16–49

Fowler, D. P. (1984) 'Sceptics and Epicureans', *OSAP* 2, 237–67

Fowler, D. P. (1986) (rev. Asmis 1984) *JHS* 106, 227–31

Fowler, D. P. (1989) 'Lucretius and politics', in Griffin & Barnes (1989) 120–50

Fraenkel, E. (1925 (1968)) 'Xenophanesstudien', *Hermes* 60, 174–92, repr. in *Wege und Formen frühgriechischen Denkens* (Munich) 335–49

Fraisse, J.-C. (1974) *Philia*. La notion d'amitié dans la philosophie antique (Paris)

Franco Repellini, F. (1985) 'Ipparco e la tradizione astronomica', in Giannantoni & Vegetti (1985) 187–224

Fraser, P. M. (1969) 'The career of Erasistratus of Ceos', *RIL* 103, 518–37

Fraser, P. M. (1972) *Ptolemaic Alexandria*, 3 vols. (Oxford)

Frede, M. (1973) (rev. Stough 1969) *JPh* 70, 805–10

Frede, M. (1974a) *Die stoische Logik*, Abhandlungen der Akademie der Wissenschaften in Gottingen. Philol.-hist. Kl. Folge 3, Nr. 88 (Göttingen)

Frede, M. (1974b) 'Stoic vs. Aristotelian syllogistic', *AGPh* 56, 1–32

Frede, M. (1977) 'The origins of traditional grammar', in Butts, R. E. & Hintikka J., edd., *Historical and Philosophical Dimensions of Logic, Methodology and Philosophy of Science* (Dordrecht/Boston) 51–79

Frede, M. (1978) 'Principles of Stoic grammar', in Rist (1978b) 27–75; repr. in Frede (1987a) 301–37

Frede, M. (1979) 'Des Skeptikers Meinungen', *Neue Hefte für Philosophie, Aktualität der Antike* 15/16, 102–29; repr. as 'The skeptic's beliefs', in Frede (1987a) 179–200

Frede, M. (1980) 'The original notion of cause', in Schofield *et al.* (1980a) 217–49; repr. in Frede (1987a) 125–50

Frede, M. (1982) 'The method of the so-called methodical school of medicine', in Barnes et al. (1982a) 1–23; repr. in Frede (1987a) 261–78

Frede, M. (1983) 'Stoics and Skeptics on clear and distinct impressions', in Burnyeat (1983) 65–93; repr. in Frede (1987a) 151–76

Frede, M. (1984) 'The sceptic's two kinds of assent and the question of the possibility of knowledge', in Rorty *et al.* (1984) 255–78; repr. Frede (1987a) 201–22

Frede, M. (1986a) 'Philosophy and medicine in antiquity', in Donagan, A., Perovich, A. N. & Wedin, M. V., edd., *Human Nature and Natural Knowledge*, Essays Presented to Marjorie Grene (Dordrecht) 211–32; repr. in Frede (1987a) 225–42

Frede, M. (1986b) 'The Stoic doctrine of the affections of the soul', in Schofield & Striker (1986a) 93–110

Frede, M. (1987a) *Essays in Ancient Philosophy* (Oxford)

Frede, M. (1987b) 'The ancient empiricists', in Frede (1987a) 243–60

Frede, M. (1988) 'The empiricist attitude towards reason and theory', in Hankinson (1988c) 79–97

Frede, M. (1990) 'An empiricist view of knowledge: memorism', in Everson (1990a) 225–50

Frede, M. (1992) 'Plato's arguments and the dialogue form', *OSAP* suppl. vol., 201–19

Frede, M. (1994) 'The Stoic notion of a *lekton*', in Everson (1994a) 109–129

Frede, M. & Striker, G., edd. (1996) *Rationality in Greek Thought* (Oxford)

Frenkian, A. M. (1958) 'Der griechische Skeptizismus und die indische Philosophie', *Bibliotheca Classica Orientalis* 3, 212–49

Freytag, W. (1995) *Mathematische Grundbegriffe bei Sextus Empiricus*, Spudasmata 57 (Hildesheim)

Frischer, B. (1982) *The Sculpted Word*: Epicureanism and philosophical recruitment in ancient Greece (Berkeley)

Fritz, K. von (1926) *Quellenuntersuchungen zu Leben und Philosophie des Diogenes von Sinope*, Philologus. Supplementband 18, H. 2 (Leipzig)

Fritz, K. von (1963) 'Pyrrhon aus Elis Skeptiker', in *Pauly Wissowa, Realencyclopädie* 24.1, cols. 89–106

Fritz, K. von (1971 (1955)) *Grundprobleme der Geschichte der antiken Wissenschaft* (Berlin)

Fritz, K. von (1972) 'Zenon (4)', in *Pauly Wissowa, Realencyclopädie* 10.A, col. 122

Fuhrmann, M. (1960) *Das systematische Lehrbuch*. Ein Beitrag zur Geschichte der Wissenschaften in der Antike (Göttingen)

Furley, D. J. (1967) *Two Studies in the Greek Atomists*, 1. Indivisible Magnitudes. 2. Aristotle and Epicurus on Voluntary Action (Princeton)

Furley, D. J. (1971) 'Knowledge of atoms and void in Epicureanism', in Anton, J. P. & Kustas, G. L., edd., *Essays in Ancient Greek Philosophy* I (Albany) 607–19

Furley, D. J. (1978) 'Lucretius the Epicurean. On the history of man', in *Lucrèce*, Fondation Hardt 24 (Vandœuvres/Geneva) 1–37

Furley, D. J. (1985) 'Strato's theory of the void', in Wiesner (1985–7) I, 594–609

Furley, D. J. (1986) 'Nothing to us?', in Schofield & Striker (1986a) 75–91

Furley, D. J. (1988) (rev. Asmis 1984) *AGPh* 70, 108–11

Furley, D. J. (1989a (1966)) 'Lucretius and the Stoics', in Furley (1989c) 183–205

Furley, D. J. (1989b (1985)) 'Strato's theory of the void', in Furley (1989c) 149–60

Furley, D. J. (1989c) *Cosmic Problems*: Essays on Greek and Roman Philosophy of Nature (Cambridge)

Furley, D. J. & Wilkie, J. S. (1984) *Galen on Respiration and the Arteries* (Princeton)

Gallo, I., ed. (1980) *Frammenti biografici da papiri* II: La biografia dei filosofi (Rome)

Garbarino, G. (1973) *Roma e la filosofia greca dalle origini alla fine del II sec. a.C.*, Studi e testi 6 (Turin)

Garofalo, I., ed. (1988), *Erasistrati fragmenta*, Biblioteca di studi antichi 62 (Pisa)

Gercke, A., ed. (1885) *Chrysippea* (Leipzig)

Giannantoni, G. (1958) *I Cirenaici. Raccolta delle fonti antiche, traduzione e studio introduttivo* (Florence)

Giannantoni, G., ed. (1981a) *Lo scetticismo antico*, 2 vols., *Elenchos* 6.1–2 (Naples)

Giannantoni, G. (1981b) 'Pirrone, la scuola scettica e il sistema delle "successioni"', in Giannantoni (1981a) I, 11–34

Giannantoni, G. (1981c) 'Il ΚΥΡΙΕΥΩΝ ΛΟΓΟΣ di Diodoro Crono', *Elenchos* 2, 239–72

Giannantoni, G. (1984) 'Il piacere cinetico nell'etica epicurea', *Elenchos* 5, 25–44

Giannantoni, G., ed. (1986a) *Diogene Laerzio storico del pensiero antico*, *Elenchos* 7 (Naples)

Giannantoni, G. (1986b) 'Socrate e i Socratici in Diogene Laerzio', in Giannantoni (1986a) 183–216

Giannantoni, G., ed. (1990) *Socratis et Socraticorum reliquiae*, 4 vols., *Elenchos* 18 (Naples)

Giannantoni, G., ed. (1992) *Sesto Empirico e il pensiero antico*, *Elenchos* 23 (Naples)

Giannantoni, G. & Gigante, M., edd. (1996) *Epicureismo greco e romano*. Atti del congresso internazionale Naples 19–26 Maggio (Naples)

Giannantoni, G. & Vegetti, M., edd. (1985) *La scienza ellenistica* (Naples)

Giannattasio Andria, R. (1989) *I frammenti delle 'Successioni dei filosofi'*, Quaderni del Dipartimento di Scienze dell'Antichità, Università degli studi di Salerno 5 (Naples)

Gigante, M. (1960) 'Il panlogismo stoico e il testo di Diogene Laerzio', *PP* 15, 415–27

Gigante, M. (1975) '"Philosophia medicans" in Filodemo', *CErc* 5, 53–61

Gigante, M., ed. (1979) *Catalogo dei papiri Ercolanesi* (Naples)

Gigante, M. (1981) *Scetticismo e epicureismo*. Per l'avviamento di un discorso storiografico, *Elenchos* 4 (Naples)

Gigante, M. (1983a) *Ricerche filodemee*, 2nd edn (Naples)

Gigante, M. (1983b) Diogene Laerzio: *Vite dei filosofi*, BUL, 3rd edn (Rome/Bari)

Gigante, M. (1983c) 'Frammenti di Ippoboto. Contributo alla storia della storiografia filosofica', in Mastrocinque, A., ed., *Studi P. Treves* (Padua)

Gigante, M. (1986) 'Biografia e dossografia in Diogene Laerzio', in Giannantoni
(1986a) 7–102

Gigante, M. (1987a) *La bibliothèque de Philodème et l'Epicuréisme Romain*. Préface de P.
Grimal (Paris)

Gigante, M. (1988) 'Prefazione alla stampa della dissertazione di A. Schober sulla
prima parte dell'opera "De pietate" di Filodemo', *CErc* 18, 65–6

Gigante, M. (1992) *Cinismo e Epicurismo* (Naples)

Gigante, M. (1995) *Philodemus in Italy: The Books from Herculaneum* (Ann Arbor)
(originally published as *Filodemo in Italia* (Florence 1990))

Gigante, M. & Dorandi, T. (1980) 'Anassarco e Epicuro "Sul regno"', in Romano, F.,
ed. (1980) 479–97

Gigon, O. (1949) Epikur: *Von der Überwindung der Furcht* (Zürich)

Gill, C. (1983) 'Did Chrysippus understand Medea?', *Phronesis* 28, 136–49

Gill, C. (1988) 'Personhood and personality: the four-*personae* theory in Cicero *De
Officiis* I', *OSAP* 6, 169–99

Giusta, M. (1964–7) *I dossografi di etica*, 2 vols., Pubblicazioni della Facoltà di lettere e
filosofia, Università di Torino vol. 15, fasc. 3–4 (Turin)

Glibert-Thirry, A., ed. (1977) Pseudo-Andronicus de Rhodes: 'ΠΕΡΙ ΠΑΘΩΝ', Corpus
latinum commentariorum in Aristotelem graecorum, suppl. 2 (Leiden)

Glidden, D. K. (1975) 'Protagorean relativism and the Cyrenaics', in Rescher, N., ed.,
Studies in Epistemology (Oxford) 113–40

Glidden, D. K. (1980) 'Epicurus and the pleasure principle', in Depew, D. J., ed. (1980)
The Greeks and the Good Life (Indianapolis) 177–97

Glidden, D. K. (1983a) 'Skeptic semiotics', *Phronesis* 28, 213–55

Glidden, D. K. (1983b) 'Epicurean semantics', in AA. VV. (1983) 185–226

Glidden, D. K. (1985) 'Epicurean *prolēpsis*', *OSAP* 3, 175–217

Glucker, J. (1978) *Antiochus and the Late Academy*, Hypomnemata 56 (Göttingen)

Glucker, J. (1988) 'Πρὸς τὸν εἰπόντα – Sources and credibility of *De Stoicorum
repugnantiis* 8', *ICS* 13, 473–89

Glucker, J. (1991) 'Images of Plato in late antiquity', in Unguru, S., ed., *Physics,
Cosmology and Astronomy, 1300–1700*: Tension and Accommodation, Boston
Studies in the Philosophy of Science 126 (Dordrecht) 3–18

Goedeckemeyer, A. (1905) *Die Geschichte des Griechischen Skeptizismus* (Leipzig)

Goetz, G. (1894) 'Aelius (144)', in *Pauly Wissowa, Realencyclopädie* 1, cols. 532–3

Goldschmidt, V. (1972) 'ὑπάρχειν et ὑφεστάναι dans la philosophie stoïcienne', *REG*
85, 331–44

Goldschmidt, V. (1977) *La doctrine d'Epicure et le droit* (Paris)

Goldschmidt, V. (1979) *Le système stoïcien et l'idée de temps*, 4th edn (Paris)

Gomperz, T. (1899) 'Platonische Aufsätze, II', *SAWW*, Philos.-hist. Kl.144.7

Göransson, T. (1995) *Albinus, Alcinous, Arius Didymus*, Studia Graeca et Latina
Gothoburgensia 61 (Gothenburg)

Görgemanns, H. (1983) 'Oikeiôsis in Arius Didymus', in Fortenbaugh (1983)
165–89

Görler, W. (1977) 'Ἀσθενὴς συγκατάθεσις, zur stoischen Erkenntnis theorie', *WJA*
NF 3, 83–92

Görler, W. (1985) (rev. Decleva Caizzi 1981a) *AGPh* 67, 320–35

Görler, W. (1989) 'Cicero und die "Schule des Aristoteles", in Fortenbaugh & Steinmetz (1989) 246–63

Görler, W. & Gawlick, G. (1994) '6. Cicero', in Flashar (1994) 991–1168

Görler, W. (1994b) 'Älterer Pyrrhonismus, Jüngere Akademie, Antiochos aus Askalon', Flashar (1994) 717–989

Gosling, J. (1987) 'The Stoics and ἀκρασία', *Apeiron* 20, 179–202

Gosling, J. & Taylor, C. C. W. (1982) *The Greeks on Pleasure* (Oxford)

Gottschalk, H. B., ed. (1965) Strato of Lampsacus: *Some Texts, Edited with a Commentary*, Proceedings of the Leeds Philosophical and Literary Society, Lit. and Hist. Sect. (11.6) 95–182

Gottschalk, H. B. (1967) (rev. Steinmetz 1964) *Gnomon* 39, 17–26

Gottschalk, H. B. (1972) 'Notes on the wills of the peripatetic scholarchs', *Hermes* 100, 314–342

Gottschalk, H. B. (1980) *Heraclides of Pontus* (Oxford)

Gottschalk, H. B. (1987) 'Aristotelian philosophy in the Roman world from the time of Cicero to the end of the second century AD', in Haase, W., ed., *ANRW* II.36.2 (Berlin/New York) 1079–174

Gottschalk, H. B. (1992) 'An errant fragment of Theophrastus', *CQ* 42, 529–33

Goudriaan, K. (1988) 'Van eerste naar tweede sofistiek', in Slings, S. R. & Sluiter, I., edd., *Ophelos* (Amsterdam) 20–39

Goudriaan, K. (1989) '*Over Classicisme*. Dionysius van Halicarnassus en zijn program van welsprekendheid, cultuur en politiek', 2 vols. (dissertation Amsterdam)

Goulet, R. (1978) 'La classification stoïcienne des propositions simples', in Brunschwig (1978a) 171–98

Goulet, R. (1989) 'Aulu Gelle', in Goulet (1989–94) I, 675–87

Goulet, R., ed. (1989–94) *Dictionnaire des philosophes antiques*, vols. I–II (Paris)

Goulet, R. (1997) 'Les références chez Diogène Laërce: sources ou autorités?', in Fredouille, J.-C. *et al.*, edd., *Titres et articulations du textes dans les oeuvres antiques* (Paris) 149–66

Goulet-Cazé, M.-O. (1982) 'Un syllogisme stoïcien sur la loi dans la doxographie de Diogène le Cynique. A propos de Diogène Laërce VI 72', *RhM* 125, 214–40

Goulet-Cazé, M.-O. (1986) *L'ascèse cynique*: un commentaire de Diogène Laerce VI 70–1 (Paris)

Goulet-Cazé, M.-O. (1992) 'Le livre VI de Diogène Laërce: analyse de sa structure et réflexions méthodologiques', in Haase, W., ed., *ANRW* II 36.5 (Berlin/New York) 3880–4048

Graeser, A. (1972) 'Zirkel oder Deduktion? Zur Begründung der stoischen Ethik', *Kant-Studien* 63, 213–24

Graeser, A., ed. (1973) *Die Logischen Fragmente des Theophrast* (Berlin)

Graeser, A. (1975) *Zenon von Kition*, Positionen und Probleme (Berlin)

Graham, D. W., ed. (1995) Gregory Vlastos, *Studies in Greek Philosophy*, vol. II: Socrates, Plato, and their Tradition (Princeton 1995)

Gregorio, L. di, ed. (1975) *Scholia vetera in Hesiodi Theogoniam*, Scienze filologiche e letteratura 6 (Milan)

Griffin, M. T. (1976) *Seneca*, a Philosopher in Politics (Oxford)

Griffin, M. T. (1986) 'Philosophy, Cato and Roman suicide', *G & R* 33, 64–77, 192–202

Griffin, M. T. & Barnes, J., edd. (1989) *Philosophia togata*. Essays on Philosophy and Roman Society (Oxford)

Grilli, A. (1963) 'Zenone e Antigono II', *RFIC* 91, 287–301; repr. in *Stoicismo, Epicureismo, Letteratura* (Brescia 1992) 405–18

Groarke, L. (1990) *Greek Scepticism* – Anti-Realist Trends in Ancient Thought (Montreal)

Grube, G. A. (1965) *The Greek and Roman Critics* (London)

Gutas, D. (1975) *Greek Wisdom Literature in Arabic Translation*: A Study of the Graeco-Arabic Gnomologia, American Oriental Series 60 (New Haven)

Guthrie, W. K. C. (1962–1981) *A History of Greek Philosophy*, 6 vols. (Cambridge, later repr.)

Guyau, M. (1910) *La morale d'Epicure et ses rapports avec les doctrines contemporaines*, 5th edn (Paris)

Habicht, Chr. (1989) 'Athen und die Seleukiden', *Chiron* 19, 7–26; repr. in id. (1994) *Athen in hellenistischer Zeit*: gesammelte Aufsätze (Munich) 164–82

Hadot, I. (1969a) *Seneca und die griechisch-römische Tradition der Seelenleitung*, Quellen und Studien zur Geschichte der Philosophie 13 (Berlin)

Hadot, I. (1969b) 'Epicure et l'enseignement philosophique hellénistique et romain', *Actes du VIIIe Congrès de l'Association Guillaume Budé*, 347–53 (1968)

Hadot, I., ed. (1990) Simplicius: *Commentaire sur les Catégories*, fasc. I: Introduction, première partie (p. 1–9, 3 Kalbfleisch). Traduction de Ph. Hoffmann (avec la collaboration d' I. et P. Hadot), Commentaire et notes à la traduction par I. Hadot, PhA 50 (Leiden)

Hadot, I. (1991) 'The role of the commentaries on Aristotle in the teaching of philosophy according to the prefaces of the Neoplatonic commentaries on the *Categories*', in Blumenthal, H. & Robinson, H., edd., *Aristotle and the Later Tradition*, OSAP, suppl. vol. (Oxford) 175–89

Hadot, P. (1957) 'De lectis non lecta conponere (Marius Victorinus, *adversus Arrium* II 7): Raisonnement théologique et raisonnement juridique', in Aland, K. & Cross, F. C., edd., *Studia patristica* I, Texte und Untersuchungen 63 (Berlin) 209–20

Hadot, P. (1969) 'Zur Vorgeschichte des Begriffs "Existenz", ὑπάρχειν, bei den Stoikern', *AGP* 13 (1969) 115–27

Hadot, P. (1979) 'Les divisions des parties de la philosophie dans l'antiquité', *Museum Helveticum* 36, 201–23

Hadot, P. (1980) 'Sur divers sens du mot *pragma* dans la tradition philosophique grecque', in Aubenque (1980) 309–19

Hadot, P. (1987) 'Théologie, exégèse, révélation, écriture dans la philosophie grecque', in Tardieu (1987) 13–34

Hadot, P. (1991) *Philosophie als Lebensform*, Geistige Übungen in der Antike (Berlin)

Hagendahl, H. (1958) *Latin Fathers and the Classics: A Study on the Apologists, Jerome and Other Christian Writers* (Gothenburg)

Hagendahl, H. (1967) *Augustine and the Latin Classics*, Studia Graeca et Latina Gothoburgensia 20 (Gothenburg)

Hager, P. (1982) 'Chrysippus' theory of pneuma', *Prudentia* 14, 97–108

Hagius, H. (1979) 'The Stoic theory of the parts of speech' (dissertation Columbia)

Hahm, D. E. (1972) 'Chrysippus' solution to the Democritean dilemma of the cone', *Isis* 63, 205–20

Hahm, D. E. (1977) *The Origins of Stoic Cosmology* (Columbus Ohio)

Hahm, D. E. (1985) 'The Stoic theory of change', in Epp (1985) 39–56

Hahm, D. E. (1990) 'The ethical doxography of Arius Didymus', in Haase, W., ed., *ANRW* II 36.4 (Berlin/New York) 2935–3055

Hahm, D. E. (1991) 'Aristotle and the Stoics: a methodological crux', *AGPh* 73, 297–311

Hahm, D. E. (1992) 'Diogenes Laertius VII: On the Stoics', in Haase, W., ed., *ANRW* II 36.6 (Berlin/New York) 4076–182

Hahm, D. E. (1995) 'Polybius' applied political theory', in Laks & Schofield (1995) 7–47

Hammerstaedt, J. (1992) 'Der Schlussteil von Philodems drittem Buch über Rhetorik', *CErc* 22, 9–117

Hankinson, R. J. (1987a) 'Evidence, externality and antecedence: inquiries into later Greek causal concepts', *Phronesis* 32, 80–100

Hankinson, R. J. (1987b) 'Causes and empiricism: a problem in the interpretation of later Greek medical method', *Phronesis* 32, 329–48

Hankinson, R. J. (1988a) 'Galen explains the elephant', in Matthen & Linsky (1988b) 135–58

Hankinson, R. J. (1988b) 'Stoicism, science, and divination', in Hankinson (1988c) 123–60

Hankinson, R. J., ed. (1988c) *Method, Medicine and Metaphysics*, Studies in the Philosophy of Ancient Science, *Apeiron* suppl. vol. 21 (Edmonton)

Hankinson, R. J. (1989) 'Galen and the best of all possible worlds', *CQ* 39, 206–27

Hankinson, R. J. (1990) 'Saying the phenomena', *Phronesis* 35, 194–215 (critical notice of von Staden 1989)

Hankinson, R. J. (1991) *Galen on the Therapeutic Method*, Books I and II (Oxford)

Hankinson, R. J. (1992) 'Galen's philosophical eclecticism', in Haase, W., ed., *ANRW* II 36.5 (Berlin/New York) 3505–22

Hankinson, R. J. (1993) 'Actions and passions: affection, emotion, and moral self-management in Galen's philosophical psychology', in Brunschwig & Nussbaum (1993) 184–222

Hankinson, R. J. (1995) *The Sceptics* (London)

Hankinson, R. J. (1998) *Galen on Antecedent Causes* (Cambridge)

Harder, R. (1960) 'Quelle oder Tradition?', in *Les Sources de Plotin*, Fondation Hardt 5 (Vandœuvres/Genève) 325–32

Hardie, W. F. R. (1965) 'The final good in Aristotle's ethics', *Philosophy* 40, 277–95

Hardie, W. F. R. (1968) *Aristotle's Ethical Theory* (Oxford)

Harris, C. R. S. (1973) *The Heart and the Vascular System in Ancient Greek Medicine from Alcmaeon to Galen* (Oxford)

Hegel, G. (1983) *Lectures on the History of Philosophy*, transl. Haldane, E. S. & Simson, F. H. (repr. London/New Jersey 1983)

Heil, J. (1992) *The Nature of True Minds* (Cambridge)

Heine, O (1869) 'Kritische Beiträge zum siebenten Buche des Laertios Diogenes', *Jahrbücher für classische Philologie* 99, 611–28

Henrichs, A. (1974) 'Die Kritik der stoischen Theologie im *PHerc.* 1428', *CErc* 4, 5–32

Henrichs, A. (1975) 'Two doxographical notes: Democritus and Prodicus on religion', *HSPh* 79, 93–123

Herbermann, C.-P. (1991) 'Antike Etymologie', in Schmitter (1991) 353–76

Hershbell, J. P. (1992a) 'Plutarch and Stoicism', in Haase, W., ed., *ANRW* II 36.5 (Berlin/New York) 3336–52

Hershbell, J. P. (1992b) 'Plutarch and Epicureanism', in Haase, W., ed., *ANRW* II 36.5 (Berlin/New York) 3353–83

Hicks, R. D., ed. (1925) Diogenes Laertius: *Lives of Eminent Philosophers*, LCL, 2 vols. (London/Cambridge, Mass.; various repr.)

Hintikka, J. & Remes, U. (1974) *The Method of Analysis*, Its Geometrical Origin and its General Significance (Dordrecht/Boston)

Hirzel, R. (1877–83) *Untersuchungen zu Ciceros philosophischen Schriften*, 3 vols. in 4 (Leipzig; repr. Hildesheim 1964)

Hobein, H. (1929) 'Sphairos (3)', in *Pauly Wissowa, Realencyclopädie* 3.A, cols. 1683–93

Höistad, R. (1948) *Cynic Hero and Cynic King*: Studies in the Cynic Conception of Man (Uppsala)

Hoenigswald, H. M. & Wiener, L. F., edd. (1987) *Biological Metaphor and Cladistic Classification*: An Interdisciplinary Perspective (London)

Hossenfelder, M. (1985) *Die Philosophie der Antike 3: Stoa, Epikureismus und Skepsis* (Munich)

Hossenfelder, M. (1988) 'Epicurus-hedonist malgré lui', in Schofield & Striker (1986a) 245–63

Hossenfelder, M. (1991a) *Epikur* (Munich)

Hossenfelder, M. (1991b) 'Epikureer', in Schmitter (1991) 217–37

Hoven, R. (1971) *Stoïcisme et stoïciens face au problème de l'au-delà*, Bibliothèque de la Faculté de Philosophie et Lettres de l' Université de Liège, fasc. 197 (Paris)

Huby, P. M. (1967) 'The first discovery of the freewill problem', *Philosophy* 42, 353–62

Huby, P. M. (1978) 'Epicurus' attitude to Democritus', *Phronesis*, 23, 80–6

Huby, P. M. & Neal, G. C., edd. (1989) *The Criterion of Truth*, Essays written in honour of George Kerferd (Liverpool)

Hülser, K.-H. (1987–8) *Die Fragmente zur Dialektik der Stoiker*. 4 vols. (Stuttgart/Bad Cannstatt)

Hülser, K.-H. (1992) 'Sextus Empiricus und die Stoiker', *Elenchos* 13, 233–76

Humbert, J. (1967) *Socrate et les Petits Socratiques* (Paris)

Hunt, H. A. K. (1976) *A Physical Interpretation of the Universe*. The Doctrines of Zeno the Stoic (Melbourne)

Hussey, E. (1990) 'The beginnings of epistemology: from Homer to Philolaus', in Everson (1990a) 11–38

Ide, H. A. (1992) 'Chrysippus's response to Diodorus's Master Argument', *History and Philosophy of Logic* 13, 133–48

Ierodiakonou, K. (1990) 'Analysis in Stoic logic' (dissertation London)

Ierodiakonou, K. (1993a) 'The Stoic indemonstrables in the later tradition', in Döring & Ebert (1993) 187–200

Ierodiakonou, K. (1993b) 'The Stoic division of philosophy', *Phronesis* 38, 57–74

Ierodiakonou, K., ed. (1999) *Topics in Stoic Philosophy* (Oxford)

Immisch, O. (1928) 'Wirklichkeit und Literaturform', *RhM* 78, 113–23

Indelli, G., ed. (1978) Polistrato: *Sul disprezzo irrazionale delle opinioni popolari* (Naples)

Indelli, G. & Tsouna-McKirahan, V. (1995) Philodemus: *On Choices and Avoidances* (Naples)

Innes, D. (1989) 'Philodemus', in Kennedy (1989) 215–19

Inwood, B. (1981) 'The origin of Epicurus' concept of void', *CPh* 76, 273–85

Inwood, B. (1984) 'Hierocles. Theory and argument in the second century AD', *OSAP* 2, 151–84

Inwood, B. (1985) *Ethics and Human Action in Early Stoicism* (Oxford)

Inwood, B. (1986) (rev. Asmis 1984) *CPh* 81, 349–54

Inwood, B. (1991) 'Chrysippus on extension & the void', *RIPh* 3, 245–66

Inwood, B. (1993) 'Seneca and psychological dualism', in Brunschwig & Nussbaum (1993) 150–83

Inwood, B. (1995) (rev. Annas 1993a) *AncPhil* 15, 647–65

Inwood, B. & Mansfeld, J., edd. (1997) *Assent and Argument: Studies in Cicero's Academic Books*, Proceedings of the 7th Symposium Hellenisticum (Utrecht, August 21–25, 1995), PhA 76 (Leiden)

Ioppolo, A. M. (1980a) *Aristone di Chio e lo stoicismo antico*, *Elenchos* 1 (Naples)

Ioppolo, A. M. (1980b) 'Anassarco e il cinismo', in Romano (1980) 499–506

Ioppolo, A. M. (1985a) 'L'astrologia nello stoicismo antico', in Giannantoni & Vegetti (1985) 73–92

Ioppolo, A. M. (1985b) 'Lo stoicismo di Erillo', *Phronesis* 30, 58–78

Ioppolo, A. M. (1986) *Opinione e scienza*: il dibattito tra Stoici e Accademici nel III e nel II secolo a. C., *Elenchos* 12 (Naples)

Ioppolo, A. M. (1990) 'Presentation and assent: a physical and cognitive problem in early Stoicism', *CQ* 40, 433–49

Ioppolo, A. M. (1992) 'Sesto Empirico e l'Accademia scettica', *Elenchos* 13, 169–200

Irigoin, J. (1994) 'Les éditions de textes', in Montanari (1994), 39–82

Irwin, T. (1986) 'Stoic and Aristotelian conceptions of happiness', in Schofield & Striker (1986a) 205–44

Isnardi Parente, M. (1974a (1983)) *Opere di Epicuro*, Classici UTET (Turin; repr. 1983)

Isnardi Parente, M. (1974b) 'Carattere e struttura dell'Accademia antica', in Zeller, E. & Mondolfo, R. *La filosofia dei Greci nel suo sviluppo storico*, a cura di M. Isnardi Parente (Florence) vol. III.2, 861–77

Isnardi Parente, M. (1980) 'Stoici, Epicurei, e il "motus sine causa"', *RSF* 35, 23–31

Isnardi Parente, M. (1985–6) 'Filosofia postaristotelica o filosofia ellenistica: storia di un concetto storiografico', *Annali dell'Istituto Italiano per gli Studi Storici* 9, 165–93

Isnardi Parente, M. (1986) 'L'Accademia antica: interpretazioni recenti e problemi di metodo', *RFIC* 114, 350–78

Isnardi Parente, M. (1987) 'Una poetica di incerto autore in Filodemo', in *Filologia e forme letterarie*, Studi offerti a Francesco Della Corte (Urbino) v 81–98

Isnardi Parente, M. (1992) 'Sesto, Platone, l'Accademia antica e i Pitagorici', *Elenchos* 13, 120–68

Jackson, H. (1920) 'Aristotle's lecture-room and lectures', *JPh* 35, 191–200

Jacoby, F. (1902) *Apollodors Chronik*: eine Sammlung der Fragmente (Berlin; repr. New York 1973)

Janko, R. (1991) 'Philodemus' *On poems* and Aristotle's *On poets*', *CErc* 21, 5–64

Janko, R. (1995) 'Reconstructing Philodemus' *On poems*', in Obbink (1995) 69–96

Jerphagnon, L., Lagrée, J. & Delattre, D., edd. (1994) *Ainsi parlaient les Anciens*: In honorem Jean-Paul Dumont (Lille)

Jocelyn, H. D. (1976/7) 'The ruling class of the Roman republic and Greek philosophers', *BRL* 59, 323–66

Joly, R. (1956) *Le Thème Philosophique des Genres de Vie dans l'Antiquité Classique* (Brussels)

Jones, H. (1989) *The Epicurean Tradition* (London/New York)

Joosen, J. C. & Waszink, J. H. (1950) 'Allegorese', in *RAC* Bd. 1 (Stuttgart) 283–93

Joseph, J. E. (1990) 'The abandonment of *nomos* in Greek linguistic thought', *HL* 17, 1–13

Kahn, Ch. (1983) 'Arius as a doxographer', in Fortenbaugh (1983) 3–14

Kahn, Ch. (1985) 'Democritus and the origins of moral psychology', *AJPh* 106, 1–31

Kahn, Ch. (1988) 'Discovering the will: from Aristotle to Augustine', in Dillon & Long (1988) 234–59

Kassel, R. (1991) 'Der Peripatetiker Prytanis', in Nesselrath, H.-G., ed., *Kleine Schriften* (Berlin/New York) 351–2

Kattenbusch, F. (1930) 'Die Entstehung einer christlichen Theologie. Zur Geschichte der Ausdrücke θεολογία, θεολογεῖν, θεολόγος', *Zeitschrift für Theologie und Kirche* N. F. 11, 161–205

Kemp, A. (1991) 'The emergence of autonomous Greek grammar', in Schmitter (1991) 302–33

Kennedy, G. A., ed. (1989a) *The Cambridge History of Literary Criticism*, vol. 1: Classical Criticism (Cambridge)

Kennedy, G. A. (1989b) 'Hellenistic literary and philosophical scholarship', in Kennedy (1989a) 200–14

Kennedy, G. A. (1994a) 'Peripatetic rhetoric as it appears (and disappears) in Quintilian', in Fortenbaugh & Mirhady (1994) 174–82

Kennedy, G. A. (1994b) *A New History of Classical Rhetoric* (Princeton N.J.)

Kenney, E. J. (1972) 'The historical imagination of Lucretius', *G&R* 19, 12–24

Kenny, A. (1992) *Aristotle on the Perfect Life* (Oxford)

Kerferd, G. B. (1971) 'Epicurus' doctrine of the soul', *Phronesis* 16, 80–96

Kerferd, G. B. (1972) 'The search for personal identity in Stoic thought', *BRL* 55, 177–96

Kerferd, G. B. (1978a) 'What does the wise man know?', in Rist (1978b) 125–36

Kerferd, G. B. (1978b) 'The problem of synkatathesis and katalepsis', in Brunschwig (1978a) 251–72

Kerferd, G. B. (1978c) 'The origin of evil in Stoic thought', *BRL* 60, 482–94

Kidd, I. G. (1971) 'Stoic intermediates and the end for man', in Long (1971a) 150–72; repr. from *CQ* 5 (1955) 181–94

Kidd, I. G. (1971a) 'Posidonius on emotions', in Long (1971a) 200–15

Kidd, I. G. (1978a) 'Philosophy and science in Posidonius', *A & A* 24, 7–15

Kidd, I. G. (1978b) 'Posidonius and logic', in Brunschwig (1978a) 273–83

Kidd, I. G. (1978c) 'Moral actions and rules in Stoic ethics', in Rist (1978b) 247–58

Kidd, I. G. (1983) '*Euemptosia* – proneness to disease', in Fortenbaugh (1983) 107–13

Kidd, I. G. (1988) Posidonius, II: *The Commentary*, 2 vols., Cambridge Classical Texts and Commentaries 14 A & B (Cambridge) (vol. I see Edelstein & Kidd 1972)

Kidd, I. G. (1989) '*Orthos logos* as a criterion of truth in the Stoa', in Huby & Neal (1989) 137–50

Kienle, W. von (1961) *Die Berichte über die Sukzessionen der Philosophen in der hellenistischen und spätantiken Literatur* (Berlin)

Kindstrand, J. F. (1976) Bion of Borysthenes: *A Collection of the Fragments with Introduction and Commentary*, Acta Universitatis Upsaliensis, Studia Graeca Upsaliensia 11 (Uppsala)

Kindstrand, J. F. (1986) 'Diogenes Laertius and the *chreia* tradition', in Giannantoni (1986) 217–44

Kindstrand, J. F., ed. (1991) *Gnomica Basileensia*, Acta Universitatis Upsaliensis, Studia Byzantina Upsaliensia 2 (Uppsala/Stockholm)

Kirk, G. S. (1955) 'Some problems in Anaximander', *CQ* 5, 21–38; repr. in Furley, D. J. & Allen, R. E., edd. (1970) *Studies in Presocratic Philosophy*, vol. 1 (London) 323–49

Kleve, K. (1963) *Gnosis Theon*. Die Lehre von der natürlichen Gotteserkenntnis in der epikureischen Theologie. Ausgangspunkt der Studie: Cicero, *De natura deorum* 1, SO suppl. 19 (Oslo)

Kleve, K. (1979) 'The Epicurean *isonomia* and its sceptical refutation', *SO* 54, 27–35

Kleve, K. (1980) 'Id facit exiguum clinamen', *SO* 55, 27–31

Kleve, K. (1983) 'Scurra Atticus. The Epicurean view of Socrates', in AA. VV. (1983) 1 227–53

Kleve, K. (1989) 'Lucretius in Herculaneum', *CErc* 19, 5–27

Kneale, W. & Kneale, M. (1962) *The Development of Logic* (Oxford; repr. with corr. 1975, 1986)

Knoepfler, D. (1991) *La Vie de Ménédème d'Erétrie de Diogène Laërce*. Contribution à l'histoire et à la critique du texte des *Vies des philosophes*, Schweizerische Beiträge zur Altertumswissenschaft 21 (Basle)

Knoepfler, D. (1995) 'Les relations des cités Eubéennes avec Antigone Gonatas et la chronologie delphique au début de l'époque étolienne', *BCH* 119, 137–59

Knorr, W. R. (1976) *The Evolution of the Euclidean Elements*: a Study of the Theory of Incommensurable Magnitudes and its Significance for Early Greek Geometry (Dordrecht)

Knorr, W. R. (1982) 'Infinity and continuity. The interaction of mathematics and philosophy in antiquity', in Kretzmann, N., ed., *Infinity and Continuity in Ancient and Medieval Thought* (Ithaca/London) 112–45

Knorr, W. R. (1986) *The Ancient Tradition of Geometric Problems* (Boston/Basle/Stuttgart)

Knorr, W. R. (1989) *Textual Studies in Ancient and Medieval Geometry* (Boston/Basle/Berlin)

Koerner, K. (1987) 'On Schleicher and trees', in Hoenigswald & Wiener (1987) 109–13

Kollesch, J. (1966) 'Zur Geschichte des medizinischen Lehrbuchs in der Antike', in Blaser, R. & Buess, H., edd., *Aktuelle Probleme aus der Geschichte der Medizin* (Basle/New York)

Kollesch, J. (1973) *Untersuchungen zu den pseudogalenischen* Definitiones medicae, Schriften zur Geschichte und Kultur der Antike 7 (Berlin)

Kollesch, J. & Nickel, D., edd. (1993) *Galen und das hellenistische Erbe*, Sudhoffs Archiv Beih. 32 (Stuttgart)

Konstan, D. (1972) 'Epicurus on "up" & "down" (*Letter to Herodotus* § 60)', *Phronesis* 17, 269–78

Konstan, D. (1973) *Some Aspects of Epicurean Psychology* (Leiden)

Konstan, D. (1979) 'Problems in Epicurean physics', *Isis*, 70, 394–418; repr. in Anton & Preuss (1983) 431–64

Konstan, D. (1982) 'Ancient atomism and its heritage: minimal parts', *AncPhil* 2, 60–75

Krämer, H. J. (1971) *Platonismus und Hellenistische Philosophie* (Berlin/New York)

Krämer, H. J. (1980) 'Epikur und die hedonistische Tradition', *Gymnasium* 87, 294–326

Krämer, H. J. (1983) 'Die ältere Akademie', in Flashar (1983) 1–174

Kraus, H.-J. (1982) *Geschichte der historisch-kritischen Erforschung des Alten Testaments* (Neukirschen-Vluyn, 3rd edn)

Kraus, M. (1987) *Name und Sache*: Ein Problem im frühgriechischen Denken, Studien zur antiken Philosophie 14 (Amsterdam)

Kristeller, P. O. (1993) *Greek Philosophers of the Hellenistic Age* (New York), transl. of *Filosofi greci dell' età ellenistica* (Pisa 1991)

Kroll, W. (1940) 'Rhetorik', in Pauly Wissowa, *Realencyclopädie* Suppl. 7, cols. 1039–138

Krumme, L. (1941) *Die Kritik der stoischen Theologie in Ciceros Schrift De natura deorum* (Düsseldorf)

Küchler, M. (1979) *Frühjüdische Weisheitstraditionen*, Orbis biblicus et orientalis 26 (Göttingen)

Kümmel, W. G. (1970) *Das Neue Testament*, Geschichte der Erforschung seiner Probleme (Freiburg/Munich, orig. edn 1958)

Kudlien, F. (1964) 'Herophilos und der Beginn der medizinischen Skepsis', *Gesnerus* 21, 1–13, repr. in Flashar, H., ed. (1971) *Antike Medizin*, Wege der Forschung 221 (Darmstadt) 280–95

Kudlien, F. (1969) 'Antike Anatomie und menschlicher Leichnam', *Hermes* 97, 78–94

Kudlien, F. (1989) 'Hippokrates-Rezeption im Hellenismus', in Baader, G. & Winau, R., edd., *Die Hippokratischen Epidemien*. Theorie – Praxis – Tradition, Sudhoffs Archiv Beih. 27 (Stuttgart) 355–76

Lachenaud, G., ed. (1993) Plutarque: *Œuvres morales*, T. 12.2: *Opinions des philosophes* (Paris)

Laffranque, M. (1964) *Poseidonios d'Apamée*, Essai de mise au point (Paris)

Laks, A. (1976) 'Edition critique commentée de la "Vie d'Epicure" dans Diogène Laërce (x, 1–34)', in Bollack & Laks (1976) 1–118

Laks, A. (1983) *Diogène d'Apollonie: La dernière cosmologie présocratique*, Cahiers de Philologie 9 (Lille)

Laks, A. & Most, G. W., edd. (1993a) Théophraste: *Métaphysique* (Paris)

Laks, A. (1993b) 'Annicéris et les plaisirs psychiques. Quelques préalables doxographiques', in Brunschwig & Nussbaum (1993) 18–49

Laks, A. (1996) 'Du témoignage comme fragment', in Most (1996) 273–88

Laks, A. & Schofield, M., edd. (1995) *Justice and Generosity*: Studies in Hellenistic Social and Political Philosophy, Proceedings of the Sixth Symposium Hellenisticum (Cambridge)

Lamberton, R. & Keaney, J. J., edd. (1992) *Homer's Ancient Readers*: The Hermeneutics of Greek Epic's Earliest Exegetes (Princeton)

Lange, F. A. (1974) *Geschichte des Materialismus und Kritik seiner Bedeutung in der Gegenwart*, Bd. 1: Geschichte des Materialismus bis auf Kant (Iserlohn 1866, [11]1921; repr. Frankfurt a. M. 1974 with introd. by A. Schmidt)

Lapidge, M. (1973) 'Archai and stoicheia: a problem in Stoic cosmology', *Phronesis* 18, 240–78

Lapidge, M. (1978) 'Stoic cosmology', in Rist (1978) 161–86

Laursen, S. (1987) 'Epicurus, *On nature* Book xxv', *CErc* 17, 77–8

Laursen, S. (1988) 'Epicurus *On nature* xxv (Long-Sedley 20, B, C and J)', *CErc* 18, 7–18

Laursen, S. (1995) 'The early parts of Epicurus, *On nature*, 25th book', *CErc* 25, 5–109

Lausberg, M. (1970) *Untersuchungen zu Senecas Fragmenten*, Untersuchungen zur antiken Literatur und Geschichte 7 (Berlin)

Le Boulluec, see: Boulluec, Le

Lebedev, A. (1984) 'Φύσις ταλαντεύουσα. Neglected fragments of Democritus and Metrodorus of Chios', *Proceedings of the Ist International Congress on Democritus* (Xanthi) vol. 2, 13–8

Lee, Tae-Soo (1984) *Die Griechische Tradition der Aristotelischen Syllogistik in der Spätantike*: eine Untersuchung über die Kommentare zu den *Analytica Priora* von Alexander Aphrodisiensis, Ammonius und Philoponus, Hypomnemata 79 (Göttingen)

Leeman, A. D. & Pinkster, H. (1981) M. Tullius Cicero: *De Oratore* libri III. Kommentar, 1. Bd.: Buch I, 1–165 (Heidelberg)

Lefèvre, F. (1995) 'La chronologie du IIIe siècle à Delphes, d'après les actes amphictioniques (280–200)', 161–208

Lefkowitz, M. R. (1981) *The Lives of the Greek Poets* (London)

Lemke, D. (1973) *Die Theologie Epikurs*: Versuch einer Rekonstruktion, Zetemata 57 (Munich)

Lennox, J. (1985) 'Theophrastus on the limits of teleology', in Fortenbaugh *et al.* (1985) 143–63

Leo, F. (1901) *Die Griechisch-Römische Biographie nach ihrer literarischen Form* (Leipzig; repr. Darmstadt 1965)

Lesher, J. H. (1978) 'Xenophanes' scepticism', *Phronesis* 23, 1–21

Lévy, C. (1978) 'Scepticisme et dogmatisme dans l'Académie: "l'ésotéricisme de Arcésilas"', *REL* 56, 335–48

Lévy, C. (1990) 'Platon, Arcésilas, Carnéade — Réponse à J. Annas', *RMM* 95, 293–306

Lévy, C. (1992) *Cicero Academicus*, Recherches sur les *Académiques* et sur la philosophie cicéronienne (Rome)

Lévy, C. (1993) 'Le concept de *doxa* des Stoïciens à Philon d' Alexandrie: essai d' étude diachronique', in Brunschwig & Nussbaum (1993) 250–84

Lévy, C. (1996) 'Doxographie et philosophie chez Cicéron', in id., ed., *Le concept de nature à Rome. La physique* (Paris) 109–23

Lilla, S. R. C. (1970) *Clement of Alexandria*: A Study in Christian Platonism and Gnosticism (Oxford)

Lloyd, A. C. (1971) 'Grammar and metaphysics in the Stoa', in Long (1971a) 58–74

Lloyd, A. C. (1978a) 'Emotion and decision in Stoic psychology', in Rist (1978) pp. 233–46

Lloyd, A. C. (1978b) 'Definite propositions and the concept of reference', in Brunschwig (1978a) 285–96

Lloyd, G. E. R. (1964) 'Experiment in early Greek philosophy and medicine', *PCPhS* n.s. 10, 50–72; repr. in Lloyd (1991a) 70–99

Lloyd, G. E. R. (1975) 'A note on Erasistratus of Ceos', *JHS* 95, 172–5

Lloyd, G. E. R. (1983) *Science, Folklore, and Ideology*: Studies in the Life Sciences in Ancient Greece (Cambridge)

Lloyd, G. E. R. (1991a) *Methods and Problems in Greek Science* (Cambridge)

Lloyd, G. E. R. (1991b) 'Galen on Hellenistics and Hippocrateans: contemporary battles and past authorities', in Lloyd (1991a) 398–416; also pr. in Kollesch & Nickel (1993) 157–64 (125–43)

Lloyd-Jones, H. & Parsons, P., edd. (1981) *Supplementum Hellenisticum* (Berlin)

Long, A. A. (1967) 'Carneades and the Stoic telos', *Phronesis* 12, 59–90

Long, A. A. (1968) 'Aristotle's legacy to Stoic ethics', *BICS* 15, 72–85

Long, A. A. (1970–1) 'The logical basis of Stoic ethics', *PAS* 71, 85–104; repr. in Long (1996) 134–55

Long, A. A., ed. (1971a) *Problems in Stoicism* (London; repr. 1996)

Long, A. A. (1971b) 'Freedom and determinism in the Stoic theory of human action', in Long (1971a) 173–99

Long, A. A. (1971c) 'Language and thought in Stoicism', in Long (1971a) 75–113

Long, A. A. (1971d) '*Aisthesis, prolepsis* and linguistic theory in Epicurus', *BICS* 18, 114–33

Long, A. A. (1974) *Hellenistic Philosophy*: Stoics, Epicureans, Sceptics (London; 2nd edn, Berkeley 1986)

Long, A. A. (1975–6) 'Heraclitus and Stoicism', *Philosophia* 5/6, 133–56; repr. in Long (1996) 35–57

Long, A. A. (1976) 'The early Stoic concept of moral choice', in *Images of Man in Ancient and Medieval Thought*. Studies Presented to G. Verbeke (Leuven) 77–92

Long, A. A. (1977) 'Chance and natural law in Epicureanism', *Phronesis* 22, 63–88

Long, A. A. (1978a) 'Timon of Phlius: Pyrrhonist and satirist', *PCPhS* 204 (n.s. 24) 68–91

Long, A. A. (1978b) 'The Stoic distinction between truth and the true', in Brunschwig (1978a) 297–316

Long, A. A. (1978c) 'Dialectic and the Stoic sage', in Rist (1978b) 101–24; repr. in Long (1996) 85–106

Long, A. A. (1981) 'Aristotle and the history of Greek scepticism', in O'Meara (1981) 79–106

Long, A. A. (1982a) 'Astrology: arguments pro and contra', in Barnes *et al.* (1982a) 165–92

Long, A. A. (1982b) 'Soul and body in Stoicism', *Phronesis* 27 (1982) 34–57; repr. in Long (1996) 224–49

Long, A. A. (1983a) 'Arius Didymus and the exposition of Stoic ethics', in Fortenbaugh (1983) 41–66; repr. in Long (1996) 107–33

Long, A. A. (1983b) 'Greek ethics after MacIntyre and the Stoic community of reason', *AncPhil* 3, 184–99; repr. in Long (1996) 156–78

Long, A. A. (1985) 'The Stoics on world-conflagration and everlasting recurrence', in Epp (1985) 13–37

Long, A. A. (1986a) 'Diogenes Laertius, life of Arcesilaus', in Giannantoni (1986a) 429–49

Long, A. A. (1986b) 'Pleasure and social utility – the virtues of being Epicurean', in Flashar & Gigon (1986) 283–316

Long, A. A. (1988a) 'Stoic eudaimonism', in Cleary & Shartin (1988) 77–101; repr. in Long (1996) 179–201

Long, A. A. (1988b) 'Socrates in Hellenistic philosophy', *CQ* 38, 150–71; repr. in Long (1996) 1–34

Long, A. A. (1988c) 'Reply to Jonathan Barnes, "Epicurean Signs"', *OSAP*, suppl. vol., 135–44

Long, A. A. (1988d) (rev. Asmis 1984) *PhR* 97, 249–51

Long, A. A. (1990) 'Scepticism about Gods in Hellenistic philosophy', in Griffith, M. & Mastronarde, D. J., edd., *Cabinet of the Muses*, Essays on Classical and Comparative Literature in Honor of Thomas G. Rosenmeyer (Atlanta) 279–91

Long, A. A. (1991a) 'Representation and the self in Stoicism', in Everson (1991a) 102–20; repr. in Long (1996) 264–85

Long, A. A. (1991b) 'The harmonics of Stoic virtue', *OSAP*, suppl. vol. 1991, 97–116; repr. in Long (1996) 202–23

Long, A. A. (1992) 'Stoic readings of Homer', in Lamberton & Keaney (1992) 41–66; repr. in Long (1996) 58–84

Long, A. A. (1993a) 'Hellenistic ethics and philosophical power', in Green, P., ed., *Hellenistic History and Culture* (Berkeley/Los Angeles) 138–56

Long, A. A. (1993b) 'Hierocles on *oikeiosis* and self-perception', in Boudouris, K., ed., *Hellenistic Philosophy* (Athens) 93–102; repr. in Long (1996) 250–63

Long, A. A. (1996) *Stoic Studies* (Cambridge)

Long, A. A. (1997) 'Theophrastus and the Stoa', in van Ophuijsen & van Raalte (1997) 357–85

Long, A. A. & Sedley, D. N., edd. (1987) *The Hellenistic Philosophers*, 2 vols.: I. Translations of the principal sources with philosophical commentary; II. Greek and Latin texts with notes and bibliography (Cambridge, various reprints)

Longo Auricchio, F. (1978) 'La scuola di Epicuro', *CErc* 8, 21–37

Longo Auricchio, F., ed. (1988) Ermarco: *Frammenti*, La scuola di Epicuro 6 (Naples)

Longo Auricchio, F. & Tepedino Guerra, A. (1981) 'Aspetti e problemi della dissidenza epicurea', *CErc* 11, 25–40

Lonie, I. M. (1964) 'Erasistratus, the Erasistrateans, and Aristotle', *BHM* 38, 426–43

Luria, S. (1932) 'Die Infinitesimaltheorie der antiken Atomisten', *QGM*, B 2, 106–85

Luschnat, O. (1958) 'Das Problem des ethischen Fortschritts in der alten Stoa', *Philologus* 102, 178–214

Lynch, J. P. (1972) *Aristotle's School*. A History of a Greek Educational Institution (Berkeley)

Maccoll, N. (1869) *The Greek Sceptics from Pyrrho to Sextus* (London)

MacKendrick, P. (1989) *The Philosophical Books of Cicero* (London; repr. 1995)

MacKim, R. (1984) 'Democritus against Scepticism: all sense-impressions are true', in *Proceedings of the 1st International Congress on Democritus* (Xanthi) vol. I, 281–90

Maconi, H. (1988) 'Nova non philosophandi philosophia', *OSAP* 6, 231–53

Malaparte, C. (1929) 'Ritratto di Pirrone', *Pegaso* 1, 44–7

Manetti, D. (1986) 'Note di lettura dell'Anonimo Londinese – Prolegomena ad una nuova edizione', *ZPE* 63, 57–74

Manetti, D. (1994) 'Autografi e incompiuti: il caso dell'Anonimo Londinese P. Lit. Lond. 165', *ZPE* 100, 47–58

Manetti, G., ed. (1995) Knowledge through Signs: Ancient Semiotic Theories and Practices (Turnhout)

Mangoni, C., ed. (1993) *Filodemo, Il quinto libro della Poetica (PHerc. 1425 e 1538)*, La scuola di Epicuro 14 (Naples)

Mannebach, E., ed. (1961) *Aristippi et Cyrenaicorum Fragmenta* (Leiden/Cologne)

Manolidis, G. (1987) *Die Rolle der Physiologie in der Philosophie Epikurs*, Monographien zur philosophischen Forschung 241 (Frankfurt a.M.)

Mansfeld, J. (1978) 'Zeno of Citium', *Mnemosyne* 31, 134–78

Mansfeld, J. (1979) 'Providence and the destruction of the universe in early Stoic thought', in Vermaseren, M. J., ed., *Studies in Hellenistic Religions*, EPRO 78 (Leiden) 129–88; repr. in Mansfeld (1989b) study I

Mansfeld, J. (1981) 'Protagoras on epistemological obstacles and persons', in Kerferd, G. B., ed., *The Sophists and their Legacy*, Proceedings of the Fourth International Colloquium on Ancient Philosophy, Hermes Einzelschr. 44 (Wiesbaden) 38–53

Mansfeld, J. (1983a) 'Intuitionism and formalism: Zeno's definition of geometry in a fragment of L. Calvenus Taurus', *Phronesis* 28, 59–74

Mansfeld, J. (1983b) '*Techne*: a new fragment of Chrysippus', *GRBS* 24, 57–65; repr. in Mansfeld (1989b) study III

Mansfeld, J. (1986) 'Diogenes Laertius on Stoic philosophy', in Giannantoni (1986a) 295–382; repr. in Mansfeld (1990b) 343–428

Mansfeld, J. (1988a) 'Philosophy in the service of Scripture: Philo's exegetical strategies', in Dillon & Long (1988) 70–102; repr. in Mansfeld (1989b) study x

Mansfeld, J. (1988b) (rev. Goulet-Cazé 1986) *CR* 38, 162–3

Mansfeld, J. (1989a) 'Gibt es Spuren von Theophrasts *Phys. op.* bei Cicero?', in Fortenbaugh & Steinmetz (1989) 133–58; repr. in Mansfeld (1990b) 238–63

Mansfeld, J. (1989b) *Studies in Later Greek Philosophy and Gnosticism*, Variorum Collected Studies Series 292 (London)

Mansfeld, J. (1989c) 'Chrysippus and the *Placita*', *Phronesis* 34, 311–42

Mansfeld, J. (1990a) 'Doxography and dialectic: The *Sitz im Leben* of the "Placita"', in Haase, W., ed., *ANRW* II 36.4 (Berlin/New York) 3056–229

Mansfeld, J. (1990b) *Studies in the Historiography of Greek Philosophy* (Assen/Maastricht)

Mansfeld, J. (1992a) *Heresiography in Context*: Hippolytus' *Elenchos* as a Source for Greek Philosophy, PhA 56 (Leiden)

Mansfeld, J. (1992b) 'A Theophrastean excursus on God and nature and its aftermath in Hellenistic thought', *Phronesis* 37, 314–35

Mansfeld, J. (1992c) '*Physikai doxai* and *problemata physika* from Aristotle to Aëtius (and beyond)', in Fortenbaugh & Gutas (1992) 63–111

Mansfeld, J. (1992d) 'The idea of the will in Chrysippus, Posidonius, and Galen', in Cleary & Wians (1992) 107–45

Mansfeld, J. (1993) 'Aspects of Epicurean theology', *Mnemosyne* 46, 172–210

Mansfeld, J. (1994a) 'Epicurus peripateticus', in Alberti, A., ed., *Realtà e ragione, Studi di filosofia antica* (Florence) 29–47

Mansfeld, J. (1994b) *Prolegomena*: Questions to be Settled Before the Study of an Author, or a Text, PhA 61 (Leiden)

Mansfeld, J. (1995) 'Aenesidemus and the Academics' in L. Ayres (ed.), *The Passionate Intellect*: Festschrift I. G. Kidd, RUSCH vol. VII (New Brunswick/London) 235–47

Mansfeld, J. (1998) 'Doxographical studies, Quellenforschung, tabular presentation, and other varieties of comparativism', in Burkert *et al.* (1998) 16–40

Mansfeld, J. & Runia, D. T. (1997) *Aëtiana*: The Method and Intellectual Context of a Doxographer, vol. I: The Sources, PhA 73 (Leiden)

Manuwald, A. (1972) *Die Prolepsislehre Epikurs*, Habelts Dissertationsdrucke, Reihe klassische Philologie 15 (Bonn)

Manuwald, B. (1980) *Der Aufbau der Lukrezischen Kulturentstehungslehre*, AAWM, Geistes- und sozialwiss. Klasse 1980.3 (Mainz/Wiesbaden)

Marco, M. di, ed. (1989) Timone di Fliunte: *Silli*, Testi e commenti 10 (Rome)

Marelli, C. (1981) 'La medicina empirica ed il suo sistema epistemologico', in Giannantoni (1981a) II, 657–76

Maróth, M. (1989) *Ibn Sina und die Peripatetische 'Aussagenlogik'*, Islamic Philosophy and Theology 6 (Leiden)

Marrone, L. (1980) 'Il mentitore nel *PHerc*. 307 (Questioni logiche di Crisippo)', in *Proceed. XVIII Intern. Congr. Papyrology* (Athens) I, 271–6

Marrone, L. (1982) 'Nuove letture nel *PHerc*. 307 (Questioni Logiche di Crisippo)', *CErc* 12, 13–18

Marrone, L. (1984) 'Proposizione e predicato in Crisippo', *CErc* 14, 135–46

Marrone, L. (1992) 'L'ambiguità verbale nel *PHerc*. 307 (Questioni logiche di Crisippo)', in *Proceed. XIX Intern. Congr. Papyrology* (Cairo) I, 261–7

Marrone, L. (1993) 'Gnoseologia stoica nel *PHerc*. 307', in Franchi dell'Orto, L., ed., *Ercolano 1738–1988. 250 anni di ricerca archeologica* (Rome) 339–41

Marrone, L. (1997) 'Le questioni logichi di Crisippo (*PHerc* 307)', *Cronache Ercolanesi* 27, 83–100

Martini, E. (1899) 'Analecta laertiana', pt. 1, *Leipziger Studien zur classischen Philologie* 19, 73–177

Mates, B. (1961) *Stoic Logic*, University of California Publications in Philosophy 26 2nd edn (Berkeley; microfilm repr. Ann Arbor 1992)

Matthen, M., ed. (1987) *Aristotle Today* — Essays on Aristotle's Ideal of Science (Edmonton)

Matthen, M. (1988a) 'Empiricism and ontology in ancient medicine', in Hankinson (1988c) 98–121

Matthen, M. & Linsky, B., edd. (1988b) *Philosophy and Biology*. Canadian Journal of Philosophy, suppl. vol. 14 (Alberta)

Mattingly, H. B. (1986) 'Scipio Aemilianus' eastern embassy', *CQ* NS 36, 491–5

Mau, J. (1954a) *Zum Problem des Infinitesimalen bei den Antiken Atomisten* (Berlin)

Mau, J. (1954b) 'Raum und Bewegung: zu Epikurs Brief an Herodot § 60', *Hermes* 82, 13–24

Mau, J., ed. (1971) Plutarchi *Moralia*, vol. V 2.1: x oratorum vitae; Placita philosophorum, Bibl. teubneriana (Leipzig)

Mau, J. (1973) 'Was there a special Epicurean mathematics?', in Lee, E. N., Mourelatos, A. P. D. & Rorty, R. M., edd., *Exegesis and Argument*. Studies presented to Gregory Vlastos (Assen) 421–30

Mauro, T. De & Formigaro, L., edd. (1990) *Leibniz, Humboldt and the Origins of Comparativism* (Amsterdam/Philadelphia)

McDowell, J., ed. (1973) Plato: *Theaetetus* (Oxford)

McDowell, J. H. (1980) 'Physicalism and primitive denotation: Field on Tarski', in Platts, M., ed., *Reference, Truth and Reality* (London) 111–30; first published in *Erkenntnis* 13 (1978) 131–52

McDowell, J. (1985) 'Functionalism and anomalous monism', in LePore, E. &
McLaughlin, B. P., edd., *Actions and Events:* Perspectives on the Philosophy of
Donald Davidson (Oxford/New York) 387–98

Méhat, A. (1966) *Etudes sur les 'Stromates' de Clément d'Alexandrie*, Patristica
Sorbonensia 7 (Paris)

Meijering, R. (1987) 'Literary and Rhetorical Theories in Greek Scholia' (dissertation
Groningen)

Mejer, J. (1978) *Diogenes Laertius and his Hellenistic Background*, Hermes Einzelschr. 40
(Wiesbaden)

Mejer, J. (1992) 'Diogenes Laertius and the transmission of Greek philosophy', in
Haase, W., ed., *ANRW* II 36.5 (Berlin/New York) 3556–602

Merlan, Ph. (1960) *Studies in Epicurus and Aristotle* (Wiesbaden)

Mette, H. J. (1984) 'Zwei Akademiker heute: Krantor und Arkesilaos', *Lustrum* 26,
7–94

Mette, H. J. (1985) 'Weitere Akademiker heute: von Lakydes bis zu Kleitomachos',
Lustrum 27, 39–148

Mignucci, M. (1978) 'Sur la logique modale des stoiciens', in Brunschwig (1978a)
317–46

Mignucci, M. (1988) 'The Stoic notion of relatives', in Barnes & Mignucci (1988a)
129–221

Mignucci, M. (1993) 'The Stoic *themata*', in Döring & Ebert (1993) 217–38

Mills Patrick, M. (1899) *Sextus Empiricus and Greek Scepticism* (Cambridge)

Mills Patrick, M. (1929) *The Greek Sceptics* (New York)

Mitsis, P. (1988a) *Epicurus' Ethical Theory*, Cornell studies in classical philology 48
(Ithaca/London)

Mitsis, P. (1988b) 'Epicurus on death and the duration of life', in Cleary & Shartin
(1988) 303–22

Moles, J. L. (1995) 'The Cynics and politics', in Laks & Schofield (1995) 129–58

Momigliano, A. (1941) (rev. Farrington 1939) *JRS* 31, 149–57, repr. in id. (1960) *Secondo
contributo alla storia degli studi classici*, Storia e letteratura 77 (Rome) 375–88

Momigliano, A. (1993) *The Development of Greek Biography*, expanded edn (Cambridge,
Mass.)

Mondolfo, R. (1934) *L'infinito nel pensiero dei Greci* (Florence)

Monet, A. (1996) '[Philodème, *Sur les sensations*] PHerc. 19/698', *CErc.* 26, 27–127

Montanari, F., ed. (1994) *La philologie grecque à l'époque hellénistique et romaine*
(Vandœuvres/Geneva)

Montoneri, L., ed. (1984) *I Megarici*: studio storico-critico e traduzione delle
testimonianze antiche (Catania)

Moraux, P. (1973) *Der Aristotelismus bei den Griechen von Andronikos von Rhodos bis
Alexander von Aphrodisias* Bd. 1, Die Renaissance des Aristotelismus im I. Jh. v.
Chr., Peripatoi 5 (Berlin/New York)

Moraux, P. (1986) 'Diogène Laërce et le Peripatos', in Giannantoni (1986a) 245–94

Moretti, L. (1967) *Iscrizioni storiche ellenistiche*, I: Attica, Peloponneso, Beozia
(Florence)

Moretti, L. (1976) 'Epigrafica. 16. Un successore di Posidonio d' Apamea', *RFIC* 104,
191–4

Morrison, D. (1987) 'On Professor Vlastos' Xenophon', *AncPhil* 7, 9–22

Morrow, G., ed. (1970) Proclus: *A Commentary on the First Book of Euclid's Elements* (Princeton)

Most, G. W., ed. (1996) *Collecting Fragments — Fragmente Sammeln* (Göttingen)

Mudry, Ph. (1982) *La préface du* De Medicina *de Celse*, Bibliotheca Helvetica Romana 19 (Rome)

Mudry, Ph. (1990) 'Le scepticisme des médecins empiriques dans le traité *De la médecine* de Celse: modèles et modalités', in *Le scepticisme antique: perspectives historiques et systématiques*, Cahiers de la Revue de théologie et de philosophie 15, 85–96

Mueller, I. (1974) 'Greek mathematics and Greek logic', in Corcoran, J., ed., *Ancient Logic and its Modern Interpretation* (Dordrecht/Boston) 35–70

Mueller, I. (1979) 'The completeness of Stoic propositional logic', *Notre Dame Journal of Formal Logic* 20, 201–15

Mueller, I. (1981) *Philosophy of Mathematics and Deductive Structure in Euclid's Elements* (Cambridge, Mass.)

Mueller, I. (1982) 'Geometry and Scepticism', in Barnes *et al.* (1982a) 69–95

Mühll, P. Von der, ed. (1922) *Epicuri epistulae tres et ratae sententiae a Laertio Diogene servatae* (Leipzig, various repr.)

Muller, R., ed. (1985) Les Mégariques: *Fragments et témoignages* (Paris)

Muller, R. (1994) 'Bryson d'Héraclée', in Goulet (1989–94) II, 142–3

Müller, H.-E. (1943) *Die Prinzipien der stoischen Grammatik*, 2 vols. (Rostock)

Müller, R. (1972) *Die epikureische Gesellschaftstheorie* (Berlin)

Müller, R. (1991) *Die Epikureische Ethik*, Schriften zur Geschichte und Kultur der Antike 32 (Berlin)

Murray, O. (1965) 'Philodemus on the good king according to Homer', *JRS* 55, 161–82

Murray, O. (1967) 'Aristeas and Ptolemaic kingship', *JThS* 18, 337–71

Murray, O. (1970) 'Hecataeus of Abdera and Pharaonic kingship', *JEA* 56, 141–71

Mutschmann, H. (1911a) 'Inhaltsangabe und Kapitelüberschrift im antiken Buch', *Hermes* 46, 93–107

Mutschmann, H. (1911b) 'Die Stufen der Wahrscheinlichkeit bei Karneades', *RhM* 66, 190–8

Nachmanson, E. (1941) *Der griechische Buchtitel. Einige Beobachtungen*, Göteborgs Högskolas Årsskrift 47.19 (Gothenburg)

Nassen Poulos, P. (1981) 'Form and function of the pronouncement story in Diogenes' *Lives*', in Tannehill, R. C., ed., *Pronouncement Studies* (Missoula) 53–64

Natali, C. (1991) *Bios theoretikos*. La vita di Aristotele e l'organizzazione della sua scuola (Bologna)

Natorp, P. (1884) *Forschungen zur Geschichte des Erkenntnisproblems im Alterthum* (Berlin; repr. Hildesheim 1965)

Nautin, P. (1976) 'La fin des *Stromates* et les hypotyposes de Clément d'Alexandrie', *VChr* 30, 268–302

Nebel, G. (1935) 'Der Begriff des Kathēkon in der alten Stoa', *Hermes* 70, 439–60

Nestle, W. (1932) 'Metrodoros (14)', in *Pauly Wissowa, Realencyclopädie* 15, cols. 1475–6

Neugebauer, O. (1975) *A History of Ancient Mathematical Astronomy*, 3 vols. (Berlin)

Niehues Pröbsting, H. (1979) *Der Kynismus des Diogenes und der Begriff des Zynismus*, Humanistische Bibliothek, Reihe 1 Bd. 40 (Munich)

Nietzsche, F. (1870) 'Analecta Laertiana', *RhM* 25, 217–31

Nuchelmans, G. (1973) *Theories of the Proposition*: Ancient and Medieval Conceptions of the Bearers of Truth and Falsity (Amsterdam/London)

Nussbaum, M. C. (1986) 'Therapeutic arguments: Epicurus and Aristotle', in Schofield & Striker (1986a) 31–74

Nussbaum, M. C. (1987) 'The Stoics on the extirpation of the passions', *Apeiron* 20, 129–77

Nussbaum, M. C. (1994) *The Therapy of Desire: Theory and Practice in Hellenistic Ethics* (Princeton)

O'Brien, D. (1981) *Theories of Weight in the Ancient World*, vol. 1: Democritus, Weight and Size, PhA 37 (Leiden/Paris)

O'Meara, D. J., ed. (1981) *Studies in Aristotle*, Studies in Philosophy and the History of Philosophy 9 (Washington)

Obbink, D. (1984) 'P.Oxy. 215 and Epicurean religious θεωρία', in *Atti del XVII Congresso internazionale di papirologia*, vol. II (Naples) 607–19

Obbink, D. (1988) 'Hermarchus, *Against Empedocles*', *CQ* 38, 428–35

Obbink, D. (1989) 'The atheism of Epicurus', *GRBS* 30, 187–223

Obbink, D. (1992) 'Epicurus 11 (?): Sulla religiosità e il culto popolare', in *Corpus dei papiri filosofici greci e latini* I, 1** (Florence) 167–91

Obbink, D., ed. (1995) *Philodemus and Poetry. Poetic Theory and Practice in Lucretius, Philodemus and Horace* (Oxford)

Obbink, D., ed. (1996) Philodemus *On Piety*, Part 1: Critical Text with Commentary (Oxford)

Ogilvie, R. M. (1978) *The Library of Lactantius* (Oxford)

Opelt, I. (1962) 'Epitome', in *RAC* Bd. 5 (Stuttgart) 944–73

Ophuijsen, J. M. van (1994) 'Where have the topics gone?', in Fortenbaugh & Mirhady (1994) 131–73

Ophuijsen, J. van & Raalte, M. van, edd. (1998) *Theophrastus: Reappraising the Sources*, RUSCH 8 (New Brunswick)

Pachet, P. (1978) 'L'imperatif stoïcien', in Brunschwig (1978a) 361–74

Pasquali, G. (1910) 'Doxographica aus Basiliusscholien', *NAWG*, Philol.-hist. Klasse 194–228; repr. in La Penna, A. *et al.*, edd., *G. Pasquali: Scritti filologici*, vol. I (Florence 1986) 539–74

Pasquali, G., (1952) *Storia della tradizione e critica del testo* (Florence, 2nd edn 1971)

Pearson, A. C., ed. (1891) *The Fragments of Zeno and Cleanthes* (Cambridge)

Pembroke, S. (1971) 'Oikeiōsis', in Long (1971a) 114–49

Pépin, J. (1976) *Mythe et allégorie*. Les origines grecques et les contestations judéo-chrétiennes, 2nd edn (Paris)

Pesce, D. (1980) *Introduzione a Epicuro* (Rome/Bari)

Pfeiffer, R. (1968) *History of Classical Scholarship from the Beginnings to the End of the Hellenistic Age* (Oxford)

Philippson, R. (1910) 'Die Rechtsphilosophie der Epikureer', *AGPh* 23, 289–337, 433–46

Philippson, R. (1911) 'Zu Ciceros erstem Buch *De finibus*', *RhM* 66, 231–6

Philippson, R. (1932) 'Das "erste Naturgemäße"', *Philologus* 87, 445–66

Philippson, R. (1935) 'Neokles (4)', in *Pauly Wissowa, Realencyclopädie* 16.2, cols. 2414–16

Piantelli, M. (1978) 'Possibili elementi indiani nella formazione del pensiero di Pirrone d'Elide', *Filosofia* 29, 135–64

Pinborg, J. (1961) 'Interjektionen und Naturlaute. Petrus Heliae und ein Problem der antiken und mittelalterlichen Sprachphilosophie', *C&M* 22, 117–38

Pinborg, J. (1975) 'Classical Antiquity: Greece', in Sebeok, T. A., ed., *Current Trends in Linguistics* 13.1: Historiography of Linguistics (Den Haag/Paris) 69–126

Places, E. des, ed. (1987) Eusèbe de Césarée: *La préparation évangélique*, Livres XIV–XV, SC 338 (Paris)

Plasberg, O. (1922) *M. Tulli Ciceronis Academicorum Reliquiae cum Lucullo*, Bibl. Teubneriana (Leipzig)

Pohlenz, M. (1934) 'Cicero de officiis III', *NGG*, Philos.-hist.Kl. 1, 1–40; repr. in Pohlenz (1965) I, 243–91

Pohlenz, M. (1939) 'Die Begründung der abendländischen Sprachlehre durch die Stoa', *NGG*, Phil.-hist. Kl. III, 6, 151–98; repr. in Pohlenz (1965) I, 39–86

Pohlenz, M. (1940) *Grundfragen der stoischen Philosophie*, Abh. der Gesellschaft der Wissenschaften zu Göttingen, Phil.-hist. Kl. 3ᵉ Folge, 26; repr. in Tarán, L., ed. (1987) *Greek & Roman Philosophy* (New York/London) 1–122

Pohlenz, M. (1959) *Die Stoa*, 2nd edn (Göttingen)

Pohlenz, M. (1965) *Kleine Schriften*, 2 vols. (Hildesheim)

Pohlenz, M. (1967) *La Stoa* [trad. it.] (Florence)

Pope, M. (1986) 'Epicureanism and the atomic swerve', *SO* 61, 77–97

Porter, J. I. (1992) 'Hermeneutic lines and circles: Aristarchus and Crates on the exegesis of Homer', in Lamberton & Keaney (1992) 67–114

Porter, J. I. (1994) 'Stoic morals and poetics in Philodemus', *CErc* 24, 63–88

Porter, J. I. (1995) 'Οἱ κριτικοί: a reassessment', in Abbenes, J. G. J., Slings, S. R. & Sluiter, I., edd. (1995) *Greek Literary Theory after Aristotle*: a Collections of Papers in Honour of D. M. Schenkeveld (Amsterdam) 83–109

Powell, J. G. F., ed. (1995a) *Cicero the Philosopher*, Twelve Papers (Oxford)

Powell, J. G. F. (1995b) 'Introduction: Cicero's philosophical works and their background', in Powell (1995a) 1–35

Pra, M. dal (1950) *Lo Scetticismo Greco* (Milano; repr. in 2 vols. Rome/Bari 1975²)

Prantl, C. von (1855) *Geschichte der Logik im Abendlande*, Bd. 1 (Leipzig; repr. Graz 1955)

Prior, A. N. (1955) 'Diodoran modalities', *PhilosQ* 5, 205–13

Puglia, E. (1980) 'Nuove letture nei *PHerc.* 1012 e 1786 (Demetrii Laconis opera incerta)', *CErc* 10, 25–53

Puglia, E., ed. (1988) Demetrio Lacone: *Aporie testuali e esegetiche in Epicuro* (*PHerc.* 1012), La Scuola di Epicuro 8 (Naples)

Puliga, D. (1983) 'ΧΡΟΝΟΣ e ΘΑΝΑΤΟΣ in Epicuro', *Elenchos* 4, 235–60

Purinton, J. S. (1993) 'Epicurus on the telos', *Phronesis* 38, 281–320

Purinton, J. S. (1994) 'Magnifying Epicurean minima', *AncPhil* 14, 115–46

Raalte, M. van (1988) 'The idea of the cosmos as an organic whole in Theophrastus' *Metaphysics*', in Fortenbaugh & Sharples (1988) 189–215

Rabbow, P. (1954) *Seelenführung*, Methodik der Exerzitien in der Antike (Munich)

Rabe, H. (1931) *Prolegomenon Sylloge*, Bibl. Teubneriana, Rhetores graeci, vol. XIV (Leipzig)

Raphael, M. (1931) 'Die pyrrhoneische Skepsis', *Philosophische Hefte* 3, 47–70

Raubitschek, A. E. (1991 (1949)) 'Phaidros and his Roman pupils', in Obbink, D. & Vander Waerdt, P. A., edd. (1991) A. E. Raubitschek: *The School of Hellas*: Essays on Greek History, Archaeology and Literature (New York/Oxford) 337–44, orig. ed. *Hesperia* 18 (1949) 96–103

Rawson, E. (1969) *The Spartan Tradition in European Thought* (Oxford; repr. 1991)

Rawson, E. (1975) *Cicero: A Portrait* (London)

Rawson, E. (1985) *Intellectual Life in the Late Roman Republic* (London)

Reale, G. (1981) 'Ipotesi per una rilettura della filosofia di Pirrone di Elide', in Giannantoni (1981a) I, 243–336

Reesor, M. E. (1989) *The Nature of Man in Early Stoic Philosophy* (London)

Regenbogen, O. (1940) 'Theophrastos', in *Pauly Wissowa, Realencyclopädie* Suppl. 7, cols. 1354–562

Reid, J. S. (1885) M. Tulli Ciceronis *Academica* (London; repr. Hildesheim 1966)

Repici, L. (1977) *La Logica di Teofrasto*: studio critico e raccolta dei frammenti e delle testimonianze (Bologna)

Repici, L. (1990) 'L' epiglottide nell' antichità tra medicina e filosofia', *HPLS* 12, 67–104

Reynolds, L. D. & Wilson, N. G. (1978) *Scribes & Scholars*: A Guide to the Transmission of Greek & Latin Literature, 2nd edn (Oxford)

Richard, M. (1964) 'Florilèges grecs', in *Dictionnaire de spiritualité ascétique et mystique, doctrine et histoire* 5, 475–512 (Paris)

Richardson, N. J. (1994) 'Aristotle and Hellenistic scholarship', in Montanari (1994) 7–28

Ridings, D. (1995) *The Attic Moses*: The Dependency Theme in Some Early Christian Writers (Gothenburg)

Rieth, O. (1933) *Grundbegriffe der stoischen Ethik*: Eine traditionsgeschichtliche Untersuchung, Problemata 9 (Berlin)

Rieth, O. (1934) 'Über das Telos der Stoiker', *Hermes* 69, 13–45

Rijk, L. M. de (1966) 'Some notes on the Medieval tract *De insolubilibus*, with the edition of a tract dating from the end of the twelfth century', *Vivarium* 4, 83–115

Rist, J. M. (1969a) *Stoic Philosophy* (Cambridge; later repr.)

Rist, J. M. (1969b) 'Categories and their uses', in Rist (1969a) 152–72; repr. in Long (1971a) 38–57

Rist, J. M. (1972) *Epicurus: An introduction* (Cambridge)

Rist, J. M. (1974) 'Pleasure: 360–300 BC', *Phoenix* 28, 167–79

Rist, J. M. (1977) 'Zeno and Stoic consistency', *Phronesis* 22, 161–74; repr. in Anton & Preuss (1983) 465–77

Rist, J. M. (1978a) 'Zeno and the origins of Stoic logic', in Brunschwig (1978a) 387–400

Rist, J. M., ed. (1978b) *The Stoics* (Berkeley/Los Angeles/London)

Rist, J. M. (1978c) ' The Stoic concept of detachment' in Rist (1978b) 259–73

Rist, J. M. (1980) 'Epicurus on friendship', *CPh* 75, 121–9

Riverso, E. (1960) 'Il paradosso del mentitore', *RScF* 12, 296–325

Robin, L. (1944) *Pyrrhon et le Scepticisme Grec* (Paris)

Robins, R. H. (1979) *A Short History of Linguistics*, 2nd edn (London)

Robinson, R. (1969) *Essays in Greek Philosophy* (Oxford)

Rohde, E. (1881) 'Ueber Leukipp und Demokrit', *Verhandlungen der 34. Philologenvers. zu Trier 1880* (Leipzig) 64–90; repr. in *Kleine Schriften* (Tübingen/Leipzig 1901) vol. 1, 205–45

Romano, F., ed. (1980) *Democrito e l'atomismo antico* (Catania)

Romeo, C. (1979) 'Demetrio Lacone sulla grandezza del sole (*PHerc.* 1013)', *CErc* 9, 11–35

Romeo, C., ed. (1988) Demetrio Lacone: *La poesia (PHerc. 188 e 1014)*, La scuola di Epicuro 9 (Naples)

Rorty, R., Schneewind, J. B. & Skinner, Q., edd. (1984) *Philosophy in History*, Essays on the Historiography of Philosophy (Cambridge)

Roselli, A. (1990) 'Appunti per una storia dell'uso apologetico della filologia: la nuova edizione di Demetrio Lacone (*PHerc.* 1012)', *SCO* 40, 117–38

Rosenbaum, S. E. (1986) 'How to be dead and not care: a defense of Epicurus', *APhQ* 23, 217–25

Rosenbaum, S. E. (1990) 'Epicurus on pleasure and the complete life', in Cooper, J., ed. *The Monist* 73, 21–41

Rubin Pinault, J. (1992) *Hippocratic Lives and Legends*, Studies in Ancient Medicine 4 (Leiden)

Ruland, H.-J. (1976) *Die arabische Fassung zweier Schriften des Alexander von Aphrodisias: Über die Vorsehung und Über das liberum arbitrium* (Saarbrücken)

Runia, D. T. (1981) 'Philo's *De aeternitate mundi*: the problem of its interpretation', *VChr* 35, 105–51

Runia, D. T. (1989) 'Xenophanes on the moon: a *doxographicum* in Aëtius', *Phronesis* 34, 245–69

Runia, D. T. (1990) *Exegesis and Philosophy*: Studies in Philo of Alexandria, Variorum CSS 332 (Aldershot)

Runia, D. T. (1992) 'The language of excellence in Plato's *Timaeus* and later Platonism', in Gersh, S. & Kannengiesser, C., edd., *Platonism in Late Antiquity* (Notre Dame) 11–37

Runia, D. T. (1993) *Philo in Early Christian Literature*: A Survey, Compendia Rerum Iudaicarum ad Novum Testamentum III.3 (Assen/Minneapolis)

Runia, D. T. (1996a) 'Additional fragments of Arius Didymus on physics', in Algra *et al.* (1996) 363–81

Runia, D. T. (1996b) 'Atheists in Aëtius. Text, translation and comments on *De placitis* 1.7.1–10', *Mnemosyne* IV.59, 542–76

Russo, A. (1978) *Scettici antichi*, Classici della filosofia 22 (Turin)

Rüstow, A. (1910) *Der Lügner*: Theorie/Geschichte und Auflösung (Leipzig)

Ryffel, H. (1949) *Der Wandel der Staatsverfassungen* (Bern)

Saffrey, H. D. & Westerink, L. G., edd. (1968) Proclus: *Théologie Platonicienne*, t. 1, Coll. Budé (Paris)

Salvadori Baldascino, L. (1990) 'Masilaos oppure Mnasilas?', *CErc* 20, 65–6

Sambursky, S. (1959) *Physics of the Stoics* (London)

Sandbach, F. H. (1930) '*Ennoia* and *prolepsis*', *CQ* 24, 45–51

Sandbach, F. H., ed. (1969) Plutarch's *Moralia*, vol. 15: Fragments, LCL (Cambridge, Mass./London)

Sandbach, F. H. (1971) '*Phantasia kataleptike*', in Long (1971a) 9–21

Sandbach, F. H. (1985) *Aristotle and the Stoics*, PCPhS suppl. vol. 10 (Cambridge)

Sandbach, F. H. (1989 (1975)) *The Stoics*, 2nd edn (Bristol (London))

Saunders, T. J. (1984) 'Free will and atomic swerve in Lucretius', *SO* 59, 37–59

Sbordone, F. (1968) 'Primi lineamenti d'un ritratto di Fedro epicureo', *P & I* 10, 21–30

Scarborough, J. (1985) 'Erasistratus, student of Theophrastus?', *BHM* 59, 515–17

Schäfer, K. Th. (1959) 'Eisagoge', *RAC* Bd. 4 (Stuttgart) 862–904

Schäublin, C. (1977) 'Homerum ex Homero', *MH* 34, 221–7

Schäublin, C. (1990) 'Philosophie und Rhetorik in der Auseinandersetzung um die Religion. Zu Cicero, De natura deorum I', *MH* 47, 87–101

Schäublin, C. (1993) 'Kritisches und Exegetisches zu Ciceros "Lucullus" II', *MH* 50, 158–69

Schenkeveld, D. M. (1964) 'Studies in Demetrius "On Style"' (dissertation Amsterdam)

Schenkeveld, D. M. (1968) 'Οἱ κριτικοί in Philodemus', *Mnemosyne* 21, 176–214

Schenkeveld, D. M. (1970) 'Aristarchus and ΟΜΗΡΟΣ ΦΙΛΟΤΕΧΝΟΣ. Some fundamental ideas of Aristarchus on Homer as a poet', *Mnemosyne* 23, 162–78

Schenkeveld, D. M. (1983) 'Linguistic theories in the rhetorical works of Dionysius of Halicarnassus', *Glotta* 61, 67–94

Schenkeveld, D. M. (1984) 'Studies in the history of ancient linguistics II: Stoic and Peripatetic kinds of speech act and the distinction of grammatical moods', *Mnemosyne* 37, 291–353

Schenkeveld, D. M. (1990a) 'Studies in the history of ancient linguistics III: The Stoic ΤΕΧΝΗ ΠΕΡΙ ΦΩΝΗΣ', *Mnemosyne* 43, 86–108

Schenkeveld, D. M. (1990b) 'Studies in the history of ancient linguistics IV: Developments in the study of ancient linguistics', *Mnemosyne* 43, 289–306

Schenkeveld, D. M. (1991) 'Figures and tropes. A border-case between grammar and rhetoric', in Ueding (1991) 149–60

Schenkeveld, D. M. (1993) 'Pap. Hamb. 128. A Hellenistic ars poetica', *ZPE* 97, 67–80

Schenkeveld, D. M. (1994) 'Scholarship and grammar', in Montanari (1994) 263–301

Schenkeveld, D. M. (1995) 'The linguistic contents of Dionysius' Παραγγέλματα', in Law, V. & Sluiter, I., edd., *Dionysius Thrax and the Technē Grammatikē* (Müster) 41–52

Schian, R. (1973) *Untersuchungen über das 'argumentum e consensu omnium'*, Spudasmata 28 (Hildesheim)

Schiesaro, A. (1990) *Simulacrum et Imago*: gli argomenti analogici nel *De rerum natura* (Pisa)

Schmid, W. (1936) *Epikurs Kritik der platonischen Elementenlehre*, Klassisch-philologische Studien 9 (Leipzig)

Schmid, W. (1939) *Ethica Epicurea, Pap. Herc. 1251*, Studia Herculanensia 1 (Leipzig)

Schmid, W. (1951) 'Götter und Menschen in der Theologie Epikurs', *RhM* 94, 97–156

Schmid, W. (1957) '*Contritio* und *ultima linea rerum* in neuen epikureischen Texten', *RhM* 100, 301–27

Schmid, W. (1962) 'Epikur', in *RAC* Bd. 5 (Stuttgart) 681–819; repr. in Erbse, H. & Küppers, J., edd. (1984) W. Schmid: *Ausgewählte philologische Schriften* (Berlin/New York) 151–266

Schmid, W. (1978) 'Lucretius ethicus', in Gigon, O., ed. *Lucrèce*, Fondation Hardt 24 (Vandœuvres/Geneva) 123–57

Schmidt, J. (1975) 'Lukrez und die Stoiker, Quellenuntersuchungen zu *De rerum natura*' (dissertation Marburg)

Schmidt, J. (1990) *Lukrez, der Kepos und die Stoiker*, Untersuchungen zur Schule Epikurs und zu den Quellen von *De rerum natura* (Frankfurt am Main)

Schmidt, P. L. (1978) 'Cicero's place in Roman philosophy: a study of his prefaces', *CJ* 74, 115–27

Schmidt, R. T. (1967 (1839)) *Stoicorum Grammatica* (Halle, repr. Amsterdam 1967), transl. by Hülser, K. (1979) 'Die Grammatik der Stoiker', with an introduction by U. Egli, Schriften zur Linguistik 12 (Braunschweig/Wiesbaden)

Schmitter, P., ed. (1991) *Sprachtheorien der Abendländischen Antike*, Geschichte der Sprachtheorie 2 (Tübingen)

Schober, A., ed. (1988) 'Philodemi *De pietate* pars prior', *CErc* 18, 67–125

Schofield, M. (1980b) 'Preconception, argument and god', in Schofield *et al.* (1980a) 283–308

Schofield, M. (1983) 'The syllogisms of Zeno of Citium', *Phronesis* 28, 31–58

Schofield, M. (1984) 'Ariston of Chios and the unity of virtue', *AncPhil* 4, 83–96

Schofield, M. (1986b) 'Cicero for and against divination', *JRS* 76, 47–65

Schofield, M. (1988) 'The retrenchable present', in Barnes & Mignucci (1988a) 329–74

Schofield, M. (1991) *The Stoic Idea of the City* (Cambridge)

Schofield, M. (1995) 'Two Stoic approaches to justice', in Laks & Schofield (1995) 191–212

Schofield, M., Burnyeat, M. F. & Barnes, J., edd. (1980a) *Doubt and Dogmatism*. Studies in Hellenistic Epistemology (Oxford)

Schofield, M. & Nussbaum, M. C., edd. (1982) *Language and Logos*: Studies in Ancient Greek Philosophy Presented to G. E. L. Owen (Cambridge)

Schofield, M. & Striker, G., edd. (1986a) *The Norms of Nature*, Studies in Hellenistic Ethics (Cambridge/Paris)

Schubert, A. (1994) *Untersuchungen zur stoischen Bedeutungslehre* (Göttingen)

Schwartz, E. (1905) 'Diogenes (40) Laertios', in *Pauly Wissowa, Realencyclopädie* 5, cols. 738–63

Searle, J. R. (1992) *The Rediscovery of the Mind* (Boston)

Sedley, D. N. (1973) 'Epicurus, *On Nature* book xxviii', *CErc* 3, 5–83

Sedley, D. N. (1974) 'The structure of Epicurus' *On Nature*', *CErc* 4, 89–92

Sedley, D. N. (1976a) 'Epicurus and his professional rivals', in Bollack & Laks (1976) 119–59

Sedley, D. N. (1976b) 'Epicurus and the mathematicians of Cyzicus', *CErc* 6, 23–54

Sedley, D. N. (1977) 'Diodorus Cronus and Hellenistic philosophy', *PCPhS* 23, 74–120

Sedley, D. N. (1981) 'The end of the Academy', *Phronesis* 26, 67–75

Sedley, D. N. (1982a) 'Two conceptions of vacuum', *Phronesis* 27, 175–93

Sedley, D. N. (1982b) 'The Stoic criterion of identity', *Phronesis* 27, 255–75

Sedley, D. N. (1982c) 'On Signs', in Barnes *et al.* (1982a) 239–72

Sedley, D. N. (1983a) 'The motivation of Greek skepticism', in Burnyeat (1983) 9–29

Sedley, D. N. (1983b) 'Epicurus' refutation of determinism', in AA. VV. (1983) 11–51

Sedley, D. N. (1984) 'The negated conjunction in Stoicism', *Elenchos* 5, 311–16

Sedley, D. N. (1985) 'The Stoic theory of universals', in Epp (1985) 87–92

Sedley, D. N. (1988) 'Epicurean anti-reductionism', in Barnes & Mignucci (1988a) 295–327

Sedley, D. N. (1989a) 'Philosophical allegiance in the Greco-Roman World', in Griffin & Barnes (1989) 97–119

Sedley, D. N. (1989b) 'Epicurus on the common sensibles', in Huby & Neal (1989) 123–36

Sedley, D. N. (1992a) 'Sextus Empiricus and the atomist criteria of truth', *Elenchos* 13, 19–56

Sedley, D. N. (1992b) 'Commentary on Mansfeld', in Cleary & Wians (1992) 146–52

Sedley, D. N. (1996) 'The inferential foundations of Epicurean ethics', in Giannantoni & Gigante (1996) 313–39

Sedley, D. N. (1997) 'Theophrastus and Epicurean physics', in van Ophuijsen & van Raalte (1998) 331–54

Sedley, D. N. (1998) *Lucretius and the Transmission of Greek Wisdom* (Cambridge)

Seel, G. (1993) 'Zur Geschichte und Logik des θερίζων λόγος', in Döring & Ebert (1993) 291–318

Sharples, R. W. (1983) Alexander of Aphrodisias: *On Fate*, Text, Translation, Commentary (London; repr. 1987)

Sharples, R. W. (1984) 'On fire in Heraclitus and in Zeno of Citium', *CQ* 34, 231–3

Sharples, R. W. (1987) 'Alexander of Aphrodisias: scholasticism and innovation', in Haase, W., ed., *ANRW* II 36.2 (Berlin/New York) 1176–243

Sharples, R. W., ed. (1993) *Modern Thinkers and Ancient Thinkers* (London)

Shields, C. J. (1994) 'Socrates among the Skeptics', in Vander Waerdt, P. A., ed., *The Socratic Movement* (Ithaca, NY) 341–66

Siebenborn, E. (1976) *Die Lehre von der Sprachrichtigkeit und ihren Kriterien*: Studien zur antiken normativen Grammatik, Studien zur antiken Philosophie 5 (Amsterdam)

Sinclair, T. A. (1951) *A History of Greek Political Thought*, 2nd edn 1968 (London)

Sluiter, I. (1988) 'On ἦ διασαφητικός and propositions containing μᾶλλον/ἧττον', *Mnemosyne* 41, 46–66

Sluiter, I. (1990) *Ancient Grammar in Context*: contributions to the study of ancient linguistic thought (Amsterdam)

Smend, R. (1984) *Die Entstehung des Alten Testaments* 3rd edn (Stuttgart)

Smith, M. F., ed. (1993) Diogenes of Oinoanda: *The Epicurean Inscription*, La scuola di Epicuro, suppl. 1 (Naples)

Smith, W. D. (1979) *The Hippocratic Tradition*, Cornell Publications in the History of Science (Ithaca, N.Y./London)

Smith, W. D. (1989) 'Notes on ancient medical historiography', *BHM* 63, 73–109

Sollenberger, M. G. (1992) 'The lives of the Peripatetics: an analysis of the contents and structure of Diogenes Laertius' "Vitae philosophorum" book 5', in Haase, W., ed., *ANRW* II 36.6 (Berlin/New York) 3793–879

Solmsen, F. (1929) 'Ancora il frammento logico fiorentino', *RFIC* 7, 507–10; repr. in Solmsen (1968–82) II, 44–7

Solmsen, F. (1941) 'The Aristotelian tradition in ancient rhetoric', *AJPh* 62, 35–50, 169–90

Solmsen, F. (1942) 'Eratosthenes as Platonist and poet', *TAPhA* 73, 192–213

Solmsen, F. (1951) 'Epicurus and cosmological heresies', *AJPh* 72, 1–23; repr. in
Solmsen (1968–82) I, 461–83

Solmsen, F. (1953) 'Epicurus on the growth and decline of the cosmos', *AJPh* 74, 34–51;
repr. in Solmsen (1968–82) I, 484–501

Solmsen, F. (1961) 'Greek philosophy and the discovery of the nerves', *MH* 18, 150–97;
repr. in Solmsen (1968–82) I, 536–82

Solmsen, F. (1968–82) *Kleine Schriften*, 3 vols. (Hildesheim)

Solmsen, F. (1977) 'Epicurus on void, matter and genesis', *Phronesis* 22, 263–81; repr. in
Solmsen (1968–82) III, 333–51

Sorabji, R. (1980a) *Necessity, Cause, and Blame*: Perspectives on Aristotle's Theory
(Ithaca, N.Y. and London)

Sorabji, R. (1980b) 'Causation, laws, and necessity', in Schofield *et al.* (1980a) 250–82

Sorabji, R. (1983) *Time, Creation and the Continuum* (London)

Sorabji, R. (1988) *Matter, Space and Motion*: Theories in Antiquity and Their Sequel
(London)

Sorabji, R., ed. (1990) *Aristotle Transformed*: The Ancient Commentators and Their
Influence (London)

Soreth, M. (1968) 'Die zweite Telosformel des Antipater von Tarsos', *AGPh* 50, 48–72

Sosa, E., ed. (1975) *Causation and Conditionals* (Oxford)

Spanneut, M. (1957) *Le Stoïcisme des Pères de l'Eglise de Clément de Rome à Clément
d'Alexandrie* (Paris)

Spinelli, E. (1986) 'Metrodoro contro i dialettici?', *CErc* 16, 29–43

Squilloni, A. (1991) *Il concetto di 'regno' nel pensiero dello ps.Ecfanto*: le fonti e i trattati
Περὶ βασιλείας (Florence)

Staden, H. von (1975) 'Experiment and experience in Hellenistic medicine', *BICS* 22,
178–99

Staden, H. von (1978) 'The Stoic theory of perception and its "Platonic" critics', in
Machamer, P. K. & Turnbull, R. G., edd., *Studies in Perception* (Columbus)
96–136

Staden, H. von (1982) 'Hairesis and heresy: the case of the *haireseis iatrikai*', in Meyer,
B. F. & Sanders, E. P., edd., *Jewish and Christian Self-Definition*, 3: Self-Definition
in the Graeco-Roman World (London) 76–100, 199–206

Staden, H. von, ed. (1989) *Herophilus*, The Art of Medicine in Early Alexandria
(Cambridge)

Staden, H. von (1991) 'Galen as historian: his use of sources on the Herophileans', in
López Férez, J. A., ed., *Galeno: Obra, pensamiento e influencia* (Madrid) 205–22

Staden, H. von (1997) 'Teleology and mechanism: Aristotelian biology and early
hellenistic medicine', in Kullman, W., & Föllinger, S., edd., *Aristotelische Biologie*
(Stuttgart) 183–208

Steckel, H. (1960) 'Epikurs Prinzip der Einheit von Schmerzlosigkeit und Lust'
(dissertation Göttingen)

Steckel, H. (1968) 'Epikuros', in *Pauly Wissowa, Realencyclopädie* Suppl. 11, cols.
579–652

Steckerl, F. (1958) *The Fragments of Praxagoras of Cos and His School*, PhA 8 (Leiden)

Steinmetz, P. (1964) *Die Physik des Theophrastos von Eresos*, Palingenesia 1
(Bad Homburg)

Steinmetz, P. (1990) 'Planung und Planänderung der philosophischen Schriften

Ciceros', in Steinmetz, P., ed., *Beiträge zur hellenistischen Literatur und ihrer Rezeption in Rom* (Stuttgart) 141–53

Steinmetz, P. (1994) 'Die Stoa', in Flashar (1994) 491–716

Steinthal, H. (1890–91) *Geschichte der Sprachwissenschaft bei den Griechen und Römern mit besonderer Rücksicht der Logik*, 2nd edn, 2 vols. (Berlin)

Sternbach, L., ed. (1963) *Gnomologium Vaticanum e codice vaticano graeco 743*; repr. from *WS* 9–11 (1887–9) (Berlin)

Stopper, M. R. (1983) 'Schizzi Pirroniani', *Phronesis* 28, 265–97

Stough, Ch.L. (1969) *Greek Scepticism* (Berkeley/Los Angeles)

Strasburger, H. (1965) 'Posidonius on problems of the Roman empire', *JRS* 55, 40–53

Strasburger, H. (1966) 'Der "Scipionenkreis"', *Hermes* 94, 60–72

Striker, G. (1974) Κριτήριον τῆς ἀληθείας, *NGG*, Philol.-hist. Klasse 2, 47–110; repr. in Striker (1996) 22–77

Striker, G. (1977) 'Epicurus on the truth of sense impressions', *AGPh* 59, 125–42; repr. in Striker (1996) 77–92

Striker, G. (1980) 'Sceptical strategies', in Schofield *et al.* (1980a) 54–83; repr. in Striker (1996) 92–116

Striker, G. (1981) 'Über den Unterschied zwischen den Pyrrhoneern und den Akademikern', *Phronesis* 26, 153–71; English version in Striker (1996) 135–50

Striker, G. (1983) 'The role of oikeiōsis in Stoic ethics', *OSAP* 1, 145–67; repr. in Striker (1996) 281–98

Striker, G. (1986) 'Antipater, or the art of living', in Schofield & Striker (1986a) 185–204; repr. in Striker (1996) 298–316

Striker, G. (1987) 'Origins of the concept of natural law', in Cleary, J. J., ed., *Proceedings of the Boston Area Colloquium in Ancient Philosophy* 2 (Lanham, MD) 79–101; repr. in Striker (1996) 209–21

Striker, G. (1988) 'Commentary on Mitsis (1988b)', in Cleary & Shartin (1988) 323–8

Striker, G. (1990) 'The problem of the criterion', in Everson (1990a) 143–60; repr. in Striker (1996) 150–69

Striker, G. (1991) 'Following nature. A study in Stoic ethics', *OSAP* 10, 1–73; repr. in Striker (1996) 221–81

Striker, G. (1993) 'Epicurean hedonism', in Brunschwig & Nussbaum (1993) 3–17; repr. in Striker (1996) 196–209

Striker, G. (1996) *Essays on Hellenistic Epistemology and Ethics* (Cambridge)

Stroux, J. (1912) *De Theophrasti Virtutibus Dicendi* (Leipzig)

Sudhaus, E. S. (1911) 'Epikur als Beichtvater', *Archiv für Religionswissenschaft* 14, 647–8

Sullivan, M. W. (1967) *Apuleian logic*: The Nature, Sources, and Influence of Apuleius's *Peri Hermeneias* (Amsterdam)

Szabó, A. (1960) 'Anfänge des euklidischen Axiomensystems', *Archive for History of Exact Sciences* 1, 38–106

Szabó, A. (1969) *Anfänge der griechischen Mathematik* (Munich)

Tardieu, M., ed. (1987) *Les Règles de l'Interprétation* (Paris)

Tarn, W. W. (1933) 'Alexander and the unity of mankind', *PBA* 19, 123–66

Tarrant, H. (1984) 'Zeno on knowledge or on geometry? The evidence of Anon. *In Theaetetum*', *Phronesis* 29, 96–9

Tarrant, H. (1985) *Scepticism or Platonism?* The Philosophy of the Fourth Academy (Cambridge)

Taylor, C. C. W. (1980) 'All perceptions are true', in Schofield *et al.* (1980a) 105–24

Taylor, C. C. W. (1990) 'Aristotle's epistemology', in Everson (1990a) 116–42

Taylor, D. J., ed. (1987a) *The History of Linguistics in the Classical Period* (Amsterdam)

Taylor, D. J. (1987b) 'Rethinking the history of language science in classical antiquity', in Taylor (1987a) 1–16

Taylor, R. (1975) 'The metaphysics of causation', in Sosa (1975) 39–43

Temkin, O. & Temkin, C. L., edd. (1967) *Ancient Medicine*, Selected Papers of L. Edelstein (Baltimore; repr. Baltimore/London 1987)

Tepedino Guerra, A. (1978) 'Il primo libro "Sulla ricchezza" di Filodemo', *CErc* 8, 52–95

Tepedino Guerra, A. (1987) 'Una testimonianza del libro "Sul fine" di Epicuro?', *CErc* 17, 85–8

Tepedino Guerra, A. (1990) 'Il contributo di Metrodoro di Lampsaco alla formazione della teoria Epicurea del linguaggio', *CErc* 20, 17–25

Tepedino Guerra, A., ed. (1991) Polieno: *Frammenti*, La scuola di Epicuro 11 (Naples)

Tepedino Guerra, A. (1992) 'Metrodoro "Contro i dialettici"?', *CErc* 22, 119–22

Tepedino Guerra, A. (1994) 'L'opera filodemea *Su Epicuro (PHerc. 1232, 1289b)*', *CErc* 24, 5–53

Thesleff, H. (1961) *An Introduction to the Pythagorean Writings of the Hellenistic Period* (Åbo)

Thesleff, H. (1965) *The Pythagorean Texts of the Hellenistic Period* (Åbo)

Thesleff, H. (1972) 'The problem of the Doric pseudo-Pythagorica', in *Pseudepigrapha* I, Fondation Hardt 18 (Vandœuvres/Geneva) 59–87

Throm, H. (1932) *Die Thesis* (Paderborn)

Tieleman, T. L. (1991) 'Diogenes of Babylon and Stoic embryology. Ps.Plutarch, *Plac.* V 15.4 reconsidered', *Mnemosyne* 44, 106–25

Tieleman, T. L. (1996) *Galen and Chrysippus on the Soul*, Argument and Refutation in the *De Placitis* Books II–III, PhA 68 (Leiden)

Tigerstedt, E. N. (1974) *The Legend of Sparta in Classical Antiquity*, vol. II (Stockholm)

Timpanaro, S. (1972) 'Friedrich Schlegel e gli inizi della linguistica indoeuropea in Germania', *Critica Storica* N.S. 10, 72–105, rev. transl. in Amsterdam Studies in the Theory and History of Linguistic Science Ser. 1, Amsterdam Classics in Linguistics, vol. I (Amsterdam) xi–lvii

Timpanaro, S. (1981 (1963)) *La genesi del metodo del Lachmann*, Saggi 5 (Padua (Florence 1963))

Todd, R. B. (1973) 'The Stoic common notions', *SO* 48, 47–73

Todd, R. B. (1976) *Alexander of Aphrodisias on Stoic Physics*. A Study of the *De mixtione* with Preliminary Essays, Text, Translation and Commentary (Leiden)

Todd, R. B. (1978) 'Monism and immanence: foundations of Stoic physics', in Rist (1978b) 137–60

Todd, R. B. (1985) 'The title of Cleomedes' treatise', *Philologus* 129, 250–61

Todd, R. B. (1989) 'The Stoics and their cosmology in the first and second centuries AD', in Haase, W., ed., *ANRW* II 36.3 (Berlin/New York) 1365–78

Todd, R. B., ed. (1990) Cleomedis *Caelestia* (ΜΕΤΕΩΡΑ) (Leipzig)

Tracy, S. (1994) *Boeotia Antiqua* (Amsterdam)

Trillitzsch, W. (1971) *Seneca im literarischen Urteil der Antike*. Darstellung und Sammlung der Zeugnisse, 2 vols. (Amsterdam)

Trompf, G. W. (1979) *The Idea of Historical Recurrence in Western Thought*: From
 Antiquity to the Reformation (Berkeley)
Tsekourakis, D. (1974) *Studies in the Terminology of Early Stoic Ethics*, Hermes Einzelschr.
 32 (Wiesbaden)
Tsouna McKirahan, V. (1992) 'The Cyrenaic theory of knowledge', *OSAP* 10, 161–92
Tsouna McKirahan, V. (1998) *The Epistemology of the Cyrenaic School* (Cambridge)
Ueding, G., ed. (1991) *Rhetorik zwischen den Wissenschaften*: Geschichte, System, Praxis
 als Probleme des 'Historischen Wörterbuchs der Rhetorik' (Tübingen)
Usener, H., ed. (1887) *Epicurea* (Leipzig; repr. Stuttgart 1966)
van Ophuijsen; van Raalte, *see*: Ophuijsen, van; Raalte, van
Vallance, J. T. (1990) *The Lost Theory of Asclepiades of Bithynia* (Oxford)
Vander Waerdt, P. A. (1987) 'The justice of the Epicurean wise man', *CQ* 37, 402–22
Vander Waerdt, P. A. (1988) 'Hermarchus and the Epicurean genealogy of morals',
 TAPA 118, 87–106
Vander Waerdt, P. A. (1989) 'Colotes and the Epicurean refutation of Skepticism',
 GRBS 30, 225–67
Vegetti, M. (1986) 'Tradizione e verità. Forme della storiografia filosofico-scientifica
 nel *De placitis* di Galeno', in G. Cambiano, ed., *Storiografia e dossografia nella
 filosofia antica* (Turin) 227–44
Vegetti, M. (1989) *L'etica degli antichi*, Manuali Laterza 4 (Rome/Bari)
Vegetti, M. (1993) 'I nervi dell' anima', in Kollesch & Nickel (1993) 63–77
Verbeke, G. (1945) *L'évolution de la doctrine du* pneuma *du Stoicisme à S. Augustin*
 (Paris/Louvain)
Verbeke, G. (1949) *Kleanthes van Assos* (Brussels)
Versteegh, C. H. M. (1980) 'The Stoic verbal system', *Hermes* 108, 338–57
Veyne, P. (1976) *Le pain et le cirque*: sociologie historique d'un pluralisme politique (Paris)
Viano, C. A. (1981) 'Lo scetticismo antico e la medicina', in Giannantoni (1981a) II,
 563–656
Vitelli, G. (1902) 'Due frammenti di Alessandro di Afrodisia', in *Festschrift Theodor
 Gomperz* (Wien) 90–3, Engl. transl. in Sharples, R. W., ed. (1994) Alexander of
 Aphrodisias: *Quaestiones 2.16–3.15* (London) 90–4
Vlastos, G. (1965) 'Minimal parts in Epicurean atomism', *Isis* 56, 121–47; repr. in
 Graham (1995) 285–314
Vlastos, G. (1966) 'Zeno of Sidon as a critic of Euclid', in Wallach, L., ed., *The Classical
 Tradition*, Literary and Historical Studies in Honor of Harry Caplan (Ithaca)
 148–59; repr. in Graham (1995) 315–24
Vlastos, G. (1991) *Socrates: Ironist and Moral Philosopher* (Cambridge)
Voelke, A.-J. (1973) *L'idée de volonté dans le Stoïcisme* (Paris)
von Arnim; von Fritz; von Kienle; von der Mühll; von Prantl; von Staden; von
 Wilamowitz-Moellendorff, *see*: Arnim, von etc.
Wachsmuth, C., ed. (1885) *Corpusculum poesis epicae ludibundae*, vol. II: De Timone
 Phliasio ceterisque sillographis commentatio (Leipzig)
Walbank, F. W. (1957) *A Historical Commentary on Polybius*, vol. I (Oxford)
Walbank, F. W. (1972) *Polybius* (Berkeley)
Walbank, F. W. (1984) 'Monarchies and monarchical ideas', in *The Cambridge Ancient
 History*, 2nd edn, vol. VII.1 (Cambridge)

Walzer, R. & Frede, M., edd. (1985) *Galen. Three Treatises On the Nature of Science*, 3 vols. (Indianapolis)

Wardy, R. (1988) 'Lucretius on what atoms are not', *CPh* 83, 112–28

Wasserstein, A. (1978) 'Epicurean science', *Hermes*, 106, 484–94

Watson, G. (1966) *The Stoic Theory of Knowledge* (Belfast)

Watson, G. (1971) 'The natural law and Stoicism', in Long (1971a) 216–38

Wehrli, F., ed. (1969a) *Straton von Lampsakos*, Die Schule des Aristoteles: H. 5, Zweite Auflage (Basle/Stuttgart)

Wehrli, F., ed. (1969b) *Eudemos von Rhodos*, Die Schule des Aristoteles, H. 8, Zweite Auflage (Basle/Stuttgart)

Wehrli, F., ed. (1969c) *Phainias von Eresos, Chamaileon, Praxiphanes*, Die Schule des Aristoteles, H. 9, Zweite Auflage (Basle/Stuttgart)

Wehrli, F., ed. (1969d) *Hieronymos von Rhodos, Kritolaos und seine Schüler*, Die Schule des Aristoteles, H. 10, Zweite Auflage (Basle/Stuttgart)

Wehrli, F. (1976) (rev. Lynch 1972) *Gnomon* 48, 128–34

Wehrli, F., ed. (1978) *Sotion*, Die Schule des Aristoteles, Suppl. Bd. 2 (Basle/Stuttgart)

Wehrli, F. (1983) 'Der Peripatos bis zum Beginn der römischen Kaiserzeit', in Flashar (1983) 459–599

Weische, A. (1961) *Cicero und die Neue Akademie*: Untersuchungen zur Entstehung und Geschichte der antiken Skeptizismus, Orbis antiquus 18 (Münster i. Westf., 2nd edn 1975)

Wellmann, M. (1895) 'Die pneumatische Schule bis auf Archigenes in ihrer Entwicklung dargestellt', *Philosophische Untersuchungen* 14 (1895)

Wellmann, M. (1901) *Fragmentensammlung der griechischen Ärzte*, vol. 1: Die Fragmente der sikelischen Ärzte Akron, Philistion und des Diokles von Karystos (Berlin)

Wendland, P. (1897) 'Eine doxographische Quelle Philos', *Sitzungsberichte der Deutschen Akademie der Wissenschaften zu Berlin*, 1074–9

Westerink, L. G., ed. (1990) *Prolégomènes à la philosophie de Platon*, Coll. Budé (Paris)

White, M. J. (1992) *The Continuous and the Discrete*, Ancient Physical Theories from a Contemporary Perspective (Oxford)

White, N. P. (1978) 'Two notes on Stoic terminology', *AJPh* 99, 111–19

White, N. P. (1979) 'The basis of Stoic ethics', *HSPh* 83, 143–78

White, N. P. (1985) 'The role of physics in Stoic ethics', in Epp (1985) 57–74

White, N. P. (1990) 'Stoic values', *The Monist* 73, 42–58

White, S. (1991) (rev. Englert 1987) *AncPhil* 11, 455–9

Wiesner, J., ed. (1985–87) *Aristoteles, Werk und Wirkung*, Paul Moraux gewidmet, 2 vols. (Berlin)

Wilamowitz-Moellendorff, U., von (1881) *Antigonos von Karystos* (Berlin; repr. 1965)

Williamson, T. (1994) *Vagueness* (London)

Wilson, N. G. (1983) *Scholars of Byzantium* (London)

Winiarczyk, M., ed. (1981) Diagorae Melii et Theodori Cyrenaei *reliquiae*, Bibl. Teubneriana (Leipzig)

Winiarczyk, M. (1984) 'Wer galt im Altertum als Atheist?', *Philologus* 128, 157–83

Winiarczyk, M. (1989) 'Bibliographie zum antiken Atheismus', *Elenchos* 10, 103–92

Winiarczyk, M. (1990) 'Methodisches zum antiken Atheismus', *RhM* 133, 1–15

Winiarczyk, M. (1992) 'Wer galt im Altertum als Atheist? 2. Teil', *Philologus* 136, 306–10

Wolff, M. (1988) 'Hipparchus and the Stoic theory of motion', in Barnes & Mignucci (1988a) 471–545

Woltjer, J. (1877) 'Lucretii philosophia cum fontibus comparata' (dissertation Groningen; repr. in Greek and Roman Philosophy 45, New York/London 1987)

Woodruff, P. (1986) 'The skeptical side of Plato's method', *RIPh* 90, 22–37

Woodward, P. G. (1989) 'Star gods in Philodemus, *PHerc.* 152/157', *CErc* 19, 29–47

Wotke, K., ed. (1888) 'Epikurische Spruchsammlung', *WS* 10 (1888) 175–201

Wright, M. R. (1991) Cicero: *On Stoic Good and Evil. De Finibus bonorum et malorum 3 and Paradoxa Stoicorum* (Warminster)

Zacher, K. D. (1982) *Plutarchs Kritik an der Lustlehre Epikurs.* Ein Kommentar zu 'Non posse suaviter vivi secundum Epicurum, Kap. 1–8', Beiträge zur klassischen Philologie 124 (Königstein)

Zacher, K. D. (1985) 'Zur Lustlehre Epikurs', *WJA* N.F. 11, 63–72

Zanker, G. (1981) 'Enargeia in the ancient criticism of poetry', *RhM* 124, 297–311

Zanker, P. (1995) *Die Maske des Sokrates. Das Bild des Intellektuellen in der antiken Kunst* (Munich)

Zeller, E. (& Wellmann, E., ed.) (1909) *Die Philosophie der Griechen in ihrer geschichtlichen Entwicklung*, III.1: Die nacharistotelische Philosophie, erste Hälfte (Leipzig; [5]1923 = Darmstadt [6]1963)

Zeller, E. & Mondolfo, R. (1969) *La Filosofia dei Greci nel suo sviluppo storico*, parte I: I Presocratici, vol. V: Empedocle, Atomisti, Anassagora, a cura di Capizzi, A. (Florence)

Index Locorum

General index